THE OXFORD HANDBOOK OF

MODERN GERMAN HISTORY

THE OXFORD HANDBOOK OF

MODERN
GERMAN
HISTORY

Edited by
HELMUT WALSER SMITH

OXFORD

UNIVERSITY PRESS

Great Clarendon Street, Oxford OX2 6DP

Oxford University Press is a department of the University of Oxford.
It furthers the University's objective of excellence in research, scholarship,
and education by publishing worldwide in

Oxford New York

Auckland Cape Town Dar es Salaam Hong Kong Karachi
Kuala Lumpur Madrid Melbourne Mexico City Nairobi
New Delhi Shanghai Taipei Toronto

With offices in

Argentina Austria Brazil Chile Czech Republic France Greece
Guatemala Hungary Italy Japan Poland Portugal Singapore
South Korea Switzerland Thailand Turkey Ukraine Vietnam

Oxford is a registered trade mark of Oxford University Press
in the UK and in certain other countries

Published in the United States
by Oxford University Press Inc., New York

British Library Cataloguing in Publication Data

Data available

Library of Congress Cataloging in Publication Data

Data available

Typeset by SPI Publisher Services, Pondicherry, India
Printed in Great Britain
on acid-free paper by
CPI Antony Rowe, Chippenham, Wiltshire

ISBN 978-0-19-923739-5

1 3 5 7 9 10 8 6 4 2

Acknowledgements

The *Oxford Handbook of Modern German History* is four years in the making, and we have accumulated many debts along the way. We would first like to thank Christopher Wheeler, who commissioned the project and helped see it to the end, and Matthew Cotton, for his sound editorial advice. We would also like to thank Emma Barber, who carefully steered the project through production, Sue Finlay, the copyeditor, and Nicola Sangster, who proofread the final manuscript with a watchful eye. As the editor, I am especially grateful to the authors, leading experts in their fields, who have taken time away from their own work to offer an interpretive reading of their research area. The chapters, as readers will see, are neither historiographical overviews nor simple textbook glosses; instead, they represent what in Germany is sometimes called mid-level synthesis: genuine attempts to make sense of the German past, and to suggest starting points for further thinking. A Handbook, we all agreed, should open, not close, a field. I would also like to thank Christine Brocks, who translated a series of chapters (5, 11, 13, 19, and part of 26), compiled the index, and helped with proof reading. At Vanderbilt, Ann Oslin, the administrative assistant at the Max Kade Center for European and German Studies, also scrutinized a number of chapters, as did my graduate students, Jeremy DeWaal, Robbie Gibson, Heather Jones, and Sonja Ostrow. Andreas W. Daum (Buffalo), Margaret Lavinia Anderson (Berkeley), James Retallack (Toronto), and Benjamin Ziemann (Sheffield) read my own chapters, and offered invaluable criticism. Finally, we owe a debt of gratitude to the German Studies Association for allowing us to present our ideas in a series of panels in Washington D.C., to the German Historical Institute in London for critical discussion of the Handbook's conception, and to the "*Verband der Historiker und Historikerinnen Deutschlands*," as it is now called, for hosting a panel at its annual meeting in Berlin to consider some of the Handbook's conclusions.

CONTENTS

PART IV: GERMANY 1945–1989

PART V: CONTEMPORARY GERMANY

List of Maps, Tables, and Illustrations

List of Maps

List of Tables

List of Figures

LIST OF CONTRIBUTORS

Celia Applegate is Professor of History at the University of Rochester.

William A. Barbieri, Jr. is Associate Professor of Ethics and Director of the Peace and Justice Studies Program at the Catholic University of America.

Ernest Benz is Associate Professor of History at Smith College.

James M. Brophy is Professor of History at the University of Delaware.

Sebastian Conrad is Professor of History at the Free University of Berlin.

Andreas W. Daum is Professor of History and Associate Dean of Undergraduate Education at the State University of New York at Buffalo.

Stephen D. Dowden is Professor of Literature at Brandeis University.

Franz Leander Fillafer is Research Associate at the University of Konstanz, Centre of Excellence focused on 'Cultural Foundations of Integration'.

Robert von Friedeburg is Chair of Early Modern History and Director of the Erasmus Center, University of Rotterdam.

Ann Goldberg is Professor of History at the University of California, Riverside.

Rebekka Habermas is Professor of Modern History at the University of Göttingen.

William W. Hagen is Professor of History at the University of California, Davis.

Donna Harsch is Professor of History at Carnegie Mellon University.

Stefan-Ludwig Hoffmann is Senior Fellow at the Center for Advanced Studies, Freiburg, and Research Director at the Center for Contemporary History, Potsdam.

Christian Jansen is Professor of History at the Technical University of Berlin.

Pieter M. Judson is Professor of History at Swarthmore College.

Lutz Koepnick is Professor of German, Film and Media Studies at Washington University in St Louis.

Thomas Kühne is Strassler Family Professor in the Study of Holocaust History at Clark University.

Thomas Mergel is Professor of Modern History at the Humboldt University in Berlin.

Jürgen Osterhammel is Professor of Modern History at the University of Konstanz.

David F. Patton is Professor of Government at Connecticut College.

Andrew I. Port is Associate Professor of History at Wayne State University.

Uta G. Poiger is Associate Professor of History at the University of Washington.

Kiran Klaus Patel is Joint Chair in History of the European Union and Transatlantic Studies at the European University Institute, Florence.

Ute Planert is Professor of History at the University of Wuppertal.

Ritchie Robertson is Taylor Professor of German at the University of Oxford and Fellow of Queen's College.

Helmut Walser Smith is Martha Rivers Ingram Professor of History and Director of the Max Kade Center for European and German Studies at Vanderbilt University.

Jonathan Sperber is Curator's Professor of History at the University of Missouri.

Philipp Ther is Professor of History, University of Vienna.

Adam Tooze is Professor of History at Yale University.

Cornelius Torp is Marie Curie Fellow at the European University Institute, Florence and Lecturer at the University of Halle.

Siegfried Weichlein is Professor of Contemporary History at the University of Fribourg.

Meike G. Werner is Associate Professor of German Literature at Vanderbilt University.

George S. Williamson is Associate Professor of History at Florida State University.

Benjamin Ziemann is Professor of Modern German History at the University of Sheffield.

Andrew Zimmerman is Professor of History at the George Washington University.

LIST OF ABBREVIATIONS

AEG	Allgemeine Elektricitäts-Gesellschaft
AG	Aktiengesellschaft (public corporation)
APO	Außerparlamentarische Opposition (Extra-Parliamentary Opposition)
BDF	Bund Deutscher Frauenvereine (Federation of German Women's Associations)
BDKJ	Bund der Deutschen katholischen Jugend (League of German Catholic Youth)
BHE	Bund der Heimatvertriebenen und Entrechteten (Federation of Expellees)
CCC	Civilian Conservation Corps
CDU	Christlich Demokratische Union Deutschlands (Christian Democratic Union)
COMECON	Council for Mutual Economic Assistance
CSCE	Commission on Security and Cooperation in Europe
CSU	Christlich Soziale Union (Christian Social Union)
DAF	Deutsche Arbeitsfront (German Labor Front)
DBD	Demokratische Bauernpartei Deutschlands (Democratic Farmers Party of Germany)
DDP	Deutsche Demokratische Partei (German Democratic Party)
DKP	Deutsche Kommunistische Partei (German Communist Party)
DNVP	Deutschnationale Volkspartei (German National People's Party)
DVP	Deutsche Volkspartei (German People's Party)
ECSC	European Coal and Steel Community
EDC	European Defence Community
EEC	European Economic Community
EFTA	European Free Trade Association
EKD	Evangelische Kirche in Deutschland
EMS	European Monetary System
FDJ	Freie Deutsche Jugend (Free German Youth)

FDP	Freie Demokratische Partei (Free Democratic Party)
FRG	Federal Republic of Germany
GATT	General Agreement on Tariffs and Trade
GDP	Gross Domestic Product
GDR	German Democratic Republic
GM	General Motors
GNP	Gross National Product
KdF	Kraft durch Freude (Strength through Joy)
KPD	Kommunistische Partei Deutschlands (Communist Party of Germany)
LDPD	Liberal-Demokratische Partei Deutschlands (Liberal Democratic Party of Germany)
LDP	Liberal-Demokratische Partei (Liberal Democratic Party)
MBFR	Mutual and Balanced Force Reductions
MfS	Ministerium für Staatssicherheit (Ministry for State Security)
MLF	Multilateral Force
MSPD	Mehrheitssozialdemokratische Partei Deutschlands (Majority Social Democratic Party of Germany)
NATO	North Atlantic Treaty organization
NCO	Non-commissioned officer
NDP	Net Domestic Product
NDPD	National-Demokratische Partei Deutschlands (National Democratic Party of Germany)
NKWD	People's Commissariat for Internal Affairs (Soviet)
NS	National socialismus (National Socialism)
NSDAP	Nationalsozialistische Deutsche Arbeiterpartei (Nazi Party)
OEEC	Organization for European Economic Co-operation
RAD	Reichsarbeitsdienst (Reich Labor Service)
RAF	Rote Armee Fraktion (Red Army Faction)
RNST	Reichsnährstand (Agricultural Agency)
SA	Sturmabteilung (Storm Troopers)
SAG	Sowjetische Aktiengesellschaften (Soviet Corporation)
SALT	Strategic Arms Limitation Treaty
SDS	Sozialistischer Deutscher Studentenbund (Socialist German Student Union)
SED	Sozialistische Einheitspartei Deutschlands (Socialist Unity Party)

SoPaDe	Sozialdemokratische Partei Deutschlands (Exile designation of the SPD)
SPD	Sozialdemokratische Partei Deutschlands (Social Democratic Party of Germany)
SRA	Statistisches Reichsamt (Statistical Office)
USPD	Unabhängige Sozialdemokratische Partei Deutschlands (Independent Social Democratic Party of Germany)
VDA	Verein für das Deutschtum im Ausland (Association for Germandom Abroad)
WWI	World War I
WWII	World War II
ZAG	Zentrale Arbeitsgemeinschaft (Association of Employers and Unions)

CHAPTER 1

INTRODUCTION

HELMUT WALSER SMITH

THE *Oxford Handbook of Modern German History* departs in significant ways from previous histories of modern Germany. It is, for one, a national history put together by an international team of scholars, with historians from Germany, Great Britain, the United States, and other nations suggesting the diversity of scholarship and the global context of the modern discipline of history. We offer neither a German history in a national key nor the view of outsiders looking in. Rather, we take into account that German history is a substantial field of study in a range of countries that have been affected by Germany's past.

The Oxford Handbook also represents a novel attempt to place German history in a deeper international and transnational setting than has hitherto been the case. This is the second important departure, and is, in this sense, indebted to the proposition, as C. A. Bayly has recently emphasized, 'that national histories and "area studies" need to take fuller account of changes occurring in the wider world.'[1] Accordingly, the Oxford Handbook is not fixed on the *Sonderweg* debate—the question of whether Germany took a special and mistaken path to modernity, resulting in World War I, World War II, and the Holocaust. Rather, the contributors emphasize the embeddedness and the impact of German history in and on wider developments, and render these qualities as central organizing principles of modern German history. This approach does not preclude showing how German history differed from other national histories, but it allows us to see these differences in a more complex and international field. It also encourages students of German history to develop a catholic sense of 'family resemblances' to other histories, seeing, as Wittgenstein would have insisted, a wider range of likeness even while retaining a concept of difference.

The third departure follows from these propositions and concerns the chronological markers of German history. As few countries have experienced political ruptures with such dramatic impact on everyday life, it has become accepted practice to demarcate historical change with the dates of regime changes. These typically include the end of the Holy Roman Empire of 1806, the Revolutions of 1848/9, the foundation of the

Second German Empire in 1871, the foundation of the Weimar Republic in 1918, the Nazi take-over of power in 1933, the collapse of the Nazi Empire in 1945, the founding of East and West Germany in 1949, and the Revolution of 1989 and the Unification of Germany in 1990. There have also been a number of attempts to emphasize the history of the everyday, or to underscore the impact of war on German society. Historians have, for example, interpreted World War I as 'the great seminal catastrophe' (George F. Kennan) of the twentieth century, and characterized the years between 1914 and 1945 as a modern Thirty Years War. This periodization separates the first half of the bellicose twentieth century from the comparatively peaceful 'belle époque,' and emphasizes the magnitude of the human tragedy—so many 'quick eyes gone under earth's lid,' as Ezra Pound put it. Yet as the historian Charles S. Maier has argued, this periodization also renders twentieth-century barbarity as a moral narrative without a convincing analytical frame.[2]

The Handbook makes nation-state sovereignty into a decisive marker as well as a problem of modern German history. A concept of the German nation reaches at least to the early sixteenth century, when the Holy Roman Empire officially added the appellation 'of the German Nation,' and the first two-dimensional images of Germany as a cultural nation were reproduced on maps.[3] If the German nation was an old category, German nationalism—the political doctrine positing the necessity of congruence between a German nation and a German state—was at best a late eighteenth century invention, which in the German lands had few adherents until the nineteenth century. In 1871, the German nation state was formed in a world of multinational and overseas empires, and the pull of empire, including dominion over peoples considered inferior, shaped the context in which Germany's subsequent political history unfolded. The nation state—the ideology behind it, the forces creating it, holding it together, and tearing it apart—thus plays a prominent role in this Handbook. Yet the sovereign nation state was not a given frame, and most of German history happened outside of it: at the communal level, in the individual states, in regions, and in transnational networks. It is also true that in the 250-year history that this Handbook covers, the sovereign nation state as the principal form of government constituted an interlude, just as on a wider stage nation states were always only one possible way of organizing the political world. In Germany, that interlude covered nearly three-quarters of a century, from 1871 to 1945. After 1990, full national sovereignty returned, if embedded in European structures.

The Oxford Handbook is divided into an introductory section and four chronological parts. The introductory section roots the Handbook in a chronologically deeper conception of German history. It also offers the reader overarching chapters on place and on people, with the former showing the changing representation of German homelands, and the latter focusing on gender as constitutive, but historically changing. The Handbook is thereafter divided by four chronological markers, which separate two long periods of time (1760–1860 and 1860–1945), and two shorter periods (1945–1989, and 1989 to the present). These markers point to central events in the economic and political history of modern Germany, and therefore remain familiar reference points:

the 1760s signaling the Seven Years War and a decisive turn in the history of Austro-Prussian dualism; the 1860s marking the industrial revolution and the events leading towards national unification; 1945, the collapse of the Nazi Empire; and 1989, the East German Revolution. To see these markers only in this way is however to stay within a primarily internal history of modern Germany. Our intention is also to signal fundamental changes in the history of nation-state sovereignty, and to evoke a wider history of war and peace, economic change, and the making of modern polities. What follows in this introduction is not a synopsis of the Handbook's contents, but an attempt to show why these transition periods suggest a possible frame for understanding modern German history.

1.1 CIRCA 1760

The first section, 1760–1860, chronicles a period in German history when the history of the German nation and the history of the state in Germany represent separate histories—not histories without relation to one another, but histories that cannot be narrated as if they were one. Circa 1760, it was not evident that a German nation state would emerge or that Prussia would be the state that placed its indelible stamp upon it; in fact, in 1762 it was entirely plausible that Prussia would cease to exist. Prussia, as is well known, was saved not by its inner strength, but by the death of Empress Elizabeth of Russia and the withdrawal of Russian troops from the Seven Years War. This fact reminds us that although German historians have tended to downplay the significance of international relations, these relations played a decisive role in the unfolding of German history. If Prussia was spared oblivion in 1762, it narrowly escaped this fate again in 1806. The next half-century witnessed the increasing centrality of a political and territorial dualism between the Hohenzollern and Habsburg dynasties. The rise of the idea of nation and the ideology of nationalism did not emanate from this dualism, but rather flourished in its shadow. For most of this period, nationalism, as John Breuilly has convincingly argued, was not an engine of national unification, but at best an ideology that made other solutions increasingly improbable.[4] At the same time, the Seven Years War, which opens our Handbook, while not the first German civil war, was the first trans-continental war, fought on three continents, and involving the great issues of the day—colonial rule, slavery, the dissolution of religiously unified states, and the balance of power. It allows us to set German history, from the very start, in a wider global history, and to emphasize the transformative impact of inter-state violence on this history.

It has been conventional to begin consideration of the second half of the eighteenth century by noting that there was no single Germany, but only 'the electoral princes, 94 spiritual and lay princes, 103 counts, 40 prelates, 51 free towns, in all some 300 separate "territories."'[5] Fewer historians pause to mention that, in the second part of the eighteenth century, and especially in the eastern parts of the Empire, the majority of people nevertheless lived in the great territorial states.[6] Take a contemporary mid-century map of the German Empire, say from the workshop of Jean Baptiste Homann in Nuremberg. If one folded it in half, creasing it at a line passing roughly through Augsburg, Erfurt, and Lübeck, then practically the whole of the east would be taken up by Prussia, Saxony, the Hereditary Crown lands of Austria, and Bavaria. To the left of the fold there would be Hanover and Württemberg. In the northern part, Western Pomerania north of the river Peene belonged to Sweden, while Holstein, including the city of Altona, belonged to the Kingdom of Denmark. In the southwest, an estimated 400,000 subjects lived in Anterior Austria, and thus under Habsburg control. Much of the map, in other words, would be covered by medium and even large-scale territorial states. In recent years, historians have rightly emphasized the importance and vitality of the Holy Roman Empire.[7] The Empire, however, was not a state; contemporaries called it a 'political system.' In the second half of the eighteenth century, it was dominated by near-sovereign, largely, but not completely autonomous territories—countries almost—with a smaller part, containing fewer people, consisting of less powerful, and therefore less sovereign, territories and cities. The German nation, in other words, constituted a framework of language and culture within a fragile political system. It did not govern politics in the elementary sense, as Carl Schmitt put it, of defining friend-foe relationships, or of regulating the state of exception.[8] In the late eighteenth century, the salient and defining friend-foe conflicts were internal: Prussia versus Austria, Austria versus Bavaria, and Prussia versus Saxony—to list a few prominent examples. These conflicts were also played out among shifting European and even global alliances.

Circa 1760, these alliances had come to center on the clash of major seagoing Empires pursuing a vast human trade transported in 'practically floating concentration camps.'[9] This was, of course, the slave trade, now nearly at its apex. Between 1760 and 1860, six times as many Africans as Europeans traversed the Atlantic, creating, as the historian David Eltis has written, 'a hemispheric "community"... for the first time in human history.'[10] Germans were largely excluded from this hemispheric community, except as migrants themselves or as mercenary soldiers. Germany did not possess an Empire that ruled over distant lands, and Germans did not own slaves, or participate, except as critical observers, in the drawn-out, often violent, abolition of the trade and the institution of slavery. It is difficult to discern the precise meaning of these facts, but in the period 1760–1860 they arguably separated Germany from the 'west' in ways far deeper than the alleged lateness of Germany as a nation state.[11]

It is commonly accepted that the period subsequent to the Treaty of Westphalia in 1648 represented an epoch of territorial states. Yet it was not until the eighteenth century that these states came to be thought of as precisely delimited territorial spaces measured by area and not just as a vertical extension of a ruler's patrimony. The position of the individual within territorial states changed as well. Not the chain of feudal obligations, but the laws, customs, and bureaucracy of the state increasingly circumscribed the everyday life of subjects. Based on binding rules, transparency, and a supposedly neutral bureaucracy, the modern state engendered an increasing depersonalization of rule. Frederick the Great's charisma notwithstanding, this depersonalization encouraged identification with the state first, and the regent as an expression of state and territory. By the end of the eighteenth century, the 'machine' had become the principal metaphor for the state, and the relationship of state to individual had changed considerably.[12] One should not over-estimate this development, still in its incipient stages. The estate (*Stand*) to which one belonged—whether noble, townsman, craftsman, or peasant—marked individual identity more decisively than public allegiance to a territorial state. Military organization reflected this fact. Circa 1760, the vast majority of soldiers remained either mercenaries or forced conscripts. Yet it is indicative that in the midst of the Seven Years War, the first political tract in the German lands encouraging citizen-subjects to die for the fatherland appeared; its author, Thomas Abbt, admonished his countrymen to sacrifice themselves for their state, Prussia, and the admonishment followed English, French, and still more decisively classical models.[13] The wider Germany, Abbt made clear, was not something to die for—but territorial states, fatherlands, were. Moreover, only men were slated for active sacrifice, a line of thinking that foreshadowed the gendered division of public and private, making, as Fichte would later write, the weapon into 'the main symbol of citizens.'[14]

There are other reasons to start the *Oxford Handbook of Modern German History* around 1760, even if they tend to confirm the Heraclitian insight that 'war is the father and king of all.' The first is demographic. Although demographers disagree on precise numbers, it took Germany roughly a century after the Peace of Westphalia to claw its way back to the population levels it had achieved in 1600. By the mid-eighteenth century, the German population was, however, finally in the midst of a demographic up-swing that would see the population of the German lands double in the next hundred years.[15] An agricultural, not an industrial, revolution drove this slow, fitful departure from a subsistence economy. Between 1760 and 1860, the agricultural constitution—the balance between large and small farms, free and unfree labor, and different methods of crop rotation—determined human possibilities as surely as industrial take-off shaped what was possible in the century thereafter. In 1860, the majority of the German population still worked in the agricultural sector, which had significantly diversified in the intervening period. Among the dynamic factors was rural industry—concentrated on the spinning and weaving of linen, cotton, and wool—and which historians have credited, perhaps too much, with causing the population explosion and bringing forth the transition from a rural to an industrial economy. The basic fact of life in 1760, and for most of the next hundred years, was nevertheless that the majority of Germans lived on the land, and accorded themselves to its rhythm, just as had been the case for hundreds of years previously, and would not change on a global scale until the second half of the twentieth century.[16] Finally, Germany was, in fact, beginning to become more urban, with the number of cities with at least 10,000 inhabitants increasing from 39 in 1750 to 62 in 1800.[17] In terms of the percentage of people living in such cities, Germany remained behind—certainly behind Great Britain, the Italian lands, and the Low Countries, but also still behind Spain and Portugal.[18]

Another reason to start circa 1760 is cultural. The Thirty Years War had devastated not only a population, but also a world of religious and humanistic learning, and one of the surest indexes of this devastation was the production of books. Remarkably, it would not be until 1765 that book production in the German lands reached the levels it had attained in 1600.[19] The language in which books were written also changed. Just after the Thirty Years War, Latin-language books outstripped German by 2:1, but by 1740, according to the catalogs of the Leipzig book fair, Latin books made up just over a quarter of the total, and by 1800 they constituted a mere four percent of the book trade.[20] The world of German learning had become a German-language world, and this allowed for the creation of a public sphere with a deeper reach. A rise in literacy corresponded to this crucial transformation from Latin to German. Historians used to place literacy in Germany far behind northern France, Holland, England, Sweden, and Scotland, seeing German literacy as crawling from roughly 10% in 1700 to 15% by 1770, and 25% by 1800.[21] Recent research places literacy rates—based on the low threshold revealed by the ability of marriage partners to sign their names—well above 50% in 1780. This literacy was higher in cities and market towns than in the countryside; higher for men than for women, with the gap closing fast by the end of the century; and marginally higher in Protestant than in Catholic territories.[22] Of the sociological indicators, class, more than gender or religion, influenced reading ability. In Koblenz, for example, the urban upper class registered literacy rates higher than 95% at a time when fewer than half of day laborers could sign their names.[23] Still, even the numbers for the lower classes remained impressive, and suggest that the take off in literacy had already begun in the second half of the eighteenth century.[24]

Accompanying the shift from Latin to the vernacular and the rise in literacy was the standardization of German and the creation of a modern German literature embedded in the wider currents of European Enlightenment. The standardization of German involved a longer history, from the first attempt to 'stabilize' the language in the sixteenth and seventeenth centuries (when throughout Europe we find the first grammatical works, rhetorical manuals, orthographies, lexica, and dictionaries in vernacular languages) to successful 'standardization'—which in Germany, unlike England or France, did not finally occur until the eighteenth century.[25] 'It was in the period between 1700 and 1775,' the literary historian Eric A. Blackall has written, 'that the German language developed into a literary language of infinite richness and subtlety.'[26] Gotthold Ephraim Lessing was at once actor and emblem of this transition, and his turn away from the French of the courts—famously in Letter Number Seventeen (1759) of *Letters Concerning the Newest Literature*—signaled the emergence of an independent literature whose bearings, like those of Lessing himself, were European and cosmopolitan, but whose authors aspired to create a genuine German and national literature. Not coincidentally, Lessing's letter has the war as its context.

Finally, it was in German, rather than Latin, that an intense, learned, and engaged debate about religion and its place in society took place. Beginning circa 1780, this debate continued for more than a century until Nietzsche mistakenly pronounced 'God is dead...and we have killed him.'[27] In fact, the century witnessed a resurgence, especially after 1815, of church-oriented and popular religious practice.[28] In Germany, this resurgence was especially evident among Catholics, who in the decades after the mid-century constituted themselves into modern religious milieus. The century also saw an intensification and clarification of religious identity, the twining of that identity with politics, and the exacerbation of conflicts between religious groups. By 1860, religion was not dead, but rather at the center of social and political life.

1.2 CIRCA 1860

The second caesura, 1860, marks the time when the history of the nation and the history of the state begin to come together, chronicling what might be called, starting in 1870/71, the 75-year experiment of the German nation state. In this period, stretching to 1945, German history was at the center of international events—World War I, World War II, and the Holocaust—that brought about mass death and population movements nearly unparalleled in human history.[29] Bringing the experience of the nation and state together, in one chronological arc, places less stress on the undeniable importance of specific governments, regimes, and revolutions. Instead, it emphasizes continuity, and sets this continuity not in the context of social structure or the history of everyday life, but in terms of the history of the nationalizing state, inter-state violence, and global war. On the other hand, it makes little sense to write German history as if only the gun of the soldier-as-executioner mattered, for this was also a period, at least until 1933, of German ascendancy in education, arts, and science, and in modernist experimentation. These developments also had a wider impact, not the least through the emigration of German intellectuals, many of them Jewish.

The German experience of the nation state was eminently international in its timing and its consequences. In the 1850s and 1860s, nation and state first came together, not just in Germany, but also in the two halves of the Habsburg Empire, as well as in Italy, Meiji Japan, and, in significant ways, the United States of America. This coincidence reveals that until the mid-century, confederations of loosely organized polities, with relatively weak central governments, remained nearly ubiquitous, and the national state, with a centralizing government, hardly foreordained.[30] Italy, for example, tried a series of confederate solutions before its partial unification in 1861 as a nation state. Even thereafter, 'legal Italy' masked a society whose attachment to the unified nation was tenuous, whose command of Italian, a written language in a significantly illiterate society, was hardly impressive; and where the new federal government, as Gramsci famously put it, lacked hegemony.[31] It was also remarkable for Japan, where the decentralized rule of the *Shogunate* had seemed viable for hundreds of years, and to which the shock of exogenous pressure helped put an end. In the United States, it was not until the post civil-war federal government occupied the Confederacy and subdued the western territories that the powers of the central government, and with it a standardization of national institutions, dramatically increased. By contrast, nation state consolidation occurred far earlier in the two great warring states of the eighteenth and early nineteenth centuries: England and France.

There was then nothing natural about national unification. The state, as John Breuilly has argued, gave form to the nation, not the reverse.[32] In fact, Germany, unlike the United States, which fought a civil war for the sake of union, achieved unity only by massively slicing through, and in fact dividing, what many contemporaries thought belonged together. A glance at August Petermann's *Handatlas of Central Europe*, which unlike Homann's atlas of a century earlier could reproduce color mechanically, underscores the dimensions of the rupture, as roughly one-quarter of the area of the German Confederation of 1815 was now excised out of Germany, along with Vienna, which in 1870 was still the largest German-speaking city.[33] The composition of religious affiliation also changed as a result of the unification and division of Germany: from a marginal majority of Catholics in the Holy Roman Empire and the German Confederation to the two-thirds majority that Protestants held in Imperial Germany. The shift had crucial consequences for the identity of the new German nation state. It fueled Prussian—and largely Protestant—foundation myths that saw the German Empire of 1871 as the apotheosis of a German history centered on Martin Luther, Gustav Adolph, Frederick the Great, and the Prussian 'Wars of Liberation.' In this context, middle class Protestants articulated a theologically-framed, religiously-inspired nationalism, which exacerbated religious conflict with Catholics and in some cases denied Jews, granted full citizenship in the imperial constitution, the status of fully-authentic Germans.[34] Finally, the ethnic composition of the German Empire of 1871 differed from the German Confederation of 1815. Here, historians have become more cautious, understanding the degree to which hardened ethnic categories are themselves the products of the late nineteenth-century politicization of ethnicity. It was, nevertheless, of considerable importance that many more Polish speakers, who had belonged to Prussia, but were outside the Confederation, were now citizens of the German Empire by virtue of being subjects of Prussia. The German Empire also included Danish and French speakers, making the population of its linguistic minorities close to 7% of the total population. This made Imperial Germany far less multi-ethnic than the Austro-Hungarian Monarchy or the Russian Empire, but more ethnically diverse, at least according to official categories, than France or Italy. In fact, it made it in some ways structurally similar to Spain, and to the Federal Republic of Germany of the 1990s.

At the time of German unification, nation states existed in an international arena still dominated by empires as the main form of political organization. In mid-century, Great Britain, Austria-Hungary, Russia, Ottoman Turkey, and Imperial China defined themselves principally as Empires.[35] Not until the 'imperial implosion' following World War I would the era of nation states predominate, and not until after World War II would national states become the principal political form organizing humanity on a global scale.[36] Precisely for this reason, Germany, a new national state in a world of empires—an experiment, in fact—tells us something about the beginning of a process that left an indelible mark on the twentieth century.

Germany was not a late nation, but a 'nationalizing state,' to use Roger Brubaker's term, whose novel homogenizing policies 'from above' provoked resistance 'from below,' and this resistance constituted one of the formative moments of post-unification

German politics.[37] In Germany, these policies remind us again that, although integrative in intent, nationalism was also a divisive force. Once political nationhood had been achieved, the divisiveness of nationalism came more strongly to the fore: dividing Protestants from Catholics (and both from Jews), liberals amongst themselves, and the majority of Germans from the Socialists, stigmatized as essentially anti-national. In all of this Germany was hardly alone. The *Kulturkampf*, for example, represented one aspect of a wider, pan-European clash between secularizing liberals who hoped to harness the transformative potential of the modern state, and Catholics, who, resisting the intrusion of modern states into networks at once more local and universal, had since the 1840s experienced a remarkable religious revival. Similar conflicts, each with lasting effects on national political cultures, played out in Italy, Spain (where it was considerably more violent), Belgium, the Netherlands (where it divided society into strict social-cultural milieus), and France.[38] Likewise, the problem of regional autonomy, and minority ethnic status within nation states, was hardly confined to Germany. In the United States, the problem was posed more sharply still, especially in the *post-bellum* South and in the new states and territories of the West, but also with respect to the recently emancipated black population. The problem of the nationalizing state was also posed sharply in the United Kingdom, where starting in the 1870s Irish home rule became a continual source of political turbulence; and in Italy, where unification exacerbated and politicized considerable disparities between north and south, city and country, and within regions.

In Germany the 'nationalizing state' was not a single, coherent entity, but rather represented the convergence of nation and state into an interdependent conception of sovereignty. In the Constitution of 1871, it was defined as an 'everlasting alliance' of states, 'which carries the name German Reich.'[39] In the German Confederation of 1815, sovereignty lay, with few if important limitations, with the states. In 1871, the individual states still carried out an enormous portion of the national work—such as raising taxes, creating infrastructure, and schooling. It was, however, the actual constitution of the Reich, not of the individual states, that delineated competencies and set the terms for the separation of power. In this sense, as the contemporary jurist Georg Jellinek argued, ultimate sovereignty lay, in fact, with the Empire.[40] Within this constellation, enormous power devolved, however, to Prussia, the largest of the states, with its king, William I, now also German Emperor, and its Minister-President, Otto von Bismarck, Chancellor of the Empire and responsible only to the monarch.

In practice, Bismarck retained significant power, with members of the imperial cabinet, the state secretaries (lower in social rank than the corresponding Prussian ministers) answering directly to him, and William I allegedly complaining that 'it was not easy to be Emperor under such a Chancellor.'[41] Bismarck also controlled foreign policy, perhaps more than any one man in Europe, and therefore exercized an important influence over the definition of the external enemy. His authority faltered, however, before the Prussian Army. In the crucial matter of who has the monopoly of violence, the King of Prussia, and his military cabinet, retained *Kommandogewalt*, and the Prussian Minister of War answered to the king, not to Bismarck. This was decisive not only for the deployment of force in inter-state conflict, but also because changes in military organization, tactics, and weaponry made the army more efficacious when it came to suppressing armed rebellion than ever before. In two crucial areas—fighting external foes and retaining the monopoly of violence during a state of exception—the German Army, dominated by the Prussian Army but also including the armies of Bavaria, Württemberg, and Saxony, remained effectively insulated from democratic pressure and constitutional control. The *Reichstag* could ask for an accounting of military policy; it could also limit the size and budget of the army when that budget was set for renewal. There its influence over the army ended, however.

Yet the Empire, based on the model of the North German Confederation that preceded it, also created a democratic institution, the *Reichstag*, whose deputies were elected by universal suffrage for men above 25 years of age. If the gender of suffrage seemed self-evident to contemporaries, habituated to structures of male superiority, it also reflected a deepening of the middle class separation of spheres, public and private, and stark divisions of labor in the new industrial factories.[42] In this way, the mid-century timing of the suffrage replicated and hardened the gendered coding of citizenship, whose discursive co-ordinates had been set a century earlier in discussions of patriotism, war, and male sacrifice. The suffrage transformed imperial Germany, as Margaret Lavinia Anderson has put it, 'into a nationalized, participatory, public culture, one in which partisan loyalties organized expectations and structured much of public life.'[43] Not democracy, but democratic practices followed.

If conventional histories have emphasized Germany's democratic deficiencies, a comparison with contemporary states reveals significant shortcomings elsewhere as well. Such a comparison would show a United States, which in 1870 had just ratified the Fifteenth Amendment to the Constitution prohibiting individual states from denying citizens the right to vote based on 'race, color, or previous condition of servitude,' but which left open the possibility of denying these rights through poll taxes and literacy tests; US elections were also marred by fraud and by staggering outbreaks of voter-intimidating violence. The comparison would further reveal a Great Britain that, even after the Reform Act of 1867, enfranchised only male householders, and thus registered as voters less than half the adult male population. It would also show a France of the Second Republic that oscillated under Napoleon III between Caesarist autocracy and the begrudged rudiments of parliamentary control, and a Third Republic, proclaimed in 1870, that featured a representative assembly based on universal manhood suffrage, but that was marred at its inception by the brutal repression of the Paris Commune. The list of democratic shortcomings does not end there. A contemporary comparison would also show a Belgium that did not embrace democratic male suffrage until 1893 and a Netherlands that did not until 1896 (and then only for about half the adult men); an Austro-Hungarian Empire that did not take this step until 1907 (and then only on the Austrian side); an Italy that desisted until 1912; and a Russian Empire that took the step in 1905, but with an elected Duma of drastically limited power.[44] Against these comparative facts of politics and suffrage, it must be noted that Germans fought for near universal manhood suffrage in the Revolution of 1848–1849, but not thereafter. Instead, Bismarck unceremoniously presented it to the North German Confederation in 1867, as an unasked for gift. Moreover, Germany remained remarkable for the many limits the Constitution placed on the power that representative institutions exercised over the monarchy. Germans practiced democracy, but with limited democratic power, and the gap, while narrowing in the years before World War I, remained wide. Within this system, historians have rightly emphasized the transformation of political culture in Imperial Germany, especially after Bismarck's departure. But precisely because this political culture flourished without ministerial responsibility, it turned political parties into lobbying groups for sectional interests and encouraged rhetorical excess or, as David Blackbourn has put it, 'an irresponsible politics of posture.'[45]

In Germany the formation of the nation state came together with industrial take-off. This confluence, which historians have called the 'double revolution', had profound consequences for subsequent developments, even if the zones of take-off remained regionally specific and often crossed political boundaries, as was true of the industrial region stretching between the Ruhr and Pas-de-Calais.[46] In Germany, the foundation of the nation state coincided with the breakthrough of a form of capitalism that was both industrial and global. Economic growth, represented by net domestic product, increased nearly four times as fast in the second half of the century as in the first. In roughly the same period, German exports, measured as the share of world exports, grew more impressively than in any other country, including the United States and Great Britain. This meant, first, that the foundation of the German Empire in 1871 coincided with the beginning of an economic take-off that in the long term brought about a modern mass consumer society in which the department store, more than the army barrack, left its imprint on everyday life.[47] Yet despite a long-term trajectory of increasing *per capita* wealth, the German experience was equally marked by calamitous economic ruptures, periodically trapping Germans in hunger and want. In material terms, these ruptures temporarily set Germans back decades, and even, as occurred at the end of World War II, a half century.[48] In the long era of the German nation state, the impact of politics and war on material life can hardly be underestimated. Between 1871 and 1945, the history of the nation state in Germany oscillated between economic progress, especially in the first half of this chronological arc, and dramatic regress. This was not the fate of Germany alone. Yet in economic terms, the deleterious impact of war proved more profound in Germany in this period than in either Great Britain or the United States, which in the same time period experienced fewer, although still significant economic ruptures. The impact of war on social and economic life conformed more closely to the experiences of France and Italy. It was not, however, as severe as in the Russian Empire and the Soviet Union.

In the 54 years after 1860, the remarkable growth of the German economy had a number of political repercussions. One involved the take-off in urbanization—so that in the half-century after the foundation of the German Empire, Germany went from being a country where nearly two-thirds of the population lived in the countryside to one in which almost two-thirds lived in urban communities of 2000 people or more, with the largest growth in the great cities, like Berlin, which more than doubled in population, Hamburg and Munich, which trebled, and Leipzig and Düsseldorf, which increased roughly four-fold in size.[49] If Germany did not yet match the urban density of England, where urban dwellers approached eighty percent of the population, it nevertheless now, unlike a hundred years earlier, was counted among the genuine urban civilizations of Europe, with a higher urban density (of cities with 20,000 inhabitants) than Italy, France, and Belgium.[50] Berlin was, in one estimate, the third largest city in the world, and Hamburg the fourteenth, with European cities still comprising half of the world's twenty largest cities—a fact that in the late twentieth century no longer pertained. A second repercussion involves the fundamental fact that in Germany, as well as the rest of industrializing Europe, the second half of the long nineteenth century up until World War I was an era wholly without political revolution—excepting the Paris Commune of 1870 and the devastating events in Russia in 1905, both products of defeat in war. Although historians usually start from a different assumption, the growth of one of Germany's most potent forces for democratic change, the Social Democratic Party, and in fact, the existence of the Second International, cannot easily be understood without this nearly Europe-wide non-revolutionary, non-bellicose, context. The third repercussion is that, in the long term, most Germans, including those organized in the Social Democratic Party, experienced the new national state as a framework for continual improvement in the material quality of life. The social insurance bills of the 1880s, early, primitive welfare measures, cemented this image, and suggested the novel role of the new state as a provider of public goods.

The deep connection between the first German sovereign nation state and the experience of material improvement and peace shaped the affective ties of Germans to the *Kaiserreich*, cementing their loyalties and constraining radicalism. The contrast with Weimar, teaming on either side of the political spectrum with demands to overturn the fundamental political order, is instructive. It is true that, in Imperial Germany, the Social Democrats—albeit an increasingly small number of them—hoped for fundamental revision of the political and economic system. In practice, the SPD, in its Erfurt Program of 1891, pursued increasingly reformist politics. Reinforced by one of the most densely unionized workforces in the world, the SPD pushed for small changes to a system that its members increasingly accepted as legitimate.[51] No other groups, excepting a small number of separatist representatives of ethnic minorities, placed the fundamental political order in question so that, however divided German society was in cultural and political terms, there remained a significant consensus about sovereignty, political comportment, and ultimate loyalties: which in matters of international politics and war were unequivocally to the German Empire. In its 1871 borders, the German Empire continued to exercise a profound emotional pull. During the Weimar Republic, so-called revisionists hoped to restore Germany to its pre-war Imperial borders (minus Alsace-Lorraine). These revisionist claims, it may be recalled, enjoyed wide consensus, reaching into the Catholic Center and the Social Democratic Party. The National Socialists, who combined ethnic and imperial ambitions, represented an exception. They wanted much more than a return to the nation state of 1871.

1.3 1945

The era of national states came to a preliminary end in 1945. It did not come to a complete end because, even after 'hour zero', Germans continued to think primarily in terms of the nation state. They also proved slow to shed the nationalist categories they had acquired in the previous century, maintaining many of the affinities, antipathies, and ideologies, including anti-Semitism, that had led to Nazism and World War II. Even after 1945, most Germans remained loath to confront the full measure of the catastrophe that they and their country had brought upon Europe and the world. Especially destructive in the last years of the war, this catastrophe culminated in an apocalyptic crescendo of violence and murder. Not resistance, but the military victory of the allies— and in particular the Soviet Union—brought it to an end. It is for this reason that 1945 must be seen as a break with the past. Moreover, the collapse in 1945 set the stage for the revolution in mentalities that occurred, however incompletely, in the 1960s.

First, the demographic trauma, now accumulated over two wars. The First World War ended with 2.5 million lives lost in Germany, and a further depletion of an estimated 4.5 million through a decline in the birth rate coupled with high rates of mortality. More devastating still, the Second World War cost (in a conservative estimation) roughly seven million German lives, or about 10% of the German population, with the German dead spread out among the soldiers (3.7 million), civilians (2 million), and expellees from the former eastern territories (1.2 million). Demographers estimate that a further population deficit, resulting from a decline in births and a general increase in mortality, accounted for another seven million.[52] These figures, especially when both wars are taken together, constitute a historical calamity by any measure. In the Second World War, the great death toll was in Eastern Europe, where the invasion of German armies and killing squads resulted in a theater of terror that ended with well over fifty million lives lost, with Poland, the Soviet Union, and Yugoslavia losing between ten and twenty percent of their populations. The comparison with pre-war populations gives a sense of the dimension of the catastrophe, and its concentration in the east: in one estimate, Poland lost one in five, Yugoslavia one in eight, the Soviet Union one in eleven, Greece one in fourteen, Germany one in fifteen, France one in seventy-seven, and Britain one in 125.[53]

The National Socialists pursued policies of annihilation that were without precedent on the continent, even if there were harbingers, as Hannah Arendt understood, in the colonial wars.[54] The German Army killed an estimated 3.3 of 5.7 million Soviet POWs in its custody, most in the first year of the war against the Soviet Union. The Nazis also targeted Roma and Sinti for extermination, and killed nearly a quarter of the population. They murdered a further 190,000 handicapped people in the course of their Euthanasia campaigns. Yet their greatest effort was focused on the eradication of the Jews, killing nearly six million, roughly half with industrial efficiency in extermination camps, the rest by brutal shootings, or by allowing them to starve or die of disease in the ghettos and concentration camps. The genocide—one should perhaps write in the plural—remains at the center of any attempt to understand modern German history, and the history of Europe in the twentieth century.[55] It may also lie at the center of one of the abiding questions of contemporary history: why, when all was lost, did German troops resist so tenaciously? Although it remains a matter of debate, good evidence suggests that knowledge of the crimes contributed to the cohesion of the Army in the last months of the war, when the death toll on the German side was simply immense.[56] In January alone, more than 450,000 soldiers fell—more soldiers than either Great Britain or the United States lost in the whole war, and nearly a million more German soldiers died in the next few months of war, until the European war finally ended on 8 May 1945.[57]

The racial war also had radical consequences for the complexion of nations and cities. The brutality of the Nazi-prosecuted war, the ruthlessness of the genocides in its wake, and the expulsions that followed, transformed central and eastern Europe from a multi-ethnic landscape into to a patchwork of nation states with a high degree of ethnic homogeneity. By 1950, when most of the displaced persons had returned, Germany counted among these homogenous states, with the foreign population of West Germany barely more than one percent.[58] The visage of European cities—such as Vienna, Vilnus, and Prague—had likewise become ethnically monotone. Berlin too was a distant shadow of its diverse inter-war self, a process the historian Karl Schlögel illuminated by analyzing the disappearance of groups, primarily Jews, in its address books.[59]

The new ethnic homogeneity of states in Central and Eastern Europe was in part purchased with one of the largest forced evacuations of a people in history: the expulsion of the Germans. The numbers are prodigious. Between 1945 and 1949, some twelve million Germans were forced to leave their homes in eastern and central Europe, with perhaps more than a million Germans not surviving the ordeal. When combined with the wartime resettlement of nearly a half a million ethnic Germans, and the three million Germans who fled helter skelter as the Red Army crossed East Prussia and approached Berlin, these forced migrations meant the end of a significant German presence in Europe east of the Oder. The center of gravity of German history would now shift geographically west, even if East Germany remained a Soviet satellite. The towns of East Prussia became 'names that no one named,' as Marion Gräfin Dönhoff put it, while such places in Silesia as the Schweidnitz Peace Church, a Protestant house of worship lined by splendid oak beams and topped by a bell-less spire, became a faint memory of a more tolerant time.[60]

When the expellees arrived in what remained of Germany after 1945, they encountered a country in utter collapse and dissolution. Transportation and communication systems were down, electricity and fuel barely available, food scarce, and disease, especially tuberculosis, rampant. In Berlin corpses rotted in the streets, and women tried desperately to save themselves from rape, of which there were well over 100,000 documented cases in Berlin, and in all of Germany upwards of two million. Children, in seeming endless number, were lost—in Berlin alone, an estimated 53,000.[61]

The collapse of the country was total, and if it had 'no parallel in modern European experience,' as George Kennan thought, it was nevertheless a shared fate.[62] Like many German cities, including Cologne, Dresden, Hamburg, and Berlin, Warsaw also lay in complete ruins; so too did Budapest and Leningrad, and to a lesser degree a string of European cities from Minsk to Rotterdam. Population transfers, undertaken with stunning brutality during the war, now commenced in peacetime as well, making what Lord Curzon in 1913 still called 'a thoroughly bad and viscous solution' to ethnic conflict into something that by the end of the twentieth century would become an international norm.[63] Within war-ravaged Europe, Poles from roughly east of the Curzon Line were forced to move west to Pomerania and Silesia while Ukranians in Polish territory were sent to the Soviet Union. Outside of Europe, the newly established Pakistan expelled some ten million Hindus and Sikhs, while India expelled roughly seven million Muslims, with the total death toll of the 'exchange' approaching a million people. The number of orphaned children throughout Europe was equally startling: in Poland, 200,000; in Yugoslavia, 300,000; in the Netherlands, 60,000. Rape, too, was not a German experience alone, with the women of Hungary, Romania, Slovakia, and Yugoslavia especially suffering.

The collapse of Germany also brought with it the end of sovereignty. This is a second, crucial reason to emphasize 1945 as decisive. After the defeat in World War I, Germans retained their government—in fact, the Weimar Constitution declared, for the first time in German history, unequivocal national sovereignty, stating, in article 1: 'The German Empire is a Republic. The power of the state emanates from the people' (In Hugo Pruess's earlier draft, the formulation had actually been 'the German people').[64] There was, in any case, little disjuncture between identity space and decision space, to use Charles Maier's terms, except that in matters of financial policy and the constitution of defense, the Treaty of Versailles saddled the new Republic with signifi-cant restrictions. Hitler saw little reason to amend the sovereignty article of the constitution.[65] His dictatorship, so it was reasoned, also drew its legitimacy from a sovereign nation. But in 1945, Germany not only lacked sovereignty, there was a serious question concerning its territorial integrity.

In the mid-1940s, the maps that mattered were no longer elegantly drawn depictions of German territory, but hasty sketches of national borders that determined the fate of millions. The most important was arguably the map of northern and eastern Europe sketched upon by Stalin and Ribbentrop in the secret appendix to the Nazi-Soviet Non-Aggression Pact of August 1939. As Stalin was not willing in 1945 to return the eastern territories he received in the secret appendix, Poland had to be compensated in the west: with Silesia, with Pomerania from Stettin eastwards, and with the Masurian plains of East Prussia. Another such fateful map belonged to Henry Morgenthau. As Secretary of the US Treasury, he conceived, in 1944, of a plan to render Germany 'primarily agricultural and pastoral in its character,' and to carve it into three lands: an inter-national zone, a North German state, and a South German state.[66] In the end, this radical dismemberment never occurred. Yet the status of Germany remained open. One possibility was a Germany aligned with one or the other camp; another Germany neutral and de-militarized; a third, as came to pass, Germany partitioned. The historic interior lines were also redrawn. The Law on the Reconstitution of the Reich of January 30, 1934 had already severely compromised the sovereignties of individual states. In the Nazi system, the Gau was meant to overlay the old states, without formally abolishing them. In the immediate postwar period, the Allied Control Council dissolved Prussia, amalgamated states, and actually redrew state borders. The final dissolution of Prussia on 25 February 1947 was especially important to this process. If hardly noticed amidst the disarray of population transfer and mass homelessness, the dissolution of Prussia meant the final burial of a military and political powerhouse, which had been the motor of national unification in 1871. The dissolution also opened a space for a more robust federalism, at least in West Germany, since Prussia no longer dominated, as had been the case from 1871 to 1918, and in attenuated measure from 1919 to 1934. Even then, the precise shape of the emergent states remained an object of intense debate. Should Baden twine with Württemberg, as almost everyone in Württemberg wanted, or should it remain separate, as especially people in south Baden hoped? In the still larger question of the division of zones, the Germans themselves would have little say— except that municipal elections in Berlin in October 1946 (where the Socialist Unity Party, a forced merger of Communist and Socialists in the east, received only 19.8 percent of the vote) made it evident that an open and fair democratic election would almost certainly prevent a pro-Soviet outcome. This general impression was powerfully reinforced by the enthusiasm with which the local population greeted the Berlin airlift of 1948–1949.

Not only was Germany divided, but decision making in matters of peace and war were made elsewhere. In essential domains, this remained true after 1949, when separate German states were founded: the Federal Republic encompassing the territories of the three western occupation zones, the German Democratic Republic the territory of the Soviet zone. Although West Germany proved more successful than East Germany in regaining elements of state sovereignty, it, too, continued to live with severe restrictions in this regard. It is even possible, as the political scientist Peter J. Katzenstein has argued, that West Germany's 'semisovereignty' was a precondition of its prosperity.[67]

This prosperity, or at least its fast take-off, was aided by the infusion of the Marshall Plan. As the emerging Cold War was a competition of economic systems, the Marshall Plan also solidified the economic division of Germany and presaged the partition of Europe. Through another remarkable flight of the population, the economic disparity between the two German countries also led directly to the building of the Berlin Wall. It seems hard to imagine a starker symbol of compromised sovereignty. Yet by the 1970s it was already becoming a given that there would, in fact, be two countries. This was also true in the east, where many East German citizens actively cultivated a sense of *Heimat* within socialism, creating, by the 1970s, a genuine if fragile sense of belonging.[68] By the 1980s the division of Germany seemed to most Germans to be a permanent state of affairs: not one, but two small German solutions.

Finally, 1945 marked the end of Empire. Perhaps too obvious to note, this fact, nevertheless, separates the end of the Second from the end of the First World War. In 1918, Germany lost its colonies, but not its historic sense that its real empire lay in the east, and that such an empire was based—so the assumption went—on the alleged cultural superiority of the Germans. If some of those prejudices persisted after 1945, they were no longer bound up with dreams of dominion. On the contrary, the collapse in 1945 meant the end of an era in which Germany made its mark on the world by territorial conquest—whether in colonial acquisition or continental hegemony. The comparison with the end of World War I is again telling. In 1918, a significant portion of the German public seethed with frustrated nationalism, and while the Weimar Republic harbored plenty of pacifists and republicans of reason, the balance of forces remained unclear. In 1945, the shift was unambiguous, and counts as one of the fundamental facts of twentieth century history. The historians Michael Geyer and Konrad Jarausch have written eloquently about the incommensurability of the man-made death worlds and life worlds of modern German history—of war, annihilation, and displacement on one side, and wealth, civil society, and consumption on the other.[69] 1945, or thereabouts, marked the end of one of these crucial strands of German history—not completely perhaps, but in a very significant sense. Henceforth, Germans, in the East and the West, measured their governments, and defined who they were, by material well-being, social stability, and the ability to prevent another war. The other history remained present, but became an object of unusually fierce and highly political conflicts over public memory. The history of Germany in this regard bore a striking resemblance to the history of Japan. In a wider view, it also suggested something of the drift of European history, in which major imperial powers, foremost France and Great Britain, eventually relinquished most of their formal dominions in the colonial world, and made well-being, not imperial grandeur, the measure of a successful country.[70]

1.4 1989

It was testimony to the degree to which German history had become enmeshed in international politics that the major events leading to the Revolution of 1989 and the subsequent reunification of Germany happened elsewhere. A listing of these events would necessarily include the Helsinki Accords of 1975, the Soviet invasion of Afghanistan in 1979, the breakthrough in Poland of *Solidarność* in 1980, the heating up of the arms race (with the stationing of nuclear arms making Germany the most heavily weaponed place on earth), and the death in rapid succession of three Soviet leaders born before World War I, and the succession of Mikhail Gorbachev as General Secretary of the Communist Party of the Soviet Union on 11 March 1985. Not for the first time in German history did a change of rulers in Russia have decisive consequences for the life and death of German states. Then there was the meltdown on 26 April 1986 of the nuclear reactor at Chernobyl, releasing more radioactive material than the combined bombs dropped on Hiroshima and Nagasaki, and accelerating the necessity of Gorbachev's recently announced policy of *Glasnost*. On the other side, there was Ronald Reagan's exhortation, at the Brandenburg Gate on 12 June 1987, to 'Mr. Gorbachov' to 'tear down this wall' (for which Reagan was more criticized than applauded in the German media). Strikes in the Gdansk shipyards in the summer of 1988 led to the roundtable talks in Poland of the following March. Then, on 2 May 1989, the Hungarian government removed an electrified fence on the border to Austria.

At this point, East Germans, upwards of 30,000, entered the story—taking off to Hungary, waiting, hoping, until 10 September, when the Hungarian Foreign Minister announced 'we will let them through without any further ado and I assume that the Austrians will let them in.'[71] What started with an exodus was, within a month, complemented by demonstrations in the city of Leipzig, which by early November swelled to hundreds of thousands of people. The story of the revolution and the unification that followed need not be recounted here. Suffice that the dual revolution—of voice and exit, of demonstrations in the street and flight to West Germany—brought about the swift collapse of the East German government. When elections were held in March, 1990, the party of Chancellor Helmut Kohl, the Christian Democratic Union, won hands down, not only against other 'western' parties, but also against the political groups—like New Forum—that played an important, organizing role in the massive demonstrations in the streets. Unlike in Poland and Czechoslovakia, Hungary and the Ukraine, the East German opposition never came close to holding power. For some East Germans, the subsequent joining of East to West felt like a sell-out, even an annexation. On the other hand, the opposition never had to face vexed constitutional and nationality questions, as in 1848, nor did they make a fateful pact with the military to eliminate armed insurrection, as in 1918. Instead, 1989—unlike 1848 and 1918—retained its innocence.

The majority of people in East Germany wanted unification, the faster the better. Mainly, perhaps, they wanted the material benefits of unification. Jürgen Habermas branded East German demands '*DM Nationalismus*,' German Mark Nationalism, and suggested that the nobler path to unity would have been a constitutionally-centered national identity, inspired anew by a constitutional convention. In fact, however, faith in the nation state and material well-being had long been entwined. This is what Bismarck understood in the 1880s. To bind loyalties, modern states, as religious communities before them, ensured welfare. Erich Hoenecker understood the lesson as well, and the last decades of East German politics were marked by anxious production for a consumer society and close surveillance of the attitudes of its citizens to their comparatively meager basket of goods.[72] In an important sense, then, unification was built on a convergence—not in the level of material well-being, but on the assumption that the state should provide the frame for it. There was, of course, a great deal more to the Revolution than that. As a Leipzig baker stated it: 'If you put a bird in a cage and give it something to eat, it still does not feel free.'[73]

Unification—more precisely five East German states joining the Federal Republic—was not for Germans to decide alone, however. Rather, it occurred as a result of the so-called two plus four agreements; in particular, it would not have happened without consent from George H. W. Bush in Washington and Mikhail Gorbachev in Moscow. East and West Germany, and the four occupying powers agreed to grant a united Germany 'full sovereignty over its internal and external affairs,' with stipulations placing a cap on the size of its armed forces (limited to 370,000 troops), the 'renunciation of the manufacture and possession of and control over nuclear, biological and chemical weapons,' and a guarantee that 'the united Germany will never employ any of its weapons except in accordance with its constitution and the Charter of the United Nations.'[74]

The agreement put an end to the 'German Question' in Central Europe, which had historically centered on the problem of German military might and territorial ambitions. By the beginning of the new millennium, German *per capita* military expenditures seemed modest for a major nation, and there were very few Germans for whom dying for one's fatherland seemed part of the social contract. It is impossible to emphasize enough the profundity of this historical sea change, which, as James Sheehan has recently shown, represented a core transformation of postwar Europe.[75] The two-plus-four agreement also involved the final recognition of the Oder-Neisse line as inviolable. In her memoirs, the former British Prime Minister, Margaret Thatcher, recounted a meeting with François Mitterrand, President of the French Republic, in which she 'produced from [her] handbag a map showing the various configurations of Germany in the past, which were not altogether reassuring about the future.'[76] Yet unification in 1990, rather than making such maps relevant, actually made them beside the point. For the first time in 150 years, Germany possessed no revisionist claims and no territorial ambitions. This was not the end of history, but it was—for the foreseeable future—the end of this history. In the 1990s, maps of political boundaries in Europe were changing with dizzying speed. Cartographers still working in print media struggled to keep up with the secession of former Soviet Republics, the divorce of the Czech from the Slovak Republic, and the break-up of Yugoslavia. German borders, however, no longer presented a challenge.

Although 1990 marks the year in which Germany recovered full sovereignty, it also saw an acceleration of supra-national organization, in which sovereignty was again dispersed. German unification in fact depended on integration into European structures, with the Maastricht Treaty of 1992 leading to the formation of a unified currency and adding political dimensions to what was principally an economic union. In the cultural realm, the shift had already begun. In the 1980s, many young Germans began to think of themselves as Europeans, sometimes rather than Germans. But if German unification seemed to occur in the context of the country's post-national identity, one should not push this insight too far. In periods of crisis, or when it comes to zero-sum questions of distribution, Germans, even in their post-national phase, are likely to think in terms of the gains and sacrifices of Germany. Moreover, the younger generation, if the patriotism shown at the soccer World Cups of 2006 and 2010 is an indication, have little difficulty waving German flags while seeing themselves as Europeans. Finally, while the European Union has become indispensable for helping to solve significant problems, it is not a state. It neither collects taxes directly nor does it prosecute war. It does not pay pensions, offer basic education to citizens, or keep the unemployed from falling into abject destitution. Nor does it ensure domestic security. Moreover, more than a third of its budget is tied to one special interest, agriculture, an economic sector in irreversible decline, and that budget, which is roughly the size of the national budget of Norway, remains far too meager to displace the major nation states of Europe as central actors in an international arena.

It is perhaps more important to appreciate the fundamentally new character of German society. Germany is now an urban civilization, with only 6 percent of its people living in communities of less than 2000 people. Yet its great cities no longer belong to the great cities of the world. In terms of population, not even Berlin, however culturally dynamic, is in the top fifty—a fact that reflects the demographic impact of war and the division of Germany, but also the more profound provincialization of Europe. Germany is also no longer an industrial civilization, as it became in the second half of the nineteenth-century and remained until the 1970s (and longer in East Germany). Instead, by 1990, trade and services had already become the largest sector (56 percent), followed by industry, including mining and construction (40 percent), and agriculture (4 percent).[77] The tectonic shift in the basic structure has made past cultural and political ideologies, centered on industrial utopias, seem as if already belonging to another age. The bursting confidence in the future, and a sense that Germany ought to shape the world, is also no longer at the center of the German sense of self—as it was, in productive and problematic ways, a century ago. There is, instead, deeper reflection on the past than almost anywhere in the modern world, and an abiding sense that the world's problems—of security, development, health, and environmental destruction—can only be solved by international co-operation, preferably through supra-national organizations, foremost the European Union and the United Nations, but also, if more hesitantly, through military deployment in NATO. No serious voice in Germany calls for an 'Alleingang,' or even suggests, as Wilhelminian subjects so self-evidently did: 'that the world should profit from the essence of Germanness.' The more cautious tone has a demographic underpinning in profound shifts in the basic structure of the population. Germany now has the oldest population, with the highest life expectancy, in its history. A brief comparison with the optimistic late Kaiserreich suggests the enormity of the change. Reflecting ratios typical of the nineteenth century, 34 percent of Germans in 1910 were fifteen or younger, and only 8 percent sixty or older. In the year 2000, however, only 15 percent of the German population was fifteen or younger, and 24 percent were sixty or older. The age pyramid is now inverted—a result of declining fertility and higher life expectancy—the latter essentially double what it was in 1865.[78] The meaning of marriage, family, occupation, and the expectation of what life will bring has changed apace.

Germany has become a multi-cultural society: as of 2005, it the third largest immigrant country in the world, only behind the United States and Russia, and is roughly equal to the United States in terms of new immigrants as a percentage of the population. The change is especially remarkable for its low starting point: in 1950, the foreign population of West Germany was barely above 1 percent. Paradoxically, this fact of immigrant country status makes Germany different from its immediate eastern neighbors and closer to the west—where in countries like Great Britain, France, Belgium, and the Netherlands, the significant numbers of immigrants (plus minorities from former colonies) give each of these nations a noticeably diverse population. It is a paradox only because Germany's putative status of late or unfinished nation allegedly placed it behind the west, and because East Central Europe was once a landscape of enormous ethnic and religious complexity. Germany is also a country of changing religious constellations. The historical splits so central to German history had been between Protestants and Catholics, and Christians and Jews. But in 2010, twenty years after unification, Christians only make up about two-thirds of the population, and nearly a third of the population is avowedly secular (including almost the entire population raised in East Germany). Islam, not Judaism, constitutes the next largest religious minority, making up about 4 percent of the population, which, if the parallel is allowed, is four times larger than the Jewish population in the era of the German nation state before the Nazi seizure of power.

Statistical compilations tell us little about attitude. A comparison may, however, be illuminating. Roughly a decade into the founding of the Second Empire, the influential historian Heinrich von Treitschke called Jews 'our misfortune', and unleashed a torrent of polemic, much of it anti-Semitic. A small group of Berlin notables, led by the historian Theodor Mommsen, charged Treitschke with attacking the tradition of tolerance established by Lessing. Otherwise there was silence or boisterous support for Treitschke, not the least by the students of the University of Berlin, nearly half of whom signed a petition to curtail the rights of the newly emancipated Jews. Historians have rightly placed the incident in its context of the 'second foundation' of the German Empire, suggesting it spoke volumes about the political culture of the *Kaiserreich*. In the early 1990s, there was a series of events that might have evoked this earlier era. An alarming rise in anti-foreigner violence culminated in vicious attacks in the communities of Rostock-Lichterhagen, Solingen, and Mölln. Unlike in the *Kaiserreich*, however, citizens of the newly united Federal Republic of Germany took to the streets, staging candle light protests against the violence. Partly, these protests were about solidarity with foreigners. Partly, they were about German sensitivity to its international image. If in 1880, a prominent few criticized Treitschke, in Germany in the early 1990s hundreds of thousands of protesters, men and women of all ages, walks of life, and political persuasions, registered their opposition, and indeed more than a million when the demonstrations in Berlin, Munich, Essen, Hamburg, and Nuremberg are tallied together. The protests did not end anti-foreigner violence or completely allay the fears of foreigners. They did however symbolically affirm that Germany now stood for tolerance and solidarity. The German past was not incidental to these protests, and there already have been, and will continue to be, setbacks to the creation of an open society. Yet these protests also suggest a popular embrace of the civic work of a society that, for all its deficiencies, has become tolerant of difference, sensitive to the disparities in life chances, and cognizant of its new role in Europe and the world.

NOTES

1. C. A. Bayly, *The Birth of the Modern World, 1780–1914: Global Connections and Comparisons* (Oxford: Blackwell, 2004), 3.
2. Charles Maier, 'Consigning the Twentieth Century to History: Alternative Narratives for the Modern Era,' *American Historical Review* 105, 3 (June 2000): 807–831.
3. The standard work is: Peter H. Meurer, *Corpus der älteren Germania-Karten. Ein annotierter Katalog der gedruckten Gesamtkarten des deutschen Raumes von den Anfängen bis um 1650* (Aalphen aan den Rijn: Uitgeverij Canaletto, 2001). On sixteenth-century conceptions of the nation, Wolfgang Hardtwig, *Nationalismus und Bürgerkultur in Deutschalnd, 1500–1914* (Göttingen: Vandehoeck & Ruprecht, 1994), 34–55.
4. John Breuilly, *The Formation of the First German Nation-State, 1800–1871* (London, Palgrave, 1996), 109.
5. W.H. Bruford, *Germany in the Eighteenth Century: The Social Background of the Literary Revival* (Cambridge: Cambridge University Press, 1935), 7.
6. Following the population estimates of territorial states in D. Anton Friderich Büsching, *Vorbereitung zur gründlichen und nützlichen Kenntniss der geographischen Beschaffenheit und Staatsverfassung der europäischen Reiche und Republiken, welche zugleich ein allgemeiner Abriss von Europa ist,* 3rd edn (Hamburg: Johann Carl Bohn, 1761).
7. For the argument that the Empire was the state of the German nation, see Georg Schmidt, *Geschichte des Alten Reiches. Staat und Nation in der Frühen Neuzeit 1495–1806* (Munich: Beck, 1999), 347–354. For a trenchant critique, Heinz Schilling, 'Reichs-Staat und frühneuzeitliche Nation der Deutschen oder teilmodernisiertes Reichssystem,' *Historische Zeitschrift* 272 (2001), 377–395.
8. Carl Schmitt, *Der Begriff des Politischen,* 7th edn (Berlin: Duncker & Humblot, 2002), 26–28; Carl Schmitt, *Politische Theologie. Vier Kapitel zur Lehre von der Souveränität,* 7th edn (Berlin: Duncker & Humblot, 1996), 13.
9. Czelsaw Milosz, *Milosz's ABCs,* trans. Madeline G. Levine (New York: Farrar, Straus and Giroux, 2001), 139.
10. David Eltis, *Coerced and Free Migrations. Global Perspectives* (Stanford: Stanford University Press, 2002), 33.
11. For a reflection on this aspect of German history, Jürgen Osterhammel, *Geschichtswissenshaft jenseits des Nationalstaats: Studien zu Beziehungsgeschichte und Zivilisationsvergleich* (Göttingen: Vandenhoeck & Ruprecht, 2001), 363–369.
12. Barbara Stolberg-Rilinger, *Der Staat als Maschine. Zur politischen Metaphorik des absoluten Fürstenstaats* (Berlin: Duncker & Humblot, 1986).
13. Thomas Abbt, 'Vom Tode für das Vaterland,' in Johannes Kunisch (ed.) *Aufklärung und Kriegserfahrung* (Frankfurt am Main: Deutscher Klassiker Verlag, 1996).
14. J. G. Fichte, 'Die Republik der Deutschen im 22 Jahrhundert', in Fichte, *Nachgelassene Schriften 1806–1807,* ed. Reinhard Lauth et al. (Stuttgart-Bad Cannstadt: Friedrich Frommann Verlag, 1994), 419.
15. Massimo Livi Bacci, *Europa und seine Menschen. Eine Bevölkerungsgeschcihte,* trans. from Italian by Rita Seuß (Munich: Beck, 1990), 20.
16. Eric Hobsbawm, *Age of Extremes. The Short Twentieth Century* (London: Michael Joseph, 1994), 9.
17. Jan de Vries, *European Urbanization 1500–1800* (Cambridge: Harvard University Press, 1984), 319, 335.

18. Ibid., 305–337.
19. Winfried Müller, *Die Aufklärung* (Munich: Oldenburg, 2002), 20–30.
20. Hans Erich Bödeker, 'Die bürgerliche Literatur-und Medienegesellschaft,' in Notker Hammerstein and Ulrich Herrmann (eds), *Handbuch der deutschen Bildungsgeschichte*, vol. 2, *18. Jahrhundert* (Munich: Beck, 2005), 501–502.
21. See, as one example, Horst Müller, *Vernunft und Kritik. Deutsche Aufklärung im 17. und 18. Jahrhundert* (Frankfurt am Main: Suhrkamp, 1986), 271.
22. Reinhart Siegert, 'Volksbildung im 18. Jahrhundert,' in Hammerstein and Herrmann (eds), *Handbuch der Bildungsgeschichte*, 446, and the literature cited there.
23. Etienne François, 'Regionale Unterschiede der Lese-und Schreibfähigkeit in Deutschland im 18. und 19. Jahrhundert', *Jahrbuch für Regionalgeschichte und Landeskunde*, 17, 2 (1990), 155–156.
24. Reinhardt Siegert, 'Zur Alphabetisierung in den deutschen Regionen am Ende des 18. Jahrhunderts,' in H. E. Bödeker and Ernst Hinrichs (eds) *Alphabetisierung und Literalisierung in Deutschland in der Frühen Neuzeit* (Tübingen: Niemeyer, 1999), 298.
25. Daniel Baggioni, *Langues et nations en Europe* (Paris: Payot & Rivages, 1997); Peter Burke, *Languages and Communities in Early Modern Europe* (Cambridge: Cambridge University Press, 2004).
26. Eric A. Blackall, *The Emergence of German as a Literary Language* (Cambridge: Cambridge University Press, 1959), 2.
27. Friedrich Nietzsche, 'Die fröhliche Wissenschaft,' in Nietzsche, *Sämtliche Werke. Kritische Studienausgabe*, vol. 3, ed. Giorgio Colli and Mazzino Montinari (Berlin: Walter de Gruyter, 1967–1977), 481.
28. Lucia Hölscher, *Geschichte der protestantische Frömmigkeit in Deutschland* (Munich: Beck, 2005), 181 ff.
29. The classic, if in detail dated work for understanding the confluence of war and migration in the modern world remains Alexander and Eugene M. Kulischer, *Europe on the Move: War and Population Changes, 1917–1947* (New York: Columbia University Press, 1948).
30. Charles S. Maier, 'Consigning the Twentieth Century to History: Alternative Narratives for the Modern Era,' *American Historical Review* 105, 3 (June, 2002), 807–131; Jürgen Osterhammel, *Die Verwandlung der Welt: Eine Geschichte des 19. Jahrhunderts* (Munich: Beck, 2009), 601; David Blackbourn, *The Long Nineteenth Century. A History of Germany, 1780–1918* (New York: Oxford University Press, 1998), 244–245. On confederations, Robert C. Binkley, *Realism and Nationalism* (New York: Harper and Brothers, 1935), 181–262.
31. Martin Clark, *Modern Italy: 1871 to the Present*, 3rd edn (Harlow, England: Longman, 2008), 37–48.
32. Breuilly, *The Formation of the First German Nation-State.*
33. Peter J. Katzenstein, *Disjoined Partners: Austria and Germany since 1815* (Berkeley: University of California Press, 1976), 227–251.
34. Michael Geyer, 'Religion und Nation—Eine unbewältigte Geschichte,' in Michael Geyer and Hartmut Lehmann (eds), *Religion und Nation—Nation und Religion: Beiträge zu einer unbewältigten Geschichte* (Göttingen: Wallstein, 2004), 23–25.
35. Jane Burbank and Frederick Cooper, *Empire in World History. Power and the Politics of Difference* (Princeton: Princeton University Press, 2010).
36. Osterhammel, *Geschichtswissenschaft jenseits des Nationalstaats*, 322–341.
37. Rogers Brubaker, *Nationalism Reframed: Nationhood and the National Question in the New Europe* (Cambridge: Cambridge University Press, 1996), 9. Brubaker defines 'nationalizing states' as 'states that are conceived by their dominant elites as nation-states, as

the states of and for particular ethnocultural nations, yet as "incomplete" or "unrealized" nation states, as insufficiently "national" in a variety of senses.'

38. Christopher Clark and Wolfram Kaiser (eds), *Culture Wars: Secular-Catholic Conflict in Nineteenth-Century Europe* (Cambridge: Cambridge University Press, 2003).

39. Dieter Gosewinkel and Johannes Masing (with the assistance of Andreas Würschinger), *Die Verfassungen in Europa 1789–1949* (Munich: Beck, 2006), 784.

40. Dieter Grimm, 'War das Deutsche *Kaiserreich* ein souveräner Staat?" in Sven Oliver Müller and Cornelius Torp (eds), *Das Deutsche Kaiserreich in der Kontroverse* (Göttingen: Vandenhoeck & Ruprecht, 2009), 98–99.

41. Ludwig Bamberger, *Bismarck Posthumus* (Berlin: Harmonie, 1899), 8.

42. Geoff Eley, *Forging Democracy: The History of the Left in Europe, 1850–2000* (Oxford: Oxford University Press, 2002), 23.

43. Margaret L. Anderson, *Practicing Democracy. Elections and Political Culture in Imperial Germany* (Princeton: Princeton University Press, 2000), 20.

44. On suffrage regimes, see ibid., 5–8; Wolfgang Reinhard, *Geschichte der Staatsgewalt. Eine vergleichende Verfassungsgeschichte Europas von den Anfängen bis zur Gegenwart* (Munich: Beck, 2002), 431–434.

45. David Blackbourn, 'Politics as Theatre,' in Blackbourn, *Populists and Patricians: Essays in Modern German History* (London: Allen & Unwin, 1987), 257.

46. Hans-Ulrich Wehler, *Deutsche Gesellschaftsgeschichte, 1849–1914* (Munich: Beck, 1995), 3–5.

47. Konrad Jarausch and Michael Geyer, *Shattered Past: Reconstructing German Histories* (Princeton: Princeton University Press, 2003), 269.

48. See the graph of Adam Tooze, on page 401 of this volume.

49. Jürgen Kocka, *Das lange 19. Jahrhundert. Arbeit, Nation und bürgerliche Gesellschaft* (Stuttgart: Klett-Cotta, 2004), 77.

50. Wolfram Fischer et al. (eds), *Handbuch der europäischen Wirtschafts-und Sozialgeschichte*, vol. 5 (Stuttgart: Klett-Cotta, 1985), 42.

51. On the comparative level of unionization, Hartmut Kaelble, *Auf dem Wege zu einer europäischen Gesellschaft* (Munich: Beck, 1987), 84.

52. Josef Ehmer, *Bevölkerungsgeschichte und historische Demographie, 1800–2000* (Munich: Oldenbourg, 2004), 13. For a higher estimation, see Hans-Ulrich Wehler, *Deutsche Geselschaftsgeshcihte, 1914–1949* (Munich: Beck, 2003), 944, who places it between 9.23 million and 10.13 million.

53. Tony Judt, *A History of Europe since 1945* (New York: Penguin, 2005), 18.

54. Hannah Arendt, *The Origins of Totalitarianism* (New York: Schocken, 1951).

55. The argument, and some of its implications, in Helmut Walser Smith, *The Continuities of German History: Race, Religion, and Nation across the Long Nineteenth Century* (New York: Cambridge University Press, 2008).

56. Thomas Kühne, *Belonging and Genocide: Hitler's Community, 1918–1945* (New Haven: Yale University Press, 2010).

57. Rüdiger Overmans, *Deutsche militärische Verluste im zweiten Weltkrieg*, 3rd edn (Munich: Oldenbourg, 2004), 239.

58. Hartmut Kaelble, *Sozialgeschichte Europas, 1945 bis zur Gegenwart* (Munich: Beck, 2007), 246.

59. Karl Schlögel, *Im Raume Lesen Wir die Zeit. Über Zivilisationsgeschichte und Geopolitik* (Munich: Carl Hanser, 2003), 329–346.

60. Marion Gräfin Dönhoff, *Namen die keiner mehr nennt; Ostpreussen—Menschen und Geschichte* (Düsseldorf: Eugen Diederichs Verlag, 1962).

61. Tony Judt, *Postwar*, 21. The best work is now Richard Bessel, *Germany 1945: From War to Peace* (New York: Harper Collins, 2009).
62. George Kennan cited in Judt, *Postwar*, 21.
63. Curzon, cited in Smith, *The Continuities of German History*, 208. For the comparison of expulsions, see Philipp Ther, *Deutsche und Polnische Vertriebene. Gesellschaft und Vertriebenenpolitik in der SBZ/DDR und in Polen 1945–1956* (Göttingen: Vandenhoeck & Ruprecht, 1998). For the broader context, Norman M. Naimark, *Fires of Hatred: Ethnic Cleansing in Twentieth-Century Europe* (Cambridge, Mass: Harvard University Press, 2001).
64. For a discussion of Preuss's earlier draft, Michael Wildt, *Volksgemeinschaft als Selbstermächtigung. Gewalt gegen Juden in der deutschen Provinz 1919 bis 1939* (Hamburg: Hamburger Edition, 2007), 42–43.
65. Charles S. Maier, 'Transformations of Territoriality, 1600–2000,' in Gunilla Bude, Sebastian Conrad, and Oliver Janz (eds), *Transnationale Geschichte: Themen, Tendenzen und Theorien* (Göttingen: Vandenhoeck & Ruprecht, 2006), 32–55.
66. Melvyn P. Leffler and Odd Arne Westad (eds), *The Cambridge History of the Cold War* (New York: Cambridge University Press, 2010), vol. 2, 146.
67. Peter J Katzenstein, *Policy and Politics in West Germany: The Growth of a Semisovereign State* (Philadelphia: Temple University Press, 1987).
68. Jan Palmowski, *Inventing a Socialist Nation: Heimat and the Politics of Everyday Life in the GDR, 1945–90* (New York: Cambridge University Press, 2009).
69. Jarausch and Geyer, *Shattered Past*, 12.
70. James J. Sheehan, *Where have all the Soldiers Gone? The Transformation of Modern Europe* (Boston: Houghton Mifflin, 2008), 171.
71. Cited in Judt, *Postwar*, 613.
72. Jonathan R. Zatlin, *The Currency of Socialism. Money and Political Culture in East Germany* (New York: Cambridge University Press, 2007).
73. Cited in Norman Naimark, '"Ich will hier raus": Emigration and the Collapse of the German Democratic Republic,' in Ivo Banac (ed.), *Eastern Europe in Revolution* (Ithaca: Cornell University Press, 1992), 86.
74. *American Foreign Policy Current Documents 1990*. Department of State, Washington, 1991.
75. Sheehan, *Where have all the Soldiers Gone?*
76. Cited in Judt, *Postwar*, 639.
77. Kocka, *Das lange Neunzehten Jahrhundert*, 49.
78. Ehmer, *Bevölkerungsgeschichte*, 34, 53–55.

BIBLIOGRAPHY

ARENDT, HANNAH, *The Origins of Totalitarianism* (New York: Schocken, 1951).
BLACKBOURN, DAVID, *The Long Nineteenth Century. A History of Germany, 1780–1918* (New York: Oxford University Press, 1998).
BAYLY, C.A., *The Birth of the Modern World, 1780–1914: Global Connections and Comparisons* (Oxford: Blackwell, 2004).
ELEY, GEOFF, *Forging Democracy. The History of the Left in Europe, 1850–2000* (New York: Oxford University Press, 2002).

GOSEWINKEL, DIETER and JOHANNES MASING (with the assistance of Andreas Würschinger), *Die Verfassungen in Europa 1789–1949* (Munich: Beck, 2006).

HOBSBAWM, ERIC, *Age of Extremes. The Short Twentieth Century* (London: Michael Joseph, 1994).

JARAUSCH, KONRAD and MICHAEL GEYER, *Shattered Past: Reconstructing German Histories* (Princeton: Princeton University Press, 2003).

JUDT, TONY, *A History of Europe since 1945* (New York: Penguin, 2005).

KOCKA, JÜRGEN, *Das lange 19. Jahrhundert. Arbeit. Nation, und bürgerliche Gesellschaft* (Stuttgart: Klett-Cotta, 2004).

LANGEWIESCHE, DIETER, *Nation, Nationalismus, Nationalstaat in Deutschland und Europa* (Munich: Beck, 2000).

NIPPERDEY, THOMAS, *Deutsche Geschichte 1800–1918*, 3 vols (Munich: Beck, 1998).

OSTERHAMMEL, JÜRGEN, *Die Verwandlung der Welt: Eine Geschichte des 19. Jahrhunderts* (Munich: Beck, 2009).

REINHARD, WOLFGANG, *Geschichte der Staatsgewalt. Eine vergleichende Verfassungsgeschichte Europas von den Anfängen bis zur Gegenwart* (Munich: Beck, 2002).

SHEEHAN, JAMES J., *German History 1770–1866* (Oxford: Oxford University Press, 1989).

STOLLEIS, MICHAEL, *Geschichte des öffentlichen Rechts in Deutschland*, 3 vols (Munich: Beck, 1999).

TIPTON, FRANK, *A History of Modern Germany since 1815* (Berkeley: University of California Press, 2003).

WEHLER, HANS-ULRICH WEHLER, *Deutsche Gesellschaftsgeschichte, 1790–1990*, 5 vols (Munich: Beck, 1987–2008).

WINKLER, HEINRICH AUGUST, *Der lange Weg nach Westen. Deutsche Geschichte vom Ende des Alten Reiches bis zum Untergang der Weimarer Republik*, 2 vols, 5th edn (Munich: Beck, 2002).

PART I

HISTORY

CHAPTER 2

....

ORIGINS OF MODERN
GERMANY

....

ROBERT VON FRIEDEBURG

2.1 INTRODUCTION

....

THE term 'origin' suggests a relation to a later outcome. But do we address as this outcome
the Western Federal (Bonn-) Republic of 1949–1989, curiously similar to the Eastern
Franconian Empire of Ludwig the German emerging with the treaty of Verdun (843),[1]
or the unified Germany with its much larger capital? In any case, the collapse of the GDR
in 1989 did not make the relationship between German-speaking culture in its broadest
sense, and the idea of a single German state or nationhood any less problematic. This, of
course, is not a problem of German history only. One could make similar introductory
remarks about the British Isles and Britishness. Nor is this a modern problem. 'Where
there is freedom and law, there is the fatherland, but where [freedom and law] is, is
unknown to us, and we to it,' said Daniel von Czepko in 1632 as the Thirty Years War raged
through German lands.[2] One-and-a-half centuries later, in 1793, Wieland found it still
impossible to identify a 'clear and orthodox' idea of German patriotism.[3]

Early modern Germans had a wide number of varying and partly contradictory ideas
about the relation of empire, nation, and fatherland. In the decade of the 1660s alone,
ideas ranged from Germany as the fatherland of town citizens, projecting the practices
and realities of the loyalty to the urban *patria* onto a more general conception of a
German fatherland, as did the Regensburg statesman and poet, Ludwig Prasch; to the
fatherland as the state that citizens had chosen for their own good to be its subjects, as
advanced by the jurist Samuel von Pufendorf; and to the fatherland as that public order
emphasizing security and welfare organized by a number of middling princes, such as
was adumbrated by the universal thinker Gottfried Wilhelm Leibniz.[4] Precisely the lack
of clarity with respect to Germany as nation and fatherland allowed for this dizzying
plurality of ideas.

Most of the authors grappling with the question of nation and fatherland were Lutheran, and their common response to the situation of the Empire shared characteristics imposed by the 1660s. They responded to the failure of the Peace of Westphalia of 1648 to provide a lasting protection against further warfare; they wrote against the background of the gradual disintegration of the confessional *politica*; and they did not take the dynastic agglomerations of princes or princely rights of majesty as their analytical starting point. Instead, they emphasized the needs of citizens in society. To most, the Holy Roman Empire, the German nation, and the common fatherland were an unproblematic unity, and they all, in various ways, developed further the Ciceronian notion of the correlation of a larger *patria communis*, the Roman Empire of the German Nation, and a smaller *patria naturalis*, a hometown or region. In utilizing these premises, they were eventually superseded by the increasing importance of a small number of powerful princely dynasties (Bavaria, Saxony, Brandenburg, later Hanover), each attempting to pursue its own reason of state as a European military power.[5]

Veritable tensions between the location of sovereign power and allegiances to nation and fatherland characterized all of the four major continental Empires of Early Modern Europe: the dynastic union of crowns of the Spanish monarchy, the Kingdom of France, the Holy Roman Empire, and the Polish-Lithuanian Commonwealth. (In contrast, such tensions were less marked in the smaller and territorially more coherent kingdoms of Portugal, England, Scotland, Norway, Denmark, and Sweden.) Of these continental Empires, only France, it might be argued, developed a unified nation state during the nineteenth century, by which time it had already been severely shaken by tensions between the demands for uniformity, and the diversity of its regions, languages, and cultures, as well as by two of Europe's most vicious civil wars between the 1560s and 1590s, and between 1792 and 1794.[6]

A considerable historiographical tradition gives particular weight to contemporary rhetoric identifying the Holy Roman Empire as a fatherland and as a house of the German Nation.[7] But while the kings in Madrid and Paris managed to enforce their royal jurisdiction and monopoly of military power over significant parts of what they claimed to be their lands, and no plurality of territorial states developed within the Polish Lithuanian Union, Germans not only hung on to envisioning a common Empire-fatherland during the fifteenth to nineteenth centuries, they simultaneously built territorial states with their own claims to medieval origins, fatherland status, and sometimes even nationhood.[8] Self-confident enlightened Germans like Justus Möser or Johann Wolfgang Goethe had little patience for Imperial patriotism, let alone the nationalist enthusiasm of some of their contemporaries.[9] Indeed, at the beginning of the nineteenth century, good German patriots could welcome French occupation and cooperate actively with the French, not least to administer further reforms that only seemed possible under a foreign protectorate.[10]

This lack of determinedness of the language of nation and fatherland reminds us that material resources and the availability of communication shaped patriotic speech. The argument that makes national identity dependent on the prior formation of a state has been discredited over the last decades. Yet it remains true that the gradual and piecemeal strengthening of institutions and resources on both the territorial and imperial level eventually led to at least two foci, the territorial state and the nation, for contemporary descriptions of fatherland.[11] Still in the sixteenth, but much less frequently in the seventeenth or eighteenth century, communities as tiny as a small ducal town were occasionally addressed as 'fatherland'[12] Right into the nineteenth century, German dynasties encouraged and developed their own historiography tracing the specific history of the unity of their family with a territorial fatherland.[13]

These considerations leave us with four main characteristics shaping Germany into the 1800s: the relation of Empire and Nation; the plurality of major princely dynasties; the confessional divide, characterizing German-speaking middle Europe right into the first half of the twentieth century; and the emergence of the territorial state with its broad administrative, police, and reform agenda. Finally, this chapter will also consider the origins of the German nineteenth and twentieth century *Rechts- und Verwaltungsstaat* (bureaucratic state based on the rule of law).

2.2 EMPIRE AND NATION

Since the 1070s, the Salic establishment of rule in Italy was accompanied by claims that the Empire of the Salic rulers was both Roman and German. The transferal of right and might from the Roman people to the Emperor; the transferal of the right to invest popes and bishops onto the kings of the Franks and Langobards, and then onto the first king of Romans of German origin; and finally the complete possession of these rights by the ruler of the Roman Empire—all these were claims supporting Salic rule in Italy against the papacy.[14] In contrast, the popes attempted to limit the rule of the Salic kings to areas north of the Alps as rule over a 'German' kingdom only.[15] In the years to come, Emperors remained interested in the Imperial title, not in ruling over Germany as such. Thus, the Golden Bull addressed the *Sacrum Imperium Romanum*, but not Germany, a German King, or a German Empire. As the historian Eckhard Müller-Mertens has demonstrated, we can no longer assume a conflation of the Roman Empire and the German Kingdom over time, or an increasing Germanness of the whole, precipitated by the gradual shrinking of the Italian and Burgundian dimension of Imperial power and a subsequent increasing identification of the remaining Empire with German-speaking lands.[16]

The papacy eventually accepted that the Roman Empire was in possession of Germans, i.e. the German princes, yet it insisted that only princely election made a king and that the papacy had the function of translating the king into the office of Emperor, thereby emphasizing the role of both the princes and the papacy.[17] As the dispute between kings and popes such as Frederick II and Gregory IX moved to arguing the constitutional role of the princes and the papacy in making the emperor, Innocence IV claimed *plenitudo potestatis* as representative of Christ, while Frederick II claimed rule over an *Imperium Romanum* that was also *Sacrum*. But a German Empire had no specific role in either argument. Addressing 'Germany' was thus deprived of such legal qualities as holding fiefs or of any specific ideological meaning. Instead, it became a name for a land, as for instance when, in 1238, Gregory IX feared that *Bohemie et Teutonie regna*, the Bohemian and the German Kingdoms, were going to be invaded by the Mongols. The sources rarely addressed Germans, whether as *Teutonici*, *Alamanni*, or *Germani* as legal entities endowed with privileges.[18] The *regnum Alamannie* was mentioned together or as a part of the *Imperium Romanum*.[19] Similarly, Henry VII, Ludwig the Bavarian, and Charles IV addressed the *Imperium Sacrum Romanum* to lay claim on their rights and honors. Popes and Emperors concentrated on the Roman empire, an Empire in the possession of Germans, and that meant of the German princes.[20]

The more important among these princes participated actively in royal rule. Historians have addressed this participation as royal *and* princely rule—*Königs- und Fürstenherrschaft*. The significant number of depositions of Emperors by the princes during the High and Late Middle Ages bears witness to their explicit claim to participation in power, quite in contrast to the attempt of English magnates to avoid or at least cover up their own hand in the fall of a king.[21] During the later fourteenth and fifteenth centuries, the kings of the Holy Roman Empire did not manage to keep or build up a net of their own officeholders across Germany, but different regions had more or less close contact with the king, and many princes began to organize networks of officeholders among their scattered jurisdictions. Kings were not able to impose taxes on their subjects as in England. They had to rely mainly on the imperial demesne (*Reichskammergut*), although they did not possess detailed listings of all the holdings it comprised. The elected kings remained feudal lords over imperial fiefs, responsible for the church and supreme judges, although most holders of fiefs also received rights to higher jurisdiction. The existence of allodial land not held as a fief from the king further strengthened the position of the princes. The princes did not possess, however, closed spatial geographical districts in any way resembling modern states, but instead a wide array of privileges and rights over persons scattered across regions. By the fifteenth century, this spread had achieved considerable geographical stability.[22]

By the Late Middle Ages, small territorial districts (*Ämter*) did emerge, although it is vital to stress that princely areas of rule were not organized into these, but built partly from such districts, which were themselves subject of being mortgaged, sold, exchanged, or given away in marriage and inheritance transactions.[23] Princely financial administration, spurred into increased activity as agricultural income was hit by the Great Plague, and the desire to draw on new sources of revenue from towns and the countryside, now became an important focus of princely rule.[24] Subsequently, estate assemblies of princely areas of influence came into being.[25]

The German lands were marked by conflicts and tensions between emperors and popes, kings and higher nobility, and among regions under varying degrees of royal influence and control. They were also characterized by a lack of dynastic continuity, and a dearth of economic or social coherence in the heterogeneous lands stretching from the belt of urban centers along the upper Rhine to the agrarian areas east of the Elbe. These structural facts encouraged, in turn, a form of rule characterized by a minimal institutional framework (the person of the king, the royal court, and with regard to the election of the king) and the reduction to a comparatively small group of princes of continuous and active participation in the politics of the Empire as a whole.[26] During the fifteenth century, the turmoil of the Hussite Wars and later the threats from the Burgundian Wars, and from the advance of the Ottoman Turks led to demands for an increase in coordinated activity and for institutional reform to deliver it. Spurred by the Humanist celebration of the recently recovered *Germania* of Tacitus (first printed in 1471), this bellicose context encouraged increasing damnation of the corruption of Rome and the grievances of the German Nation at the Church councils. It was in this context, too, that the rhetoric of nation and fatherland was massively utilized for the first time.[27]

The degree to which these issues could be informed and articulated by humanist learning with an emphasis on nation and *patria* is already reflected in Enea Silvio Piccolomini's *Pentalogus* (1443) and the *oratio* he proposed for Emperor Frederick to address the princes, counts, and cities of the Empire of the German Nation, as the Empire was increasingly called. Emperor Frederick's *oratio* to the assembled estates is full of references to German honor (*honor Germanico*), the German nation (*nacio Germanico*), and our nation (*nostra nacio*). He also justified the imperial government as serving the fatherland, rather than his own honor, and as embodying the ancient virtues of Germans.[28] To Frederick, specific group interests mattered just as much. He reminded the cities about their vested interest in a strong Empire that could defend their liberties against the incursions of princes; and he reminded princes that the electoral character of the monarchy protected their privileges, while opening up the possibility of gaining the imperial title for their own dynasty. Frederick compared his appeal to utility and the conservation of common honor with Alexander the Great's appeal to the Macedonians after his father's death. But the appeal also reflected the need to hide from suspicious electoral princes his own plans to increase imperial power and ensure the election of his own dynasty.[29]

Debates eventually led to and coincided with agreements on major institutional reforms from 1495 onwards, mainly encompassing the German-speaking areas of the Empire or eventually not becoming effective elsewhere, as in Burgundy or Bohemia. At the Imperial Diet of 1495, an agreement was reached on an enforceable peace (*Reichslandfrieden*) and a supreme court (*Reichskammergericht*) to determine the Imperial ban (*Reichsacht*) against offenders, and to coerce them into submitting to the punishment.[30] In 1500, six regional districts were created as electoral districts for the *Reichsregiment*, a governing council comprising representatives from the estates and the emperor for periods of the latter's absence. The *Regiment* failed, but between 1512 and 1522 the number of districts was enlarged to ten Imperial circles (*Reichskreise*), serving as regional executive machinery to execute the imperial ban as determined by the *Reichskammergericht*. The elected king remained dependent on the Imperial Diet in matters of legislation, the jurisdiction of the Imperial Chamber Court, taxation, and decisions concerning war and peace. In the 160 years between 1495 and 1655, the Diet, convened by the king with the assent of the electoral princes, assembled between 40 and 45 times (depending on definition) for a period of five weeks (Nuremberg 1522) to 10 months (Augsburg 1547–1548).[31]

In the period before the Peace of Westphalia, the Burgundian lands and Bohemia effectively ceased to be administered via these new institutions. Conversely, the areas subject to the legislation of the Diet were consistently addressed as the German fatherland, while Martin Luther, for example, addressed the dynasties of knights, counts, and princes subsequently represented at the Imperial Diet as the nobility of the German nation. Together with the free cities and ecclesiastical corporations represented at the Diet, these estates were understood to be simultaneously the citizens of the Empire and magistrates over their subjects, although it remained anything but clear which counts, cities, knights, and ecclesiastical corporations, such as abbeys and monasteries, were immediate or only mediate to the Emperor. The 1555 Peace of Religion at Augsburg did not complete, but only brought into full swing the process of the territorialization of the personal and jurisdictional rights of those represented at the Diet, a process anything but finalized by 1648.[32] Nor should we overestimate the Germanness of the whole. Take the case of the Church of the Empire (*Reichskirche*), which was comprised of prelates with jurisdictions and lands extending into Italy and France. It included Giovanni Ludovico Madruzzo (1532–1600), Bishop of Trento, and a member of the *congregatio germanicae* of the papal administration in Rome, who dealt through the 1560s with the Imperial Aulic Court and the Imperial Diet. It also comprised the Archbishopric and Electorship of Trier, which was also the Metropolitan archbishopric over the suffragan-bishoprics of Metz, Toul, and Verdun and the Chancellorship for Gallia and Arelat.[33] Since the 1590s, the reception of the French jurist Jean Bodin had not only sparked a vigorous debate about the character of the Empire as a state and the location of its sovereignty, but also a new discipline, the *Reichspublizistik* on the public law of the Empire and its emerging territories. From the 1620s and all over Europe, the search for the legitimacy of public law shifted from interpretation of Roman Law to the search for alleged historic ancient laws specific to a given realm. Research on medieval Germany, its history and constitution, moved to center-stage, with commentators from Hermann Conring to Samuel von Pufendorf now questioning the holiness and the Romanness of the Empire. As a result, the Germanness of the Empire came to represent a new cornerstone of the legal order.[34]

In the wake of the Peace of Westphalia, the Imperial Diet became a permanent meeting place for the representatives and diplomats of the dynasties as well as of the cities and ecclesiastical principalities.[35] Although decreasingly understood to be a proper state in the eyes of its own contemporaries, the Empire's tools for the enforcement of the findings of its courts had anything but exhausted its role. Right into the 1730s, Lutheran territories, such as Brunswick Lüneburg and Wolfenbüttel assisted the Imperial Courts and Vienna in protecting German freedoms against absolutist territorial princes, as in the case of Mecklenburg. Until the 1740s, neither the confessional divide nor the militarization and European pretensions of some of the major dynasties had entirely eroded the viability of the economic, political, and cultural umbrella the Empire still provided for the German people.

2.3 DYNASTIC PLURALITY IN A
SOCIETY OF PRINCES

Besides the Emperor, princely dynasties were the major players in the Empire. As Piccolomini's *Pentalogus* suggested, it was the balance between their co-operation and competition among each other and with the Habsburg Emperors that held the Empire together. There was, first of all, the dynasty of the German Habsburgs; it possessed lands in Austria and Upper Germany, and substantial lands outside the Empire, as well as possessing the ability to maintain considerable armed forces. Beyond the Habsburgs, there were the Palatinate and Bavarian branches of the Wittelsbach dynasty (bitterly divided over the electoral honor of the Palatinate, and both becoming particularly aggressive representatives of their respective confessional camp, the Roman Catholic and the Reformed one); the Ernestine and Albertine branch of the Wettin dynasty in electoral and ducal Saxony; and the Welfs in Calenberg and Brunswick. Throughout, there were considerable differences in the power and status of these dynasties, and these differences did not necessarily reflect the possession of electoral dignity. Already by 1500, for instance, the ecclesiastical electorates of Mainz or Trier were hardly more powerful than the princes of Hesse, who were not electors. Conversely, the other electoral princes had every reason to preserve the exclusiveness of this group against the pretensions of newcomers among the other princely dynasties.[36]

Since the Reformation, the web of marriages and its function as a means to distribute lands and rights, and as a token of social recognition, began to be reorganized along confessional lines. In this context, competition between dynasties took on new forms, and involved strategies such as placing family members as prelates in the ecclesiastical elective principalities of the Empire; the pursuit of marriages with prestigious same-confession spouses and options for later inheritance claims; the accumulation of new—and alleged ancient—rights and privileges over vassals and weaker neighbors in order to extend influence and eventually gain or consolidate new dependencies by exploiting favorable constellations; and the division of lands to provide for male offspring and the subsequent production of new branches with their own and competing ambitions.[37] More spectacular both in success and failure was the pursuit of electoral (e.g. the Bavarian Wittelsbach, the Hanoverians, and the house of Hesse) or even royal dignities (e.g. the Palatinate Wittelsbach in Bohemia, the Wettins of Electoral Saxony in Poland, the Hohenzollern of Electoral Brandenburg in Prussia), and of marriage or diplomatic relations to Europe's Royal dynasties in order to gain subsidies or play some role on the wider European theatre. During struggles for inheritance, such as those over the Julich-Cleve principalities, or during conflicts with the Emperor, such alliances could provide much-needed resources. For dynasties who dared, challenging the Emperor was a dangerous gamble. Johann Friedrich of Electoral Saxony (1547), Frederick III of the Palatinate (1620), and the Wittelsbach in Bavaria and Cologne (1704) failed, and lost all or part of their lands and titles. Conversely,

Maximilian I of Bavaria (1623) and Frederick II Hohenzollern in Prussia (1742/63) succeeded, and gained electoral dignity or even near-parity with the Habsburgs.

The confessionalization of politics since the 1580s brought in its wake a stronger willingness to make deals with foreign powers, and the (first) Confederation of the Rhine (*Rheinbund*) with France (1658–1668) seemed to bring about a transformation of the Empire into a federation of dynasties. But as the Thirty Years War showed, European princes remained overly powerful and unreliable allies, and by the 1670s, most German princes re-oriented toward loyalty to the Empire, and Emperor Leopold I of Austria became 'The Other Sun.'[38] By that time, however, several dynasties had begun to lay the ground for their own standing armies. Contemporaries remarked that dynastic agglomerations increasingly assumed the characteristics of states. Yet with the single if important exception of the Hohenzollern agglomeration, which emerged by the middle of the seventeenth century between Cleves in the west and Prussia in the east, most projects for dynastic enhancement and European pretensions proved overly ambitious and ended in disaster. This included the bid of the Bavarian Wittelsbachs, which only superficially succeeded with the election in 1742 of the Bavarian King Charles Albert to the imperial throne.

Two issues should be kept in mind. First, dynastic power shaped politics in the Empire to a significant extent. Decisive, however, was the existence of not one, but of several competing dynasties. Leagues and associations, of which the kings and emperors were themselves members, remained an important feature of imperial politics. Because of the competition of these dynasties among each other, no single one could ever impose its will. Therefore, arguments from law remained an important part in the politics of the Empire. Secondly, the Empire existed independently of the king, but was not entirely an aristocracy of dynasties either. In 1582, the Diet ruled that representation would be linked neither to lineages nor to all noblemen given princely dignities by the emperor, but rather to the principalities so far acknowledged.[39] By the 1550s, princely rule itself was addressed as monarchical, and corresponded to jurisdictions that between the 1540s and 1600s were increasingly understood to be spatial units, without denying the monarchical character of the Empire. Since the Reformation, these territorial spaces were beginning to claim their own church and beginning to develop their own confessional identity.

2.4 THE CONFESSIONIAL DIVIDE

The Church of Rome remained, with its ecclesiastical corporations and the three electoral princes, inextricably intertwined with the constitutional architecture of the Empire. In contrast to the kings of England and France, who exerted considerable control over the investiture of bishops and the revenues of the church, major princes within the Empire concluded their own concordats with the papacy, and asserted their duty to reform and discipline where Rome had failed to do so.[40] Simultaneously, the German nation at the councils had urgently demanded reform, since the fiscal practices of Rome had scandalous consequences, primarily in Germany. As the Reformation spread, Luther consciously attempted to use the rhetoric of the grievances of the German nation for his own purposes. But as the urge for a general reform of the church increasingly gave way to the confessionalization of the Christian faith, the tensions between Emperors and the papacy, between princes and Emperors, and among the princely dynasties were reconfigured, although not entirely transformed, by the confessionalization of almost all aspects of daily life.

Paradoxically, while the development of irreconcilable confessional theologies did, to some extent, start on German soil, political and practical considerations initially overshadowed and informed the developing confessional divide. The nature of the Empire as a society of princely dynasties and the openness of its constitutional development allowed for many compromises among princes of different religious persuasions. Still, in the 1510s the papacy was willing to wait with prosecuting Luther in order to commit his protector, Elector Frederick (The Wise) of Saxony, to compete with Charles V for kingship, while Frederick himself, a devout Catholic, protected Luther not least because he wished to limit imperial power and shared the general resentment against the fiscal outrages of Rome. Bitter confessional dispute, political interest, and common points of view on malpractices in need of reform went hand-in-hand.

Barely implemented, the new institutions of the Diet and Imperial Chamber Court had to deal with the intractable problem of religious division, especially as neither side envisioned or accepted a principled or long-term toleration of what they saw as heretics, and the theologians were unable or unwilling to come to a compromise.[41] Charles himself did eventually attempt to force the Lutherans to the negotiating table by removing the Smalkaldic league, their instrument of defense, from the political equation. He then summoned the imperial estates under his command in a new league to circumvent the burdensome institutions of the Empire that enshrined estate participation.[42] Yet even the Catholic estates neither accepted the intermediate compromise formula of the Interim, nor did they back up Charles when some of the Protestant princes, supported by France, rebelled and eventually achieved, together with Charles' younger brother Ferdinand, the Treaty of Passau of 1552 and the eventual Peace of Augsburg in 1555.[43] Moreover, a sizeable group of estates had opposed the use of force in religious questions from the start. Practically all of them preferred to tolerate their heretical princely neighbors over accepting an increase in the power and influence of the Emperor.[44] Although deeply disputed in its interpretation from the beginning, the eventual compromise of 1555 nevertheless remained a common background for debate until its more precise and re-weighted re-implementation at the Peace of Westphalia of 1648.[45]

Across the confessional divide, princes and estates had been striking compromise after compromise, and had secured necessary legislation at the Imperial Diets in matters of police, crime and punishment, and the economy. Along the lines of the compromise among the imperial estates in 1526 and subsequent attempts to come to some agreement, reforming lay magistrates were eventually allowed to proceed in their lands according to either the Church of Rome or the Augsburg Confession (Treaty of

Passau 1552, the Peace of Augsburg 1555). Ecclesiastical authorities immediately below the Emperor had to be left alone, however, and ecclesiastical princes choosing to convert were meant to lose lands and titles entirely (*Geistlicher Vorbehalt*). This *reservatum ecclesiasticum* was never fully accepted by all Protestant princes, who in return demanded that Lutheran estates and cities subject to a Catholic prince should be allowed to profess their faith, as they *de facto* did throughout the sixteenth century in several Catholic jurisdictions. Catholics never accepted this proviso (*declaratio ferdinandeae*) either. Alternatively, or in conjunction with insisting on the *declaratio ferdinandeae*, Lutherans also attempted to interpret the *ius emigrandi*, the provision for subjects to leave their jurisdiction should the choice of its prince in matters of faith be not that of the subject, as a right to private or public worship.[46]

Above and beyond these matters of dispute, the range and nature of a given 'land' or 'jurisdiction' was anything but clear. Indeed, it was in the many legal disputes before the Imperial Chamber Court, set in motion by the Reformation, that the precise status of a given town, knight, monastery, or count as subject or lord immediate to the Emperor was debated and the tools of analysis argued, defined, and sharpened. Only from the 1540s did the suggestion emerge that princely possessions consist of spatial districts within which the power of a given prince was supreme, and only from the 1580s did commentators on these disputes suggest that rule over such a district included a right to reform the church within the district's spatial boundaries and the formula *cuius regio eius religio* (Whose district his religion) gradually began to assert a— disputed—meaning. But right into the 1620s, a family or institution could be thought of as being geographically situated within, yet *not* being a part of a territory.[47] Only gradually were princely jurisdictions understood to be spatial districts and physical location within them proof of legal subjecthood, although different areas in the Empire developed different patterns of territory formation and Protestant lawyers were more likely than Catholic to assert the rights of civil princes in order to extend the grip of the Reformation on as many Catholic corporations allegedly 'laying in' princely lands as possible. In contrast, both in terms of the more personal nature of legal relations addressed in the 1555 Peace of Augsburg and in terms of the interpretation of the *ius reformandi*, Catholic lawyers attempted to stick much more to the letter, rather than the spirit of the text.[48] But still in 1629, Christoph Besold, the towering legal authority of Lutheran Germany, ruled that significant parts of the ecclesiastical possessions of the Dukes of Württemberg had been illegally reformed after 1552 and had to be given back to the church of Rome, much to the dismay of the Habsburg successors, who would have liked to have captured the territory with its ecclesiastical possessions intact.

Under Emperors Ferdinand I (1558–1564) and Maximilian II (1564–1575), concili-atory politics had helped to keep the peace. Yet the accession of Rudolf (1576–1612), and the more aggressive stance of some Calvinist and Catholic dynasties—not least the Wittelsbachs with their mutually hostile branches in the Palatinate and Bavaria—led to a number of clashes. The disputes centered on such issues as whether the Archbishop of Cologne, who had converted to Calvinism in 1582, could legally keep his lands, or whether a Lutheran could administer the secular holdings of the Diocese of

Magdeburg. They also included issues concerning the disintegration of the Imperial Chamber Court (in 1567, 1582, and 1588) and the capture of the Lutheran city of Donauwörth by the Bavarian Wittelsbach in 1607. As Catholic and Calvinist estates increasingly chose confessional confrontation and oriented themselves toward allies outside the Empire, and Counter-Reformation princes attempted to eradicate Lutheran worship within their spheres of influence, dynastic inheritance disputes like those over Jülich-Kleve were re-enforced by confessional enmity and external military support from Europe's main antagonists, Spain, France, and the Netherlands.[49] The formation of the Protestant Union and the Catholic League in 1608–1609 concluded this development. But only the acceptance of the election of Frederick III of the Palatinate as King of Bohemia set in motion the Spanish suggestion to recapture Bohemia with the help of the Bavarian-led Catholic League and the transfer of the Palatinate electorate to the Bavarian branch of the Wittelsbachs. In turn, these developments led to the campaigns in Bohemia and Germany in the 1620s, followed by Danish, Swedish, and French intervention, with the bloodshed eventually turning into what contemporaries subsequently addressed as the Thirty Years War.[50]

These foreign powers also guaranteed the Peace of Westphalia in 1648, whose stipulations sought to provide a lasting compromise, including provisions to make it impossible for one religious group to outvote another in imperial elections, which sealed the military defeat of the Habsburgs as Emperors and the further territorial consolidation of the major dynasties. Thereafter, dynastic competition and alliances with other powers increasingly overshadowed the confessional divide. By the end of the century, Lutheran princes supported the Habsburg emperor against the Catholic king of France, Louis XIV, while the Catholic Wittelsbach in Bavaria and Cologne supported the 'Sun King,' and were evicted by the Habsburgs and their Protestant allies. To be sure, fears about the potential consequences of a triumph of the Habsburg emperors over Protestant guarantees of the Peace of Westphalia still emerged in 1759/1760. Although the confessional divide did not directly inform power politics to the extent it had during the first part of the seventeenth century, German society had been thoroughly confessionalized.

Already by the 1620s, the territorial churches with their parishes in town and countryside, their court preachers and princely advisors, their faculties of theology, and their tools of ecclesiastical discipline and censure, counted in terms of local embeddedness and supra-local organization as one of the most pervasive forces in all of Germany. The change profoundly affected politics. During the 1560s, princes could still carry their subjects along to another faith.[51] The military pressure of the Counter-Reformation had allowed Catholic princes to change the confessional landscape in Bohemia, Austria, and elsewhere. But by the mid-seventeenth century, confessional identity had sufficiently reinforced and redefined the confessional allegiances of Germans to a given church, so that these allegiances existed independently of princely pressure. From Catholic Paderborn or Fulda to Lutheran Württemberg or Brandenburg, the cooperation of magistrates and churches had managed to build deep-rooted allegiances of confessional territorial identity. Throughout the German lands, this process divided private and social contacts on all levels of life, from the varying orientation of noblemen to university life and the movement of scholars.

Within closed territorial units, this process of confessionalization proved a decisive boost for the transformation of a large variety of personal and jurisdictional rights, permeating towns and countryside with the sinews of church and state, and transforming lordly rule in a slow, contradictory, and piece-meal process into territorial rule. This transformation was mirrored in a prodigious number of agreements within dynasties, such as house laws governing succession and among princes, territorial estates, and imperial courts, such as recesses, parliamentary ordinances, and judgments of the imperial courts. The transformation also witnessed the emergence of territorial churches as a major means of consolidating territories.[52] That consolidation brought about the *ius publicum territoriale*, which was defended by the Empire as a whole. Eventually, its regulations allowed territorial estates to defend their own ideas about the constitution and the faith of the land. To a significant degree, the resulting territories developed their own lives distinct from the dynasties that had tried to consolidate them for their own interests. Territorial estates and territorial churches were eventually able to resist further changes attempted by their dynastic rulers.[53] Confessionalization of society and its boost to state-building had brought about a new and nearly permanent confessional landscape. Until the wave of secularization in the 1960s, Germany remained fundamentally characterized by different confessions organized along spatial districts, for which peaceful coexistence in the sixteenth and seventeenth century Empire had provided ground-breaking legal and political thought.

2.5 THE TERRITORIAL STATE

By and large, whether the Bonn or Berlin Federal Republic is seen to be the true representative of modern Germany, the territorial state seems to remain unavoidably at center stage. Yet it need not be projected back into a medieval past, hailed as the ethical goal of the Lutheran Reformation,[54] or serve as the scapegoat for modern nationalist mass mobilization.[55] As the dynasties have disappeared and even confessionalization has lost its grip in the face of unprecedented secularization, the specific characteristics of the German territorial state can rightly be regarded as the roots of the German *Verwaltungs-* and *Rechtsstaat* (a state governed by administration and the rule of law).[56] These roots reach back to the sixteenth century *Confessions-* and *Policey-staat* and its transformation into the eighteenth-century '*Verwaltungs-, Wohlfahrts- und Toleranz-staat*' (administrative, welfare, and toleration state).[57]

Three crucial features need to be considered in order to understand this transformation and its influence on the nineteenth century. One feature concerns confessionalization and the context of the Empire. As should be clear from the preceding section, the concept of the German territorial state as a spatially demarcated legal district did not emerge in the Middle Ages. Instead, it came about through the consolidation of scattered personal and jurisdictional rights into spatial districts in the wake of the Reformation, and thus became intrinsically linked with a certain confessional identity, defended not just by local territorial churches, but also by the large majority of the estates. Despite several cases of enforced change of confession by successful counter-reformation campaigns, Bavaria and Brandenburg, Saxony and Lower Hesse acquired confessional identities enshrined in the allegiances of local people and estates, and in institutional bonds embedded in a multitude of agreements. Territorial churches and territorial laws became cornerstones of these new entities, and neither were entirely dependent on the whim of a prince.

The second feature concerns economy of scale and social cohesion: in the German lands, even the larger emerging territories, such as Brandenburg or Saxony, were small in comparison with the smaller European kingdoms, such as Denmark or Portugal. Up to the middle of the eighteenth century, Stuttgart, Kassel, Berlin, and even Vienna were hardly comparable with London, Paris, or Naples. There remained often few or even no higher aristocracy in these lands. In most cases, the higher nobility had moved out of princely or ecclesiastical jurisdiction in order to become imperial estates themselves. The Reformation had spurred this process, as in the Palatinate.[58] This meant that territorial estate assemblies were mainly manned by relatively humble—although sometimes ancient—lower nobility and small-town folk. Here, as elsewhere, the nobility normally led the political initiatives of the estates and attempted to burden their fellow estates, much to their chagrin and subsequent inner back-fighting, with financial obligations. But larger political ambitions played a significantly smaller role for them than for the great dynasties of the English, Castilian, or French higher aristocracy. Rather, issues of local economy and taxation provided a common horizon to local elites. Among them, kinship networks connected princely councilors, district supervisors (*Amtsleute*), and families simultaneously serving the territory's princely and estate administration. With few exceptions, sons attended the territorial university to gain employment in the territorial administration. To a degree, the emergence of a 'county community' in English counties around attendance and service at the Assize Courts and Quarter Sessions provides a comparison with the making of social networks that would eventually identify with the spatial unit of the territory. But while in England or France seventeenth-century noblemen and burghers would increasingly look for patronage and placement within national networks run by the higher aristocracy, or even the crown within the kingdom as a whole, the emerging territorial elites looked increasingly toward territorial sources of influence and income, from the territorial church and university via the territorial civil administration and courts to the armed forces of the prince, all providing for a re-enforcement of their territorial orientation and network-building. Again, the main patron remained the prince, but in particular in issues of religion—as in Hesse or Cologne, Mecklenburg or Württemberg—and with regards to taxation, the constitution, and foreign policy, princely patronage did not manage to carry nor were princely resources regularly strong enough to enforce princely will.

Under the pressure of the Thirty Years War and subsequent conflicts, small-town elites and territorial nobility consolidated their networks among each other on the territorial, rather than on a German or imperial level. Estate assemblies throughout Germany thus continued to represent the interests of local and regional petty elites, and, in times of acute threat by foreign armies, the interests of subjects for protection against the harmful consequences of princely war politics. In contrast, elites in English counties, such as Essex or in the French principality of Brittany were gradually integrated into larger national frameworks. During the seventeenth century, even where regional assemblies of representative institutions did survive, their members looked increasingly for advancement within networks comprising the whole kingdom, with the result that the specific regional interests of Essex or Brittany townsfolk or rural people counted for less and less, and regional protest gradually lost its noble leadership. In contrast, territorial state-making in the Empire, spurred by the specific devastation of the Thirty Years War and characterized by the long-term establishment and routinization of territorial estate cooperation and partly even co-government and the lack of any national center, was backed and accompanied by the establishment of a regional, rather than national framework for patronage and networks. Prominent scholars and famous enlightened spirits, imperial counts, and Catholics and Protestants seeking further advancement in Berlin or Vienna were exceptions, rather than the rule.

The third feature to consider involves the orientation within the German lands toward *Gemeinnutz* and *policey*, all-encompassing regulation for the sake of the common good. Territories came in all sorts of shapes and governments. Imperial cities like Frankfurt and Nuremberg built their territories just as elective ecclesiastical corporations and hereditable princely dynasties. But all took on board the lessons of government developed since urban magistrates had faced the Black Death in the fourteenth century and were forced to intervene in and actively shape society and economy. German *policey* and territorial government were modeled to a significant extent after recipes of urban rule.[59]

Reading the blueprints by and for territorial administrators of what they thought they were serving, from Johannes Ferrarius to Christoph Besold, and from Veit Ludwig von Seckendorff to Samuel von Pufendorf, one is struck by the relative lack of stress on the dynastic agglomerate fueled by dynastic aggrandizement and honor. In contrast, their sources of orientation, from Aristotle via Cicero to the Bible, insisted on the commitment of any public government to the common good, the true faith, the administration of justice, and the welfare of the people. The Bible provided ample evidence for the wrath of God against rulers abusing their proper office. When, for example, Moritz of Hesse plunged the country into war during the 1620s and was eventually forced to abdicate, sermons from pulpits compared his abdication with that of David, stressing the misery of the country for the prince's sins. If there was a shared ideal of the prince; it was the pious, prudent, and economical housefather,[60] not the Machiavellian entrepreneur in fortune, war, and glory. To Germany's petty noble and small-town territorial elites, Machiavelli was nothing but the epitome of the evil and dangerous pursuit of power and prestige. Luxury at court, hunting or the glory of war, found nothing but spite and resentment. Occasionally, when push came to shove, this showed. Frightened by the specter of religious war, and Spanish intervention in the

Netherlands and France, the territorial estates of Hesse Cassel had urged their prince to stay out of conflict, and keep peace with his neighbors and the Emperor. As the prince and his son refused to listen and the country was plunged into what became the Thirty Years War, bloodshed and plunder turned Hesse into the model for Grimmelshausen's description of what war meant for local people. In this context, members of the states styled themselves as patriots, accused the princes of being traitors to their vassals and people, and claimed that in the Empire, only a *regimen politicum* was valid, and, moreover, that it was viable only through the participation of patriots in the affairs of the territorial fatherland. These patriots also insisted that princely rule without the estates was despotic and had to be resisted, just as with the tyrant Caesar, who had raped Rome.[61]

While in the 1640s the hardships of war also led in England and France to regional denouncements of war politics and even to armed neutralism, a county like Essex or a principality like Brittany was hardly addressed as a fatherland. Their regional leadership did not describe themselves as patriots of such a fatherland, for these elites were increasingly integrated in national networks seeking profit and advancement beyond the world of their own county or principality. In contrast, the minor nobility in Pomerania, Cleve, Jülich, or Hesse had no such ambitions or prospects. Faced with the utter devastation brought about by the Thirty Years War, they rather identified with the plight of their own tenants, the very basis of their own income, and opposed princely politics as patriots for their territorial fatherland. As late as 1813, the backbone of the so-called *Preussische Erhebung*, or Prussian Liberation, were, apart from the small surviving Prussian rump army, the Eastern Prussian and Silesian territorial estates, and their backing by townsfolk and peasants, opposing further French occupation under the rather lose banner of throne and altar. Although dynastic politics almost habitually collided with regional territorial interests, German princes remained squeezed between meager resources, territorial church and estates, and princely neighbors, and an Emperor only too eager to intervene on behalf of 'poor subjects' for his own purposes. From Duke Ulrich of Wüerttemberg and Moritz of Hesse-Cassel to Elector Joseph Clemens of Cologne and Duke Karl Leopold of Mecklenburg, princes learned that lesson when being evicted from their lands or forced into abdication.

Territories were no *Heimat*, harmonious in its social setting or institutional make-up. The burden of services and dues on the rural population and later also the hierarchy of ranks and offices became icons of social complaint and bitter satire. The social and political integration of German Jews, for instance, came with the Napoleonic invaders and their *Code Civile*, and eventually thrived in the larger cities and their emerging liberal bourgeoisie, both remaining comparatively alien to the home-town milieu of the territorial state.[62] Many citizens and subjects to a patria and territory, such as the Free Imperial City of Frankfurt, for example, identified burdens and misfortunes with their Jewish neighbors, and still tried to expel them (although the Emperor functioned as protection for his Jewish subjects), defended the city against the French Revolution in the 1790s, and resented Prussian occupation in 1866, even though Prussia brought many liberal and social reforms.

But we should beware of concluding from this the veracity of Heinrich Heine's cliché of the narrow and oppressive *Vormärz*, or the equally mistaken view of the petty absolutist state, defined by religious homogeneity. From the 1690s, the German Enlightenment, even where it was critical of princely rule and hostile to confessional exclusion, remained rooted and entrenched in service to the territorial church and state, and based both on wider German and on territorial networks. Lessing and Jean Paul, Goethe and Wieland, Matthias Claudius and Friedrich Schiller—they were all in their various ways embedded in this milieu, an *Ancien Regime* peculiarly German in that it was emphatically both part of a wider German culture and part of the life of the relatively small territorial state.

Notes

1. Wilfried Hartmann, *Ludwig der Deutsche* (Darmstadt: Primus, 2002).
2. Daniel van Czepko, 1632, quoted in Georg Schmidt, *Der Dreissigjährige Krieg* (Munich: C.H. Beck, 1995), 7.
3. Christoph Martin Wieland, 'Über deutschen Patriotismus. Betrachtungen, Fragen und Zweifel,' in: *Christoph Martin Wielands Werke*, 1879, 34, 318; quoted after Reinhardt Koselleck, 'Patriotismus. Gründe und Grenzen eines neuzeitlichen Begriffs', in: Robert von Friedeburg (ed.), *Patria und Patrioten vor dem Patriotismus. Pflichten, Rechte, Glauben und die Rekonfigurierung europäischer Gemeinwesen im 17. Jahrhundert* (Wiesbaden: Harrassowitz, 2005), 535–552, 535.
4. Horst Dreitzel, 'Zehn Jahre Patria in der politischen Theorie in Deutschland: Prasch, Pufendorf, Leibniz, Becher 1662–1672,' in Friedeburg (ed.), *Patria und Patrioten*, 367–534, 491.
5. Dreitzel, 'Zehn Jahre,' 369–372.
6. See further, Robert von Friedeburg, *Europa in der frühen Neuzeit* (Frankfurt am Main: Fischer, 2012).
7. For a nineteenth century confessional perspective, see for instance Johannes Janssen, *Geschichte des Deutschen Volkes seit dem Ausgang des Mittelalters* (Freiburg in. Br.: Herder, 1876–94); more recently, Georg Schmidt, *Geschichte des Alten Reiches. Staat und Nation in der frühen Neuzeit, 1450–1806* (Munich: C.H. Beck, 1999); for the state of debate, see Heinz Schilling, 'Reichs-Staat und frühneuzeitliche Nation der Deutschen oder teilmodernisiertes Reichssystem. Überlegungen zu Charakter und Aktualität des Alten Reiches,' *Historische Zeitschrift* (2001), 272, 377–396; Matthias Schnettger (ed.), *Imperium Romanum—Irregulare Corpus—Teutscher Reichs-Staat: das Alte Reich im Verständnis der Zeitgenossen und der Historiographie* (Mainz: Philipp von Zabern, 2002); Georg Schmidt and Dieter Langewiesche (eds), *Föderative Nation. Deutschlandkonzepte von der Reformation bis zum Ersten Weltkrieg* (Munich: C. H. Beck, 2000).
8. For instance Wilhelm Kühlmann and Horst Langer (eds), *Pommern in der frühen Neuzeit* (Tübingen: Walter de Gruyter Verlag, 1994); Thomas Fuchs, *Traditionsstiftung und Erinnerungspolitik. Geschichtsschreibung in Hessen in der Frühen Neuzeit* (Kassel: Hessische Forschungen zur geschichtlichen Landes-und Volkskunde, 2002).

9. Wolfgang Roth, *Der Politische Goethe* (Göttingen: Vandenhoeck, 1992), 216–236; Karl H. Welker, *Rechtsgeschichte als Rechtspolitik. Justus Möser als Jurist und Staatsmann,* (Osnabrück: Osnabrücker Verlag, 1996), 213.

10. See Robert D. Billinger Jr., 'Good and True Germans: the Nationalism of the Rheinbund Princes, 1806–1814,' in Heinz Duchhardt and Andreas Kunz (eds), *Reich oder Nation? Mitteleuropa 1780–1815* (Mainz: Philipp von Zabern, 1998), 105–140.

11. One of the most important contributions on the importance of national sentiments on large segments of the political nation in the English, French and Prussian monarchies is Tim Blanning, *The Power of Culture and the Culture of Power. Old Regime Europe 1660–1789* (Oxford: Oxford University Press, 2002).

12. Monika Spicker-Beck, *Räuber, Mordbrenner, umschweifendes Gesinde. Zur Kriminalität im 16. Jahrhundert* (Freiburg, Rombach, 1995), 157.

13. Manfred Hanisch, *Für Fürst und Vaterland. Legitimitätsstiftung in Bayern zwischen Revolution und deutscher Einheit* (München: R. Oldenbourg, 1991); Abigail Green, *Fatherlands: State-building and Nationhood in Nineteenth Century Germany,* (Cambridge: Cambridge University Press, 2001).

14. Eckhard Müller-Mertens, 'Römisches Reich im Besitz der Deutschen, der König an Stelle des Augustus. Recherche zu der Frage: seit wann wird das mittelalterlich-frühneuzeitliche Reich von den Zeitgenossen als römisch und deutsch begriffen?,' *Historische Zeitschrift* 282 (2006), 1–57, 17, 28, 37–39. On the terminology addressing a German people, see Bernd Schneidmüller, 'Reich—Volk—Nation: Die Entstehung des deutschen Reiches und der deutschen Nation im Mittelalter,' in Almut Bues and Rex Rexheuser (eds), *Mittelalterliche Nationes—neuzeitliche Nationen?* (Wiesbaden: Harrassowitz, 1995), 73–111, 94.

15. Müller-Mertens, 'Römisches Reich', 56–57. For a concise summary see Wilfried Hartmann, *Der Investiturstreit* (Munich: R. Oldenburg, 1996), 36–43.

16. Eckard Müller-Mertens, 'Imperium und Regnum im Verhältnis zwischen Wormser Konkordat und Goldener Bulle,' *Historische Zeitschrift* 284 (2007), 561–595, 561–562.

17. Ibid., 567–569.

18. Ibid., 569–576.

19. Ibid., 582–586.

20. Ibid., 588–590.

21. See Arno Buschmann, 'Heiliges Römisches Reich. Reich, Verfassung, Staat,' *Der Staat* 16 (2006), 9–38, 13; Ernst Schubert, *Königsabsetzung im deutschen Mittelalter. Eine Studie zum Werden der Reichsverfassung* (Göttingen: Vandenhoeck & Ruprecht, 2005); Christine Carpenter, 'Resisting and Deposing Kings in the Thirteenth, Fourteenth and Fifteenth Century,' in Robert von Friedeburg (ed.), *Murder and Monarchy. Regicide in European History 1300–1800* (Basingstoke: Palgrave Macmillan, 2004), 99–121.

22. Ernst Schubert, *Fürstliche Herrschaft und Territorium im späten Mittelalter* (Munich: R. Oldenburg, 1996), 107.

23. Christian Hesse, *Amtsträger der Fürsten im spätmittelalterlichen Reich: Die Funktionseliten der lokalen Verwaltung in Bayern-Landshut, Hessen, Sachsen und Württemberg 1350–1515* (Göttingen: Vandenhoeck & Ruprecht, 2005), 192, refering to Walter Schlesinger, 'Zur Geschichte der Landesherrschaft in den Marken Brandenburg und Meissen während des 14. Jahrhunderts,' in: Hans Patze (ed.), *Der deutsche Territorialstaat im 14. Jahrhundert,* 2 vols (Sigmaringen: Thorbecke, 1970), vol 2, 101–126, 120.

24. Hesse, *Amtsträger der Fürsten im spätmittelalterlichen Reich,* 192.

25. Schubert, *Fürstliche Herrschaft*, 92–95.

26. For a concise summary, see Karl-Friedrich Krieger, *König, Reich und Reichsreform im Spätmittelalter* (Munich: R. Oldenburg, 1992); Peter Moraw, *Von offener Verfassung zu gestalteter Verdichtung: Das Reich im späten Mittelalter 1250 bis 1490* (Berlin: Propylaen, 1985).

27. Caspar Hirschi, *Wettkampf der Nationen. Konstruktion einer deutschen Ehrgemeinschaft an der Wende vom Mittelalter zur Neuzeit* (Göttingen: Wallstein, 2005); Claudius Sieber-Lehmann, *Spätmittelalterlicher Nationalismus. Die Burgunderkriege am Oberrhein und in der Eidgenossenschaft* (Göttingen: Vandenhoeck & Ruprecht, 1995).

28. Enea Silvio Piccolomini, 'Pentalogus (1443),' (no 31); in Lorenz Weinrich (ed.) *Quellen zur Reichsreform im Spätmittelalter* (Darmstadt: Wissenschaftliche Buchgesellschaft, 2001), 257–260. See Johannes Helmrath and Heribert Müller (eds), *Die Konzilien von Pisa (1409), Konstanz (1414–1418) und Basel (1431–1449)* (Sigmaringen: Thorbecke, 2007); Johannes Helmrath, 'Diffusion des Humanismus und Antikenrezeption auf den Konzilien von Konstanz, Basel und Ferrara/Florenz,' in Ludger Grenzmann et al. (eds), *Die Präsenz der Antike im Übergang vom Mittelalter zur frühen Neuzeit* (Göttingen: Vandenhoeck & Ruprecht, 2004), 9–54.

29. Enea Silvio Piccolomini, "Pentalogus (1443)," 285, 289.

30. Bernhard Diestelkamp, (ed.) *Das Reichskammergericht. Der Weg zu seiner Gründung und die ersten Jahrzehnte seines Wirkens (1451–1527)*, (Cologne: Böhlau, 2004).

31. Helmut Neuhaus, *Das Reich in der frühen Neuzeit* (Munich: Oldenbourg, 1997), 40.

32. Dietmar Willoweit, *Rechtsgrundlagen der Territorialgewalt* (Cologne: Böhlau, 1975); Robert von Friedeburg, '"Officium in rempublicam": Fürstliche Herrschaft und Territorialstaat in politischen und rechtlichen Reflektionen und Projektionen im Jahrhundert der Reformation,' in Robert von Friedeburg and Louise Schorn-Schütte (eds), *Politik und Religion: Eigenlogik oder Verzahnung?* (Munich: R. Oldenbourg, 2007), 33–70, 33–51.

33. Bernhard Steinhauf, *Giovanni Ludovico Madruzzo (1532–1600): katholische Reformation zwischen Kaiser und Pabst: das Konzept zur praktischen Gestaltung der Kirch der Neuzeit im Anschluß an das Konzil von Trient* (Münster: Aschendorff, 1993).

34. See for instance Constantin Fasolt, 'Author and Authenticity in Conring's "New Discourse on the Roman-German Emperor": A Seventeenth Century Case Study,' *Renaissance Quarterly* 54 (2001), 188–220, and the literature cited there.

35. See, for example, Matthias Schnettger, *Principe sovrano oder civitas imperialis? Die Republik Genua und das Alte Reich in der Frühen Neuzeit (1556–1797)* (Mainz: Philipp von Zabern Verlag, 2006); for an overview see Karl Otmar von Aretin, *Das Alte Reich 1648–1806*, 4 vols (Stuttgart: Klett-Cotta, 1992–2000).

36. Christine Roll, *Das zweite Reichsregiment 1521–1530* (Cologne: Böhlau, 1996), 66–69; Helmut Neuhaus, 'Die rheinischen Kurfürsten, der Kurrheinische Kreis und das Reich im 16. Jahrhundert,' *Rheinische Vierteljahrsblätter* 48 (1984): 138–160.

37. Friedrich Edelmeyer, *Söldner und Pensionäre: Das Netzwerk Philipps II im Heiligen Römischen Reich* (Vienna: Böhlau, 2002).

38. Jutta Schumann, *Die andere Sonne. Kaiserbild und Medienstrategien im Zeitalter Leopolds I* (Berlin: Akademie, 2003).

39. Thus, neither the multiplication nor the extinction of dynastic lineages led to more or less seats in the Diet. While there were *c.* 160 cases of imperial endowments with princely status between 1582–1806, only 19 new princes made it into the Diet between 1653 and 1754. See Neuhaus, *Das Reich*, 17.

40. Heinz Angermeier, *Reichsreform und Reformation* (Munich: R. Oldenbourg, 1983), 15–25; Christoph Volkmar, *Reform statt Reformation. Die Kirchenpolitik Herzog Georgs von Sachsen 1488–1525* (Tübginen: Mohr Siebeck, 2008).

41. See for instance Volkmar Ortmann, *Reformation und Einheit der Kirche. Martin Bucers Einigungsbemühungen bei den Religionsgesprächen in Leipzig, Hagenau, Worms und Regensburg 1539–1541* (Mainz: Philipp von Zabern, 2001).

42. Horst Rabe, *Reich und Glaubensspaltung. Deutschland 1500–1600* (Munich: C.H. Beck, 1989).

43. Luise Schorn-Schütte (ed.), *Das Interim 1548–50. Herrschaftskrise und Glaubenskonflikt* (Gütersloh: Gütersloher Verlagshaus, 2005).

44. Maximilian Lanzinner, *Friedenssicherung und politische Einheit des Reiches unter Kaiser Maximilian II* (Göttingen: Vandenhoeck & Ruprecht, 1993).

45. Heinz Duchhardt (ed.), *Der Westfälische Frieden* (Munich: R. Oldenburg, 1998).

46. Heinz Schilling and Heribert Smolinsky (eds), *Der Augsburger Religionsfrieden* (Münster: Aschendorff, 2007); Robert von Friedeburg, 'The Juridification of Natural Law: Christoph Besold's Claim for a Natural Right to Believe what One Wants,' *The Historical Journal* 53 (2010), 1–19.

47. See, in particular, the reasoning of Christoph Besold; Bernd Christian Schneider, *Ius Reformandi: Die Entwicklung eines Staatskirchenrechts von seinen Anfängen bis zum Ende des Alten Reiches* (Tübingen: Mohr Siebeck, 2001).

48. Christoph Strohm, 'Konfessionsspezifische Zugänge zum Augsburger Religionsfrieden,' in Schilling and Smolinsky (eds), *Augsburger Religionsfrieden*, 127–156.

49. On the overriding dynamics of confessionalisation in this period, and not just within the Empire, see Heinz Schilling, 'Gab es um 1600 in Europa einen Konfessionsfundamentalismus? Die Geburt des internationalen Systems in der Krise des konfessionellen Zeitalters,' *Jahrbuch des Historischen Kollegs* (2005), 69–94.

50. G. Mortimer, 'Did Contemporaries Recognize a "Thirty Years' War"?' *The English Historical Review* 116, no. 465 (February, 2001), 124–136.

51. Ernst Walter Zeeden, *Die Entstehung der Konfessionen* (Munich: C.H. Beck, 1965), 96.

52. This decisive insight and subsequent reordering of the chronology and meaning of territorial state building is mainly due to Heinz Schilling. See for instance his 'Die Konfessionalisierung im Reich. Religiöser und gesellschaftlicher Wandel in Deutschland zwischen 1555 und 1620,' *Historische Zeitschrift* 246 (1988), 1–45.

53. See for this re-evaluation of the role of the Lutheran church and clergy, Wolfgang Sommer and Luise Schorn Schütte, 'Politische Kommunikation in der frühen Neuzeit: Obrigkeitskritik im Alten Reich,' *Geschichte und Gesellschaft* 32 (2006), 273–314; Wolfgang Sommer, 'Obrigkeitskritik und die politische Funktion der Frömmigkeit im deutschen Luthertum des konfessionellen Zeitalters,' in Robert von Friedeburg (ed.), *Widerstandsrecht in der frühen Neuzeit. Erträge und Perspektiven der Forschung im deutsch-britischen Vergleich* (Berlin: Duncker & Humblot, 2001), 245–264.

54. For example Walter Sohm, *Territorium und Reformation in der hessischen Geschichte 1526–1555* (Marburg: Elwert, 1915).

55. A good example of making this distinction between the early modern and nineteenth century territorial state and the effects of modern mass mobilization is Christopher Clark, *Iron Kingdom. The Rise and Fall of Prussia, 1600–1947* (London: Penguin, 2006), 561–640, 685.

56. Otto Bähr, *Der Rechtsstaat* (Kassel und Göttingen: Georg H. Wigand, 1864). The author, a liberal jurist, makes the explicit link between the supervision of legal proceedings in the Empire's early modern principalities by the Imperial courts and his own vision of a judiciary independent from princely control.

57. Heinz Schilling, in Luise Schorn Schütte and Olaf Mörke (eds), *Ausgewählte Abhandlungen zur europäischen Reformations-und Konfessionsgeschichte* (Berlin: Duncker and Humblot, 2002), 699.
58. Volker Press, *Calvinismus und Territorialstaat* (Stuttgart: Klett-Cotta, 1970).
59. For example Monika Hagenmeier, *Predigt und Policey: Der gesellschaftspolitische Diskurs zwischen Kirche und Obrigkeit in Ulm 1614-1639* (Baden-Baden: Nomos, 1989).
60. Manfred Rudersdorf, 'Die Generation der lutherischen Landesväter im Reich. Bausteine zu einer Typologie der deutschen Reformationsfürsten,' in Anton Schindling and Walter Ziegler (eds), *Die Territorien des Reichs im Zeitalter der Reformation und Konfessionalisierung. Land und Konfession 1500-1600* (Münster: Aschendorff, 1989), vol. 7, 137-170.
61. For this re-evaluation of the politics of German territorial estates, see Robert von Friedeburg, *Self-Defence and Religious Strife in Early Modern Europe: England and Germany, 1530-1680* (Aldershot: Ashgate, 2002); von Friedeburg, 'The Making of Patriots: Love of Fatherland and Negotiating Monarchy in Seventeenth Century Germany,' *Journal of Modern History* 77 (2005), 881-916.
62. See now Stephan Laux, *Gravamen und Geleit. Die Juden im Ständestaat der Frühen Neuzeit (15-18 Jahrhundert)* (Hannover: Hahn, 2010). On the 'Bürgertum' of German lands see Wolfgang Mager and Robert von Friedeburg, 'Learned Men and Merchants: The Rise of the "Bürgertum", 1648-1806,' in Sheilagh Ogilvie, Richard Overy, and Robert Scribner (eds), *Germany: A New Social and Economic History 1300-1800*, vol. 2 (London: Hodder Arnolds, 1996), 164-195.

BIBLIOGRAPHY

ARETIN, KARL OTMAR VON, *Das Alte Reich 1648-1806*, 4 vols (Stuttgart: Klett-Cotta Verlag, 1992-2000).

BRADY JR., THOMAS A., *German Histories in the Age of Reformations, 1400-1650* (New York: Cambridge University Press, 2009).

DUCHHARDT, HEINZ (ed.), *Der Westfälische Friede* (Munich: Oldenbourg, 1998).

EVANS, ROBERT J.W., The Making of the Habsburg Monarchy (Oxford: Clarendon Press, 1979).

FRIEDEBURG, ROBERT VON, *Self-defence and Religious Strife in Early Modern Europe: England and Germany, 1530-1680* (Aldershot: Ashgate, 2002).

FRIEDEBURG, ROBERT VON, 'The Making of Patriots: Love of Fatherland and Negotiating Monarchy in Seventeenth Century Germany,' *Journal of Modern History* 77 (2005), 881-916.

MORAW, PETER, *Von offener Verfassung bis zu gestalteter Verdichtung: Das Reich im späten Mittelalter, 1250 bis 1490* (Berlin: Propylaen, 1985).

PRESS, VOLKER, *Kriege und Krisen. Deutschland 1600-1715* (Munich: C. H. Beck, 1991).

RABE, HORST, *Reich und Glaubensspaltung. Deutschland 1500-1600* (Munich: C. H. Beck, 1989).

SCHILLING, HEINZ, *Aufbruch und Krise: Deutschland 1517-1648* (Berlin: Siedler, 1994).

SCHILLING, HEINZ, *Höfe und Allianzen: Deutschland 1648-1763* (Berlin: Siedler, 1998).

SCHILLING, HEINZ, *Konfessionskonflikt und Staatsbildung: Eine Fallstudie über das Verhältnis von religiösem und sozialem Wandel in der Frühneuzeit am Beispiel der Grafschaft Lippe* (Gütersloh: Mohn, 1981).

SCHILLING, HEINZ and HERIBERT SMOLINSKY (eds), *Der Augsburger Religionsfrieden* (Münster: Aschendorff, 2007).

CHAPTER 3

··

SENSES OF PLACE

··

CELIA APPLEGATE

A few decades before the start of Germany's first Thirty Years' War, the Swiss-German geographer Johann Rauw wrote that the German landscape made him think of 'a great and splendid city with its suburbs, the city itself located within its walls and fortifications, the suburbs without.'[1] The image, an elegant way of evading the muddle of borders, contrasts to his equally vivid image of walking the 'circumference of Germany, as far as the German language is spoken,' a voyage marked by the cities and regions one would pass through ('from there to Ghent, Maastricht, . . . Hamburg, Rostock, . . . Dantzig, Königsberg . . . Breslau, Vienna . . . .') and lasting, he estimated, some ninety-three days at a pace of 5 miles a day. Three-hundred-and-fifty-five years later and less than a decade after the end of Germany's second Thirty Years' War, a German man named Otto Schmitt sent a book of urban and rural landscape photographs called *This is Germany* to his brother in the United States, with the hope that it would 'keep your beautiful land of birth before your eyes and awaken the wish to visit it again soon.'[2] Adrian Mohr, author of the text accompanying these photographs, identified Germany's actual boundaries as elusively as had Rauw. The north and south were easy enough to name (Baltic and North Sea, Alps), but to the east and the west the boundaries 'correspond to a line beyond which manifestations of German life cease.'[3] In between lay Germany, 222 places defining it, from belching smokestacks in the Ruhrgebiet to the statues of Ekkehard and Uta in the cathedral at Naumburg, from the vineyards of the Pfalz to the chalk cliffs of Rügen. The compilers and consumers of this book, like Rauw and his *Cosmographia*, sought to capture Germany's essence by cataloguing its places. They understood place not as would the single-minded hedgehog or the multi-visual, inattentive fox, but as some hybrid creature who knows the one through the many.

Knowing place has been a way of knowing Germany for the many hundreds of years in which some concept of Germany existed. The ways of knowing place have shifted and varied, but the inclination to sense and to experience Germany as place-dependent—*ortsbezogen*—has remained. Place gives one an identity in the world, or what Mack Walker once described as 'a silhouette projected on community' which can be 'rendered and reflected only by community.'[4] Lacking place, one becomes like Adalbert Chamisso's Peter Schlemiel, who gave the 'grey man' his shadow in return for riches and soon found that, no matter where he went, he could no longer properly live in the world. To be German is to claim a place and to declare one's dependence on it. This claim could be made in exile, as well as at home, in retrospect as well as in the present. The German-Jewish poet Mascha Kaleka wrote in exile on the Hudson that:

> Sometimes in the middle of those nights, / That each of us has known,/ . . . ,/ I think about the Rhine and the Elbe,/ And smaller, but my own, the Spree./ And always the same:/ thinking brings pain.'[5]

As Johannes Rauw, the Swiss-German cartographer, and Otto Schmitt, the German man visiting family members in the United States, as well as countless others, reveal attachment to place was not the result of staying in one place or of the notorious inward-turning of the 'German mind,' but rather a cultural trait that comes from, as often as not, mobility, travel, and distance, from looking in the rear-view mirror.

The notion of place is, of course, no more self-evident in its meanings than those many other laden terms—culture, nation, class, race—by which we try to capture aspects of reality that have powerfully determinative roles in historical development. It is a truism to say that people give meaning to place, but in the case of places associated with nation and identity, these meanings are often formulaic, stating and re-stating notions of beauty, security, familiarity. Danger and excitement would seem to reside elsewhere, yet for all travelers—and the Germans are no exception—the experience of strangeness and unknown places also casts light on the mental operations of place-making. In 1932, a party of German climbers, making their way to the foot of Nanga Parbat on the Kashmiri frontier of the British Raj, came upon what they subsequently named the *Märchenwiese* or fairy tale meadow. In the words of expedition leader Willy Merkl of Munich, it lay before them 'in sublime charm among the light green of the pasture, covered with the stars of the edelweiss and embraced by the trunks of ancient timber forest . . . with mighty fir trees and glowing birches.' As he recounted the experience to his audience in Germany and Austria, 'we felt deeply the kinship with the mountains of our homeland [*Heimat*], only here the feelings and impressions of the Alps were magnified in the unimaginable massiveness of the Himalaya, *Heimat* for the Indo-Germanic peoples, who were born in these mountains and fell under their power.'[6] They had 'uncannily found themselves at home,'[7] and in recognition of it, the men sang an old hikers' song, 'Dear *Heimat*, We Greet You,' broke out their store of *Geselschtes*, a Bavarian smoked ham, and soundly rebuked a 'Saxon comrade' for picking the edelweiss.[8]

Heimat is the word Germans reach for to express the attachments of place, and as those who claim one usually say, *Heimat* is a particular place and landscape, a particular set of associations in both spatial and temporal terms. However, such particularity does not amount to fragmentation, neither experientially nor cognitively. When thinking of or attempting to feel Germany as a whole, the impulse has been to collect particular places. The collection of the particularities that constitute Germany are, to borrow Simon Schama's biological metaphor, the 'homology of people's own idea of themselves.' The 'primal cultural sense' by which 'landscape and people are morphologically akin' in the German case has put great emphasis on the multiplicity of German places and, therefore, on the variety of both people and of their attachments.[9] This sense has been both inclusive in its embrace of places in the plural and profoundly exclusive of those who are deemed placeless. Such a sense of place nevertheless leaves open the possibility for involuntary outsiders, like Kaleko, to assert their German identity by claiming some particular place as 'my own.' Place has been the most intimate form of national self-understanding.

The main purpose of this essay is, then, to focus on a few narratives and representations of German places that bring together multiplicity and familiarity. It looks at compendiums of places and travels among places in which the inventory of variety constitutes the wholeness of the culture. In many of these inventories, the particularities of place serve as rebukes to the universalist claims of others, usually the heirs of ancient Rome with Rome's imperialist ambitions and monotonizing designs. Many-sidedness (*Vielfältigkeit*) became the battle cry of place claims in Germany. 'See, this is Germany!' (*Seht, das ist Deutschland!*) was the imperative title of a children's 'multi-colored' (*bunt*) treasury of information on German places prepared during the Third Reich, and even the language conspired in the making of this mentality, providing a single syllable, *bunt*, for the phenomenon of multiplicity.[10] Coming to appreciate multiplicity is, of course, a simpler matter in the case of colors than places. The links between the *Cosmographia* of 1597 to *This is Germany* of 1953 were formed through accounts of German places that ranged from maps to poems to novels to travelogues to atlases to organized expeditions to a veritable flood of books of photography in the inter-and post-war periods. They consisted, in other words, of eye-work and leg-work, of reading and writing, of looking, hearing, and walking, with an increasingly self-conscious emphasis on the latter as Germany came into sharper focus by the end of the eighteenth century.

Among the earliest and least appreciated of the representations of multiplicity of place in German-speaking Europe were the picaresque novels of the late seventeenth and early eighteenth century, of which only the sprawling *Adventures of Simplicius Simplicissimus the Vagabond* by Hans Jacob von Grimmelshausen of 1669 remains well-known. *Simplicissimus* spawned a host of imitators, and many of these novelists found their heroes and anti-heroes in the figure of the musician, perhaps because musicians spent so much time on the road and thus could easily stand in for a human condition of wandering and loss of place. The novels were popular in their day, but forgotten after it; most were rediscovered only in the early twentieth century.[11] Literary historians have found in them a kind of proto-realism, with dashes of the magical-realistic thrown in, and preposterous though these characters and plot-lines can be, even the strangest of them remain powerfully grounded in the circumstances of the late seventeenth century.[12]

In the musician novels, two closely-related aspects of Germany come to the fore repeatedly—the problem of the social identity of the wanderer within a world of fixed places and the problem of national identity within a world of diffuse and contrary power. Both are worked out in the novels through the thematic device of travel and encounters with travelers. In Johann Beer's derivative *Der simplicianische Welt-Kucker oder abentheuerliche Jan Rebhu* (The Simplician World-Observer or the Adventurous Jan Rebhu), the title character, an orphan, becomes a soprano at a court dominated by Italian musicians, is taught by a castrato, barely escapes becoming one himself, and then wanders in and out of dangerous political and love affairs in the small courts of Germany and beyond, never finding a settled place. In Daniel Speer's *Haspel-Hanss*, the main character, a deformed orphan, half learns the musical trade and practices it badly in university towns all across Germany. In Speer's *Dacianische Simplicissimus*, the main character, a religiously persecuted orphan, takes to the road, learns to play the drum and the trumpet, then serves as a military musician in the wars against the Turks, traveling through Galicia, Bohemia, Hungary, and Austria, ending up ultimately an exile in the Ottoman Empire.

In Johann Kuhnau's novel *The Musical Charlatan* [*Der musikalische Quacksalber*], one finds one of the few sustained depictions of an actual community into which the wandering, displaced person tries to place himself.[13] The charlatan of the work is 'the so-called Caraffa,' a German from Swabia with a false name who 'for approximately a year had carried the instruments of some famous musicians in Italy.' He returns to a town in Germany (clearly Kuhnau's Leipzig), sure that he will be able to fool people in a way he could not have either in Italy or in his particular place. He gets away with his deception for a little while, because so many Germans belong to 'that silly company who think a composer or *musicus* who hasn't seen Italy is a foolish dunderhead.'[14] However, whatever the limits of local knowledge, a man without a shadow, as Caraffa is, cannot survive for long. The members of the well-educated *Collegium Musicum*, not bumpkins, but Germans of broad experience and 'old German probity and honesty' [*alte teutsche Redlichkeit und Aufrichtigkeit*], quickly identify Caraffa as a fraud through reports of a member who knows someone who comes from Swabia and so knows the 'real' Caraffa. The charlatan, moreover, continually interrupts a performance by taking snuff 'in the French style' at difficult passages in the music. The *Collegium* members pass judgment on Caraffa in the course of a conversation about people who change their names: 'All those who are ashamed of their German names and commit a fraud by changing them deserve to have Germany be ashamed of *them* and expel them from its borders along with other frauds,' says one musician, and another adds, 'because he prefers the Italian language, manners, and names to the Swabian and thus disdains his good fatherland, I cannot recognize him as an honest fellow.'[15] The rest of the novel consists of the so-called Caraffa's travels through other places of Germany, in each of which his lack of authentic identity, of a shadow, a place, leads to eventual failure and return to the road. The only place where he lingers and prospers is the castle of a petty prince, a kind of non-place from which people are always coming and going, always ripe for the fooling, shadowless themselves.

As a novel, the *Musical Charlatan* is repetitive and predictable, and as a travelogue, its 'proto-realism' did not extend to sustained descriptions of either landscapes or customs. However, such was not the nature of the baroque picaresque. The marginality of all its characters allowed them to serve a common admonitory purpose. All suffered from deficient craft knowledge because they lack a settled place in their native land. Buffeted by fate, alternatively exploited and abandoned by nobles and courtiers, these characters embodied the displacements and sufferings of a Germany victimized by its more powerful neighbors, and by its selfish or clueless rulers. Their travel, as much a symptom as a cause of their vulnerability, could produce no worldly experience that would make up for what it took away; a life of adventure was no substitute for a craft well-learned in a place well-known. Their problems could only be solved by thorough education in a craft, which in turn required that Germans—musicians especially— resist the siren call of foreign names and foreign ways, learn their trade, and practice it well. It required, in short, not that Germans cease to travel, but that they cease to wander aimlessly.

Aimless wandering was the last thing on Friedrich Ludwig Jahn's mind when in 1810 he devoted the final chapter of his treatise on the national character of Germans to 'walks in the Fatherland' or *vaterländische Wanderungen*—a term that might just as well be translated as 'patriotic hiking.'[16] When he was writing his book in the first decade of the nineteenth century, Jahn was by no means the most famous German walker. That tribute had been earned by men like Ernst Moritz Arndt or Johann Gottfried Seume, who had walked through many lands, German and otherwise, and in Seume's case as far as Syracuse.[17] Travel writing was one of the central literary genres of the Enlightened century, but in the work of these German 'Master Wayfarers' [*Meisterwanderer*], walking, observing, comparing, and recording life in the towns of Germany and its neighbors acquired a defensive tone, at once appreciative of the virtues and exasperated by the irritations of hometown life. Jahn, for his part, held up Arndt and Seume as exemplars of something essential to national character, what he called the 'ancient German compulsion to travel' [*Urdeutsche Reisetrieb*]. Travel was a 'necessity' for Germans, he thought; one needed to see the world 'with one's own eyes,' learn from it, and 'transplant into the *Heimat* the good and noble things' to be found in it. 'Mere desk work' could not achieve such improving experience, and citing the 'old complaint' about Germans, that 'in foreign lands they could see, but at home they were either blind or idiotic [*blödsichtig*],' he urged Germans to get out on the road. Instead of eating and drinking one's way from one roadside inn to the next (presumably also an *urdeutsche* compulsion), they needed to experience the many places of their Fatherland and thereby bind together the 'limbs of an outstretched people, who do not know each other personally, who live divided one from the other across a great distance, and so live as though each other do not even exist.'[18]

However, Jahn's more abstract pronouncements led to a practical set of recommen- dations, which he urged the German states to make in order to improve traveling conditions for all patriotic walkers. They included signposts and public hospitals, 'instruction in good manners for post-men' and 'strict penalties for innkeeper dishon- esty,' and they culminated in a suggestion that all travelers be required to submit to a 'state authority or Reich academy' a written account of their travels upon their return.

The notion has a breathtakingly authoritarian ring to it, but should remind us of the extent to which, as Ian McNeely has argued, the creation of civil society and ultimately the German national community came from the interactions of citizens with states, in precisely the period in which Jahn was struggling to understand what it meant to be German. His book is, in a sense, one of the 'textual encounters' between citizens and states that transformed German civic culture in the course of the 'traumatic reshufflings of territory and populations' that accompanied Napoleon's 'rampage through Germany'. McNeely writes metaphorically of the new 'road maps' that were required to 'envision new prospects', and in a very literal way, Jahn was demanding these new roads and sending out young Germans onto the old ones in order to establish a new national community in the presence of universalizing, denaturing French authority in much of the old Reich.[19] 'Patriotic hiking,' like the gymnastics and the Lützow Free Corps for which he was more famous then and since, seemed a means both of education in an enlightening sense and mobilization in a nationalizing one.

Moreover, again relying on McNeely's terms, Jahn and his generation of chroniclers of the landscapes and townscapes of Germany established the practices of 'sociography,' by which Germans 'actively came to know and understand the social networks'—and the places—in which they participated.[20] Sociography was 'intimately bound up with a sense of place' and was all about making them legible, writes McNeely, but as Jahn's work indicated, a great deal of walking and looking preceded the writing and the reading—and the former activities, more about visibility than legibility, proved just as significant for how Germans in the future would sense their place. The civic cultures of nineteenth century Germany soon filled up with associations and institutions that were dedicated, through a variety of means, to the understanding of their particular places and beyond, and much of this involved tramping about and recording. Whether the subject was the history of a place, its flora and fauna, or its traditional customs and styles of dress, building, or food, place was something to be scrutinized and catalogued, celebrated and felt. Even singing associations, which would seem, on the face of it, to have the least to do with place, dedicated themselves quite explicitly to filling German space with sound. Local, regional, national, and indeed international song festivals were moveable feasts of sound, taking place first in one German city, then another, and always including in their programs some musical homage to the locality. Individual music clubs would have a yearly roster of activities that included at least one expedition or *Ausflug* to a neighboring town, on which occasion walks would be taken, toasts would be made, local folk songs would be exchanged, and in general the pleasures of German diversity celebrated. The intense localness of associational life as it developed in the nineteenth century included consciousness of some collectivity composed of others who were different, but alike.

These activities tended, moreover, to go with the grain of state-building and governance, at local, regional, and national levels, and in part because the units of place were so variable, their combinations could be flexible as well. Thus, Wilhelm Heinrich Riehl, the great mid-century representative of sociography—what he called *Sozialpolitik*, or social politics—wrote to his patron and employer, King Ludwig I of Bavaria, that 'the most important requirement for a reasonable administration of the land ... is for all authorities to possess knowledge of the land and its people—everything that promotes this knowledge is a victory for the whole state.'[21] Together Riehl and Ludwig became the collectors and cataloguers of the places of Bavaria, gathering them together in a complete 'statistical, historical, topographical, and ethnographic description' of the 'land and people of Bavaria.' Not uniformity, but variety was the watchword of the flexible administration Riehl advocated, and his favorite metaphor was the rainbow, in which all the shades of geographic and ethnographic variation—the *Volkseigenthüm-lichkeit* or individual characteristics of all—could be imagined. Like Gropius, *bunt* was his favorite color.

Listening, looking, and hiking were his favorite methods; indeed, the best methods for understanding places and their people, or so he advised others. As a child, he wrote in the introduction to an ethnology of the Pfalz and its people, he had sat at his Pfälzer grandfather's feet listening to stories; as a student, he had hiked through the country-side; as ethnographer to the King, he had spent months walking from village to village and speaking with local people. His *Natural History of the German People* began with what he called the 'trade secrets for the study of folklore' and Germany's essential diversity; what they amounted to was a recommendation that all Germans get them-selves a good pair of boots and go walking around their native towns and countryside. Railroads were okay—they did perform the important function of making the diversity of German place and life 'obvious and apparent to all'—but back roads were better. Riehl wrote and published his immensely popular *Natural History* in the two decades between the disappointments of 1848 and the achievement of a political unity of sorts in 1871. It was not a history at all, but a conglomeration of descriptions, anecdotes, and sometimes cranky generalizations that were to add up to the 'foundation for a German sociopolitics' and, indeed, for German unity, as compared with a hateful French uniformity. The 'very nature of the German community,' he thought, 'precludes attempts at homogenization,' and 'if we are to become mature enough for national unification, we must first mature in our understanding and appreciation of differences in national character.' These were, in turn, grounded in the diversity of places—'the most persistent differences of region and landscape,' he thought, had 'embedded themselves' in the German peasant and the German burgher. The task of the writer or the schoolteacher or the statesmen was to assist people 'in realizing their own authentic character.'[22]

At nearly the same time, Theodor Fontane was walking around the Mark Branden-burg producing his own very different account of diversity within unity. The literary and historical merits of Fontane's famous *Wanderungen* are, in retrospect, much greater than those of Riehl's social-political descriptions, but the comparison is a fair one, given that Fontane, far more than the unsubtle Riehl himself, embraced the task Riehl had set for Germans of exploring their homeland by foot and taking full stock of the diversity of Germany's individual places. Fontane began his account of the Mark in a boat on Loch Leven in Scotland, like Willy Merkl in the Kashmiri borderlands gazing on a place far from home and finding his thoughts turning back to where he had come from—'Foreign lands first teach us what we possess in our *Heimat*.'[23] Unlike Merkl, Fontane had not absorbed the pseudo-scientific fantasies of a largely twentieth-century racialist ethnography, and so he thought less of unknowable primeval origins than of an actual past whose traces were everywhere to be found in the many aspects of the infinitely complex and intertwining landscapes of the present, if one only looked closely for them and studied them. 'When I returned to the Mark,' he wrote, 'I found it richer than I could have dared to hope.' 'Each foot-breadth of earth was full of animation and gave forth images and shapes of life,' which his own prose could barely express, even after five volumes of unsparing attention to the historical and physical details of the land and its peoples. Moreover, as if speaking into the future to the devotees of extreme exploration, he suggested that for those who needed 'glaciers or storms at sea' to appreciate nature, his footways would not give pleasure. The dramas of the Mark were not spectacular and, such as they were, largely in the past: it required love, hard work, and imagination to experience them, and even then the drama lay in the discovery of forgotten details, in the pathos of distances, both spatial and temporal, and above all in the endless variety.[24] 'Look here,' he recalled saying to himself as he toured around Scotland after his moment of revelation on Loch Leven, 'one finds this much also in the Mark Brandenburg—get yourself back there and show this to be so' [*Geh hin und zeig es*]. The motto of his *Wanderungen* could be found in his closing words, 'see how the good lies so near at hand' [*Sieh, das Gute liegt so nah*].[25] 'This is a multicolored, many-faceted thing [*ein Buntes, Mannigfaches*] that I have brought together,' he concluded, 'born of love and attachment to the *Heimat*.'[26]

Fontane was probably more successful at the 'animation of locality' than any German writer before or since, and for every professional critic or historian who accused him of creating little more than a 'local historical junk room,' his capacity to describe things in their uniqueness and variety led thousands to follow his pathways, through an increasingly unrecognizable land- and cityscape.[27] Fontane was to the travel literature of his time what Richard Wagner was to its opera, although unlike Wagner, Fontane expended no effort in re-naming and proclaiming the genre that he had redefined through his contribution to it. In any case, the advent of the illustrated newspaper and soon the invention and diffusion of photography, transformed the ways that Germans perceived the diversity of place in what was becoming, for better or for worse, the unity of polity and fixity of borders in their nation. In 1843, Leipzig publisher Johann Jacob Weber founded the first illustrated weekly paper in central Europe, the *Illustrirte Zeitung*, in imitation of the *Illustrated London News* and Paris's *L'Illustration*. It and others like them made the world visible to their readers, initially through wood engravings, the capacity of which to depict detail had been enhanced through new techniques in engraving and printing, and after 1883 in Germany, through direct photographic reproduction, not just engravings based on photographs.

The illustrated weeklies devoted considerable space to the depiction of places. The masthead of the *Illustrirte Zeitung* showed Leipzig, unidentified and thus more as a generic German cityscape than a particular place, but engravings and photographs were otherwise dedicated to the principle of the unique and specific. 'Illustration' did

travel photography generally embodied the touristic gaze, as cultural critics have suggested, then Germans appropriated their own lands through these books, embarking on journeys that have less of discovery than of re-affirmation about them—or perhaps recovery of nerve. Susan Sontag famously wrote of photography that 'photographed images do not seem to be statements about the world so much as pieces of it, miniatures of reality that anyone can make or acquire.' They fiddle with the scale of the world, and to own a book of them, to collect them, is 'to collect the world.' The act of photography and, to a lesser extent, the act of looking at the photographs, establishes a 'certain relation to the world that feels like knowledge, and therefore like power.'[34]

It is, nevertheless, too simple to conclude that the knowledge these books conveyed to their readers was of the one true Germany and their power that of defying those who would chop off bits of it. The books of German places did, to be sure, include places that had been lost, occupied, and diminished as the consequence of defeat. Defiance, even revanchism, is one possible meaning one can find in these 'miniatures of reality.' However, the introductory texts that usually accompanied them conveyed additional and sometimes different meanings. In 1929, Kurt Hielscher, a German photographer born in Silesia, published a lavish collection of his black-and-white photographs of German landscapes, villages, and buildings of various sorts. It began with a fulsome dedication to the painter Hans Thoma, the old man of the Black Forest whose ingratiatingly pretty landscapes and scenes of attractive, charmingly-dressed rural people evidently inspired Hielscher to call him the 'truest representative of Germany's essential being.' Hielscher had traveled the world photographing it and his reputation today largely rests on beautifully composed black-and-white images of Spanish villages, natives in native dress, haunting landscapes, in short, places exotic and far away. His images of Germany were not so different from this, although in them the distant becomes the provincial, and the exotic the familiar. There is not a single modern building or person to be found in these hundreds of photographs of thatched roofs, provincial town squares, interesting rock formations, and the like.[35] His fellow Silesian Gerhart Hauptmann underscored this impression with an introduction in full neo-romantic mode, the naturalist dramatist and social critic submerged beneath a torrent of invocations of German soul, spirit, essence, and fate. Fire and war, ironworks, and Americanization threatened the 'last Gothic, the last Romanesque, the last Renaissance building' still standing in Germany, and when they were gone, what of Germany would be left? Hauptmann's rhetoric might have made more sense in 1945; in the context of 1928, it sounds overwrought, the wartime pacifist turned peacetime neurasthenic. The book's placid imagery contrasts oddly to Hauptmann's dire predictions, yet in light of them, these places look like refuges that no longer exist, rather than representations of a present Germany. Variety of place, so Hauptmann's introduction seems to suggest, will soon disappear, and only this book will remain, 'sent out into the world,' as Hielscher writes in his own introduction to the book, 'to the farthest eastern reaches of Asia and the farthest western reaches of America' to 'sow love and awaken a sense of beauty.' The final image he provided was of an ancient gnarled oak tree, his composition and his message of endurance a near copy of the famous Caspar David Friedrich painting of

1822, *The Solitary Tree*. The tree was, of course, Germany, as Hielscher explained; it was the essence beneath the surface variations his other photographs chronicled.

A few years later, the *Orbis Terrarum* series of landscape photobooks in which Hielscher's work had appeared passed into the hands of Martin Hürlimann, the Swiss photographer and founder of the Atlantis Verlag, and he brought out another lavish *Germany*. His Germany was a rather different place than Hielscher's, not unrecognizably so, but different enough to confound simple generalizations about inter-war nostalgia. Hürlimann's artistic aspirations for the book led him to seek out a wide range of contemporary photographers, some like Walter Hege associated with the Bauhaus, others like Lendvai-Dircksen well-known portraitists, and many, like Emil Otto Hoppe and Albert Renger-Patzsch, celebrated for their work outside Germany, photographing the world. The images he gathered took one on a circuitous route around Germany in much the same way as had other books of this kind, but he included a range of places, from wide coastal vistas to allotment gardens, from monuments to family homes, from small towns to metropolises, from castles on the Rhine to mines in Silesia. Many photographs are of places associated with cultural heroes—Bach's organ in the Thomaskirche, Schiller's birthplace, Wagner's Festspielhaus, the house in Regensburg where Kepler died, the Weimar National Theater. In a way, he anticipated the eclecticism and the purpose of the early twenty-first century investigations of 'sites of memory' or *Erinnerungsorte*.[36]

Two aspects in particular complicate the book's rendering of place—its photographs of modernist architecture and modern industry, and its introduction by the *grande dame* of German letters, Ricarda Huch. The inclusion of the former represents the dynamic and forward-moving aspects of diversity alongside tradition and an unchanging natural world (which was, of course, nothing of the sort). Department stores designed by Erich Mendelssohn in Chemnitz and Phillip Schaefer in Berlin; the 1924 modernist memorial at Kant's gravesite; modern housing by Bruno Taut and Karl Schneider; steel works in the Ruhr, smokestacks in Essen, the I. G. Farben headquarters in Frankfurt: these are interspersed among townscapes of medieval bridges, Benedictine abbeys, and Danubian valleys. Yet with the single exception of the smokestacks in Essen, which we glimpse through narrow streets, the images of Germany's multiplicity of place depict no blending of old and new; there are no cars in the old cities (not unlike their restored Federal Republic versions). The photographs themselves do not account for their stark juxtaposition, one image after another, page after page, and the extensive descriptions of each photograph do little more than provide the reader with a fuller version of the many-sidedness of past and present in contemporary Germany. The only sense that the whole makes is the sequential one of proximity in space.

It fell then to Ricarda Huch, the woman whom Thomas Mann had recently proclaimed to be 'the first woman of Germany, and probably of Europe also,' to articulate the sense of place this volume encapsulated, and articulate it she did, in an ambitious introduction which is in some ways its most impressive feature.[37] Huch has received much less attention since her death in 1947 than the extent of what she achieved in life and what she stood for would suggest she merits.[38] At the time

Hürlimann recruited her to his project, she was at the peak of her eminence. In 1926, she had become the first female member of the writers' section of the Prussian Academy of the Arts; she was the author of a much-admired history of German romanticism, lyric poetry, novels, and a number of works of popular history in a novelistic mode. Most relevant to Hürlimann, in 1927 she had published the first of several volumes on German cities, called *Im alten Reich: Lebensbilder deutscher Städte* [In the Old Reich: Living Portraits of German Cities]. These volumes, and the introduction she wrote for the *Germany* photographs, articulated an understanding of Germany's past and present in which the diversity of place encapsulates what for her was the essential character of the German people, its individuality and its creative drive. As far as she was concerned, the Holy Roman Empire of the Middle Ages had been the last time in German history in which these qualities had been allowed to develop freely. Huch believed in a German *Sonderweg*, but it was hardly the triumphal forward march that many of her contemporary historians had seen before the defeat. She, like them, was not enthusiastic about the state of Germany under its new Republic, but unlike other conservatives, she thought things had been going wrong for centuries and, hence, did not resort, either in this introduction or her other works, to blaming Americanization or the Jews. Germany's problems were deeper; they stemmed from a centuries-long struggle against centralizing, rationalizing power, some of which came from outside Germany, but most from within, in the form of centralizing, territorially predatory princes. Every expression of the German creative, productive genius—in economic life, in architecture, in literature, above all in music—had emerged in cities and towns under siege. Her heroes were not just *Dichter* and *Denker*, but composers and builders, townsmen and peasants, and emperors like Siegmund (1368–1437) who healed schisms and struggled against princes. In her account, 'the blood of many races mixed in him and yet he was completely German and felt himself to be so.'[39] In her 1923 biography of her most unexpected hero, the Russian anarchist Mikhail Bakunin, she praised his recognition that human affairs required the greatest possible political decentralization, which would, in turn, foster the spirit of voluntariness [*Freiwilligkeit*], the possibility of self-determination, and ultimately a productive, self-actualizing creative, *working* life. The notorious anarchist who had led Richard Wagner down the path of revolution became a latter-day Baron vom Stein (one of the few actual statesmen she admired), whose recognition of Germany's many-sidedness (*Mannigfaltigkeit*) lay at the foundation of his plans for self-government.

These essential ideas shaped her introduction to Hürlimann's *Germany*. It consists of an extended description of a journey through Germany that integrates movement in time and in place, as the observer travels ancient routes, finding everywhere layers of creativity, diversity, human labor. The grey and swampy land with which her journey begins, in Tacitus's time, retreats farther and farther from memory as her description accumulates a kaleidoscopic array of places and histories, but she returns to it at the end. 'Under their grey skies and through their unrelenting winters,' she wrote, 'the Germans have had to earn their daily bread through hard work.' They have had 'an abundance only of mental and spiritual goods.' However, these too 'have been inextricably bound up with work,' the 'life's breath of the people.' The greatest curse of the present day was thus not the machine or industrialization, but unemployment and exploitation. Huch was not someone always looking back to better times; nor was she inclined to believe that Germany, to paraphrase Karl Scheffler's famous remark about Berlin, 'was condemned forever to becoming and never to being.'[40] These times, she thought, could be like those following the Thirty Years' War, a catastrophe that had been the subject of a three-volume popular history she wrote before the war and published in 1914. Just as 'out of misery and suffering,' 'the wonder of music and a new cultural flowering' had emerged, so too could the present bring about a new vitality in German life.[41]

Evocative though such phrases may be of the regime that would soon seize power in Germany, Huch's own views of the National Socialists were to see them as yet another manifestation of the centralizing impulses of power-seeking princes. In her famous letter resigning from the Prussian Academy of the Arts in 1933, she wrote that 'of course all Germans feel themselves to be German,' but 'what *is* German [*was deutsch ist*] and how Germanness [*Deutschtum*] applies itself,' well, 'about that there are many opinions.' 'What the current regime promotes as the national ethos is not my Germanness,' she wrote, and its qualities—'centralization, force, brutal methods, defamation of those who think otherwise, limitless self-praising'—she held to be 'neither German nor healthy.'[42] Her analysis was powerful, but partial. Huch seemed unable to acknowledge Nazism's largely successful appeal to Germany's diversity of place and ethic of work, especially after the seizure of power. After all, what was more central to Nazi propaganda than its promise to put Germans back to work? What are the early scenes from Riefenstahl's *Triumph of the Will*, with the bird's eye view of Germany from above, the peasant costumes, young working men calling out the name of their *Heimats*, other than a paean to the unity in diversity of German place?

Both the celebration of place diversity and the glorification of German labor had an apogee of sorts in the hype surrounding the building of the autobahn. The propagandizing of the autobahn to the German public drew on long-established traditions of place representation and pitched this new infrastructural wonder as the means by which German, indeed *ur*-German, love of home and of travel would be reconciled and fulfilled.[43] The autobahn's director, Inspector-General for German Roadways Fritz Todt, could sound remarkably like Father Jahn trying to bind together the 'the limbs of an outstretched people'—in Todt's formulation, the linked motorways were a 'clasp around the national community.' The roads would support German *Wanderlust* and make visible German *Lebensraum*. They would unveil a 'colorful succession of alternating landscape images,' and in places where 'beauty has already disappeared,' the road-builders would reconstruct it.[44] 'The German landscape is full of character,' said Todt to Hitler in January 1934, and 'the motor roadway, too, must be given German character.'[45] The autobahn, its sweeping curves connecting all parts of the fatherland, would be the technology that embedded race and place, blood and soil, into the consciousness of all Germans.

However, a funny thing happened in the process of building the autobahn and selling it to the German people—place itself disappeared. In the struggles for influence among a bewildering, typically National Socialist array of conservationists, landscape architects, engineers, finance officials, and party men, the autobahn became the means by which German particularity was erased, not celebrated. Part of the reason for this was practical. Too many 'diversions' in the form of 'villages, cities, sharp curves, wild ascents, switchbacks, the alternation of good and not-so-good roads, bicyclists, horse-drawn carts, herds of sheep' would slow the movement of the motorized nation.[46] Rhetoric aside, most of Todt's engineers came from the railway world, where straight lines and level plains overcame curves, contours, and all the little quirks that actual places present. Meanwhile, the regime's photographers themselves contributed to the task of erasure even while celebrating the 'new' landscapes the autobahn created. The glossy photography books of Erna Lendvai-Dircksen and Wolf Strache, among others, were remarkably inadequate in their portrayal of Germany's distinctive 'placeness'.[47] In the case of Lendvai-Dircksen, this tendency is hardly surprising: her work had always focused on the peculiarities of human face and form, not place. For Strache, for whom the autobahn photography began a long and largely post-war career of publishing photobooks on German cities (Stuttgart, Berlin, Oldenburg, Wurzburg, Schweinfurt, etc.), waters (Weser, Bodensee, Neckar), and roads (the *Romantische Strasse*, the *Burgstrasse*, the auto-friendly Alpine crossings), the blandness of his images seemed to emphasize photography's capacity to abstract from the world, not capture it. The details of place disappear in vistas of landscape that could be anywhere in the northern temperate zone.

The emptiness of these images—empty roads, empty landscapes, maybe even empty cars given how few Germans owned one—suggested something more, however, than the Potemkin-village character of the whole enterprise.[48] As we now know, for all its attention to soil, what mattered to the regime was blood. Despite its lip-service to German diversity and its chaos of administration that can look like decentralization, Huch was not wrong to regard centralization—'working toward the Führer'—as the essence of the Third Reich. The impact of the Third Reich on the German sense of place and on the sense of German places was, then, two-fold. It left behind a legacy of 'evil places' and submerged memories of associations among particular places and acts, memories that surfaced only gradually as the years went by. 'Germany [today] is an open-air museum, filled with exhibits from the time of terror,' as a recent anti-guide to a handful of the most notorious sites put it.[49] Furthermore, as the autobahn suggested and the war made actual, the Third Reich brought about an unprecedented destruction and loss of German places, and the people in them. One need not recapitulate the statistics on bombed-out cities, displaced persons, and death to recognize that whatever of the old feeling for German places was able to survive, it could not be other than changed.

The post-war period in both Germanies did, nevertheless, see an outburst of localist activism. With something of that ant-like vitality that Huch had once seen in German city life, people pulled their sense of *Heimat* out of the rubble as though it had never been an accessory, but only a victim of the crimes of the past 12 years. 'Out of our spiritual and material distress,' observed a Bavarian historian in 1949, 'has been born a new animation of *Heimat* thoughts.'[50] In those first years after the war, it seemed to

Germans that their wartime suffering had been punishment enough for their misjudgments, ambitions, and sins. Locally-grounded spiritual meditation and the hard labor of rebuilding ruined places might somehow bring about rehabilitation; the 'song of the soul's path homeward' [*das Lied von dem Heimweg der Seele*] was the closing line of one of thousands of post-war lyrical tributes to the enduring and beneficent power of place.[51] Yet it was all so very false in its heartfelt sincerity. The books of photographs produced in the decades after the war—and there were hundreds of them, in every city and region—made German places look as though the path to the present had consisted only of building, never re-building. Cities and landscapes seemed not so much unchanged as untroubled, with both bustle and tranquility a tribute to hard work. The reality behind these formulaic catalogues of German variety was a pervasive loss of place and the possibility that, in the west at least, rootedness was gone from German life, and only *Wanderlust* remained. Every West German place of any size recovered and soon flourished with the help of thousands of refugees and then later 'guest workers'. For the former, some kind of absorption into a new place seemed at least possible, though in Siegfried Lenz's novel *Heimatmuseum*, the hero, a displaced person from the eastern provinces, ultimately sets fire to the museum of his Masurian homeland that he had painstakingly assembled in Schleswig-Holstein after the war.[52] For the latter, a German place was not meant to be available at all.

However, whatever else they are, humans are place makers, ever engaged in the effort to define and control the space around them. After so enormous a catastrophe as the Second World War, the cultural idioms of place-making were bound to change, just as predictably as many were bound to look the same. Certainly, both Germanies suffered from various forms of the bungled social engineering that created, in social critic James Howard Kunstler's term, a 'geography of nowhere.'[53] Whether tower blocks popped up in the middle of cities or on their edges or way out in the formerly agricultural countryside, they seemed to embody the threat of the word utopia itself—no place. The East Germans had a particular genius for creating no-places. One can scarcely imagine less of a place than Kella. No maps located this village in the German-German border's prohibited zone (*Sperrgebiet*), no road signs pointed to it, and no glossy books of photographs displayed it.

Yet it was there, and as anthropologist Daphne Berdahl has described, Kella's inhabitants made it a place in all the ways that people do, with collective rituals like the Palm Sunday procession, with private encounters, with all the coming and going of everyday life, however restricted it had become.[54] The restrictions themselves gave meaning to the place, but Berdahl's point, which captures the perspective of the inhabitants themselves, is that the meanings of place generated by the state and, indeed, the outside world were no more, nor less, constitutive of it than the place-work of the people who lived there. Likewise East German citizens, especially in the decade before it all came to an end, had learned how to 'game the rules' of the state, as historian Brian Campbell has put it, in order to preserve and beautify their own little corners of the East German dystopia.[55]

Mutatis mutandis, similarly transgressive efforts characterized the German placemaking of Turkish immigrants. Emine Sevgi Özdamar's coming-of-age novel, *The*

Bridge of the Golden Horn, begins with a gesture toward place—'On Stresemannstrasse at that time, it was 1966, a baker's shop was there'—then piece by piece, she (her heroine) tries to assemble a coherent life out of the dispersed, partial, and always disrupted experiences of many different places. At one point, she writes that Germany seemed to her as though it were a single building made up of long corridors and many doors. At another, comparing her perceptions to her work on the factory assembly line where vision narrowed down to one small piece of reality, she depicts her surroundings in tiny fragments, a bathroom, a bed, a pair of knees, a phone booth, the ruins of the Anhalter Bahnhof, a train, a boat, a bridge. 'Homeland,' say the men of the Turkish Workers' Association in Berlin, 'is where work is.' However, for her the phone booth, with the voices of her parents, is Turkey, and the Anhalter Bahnhof—the 'offended station,' she calls it, in a deliberately naïve transliteration from German to Turkish and back again—is her German *Heimat*, sort of. 'We were like birds,' she wrote, 'who flew somewhere and from time to time came down to earth, before flying away again.'[56]

Seventy years earlier, Joseph Roth had said of Berlin that it 'exists outside Germany, outside Europe, . . . obtains nothing from the earth on which it is built, [and] converts this earth into asphalt, brick, and walls.' It has 'no culture of its own, as have Breslau, Cologne, Frankfurt, Königsberg,' he continued; 'it is an aimlessly sprawling stone emblem for the sorry aimlessness of our national existence.'[57] In Özdamar's Berlin, the bleakness remains and the sense of no-place lingers, but both are now overlaid with something ever so slightly more hopeful. The possibility exists—as we know, and Roth did too, it would never exist for him—to make something real in these stone corridors. Perhaps this is what literary theorist Leslie Adelson means when she distances her analysis of the 'Turkish turn' in German literature from the concept of diaspora. In her 'new grammar of migration,' she suggests that our tendency to believe in a distinction between the rootlessness (Roth's aimlessness) of the 'here and now' in German places and the rooted authenticity of the 'then and there' in the place left behind does not adequately account for immigrant experiences in Germany. We need, she argues, a new topography of citizenship—multi-layered, multi-referential, post-national.[58] Undoubtedly, that topography will not consist only of compendiums and catalogues, and panoramic views of some presumed whole that seemed to encompass so much, including the variegated details, but left out even more. Perhaps this new topography will bear more resemblance to the one imagined in Robert D. Sack's *Geographical Guide to the Real and the Good*. There he describes the place-character of the death camps and the moral blindness they engendered, but argues for the possibility of something wholly different. For Sack, sheer moral goodness exists in places that expand our awareness of complexity and open our eyes to variety.[59] Many Germans before 1933 and after 1945 thought that their sense of place had, in fact, opened their eyes to complexity and provided them, as Huch argued, with the moral foundation for freedom in public and private life. Their experiences, of place and all else, had unfortunately taught them less than they thought, but so it could be said of all of us.

NOTES

1. From the *Cosmographia* of 1597, cited in Gerald Strauss, *Sixteenth-Century Germany: Its Topography and Topographers* (Madison: University of Wisconsin Press, 1959), 41.

2. Otto Schmitt to his brother, 2 November 1953, handwritten inscription in *This is Germany* (Munich: Ludwig Simon, 1952), copy owned by grandson Benjamin Schmitt and loaned to this author.

3. Adrian Mohr, text introduction to *This is Germany*, 1.

4. Mack Walker, *German Home Towns: Community, State, and General Estate* (Ithaca: Cornell University Press, 1971), 2–3.

5. Mascha Kaleko, *Verse für Zeitgenossen* (Cambridge: Schoenhof, 1945), translation my own.

6. Willy Merkl, 'Die Deutsche-Amerikanische Himalaja Expedition 132,' *Zeitschrift des Deutschen und Österreichischen Alpenvereins* (1933), 65, translation my own; cited in Maurice Isserman and Stewart Weaver, *Fallen Giants: A History of Himalayan Mountaineering from the Age of Empire to the Age of Extremes* (New Haven: Yale University Press, 2008), 152.

7. Isserman and Weaver, *Fallen Giants*, 152. For a discussion of similar ephiphanic moments of *Heimat* recognition in the less exotic valleys of Pennsylvania and the American midwest, see Thomas Lekan, 'German Landscape: Local Promotion of the *Heimat* Abroad,' in Krista O'Donnell, Renate Bridenthal, and Nancy Reagin (eds), *The Heimat Abroad: the Boundaries of Germanness* (Ann Arbor: University of Michigan, 2005), 141–166.

8. Merkl, *Deutsche-Amerikanische Expedition*, 65.

9. Simon Schama, 'Homelands,' *Social Research* 1991, 58, 11.

10. The most-quoted instance of this is Walter Gropius's memory of telling his parents that '*Bunt ist meine Lieblingsfarbe*'–multi-colored is my favorite color: Peter Gay, *Art and Act: On Causes in History* (New York: Harper & Row, 1976), 133. The children's book is Bernhard Klaffke, *Seht das ist Deutschland! Ein buntes Kartenbilderbuch* (Leipzig: Bibliographisches Institute, 1936).

11. The key figure in the rediscovery was Hans Menck, *Der Musiker im Roman* (Heidelberg: Carl Winters Universitätsbuchhandlung, 1931), 28. Since his time, miscellaneous work on individual authors has appeared, most notably Richard Alewyn's *Johann Beer: Studien zum Roman des 17. Jahrhundert* (Leipzig: Mayer & Müller, 1932), which rescued the great bulk of Beer's work from anonymity; and in English, George Schoolfield, *The Figure of the Musician in German Literature* (Chapel Hill: University of North Carolina Press, 1956), which begins only with the Romantics. Beer has had a renaissance lately: see Andreas Brandtner and Wolfgang Neuber (eds), *Beer 1655–1700, Hofmusiker, Satiriker, Anonymus: eine Karriere zwischen Bürgertum und Hof* (Wien: Turia & Kant, 2000).

12. Steven Rose, 'The Musician-Novels of the German Baroque: New Light on Bach's World,' *Understanding Bach* 3 (Bach Network UK), http://www.bachnetwork.co.uk/ub3/ROSE.pdf, 363–364.

13. Kuhnau was Johann Sebastian Bach's predecessor as the Kantor of the Thomaskirche in Leipzig, and his novel, a sort of *jeu d'esprit* on the part of a famously scholarly musician, was first published in Dresden in 1700: Johann Kuhnau, *The Musical Charlatan*, trans. John R. Russell, intro. James Hardin (Columbia: Camden House, 1997).

14. Kuhnau, *Musical Charlatan*, 4.

15. Kuhnau, *Musical Charlatan*, 7–8, 20–21.

16. Friedrich Ludwig Jahn, *Deutsches Volkstum* (1810; Berlin and Weimar: Aufbau-Verlag, 1991), 301–305.

17. Seume's *Spaziergang nach Syrakus in 1802*, was reprinted countless times, in German and in translation, throughout the 19th century. It ended with a famous paean to his sturdy German boots. The most modern edition is in Volume I of his *Werke in zwei Bände*, Jörg Drews (ed.), (Frankfurt am Main: Deutscher Klassiker Verlag, 1993).

18. Jahn, *Volkstum*, 301–302.

19. Ian F. McNeely, *The Emancipation of Writing: German Civil Society in the Making, 1790s–1820s* (Berkeley: University of California Press, 2003), 239–240.

20. McNeely, *Emancipation*, 7.

21. Celia Applegate, *A Nation of Provincials: the German Idea of Heimat* (Berkeley: University of California Press, 1990), 35.

22. See the fuller discussion in 'The Mediated Nation: Regions, Readers, and the German Past,' in J. Retallack (ed.) *Saxony in German History: Culture, Society, Politics, 1830–1933* (Ann Arbor: University of Michigan Press, 2000), 33–50.

23. Theodor Fontane, *Wanderungen durch die Mark Brandenburg: Erster Teil* (Stuttgart: Cotta Buchhandlung, 1917), vii.

24. Fontane, *Wanderungen: Erster Teil*, x–xi.

25. Fontane, *Wanderungen durch die Mark Brandenburg: Vierter Teil* (Leipzig: Cotta Buchhandlung, 1914), vii.

26. Fontane, *Wanderungen: Erster Teil*, viii.

27. This was Fontane's term—'*Belebung des Örtlichen.*' Herbert Roch called the *Wanderungen* a '*lokalgeschichtlichen Rumpelkammer,*' in Fontane (ed.), *Berlin und das 19. Jahrhundert* (Berlin-Schöneberg: Gebrüder Weiss, 1962), 132. Among Fontane's most fervent recent admirers was Gordon Craig, whose chapter on the *Wanderungen* in his Fontane biography consists mainly of Craig's travels through the same places in the 1970s under the government of the SED (see Craig, *Theodor Fontane: Literature and History in the Bismarck Reich* [New York: Oxford University Press, 1999], 48–69).

28. See 'Was Wir Wollen,' *Illustrirte Zeitung* Nr. 1 (1 July 1843).

29. 'An unsere Freunde und Leser!' *Die Gartenlaube* 1 (1853). See also Kirsten Belgum, *Popularizing the Nation: Audience, Participation, and the Production of Identity in Die Gartenlaube, 1853–1900* (Lincoln: University of Nebraska Press, 1998).

30. Ulrich Keller, 'The Art Photography Movement Around 1900: Painting as a Model,' in Klaus Honnef, Rolf Sachsse and Karin Thomas (eds), *German Photography 1870–1970: Power of a Medium*, trans. Paulin Cumbers, Ishbel Flett (Bonn: Kunst-und Austellungshalle der Bundesrepublik Deutschland, 1997), 31–40.

31. In the interwar period, Swiss photographer Martin Hürliman founded the magazine *Atlantis* in Berlin, which published high quality photography of peoples and places around the world; in 1930 he established the Atlantis Verlag and took on the Wasmuth Verlag's series of place photography books called *Orbis Terrarum*. One finds among them an *Eternal France* and *Eternal Greece*, but Germany remains simply *Germany*.

32. Andres Mario Zervigon, 'Modernity Inverted: Looking Closely at Erna Lendvai-Dircksen's *Face of the German Race,*' unpublished paper delivered at the Shelby Cullom Davis Center for Historical Studies, Princeton University, February 20, 2009.

33. August Sander, *Face of our Time: Sixty Portraits of Twentieth-Century Germans*, intro. Alfred Döblin, trans. Michael Robertson (1929) (New York: Schirmer Art Books, 1997), 7, 10.

34. Susan Sontag, *On Photography* (New York: Farrar, Straus, and Giroux, 1978), 4.

35. Kurt Hielscher, *Deutschland: Baukunst und Landschaft*, intro. Gerhart Hauptmann (Berlin: Ernst Wasmuth Verlag, 1928), vii–x.

36. Etienne François and Hagen Schulze (eds), *Deutsche Erinnerungsorte*, 3 vols (Munich: C. H. Beck Verlag, 2001).

37. He wrote on the occasion of her sixtieth birthday: 'Dies sollte ein Deutscher Frauentag sein, und mehr als ein deutscher. Denn nicht nur die erste Frau Deutschlands ist es, die man zu feiern hat, es ist wahrscheinlich heute die erste Europas.' Mann, 'Zum sechzigsten Geburtstag Ricarda Huch,' *Gesammelte Werke*, 13 vols (Frankfurt: Fischer, 1960), 10: 429.

38. Exceptions are the excellent study by James M. Skidmore, *The Trauma of Defeat: Ricarda Huch's Historiography during the Weimar Republic* (Bern: Peter Lang, 2005); Susan C. Anderson, 'Against modernity and historicism: Ricarda Huch's representation of the Thirty Years' War,' *Colloquia Germanica* 27 (1994); and Jutta Bendt and Karin Schmid-gall, *Ricarda Huch 1864–1947: Eine Ausstellung des Detuschen Literaturarchivs im Schiller-National-Museum Marbach am Neckar* (Marbach am Neckar: Deutsche Schillergesellschaft, 1994).

39. '. . . sich das Blut verschiedener Rassen in ihm mischte und dass er doch ganz Deutscher war, sich ganz als Deutscher fühlte': quoted in Skidmore, *Trauma of Defeat*, 126; see also 116–117.

40. *Verdammt dazu, ewig zu werden, niemals zu sein*: Karl Scheffler, *Berlin: ein Schicksalstadt 1910* (Berlin: Fannei and Walz, 1989), 219.

41. Huch, Einleitung, in Hürlimann, *Deutschland*, v, xxviii–xxix.

42. Huch, *Briefe*, 225–226.

43. On the propaganda and the place of the autobahn in traditions of landscape preservation, see Thomas Zeller, *Driving Germany: the Landscape of the German Autobahn, 1930–1970*, trans. Thomas Dunlap (New York: Berghahn Books, 2007), esp. 62–65, 80–179.

44. Quoted in Peter Reichel, 'Images of the National Socialist State: Images of Power; Power of Images,' in Honnef, Sachsse, and Thomas (eds), *German Photography*, 76–77.

45. Zeller, *Driving Germany*, 128.

46. Oskar Weller, writing in Todt's journal *Die Strasse* in 1935: quoted in Zeller, *Driving Germany*, 129.

47. See Erna Lendvai-Dircksen, *Reichsautobahn: Mensch und Werk* (Bayreuth: Gauverlag, 1939, 1942); Wolf Strache, *Auf allen Autobahnen: Ein Bildbuch vom neuen Reisen* (Darmstadt: L.C. Wittich, 1939); Strache, *Donnernde Motoren* (Stuttgart: Tazzelwurm, 1942).

48. The Germans were, in fact, among the least motorized people in the industrial world. In 1935, there were 204 motorized vehicles per thousand inhabitants in the United States; in France, 49; in Great Britain, 45; in Germany, 16. As an American official described the situation, 'Germany has the roads while we have the traffic.' See Zeller, *Driving Germany*, 48–52.

49. Stephan Porombka und Hilmar Schmidt, *Böse Orte: Stätten nationalsozialistischer Selbstdarstellung—heute* (Berlin: Claasen Verlag, 2005), vi.

50. Max Spindler, 'Zur Lage der bayerischen Geschichtsvereine,' *Zeitschrift für bayerische Landesgeschichte* 15 (1949), 263. See also Applegate, *Nation of Provincials*, 228–246.

51. Kurt Kölsch, 'Abendländlische Elegie,' *Pfalz und Pfälzer* 13 (January 1952), 1.

52. Lenz's work, published in 1978, contributed to a post-war genre of what one might call the anti-*Heimat* novel or the novel of placelessness. Günter Grass's *Tin Drum* is another example. In them, the sense of place and locality no longer provides consolation or identity.

53. James Howard Kunstler, *The Geography of Nowhere: the Rise and Decline of America's Man-Made Landscape* (New York: Free Press, 1994).

54. Daphne Berdahl, *Where the World Ended: Re-Unification and Identity in the German Borderland* (Berkeley: University of California Press, 1999).

55. Brian W. Campbell, 'Resurrected from the Ruins, Turning to the Past: Historic Preservation in the SBZ/GDR, 1945–1990.' PhD diss., University of Rochester, 2005.

56. Emine Sevgi Özdamar, *The Bridge of the Golden Horn*, trans. Martin Chalmers (London: Profile Books Ltd, 2007), 3, 7, 9, 14, 25, 31.

57. From his *Flight Without End* (1927), quoted by Michael Hofmann, introduction to Joseph Roth, *What I Saw: Reports from Berlin 1920–1933*, trans. Michael Hofmann (New York: W. W. Norton, 2003), 13.

58. Leslie A. Adelson, *The Turkish Turn in Contemporary German Literature: Toward a New Critical Grammar of Migration* (New York: Palgrave Macmillan, 2005), 1–30.

59. Robert D. Sack, *The Geographical Guide to the Real and the Good* (New York: Routledge, 2003), passim.

BIBLIOGRAPHY

APPLEGATE, CELIA, *A Nation of Provincials: The German Idea of Heimat* (Berkeley: University of California Press, 1990).

BERDAHL, DAPHNE, *Where the World Ended: Re-Unification and Identity in the German Borderland* (Berkeley: University of California Press, 1990).

BLACKBOURN, DAVID. *The Conquest of Nature: Water, Landscape, and the Making of Modern Germany* (New York: W. W. Norton & Co., 2006).

BLACKBOURN, DAVID, and JAMES RETALLACK, *Localism, Landscape, and the Ambiguities of Place: German-Speaking Central Europe, 1860–1930* (Toronto: University of Toronto Press, 2007).

CRESWELL, TIM, *Place: a Short Introduction* (London: Blackwell Publishing, 2004).

KOSHAR, RUDY, *From Monuments to Traces: Artifacts of German Memory, 1870–1990* (Berkeley: University of California Press, 2000).

LEKAN, THOMAS M., *Imagining the Nation in Nature: Landscape Preservation and German Identity, 1885–1945* (Cambridge: Harvard University Press, 2004).

LOWER, WENDY, *Nazi Empire-Building and the Holocaust in Ukraine* (Chapel Hill: University of North Carolina Press, 2006).

LUMANS, VALDIS O., *Himmler's Auxiliaries: the Volksdeutsche Mittelstelle and the German National Minorities of Europe, 1933–1945* (Chapel Hill: University of North Carolina Press, 1993).

MURDOCK, CAITLIN E., *Changing Places: Society, Culture, and Territory in the Saxon-Bohemian Borderlands, 1870–1946* (Ann Arbor: University of Michigan Press, 2010).

O'DONNELL, KRISTA, RENATE BRIDENTHAL, and NANCY REAGIN (eds), *The Heimat Abroad: The Boundaries of Germanness* (Ann Arbor: University of Michigan Press, 2006).

PALMOWSKI, JAN. *Inventing a Socialist Nation: Heimat and the Politics of Everyday Life in the GDR, 1945–90* (New York: Cambridge University Press, 2009).

SCHLÖGEL, KARL, *Im Raume lesen wir die Zeit: Über Zivilisationsgeschichte und Geopolitik.* (Munich: Carl Hanser, 2003).

STRAUSS, GERALD, *Sixteenth-Century Germany: Its Topography and Topographers* (Madison: University of Wisconsin Press, 1959).

TUAN, YI-FU, *Space and Place: the Perspective of Experience* (Minneapolis: University of Minnesota Press, 1977).

CHAPTER 4

....

WOMEN AND MEN:
1760–1960

....

ANN GOLDBERG

THIS essay is about the power of a norm and its mutation over time: the gender role division of the private nuclear family composed of a male provider and protector, and his dependent children and homemaker wife. Those roles corresponded to rigid distinctions that were made between a male public world of work, money, and politics, on the one hand, and a female private sphere of reproduction and nurturance, on the other. These were prescribed ideals of gender, not objective reality. However, as such, the ideals, over two centuries, have had tremendous power, shaping personal identity and the daily lives of men and women, as well as influencing the development of the state, civil society, politics, and the economy, according to a vast and growing scholarship.[1] The power of the separate spheres norm came from how it modeled gender relations within the family and society, determining the rights, roles, and status of women and men. It also came from the way it functioned as a symbolic language of power, a language that was easily adaptable to a range of institutions and public debates—about freedom, state power, citizenship, and the nation. Nothing about the separate spheres paradigm was unique to Germany. Indeed, much of the history described in this essay applied throughout the western world. Yet, gender history—its norms, roles, institutions, and debates—was also deeply inflected by the German context, a fact also emphasized. This essay discusses the rise of separate spheres in the eighteenth century, its role in the rise of liberalism and the development of the *Rechtsstaat*, and its incorporation into industrial capitalism. It moves subsequently to challenges to the gender order in the late nineteenth and early twentieth centuries, and the backlash of Nazism. It ends with German reconstruction in the 1940s and 1950s, and the differing ways that gender roles were re-established in West and East Germany.

What would eventually become a universal norm in Germany and the West—the private, patriarchal nuclear family—first arose within bourgeois circles in the late eighteenth century as a radical re-invention of both family and gender relations. Before this time, families in pre-industrial Germany were neither 'private' nor, strictly speaking, nuclear. This was because the functions of reproduction and consumption that later came to be identified with the modern family were not yet separated from production. Peasant and urban artisan households raised children and consumed goods, but they were also institutions that produced goods and drove the economy. This meant that, in addition to the marital couple and its offspring, households often included servants, apprentices, and journeymen, all of whom were engaged in the household economy of agriculture, craft production, or proto-industrialized work.[2] Subject to external regulations and exigencies, these households ("*Ganzes Haus*") were inextricably linked to the economy, family alliances, and property transfers, as well as to the tax interests of the state. Marriage was a privilege, not a right, joining together the property, labor, and alliances of two families at the point where a couple had acquired the independent means to support a family. Given the material stakes at issue in marriage alliances, sexuality and courtship were strictly regulated by families, communities, and the state. Marriages between social unequals were severely frowned upon, and those across estates (*Stände*) were illegal in Prussia's law code of 1794. The relationship between husband and wife was, legally and socially, a hierarchical one, the husband or *Hausvater*, being the head and master of the household, the one with full political and civic rights in the commune/town, and, normally, the person in master artisan families with official training and full rights in the guild. Yet, husbands and wives were also economic partners, whose labor tasks were usually structured, in turn, by their gender. Men performed most of the field work and headed the craft workshop. Women, by contrast, performed duties in and around the house: cooking, caring for the garden and domestic livestock, or helping out in an unofficial capacity in the family workshop, as well as producing many of the consumer goods that later, post-industrial peoples would buy in stores, such as clothing, candles, and soap. Children of both sexes were put to work at an early age, and were often sent away to work as servants and apprentices in their teens.

In the late eighteenth century, a radically different sort of family model began to emerge among middle class groups of civil servants, professionals, and entrepreneurs. This family, embodying Enlightenment and Romantic ideas, was reconceived as a space of affection, nurturance, and self-expression—a private and reproductive space separated from the world of production and money-making, and centered on the raising of children. Accordingly, childhood itself, influenced by the writings of Jean Jacques Rousseau, was being reconceived as a special, psychologically distinct phase of life requiring attentive care-giving and intellectual training. Marriage, in turn, was to be grounded in mutual affection and companionship. It was to be the result of a free, personal choice between husband and wife, and the hierarchical relations between them replaced by a new polarized notion of gender difference and complementarity: the husband as protector and breadwinner; the wife in the domestic sphere taking care of the home and children. The polarization of gender roles in the bourgeois family was, in turn, accompanied by a dichotomized view of the nature of the sexes as opposites.

Women were seen as biologically fitted solely for domestic and reproductive roles within the family because of their passive, emotional, nurturing, and spiritual natures, while men possessed the rationality, independence, strength and self-control that equipped them for roles in the public sphere.[3]

To be sure, this new separate-spheres model of the family—its radical distinction between work and home, and its dichotomized view of male and female roles—was far from the reality for the majority of Germans in the late eighteenth and nineteenth centuries. Most working-class women worked for wages and their lives, devoted to problems of survival, left little room for anything resembling domesticity in the bourgeois sense. Indeed, according to new research in the social history of gender, as late as the 1840s, the separate spheres model of the family did not yet exist, even among the bourgeoisie. In a study of one such family in the 1820s and 1830s, the Munich Roth household, the lives of wife and husband (Käthe and her jurist husband Friedrich) were actually becoming closer and more intertwined, not rigidly separated. Unlike their parents' generation, both husband and wife dedicated themselves with a new intensity and sense of mission to childrearing. While Käthe, unlike her mother, consciously distanced herself from the marketplace, she brought to her domestic role a moral-religious vision that paralleled her husband's ethic in his professional and personal life, an ethic dedicated to the cultivation of *Bildung* and non-economic pursuits. Likewise, there was a fluidity of gender boundaries in the practice of 'domestic sociability'—an almost daily round of often mixed-gender visiting, and conversation on topics ranging from the personal to the cultural and political. Domestic sociability, in turn, fostered social networks and the diffusion of bourgeois values that were crucial to bourgeois class formation, a fact unrecognized in the earlier, pre-gender historiography.[4]

While limited in daily life, separate spheres as an ideal and norm played an important role in the development of liberal thought and civil society in the late eighteenth and early nineteenth centuries. It was not accidental that the bourgeoisie, the group leading the fight against corporate privileges and absolutist government, developed the separate spheres gender norm. The two spheres—politics and gender/sexuality—went hand in hand. For philosophers, jurists, and pedagogues of the late Enlightenment and early liberal movements, the political vision of individual autonomy and self-rule had its necessary counterpart in a privatized sphere of marital sexual self-expression divorced from the state and other outside interference. They made claims for self-rule and citizenship rights on the basis of men's inherent rationality, arguing that their ability for self-mastery, free from the state, extended as well to a privatized sphere of sexual freedom and self-expression within marriage and the family. Women, by contrast, because of their passivity and lack of self-control, would fulfill their destinies not as autonomous agents, but as dependents, their sexuality serving the ends of reproduction and pleasing their husbands.[5]

Meanwhile, the separate spheres ideal was shaping the very notion, at its inception, of the modern German nation. German nationalism was born of defeat by and resistance to the French enemy during the Napoleonic Wars. After Prussia's defeat in 1806–1807, government officials and publicists of the Prussian reform movement sought to mobilize subjects to patriotic resistance against French occupation with the vision of a unified German *Volk*, a concept that recast the relationship of state and society along lines modeled after the bourgeois family. In this familial model, the 'fear and obedience' that earlier characterized the relationship of the monarchy and its subjects were replaced by the idea of the king and queen as benevolent parental figures leading a proud, free nation in defense of the fatherland. The self-sacrificing patriotism of both men and women was crucial to the national cause, but this patriotism was conceived differently, in terms of complementary opposites, for men and women. Men would serve as a 'brotherhood' of soldiers defending home, hearth, and fatherland. Women's patriotism, by contrast, would be fulfilled by their maternal roles: raising German children, giving emotional sustenance, and providing charity to the sick and needy. Masculinity thus, in effect, began to be militarized, a fact institutionalized in the introduction of universal male conscription in 1814. In turn, the militarized male—the German brothers-in-arms defending (or potentially capable of defending) the nation— was coming to be seen as the basis for full citizenship rights. The new male ideal of the citizen-soldier, which would take on great significance in the twentieth century (below), symbolically, if not in actual social relations, leveled age-old distinctions between men (class, religion, geography) while intensifying those between men and women.[6]

The norm of separate spheres had far-reaching consequences for the lives of women and men. Enlightenment claims for male sexual autonomy, self-expression, and rationality were implicated in the promotion of a more dynamic and self-regulating conception of civil society that accompanied the shift toward a world of market relations, consumption, and, eventually, parliamentary institutions in the nineteenth century. However, this occurred through widening and intensifying the gap between the lives and roles of men and women. Legal codes preserved and sharpened the subordinate status of women, and the patriarchal rights of husbands and fathers. The Napoleonic Code (1804), which remained in effect after 1814 in the Rhineland and, in modified form, in Baden, required women to 'obey' their husbands and placed women under their husband's guardianship. Prussia's 1794 civil code was unusually progressive in two areas: it provided comparatively greater rights to illegitimate children and single women, and relatively easy access to divorce. However, those clauses were whittled away in the course of the nineteenth century as Prussian law was aligned more closely with other German and European law codes.[7] Germany's national civil code—the *bürgerliches Gesetzbuch*—which came into effect in 1900, maintained for decades to come the rule of husbands over wives, giving the former authority in matters related to the children, administrative rights over his wife's property and earnings, and power over his wife's legal contracts.

The gap also widened between the rights and opportunities of men and women in the spheres of education, work, civil society, and politics. Bourgeois men made extraordinary gains in higher education, business, the professions, and the civil service. They created a vigorous, all-male associational life of literary clubs, museum associations, and Masonic lodges. They joined reform movements, participated in local and regional parliaments, and, together with working-class men, were given the franchise at the national level in 1871. Women, because of their alleged maternal roles and fragile, less rational natures, were denied access to all of these things. Thus, at a time when ideas about natural rights were undermining old hierarchies, these hierarchies were maintained, and made rigid, within relations between men and women on the basis of a new polarized conception of masculinity and femininity.

This fact had profound consequences, in turn, for the development of the economy, labor politics, and the state in the era of industrial capitalism. Far from undermining traditional inequalities between men and women, industrial capitalism, which took off after the mid-century, built upon, incorporated, and, in some ways, intensified those inequalities. The mechanization of industry and mass migration to cities and factory towns began to replace the *Ganzes Haus* of small artisans and peasant farmers with an urban proletariat that worked in the factories, coal mines, shipyards, and the workshops of newly industrialized areas like the Ruhr. There, women and men were integrated into the industrial economy quite differently. Until recently, labor historians, focused on class issues and the rise of a primarily male labor movement, rarely wrote about women's labor. Generally, in such accounts, women appeared merely in terms of the nineteenth-century problem of intensified capitalist exploitation—of employers in sectors of the economy undergoing mechanization and deskilling, who intentionally undercut male wages and autonomy by substituting the lower-paid, unskilled work of women and children. More recent feminist labor histories, integrating gender, have brought a new understanding of both women's roles in the industrial economy and the close interconnections—despite the ideology of separate spheres—between production, reproduction, and consumption, i.e. work and family.[8]

We now know that what developed in the nineteenth century was a sex-segregated economy in which women were tracked into the lowest paid, lower skilled jobs, and into female sectors of industry, such as textiles, garment-making, and food processing. Women also disproportionately worked in less modern and non-unionized sectors of the economy, such as domestic service and industrial homework. While working for wages to help support their families, women continued to be responsible for domestic tasks. However, as production moved outside of the home, it became increasingly difficult to combine the two. The modern phenomenon of the 'double burden' came into existence. One solution for women was to perform wage labor in the home, piecework that was paid at extremely low rates. There were other factors disadvantaging women in the workforce: limited formal training in work skills (the inheritance of the pre-industrial guild system); constant interruptions of their work lives as they withdrew from waged labor for childbirth and other family matters; and outright discrimination. That discrimination on the part of employers was based on the norm of separate spheres, namely, that men were the primary breadwinners of the family and, hence, women were only subsidiary workers, as well as ones fit for certain female jobs and tasks. The male breadwinner—an identity strongly embraced by many male workers themselves—justified paying women lower wages, keeping them out of higher paid, unionized 'male' jobs in heavy industry, and withholding promotions to managerial positions. It also affected skill definitions (and, hence, wage scales) themselves.

Even within the same workplace, tasks performed by women could be classified as unskilled, whereas the same or similar male tasks were labeled as semi-skilled.[9] Skill, in other words, was in part a social construct, the result both of employer exploitation and the demands of many male workers, whose work and family identities (as breadwinners and heads of households), we now know were closely intertwined.

Labor unions and the Social Democratic Party (SPD), the political voice of the independent labor movement, had a fraught and ambivalent relationship to women workers. On the one hand, Socialist writers, such as Friedrich Engels and August Bebel, developed extremely important and influential critiques of patriarchy.[10] Women under capitalism, they argued, were doubly oppressed: as domestic slaves within the bourgeois family and as exploited workers in capitalist industry. Women would not be truly emancipated, therefore, until the advent of socialism. The SPD built on these ideas, becoming the only political party before 1918 that advocated women's suffrage and the 'abolition of all laws which place women at a disadvantage to men in public and civil law.'[11] The party, moreover, contained its own massive women's section (200,000 on the eve of WWI), led by the socialist-feminist Clara Zetkin and devoted to women's issues.[12] On the other hand, women were perceived as threats to many trade unionists and male, especially skilled, workers—as unskilled replacement workers, illegitimate usurpers, and violators of proper gender roles.

The German welfare state was likewise shaped by and institutionalized a separate-spheres ideal of gender roles. Bismarck's introduction of social insurance (disability, health, and old-age) in the 1880s is well known and usually seen in terms of the history of class, as the state's attempt to appease and buy off an increasingly organized and radicalized working class. Less well known is that this legislation was crafted specifically with male workers in mind. Predicated upon the norm of the male breadwinner, this form of welfare assumed the active, politically-enfranchised citizenship of its recipients. At the same time, a quite different form of welfare applied to women and children: poor relief and protective legislation.[13] First introduced in the 1878 labor code, the latter forbade women from working in mines and provided childbearing women with 3 weeks maternity leave. The revised 1891 labor code, expanding this, 'excluded women from night work, mandated an eleven-hour day for women workers, and expanded maternity leave' to 6 weeks.[14] It also gave women extra time at lunch and on Saturdays to perform domestic duties at home. Protective legislation was helpful to and embraced by many women. However, it was predicated on and reinforced the notion of women's dependent and subordinate status in the family, and their lack therefore of active political rights. It was the product of fears on the part of social reformers and legislators about the rapid expansion of married women factory workers in the last decades of the century, which was thought to be endangering the health of the family and the nation. Causing infant mortality, miscarriage, the break-up of the family, and the displacement of male workers, women's bodies came to be a central arena for debates about work, society, and nation. The result for men and women was to 'codify a sexual division of labor' in the workplace and the family.[15]

While the notion of separate spheres shaped laws and institutions, economic, political, social, and cultural developments were working to erode sexual inequalities and the dominance of fathers and husbands in the family. Industrialization, while re-inforcing sex-segregation in the workplace, also, in undermining the patriarchal *Ganzes Haus*, freed the sexual and marital choices of youths.[16] The dispossessed urban working classes were no longer bound in their sexual and marital choices by the constraints of inheritance and property. For former pre-industrial laborers, servants, and journeymen now-turned industrial workers, the personalized, familial authority of the *Hausvater* was being replaced by the more distant and impersonal authority of the mill owner. Likewise, hierarchical links between the various estates were gradually supplanted by horizontal relations of class. A similar process was taking place in some rural areas, the result of changing agricultural practices and family strategies.[17]

An organized bourgeois feminist movement emerged in the 1860s that, by the turn of the century, was connected to a massive women's movement under the umbrella organization of the Federation of German Women's Associations (BDF). Building upon decades of organizational experience in women's charity and philanthropic associations, feminists based their demands for women's rights on both liberalism and a revised version of separate spheres. Appropriating a liberal political culture of rights, they demanded the end to women's second class status, to improvements in women's legal status, and to access to higher education, better jobs, and, finally, the vote. Feminists, however, often made these arguments within the language of matern-alism and gender difference, arguing that precisely because of their value as caregivers and 'spiritual mothers,' women should be given expanded rights and roles outside the home. They also argued for the special needs and rights (e.g. maternity leave) of women as mothers and housewives.[18] This discourse, in effect, turned separate spheres on its head, while at the same time accommodating its notion of gender difference. Bourgeois feminism was a movement that was less developed and, in some historians' minds, more conservative than its counterparts in England and the USA (one important reason was the ban on women's political activities that was in effect in Prussia and most of Germany from 1850 to 1908). It nevertheless posed a radical threat to the patriarchal order of separate spheres. This was particularly the case after the movement began to see practical results in gaining women entrance into the male bastions of the universities and some professions. These developments coincided in time with a sex reform movement that, together with the radical wing of the feminist movement (*Bund für Mutterschutz*), were agitating for women's reproductive rights, and for the rights of homosexuals, single mothers, and their children.

The most important single event undermining separate spheres was World War I. In fundamental ways, the war and its aftermath challenged and weakened the patriarchal bourgeois family and its system of gender relations. This was not supposed to be so. At the outbreak of war in 1914, as men heroically marched off to war, leaving their wives to care for home and hearth, and as feminists rallied to the flag, it looked like a godsend for antifeminists and supporters of separate spheres. However, months and years of stalemated industrial warfare turned the Great War into something altogether new:

a total war requiring the mobilization and co-ordination on an unprecedented scale of the country's resources. With large numbers of men away at the war and a growing labor shortage, women began entering *en masse* male jobs in the armaments industry (chemicals, iron, steel, engineering), and in transportation and the postal service, all of which were crucial to the war economy. It is not, as previously believed, that there was a large increase in the numbers of women working for the first time outside of the home;[19] it was *what* they were doing, the symbolism of women 'wielding pneumatic drills'[20] and manning railway stations, that struck contemporaries. With their husbands and fathers away at the war, many women themselves experienced a new sense of freedom, responsibility, and importance in their new roles as the primary breadwinners, heads of households, and contributors to the war effort. They were now appealed to as nationally valued workers and as 'mothers of the nation,' whose reproductive functions would help save the nation from demographic death. Domesticity itself was transformed. In the extremely harsh economic conditions of the war, it meant scrounging for food, waiting in long lines, rationing, and, for the poor and lower middle class, welfare support. Reproduction and consumption, the traditional roles of women, were becoming nationalized and militarized.[21]

A similarly transformative experience was taking place among men. On a massive scale, husbands and fathers were inducted into the war, a fact that greatly intensified the identification, begun in the early nineteenth century, of masculinity with warfare. Male gender authority, legitimized earlier by the masculine role of family breadwinner, came to be based on the ideal of the militarized soldier. Trench warfare on the western front, at the same time, was a new phenomenon: far from offering the experience of heroic combat, it was a mechanized, depersonalized killing field. It offered terror and disempowerment, the rates of 'shell shock,' a newly discovered psychiatric illness, being one symptom of that.[22] There was resentment and alienation from the allegedly cushy and feminized home front. In this situation, many soldiers found solace and meaning with their fellow soldiers. Their same-sex bonding in comrade associations and *Männerbunde*, which celebrated a militarized ideal of group loyalty as the basis for manhood, would remain after the war, shaping political movements and offering a ready model for a new fascist politics.[23]

A sense of gender crisis continued into the post-war years under the Weimar Republic. Returning soldiers, many emotionally and physically damaged, found their country in upheaval: the abdication of the Kaiser, revolutionary uprisings, and economic chaos. Gender roles seemed to be turned on their heads. Feminists saw the realization in 1918 of a long-sought goal: woman's suffrage. Thousands of women were entering political office and public life. War widows were heading their households. A new and, for many disquieting, modern woman was emerging. Young, single, urban, the New Woman, who typically worked in white-collar jobs, was, unlike her mother's generation, independent, sexually active, a frequenter of nightclubs, and a consumer of mass culture, whose androgynous appearance—bobbed hair, athletic lean body—physically embodied the way she blurred and transgressed the boundaries of traditional femininity.[24]

The alleged undermining of the patriarchal family—the rise of 'double earners' (married women performing paid labor outside the home), and sexually liberated New Women—became a powerful symbol of the breakdown of the social fabric in the chaotic years of the Weimar Republic, subject to intense political debate, social policy interventions, and efforts to resurrect the traditional gender order. The Nazis played directly on these gender anxieties as they built their movement in the Weimar years. Together with Jews and leftists, feminists and New Women became symbols in Nazi propaganda of the decadence and weakness of liberal democracy and modern urban life. Railing against the 'soulless' and 'egotistical' modern woman, National Socialists called for their return to the home and for the restoration of the patriarchal family—for, as the slogan went, 'emancipation from emancipation'.

At the same time, the Nazis built upon the militarized masculinity and culture of comradeship that had evolved in WWI, glorifying the ideal of a brotherhood of self-sacrificing soldier-comrades, and turning it into an extreme cult of violence, hardness, and duty to the racial *Volk*.[25] A study of the writings of members of the *Freikorps*—right-wing paramilitary groups of ex-soldiers and officers formed in the aftermath of WWI—explores the unconscious fears and desires of this fascist masculinity. It shows the deep misogyny of men who possessed weak, fragmented egos, whose terrors of psychic dissolution were associated with feminization and female sexuality, and who, as a result, embraced a cult of masculine hardness and violence as an emotional defense mechanism.[26] The extraordinary loyalty of most German soldiers to the war effort during WWII suggests how deeply and widespread the militarized ideal of masculine comradeship had been internalized. The historian Thomas Kühne ascribes the low level of desertions—despite genocide, catastrophic military setbacks, and the growing realization that the war was lost—to an ingrained pressure to conform and persevere, even in the face of death, in soldiers for whom displays of cowardice and disloyalty to the group were, according to their sense of manhood, the equivalent of social death.[27]

To what extent did the Nazis' anti-emancipationist and antifeminist message resonate with women voters? Women came late to voting for the Nazis (only when the Great Depression set in after 1929). However, even before this, the majority of them did not vote along gender lines in the interest of women's emancipation. Instead, many voted for conservative and antifeminist parties—DNVP and Catholic Center party—whose gender messages were similar to the Nazis. These women seemed to have voted their class over their gender interests. To be sure, this situation was not unique to Germany; across the western world, newly-enfranchised women refused to vote as a woman's bloc, to the great disappointment of suffragists. However, given the political stakes involved, the phenomenon in Germany has been the subject of great interest and controversy among historians.

A number of historians fault German feminism itself, arguing that the movement possessed certain characteristics—it was more conservative, nationalist, and maternalist relative to its counterparts in England and the USA—that played into the antifeminist message of the right and that paved the way for the capitulation of feminist leaders to the Nazis in 1933.[28] More recently, this *Sonderweg* view has been refuted by studies showing both the ubiquity of maternalism in western feminism, and its empowering and emancipatory aspects.[29] Whatever the role of feminism, there is a broader social explanation for women's voting patterns. They voted for antifeminist parties, including the Nazis, because 'emancipation' in the Weimar years had brought so few gains to the majority of women. Gender equality, enshrined in the Weimar constitution, remained merely on paper. Women continued to experience massive discrimination and hostility in the workplace. Most women worked in menial, dead-end jobs. The double burden of waged work and domesticity, far from disappearing, was intensified by Weimar's ruined economy. Conservatives and Nazis appealed to the anxieties caused by these and other problems, promising protection and support to women as mothers and housewives, while 'upgrading' those traditional roles into a calling crucial to the well-being of the nation and *Volk*.[30]

Conservative women activists played an important role in the backlash against Weimar democracy and the propagation of a nationalist and *völkisch* (racialist) discourse that helped pave the way for the Nazi takeover in 1933. However, they did so, unlike their male counterparts, by marshalling maternalist rhetoric about women's special nurturing natures in order, paradoxically, to argue for women's inclusion in public life. They asserted that, precisely because of their motherly qualities, women were essential to the cause of defending Christian traditions and championing national harmony. In doing so, they mobilized thousands of like-minded women and succeeded in building a separate 'female-dominated, conservative sub-milieu' that has been the focus of recent historical research.[31]

In the sphere of gender relations, the Third Reich constituted an extreme antifeminist backlash aimed at restoring male authority in the family and society. Once in power, the National Socialists banned or Nazified all feminist and women's groups. They dismissed women from government posts, fired married female civil servants, forbade women from the legal professions and, in effect, from practicing medicine. Other measures to force or induce women back into the home included the slapping of a 10% quota on women's admissions to universities and offering interest-free family loans to young 'Aryan' couples with the proviso that the wife abstain from paid employment.[32] (These policies were later reversed when re-armament and war led to massive labor shortages.)

Yet, at the same time, much of National Socialist gender and reproductive policy was built upon radically new ideas whose effect was essentially the destruction of the private bourgeois family. It disappeared under the Third Reich because the liberal values on which it had been based—the separation of private and public spheres; an autonomous civil society—ceased to exist. They were replaced by an extreme nationalization and militarization of life for the purposes of racial purification and world domination. Nazi masculinity, revolving around a cult of violence and the man-of-steel soldier dedicated to race, nation, and *Volk*, was a far cry from the bourgeois paterfamilias. Similarly, the domestic roles of women were utterly transformed by their new mission to breed and raise the master race. This, unlike nineteenth-century femininity, required both racial and physical fitness. It involved the mass mobilization of women in groups like the

League of German Maidens and the National Socialist Womanhood, whose purpose was bringing women into the party state through indoctrination and the organization of daily life—in leisure activities, housekeeping, and childrearing courses, and so forth. As settlement advisors and teachers, it also involved women in the violent Germanization of occupied Poland during WWII.[33] Equally extreme were Nazi eugenic policies that brought under state control the deepest private matters of bourgeois culture: marriage, sexuality, and reproduction. For the 'racially fit,' this involved pro-natalist policies ranging from a crackdown on abortions, generous family loans, genetic 'counseling centers,' and the *Lebensborn* program, in effect, breeding centers that encouraged for the good of the Reich out-of-wedlock sexuality between racially super-ior SS officers and their female counterparts. An opposite set of policies—anti-natalism—were implemented on the 'racially unfit'—Jews, the mentally ill, physically impaired, alcoholics, prostitutes, and other undesirables. These policies included forced sterilization, 'euthanasia,' and, finally, mass murder in the death camps.

Gender roles influenced men's and women's experiences of persecution, incarcera-tion, and, even, death. Among Jews in post-1933 Germany, women, because of their more direct involvement as housewives in neighborhoods and communities, were often more in touch with the pervasiveness of anti-Semitism in daily life, and were more likely, on this basis, to be advocates of emigration. Their husbands, on the other hand, were more likely to be the first ones in the family to emigrate because of the belief that as men they were in greater physical peril; that women, on the other hand, had a better chance of finding work in Germany (in Jewish welfare organizations); and that girls should remain as caretakers for elderly parents and grandparents who were unable to leave Germany.[34] In the concentration camps, there is evidence that women utilized certain gender-specific survival skills from their former lives, such as social-networking and care-giving skills that helped women inmates create support networks and without which any chance of survival was impossible.[35] Gender, on the other hand, made women more vulnerable in the camps—from rape and pregnancy, the latter of which was a death sentence. In the inverted world of Auschwitz, women's traditional maternal roles put them at greater risk of being murdered: women arriving in the camp with young children were often sent immediately to the gas chambers, the camp authorities not wanting to deal with the problems of separating mother and child. Here, in the camps, in the name of a hypermasculinist racialist state, the idea of protecting the 'weaker sex' no longer held any meaning. Race had come to entirely consume traditional gender distinctions along with the other values that had constituted civilized life.

Gender—as both a set of social relations between the sexes and as a symbolic system of thought—was crucial to the reconstitution of post-war national identities in West and East Germany after the devastations of war, defeat, occupation, and division. For Germans, part of the devastation, we now know, came from the chaos wrought within families and gender relations. Germany in these years was characterized by large numbers of female-headed households, their husbands and fathers having perished in the war or been incarcerated in POW camps. Traumatized returning soldiers found ruined cities and homes, wives and girlfriends used to fending for themselves and fraternizing, to this end, with occupying soldiers in the western zones. In the Soviet zone there was mass rape of German women. In both cases, German men found themselves unable or unwilling to perform as 'men,' namely supporting and providing for their families. Divorce rates climbed, and a sense of anxiety and crisis surrounded this apparent breakdown in masculinity, gender, and the family.[36]

That anxiety was incorporated into the stories West Germans began to tell themselves as they sought to process (and repress) the past and construct a new national identity. There was the widespread notion that emerged of German victimization, which was constructed out of women's experiences as victims of allied bombing and Red Army rapes. There was the heroic German symbolized by the 'Rubble Women'— the hardworking women, standing alone, successfully facing adversity in the bombed out cities. There was the sexually promiscuous woman fraternizer, symbol of Germany's 'moral decline' and degradation under foreign occupation.[37]

Well into the 1950s, in both West and East Germany, there continued to be intense fears about 'overly powerful women and weak men'.[38] Yet efforts to reassert male authority in both Germanies were constructed quite differently. West Germany built its state and civil society around obsessive concerns about restoring the private nuclear family of traditional gender roles. Its program of benefits to children (*Kindergeld*), for example, was set up with the norm of the male wage earner supporting dependent wife and children, despite the large numbers of needy families headed by women. These alternative families were shut out of the program because benefits went to wage earners with at least three children, and most single or widowed women had fewer offspring. Likewise, the Pension Reform Act of 1957, which greatly improved benefits, continued the practice since the inception of pension insurance in the 1870s of tying benefits to earnings and the wage contract. This again disadvantaged women workers (not to mention non-wage-earning women), because they earned less due to differential gendered wage scales and the complex ways that women's domestic duties in the family impacted their work lives (e.g. part-time work and interruptions for child-rearing).[39]

There were, on the other hand, more gender-equitable models for the welfare state in contemporary Europe. The French system, supported by the French labor movement, had long accommodated and supported the fact of high numbers of married women in the workforce.[40] Sweden's egalitarian policies, most strikingly, were crafted on the 'assumption that all adults would work outside the home and that [therefore] single women with children needed particular assistance' (e.g. daycare facilities).[41] The obsession in West Germany with restoring the 'normal family' was not only about overcoming the war. It was also deeply linked with cold war politics and the dominance of the conservative CDU/CSU coalition in these years. The 'normal family' became a marker of liberal democracy, distinguishing West Germany from the authoritarian statism of both National Socialism and socialist East Germany. In this thinking, not state interference, but the private family would be the basis of West German democracy and a 'bulwark against communism.'[42] The historically strong maternalist strain in German feminism, as well as organized labor's ambivalence toward women workers, made both these groups less effective in countering conservative West German gender policies.

In this sense, continuity across multiple divides of German history—1871, 1914, 1918/ 1919, and 1945—characterized gender ideals in the West. To be sure, formal legal equality of the sexes became law in the West German Basic Law (1949). However, it was not until the introduction of a revised civil code in 1957 that wives were granted legal equality with their husbands. Even then, it took a 1959 Constitutional Court ruling to strike down as unconstitutional a provision that had continued to grant fathers authority over matters related to a couple's children.[43]

Building state socialism in East Germany had quite different consequences for gender. Instead of the 'family-centered citizenship' of West Germany, the SED (Socialist Unity Party) state substituted the 'state-citizen' model.[44] This downplaying of the family unit combined with economic and ideological factors—the socialist critique of gender inequality and the bourgeois family—to underpin a new gender ideal of the citizen worker, both male and female. State policies, accordingly, greatly encouraged women to enter and stay in the workforce. Those policies favoring women's employment included recruitment and training programs, opening up formerly male jobs, equal pay for equal work, numerous social services for working mothers, which, in the 1970s, were expanded to include generous daycare facilities and maternity leave. The result was that in East Germany, in contrast to both the contemporary West and to previous eras, women did not face in the same way the need to choose between motherhood and a career. Yet, the division of labor in the East German family remained largely what it had always been: the burden fell almost exclusively on women, which continued to disadvantage them in their work and political roles.[45] The political trade-off, moreover, for policies of gender equality was very high indeed.

This chapter has shown the powerful role played by the norm of separate spheres over two centuries of German history. As an asymmetrical ideal of gender relations, separate spheres shaped not only social roles within the family, but wage scales and industrial labor relations, the development of civil society, political rights and movements, national identities, and the welfare state. Private and public identities, from this historical perspective, were deeply intertwined. Given this insight, which derives from a rich and growing historiography, it is no longer possible, as it was in the early days of women's history in the 1970s, to marginalize gender history as a field 'merely' about adding women's voices and experiences to the existing historical record. Gender has become a tool of historical analysis that is allowing historians of Germany and other nations to challenge and rethink that historical record. For, in historian Joan Scott's influential formulation, gender lays at the heart of the way societies organize social and power relations, being a 'constitutive element of social relationships based on perceived differences between the sexes . . . and a primary way of signifying relationships of power.'[46] This insight in German history has opened up new understandings of the lives of women and men. It is also, as this essay has shown, providing new insights and perspectives on traditional historical topics, from the nature of industrialization to war, fascism, and the post-war division of Germany.

Notes

1. A recent collection of essays offers the best introduction to the newest scholarship on the way historians have been rethinking German history from the point of view of gender: Karen Hagemann and Jean H. Quataert (eds), *Gendering Modern German History: Rewriting Historiography* (New York: Berghahn Books, 2007).

2. For one overview of the era, see Heide Wunder, *He Is the Sun, She Is the Moon: Women in Early Modern Germany* (Cambridge: Harvard University Press, 1998).

3. Karin Hausen, 'Family and Role-Division: the Polarization of Sexual Stereotypes in the Nineteenth Century—An Aspect of the Dissociation of Work and Family Life,' in R. Evans and W. R. Lee (eds), *The German Family* (London: Barnes and Noble, 1981), pp. 51–83. Hausen's essay remains influential, despite challenges. See, e.g., Ulrike Gleixner and Marion W. Gray (eds), *Gender in Transition: Discourse and Practice in German-Speaking Europe, 1750–1830* (Ann Arbor: University of Michigan Press, 2006).

4. Rebekka Habermas, *Frauen und Männer des Bürgertums* (Göttingen: Vandenhoeck & Ruprecht, 2000). See also Anne-Charlott Trepp, *Sanfte Männlichkeit und selbstständige Weiblichkeit* (Göttingen: Vandenhoeck & Ruprecht, 1996).

5. Isabel V. Hull, *Sexuality, State, and Civil Society in Germany, 1700–1815* (Ithaca: Cornell University Press, 1996).

6. Karen Hagemann, 'A Valorous *Volk* Family: The Nation, the Military, and the Gender Order in Prussia in the Time of the Anti-Napoleonic Wars, 1806–15,' in I. Blom, K. Hagemann, C. Hall (eds), *Gendered Nations: Nationalism and Gender Order in the Long Nineteenth Century* (Oxford: Berg, 2000), 179–205; idem, *'Mannlicher Muth und teutsche Ehre': Nation, Militär und Geschlecht zur Zeit der antinapoleonischen Kriege Preussens* (Paderborn: F. Schöningh, 2002); Ute Frevert, *A Nation in Barracks: Modern Germany, Military Conscription, and Civil Society* (Oxford: Berg, 2004).

7. Harry Willekens, 'Die Geschichte des Familienrechts in Deutschland seit 1794: Eine Interpretation aus vergleichender Perspektive,' in Stephan Meder et al. (eds), *Frauenrecht und Rechtsgeschichte* (Cologne: Böhlau, 2006), 137–168.

8. Laura L. Frader and Sonya O. Rose (eds), *Gender and Class in Modern Europe* (Ithaca: Cornell University Press, 1996).

9. The classic work on this subject was done in reference to British labor history: Anne Phillips and Barbara Taylor, 'Sex and Skill: Notes Towards a Feminist Economics,' *Feminist Review* 6 (1980), 79–88. On German working-class women and labor, see Kathleen Canning, *Languages of Labor and Gender: Female Factory Work in Germany, 1850–1914* (Ithaca: Cornell University Press, 1996).

10. Friedrich Engels, *The Origin of the Family, Private Property, and the State*, first published in German in 1884. August Bebel's widely-read *Woman Under Socialism* (German original, 1879).

11. Quoted in Frevert, *Women in German History*, 141.

12. Stefan Berger, 'Labor Movements,' in: idem (ed.), *A Companion to Nineteenth-Century Europe* (Malden, MA: Blackwell Pub, 2006), 173–174.

13. This section summarizes the argument of Kathleen Canning, 'Social Policy, Body Politics: Recasting the Social Question in Germany, 1875–1900,' in Frader (ed.), *Gender and Class in Modern Europe*.

14. Ibid., 224.

15. Ibid., 234.

16. Annette F. Timm and Joshua A. Sanborn, *Gender, Sex and the Shaping of Modern Europe: A History from the French Revolution to the Present Day* (Oxford: Berg, 2007).

17. David Warren Sabean, *Property, Production, and Family in Neckarhausen, 1700–1870* (Cambridge: Cambridge University Press, 1990).

18. For an introductory overview, see Angelika Schaser, *Frauenbewegung in Deutschland, 1848–1933* (Darmstadt: WBC Wissenschaftliche Buchgesellschaft, 2006). On German feminism in comparative and international context, see Ann Taylor Allen, 'Feminist Movements in the United States and Germany: A Comparative Perspective, 1848–1933,' in Manfred Berg and Michael Geyer (eds), *Two Cultures of Rights: The Quest for Inclusion and Participation in Modern America and Germany* (Cambridge: Cambridge University Press, 2001), 231–247; Ute Gerhard, 'The Women's Movement in Germany in an International Context,' in Sylvia Paletschek and Bianca Pietrow-Ennker (eds) *Women's Emancipation Movements in the Nineteenth Century* (Stanford: Stanford University Press, 2004), 102–122; Karen Offen, *European Feminisms, 1700–1950* (Stanford: Stanford University Press, 2000).

19. Ute Daniel, 'Women's Work in Industry and Family: Germany, 1914–18,' in Richard Wall and Jay Winter (eds), *The Upheaval of War* (Cambridge: Cambridge University Press, 1988), 267–296. See also, Ute Daniel, *The War From Within: German Working-Class Women in the First World War* (Oxford: Berg, 1997).

20. Frevert, *Women in German History*, 157.

21. Elisabeth Domansky, 'Militarization and Reproduction in World War I Germany,' in Geoff Eley (ed.) *Society, Culture, and the State in Germany, 1870–1930* (Ann Arbor: University of Michigan Press, 1996), 427–463. Belinda J. Davis, *Home Fires Burning: Food, Politics, and Everyday Life in World War I Berlin* (Chapel Hill: University of North Carolina Press, 2000); Ute Daniel, *The War From Within*.

22. Paul Lerner, *Hysterical Men: War, Psychiatry, and the Politics of Trauma in Germany 1890–1930* (Ithaca: Cornell University Press, 2003).

23. Domansky, 'Militarization,' in Thomas Kühne (ed.) *Kameradschaft: Die Soldaten des nationalsozialistischen Krieges und das 20. Jahrhundert* (Göttingen: Vandenhoeck & Ruprecht, 2006).

24. Atina Grossmann, 'The New Woman and the Rationalization of Sexuality in Weimar Germany,' in Ann Snitow et al. (eds), *Powers of Desire: The Politics of Sexuality* (New York: Monthly Review Press, 1983), 153–171; Ann Goldberg, 'The Black Jew with the Blond Heart: Friedrich Gundolf, Elisabeth Salomon, and Conservative Bohemianism in Weimar Germany,' *Journal of Modern History* 79, no. 2 (June 2007), 306–334.

25. Thomas Kühne, *Kameradschaft: Die Soldaten des nationalsozialistischen Krieges und das 20. Jahrhundert* (Göttingen: Vandenhoeck & Ruprecht, 2006).

26. Klaus Theweleit, *Male Fantasies* 2 vols (Minneapolis: University of Minneapolis Press, 1987, 1989).

27. Kühne, *Kamaradschaft*.

28. Richard Evans, *The Feminist Movement in Germany, 1894–1933* (London: Sage Publications, 1976); Claudia Koonz, *Mothers in the Fatherland: Women, the Family, and Nazi Politics* (New York: St. Martin's Press, 1987).

29. See, for example, Ann Taylor Allen, *Feminism and Motherhood in Germany, 1800–1914* (New Brunswick: Rutgers University Press, 1991); Karen Offen, *European Feminisms*.

30. Renate Bridenthal and Claudia Koonz, 'Beyond Kinder, Küche, Kirche: Weimar Women in Politics and Work,' in R. Bridenthal et al. (eds), *When Biology Became Destiny: Women in Weimar and Nazi Germany* (New York: Monthly Review Press, 1984), 33–65.

31. Adelheid von Saldern, 'Innovative Trends in Women's and Gender Studies of the National Socialist Era,' *German History* 27, no. 1 (January 2009), 89. For example, Raffael

Scheck, *Mothers of the Nation: Right-Wing Women in Weimar Germany* (Oxford: Berg, 2004). For a broader study of the link between women, ideas of domesticity, and nationalist politics, see Nancy Reagin, *Sweeping the German Nation: Domesticity and National Identity in Germany, 1870–1945* (Cambridge: Cambridge University Press, 2007).

32. Overviews of these and other Nazi gender matters can be found in Matthew Stibbe, *Women in the Third Reich* (London: Arnold, 2003); Jill Stephenson, *Women in Nazi Germany* (Harlow, England: Longman, 2001).

33. Elizabeth Harvey, *Women and the Nazi East: Agents and Witnesses of Germanization* (New Haven: Yale University Press, 2003).

34. Marion Kaplan, 'Jewish Women in Nazi Germany: Daily Life, Daily Struggles, 1933–1939,' in Carol Rittner and John K. Roth (eds), *Different Voices: Women and the Holocaust* (St. Paul, Minn.: Paragon House, 1993), 187–212.

35. A number of articles and primary sources in Carol Rittner and John K. Roth (eds), *Different Voices* suggest or claim this.

36. Frank Biess, *Homecomings: Returning POWs and the Legacies of Defeat in Postwar Germany* (Princeton: Princeton University Press, 2006).

37. Elizabeth Heineman, 'The Hour of the Woman: Memories of Germany's 'Crisis Years' and West German National Identity,' *American Historical Review* 101, no. 2 (April 1996), 354–395.

38. Uta Poiger, *Jazz, Rock, and Rebels: Cold War Politics and American Culture in a Divided Germany* (Berkeley: University of California Press, 2000).

39. Robert Moeller, *Protecting Motherhood: Women and the Family in the Politics of Postwar West Germany* (Berkeley: University of California Press, 1993).

40. Susan Pedersen, *Family, Dependence, and the Origins of the Welfare State: Britain and France, 1914–1945* (Cambridge: Cambridge University Press, 1993).

41. Moeller, *Protecting Motherhood*, 135.

42. Robert Moeller, 'Reconstructing the Family in Reconstruction Germany: Women and Social Policy in the Federal Republic, 1949–1955,' in idem (ed.), *West Germany Under Construction* (Ann Arbor: University of Michigan Press, 1997), 133.

43. Ibid.

44. Thomas Lindenberger quoted in Biess, *Homecomings*, 151.

45. Elizabeth Heineman, *What Difference: Women and Marital Status in Nazi and Postwar Germany* (Berkeley: University of California Press, 1999). For a recent study of gender politics in the GDR, see Donna Harsch, *Revenge of the Domestic: Women, the Family, and Communism in the German Democratic Republic* (Princeton: Princeton University Press, 2007).

46. Joan Scott, 'Gender: A Useful Category of Historical Analysis,' in idem (ed.), *Gender and the Politics of History* (New York: Columbia University Press, 1988), 42.

Bibliography

ALLEN, ANN TAYLOR, *Feminism and Motherhood in Germany, 1800–1914* (New Brunswick: Rutgers University Press, 1991).

BRIDENTHAL, RENATE, ATINA GROSSMANN, and MARION KAPLAN (eds), *When Biology Became Destiny: Women in Weimar and Nazi Germany* (New York: Monthly Review Press, 1984).

Canning, Kathleen, *Languages of Labor and Gender: Female Factory Work in Germany, 1850–1914* (Ithaca: Cornell University Press, 1996).

Dudink, Stefan and Karen Hagemann, John Tosh (eds), *Masculinities in Politics and War: Gendering Modern History* (Manchester: Manchester University Press, 2004).

Forth, Christopher, *Masculinity in the Modern West: Gender, Civilization, and the Body* (New York: Palgrave Macmillan, 2008).

Frevert, Ute, *Women in German History: From Bourgeois Emancipation to Sexual Liberation* (Oxford: Berg Publishers, 1990).

Habermas, Rebekka, *Frauen und Männer des Bürgertums: Eine Familiengeschichte (1750– 1850)* (Göttingen: Vandenhoeck & Ruprecht, 2000).

Hagemann, Karen, *'Mannlicher Muth und teutsche Ehre': Nation, Militär und Geschlecht zur Zeit der antinapoleonischen Kriege Preussens* (Paderborn: F. Schöningh, 2002).

—— and Jean H. Quataert, *Gendering Modern German History: Rewriting Historiography* (New York: Berghahn Books, 2007).

—— and Stefanie Schüler-Springorum, *Home/Front: The Military, War and Gender in Twentieth-Century Germany* (Oxford: Berg Publishers, 2002).

Heineman, Elizabeth D., *What Difference Does a Husband Make? Women and Marital Status in Nazi and Postwar Germany* (Berkeley: University of California Press, 1999).

Herzog, Dagmar (ed.), *Sexuality and German Fascism* (New York: Berghahn, 2005).

Moeller, Robert, *Protecting Motherhood: Women and the Family in the Politics of Postwar West Germany* (Berkeley: University of California Press, 1993).

Stibbe, Matthew, *Women in the Third Reich* (New York: Oxford University Press, 2003).

Timm, Annette F. and Joshua A. Sanborn, *Gender, Sex and the Shaping of Modern Europe: A History from the French Revolution to the Present Day* (Oxford: Berg, 2007).

Wunder, Heide, *He is the Sun, She is the Moon: Women in Early Modern Germany* (Cambridge, MA: Harvard University Press, 1998).

PART II

STATES, PEOPLE, AND NATION, 1760–1860

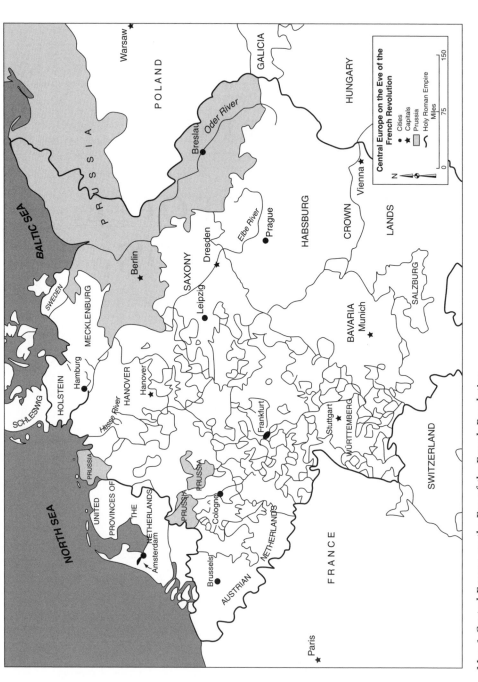

Map 1 Central Europe on the Eve of the French Revolution

Source: Jonathan Sperber (ed.), *Short Oxford History of Germany: Germany 1800–1870* (Oxford: Oxford University Press, 2004) 286.

CHAPTER 5

....

INTERNATIONAL CONFLICT, WAR, AND THE MAKING OF MODERN GERMANY, 1740–1815

....

UTE PLANERT

In the beginning was not Napoleon, but war. 'War made the state, and the state made war,' as Charles Tilly pithily summarized one of the core processes of European nation state building.[1] This was also true for the German states and for what would later emerge as the German nation state. Unlike in France and England, political loyalties in Germany oscillated between the Reich, the nation, and individual states, as well as between different confessions. For this reason, problems in the course of state and nation building were more complex than in those European neighbor states where centralized power was established earlier and on a mono-confessional basis. German-language research literature usually dates the beginning of the modern age to the fall of the Old Reich and the wars against the French Emperor. 'In the beginning was Napoleon': There is hardly any other expression which has been quoted more often than the suggestive first sentence to Thomas Nipperdey's *German History 1800–1866*. Like the declaration of independence in the USA and the revolution in France, the wars against the French Emperor served as a national foundation myth. However, the impact of the anti-Napoleonic wars as the threshold of a new era is often overestimated. In the following chapter, therefore, the transformation of the German states shall be discussed in the context of global developments. An emphasis will be put on the question of how international conflicts expedited the processes of state building and nationalization in Central Europe.

To this end, the developments in the Reich will first be embedded in the context of the shift in the international balance of power and the colonial rivalry between Great Britain and France, a conflict that marked the first nationally justified mobilization for war. From then on, wars were increasingly seen as being between nations, not states.

Even in the Old Reich, nationalization tendencies are traceable in Prussia, which on the eve of the French Revolution was on the cusp of becoming a nation. Secondly, the transformation of Europe through the wars of the French Revolution and the rise of the Napoleonic Empire shall be examined. It will be shown that Napoleon's policy can only be comprehended against the background of the global rivalry of France with Great Britain. This chapter will describe power politics on the continent and the fall of the Old Reich in four different spheres of influence according to their level of assimilation into the French system of rule, and will elaborate on the transnational integration and interdependences of this era. This will reveal the extent to which the French epoch pre-formed future developments in Central Europe—in territorial and political terms, but also in the formation of political loyalties. Seen from this perspective, the German states of the nineteenth century appear as the result of a long-lasting phase of international wars and conflicts from the middle of the eighteenth century until 1815. In the context of these conflicts, national ideas became increasingly prevalent, even though these ideas neither reached all strata of the population, nor all regions. In the Rhineland and the states of the former Confederation of the Rhine, the heritage of French rule accounted for the formation of a type of liberal and democratic national identity, which considered France as a role model rather than an opponent.

5.1 EUROPE AND THE WORLD: GLOBAL RIVALRY OF POWER AND CONTINENTAL POLITICS

The international rivalry of power played a pivotal role for European developments in the eighteenth century. Several German language territories strove to outgrow the constraints of the Holy Roman Empire, or Old Reich, and gain influence and importance. A number of dynasties had achieved a considerable increase in their political power: The Saxon Elector gained the Polish elective kingship, Welfs ruled in Great Britain, and the Bavarian Wittelsbachs tried to get involved in European politics by establishing close ties with France. To an even greater extent, Austria and Brandenburg-Prussia also tried to pull out of the Reich confederation. Both countries evolved during the eighteenth century from Reich territories into modern states: the Habsburgs from the reign of Charles VI (1711–1740) by giving priority to Austrian power politics instead of the Reich; Prussia by systematically breaking the power of the *Landstände* (provincial diets) and militarily forcing its way on to the European stage. The hitherto latent rivalry between the two great powers became virulent when Frederick II became king in 1740. From then on, the developing dualism between Prussia and Habsburg over Central European supremacy shaped the final stage of the Old Reich.[2]

In a calculated political maneuver, the young Prussian King Frederick invaded the Habsburg province of Silesia in December 1740, deploying an army that had been established by his father and that was said to be the best in Europe.[3] The international circumstances could not have been better for the realignment of Prussia's boundaries. In the recent war with Russia against the Ottoman Empire, the Habsburg monarchy accepted heavy losses and an expensive defeat. As Austria was also politically weakened through the death of Charles VI and Maria Theresia's controversial accession to the throne, it proved unable to defend Silesia. Its ally Russia, meanwhile, suffered from succession conflicts after the death of Tsarina Anna. While a new emperor of the Holy Roman Empire was being sought, England, France, and Spain tested their influence, while being bound by naval warfare in the Caribbean.[4] Frederick's calculations not-withstanding, the occupation of the profitable and strategically significant Silesian provinces turned into a long-lasting Europe-wide conflict. There were, above all, two reasons for this. First, Prussia's breach offered a welcome excuse for other countries to pursue their own agenda against Austria by entering the war. Secondly, the three wars over Silesia were part of a long-standing shift in the balance of power in Europe. In the course of this shift, conflicts and alliances occasioned by colonial interests increasingly influenced Central European politics according to overseas interests.

The Austro-Prussian conflict had as its backdrop the changing balance of global power. In the seventeenth century, the Netherlands had superseded Spain and Portugal as the leading trading and colonial power. After the gradual decline of the Spanish Empire and the fall of Dutch trading power, colonial antagonisms between Britain and France became a political constant of international relations.[5] During a number of 'cold' and 'hot' wars in North America from 1689 on, the situation increasingly changed in England's favor. Although the French were more successful than their opponents in mobilizing their Indian allies, the sparsely populated New France was, in the long run, unable to cope with the influx of settlers in the English territories and the pressure of their powerful trading companies. This was not least because it lacked support from the home country, which in terms of economic interests was increasingly oriented to the more profitable properties in the Caribbean. The War of the Spanish Succession, which marked the beginning of a new balance of power in Europe, was another conflict from which England (joined with Scotland in 1707 as the Kingdom of Great Britain) emerged victorious. The remaining disagreement between Britain and Spain over the control of the Mediterranean Sea, the Caribbean, and the profitable business from the trilateral trade—as well as the Austrian attempt to take part in the race for the oceans after acquiring the Austrian Netherlands—kindled several crises and wars between the European powers after 1718. However, like the conflicts between France and England in North America, these did not initially affect the European mainland. It was not until the Anglo-Spanish 'War of Jenkin's Ear,' officially declared in 1739 and conducted until 1742 in the Caribbean and the southern colonies of North America, that a colonial crisis affected Europe, creating an internationally favorable environment for Prussia to invade Silesia. In the War of the Austrian Succession, Naples, Spain, France, Sweden, and some German states fought on Prussia's side, while Great Britain, the Netherlands, and an aspiring Russia were Austria's allies. The British involvement in the continental war weakened British engagement in the Caribbean. Thus, Spain was initially able to hold its American positions. At the same time, Great Britain clashed with France in India, with the French temporarily prevailing against British interests.[6]

Although the War of the Austrian Succession concerned far more than just Silesia and was fought simultaneously on different continents, it would be inappropriate to call it a 'world war'.[7] Rather, it was a conglomerate of international conflicts fought between disciplined armies with regular soldiers over different dynastic claims to power. The civilian population and the political public sphere were hardly involved at all.[8] Frederick succeeded in enforcing his claim to the Silesian provinces, while Maria Theresia was able to gain the acceptance of the European powers for her succession to the throne. Yet the Second Treaty of Aix-la-Chapelle, which seemed to settle the matter, did not dampen the potential for international conflict. Austria had not accepted Prussia's annexation of Silesia, and nor had the colonial antagonism between Great Britain and France been defused. Starting in 1751, troops of the British East India Company battled with the armed forces of the French *Compagnie des Indes orientales* in India in an undeclared war. In North America, settlers skirmished again with soldiers from as early as 1750. These intermittent battles led to a European war four years later, which was not officially declared until 1756 with the beginning of the Seven Years' War between France and Great Britain. It was the first time that the colonial rivalry between both Western European powers affected European politics.

On the European continent, renewed armed conflict began when Prussia attacked Saxony in August 1756. Frederick had hoped to forestall a feared encirclement, the background of which was a diplomatic revolution, the so-called *renversement des alliances*. After the costly Peace of Aix-la-Chapelle, the Austrian State Chancellor, Wenzel Anton von Kaunitz, had prepared a new conception of foreign policy, which Maria Theresia subsequently approved. Contrary to the rather limited war aims typical of the *Ancien Régime*, Kaunitz proposed to cut back Prussia's territory to what it had been before the Thirty Years' War. To this end, France changed sides and on Kaunitz's instigation give up its century-long role as Austria's opponent and become a Habsburg ally.[9] The fact that Brandenburg-Prussia and Great Britain signed the Convention of Westminster in 1756, in order to secure Hanover, possibly eased this decision for France. Even if it came as a surprise for both contemporary and later observers, the new constellation of alliances in Europe only confirmed the colonial opposition between Great Britain and France as it had applied in North America and Asia.

5.2 Structural characteristics of the Seven Years' War as the initial point of modern processes of nationalization in Europe

The Seven Years' War was the first time that the great powers' interests outside Europe affected the European system of alliances. Battles were conducted simultaneously on different continents. Non-European events—first and foremost in the New World—played a crucial role by influencing the overall course of war. From a British perspective, the war in North America was, in fact, won in Silesia. London merely had to pay subsidies to the victorious Prussian army, whereas the military clout of the French troops overseas and France's financial strength suffered under the new circumstances in Europe. Therefore, there is good reason to perceive the Seven Years' War, as opposed to the War of the Austrian Succession, as the 'first world war'.[10]

Even the form of warfare changed: a larger number of soldiers now faced each other on the battlefield; traditional forms of warfare were superseded by decisive battles with heavy losses; small and unregulated combats and ambushes conducted with light units gained importance against large troop maneuvers. The Seven Years' War ushered in a new era in which wars were no longer limited to the battlefield. No longer a matter of cabinet policy alone, war absorbed great amounts of resources and involved civilians more than had hitherto been the case.[11] With the emergence of a politicized public sphere, conflicts were perceived as being fought between nations, not just states. In return, media coverage of the war affected the warring societies and accelerated the process of nationalization. Historians are accustomed to classifying the Seven Years' War as the last Cabinet War and to perceiving the Napoleonic Wars as the first people's wars.[12] A closer look, however, shows how debatable such a clear distinction is. If both wars represented the gradual transition towards a form of warfare without boundaries, increasingly involving the population of the territories, this process was never a straight line, and the new model was not fully realized until the twentieth century.[13]

The nationalization of publics was enabled by a process that had started in the first half of the eighteenth century and had gradually emerged among Western and Central European societies. The educated elites started to secure their national identity by looking at the past and, in so doing, legitimized their demand for political participation—albeit initially in limited forms. Several factors contributed to this process: the rise of the bourgeoisie, a growing tendency towards reform on the part of the aristocracy, a widening impact of Enlightenment ideas, intensified market integration, and the dissemination of new forms of communication and knowledge. From London to Paris, and not only in the larger cities, patriotic associations were founded. New newspaper journals offered the opportunity for lively discussions. The objectives in the long run were to establish a political public sphere, to limit the monarchs' power and to consider alternate political sovereignties. In France, the endemic disputes between the crown and the parliaments, newly-developed political theories, and the monarchy's crisis of legitimacy had encouraged the emergence of a large number of pamphlets written by the educated elites. For them, the sovereignty of the people and the political nation state increasingly became an alternative to monarchic rule. The number of publications with titles containing terms such as 'patriotic' and 'national' exploded during the eighteenth century. Up to the year 1700, there were only about 120 such tracts to be found; yet from 1700 until the beginning of the French Revolution, more than a thousand were published.[14] The flood of patriotic and national publications originated from domestic disputes. However, it was the war against the external rival that popularized the idea of being part of a politically active community. Thus, there is good reason to consider the Seven Years' War as the initial point of a transition period lasting into the *Vormärz* era. During this time, the already-existing awareness of a common German identity became politically charged by wars, conflict, and crisis, and gained in importance for more and more people.[15]

In both France and England, ideas of a common identity can be traced back to the High Middle Ages. The development of integrated markets and political centralism strengthened these ideas in the course of early modern times. Armed conflicts that flared up time and again intensified the processes of internal integration and of external differentiation. The religious antagonism between both countries, which perceived themselves as the protector of Catholic statehood, on the one hand, and as the representative of Protestant Christianity on the other, increased in equal measure. The multilayered rivalry between Great Britain and France was not at all new, and neither was its homogenizing internal impact. What was new, however, was that during the Seven Years' War, the military conflicts overseas caused a flood of newspaper articles, pamphlets, etchings, songs, and eye-witness reports on an unprecedented scale on both sides of the English Channel. These publications were supposed to demonstrate graphically the atrocities of the respective opponents. They mostly focused on the cruel behavior of the opposition towards the settlers in North America. Common themes, such as anti-Catholic resentments on the part of the British, and royalist attitudes on the French side, played a significant role. However, this international conflict was no longer staged as a religious war or as a conflict between states, but as a war between two irreconcilable nations. By this means, the colonial and economic rivalry between the two great Western European powers was turned into a mobilization for war which was, for the very first time, justified by the idea of the nation.[16]

Domestic and foreign policy motives were closely intertwined. In both Great Britain and France, the media mobilization of the masses was aimed at overcoming domestic problems. In France, war propaganda served as a means of legitimizing the continuation of the war in spite of the continual losses of battles and territories. Against the background of the empty state coffers and the desolate condition of the French navy, citizens were, for the first time, called upon to participate in the war and asked to give their silver tableware as a patriotic sacrifice in the national interest. Even without general conscription, the transition from a cabinet war to a national war began to show.[17]

British war propaganda followed a similar domestic strategy. During the previous decades, Jacobitism had been defeated and Scottish riots quelled. A tense relationship between England and Scotland remained, as did the widespread belief that the internal division of the country had to be overcome by developing a united national spirit. Initially, the British military proved to be one of the most important instruments of integration, because ambitious Scottish officers were able to make their career in the army. In addition, several patriotic associations emerged in the middle of the eighteenth century. They reflected the impressive alliance between economic and cultural nationalism, and an ambitious bourgeoisie demanding social influence. These associations were committed to keeping French influence at a distance, to supporting the idea of

'Britishness,' and to strengthening Britain's position in world markets. The Seven Years' War offered two opportunities at the same time: first, to expand Britain's economic and political dominance against its eternal rival, France, and secondly, to overcome the antagonism between England and Scotland by fighting an external enemy. For the sake of a domestic closing of ranks between the English and the Scottish, the confessional dimension was emphasized. English and Scottish Protestants could find common cause against French Catholicism. This patriotic attitude turned into active support for the war: patriotic organizations helped to provide British soldiers with clothing and consumer goods, and more than 10,000 soldiers were enlisted for service in the British navy.[18]

From the middle of the eighteenth century onwards, war left the arcane field of cabinet politics, taking place not only on the battlefield, but also as a matter of public opinion. Against the background of global political and economic rivalry, it turned from a dynastic conflict into the common interest of the entire nation.

5.3 Beginning of nationalization in the Reich

In the Old Reich with its multiple levels of legal relationships and loyalties, which oscillated between the Reich and individual states, the process of nationalization turned out to be much more complex than in the centralized states of Western Europe. Aware of the blur and overlap of empirical findings, I shall therefore distinguish between the notion of 'national consciousness' as the conceptualization of German self-awareness (to the exclusion of others) and of 'patriotism' as a demand for participation focused on the narrow fatherland. Nationalism is premised on the complex imagination of a common ontological entity, a concept of an ineluctable community affecting every single individual. It was often, but not necessarily, associated with xenophobia and claims of superiority. The term 'modern nationalism' applies when the nation is considered to be the greatest good, often with deadly implications.[19]

In the Reich, there had temporarily emerged a humanistic discourse of the nation at the beginning of the sixteenth century, which, however, remained limited to a small part of society. Religious confession still dominated the contemporary mindset; phases of national thinking came and went. The Christian-Muslim antagonism in the Reich wars against the Ottomans, and the intensive anti-French agitation of the Austrian court in the War of the Spanish Succession, served, by contrast, to generate a concept of the nation and to politicize the public sphere.[20] At the same time, so called 'patriotism' emerged at the level of the individual states, a certain 'moral and political' attitude of educated and propertied men who began 'to overcome their previous existence as subjects and to actively participate in the community' out of their love of fatherland.[21] Loyalty and participation legitimized political debates. The fact that even ruling monarchs ultimately began to call themselves 'patriots,' and justified their actions with reference to their love of fatherland, indicates how successful this concept had become. With this, the notion of birth and the doctrine of divine right as sources of monarchic sovereignty gradually gave way to a supposed common good.[22] The discourse on the fatherland contained a distinctly political element of participation, although it referred to the individual state.

In the middle of the eighteenth century, several new developments occurred that give us good cause to understand the following decades as a laboratory for the gradual formation of national consciousness, territorial patriotism, and even flickers of modern nationalism. The beginning of this national *Sattelzeit* saw the establishment of a national sphere of culture and communication, the popularization of war heroes, and the theoretical linking of the opportunity for participation with the willingness to die in the name of the nation, although that notion of nation referred to the territorial state (esp. Prussia), not to Germany as such. The War of the Austrian Succession started this process. A small number of authors seized upon the myth of Arminius and portrayed the French as 'Germany's oppressors' by referring to them as 'Gauls.' In so doing, they took up the critique of French cultural hegemony. By linking death to the love of the fatherland, a structural principle was adumbrated, if still only in the aesthetic sphere. This principle is, nevertheless, constitutive for modern nationalism. It holds that every man must be willing to sacrifice his life on the 'altar of the fatherland.' The martyrdom of Christ is thereby turned into the sacrificial death for the fatherland, and religious hopes of salvation and fantasies of eternity are transferred to the political collective.

During the Seven Years' War, Thomas Abbt was the first prose writer to divest this credo of its aesthetic aura and to demand from his contemporaries a willingness to 'die for the fatherland.' In this text, a forerunner of modern nationalism, war was completely re-evaluated. No longer seen as a horrific event, and even less as a judgment from above, war appeared as an instrument of purification both for the individual and the national community. To this effect, war atrocities were aestheticized, heroic death eroticized, and primordial affiliations to the family transferred to the national collective. The ultimate love of fatherland was closely linked to the idea that citizens could voluntarily commit themselves to a state based on reason, on a legal system, and on a voluntary limitation of power. Every individual, according to Abbt, would happily bow to such a state. Abbt, however, did not concede extensive political participation. Instead, equality in death was prior to political rights of equality, and willing acceptance of one's own physical extermination justified the right to participate, in the form of service, in the mission of the fatherland—which for Abbt was Prussia.[23]

Like Abbt's pamphlet, Johann Wilhelm Ludwig Gleim's war-glorifying military songs (*Grenadierlieder*) from 1758 were created in the context of an unprecedented Prussian propaganda campaign, which was far more successful then the Austrian effort.[24] Although King Frederick's concern was not the Reich, but Prussia, Prussian war propaganda, its structure and function, met all criteria on which the term 'nationalism' is usually based. In the wars against Austria, Prussia crossed the threshold not only of state building, but also of nation building—this included the emergence of war heroes, preachers of the fatherland, and the cult of the fallen. Here, a Prussian 'territorial nationalism' (Burgdorff) evolved, which remained dynastically based and tailored to King Frederick, even expressing itself in the merchandizing of the royal portrait on plates and tobacco pipe bowls.[25] The Seven Years' War was, to some extent, the foundation on which Prussia was able to build during the era of the 'wars of liberation' by mobilizing the public and engaging writers.[26]

National consciousness in the Reich was a different matter. It was threatened by the hegemony policy of its two great powers, with Austrian claims, as became apparent in the conflict over Bavarian succession, no less pronounced than Prussian demands. In the last third of the eighteenth century, the threat to the Empire fuelled intensive debates on the unity of the nation and the ability of the Reich to transform itself. The resulting plans, representing a wide range of opinion, addressed the question of whether it was possible to find a new organizing principle of the German nation.[27] Since the 1770s, poets and writers linked the nation to an inescapable speech and cultural community with a common 'national character.' The discussions in the media in the wake of Prussian and Habsburg attempts to increase their dominance had made significant contributions in this respect, so that, on the eve of the French Revolution, the Reich, like other European regions, featured several elements constitutive of national consciousness, even if it co-existed in the Reich with a territorial patriotism.[28] Taken together, these ideas contained:

- a specific identity of all Germans as a community of descent, with a common culture and language as well as a common history expressed in myths;
- the conscious opposition to and exclusion of different social collectives through war and propagandistic mobilization, first and foremost France, perceived as a hegemonic power;
- the transfer of primordial and emotional relationships to the national collective, especially, but not exclusively in the concept of fatherland. Indeed, in German sources, there was often a distinction between '*engeres*' (narrower, regional) and '*weiteres*' (expanded, German) Fatherland;
- the sacralization of the fatherland and the demand that citizens be willing to die for it—cultivated in the Prussian context, but not as prevalent elsewhere;
- a social group that not only articulated national ideas, but also possessed a communications infrastructure, enabling a nationwide discourse;
- the discussion on the political formation of the community in which the monarchs would be bound by law and their power limited—a process that occurred at both the level of the Empire and of the territorial fatherlands.

These national discourses were not about bourgeois demands for representation in constitutional and parliamentary terms. From a contemporary perspective, political participation could be expressed either through representation of the estates (*Stände*) or through the medium of the public sphere. Even Kant's draft of a representational government, developed in his writings on 'perpetual peace' six years after the French Revolution, did not provide for a parliament, but for a public sphere.[29]

5.4 Reshaping Europe through the wars of the French Revolution and the rise of the Napoleonic Empire

The French Revolution marked a deep caesura in European history. The fact that the French people declared themselves a sovereign nation, and disempowered the ruling aristocracy, fascinated the enlightened bourgeoisie of the neighboring countries, raised hopes among the lower classes and frightened the traditional elites. Although European rulers feared the expansion of the revolution, the war of the Reich against France quickly turned into a debacle. However, new forms of warfare and Napoleon's military genius were not the only reasons for France's military success. It was equally significant that, for many years, its European opponents were incapable of agreeing on a common strategy consistently applied. Accordingly, the coalition wars against France were characterized by changing participation and responsibilities. Great Britain and Austria were involved in most acts of war, either directly or indirectly. The great European powers were, however, only able to agree on a concerted operation after the downfall of the Russian army in the so called 'wars of liberation.' Before that, they merely pursued their own interests.

Whereas on the continent, the front line of the conflict ran between Paris and Vienna, the global rivalry between France and Great Britain over the colonies persisted.[30] Great Britain had realized the dangerous impact of the revolution on the other side of the English Channel, when France supported the Irish uprising, even though this upheaval was rapidly quelled. France also tried to expand its position in the Mediterranean area and in the Levant. After Napoleon had dismissed the idea of invading England directly, he received the order to conduct a campaign in Egypt. This was for internal political reasons, but also to interrupt British trade with India through a war in the Middle East and the occupation of the Isthmus of Suez. At the same time, this strategy was supposed to create a base of operation in order to acquire colonies in the Levant and, first and foremost, to re-establish French rule over India which had been lost during the Seven Years' War.

The defeat of the French fleet at Abukir was the first of several blows. English naval power destroyed the dream of restoring the French colonial empire. The declaration of 'Nouvelle France' in Louisiana proved just as impossible to realize as the plans for an empire in the Caribbean or the joint plan with Russia to take action against British India. Here, local groups had attempted to win over the French as allies against the British colonial rulers. In so doing, however, they had given welcome cause for further military expansions to the English 'men on the spot.' This meant that, by 1806, the British controlled two-thirds of the Indian subcontinent. At the same time, Great Britain exploited every possibility of acquiring the former Dutch territories in South Asia and the French islands in the Indian Ocean. Whereas British ships blockaded French ports, France was never able to seriously threaten the British Isles. The naval battle of Trafalgar finally defeated the combined fleet of Spanish and French ships, and guaranteed British domination of the seas for another century. Hence, from a global point of view, the Napoleonic Wars reinforced the colonial dualism between Great Britain and France.[31]

Apart from the short-lived peace of Amiens, both countries were in a state of permanent war during the years around 1800. As in the Seven Years' War, Great Britain was again focused on the situation overseas and involved itself on the continent only by paying subsidies—a fact that allowed the seemingly unstoppable expansion of Napoleon's armies on the mainland. British troops did not intervene in the continental war on the Iberian Peninsula before 1808. At this time, Napoleon had already begun to resort to economic warfare, having failed to beat Britain at sea or by conducting a land invasion. In 1806, Napoleon decreed the Continental System, a large-scale embargo against British trade, and forced his allies to control all European mainland ports. However, the embargo never achieved its target. Despite economic problems and domestic crises, the British Empire was never in substantial danger—unlike the Reich, which ultimately collapsed under the attacks of the revolutionary troops.[32]

In the course of the French Revolution and the turbulent international climate, Austria and Prussia attempted to expand their own territory while the middle states followed this example, attempting to achieve greater sovereignty from the Reich. In order to weaken his Austrian rival, on the verge of gaining victory over the Turks in 1788, the Prussian King Frederick William II welcomed the uprisings in Brabant, in Hungary, and in other fringe areas of the Habsburg monarchy in the summer and autumn of 1789. The two German states came to an agreement in 1790, which paved the way for joint action against revolutionary France. Despite its tradition as a military power, Prussia provided only a fraction of its resources for the campaign in the West. It hoped for new opportunities for expansion in the East, where Prussia, Austria, and Russia had acquired territories of the Kingdom of Poland in 1772. Like Prussia, Russia had become a European great power during the eighteenth century, catching up with Western European developments and superseding Sweden in the Northern War as the new dominant power in the Baltic area. In several Imperial wars against the Ottoman Empire, Russia expanded its territory ever further toward the West and the Black Sea. The ambitious tsardom also gained enormous influence in Poland and subsequently became a sought-after coalition partner of the great European powers.

In order to inhibit a domestic consolidation of Poland, and to avoid tensions between them after the declaration of the first European constitution, Prussia, Austria, and Russia further divided the territory. Finally, an uprising by Polish patriots came as a welcome excuse to dissolve the Polish state for good. In the third Partition of Poland in 1795, Austria annexed the whole of Galicia and Prussia increased its territory by a third, gaining more than two million new subjects. After this victory, Prussia withdrew as quickly as possible from the anti-French coalition in the west of the Reich. In the Peace of Basel in spring 1795, France and Prussia agreed to respect North Germany's neutrality. This led to a quiet decade for the inhabitants who lived in the eye of the storm. Prussia, on the other hand, was able to expand its influence in North Germany. Following a Prussian proposal, several North German territories joined Prussia's policy of neutrality and abandoned their duty to defend the Reich. A secret additional treaty of the Peace of Basel promised the King of Prussia the territories on the right bank of the River Rhine as compensation, if France were to lay permanent claim to the left bank and its Prussian territories.

The Peace of Basel had drawn a transverse demarcation line right through Germany. Austria and a rump coalition were the only states responsible for defending the South, and they proved too weak to carry out this task. Baden and Württemberg likewise left the coalition. Moreover, Vienna pursued its own agenda and hoped, for instance, to lay claim to Bavaria. The theatre of war moved to northern Italy, where Napoleon Bonaparte had, in the meantime, become the supreme commander of the French army. Sardinia-Piedmont and Austria had to accept defeat. In the Peace Treaty of Campo Formio, Francis II ceded the Austrian Netherlands and parts of northern Italy to France, and received, in exchange, the Republic of Venice which in the meantime had been plundered by French troops, and the prospect of acquiring Salzburg and parts of Bavaria at a later date. At the same time, Francis accepted the establishment of the Cisalpine and the Ligurian Republic in northern Italy. Hence, France had added several more satellite states to its wreath of client republics to which the Batavian and the Helvetic Republics already belonged.

The left bank of the Rhine, from the Palatine to the Lower Rhine, was also under French control. Therefore, it was of the utmost importance for the Reich that Francis II accepted the Rhine as France's eastern border in the secret additional protocol of the treaty of Campo Formio. As had happened in the Peace of Basel with Prussia, the Campo Formio agreement in principle stipulated that those *Reichsstände* affected would be compensated for their losses by gaining territories on the right bank of the Rhine. This was finally agreed at the negotiations between the Reich and France in Rastatt, much to the dismay of the ecclesiastical princes and territories. Under the circumstances, this compensation could only mean shattering ecclesiastical and less powerful secular regimes. During the previous decades, larger territories—first and foremost Prussia and Austria—had increasingly developed into modern states, sovereign and acquisitive, and smaller neighboring territories stood in their way. Negotiations after the beginning of the Second Coalition War could not be continued, and almost another decade went by before the Reich was ultimately dissolved. However, from this point on, the structure of the Reich was severely damaged.

After the Second Coalition War was lost, the Peace of Lunéville confirmed the conditions of Campo Formio and the process of dissolution continued. What had started in Rastatt ended with the *Reichsdeputationshauptschluss* (Principal Conclusion of the Extraordinary Imperial Delegation) in 1803. This treaty was largely oriented towards a Franco-Russian compensation plan: Russia had superseded Sweden as the guarantor power of the Reich in 1779. This last significant Reich law decreed nothing less than territorial revolution through secularization and mediatization. All free Imperial cities were abolished with the exception of six. Ecclesiastical princedoms and monasteries were dissolved and added to secular territories. Because Napoleon intended to create a system of independent middle states between France and Austria, and to strengthen the North German hegemony against Habsburg, Prussia and the South German states benefited the most from the geographical restructuring process in Central Europe. Prussia's new territories realigned the borders in North Germany and were five times larger than its lost regions on the left bank of the Rhine. Baden and Württemberg were able to point not only to their strategic location, but also to their family relations with the new Tsar Alexander I, and were bestowed even more generously. The Reich knights were not able to hold their ground without a powerful Reich for support, and had to accept the unlawful annexation of their territories by more powerful neighbors in the so called 'Rittersturm' of 1803.

All in all, the *Reichsdeputationshauptschluss* ended the existence of 112 territories with around three million inhabitants. At least 350 knights lost their imperial immediacy (*Reichsunmittelbarkeit*) by 1806. In 1804 the Habsburg monarch reacted to Napoleon's self-proclamation as Emperor of France by declaring himself Emperor of Austria in violation of Reich law. This event made it even clearer that not only Prussia's, but also Austria's interests, were beyond the Reich.

French military successes in Upper Italy, an area under Habsburg control, led the Austrian Emperor to join the Anglo-Russian coalition against France in the following year. This Third Coalition War revealed considerable deficiencies in Austrian warfare. Baden, Württemberg, and Bavaria already fought on the side of France and gained state sovereignty after the Peace of Pressburg. Napoleon had accomplished his goal of creating middle states capable of acting as the core of a 'Third Germany' and as a counterbalance against Prussia and Austria. Half a year later, sixteen southern and south-western German states left the Reich and formed the alliance of the Confederation of the Rhine (*Rheinbund*) under Napoleon's protectorate. On 6 August 1806, the Austrian Emperor declared the Reich dissolved. An institution with a history of nearly 1000 years had ceased to exist.[33]

Apart from the areas ruled by Austria, Prussia, Denmark, and Sweden, nearly all German territories joined the Confederation of the Rhine. The German-French military alliance reached from the Alps to the Baltic Sea. Prussia's hopes of a North German Empire, which Napoleon had fuelled by assigning the Electorate of Hanover to Prussia, were now obsolete. When Napoleon then offered to return Hanover to the English King— Nelson had recently devastated the French-Spanish fleet at Trafalgar—Frederick William III of Prussia declared war against France. After several crushing defeats, Prussia only narrowly escaped complete dissolution thanks to the backing of its Russian ally, and lost half of its territory. French occupation and large financial demands plunged the country into a severe crisis, which triggered expansive domestic reforms. Prussian territories on the western bank of the River Elbe were added to the newly created Kingdom of Westphalia ruled by Napoleon's brother Jerome. Prussia's former Polish territories became the Duchy of Warsaw and were joined in personal union with the new Kingdom of Saxony (a former Electorate) following the old tradition of Polish-Saxon relations.

Although he never succeeded in defeating his arch rival Great Britain, Napoleon was at the zenith of his continental power. As Emperor of France and King of Italy he turned the Netherlands, Naples, and smaller Italian areas into princedoms which were ruled by his siblings. Only Switzerland remained spared from the feudalization of the French satellite states. After the Spanish Bourbons had abdicated, a Napoleonic ally held the throne even in Spain. Family marriages consolidated the alliance with the princes of the Confederation of the Rhine. The Swedish Estates elected Jean Baptiste Bernadotte, one of Bonaparte's intimates, as crown prince. In 1809 Austria for the last time attempted to take military action against Napoleonic hegemony in Europe and had to pay a high price, losing substantial territories to the southern states of the Confederation of the Rhine. After that, the marriage between Napoleon and the Emperor's daughter, Marie Louise, would not only consolidate the relations between France and Austria, but also add some aristocratic prestige to the French throne.[34]

After the fall of the Reich, the German territories divided into four different spheres of influence, each developing in a different way: Prussia, Austria, France, and the Confederation of the Rhine. In Prussia, French occupation plunged the territory into an unprecedented economic and financial crisis. In addition to this came pressure from the French military that, in satisfying its own needs, attended little to the necessities of the Prussian people. Even after the withdrawal of the occupation army, however, the situation failed to improve, since Paris demanded large payments that raised the tax burden. The Continental System added to the economic collapse. Without export markets, food prices declined. Several landlords had to file for bankruptcy. The state, impoverished and diminished in size, had no use for many of its civil servants. The scaled-down army had to dismiss soldiers and officers who had difficulty returning to civilian life in the midst of the economic crisis. Even though the reform policy induced by Baron vom Stein and Karl August von Hardenberg modernized the state and laid the foundations of the dominant role Prussia would play in the nineteenth century, many people suffered and had reason enough to blame French politics for their misery.[35]

The situation on the left bank of the Rhine was completely different. The area between Basel and the Lower Rhine had been conquered in 1794. Four years later, it was integrated into France as four departments. For two decades around 1.5 million German-speaking people became French citizens. The old feudal system was replaced by equality before the law, with the introduction of the *Code Napoléon* paving the way for the development of the bourgeois society of proprietors. The economy of the left bank of the Rhine benefited from the new sales markets of the French Empire and could expand its lead substantially and perceptibly over the areas on the right bank. The Rhineland had, in fact, already been one of the most prosperous regions of the Reich, thanks to its proximity to England and the early industrialized areas of the Netherlands. There is good reason to assume that this economic dynamic would have caused political change anyway in the long run. However, the boom that started around 1800 would have been impossible without the new markets of greater France, without new legal relationships, and without the expansion of infrastructure forced by Napoleon. Once the chaotic situation following the invasion of the revolutionary troops had calmed down, the bourgeoisie of the Rhineland tended to regard the Napoleonic regime with favor.

Despite some unrest, wealthy parts of the population reconciled themselves with the Napoleonic system of conscription since they were able to buy their way out of military service. Although up to 60 per cent of young men from each age cohort were drafted, the number of deserters was even lower than the French average. It was not until the latter years of Napoleonic rule that, here as elsewhere, opposition to the conscription system grew. Even in the Rhineland, there was resentment at the Continental System that had caused the economic crisis. However, the invasion of allied troops in 1813 did not lead to the extensive anti-French feeling that the new Prussian administrators had expected. Instead of national sentiments, hopes were expressed in some cases for a return to the Old Reich. Still more evident was a pronounced regional identity.[36]

After the decline of the Old Reich, the manifold forms of rule such as involved Catholic dignitaries, lower aristocrats, free Reich cities, and Reich knights all vanished. These had earlier shaped the geography in the southern and western parts of German central Europe. Now, however, larger territorial states grew into kingdoms and grand duchies. In the northwest, the newly-created states of Berg and Westphalia were buffer zones between France and Prussia. Following the French model, many rulers and ministers forged modern states out of their territories, some achieving a degree of modernization equal, if not superior, to the Prussian reforms. Feudal privileges were abandoned, or at least limited, and the power of the state was extended. Judicial reform paved the way for the civil society. Units of weights and measures were standardized, the power of the guilds was reduced, trade and industry were promoted, and a single economic area was created. The model state of Westphalia, ruled by Napoleon's brother Jerome, was supposed to generate enthusiasm among people living on the right bank of the Rhine for the new French achievements. Westphalia introduced the *Code Napoléon*, a constitution, and the first parliament on German soil.[37]

Through the loss of the Austrian Netherlands and its hereditary lands in southern Germany, the Habsburg monarchy had lost its dominant position in Central Europe and permanently shifted its geographical focus towards the East. In the wake of Joseph II's unpopular reform policy further reform efforts became almost impossible. Only the military system was adjusted to meet the new demands. Five years before Prussia, Austria had established, as part of a sweeping military reform, a *Landwehr* for all men between 18 and 45 years of age (regular troops of conscripts in addition to the Austrian army), which also served as an instrument to politicize the people.[38]

5.5 Wars and Crises: the Decline of Napoleonic Rule in Europe

At the same time that Napoleon absorbed the German middle states into the Empire, he expanded his rule in Southern and Western Europe. Former French client republics and newly-conquered territories were transformed into vassal states and assigned to

Napoleon's siblings or loyalists. In Italy and Holland, these neo-aristocratic tendencies initially met little open opposition. In Spain, by contrast, resistance took shape against the forced abdication of the Spanish dynasty in favor of Napoleon's brother Joseph. With the help of the British army and the ideological support of Catholic clerics, Napoleon's men were routed by regular and guerrilla troops.[39]

The Spanish rebellion had raised hopes in Vienna that, in Central Europe too, an anti-Napoleonic uprising could be initiated in a similar way.[40] Austria had learned its lessons from the Seven Years' War and sought to lead the national movement by disseminating pamphlets and patriotic poetry. Vienna made every effort to mobilize its population nationally and to emphasize not only the idea of the Reich, but also the congruence of German and Austrian interests. However, Austrian war propaganda was successful only in the Tyrol, in the Vorarlberg, and in a few other regions in the south of the Old Reich, which were traditionally in favor of the Emperor—such as Anterior Austria, the former imperial cities, and the territories of smaller aristocrats and secularized Church estates. Historians have in the past interpreted the year 1809 as the beginnings of a national 'war of liberation.' A closer look, however, reveals that the uprisings in the German language areas, inspired by the traditionalist upheaval in Spain in 1808, were almost without exception aimed at the restoration of the *status quo ante*. In most cases, they represented attempts to avert modernization policies initiated by the annexing states and in particular to fend off conscription. Political loyalty played a role, too. These rebellions were based neither on a political program, nor on a national objective which promised anything more than the restoration of previous power relations. This was also shown at the level of symbolic politics in the South, where people removed the signs of rule of the new potentates and substituted them with the double-headed eagle of the Old Reich.[41]

In the northwest, the model states of Westphalia and Berg in particular turned out to be prone to crisis. Here, riots due to recruitment for the Spanish campaign coincided with putsch attempts by Prussian officers who aimed to restore the former territorial situation. Only a few activists intended more than a mere restoration: Justice of the Peace, Siegmund Peter Martin from Hornberg, for instance, envisioned the beginnings of a liberal constitutional state while the Prussian hussar officer, Ferdinand von Schill, hoped for a people's uprising initiated by *franc-tireurs*. It was notable that the urban bourgeoisie kept away from the turmoil; they often had better opportunities in the states of the Confederation of the Rhine than in the Ancien Régime. Fear of violence and attacks on bourgeois property were additional reasons for their reluctance to become involved.[42]

In Tyrol alone, the opposition against rigid Bavarian policies of centralization, anticlericalism, and modernization mobilized large groups of the predominantly rural society. Tyrol had formerly belonged to Habsburg for centuries and had enjoyed a largely autonomous position with its own system of defense, its own estate-based constitution, and a low tax burden. However, even here, the urban bourgeoisie, few in number, remained skeptical. The Tyrolean rebellion was also far from being a spontaneous uprising of the people. It was prepared well in advance with the full knowledge, consent, propaganda, and financial support of Vienna. References to 'Germanness' played a significant role in the accompanying rhetoric. However, the Tyroleans were far from advocating a modern nation. Rather, they hoped for a return to their privileges of the *status quo ante* combined with their commitment to the Habsburg monarchy. Overall, the riots of the year 1809 were unable to affect Napoleonic hegemony in Europe.[43]

It was the old rivalry with Great Britain that paved the way for the decline of the French Empire. As France was unable to defeat Great Britain in military terms, and as its colonial policy stood no chance, Napoleon planned to bring the nascent industrial country to its knees with economic warfare. Decrees prohibited trade to and from Great Britain and a wall of protective duties surrounded the continent. However, whereas England was able to open up new sales markets with transatlantic trade, the continent, from 1810 at the latest, suffered from a drastic slump of economic prosperity caused by the embargo and ever increasing taxes. Although the Continental System induced a temporary boom in the textile industries of France, Saxony, and the Rhineland, agrarian East Elbia and Russia as well as trading cities in Central Europe and some manufacturing (proto-industries) were cut off from international markets. In reaction to the recession in the French economy, Napoleon introduced a complex system of trade treaties and customs tariffs in order to secure sales of French products on the continent at the expense of the economies of his allies. The spectacular burning of confiscated English goods became a symbol of the arbitrary nature of the Napoleonic Continental System.[44]

German and Dutch coastal cities—first and foremost Amsterdam, Hamburg, and Bremen—suffered considerably from the decline of maritime trade and the shift of prosperity to areas on the Rhine. Initially, well-organized smuggling was able partly to make up for the losses caused by the embargo and high tariffs. The military annexation of the North Sea coast in 1810—in order to enforce the Decree of Trianon—ultimately brought the once thriving economies of the coastal cities to a standstill. Cut off from international and French markets, unemployment, poverty, and bankruptcies increased. High taxes, military suppression, and the introduction of conscription added to the resentment of the French occupying power. Widespread anti-French feeling found expression in attacks on tax collectors and customs policemen, as well as in rebellions by the lower classes and the formation of a militia in cities of the Hanseatic League, such as Hamburg, Lübeck, and Bremen in 1813. French rule was hated, however, not for national reasons (for that, city-state republicanism remained too prominent), but because it had caused hardship and misery for the people.[45]

The uncompromising attempt to defeat Great Britain in an economic war overextended the French sphere of influence and marked the beginning of the end of Napoleonic rule in Europe. In order to enforce the Continental System, Napoleon was compelled to go to war and to annex territories when diplomatic and political pressure was unsuccessful. In so doing, he extended his sphere of influence and antagonized the French people and (forced) allies. After Sweden, Portugal, the Vatican State, and the people of the North Sea coast had been forced to comply with the Continental System,

Napoleon intended to coerce the Russian Tsar into cooperation by a military invasion. The events of the year 1809 had shaken the French Empire, but had not been able to bring it down. The fall of the great French army in Russia, however, became a beacon of hope for all those who had worked toward putting an end to Napoleonic rule.[46]

Tensions between Russia and France grew ever greater after the Duchy of Oldenburg, which belonged to a relative of Alexander I, passed in the course of the annexation of the German North Sea coast to the sphere of French influence. The Tsar no longer complied with the Continental System, and closed Russian markets and harbors for the majority of French products. In response, Napoleon deployed his army in East Prussia, and forced the Prussian government to provide for the French troops and to make additional armies available. Under the pressure of the largest number of troops Napoleon had ever commanded, the supply system completely collapsed, leaving the troops to take care of themselves. The experience of hunger, pillaging, looting, extortion, and abuse constituted the social-historical background for the enmity shown toward the French army on their way back from the disaster in Russia. It was also the precondition for the mobilization of Prussian troops, which later went down in history as the 'War of Liberation.'[47]

Sweeping army reforms had created the institutional framework for this to happen. Along with measures to modernize the economy, administration, and education, they were supposed to make a fresh start in Prussia after the bitter defeat of 1806/7. Reformers such as Gerhard von Scharnhorst and August Neidhardt von Gneisenau expected a French-style army to be the school of the nation. To them, conscription was the patriotic duty of every citizen. This sort of Jacobin mindset, however, was unable to prevail in the Prussian Court. Gneisenau's plans from before the war, which he based on the Spanish model and which included the idea of deploying clerics to mobilize the masses, met with the King's disapproval. Like most of his aides and officers, Frederick William III saw the paramilitary and egalitarian experiments—such as the gymnastic events initiated by Ludwig Jahn on the Hasenheide in Berlin—as a dangerous force, capable of unleashing powers that the regular army and the feudal state would ultimately be unable to control. Nevertheless, the Prussian reserve system, the 'Krümper system,' involved the alternating call-up of all men fit for military service. The men were retained in the army for a few months, trained intensively, and then released into the reserves. This was the foundation for introducing general conscription and enabled Prussia to organize 270,000 soldiers against Napoleon.[48]

For a long time, the King had hesitated to break with France. Eventually, however, he was overtaken by events and yielded to the pressure of the 'Patriots' Party' in his court. His famous appeal, 'To my people,' hardly attested to devout nationalism, but was rather an attempt to mobilize Prussian provinces. He was careful to use only the traditionalist uprisings as his model, such as those in the Vendée, Spain, and Tyrol. The extent of the donations to his cause and the mobilization of volunteers showed how much this allegedly first national war was influenced by dynastic loyalties. People were most willing to donate and volunteer in the 'Old Prussian provinces', which were mainly Protestant, and in war-plagued East Prussia, whereas this favorable attitude was considerably less widespread in the younger Prussian provinces, and especially in Catholic areas.[49]

The oft-quoted nationalist enthusiasm was predominantly a media event created by the educated elite. Politicized by the dramatic developments from 1789 on, the more radical representatives of this elite placed their hopes in the nation to overcome the feudal system. For them, to serve as a soldier of the nation was the first step toward political participation. The majority of publications featured a mixture of Prussian patriotism, vague incantations of national unity in the fight against Napoleon, and pure hatred for France. Around 500 writers, most of them Prussians, took part in the national discourse.[50] Only among students was nationalist enthusiasm common in all German speaking areas. Students were highly motivated to join up. Equally remarkable, however, was the number of desertions, which was much higher among voluntary than among regular troops.[51]

Most of the nationalist publications could be chalked up to Prussian war propaganda, which built on experiences of the Seven Years' War. As early as 1809, the reformer Baron vom Stein had suggested 'maintaining as great a tension as possible across the nation by issuing pamphlets [. . .] and stirring up hatred against the French by means of processions, sermons, target shootings, gymnastic exercises in every school, etc.'[52] Upon Napoleon's insistence, von Stein was dismissed, but later realized these plans after moving to the Tsar's court, which was then evolving into a center for anti-Napoleonic propaganda. It was in Russia where the war and hate pamphlets of Ernst Moritz Arndt were made public, before the allied headquarters in Frankfurt took over this task during the 'Wars of Liberation.' 10,000 copies of Arndt's war catechism were printed, field newspapers were filled with anti-French poems, and existing press organs such as Karl von Rotteck's 'Teutsche Blätter' were published in high print runs.[53] Cartoons and lithographic prints from England contributed to the dissemination of political journalism on an unprecedented scale.

However, one should be wary of extrapolating from a well documented flood of material to a collective consciousness among a wide strata of the population. Even though French rule was hated because of its system of imperial exploitation, political loyalties were too manifold to be subsumed under the common denominator of 'nationalism,' particularly beyond Prussian borders.[54] German soldiers persistently perceived themselves as Saxons, Bavarians, and Württembergers.[55] Indicative is that the wars against Napoleon did not create a German national hero. Instead, songs and poems created a transnational pantheon of heroes, including not only Tsar Alexander and Prince Bernadotte, but also the King of Great Britain and the Generals Blücher, York, and Wellington. This reflected the reality of international war efforts. Only from the perspective of nineteenth century nationalism could these be interpreted as German 'Wars of Liberation.' The influential merchant princes of Augsburg, on the other hand, whose banks and trading companies had suffered under the Continental System, did not erect memorials in honor of the international heroes, but only of the Bavarian General Wrede who only recently had fought on Napoleon's side.[56] Controlled by the authorities, Bavaria developed a special type of Bavarian nationalism. Unlike in the Protestant regions of Franconia under the lasting influence of Prussia, in many other areas in the South and West of Germany Prussia's 'treason' of the Reich in accepting the treaty of 1795 was not forgotten. These areas were not prepared to approve a Protestant power as the new leading national authority. In Saxony, too, the mood was against Prussia's hegemonic policy. Pietist pastors in Southern Germany did not appreciate the nationalist turn, but were inspired by the religious renewal, which seemed to have had a beacon in the Tsar's demonstrative piety. In the Catholic regions of the south, and also in Anterior Austria, people hoped for the return of the Habsburg monarchy or even the restoration of the Old Reich.[57]

During the anti-Napoleonic wars, however, the number of desertions increased as quickly as the population's tax burden. The well-known accompaniments of battles and campaigns went on. As had already happened during the revolutionary wars, there were more complaints in the South of Germany about the behavior of the Russian allies than there were about the French enemy. For many people, it made no difference whether they fought with or against Napoleon. Some peasants' writings do not even mention the change of sides of 1813. It was not national or global politics, but the hope for peace that played a crucial role for those outside the educated elites. After more than twenty years of war, even those who were not nationally oriented hoped for an end to the Napoleonic era. This was not because Napoleon was French, but because he had proved himself an insatiable warmonger with whom peace seemed to be impossible.[58]

5.6 The Aftermath

The era of the French Revolution and of Napoleon had smashed the Old Reich and had turned it into an assemblage of modern territorial states. National currents, which had already become noticeable from the middle of the eighteenth century, substantially intensified during the anti-Napoleonic wars without, however, prevailing completely. The guns had hardly fallen silent when the competition for the hegemony of remembrance followed the French era after 1815. From an early stage on, this struggle would be decided in the field of terminology and concepts. The older notion of the 'wars of freedom' (Freiheitskriege) for the anti-Napoleonic wars referred semantically to the processes of bourgeois emancipation in France and North America. Any mention of the 'wars of freedom' put German events into the context of global history. Early liberal intellectuals and left-wing historians of the Kaiserreich perceived the anti-Napoleonic wars as a struggle for constitutional rights, for accomplishing a policy of reform in Prussia and in the states of the Confederation of the Rhine, and as a fight against the obstructionism of the aristocracy and the monarchs. According to this understanding, the desire for unity and the pursuit of freedom were inextricably linked with each other.

This emancipatory element was, however, absent in contemporary interpretations of the anti-Napoleonic uprising. Even the term 'Wars of Liberation' (Befreiungskriege) can only be traced from 1816 onwards. For conservatives and monarchists, the war was not about national unity and liberal rights of freedom, but about devotion to the ruling monarchy and fending off French foreign rule. From as early as the Vormärz, these two competing interpretations—the 'wars of freedom' versus the 'wars of liberation'—held their ground in various forms until the late twentieth century. In Prussia, the antagonism between the dynastic and conservative concept, on the one hand, and the national liberal interpretation on the other, was even reflected in the culture of remembrance.[59]

On the left bank of the Rhine, by contrast, French influence was dominant well into the nineteenth century. This was true not only with regard to the preservation of Rhenish law wrested from Prussia, but also with regard to the political culture and a notable Francophilia. In their writings, Rhenish and Palatine soldiers often mentioned their connection to the Napoleonic army and the Emperor. In the *Vormärz*, this was reflected by the foundation of several veterans' associations. They stood firm and erected memorials in Napoleon's honor, even after the press had started to stir up hatred against France in the context of the Rhine crisis. In 1840 there were still newspapers that saw Germans and French as 'brethren peoples' (*'Brudervölker'*), dependent on one other and destined to fight despotism together.[60]

Rhinelanders were used to a tradition of local administration and autonomy. They did not see themselves as an integral part of the Prussian monarchy, but as an independent region—administered by Prussia, but having more in common with France than with the government in Berlin. Even the Prussian Minister of the Interior, Gustav Adolf Rochow, could not avoid the impression of being 'in a foreign country occupied by Prussia' when he visited the area in 1837. Here, as well as in the Palatinate, the French experience strengthened the opposition against territorial authorities after Napoleonic rule had ended.[61]

The French era likewise left its marks on the right bank of the Rhine. During the *Vormärz* period, the process of constitutional transition took place, in the former states of the Confederation of the Rhine in Southern and Central Germany where French influence had been strongest. Although the former states of the Confederation of the Rhine—first and foremost Bavaria—made every effort to create a new kind of memory politics in order to forget their French misalliance, the liberal democratic bourgeoisie tended to see the era of the French Revolution as the midwife of a new, progressive present.[62] Hence, Baden, Württemberg, and Bavaria became the experimental laboratory of early constitutionalism. They were joined by states like Electorate Hesse and Saxony after the French and the Belgian Revolutions of 1830, which provided a further boost to liberal ideas.[63] Here, a form of nationalism emerged, which considered France not as an enemy, but as a role model. Even though the European revolutions of 1848/9 failed in no small part due to national differences, many democrats and liberals thought in transnational, rather than in national terms until the late 1840s.[64] Popular historical accounts from the 1860s still characterized Napoleon as the man who had freed the bourgeoisie from the chains of the *Ancien Régime*.[65] Representatives from the South and the West ostentatiously stayed away from the Prussian nationalist celebration of the fiftieth anniversary of the battle of Leipzig in 1863.[66] It was not until the *Kaiserreich* that professional custodians of history succeeded in characterizing the era of Napoleon as one of doom and gloom, and placing it against the background of a new war with France. They did so in order to provide a historical legitimization for the leading position of Prussia, to secure the inner unity of the new nation by demarcating it from France, and to actively forget that it was the recent 'civil war' between Prussia and Austria that had actually created the preconditions for the unification of the small German Reich.

[Translated from German by Christine Brocks.]

Notes

1. Charles Tilly, 'Reflections on the History of European State-Making,' in Charles Tilly (ed.), *The Formation of National States in Western Europe* (Princeton: Princeton University Press, 1975), 42.

2. Karl Otmar von Aretin, *Das Alte Reich 1648–1806*, vol. 3, *Das Reich und der österreichisch-preußische Dualismus* (Stuttgart: Klett-Cotta, 1997); Helmut Neuhaus, 'Hie Österreichisch—hier fritzisch. Die Wende der 1740er Jahre in der Geschichte des Alten Reiches,' in Helmut Neuhaus (ed.), *Aufbruch aus dem Ancien Régime. Beiträge zur Geschichte des 18. Jahrhunderts*, (Cologne: Böhlau, 1993), 57–77.

3. Christopher Clark, *Iron Kingdom: The Rise and Downfall of Prussia, 1600–1947* (Cambridge, Mass.: Belknap Press, 2006); Johannes Kunisch, *Friedrich der Große. Der König und seine Zeit* (Munich: Beck, 2004).

4. Johannes Kunisch, *Staatsverfassung und Mächtepolitik. Zur Genese von Staatskonflikten im Zeitalter des Absolutismus* (Berlin: Duncker und Humblot, 1979), 66.

5. Peter Krüger (ed.), *Das europäische Staatensystem im Wandeel* (Munich: Oldenbourg, 1994); John Darwin, *After Tamerlane, The Rise and Fall of Global Empires, 1400–2000* (London: Penguin Books, 2008); Heinz Duchhardt, *Balance of Power und Pentarchie. Internationale Beziehungen 1700–1785* (Paderborn: Schöningh, 1997).

6. Betsy Maestro, *Struggle for a Continent: The French and Indian Wars, 1689–1763* (New York: Harper Collins, 2000); Frederick Quinn, *The French Overseas Empire* (Westport, Conn.: Praeger, 2000); Fred Anderson, *Crucible of War: The Seven Years' War and the Fate of Empire in British North America, 1754–1766* (New York: Knopf, 2000); Francis Jennings, *Empire of Fortune: Crowns, Colonies, and Tribes in the Seven Years War in America* (New York: W. W. Norton, 1988); Walter R. Borneman, *The French and Indian War: Deciding the Fate of North America* (New York: Harper Perennial, 2007).

7. Reed Browning, *The War of the Austrian Succession* (New York: St. Martin's Press, 1993); Nicholas A. M. Rodger, *The Command of the Ocean: A Naval History of Britain, 1649–1815* (London: Penguin Books, 2006). Brendan Simms, *Three Victories and a Defeat: The Rise and Fall of the First British Empire* (London: Penguin Books, 2008).

8. Jürgen Luh, *Kriegskunst in Europa 1650–1800* (Cologne: Böhlau, 2004); Siegfried Fiedler, *Kriegswesen und Kriegführung im Zeitalter der Kabinettskriege* (Koblenz: Bernard & Graefe, 1986).

9. Lothar Schilling, *Kaunitz und das Renversement des alliances* (Berlin: Duncker und Humblot, 1994).

10. Franz A. J. Szabo, *The Seven Years War in Europe, 1756–1763* (Munich: Pearson Longman, 2008); H. M. Scott, *The Emergence of the Eastern Powers, 1756–1775* (Cambridge: Cambridge University Press, 2001); Sven Externbrink (ed.), *Der Siebenjährige Krieg (1756–1763): Ein europäischer Weltkrieg im Zeitalter der Aufklärung* (Berlin: Akademie-Verlag, 2010).

11. Horst Carl, *Okkupation und Regionalismus. Die preußischen Westprovinzen im Sieben-jährigen Krieg* (Mainz: Verlag Philipp von Zabern, 1993).

12. Rolf-Dieter Müller, *Militärgeschichte* (Cologne: Böhlau, 2009).

13. Ute Planert, 'Innovation or Evolution? The French Wars in Military History,' in Roger Chickering and Stig Förster (eds), *Wars in an Age of Revolution: 1775–1815* (New York: Cambridge University Press, 2010), 69–84.

14. David A. Bell, *The Cult of the Nation in France. Inventing Nationalism, 1680–1800* (Cambridge: Harvard University Press, 2001), 12.

15. For the German case, see Ute Planert, 'Wann beginnt der 'moderne' deutsche Nationalis-mus? Plädoyer für eine nationale Sattelzeit,' in Jörg Echternkamp and Sven Oliver Müller (eds), *Die Politik der Nation. Deutscher Nationalismus in Krieg und Krisen, 1760–1960* (Munich: Oldenbourg, 2002), 25–59.

16. Adrian Hastings, *The Construction of Nationhood: Ethnicity, Religion and Nationalism.* (Cambridge: Cambridge University Press, 1997); Christopher A. Bayly, *The Birth of the Modern World, 1780–1914* (Malden, Mass., Blackwell, 2004).

17. Bell, *Cult of the Nation*, 80; Edmond Dziembowski, *Un nouveau patriotisme français, 1750–1770: La France face à la puissance anglaise à l'époque de la guerre de Sept Ans* (Oxford: Voltaire Foundation, 1998); Hélène Dupuy, *Genèse de la patrie moderne: La naissance de l'idée moderne de patrie en France avant et pendant la Révolution* (University Dissertation Université de Paris-I, 1995).

18. Linda Colley, *Britons. Forging the Nation, 1707–1837* (New Haven/London: Yale Univer-sity Press, 2005), 91, 95.

19. Planert, 'Wann beginnt der, moderne deutsche Nationalismus?'

20. Ibid.; Jörg Echternkamp, *Der Aufstieg des deutschen Nationalismus, 1770–1840* (Frankfurt am Main: Campus, 1998); Dieter Langewiesche, *Nation, Nationalismus, Nationalstaat in Deutschland und Europa* (Munich: Beck, 2000); Wolfgang Burgdorf, '"Reichsnationalis-mus" gegen "Territorialnationalismus": Phasen der Intensivierung des nationalen Be-wußtseins in Deutschland seit dem Siebenjährigen Krieg,' in Dieter Langewiesche and Georg Schmidt (eds), *Föderative Nation. Deutschlandkonzepte von der Reformation bis zum Ersten Weltkrieg* (Munich: Oldenbourg, 2000), 158; Martin Wrede, *Das Reich und seine Feinde. Politische Feindbilder in der reichspatriotischen Publizistik zwischen West-fälischem Frieden und Siebenjährigem Krieg* (Mainz: Zabern, 2004).

21. Rudolf Vierhaus, 'Patriotismus—Begriff und Realität einer moralisch-politischen Hal-tung,' in Vierhaus (ed.), *Deutschland im 18. Jahrhundert. Politische Verfassung, soziales Gefüge, geistige Bewegungen* (Göttingen: Vandenhoeck und Ruprecht, 1987), 96–109.

22. Christoph Prignitz, *Vaterlandsliebe und Freiheit. Deutscher Patriotismus von 1750 bis 1850* (Wiesbaden: Steiner, 1981); Vierhaus, 'Patriotismus.'

23. Hans-Peter Herrmann, '"Ich bin fürs Vaterland zu sterben auch bereit." Patriotismus oder Nationalismus im 18. Jahrhundert? Lesenotizen zu den deutschen Arminiusdramen 1740–1808,' in Hans-Peter Herrmann, Hans-Martin Blitz and Susanna Moßmann (eds), *Machtphantasie Deutschland. Nationalismus, Männlichkeit und Fremdenhaß im Vater-landsdiskars deutscher Schriftsteller des 18. Jahrhunderts* (Frankfurt am Main: Suhrkamp 1996), 32–65; Wolfgang Adam and Holger Dainat (eds), *'Krieg ist mein Lied.' Der Siebenjährige Krieg in den zeitgenössischen Medien* (Göttingen: Wallstein, 2007); Peter Berghoff, *Der Tod des politischen Kollektivs. Politische Religion und das Sterben und Töten für Volk, Nation und Rasse* (Berlin: Akademie-Verlag, 1997).

24. Manfred Schort, *Politik und Propaganda. Der Siebenjährige Krieg in den zeitgenössischen Flugschriften* (Frankfurt am Main: Peter Lang, 2006); Adam and Dainat (eds), *Krieg ist mein Lied*; Ewa Anklam, *Wissen nach Augenmaß. Militärische Beobachtung und Berichterstattung im Siebenjährigen Krieg* (Berlin: Lit-Verlag, 2007); Silvia Mazura, *Die preußische und österreichische Kriegspropaganda im Ersten und Zweiten Schlesischen Krieg* (Berlin: Duncker und Humblot, 1996).

25. Burgdorf, *Reichsnationalismus*; Carl, *Okkupation und Regionalismus*.

26. Schort, *Politik und Propaganda*; Karen Hagemann, *Mannlicher Muth und teutsche Ehre. Nation, Militär und Geschlecht zur Zeit der antinapoleonischen Kriege Preußens* (Paderborn: Schöningh, 2002).

27. Wolfgang Burgdorf, *Reichskonstitution und Nation. Verfassungsreformprojekte für das Heilige Römische Reich Deutscher Nation im politischen Schrifttum von 1648 bis 1806* (Mainz: Zabern, 1998); Wolfgang Frühwald, 'Die Idee kultureller Nationsbildung und die Entstehung der Literatursprache in Deutschland,' in Otto Dann (ed.), *Nationalismus in vorindustrieller Zeit* (Munich: Oldenbourg, 1986), 129–142; Nicholas Vazsonyi, 'Montesquieu, Friedrich Carl von Moser, and the "National Spirit Debate" in Germany, 1765–1767' *German Studies Review*, 1999, 22, 225–246.

28. Otto Dann (ed.), *Nationalismus in vorindustrieller Zeit* (München: Oldenbourg, 1986); Otto Dann and John Dinwiddy (eds), *Nationalism in the Age of the French Revolution* (London: Hambledon, 1988); Otto Dann, Miroslav Hroch, and Johannes Kroll (eds), *Patriotismus und Nationsbildung am Ende des Heiligen Römischen Reiches* (Cologne: SH-Verlag, 2003).

29. Immanuel Kant, *Zum ewigen Frieden. Ein philosophischer Entwurf* (Königsberg: Nicolovius, 1795).

30. Paul W. Schroeder, *The Transformation of European Politics, 1763–1848* (Oxford: Clarendon Press, 1994); Paul Kennedy, *The Rise and Fall of the Great Powers* (New York: Random House 1987); Michael Erbe, *Revolutionäre Erschütterung und erneuertes Gleichgewicht. Internationale Beziehungen 1785–1830* (Paderborn: Schöningh, 2004); Brendan Simms, *The Struggle for Mastery in Germany, 1779–1850* (Basingstoke: Palgrave Macmillan 1998).

31. Vgl. Stig Förster, 'Der Weltkrieg, 1792–1815. Bewaffnete Konflikte und Revolutionen in der Weltgesellschaft,' in Jost Dülffer (ed.), *Kriegsbereitschaft und Friedensordnung in Deutschland, 1800–1814* (Münster: Lit-Verlag, 1994), 17–38; Paul Fregosi, *Dreams of Empire. Napoleon and the First World War, 1792–1815* (London: Hutchinson, 1989); A. D. Harvey, *Collision of Empires. Britain in Three World Wars, 1793–1945* (London: Hambledon Press, 1992), 3–201.

32. Jacques-Olivier Boudon, *La France et l'Europe de Napoléon* (Paris, Armand Colin, 2006); Bernd Wunder, *Europäische Geschichte im Zeitalter der Französischen Revolution* (Stuttgart: Kohlhammer, 2001).

33. Walter Demel, *Reich, Reformen und sozialer Wandel, 1763–1806* (Stuttgart: Klett-Cotta, 2005); Alan Forrest and Peter Wilson (eds), *The Bee and the Eagle: Napoleonic France and the End of the Holy Roman Empire 1806* (Basingstoke: Palgrave Macmillan, 2009); Karl Otmar von Aretin, *Das Alte Reich 1648–1806*, vol. 3.

34. Stuart Woolf, *Napoleon's Integration of Europe* (London/New York: Routledge, 1991); Michael Broers, *Europe under Napoleon, 1799–1815* (London: Arnold, 1996); Jonathan Sperber, *Revolutionary Europe, 1780–1850* (Harlow: Longman, 2000); Annie Jourdan, *L'Empire de Napoléon* (Paris: Flammarion, 2000); Philipp Dwyer (ed.), *Napoleon and*

Europe (Harlow: Longman, 2001); Geoffrey Ellis, *The Napoleonic Empire* (Basingstoke: Palgrave Macmillan, 1991); Alexander Grab, *Napoleon and the Transformation of Europe* (Basingstoke: Palgrave Macmillan, 2003); Michael Broers, *Napoleonic Imperialism and the Savoyard Monarchy 1773–1821. State-Building in Piedmont*. (Lewiston: Mellen, 1997); John Anthony Davis, *Naples and Napoleon: Southern Italy and the European Revolutions, 1780–1860* (Oxford/New York: Oxford University Press, 2006); Alain Pillépich, *Napoléon et les Italiens: Republique italienne et royaume d'Italie 1802–1814* (Paris: Nouveau Monde Éd., 2003); Simon Schama, *Patriots and Liberators. Revolution in the Netherlands, 1780–1813* (New York: Knopf, 1977); Johan Joor, *De adelaar en het lam: Onrust, opruiing en onwilligheid in Nederland ten tijde van het Koninkrijk Holland en de inlijving bij het Franse keizerrijk, 1806–1813* (Amsterdam: Bataafsche Leeuw, 2000).

35. Bernd von Münchow-Pohl, *Zwischen Reform und Krieg. Untersuchungen zur Bewußtseinslage in Preußen 1809–1812* (Göttingen: Vandenhoeck und Ruprecht, 1987); Clark, *Iron Kingdom*.

36. Josef Smets, *Les Pays Rhénans (1794–1814). Le comportement des Rhénans face à l' occupation française* (Bern: Lang, 1997); Roger Dufraisse, *L'Allemagne à l'époche napoléonienne. Questions d' histoire politique, économique et sociale* (Bonn/Berlin: Bouvier, 1992); Hansgeorg Molitor, *Vom Untertan zum Administré. Studien zur französischen Herrschaft und zum Verhalten der Bevölkerung im Rhein-Mosel-Raum von den Revolutionskriegen bis zum Ende der napoleonischen Zeit* (Wiesbaden: Franz Steiner, 1980); Michael Rowe, *From Reich to State. The Rhineland in the Revolutionary Age, 1780–1830* (Cambridge: Cambridge University Press, 2003); Timothy C. Blanning, *The French Revolution in Germany: Occupation and Resistance in the Rhineland, 1792–1802* (Oxford: Clarendon Press, 1983); Sabine Graumann, *Französische Verwaltung am Niederrhein. Das Roerdepartement, 1798–1814* (Essen: Klartext-Verlag, 1990).

37. Helmut Berding, *Napoleonische Herrschafts-und Gesellschaftspolitik im Königreich Westfalen 1807–1813* (Göttingen: Vandenhoeck & Ruprecht, 1973); Burkhard Dietz (ed.), *Das Großherzogtum Berg als napoleonischer Modellstaat. Eine regionalhistorische Zwischenbilanz* (Cologne: Landschaftsverbund, Rheinland, 1995); Bettina Severin-Barboutie, 'Modellstaatspolitik im rheinbündischen Deutschland. Berg, Westfalen und Frankfurt im Vergleich,' *Francia* 1997, 24, 181–203; id., *Französische Herrschaftspolitik und Modernisierung. Verwaltungs-und Verfassungsreformen im Großherzogtum Berg, 1806–1813* (Munich: Oldenbourg, 2008); Gerd Dethlefs, Armin Owzar, and Gisela Weiß (eds), *Modell und Wirklichkeit: Politik, Kultur und Gesellschaft im Großherzogtum Berg und im Königreich Westphalen 1806–1813* (Paderborn: Schöningh, 2007); Michael Hecker, *Napoleonischer Konstitutionalismus in Deutschland* (Berlin: Duncker and Humblot, 2005); Hartwig Brandt and Ewald Grothe (eds), *Rheinbündischer Konstitutionalismus* (Frankfurt am Main: Lang, 2007).

38. Ernst Zehetbauer, *Landwehr gegen Napoleon. Österreichs erste Miliz und der Nationalkrieg von 1809* (Vienna: öbv & hpt, 1999).

39. Michael Rowe (ed.), *Collaboration and Resistance in Napoleonic Europe: State Formation in an Age of Upheaval, c. 1800–1815* (Basingstoke: Palgrave Macmillan, 2003); Charles J. Esdaile, *The Peninsular War: A New History* (Basingstoke: Palgrave Macmillan 2003); Charles J. Esdaile, *Fighting Napoleon: Guerillas, Bandits, and Adventurers in Spain, 1808–1814* (New Haven: Yale University Press, 2004); Michael Broers, *Napoleon's other War. Bandits, Rebels, and Their Persuers in the Age of Revolutions* (London: Peter Lang, 2010).

40. Rainer Wohlfeil, *Spanien und die deutsche Erhebung* (Wiesbaden: Franz Steiner, 1965).

41. Sandro Guzzi-Heeb, 'Logik des traditionalistischen Aufstandes. Revolten gegen die Helvetische Republik (1798–1803),' *Historische Anthropologie* 2001, 9, 233–253; Ute Planert and Tobias Kies in Ute Planert (ed.), *Krieg und Umbruch in Mitteleuropa um 1800. Erfahrungsgeschichte(n) auf dem Weg in eine neue Zeit*, (Paderborn: Schöningh, 2009).

42. Jens Flemming (ed.), *Fremdherrschaft und Freiheit. Das Königreich Westphalen als napoleonischer Modellstaat* (Kassel: Kassel University Press, 2009).

43. Laurence Cole, 'Religion und patriotische Aktion in Deutsch-Tirol, 1790–1814,' in Otto Dann et. al. (eds), *Patriotismus und Nationsbildung am Ende des Heiligen Römischen Reichs* (Cologne: SH-Verlag, 2004), 345–378; Martin P. Schennach, *Revolte in der Region. Zur Tiroler Erhebung von 1809* (Innsbruck: Universitätsverlag Wagner, 2009).

44. Jacques Wolff, *Napoléon et l'économie: L'impuissance du politique* (Paris: Jas Ed., 2007); Bertrand de Jouvenel, *Napoléon et l'économie dirigée. Le blocus continental* (Paris: Les Ed. de la Toison d'Or, 1942); François Crouzet, 'Wars, Blockade, and Economic Change in Europe, 1792–1815,' *Journal of Economic History*, 1964, 24, 567–588; Roger Dufraisse, 'Französische Zollpolitik, Kontinentalsperre und Kontinentalsystem im Deutschland der napoleonischen Zeit,'; Robert Beachy, *The Soul of Commerce. Credit, Property, and Politics in Leipzig 1750–1840* (Leiden: Brill, 2005).

45. Burghart Schmid, *Hamburg im Zeitalter der Französischen Revolution und Napoleons, 1789–1813* (Hamburg: Verein für Hamburgische Geschichte, 1998); Katherine Aaslestad, *Place and Politics: Local Identity, Civic Culture, and German Nationalism in North Germany during the Revolutionary Era* (Leiden: Brill, 2005).

46. Wunder, *Europäische Geschichte*, 114–121.

47. Münchow-Pohl, *Zwischen Reform und Krieg*.

48. Clark, *Iron Kingdom*; Rudolf Ibekken, *Preußen 1807–1813. Staat und Volk als Idee und Wirklichkeit* (Cologne: Grote, 1970).

49. Hagemann, *Mannlicher Muth*.

50. Ibid.

51. Peter Brandt, 'Die Befreiungskriege von 1813 bis 1815 in der deutschen Geschichte,' in Michael Grüttner et. al. (eds), *Geschichte und Emanzipation. Festschrift für Reinhard Rürup* (Frankfurt am Main: Campus-Verlag, 1999) 17–57; Peter Brandt, 'Einstellungen, Motive und Ziele von Kriegsfreiwilligen 1813/14: Das Freikorps Lützow,' in Jost Dülffer (ed.), *Kriegsbereitschaft und Friedensordnung in Deutschland* (Münster: Lit-Verlag, 1995), 211–233.

52. Stein to Graf Götzen, Brünn, 8.6.1809 and to Graf Stadion, 3.8.1809; cited in E. Botzenhart and Walther Hubatsch (eds), *Freiherr vom Stein. Briefe und amtlicher Schriftwechsel. Vol. 3: In Brünn und Prag. Die Krise des Jahres 1811. In Moskau und Petersburg. Die große Wendung. 1809–1812* (Stuttgart: Kohlhammer, 1961), 148 and 161f.

53. Ernst Weber, *Lyrik der Befreiungskriege (1812–1815). Gesellschaftspolitische Meinungs-und Willensbildung durch Literatur* (Stuttgart: Metzler, 1991); Gerhard Graf, *Gottesbild und Politik. Eine Studie zur Frömmigkeit in Preußen während der Befreiungskriege 1813–1815* (Göttingen: Vandenhoeck und Ruprecht, 1993); Jean-Paul Bertaud and Alan Forrest, Annie Jourdan, *Napoléon, le monde et les Anglais. Guerre des mots et des images* (Paris: Editions Autrement, 2004).

54. Ute Planert, *Der Mythos vom Befreiungskrieg. Frankreichs Kriege und der deutsche Süden. Alltag, Wahrnehmung, Deutung, 1792–1841* (Paderborn: Schöningh, 2007); James J. Sheehan, 'State and Nationality in the Napoleonic period,' in John Breuilly (ed.), *The State of Germany. The National Idea in the Making, Unmaking and Remaking of a Modern*

Nation-State (London/New York: Longman, 1992), 47–59; John Breuilly, 'The National Idea in Modern German History', ibid., 1–28.

55. Carl Buhle, *Erinnerungen aus den Feldzügen von 1809 bis 1816 entlehnt aus den Papieren eines Veteranen der sächsischen Armee* (Bautzen: Schlüssel, 1844).

56. Bayerisches Hauptstaatsarchiv München, Ministerium des Inneren, 45770.

57. Planert, *Mythos*, 207; Police Reports, Augsburg, 22 September 1814 and 3 October 1814.

58. Ibid.; Michael Sikora, 'Desertion und nationale Mobilmachung. Militärische Verweigerung 1792–1815,' in Ulrich Bröckling and Michael Sikora (eds), *Armeen und ihre Deserteure. Vernachlässigte Kapitel einer Militärgeschichte der Neuzeit* (Göttingen: Vandenhoeck und Ruprecht, 1998), 112–140.

59. Helmut Berding, 'Das geschichtliche Problem der Freiheitskriege 1813–1814,' in Karl Otmar von Aretin and Gerhard A. Ritter (eds), *Historismus und moderne Geschichtswissenschaft. Europa zwischen Revolution und Restauration 1797–1815* (Stuttgart: Steiner, 1987), 201–215; Christopher Clark, 'The Wars of Liberation in Prussian Memory: Reflections on the Memorialization of War in Early Nineteenth-Century Germany', *Journal of Modern History*, 68(1996), 550–576.

60. Irmeline Veit-Brause, *Die deutsch-französische Krise von 1840. Studien zur deutschen Einheitsbewegung* (Ph.D Dissertation, University of Cologne, 1967), 198f.; Roland Bauer, *Die Rheinkrise von 1840 in der deutschen Öffentlichkeit—eine Zeitungsanalyse* (Masters Thesis: Tübingen 2001); Walther Klein, *Der Napoleonkult in der Pfalz* (Munich and Berlin: Beck, 1934); Johann F. H. Cantzler, *Gesänge der unter Napoleon's Fahnen in der ehemaligen kaiserlich französischen Armee gedienten Veteranen Frankenthals und Umgebung* (Frankenthal: Enderes, 1842).

61. James M. Brophy, *Popular Culture and the Public Sphere in the Rhineland, 1800–1850* (Cambridge: Cambridge University Press, 2007), 308f.

62. *Das Veteranenfest des Oberamtsbezirks Tübingen am 27 September 1839,* (Tübingen: Fues, 1839).

63. Dieter Langewiesche, *Liberalismus in Deutschland* (Frankfurt am Main: Suhrkamp, 1988).

64. Ulrike Ruttmann, *Wunschbild—Schreckbild—Trugbild: Rezeption und Instrumentalisierung Frankreichs in der deutschen Revolution von 1848/49* (Stuttgart: Franz Steiner, 2001).

65. Karl von Rotteck, *Allgemeine Geschichte vom Anfang der historischen Kenntniß bis auf unsere Zeiten*, 24th ed. (Braunschweig: Westermann, 1863); Friedrich Christoph Schlosser, *Geschichte des 18. Jahrhunderts und des 19. bis zum Sturz des französischen Kaiserreiches.* 8 vols. 3rd ed. (Heidelberg: Mohr, 1864–1866); Hans Schmidt, 'Napoleon in der deutschen Geschichtsschreibung,' *Francia*, 14(1986), 530–560.

66. Friedrich Lenger, 'Die Erinnnerung an die Völkerschlacht bei Leipzig im Jubiläumsjahr 1863,' in: Manfred Hettling (ed.), *Figuren und Strukturen. Historische Essays für Hartmut Zwar zum 65. Geburtstag* (Munich: Saur, 2002), 25–41.

Bibliography

ARETIN, KARL OTMAR VON, *Das Alte Reich 1648–1806*, 4 vols (Stuttgart: Klett-Cotta, 1997–2000).

BELL, DAVID A., *The Cult of the Nation in France. Inventing Nationalism, 1680–1800* (Cambridge: Harvard University Press, 2001).

BROERS, MICHAEL, *Europe under Napoleon, 1799–1815* (London: Arnold, 1996).

CHICKERING, ROGER and STIG FOERSTER (eds), *War in an Age of Revolution 1775–1815* (Cambridge: Cambridge University Press, 2010).

COLLEY, LINDA, *Britons. Forging the Nation, 1707–1837* (New Haven: Yale University Press, 2005).

DANN, OTTO and JOHN DINWIDDY (eds), *Nationalism in the Age of the French Revolution* (London: Hambledon, 1988).

DANN, OTTO, MIROSLAV HROCH, and JOHANNES KOLL (eds), *Patriotismus und Nationsbildung am Ende des Heiligen Römischen Reiches* (Cologne: SH-Verlag, 2003).

DARWIN, JOHN, *After Tamerlane, The Rise & Fall of Global Empires, 1400–2000* (London: Penguin Books, 2008).

DEMEL, WALTER, *Reich, Reformen und sozialer Wandel, 1763–1806* (Stuttgart: Klett-Cotta, 2005).

ECHTERNKAMP, JÖRG, *Der Aufstieg des deutschen Nationalismus, 1770–1840* (Frankfurt am Main: Campus, 1998).

EXTERNBRINK, SVEN (ed.), *Der Siebenjährige Krieg (1756–1763): Ein europäischer Weltkrieg im Zeitalter der Aufklärung* (Berlin: Akademie-Verlag, 2010).

FREGOSI, PAUL, *Dreams of Empire. Napoleon and the First World War, 1792–1815* (London: Hutchinson, 1989).

FORREST, ALAN and PETER WILSON (eds), *The Bee and the Eagle: Napoleonic France and the End of the Holy Roman Empire 1806* (Basingstoke/New York: Palgrave Macmillan, 2009).

KENNEDY, PAUL M. *The Rise and Fall of the Great Powers. Economic Change and Military Conflict from 1500 to 2000* (New York: Random House, 1987).

PLANERT, UTE, *Der Mythos vom Befreiungskrieg. Frankreichs Kriege und der deutsche Süden. Alltag, Wahrnehmung, Deutung, 1792–1841* (Paderborn: Schöningh, 2007).

SCHENNACH, MARTIN P., *Revolte in der Region. Zur Tiroler Erhebung von 1809* (Innsbruck: Universitätsverlag Wagner, 2009).

SCHROEDER, PAUL W., *The Transformation of European Politics, 1763–1848* (Oxford: Clarendon Press, 1994).

WOOLF, STUART, *Napoleon's Integration of Europe* (London/New York: Routledge, 1991).

CHAPTER 6

....

COSMOPOLITANISM AND THE GERMAN ENLIGHTENMENT

....

FRANZ LEANDER FILLAFER AND
JÜRGEN OSTERHAMMEL

THE European Enlightenment has long been regarded as a host of disembodied, self-perpetuating ideas typically emanating from France and inspiring apprentices at the various European peripheries. Historians have demonstrated the scope and depth of the Enlightenment's reach and have painted a variegated picture of a decentralized intellectual system with fulcrums as remote as Lima, Calcutta, and Batavia. There clearly was a set of overarching purposes of emancipation and improvement, but elaborating and pursuing 'the Enlightenment' also involved a 'sense of place.' We encounter sentimentalist empiricists, atheist republican hacks, Leibnizian metaphysicians, Kantian defenders of enlightened kingship, and Anglican Newtonians. Enlightened premises were reconfigured by translation, showing the disparities of audience and purpose. The German translators of Adam Ferguson's *Essay on the History of Civil Society*, for example, diluted his civic humanism and praise of commerce and placed it in the service of an advocacy of spiritual freedom and aesthetic inwardness. Civic participation was in this way transmuted into the striving for individual perfection.[1] By its very nature, the Enlightenment imposed identifiable modes of thought on those who used it, while it always remained an expression of particular desires and meanings, and a response to particular conditions.

What difference did the Enlightenment make? It maintained that human reason was able to understand nature unaided by divine revelation, but attuned to its truths;

many Enlighteners agreed that God, like Newton's divine clockmaker, had created the universe, but thereafter intervened no more. John Locke's critique of primordialism challenged the existence of innate ideas and original sin. He also mounted a pervasive argument in favor of government based on public support. Pierre Bayle maintained that a society of atheists would not relapse into internecine violence. German scholarly pursuits contributed to the force and panache of this intellectual revolution, both in Protestant territories and in the Catholic South, which was, contrary to long-held opinions, not stifled by Baroque piety. Religion and religiosity did not simply 'adjust' to 'modernity,' but theological preoccupations fed into enlightened interests. References to Hobbes, Spinoza and Toland were often concealed with erudite codes.[2] Contrary to England and France where universities receded into insignificance during the eighteenth century, German universities became the power nodes of intellectual and political rejuvenation. They played a key part in displacing Aristotelianism, and later heralded innovation when Leibnizian-Wolffian philosophy fell into disrepute. Structurally similar to the Scottish Enlightenment, the German *Aufklärung* initially revolved around two pivot institutions, school and church; it was rooted in learned societies, and flourished among the Protestant and Catholic clergy alike. The rarity of gentleman scholars accounts for this; almost all successful writers of the German Enlightenment had to earn their living as teachers or civil servants. By and large, the general political climate in the German lands was not an impediment to public intellectual activity. If German Enlighteners proceeded with caution, they were rarely exposed to full princely caprice.

Around 1750, German was not yet established on the map of Europe as a language of scholarship and high culture. It is difficult to chart the evolution of the German language, from the rustic and recondite idiom used by scribes and preachers and despised by Frederick II, to the subtle instrument it had become by 1780.[3] While the genius polymath Gottfried Wilhelm Leibniz or the firebrand professor of law Christian Thomasius had made occasional forays into the vernacular, Christian Wolff was the first to propagate German as a language of instruction. After the mid-century, Gotthold Ephraim Lessing, a man of many talents, heralded a cultural transformation of unprecedented magnitude. In the years around 1760, German became the main language of Enlightenment in the principalities and free cities of the Holy Roman Empire. At the same time, German-speaking scholars and intellectuals remained deeply enmeshed in the networks of philosophical discourse that had spanned Europe since the radical early Enlightenment.

In the German lands, patriotism as a sentiment of solidarity can be found among Enlighteners, as well as among their opponents. It was often colored by resistance against French hegemony in the realm of culture and motivated by a struggle against cultural inferiority. Eighteenth-century Germans began to grapple with alternative objects of their patriotism, be it the Reich, their principality, or their hometown. For those in the mainly Catholic South, the focus lay on a centripetal agglutination of territories, the Habsburg Monarchy. However, even throughout Germany, few committed themselves to a vague overarching unit of German culture. Conservative critics, like Friedrich Karl von

Moser in his *Of German National Spirit* (*Vom deutschen Nationalgeist*, 1765) tended to favor the Reich or smaller regional and local communities, engendering brotherhood and calling for a reform of the Reich's constitution.

Thomas Abbt, who in 1761 published *On Dying for the Fatherland* (*Vom Tode für das Vaterland*), elaborated his stance within the enlightened debate on the moral prerequisites of politics and the genius of nations. In a time of dispersed territories and mercenary recruitment, Abbt posited that martial patriotism countervailed individual selfishness; it was aroused by an inborn aesthetic admiration for beauty and order, and by the emulation of incarnate virtue as epitomized by the just ruler, Frederick II. Abbt's theory wedded reason and sentiment. Arguing in the vein of the Earl of Shaftesbury's and Moses Mendelssohn's aesthetics, Abbt hoped for moral renewal centered on altruistic patriotism, which he believed yielded pleasurable affections as well as rich intellectual and emotional delights.[4]

A conceptual centerpiece of the Enlightenment agenda of self-cultivation, cosmopolitanism possessed protean meanings and associations. The archetypical 'polite' cosmopolitan would have travelled, mastered foreign languages, and displayed refined manners. He would be acquainted with the recent outpouring of the European republic of letters and conversant with the political, economic, and social state of the various corners of the world. He would also evince tolerance and curiosity, and harness his knowledge to a particular end—the reform of his fatherland.

Modern forms of cosmopolitanism developed in Europe from about the middle of the seventeenth century, especially in its earliest cradle—the Dutch Republic with its double face as sanctuary of religious toleration and pivot of a global commercial empire.[5] In a world of merchants, 'cosmopolitanism' mainly referred to the enlarged scope of one's own business interests. However, other milieus on the European continent cultivated a self-image that transcended mercantile egoism and repudiated the haughty exclusiveness of privileged elites. This kind of cosmopolitanism flourished in a shadowy sphere of semi-secrecy, especially in Masonic lodges that encouraged social mixing and pursued emancipatory aspirations. During the latter half of the eighteenth century, cosmopolitanism gradually lost its tinge of unorthodoxy and dissidence and developed into an openly proclaimed identity and style of life, which was frequently associated with the French cultural model of the '*gentilhomme*'.[6] By the end of the century, complaints abounded that cosmopolitanism meant little more than fashionable rhetorical frills, an attitude of irresponsible armchair travelers. At the same time, however, the growth of nationalist sentiments lent a new urgency to any serious attempt at overcoming a spirit of selfishness and confrontation. Cosmopolitanism was an ambiguous concept; it could possess strong imperial contours, encapsulating a civilizing and pacifying mission; in the German context, it could also refurbish the *Reichsidee* in the sense of a *translatio imperii*.

German states did not pursue imperial projects. Although Joseph II contemplated a Pacific voyage, Germans eager to visit other continents sought employment abroad, joining voyages, expeditions, or diplomatic missions organized by the Dutch East India Company, the British Admiralty, the Tsarist Crown, or the Royal Danish government.

Indeed, their political unobtrusiveness, as well as their philological, naturalist and medical qualifications, endeared Germans abroad. At another level, German intellectuals engaged with the world through a vibrant culture of translation. Philosophical treatises, historical surveys, novels, and travel reports from all over the world were translated soon after their first publication, and were frequently adorned with lengthy disquisitions and corrections by the editors. Several large-scale publishing projects acquainted German readers with an unprecedented wealth of material; foremost among them was the *Allgemeine Historie aller merckwürdigen Reisen, zu Wasser, und zu Lande* (The General History of Curious Travels on Water and Land), which appeared in twenty-one volumes between 1747 and 1774. Marvelous material objects from the remotest corners of the world found their way into German curiosity cabinets (*Wunderkammern*) and other, more specialized, collections—the forerunners of the ethnological museums of the nineteenth century.[7] None of the German libraries could equal the enormous repositories of oriental manuscripts that were now accumulating in Paris, Leiden, London, or St. Petersburg, but the Arabic, Ottoman, or Chinese texts in German and Austrian possession sufficed as the material basis for the oriental philologies as they emerged, with only a minor time lag behind France, at places like Vienna, Leipzig, or Göttingen.

To summarize, German scholars were well integrated both into the intellectual networks within Europe and into the circuits of information about the extra-European world that were fully developed in the wake of Captain Cook's three circumnavigations. To some degree, the lack of direct access to exploration and colonial conquest was compensated by a heightened attention to all kinds of systematic knowledge about the 'East' and about the peoples labeled 'savages' in the language of the eighteenth century. When German authors reasoned about anthropology or the patterns of world history, they drew heavily on evidence provided in travel accounts. Immanuel Kant and Johann Gottfried Herder, Johann Wolfgang von Goethe and Georg Wilhelm Friedrich Hegel, were thoroughly familiar with this kind of material.

We need a conceptual grid to grasp the complexities of enlightened cosmopolitanism in the German lands, and to explain how the global and the local were interrelated. Our chapter will first delineate four analytical facets of the cosmopolitan agenda. In a second step we will introduce selected fields of enlightened cosmopolitan reasoning. In a third subsection, we will survey the multiple transformations of cosmopolitanism around 1800, following some of its guiding threads into the nineteenth century.

6.1 Facets

First, the world could figure as Europe's mirror. In enlightened literature, most prominently Montesquieu's influential *Persian Letters* (1721), the external perspective of the puzzled alien observer is adopted to lay bare what was considered reprobate and decrepit in Europe. European literature of the eighteenth century is replete with travelling Chinese or Turkish spies, modeled on Montesquieu's Persian visitors, who tell the satirical 'truth' about the West.[8] These were often critical tracts informed by an increasingly profound acquaintance with the political, religious, economic, and cultural past and present of other continents. Some Enlighteners clearly saw that 'oriental despotism' was a mirage, a reverse reflection of intra-European grievances.[9] Conversely, another genre preferred the direct juxtaposition of flawed European reality with an idealized East. An example is Johann Heinrich Gottlob von Justi's *Vergleichungen der Europäischen mit den Asiatischen und anderen vermeintlich Barbarischen Regierungen* (Comparisons of European with Asian and other Supposedly Barbaric Governments), published in 1762. A prominent cameralist, Justi contrasted the alleged wisdom and rationality of China and other Asian countries with the backwardness and folly of the social and political arrangements prevailing in the German lands. Justi's favorable views on Asia, not entirely unfounded, were based on the reading of travelogues and Jesuit 'relations,' a common source of eighteenth-century visions of other civilizations.

Secondly, pivotal concepts of eighteenth-century theorizing were elaborated against the backdrop of perceptions of America, Asia, Africa, and the South Seas. A discipline of 'comparative government' arose at the moment in history when the 'great map of mankind' (Edmund Burke) unfolded before the eyes of European observers. A broad range of varieties of political experience far beyond the confines of Christendom and the Greco-Roman tradition became visible for the first time and enabled Europeans to define their own place in the world. The very concept of 'civilization,' a key term of the age, was predicated on semantic opposition and contrast. Earlier notions of 'barbarism' and 'savagery' could now be refined in the light of new ethnographic information, and comparative reasoning threw new light on the historical specificity of modern Europe. The 'comparative method' was a favorite with Enlightenment thinkers. One of its foremost applications was the devising of ambitious matrices and graded scales of social and cultural forms around the globe.

Thirdly, connections within a planetary space were very much on the minds of eighteenth century readers and writers, especially during the second half of the century. In an age of expanding inter-continental shipping and commerce and especially during and after a war—the Seven Years War (1756–1763)—that was fought for global maritime hegemony, Europeans clearly recognized that the different parts of the world were interwoven and interconnected to an unprecedented degree. The 'spirit of commerce' (*Handelsgeist*) would create bonds of mutual interest that would overcome the traditional ignorance and suspicion between peoples living in different countries. A number of German *Staatswissenschaftler* and geographers specialized in observing and interpreting the momentous changes taking place in the world. One of them was Matthias Christian Sprengel (1746–1803), who edited, among other such projects, a massive collection of news and data on all parts of the world, entitled *Auswahl der besten ausländischen geographischen und statistischen Nachrichten zur Aufklärung der Völker- und Länderkunde* (Selection of the Best Foreign Geographical and Statistical Reports for Illuminating the Knowledge of Peoples and Countries), which appeared in fourteen volumes between 1794 and 1800. Another manifestation of an acute sense of interconnectedness was a series of lectures given by August Ludwig Schlözer at Göttingen in 1795/96 on global travel and its impact on Europe.[10]

Fourthly, the anthropological study of human 'nature' and a broadly-conceived 'conjectural' history operating on a level far above the plurality of peoples and nations seemed to validate the enlightened adage of the unity of mankind. The idea of *Menschheit* (Humanity) served several functions in German Enlightenment thought, and two of them are of particular importance.[11] On the one hand, the concept carried the meaning of utopian emancipation. *Menschheit* as a concept was deliberately opposed to 'Christendom' and the theological model of man linked with it; in this sense, *Menschheit* referred not to a given order in which human beings were supposed to integrate themselves, but to a common task to be accomplished by activity and a conscious development of human capabilities. Humanity as a condition of liberty and (though far from absolute) equality had to be achieved through autonomous human action in pursuit of moral purposes. The idea itself could be used as a critical yardstick by which to measure all social, political, and cultural arrangements that stood in the way of human progress and perfection. On the other hand, many Enlightenment thinkers also had in mind the empirical collective of human beings co-existing on the face of the earth. As Christoph Martin Wieland put it in 1788: cosmopolitans 'regard all peoples of the earth as just so many branches of a single family, and the universe as a state in which they are citizens, together with innumerable other rational beings, in order to promote the perfection of the whole.'[12] Crucial for Wieland as for many others was the idea of unity in diversity. Many Enlightenment intellectuals not only assumed a common natural right possessed by human beings on all levels of 'refinement,' but also shared cognitive and bodily capacities that made it possible to acknowledge the other's humanity in situations, rare as they were, of direct personal contact.

6.2 FIELDS

6.2.1 History

Enlightened historians did not fret about the expansive range of their subjects; indeed, the subject of the history they wrote was no less than the world. According to the two pundits of German *Aufklärungshistorie* who taught at Göttingen, Johann Christoph Gatterer and August Ludwig Schlözer, all particular histories had to be constructed bearing this global angle of significance in mind: This '[...] powerful gaze turns the aggregate into a system, a system in which world and humanity form a unit.'[13] Universal history was written 'with the intention of creating world citizens' (*in weltbürgerlicher Absicht*). Enlightened historians operated in the aftermath of the so-called 'Pyrrhonian Crisis' around 1700 when the knowledge of the past provided by elder 'antiquarian' or 'erudite' scholarship had come under severe attack. What the best of eighteenth-century German historical scholarship aimed at was no mere enumeration of data, but the critical-systematic (and necessarily selective) establishment of a '*nexus rerum universalis*,' a universal connection of things in the world, in order to retrieve a universal connection between events.[14] When tied to source-criticism, as it was in the Göttingen school, this emphasis on 'structures' replaced an earlier focus on rulers and warfare. In a somewhat less empirical vein, 'conjectural' or 'philosophical' history chiseled out a sequence of developmental stages through which mankind passed on its way towards refinement. The works of the Basel-born Isaak Iselin (1728–1782) exemplified this approach.[15] Schlözer's own major works, *Vorstellung seiner Universal-Historie* (The Conception of Universal History), published in two volumes in 1772–1773, and *WeltGeschichte nach ihren HauptTheilen im Auszug und Zusammenhange,* (World History in its Main Outlines in Selections and Connections, two volumes, 1785–1789) strove to supersede both Iselin's lofty design and purely compilatory collections, such as the gargantuan English *Universal History,* which was translated and assiduously annotated by a consortium of staunchly Lutheran scholars from Halle headed by Sigmund Jacob Baumgarten.[16] Schlözer's works represent path-breaking attempts to delineate the parameters of a non-providential history of mankind: space, time, and the plurality of ethnic groups or civilizations ('Völker') who, due to contingent constellations of factors, had experienced different historical trajectories.[17]

All comprehensive histories invariably included reflections on ancient history and the biblical narrative, on Chinese history (introduced through Jesuit missionaries) and on the customs of 'savage societies.' A way to reconcile universalism with diversity on an analytical level was to survey gradations of 'progress.' This problem was tied to a broader question about the course of history, whether it proceeded in a cyclical fashion or rather in a linear manner? For Enlighteners, the circular motion of history became applicable to the non-European world *and* to Europe's internal peripheries, whereas the linear arrow was the discernible trait of the advanced, cultivated nations. Nevertheless, a set of concentric perimeters or orbits with different degrees of approximation to the European standard was not constructed before the end of the eighteenth century. Enlighteners relished in viewing the savage cultures of the age as their 'contemporary predecessors' consigned to earlier stages of European history. Intimate knowledge of 'primitive' societies would shed new light on antiquity and the early civilizations. Associations binding together the history of the mind, religious cults, and social organization became prevalent. This way of thinking correlated monotheism with reason and civilization, the predominance of the imagination with mythology and 'barbarism,' or the 'uncultured' mind with poetic, sensual-allegorical concepts and pantheist leanings. Johann Gottfried Herder and Christoph Gottlieb Heyne likewise conducted horizontal and vertical comparisons. As the Prussian cleric Friedrich Gedike put it: '[T]here was a time when the Greeks were no more prudent [...] than the Greenlanders or Kamtchatkans whose mythology is strikingly similar to that of the Greeks.' Under the auspices of a history of human reason, the ontogenesis of the human being was tied to the phylogenesis of mankind: 'Observations about the development of a child's soul give insights about the pace of development of an entire uncultivated people,' Gedike argued.[18]

This anthropological design co-existed with a bold re-envisaging of the German lands' place in the history of Europe. Since Johann Jacob Mascov's *Geschichte der Teutschen* (two volumes, 1726–1734), the migrations of late antiquity acquired prominence as a axial period in Europe's progress toward enlightenment. Barbaric German tribes, forest transhumants pasturing their cattle on glades in the immense woodlands, initially lacked sociability and law before nomadic invasions originating at the inner Asian boundaries of China set off snowball effects with repercussions reaching to the frontiers of the Roman Empire. German barbarians, converts to the Arian variety of Christianity, conquered Rome and, submitting to its legal culture, forged a blend of Roman law with their models of allodial and proprietorial tenure: it was Montesquieu who famously exclaimed in his *Spirit of the Laws* (1748) that 'this beautiful system was invented in the woods.'[19] In this way, the Germans became key agents in the transformation that gave rise to the medieval European system of state and Church. The formerly barbarian, acculturated *legalis homo* would emerge from their cisalpine and transalpine feudal kingdoms, shattered by their conflict with the papacy, as the first *Bürger* of flourishing cities. This marriage of German liberty and Roman legality was thus taken to encapsulate the germ of the eighteenth-century European order.

6.2.2 Religion

Enlighteners, as is well known, propagated religious toleration. Notwithstanding this practice of openness, a comparative study of non-Christian religions had to wait for the Romantic fascination with mythology to grow into a scholarly field of some importance. Under the influence of the Jesuits, Confucianism did not count as a religion, but as an inner-worldly system of ethics. Buddhism was discovered in Europe only around the middle of the nineteenth century. Hinduism (a collective label covering a broad range of Indian religious creeds and practices) became visible to European eyes as a result of early Sanskrit studies in Bengal and in Paris from the 1780s onwards. At first linguistic and mythological aspects of Indian civilization received more attention than its religious side. This remains true until Friedrich Schlegel's essay *Über die Sprache und Weisheit der Indier* (On the Language and Wisdom of the Indians), published in 1808, which marks a decisive shift from the sensualist study of imagination to the philological and symbolic penetration of myth. During the Enlightenment, however, the religious practices of 'savages' continued to be lumped under the old catch-all notion of 'idolatry.'

For several decades, the European debate about Islam left few traces in Germany. The outstanding German-language contribution was the sympathetic description of tribal Arabia by the traveler and proto-ethnographer in Danish service, Carsten Niebuhr (1733–1815), whose *Reisebeschreibung nach Arabien und anderen umliegenden Ländern* (Descriptions of Travels to Arabia and other Nearby Lands) appeared in three volumes between 1774 and 1837. Most writers of the German Enlightenment took a detached attitude towards Islam, a religion that had few adherents in Germany and was no longer, following the decline of the Ottoman Empire, considered a menace to Christendom. Few major German intellectuals, apart from Lessing, engaged with Islam, which does not diminish the importance of orientalist scholarship.[20] The rediscovery of Islam during the first half of the eighteenth century led to subversive consequences,[21] but 'Mohamedanism' presented no religious threat and little of an intellectual challenge, even though much ink was spilled on the rise of Islam as a peculiarly 'Asiatic revolution.'

Orientalist scholarship was bolstered by biblical hermeneutics and Pietism, a prose-lytizing, evangelical movement, which emphasized heartfelt sincerity of belief over formulaic professions of faith. Excellent Pietist language schools at Halle (*Collegium Orientale Theologicum, Collegium Judaicum*) designed to train missionaries saw many students abort their theological careers. A trailblazer of biblical criticism emerging from this very milieu was Johann David Michaelis (1717–1791), who moved from the then-conventional Protestant view of Hebrew as an immutable, divinely inspired tongue to a naturalist notion of the emergence of language. In 1761, he prompted the Danish court to send a scholarly expedition to the Arabian Peninsula, which Michaelis considered a static polity where one could still study the customs and rites related in the Bible. Although antediluvian chronologies became available, the scope of sacred history was not constricted, and the pedigree of Confucianism was even traced back to the Ark of Noah (vice-versa, Jesus was cast by Chinese writers as a disciple of Confucius' equilibrist doctrine).

Eager to end vindictive persecution, most German Enlighteners defended the toler-ation of Jews—with Christian Wilhelm Dohm's *Über die bürgerliche Verbesserung der Juden* (On the Civic Improvement of the Jews, 1781) prominent among them. The desirability of Jewish 'emancipation,' and civic integration was however also contested among Jewish *Maskilim*, scholars and adherents of *Haskalah*, Jewish Enlightenment. What Christian Enlighteners perceived as rebarbative traits of the Jews' behavior was explained as a result of their ignominious humiliation over centuries. Positions vis-à-vis Jewry thus oscillated between patronizing 'betterment,' calls for conversion, and anthropological curiosity.

6.2.3 Empire

The critique of Empire was a discourse of its own that bore a discernibly German imprint, since the German states took no part in the colonial expansion of the time.

Colonialism was not a domestic political issue, and nothing ever came close to such great public events as the process of impeachment against Warren Hastings, the first Governor General of India, in the House of Commons in the years 1788–1795, or the debates in the French National Convention preceding the abolition of colonial slavery in February 1794. The Germans were keen, but detached observers of other people's empires and colonialism.

Racist remarks directed at Africans by Christoph Meiners (1747–1810), a prolific professor of *Weltweisheit* (Worldly Wisdom) at the University of Göttingen, have given the German Enlightenment a bad reputation, and even in Herder, rightly considered the paragon of cultural diversity, one comes across occasional comments on non-Europeans, Mongols for example, of a blatantly offensive nature.[22] On the whole, however, the German Enlighteners in the second half of the eighteenth century were outspoken critics of imperialism and colonialism. This holds true for Immanuel Kant, Herder, Georg Christoph Lichtenberg, Georg Forster, and many less well-known authors, such as August Hennings (1746–1826), a Danish civil servant writing in German.[23] However, the German critique of empire responded less to specific abuses and outrages than anti-colonial agitation in Britain or France. It argued on principal grounds, and discussed conquest and subjugation in fundamental terms of justice, legitimacy, and the tolerance of diversity. Immanuel Kant put forward the strongest objection to colonialism; he rejected the right to settle on another people's soil except when permitted through a treaty, and he left no doubt that even 'savages' had rights and were capable of acting as legal subjects. The most powerful enlightened critique of empire was the detailed analysis of the Spanish colonial system in Mexico composed by Alexander von Humboldt after his extended visit to the country (*Essai politique sur le Royaume de la Nouvelle-Espagne*, 1808–1812), a book written in French, the principal language of enlightened cosmopolitanism. Here, and in his later work on Cuba (*Essai politique sur l'île de Cuba*, 1831), Humboldt did not limit himself to moral or legal denunciation. Through careful examination, he uncovered the inherent irrationality of the colonial system and questioned its long-term capacity for survival.

Post-modernist critics belittle enlightened interest in the world as a mere soliloquy, give short shrift to Enlighteners' recognition of diversity and calls for toleration, and see eighteenth-century universalism as a smokescreen of benevolence to camouflage Europe's rise to world supremacy. According to these critiques, genuinely European categories have been ruthlessly grafted onto the world in the guise of 'universal' characteristics of mankind by means of expropriation and colonial oppression.[24] However, we must be careful not to read back into the *ancien régime* nineteenth-century commonplaces. German Enlighteners who subscribed to a *weltbürgerlich* or cosmopolitan agenda by no means licensed a *mission civilisatrice*. Moreover, they did not exculpate the destruction of primitive cultures as a prerequisite for their advancement. Although Enlighteners' criticism of exploitative colonialism did not entail a full recognition of cultural equality irrespective of place, most Enlighteners preserved the unity of mankind as a pivotal idea. 'All men,' Herder insisted, 'are endowed with the power of attaining' superior reason.[25] Foreign cultures should be treated with respect, not lured into exploitative treaties. However, he also wondered whether, when under European dominion, foreign cultures should be given laws adjusted to their moral customs and intellectual capacity, In the early nineteenth century, the idiom of enlightened benevolence lingered on, but it was gradually interspersed with more disparaging attitudes toward other cultures arrested in their respective stages of development. This left little doubt about the progress of Europe as a guiding beacon for the world. Whereas in the eighteenth century the propensity for despotism was ascribed to malleable traits, habits, or oppression, a new explanatory model lodged it in the intrinsic indolence and servility of non-Europeans from the early nineteenth century onwards. In his *Principles of Political Economy* of 1848, John Stuart Mill famously lamented the recent tendency of 'attributing the diversities of conduct and character to inherent national differences.'[26]

6.2.4 Commerce and the law of nations

The eighteenth-century European order was built on a system of treaties and on the mollifying benefits of commerce. According to Emmerich de Vattel's classic on the *Law of Nations* (1758), this *res publica* was based on a common interest in the maintenance of order and in the preservation of liberty.[27] It was a 'balanced' commonwealth of self-governing entities, interconnected to a degree of interdependency where one state could not dispense with the other. The republic of letters spread enlightened reasoning and polite morals, multiplying advancement beyond the narrow circle of its accredited members.[28] This system was deemed incompatible with assertions of empire, of a *monarchia universalis* on the continent itself,[29] even if, at the same time, Europe hosted several metropolitan centers of maritime empires. Obviously, the conceptual distinctions drawn within Europe as well as between Europe and the rest of the world were crucial here. The new notion of Europe as a balanced stable system of enlightened states that mutually enhanced the commonweal increasingly provoked doubts, also from a cosmopolitan perspective. If a state failed to fulfill its duties to its subjects, by investing them with liberty and to ensuring justice, could it, some asked, forfeit its right to self-preservation? The three partitions of Poland (1772, 1793, 1795), when Europe's second-largest state disappeared from the map within twenty years, aroused fierce debates, and so did Joseph II's plan of 1785 to trade off the Austrian Netherlands for Bavaria. The Polish case could be seen as an example of morally responsible absolutism repressing a myopic movement of Catholic-aristocratic resistance to the modern state.[30] Anarchy could spill over Poland's boundaries and would be in need of containment. This issue threw into relief the co-existence of alternative models that inhabited the enlightened sphere of political legitimacy. To quite a few authors reforming monarchies were superior to the sturdy, but ramshackle republics so dear to the defenders of ancient public virtue. On this reasoning, the monarchy's function as warrantor of public welfare and felicity justified inter-state intervention, even occupation. This was precisely the argument advanced in the Polish case to brush aside claims of autarky and self-determination, which had been eloquently rephrased by Jean-Jacques Rousseau in his *Considerations on the Government of Poland* (1770–1771). In their acerbic reports, Prussian bureaucrats meticulously took stock of the alleged moral destitution of the newly acquired territories.

By the late eighteenth century, the 'cosmopolitan regime' came under attack for propagating vapid and abstract legal and moral norms. Enlightened cosmopolitanism could then be seen as tantamount to the perilous symptoms of (ostensibly) *doux commerce* (marked, e.g., by counterfeit coins and *cordons sanitaires*, which impeded trade and thus severed bonds between regional economies). Among these supposedly perilous symptoms were emotional depravation, individual self-aggrandizement, prod-igality, and avarice, together forming a system of 'interactive greed.'[31] Critics put forward a non-utilitarian notion of morals, tilting a lance at Kant's 'unsociable sociability.' Writers like Thomas Abbt challenged the significance of egoistical self-gratification and rehabilitated sacrifice for the common good and for posterity, envisaging moral self-regeneration through sublime, patriotic virtue. Moral perfection thus served as a scaffold for common welfare (*allgemeines Bestes*). This was the critical juncture where Kant felt obliged to take up the gauntlet flung down by his former student Herder in the *Ideas for a Philosophy of the History of Mankind* (1784–91). Herder, as Kant argued in a famous review, adhered to fallacious sensationalist principles in order to prove a speculative presumption about the benign harmony between the individual and society. The attain-ment of harmony, Kant argued, was a vain hope in light of natural human antagonisms, which surreptitiously contributed to happiness and perfection.[32]

In the last quarter of the eighteenth century, the whole idea of a regulated polite and commercial advancement could seem a decoy, a prevarication of glib enlightened parlance. Students of national economy had argued for some time that the subjugation (by means of spreading law and morals) and cultural evisceration of peoples were the by-products of commercial domination within as well as outside Europe.[33] Commerce meant coercion and conquest. In 1807, the Berlin publicist Friedrich Buchholz called for a Franco-Prussian alliance against the universal monarchy of British mercantile dominance.[34] Reiterating tenets from Rousseau's *Social Contract*, Johann Gottlieb Fichte's *Closed Commercial State* (1800) likewise urged the abandonment of inter-national trade.[35] A disdain for the overtly paternalistic state-economies of the static Eastern Empires, held responsible for distortions of commerce, also began to over-shadow the erstwhile appreciation for the fine-tuned checks and balances which domesticated despotism.

Fifthly, philosophy of history and *Weltbürgertum*. Common to Enlighteners' view of progress was the ascertaining of three particular qualities: economic activity (dyna-mism and competitive entrepreneurship), sociability (translating private virtues into social modes and collective habits of comportment or channeling private vices into public benefits) and public governance (as opposed to the arbitrary use of power). These three traits shaped enlightened attempts to come to terms with Europe's place in history.

Two of the shorter writings of the greatest German philosopher of the eighteenth century, Immanuel Kant, are of particular relevance here: '*Idee zu einer allgemeinen Geschichte in weltbürgerlicher Absicht*' (Ideas for a Universal History with a Cosmopolitan Aim, 1784)[36] and '*Zum ewigen Frieden. Ein philosophischer Entwurf*' (Perpetual Peace: A Philosophical Sketch, 1795).[37] Kant's treatise on perpetual peace stands not only in a tradition of irenic writings since Erasmus' *Querela Pacis* (The Complaint of Peace) of 1517, but should also be seen as part of a debate on the contemporary condition of Europe in an age of large-scale war.

Immanuel Kant's essay 'Idea for a Universal History with a Cosmopolitan Aim' proposes a regulative idea of the improvement of mankind that allows for the full development of man's predispositions (*Anlagen*) for the use of reason. Similar to the Göttingen historians, Kant's regulative idea serves to make the 'complex and disorderly' material of history reveal order, allowing the historian to see the 'system' behind the 'aggregate' of disparate and arbitrary facts.[38] The teleological idea of a providential plan of nature is a 'maxim' and 'guiding principle' necessary to organize empirical material.[39] The presupposition of 'progress' does not serve as a causal explanation or as an absolute truth, but as a heuristic principle capable of empirical confirmation, revealing a 'regular cause of improvement.'[40] Kant's conjectural axiom, the improvement of mankind, organizes the process of history 'as if,' prefiguring man's further development *and* encouraging social and political reform. The axiom prepares its own decrease of importance without ever being dislodged. As soon as man is emancipated from the 'rule of instincts,' the toil endured to achieve this stage will be retrospectively justified. Kant's *a priori* thus saves mankind from despair in the face of injustices that are man-made and therefore changeable. Kant is concerned with a species-wide rational and moral advancement through social 'antagonism.' This irresolvable state of competition, in turn, precludes men from developing the self-discipline necessary for moral agency, a function fulfilled by public law with its threat of sanction.

Perfect justice remains an illusion and even the state's approximate justice is, in Kant's view, constantly imperiled by warfare and inter-state conflict. A cosmopolitan federation with legislative powers, inaugurating a world senate for universal jurisdiction and a court of international arbitration, is the prerequisite for the further advancement of mankind. We need to situate Kant's 'perpetual peace' of 1795 in its context: the idea that the international cohabitation of nations could be described as a natural society—subject to natural law, as was the community of men within a state—was common to enlightened thought.[41] Accordingly, international law had aimed at preventing individual states from destroying this (fictional) 'natural order.' Kant envisages a global legal community of equal citizens who assent to their polity's laws and are not forced into arms. He favors a voluntary league of nations over a regime of universal jurisdiction with coercive powers. Predestination forecloses the total 'confluence' of peoples, but there exists a mechanism, based on shared instincts, which connects and at the same time separates them: 'National pride and national hatred are necessary to separate nations' and, Kant adds, governments 'like this folly.' Moral perfection will surmount the instinctual state through 'maxims of reason,' which will enable men to 'eradicate *Nationalwahn*' (national delusion) whose place will be taken by 'patriotism and cosmopolitism.'[42]

Johann Gottfried Herder, Kant's former student, repudiated the 'spirit of the times,' which he saw as a presumption of uniformity based upon self-adulatory parochialism. Herder's unease with 'facile, grandiose' generalities and his emphasis on the contingency of history were reinforced by his studies on the origins of language.[43] Subscribing to a nominalist approach, Herder highlighted how particular, descriptive notions were transmuted into universal denominators.[44] Generalized claims that fitted entire peoples into an overall scheme were perilous and unfounded as no universal standard to measure 'progress' existed. This absence of parameters resulted as much from the fallibility and finitude of human capacities as from the circumstantial conditions of every specific situation. The notion of 'deviation' from a given 'standard' is therefore erroneous. According to Herder the force of knowledge imprinted by concrete circumstances leads to moral incommensurability across time and place. 'Why do we not realize that if we do not have all the vices and virtues of former ages?', Herder asked in his 1774 *Auch eine Philosophie der Geschichte der Menschheit* (Also a Philosophy of History), it is 'because we are not in their position [. . .] nor breathe the same air.'[45] 'The philosopher,' according to Herder's poignant appraisal, 'is never more of an ass than when he [. . .] pronounces on the perfection of the world, wholly convinced that everything moves just so, in a [. . .] straight line, that every succeeding generation reaches perfection in a [. . .] linear progression, according to *his* ideals of virtue and progress.'[46] Indeed, the self-serving teleology that pervades all the countless 'pragmatic histories' of the age fuels a complacent trust in *general* progress. This basic conviction makes it impossible to properly appreciate minor, but *concrete* and overdue reforms. According to Herder, conjuring up the 'opium dream' of the superiority of eighteenth-century Europe served as a pretext for cowardice and inactivity. Adorning man's chains with flowers, the 'uniformity of progress' sapped the cosmopolitan project by setting up a complacent notion of 'humanity,' tied to the alleged benefits of commerce.[47]

By emphasizing the uniqueness of situations and the incomparability of different sociopolitical configurations, Herder does not assign intrinsic, inalienable characteristics to peoples. In his *Ideen zu einer Philosophie der Geschichte der Menschheit* (1784–1791). he claimed that all individuals and nations are expressions of a single human nature, all gravitating toward the fullest expression of their potentialities. The 'New Zealand cannibal and a Fénelon, a Newton and the wretched Pesheray, are all creatures of one and the same species,' he insisted.[48]

6.3 TRANSITIONS AROUND 1800

The period around 1800 was a time of multiple transitions and of the fragmentation of enlightened agendas and claims. New, ostensibly self-contained 'currents' surfaced: liberalism, conservatism, romanticism. The conventional taxonomy suggests that

Enlightenment's demise neatly coincided with the centennial divide. This oversimplifies the ways by which enlightened objectives and methods were reconfigured and built into newly available idioms; also, partisans of late Enlightenment, *Spätaufklärung*, did not simply acquiesce to this polemical and selective re-tailoring. The engrained view of Enlightenment's decline also tends to portray the available agendas around 1800 in isolation from each other.

This chapter can only hint at the changes the concept of *Weltbürgertum* underwent around 1800. Let us single out two epistemological dislocations: a sanguine eighteenth-century debate about the history of writing came to an end with the disenchanted realization that Chinese and Egyptian civilizations did not possess scripts reproducing reality in pictorial or symbolic signs beyond phonetic and alphabetical notation. Jean-François Champollion's decipherment of the Rosetta Stone and Wilhelm von Humboldt's studies on Chinese language are pivotal here. Also, the belief in the pristine African and Oriental progenitors of Greek Antiquity rapidly lost prestige by the early nineteenth century, being replaced by a notion of indigenously European or Indo-European 'Aryan' origins. A renewed sentiment of European solidarity, culturally validated by an invoked shared 'heritage,' went hand in hand with an increasing disregard for the fate of peoples outside Europe.

In the realm of politics, three processes come to mind: the years around 1800 brought a redistribution of global power, with the Napoleonic wars heralding British ascendancy. Distances between the continents shrunk further and Europe's mercantile empire was consolidated. After a marked decline before 1800, European missionary aspirations again began to soar.[49] In a more narrowly German setting, the unmasking of the Illuminati order in 1784–1785 and the spread of revolutionary conflagration after 1789 allowed cosmopolitanism to acquire yet another layer of meaning—while tarnishing, for some, the process of Enlightenment further still.[50] The Enlightenment could now, in the wake of Napoleonic 'despotism' and belligerent expansionist zeal, be denounced as universalist, French, and as a potential menace.[51] The divorce between the cosmopolitan (in a disparaging sense), superficial and vapid French ideas and an ostensibly deeper German national 'spirit' became a much-labored theme of cultural self-recognition in the German lands, one which still resonated in Friedrich Meinecke's magisterial *Weltbürgertum und Nationalstaat* (1908). In fact, the rejection of Napoleon's German politics was far less pervasive than usually assumed. The shifts in political sensibilities and rhetoric are difficult to gauge, but the Masonic lodges provide revealing evidence. Around 1800 cosmopolitan rhetoric was readjusted and realigned to fit an agenda more straightforwardly alloyed to a 'nation.'[52] In 1809, a few days after the foundation of the *Rheinbund*, Prussian Masons of Erlangen dispatched a circular to fraternal lodges in which they insisted that 'the cosmopolitan interest can and should coexist with the patriotic [*vaterländischen*] in complete harmony.'[53]

The 'nation' frequently invoked around 1800 was not a concept developed in clear contradistinction to cosmopolitism. It rather seems that cosmopolitanism and hyperbolic 'nationalism' carved out separate channels. The early nineteenth century did not bring a backlash of stubborn nationalism traditionally attributed to popular revolts against Napoleon. Fraternal bonds to other peoples were reinforced and praise for the Revolution in France remained strong. German Philhellenism in the 1820s also rested on a cosmopolitan scaffold, as Greek patriots modeled their pedigree on what they considered to be the ancient ancestors of all civilized mankind. Notwithstanding the nationalist harangues of Joseph Görres and Ernst Moritz Arndt, many of Germany's foremost men of letters retained a distinctly cosmopolitan perspective and refrained from adulating the *Vaterland*. During the last years of his life, Friedrich Schiller collected materials on several plays with oceanic and exotic subject matters. Only fragments indicate the direction in which his interest in pirates, emigration, and the New World might have taken the great dramatist.[54] Cosmopolitanism survived powerfully in Goethe's idea and program of *Weltliteratur*, which he began to adumbrate in 1827. He did not, in the first place, mean the formation of an extended literary canon to be enjoyed and contemplated quietly by readers in the Germany of the *Biedermeier* years, but rather a constant, and well-organized, activity of awareness and mediation, translation and transfer, a process of linking intellectual communities in distant parts of the world, encouraging the educated to transcend parochialism or national bigotry. *Weltliteratur*, as the cultural underpinning of world society, had not just to be assembled and displayed, it had to be created.[55] In his last years, the ever-attentive Goethe hailed the advent of the steamship, predicted a great future for the railway and understood that cross-border cultural communication would be facilitated by the logistics of the dawning industrial age. While the old enlightened republic of letters was dilapidated after 1815, a pan-European community of scholars was not torn apart by the Napoleonic wars. German scholars were actively involved in the many networks tirelessly spun by that indefatigable survivor and defender of the late Enlightenment, Alexander von Humboldt.

The desirability of 'Enlightenment' as moral and political advancement remained forceful. From the early nineteenth century onwards, its universal thrust became more and more unequivocally tied to a distinct, tangible 'national' community, which was portrayed as both the target and agent of enlightening in the sense of a 'national renaissance.' A double-threaded process can be observed. On the one hand, one relished Germany's alleged role as intellectual *primus inter pares*, which encouraged the wish to bestow to others one's pioneer accomplishments. On the other hand, and this is particularly salient well into the *Vormärz*, Germans gave themselves pride of place in their solitary cosmopolitanism: cosmopolitanism was thus emblazoned as a key cachet of German national character, as a quality which potentially superseded that of other peoples.[56]

In the Habsburg monarchy after 1800, the conceptual triad of cosmopolitan universalism, territorial patriotism and an incipient stress on national distinctiveness was equally significant. In its multilingual milieus, rival conceptions of the nation contended for legitimacy. As in the non-Habsburg German context, cosmopolitanism could become a term of vituperation directed against an irresponsibly 'rootless' (in the Central European case: 'Germanized') aristocracy with its outdated taste and opinions, whose legally sanctioned predominance had to be curtailed.[57] In addition, a 'cosmopolitan' proclivity could be accused of enticing consent to Joseph II's reforms of the

1780s, which rode roughshod over inherited constitutions and an ostensibly 'natural' diversity. This linkage did not deter early conservatives from decrying liberalism as a reincarnation of the enlightened cosmopolitan ideal, or from seeing liberalism as expressing abstract legalism and encouraging self-love. This was a key moment in the fragmentation of enlightened cosmopolitanism.[58] However, while agents of the Bohemian and Hungarian 'national renaissance' rejected antiquated and detrimental 'cosmopolitanism,' they strongly emphasized the brotherhood and interdependency of peoples who were entitled to aspire and achieve freedom. This again clearly evinces traits of the late-enlightened model of a European equilibrium, and of eighteenth-century universalism reoriented toward the 'people' as the agent of emancipation and refinement. Moreover, the 'cosmopolitan patriotism' inculcated by the imperial state explicitly situated itself in the dignified ancestry of the Roman Empire.[59]

Another shift relevant to the reconfiguration of cosmopolitanism both in the Habsburg Monarchy and in the German lands occurred around 1800. During the eighteenth century, the European Republic of letters was involved in charting an imaginary boundary between 'East' and 'West,' portraying the former as exotically backward and the later as progressive and enlightened. The debate over Poland sketched above was a critical point in this drift. These clichés were often reinforced by intellectuals from 'the East' for reasons of polemical purchase in order to spur their audiences' will to reform. However, with the Revolutionary Wars this sliding frontier between East and West became more tangible and politically charged. While Germany was not squarely placed on the Eastern side of this divide, German educated citizens' self-recognition acquired a certain gravitational pull in that direction after 1800. The conventional wisdom about the renunciation of enlightened ideas and methodological devices after 1800 is heavily colored by hindsight. The disavowal of cosmopolitanism was a convenient exit from the Enlightenment. Later in the nineteenth century, liberal nationalists wished to efface the cosmopolitan blot on their shield and, in doing so, they diluted the intellectual force of enlightened dispositions after 1800. Posterity has accepted this liberal-nationalist image of German cosmopolitanism and connected it to assumptions about Germany's purported 'special path.' As a consequence, cosmopolitanism has been frequently treated as a typically German idealist pipe dream that hampered political realism and reinforced escapism, thus buttressing pusillanimous state-obedience.[60] Those who deplored Germany's status as a 'belated nation' could hold cosmopolitanism responsible for this delay. The dissociation from questionable *Spätaufklärung* with its asserted revolutionary potential thus served a central purpose. In retrospect, it irrevocably attuned liberal aspirations to the nation state already during the *Vormärz*.[61] This claiming and realigning of intellectual predecessors has also colored basic assumptions of German history, with liberal nationalists later maligning the bureaucrats who had supported Napoleonic rule. In fact, those civil servants were eager to level the privilege-based society of orders and inherited prerogative including what remained of the estates (*Stände* or *Landtage*) that had not been entirely subverted by the enlightened despots of the eighteenth century. Later liberal nationalists essentially erased the patriotic activities of enlightened bureaucrats where they had succumbed to pro-Napoleonic sentiments. In the former *Rheinbund* states, liberal nationalists slighted the long-standing effects of bureau-cratic reform, whereas in Prussia the reconstruction of the state after the crushing defeat of 1806 was conceived as the foundational moment for 'liberal' statehood. As for the intellectual genesis and antecedents of Prussia's rebirth, their 'cosmopolitan' purview was disputed. Around 1900, this would spark a veritable *Historikerstreit* about Baron vom Stein, Karl August von Hardenberg, and other Prussian heroes. The debate focused on their reliance on eighteenth-century French reforming schemes that had been thwarted or distorted by the Revolution of 1789 and, of course, on their debt to Kant.

The Romantics' cosmopolitan schemes are difficult to square with the conventional image of their inveterate repudiation of Enlightenment. Romantics joined in the disavowal of the paradigms of commerce and 'unsocial sociability.' They wished to resuscitate a world of fraternity marked by—in Novalis' words—'faith and love,' not by 'knowing and having.'[62] They tacitly endorsed enlightened ideals of individuality, freedom, and equality, but accused the Enlightenment of having devaluated them, ridiculing sacrifice for the best of mankind and supplanting true charity with greed. The Romantics took issue with contractualism, which stipulated the self-subjugation of individuals to the state's laws. Joseph von Eichendorff, for example, tried to strip the prejudicial incrustations of 'Enlightenment' in order to retrieve the true core of cosmopolitanism, which he saw as a Catholic universalism beyond confessional hostil-ity.[63] Similarly, Johann Gottlieb Fichte had initially aspired to the cosmopolitan unification of 'Neo-Europeans'—unflinchingly rejecting Arab-Muslim culture—under the aegis of a 'science of reason' [*Vernunftwissenschaft*]. He devised a heliotro-pism which irresistibly attracted the cosmopolitan mind to the 'sun' of the most refined culture.[64] Fichte's crestfallen response to Napoleonic victory first in Austerlitz, then in Jena, made him pronounce that 'in reality cosmopolitism should necessarily become patriotism'.[65] In his *Addresses to the German Nation*, delivered in Berlin between December 1807 and March 1808, Fichte even claimed that the German nation should excel as the 'rebirthing mother and conceiver of the World' (*Wiedergebärerin und Wiederherstellerin der Welt*).[66] Indeed, the criticism of what the Romantics took to be the enlightened conception of the state, an aggregate of individuals detached from each other, re-invigorated their cosmopolitan view of mankind as a family united in spiritual harmony: The 'poetic state' would dispense with coercive laws to the degree it suc-ceeded in educating its citizen to emotional, spiritual, and moral perfection.[67]

At the very time the divide between 'East' and 'West' underwent a reconfiguration, there also occurred a refashioning of the conceptual arbitrator between the 'universal' and the 'particular.' The 'nation' increasingly came to replace the 'citizen of the world' as the epistemological interface between the 'whole' and the 'parts.' The character of this seismic shift can best be studied in historical writing: the decades immediately preceding 1800 witnessed the last heyday of cosmopolitan world history, for example, with Johann Gottfried Eichhorn's *Weltgeschichte* (2 vols, 1799–1800).[68] The 'cultural history of the human race' (*Kulturgeschichte des Menschengeschlechts*) was losing academic significance within Germany, and the same applies to the 'history of the European system of states,' whose main practitioner had been Arnold Hermann

Ludwig Heeren at Göttingen. However, both did not simply peter out. We know little about how the *science de l'homme*, which furnished the Napoleonic Empire with its key tools of knowledge, was received in the German lands. A philosophical history of the Scottish type found new acolytes among Hegelians.[69] The large-scale historical enterprises of this 'threshold period' (*Schwellenzeit*), mocked as insipid and anodyne by a younger generation, refused to vanish.[70] Notable examples are Alexander von Humboldt's far-flung œuvre based on his American voyage of 1799–1805 or Carl Ritter with his monumental *Die Erdkunde im Verhältniß zur Natur und Geschichte des Menschen* (1817–1859). Nevertheless, impermeable disciplinary dispensations emerged and a contraction of the gaze replaced the far less prejudiced enlightened global perspective. With specialization came claims to European omniscience. Axiomatic and aprioristic Eurocentrism retained the enlightened *terminus ad quem*, the apogee of refinement, but tended to identify this stage with the situation of early nineteenth century Europe. The sliding scale of progress designed by eighteenth century historians-cum-anthropologists was a heuristic grid and elastic model, which atrophied into a teleological model, with Europe as its implicit parameter, pinnacle, and destination. In practice, this superior stage of civilization was identified with *western* Europe.

These shifts had far-ranging implications for the purpose and purview of the historian's craft: enlighteners enjoyed the unraveling of evil intentions resulting in beneficial effects. With a fine sense of irony, Enlighteners pinpointed how fallacious doctrines and 'salutary nonsense' spurred societal progress. These tools were gradually replaced with new explanatory devices, most saliently by an appeal to moral powers (*sittliche Mächte*) and their earth-bound protagonists, notable individuals (mostly 'great men'), who served as the significant agents of history. Here, of course, lies the much-betrodden threshold between Enlightenment and 'Historicism.'[71] The recognition of the artificiality of the units and entities of historical enquiry stressed by the Enlighteners gave way to a new authentication of the intrinsic qualities of 'identity' and 'individuality'—be it of states, peoples, nations, or guiding 'ideas.' The discontinuities of history that Enlighteners had stressed were now increasingly glossed over. Enlighteners had argued that the linchpin of historical refinement wandered. Peoples replaced each other at the helm of progress. By the early nineteenth century, 'culture' was divested of this typological, Linnéan mould and imparted with a new immanent thrust and a set of diachronic, organicist-ontological metaphors: a cataract-or glacier-like 'world historical stream of peoples' rolls along and nations are likened to the peaks of a 'primeval mountain range.'[72] When scholars after 1800 subverted the eighteenth-century system of world history, this involved a redistribution of emphasis, allotting more significance to the 'interior,' to intrinsic pulls and qualities.

Anthropology, with its classificatory schemes, held in the highest esteem in the eighteenth century, was discarded in the long run as far as it did not serve to justify material exploitation. Accounts of the stages of civilization proved superfluous once the savage was regarded as markedly less 'noble' and ultimately incomprehensible. Historical writing, then, came to lend credence to two basic convictions: Europe's superiority was taken to consist in the division of its land mass into nation states whose global destiny and mission only now, after 1800, unfurled fully. The second prerequisite was the role of the rational state as the ultimate agent of historical progress. The absence of these engines of reform elsewhere made the study of extra-European constitutional regulations and customs expendable. Acquitting the historian of his responsibility to forge the global *'nexus rerum'* stressed by Gatterer, the cosmopolitan synoptic vision was surrendered to God, who adjudicated *sub specie aeternitatis*. States could now be portrayed as the 'thoughts of God.'[73] The re-entrance of God into history was also predicated upon the late-eighteenth century break with the old pragmatic universal history. Now, given the asserted self-actualization of a *deus absconditus*, progress could be retrieved in the most diverse shapes and figurations of an 'inner history' and 'inner meaning': one could see all epochs—following Ranke—as 'immediate to God.'[74] This radicalized the eighteenth century's appreciation of diversity.[75] The new mode of historiographical 'depiction' implied a reverential reluctance to decipher the innermost 'hieroglyphic' forces of history: a new idiom of disclosure and revelation emerged.

NOTES

1. Fania Oz-Salzberger, *Translating the Enlightenment: Scottish Civic Discourse in Eighteenth-Century Germany* (Oxford: Oxford University Press, 1995), 48, 138–166; László Kontler, 'William Robertson's History of Manners in German,' *Journal of the History of Ideas* 58 (1997), 125–144.
2. Martin Mulsow, *Moderne aus dem Untergrund: Radikale Frühaufklärung in Deutschland 1680–1720* (Hamburg: Meiner, 2002).
3. Eric A. Blackall, The *Emergence of German as a Literary Language, 1700–1775*, 2nd edn (Ithaca: Cornell University Press, 1978).
4. Notker Hammerstein, 'Das politische Denken Friedrich Carl von Mosers,' *Historische Zeitschrift* 212 (1971), 316–338; Eva Piirimäe, 'Dying for the Fatherland: Thomas Abbt's Theory of Aesthetic Patriotism,' *History of European Ideas* 35 (2009), 194–208; the best available edition of Abbt's treatise is in Johannes Kunisch (ed.), *Aufklärung und Kriegserfahrung: Klassische Zeitzeugen zum Siebenjährigen Krieg* (Frankfurt am Main: Deutscher Klassikerverlag, 1996), 589–650.
5. Margaret C. Jacob, *Strangers Nowhere in the World: The Rise of Cosmopolitanism in Early Modern Europe* (Philadelphia: University of Pennsylvania Press, 2006).
6. On the main varieties of cosmopolitanism see Axel Horstmann, 'Kosmopolit, Kosmopolitismus,' in Joachim Ritter and Karlfried Gründer (eds), *Historisches Wörterbuch der Philosophie* (Basel: Schwabe, 1971–2007), iv (1976), column 1155–1167, 1159–1162.
7. Dominik Collet, *Die Welt in der Stube: Begegnungen mit Außereuropa in Kunstkammern der Frühen Neuzeit* (Göttingen: Vandenhoeck & Ruprecht, 2007).
8. Winfried Weisshaupt, *Europa sieht sich mit fremdem Blick: Werke nach dem Schema der 'Lettres persanes' in der europäischen, insbesondere der deutschen Literatur des 18. Jahrhundert*, 3 vols (Frankfurt am Main: Lang, 1979).
9. Franco Venturi, 'Despotismo orientale', *Rivista storica italiana* 72 (1960), 117–126; Joan-Pau Rubiés, 'Oriental Despotism and European Orientalism: Botero to Montesquieu', *Journal of Early Modern History* 9 (2005), 109–180; Jürgen Osterhammel, *Die Entzauberung Asiens: Europa und die asiatischen Reiche im 18. Jahrhundert*, 2nd edn (Munich: Beck, 2010), 271–309.

10. August Ludwig Schlözer, *Vorlesungen über Land-und Seereisen: Nach dem Kollegheft des stud. jur. E. F. Haupt (Wintersemester 1795/96)*, ed. Wilhelm Ebel (Göttingen: Musterschmidt, 1962).

11. See Hans Erich Bödeker, 'Menschheit, Humanität, Humanismus,' in Otto Brunner, Werner Conze and Reinhart Koselleck (eds), *Geschichtliche Grundbegriffe: Historisches Lexikon zur politisch-sozialen Sprache in Deutschland* (Stuttgart: Klett-Cotta, 1972–1997), iii (1982), 1063–1128, 1079–1090.

12. 'Das Geheimnis des Kosmopolitenordens [1788],' in Christoph Martin Wieland, *Werke*, Fritz Martini and Hans Werner Seiffert (eds), (Munich: Hanser, 1967), iii. 553–575, at 556. Translation: Pauline Kleingeld, 'Six Varieties of Cosmopolitanism in Late Eighteenth-Century Germany,' *Journal of the History of Ideas* 60, no. 3 (1999), 505–525, at 508.

13. August Ludwig Schlözer, *Vorstellung seiner Universal-Historie* (Göttingen and Gotha: J. C. Dieterich, 1772), 18–19, 86, idem, *Weltgeschichte nach ihren Haupttheilen im Auszug und Zusammenhange*, 2 vols (Göttingen: Vandenhoeck & Ruprecht, 1785–1789), i. 1, 70.

14. Johann Christoph Gatterer, 'Vom historischen Plan und der sich darauf gründenden historischen Erzählung,' *Allgemeine historische Bibliothek* 1 (1767), 15–89.

15. Isaak Iselin, *Ueber die Geschichte der Menschheit*, 2 vols. (Frankfurt am Main: J. H. Harsche 1764). Another important author was the librarian Johann Christoph Adelung (1732–1806) with his *Versuch einer Geschichte der Cultur des menschlichen Geschlechtes* (Leipzig: Hertel, 1782).

16. *An Universal History from the Earliest Account of Time; Compiled from Original Authors and illustrated with Maps, cuts, notes, chronological and other tables*, 44 vols. + 16 folio vols., (London: various printers), 1736–1765); *Uebersetzung der Algemeinen Welthistorie, die in England von einer Geselschaft von Gelehrten angefertiget worden*, i (Halle: Gebauer, 1744).

17. Martin Peters, *Altes Reich und Europa: Der Historiker, Statistiker und Publizist August Ludwig (v.) Schlözer (1735–1809)* (Münster, Lit, 2003), 180.

18. Friedrich Gedike, 'Ueber die mannigfaltigen Hypothesen zur Erklärung der Mythologie: Eine Vorlesung an der Akademie der Wissenschaften,' *Berlinische Monatsschrift* 17, no. 1 (1791), 333–370, at 336, 364.

19. Charles le Secondat de Montesquieu, *The Spirit of Laws*, Book XI, chapter 6, tr. by Thomas Nugent (4th edn, London: Nourse, 1766), 237, cf. Erwin Hölzle, *Die Idee einer altgermanischen Freiheit vor Montesquieu* (Munich: Oldenbourg, 1926).

20. Karl-Josef Kuschel, *Vom Streit zum Wettstreit der Religionen: Lessing und die Herausforderung des Islam* (Düsseldorf: Patmos, 1998). We cannot here discuss pioneers of Arabic studies like Johann Jacob Reiske (1716–1774).

21. Jonathan I. Israel, *Enlightenment Contested: Philosophy, Modernity, and the Emancipation of Man 1670–1752* (Oxford: Oxford University Press, 2006), 615–639.

22. Christoph Meiners, *Ueber die Natur der afrikanischen Neger und die davon abhangende Befreyung, oder Einschränkung der Schwarzen* [1790] (Hanover: Wehrhahn 2000); see also id., *Grundriß der Geschichte der Menschheit* (Lemgo: Meyer, 1793), 58–128.

23. August Hennings, *Gegenwärtiger Zustand der Besitzungen der Europäer in Ostindien*, 3 vols. (Hamburg: Bohn, 1784–86).

24. Gayatri Chakravorty Spivak, *A Critique of Postcolonial Reason: Toward a History of the Vanishing Present* (Cambridge, Mass.: Harvard University Press, 1999), 7. For an incisive critique see Daniel Carey and Sven Trakulhun, 'Universalism, Diversity, and the Postcolonial Enlightenment,' in Daniel Carey and Lynn Festa (eds), *The Postcolonial Enlightenment:*

Eighteenth-Century Colonialism and Postcolonial Theory (Oxford: Oxford University Press, 2009), 240–280.

25. Johann Gottfried Herder, *Outlines of a Philosophy of the History of Man*, trans. Thomas O. Churchill (London: Johnson, 1800), 231, an abridged translation, with certain idiosyncrasies, of Herder's *Ideen zur Philosophie der Geschichte der Menschheit* (1784–1791).

26. John Stuart Mill, *Principles of Political Economy* [1848], in *Collected Works of John Stuart Mill*, ed. John M. Robson (Toronto: University of Toronto Press, 1965–1991), ii (1965), 319.

27. Emmerich de Vattel, *Le droit des gens, ou principes de la loi naturelle* (London [i.e. Neuchâtel] 1758).

28. Jean Paul speaks of a 'geistige Gütergemeinschaft mit allen Völkern': 'Friedens-Predigt an Deutschland' [1808], in *Sämtliche Werke*, ed. Norbert Miller (Munich: Hanser, 1959–1963), series I, v (1962), 877–916, at 889.

29. It is in precisely this sense that Karl von Rotteck identifies the Holy Alliance as an 'die Schrecken der Universalmonarchie in sich beherbergende Macht': *Allgemeine Weltgeschichte* (Stuttgart: Hoffmann, 1831–1845), iv. 291.

30. Friedrich von der Trenck, *Beantwortung auf die in französischer Sprache erschienene Schmähschrift: Anmerkung über die Erklärung der Wiener, Petersburger und Berliner Höfe, die Zergliederung der Republik Pohlen betreffend* (Aachen, 1773); Johann Erich Biester, *Abriß des Lebens und der Regierung der Kaiserinn Katharina II. von Rußland* (Berlin: Nicolai, 1797), 128; see also David Pickus, *Dying with an Enlightened Fall: Poland in the Eyes of German Intellectuals 1764–1800* (Oxford: Lexington Books, 2001), 71–156.

31. István Hont, *The Jealousy of Trade: International Competition and the Nation-State in Historical Perspective* (Cambridge: Cambridge University Press, 2005).

32. Immanuel Kant, *Political Writings*, trans. H. B. Nisbet (Cambridge: Cambridge University Press, 1991), 209.

33. See Kenneth E. Carpenter, *Dialogue in Political Economy: Translations From and Into German in the 18th Century* (Boston: Kress Library Publications, 1977). This line of critique still informs Karl Marx's reading: 'The bourgeoisie has through its exploitation of the world market given a cosmopolitan character to production and consumption in every country. [. . .] In place of the old local and national seclusion and self-sufficiency, we have intercourse in every direction, universal inter-dependence of nations.' Karl Marx and Friedrich Engels: "Manifesto of the Communist Party" [1848],' in id., *Collected Works* (New York: International Publishers, 1976), vi. 488.

34. Friedrich Buchholz, *Rom und London oder über die Beschaffenheit der nächsten Universal-Monarchie* (Tübingen: Cotta, 1807).

35. Johann Gottlieb Fichte, 'Über den geschlossenen Handelsstaat,' in id., Reinhard Lauth et al. (eds), *Gesamtausgabe der Bayerischen Akademie der Wissenschaften* (Stuttgart—Bad Cannstatt: Friedrich Frommann Verlag 1962), series I, vii (1988); id., 'Prüfung der Rousseauschen Behauptungen über den Einfluss der Künste und Wissenschaften auf das Wohl der Menschheit' in *Gesamtausgabe*, series I, iii (1966) 59–68.

36. Translated in Amélie Oksenberg Rorty and James Schmidt (eds), *Kant's Idea for a Universal History with a Cosmopolitan Aim: A Critical Guide* (Cambridge: Cambridge University Press, 2009), 9–23.

37. For a translation see Immanuel Kant, *Toward Perpetual Peace and Other Writings on Politics, Peace, and History*, ed. Pauline Kleingeld, (New Haven: Yale University Press, 2006), 67–109.

38. Immanuel *Kant*, 'Idee zu einer allgemeinen Geschichte in weltbürgerlicher Absicht,' in: Kant, *Gesammelte Schriften*, ed. Preußischen/Deutschen Akademie der Wissenschaften

zu Berlin/Göttingen (Berlin: de Gruyter, 1902), viii (1912), 17–18; id. 'Streit der Fakultäten,' in Kant, *Gesammelte Schriften*, vii (1907), 83.

39. Id., *Kritik der Urteilskraft*, in Kant, *Gesammelte Schriften*, v (1908), 360.

40. Id., *Idea*, 29.

41. For example, Christian Wolff, *Jus Gentium Methodo Scientifica Pertractatum* [1749], trans. Joseph Drake (Oxford: Clarendon Press, 1934), ii. 16–17, § 19–20.

42. Kant, *Gesammelte Schriften*, xv (1913), no. 1353.

43. *Auch eine Philosophie der Geschichte der Menschheit* [1774], cited after *J. G. Herder on Social and Political Culture*, ed. and trans. F. M. Barnard (Cambridge: Cambridge University Press, 1969), 198.

44. 'Abhandlung über den Ursprung der Sprache (Berlin: Voss, 1772)' in all languages the same type of searching reason is conspicuous. See also Herder, *Outlines*, 251.

45. *J. G. Herder on Social and Political culture*, 212, see also 187.

46. Ibid., 214.

47. Ibid., 213–14, Herder, *Outlines*, 92.

48. J.G. Herder, *Sämmtliche Werke* ed. Bernhard Suphan (Berlin: Weidmann, 1877–1913), xiii (1887), 147.

49. Stuart Woolf, 'The Construction of a European World-View in the Revolutionary-Napoleonic Years,' *Past and Present* 137 (1992), 72–101.

50. Ernst August von Göchhausen, *Enthüllung des Systems der Weltbürger-Republik: In Briefen aus der Verlassenschaft eines Freymaurers: wahrscheinlich manchem Leser zwanzig Jahre zu spät publiziert* (Rome, [Leipzig: Göschen] 1786) and *Einige Originalschriften des Illumina-tenordens, welche bey dem gewesenen Regierungsrath Zwack[h] durch vorgenommene Hausvisitation [. . .] vorgefunden worden*, 3 vols (Munich: Stroll, 1787), i, 3–56.

51. Gerhard Schuck, *Rheinbundpatriotismus und politische Öffentlichkeit zwischen Aufklärung und Frühliberalismus: Kontinuitätsdenken und Diskontinuitätserfahrung in den Staatsrechts- und Verfassungsdebatten der Rheinbundpublizistik*, (Stuttgart: Franz Steiner, 1994).

52. See Robert Beachy, 'Recasting Cosmopolitanism: German Freemasonry and Regional Identity in the Early Nineteenth Century,' *Eighteenth-Century Studies* 33 (2000), 266–274.

53. Julius R. Haarhaus, *Deutsche Freimaurer zur Zeit der Befreiungskriege* (Jena: Eugen Diederichs, 1913) 71–74; see also Jörg Echternkamp, *Der Aufstieg des deutschen Nationa-lismus 1770–1840* (Frankfurt: Campus, 1999), 577, note 105.

54. *Schillers Werke. Nationalausgabe* (Weimar: Böhlau, 1943), xii (1982), 303–320.

55. See Karl S Guthke, *Goethes Weimar und 'Die große Öffnung in die weite Welt'* (Wiesbaden: Harrassowitz, 2001).

56. For example: Johann Gottlieb Fichte, 'Der Patriotismus und sein Gegenteil: Patriotische Dialoge,' in id., *Gesamtausgabe*, series II, ix (1993), 387–445, 405.

57. Maciej Janowski, 'Wavering Friendship: Liberal and Nationalist Ideas in Nineteenth-century East Central Europe', *Ab Imperio* 3-4 (2000), 69–90.

58. See Anton Klement, *Die Prager Monatsschrift Kronos: Ein Beitrag zur Geschichte der deutschen Journalistik während der Befreiungskriege* (PhD, University of Vienna, 1908); Maria Kleffer, *Beiträge zur Geschichte der kosmopolitisch gerichteten Zeitschriften um die Wende des 18. und 19. Jahrhunderts* (PhD, University of Münster, 1923).

59. For example: Johann Berényi, *Das große Zeitalter Franz I.* (Pesth: Landerer, 1831), 14–15.

60. See Irmtraud Sahmland, *Christoph Martin Wieland und die deutsche Nation: Zwischen Patriotismus, Kosmopolitismus und Griechentum* (Tübingen: Niemeyer 1990), 269–270.

61. On this liberal-national retailoring of the past see Wolfgang Hardtwig, 'Von Preußens Aufgabe in Deutschland zu Deutschlands Aufgabe in der Welt: Liberalismus und

borussianisches Geschichtsbild zwischen Revolution und Restauration' in id., *Geschichts-kultur und Wissenschaft* (Munich: Beck, 1990), 103–160.

62. Novalis, *Die Christenheit oder Europa* [delivered 1799, first published 1826], in Richard Samuel et al. (eds) *Novalis: Schriften: Die Werke Friedrich von Hardenbergs*, 6 vols, ed. (Stuttgart: Kohlhammer, 1960–2008), iii. 510 (§ 64). This, however, did not amount to a nostalgia for the ancién regime, see ibid., 522, (§ 76).

63. Joseph von Eichendorff, *Zur Geschichte des Dramas* [1855], in id., Jost Perfahl et al. (eds) *Werke*, 5 vols (Munich: Winkler, 1970–1988), iii (1976), 379–527, at 525.

64. Johann Gottlieb Fichte, 'Grundzüge des gegenwärtigen Zeitalters [1804/1805]' in id., *Gesamtausgabe*, series I, viii (1991) 141–396, at 199, 351–352, 363.

65. Id, 'Patriotismus und sein Gegentheil,' 399.

66. Fichte, *Reden an die deutsche Nation*, Reinhard Lauth (ed.) (Hamburg: Felix Meiner, 1978), 233. The standard account is Stefan Reiß, *Fichtes 'Reden an die deutsche Nation' oder: Vom Ich zum Wir* (Berlin: Akademie Verlag, 2006).

67. See Hans-Joachim Mähl, 'Der poetische Staat', in Wilhelm Voßkamp (ed.), *Utopie-forschung: Interdisziplinäre Studien zur neuzeitlichen Utopie*, 3 vols (Stuttgart: Metzler, 1985), iii. 273–302.

68. See Giuseppe D'Alessandro, *L'Illuminismo dimenticato: Johann Gottfried Eichhorn (1752–1826) e il suo tempo* (Naples: Liguori Editore, 2000).

69. Norbert Waszek, 'Adam Smith in Germany, 1776–1832,' in Hiroshi Mizuta and Chuhei Sugiyama (eds), *Adam Smith: International Perspectives* (Basingstoke: Palgrave Macmillan, 1993), 163–180.

70. See Mihály Horváth, 'Az államelméleti teóriák eredete, kifejlése és befolyása az újabb Euró-pában, Heeren után [The Origins, Development and Influence of State Theories in Modern Europe after Heeren] [1841],' in id., Pál Lányi (ed.) *Polgárosodás, liberalizmus, függetlenségi harc: válogatott írások* (Budapest: Gondolat, 1986), 64–103; Horst-Walter Blanke, 'Verfassun-gen, die nicht rechtlich, aber wirklich sind: A. H. L. Heeren und das Ende der Aufklärung-shistorie,' *Berichte für Wissenschaftsgeschichte* 6 (1983), 143–164. The most popular authors in this vein were Karl von Rotteck (1775–1840) and Friedrich Christoph Schlosser (1776–1861).

71. See Ernst Schulin, 'Die Epochenschwelle zwischen Aufklärung und Historismus,' in Wolfgang Küttler et al. (eds), *Geschichtsdiskurs*, iii: *Die Epoche der Historisierung* (Frank-furt am Main: Fisher, 1997), 17–26; on institutionalization see Wolfgang Hardtwig, 'Die Verwissenschaftlichung der Geschichtsschreibung zwischen Aufklärung und Historis-mus,' in id., *Geschichtskultur und Wissenschaft*, 58–91.

72. '"Weltgeschichtlicher Völkerstrom": Friedrich Schlegel, Philosophie der Geschichte [1828],' in Ernst Behler et al. (eds) *Kritische Friedrich Schlegel-Ausgabe*, 35 vols (Paderborn: Schoningh, 1959–2002), ix (1971), 4, 55. 'Urgebirgskette': Heinrich Luden, *Allgemeine Geschichte der Völker und Staaten*, 3 vols. (Jena, 1814–1822), i (1814), 30. See also Hans Erich Bödeker, 'The Debates About Universal History and National History, c. 1800: A Problem-Oriented Historical Attempt,' in T. C. W. Blanning and Hagen Schulze (eds), *Unity and Diversity in European Culture c. 1800* (Oxford: Oxford University Press, 2006), 135–170.

73. Leopold von Ranke, 'Die sittlichen Mächte,' in id., *Sämtliche Werke*, 54 vols (Leipzig: Duncker & Humblot, 1867–90), xxiv (1872) 8, 11.

74. Id., *Aus Werk und Nachlaß*, ii: *Über die Epochen der neueren Geschichte*, ed. Theodor Schieder and Helmut Berding (Munich: Oldenbourg, 1971), 9.

75. For the shaky foundations of the Romantic disavowal of Enlightenment's sense for the unique see Ernst Cassirer, *The Philosophy of the Enlightenment*, trans. Fritz C. A. Koelln and James P. Pettegrove (Princeton: Princeton University Press, 1951), 197–199.

BIBLIOGRAPHY

ALBRECHT, ANDREA, *Kosmopolitismus: Weltbürgerdiskurse in Literatur, Philosophie und Publizistik um 1800* (Berlin: de Gruyter, 2005).

BEISER, FREDERICK C., *Enlightenment, Romanticism and Revolution: The Genesis of Modern German Political Thought 1790–1800* (Cambridge: Cambridge University Press, 1992).

CHENEVAL, FRANCIS, *Philosophie in weltbürgerlicher Bedeutung: Über die Entstehung und die philosophischen Grundlagen des supranationalen und kosmopolitischen Denkens der Moderne* (Basel: Schwabe, 2002).

GAY, PETER, *The Enlightenment: An Interpretation*, 2 vols (New York: W. W. Norton, 1966 and 1969).

GISI, LUCAS MARCO, *Einbildungskraft und Mythologie: Die Verschränkung von Anthropologie und Geschichte im 18. Jahrhundert* (Berlin: de Gruyter, 2007).

HARDTWIG, WOLFGANG (ed.), *Die Aufklärung und ihre Weltwirkung* (Göttingen: Vandenhoeck & Ruprecht, 2010).

KLEINGELD, PAULINE, 'Romantic Cosmopolitanism: Novalis, Christianity or Europe,' *Journal of the History of Philosophy* 46 (2008), 269–284.

KLEINGELD, PAULINE, 'Six Varieties of Cosmopolitanism in Late Eighteenth-century Germany,' *Journal of the History of Ideas* 60, no. 3 (1999), 505–524.

MEINECKE, FRIEDRICH, *Cosmopolitanism and the National State* [1908], trans. Robert B. Kimber (Princeton: Princeton University Press, 1970).

MUTHU, SANKAR, *Enlightenment against Empire* (Princeton: Princeton University Press, 2003).

O'BRIEN, KAREN, *Narratives of Enlightenment: Cosmopolitan History from Voltaire to Gibbon* (Cambridge: Cambridge University Press, 1997).

OSTERHAMMEL, JÜRGEN, *Die Entzauberung Asiens: Europa und die asiatischen Reiche im 18. Jahrhundert*, 2nd edn (Munich: C.H. Beck, 2010).

POCOCK, J. G. A., *Barbarism and Religion*, 4 vols (Cambridge: Cambridge University Press, 1999–2005).

PONSO, MARZIA, *Cosmopoliti e Patrioti: Trasformazioni dell'ideologia nazionale tedesca tra Kant e Hegel (1795–1815)* (Milan: Franco Angeli, 2005).

PORTER, ROY and TEICH MIKULAŠ (eds), *The Enlightenment in National Context* (Cambridge: Cambridge University Press, 1981).

REED, TERENCE JAMES, *Mehr Licht in Deutschland: Eine kleine Geschichte der Aufklärung* (Munich: C.H. Beck, 2009).

REILL, PETER HANNS, *The German Enlightenment and the Rise of Historicism* (Berkeley: University of California Press, 1975).

TORTAROLO, EDOARDO, *L'Illuminismo: Ragioni e dubbi della modernità* (Rome: Carocci, 1999).

WOLFF, LARRY, *Inventing Eastern Europe: The Map of Civilization on the Mind of the Enlightenment* (Stanford: Stanford University Press, 1994).

ZEDELMAIER, HELMUT, *Der Anfang der Geschichte: Studien zur Ursprungsdebatte im 18. Jahrhundert* (Hamburg: Meiner, 2003).

CHAPTER 7

....

THE ATLANTIC REVOLUTIONS IN THE GERMAN LANDS, 1776–1849

....

JONATHAN SPERBER

A discussion of the Atlantic revolutions in the German lands can begin with a consideration of the connections between those lands and the Atlantic world. On the eve of the age of revolution, these connections were modest, at best. The German lands had few direct ties to the Atlantic economy; social and cultural connections were sparse as well. New forms of political organization and action, as well as new ideas about the nature of politics were developing in some of the Atlantic countries during the third quarter of the eighteenth century, all of which would lead into the revolutions of 1776 and 1789. While these new political structures and political ideas were not unknown in central Europe, they were less prevalent, still outweighed by older versions of political life and political ideology.

Given the lack of contacts between the German lands and the Atlantic world, the Atlantic revolutions there took the form of an incursion, of a drastic and painful imposition from outside of new ways of thinking, new ways of acting, and new ways of governing. This process began gently, with the American Revolution of 1776, whose influence on central Europe was primarily an intellectual one. Following 1789, the world of the German states was turned upside down by the impact of the French Revolution. This great revolution's influence was transmitted in many forms, but one stands out above all, namely warfare. The French Revolutionary and Napoleonic armies defeated, repeatedly, the forces of the German Great Powers, Austria and Prussia, leading to the radical transformation of the map of central Europe and to the implementation of a wide variety of political experiments, inspired by the ideas of the revolution. This formulation, though, does not do justice to the dramatic, catastrophic nature of the impact of the French Revolution on central Europe—violent warfare with hundreds of thousands of casualties, extreme economic disruption, including the breaking of Germany's ties to the Atlantic economy, all combined with extortionately high levels of taxation. Such treatment generated enormous opposition, and the surge in political mobilization and political participation, particularly in Prussia, as Napoleon's war machine faltered, following his disastrous invasion of Russia in 1812, was, in part, directed against the basic ideas and principles of the Atlantic Revolutions. The end of Napoleonic rule in Germany and the political reorganization of the Congress of Vienna in 1814–1815 seemed to have brought with them a repudiation of the revolutionary initiatives of the previous four decades and a determination to repress any future manifestation of these initiatives.

This repudiation and repression continued over the subsequent thirty-five years, in the policies of the German states and in the main currents of political thought. Yet, in what Freudians would call the return of the repressed, the political ideas, forms of organization, and action, as well as the trans-Atlantic influences of the Atlantic revolutions, steadily found their way back into Germany. At the same time, political, economic, social, and cultural connections between the German lands and the Atlantic world gradually increased. The revolutions of 1830, and, especially, of 1848–1849, would show the powerful influence of the earlier phase of the age of revolution on German political life. Still, it would only be after the end of the age of revolution, in the decade of the 1850s, that integration of the German states into the Atlantic world made its greatest strides forward.

7.1 Central Europe on the Eve of the Atlantic Revolutions

In eighteenth century Europe, one of the major engines of economic growth was trans-Atlantic commerce, but lacking Atlantic seaports, overseas empires, or a large-scale Atlantic merchant fleet, the German states' economic connections with the Americas were at best modest, and usually indirect, via Great Britain. As late as 1830, direct trade with the United States made up just two percent of the total commerce of the German states (excluding the Austrian Empire)—about half as much as German trade with Belgium.[1]

Germany was tied into the Atlantic world through the process of emigration, with the 'Pennsylvania Dutch' of British North America a living trans-Atlantic link. There certainly was substantial long-distance migration occurring in central Europe during the eighteenth century, in the course of which around 900,000 people permanently relocated over distances of hundreds and thousands of miles. The bulk of it was to the eastern European territories of Prussia, Austria, or Russia, however. About 800,000 long-distance migrants moved in this eastern direction, a 'dry' emigration as contemporaries said, as opposed to the approximately 100,000 who took the westward, trans-Atlantic, 'wet' route to North

America. The predominance of, 'dry' over 'wet' emigration from central Europe continued through the 1820s.[2] These migratory flows show a central Europe with its back to the Atlantic world, a place where the Banat and the Volga River were more familiar than the 'island of Pennsylvania,' as one official of Baden-Durlach described the destination of a group of emigrants in 1752.[3]

Intellectual and cultural ties between the German lands and the nations of the Atlantic world were closer. The presence of the ideas of the Enlightenment, the enthusiasm of Evangelical Protestantism, or Classicist and Romantic artistic ideals in the German-speaking world was part of a broader trans-European and trans-Atlantic interchange. When we look at the political implications of common ideas, though, and their relationship to forms of political organization, action, and conflict, we discover a somewhat different state of affairs. Newer ideas about politics—ones that would be crucial to the Atlantic revolutions—were rarely present in the German lands; newer forms of political organization were few and far between; newer forms of political conflict were absent.

The dominant form of political conflict in pre-revolutionary, eighteenth century Europe pitted the claims to absolute rule of a monarch, supported by his state officials, organized in more or less bureaucratic fashion, against the constituted bodies of the society of orders—a form of social organization based on distinctions acquired at birth—and the defense by these bodies (in German *Stände* or *Landtag*) of the chartered privileges and freedoms, pertaining to members of specific social groups. Adherents of newer, Enlightened ideas, and supporters of older, often religiously based, conceptions of politics could be found on both sides.[4] While these conflicts had a particular impact on the German lands—since the Holy Roman Empire, the overarching political organization into which the German states were incorporated, guaranteed, at least in theory, chartered privileges—similar conflicts between the king and the estates occurred, among other places, in eighteenth century Sweden, Poland, France, and the United Netherlands.

Although the French Revolution began as such an old regime conflict, it ended up quite differently, a result of new political principles and new forms of political action developing in the Atlantic world during the second half of the eighteenth century. One such new political principle was the concept of popular sovereignty, the proposal that the ultimate basis for the legitimate exercise of political power resided in the body of the people, not in a monarch, ruling by the grace of God, nor in written charters of privilege. Another new principle was the idea of legal equality, and that basic rights and liberties, and the laws that flowed from these rights, were universal in application, and should apply to all people (at least all males) equally, rather than having different rights and different laws for members of different religions or different groups in the society of orders.

Paralleling the gradual development of this new understanding of the bases of politics was the development of a new vehicle for political activism, the voluntary association, club, or society. Such associations, whose actions were outside the rules of the society of orders and whose membership crossed the social boundaries of this society, were increasingly common in eighteenth century Europe. Examples would include Masonic Lodges, reading clubs, and organizations devoted to charity and public moral improvement. The Committees of Correspondence in pre-revolutionary North America or the Society of the Supporters of the Bill of Rights, in 1760s England, employed this new form of association to mobilize public support for their ideas, and to influence government policy and elections to legislative bodies, their activities in doing so often being inspired by the new political principles emerging at the time.

In the German states these new political principles and political organizations had only a marginal appearance. Older conceptions of politics continued to dominate public thought and ideas through the 1780s. While there were certainly a rapidly growing number of voluntary associations in central Europe, explicitly political versions of them were few in number, and, to the extent that they existed, did not articulate new political principles.[5] Admittedly, before the 1780s, such new political conceptions and forms of political organization were found primarily in Great Britain and its American colonies, so the German states were not, in this respect, all that different from France, Switzerland, or the Low Countries, where new features of political life only began to appear sporadically in that decade.

7.2 INITIAL IMPACT OF THE REVOLUTIONARY ERA, 1776–1792

Reports of the uprising of American colonists against their British overlords was big news in Germany; as early as February 1776, the *Leipziger Zeitung* could tell its readers that 'England's dispute with its colonies is at present undoubtedly the most important public topic. Everyone participates in it, and everyone judges it as he sees fit.'[6] Certainly in the German-language periodical literature, the American Revolution was hotly debated, with partisans of the colonies and those of the crown firing polemics at each other. There were even some 200 Germans, from all walks of life, who wrote personal letters to the American statesman, Benjamin Franklin, a remarkable occurrence, evidence of the impact of the American Revolution beyond the usual suspects of professional authors, with opinions on many different matters.

While the interest and excitement generated by the American Revolution and subsequent war in central Europe is not in doubt, the meaning Germans attributed to these events might be open to question. Horst Dippel, author of the definitive account of Germans' perception of the American Revolution, has emphasized the extent to which the new political developments of the event were assimilated into older concepts. 'Liberty,' a very popular phrase used to describe the colonists' demands, was often understood in terms of chartered corporate privileges, or, by German proponents of the English Crown, as a state of anarchy and lawlessness. References to the basic political documents of the revolution, the Declaration of Independence or the US Constitution of 1787, with their principles of universal human rights and popular sovereignty, were few and far between.[7]

Another way to trace the ideological appeal of the American Revolution is to see its impact on the German mercenaries, whose rulers, most prominently the Landgrave of Hessen-Kassel, sold their services to the British Crown, to help suppress the colonists' insurrection. This policy acquired a very bad press in Germany. Frederick the Great, King of Prussia, swimming with the tide of public opinion, denounced the Landgrave for '[selling] his subjects to the English as one sells cattle to be dragged to the slaughter.'[8] Yet these Hessian soldiers, in spite of considerable exposure to propaganda offers by the American revolutionaries to join their cause, deserted at rates much lower than European armies typically experienced in eighteenth century campaigns. Indeed, the Hessians often scornfully rejected the claims of the Americans to be fighting for freedom, noting that many of these self-same freedom fighters saw nothing wrong with keeping slaves.

What this discussion suggests is that the external political and intellectual impulses of the American Revolution were, at best, supplemental to trends generated within the German lands themselves. Contemporaries, and, following them, some historians, have suggested that such trends in the 1770s and 1780s were moving in the direction of peaceful reforms, a progression disrupted by the impact of the French Revolution.[9] There certainly were reforms ongoing in a number of the German states during the 1770s and 1780s, particularly directed at education and religion, but both their potential for broader social and political change, and their long-term continuance were very much in doubt.

The very idea of a reform program is a retrospective judgment, developed after the outbreak of the French Revolution, and designed to be an alternative to it. Contemporaries saw many of these reforms in terms of existing political conflicts, as another means for rulers to increase their authority, so that they were resisted—sometimes quite fiercely—by the constituted bodies of the society of orders.[10] The reforms never touched crucial elements of the society of orders: serfdom, seigneurialism, and noble privilege; the craft monopolies of the guilds; the elaborate restrictions on the social, economic, and civic position of the Jews—to mention three characteristic features of the social and economic system of old regime Germany. Reluctance to deal with these issues was typical for Frederick the Great, often seen as the model of a reforming German ruler. The Holy Roman Emperor Joseph II did attempt reforms striking at these aspects of the society of orders in the territories directly under his rule—earning him the sobriquets of the 'peasants' emperor' and the 'Jews' emperor'—but vehement opposition, mobilized by the provincial estates of his realm, forced him to revoke many of his reforming decrees in the last years of his rule.

This opposition to reform, so evident in the Habsburg territories, was increasingly common in the 1780s. Such opposition could become official policy with the death of a ruling prince who had been patron of reform efforts: this is precisely what happened in the central European great powers of Prussia and Austria following the deaths in 1786 and 1790, respectively, of their reforming monarchs. Supporters of Enlightened reform, among the officials of a number of the smaller German states, were aware of this problem and had, as early as 1776, attempted to overcome it by creating a political association, the secret 'Society of the Illuminati.' From the 1780s down to the present day, stories about the Illuminati as a dangerous, even satanic group of conspirators have circulated, but the organization, for all its elaborate ritual and mystery (largely taken from Masonic sources), was fundamentally a lobbying group, pressing for the continuation of Enlightened reforms. The dissolution of the Illuminati, following its prohibition in Bavaria by the Elector in 1785, was another example of the waning strength of reform—admittedly of the most extreme wing of reform aspirations—in central Europe.[11]

The French Revolution of 1789 thus did not so much interrupt a process of successful, peaceful reform in central Europe as it appeared in the context of two interrelated political controversies: between the adherents of monarchical power and the constituted bodies of the society of orders, and between the proponents and opponents of Enlightened government measures. Early reactions to the revolution tended to follow the lines of these debates; the dying Joseph II, for instance, despairing at the failure of all of his reforming initiatives due to opposition from the society of orders, greeted the revolution as the successful implementation of his reforms. Germany's intellectuals were very favorable to the Revolution at its outset; characteristically, the major exception was the north German legal theorist, Justus Möser, a prominent defender of the society of orders and public critic of the Enlightenment.[12]

The initial German responses to 1789 were rather similar to the responses to 1776, albeit with the difference that the French Revolution inspired a number of riots, demonstrations, and uprisings, aimed at high taxation or seigneurial privilege, particularly common in western Germany, near the French border, but reaching their greatest extent in Saxony, where insurgent peasants forced nobles to flee and where a large deployment of troops was required to suppress the insurrection. Yet riots and disorders of the lower classes had not been uncommon earlier in the eighteenth century, and it is unclear just how post-1789 rioters interpreted the events in France. When, in 1791, there was a general strike of all journeymen artisans in Hamburg and they shouted, 'Long live the consvolution!'—what, exactly, were they thinking?[13]

7.3 TWO DECADES OF WAR AND COERCED UPHEAVAL, 1792–1812

What completely changed the relatively modest political, material, and intellectual impact of the Atlantic Revolutions on central Europe was the outbreak of war in 1792 between France and almost all the European powers, and certainly all the German ones. Impetus for the wars did not come from the German side. The one German prince with an anti-revolutionary policy, the Archbishop Elector of Trier, was a minor one; the great powers, Prussia and Austria, were too busy at the beginning of the 1790s partitioning Poland to pay much attention to France.[14]

The war emerged from the internal revolutionary dynamics of a struggle between moderates and radicals in France. No one could quite foresee just how the war would, as French historians say, 'revolutionize the revolution,' leading to the unprecedented experiment of a radical, revolutionary republic. One of the many revolutionary features of this revolutionary republic was the way it conducted warfare. Its very large conscript armies, with their tactics of columns of infantry charging enemy positions, bayonets extended, while skirmishers provided covering fire, proved to have a decisive advantage over the less mobile forces of old regime armies arrayed in battle lines. One of the officers of the revolutionary army, Napoleon Bonaparte, mastered these tactics and combined them with the strategic principle of rapid movement, to create a seemingly invincible armed force, which he could use at his will, following his seizure of power in 1799. An initial series of French victories in 1793–1794 led to the Prussians abandoning the war; another series in 1799–1801 brought about the Peace of Lunéville, which completely transformed the map of Germany. Efforts by the Austrians to resume the war, in 1803–1805, and again in 1809, and by the Prussians to do so in 1806, resulted in some of Napoleon's most crushing victories, making him the master of the German lands.

In the wake of these successes of the French armies, the full weight of the changes stemming from the Atlantic Revolutions reached the German lands. We can distinguish two attempts at political and socio-economic transformation, one in the 1790s and the second during the decade following 1802. The former was politically more radical, closely linked with the advocacy of democratic and republican ideas, but geographically more limited, primarily to the lands on the west bank of the Rhine river. By contrast, the latter was undertaken in a monarchical framework and aimed at less drastic changes, but was more widespread, encompassing virtually the entirety of the German lands, with the exception of the core territories of the Prussian kingdom and the Austrian Empire. Both attempts at transformation involved co-operation between militarily dominant French forces and indigenous German political movements. The military domination making possible such a radical transformation also created considerable antipathy towards it, and limited both its support and success.

The capture of the Rhineland city of Mainz by French troops in October 1792 initiated the first effort at revolutionary transformation of Germany. The occupying forces sponsored the creation of a Jacobin club, a radical political association affiliated with the ruling party in Paris. This was a dramatic entry of the new political world of the Atlantic revolutions onto the German scene, and the Mainz Jacobins, or at least the activists among the 400 club members, lived up to their revolutionary reputation by sending out emissaries into the countryside to plant trees of liberty, to raise tricolor flags, to administer oaths of allegiance, and, ultimately, to hold elections for a 'Rhenish-German National Convention.' Their project collapsed with French military reverses, but radical political clubs under various names continued to exist in the Rhineland throughout the rest of the decade of the 1790s. Similar groups—generally clandestine, since the democratic and republican political program they advocated was not tolerated by the authorities of the German states at war with revolutionary France—and individual sympathizers could be found throughout the German-speaking world.

These German Jacobins have generated a substantial amount of controversial litera-ture, but recently something of a consensus has emerged about their origins, ideas, supporters, and possibilities for action. German Jacobin activists had generally been adherents of reforming and Enlightened ideas before 1789; in the Habsburg Monarchy, many of these Jacobins were government officials who had been strong supporters of the reforming emperor Joseph II, and were left high and dry after his death, with the succession of conservative monarchs. They do seem to have been the first group in central Europe to recognize and advocate the revolutionary ideas of popular sovereignty and equality before the law. Most of the active Jacobins were government officials, clergy, university professors and secondary school teachers, attorneys, and other intellectual figures, either working for the government, or in heavily state-regulated occupations. Some craftsmen and shopkeepers supported them and there were a few sympathizers in rural areas. However, any influence they could exercise depended on the active support of French revolutionary troops. All the Mainz Jacobins' actions and initiatives took place under French military protection.

This necessity for French support was the undoing of the German radicals' new government, as the experience of French military rule proved powerfully disillusioning. The new strategic doctrines of the revolutionary armies favored a war of rapid movement, so in place of clumsy supply trains, slowing down an army's progress, the French armies just seized their food, clothing, horses, and other supplies from the civilian population of the occupied territories. Whether through newly-instituted taxes, formal requisitions (with a dubious promise to repay), or simple confiscation, the revolutionary troops took everything that was not nailed down. Their frequent expres-sions of anti-clericalism, ranging from the verbal to using churches as stables, alienated the Catholic population of western Germany in particular. Increasingly, the German radicals appeared as the front men for a brutal, exploitative, and oppressive foreign military occupation.[15]

The attempt to restructure a part of the German lands in a revolutionary direction during the 1790s was thus a failure, leaving little result behind. The second, more moderate and widespread effort of the following decade would have more long-lasting consequences. This restructuring effort was a direct consequence of the drastic territor-ial changes following the Peace of Lunéville in 1801. With this peace, the lands on the west bank of the Rhine River were formally ceded to France. As compensation to the rulers of these territories, the 'Main Recess of the Imperial Diet' (*Reichsdeputations-hauptschluss*) of 1803 granted them rule over the many petty principalities, ecclesiastical states, and imperial free cities to the east of the river. Renewed defeats of the Austrians and the Prussians, between 1805 and 1809, brought still more territorial changes: the dissolution of the Holy Roman Empire, the expansion of medium-sized German states who had become French allies, such as Bavaria, Baden, or Württemberg, and the creation of new states, particularly out of former Prussian territory.

By 1810, these developments had reached their climax. As part of his campaign of economic warfare against England, Napoleon annexed additional portions of northern Germany and the North Sea coast as far as the port city of Hamburg to France. The remaining German territories were grouped into a Confederation of the Rhine, another Napoleonic creation. Members of this confederation included Napoleon's German allies, the medium-sized states, and the newly-created Grand Duchy of Berg, the Kingdom of Westphalia, and the Duchy (later Grand Duchy) of Frankfurt, the 'model states,' created by Napoleon as a central European showcase for his policies. A considerably shrunken Austria and Prussia were not a part of Napoleon's system of domination in central Europe, yet they too were, at least in foreign policy terms, not independent of Napoleon, as can be seen most explicitly in the marriage of the Austrian emperor's daughter, Marie Louise to Napoleon in 1810.[16]

All parts of Napoleonic Germany saw efforts to implement an ambitious and wide-reaching program of reform, characterized by three broad aspirations. One was governmental: the elimination of the constituted bodies of the society of orders, and the creation of a centralized government administered by bureaucratically organized state officials. The second was the replacement of the society of orders with a civil society of property owners, interacting in a free market, by abolishing seigneurialism and serfdom in agriculture, eliminating the craft guilds, and secularizing—that is, selling on the free market—the landed property of the Catholic Church. The third was legal and constitutional: the implementation of a new law code, characterized by public, oral, and jury trials, and the equality of all individuals under the law, as well as the written guarantee of these changes by means of a constitution, including an elected legislature.[17]

In terms of the ideas of the Atlantic revolutions, these reforms, carried out by monarchical regimes in an authoritarian and bureaucratic fashion, lacked the element of popular sovereignty, but the principle of equality before the law was certainly present. If not so self-consciously revolutionary as the plans of the German Jacobins, there can be no doubt that the Napoleonic-era reforms marked a sharp, indeed, revolutionary break in government and public life in much of Germany. The motives behind these reforms were a mixture of pragmatic and more ideological considerations. The new bureaucracies, constitutions and legal codes would encourage the integration of the new subjects of the expanded German states, to say nothing of other practices of integration, such as the Oktoberfest in Munich, initiated in 1811, to allow all the subjects of the king of Bavaria to drink together. The new royal bureaucracies, and, especially, the armed forces that needed to be raised by Napoleon's allies to fight in Napoleon's wars, were expensive, and seizing the lands of the Catholic Church helped to pay for them.

There were more ideal motives involved, as well. Napoleonic administrators in the German territories annexed to France included many former Jacobins, both French and German, who saw the emperor's reform program as an attempt to implement some of their political ideals. Reformers in the German states were often former determined proponents of Enlightened government measures, like Maximilian Count Montgelas, the Bavarian Prime Minister, who had once been a member of the Society of the Illuminati.[18] Napoleon himself combined these motives, seeing the creation of reformed German states as a key to maintaining his dominant position in German politics. In a letter to his brother Jérôme, whom he was sending off to be King of Westphalia, the largest of his model states, Napoleon informed him:

What the people of German impatiently desire is that individuals who do not belong to the nobility, yet are capable and talented, have an equal right to your consideration for employment, that all kinds of servitude and any intermediary bodies between the sovereign and the common people be completely abolished ... What people would want to return to the arbitrary Prussian government when they have enjoyed the benefits of a wise and liberal administration?[19]

These very large aspirations did not fully translate into accomplishments. The governmental reforms were the ones most thoroughly implemented. The centralized Bavarian state created then has existed continuously—admittedly, with some interruptions in the Nazi era—down to the present day. Property of the Catholic Church was duly seized and sold off. Devout Catholics in central Europe are still angry about this secularization, but, in many ways, it was a blessing in disguise, as the Catholic clergy no longer needed to concern themselves with running small principalities, competing for the seigneurial benefits of membership in cathedral chapters, or collecting tithes, but could devote their time and energy to the pastoral care of the faithful. The remarkable expansion of Catholic piety in the German lands during the nineteenth century goes back to the church's response to the challenges it faced following secularization.

By contrast, the social and economic reforms never did get very far. Seigneurialism and guilds survived largely untouched; it was only in the Rhineland, directly part of France, that they were abolished, helping to make the region a center of free-market activity, pro-*laissez faire* ideology and economic growth for much of the nineteenth century. Constitutional and legal reforms were a more mixed bag. Those parts of Germany directly incorporated into the Napoleonic Empire did get to participate in the representative institutions of the empire, for what that was worth; they also enjoyed the benefits of the Napoleonic Code that the new legal system introduced, which incorporated many of the reforms of the French Revolution.[20] The model states also received admirable, up-to-date constitutions; in the most important of those states, the Kingdom of Westphalia, the principle of full equality under the law for members of all religious confessions was implemented, abolishing all the many restrictions on and discriminations against the Jewish population—the only place in central Europe where this happened at the time.[21] The model states, however, vanished with the end of Napoleonic rule. Legal and constitutional reforms in Napoleon's German allies moved ahead more slowly, but would continue after the emperor's final defeat in 1815.[22]

The reform process was much less drastic than the revolutionary aspirations of the 1790s, and that helps explain some of the problems with its implementation. After seizing the properties of the Catholic Church, consisting of land with seigneurial rights, the Bavarian government found itself the largest seigneurial landlord in its kingdom, making it reluctant to go ahead with abolishing seigneurial obligations. Napoleon distributed estates in the Kingdom of Westphalia to his top generals and state officials, land that came with seigneurial obligations, making it difficult for the kingdom's government to abolish seigneurialism.[23]

Another, and the chief reason why the Napoleonic reform program was not success-fully and completely implemented was one closely related to the difficulties the German Jacobins experienced in the 1790s, namely the close connection between French-sponsored political upheavals and the wars inspired by France. Napoleon's quest for victory over his elusive British adversary by means of economic warfare, the 'Conti-nental System,' with its embargo on commerce with England, proved economically disastrous in central Europe. Recession spread inland from port cities and manufacturing opportunities opened up by the absence of British goods could not make up for it. The trans-Atlantic element of commerce was particularly important. Tropical goods had always reached central Europe from the Americas via Britain; with Napoleon's embargo, their lack was felt particularly painfully. Decades later, Karl Marx and Friedrich Engels in *The German Ideology* would make fun of German resistance to Napoleonic rule, asserting that it was based on the lack of coffee and sugar, not on elevated nationalist ideals. Marx and Engels were more right, perhaps, than they knew, because smuggling to evade the embargo became a massive enterprise in Germany's sea- and river-ports. All elements of the population participated, from wealthy bankers, who actually wrote insurance policies on smugglers, guaranteeing against seizure of their goods, to day laborers, who fought it out with Napoleon's customs agents. The clash between the population and the *douaniers*, the French customs agents, was long and bitter; the bonfires of confiscated contraband, and the many smugglers put in jail by the Napoleonic officials powerfully undermined support for or even tolerance of Napoleonic rule.[24]

However, even more oppressive than the interruption of commerce was the price, paid in blood and treasure, for participation in Napoleon's wars. German allies provided almost half of the contingent of the *Grande Armée* that invaded Russia in 1812; the vast majority never returned. Taxes, going above all to military expenditures, increased steadily throughout the period of Napoleonic domination, reaching unbear-able levels in the empire's last desperate years, following his invasion of Russia. In the once imperial free city of Wetzlar, incorporated into (Grand) Duchy of Frankfurt, direct taxes that had been around 10,000 fl. per year in the first years of the city's incorporation, doubled to 21,353 fl. in 1812—most of which, in spite of the most diligent of efforts, could not actually be collected.[25]

With the defeat of Napoleon's armies in 1813–1815, his German system collapsed: both the model states and the Rhineland ended up largely, although not exclusively, as Prussian possessions. In view of the upheavals, economic crisis, burdens of taxation, and bureaucracy that it brought, there were relatively few who regretted the end of Napoleonic domination. However, the territorial expansion of Napoleon's German allies largely survived—especially as most of those states were quick to change sides when the fortunes of war went against the emperor—as did the administrative and legal changes and the secularization of church property implemented under Napoleonic rule. The aspirations of Napoleonic reform would remain a guideline to the demands of German liberalism for the next half-century.

7.4 REACTIONS, 1806–1815

The leaders of the central European great powers, Austria and Prussia, marginalized by military defeat and territorial excisions, sought to respond to the Napoleonic reforms with their own counter-reforms, and to deal with the political claims of the Atlantic revolution, by their own assertions of new political ideas. The counter-claims and counter-reforms involved a complex interaction with those raised by the Atlantic revolutions, simultaneously accepting, reshaping, and rejecting them. In the end, the Prussian kingdom, in part because its situation was more desperate and in part because its statesmen were ideologically more flexible than their Austrian counterparts, proved more successful at both these tasks, a development that would reverberate through the nineteenth century until Prussia's war with Austria in 1866.

The least populous of the European great powers, and the one with the most precarious hold on great power status, the Prussian kingdom had maneuvered very carefully in the wars of the French Revolution and Napoleon, leaving the war against France in 1795, and using the continued conflict between the French and the Austrians to turn northern Germany into a *de facto* Prussian protectorate. This position could only continue as long as the military power of France was approximately balanced by its continental enemies, but Napoleon's victories upset this balance, and his demands on Prussia forced it into war, resulting in a crushing defeat at the battle of Jena and Auerstedt in 1806.[26] The Peace of Tilist, signed the following year, deprived Prussia of half its territory, and levied an enormous war indemnity, equal to about sixteen years of the government's annual pre-war income. French troops occupied Berlin and the king, Frederick William III, with his court and ministers, were camped out in Memel, in today's Lithuania.

This desperate situation opened the way to drastic reforms in Prussian state and society, carried out by the two great reforming Chancellors, Karl Freiherr vom Stein, and August Prince von Hardenberg. Stein's reforms seem most clearly to involve a political program opposed to the Napoleonic one. Stein wished to revive the society of orders rather than eliminate it: abolishing serfdom to bring the peasantry into this society, creating municipal self-government to do the same for urban craftsmen and their guilds. Both reforms would weaken the position of the bureaucracy, which Stein saw as responsible for many of Prussia's problems.

By contrast, Hardenberg's course was much closer to that of the policies carried out in the states of the Confederation of the Rhine, and he paid careful attention to the reforms there. Hardenberg continued Stein's agrarian reform, setting in progress the abolition of labor services and seigneurial dues, thus creating a free market in agricultural land and labor, albeit on terms that were quite favorable to Prussia's landholding nobility—none of which stopped noblemen from denouncing Hardenberg as a Jacobin subversive. In contrast to Stein's efforts to reform a guild-based urban life, Hardenberg stripped the guilds of their powers, allowing craftsmen to purchase a trade license to practice the crafts. He eliminated many of the discriminatory measures directed at the Jews, allowing Jews to practice any occupation they wished, a proposal that Stein, who was a vehement anti-Semite, and believed Jews should continue in the subordinate position they had in the old regime society of orders, found appalling. Far from opposing bureaucracy, Hardenberg tried—with only partial success—to make Prussia's existing bureaucracy more efficient and more encompassing.

For all the differences between Stein and Hardenberg, the contrast between their energetic reforms and the policy of Austria's leaders is particularly apparent. While being forced to cede its southwest German, northern Italian and Balkan possessions following military defeats, the Habsburg monarchy retained its core territories, neatly registering the circumstances by proclaiming the end of the Holy Roman Empire and the creation of a new, Austrian Empire. Austrian statesmen made no changes in either the society of orders or state administration. The one 'reform' they did undertake was to declare a state bankruptcy in 1812, the beginning of a five-decade-long condition in which Austrian government finances remained on a chronically unsound basis.[27]

If the contrast between Prussia and Austria in reform measures was very great, the counter-ideology they developed had important similarities. Its central feature was nationalism, a transformation of the conflict between Napoleonic France, on the one hand, and the European great powers, on the other, into a struggle between nationalities, pitting alien and pernicious Frenchmen, against true and virtuous Germans. The major anti-Napoleonic military initiatives of the two great powers, the Austrian declaration of war in 1809, and the Prussian in 1813, were accompanied by a barrage of nationalist propaganda, proclaiming the monarchs' war to be the national cause of all Germans. Perhaps more than in any other respect, the rise and development of nationalism shows the complexity of the response of the German lands to the Atlantic revolutions.

Scholars have been hotly debating the historical roots of nationalism in general, the extent to which it is a sentiment reaching back to medieval times and even earlier, or largely a product of the age of the Atlantic revolutions.[28] The anti-French German nationalism of the Napoleonic era has sometimes been portrayed as a continuation of old regime loyalties to the Holy Roman Empire and to the individual dynasties. Although possessing a certain superficial attractiveness, this notion seems basically incorrect. The Holy Roman Empire was not a nation state, but a political body of the society of orders, where sovereignty and political authority did not reside in the nation, but in monarchical claims of divine blessing and individual charters of privilege. There was a group of late eighteenth century reformers, who propounded what they called 'patriotism of the empire,' [Reichspatriotismus], which might seem like German nationalism, only these imperial patriots were not the nationalists of the 1806–1815 period, but mostly supporters of the Napoleonic Confederation of the Rhine.[29]

German nationalists of the Napoleonic era, by contrast, exalted the nation as the highest political authority, subordinating the princes to it and, while not unsympathetic to the political institutions of the society of orders, had no problem in vehemently rejecting them if they conflicted with the claims of the nation. Freiherr vom Stein, who became a leading political advocate for nationalism after his dismissal from the post of chancellor in Prussia, described his opinions at the end of 1812, as the Napoleonic debacle in Russia was becoming clear, and possibilities of dismantling French hegemony were opening:

> In this current moment of great developments, I am completely indifferent to the fate of the dynasties; my wish is that Germany may become great and strong, to achieve once again its self-determination, its independence and its nationality . . . this is the interest of the nation . . . it cannot be preserved on the path of old, rotting forms that are falling apart.[30]

Such an exaltation of the nation raises the question of the connection of the nationalist conceptions of the period to the ideals of the Atlantic Revolutions, in particular to the concept of popular sovereignty, and whether early nineteenth century German nationalism could be seen as a version of it. Rather like the identification of early nineteenth century nationalism with earlier forms of loyalty to the Holy Roman Empire, this conflation of the nationalists' cause with that of the French Revolution misses one fundamental distinction. Popular sovereignty in the Atlantic Revolutions was integrally linked to the creation of a nation of equal citizens, repudiating the distinctions of the old regime society of orders. German nationalists made no such repudiation, embracing social hierarchies, envisaging a nation divided into different orders of knights, clergy, and commoners, linking their nationalist future with a glorified version of the Middle Ages or of the ancient Germanic tribes, often making religious distinctions for membership in the nation—typically excluding Jews, but sometimes also identifying being German with Protestantism or Catholicism, and denying truly national status to members of the other Christian confession.

One does need to be careful in interpreting all opposition to Napoleonic domination as an expression of German nationalism. In going to war against Napoleon in 1809, the Austrian government had relied heavily on nationalist appeals, hoping for anti-Napoleonic uprisings throughout central Europe. The results were disappointing, for no such insurrections broke out, except in the mountainous province of Tyrol, against the rule of Napoleon's Bavarian allies. There, the appeal was not so much to German nationalism, as to Habsburg dynastic loyalties, given the province's long connection with the Austrian ruling family, and to opposition to the anti-clerical policies of the Bavarian occupiers. This was perhaps to be expected in a province, whose estates had consecrated it to the Sacred Heart in 1796, as a response to the threat of French invasion.[31]

The Prussian government, when it went to war with Napoleon in 1813, had much greater success in mobilizing nationalist sentiment. Thirty-thousand volunteers responded to its appeals, including Lützow's Free Corps, the black, red and gold of whose uniforms would become the German national colors. Yet the Prussian government's pro-war propaganda stressed dynastic loyalties, with memories of Frederick the Great. The Prussian motto, 'With God for king and fatherland,' carefully and deliberately obscured what the fatherland was—Germany or Prussia.[32] Certainly, in the states of the former Confederation of the Rhine, opposition to Napoleonic rule and celebration of its end generally took the form of a desire for the return of old regime rulers, rather than the creation of a German nation state, as nationalists wanted.[33] More generally, we can say that understanding the overthrow of Napoleonic rule in nationalist terms, as a nationalist uprising against foreign domination, and the prelude to a German nation state, was more common in the north of Germany than in the south, and among the urban population, particularly educated young men, but artisans as well, than in the countryside. For Germans less influenced by the new ideas of the nationalists, the rejection of the Napoleonic version (or perversion, depending on your point of view) of the ideas of the Atlantic revolutions meant a reaffirmation of the dynastic and religious bases of political loyalties as had existed in central Europe before the onset of the revolutionary era.

7.5 Repression and return of the repressed: 1815–1850

At first glance, Napoleon's defeat meant the complete repression of the ideas and consequences of the Atlantic revolutions in the German lands. The celebrated Congress of Vienna, the international peace conference in 1814–1815 that ended the Napoleonic Wars, marked the onset of the Restoration, the effort to restore Europe to its pre-1789 condition. Central to the political theory of the Restoration was the rejection of revolutionary principles of popular sovereignty and equality under the law. Friedrich von Gentz, close adviser to Austrian Chancellor Clemens von Metternich, the leading statesmen of Restoration Europe, vehemently denounced the 'perverted concept of the supreme sovereignty of the nation,' and asserted that constitutional governments had a:

> [c]onstant tendency to set the phantom of so-called freedom of the people (i.e. universal arbitrariness) in the place of civil order and subordination; and to set the delusion of equality of rights or (what is no better) universal equality before the law, in the place of the ineradicable distinctions between the orders that were established by God Himself.[34]

Even most German liberals, who opposed the Restoration era governments, endorsed the so-called 'monarchical principle' of the Congress of Vienna that located sovereignty in the person of the monarch. Liberals hoped to combine this predominance of the monarchy with some sort of representative legislature. In searching for foreign models by which this might be accomplished, they explicitly rejected France and the United States, looking instead to—a rather badly misunderstood—Great Britain.[35]

In the decade following 1815, Germany's monarchs and their government ministers, especially the authorities of the kingdom of Prussia, broke their ties with the nationalist movement, which they had cultivated during the wars against Napoleon. The gymnastics societies, in which nationalists had organized their followers, and the fraternities, where nationalist student volunteers of the post-1812 wars against Napoleon had gathered on their return to university studies, were prohibited. Leading nationalists, such as the author Ernst Moritz Arndt, Friedrich Ludwig Jahn, the leader of the gymnastics societies, or Joseph Görres, the one-time Rhineland Jacobin turned fiery nationalist newspaper editor, were dismissed from their official positions and threatened with imprisonment, forcing Görres to seek refuge in France, in the territory of the hated national enemy. In spite of the nationalists' considerable differences with the principles of the Atlantic revolution, their appeal to the nation as the highest authority was far too subversive for the statesmen of the Restoration.[36]

Yet the increasingly strenuous efforts to banish the heritage of the Atlantic revolutions from the German lands proved to be ultimately unavailing. One prime reason, long emphasized by historians, is that the Restoration did not really restore pre-1789 conditions in central Europe. The old regime rulers did not return; most of the territorial acquisitions of Napoleon's German allies remained intact, and the centralized administrations they had built in the first decade of the nineteenth century continued to function.[37] The Napoleonic constitutional reform project, including an elected legislature, went forward after 1815, albeit sometimes under somewhat different auspices. The largest states, Prussia and Austria, remained absolutist regimes without a constitution, and they used their powerful position in the German Confederation, the league of sovereign states created by the Congress of Vienna, to pressure the smaller ones into limiting still further the constitutional powers of legislatures, which were not very great to begin with. Still, by the 1830s, constitutional governments were found virtually everywhere in central Europe outside of Prussia and Austria. The legislatures these constitutions authorized became a forum for the articulation of public opinion.[38]

A less well-known legacy of the revolutionary and Napoleonic period was the continued validity of the Napoleonic law codes in the Rhineland after the end of French rule. Renamed 'Rhenish Law,' to suit nationalist opinion, this legal system provided a rallying point for opponents of the 'monarchical principle' and supporters of the ideals of the Atlantic revolutions.[39]

Another destabilizing feature of the period was the increasing contact between German lands and the Atlantic world. After being almost eliminated during the Napoleonic Wars, German trans-Atlantic commerce grew in the first half of the nineteenth century. Trade with North America, just 2.2% of the total foreign trade of the German states as late as the beginning of the 1840s, almost doubled to 3.8% of German foreign trade a decade later. Complementing this flow of goods was one of people. The 1830s was the first decade in which 'wet' emigration across the Atlantic exceeded 'dry' emigration to eastern Europe. Still at relatively modest levels in that decade, trans-Atlantic migration from Germany soared to over 400,000 in the 1840s, a period of economic crisis.[40]

The New World was a refuge for opponents of the Restoration regimes and a secure sanctuary from which they could combat the regimes' authoritarian rule, but before the revolution of 1848 German political émigrés were few and far between in North America. More important were the hundreds of thousands of ostensibly non-political emigrants. The

German states certainly took their leaving as an implicit criticism, and sponsored endless warnings of the dangers of life in North America, or publicized widely cases of individuals who had returned from the United States, after failing to make a go of it. And the governments were right to do so, for emigrants made no secret of their expectations of an America lacking noble landlords, government bureaucrats, high taxes, and other unpleasant aspects of social and political structures in the German lands during the 1830s and 1840s. As an emigrants' song asserted, in America 'taxes are not yet invented . . . we recognize no princes who drive us to despair . . . the nobility is despised . . . even the proud Herr Baron is worth no more than the peasant's son.'[41]

In the three decades between the signing of the Vienna settlement and the outbreak of the mid-nineteenth century revolutions in 1848, direct political impulses generally reached the German lands less from North America than from somewhat closer in the Atlantic world. James Brophy's excellent study of popular culture and nascent political opinion in the Rhineland has uncovered a veritable flood of political and proto-political pamphlets, almanacs, fliers, cartoons, traveling balladeers, and hurdy-gurdy men from France and, after 1830, Belgium, influencing the lower-class inhabitants of western Germany and inspiring Rhinelanders themselves to produce such materials.[42]

As the westernmost part of Germany, the Rhineland was physically close to western Europe, but if western Europe would not come to the Germans, the Germans would come to it. By the 1840s, there were at least 50,000 Germans living in Paris, mostly artisans looking for an economically favorable place to practice their crafts, but also émigré intellectuals, such as Karl Marx, Heinrich Heine, or Georg Herwegh. There, and elsewhere in western Europe, German craftsmen and intellectuals came into contact with the most up-to-date versions of the radical ideas of the Atlantic revolutions, including the novel concepts of socialism and a labor movement, so that the German labor and socialist movements began among German craftsmen in Paris, London, Zurich, and Brussels.[43]

This increasing influence of the ideas of the Atlantic Revolutions became apparent in the German lands during the 1830s and, especially, the 1840s. Political conflicts came to be articulated in the language of the Atlantic revolutions. "Inhabitants of small towns and villages of southwestern Germany opposed tax-collecting and regulatory policies of government bureaucrats as they had in the past, but no longer used the language of the society of orders, counter posing their chartered privileges to the prince's claims to power. Instead, they demanded their constitutional rights, and even asserted the sovereign power of the people."[44] With a bit of a delay, this same configuration appeared in the kingdom of Prussia, when the monarch Frederick William IV, a rather eccentric and particularly vehement proponent of a government based on the society of orders, summoned the kingdom's provincial estates, or diets, into a common session in Berlin, the 'United Diet' of 1847. Instead of following their royal master's ideas about the appropriate behavior of a constituted body of the society of orders, most of the deputies to this United Diet acted like parliamentary representatives and demanded the establishment of a constitution in Prussia. The echoes of the events of 1789, when the French monarch had summoned the estates of his realm, only to see them turn into a parliamentary national assembly were all too evident.[45]

Another feature of the 1840s was the re-emergence of nationalist ideas and associations. Sometimes, this re-emergent nationalism followed along the ideological lines of the Napoleonic era—anti-French and pro-society of orders—particularly during the 'Rhine crisis' of 1840, or in Frederick William IV's efforts to articulate nationalist ideas.[46] In this later period, though, nationalist ideas and nationalist associations were increasingly linked to the concepts of the Atlantic revolutions, rather than opposed to them. Student fraternities and gymnastics associations, revived in the 1840s, tied their nationalism to the creation of a constitutional, or even democratic and republican German nation state, with equal rights for all its citizens, rather than, as had been the case in 1813–1815, to a glorified medieval era, with old regime forms of social stratification and religious discrimination. Characteristic of this new orientation of nationalism was the composition of the *Deutschlandlied*, the future national anthem, by the radical poet Hoffmann von Fallersleben in 1841.

Their origins, international connections, political aspirations, and forms of political action and political participation in the revolutions of 1830 and 1848 all demonstrated how Germans had made the principles of the Atlantic Revolutions their own. The ultimate failure of these revolutions, their inability to permanently change structures of political power in Austria and Prussia, the two central European great powers, also demonstrated the strength of the forces lined up against the principles of the Atlantic revolutions.

French impulses, the Parisian uprisings of June 1830 and February 1848, led to the revolutionary actions in central Europe, more scattered in 1830, affecting primarily two of the mid-sized states, the duchy of Braunschweig and the kingdom of Saxony. In 1848, these actions became almost universal, including spectacular barricade fights in Berlin and Vienna, and led to the creation of new liberal governments in all the German states, the suspension of the German Confederation and the election of a National Assembly, to create a united German nation state.

Political life in the revolutions showed a strong orientation toward the Atlantic world. Francophilia, already evident in the Hambach National Festival of 1832, a large-scale mass meeting and offshoot of the 1830 revolutions, was common among German leftists in 1848, and even among liberals, at least for a while. Admittedly, Germany's conservatives, opposed to the 1848 revolutions, continued the anti-revolutionary Francophobia of the Napoleonic era—the affinities of the right were with the Tsar's Empire—but the mid-century revolutions marked a high-point of Franco-German relations over the entire period 1789–1945.[47]

Of all the major powers of the mid-nineteenth century world, the United States was the one most favorable to the Germans' revolutionary aspirations in 1848. American public opinion and American foreign policy supported the German revolutions, the US being the only major government to recognize diplomatically the provisional German central government set up by the Frankfurt National Assembly. Of course, American sympathies for the revolution had little practical effect at the time—certainly when compared with Russian antipathies, backed by the armed forces of the tsar—but the revolution marked a stage in greater diplomatic connections between the major German states and the USA, connections that, unlike the Francophilia of 1848, would not dissolve in subsequent decades.[48]

It is in the political aspirations and forms of action of the nineteenth century German revolutions, especially those of 1848, that we can see most clearly the influence of the ideas of the Atlantic revolutions of the previous century. While parliamentarians were debating American models of federalism in the Frankfurt National Assembly, radical agitators were informing participants at mass meetings that the United States, a country without a monarch, large bureaucratic apparatus, or noble landlords, and blessed with low taxes (note the close connections between these assertions and the aspirations of German emigrants), was an ideal model for a future republican and democratic Germany. American influences, though, rather faded before French ones. Occasionally, in 1830, but on a large scale in 1848, Germans waved tricolor flags and planted trees of liberty, called for liberty, equality, and fraternity, formed political clubs (on an enormous scale—probably fifteen percent of all adult men in central Europe belonged to such a club in 1848–1849)—and, at moments of crisis, committees of public safety. All these actions demonstrated the incorporation and internalization of the ideals and forms of action of the French Revolution of 1789 on a massive scale.[49]

In the end, the supporters of the ideals of the Atlantic revolutions did not have their way. Only marginally affected by the revolutionary events of 1830, Prussia and Austria were able to limit its consequences in central Europe. In 1848, by contrast, the revolutionary movement reached those central European Great Powers, leading to liberal governments and the legalization of radical political movements, but, ultimately, conservative forces in those realms, relying on loyal peasant soldiers from the provinces furthest from the Atlantic world, backed, in crucial situations, by the diplomatic and military support of the tsar, triumphed over the revolution, a victory of an eastward orientation over a westward one.

After the revolutionaries' defeat in 1849–1851, connections between central Europe and the Atlantic world would grow: commerce would increase during the 1850s, and about 1.1 million Germans would emigrate to North America in that decade. As a result both of the Crimean War and the U.S. Civil War, trans-Atlantic diplomatic contacts would become closer. Political refugees from the 1848 revolutions, reaching North America in considerable numbers, would come to have an influence on domestic politics in the United States, particularly the conflict over slavery and the run-up to the Civil War, and would be able to intervene, from across the Atlantic, in German affairs, after the end of the era of reaction in 1859. Yet these new trans-Atlantic connections occurred after the age of the Atlantic revolutions had come to an end.[50]

Looking back at the entire period from 1776 to 1849, three main features stand out. One is that the intellectual, economic, and political networks of the Atlantic world existed alongside an eastern-facing, continental network, leading toward Russia, rather than North America. This eastern orientation made itself felt in 'dry,' eighteenth century emigration, the Treaty of Vienna, or political influences on the 1848 revolutions. It may be that the influence of the Atlantic world in central Europe was growing, both absolutely and relatively, over time, but the inland influences remained powerful.

Another, and rather obvious, point is that the ideas and practices of the Atlantic revolutions had their most positive effect in the German lands when they arrived in peaceful and non-coercive form. Germans enthusing about the American Revolution during the 1770s and 1780s, or being inspired by French or Belgian examples to sing revolutionary songs or publish almanacs with a subversive message in the 1830s and 1840s, were more likely to generate approval than Germans planting trees of liberty in the 1790s with a French military escort (composed of soldiers who had just finished requisitioning peasant families' horses or their grain) or German officials from states that were Napoleon's allies seizing a monastery and turning monks out into the snow.

Yet the long-term effect of the years 1792–1812 on central Europe should not be underestimated. In particular by destroying the political institutions of the old regime society of orders, the Napoleonic regimes made possible new forms of political thought and political action. The harsh fiscal exactions, the severe economic depression and the endless demands for military manpower Napoleon inflicted on his German allies ensured that such new forms would not appear right away. However, their return, between the revolutions of 1830 and 1848, showed the long-term effects of the Napoleonic transformation of German politics.

Finally, one of the key questions of the entire period was the relationship of the Germans to the new political principles articulated in the Atlantic revolutions—whether they would affirm these principles, adopt, and transform them, or reject them altogether. In many ways, the crucial workshop for this question was the kingdom of Prussia, the more flexible and adaptable of the two central European Great Powers. By the end of the period, there was still no definitive answer to this question; a very tentative one would only emerge over the following quarter century.

NOTES

1. Martin Kutz, *Deutschlands Aussenhandel von der Französischen Revolution bis zur Gründung des Zollvereins* (Wiesbaden: Franz Steiner Verlag, 1974), 364. Admittedly, German commerce with the West Indies and Latin America was larger, at six percent of the foreign trade of the German states, but still not a particularly important part of total commerce.

2. An overview of migration in Hans Fenske, 'International Migration: Germany in the Eighteenth Century,' *Central European History* 13 (1980), 332–347. On the different forms of emigration, see Aaron Spencer Fogleman, *Hopeful Journeys: German Immigration, Settlement, and Political Culture in Colonial America, 1717–1775* (Philadelphia: University of Pennsylvania Press, 1996) and Mathias Beer and Dittmar Dahlmann (eds), *Migration nach Ost-und Südeuropa vom 18. bis zum Beginn des 19. Jahrhunderts* (Stuttgart: Jan

Thorbecke Verlag, 1999). Figures from the 1820s according to Wolfgang Hippel, *Auswanderung aus Südwestdeutschland* (Stuttgart: Klett-Cotta, 1984), 250–264.

3. Quoted in Georg Fertig, '"Man müßte es sich schier fremd vorkommen lassen": Auswanderungspolitik am Oberrhein im 18. Jahrhundert,' in Beer and Dahlmann (eds), *Migration nach Ost-und Südeuropa*, 75.

4. An elegant discussion of the intellectual universe behind these conflicts is in Rudolf Vierhaus, 'Politisches Bewußtsein in Deutschland vor 1789,' in Helmut Berding and Hans-Peter Ullmann (eds), *Deutschland zwischen Revolution und Restauration* (Königstein/Ts: Athenäum, 1981), 161–83.

5. On these points, see the essays in Eckhart Hellmuth (ed.), *The Transformation of Political Culture: England and Germany in the Late Eighteenth Century* (Oxford: Oxford University Press, 1990).

6. Cited in Horst Dippel, *Germany and the American Revolution 1770–1800: A Sociohistorical Investigation of Late Eighteenth-Century Political Thinking* (Wiesbaden: Franz Steiner Verlag, 1978), 206.

7. Ibid., 90–92, and passim.

8. Cited in Charles Ingrao, *The Hessian Mercenary State: Ideas, Institutions, and Reform under Frederick II, 1760–1785* (Cambridge: Cambridge University Press, 1987), 139. Other information on the Hessians comes from this excellent monograph.

9. A forceful assertion of this thesis can be found in the works of T. C. W. Blanning, in particular, *Reform and Revolution in Mainz, 1743–1803* (Cambridge: Cambridge University Press, 1974) and *The French Revolution in Germany: Occupation and Resistance in the Rhineland, 1792–1802* (Oxford: Oxford University Press, 1983).

10. The intellectual contours of the increasing opposition to reform are outlined by Klaus Epstein, *The Genesis of German Conservatism* (Princeton: Princeton University Press, 1966), 4–338, an older but still very helpful work.

11. Norbert Schindler, 'Der Geheimbund der Illuminaten: Aufklärung, Geheimnis und Politik,' in Helmut Reinalter (ed.), *Freimauer und Geheimbünde im 18. Jahrhundert in Mitteleuropa* (Frankfurt: Suhrkamp Verlag, 1983), 284–318.

12. Epstein, *Genesis*, 434–502.

13. Andreas Grießinger, *Das symbolische Kapital der Ehre: Streikbewegungen und kollektives Bewußtsein deutscher Handwerksgesellen im 18. Jahrhundert* (Frankfurt am Main: Verlag Ullstein, 1981), 117.

14. Michael Rowe, *From Reich to State*, 43–45.

15. For just a selection from the increasingly large literature on the German Jacobins, see Blanning, *The French Revolution in Germany*; Axel Kuhn, *Jakobiner im Rheinland. Der Kölner Konstitutionelle Zirkel von 1789* (Stuttgart: Ernst Klett Verlag, 1976); Ernst Wangermann, *From Joseph II to the Jacobin Trials: Government Policy and Public Opinion in the Habsburg Dominions in the Period of the French Revolution* (Oxford: Oxford University Press, 1959); Franz Dumont, *Die Mainzer Republik von 1792/93. Studien zur Revolutionierung in Rheinhessen und in der Pfalz* (Alzey: Verlag der Rheinhessischen Druckwerkstätte, 1982).

16. An overview of the territorial and constitutional changes in James Sheehan, *German History 1770–1866* (Oxford: Clarendon Press, 1989), 235–250.

17. Elisabeth Fehrenbach, 'Verfassungs-und sozialpolitische Reformen und Reformprojekte in Deutschland unter dem Einfluss des napoleonischen Frankreich,' in Berding and

Ullmann (eds), *Deutschland zwischen Revolution und Restauration*, 65–90, has an excellent comparison of Napoleonic and Prussian reforms.

18. Eberhard Weis, *Montgelas*, 2 vols (Munich: Beck, 1971–2005).

19. Quoted in Helmut Berding, *Napoleonische Herrschafts-und Gesellschaftspolitik im Königreich Westfalen* (Göttingen: Vandenhoeck & Rupprecht, 1973), 116–117.

20. For a discussion of these institutions in practice, see Rowe, *From Reich to State*, 87–116.

21. Michael Hecker, *Napoleonischer Konstitutionalismus in Deutschland* (Berlin: Duncker & Humblot, 2005) is a thorough analysis of the constitutions of the model states, including the emancipation of the Jews, by a legal historian.

22. The difficulties of legal and constitutional reform are illuminated in the classic account of Elisabeth Fehrenbach, *Traditionale Gesellschaft und revolutionäres Recht: die Einführung des Code Napoléon in den Rheinbundstaaten* (Göttingen: Vandenhoeck & Ruprecht, 1974).

23. The study of Berding, mentioned above in note 19, has an excellent account of this issue.

24. Karl Marx and Friedrich Engels, *The German Ideology* (New York: International Publishers, 1966), 38–39. On economic consequences of the continental system, smuggling and conflicts resulting from it, cf. Katherine Aaslestad, *Place and Politics: Local Identity, Civic Culture, and German Nationalism in North Germany during the Revolutionary Era* (Boston: Brill, 2005) or Norbert Finzsch, *Obrigkeit und Unterschichten: Zur Geschichte der Rheinischen Unterschichten Gegen Ende des 18. und zu Beginn des 19. Jahrhunderts* (Stuttgart: Franz Steiner Verlag, 1990), 199–240.

25. Hans-Werner Hahn, *Altständisches Bürgertum zwischen Beharrung und Wandel: Wetzlar, 1689–1870* (Munich: Oldenbourg Verlag, 1991), 258.

26. On Prussian foreign policy in this era, Brendan Simms, *The Impact of Napoleon: Prussian High Politics, Foreign Policy and the Crisis of the Executive, 1797–1806* (Cambridge: Cambridge University Press, 1997), is authoritative.

27. On Austrian government finances, Harm-Heinrich Brandt, *Der österreichische Neoabsolutismus: Staatsfinanzen und Politik, 1848–1860*, 2 vols (Göttingen: Vandenhoeck & Ruprecht, 1978), 1: 103–106 and passim.

28. On this issue, see Len Scales and Oliver Zimmer (eds), *Power and the Nation in European History* (Cambridge: Cambridge University Press, 2005).

29. Anke Waldmann, 'Reichspatriotismus im letzten Drittel des 18. Jahrhunderts,' in Otto Dann and Miroslav Hroch (eds), *Patriotismus und Nationsbildung am Endes des Heiligen Römischen Reiches*, (Cologne: SH-Verlag, 2003), 19–61.

30. Cited in Karen Hagemann, *'Mannlicher Muth und Teutsche Ehre': Nation, Militär und Geschlecht zur Zeit der Antinapoleonischen Kriege Preußens* (Paderborn: Ferdinand Schöningh, 2002), 192.

31. Lawrence Cole, 'Religion und patriotische Aktion in Deutsch-Tirol (1790–1814),' in Dann and Hroch (eds), *Patriotismus und Nationsbildung* 345–377.

32. On the purposes of this ambiguity, see Matthew Levinger, *Enlightened Nationalism: The Transformation of Prussian Political Culture 1806–1848* (New York: Oxford University Press, 2000), 63–68.

33. On this point, see Ute Planert, *Der Mythos vom Befreiungskrieg: Frankreichs Kriege und der deutsche Süden. Alltag-Wahrnehmung-Deutung 1792–1841* (Paderborn: Schöningh Verlag, 2006).

34. Cited in Levinger, *Enlightened Nationalism* (author's translation slightly revised), 150–151.

35. Hermann Wellenreuther, 'Die USA. Ein politisches Vorbild der bürgerlich-liberalen Kräfte des Vormärz,' in Jürgen Elvert and Michael Salewski (eds), *Deutschland und der*

Westen im 19. und 20. Jahrhundert 2 vols. (Stuttgart: Franz Steiner Verlag, 1993), 1, 23–41, esp. 34. More generally, see Uwe Backes, *Liberalismus und Demokratie—Antinomie und Synthese. Zum Wechselverhältnis zweier politischer Strömungen im Vormärz* (Düsseldorf: Droste Verlag, 2000).

36. Dieter Düdung, *Organisierter gesellschaftlicher Nationalismus in Deutschland (1808–1847)*, (Munich: Oldenbourg Verlag, 1984); Jon Vanden Heuvel, *A German Life in the Age of Revolution: Joseph Görres 1776–1848* (Washington, DC: Catholic University Press of America, 2001).

37. On the Congress and its settlement, Sheehan, *German History 1770–1866*, 393–404.

38. On the workings of such a constitution and the parliament it authorized, see Dirk Götschmann, *Bayerischer Parlamentarismus im Vormärz: die Ständeversammlung des Königreichs Bayern, 1819–1848* (Düsseldorf: Droste Verlag, 2002).

39. Karl Georg Faber, *Die Rheinlande zwischen Restauration und Revolution* (Wiesbaden: Franz Steiner Verlag, 1966).

40. Trade statistics (very approximate) are calculated from Bodo von Borries, *Deutschlands Außenhandel 1836 bis 1858* (Stuttgart: Gustav Fischer Verlag, 1970), Table 42, 192. Figures on emigration from Peter Marschalk, *Deutsche Überseewanderung im 19. Jahrhundert* (Stuttgart: Ernst Klett Verlag, 1973), 48.

41. Cited in Albin Gladen, *Der Kreis Tecklenburg an der Schwelle des Zeitalters der Industrialisierung* (Münster: Aschendorff, 1970), 215–218. On emigrants' expectations and the politics of emigration, see Wolfgang Helbich, 'Land der unbegrenzten Möglichkeiten? Das Amerika-Bild der deutschen Auswanderer im 19. Jahrhundert,' in Elvert and Salewski (eds), *Deutschland und der Westen* 1: 295–321. For emigrants' own opinions, see the admirable collection of letters, in Walter Kamphoefner, Wolfgang Helbich, and Ulrike Sommer (eds), *News from the Land of Freedom: German Immigrants Write Home*, trans. Susan Carter Vogel (Ithaca: Cornell University Press, 1991).

42. James Brophy, *Popular Culture and the Public Sphere in the Rhineland 1800–1850* (Cambridge: Cambridge University Press, 2007).

43. On these points, see Wolfgang Schieder, *Anfänge der deutschen Arbeiterbewegung: die Auslandsvereine im Jahrzehnt nach der Julirevolution von 1830* (Stuttgart: Ernst Klett Verlag, 1963); Christine Lattek, *Revolutionary Refugees: German Socialism in Britain, 1840–1860* (London: Routledge, 2006).

44. Paul Nolte, *Gemeindebürgertum und Liberalismus in Baden 1800–1850: Tradition, Radikalismus, Republik* (Göttingen: Vandenhoeck & Rupprecht, 1994) or Ian McNeely, *The Emancipation of Writing: German Civil Society in the Making, 1790s–1820s* (Berkeley: University of California Press, 2003).

45. Herbert Obenaus, *Anfänge des Parlamentarismus in Preussen bis 1848* (Düsseldorf: Droste Verlag, 1984), 649–716 and passim.

46. On the impact of the Rhine crisis, cf. Brophy, *Popular Culture*, 90–96; on Frederick William IV and nationalism, see David Barclay, *Frederick William IV and the Prussian Monarchy, 1840–1861* (Oxford: Oxford University Press, 1995), 31–32, 49–50.

47. On the Hambach festival, see Cornelia Foerster, *Der Preß-und Vaterlandsverein von 1832/33. Sozialstruktur und Organisationsformen der bürgerlichen Bewegung in der Zeit des Hambacher Festes* (Trier: Verlag Trierer Historische Forschungen, 1982); for Franco-German relations, see Ulrike Ruttmann, *Wunschbild, Schreckbild, Trugbild: Rezeption und Instrumentalisierung Frankreichs in der Deutschen Revolution von 1848/49* (Stuttgart: Franz Steiner Verlag, 2001).

48. Günter Moltmann, *Atlantische Blockpolitik im 19. Jahrhundert. Die Vereinigten Staaten und der deutsche Liberalismus während der Revolution von 1848/49* (Düsseldorf: Droste Verlag, 1973); Herbert Kleinlercher, 'Diplomatisch-politische Beziehungen zwischen Österreich und den USA: Antagonismen und Konflikte in der ersten Hälfte des 19. Jahrhunderts,' *Wiener Zeitschrift zur Geschichte der Neuzeit* 5 (2005), 36–50; Timothy Roberts and Daniel Howe, 'The United States and the Revolutions of 1848,' in R. J. W. Evans and Hartmut Pogge von Strandmann (eds), *The Revolutions in Europe 1848–1849: From Reform to Reaction* (Oxford: Oxford University Press, 2000), 157–179; Enno Eimers, *Preußen und die USA 1850 bis 1867* (Berlin: Duncker & Humblot, 2004).

49. Generally, on the revolution of 1848/49 in Germany, see Wolfram Siemann, *The German Revolution of 1848/49*, trans. Christiane Banerji (New York: St. Martin's, 1998). Two monographic studies that emphasize the importance of the heritage of the Atlantic revolutions for the German revolution of 1848/49 are: Jonathan Sperber, *Rhineland Radicals: The Democratic Movement and the Revolution of 1848–1849* (Princeton: Princeton University Press, 1991) and Rüdiger Hachtmann, *Berlin 1848. Eine Politik-und Gesellschaftsgeschichte der Revolution* (Bonn: Verlag J. H. W. Dietz Nachf, 1997).

50. Besides the works of Enno Enders, cited above, and of Peter Marschalk, in note 40, cf. Angsar Reiß, *Radikalismus und Exil: Gustav Struve und die Demokratie in Deutschland und Amerika* (Stuttgart: Franz Steiner Verlag, 2004) and Bruce Levine, *The Spirit of 1848: German Immigrants, Labor Conflict, and the Coming of the Civil War* (Urbana: University of Illinois Press, 1992).

BIBLIOGRAPHY

BLANNING, T.C.W., *The French Revolution in Germany: Occupation and Resistance in the Rhineland, 1792–1802* (Oxford: Oxford University Press, 1983).

BERDING, HELMUT and HANS-PETER ULLMANN, (eds), *Deutschland zwischen Revolution und Restauration* (Königstein/Ts: Athenäum Verlag, 1981).

BROPHY, JAMES, *Popular Culture and the Public Sphere in the Rhineland 1800–1850* (Cambridge: Cambridge University Press, 2007).

DIPPEL, HORST, *Germany and the American Revolution 1770–1800: A Sociohistorical Investigation of Late Eighteenth-Century Political Thinking*, trans Bernhard A. Uhlendorf (Wiesbaden: Franz Steiner Verlag, 1978).

EPSTEIN, KLAUS, *The Genesis of German Conservatism* (Princeton: Princeton University Press, 1966).

HAGEMANN, KAREN. *'Mannlicher Muth und Teutsche Ehre': Nation, Militär und Geschlecht zur Zeit der Antinapoleonischen Kriege Preußens* (Paderborn: Ferdinand Schöningh Verlag, 2002).

HELLMUTH, ECKHART (ed.), *The Transformation of Political Culture: England and Germany in the Late Eighteenth Century* (Oxford: Oxford University Press, 1990).

JEISMANN, MICHAEL, *Das Vaterland der Feinde: Studien zum nationalen Feindbegriff und Selbstverständnis in Deutschland und Frankreich 1792–1918* (Stuttgart: Klett-Cotta Verlag, 1992).

LEVINGER, MATTHEW, *Enlightened Nationalism: The Transformation of Prussian Political Culture 1806–1848* (New York and Oxford: Oxford University Press, 2000).

PLANERT, UTE, *Der Mythos vom Befreiungskrieg: Frankreichs Kriege und der deutsche Süden. Alltag-Wahrnehmung-Deutung 1792–1841* (Paderborn: Schöningh Verlag, 2006).

ROWE, MICHAEL, *From Reich to State: The Rhineland in the Revolutionary Age 1780–1830* (Cambridge: Cambridge University Press, 2003).

SIEMANN, WOLFRAM, *The German Revolution of 1848/49*, trans Christiane Banerji (New York: St. Martin's, 1998).

SPERBER, JONATHAN, *Rhineland Radicals: The Democratic Movement and the Revolution of 1848–1849* (Princeton: Princeton University Press, 1991).

CHAPTER 8

....

THE END OF THE
ECONOMIC OLD ORDER:
THE GREAT TRANSITION,
1750–1860

....

JAMES M. BROPHY

ALFRED Rethel's oil canvas, *The Harkort Factory at Castle Wetter on the Ruhr* (1834), marks one of the first aesthetic evocations of industrial culture in Germany. In bright clarity, Rethel depicts a castle, with both its medieval keep and neoclassical additions, amidst an array of tall industrial smokestacks, putting forth fire and smoke.[1] Men and draft horses labor near the converted workshops of the castle's courtyards, whose brick chimneys dwarf the presence of animate life. The artist's juxtaposition of one economic order yielding to another is hard to miss. Friedrich Harkort himself celebrated the castle's makeover. The workshop, he wrote, 'conquered the *Burg*, thus creating an enduring site in which iron and steel could be transformed into the mightiest weapons of industrial diligence.' 'The battle of the old and new age,' he continued, 'was decided here to the obvious advantage to the latter.'[2]

Harkort's triumphalism needs a footnote. His workshop opened in 1816 to make machinery and, soon thereafter, to puddle steel and roll metal, but it closed in the early 1830s because of debt. Harkort's castle-factory is thus less a symbol of decisive change than a lesson about the risks of innovation. Rather than embrace Harkort's rhetoric of dramatic rupture, we should interpret the painting's multiple worlds of agriculture, early industry, and corporatist society as more emblematic of the early nineteenth century. The period 1750–1860 presents both varied and hybrid economic worlds. Innovation and expansion existed alongside local handicrafts and subsistence farming. As Friedrich Engels, the son and future partner of a textile manufacturer in near-by Barmen, noted in 1847: 'no single class has hitherto been strong enough to establish its line of work as the national branch of production . . . All the estates and classes that have emerged in history since the tenth century—nobles, serfs, peasants subject to corvée labor, free peasants, petty bourgeoisie, journeymen, manufactory workers, bourgeoisie, and proletarians—exist alongside one another.'[3] For Engels, the simultaneity of several economies best characterized Germany's condition.

These three views of economic activity by Rethel, Harkort, and Engels instruct us to acknowledge the enduring presence of the old, but to recognize the transition toward a new order by the mid-nineteenth century. The industrial 'take-off' of the 1840s and 1850s introduced a scale of production that forever changed the material conditions of Germany. The belching smokestacks of factories and locomotives might have tokened swift change, but the foundations for industrial capitalism were long in preparation. This essay focuses on this long-term transition toward Germany's modern economy, examining how agriculture and market economies shaped the socioeconomic formations of proto-industrialization, urbanization, and industrialization. No one factor or sector suffices as an interpretive key to explain Germany's transformation.

A number of premises frame this discussion of Germany's evolving economic order. First, the impact of economic change in this period remained highly uneven. In 1860, Germany still remained more rural and agricultural than urban and industrial. Even in the realm of manufactures, artisanal work thrived into the second half of the nineteenth century. Furthermore, this unevenness of economic change has a pronounced regional diversity. Industrial centers unfolded in specific areas, but left other regions and lives largely untouched. More crucially, the regional variations of economic change correspond poorly with political frontiers or conceptions of national economy. The textile and metallurgical industries of the Rhineland are better linked with the first phase of industrialization in Belgium and France than with those of central Germany. The agrarian capitalism of East-Elbian estates fits well with the grain-exporting economies of Eastern Europe, but bears little relation to farming in southwestern Germany, whose partible inheritance, regional markets, and specialized cash crops are better compared with French or Swiss farmers. Hanseatic merchants were more closely knit in marriage and financial affairs with shipping elites from Amsterdam, London, and Baltimore than with businessmen from Munich or Vienna.[4] Simply put, there was no single economy in Germany, least of all a German economy. Examining long-term regional developments of Saxony, Silesia, or the Rhineland reveals neither national cohesion nor a latecomer status to industrialization.[5] This point leads to the final premise: the emerging modern economy of Central Europe did not prefigure the German nation-state created by Prussia in 1870–1871. Rather, German economies participated as European components of world markets that touched on agrarian, market, and industrial economies. Although significant, the impact of the state on economic development was not determinative.

8.1 AGRARIAN SOCIETY

In the early modern period, agriculture was not a 'sector'—it constituted a way of life and framed virtually all other forms of economic activity.[6] In this regard, historians speak of an agrarian order (*Agrarverfassung*) and view two principal forms in which German peasants lived and tilled the soil since the sixteenth century: *Gutsherrschaft* and *Grundherrschaft*. The former refers to a manorial system that predominated in eastern Germany, especially the latifundia east of the Elbe river. In this region, lords exercised dominion over both soil and the personal liberty of peasants. This type of hereditary personal servitude reasserted itself during the 'second serfdom' of the early modern period, when the principal eastern states of Russia, Austria, and Prussia permitted aristocratic estate holders to strengthen their legal and economic control over peasants in return for recognizing state sovereignty over taxation and standing armies. In this social order, serfs provided extensive labor services for their lords; their children served as domestic servants for lords until adulthood; and lords presided over forms of patrimonial justice that assigned them the roles of judge, prefect, and sheriff over their peasants. Peasants needed permission to move or marry, and the Prussian law code of 1794 prohibited peasants from adopting a different trade. This agrarian system confined peasants on vast estates with little contact to thinly dispersed cities and towns. The presence of lords on these estates was common, and they supervised economic activity in close physical proximity with their serfs.

Grundherrschaft, the second major form of peasant servitude, predominated in western Germany. Less restrictive than the East-Elbian system, this form of rule centered on land tenancy; lords leased land, demanding both money rents and in-kind payments. Additional burdens on peasants also existed, such as milling and distilling monopolies, as well as a variety of tithes on agricultural products, but this form of lord-peasant relations generally did not involve labor services or patrimonial justice. In this system, the lord was generally absent, relying on agents to collect rents. Because this agrarian system demanded few, if any, labor services, historians are wont to see a latent liberalism in this share-cropping system. Farmers were relatively free to dispose of their labor and land as they saw fit, and many grew crops to sell in the numerous towns and cities in southwestern and western Germany. Rural domestic industry also took hold in these regions, further connecting farmers to market life.

Of course, this schema begs for qualification. In western Germany, one should first note that peasants owned almost two-thirds of the land by the late eighteenth century, and many merely subsisted rather than flourished from commercial agriculture.[7] Furthermore, forms of *Gutsherrschaft* existed in certain areas of Westphalia and Bavaria, just as forms of servitude in Franconia and Hesse conform to neither type. Because of such exemptions, Heide Wunder has suggested the overarching term of 'economic dominion' (*Wirtschaftsherrschaft*), which scholars use to describe peasant servitude on Bavaria's large estates.[8] More importantly, perhaps, recent scholarship has softened the stark contrast of eastern and western forms of agricultural life. While the western system of cash rents might appear to modern eyes as a greater freedom, one must recognize the inherent tyranny of generating annual cash payments, which peasants did not always prefer over labor service. Conversely, the life of eastern peasants might not have been as constrained and regimented as once held. By the end of the eighteenth century, 13,000 out of 61,000 East Prussian peasant farms were owned by free tenant farmers. Even serfs, in spite of labor services, enjoyed a latitude of socio-economic freedom not previously emphasized, earning money outside of the demesne economy, renegotiating labor burdens with seigneurs, and using the courts to their advantage.[9] William Hagen's research on the Brandenburg estate of Stavenow underscores the ability of peasants to petition and protest, lower the value of labor service, and secure material and security assets. Their condition, Hagen argues, was characteristic of the 'agrarian western world of the eighteenth and nineteenth centuries.'[10] In Saxony, too, new categories of workers, such as *Gärtner* or *Häusler,* emerged because of home industry, which fell outside the estate economy. Puncturing a number of clichés, this new view of eastern agricultural life is instructive and significant, yet one should also not fall prey to the drastic pendulum swings of historiographical trends. Whether the rural life of eastern peasants produced an assertive, rights-bearing political culture equal to that of Germany's western territories still demands more research.

Nonetheless, both systems acted as solvents of traditional agriculture under the *ancien régime.* While independent peasants and lease-holding farmers in western Germany pursued market gardening for urban centers in Germany, Holland, and France, some forms of eastern *Gutsherrschaft* promoted domestic industry for their serfs, as witnessed by the prominent example of Silesia's linen industry. Cloth merchants paid Saxon and Prussian lords for the privilege of penetrating villages and utilizing serf labor, thus linking exogenous market relations to the lives of eastern peasants. Equally crucial, Prussian Junkers embraced agrarian capitalism. Their latifundia produced surpluses of rye and other grains for urban centers in the west. They negotiated with banks in London and Amsterdam, and deftly used state-backed credit institutes founded in the 1770s (*Landschaften*) to improve land, enclose commons, and experiment in new crop rotations. The *Landschaften* in turn used the value of these mortgages to float bonds on the financial markets at competitive rates. Carried out with the aim of retaining corporatist privilege and rank, these agrarian and financial reforms were nonetheless distinctly modern in character. The term 'feudalism' consequently explains little about East-Elbian agribusiness after 1750.

In spite of such reforms, *Gutsherrschaft* remained economically inefficient. Taking 100 as the Prussian average yield per acre in the early nineteenth century, the small-scale agriculture of the Rhineland measured 175 to East Prussia's 57. Overall, the agricultural revolution came more slowly to German lands than it did in Western Europe. By 1800 a mere quarter of German fields followed modern crop rotations. In 1820, only East Friesian yields of 12 bushels of grain to 1 of seed compared favorably with Holland and Britain (11.3:1), whereby the German average of 5.4:1 manifested Central Europe's relative backwardness—in spite of Friedrich II's and Joseph II's model farms. Yet Central Europe did not experience France's general crisis of bad harvests and famines in the late eighteenth-century. (By contrast, hunger years in German territories occurred in 1817–1819 and most notably in the 1840s.) In view of the secular trend of rising prices (and general stability) in German agriculture between 1740 and 1820, insufficient growth better explains Germany's need for reform than any one revolutionary crisis.[11]

Efficiency rose rapidly over the course of the nineteenth century with increasing investments of capital and technology. Between 1820 and 1860, arable land in Germany increased 40 percent. Land drainage, rail transport, better animal breeds, chemical fertilizers, and new crops like potatoes, sugar beet, and clover all improved harvests. Between 1800 and 1870, agrarian production rose by 174 percent, thus exceeding the 66 percent rise in population. By the last quarter of the nineteenth century, most areas of Germany matched yields per acre with the most advanced regions in Holland, Denmark, and England.[12] In terms of investment, agriculture was the clear leader. To draw on one series for 1830–1840, agriculture attracted 58 percent of the Zollverein's investment, followed by construction (27 percent), infrastructure (12 percent) and industry (3 percent).[13] If agriculture remained the dominant economic sector through 1860, was Germany's agricultural capitalism a critical catalyst for the onset of industrialization?[14] Historians are cautious about causal arguments, noting that the heavy industries—the backbone of early industrialization—did not rely on domestic rural demand.[15] What perhaps deserves emphasis is the link between Germany's agricultural capitalism and the industrializing centers in western Europe, whose need for imported grain restructured German agriculture.

Agriculture's new-won efficiency stems primarily from the emancipation of serfs in the first half of the century. Faced with the threat of Napoleonic conquest, Prussia and other German states reformed their agrarian orders, striving to tap new economic energies from their subjects. Between 1807 and the 1820s, German states began the legal process of emancipating their serfs, thus inaugurating a transition toward market labor conditions that reached completion in the 1850s. The most famous of these laws is Prussia's October Edict of 1807, which abolished serfdom in its provinces and enabled non-aristocratic classes to purchase land. Further decrees in 1811 and 1816 framed the specific terms for emancipation, restitution of lords, and the distribution of common lands. These laws determined which strata of the peasantry received property, and prosperous farmers who owned plow teams (*spannfähige Grossbauern*) emerged as the clear winners. Peasants with meager holdings, however, did not attain independence and skidded into the class of landless rural laborers. They now worked others' land for wages, though they possessed the freedom of mobility to find work in towns or other agricultural regions. Overall, these settlements greatly favored the Junker landowning class, which by mid-century repossessed over three million acres of peasant land, as well as 86 percent of all common land—over fifteen million acres.[16] The Prussian state also failed to extend credit to common farmers in the way it had previously aided noble landholders. In spite of such iniquities, peasant farmers survived in the modern era and even increased in number. The liberalization of agriculture also set off tumultuous change in the ownership of Prussia's great estates. Between 1800 and 1805, one in six Junkers sold his property; between 1830 and 1835, the average Prussian noble estate changed hands more than twice.[17]

The impact of agrarian change on German lands outside of Prussia was no less significant, although complex in its regional diversity. How states adjudicated the secularization of ecclesiastical lands, the reallocation of village commons, communal meadows and forests, and the restitution of seigneurial privileges differed among the thirty-nine states of the German Confederation. Some general trends, however, arose. In many instances, the process toward complete transition to peasant ownership was dilatory and fitful. Through the 1840s, numerous laws, edicts, and acts throughout the German Confederation enacted the partial end of labor services and transfer of property. Yet nobles wielded great political influence and feudal dues persisted. In Hesse, Württemberg, Nassau, and Baden, for example, it was not until the Revolution of 1848–1849 that states abolished all dues and completed compulsory conversion. The exception to this rule was Saxony, whose early and relatively painless transition encouraged industrial growth. Amidst this overall slow transition, however, the presence of the state in the common farmer's life stood prominent. In Bavaria, the state took over vast church holdings, making it the seigneurial overseer for roughly two-thirds of Bavaria's farmers. In the Rhineland, the secularization of ecclesiastical lands benefited some farmers, but the Napoleonic state and their successors burdened village life with new levels of taxation, conscription, and social controls from a centralized administration. Rhenish farmers grudgingly tolerated the state's appropriation of common lands, communal forests, and other usufruct privileges. In Baden, to cite another example, the state offered loans to peasants to pay off their seigneurial obligations. The loans were intended to aid Baden's peasantry, but farmers came to resent the interest payments, which in the depressed economy of the 1830s and 1840s aroused antipathy toward the state. In regard to taxation, conscription, and social disciplining, western post-Napoleonic states assumed similar roles to those of previous aristocratic landlords and absolutist states, thereby eliciting deep-seated resentment in village and countryside. All these examples shed critical light on farmers' aims, interests, and opposition to the state in the Revolution of 1848–1849.

Perhaps the most significant consequence of land reforms was the trend of pulling farmers into the 'cash nexus' of the market economy. Taxation, fixed debt, and fluctuating market prices irrevocably linked farmers to the full pressures of the market economy. In western Germany, a swelling rural population and laws of partible inheritance produced a number of responses that altered social structures. Farmers, both men and women, intensively worked less land for greater efficiency; men became long-distance itinerant workers for more cash; and women raised animals for sale, tended market crops, and sought domestic work in towns. Such changes recast the household economy. David Sabean has documented how it strained marital relations in Swabia, with dramatic increases in violence and divorce.[18] In other instances, the altered work pattern eroded village social controls, encouraging a rise in illegitimate births.

8.2 PROTO-INDUSTRY

In any discussion on the transition from 'traditional' to 'modern' economies, the role of rural industry is paramount. Rural industry refers to the goods that farmers or village artisans produced in their homes to supplement their income. Over the course of the early modern period, a class of cottage workers disengaged from agriculture altogether and turned to home crafts as their principal form of income. This rural form of domestic industry produced such goods as the wooden toys of southern Saxony, the clocks of the Black Forest, or the knives and swords of Solingen and Remscheid cutlers, but the predominant sector was clearly that of textiles—primarily linen, cotton, and wool. For decades, economic historians have debated the relationship of rural spinning and weaving to the growth of commodity markets, the decline of the guild system, the rise of merchant capitalism, and to the labor skills that promoted early industrialization.

In 1972, Franklin Mendels coined the term 'proto-industry' to show how rural domestic manufactures provided critical socio-economic structural changes to push western Europe toward population growth and commodity markets that prepared both the demand and labor skills for industrialization.[19] By the late 1970s, other historians presented proto-industrialization as a central model for explaining the great transition from early modern to modern industrial economy.[20] Family historians became equally animated about the term's potential to explain both population growth and the transition of the traditional household to the modern family. The claim that rural industry freed workers from the restraints of property inheritance and guild restriction, thus enabling them to marry early and bear more children, offered a simple logical explanation for dramatic population growth after 1750.[21] Subsequent research has, however, qualified the claims of proto-industrialization as an all-encompassing explanation of change. The correlation between domestic industry and large families is, for example, increasingly tenuous. Industrialization, scholars further argue, took place outside typical patterns of proto-industrialization. Recent research has simply uncovered too much diversity and too many exceptions to view economic growth as a single, stage-like pattern of development. Karl Heinrich Kaufhold has painstakingly located 39 areas of industrial concentration in Germany, whose heterogeneous conditions for growth by 1800 do not conform to Mendel's model.[22] More recently, Jan de Vries has criticized the narrow analytical lens of proto-industrialization. In addition to proto-industry, he argues, the features of waged labor, commercial service, agricultural specialization, and, above all, the relationship between household production and consumption must be weighted. For de Vries, the altered consumer behavior of the early modern period—the desire of domestic producers to buy and consume the goods of others—is as critical as production.[23]

The weaknesses of proto-industrialization as a model notwithstanding, we should nonetheless recognize it as a rich descriptive term whose broader ramifications warrant our attention. Domestic production, for example, enabled merchants to supply larger and more distant markets, thus expanding Germany's handicraft activity to European, Asian, and overseas markets. A few examples can illustrate this growing sector. By the end of the eighteenth century, 40,000 metal workers of the Duchy of Berg's 260,000 residents produced swords, scissors, knives, and textiles principally for export markets.[24] The fine wool garments of Eupen and Monschau were similarly sold not only throughout Europe, but also in Turkey, Africa, and the new world. Through the trade fairs of Frankfurt and Leipzig, Aachen's black wool found lucrative markets in Russia and the Levant.[25] The domestic weavers of Elberfeld and Silesia supplied mid-grade linen and cotton for both the Atlantic economy and the East India market, while Upper Lusatian weavers provided cottons for Viennese merchants finding new markets in the Ottoman Empire and the Orient. 'Oberlausitz [Upper Lusatian] linen wares produced by these rural cottagers,' writes Jean Quataert, 'became an essential part of the flowing colonial trade of cloth, cutlery, and hardware from Central Europe in exchange for indigo, rice, sugar, and tobacco.'[26] Circulating in Middle-Eastern markets as well as in the slave economies of the Americas, Upper Lusatian cloth followed a route through the *entrepôt* of London and Vienna to far-flung distribution points in the eighteenth-century world economy.

Secondly, proto-industry offers a window on the expansion of market relations. Urban merchants usually supplied the material and the equipment, such as looms and thread, thus encouraging rural villagers to participate in the ever widening activity of earning additional income. Because agricultural households usually stopped weaving after attaining a certain level of income, the putting-out merchant-capitalists found themselves compelled to employ additional rural households to meet demand. Proto-industry thus possessed an inherent growth dynamic to penetrate ever wider swathes of rural life. The crafts of carding, shearing, spinning, weaving, bleaching, dying, finishing, dressmaking, and button-making not only altered the rhythm and pace of rural life, but also connected villagers to market networks. The manufacture of clocks, furniture, and a variety of metal goods offer similar windows for understanding the hybrid economies of agriculture, cottage industry, and early industrial work.[27] Of course, some regions welcomed home industry more than others. The opportunity costs of hilly regions with poor soil, such as the Wupper valley or the Saxon uplands, was correspondingly low, thus developing sustained traditions of domestic industry that forever changed the regions. By 1799, reports Sidney Pollard, Chemnitz merchants employed 15,000 rural spinners within four miles of their city.[28] The early developed linen industry in Elberfeld in the Wupper valley, which later branched out into silk, cottons, and woolens, numbered over 33,000 workers in 1767, many of whom included domestic spinners and weavers.[29] By 1816, 75 percent of Bavaria's registered industrial population lived in the countryside, suggesting the long arm of proto-industry. In response to steam-driven spinning mills producing more thread and yarn, home weavers in the Prussian Rhine province actually increased over the first half of the nineteenth century. In 1849, between 12,000 and 15,000 workers toiled in textile factories, but 60,000 to 63,000 weavers worked at home; only gradually in the decades after 1850 did handloom weaving decline in the region. Cottage workers' relative dependency on cash for food and goods increasingly insinuated market economies into rural life, though rural demand should not be overestimated. Whether rural families concentrated on one task or strategized with many waged jobs is a current point for debate, but, regardless of such details, we should generally acknowledge proto-industry's role in expanding export markets, generating modest domestic demand, and in drawing rural regions into the maw of merchant capitalism, the dynamic of which was international in scope.

Hence, when Silesian linen weavers starved in 1844, the larger explanation involved a world-wide shift toward cotton, English mechanized spinning and weaving, and the slow response of German merchant-capitalists to consumer taste.

Although scholars have corrected the notion that proto-industry axiomatically led to mechanized industry, the correlation between dense domestic manufacture, centralized mechanization, and the spawning of urban centers should still be noted. The industrial clusters of Saxony, Silesia, and the Rhineland were early leaders in mechanized production after 1820 because entrepreneurs logically situated their factories near dense areas of spinning and weaving, which centralized production sought to replace or supplement. J. G. Brügelmann introduced the first water-powered loom in Düsseldorf in 1783 because of the region's weaving skills. Thereafter mechanization transformed the extensive network of domestic manufacture in Barmen and Elberfeld. By 1799, 10 spinning mills drew on water; in 1821, the first steam-driven cotton mill began; and by 1834, 10 steam engines were in operation, thus recalibrating merchants' need for domestic industry. In 1861, 116 steam engines existed in the towns, with 60 percent of the work force toiling in genuine factories. The mechanization of the woolen industry of the Aachen-Eupen-Monschau belt also occurred in the 1820s. To keep pace with British competition, manufacturing merchants slowly phased out its vast hinterland of rural production, which fanned into Limburg, the lower Rhineland, and present-day Belgium. By the 1830s, Aachen factories worked 1850 mechanized looms, employing 6500 workers. Of the 7000 textile workers engaged in Eupen, 5000 worked within the closed factory system. In 1850, the Aachen area employed 17,800 textile workers, making it by far the regional leader. The upland Saxon textile workers of the Vogtland and Erzgebirge, whose domestic spinning was supplanted by the mills of Chemnitz and Crimmitschau, followed a similar pattern. Chemnitz saw its first water-driven mule in 1799; by 1831, there were 84 spinning mills counting 321,000 spindles.[30] In summary, the textile industry largely pioneered mechanization, mostly because fierce competition in export markets necessitated innovation. Of course, technological change also meant the de-skilling of laborers and, with that, the exploitative use of women and children as factory 'hands.' The horrendous work conditions of early factories opened a new chapter in labor history.

Was proto-industrialization the principal solvent of the guild system? Such an assertion should be qualified. With or without domestic industry, state mercantilism already compromised the integrity of guilds. In the sixteenth and seventeenth centuries, German states not only stripped guilds of their legal jurisdiction over workers, but also permitted their state-subsidized manufactories to flout guilds' privileges. By 1783, for example, Berlin-Brandenburg suspended guild restrictions for silk, cotton, and wool production.[31] By 1800, over 100,000 workers were employed in German manufactories, which included both state workshops, as well as those merchants who needed to inspect and finish materials made in different places. Austria's state manufactory at Linz also undermined traditional craft traditions; wool cloth was finished by 5000 weavers, who were fed by 30,000 home spinners, many of whom resided in Bohemia. However, even when merchants moved beyond city walls—the medieval marker between industry and agriculture—to hire rural producers for low-wage piece-work, one should note that this often took place in regions whose urban centers had weak holds on the surrounding countryside. The textile industry of the Rhineland, a region whose urban-rural relationship historians liken more to England than to the strong home-town traditions of southern Germany, is a good example. Likewise, Limburg's wool industry and Krefeld's rural silk-weaving production arose where they did because merchants encountered little resistance in introducing a putting-out system.[32]

There is no shortage of evidence to portray guilds as an archaic form of production. To cite a famous example, Aachen's woolen industry, one of the first industrialized sectors in the German economy, did not fully exploit its contiguous proximity to the Liége-Verviers textile belt or its gateway role to the Rhine until the medieval guild, *die Wollenambacht*, and the patrician oligarchy that preserved it, were swept away in 1790, when it could start to compete with putting-out merchants in nearby Monschau and Eupen.[33] However, guilds also adapted and persisted in small southern and southwestern cities, retaining their hinterlands and continuing to determine who entered crafts, and who married. In some cases, such as with Zürich, guilds even oversaw the production of rural industry, thus blending two forms of production.

It is particularly instructive that, even after the French and Prussian states abolished guilds, they returned as weakened craft associations. The freedoms of movement and occupation undermined their economic force, but these agencies nonetheless affected the world of nineteenth-century work. Earlier controls on quality, distribution, and social behavior disappeared in the traditional crafts, but the dissolution process was slow, uneven, and enmeshed with modern capitalism. In 1835, for example, Württemberg guilds controlled only 17 percent of the state's manufacturing sector, yet 80 percent of their masters and apprentices worked in non-guild enterprises, suggesting how traditional skills bolstered a modern work force. Some trades held on to guild traditions more than others. In Berlin, only 19 percent of shoemakers and 14 percent of plumbers belong to their guilds in 1845, yet 80 percent of bakers and 65 percent of tailors did.

With the exception of tailors, the above figures illustrate the steady decline of guild influence. In the decades prior to the Revolution of 1848–1849, the most pressing problem facing guilds was career advancement: apprentices had less opportunity to attain master status. Masters in Prussia grew by 65 percent, but apprentices by 124 percent, thus leading to desperate young craftsmen to fight on barricades in 1848 for the 'right to work.'[34] Overall, one sees the market forces of waged labor straining traditional claims of workers' sustenance (*Ernährungsrecht*) during a time when city governance lost its corporate rights to bar outsiders to trades. The freedom of mobility exerted pressure on cities to receive workers who had ties neither to local soil nor to traditional crafts, thus forming the basis of a modern work force. Proletariat wage earners slowly, but ineluctably, altered the politics of production and social relations for the modern era.[35]

Yet the staying power of craft associations into the nineteenth century is noteworthy. Saxon towns' control over industrial rights persisted into the late 1850s and the North German Confederation intervened in 1869 to ban Mecklenburg's guild restrictions. In the age of steam, these craft guilds still provided frameworks for training and enabled

Table 8.1 Non-guild masters in Berlin, 1826–1845 (%)

	1826	1845
Bakers	5.1	19
Plasterers	0	65.4
Shoemakers	35	81.7
Plumbers	54	86
Tailors	59	35
Joiners	62	86

Source: Sidney Pollard, *Peaceful Conquest: The Industrialization of Europe, 1760–1970* (Oxford: Oxford University Press, 1981), 62.

the specialization of high-quality goods to flourish. The economy still demanded artisans for finished goods in leather, wrought iron, wood, glass, stone, and textiles. Indeed, with the exception of Saxony and the Rhineland, craft production still employed more workers than factory industry. In political terms, too, artisanal guilds also provided critical transnational links among European workers. During their wander years, German journeymen in France, Switzerland, and Belgium provided a subversive conduit for news and opinions about constitutions and participatory politics, thus creating problems for Metternichean Europe during the years 1815–1848. However, other political legacies of these hybrid craft associations merit attention. While certain branches of labor bridged guild traditions with union building, other lines of work provided skilled craftsmen of the lower middle class with a proud identity to differentiate themselves from the proletariat. The qualities that distinguished a 'craftsman' from a 'worker' resonated into the twentieth century.

The bloc politics of Wilhelminian conservatism turned on this distinction. Its antisocialist rhetoric of 'productive estates' invoked a skilled craftsman whose loyalty to nation and trade ostensibly opposed the interests of unionized workers. Of course, such conservative tactics furthermore relied on the social stability of rural communities, whose traditional suspicion of state reform and the urban voices of liberalism and social democracy endured throughout the century. Indeed, urban politics was often out of step with rural political culture, whose social conservatism took on an array of political hues. As Robert von Friedeburg has suggested, traditional rural attitudes and prejudices, in spite of market forces and proto-industry, lingered well into the twentieth century. Consequently, one should note cultural continuities alongside discussions of rupture and change.[36]

8.3 Urbanization

Germany's overall population grew from 30.7 million in 1816 to 47.6 million in 1865. Such population growth was the critical force that diversified rural work, intensified agricultural farming, and thickened market relations. Because modern urban growth only set in after 1870, when urban populations boomed, rural regions mostly absorbed the growing population. In 1830, only 4.5 percent of Germans lived in cities with a population above 20,000, a figure that rose to 12.5 percent in 1871, 21.9 percent in 1890, and to 34.7 percent in 1910. In Prussia, population rose 88 percent between 1815 and 1865, but urban centers with a population exceeding 2000 only grew from 27.9 percent of the total population in 1816 to 32.5 percent in 1871.[37] Because rural economies simply accommodated greater numbers, the entrepreneurial character of rural society—a site of commercial agriculture, land reclamation, domestic manufacture, emigration—must remain in the foreground of any discussion on mid-century social change.[38] In the 1850s, however, a new dynamic set in. Urban growth in Prussia began to outstrip overall population growth; cities grew from 4.07 to 8.79 million, whereas the kingdom's population increased from 14.96 (of a population of 20,000 or more) to 25.7 million.[39] In short, Prussia, and Germany as a whole, inaugurated a new phase of urbanization between 1800 and 1870, but only became an urban society sometime at the end of the century.[40]

If the most dramatic growth rates of German cities occurred after 1870, one should still view prior urban growth in Germany as significant and part of larger European trends (see Table 8.2). Berlin and Vienna joined Paris and London as large, fast-growing capitals. The expansion of such British industrial towns as Manchester, Sheffield, and Birmingham is daunting, but the exponential growth of Essen (twelve-fold), Duisburg (seven-fold), Dortmund (eleven-fold) merits comparison, if adjusted for proportion. The growth of Barmen and Elberfeld, the twin cities of Wupper valley, from 16,000 in 1800 to 146,000 in 1870, attests the explosive rise of an early German industrial center. The growth of Bremen and Hamburg lagged behind Liverpool or Marseille, but nonetheless marked their ascendancy as world ports. The impressive growth of middle-sized capitals, such as Munich or Hanover, or of traditional commercial centers, such as Frankfurt or Leipzig, further point to rapid expansion. By 1861, the greater Berlin region and the Prussian Rhine province had over 10 percent of their populations living in cities over 50,000—one threshold figure for irreversible urbanization.[41] Similarly, Saxony, with Chemnitz and Dresden, was well on its way to becoming one of the most densely urbanized regions in Europe.

More important than sheer growth, however, are structural changes. The first of these is the free movement of people: after 1800, rural migrations to urban centers altered social composition. Of the some 26,000 new residents in Cologne in the 1840s, 14,000 were born outside the city. The population boom in Berlin between 283,000 in 1837 to 459,000 in 1856 is attributed partially to natural increase (58,000), but mostly to immigration (118,000). This trend of surplus labor obviously contributed to the proletarianization of urban work. Migration patterns, however, differed from region to region. Movement from countryside to city constitutes one dominant pattern, but eastern agricultural laborers continued to migrate to other rural areas offering better economic circumstances. Similarly, transnational migration trends merit more scholarly attention. Even though migrations only ranged between 50 and 100 miles in this period, workers often crossed 'national' borders. Bohemian weavers crossed borders to

Table 8.2 City growth in Germany and Europe, 1800–1870 (in 000s)

	1800	1850	1870	% of growth, 1800–1870
Aachen*	32	51	74	131
Amsterdam	201	224	264	31
Barcelona	115	175	180	57
Berlin	172	419	826	380
Birmingham	74	233	344	364
Braunschweig*	33	39	58	76
Bremen	40	53	83	107
Breslau*	75	111	208	177
Brussels	66	251	314	376
Budapest	54	178	202	274
Cologne	50	97	129	158
Chemnitz*	15	34	68	353
Dortmund	4	11	44	1000
Dresden	60	97	177	195
Duisburg	4	9	31	675
Essen	4	9	52	1200
Frankfurt	48	65	91	89
Glasgow	77	357	522	577
Hamburg	130	132	240	85
Hanover	18	29	88	388
Leipzig	30	63	107	256
Liverpool	80	376	493	516
London	1,117	2,685	3,890	248
Madrid	160	281	332	108
Manchester	90	303	351	290
Marseille	111	194	313	182
Moscow	250	365	612	145
Munich	40	110	169	323
Nuremberg	30	54	83	177
Paris	547	1,053	1,696	210
Rome	163	175	244	50
Sheffield	31	135	240	674
St. Petersburg	220	485	667	203
Stettin*	25	47	76	204
Vienna	247	444	834	411
Wuppertal	16	80	146	813

Source: B.R. Mitchell, *European Historical Statistics, 1750–1970* (New York: Columbia University Press, 1975), 75–79; Jürgen Reulecke, *Geschichte der Urbanisierung in Deutschland* (Frankfurt: Suhrkamp, 1985), 203; Walter Demel, *Reich, Reformen und Sozialer Wandel 1763–1806* (Stuttgart: Klett-Cotta, 2005), 85.

* 1800 column cites 1815 data.

work in Lusatia and Saxony; Polish workers sought better wages in eastern Prussia; and Flemish, Dutch, French, and Rhenish textile workers followed pre-national work patterns in Belgium, Holland, Limburg, Luxemburg, and in the Rhineland valley. The mining and metallurgical industries in Belgium, Aachen, and the Ruhr valley also attracted foreign workers. In the second half of the nineteenth century, migration routes became longer; for instance, Poles now flocked to Essen and Duisburg for work in coal mines. The material and cultural frameworks of these workers bore little relation to a national economy. How such transnational work patterns affected the political attitudes and identities of ordinary Europeans remains insufficiently researched.

Urban political structures also underwent significant change. Not only did guilds gradually lose their grip on social and economic controls, but less restrictive voting criteria widened political participation. After 1800, state authorities no longer tied the right of urban citizenship to social status, religion, or occupation, but, rather, to property taxes. In Prussia, for example, the municipal ordinance of 1808 (*Stein'sche Städteordnung*) enfranchised those who paid more than fifteen talers in property tax. By using propertied wealth as a criterion for entry into the political class, this reform swept aside the corporate representation that ensured the early dominance of patricians, prelates, and guild masters over newcomers. To be sure, the liberalism of the Prussian reform had its limits; the state appointed mayors and, furthermore, introduced active and passive voting rights in its revised ordinance of 1831. Yet the shift toward modern urban self-administration had taken place. Contributing to this was the survival of Napoleonic Law in western Germany after 1815. Its new institutions of chambers of commerce and commercial courts promoted urban industry and dissolved remaining legal restraints for the expansion of industry into the countryside. The Civil Code further chipped away at confessional differences. Protestant capitalists penetrated the Catholic bastions of Cologne and Aachen in the 1840s, thus enabling such entrepreneurs as Ludolf Camphausen, Gustav Mevissen, and David Hansemann to advocate commercial and industrial innovation.[42] Overall, these forms of urban citizenship redefined the political elite of German cities, widening the field of bourgeois notable politics. The age of expanded urban administration and an urban technical expertise would come later in the century, but these reforms opened a new era in bourgeois politics and market economies.

The spirit of municipal reform was liberal, but not democratic. The Rhenish municipal ordinance of 1845, which instituted the Three Class Voting System, was emphatically plutocratic. Although this system practiced universal manhood suffrage, it divided tax payers among three income brackets, which accorded each voting class one third of political influence. Consequently, the wealthiest voters received a disproportionate degree of political influence, thus enabling new and old money to dominate city politics. Of the 83,195 residents of Cologne in 1845, only 533, 1262, and 2304 persons voted in their respective brackets.[43] (These low numbers are additionally explained by women lacking the vote as well as high birth rates that left 50 percent of the male population as minors.) In 1849, the Prussian state borrowed this principle from Rhenish liberals, introducing a franchise to Landtag elections that crippled the political influence of ordinary voters until 1918.[44]

Viewed from the standpoint of the *ancien régime* and its entangled hierarchies, such plutocratic criteria provided an aspirational middle class with a more porous political structure. For the bourgeoisie, the legal equality of property constituted the great equalizer in the modern era. As Jonathan Sperber has insightfully argued, the civic relationships that grew out of property relations encompassed a surprisingly wide range of social groups, whose material relationships affected an array of other social networks that bound together nineteenth-century civil society. The networks of social influence that families developed through property relations constitutes a central interpretive key for explaining bourgeois behavior. In fact, the transition of a corporatist society, with entrenched and limited rights of ownership and liberties, toward a civil society with legal equality and unrestricted property rights is foundational for understanding the nineteenth-century liberal order.[45] To be sure, equal property rights do not obtain in parts of central and eastern Germany, but the 'property regimes' of western and southwestern Germany are highly comparable to developments in Holland, Belgium, France, and other western states. Indeed, the Napoleonic Code (and its property rights) ranks as a leading transnational institution of modern civil society.

Finally, voluntary associations in the post-corporatist German cities also merit attention, for they transformed nineteenth-century public life. Although the principle of voluntary association certainly thrived in the *ancien régime*, its use for self-administration in the fledgling civil society of post-Napoleonic Germany was critical. The thicket of urban associations that mushroomed in German cities after 1815 provided burghers with a means for replacing corporatist institutions to address education, poor relief, orphanages, and medical care, while also organizing the social and cultural program of the middle classes: choirs, symphonies, theaters, reading circles, libraries, improvement societies, and even zoos. The completion of the Cologne Cathedral was, for example, organized through a central Cathedral Association that possessed an impressive network of national affiliates. Hunger relief during the hungry forties was organized in the same manner. These associations mobilized an ideal of civil society: independent citizens organizing and regulating their own public affairs. Lothar Gall and others have stressed the communitarian ideal of these social formations: a 'classless' society committed to the common good. Yet such citizenship ideals foundered on the bourgeoisie's harsh treatment of beggars, vagabonds, and unemployed. 'Beggar hunts and the establishment of penitentiaries and workhouses,' writes Gisela Mettele, 'aimed at the exclusion of these poor people from city society, not their integration.'[46] A similar criticism can be offered in regard to civil society's vision of women's public lives, whose 'free association' was mediated through father, husband, and the social standing of patriarchal families.[47]

8.4 INDUSTRIALIZATION

The year 1845 marks the transition toward an industrial society by displaying in bold relief the presence of two business cycles. On the one hand, central Europe witnessed widespread harvest failures that set off the last of the old regime hunger crises; high food prices throttled consumer demand, thus producing a general downward spiral in handicrafts and commerce. The privation and hardship of the hungry forties set the stage for the Revolution of 1848 and its economic agendas. On the other hand, the year inaugurates the modest start of a robust industrial business cycle. Although the revolution and its attending socio-economic crises disguised and retarded the growth of the coal, iron, and railroad industries, the mid-1840s prepared the basis of a long upward business cycle (1850–1873) that redefined Germany as an industrialized nation. Even in the early 1840s, having witnessed the rapid industrialization of the Rhineland, the banker-industrialist Gustav Mevissen could confidently state: 'Industry has strengthened to become an independent power in German life. It is not an ephemeral activity of trade and export but, rather, a more sustained, domestic-oriented manufacturing industry . . . With this newly-created social power in its midst, Germany undeniably approaches a new era.'[48]

Driving this 'independent' industrial cycle were railroads. Its influence stretched in two principal directions, what economists call backward and forward linkages. The former refers to the massive demand for building materials and its ability to develop industries affiliated with railroad construction. Laying rail, forging locomotives, assembling freight and passenger cars, blasting tunnels, landscaping rail beds, and building stations, platforms, and roundhouses created a soaring demand for iron, steel, wood, brick, machinery, and labor. Coal not only powered locomotives, but also stoked the forges, hammer works, blast furnaces, and pumps required for mining and metallurgical industries. Forward linkages refer to the commercial growth that rail transport created. By connecting regions with long-distance markets, railroads carved out wider and denser hinterlands for merchants and manufacturers; rail lines particularly opened up east-west trade networks in Germany. For centuries, European trade had traveled at the speed of horses and wind. Now, with astonishing velocity and precise calculability of arrival, the railroad seemingly conquered time and space. It introduced a new scale of economy, widening the scope of continental and intercontinental trade to flourish as never before.

After the first railroad appeared in Bavaria in 1835, railroad construction took off. In the 1840s, the length of German rail grew from 579 to 7123 km. During the 1840s, railroads attracted between 20–30 percent of the economy's entire investment, growing from 22.5 million gold marks in 1841 to 177.6 million in 1846—a net worth that would only be surpassed in 1859. Using the Prussian state debt in 1850 of 156 million talers as a yardstick, one can appreciate the magnitude of this enterprise. In the 1840s the number of passenger kilometers rose from 62 million to 782 million; with freight, from 3.2 to 302 million tons per kilometer. By 1846, railroads employed 178,000 workers and boasted an income of 63.78 million gold marks.[49] In the 1850s the length of German rail nearly doubled from 5475 to 10,337 km, exponentially expanding the scope of industry and trade. Table 8.3 indicates the overall surge in German railroad growth in comparison with other leading industrial countries, as well as showing the rail density for such industrial centers as Silesia, the Rhineland, Brandenburg, Saxony, and Bavaria.

Table 8.3 Railroad development in Germany, 1839–1865 (km)

	1839	1845	1850	1855	1860
Prussia	69.5	1042.20	2649.60	3482.10	5200.20
Silesia	40.6	355	646.8	711.9	1056.50
Rhineland	15.8	180.2	321.1	493.8	944.5
Brandenburg	26.4	271	642.9	653.7	784.7
Saxony	27.3	193	502	505.6	685.3
Prussia	3.8	285	455.6		
Westphalia	183.4	342.2	472.8	606.9	
Bavaria	28	160	610.2	1151.70	1769.20
Saxony	115.5	218.6	436.1	529.6	689.3
Württemberg	10.3	250	283.9	318.1	
Hanover	7.3	85.6	359.6	538.7	716.9
Baden	19	223.2	302.6	333.6	400.1
Hessen-	8	110.6	175.7	274.4	
Darmstadt*	14.7	35.7	352.8	361	447.7
Schleswig-Holstein	106.1	154.5	159.8	272	295.7
Mecklenburg-Schwerin	81.1	226.2	226.2	226.2	
Total	360.1	2019.20	5457.50	7354.20	10,337.80
Austria-Hungary	144	728.00	1357.00	1588.00	2927.00
Belgium	312	577.00	854.00	1333.00	1729.00
France	224	875.00	2915.00	5037.00	9167.00
United Kingdom**	1562	3931.00	9797.00	11,744.00	14,603.00

* Includes Electoral Hessen, as well as Nassau and Frankfurt a.M.
** 1839 and 1845 includes Ireland.

Sources: Hubert Kiesewetter, *Die Industrialisierung Sachsens* (Stuttgart: Klett-Cotta, 2007), 476; B. R. Mitchell, *European Historical Statistics, 1750–1970* (New York: Columbia University Press, 1975), 581–582.

Between 1850 and 1873, railroads continued to absorb one-quarter of all investment in Germany, whose absolute numbers dwarfed those of the 1840s. In 1866, for example, Prussian private railroads presided over 499.5 million talers of capital, yielding profits of 65.8 million talers.

Economic historians customarily measure railroad development in national categories (see Table 8.3), but it is equally apposite to view railways as exemplary border-crossing institutions.[50] No railway company wished to terminate service at national frontiers; co-operation with foreign railway companies was imperative.[51] The principal aim for creating the Rhenish Railway (1837) was, for example, to connect passengers and freight of the Rhine valley with Belgium's Antwerp and its world-class harbor. The price share of stocks for the Upper and Lower Silesian railway companies hinged on connections to Austria's network. The profitability of Germany's eastern lines similarly depended on its links to Russia. French, Baden, and Württemberg railways competed for northern European freight seeking the most efficient route over the Alps. Such contests between railway companies centered on time, distance, and freight rates, not on the abstraction of national economy. Of course, state ministers and railroad directors deployed patriotic rhetoric, alternately stirring or ominous, when seeking state subventions or stock subscriptions, but railroads existed for profits, not national aggregates. Military considerations certainly affected rail development, but international transit was a principal goal of railroad directors, who created such associations as the Norddeutscher Eisenbahn-Verband (1848–1852) and the Westdeutscher Eisenbahn-Verband (1857) to co-ordinate timetables, fares, and freight rates independent of government treaties.[52] Before individual states within the German Empire bought out private railroads in 1878–1879, these associations validated the liberal argument that private commerce could handle the international scope of the industrial age without state intervention.

The continental dimension of European railroads notwithstanding, they nonetheless remained a central motor of national economic growth. The German locomotive factories of Borsig (Berlin), Maffei (Munich), and Kessler (Karlsruhe) all constructed their hundredth locomotive by 1847; Borsig built 1000 by 1858.[53] In general, German machine shops assumed mass numbers; in Prussia alone in the 1850s there were 399 factories building machinery, employing 26,000 laborers. The number of steam engines in the Zollverein grew from 1416 in 1850 (26,354 horsepower) to 10,113 in 1860 (184,649 horsepower). Coal consumption is perhaps the best index of industrial growth. In the 1840s, coal output grew from 3900 to 6900 metric tons (see Table 8.4), but soared to 16,731 tons by 1860, a figure that doubled France's yield and outstripped Belgium.

The demand for coal and coke transformed the Ruhr valley between 1850 and 1870. The Ruhr river had been rendered navigable earlier in the century, but railroad lines now connected coal fields with the Rhine and Weser rivers, as well as with points eastward, above all with Berlin. Railroad lines connecting Upper Silesia with Berlin and Vienna also expanded its markets. Saxony, the other major coal region, raised its output from 441,816 tons in 1845 to 2,412,580 tons in 1865. Linked with these figures is the growth of iron and steel production. The demand for metal—rods, bars, sheets, wire—was enormous, which domestic producers met over the period 1850–1870. Whereas German lands in 1850 still imported steel to meet its need of 207,311 tons, by 1870 they were exporting 57 percent of the 1,322,674 tons that it produced. Viewing these leading sectors as a composite whole, one can appreciate W. W. Rostow's metaphor of an economy's

Table 8.4 Output of coal (000s metric tons)

	1835	1840	1845	1850	1855	1860
Belgium	2,639	3,930	4,919	5,821	8,409	9,611
France	2,506	3,003	4,202	4,434	7,453	8,304
Germany*	2,100	3,900	5,600	6,900	12,800	16,731
U.K.	28,100	34,200	46,600	50,200	65,487	81,327

* Hard and brown coal combined for Germany.

Source: B.R. Mitchell, *European Historical Statistics, 1750–1970* (New York: Columbia University Press, 1975), 360–361.

'take-off' phase to industrialization. Sometime in the 1850s, mechanization and heavy industry propelled Germany's robust economy to airborne status.

No less important than coal or iron was the overhauling of the financial sector during the 1850s. During the railroad boom of the 1840s, entrepreneurs complained of a lack of sufficient money in circulation and further criticized the reluctance of the Prussian state to overhaul its banking principles, not only with the Seehandlung, its cautious investment bank, but also with chartering new banks. Between 1848 and 1856, however, the joint-stock bank emerged in Germany. This new kind of commercial bank, capitalized through stock issues, sought to offer long-term loans to large-scale industrial enterprises. During the financial crisis of 1848, the Schaaffhausen Bank's lending capacity was expanded through the joint-stock principle, a precedent that spawned the founding of the Disconto Gesellschaft (1851–1856), the Darmstädter Bank für Handel und Industrie (1853), the Berliner Handelsgesellschaft (1856), and the Mitteldeutsche Kreditbank (1856). Their combined capitalization of 103.5 million marks enabled these banks to offer direct loans to industrial enterprises as well as subscribe large blocks of their stocks and bonds. The real model for this new kind of bank was France's Crédit Mobilier (1852). Its principle of extending long-term credit to businesses—and high dividends to its investors—extended the transnational circulation of capital from Russia to Spain, thus raising the influence of investment capital to new heights—a sphere of public life not always within the purview of the state. It is noteworthy that the Prussian state staunchly opposed this innovation. Shedding its mercantilist attitudes reluctantly, the state ministry looked askance at this independent financial lever, which it did not control. Although the Prussian government refused to charter joint-stock banks in the 1850s, entrepreneurs exploited a legal loophole to found a passing alternative: commandite banks, which also amassed capital through shares but did not offer limited liability.[54]

The Prussian state's skeptical rejection of this financial innovation introduces an important subject: the role of the state in promoting industrialization. There is a long and well-developed historiography that stresses the importance of state participation in economic development, from early modern mercantilism to nineteenth-century national economy. Governments constructed model manufactories, developed overseas markets, invested in private enterprise, set tariff policies to protect domestic industry, and founded universities and institutes to hone technical expertise. Certainly, the economic liberalism that underpinned Prussia's reforms in the years 1807–1816 remains a signal example of state influence. In the area of infrastructure, one can point to clear gains made by states. Between 1816 and 1831 the Prussian state doubled its highways to accommodate trade and communication; in the same time period, it worked with an international consortium to secure free navigation on the Rhine, doubling its traffic between 1836 and 1840. Of course, state reforms did not always produce the intended effects: model locomotives failed to work; royal manufactories harmed private enterprise; tariff policies stagnated technological innovation; and the legal settlements of peasant emancipation produced as many have-nots as beneficiaries. However one interprets the balance sheet, state policies impinged on economic activity. Whether effective or not, contemporaries furthermore viewed the state as an entitled, even necessary, component of commerce and industry.

The impact of the French era on the German economy is a favorite chestnut for economic historians. In the short term, historians emphasize the varied regional experiences. During the Napoleonic Era, the western bank of the Rhineland generally benefited from its absorption into the *grande nation* and its commercial ties to Paris and its empire, while manufacturing and commerce east of the Rhine suffered under the Rhenish Confederation and its role as a client state supplying tribute, materiel, and soldiers to Napoleon's insatiable war economy. The continental blockade of English products (1807–1814) also brought about shifts in manufacturing that were not advantageous. To take one example, cotton spinning prospered briefly, but quickly collapsed when English textiles returned to continental markets after 1815. In agricultural sectors, the southern states of Württemberg, Baden, and Bavaria certainly sustained economic setbacks from two decades of war. Württemberg herds of cattle and swine diminished by half a million animals, and only in the 1830s did farmers reach pre-war levels. Overall, historians view farmers and their rural economies as the principal victim of Napoleon's policies.[55]

For the long run, however, historians point to the commercial and industrial courts that Napoleonic law introduced, as well as modern chambers of commerce, all of which offered a more efficient means for negotiating the needs of business with the state. Previously existing machinery under the *ancien régime* beggars comparison with these commercial codes. By banning guilds and lingering restrictions on rural manufacturing, the growth of merchant capitalism became less encumbered. It is understandable, then, that the Rhenish bourgeoisie fought hard to retain Napoleonic law after the Prussian state absorbed the Rhineland at the Congress of Vienna in 1815. Its legal and political machinery facilitated the rapid industrialization of western Germany during the 1840s.

Prussia's creation of the *Zollverein* (1818–1834) looms especially important for political economists. This customs union not only minimized confusion with the weights, measures, and currencies that had handicapped trade during the Holy Roman Empire, but also created a domestic market free of tariffs that fostered Germany's industrial take-off. More recent scholarship has played down the heroic accents of this narrative, especially with regard to the logic of the *Zollverein* as a framework for national industries that prefigured political unification. For instance, excluding the vast market of Austria and its southeastern hinterlands from German domestic trade certainly made little economic sense, nor did it reflect actual practice. In spite of tariff barriers, regional trade continued between southern Germany and the Habsburg Empire. Austrian railways bought Bavarian locomotives, just as Mannheim traded Hungarian wheat on its grain market.[56] Addressing the point of economic growth, Hans-Joachim Voth marshaled data to argue that the union did little to attract investment and enhance industrial performance, which lagged comparatively. He further questions whether the *Zollverein*'s intra-German trade was necessarily positive; it forced Germans to buy Prussian products, thus preventing Germans from exploiting their own comparative advantages as fully as they might have in a free market. 'The idea of a customs union,' he concludes, 'may have excited the hearts and minds of contemporary bourgeois commentators, but did little to boost economic performance.'[57] In short, Prussia's aims were ultimately more political than economic. The union pulled middle-German states into the orbit of Prussian commerce, while minimizing the role of Austrian participation in German trade and industry. In doing so, the Zollverein augmented Prussian political power, but not necessarily the prowess of the German economy. And even in the realm of political power, Prussian success must be qualified. After all, many Zollverein states sided with Austria during the Austro-Prussian war of 1866.

The Prussian state's early unwillingness to promote railroads, the leading sector of the first industrial revolution, illustrates well the state's secondary role in promoting industrialization. During the fledgling decades of railroad construction, the Prussian state proved too inflexible to provide leadership.[58] Restrained by a law that forbade the Prussian state to authorize loans over twenty million talers without calling a parliament, the Prussian state failed to offer initiative. Peter Beuth, Christian von Rother, and Friedrich von Nagler, Prussia's leading economic advisors, saw little benefit in railways, viewing them as unprofitable projects that threatened the attraction of state bonds as well as the future of its toll roads and canals. Although entrepreneurs from various regions of Prussia pressed for state ownership in the early 1830s, they reluctantly founded private companies to meet the challenge of the new age. After the creation of four railroad companies, the Prussian state issued a Railroad Law in 1838 and, following this law's poor market reception, created the Railroad Fund in 1842. Both displayed the state's defensive posture. The 1838 law secured privileges and rights for state intervention, but offered little assurance and support to prospective investors. The Railroad Fund strove to emend this, offering dividend guarantees for five essential railway lines in the kingdom, one of them the *Ostbahn*, an eastern line to connect Berlin and Königsberg. What the state gave with one hand, however, it took with another. The state's six-million taler account guaranteed minimum rates of return on stocks yet instituted a tax on railroad profits to fund eventual state ownership. Not surprisingly, neither law attracted capital to build the eastern railway—a signal failure of state policy. In summary, what should have been a clinching argument for economic leadership proved a fitful, defensive half-measure. When King Friedrich Wilhelm IV convened a United Diet in 1847 to authorize a state loan for the *Ostbahn*, the deputies defiantly rejected it. The failed vote showed Prussia's political framework to be incapable of serving the needs of a modernizing industrial society.[59] The private sector thus ushered Prussia into the railway age.[60]

To be sure, one can offer a more positive interpretation of state guidance. In the 1850s, the Prussian state chartered 201 joint-stock enterprises, thus encouraging industrial expansion. It also increased money circulation in the 1850s to accommodate the growing economy and its need for specie. Between 1850 and 1861, the Prussian state further abolished its controls over the coal mining industry, including its restraints on the mobility of miners, thus ending its mercantilist paternalism. Mine owners could now pursue unrestrained economic growth and consolidate their enterprises into the vertically integrated behemoths that characterized the *Kaiserreich*'s coal industry. In

1861, the Prussian state additionally abolished exemptions on property taxes for East Elbian estates, which partially redressed the disproportionate tax burden of the business class. In doing so, it offered important evidence that this state could balance the needs of industry and agriculture. Yet the larger point remains salient: the role of the state in the industrialization of Germany remained secondary. German states encouraged economic growth but did not supplant the more elemental criteria of international markets, natural resources, and entrepreneurial initiative.

Underpinning Germany's boom business cycle was greater access to world markets. In the *Manifesto of the Communist Party*, Marx and Engels underscored the 'cosmopolitan character' of the bourgeoisie's 'exploitation of the world market,' observing that 'the need of a constantly expanding market for its products chases the bourgeoisie over the whole surface of the globe. It must nestle everywhere, settle everywhere, establish connections everywhere.'[61] In this statement from 1848, Marx and Engels referred more to the English, French, and Dutch mercantile empires than to any paradigmatic German experience, but the integration of German industry and commerce into the world economy became more pronounced during the 1850s and 1860s. Germany's financial crisis of 1857–1859, for instance, stemmed from bank failures in the American Midwest. Following the Cobden-Chevalier treaty between England and France in 1860, which opened up France to free trade, the Franco-Prussian trade treaty of 1862 integrated the *Zollverein* economy into the broader commercial expanses of Britain, western Europe, and the world imperium of free trade. No longer a 'backward economy,' northern German industry found itself in the central arena of industrial leadership, competing for markets and profits. Although these treaties are only referents of more complex economic contexts, they nonetheless point to entwined continental industrial development. They marked a momentum in productivity that hurled German society toward high industrialization in the last third of the nineteenth century.

Germany's accelerated pace of industrialization after 1860, and its leading role in Wilhelminian aspirations for presence and power in the world, put politics in a new key that challenged the German empire to redefine itself as an urban, industrial society. The drama of surging industrial power is indeed a cornerstone of the *Sonderweg* thesis; its exceptionally rapid pace ostensibly contributed to Germany's perilous political instability.[62] But the great transition, this essay argues, is more accurately understood as a protracted process, stretching back into the early modern period. Entangled in continuity, as much as in change, the deeper roots of this long transformation reveal the social forces, both domestic and external, that formed Germany's modern economic order.

Notes

1. The author thanks Walter Rummel, Helmut Walser Smith, and Jonathan Sperber for their generosity in reading and commenting on an earlier draft of this chapter.

2. Friedrich Harkort, *Geschichte des Dorfs, der Burg und der Freiheit Wetter als Beitrag zur Geschichte der Grafschaft Mark*, Reprint (Wetter: Kulturamt, 1980), 39.

3. Quoted in James J. Sheehan, *German History, 1770–1866* (Oxford: Clarendon Press, 1989), 452.

4. Lars Maischak, 'A Cosmopolitan Community: Hanseatic Merchants in the German-American Atlantic of the Nineteenth Century' (PhD thesis, John Hopkins University, 2005).

5. Gary Herrigel, *Industrial Constructions: The Sources of German Industrial Power* (Cambridge: Cambridge University Press, 1996); Hubert Kiesewetter, *Die Industrialiserung Sachsens. Ein regional-vergleichendes Erklärungsmodell* (Stuttgart: Steiner, 2007).

6. Heide Wunder, 'Agriculture and Agrarian Society,' in Sheilagh Ogilvie (ed.), *A New Social and Economic History of Germany*, vol. 2, 1630–1800 (London: Arnold, 2003), 63, 71.

7. Sidney Pollard, *Peaceful Conquest: The Industrialization of Europe, 1760–1970* (Oxford: Oxford University Press, 1981), 55.

8. Wunder, 'Agriculture and Agrarian Society,' 75.

9. Christopher Clark, *Iron Kingdom: The Rise and Downfall of Prussia, 1600–1947* (Cambridge, MA: Belknap Press, 2006), 163–166.

10. William Hagen, *Ordinary Prussians: Brandenburg Junkers and Villagers, 1500–1840* (Cambridge: Cambridge University Press, 2002), 279.

11. For Wilhelm Abel's serial data on prices and secular trends, see Karl Heinrich Kaufhold, 'Deutschland, 1650–1850,' in Wolfram Fischer et al., *Europäische Wirtschafts-und Sozialgeschichte*, vol. 4 (Stuttgart: Klett-Cotta, 1993), 558–560.

12. Pollard, *Peaceful Conquest*, 57–58.

13. Hans-Joachim Voth, 'The Prussian Zollverein and the Bid for Economic Superiority,' in Philip Dwyer, (ed.), *Modern Prussian History 1830–1947* (Harlow: Longman, 2001), 123.

14. Friedrich Lenger, *Industrielle Revolution und Nationalstaatsgründung (1849–1870er Jahre)* (Stuttgart: Klett-Cotta, 2001), 80.

15. Hartmut Harnisch, *Kapitalistische Agrarreform und Industrielle Revolution. Agrarhistorische Untersuchungen über das ostelbische Preußen zwischen Spätfeudalismus und bürgerlich-demokratischer Revolution von 1848/49 unter besonderer Berücksichtigung der Provinz Brandenburg* (Weimar: Böhlau, 1984); for critiques of this thesis see Joseph Mooser, 'Preußische Agrarreformen, Bauern und Kapitalismus. Bemerkungen zu Hartmut Harnischs Buch "Kapitalistische Agrarrefrom und industrielle Revolution",' *Geschichte und Gesellschaft* 18 (1992), 533–554; Toni Pierenkemper, (ed.), *Landwirtschaft und industrielle Entwicklung. Zur ökonomischen Bedeutung von Bauernbefreiung, Agrarreform und Agrarrevolution* (Stuttgart: Steiner, 1989).

16. Friedrich Lenger, 'Economy and Society,' in Jonathan Sperber, *Oxford Short History of Germany, 1800–1870* (Oxford: Oxford University Press, 2004), 94.

17. Sheehan, *German History*, 481.

18. David W. Sabean, *Property, Production, and Family in Neckerhausen*, 1700–1870 (Cambridge: Cambridge University Press, 1990), 126; Jonathan Sperber, *Revolutionary Europe, 1780–1850* (Harlow: Longman, 2000), 239.

19. Franklin Mendels, 'Proto-Industrialization, the First Phase of the Industrialization Process,' *Journal of Economic History* 32 (1972), 241–261.

20. Peter Kriedte, Hans Medick, and Jürgen Schlumbohm, *Industrialization before Industrialization*, trans. Beate Schempp (Cambridge: Cambridge University Press, 1981); Hans Medick, *Weben und Überleben in Laichingen, 1650–1900*, 2nd edn (Göttingen: Vandenhoeck & Ruprecht, 1997).

21. Michael Mitterauer and Richard Seider, *Historische Familienforschung* (Frankfurt a.M.: Suhrkamp, 1982).

22. Karl-Heinrich Kaufhold, 'Gewerbelandschaften in der frühen Neuzeit,' in Hans Pohl, (ed.), *Gewerbe-und Industrielandschaften vom Spätmittelalter bis ins 20. Jahrhundert* (Stuttgart: Steiner, 1986), 112–202; Sheilagh Ogilvie, 'The Beginnings of Industrialization,' in Sheilagh Ogilvie and Bob Scribner (eds), *Germany: A New Social and Economic History. Vol. 2, 1630–1800* (Göttingen: Arnold, 2003), 269–271.

23. Jan de Vries, *The Industrious Revolution: Consumer Behavior and the Household Economy, 1650 to the Present* (Cambridge: Cambridge University Press, 2008), 71.

24. Hans-Werner Hahn, *Die Industrielle Revolution in Deutschland* (Munich: Oldenbourg, 1998), 9.

25. Herbert Kisch, *From Domestic Manufacture to Industrial Revolution: The Case of the Rhineland Textile Districts* (Oxford: Oxford University Press, 1989), 178, 201.

26. Jean H. Quataert, 'Survival Strategies in a Saxon Textile District during the Early Phase of Industrialization, 1780–1860,' in Daryl M. Hafter (ed.), *European Women and Preindustrial Craft* (Bloomington: Indiana University Press, 1995), 153.

27. Myron P. Gutmann, *Toward the Modern Economy: Early Industry in Europe, 1500–1800* (New York: Knopf, 1988), 180–188.

28. Sidney Pollard, *Silent Conquest*, 66.

29. Herbert Kisch, *From Domestic Manufacture*, 131.

30. For this discussion on domestic mechanization, see Pollard, *Peaceful Conquest*, 61–102; David S. Landes, *The Unbound Prometheus: Technological Change and Industrial Development in Western Europe from 1750 to the Present* (Cambridge: Cambridge University Press, 1982), 137ff.

31. Pollard, *Peaceful Conquest*, 61.

32. Peter Kriedte, *Eine Stadt am seidenen Faden. Haushalt, Hausindustrie und soziale Bewegung in Krefeld in der Mitte des 19. Jahrhunderts* (Göttingen: Vandenhoeck & Ruprecht, 1991); Kisch, *From Domestic Manufacture*.

33. Kisch, *From Domestic Manufacture*, 153–188.

34. Sheehan, *German History*, p. 492; Friedrich Lenger, *Sozialgeschichte der deutschen Handwerker seit 1800* (Frankfurt a.M.: Suhrkamp, 1992).

35. Jürgen Kocka, *Lohnarbeit und Klassenbildung: Arbeiter und Arbeiterbewegung in Deutschland 1800–1875* (Bonn: Dietz, 1993).

36. Robert von Friedeburg, *Ländliche Gesellschaft und Obrigkeit. Gemeindeprotest und politische Mobilisierung im 18. und 19. Jahrhundert* (Göttingen: Vandenhoeck & Ruprecht, 1997), 277ff.

37. Wolfram Fischer et al, *Sozialgeschichtliches Arbeitsbuch*, vol. 1, *Materialen zur Statistik des Deutschen Bundes 1815–1870* (Munich: Beck, 1982), 38.

38. See the following chapter for a complete discussion on population growth.

39. John Breuilly, 'Urbanization and Social Transformation,' in Sheilagh Ogilvie and Richard Overy (eds), *Germany: A New Social and Economic History. Vol. 3, Since 1800* (London: Arnold, 2003), 219, n. 5.

40. Klaus Tenfelde, 'Urbanization and the Spread of Urban Culture in Germany in the Nineteenth and Twentieth Centuries,' in Friedrich Lenger (ed.), *Towards an Urban Nation: Germany since 1770* (Oxford: Berg, 2002), 16.

41. Jürgen Reulecke, *Geschichte der Urbanisierung in Deutschland* (Frankfurt a.M.: Suhrkamp, 1985), 42.

42. The civic equality of Jews waited until after 1848, but it is worth noting that the religious-neutral ground of capitalism engendered a Judeophilic pragmatism among businessmen that encouraged support of Jewish equality. Shulamit S. Magnus, *Jewish Emancipation in a German City: Cologne, 1798–1871* (Stanford: Stanford University Press, 1997), 135.

43. Reulecke, *Geschichte der Urbanisierung*, 19.

44. Heinz Boberach, *Wahlrechtsfragen im Vormärz. Die Wahlrechtsanschauung im Rheinland 1815–1849 und die Entstehung des Dreiklassenwahlrechts* (Düsseldorf: Droste, 1959); Thomas Kühne, *Dreiklassenwahlrecht und Wahlkultur in Preussen 1867–1914: Landtagswahlen zwischen korporativer Tradition und politischem Massenmarkt* (Düsseldorf: Droste, 1994).

45. Jonathan Sperber, *Property and Civil Society in South-Western Germany, 1820–1914* (Oxford: Oxford University Press, 2005).

46. Giesela Mettele, 'Burgher Cities on the Road to a Civil Society: Germany, 1780 to 1870,' in Friedrich Lenger (ed.), *Towards an Urban Nation: Germany since 1780*, 52; for research trends on the German middle classes, see Jonathan Sperber, '*Bürger, Bürgertum, Bürgerlichkeit, bürgerliche Gesellschaft*: Studies of the German (Upper) Middle Class and its Sociocultural World,' *Journal of Modern History* 69 (1997), 271–297.

47. See Chapter 4.

48. Quoted in Hahn, *Industrielle Revolution*, 25.

49. Hahn, *Industrielle Revolution*, 26.

50. Railroad maps display well the continental transnational logic of rail lines; see, for example, Hermann Berghaus, *Deutschland und anliegende Länder zur Übersicht der Eisenbahnen und Hauptstrassen* (Gotha: Perthes, 1860).

51. For a similar argument about railroads' integrative capacity at regional and national levels, see Siegfried Weichlein, *Nation und Region. Integrationsprozesse im Bismarckreich* (Düsseldorf: Droste, 2004), 44ff.

52. James M. Brophy, *Capitalism, Politics, and Railroads in Prussia, 1830–1870* (Columbus: Ohio State University Press, 1998), 68.

53. Kiesewetter, *Industrielle Revolution in Deutschland 1815–1914* (Frankfurt a.M.: Suhrkamp, 1989), 216.

54. James M. Brophy, 'The Political Calculus of Capital: Banking and the Business Class in Prussia, 1848–1856,' *Central European History* 25 (1992), 149–176.

55. Ute Planert, *Der Mythos vom Befreiungskrieg. Frankreichs Kriege und der deutsche Süden: Alltag-Wahrnehmung-Deutung 1792–1841* (Paderborn: Schöningh, 2007), 231ff.; Roger Dufraisse, 'L'influence de la politique économique napoléienne sur l'économie des états du rheinbund,' in Eberhard Weis, (ed.), *Reformen im rheinbündischen Deutschland* (Munich: Oldenbourg, 1984), 75–95.

56. Lenger, *Industrielle Revolution und Nationalstaatsgründung*, 91.

57. Hans Joachim Voth, 'The Prussian Zollverein,' 124.

58. Cf. Eric Dorn Brose, *The Politics of Technological Change: Out of the Shadow of Antiquity, 1809–1848* (Princeton: Princeton University Press, 1993).

59. James M. Brophy, 'Eisenbahnbau als Modernisierungsstrategie? Staatliche Wirtschaftspolitik in der ersten Industrialisierung,' in Thomas Stamm-Kuhlmann, (ed.), *Pommern im 19. Jahrhundert. Staatliche und gesellschaftliche Entwicklung in vergleichender Perspektive* (Cologne: Böhlau, 2007), 253–274.

60. Rainer Fremdling, *Eisenbahnen und deutsches Wirtschaftswachstum 1840–1879. Ein Beitrag zur Entwicklungstheorie und zur Theorie der Infrastruktur*, 2nd edn (Dortmund: Gesellschaft für Westfälische Wirtschaftsgeschichte, 1985); Dieter Ziegler, *Eisenbahnen*

und Staat im Zeitalter der Industrialisierung. Die Eisenbahnpolitik der deutschen Staaten im Vergleich (Stuttgart: Steiner, 1996).

61. Karl Marx and Friedrich Engels, *The Communist Manifesto* (New York: International Publishers, 1948), 12.

62. Contra this thesis, see Hartmut Kaelble, 'Der Mythos der rapiden Industrialisierung in Deutschland,' *Geschichte und Gesellschaft* 9 (1983), 106–118.

Bibliography

ABEL, WILHELM, *Agrarkrisen und Agrarkonjunktur. Eine Geschichte der Land-und Ernährungswirtschaft Mitteleuropas seit dem hohen Mittelalter* (Hamburg: Parey, 1966).

BOCH, RUDOLF, *Grenzenloses Wachstum? Das rheinische Wirtschaftsbürgertum und seine Industrialisierungsdebatte 1814–1857* (Göttingen: Vandenhoeck & Ruprecht, 1991).

DE VRIES, JAN, *The Industrious Revolution: Consumer Behavior and the Household Economy, 1650 to the Present* (Cambridge: Cambridge University Press, 2008).

DIPPER, CHRISTOPH, *Die Bauernbefreiung in Deutschland* (Stuttgart: Kohlhammer, 1980).

GOOD, DAVID F., *The Economic Rise of the Habsburg Empire, 1750–1914* (Berkeley and Los Angeles: University of California Press, 1984).

HAGEN, WILLIAM, *Ordinary Prussians: Brandenburg Junkers and Villagers, 1500–1840* (Cambridge: Cambridge University Press, 2002).

HAHN, HANS-WERNER, *Die Industrielle Revolution in Deutschland* (Munich: Oldenbourg, 1998).

HENNING, FRIEDRICH-WILHELM, *Deutsche Wirtschafts-und Sozialgeschichte im 19. Jahrhundert* (Paderborn: Schöningh, 1996).

KAUFHOLD, KARL HEINRICH, 'Deutschland, 1650–1850,' in Wolfram Fischer et al. (eds), *Europäischen Wirtschafts-und Sozialgeschichte*, Vol. 4 (Stuttgart: Klett-Cotta, 1993).

KIESEWETTER, HUBERT, *Die Industrialiserung Sachsens. Ein regional-vergleichendes Erklärungsmodell* (Stuttgart: Steiner, 2007).

KISCH, HERBERT, *From Domestic Manufacture to Industrial Revolution. The Case of the Rhineland Textile Districts* (Oxford: Oxford University Press, 1989).

LANDES, DAVID, *The Unbound Prometheus: Technological Change and Industrial Development in Western Europe* (Cambridge: Cambridge University Press, 1969).

LENGER, FRIEDRICH, *Sozialgeschichte der deutschen Handwerker seit 1800* (Frankfurt am Main: Suhrkamp, 1988).

MEDICK, HANS, *Weben und Überleben in Laichingen, 1650–1900*, 2nd edn (Göttingen: Vandenhoeck & Ruprecht, 1997).

OGILVIE, SHEILAGH, and BOB SCRIBNER (eds), *A New Social and Economic History of Germany*, 3 Vols (London: Arnold, 2003).

POLLARD, SIDNEY, *Peaceful Conquest. The Industrialization of Europe, 1760–1970* (Oxford: Oxford University Press, 1981).

SABEAN, DAVID WARREN, *Property, Production, and Family in Neckerhausen, 1700–1870.* (Cambridge: Cambridge University Press, 1990).

SPERBER, JONATHAN, *Property and Civil Society in South-Western Germany, 1820–1914* (Oxford: Oxford University Press, 2005).

WEHLER, HANS-ULRICH, *Deutsche Gesellschaftsgeschichte*, Vols 1 and 2 (Munich: Beck, 1989).

CHAPTER 9

ESCAPING MALTHUS: POPULATION EXPLOSION AND HUMAN MOVEMENT, 1760–1884

ERNEST BENZ

9.1 MALTHUSIAN TRAPS

BOTH Germans in the past and researchers in the present have found it difficult to escape Thomas Robert Malthus (1766–1834). The arguments of his *Essay on the Principle of Population* colored the thinking and actions of nineteenth-century householders and policy-makers. Vulgar Malthusian ideology missed the mark through over-simplification of complex human behavior, but general practice embodied his norms from 1760 to 1884. Even as the accuracy of the Malthusian model waned as a description of marriage and reproduction at the end of the 1800s, its hold on the popular imagination persisted.

Malthus bewitched with a picture. Criticizing the Enlightened hubris of the Marquis de Condorcet (1743–1794) and William Godwin (1756–1836), Malthus in 1798 proffered a schematic objection to their blueprints for perfecting humanity. Malthus postulated that the 'passion between the sexes' could unleash human 'prolifick powers' to reproduce at geometric rates, while technology generated merely arithmetic increases in the quantities of food necessary for human survival. Mathematics did the rest: sooner or later, any utopia would run up against ineluctable natural limits to growth, with its inhabitants doomed to mass starvation unless war or disease claimed them first. Means to stave off these positive checks were attractive only by comparison, resolving themselves into 'some species of misery or vice.'[1] The human race seemed condemned to a dismal existence, with any brief sparks of happiness soon doused by the cold water of want.

Small wonder so many commentators have written of a 'Malthusian trap'[2] or 'Malthusian nightmare.'[3] Populations could only oscillate within narrow limits. Increases above carrying capacity would be choked off, while decreases would stimulate reproduction to restore the original melancholy equilibrium. Logically neat, if personally unpleasant, such stability makes a tempting first approximation in population studies. The temptation is especially great when summarizing experiences over expanses of time or territory for which hard data are scarce. For example, post-war literature on development evinced great fear of a 'low-level equilibrium trap,' conceived in vulgar Malthusian terms.[4] If such conditions obtained in the developing world, gains in production would be literally eaten up by the rising population, blocking any take-off from subsistence into sustained prosperity. The bulk of humanity would be trapped in poverty, with the quantity of life rising, rather than its quality.

As it happened, this scenario bore little resemblance to actual events.[5] 'The low-level equilibrium trap shuts so slowly that escape seems inevitable,' Malthus wrote[6] Far from oscillating around equilibria, both population and income per head exploded worldwide after 1945, and rose faster in poorer economies. At the same time, mortality rates fell dramatically. Indeed, population increase may be the key trigger permitting more intensive exploitation of human and natural resources to create an abundance of commodities.[7] The implausibility of the trap applies to all historic societies, which have left agrarian subsistence far behind.

All the same, the lives of Germans in the past can be characterized as Malthusian in a less controversial and more informative sense. Let us turn back to what Malthus actually said, especially in the second (1803) edition of *An Essay on the Principle of Population*.[8] The most vivid arguments of the original *Essay* had depicted population inexorably overtaking food supply, loosing the Four Horsemen to trample the bleak future landscape. Yet Malthus did not predict such a distant apocalypse. In an even more direct challenge to the optimism of contemporary radicals, he insisted that pressures to avert demographic catastrophe were already operating in the present.[9] This meant not only that scarcity obtained, but also that active measures were being taken to mitigate it.

'If we can persuade the hare [population] to go to sleep, the tortoise [food] may have some chance of overtaking her.'[10] Social expectations, which Malthus generically termed 'customs,'[11] led many human beings to strive for standards of living that they regarded as suiting their stations in life. Such judgments of appropriateness varied by class and culture, and could be elevated. 'Supposing the people to have been before [a sudden bout of deaths] in a very depressed state, and much of the mortality to have arisen from the want of foresight which usually accompanies such a state, it is possible that the sudden improvement of their condition might give them more of a decent and proper pride.'[12] In that case, the additional nourishment *per capita* made available might be devoted to increasing longevity, rather than to multiplying the number of fatal marriages.

Malthus came to attach decisive importance to rational human foresight. The major addition to the model in the second edition of his *Essay* was the highlighting of moral restraint as a preventive check to limit population without misery or vice. In particular, would-be spouses could anticipate that beginning procreation in youth would subject their offspring to physical torment, and would subject themselves to emotional torment and downward mobility. They could diminish that prospect by postponing marriage and childbearing. Accepting sexual privation in the short term would forestall long-term privation of food and status. Malthus believed that such prudence was already widespread among his contemporaries and could spread still more widely, to the general benefit.

On the factual point at least, Malthus was right, and right for German as well as English population history. As far back as reliable records run, both countries fell within the west European marriage pattern, which dominated life west of a line from Trieste to Saint Petersburg—roughly distinguishing Germanic from Slavic populations, whose women married younger.[13] German women, like other west Europeans, separated the physiological event of menarche from the social event of wedding. Prudent Malthusian sweethearts postponed their nuptials until they were in a position to support an independent household.

By delaying the onset of marital relations for a decade after puberty, couples reduced the number of their offspring by three—that is, they did so provided premarital sex and births out of wedlock were rare, as indeed they were. Only a couple of percent of German births took place outside marriage for much of the eighteenth century.[14] In this era, even the small minority of unwed mothers conformed more to Malthusianism than they rebelled against it. Their average ages at first birth fell just below the average entry into marriage, say age twenty-four where first-time brides averaged twenty-six. While some of those brides had engaged in intercourse before marriage, they had not done so in great numbers or for long periods; only an eighth gave birth within eight months of the wedding.

This was a world Malthus recognized. 'The sons of tradesmen and farmers are exhorted not to marry, and generally find it necessary to pursue this advice, till they are settled in some business, or farm, that may enable them to support a family. These events may not occur till they are far advanced in life.'[15] In other societies around the world circa 1800, such as China or India or Russia or Brazil, almost all females had wed by age twenty-three, while fewer than half their German counterparts had done so. In short, west European females became women before they became wives, and a considerable portion—at least five percent and as much as twenty percent—never took the latter step at all.

Malthusian controls restricted marital fertility from the outside. There was no contraception to limit births within marriage;[16] rather, marriage itself was limited, and the duration of childbearing compressed by delaying its onset. Moral restraint reflected not only prudence on the part of the adolescent couples directly involved, but also pressure from their parents and communities. The old demanded patience from the young.

9.2 MALTHUSIANISM IN PRACTICE

Even so, German marriage patterns were far from uniform, as nuptiality varied extensively by era, region, and class. Much as Malthus supposed, customs and contested estimates of economic prospects characterized a range of individual choices and group constraints on marriage.

That marriage rates fluctuated over time was clear already to eighteenth-century observers. When Malthus turned his attention to data for central Europe, he had little difficulty fitting them into his overall argument. For example, Johann Peter Süssmilch's *Die göttliche Ordnung in den Veränderungen des menschlichen Geschlechts aus der Geburt, dem Tode und der Fortpflanzung desselben* (1761–1762) provided Malthus with the numbers of weddings celebrated in Halle, Leipzig, Augsburg, Danzig, the duchies of Magdeburg and Cleves, the principality of Halberstadt, and the Kurmark of Brandenburg, together with estimates of their total populations. In all these territories marriage rates had decreased between 1700 (or earlier) and the mid-century. Malthus maintained that the more frequent weddings in the early years reflected the taking up of new employments made available by previous high mortality in an area, or by improving cultivation and trade.[17] Where such means of livelihood were fully subscribed, he predicted rough constancy in marriage rates, at a lower level.

In other words, because marriage was under voluntary control in west Europe, it regulated population. A string of bountiful harvests encouraged younger weddings, with more births to follow, but ages at marriage and conception rates fell back during the recurrent food crises built into the old agrarian order. Likewise, an increase in deaths opened places for the young survivors, who hastened to wed and reproduce, making up the losses.[18] Conversely, fewer deaths meant that incumbents controlled resources longer, requiring heirs-to-be to wait to marry, and thereby postponed their reproduction. In both cases, nuptiality adjusted homeostatically to other demographic and economic realities.

A similar Malthusian summary holds for long-term trends in the German population as a whole. A century of repeated catastrophes from the Thirty Years War to the expansionist campaigns of Louis XIV, coinciding toward the end with the Great Northern War of 1700–1721, had cut the German population back considerably (see Table 9.1). Not until well after 1700 did the population of the future Imperial Germany exceed the sixteen million attained around 1600. Growth resumed when and where the return of extended peace brought a boom in weddings and births. Thereafter, through the rest of the eighteenth century and into the nineteenth, aggregate population rose by roughly one percent per year. That increase compounded to a doubling over a century and a half to twenty-three million in 1816 and then a rapid re-doubling by 1884.

This rise was by no means limited to Germans, but was general across Europe in 'the Malthusian moment' around 1800.[19] Especially in England, a higher percentage married, and at a younger age. Those youthful marriages emerged from still more youthful courtships, which generated more births out of wedlock and more births just within wedlock than previously. All these shifts combined to send the population soaring. Although initially skeptical that such an explosion was possible in the Old World, Malthus came to acknowledge it. In 1825, he noted that the vital rates reported in the 1817 Prussian census would double its population of 10.5 million over a period of forty-three years.[20] In the event, Germans as a whole kept to that pace, leaving forty-one million subjects under the Prussian king as German emperor in 1871, with several million more descendants scattered abroad.

Table 9.1 Population within Germany's 1871 borders

Year	Millions of people
1500	9
1550	13
1600	16
1650	10
1700	14
1750	17
1800	22
1850	35
1900	56

Based on Christian Pfister, *Bevölkerungsgeschichte und histor-ische Demographie 1500–1800* (Munich: Oldenbourg, 1994), 10

Germans observed analogous trends on the smaller scale of their local *Heimat*, and with more immediate concern. Already in the late 1700s, municipalities grew more hostile to newcomers. Increases in entry fees and other rising barriers to local citizenship marked a consciousness of population pressure. In the first half of the nineteenth century, that concern grew to a crescendo of complaints concerning overpopulation.[21] One response was the intensification of customary Malthusian controls to restrict reproduction even more stringently. Average marriage ages drifted up a couple of years over the first few decades of the 1800s, to twenty-eight where brides had once averaged twenty-six.

Fear of mushrooming poverty moved not only individual couples and local elders, but also central governments to action. Malthus's warnings penetrated the conscious-ness of the élite all over Europe, often severed from the British liberal framework of classical economics. Although Malthus preferred to leave individuals and families free to suffer or benefit from choices they made themselves,[22] conservative German civil servants were more inclined to enforce the behavior that they judged correct. In particular, they sought to impose prudence from the top down. From the 1820s to the 1860s, in south German States such as Bavaria, Württemberg, and Baden, and also in parts of the north, such as Hanover and Mecklenburg, officials refused marriage licenses to couples who could not demonstrate that they possessed sufficient means to provide for a household on their own.[23] This hard line did reduce marriage rates, but it was less than fully successful in reducing birth rates. Couples denied access to legal marriage went ahead and produced about half as many progeny as they would have, had they been permitted to wed. Because these children were born out of wedlock, their economic circumstances and those of their families were all the more dire. Property qualifications for marriage bred the very proletariat they were meant to forestall. This was no way to escape Malthus.

Variations across space were no less extensive than variations over time, as a comparison of geographic extremes illustrates.[24] Frisian mothers in the northwest and Bavarians well to the southeast differed dramatically in how much and how long they breastfed their infants. In large numbers, Frisians nursed their offspring for over a year, while breastfeeding was rare or perfunctory in much of Bavaria. Extended nursing had two direct consequences: infants survived in greater numbers and their mothers were slower to resume ovulating. Only a sixth of Frisian children died under the age of one, and the next child following a survivor did not arrive for two and a half years on average. By contrast, Bavaria saw infant mortality at twice the Frisian level and birth intervals a year shorter—even when the child whose birth began that interval had survived. These striking geographic differences endured for centuries, based on breast-feeding norms entrenched in popular women's lore.

Regional discordances were mitigated by marriage patterns. The slower pace of childbearing in Frisia meant that women there could wed younger than Bavarians without being overwhelmed by as many pregnancies. The net effect was a rough Malthusian balancing. The average Frisian couple whose marriage endured through menopause produced six offspring, one of whom would die in infancy, leaving the parents to raise five children. A typical Bavarian couple likewise raised five surviving children, but might do so by giving birth to eight and watching three of them perish before reaching their first birthdays. Yet such was the rapidity of Bavarian reproduction in the absence of breastfeeding that holding the number of survivors to five required not only a higher infant mortality, but also a more extended delay of marriage. In the late 1700s and early 1800s, first-time Frisian brides averaged twenty-five years of age, while the figure for their Bavarian counterparts was four years higher, at twenty-nine.

Such an average did not represent a uniform experience throughout a population, even one restricted to a specific location and era. Malthusian fertility control rested essentially on social differentiation; flexibility and restraint were enforced on the lower orders. Insisting that a couple possess the requisite resources before marrying pressed more sharply on the poor, who began with less and came by less as they aged. They took longer to accumulate sufficient wealth to maintain a household, and therefore wed older, if at all.

These constraints tightened in the nineteenth century as the population rose and resources grew scarcer. An obvious contrast in agrarian societies lies between proprie-tors with sufficient land to maintain themselves independently and laborers obliged to hire themselves out to work the land of others. In the eighteenth century, women joining these occupational classes in the southwest might wed just a couple of years apart, but during the hard times of 1825–1849, the gap between farming and laboring brides' ages widened to half a decade.[25] The difference derived entirely from an additional postponement of marriage among the poor. Rich brides, standing to inherit considerable property or to marry into it, usually both, were insulated against immis-eration. In the 1800s, these heiresses continued to wed in their early to mid-twenties as their foremothers had. The poor could not give their children the same start in life, as aging parents clung to their holdings for their own support. The younger generation among the poor only slowly amassed the customary and legal underpinnings for a life together, and in the meantime had to put off weddings until their late twenties or even their thirties.

The situation was complicated, but not transformed, by additional opportunities to secure a livelihood that did not depend directly on farming the land. Germans had long ceased to inhabit a purely agrarian economy, although artisanal pursuits tended to be by-employments, especially in the countryside. Where foodstuffs could be imported, crafts such as smithing, tailoring, or carpentry could supplement earnings and support a wider population. The same logic applied to raising cash crops for sale beyond the local market, such as wine, chicory, and later tobacco. Households pursuing such activities typically enjoyed wealth and marriage ages somewhere between those of landed proprietors and land-poor laborers, in keeping with Malthusian reasoning.

Perhaps the most interesting occupational differentiation in the eighteenth century came from weaving and spinning, first linen and later cotton or wool as well.[26] Regions such as Saxony saw disproportionate increases in manufacturing and striking growth in the parts of the population relying on that sector of the economy.[27] Although sometimes labeled proto-industrialization or early industrialization or proletarianization, such trends did not overthrow traditional Malthusian calculations. True, producing textiles did not require the same expanse of land as farming, and true again, weavers reached their maximum earning capacity younger. In that sense, the introduction of weaving permitted extra local marriages—by no means necessarily youthful marriages, as that maximum earning capacity might be low. The point was that weaving allowed couples to wed who otherwise might not have done so at all, both weavers and their neighbors who were not engaged in weaving, for whom more agricultural resources now remained. That outcome was fully Malthusian and marked no dramatic break with the past. Gender relations were not revolutionized through contraception, nor were class relations revolutionized through wage labor for a capitalist boss.[28]

A better way to make sense of this aspect of German history may be to compare it with the high-level equilibrium trap postulated for early modern China.[29] The Chinese model allows for sustained population growth over centuries without dramatic decreases in standards of living—but also without dramatic increases. Population advancing without technological or social revolution, according to some scholars, renders this prospect a trap. In the most pessimistic portrayal, the outcome is involution, as social controls intensify in the effort to wring ever greater output from finite human and natural resources.[30] In the German case, new burdens fell on nineteenth-century women. Their labor, cheap both because they were numerous and because they were subordinates within patriarchal households, was exploited more intensively.[31] These wrenching demands may have sparked a crisis in marriage, as wives fought with husbands and separated from them more frequently.

9.3 GERMANS ON THE MOVE

The problem was quite general. However well or ill Europe's thousands of local economies might each have supported a rising number of inhabitants, all experienced some form of Malthusian strain. In general, one can distinguish at least three responses to the quantitative pressure of population on resources:

1. Reproduction might be limited in qualitatively new ways that went beyond Malthusian controls;
2. resources, or their utilization, might be expanded in qualitatively new ways; or
3. part of the population might come to draw its sustenance, temporarily or permanently, from more distant resources.

Stereotypically, three west European societies diverged around 1760, one following each of these three paths. The eighteenth-century French took up family limitation, applying contraception within marriage to re-make the family. At much the same time, Britons re-made their economy, creating the first industrial society.[32] Germans meanwhile pursued the less imaginative third route, through emigration.

Forsaking hearth and home, even forsaking the German lands entirely, of course hardly constituted an escape from Malthus. Migration formed part and parcel of the old demographic order. The attenuation of adolescence that marked west European lives corresponded to equally distinctive social roles for adolescents.[33] Until they could become independent married adults, young women and men pursued other activities, as farmhands, servants, apprentices, nannies, soldiers, and so on. Most of these occupations involved at least temporary movement out of their original households. In that sense, mobility was as Malthusian as delayed marriage.

The Malthusian character of migration can also be seen in its link to inheritance, which regularly recalibrated the local ratio of population to resources. From Niccolo Machiavelli, Malthus took over a tale by the eighth-century historian, Paul the Deacon, about future Lombards drawing lots to split wealth two ways, with the one third who came out empty-handed assigned to emigrate.[34] The tale rang true a millennium later, as Germans followed two broad systems for transmitting wealth between generations, each giving its own impulse to out-migration. In the most straightforward model, impartible inheritance, an unbreakable chunk of resources, such as a homestead, passed as a unit from a father to one of his sons. The unfortunate siblings had few options: to wed the heir to some other homestead, to acquire by some means a holding where there was no heir, or to leave for some more hospitable locale. In other words, impartible inheritance guaranteed livelihoods for a favored few by leaking a steady stream of emigrants, generation after generation.

Partible inheritance, under which each son, and often each child regardless of sex, received a share of the parents' wealth, set up a more dynamic game. All the children of the rich might be wealthy enough to wed and remain in their birthplace. The shrinking of average holdings whenever a population rose under partibility gave a general incentive to innovate in order to extract more livelihoods from existing resources. Only where innovation consistently lagged would population growth provoke emigration, which would come flooding forth after a prolonged build-up. Regions following partible inheritance therefore took longer to begin to shed emigrants, but when they did so, it happened in large numbers and quickly.

Malthus himself took account of movement in analyzing regions that by his day no longer fell under the Holy Roman Empire. With regard to a locale in Jura, he remarked: 'it seems to have acted the part of a breeding parish for the towns and flat countries; and the annual drain of a certain portion of the adults made room for all the rest to marry, and to rear a numerous offspring.'[35] A similar analysis noted that pasturage can produce a surplus with relatively little work. Low demand for labor at home then led the Swiss into foreign military service 'or to emigrate in some other way, as the only chance of enabling them to marry.'[36]

Malthus also anticipated more recent understandings of urbanization. German cities, like those elsewhere in Europe, featured higher death rates than the surrounding countryside. (Malthus himself noted this phenomenon for Ducal Prussia, Pomerania, and the Kurmark and the Neumark of Brandenburg as of 1756, again following Süssmilch.[37]) Yet urbanites' total birth rates were lower than rustics'. Overall then, towns were marked by natural decrease, while rural births exceeded deaths. Maintaining town size, let alone increasing it, therefore involved a doomed influx from the country, over and over. The conventional treatment of these dynamics epitomizes vulgar Malthusianism: peasants generated big families, too large to feed all their mouths, and so dispatched them to the towns, where higher urban mortality consumed them.

An alternative explanation of these patterns reassigns causal primacy to migration.[38] In this account, Malthusian Germans, especially rural-born females, moved to towns to work as servants. They remained poor and unmarried during their sojourns there, which occasionally lasted all their adult lives. The births of such migrants would then be credited to the countryside and their deaths to the town's ledger, making the former seem to burgeon and the latter seem noxious. The effect would be all the greater as the presence of these celibate women reduced urban birth rates. Seeing metropolis and hinterland as parts of one population removes the illusion. The apparent urban-rural difference in vital rates arose not from any distinctive medical condition of town or country, but from migration between two sectors of one demographic unit. How far Malthus himself appreciated this can be gauged from occasional remarks. In connection with *Hollandgängerei* (going down the road by the scores of thousands to work in the Low Countries, notably to mow meadows and dig peat bogs), he noted 'Holland, indeed, has been called the grave of Germany.'[39]

The great mobility among early modern Germans runs counter to lingering stereotypes of isolated and static communities with limited horizons—traps, one might say. In fact, they were open, or at least porous. Whether obtaining seasonal employment, taking up a fresh one-year contract as a farmhand, tramping byways as a journeyman, leasing a mill for a nine-year term, accepting a posting as a teacher, cleric, or railway worker, moving in with a bride or groom, or seeking their fortunes less systematically, millions of Germans moved. Indeed, the best statistics suggest that they changed domicile more frequently in the mid-1800s than after the two world wars.[40] In 1830, three percent of inhabitants in the almost 200 villages and towns of the Düsseldorf district had established residence that year; by 1865, 10 percent were newcomers each year, with almost as many leaving just as abruptly. The 1871 census found nearly half of

Prussians dwelling outside the municipality where they had been born. The maximum mobility came a couple of decades later at the high tide of industrialization and urbanization. As the nineteenth century drew to a close, one-sixth of city-dwellers had resided in their city for less than one year—and would move on almost as rapidly. Yet even then, much migration followed traditional motives and patterns, simply taking advantage of new transportation to play out old social relations over a broader geographic expanse.

This mobility attracted the attention of officials, who sought to monitor its extent. Indeed, police files provide the basis for observations of the kind summarized in the preceding paragraph.[41] As the ambitions of the modern state grew, it went beyond recording movement to directing and restricting it. A particular concern in the early 1800s was the loose population of vagabonds.[42] As long as the easing of population pressure following the wars of the seventeenth century had endured, families of non-citizens had drifted easily from municipality to municipality, scrounging odd jobs and then moving on. A rag-tag population of tinkers, knife-grinders, basket-weavers, peddlers, and theatrical troupes circulated around more settled citizenries. Although their wanderings launched itinerant families on eccentric orbits far from their original jurisdictional circuits, they repeatedly returned to familiar sites, where they might even acquire second-class citizenship as *Insassen* or *Hintersassen*, squatters.

To conservative bureaucrats, such labor mobility represented not liberty, nor even a makeshift adaptation to Malthusian circumstances, but a social problem calling for regulation. They set out to reform the wanderers from above, to convert them into useful subjects of the state, much as they undertook to improve Jews around the same time. The key step, implemented in the wake of the Napoleonic Wars, was to fix the itinerant in place in the hope of giving them artificial roots. In practice, resident aliens won only grudging acceptance from their new neighbors. Without local assets to inherit, they often fell foul of property qualifications for marriage. The first half of the nineteenth century then saw the rise of illegitimate dynasties, as one generation and then another reproduced out of wedlock. Through their efforts, the proportion of births taking place out of wedlock surged to ten or more times the eighteenth-century norm. Pregnant brides also grew more frequent. The net result was that by 1850 half of first births were being conceived outside marriage in many regions.

The pile-up was eased by emigration in the 1840s and 1850s, typically to the United States, but resolved only by the abolition of the property qualifications for marriage in the 1860s. In the end, tighter legislation had offered no escape from Malthus. The solution was rather re-integration in Malthusianism, through marriage in the more laxly administered United States or in the new, more open German Empire.

Detailed patterns of long-distance, terminal emigration bring out the Malthusian dynamics sketched above. Although the eighteenth century saw 100,000 Germans cross the Atlantic, far more found abundant land closer to home, in eastern Europe.[43] Frederick the Great promoted settlement, especially of his desolated Silesian prize, drawing a quarter-million colonists before his reign ended in 1786. From 1760 to 1803, at least 100,000 pioneers made their way to Hungary, doubling the number of its German immigrants. Still others departed for more distant territories as the borders of the Ottoman Empire were rolled farther back. In the 1760s, Catherine the Great attracted 27,000 German settlers to the Volga, and a generation later welcomed 10,000 Mennonites to the Crimea. Still more Germans settled in Russian Poland. On these frontiers, where land abounded, youths entered into marriage easily and produced large families—just as Malthus predicted.

Similar abundance awaited in the United States, which drew an even larger number of immigrants in the following century, one million in the 1850s alone. (See Table 9.2.) In a tempo that paused only for the Civil War and economic recessions, America skimmed off wave after wave of the population growth generated by German villages and towns. Graphs of local population totals that had arced upward for a century before 1850 thereafter resembled saw-teeth, repeatedly rising from natural increase only to fall back as batches of emigrants departed. Even averaged across wider expanses, the number of exits remained substantial, often hitting more than one percent per year, sustained over decades.[44] Millions of Germans made their way to Antwerp and LeHavre, and later to Bremen and Hamburg, whence they embarked for the New World. Five million stayed there permanently.

Table 9.2 Emigrants from Germany, 1816–1914

Years	Thousands of people
1816–1819	25
1820–1824	10
1825–1829	13
1830–1834	51
1835–1839	94
1840–1844	111
1845–1849	308
1850–1854	728
1855–1859	372
1860–1864	226
1865–1869	543
1870–1874	485
1875–1879	143
1880–1884	864
1885–1889	498
1890–1894	462
1895–1899	142
1900–1904	141
1905–1909	136
1910–1914	104

Based on Peter Marschalck, *Deutsche Überseewanderung im 19. Jahrhundert* (Stuttgart: Klett, 1973), 35–37, in turn following Wilhelm Mönckmeier and Friedrich Burgdörfer.

American census records of place of birth make it possible to determine regional variations in emigration rates. In 1871 ten districts of the new German Empire had lost one-tenth or more of their natives to the United States.[45] Most belonged to a belt in the southwest: Karlsruhe, Mannheim, and Freiburg in Baden, the Schwarzwaldkreis in Württemberg, Sigmaringen, the Palatinate, and Trier. All gave easy access to the Rhine River, as did the other three districts of high emigration: Oberhessen, Minden, and Osnabrück. The variety of inheritance customs and religions in these districts left no obvious match between such characteristics and emigration.

Nor, contrary to vulgar interpretations of Malthus, was emigration directly linked to fertility or to population density. Migration was not a matter of scraping off the excrescence of biologically uniform reproduction. Rather, the local peculiarities and individual calculations that had long made the German realm a patchwork continued to operate. Nineteenth-century emigration was high where weaving and other by-employments had become prominent in the 1700s, and for the same Malthusian reasons.[46] The ranks of the emigrants bulged with disproportionate numbers of the usual suspects: female servants, journeymen, indebted families, engaged couples with enough money to pay for their transport but not enough to meet the property qualification, and the like.

As in the eighteenth-century drive to the east, connections between old and new homelands remained much closer than the vast intermediate expanses on the map might suggest. Migrants did not move at random, but followed paths blazed by relatives and neighbors. Over time, this chain migration transplanted clusters of houses and even whole neighborhoods. Agents did a roaring business, returning over and over to the same endpoints of transcontinental networks. Malthus would not have been surprised. The 'habit of emigration,' he had written, can arise from 'three or four very successful emigrations' giving 'a spirit of enterprise to a whole village.'[47]

In such an atmosphere, families rapidly worked out and shared practical strategies for getting around legal obstacles. If officials had to certify that a young man's motive for departing was not dodging the draft, it was easy enough to be circumspect in interviews. Simply sending his sisters ahead, who could write back to report that jobs were to be had, provided a convincing cover story—precisely because it was part of the truth.

To be sure, the state was hardly powerless, and made its own contributions to emigration in the nineteenth century. The revolutions of 1848–1849 persuaded governments to reverse their previous policy of tying those without property to definite addresses. In the 1850s they deported political activists and encouraged the departure of dangerous classes susceptible to proletarianization and radicalization. Between 1851 and 1855, the progressive southwest, namely Baden, Württemberg, and the Palatinate, bade farewell to over 10 percent of its population, up from just 2 percent in 1841–1845.[48] Solid taxpayers happily joined in removing undesired elements. Seeing a chance to reduce welfare payments in future generations, municipalities underwrote the travel costs of unwed mothers and their illegitimate children.

The calculations of all concerned altered somewhat with the creation of the German Empire of 1871. On the one hand, domestic free trade permitted any German citizen to settle anywhere within the Reich, to wed and to take up any profession there, constrained only by economic forces—now including expanding industry. Germans hastened to take advantage of their new opportunities, crowding into cities and raising their production even faster than their numbers. On the other hand, Otto von Bismarck's neo-mercantilist program of protectionism and social insurance, initiated from 1878 to 1884, discouraged movement beyond the borders of Imperial Germany. Those borders hardened as Germans were freed from the land, but bound to the nation state. The 1880s also brought more rigorous exclusion of eastern Jews and Catholics from gaining naturalization in Prussia through marriage. In much the same way, the onrush of voluntary birth control combined in the twentieth century with eugenics, as the German state once more attempted to do from above what others had done from below.

However, before that, throughout the eighteenth and nineteenth centuries, the Malthusian system, including migration as an essential component, was in full swing. When it did give way among Germans, it was supplemented, rather than supplanted. The new elements came from abroad, from the industrial revolution and the contraceptive revolution that Britons and French, respectively, had undertaken a century earlier. In both cases, the new Germany took up the foreign innovations with a vengeance. Economically, it accelerated to overtake Britain in heavy industry by 1900. Demographically, it accelerated to plummet below France in birth rates by the 1920s.

These developments were superimposed on an essentially Malthusian society. A few German couples had taken up family limitation early in the 1800s, but their isolated efforts proved insufficient to reduce aggregate birth rates in any noticeable way. Not until 1888 did overall German marital fertility drop by 10 percent, and not one district posted such a sustained decline before 1879.[49] These portents were misread by contemporaries steeped in Malthusianism. Reporting falling birth rates in the 1870s and 1880s, the Baden Statistical Bureau year after year persisted in attributing them to a cyclical fall-off in weddings, which the Bureau confidently predicted should reverse in time.[50] For the statisticians, as for Germans as a whole over the preceding century, there was no escaping Malthus.

NOTES

1. Anthony Wrigley and David Souden (eds), *The Works of Thomas Robert Malthus*, Vol. 1 (London: Pickering, 1986), 119.
2. Alan Macfarlane, *The Savage Wars of Peace: England, Japan, and the Malthusian Trap* (New York: Palgrave Macmillan, 2003).
3. Klaus Bade, *Migration in European History* (Malden: Blackwell, 2003), 39.
4. Richard Nelson, 'A Theory of the Low-level Equilibrium Trap in Underdeveloped Economies,' *American Economic Review* 46 (1956), 894–908.
5. Julian Simon, 'There is no low-level fertility and development trap,' *Population Studies* 34 (1980), 476–486.

6. Samuel Preston, 'The Changing Relation between Mortality and Level of Economic Development,' *Population Studies* 29 (1975), 241.

7. Ester Boserup, *The Conditions of Agricultural Growth* (Chicago: University of Chicago Press, 1965). Compare Jan de Vries, *The Industrious Revolution: Consumer Behavior and the Household Economy, 1650 to the Present* (Cambridge: Cambridge University Press, 2008).

8. Reprinted with comparisons to subsequent editions through 1826 as volumes two and three of Anthony Wrigley and David Souden (eds), *The Works of Thomas Robert Malthus* (London: Pickering, 1986).

9. Compare *Works of Malthus*, I, 56.

10. *Works of Malthus*, III, 486.

11. *Works of Malthus*, II, 14–15.

12. *Works of Malthus*, II, 196.

13. John Hajnal, 'European Marriage Patterns in Perspective,' in David Glass and David Eversley (eds), *Population in History* (London: Arnold, 1965), 101–143.

14. Ernest Benz, *Fertility, Wealth, and Politics in Three Southwest German Villages 1650–1900* (Boston: Humanities Press, 1999), 69–72.

15. *Works of Malthus*, I, 27. Compare *Works of Malthus*, II, 236–238.

16. *Works of Malthus*, I, 57 and 119.

17. *Works of Malthus*, II, 195.

18. For death rates, see Arthur Imhof (ed.), *Lebenserwartungen in Deutschland, Norwegen und Schweden im 19. und 20. Jahrhundert* (Berlin: Akademie Verlag, 1994).

19. David Levine, *Reproducing Families: The Political Economy of English Population History* (Cambridge: Cambridge University Press, 1987), 68–72 and 137–141.

20. *Works of Malthus*, II, 201.

21. Edward Shorter, 'Middle-Class Anxiety in the German Revolution of 1848,' *Journal of Social History*, 2 (1969), 200–205.

22. *Works of Malthus*, III, 515–517.

23. John Knodel, 'Law, Marriage, and Illegitimacy in Nineteenth Century Germany,' *Population Studies* 20 (1967), 279–294.

24. John Knodel, *Demographic behavior in the Past: A study of Fourteen German Village Populations in the Eighteenth and Nineteenth Centuries* (Cambridge: Cambridge University Press, 1988), 44–53, 275–280, 362–367, 542–549.

25. Benz, *Three*, 113–114.

26. Sheilagh Ogilvie, 'Proto-industrialization in Germany,' Ulrich Pfister, 'Proto-industrialization in Switzerland,' Markus Cerman, 'Proto-industrial development in Austria,' and Milan Myska, 'Proto-industrialization in Bohemia, Moravia, and Silesia,' all in Sheilagh Ogilvie and Markus Cerman (eds), *European proto-industrialization* (Cambridge: Cambridge University Press, 1996), 118–136, 137–154, 171–187, and 188–207, respectively.

27. Volkmar Weiss, *Bevölkerung und soziale Mobilität: Sachsen 1550–1800* (Berlin: Akademie Verlag, 1993).

28. Friedrich Engels, 'The Condition of the Working Class in England,' in *Marx Engels Collected Works*, vol. 4 (New York: International Publishers, 1975), 307–310.

29. Mark Elvin, *The Pattern of the Chinese Past* (Stanford: Stanford University Press, 1973), 298–316.

30. Clifford Geertz, *Agricultural Involution: The Processes of Ecological Change in Indonesia* (Berkeley: University of California Press, 1963).

31. David Sabean, *Property, Production, and Family in Neckarhausen, 1700-1870* (Cambridge: University of California Press, 1990), 52–65 and 146–156.

32. Contrast John Komlos, 'The Industrial Revolution as the Escape from the Malthusian Trap,' *Journal of European Economic History* 29 (2000), 307–331.

33. John Hajnal, 'Two Kinds of Pre-Industrial Household Formation System,' *Population and Development Review* 8 (1982), 449–494.

34. *Works of Malthus*, II, 67–68.

35. *Works of Malthus*, II, 208.

36. *Works of Malthus*, II, 213.

37. *Works of Malthus*, II, 199.

38. Allan Sharlin, 'Natural Decrease in Early Modern Cities: A Reconsideration,' *Past and Present* 79 (May 1978), 126–138.

39. *Works of Malthus*, II, 193. Compare Jan Lucassen, *Migrant Labour in Europe 1600-1900: The Drift to the North Sea* (London: Croom Helm, 1987).

40. Steve Hochstadt, *Mobility and Modernity: Migration in Germany 1820-1989* (Ann Arbor: University of Michigan Press, 1999), 68, 78, 117.

41. Ibid. See also John Brown, Timothy Guinnane, and Marion Lupprian, 'The Munich *Polizeimeldebögen* as a Source for Quantitative History,' *Historical Methods* 26 (1993), 101–118.

42. Eli Nathans, *The Politics of Citizenship in Germany: Ethnicity, Utility, and Nationalism* (Oxford: Berg, 2004).

43. Hans Fenske, 'International Migration: Germany in the Eighteenth Century,' *Central European History* 13 (1980), 332–347.

44. Walter Kamphoefner, *The Westfalians: From Germany to Missouri* (Princeton: Princeton University Press, 1987), 15.

45. Kamphoefner, *Westfalians*, 208.

46. Kampfhoefner, *Westfalians*, 23. Hochstadt, *Mobility*, 71, 184.

47. *Works of Malthus*, II, 208.

48. Peter Marschalck, *Deutsche Überseewanderung im 19. Jahrhundert* (Stuttgart: Klett, 1973), 104.

49. Ansley Coale and Roy Treadway, 'A Summary of the Changing Distribution of Overall Fertility, Marital Fertility, and the Proportion Married in the Provinces of Europe,' in Ansley Coale and Susan Watkins (eds), *The Decline of Fertility in Europe* (Princeton: Princeton University Press, 1986), 38. Compare John Knodel, *The Decline of Fertility in Germany, 1871-1939* (Princeton: Princeton University Press, 1974), 62, which dates the 10% decline for all Germany to 1895.

50. 'Die Bewegung der Bevölkerung im Jahre 1884,' *Statistische Mittheilungen über das Grossherzogthum Baden*, IV (1884–1885), 294. Compare similar statements for the surrounding years.

BIBLIOGRAPHY

BADE, KLAUS, *Migration in European History* (Malden: Blackwell, 2003).

DE VRIES, JAN, *The Industrious Revolution: Consumer Behavior and the Household Economy, 1650 to the Present* (Cambridge: Cambridge University Press, 2008).

FENSKE, HANS, 'International Migration: Germany in the Eighteenth Century,' *Central European History* 13 (1980), 332–347.

HOCHSTADT, STEVE, *Mobility and Modernity: Migration in Germany 1820–1989* (Ann Arbor: University of Michigan Press, 1999).

IMHOF, ARTHUR (ed.), *Lebenserwartungen in Deutschland, Norwegen und Schweden im 19. und 20. Jahrhundert* (Berlin: Akademie Verlag, 1994).

JACKSON, JAMES, *Migration and Urbanization in the Ruhr Valley 1821–1914* (Boston: Humanities Press, 1997).

KAMPFHOEFNER, WALTER, *The Westfalians: From Germany to Missouri* (Princeton: Princeton University Press, 1987).

KNODEL, JOHN, 'Law, Marriage, and Illegitimacy in Nineteenth Century Germany,' *Population Studies* 20 (1967), 279–294.

—— *Demographic Behavior in the Past: A Study of Fourteen German Village Populations in the Eighteenth and Nineteenth Centuries* (Cambridge: Cambridge Univertsity Press, 1988).

LUCASSEN, JAN, *Migrant Labour in Europe 1600–1900: The Drift to the North Sea* (London: Croom Helm, 1987).

MACFARLANE, ALAN, *The Savage Wars of Peace: England, Japan, and the Malthusian Trap* (New York: Palgrave Macmillan, 2003).

MOCH, LESLIE PAGE, *Moving Europeans: Migration in Western Europe since 1650* (Bloomington: University of Indiana Press, 2003).

OGILVIE, SHEILAGH and MARKUS CERMAN (eds), *European Proto-Industrialization* (Cambridge: Cambridge University Press, 1996).

SABEAN, DAVID, *Property, production, and family in Neckarhausen, 1700–1870* (Cambridge: Cambridge University Press, 1990).

WRIGLEY, ANTHONY and DAVID SOUDEN (eds), *The Works of Thomas Robert Malthus* (London: Pickering, 1986).

CHAPTER 10

PROTESTANTS, CATHOLICS, AND JEWS, 1760–1871: ENLIGHTENMENT, EMANCIPATION, NEW FORMS OF PIETY

GEORGE S. WILLIAMSON

'No love and no hate is stronger than that which is grounded in religion, or in which religion is intermixed. Germany has had terrible experiences of this.' Friedrich Karl von Moser's lament in *On the German National Spirit* (1765) is vivid testimony to the fact that, from the beginning, the German question was a question of religion. According to Moser, the notion of a 'Catholic' Germany opposing a 'Protestant' Germany was so deeply embedded that even two quite open-minded individuals, if they were of differing confessions, had to overcome a 'strongly rooted revulsion' in order to associate with each other.[1] Yet while Moser spoke only of Catholics and Protestants, the confessional divide was complicated by a third presence: Germany's Jewish population, which, despite its small numbers, figured largely in the imaginary of all Christian communities. For this reason, any account of the religious history of Germany must necessarily be 'triconfessional' in its approach, taking into account the experiences of Protestants, Catholics, and Jews, while exploring the dialectical relationships among them.

This chapter examines some of the major shifts in German religious life in the eighteenth and nineteenth centuries. Until quite recently, scholarship tended to present religion in this era as first accommodating, then resisting, and ultimately succumbing to the forces of modernity. Yet, as Jonathan Sheehan writes, 'religion has never been left behind, either personally or institutionally. Instead it has been continually remade and given new forms and meanings over time.'[2] Indeed, while the social, cultural, and political shifts of the *Sattelzeit* led to the demise of certain religious formations, they gave rise to (and were, in turn, influenced by) new modes of piety and new forms of religious affiliation. This was very much a European-wide process, shaped by movements and institutions that were international and even transnational in nature. In Germany, however, these transformations tended to be interpreted through the lens of confessional identity, a situation that reinforced antagonisms among Protestants, Catholics, and Jews while obscuring the degree to which theirs was, in fact, a 'shared history.'[3]

10.1 The religious landscape before 1760

For most of the eighteenth century, the religious map of the Holy Roman Empire looked much as it had at the conclusion of the Thirty Years War. A line of Protestant territories stretched from Württemberg in the southwest through Franconia, Thuringia, and Saxony and up to a solidly Protestant northern region formed by the Kingdoms of Prussia and Hanover and the Duchy of Mecklenburg. This Protestant *bloc* was broken up by the ecclesiastical territories that made up the *Reichskirche*, which included, in the west, the archbishoprics of Trier and Cologne and the bishoprics of Münster and Paderborn, and, toward the center, the archbishopric of Mainz and the bishopric of Würzburg.[4] The confessional allegiances of dozens of smaller territories further complicated this picture, as did the existence of religious minorities in most of the larger territories. In many cases, Protestant towns were surrounded by Catholic countryside, a religious difference that would have been immediately perceptible to a traveler thanks to contrasting styles of architecture, monuments, and dress.[5]

The Peace of Westphalia had recognized the existence of three confessions in the Holy Roman Empire: Lutheran, Calvinist (or 'Reformed'), and Catholic. While it allowed rulers to dictate the dominant religion in their territories, it prevented them from forcing members of other confessions to convert or emigrate. According to the Westphalian system, adherents of the dominant religion had the right to worship in churches with spires and bells, and to take part in public processions, holidays, and the like. But members of confessional communities that had owned property and worshipped publicly before the 'normal year' of 1624 retained the right to worship in chapels, while members of confessions that had not been established in 1624 were allowed to worship in their homes.[6] To be sure, these religious minorities faced all manner of hardships: they were often ineligible for full citizenship, they were typically excluded from town and territorial government, and they were usually not admitted to the guilds. Moreover this system provided no relief to members of non-recognized Christian sects, such as Anabaptists, or to non-Christians, notably Jews, who were forced to negotiate cash payments for the right to reside on the margins of individual towns and territories. Their existence remained precarious, subject to the whims of state authorities and periodic outbreaks of anti-Jewish violence. Nonetheless, the Peace of Westphalia introduced the principle of parity between the Christian confessions, which was reflected in the legal institutions and governing spirit of the Reich. As a result, the Holy Roman Empire exhibited a degree of religious co-existence that, in the seventeenth and eighteenth centuries at least, would have been unimaginable in either Great Britain or France.[7]

The rise of absolutism would challenge the equilibrium of the Empire while under-mining the premises of the confessional state. In Brandenburg-Prussia, where the Calvinist Hohenzollerns ruled over a largely Lutheran population, a form of absolutism emerged that was predicated not on confessional uniformity, but rather on what has been aptly described as a 'multireligious estate society.'[8] Beginning in the 1680s, Prussian rulers opened their borders to persecuted religious minorities (Huguenots from France, Socinians from Poland). In addition, they took steps to curtail the power and authority of Lutheran Orthodoxy, whose adherents controlled the church consistories and there-fore Protestant religious life in most of Prussia. This was accomplished in part through state sponsorship of Pietism, a revival movement within Lutheranism that deempha-sized doctrinal differences among Protestants in favor of what it termed 'practical Christianity' and an emphasis on a personal experience of rebirth and renewal. By the early eighteenth century, Pietism had emerged as the *de facto* state religion of Prussia. In Württemberg, by contrast, Pietism served to anchor the power of the territorial estates against the absolutist pretensions of the ruling dynasty (which became Catholic in 1733). Meanwhile, other Pietist communities operated outside the control of any single ruler or territorial government. Over the course of the eighteenth century, the Moravian Breth-ren, based in the Saxon village of Herrnhut, would develop a global missionary network that Gisela Mettele has described as an 'imagined community beyond the nation.'[9]

The retreat from militant confessionalism was more gradual in the Catholic terri-tories, especially those belonging to the Habsburg monarchy.[10] Baroque Catholicism, with its dense web of festivals, processions, and pilgrimages, continued to dominate religious life in Catholic Germany well into the eighteenth century. These practices were supported by the Jesuit and Capuchin orders and by the rulers of Bavaria and Austria, who sought to promote them through the examples of their own piety known, respectively, as *Pietas Bavarica* and *Pietas Austriaca*. By the mid-eighteenth century, however, these practices were being met with increasing skepticism from urban elites, many of whom favored a simpler, more private form of Christianity, by Catholic rulers, who saw the proliferation of religious holidays as extravagant and wasteful, and by older religious orders like the Augustinians and Benedictines, which resented the Jesuits' monopoly over education and public piety. Contributing to this critical mood was the growing influence of Jansenism, a Catholic theological movement that rejected the teaching methods and moral philosophy of the Jesuits and promoted a religiosity centered around the parish clergy. This shifting stance among both educated elites and secular rulers toward Baroque piety would be a crucial precondition for the spread of enlightened ideas in Catholic Germany and paralleled developments in the eighteenth century among both Protestants and Jews.

10.2 ENLIGHTENMENT

For many years, historians treated the *Aufklärung* as an early, but crucial indication of Germany's deviation from Western norms. In comparison with the French Enlightenment of Diderot and Voltaire, it was argued, German (Protestant) *Aufklärer* were overly confident in the state and much too favorable to organized religion. Yet, as Roy Porter has argued, it was the *philosophes'* unyielding hostility to the churches and the absence in France of a state-sponsored project of enlightened reform that was the true exception in Europe.[11] By contrast, German Enlightenment thought, with its orientation to a reforming state and reformable religious institutions, paralleled trends elsewhere in Western Europe. In David Sorkin's view, this 'religious enlightenment' was not only more moderate than its French counterpart, but also more tolerant. Yet the *Aufklärung* was not without its immoderate impulses. Indeed, the decade before the French Revolution witnessed a radicalization of theological debate in Germany, which would contribute in turn to an intensification of Protestant-Catholic and Jewish-Christian polemics.

From the very beginning, the *Aufklärung* was bound up in religious concerns and contexts, as can be seen in the case of the Prussia. The University of Halle, founded in 1694 to serve as the intellectual bastion of Pietism, soon became home to some of the key figures in the early Protestant Enlightenment, including the jurist Christian Thomasius, the philosopher Christian Wolff, and the theologian Siegmund Jacob Baumgarten. Halle Pietism and the early Enlightenment shared a common mission, which was the 'regeneration' of the individual and of civil society, and neither questioned that Christianity (rightly understood) would be central to that process. Indeed, as Christopher Clark notes, there was considerable continuity between some of the charitable missions launched at Halle (an orphanage, a spinning house to employ the poor) and the broader enlightenment project of unleashing the productive energies of civil society for the benefit of the state. These ideas also undergirded Halle's mission to the Jews (founded 1728): not only were Jews' souls to be won for Christ, but their bodies were to be engaged in socially useful activity, rather than the begging and petty trade that were seen by most Christians as typically Jewish. Such missionary efforts, it should be noted, were predicated on persuasion, rather than compulsion. Indeed, while Baumgarten hoped for the eventual conversion of the Jews, he argued for freedom of conscience as a political principle and authored several opinions defending Jews against spurious accusations of wrongdoing.[12]

By the 1760s, the fortunes of Pietism were in decline and the Neologists had emerged as the dominant school of theology in Prussia. Although many of the Neologists were students of Baumgarten, they found it more and more difficult to sustain his delicate balance between history and scripture, revelation and reason, church and civil society. Johann Salomo Semler, the most influential of the Neologists, drew a sharp distinction between 'church religion,' which referred to the inherited dogmas and rituals of the

Christian churches, and 'private religion,' which was essentially a matter of personal conviction. By 'private religion,' Semler did not mean a purely natural theology or deism (which was condemned by all but the most radical *Aufklärer*), but rather a practical Christian morality grounded in faith in the word of God. Nonetheless, his stance suggested a growing tension between ecclesiastical doctrine and individual belief, as well as between the outward biblical form of revelation and its inner moral core, which could only be discovered through the methods of historical-critical exegesis.

The principles of Semler's theology resonated within enlightened circles because they reflected the experiences of an educated elite that, although it still considered itself Christian, no longer felt beholden to either church doctrine or the churches themselves. The rise of a literary public sphere and the emergence of new forms of sociability in the late eighteenth century have been well documented. These trends coincided with a growing reluctance on the part of state magistrates to enforce the older system of church discipline, which mandated fines and punishments for missing Sunday services or other offenses to morality and decency. Lucian Hölscher cites statistics suggesting that in northern Protestant cities like Hanover and Berlin rates of church attendance had begun to fall markedly in the last third of the eighteenth century.[13] All of this contributed to a decline in the social prestige of the Protestant pastorate, which already faced a rather precarious economic existence. Some clergymen responded by trying to redefine their vocation: in *On the Usefulness of the Preaching Office* (1772), the Neologist J. J. Spalding defended the clergy as 'teachers of virtue' and promoters of civic welfare in an attempt to align their mission with that of a reforming state. Others promoted new hymnals and liturgies that were designed to reflect the values of a purified, practical Christianity. In the end, however, the long-term trend was toward a split within Protestantism: while educated urban elites (especially men) distanced themselves from formal church life, parishioners in smaller towns and villages continued to attend services, and to resist the imposition of enlightened reforms.

A parallel process took place among German Jews. The *Haskalah* originated in the early eighteenth century as a reform movement within orthodox Judaism whose goal was to revitalize rabbinic scholarship through contact with European philosophy and science.[14] The spread of the *Haskalah* was facilitated, paradoxically, by the decline in the prestige and authority of the rabbis and the rise of a new Jewish mercantile elite. In Prussia, Frederick the Great stripped the rabbis of their traditional jurisdiction over civil affairs and subordinated the Jewish community to the Prussian state. This created an opening, however, for the career of Moses Mendelssohn, who was destitute and poor when he arrived in Berlin in 1743 but in twenty years had established himself as an intellectual of European stature. Mendelssohn benefited, on the one hand, from the patronage of a handful of wealthy Jewish merchants who had attained the coveted status of 'protected Jew.' At the same time, his extensive knowledge of European philosophy granted him entrée into the circle of local *Aufklärer*, which included Friedrich Nicolai and Gotthold Ephraim Lessing.

In his religious writings, Mendelssohn attempted to rejuvenate Judaism by bringing it into contact with the philosophies of Leibniz and Wolff, who had suggested the compatibility between reason and religion. In this regard, he saw himself less as a modernizer than as a scholar recapturing a lost world of medieval exegesis. Mendelssohn insisted repeatedly on the historical accuracy of the Bible, the continued validity of Jewish law, and the Jews' status as a chosen people. At the same time, he argued against gentile critics that Judaism was not merely compatible with an enlightened ideal of religion but, in fact, more compatible than Christianity. Although these types of polemics were conducted in German, most of Mendelssohn's publications were in Hebrew. Indeed, one of his major goals was to establish a Hebrew-language public sphere, which he saw as key to the revitalization of Judaism. This project would be pursued by the young men who followed Mendelssohn to Berlin in the hopes of becoming Jewish literati themselves. In many cases, they would go well beyond Mendelssohn in their accommodations to natural religion. But while this has sometimes been construed as a capitulation to gentile culture, it can also be seen as a forceful bid for the civic rights that even the most enlightened Jews were still denied.[15]

In comparison to the Protestant and Jewish Enlightenments, the Catholic *Aufklärung* has remained something of a stepchild of historiography, not least because of the long-standing assumption among both Catholic and non-Catholic scholars that Catholicism and Enlightenment were fundamentally incompatible. Yet the case of Habsburg Austria demonstrates that reform absolutists could draw considerable support from trends within Catholic theology. Maria Theresa, who initiated many of the reforms associated with 'Josephinism,' was deeply influenced by Jansenism, a theological movement whose emphasis on moral purity and pastoral care offered an alternative to the Jesuits' emphasis on Baroque display and obedience to papal authority. During her reign, Maria Theresa slashed the number of religious holidays and pilgrimages, pushed Austrian Catholicism toward a Gallican model of church-state relations, and ended the Jesuit monopoly over theological education. Joseph II, while less orthodox than his mother, built on her reforms, while accelerating their pace: during the ten years of his reign, he secularized some 800 Catholic monasteries and religious foundations, forbade contact between Austrian bishops and the papal curia, and moved clerical education to state-supervised seminaries. In addition, he issued a series of toleration patents that granted greater religious freedoms to Jews, Protestants, and Greek Orthodox in the Habsburg lands. Although no other German prince went as far as Joseph II on the question of toleration, several Catholic rulers (most notably the electors of Bavaria) adopted various aspects of the Austrian reformist agenda, including scaling back holidays and pilgrimages, dissolving and seizing the assets of monasteries, and asserting control over bishops and clergy in their territories.

While these measures sparked resistance in many quarters, they found strong backing among educated elites, particularly those influenced by Wolffian philosophy, which many Catholics encountered in Protestant universities and which, by the 1740s, had begun to be incorporated into the curricula of some Austrian universities.[16] Supporters of the Enlightenment argued that these types of reforms were necessary in order to purify the faith, to demonstrate the coincidence between reason and religion, and to bridge the divide between clergy and laity. According to Joseph von

Eybel, a canon lawyer and an outspoken supporter of Joseph's reforms, 'right-thinking pastors are concerned to give their people a clear, comprehensible, and congenial instruction that is genuine and distinct, that pertains only to actual doctrines of belief and morality, and that are necessary for a good Christian and a good subject to know.'[17] To this end, a number of clergy proposed German-language hymnals and ritual books and, like their Protestant counterparts, promoted the sermon as a medium of moral instruction. Other Catholics argued along more practical lines, insisting that these measures were necessary to close the already perceptible gap in education and wealth between Catholic and Protestant areas of the Reich. For many observers, future prosperity entailed dealing with what appeared to be a bloated, unproductive, and ungovernable monastic system. In 1783, the ex-Benedictine Adolf Winkopp published *On the Civil and Spiritual Improvement of Monasticism* (1783), whose title linked the cause of monastic reform to Christian Wilhelm Dohm's influential tract on the 'civic improvement' of Jews.[18] In both cases, Winkopp suggested, it was a matter of simultaneously emancipating and reforming the behavior of a religious minority whose current practices were harmful to the welfare of society as a whole.

Although an older historiography tended to posit an axiomatic connection between the *Aufklärung* and religious toleration, recent scholarship has complicated that picture somewhat. For one thing, historians have emphasized the degree to which a framework for limited religious toleration was already built into the Westphalian settlement, even if its implementation remained scattered and incomplete. Hamburg, a predominantly Lutheran city with a reputation for tolerance, was the site of repeated efforts over the eighteenth century to extend religious rights to Catholics and Calvinists, yet the 'Toleranz-System' adopted in 1785 merely codified a right of 'private worship' without granting political rights to either group. According to Joachim Whaley, 'All that the "party of humanity" achieved in Hamburg, as elsewhere in Germany, was the clarification and limited implementation of the guidelines laid down in 1648. For that was all that trade and commerce, and Christian charity, demanded of magistrates who were neither philosophers nor utopian reformers.'[19]

In addition, however, recent work on the Enlightenment has highlighted the degree to which even prominent *Aufklärer* embraced forms of universalism that excluded or downgraded members of other religions or races. These exclusionary tendencies came to the fore during the 1780s, at a time when the more moderate impulses of the mid-century had given way to a radical and polarizing 'late enlightenment.' Wolfgang Altgeld has shown, for example, that the radicalism of some *Aufklärer* led a number of Catholics and more conservative Lutherans to contemplate a reunion of the confessions on a common basis of religious orthodoxy. These moves incited Friedrich Nicolai and other prominent figures in the Berlin Enlightenment to launch a series of attacks against the supposed backwardness, ignorance, and superstition of the Catholic religion, while accusing Protestants interested in accommodation with the Church of 'Crypto-Catholicism.'[20] Yet it was Nicolai's press that published Dohm's *On the Civic Improvement of the Jews* (1781), which went well beyond earlier calls for religious toleration to argue for granting full civic rights to Prussia's Jews.

In his treatise, Christian Wilhelm Dohm blamed the present 'depravity' of the Jews on the disabilities they had suffered over the years. By granting them the same rights enjoyed by other subjects, he argued, they would become 'happier, better people, more useful members of society.'[21] But although Dohm was prepared to admit Jews directly into civil society without requiring their conversion to Christianity, his arguments reveal a striking continuity with those of the Pietist mission to the Jews. This is not wholly surprising, since both Dohm and the missionaries saw their goal as not merely the integration, but also the regeneration of the Jews. The difference, Jonathan Hess has argued, was Dohm's adherence to a colonialist model of state-building.[22] By accepting Jews as candidates for internal colonization and allowing them to become full citizens engaged in useful (i.e. manual) occupations, Prussia would enable Jews to revitalize their body and spirit, while bringing about a transformation of Judaism into a fully rational religion.

It was precisely this transformation that the rationalist theologian Johann David Michaelis declared impossible. Drawing on his expertise in biblical history, Michaelis argued that Jews were physically unfit for military service and thus could never become full citizens. Instead, he proposed that they be deported to one of the West Indian sugar islands, where they would work alongside African slaves. It was left to Moses Mendelssohn to argue against both Dohm and Michaelis that Jews were not in need of 'civic improvement' and that Judaism did not need to be Christianized. Instead, Judaism contained within its core a rational religion that, in the Noachian laws, respected the rights of other faiths. Mendelssohn's argument went largely unheard, however, and even Dohm's views were embraced by only a small minority of *Aufklärer*, most of whom preferred that Jews demonstrate their capacity for citizenship before being granted civil rights. In the end, it was the logic of state-building, rather than the preponderance of enlightened opinion, that would make Jewish emancipation a reality in Germany.

10.3 THE FRENCH REVOLUTION
AND ITS IMPACT

The spectacle of the French Revolution evoked both sympathy and horror among observers in Germany, not least because of its impact on religious life. Many *Aufklärer* approved of the attempt by the National Assembly to remake the Catholic Church in its own image.[23] A radical few even approved the Jacobins' policy of 'dechristianization,' which led to the closing of churches, the imprisonment and execution of refractory clergy, and the institution of a new set of religious cults dedicated to liberty, reason, and other revolutionary virtues. Yet the vast majority condemned Jacobin excesses, with Protestants predictably linking them to Catholic 'corruption' and Catholics tracing them to the Protestant spirit of 'rebellion.' Among religious conservatives, in particular, the Revolution's campaigns against the Church, the monarchy, and the nobility stirred up anxieties that bordered on the apocalyptic. In his best-selling novel *Heimweh* (1794–1796), for example, the Pietist writer Johann Heinrich Jung-Stilling represented France as a pregnant woman giving birth to the Antichrist.[24]

Such fears were, in a sense, realized when revolutionary armies launched a series of invasions into German territory. France's conquest and subsequent annexation of the left bank of the Rhine resulted in the imposition of the Directory government's religious policies in the Rhineland. These included the abolition of tithes, the banning of religious processions and pilgrimages, the introduction of compulsory civil marriage, and the removal of civil disabilities against religious minorities, such as those against Protestants in majority Catholic cities like Cologne and Münster.[25] That religious toleration should also include civic equality for Jews was not universally agreed upon, even amongst the French revolutionaries, and came into effect only in 1791, thanks in part to the reception of Dohm's ideas among revolutionaries like Mirabeau and Henri Grégoire. In light of this, the introduction of Jewish emancipation into the Rhineland by French authorities, along with subsequent moves toward Jewish emancipation in Württemberg (1807), Baden (1809), Frankfurt am Main (1811), Prussia (1812), and Bavaria (1813), represents a striking example of the circulation of political ideas between Germany and France in this era.

The French takeover of the Rhineland initiated a years-long process of territorial realignment in Germany that would lead to the destruction of the *Reichskirche*. This outcome was effected through the *Reichsdeputationshauptschluss* (1803), which resulted in the 'secularization' of three archbishoprics (Mainz, Trier, and Cologne), 19 bishoprics, and 44 abbeys, and the annexation of their territory by surrounding dynastic principalities, as well as the 'mediatization' of hundreds of smaller (non-ecclesiastical) imperial territories. Secularization also entailed the dissolution of dozens of Catholic monasteries and charitable foundations, resulting in the dispersal of their artworks and the elimination of an extensive network of church-sponsored welfare. In the long run, the elimination of the ecclesiastical territories, the disappearance of hundreds of other imperial territories, and the final collapse of the Holy Roman Empire in 1806 brought about an intensified intermingling of the confessions in Germany. For example, Catholics who had resided in the former Archbishopric of Cologne or in the Bishopric of Speyer now found themselves subject to Protestant rulers in Prussia and Baden, while Protestants in Franconia and the Palatinate were now subjects of the Bavarian crown.

In the short term, however, the chaos and upheaval of the revolutionary and Napoleonic wars sparked an intense religious reaction among the affected populations in Germany. As Ute Planert has noted, the sheer unpredictability of war served as a stark reminder of the old theological dictum that humans are not the masters of their own destinies. As a result, the 1790s witnessed an upsurge in popular practices designed to invoke divine protection from marauding armies or to offer thanks for disaster averted. Catholic communities restored formerly banned pilgrimages and religious holidays (often in defiance of government and church authorities) and dedicated votive images depicting the Virgin Mary saving their villages from destruction. Meanwhile,

Württemberg Pietists saw the wars as evidence that the millennium was at hand: in their eyes, the phonetic similarity of Napoleon's name to that of Apollyon the Destroyer was no accident, while Tsar Alexander bore a striking resemblance to the judge on a white horse mentioned in Revelations 11. In 1801, stirred by the ecstatic prophecies of Maria Kummer, a group of about twenty Pietists attempted to emigrate from Württemberg to the Holy Land before being turned back in Vienna by government authorities. Over the next two decades, however, thousands of Pietists would emigrate successfully from Württemberg to southern Russia, where they were driven not only by economic privation in their homeland, but also by the promise of religious freedom under Tsar Alexander.[26]

This popular religious ferment helped to shape the nationalist sentiment that took hold among the north German educated elites in the wake of Prussia's humiliating defeat in 1806. Reacting in part to the perceived irreligiosity and atheism of their French occupiers, Ernst Moritz Arndt, Johann Gottlieb Fichte, and Friedrich Schleiermacher adopted a self-conscious piety, which combined rationalist theological principles with a newfound reverence for the German *Volk*. For these Prussian nationalists, it was self-evident that a united Germany should have a single national religion and that this religion should be Protestant. 'All of Germany is the land of Protestantism,' Arndt declared famously. On this view, Catholicism was essentially an alien presence on German soil, an occupying force that needed to be expelled along with the French invaders. Indeed, Friedrich Schleiermacher called on his fellow Protestants to 'spread the Reformation to all the Germanic peoples as the form of Christianity most appropriate to them,' while leaving Catholicism to the 'Romanic peoples.' This vision of a national religion left little room for non-Protestants, leading the Hamburg publisher Friedrich Perthes to note the obvious contradiction between the Protestant nationalists' calls for unity and their vigorous attacks on Catholics and Jews.[27]

The debates about the relationship between the confessions in post-Napoleonic Germany reached a peak of intensity in 1814–1815, as the Congress of Vienna discussed the organization and founding articles of the German Confederation. Article 16 declared that differences among the 'Christian religious parties' in the lands and territories of Germany could 'not be the basis of differences in the enjoyment of civil and political rights.' Instead, confessional relations were to be governed henceforth by the principle of 'parity.' Metternich hoped to resolve the Jewish question, too, by extending the principle of civic equality to the entire German Confederation. But this effort foundered on the resistance of Frankfurt, the Hanseatic cities, and other smaller territories, which insisted on retaining control over their Jewish populations. In the end, Article 16 left it to the states to regulate their own Jewish affairs. Meanwhile, the debate over this issue inspired a series of vicious pamphlets by Protestant nationalists attacking the very possibility of Jewish citizenship. In 1819, the attempt to implement Bavaria's relatively liberal Jewish law in the recently annexed territory of Würzburg helped spark the anti-Semitic 'Hep-Hep' riots, which spread to cities and towns across Germany. There would be no return to the ghetto for Germany's Jews, but emancipation remained an elusive goal.

10.4 VARIETIES OF PIETY IN
AN AGE OF REVIVAL

One of the most distinctive features of European life in the years after 1815 was a widespread and, to some degree, spontaneous outpouring of Christian religious engagement and activity. The intellectual roots of this revival in Germany can be traced back to the 1780s, when the Pietist writings of Jung-Stilling and Johann Kaspar Lavater, and the Catholic circles around Amalie Gallitzin and Johann Michael Sailer provided a counterpoint to the *Spätaufklärung*'s rationalism and religious skepticism. Yet it was the destruction, suffering, and economic upheaval of the Napoleonic Wars, combined with the ensuing expansion of state authority over religious life that defined the basic tendencies of the revival in Germany, which was hostile to the Enlightenment and its perceived agents in the state and the church. The Catholics and Protestants who joined the revival did so out of a profound sense of the reality of evil in the world and of sin in their hearts, which could only be cleansed through the saving grace of Jesus Christ.

The Protestant 'Awakening' was part of a broader revival that gripped not only Germany, but also Switzerland, Scandinavia, the Netherlands, Great Britain, and the United States. In Germany, this took the form of a popular Pietistic movement, which drew its energies from farmers, craftsmen, traders, Moravian missionaries, and a series of wandering preachers who conveyed their message in a folksy, colloquial, and highly effective idiom.[28] In Prussia, however, the Awakening garnered considerable support from a group of aristocrats and officers who were motivated not only by religious conviction, but also by their hostility to the centralizing reforms of Stein and Hardenberg and by their anger at Friedrich Wilhelm III's forcible union of the Lutheran and Reformed Churches in 1817. Suspicious of the teachings of the official pastorate, many nobles took it on themselves to conduct revivals on their estates. Christopher Clark relates the case of Heinrich von Below, who permitted a peasant to strike him for not bowing deeply enough during prayer, but who loudly denounced the local superintendent for his rationalism and urged parishioners to stop attending his services. These activities aroused the attention of the Prussian authorities, who denounced them as a form of ecclesiastical 'Jacobinism.'[29]

Although the Protestant Awakening saw its goal as a renewal of the Lutheran churches, the decisive locus of its work was outside the regular church liturgy. Instead, the faithful gathered together for conventicles, Bible study, and 'hours of edification' that were usually organized by laypeople, but might also include sympathetic clergy. While these activities evoked the heyday of Pietism under Spener, Francke, and Zinzendorf, they were amplified and expanded through an aggressive engagement with the media and institutions of the nineteenth-century public sphere. The theological emphasis on the authority of Holy Scripture was reinforced by the availability of inexpensive copies of the Bible, which were distributed first by the British and Foreign Bible Society, and later by the two dozen or so Bible societies that sprang up across

Germany in the 1810s and 1820s. The evangelical impulse was renewed through the foundation in 1815 of the Basel Missionary Society, which trained individuals for overseas missions while providing funding and an organizational model for similar societies in Berlin, Leipzig, Bremen, and elsewhere. Pietists directed some of their missionary energies on behalf of the 'heathens in the fatherland' to the creation of poor schools, factories, workshops for the unemployed, and, most explicitly, Johann Heinrich Wichern's 'Inner Mission' (founded in 1848), which coordinated these efforts on a national scale.[30]

Among the more influential graduates of the Basel Missionary school was the theologian Ernst Wilhelm Hengstenberg, whose *Evangelische Kirchenzeitung* (founded in 1827) was dedicated to promoting Lutheran orthodoxy and attacking rationalist theology. As editor of the *EKZ*, Hengstenberg presided over a far-flung network of correspondents (including 16 in the USA) who provided tabloid-style reports designed to expose the baseness and immorality of rationalism and of individual rationalists wherever they might threaten the true faith. The *EKZ* was crucial also to the transformation of the formerly separatist Awakening into a party of Lutheran orthodoxy and political conservatism, whose sustained patronage of "right thinking clergymen" succeeded in challenging the predominance of theological liberalism in Prussia's university faculties and Protestant pastorate.[31]

The Catholic revival followed a similar path from an intellectual awakening with decidedly ecumenical tendencies to a more strictly confessional movement. Already during the Napoleonic Wars, circles of Catholic intellectuals had arisen in Münster, Landshut, and Vienna that were committed to challenging the *Aufklärung* and recovering the historical traditions of the Church. This movement was influenced by impulses from Romantic writers like Friedrich Schlegel, who helped redeem medieval art and literature from the hostile judgments of enlightened critics and who eventually embraced the Catholic Church as a bedrock of 'positive' religious truth (Schlegel would convert to Catholicism in 1808). Nonetheless, the most influential figure of the early Catholic Awakening was probably the pastoral theologian Johann Michael Sailer, who sought to overcome the limitations of enlightenment rationalism without rejecting reason itself. From his professorial chair in Landshut, Sailer supervised the training of over 1000 Catholic priests while cultivating contacts with both Catholic and Protestant intellectuals, including many close to the Awakening.

Sailer's influence was most readily felt in Bavaria, due in part to his close contact with the Crown Prince. When Ludwig I ascended to the throne in 1825, the Catholic Restoration became official policy, reversing many of the Josephinist policies of his father Maximilian I Joseph.[32] Under Ludwig, the Bavarian state relaxed some of its former restrictions on pilgrimages and confraternities, a step that conformed to the growing popular demand for such public forms of piety. Meanwhile, the collapse of the *Reichskirche* encouraged a resacralization of the priesthood, as more and more candidates entered seminary out of purely religious motives, rather than in search of a sinecure or in hopes of exercising political power. Nonetheless, as Werner Blessing notes, the extent of this Catholic Restoration remained limited to the needs of the

Bavarian monarchy, which promoted the Church only to the extent that it served as a buttress to royal authority. Nor should the reach of the Catholic revival in 1820s and 1830s be overestimated. There were numerous areas in Bavaria, the Rhineland, and elsewhere where religious indifference prevailed among large sectors of the Catholic population, often as a result of the breakdown of the traditional social order. In addition, a form of enlightened bourgeois piety held a strong appeal for many members of the urban middle classes as well as key elements of the clergy itself.[33]

Both the nature of the Catholic revival and the extent of its reach altered dramatically between 1840 and 1871. These decades coincided with the triumph in the Catholic Church of Ultramontanism, a theological and ecclesiastical tendency characterized by a strict obedience to papal authority, a revival of Neo-Thomist scholasticism, and a renewed emphasis on popular religiosity. Ultramontanist clergy organized a series of large-scale pilgrimages, typically to sites of Marian piety, which could involve hundreds of thousands of people. They also encouraged the spread of new, clerically led religious associations, many of which were oriented to the needs and interests of specific occupational groups (such as miners or weavers). At the heart of the Ultramontanist revival, however, were a series of missions, led typically by members of religious orders like the Redemptorists, the Jesuits, and Franciscans, that were intended to inspire popular devotion and more moral living among the laity. As Jonathan Sperber shows, these were major events in the life of a community, in which all work might stop for a week. 'Extraordinary scenes were commonplace: skeptics who had not been to church in decades returned to the fold; bitter personal and family quarrels were resolved; great quantities of stolen goods were restored. Religious intensity was at a fever pitch.'[34] What made the Ultramontanist revival possible was the decision of Bavaria, Prussia, and other states in the wake of the 1848 Revolution to give the Catholic clergy a free hand in church affairs and elementary education, since they were considered useful allies in the fight against subversion. Indeed, many of the revivals included an explicit political message of counter-revolution, which declared liberalism and democracy works of the devil and preached obedience to legitimate monarchs.

To Protestant critics (especially liberals), the Ultramontanist revival appeared to be the work of reactionary foreign agents sent by the Vatican to preach superstition and unquestioning obedience to the pope. But this characterization ignores the degree to which the revival tapped into a pent-up demand among German Catholics for participation in large-scale forms of piety, and a desire among younger clergy to challenge the authority of their more rationalist and accommodationist colleagues.[35] Indeed, like the Pietist Awakening, much of the fervor of the Ultramontanist revival was sparked by confrontation with a state that was perceived as hostile to religion, most notably in the case of the Cologne affair (to be discussed below). Moreover, the role of the Jesuits and Redemptorists in the Catholic revival was not unlike that played by missionaries from London, Basel, and Geneva in the German Protestant Awakening. When combined with the growth of an Ultramontanist press, however, these intra-European connections helped foster a transnational sense of 'Catholicness,' in which the struggles of the Church in Germany were linked to the struggles of Catholics in Italy, Poland, and Ireland.

Although the Pietist Awakening and the Catholic Revival were among the most dynamic factors in post-Napoleonic religious life, the early nineteenth century also witnessed the expansion of an enlightened-bourgeois style of piety that had its roots in the eighteenth century. This form of religious practice tended to be oriented around the individual and the family, building on the notion that religion was essentially a private affair, whose purpose was to elevate the soul to God and to reaffirm a sense of moral obligation to one's neighbor and to civil society at large. A classic expression of this type of piety was Heinrich Zschokke's enormously popular *Hours of Devotion for the Promotion of True Christianity and Family Worship of God* (1809–1816). In a series of brief sketches on themes such as 'domestic happiness,' 'the art of achieving happiness in old age,' and 'civil harmony,' Zschokke painted an image of familial devotion in which fathers and mothers taught their children belief in a Christian God who was wise, tolerant, and benevolent.[36] This was a book that appealed above all to the Protestant middle classes, yet its non-sectarian version of Christianity, in which inward faith, rather than adherence to outward formulas, was the mark of true religiosity, won it a substantial following among Catholics, too.[37]

The popularity of *Hours of Devotion*, enough to sustain twenty-seven editions, reflected what Rebekka Habermas has described as a 'familiarization' of religion among the middle classes in the late eighteenth and early nineteenth centuries, in other words a shift of religiosity from public rituals to family celebrations, seen perhaps most classically in the 'German Christmas' that emerged in these years.[38] Moreover, while Zschokke typically described the father as leading the family in prayer, the displacement of middle-class religion into the home had the effect of a feminization of religion—not just in the sense that more women than men were active in religious organizations, but also in that 'religion' itself came to be figured as feminine. Nor was this a phenomenon confined to Christianity: Benjamin Maria Baader has described a parallel process within nineteenth-century Judaism. Not only was there an increased emphasis on domestic piety among middle class Jews, but the growing inclusion of women in the synagogue and in the Jewish public sphere had the effect of feminizing Judaism. Indeed, in 1855 Fanny Neuda would publish her own version of *Hours of Devotion*, this time as a prayer book aimed at increasing piety among 'Israel's women and maids.'[39] These developments paralleled and to some degree grew out of the attempts within Reform Judaism to make worship services conform to bourgeois norms of education, taste, and decorum.

Yet if in one sense religion became feminized as an intimate realm, there were also attempts within the educated classes to infuse the public—and non-ecclesiastical—realms of art, scholarship, and politics with religious values. Again, this was a process that had begun in the late eighteenth century and that was reflected in a programmatic sense in the writings of the early Romantics and Goethe, who declared that 'whoever has scholarship and art, also has religion; whoever has neither, let him have religion.'[40] But if Goethe's quote implied a rejection of Christianity, many educated Protestants preferred to view scientific progress, artistic culture, and political freedom as the result of impulses emanating from within their own confessional tradition. By the 1830s, the basic features of what became known as *Kulturprotestantismus* were already evident in the writings of Hegel and Schleiermacher, among others. After 1848 this standpoint became fused onto a liberal nationalism that would serve to legitimate the 'small German' solution to the national question in Germany.

The identification of Protestantism with 'modern' culture was reinforced by the tendency among Catholic clergy to reject German classical culture as 'atheist' or 'pagan' and to encourage their parishioners to retreat into a relatively insulated Catholic reading culture.[41] By contrast, educated Jews, immersed as they were in the German culture of *Bildung*, were critical of attempts to trace modern aesthetic and scientific culture back to Protestant Christianity or, even more problematically, the inherent superiority of the Aryan race. Indeed, during the 1860s the linguist Heymann Steinthal articulated a kind of *Kulturjudentum* as he sought to identify the roots of modern science and literature in modes of thought and expression found in the Hebrew Bible.[42] In other words, the realms of art and scholarship, while increasingly free from direct clerical influence, were by no means 'secular,' but instead served as alternative sites for the articulation of religious and confessional standpoints and antagonisms.

10.5 CONFESSIONAL AND THEOLOGICAL CONFLICT

In an influential and provocative article, the historian Olaf Blaschke posited the thesis that the nineteenth century marked a 'second confessional era.'[43] Taking stock of a decade of new scholarship on religious history, Blaschke effectively inverted the secularization paradigm, asserting instead that this era witnessed the formation and mobilization of powerful confessional cultures in Germany, which clashed repeatedly and frequently in the years 1815–1914. As evidence for his case, Blaschke cited the expansion of Ultramontane Catholicism and the equally militant confessionalism of liberal Protestantism—a rivalry that reached its apogee during the *Kulturkampf*. Yet Blaschke's argument is undercut somewhat by the ongoing theological and cultural divisions within Protestantism and Judaism (which *Kulturkampf* rhetoric tended to mask), as well as by the uneven and episodic nature of confessional conflict in the nineteenth century. On the one hand, confessional tensions were a persistent feature of everyday life—a reflection of the 'invisible boundary' that divided Catholics, Protestants, and Jews into separate mental worlds even when they lived, as they increasingly did after 1815, in close proximity to each other.[44] On the other hand, confessional conflict could also serve as a political strategy, especially when it articulated a series of overlapping and mutually ramifying grievances or to marginalize rival factions within one's own confession. For that reason, it tended to achieve particular prominence at certain moments only to fade into the background as a low-grade rumble of discontent and distrust.

The Cologne Controversy of 1837 is a case in point. Since its incorporation of the Rhineland, the Prussian monarchy had seen confessionally-mixed marriages as an opportunity to fuse the Protestant and Catholic populations into a single state. Since many of these marriages involved Protestant state officials marrying daughters of the local Catholic nobility and upper *Bürgertum*, the Prussian monarchy introduced a cabinet order requiring that the children of such marriages be raised in the faith of the father. Although this regulation flew in the face of Roman Catholic canon law, the Church leadership in Prussia attempted to work out an arrangement that would satisfy both parties. This changed with the appointment of Clemens August von Droste-Vischering as archbishop of Cologne. Droste-Vischering invalidated the prior agreements and declared that priests would only bless mixed marriages where it was agreed that the children would be raised as Roman Catholics. The heavy-handed response by the Prussian state—to arrest Droste-Vischering and imprison him in the fortress of Minden—was greeted with outrage within Ultramontanist circles, who succeeded in mobilizing public opinion in favor of the archbishop. Joseph Görres summed up the controversy in his typically inflammatory style, declaring 'under no circumstances can the church be forced to bear mongrel bastards for another confession which has become powerful in the secular world, and whoever wants to force her to do this is intending to rape her.'[45] Yet Protestant writers maintained that it was the Catholic Church that was violating the sexual rights of (male) individuals to form unions based not on confession, but love. In this way, Dagmar Herzog has argued, the Cologne Controversy became an issue not only of church-state relations, but also about the emerging definition of the bourgeois family.

In at least one instance, the roles were reversed and Protestants found themselves confronting a Catholic state. This happened in Bavaria in 1838, when Ludwig I introduced a regulation requiring militiamen to kneel before the eucharistic host if it passed by not only during church services, but also in public processions like Corpus Christi. This led to an outcry among Protestants and, as Franz Schnabel notes, parliamentary debates about such delicate theological matters as the doctrine of transubstantiation.[46] Yet because a relatively small proportion of Protestants lived under Catholic rulers, they were more likely to feel threatened by Catholic majority populations in their own towns or villages. Rebecca Ayako Bennette has detailed numerous cases from Westphalia and the Rhineland in which Protestants complained that local Catholics had denied them proper burials or fair access to a town's only church. In other cases, Catholics organized their religious processions to pass through Protestant parts of town and, in at least one instance, to wind around the Lutheran church.[47] For their part, Protestants often jeered at or made fun of such processions, in some cases trying to interrupt their paths or, when they held the reins of local power, ban them outright.

Jews almost never held the reins of power in their conflicts with Christians, but historians remain divided about the relative importance of ideology vs. economic interest in the periodic outbreaks of violence against them during the *Vormärz* era. Stefan Rohrbacher has suggested that the anti-Jewish violence seen in 1819, 1830, and 1848–1849 was motivated primarily by hostility to Jewish emancipation, particularly among those classes who viewed Jewish equality as a threat to their own status. Certainly the massive 1849 petition drive in Bavaria against Jewish civil rights, which was organized by conservative Catholic clergy and resulted in the Bavarian Upper

House rejecting emancipatory legislation that had already been approved by the Lower House, would fit into this pattern.[48] Other historians, however, have stressed the degree to which Jewish-Christian conflict was embedded in local contexts and concerns. Manfred Gailus, for examples, has shown that already in 1846 and 1847 bread riots had targeted Jewish merchants and creditors identified as 'profiteers,' particularly those who had acquired a measure of wealth or property.[49] In addition, even the violent responses to proposals for Jewish emancipation in 1819 and again in 1848–1849 reflected a broader concern about loss of communal rights in the face of a liberalizing and rationalizing state. Whatever their proximate causes, however, these conflicts tapped into established narratives about Jewish 'greed,' 'usury,' and 'betrayal,' which persisted within large elements of the Christian population and shaped the understanding of even the most well-educated Germans during this era.

While confessional conflict was a constant feature of nineteenth-century religious life, so also was intra-confessional conflict grounded in theological and political divisions. The 1830s, in particular, witnessed a wide-ranging assault on the predominance of rationalists and liberals in university theological faculties and, to some extent, the clergy as a whole. In Prussia, the *Evangelische Kirchenzeitung* launched a campaign against the rationalist spirit prevailing at the University of Halle, which Hengstenberg accused of having betrayed the mission of its Pietist founders. With rationalism backed into a corner, the *EKZ* next targeted the Hegelian school in Berlin, which had sought a compromise stance between idealist philosophy and Christian revelation. In the Rhineland, Droste-Vischering worked to eliminate the influence of Hermesianism, a rationalist form of Catholic theology, at the University of Bonn, drawing up a list of anti-Hermesian theses that all candidates for the priesthood were required to sign. At the height of the Cologne Affair, Ultramontanists accused the Hermesians of having a hand in the arrest of Droste-Vischering, a charge that helped undermine support for rationalism in the clergy and the population at large.[50] Meanwhile, the desperate efforts of both Protestant and Catholic rationalists to present themselves as loyal servants of state and church were undercut by the publication of a series of radical tracts by David Friedrich Strauss, Bruno Bauer, and Ludwig Feuerbach that rejected the most central tenets of Christianity, including the veracity of the gospel narratives and the existence of God.

These were not merely academic disputes. Developments in the 1840s would show that they had the potential to cause real and lasting splits among Jews, Protestants, and Catholics. Beginning in 1841, crackdowns by the Prussian Protestant church hierarchies in Prussia and Saxony against rationalist clergy led to the formation of a series of breakaway congregations, the so-called 'Friends of Light.' Four years later, liberal Catholics upset with the Church's turn to Ultramontanism—and especially the organization of a massive pilgrimage to the 'Holy Coat' of Trier in 1844—formed the 'German Catholics.' The *Deutschkatholiken* soon became a gathering place for Catholic and Protestant radicals, who were attracted to the movement's ecumenicism, its promise of sexual liberation, its open identification with the working classes, and its embrace of radical theology (including Feuerbach's call for a 'religion of love'). Divisions among Jews in many ways paralleled those among Christians.[51] By the 1840s, communities of reform-minded Jews in Breslau, Hamburg, and Berlin had acquired sufficient backing to break from the Orthodox community as a whole, often building separate worship spaces in the process. On the far left fringe of these groups was the Association for Reform in Berlin, which patterned itself on the German-Catholic congregations, identifying itself as a 'German-Jewish church.' While the reformers embraced the use of hymns, organs, and the German-language in services, the radicals called for an outright rejection of Jewish ritual laws and a shift of the Sabbath to Sunday. This type of splintering, whether in Judaism or in the Christian confessions, paralleled similar divisions along political and economic lines in the late 1840s.

In the aftermath of the 1848–1849 revolution, the various Christian dissident groups united to form the 'Union of Free Religious Congregations,' which initially took as its credo 'free self-determination in all religious matters,' but which by 1870 had begun moving toward a self-consciously materialist (or 'monist') standpoint. As Todd Weir has noted, this marked a reversal of the long-term trend in bourgeois religiosity toward greater inwardness, since materialism called the very existence of the individual conscience into question. Indeed, the movement would receive greatest support from those elements of the old middle class (*Mittelstand*) that were no longer considered *bürgerlich* and that had become disconnected from traditional church and confessional life.[52] At the same time, this materialist turn created the basis for a rapprochement with the socialist milieu, which in the 1860s and 1870s sought to address the 'religious question' by embracing the results of natural science as an alternative to both Christianity and upper-middle class *Bildung*. But despite the opposition of Marxists within the movement, many socialists continued to draw on the tropes and images of Christianity. One working class newspaper declared that 'everyday there are more and more signs that the poor and dispossessed, in the proper understanding of the doctrine of the Nazarener, are building the kingdom of human love, equality, and justice on earth.'[53] On this reading, Jesus was a socialist, the original Christians were communists, and the Social Democrats were the true heirs to this legacy.

The emergence of Social Democracy, as Michael Gross has argued, would form a crucial context for the outbreak of the *Kulturkampf*, which was motivated not simply by liberal Protestant fears of the Catholic Center party, but also by anxieties within the liberal camp about the political implications of mass democracy (a reality in the North German Confederation since 1867) and the growth in women's activism.[54] Supporters of the *Kulturkampf* routinely linked the 'Red International' with the 'Black International' of the Catholic Church. Meanwhile, Protestant polemicists directed a steady stream of invective toward female religious orders and congregations, which had exploded under the impact of the Catholic revival (ignoring the parallel growth of the *Diakonissenhäuser*, which provided a religious community for unmarried Protestant women while training them to work as nurses, teachers, and social workers).[55] That is not to say that the threat of political Catholicism was purely a product of the liberal imagination. After the upheavals of 1848–1849, the Prussian government had given the Catholic Church a free hand in its internal affairs, allowing it to bring in Jesuit missionaries from abroad and granting it control over the formerly contested areas of education, priestly appointments, and mixed marriages. In return, Catholic clergy had thrown their weight against political liberalism, a stance that intensified in the wake of Prussia's defeat of Austria in 1866. In other words, behind the aggressive legislation and inflated rhetoric of the *Kulturkampf* lay not only liberal anxieties about a coming age of mass politics, but also a history of political conflicts with conservative Catholic clergy dating back to the 1840s.

10.6 CONCLUSION

The political unification of Germany in 1871 under Prussian auspices did little in the short term to overcome the religious divisions that Friedrich Karl von Moser had lamented in 1765. The *Reichsgründung* did give rise to a flurry of proposals for new, national religions that were designed to unite Catholics and Protestants under a single common 'faith.' But none of these schemes was particularly plausible and what dim prospect for success any of them might have had was eliminated by the experience of the *Kulturkampf*. Yet there is evidence that by the 1890s a sizeable number of Protestants and Catholics had begun to move toward a form of mutual accommodation based on a common sense of nationality and a belief that Germany was a 'Christian state.' This shift cannot be understood, however, without reference to the emergence of an avowedly atheist socialist movement, a 'fourth confession' that in the minds of many Christians became conflated with the third confession, i.e. that of the Jews, and that served as a religious 'other' against which religious-minded Germans increasingly identified themselves.[56] Nor were these types of cross-confessional coalitions particularly stable: indeed, confessional and theological conflict would remain a dynamic and destabilizing force throughout the life of the German Empire.

Since the eighteenth century, Protestantism, Catholicism, and Judaism had undergone a series of dramatic transformations, bringing forth new forms of piety and new forms of self-understanding even as older beliefs and institutions were challenged or destroyed. What remain unchanged, however, was a tendency among Germans to define their religious situation in relation to that of their confessional rivals, and to read the political, social, and cultural shifts of their day through the lens of confessional envy, hostility, attraction, and co-existence.

NOTES

1. [Friedrich Carl von Moser], *Von dem Deutschen National-Geist* (Frankfurt a.M.: Franz Varrentrapp, 1765), 28–33.
2. Jonathan Sheehan, 'Enlightenment, Religion, and the Enigma of Secularization,' *American Historical Review* 108, no. 4 (October 2003), 1072.

3. On 'shared history' in this context, see Friedrich Wilhelm Graf, *Die Wiederkehr der Götter: Religion in der modernen Kultur* (Munich: C. H. Beck, 2004), 30–50.

4. This description is derived from Lucian Hölscher, *Geschichte der protestantische Frömmigkeit in Deutschland* (Munich: C. H. Beck, 2005), 45–46.

5. cf. Frank Eyck, *Religion and Politics in German History: From the Beginnings to the French Revolution* (Basingstoke: Macmillan; New York: St. Martin's, 1998), 340.

6. Joachim Whaley, *Religious Toleration and Social Change in Hamburg, 1529–1819* (Cambridge: Cambridge University Press, 1985), 5–7. It should be noted that this system did not include the Habsburg rulers, who retained the right to expel non-Catholics from their territories and continued to do so up through the reign of Maria Theresa.

7. On this point, Michael Maurer, *Kirche, Staat und Gesellschaft im 17. und 18. Jahrhundert* (Munich: Oldenbourg, 1999), 17.

8. David Sorkin, *The Religious Enlightenment: Protestants, Jews, and Catholics from London to Vienna* (Princeton: Princeton University Press, 2008), 119.

9. Gisela Mettele, 'Eine "Imagined Community" jenseits der Nation: Die Herrnhuter Brüdergemeinde als transnationale Gemeinschaft,' *Geschichte und Gesellschaft* 32, no. 1 (Jan–Mar, 2006), 44–68.

10. On this topic, see Marc R. Forster, *Catholic Germany from the Reformation to the Enlightenment* (Houndsmills, Basingstoke: Palgrave Macmillan, 2007), 104–198.

11. Roy Porter, *The Enlightenment* (Basingstoke: Macmillan, 1990), 55; also Sorkin, *Religious Enlightenment*, 10–11.

12. Christopher Clark, *The Politics of Conversion: Missionary Protestantism and the Jews of Prussia 1728–1941* (Oxford: Clarendon Press, 1995), 9–82; Sorkin, *Religious Enlightenment*, 153–158.

13. Hölscher, *Geschichte der protestantischen Frömmigkeit*, 101–106.

14. David Sorkin, *The Transformation of German Jewry, 1780–1840* (Oxford: Oxford University Press, 1987).

15. This particularly applies to David Friedländer, who in 1799 proposed that all Jews be baptized without their recognizing the divinity of Jesus Christ. On this proposal and its near universal rejection by Christians, see Jonathan M. Hess, *Germans, Jews and the Claims of Modernity* (New Haven: Yale University Press, 2002), 169–204.

16. David Sorkin, 'Reform Catholicism and Religious Enlightenment,' *Austrian History Yearbook* 30 (1999), 187–219, here 197–199.

17. *Was ist ein Pfarrer?* (1782), cited in Sorkin, *Religious Enlightenment*, 243–244.

18. The reference is from Michael Printy, *Enlightenment and the Creation of German Catholicism* (Cambridge: Cambridge University Press, 2009), 150.

19. Whaley, *Religious Toleration*, 209.

20. Wolfgang Altgeld, *Katholizismus, Protestantismus, Judentum: Über religiös begründete Gegensätze und nationalreligiöse Ideen in der Geschichte des deutschen Nationalismus* (Mainz: Matthias-Grünewald-Verlag, 1992), 77–91.

21. Cited in Stefi Jersch-Wenzel, 'Legal Status and Emancipation,' in Michael A. Meyer, ed., *German-Jewish History in Modern Times*, vol. 2, *Emancipation and Acculturation, 1780–1871* (New York: Columbia University Press, 1997), 12.

22. This paragraph and the next follow Hess, *Germans, Jews and the Claims of Modernity*, 25–135.

23. Hugh McLeod, *Religion and the People of Western Europe, 1789–1989*, revised ed. (Oxford: Oxford University Press, 1997), 1.

24. Kurt Nowak, *Geschichte des Christentums in Deutschland: Religion, Politik und Gesellschaft vom Ende der Aufklärung bis zur Mitte des 20. Jahrhunderts* (Munich: C. H. Beck, 1995), 39–40.

25. T.C.W. Blanning, *The French Revolution in Germany: Occupation and Resistance in the Rhineland, 1792–1802* (Oxford: Oxford University Press, 1983), 225–230.

26. Ute Planert, *Der Mythos vom Befreiungskriege. Frankreichs Kriege und der deutsche Süden. Alltag-Wahrnehmung-Deutung, 1792–1841* (Paderborn: Schöningh, 2007), 336–382.

27. Altgeld, *Katholizismus, Protestantismus, Judentum*, 133–135.

28. Nicholas Hope, *German and Scandinavian Protestantism, 1700–1914* (Oxford: Oxford University Press, 1995), 364–365.

29. Christopher Clark, 'The Politics of Revival: Pietists, Aristocrats, and the State Church in Early Nineteenth-Century Prussia,' in Larry Eugene Jones and James Retallack (eds), *Between Reform, Reaction, and Resistance: Studies in the History of German Conservatism* (Providence: Berg, 1993), 31–60, here 45–48; David Ellis, 'Erweckungsbewegung und Rationalismus im vormärzlichen Brandenburg und Pommern,' in Nils Freytag and Diethard Sawicki (eds), *Wunderwelten: Religiöse Ektase und Magie in der Moderne* (Munich: Wilhelm Fink, 2006), 53–82.

30. On the term, 'heathens in the fatherland,' see Clark, 'Politics of Revival,' 50.

31. Friedrich Wilhelm Graf, 'Die Spaltung des Protestantismus: Zum Verhältnis von evangelischer Kirche, Staat und 'Gesellschaft' im frühen 19. Jahrhundert,' in Wolfgang Schieder (ed.), *Religion und Gesellschaft im 19. Jahrhundert* (Stuttgart; Klett-Cotta, 1993), 157–190, esp. 186–187; Robert M. Bigler, *The Politics of German Protestantism: The Rise of the Protestant Church Elite in Prussia, 1815–1848* (Berkeley: University of California Press, 1972), 74.

32. On this and the following, see esp. Werner Blessing, *Staat und Kirche in der Gesellschaft: Institutionelle Autorität und mentaler Wandel in Bayern während des 19. Jahrhunderts* (Göttingen: Vandenhoeck & Ruprecht, 1982), 84–98.

33. Thomas Mergel, *Zwischen Klasse und Konfession: Katholisches Bürgertum im Rheinland 1794–1914* (Göttingen: Vandenhoeck & Ruprecht, 1994); Rudolf Schlögl, *Glaube und Religion in der Säkularisierung. Die katholische Stadt—Köln, Aachen, Münster—1740–1840* (Munich: Oldenbourg, 1995).

34. Jonathan Sperber, *Popular Catholicism in Nineteenth-Century Germany* (Princeton: Princeton University Press, 1984), 57.

35. On this point, see esp. Christopher Clark, 'The New Catholicism and the European Culture Wars,' in Clark and Wolfram Kaiser (eds), *Culture Wars: Secular-Catholic Conflict in Nineteenth-Century Europe* (Cambridge: Cambridge University Press, 2003), 11–46.

36. [Johann Heinrich Zschokke], *Stunden der Andacht, zur Beförderung des wahren Christentums*, 10th edn (Aarau: Heinrich Remigius Sauerländer, 1825).

37. cf. Blessing, *Staat und Kirche*, 85.

38. Rebekka Habermas, 'Weibliche Religiosität—oder: Von der Fragilität bürgerlicher Identitäten,' in Klaus Tenfelde and Hans-Ulrich Wehler (eds), *Wege zur Geschichte des Bürgertums* (Göttingen: Vandenhoeck & Ruprecht, 1994), 125–148, here 128; Joe Perry, *Christmas in Germany: A Cultural History* (Chapel Hill: University of North Carolina Press, 2010).

39. Benjamin Maria Baader, *Gender, Judaism, and Bourgeois Culture in Germany, 1800–1870* (Bloomington: Indiana University Press, 2006), 114.

40. Cited in Hans Erich Boedeker, 'Die Religiosität der Gebildeten,' in Karlfried Gründer and Karl Heinrich Rengstorf (eds), *Religionskritik und Religiosität in der deutschen Aufklärung* (Heidelberg: Lambert Schneider, 1989), 145–195, here 184.

41. See on this Jeffrey Zalar, 'The Process of Confessional Inculturation: Catholic Reading in the "Long Nineteenth Century",' in Helmut Walser Smith (ed.), *Protestants, Catholics, and Jews in Germany, 1800–1914* (Oxford: Berg, 2001), 121–152, here 126.

42. George S. Williamson, *The Longing for Myth in Germany: Religion and Aesthetic Culture from Romanticism to Nietzsche* (Chicago: University of Chicago Press, 2004), 230–233.

43. Olaf Blaschke, 'Das 19. Jahrhundert: Ein zweites konfessionelles Zeitalter?,' *Geschichte und Gesellschaft* 26, no. 1 (Jan–Mar, 2000), 38–75; Anthony Steinhoff, 'Ein zweites konfessionelles Zeitalter? Nachdenken über die Religion im langen 19. Jahrhundert,' *Geschichte und Gesellschaft* 30, no. 4 (Oct–Dec, 2004), 549–570.

44. cf. Etienne François, *Die unsichtbare Grenze: Protestanten und Katholiken in Augsburg, 1648–1806,* trans. Angelika Steiner-Wendt (Sigmaringen: Jan Thorbecke, 1991).

45. Cited in Dagmar Herzog, *Intimacy and Exclusion: Religious Politics in Pre-Revolutionary Baden* (Princeton: Princeton University Press, 1996), 41.

46. Franz Schnabel, *Deutsche Geschichte im neunzehnten Jahrhundert*, vol. 4, *Die religiöse Kräfte*, 3rd edn (Freiburg i.B.: Herder, 1955), 163.

47. Rebecca Ayako Bennette, 'Threatened Protestants: Confessional Conflict in the Rhine Province and Westphalia during the Nineteenth Century,' *German History* 26, no. 2 (April 2008), 168–194.

48. Stefan Rohrbacher, 'The 'Hep Hep' Riots of 1819: Anti-Jewish Ideology, Agitation, and Violence,' in Christhard Hoffmann, Werner Bergmann, and Helmut Walser Smith (eds.) *Exclusionary Violence: Antisemitic Riots in Modern German History* (Ann Arbor: University of Michigan Press, 2002), 23–42; idem, *Gewalt im Biedermeier. Antijüdische Ausschreitungen in Vormärz und Revolution (1815–1848/49)* (Frankfurt a.M.: Campus, 1993); James F. Harris, *The People Speak! Antisemitism and Emancipation in Nineteenth-Century Bavaria* (Ann Arbor: University of Michigan Press, 1994).

49. Manfred Gailus, 'Anti-Jewish Emotion and Violence in the 1848 Crisis of German Society,' in Hoffmann et al., *Exclusionary Violence*, 43–65.

50. Bigler, *Politics of German Protestantism*; Christoph Weber, *Aufklärung und Orthodoxie am Mittelrhein, 1820–1850* (Munich: Schöningh, 1973), 85–86.

51. Michael Meyer, 'Jewish Self-Understanding,' in Michael Meyer (ed.), *German-Jewish History*, vol. 2, 128–167.

52. Todd H. Weir, 'Toward a History and Sociology of Atheistic Religious Community: The Berlin Free Religious Congregations 1845–1921,' in Michael Geyer and Lucian Hölscher (eds), *Die Gegenwart Gottes in der modernen Gesellschaft: Transcendenz und Religiöse Vergemeinschaftung in Deutschland* (Göttingen: Wallstein, 2006), 197–228.

53. Sebastian Prüfer, *Sozialismus statt Religion: Die deutsche Sozialdemokratie vor der religiösen Frage 1863–1890* (Göttingen: Vandenhoeck & Ruprecht, 2002), 286.

54. Michael B. Gross, *The War Against Catholicism: Liberalism and the Anti-Catholic Imagination in Nineteenth-Century Germany* (Ann Arbor: University of Michigan Press, 2004).

55. On 'Catholic' features of the Protestant Diakonissenhäuser, see Habermas, 'Weibliche Religiosität,' 136–137.

56. Oliver Zimmer, 'Beneath the "Culture War": Corpus Christi Processions and Mutual Accommodation in the Second German Empire,' *Journal of Modern History* 82 (June, 2010), 288–324; cf. Todd Weir, 'The Fourth Confession: Atheism, Monism and Politics in the *Freigeistig* Movement in Berlin, 1859–1924' (PhD thesis, Columbia University, 2005).

BIBLIOGRAPHY

ALTGELD, WOLFGANG, *Katholizismus, Protestantismus, Judentum. Über religiös begründete Gegensätze und nationalreligiöse Ideen in der Geschichte des deutschen Nationalismus* (Mainz: Matthias-Grünewald-Verlag, 1992).

BAADER, BENJAMIN MARIA, *Gender, Judaism, and Bourgeois Culture in Germany, 1800–1870* (Bloomington: Indiana University Press, 2006).

BLESSING, WERNER K., *Staat und Kirche in der Gesellschaft: Institutionelle Autorität und mentaler Wandel in Bayern während des 19. Jahrhunderts* (Göttingen: Vandenhoeck & Ruprecht, 1982).

CLARK, CHRISTOPHER, *The Politics of Conversion: Missionary Protestantism and the Jews in Prussia, 1728–1941* (Oxford: Clarendon Press, 1995).

GROSS, MICHAEL B., *The War against Catholicism: Liberalism and the Anti-Catholic Imagination in Nineteenth-Century Germany* (Ann Arbor: University of Michigan Press, 2004).

HABERMAS, REBEKKA, 'Weibliche Religiosität—oder: Von der Fragilität bürgerlicher Identitäten,' in Klaus Tenfelde and Hans-Ulrich Wehler (eds), *Wege zur Geschichte des Bürgertums* (Göttingen: Vandenhoeck & Ruprecht, 1994).

HERZOG, DAGMAR, *Intimacy and Exclusion: Religious Politics in Pre-Revolutionary Baden* (Princeton: Princeton University Press, 1996).

HESS, JONATHAN M., *Germans, Jews and the Claims of Modernity* (New Haven: Yale University Press, 2002).

HÖLSCHER, LUCIAN, *Geschichte der protestantischen Frömmigkeit in Deutschland* (Munich: Beck, 2005).

LIEDHEGENER, ANOTONIUS, *Christentum und Urbanisierung: Katholiken und Protestanten in Münster und Bochum 1830–1933* (Paderborn: Schöningh, 1997).

MERGEL, THOMAS, *Zwischen Klasse und Konfession: Katholisches Bürgertum im Rheinland 1794–1914* (Göttingen: Vandenhoeck & Ruprecht, 1994).

NOWAK, KURT, *Geschichte des Christentums in Deutschland. Religion, Politik und Gesellschaft vom Ende der Aufklärung bis zur Mitte des 20. Jahrhunderts* (Munich: Beck, 1995).

SCHLÖGL, RUDOLF, *Glaube und Religion in der Säkularisierung. Die katholische Stadt—Köln, Aachen, Münster—1700–1840* (Munich: Oldenbourg, 1995).

SHEEHAN, JONATHAN, *The Enlightenment Bible: Translation, Scholarship, Culture* (Princeton: Princeton University Press, 2005).

SMITH, HELMUT WALSER (ed.), *Protestants, Catholics and Jews in Germany, 1800–1914* (Oxford: Berg, 2001).

SORKIN, DAVID, *The Transformation of German Jewry, 1780–1840* (Oxford: Oxford University Press, 1987).

——*The Religious Enlightenment: Protestants, Jews, and Catholics from London to Vienna* (Princeton: Princeton University Press, 2008).

SPERBER, JONATHAN, *Popular Catholicism in Nineteenth-Century Germany* (Princeton: Princeton University Press, 1984).

CHAPTER 11

THE FORMATION OF GERMAN NATIONALISM, 1740–1850

CHRISTIAN JANSEN

RECENT research considers the development of peoples and nations ('Ethnogenesis') to be a political and cultural process. According to this basic approach, a nation emerges from pre-existing national consciousness and nationalism. This view reversed the old paradigm and nationalist dogma—which also used to be a theoretical core assumption of many scholars—that peoples are 'primordial.'[1] Current definitions of concepts such as nation and people have taken leave of such assumptions. Some definitions are pragmatic, such as was suggested by Karl W. Deutsch ('A nation is a people in possession of a state. [...] A people is an extended all-purpose communication network of human beings.')[2] Others are political and constructivist, as in Benedict Anderson's terminology: a nation is an 'imagined political community—and imagined as both inherently limited and sovereign.'[3] These definitions imply that nations, and also nationalism, are modern phenomena. Neither the concept of the state in Deutsch's definition, nor the presumptions introduced by Anderson (limitation and sovereignty) are compatible with medieval or early modern societies with their characteristic forms of rule. Other theorists of nation and nationalism, such as Ernest Gellner or Eric Hobsbawm, define nations and nationalism from the outset as phenomena of modern times or of industrial societies.[4]

Nation and nationalism shall be looked at in the following as modern phenomena whose roots, however, can be traced back to pre-modern times. As early as the Middle Ages, some intellectuals started to think about the differences between European peoples. They collected and brought into systematic fashion prejudices and stereotypes about the characteristics of these peoples, from which they derived 'national charac-ters.'[5] During the fifteenth and sixteenth century, this development intensified when the discourse on 'nationes'—the Latin term for nation—became more and more exclusive. This transformation was set in the context of profound intellectual, cultural, economic, and political upheavals from the era of humanism and the 'discovery' of the 'New World,' to the Reformation, the fear of the Turks, and also the rediscovery of the 'Germania,' a work about the Germanic tribes written by the Roman author Tacitus around 98 AD.[6] After the conquests of Louis XIV, the French, in addition to the Turks, were perceived as 'hereditary enemies' of the Germans.[7] Ute Planert has pointedly summarized these developments for the German-speaking area and suggested that 'modern' nationalism emerged between 1740 and 1830. This period has long been known as a time of dramatic upheaval marked by the decline and disintegration of the old Holy Roman Empire, the development of civil society, the Enlightenment, and its mental, cultural, and political repercussions from the decreasing cohesion of the Christian confessions to the development of liberalism and, not least, the impact of the revolutions in the United States of America and in France. The argument that German nationalism emerged between 1740 and 1830 revises an older paradigm, which claimed that this development was a reaction to the American and French Revolutions.[8]

Historical research has traditionally considered the years from 1800 onwards to mark the era of the development of German nationalism. Yet, up until 1848, nationalism in Germany evolved into a political movement only partially and, locally, in some parts of Prussia from 1813 to 1815, in the southwest of Germany in 1832, and in the Rhineland in 1840. It was not until the founding of Imperial Germany in 1871 that continuous national political movements started to develop.

This means that when recent research shifts the beginnings of nationalism to an earlier date, it also prolongs the incubation period during which nationalist *topoi* and patterns of argumentation, as well as a nationalist culture, are argued to have developed. Nevertheless, this does not place the incubation period as far back as medieval times or those of the Reformation or of humanism. During these times there existed a sense of national affiliation among parts of the elites, as well as national stereotypes and clichés. However, several necessary preconditions were missing to turn them into nationalism: first, there were not yet many people who considered national solidarity an ultimate cause worth dying for.[9] Second, national consciousness had not yet become an ersatz religion. Third, allegiances towards the ruler of a duchy or principality—a relationship characterized by a particular form of deference—were more important than national affiliations. The inclusion offered by the concept of nationalism and nation states as a specifically modern feature is based on civic equality. In feudal societies, ordered in hierarchical terms along the lines of different estates, nationalist movements, and nations, as described by Deutsch and Anderson, were not possible because the necessary structural conditions were missing. In particular, these societies lacked modern statehood, demands for political participation by citizens, a public sphere, and widespread literacy as a precondition for political participation.

It has always been a complex task to explain the formation of German nationalism. For one thing, it was not quite clear to which geographic or ideational entities the developing nationalism should apply: whether the large territorial states, such as Prussia, Bavaria, or Austria, the 'whole of Germany' (which raised a question of borders), or merely some of the 'German' states? Secondly, there were periods between 1740 and 1850 when nationalist thought and culture were on the increase, but also some when they were in decline. The formation of the German nation was a discontinuous process.

Earlier research attempted to reduce the complexity of German nationalism by sub-dividing it into two variations. An early version was often called 'patriotism.' It supposedly started in the late eighteenth century, ended at the time of the foundation of Imperial Germany in 1871, and was characterized as 'progressive,' liberal, and modernizing. Compared with this, the later version of nationalism was regarded as anti-democratic, chauvinistic, racist, and anti-modern.[10] This view of a 'good' early nationalism ignored the aggressive, segregating, expansive, and at least potentially imperialistic characteristics, which are immanent in *every* kind of nationalism. Therefore, recent research assumes that all forms of 'national' and 'patriotic' thought are Janus-faced.[11] Every kind of nationalism aims not only for political emancipation, but also to gain power at the expense of other nations. Nationalist thought always considers one's own nation to be of higher value than others.

In the following, I will consistently use the terms 'nationalism' and 'nationalist,' even in those cases when they apply to one of the German territorial states such as Prussia or Bavaria. There was, after all, also Prussian and Bavarian nationalism. Moreover, when I use the term 'nationalism,' I am usually referring to individual nationalists. The spreading of national discourses can scarcely be proved, because it has hardly been examined. Like all political discourses, nationalist discourse is also gendered, an aspect which I will discuss here only in passing.[12]

11.1 Nationalist thought before nationalism

Three texts published during and immediately after the Seven Years' War were particu-larly important for the development of German nationalism. The first is: '*Vom Natio-nalstolz*' (On National Pride) by Johann Georg Zimmermann, a physician and publicist from the Swiss Canton of Aargau, published in 1758. Thomas Abbt, a professor for philosophy in Berlin, reacted to Zimmermann with the publication of '*Vom Tode für das Vaterland*' ('On Death for the Fatherland') in 1761.[13] In addition to these two antipodes of a democratic-republican nationalism, on the one hand, and a Prussian monarchist nationalism, on the other, a third publication shall be presented here: It is Friedrich Carl von Moser's '*Von dem Deutschen Nationalgeist*' ('On the German National Spirit'), written in 1765. It serves as an example of patriotism that referred to the Holy Roman Empire ('*Reichspatriotismus*'), a strand that some researchers have stressed and prob-ably exaggerated more recently as a special type of modern nationalism.

These three texts prove that certain arguments were, indeed, possible and discussed by an (admittedly very limited) public during the eighteenth century. There was a debate as to whether love of fatherland was only possible in free democratic republics, or could also exist in monarchies, which turned on the question of whether monarchies supported the process of identification between the citizen and the community. The Swiss author Johann Georg Zimmerman championed the republican position. He defined national pride from the perspective of the individual, the citizen, whereas allegedly 'inherent' national qualities were insignificant: 'The just, proper, and reasonable national pride is the love of one's fatherland in a republic, and the love of one's fatherland is the real national pride.'[14] Zimmermann, who in 1762 was a co-founder of the 'Helvetian Society,' the first nationalist organization in Switzerland, did not take part in attempts to substantiate the concept of the nation using the idea of ethnicity.[15] In his definition, with its focus on the individual, Zimmermann instead postulated a political nationalism.

Zimmermann considered freedom and law to be consistent with human 'nature,' and, hence, to be necessary conditions for the citizens' love of their fatherland. Therefore, 'true' national pride could only emerge in republics. In his view, all monarchies were examples of despotism. Their inhabitants were subjects of a sovereign and lacked a necessary condition for the love of fatherland: that of freedom. The citizens of republics, on the other hand, were subjects 'merely to the law, for in a republic, only the law is sovereign.' Thus, the political character of Zimmermann's concept of nationalism is clear once again. Although he considered national pride to be necessary for cohesion within a republican state, he was aware of its negative side effects. For him, national pride was also a 'prejudice' and a product of collective 'imagination:' 'National hatred arises from the very same sources which create national pride [...], and it is based very often on equally imagined rights.'[16] When Zimmermann nonetheless praised national pride as a virtue, he did so by taking recourse to antiquity and on the basis of an enlightenment belief in reason. Just as it had in the ancient republics, which were so much glorified by Zimmermann, republican national pride would prevent 'mean,' 'harmful,' and 'depraved' thoughts—for example 'national hatred'—'as soon as we judge our drives from the perspective of reason.' The decidedly political point of view in Zimmermann's 'On National Pride' is quite remarkable. It also provided the basis for his differentiation between a 'true,' 'just,' 'proper,' and 'reasonable' 'national pride,' which was only possible in free democratic republics, and an 'imagined' and unjustified one in monarchies. 'Just national pride' could legitimately demand every sacrifice from the citizens, and even turned 'death, bitter death, into something easy, calm and pleasant.'[17] Since nationalism can be seen as an ersatz religion during a period in which practised piety declined, Zimmermann's version of nationalism can be described as one that was based on a civil religion.

In his text 'On Death for the Fatherland,' the Berlin-based professor Thomas Abbt already referred to the classical topos of the sweetness of dying for one's fatherland. Abbt essentially presented a monarchical counterpart to Zimmermann's argument.[18] Zimmermann had written his book on his own initiative and lived in a country that was not involved in the wars of the second half of the eighteenth century. Abbt's tract, on the other hand, was part of Prussian war propaganda. His general value system was quite similar to that of the Swiss author. Like Zimmermann, Abbt considered the love of one's fatherland and basic rights of freedom to be the constituent parts of national pride. However, his emphasis was distinctively different, as can be gleaned from the following definition: 'If by accident of birth or by my free will I am united with a state to whose beneficial laws I subject myself, laws which do not deprive me of my freedom to a larger extent than necessary for the good of the entire state: then I will call this state my fatherland.'[19] In his book, Abbt argued in accordance with contemporary philosophical discourse—rationally balanced and at first glance enlightened. At the same time, he coined several *topoi*, which have subsequently turned up time and again in radical nationalist texts. The fatherland, according to Abbt, became an ultimate value, which could even overcome the fear of death. Therefore, all other human and moral values were deemed inferior to it: 'The love of fatherland convinces us that no pleasure is as relevant as the pleasure to have served one's country [on the battlefield], and that such a death adds more to the sum of our pleasures than we ever would receive in the course of a longer life.' Abbt's argument was predicated on the reason of state, not on the preconditions for a civil society. Thus, he demanded that the Church, which was close to the Prussian state, should promote the idea of dying for the fatherland.[20] Like Zimmermann, Abbt exemplified a crucial paradigm shift that occurred during the European wars of the eighteenth century and was one of the conditions for the militarization of civil societies in the nineteenth century: the heroicization of the soldier's death.[21] Since the Thirty Years' War, literary representations and popular remembrances had focused on the horrors of war. Abbt, on the other hand, aestheticized, eroticized, and—with far reaching consequences—politicized the act of killing and dying for the fatherland. For this purpose he used a metaphorical language of 'blood,' which characterized radical nationalist texts in the nineteenth and twentieth centuries: those warriors who sacrificed themselves would 'soak the soil of the groaning fatherland with the blood which spilled from our veins, in order to resurrect it.' Ultimately, this particular love of fatherland makes the citizens of a particular nation stand out from other nations.[22] In a circular argument, the pronounced love of one's fatherland increases the value of the nation and, in so doing, further strengthens the love of fatherland.

The fatherland in Abbt's book, which demanded that young men should sacrifice themselves and mothers give away their sons for this ultimate sacrifice, was Prussia, not 'Germany.' Abbt's text was in fact one of the first examples of a current of nationalism in Germany that supported a Greater Prussia.[23] In the late eighteenth century, we see a similarly aggressive tone in the war propaganda of other countries, such as Great Britain. French nationalism during the time of the Revolution was notably more aggressive than the German or the Prussian variety. From 1797, the fateful alliance of nationalism and militarism came about in France.[24]

The texts by Zimmermann and Abbt represent early versions of a republican and of a Greater Prussian nationalism. Alongside them, I would like to present another text as an example of 'Reichsnationalismus' (imperial nationalism).[25] This third current I consider to be the predecessor of a Greater German nationalism. My juxtaposition of these three different versions of nationalism represents them as ideal types. In their historical context they interacted in many ways. Not only did they use political arguments and images from the same sources (from classical writers of Antiquity, from the Christian canon, from humanism and from the Enlightenment), they also explicitly referred to each other. In addition, a paradox may be mentioned: although each nationalism focuses on the exclusiveness and superiority of its particular nation, nationalism itself is a transnational phenomenon. Nationalist images, arguments, phobias, and paranoid projections are similar; if one has studied a particular nationalism, all others seem to be familiar. Nationalists of different countries, it may even be said, have far more in common than nationalists and their opponents in their own country.

The tract 'On the German National Spirit' was published anonymously in 1765, that is, *after* the Seven Years' War. Its author was a convert (or, depending on the perspective, a renegade). During the Seven Years' War he had supported Prussia; however, from 1764 he worked in the Emperor's service. He had drawn an annual salary of 1500 guilders since 1765—a decent pay in order through his writings to 'create a spirit of loyalty to the Emperor in the country.' In 1767 the Emperor appointed him as Aulic Councillor and ennobled him as a baron in 1769. The author was Friedrich Karl Moser, who had his roots in Württemberg pietism.[26] His contribution to the debate on nationalism not only payed a dividend for Moser himself; it is also said to have been by far the most widely read text on these issues at the time.[27] Moser started his pamphlet of 108 pages with a sentence both sparkling and baroque, which also presents the core thesis of the entire text:

> We are one people with one name and language. We live under a common leader, under one set of laws that determine our constitution, rights, and duties, and we are bound together by a common and great interest in freedom [. . .] In our internal power and strength we are the first Empire in Europe [. . .] and yet, as we are now, we still remain a puzzle as a political system, the prey of our neighbours, the subject of their mockery, [. . .] disunited among ourselves, enfeebled by our divisions, strong enough to hurt ourselves, powerless to save ourselves, phlegmatic towards the honor of our name, indifferent to the dignity of the law, envious of the leader, suspicious of each other, [. . .] a great and, at the same time, despised people, one who has the potential to be happy, but is, in reality, much to be pitied.'[28]

Moser did not use the terms 'nationalism' and 'nationalist.' Instead, he championed the patriotic 'citizen' as an anti-feudal and 'Reichs' nationalist model. Yet at the same time, he anticipated some core arguments, which reappeared later in constructs such as the *Sprachnation* (a people unified by the same language), the *Kulturnation* (a people unified by the same culture) and the nation as an *Erinnerungsgemeinschaft* (community of remembrance). Since Moser considered 'the Germans' to share the same language, culture, and historical experiences, he opposed the particularism of the German states and their 'spirit of selfishness.' Compared with 'the British, Swiss, Dutch, or Swedish', he stated, Germans lacked a 'national way of thinking.'[29] Moser referred here explicitly to ordinary people ('charcoal burners, cart-men, peasants, shepherds') who in other countries would have talked about 'national rights in a reasonable and enthusiastic manner.' In Germany, on the other hand, there was merely 'here and there the occasional citizen of a free Imperial city (*Reichsstadt*) interested in the fate of Germany.' Moser's suggestions on how to strengthen the national spirit and the 'patriotic drive for the whole' in the Reich were moderate and appear quite naive in view of the enormous domestic problems of the Reich: the rulers of the German states were supposed to renounce their power 'for the good of all' and to obey all applicable laws. Because the 'source of our own evil lies right within us,' as he stated, everything depended solely on 'one's own good, decent and serious will.'[30] Moser took a firm stand against the German rulers, their cabinets, their militaries, and their bureaucracies, and championed a bourgeois and anti-feudal canon of values. Often he referred to Switzerland as a role model. It was also quite characteristic of Moser's argumentation that he repeatedly mentioned the 'constitution' and the laws of the Reich, as well as the 'rights' of the Germans.[31] This was the beginning of a constitutional patriotism—namely a national pride based on the identification with political institutions and feudal rights, as it was expressed by Wieland in the 1790s, but not on language, culture, religion, and '*Volkstum*' (the concept of ethnicity as the definition of a *Volk*).[32]

11.2 THE DISCOVERY OF THE VOLK, COMMONALITY OF LANGUAGE TO DEFINE A NATION

Napoleon's conquests, which led to reforms of society and law in the occupied territories, accelerated the increasing dissemination of enlightenment ideas and the general decline of feudal society. This process caused a new kind of social division, which announced the development of a class society. Due to the manifold fragmentations of the old Holy Roman Empire, it was not only the potential borders of a German nation state that were ambiguous and contentious. In addition, religion was no longer a means of cohesion. At the end of the eighteenth century, some intellectuals tried to inculcate a 'German' national consciousness, which went beyond loyalty to an individual German territorial state. In so doing, they considered language, as well as literary and intellectual culture mediated by language, to be the only commonality. This Archimedean point, which became more and more important for early nationalism, was also, however, the initial point for an ethnic substantiation of the German nation.

Until the late eighteenth century, '*Volk*,' a term derived from a political terminology, signified the lower classes and contained a pejorative undertone. From the 1770s, three different interconnected lines of development re-evaluated the concept of 'Volk' and added an emphatic quality to the term. First, some enlightenment scholars considered (even before the French Revolution!) education of ordinary people to be an effective driving force for political progress. Rudolf Zacharias Becker, who wrote one of the most successful tracts on the education of the people, believed that 'the true practical education [. . .] first takes root with the country man and spreads from the bottom up.'[33] In so doing, he relativized the claim to cultural leadership of the contemporary elites, a line of thought which the Romantics—and this is the second point—turned into an agenda. In their view, true poetry was only to be found among unspoilt people; that is, among ordinary people and children. They were anxious to preserve the language and traditions of the people, and initiated a cult of the natural and the primordial, which was to become a permanent companion of nationalism. Collections of fairy tales and traditional folk songs were created out of this impulse. Both of these played a significant role for German nation-building during the nineteenth century: fairy tales in bourgeois education, folksongs as part of the regular repertoire of Sängerbünde (choral societies), and national festivals in the nationalist movement during the nineteenth century.

The achievement of Johann Gottfried Herder, who followed Johann Georg Hamann's suggestions, was to find a new and fundamental definition of the term 'Volk.' When Herder used the terms 'nation-building' or 'building' of the German nation in his texts, he was playing on words.[34] In German, the word Bildung has two meanings: on the one hand, it expresses the idea of 'building,' as in nation-building; on the other, it can also represent the individualized appropriation of classical high-culture, which was the characteristic basis for the self-formation of a certain part of the middle class, the Bildungsbürgertum. Thus, Herder combined this second meaning of 'Bildung,' which was highly normative and laden with the bourgeois desire for emancipation, with the issue of nation-building in a modern sense.

Herder identified three preconditions that were, in his eyes, crucial for the process of nation-building. The first key issue was the ability of a people to be proud of 'its own' (sein Eigenes). On the one hand, he was looking for this authentic 'own' within the 'Volk,' the ordinary people, in their folksongs and dances, and in their traditions and customs. In defining the authentic 'national self,' Herder and his followers in the period of Sturm und Drang (Storm and Stress), as well as in the Romantic Movement, wanted to enhance the status of the German language. At the same time, they were interested in other Germanic languages and traditions, particularly English and Scandinavian myths and legends, but also more recent literature from Shakespeare to Walter Scott. Herder was a great admirer of the legendary Scottish bard 'Ossian.'[35] His poetry was widely received by German intellectuals, although they were later exposed as a forgery of the contemporary author James Macpherson. The educational journeys of young German intellectuals took them ever more frequently to England and Scotland, instead of Italy and Greece. In spatial terms, their early nationalism was oriented to the west and the north, and was often explicitly anti-southern. Searching for what cohered and unified peoples, Herder and other intellectuals were also interested in what created power and vitality. This search for the 'own' was in a manner of speaking a '*völkisch*' undertaking, and its broad effect, and political and cultural influence have hardly been examined. There is some evidence, such as Heinrich Heine's dispatches from Berlin in the 1820s, or the first wave of studies on the history of the '*Volk*' in the *Vormärz*, suggesting that it became highly popular in the context of developing nationalism.[36]

Herder's concept of nationality not only influenced German-speaking areas, but had an impact far beyond. Nationalists from southern and eastern Europe consistently referred to Herder, in particular his assumption that poetry and language constituted a people as a spiritual community and created the harmony of inner values.[37] According to Herder, individuals acquire their affiliation with a '*Volk*' by means of the native language; that is, during an early phase of their development. By equalizing and appreciating primordiality and naturalness, he turned the affiliation with a '*Volk*' into a quasi-natural and positive quality, which could hardly be relinquished. The German people, 'have kept their language since ancient times [...] pure and unmixed with others, as they themselves have never been ruled over by other peoples.'[38] Even though Tacitus could be quoted as evidence for the idea that the Germans and their language were particularly pure and unmixed, this view completely ignored the many migrations since antiquity. Nevertheless, it was later picked up by Johann Gottlieb Fichte and became one of the most effective arguments of radical nationalism. The fear of mixture primarily concerned a Roman influence and was therefore oriented against humanistic education and the cult of antiquity, against France and against Catholicism.[39] Influences from the 'Germanic' north and west of Europe (Great Britain, the Netherlands, and Scandinavia) were considered enriching and fertilizing. In the French and American Revolutions, historical and political categories (such as territorial borders or citizenship) defined peoples. By contrast, using language and organological imagery to identify and differentiate peoples caused ethnic exclusion and a negative judgment on the mixture of peoples, which can already be found in Herder's thought. Herder also implied a form of nationality, which was religiously charged and thus represented the beginning of the transformation process that turned German nationalism into a political religion.

The revaluation of the notion of '*Volk*' in the German speaking areas was induced both by Herder's 'Copernican turn in the semantic development of the term "*Volk*"' and by Abbé Sieyès's definition of a nation as 'le grand corps du peuple' (the grand body of the people).[40] Following Rousseau's interpretation of natural law, the existence of a people came, for Sieyès, prior to the state. This categorical differentiation also entered into German political theory. According to this view, the state was an association of the inhabitants of a territory who were led by common interest. The concept of '*Volk*,' on the other hand, was understood as a quasi-natural connection of people with the same background, in terms of descent, language, and character. Due to the different historical circumstances, the French definition of the nation was, compared with the German, always lacking a 'mysticism of language, of people, of common descent,' as the historian Elisabeth Fehrenbach states. According to the French understanding, it was 'not common language or descent, not a people in an ethnic sense, but the common state and the rights of citizens,' which defined the unity of the nation. That does not mean that the French definition was more rational and the German more irrational, or that French nationalism was less aggressive than the German. The difference was rather based on a fundamentally different definition of affiliation. The German understanding of nations as entities separated according to 'natural' characteristics and qualities biologized a core category of nationalism.[41]

Around 1800, a type of German nationalism emerged that was different from the currents in western and northern Europe, and even distanced itself from them. However, it was not individuals or particular groups of people who were responsible for this particular development, but structural conditions and historical and political constellations. Many ideas of Herder and the Romantics were politically enhanced by the later nationalist discourses in a manner that did not accord with their original intentions. It was significant for the formation of German nationalism that it first became popular during the anti-Napoleonic wars; that is, when fighting against a country that was easy to blame for the decline of German greatness. Napoleon's foreign rule, which championed the universal program of the French Revolution, strengthened anti-universalist tendencies in German nationalist discourse. Here, then, the fundamental differentiation between the peoples was highlighted and their walling-off against each other was as much appreciated as their 'individual' and 'organic' development. German national historical teleology was marked by the assumption of an individual 'national character,' which set out the special path of every nation for freedom and self-determination, and which could be harmed by implementing 'foreign' ideas.

After the victory against Napoleon and the Congress of Vienna in 1815, institutions of the German nation were established, such as the German Confederation and its bodies. However, the liberal and democratic opposition perceived these organizations merely as a new foreign rule, which had its center in Vienna instead of Paris. Compared with the cases of western or northern Europe, oppositional nationalists in Germany scarcely identified themselves with the institutions of the state, particularly after the Prussian Reforms and after the Carlsbad Decrees of 1819. As a result, the assumption of the 'Volk' as an authentic force, as the incarnation of 'Germanness' (*Deutschtum* or *Deutschheit*) deepened, causing 'a mystifying cult of the "*Volk*." The reorganization of the existing 'un-German' political system, was, in their view, supposed to be based on this apolitical concept of the 'Volk.'

Essential components of early nationalism were, then:

1. the understanding of the German 'Volk' or the German nation as an ethnic entity, given by nature and based on common descent;
2. a sense of superiority over other peoples;
3. extensive territorial ambitions which were bound to cause wars with neighboring states;
4. a revaluation of nationalism turning it into an ersatz religion;
5. strong resentments towards France.

These features did not first appear after the foundation of Imperial Germany in 1871. Rather, they already marked nationalist discourse by 1810. At the end of the nineteenth century, it was not the radical arguments which were new, but the public response to them. At the beginning of the nineteenth century, only a few people championed nationalist positions in public. But in the course of the nineteenth century, whenever a significant political public sphere emerged, these views met a major response even beyond the *Bildungsbürgertum*. Like Moser's writings from the eighteenth century, the hate pamphlets and tracts by Ernst Moritz Arndt and Friedrich Ludwig Jahn were published in high print runs.[42] There were cosmopolitan voices as well. Yet overall, the liberal and democratic opposition during the nineteenth century exhibited an 'elected affinity' with nationalism. Only the connection of nationalism and liberalism enabled the resounding success of both ideologies.[43]

11.3 BEGINNINGS OF ORGANIZED NATIONALISM

After the end of the Holy Roman Empire and the defeat of Napoleon, organized German nationalism gradually emerged, and turned into a social movement: during the 1810s, between 1830 and 1832, and during the years of the Revolution 1848–1849. From 1860 onwards, nationalism was continuously and significantly involved in the process of nation-building. As a social movement, German nationalism was based on two types of interrelated organizations: manifestly and latently political.[44] Until 1867, the prototype of a nationalist organization in Germany was not the party, but publicly operating clubs and societies, with the national festival becoming one of the most significant expressions of organized nationalism.

At the beginning of the nineteenth century, organized nationalism appealed to intellectuals and the portion of the student body that created fraternities (*Burschenschaften*), the first explicitly nationalist organizations. In the so-called 'wars of the people,' which is how Ernst Moritz Arndt stylized the struggle against Napoleon, and in the crypto-political gymnastic associations initiated by Friedrich Ludwig Jahn, organized nationalism found a rapidly increasing number of followers. It remains, however, that terms such as 'national uprising' exaggerated the actual extent of the movement, and for most German subjects, material rather than ideological factors motivated opposition to Napoleon. During the French occupation, the economic situation grew worse each year. The Continental Blockade caused severe constraints on private consumption, and persistent warfare entailed quartering, looting, rape, and epidemics. The recruitment of ever more armies in the name of general conscription also provoked opposition.[45]

The first fraternity, and thus the first nationalist organization, was founded by 150 nationalist students in Jena in June 1815. After three years, around 4000 members of fraternity associations from fourteen German universities joined the 'General Association of German Fraternities' (*Allgemeine Deutsche Burschenschaft*). At the same time, gymnastic associations were founded, primarily in Prussia. They contributed, on the one hand, to the formation of a nationalist political will, on the other to paramilitary training. There were 150 gymnastic associations in 1818 with 12,000 active members and 6000 additional members. The personnel of gymnastic associations and fraternities were tightly knit. Both organizations recruited their young followers from the milieu of the *Bildungsbürgertum*.[46] In October 1817, a large number of organized nationalists from all regions gathered for a festival on the Wartburg at Eisenach. They openly opposed the existing political system by symbolically staging the nation, with students even burning books supposedly hostile to the movement.[47] The authorities soon took drastic measures against this nationalist movement—which overall was rather small, but included a large part of the academic elite—and its revolutionary program. After one of the participants of the Wartburg festival had murdered the poet, August von Kotzebue, an alleged 'traitor of the fatherland,' the *Bundestag* (Federal Assembly, the only central institution of the German Confederation and a congress of envoys) enacted the Carlsbad Decrees with a stricter censorship, and a ban of all gymnastic associations and student fraternities. This meant the (preliminary) end for organized nationalism after just a couple of years.

Here, we can hint at the social and historical reasons why the nation became an attractive concept, even an experience, which, from the beginning of the nineteenth century onwards, found expression in festivals and associations, and in fashion and hairstyles. Alongside the influence of the French Revolution and the anti-Napoleonic wars, the most significant reasons for the dissemination of nationalist thought were:

1. the formation of the educated elite without a fixed position within the feudal system of estates;
2. the development of a literary market, of new social organizations, and communication networks
3. the concept of progress in terms of a philosophy of history.

The ideas of five men may stand as representative of the range of early German nationalism: apart from Friedrich Ludwig Jahn, these were Ernst Moritz Arndt, Johann Gottlieb Fichte, Friedrich Daniel Schleiermacher, and Heinrich Luden. During the time of the anti-Napoleonic wars and during the following years, not only the intellectual elites, but also parts of the growing bourgeoisie became enthusiastic about their ideas.[48] Their ethnic definition of Germanness implied not only hatred for the French, but also a manifest anti-Semitism. Arndt, for instance, published anti-French hate lectures and anti-Semitic tirades.[49] Jews and cosmopolitans were excluded from the community of good Germans.

The nationalists' opposition to the emancipation laws of several German states was one example of how anti-Semitism was already prevalent in the early nineteenth century.[50] It was not political engagement by any social movement that caused the improvement in the Jews' legal position, but rather the French occupiers and the bureaucracy who implemented this emancipation. In most cases nationalist-inclined liberal members of the *Landtage* (state diets) voted against it, justifying their decision with the concept of ethnic purity. Emancipation should only be allowed in the case of Jews who were entirely assimilated, which implied conversion to Christianity. Leading nationalists, such as Jakob Friedrich Fries, a professor who was suspended because he had participated in the Wartburg festival, demanded the extradition of all Jews who were not prepared to assimilate. He based this claim on the idea that a nation should be ethnically and religiously homogeneous.[51] The anti-Semitism of many nationalists was caused by substantiating the nation in ethnic terms. More and more frequently, since the 1810s, common language was considered the 'testimony of common descent,' the descent of modern peoples was extended into ancient times, and ethnicity (*Volkszugehörigkeit*) understood as an inheritable quality.

The term '*Volksthum*' introduced by Jahn was supposed to signify the specific characteristics of a nation. It became widely accepted during the early nineteenth century. By highlighting the homogeneity of all members of a people and attributing characteristics to a *Volk*, Jahn—like Herder before him—drew on one of the key concepts of idealistic philosophy: the parallelization of onto- and phylogenesis, which meant equating the development of individuals with the development of peoples. The individualized collective notion of '*Volk*' was meant in a concrete physical sense. As in the human body, every organ was understood as having a certain function. At the same time, there was supposed to be a 'natural' hierarchy of body parts. This imagery had far reaching political implications: the nation should be put before the fulfilment of individual wishes and needs. The nation in this understanding was stylized into a higher form of individuality and offered to the members of the nation as an ersatz-identity. By this means, it was possible to legitimize political inequality and to suggest that social differences should not be contested. Finally, by individualizing peoples, the physical perceptions of 'inner' and 'outer' were projected on the antagonism of friend and foe.

In combination with the wars against France, there were two further new elements that made nationalism more aggressive and also more appealing to the masses. For one thing, the superiority of the German people above other nations was suggested more and more frequently and this superiority allegedly legitimized the cultural mission of the Germans. Alongside countless popular appeals by Arndt, Jahn, Luden, and others, this sense of superiority also applied to two philosophical ideas: the first of these ideas came from Fichte who, in his 'Addresses to the German Nation,' characterized the German people as 'primordial people' (Urvolk), and therefore as hardly spoilt by civilization and foreign influences. The second came from Georg Wilhelm Friedrich Hegel who suggested that the coming era of world history would be the time of the Germanic peoples.[52] Both ideas were supposed to justify the superiority and the special mission of the German nation in distinguishing it from others. Fichte, for instance, stated that 'only the German—the original man, who has not become dead in an arbitrary organization [here, Fichte is referring to the French]—really has a people' and that he alone 'is capable of real and rational love for his nation.' With this, Fichte distinguished his own nation from others as having a model character.[53]

There was a second new element that multiplied the mobilizing power of nationalism: its religious character. Many contemporary nationalist intellectuals were concerned about the process of secularization—not least because some of them had studied theology.[54] They hoped that a religiously charged nationalism could counteract this development. According to their view, the confessional divide was one of the main reasons for the loss of unity and power, and thus had to be overcome by installing a 'united German Church without the boundaries of confession (*freigläubig*)' (Jahn). However, although the religiously charged character of nationalism was supposed to have an integrative impact, anti-Catholic and anti-Semitic currents were highly visible. By means of similar arguments, both religions were declared as opponents of the unification process in terms of a national church and a nation state. Catholics, Jews, and all cosmopolitans were accused of allegedly orienting themselves towards trans-national religious authorities. Since the nationalists had posited the nation state as the perfect collective, any attempt to reach beyond it was seen to jeopardize not only the political autonomy of the nation state, but also the rights of freedom guaranteed by it.[55]

Collections of nationalist songs are good examples with which to demonstrate the religiously charged character of nationalism. Theodor Körner, for instance, called the war against Napoleon a 'crusade' or a 'holy war.' The choral and gymnastic societies (*Sänger- und Turnerbewegung*) took up his songs, as well as some verses by Arndt and by other nationalists who used the medium of song to popularize their ideas. These songs were publicly performed on numerous occasions. Religious elements are also highly visible in the rituals of early nationalism: for instance in memorials to the so-called 'Battle of Nations' (*Völkerschlacht*), celebrated since 1814, and in gymnastic festivals.[56] In addition to Christian traditions, these rituals integrated allegedly Germanic customs of natural religion. The festivals took place outdoors and preferably under large trees. The participants garlanded themselves with oak leaves, and showed great enthusiasm for singing Protestant and nationalist hymns. The entire event resembled a church service: the sermonic speech of one of the senior members of the movement, with the speaker addressing the audience with short appeals, and the congregation chorusing ritualized formulas.[57] Popular nationalist texts were geared toward religious patterns and often had the same structure as a catechism.

To summarize the beginnings of organized nationalism, three conclusions can be emphasized. Firstly, this development was not linear, but proceeded in different waves marking temporary peaks and deep ruptures. In regard to the genuine political organizations, these ruptures can be clearly observed in the disappearance of associations and the emergence of new ones. On the crypto-political level, these breaks are marked by sudden declines in the number of clubs and societies, as well as falling membership figures. Secondly, the attitude of the authorities was a key factor in this development. They reacted on the one hand by implementing repressive measures such as bans and censorship, on the other by instrumentalizing the concept of nationalism as a means for their own power politics. Nevertheless, organized nationalism reached all three of its peaks (1811–1819, 1830–1832 and 1848–1849) by opposing governmental policy. Thirdly, it should be emphasized that crypto-political associations became less and less significant compared with explicitly political organizations.

The thirty years between the Congress of Vienna and the Revolution were characterized by the radicalization of nationalist opposition following its disappointment in the rulers who had not advanced German unification and had largely failed to keep their promise of freedom. However, after a period of broad politicization and organization, the Carlsbad Decrees restricted the political public sphere to an increasing degree. It was only a decade later, and after the July Revolution, that organized nationalism operated publicly and openly again.

11.4 DISSEMINATION AND DIFFERENTIATION OF NATIONALIST MOVEMENTS IN THE VORMÄRZ AND IN 1848–1849

The nationalist movement in southwest Germany hit its peak with the Festival of Hambach (*Hambacher Fest*) in May 1832, the biggest national festival before the Revolution with about 25,000 people participating. But the short period of success soon ended with strict persecution of fraternity students and other political activists. Due to the discrimination against openly political organizations, associations with a crypto-political character, such as male choral societies, which had been expanding since the early 1830s, and gymnastic clubs revived in the early 1840s, gained increasing significance. Under the guise of sociability, nationalist organizations were spared from immediate persecution. On the eve of the Revolution, there were almost 300 German gymnastic associations with 80,000 to 90,000 members, and more than 100,000 singers were organized in over 1,100 male choral societies. From 1830, the core area of these organizations was located in Southwest Germany (Württemberg, Baden, the Rhenish Palatinate and Hesse). Up to the 1840s, national festivals beyond local boundaries were still the most important form of public expression of the nationalists.[58] But neither gymnasts nor singers were successful in establishing permanent nationwide organizations. There was no apparent hierarchic structure operating beyond local boundaries. The gymnastic and choral societies did indeed help to spread the idea of the nation as a concept of order during the 1840s. But their political objectives remained vague. They understood their demand for unity in different ways. There is no confirmed reference to the nation state in the period before 1848.

The organized nationalists were not prepared for the events of the year 1848. It was the lower classes, driven by social misery, who dominated the battles of March 1848. The revolutionary protest paved the way for a new development in regard to the clubs and societies. It is clear that crypto-political associations suddenly became less significant. During the Revolution, the law concerning clubs and societies was abrogated so that it was possible to found overtly political organizations, whose importance now increased fundamentally. On the territory of the German Confederation (without

Austria), up to 1.5 million men became members of liberal and democratic societies, which, however, in 1849 fell victim to the reaction.[59]

The Revolutions of 1848/49 reopened a broad political debate about Germany. Arndt and Jahn, both ideologists of early nationalism, as well as several former fraternity students, were members of the first democratically elected parliament of the German people, the 'German National Assembly' (*Deutsche Nationalversammlung*), which was in session at the Paulskirche at Frankfurt upon Main. This suggests that there were continuities between the movements of the 1810s and the early 1830s. However, unlike during the 1830s, when the movement was more internationally oriented due to the enthusiasm for Poles and Greeks, in 1848, and after the escalation of the German-French conflict during the 'Rhine Crisis,' the 'dominant principle was not, thank God, freedom,' but 'nationality,' as Christian Friedrich Wurm, a member of the Assembly, put it.[60]

The arguments about the borders of a future nation state put forward during the debates in the Paulskirche were highly contradictory. The members of the Assembly could only agree on the claim that the future German state should become a dominant power in Central Europe and—as many hoped—a world power. Initially, the majority of MPs in the Paulskirche assumed that the nation state would contain the entire territory of the German Confederation, as well as Schleswig, East and West Prussia, and large parts of the province of Posen. Due to its liberal constitution and its prosperity, they believed, the new state would attract German people who lived in territories beyond these borders, such as Alsatia, the Netherlands, the German speaking cantons in Switzerland, and the Russian Baltic provinces. In addition, colonies all over the world were supposed to be conquered by establishing a strong navy. The majority of the National Assembly wanted only three great powers in Europe, aside from England, Scandinavia, and the Iberian Peninsula. These three powers were to be France, Germany, and Russia, each of them unifying one of the three main peoples: the Romans, the Germanic peoples and the Slavs.[61] With its similarities to the ideas developed by Arndt and Fichte at the beginning of the nineteenth century, this provides another example of the continuities of nationalist thought.[62]

In order to achieve this ambitious objective, the members of the Frankfurt Parliaments argued opportunistically: they laid claim to territories without a German speaking majority such as Bohemia and Moravia, Trieste and the southern Tyrol by suggesting that these places had a historical affiliation with the German Confederation. Franz Schuselka, an Austrian democrat, emphasized: 'A great people needs space in order to fulfil its mission in the world.'[63] Meanwhile, where territories which did not belong to the German confederation were concerned, the majority of parliamentarians used the idea of ethnicity to argue that all ethnic Germans should be integrated into the future state. Only the representatives of the Democrats, the political minority of the Assembly, championed in part a political understanding of the term nation and favored a democratic vote in the multilingual areas to decide whether they belonged to the new German state.

The differences among the Assembly in the Paulskirche became highly visible as Poland was debated from the 24th to 27th July 1848.[64] Only a small minority argued in favor of peaceful co-operation between nations and these members were defeated with

342 to 31 votes by those who considered war to be inevitable in solving clashes of national interest. The political debates on Germany held in the Paulskirche also show that several elements of ethnically-based nationalism were inconsistent. The contradiction between the two objectives of ethnic homogeneity, on the one hand, and the integration of all German-speaking areas on the other, was most striking. Putting into practice the line 'where the German tongue is spoken' from Arndt's famous poem, which became the unofficial anthem in 1848, and unifying Germany in this sense would have meant including millions of people with different languages in a Greater German Empire. In order to solve this contradiction, National Democrats such as Moritz Mohl, like Marx and Engels after him, appropriated the Hegelian argument about the privilege of 'great' peoples. The minorities belonging to the future nation state of Greater Germany would, according to this view, merely become 'crumbled and small nationalities.'[65] Just like the Jews, they were to be assimilated.

There were two conflicting positions in the National Assembly: a small minority favored a political concept of the nation, referring to the Republican nationalism of the eighteenth century and to the ideas of 1789. The large majority, however, represented an ethnic concept of the nation. These differences can be exemplified by analyzing the views of two prominent members of the Assembly: Ludwig Bamberger and Jakob Venedey. Both were opinion leaders and publicists of the bourgeois left wing until 1871 and beyond. In an article written shortly after the suppression of the Revolution, Bamberger picked up on an argument that the advocates of the nation state had used before in order to deny the 'smaller peoples' the right to national unity. Bamberger then applied this argument to the German people: They had 'no history' themselves. 'Germany as a political unit,' he suggested, was 'unknown in history.' Bamberger not only dismissed the idea of legitimizing German unification in historical terms, but also rejected the ethnic arguments of the majority. 'I deny that kind of unity, which is the object of an idealizing cult, a mystic religion, a romantic love. In a word, I deny it as an issue of nationality. But I approve of it as our first revolutionary task, as the fundamental condition of our existence. In a word: I approve of it as an urgent political and administrative reform.' It became obvious in 1848–1849 that the historical and ethnic justification of the German borders would lead to a permanent clash of interest with other nations, which would likewise claim their right to self-determination. Thus, in 1850, Bamberger rejected attempts to integrate the entire territory of the German Confederation—and potentially even territories where 'Germans' lived—into a nation state by referring to historical, romantic, or 'mystic' arguments.

Only a few contemporaries agreed with Bamberger when he justified the necessity of state unity in a categorically political manner. They considered it a fatal mistake that nationalists in Italy, Poland, Bohemia, and Hungary perceived nation-building as a matter of nationality. According to Bamberger, in these countries, as well as in Germany, it was not a question of 're-establishing national unity,' which was nothing more than an ideological mystification, but a matter of 'creating political unity.' This meant that the German Confederation should 'chase away the 34 sovereigns and unify Germany into one single state.' Appealing to nationalist emotions, on the other hand, would distract from politically more significant concerns and would only be in the interest of the reaction. Bamberger followed the Anglo-Saxon tradition and opposed the religious and revolutionary voluntarism of Mazzini or Kossuth, which was highly popular among his colleagues.[66]

In common with prominent leaders of the Italian and Hungarian movements of unification, Jakob Venedey, the left-wing liberal from the Rhineland, used the emotionally charged issue of Schleswig-Holstein as an opportunity to declare 'the issue of nationality' as the guiding principle for his German policy. Venedy criticized the fact that moderate liberals did not want to touch the historically grown borders and therefore intended to integrate the entire territory of Schleswig-Holstein into the German nation state, even though only parts of the country had a German-speaking majority. This would, according to Venedey, only create new forms of injustice, as the Danes would become a minority in a German Schleswig-Holstein just as the Germans were a minority in Denmark. Venedey advocated ethnic and linguistic borders, instead of historical ones. He therefore accepted the loss of North Schleswig, as well as parts of the province of Posen with a mainly Polish population, and as a result encouraged the hostility of more power-oriented liberals. Although the ethnically justified demarcation was supposed to be a rational solution to the conflict over Schleswig-Holstein, Venedey's argumentation shifted to exactly the same terminology that mystified the term 'Volk' and which was opposed by Bamberger. Venedey declared the north German 'tribes' to be 'the most precious and noble' people of 'German descent.' They had 'renewed the blood baptism of their Germanness' in 'unprecedented battles.'[67]

These two opinions were both based on the concept of 'Volk,' but in different ways. In addition, there was a third view that argued in historical terms and that preferably did not want to touch territorial borders, but instead intended a closer association between the existing states. In characterizing the various currents of nationalism, the differentiation between political, ethnic, and historic nationalism serves much better than the differentiation between patriotism and nationalism, or between liberal and radical nationalism, as these latter two approaches distort the structural discrepancies within the national movement and its development. In following this terminology, there is a fundamental difference between the ethnic concept of the nation on the one hand, and the historical and political understanding of the term on the other. In this perspective, historical nationalism appears as a version of political nationalism.

Venedey's argumentation shows the dilemma of ethnic nationalism: it proved to be rather difficult to define the terms 'Volk' or 'nation' as ethnic and linguistic concepts in central Europe with its mixture of different languages, religions, and cultures, its wars and its repeatedly changing territorial borders. It clashed with the liberal utopian dream of people co-existing in peace and freedom. Creating ethnically homogeneous states and ethnically justified borders necessarily meant forced assimilation, resettlement, and war for the territories in question. In Great Britain and France, outer borders were largely undisputed. For Central Europe, where the process of nation-building preceded the foundation of nation states, it was a different story. Here, it was also impossible to re-educate a heterogeneous population of a state by means of nationalist ideas, historical policy, and compulsion, and to turn it into a homogeneous nation in terms of language and culture.

The only chance of solving the German question in a sustainable manner in 1848–1849 would have been the decision in favor of Bamberg's political nationalism combined with a realistic assessment of Germany's own capabilities and constellations of power in Europe. This could have been, for instance, an association of the states of a 'Third Germany;' that is, a territory without the great powers of Prussia and Austria and based on the Imperial Constitution of 1849. However, a solution like this would have required a measure of restraint incompatible with the nationalist aspirations of the vast majority of the Assembly. The resolution was taken into consideration no earlier than the final weeks of the session when the defeat of the Revolution was already inevitable.

To put it pointedly: it was one of the major achievements of the Revolution of 1848 in the German Confederation to have prevented the formation of an independent Prussian nation state on the model of France, Great Britain, or Sweden. In 1848 at the latest, the ethnic definition of the nation was so deeply rooted that a Prussian nation state was unthinkable. The assumption that the *mother* tongue would create the spirit of the *father*land, the tendency of German idealism to use organological imagery, the double meaning of the German word '*Volk*'—all these circumstances, combined with specific historical conditions, caused the early ethnicization of German national consciousness. Pan-European developments, such as the paradigm shift towards scientific explanatory models intensified the biologization of the political sphere, which was at the core of *völkisch* thought. After all, not all currents following the concept of the history of ideas, which promoted a *völkisch* mentality in Germany were, in fact, specifically German. And there was, indeed, also a strong counter movement within German nationalism. Compared with other countries in Europe, however, none of this was sufficient nor the circumstances favorable enough to enforce a political definition of the term 'German' and to prevent a further dissemination of *völkisch* mentality.

In Germany, it was not just a few *völkisch* extremists and outsiders, but the center of society, above all the *Bildungsbürgertum*, who championed a concept of the nation based on ethnicity and endorsed the further biologization of the term *Volk* during the last third of the nineteenth century, culminating in its racist definition. There are highly visible continuities between the territorial dreams of German nationalists from the 1810s, to the members of the National Assembly in the Paulskirche and the movement of unification during the 1860s, to the pan-German fantasies at the end of Imperial Germany. These continuities require further research.

Summary

1. In contrast to the findings of previous research, the initial stirrings of German nationalism should be situated around 1740. There was, indeed, a national pride

before 1800, and important arguments and stereotypes belonging to the repertoire of national ideology had been developed since early-modern times. Nationalism is more than an ideology, however; it is also a social movement. And this movement did not emerge until circa 1810, and even then only in a limited number of places in the German lands. By 1850, there were only three short periods (1811–1819, 1830–32 and 1848–49) when German nationalism achieved a resonance beyond intellectual elites.

2. Literary movements such as Storm and Stress and romanticism increased the already rapidly growing interest in the '*eigenen*,' the imagined authentic self. This intellectual fashion, with its latent *völkisch* content, was a renunciation of classical antiquity and its educational ideal. Early German nationalism was anti-southern, rather than anti-western in its orientation. The most important internal and external enemies of nationalism (French, Jews, and Catholics) were considered to be representatives of the south and of advanced Mediterranean civilizations alien to 'German nature' (*Deutsches Wesen*). Only the Greeks were seen as related and as a model for Germany thanks to their federalism and republicanism (in addition, there was an enthusiasm for Greece that can be traced back to Winckelmann, as well as the Greek War of Independence against the Ottoman Empire during the 1820s). France, on the other hand, was considered the successor to the Roman Empire for linguistic reasons and due to its political centralism.[68] Catholicism, controlled by Rome, was seen as 'ultramontane,' and Jews were excluded from the nation as an alien culture and religion. Even the assumption that a nation state needed a united national religion and church was directed against Catholicism and was, sometimes openly, sometimes implicitly, anti-Semitic.

3. Political role models for German nationalists came mainly from western Europe: Great Britain, Switzerland, the USA, and after the French Revolution, sometimes even from France and, from 1830 from Belgium as well.

4. In 1848, it had not yet been decided if there were to be one or several German nation states, for instance, a Prussian or Bavarian state. Often, political nationalism relating to a single German state and pan-German ethnic nationalism overlapped.[69]

5. During the second half of the eighteenth century, three versions of nationalism can be differentiated as ideal types: republican, Prussian and 'Reich' nationalism. In terms of the history of ideas, they are related to three tendencies that occurred after 1848: political, ethnic, and historical nationalism. Alongside the controversial positions between the 'Greater German' and the 'Smaller German' solution, they dominated the debates in the Paulskirche. Political nationalism from the middle of the nineteenth century focused, like Johann Georg Zimmermann from Switzerland, on the democratic and republican constitution of the fatherland. The ethnic nationalism strove for a Greater German solution and was thus in the tradition of the 'Reich' nationalism. The type of nationalism, which favored a Smaller German solution, sometimes even a greater Prussian nation state, had already been the most influential current in the National Assembly. It increasingly prevailed after

1849. In the end, Imperial Germany was, indeed, in accordance with the constitutional compromise of Frankfurt in terms of its territorial extension. It also satisfied the demands of ethnic nationalism in re-conquering Alsace and Lorraine. However, the new Empire was not a constitutional monarchy and did not have a canon of basic rights as planned in the constitution of 1849. Furthermore, it failed to meet the vast expectations of political nationalism to initiate a process of democratization.[70]

6. Nationalism before and after 1871 did not differ in terms of being more or less radical or 'integrative.' Hardly any new nationalist arguments emerged after the foundation of Imperial Germany. But nationalism did have a completely different position within the system of rule: it was no longer an opposition (with sometimes even revolutionary tendencies), but for the first time in the history of nationalism and liberalism it supported a government, even though there was hardly any enthusiasm for Bismarck until 1890.[71] From now on, nationalism was established in all strata of society by means of the state and its institutions—from history lessons in schools, to training courses for conscripts, to the historical policy of the government. Former bonds of loyalty finally dissolved in favor of the ultimate value of the 'nation.'

Different factors in terms of geography, politics, and the history of ideas determined the specific development of German nationalism. 'Germany' was extremely heterogeneous. A deep confessional divide reshaped former regional and local differences after the Reformation and the Wars of Religion. The modern process of nation-building increased the divergences in Imperial Germany. After the end of the former Holy Roman Empire and due to the French occupation, countless ruling governments vanished. Viable middle states, some with the potential for nation-building, emerged. But there had always been more than just one 'German' state. Within the German Confederation, there were forty-one separate states; from 1871, there was the Greater Prussian Empire and the Habsburg Monarchy, part of which was German; and after 1918, there was Austria and the Weimar Republic, excluding, for the moment, German-speaking parts of Switzerland. It was only the Nazis who forcefully tried to realize a single 'Greater Germany.' After the allied coalition against Hitler put an end to this policy and its dreadful results, there were three, and since 1990 just two, German-speaking states again.

[Translated from German by Christine Brocks.]

Notes

1. Bernhard Giesen, *Die Intellektuellen und die Nation* (Frankfurt am Main: Suhrkamp, 1993), 29; Karl R. Popper, *The Open Society and Its Enemies*, vol. 2 (Princeton: Princeton University Press, 1966), 49–51.

2. Karl W. Deutsch, 'Nation und Welt,' in Heinrich A. Winkler (ed.), *Nationalismus* (Cologne: Kiepenheuer & Witsch, 1985), 50.

3. Benedict Anderson, *Imagined Communities. Reflections on the Origin and Spread of Nationalism*, 2nd ed.(London: Verso, 1996), 6.

4. Ernest Gellner, *Nations and Nationalism* (Oxford: Basil Blackwell, 1983); idem, *Nationalismus. Kultur und Macht* (Berlin: Siedler, 1999); Eric J. Hobsbawm, *Nations and Nationalism since 1780. Programme, Myth, Reality* (Cambridge: Cambridge University Press, 1990). Gellner's definitions are very debatable because of their implications in terms of modernization theory. Cf. on recent theoretical discussion Christian Jansen and Henning Borggräfe, *Nation-Nationalität-Nationalismus* (Frankfurt a.M.: Campus, 2007), 7–32 and 82–117.

5. Cf. on the European debate on 'national character,' see Wolfgang Burgdorf, '"Reichsnationalismus" gegen "Territorialnationalismus." Phasen der Intensivierung des nationalen Bewußtseins in Deutschland seit dem Siebenjährigen Krieg,' in Dieter Langewiesche and Georg Schmidt (eds), *Föderative Nation* (Munich: Oldenbourg, 2000), 159–160.

6. See Ute Planert, 'Wann beginnt der "moderne" deutsche Nationalismus?,' in Jörg Echternkamp and Sven-Oliver Müller (eds), *Politik der Nation. Deutscher Nationalismus in Krieg und Krisen 1760–1960* (Munich: Oldenbourg, 2002), 25–59; Planert, 'Nationalismus,' 28–43; Dieter Langewiesche, '"Nation," "Nationalismus," "Nationalstaat" in der europäischen Geschichte seit dem Mittelalter—Versuch einer Bilanz,' in Langewiesche and Schmidt (eds), *Föderative Nation*, 9–32.

7. Ute Planert, *Der Mythos vom Befreiungskrieg. Frankreichs Kriege und der deutsche Süden: Alltag-Wahrnehmung-Deutung 1792-1841* (Paderborn: Schöningh, 2007), 477–482.

8. For references see Planert, 'Nationalismus,' 26–27; Burgdorf, 'Reichsnationalismus,' 158. In my opinion, there is no need to use the adjective 'modern' for nationalism since nationalism, as such, is a modern phenomenon.

9. Langewiesche, 'Nation,' 12–13.

10. Otto Dann, *Nation und Nationalismus in Deutschland 1770–1990* (Munich: Beck, 1996), 16–20; similarly Heinrich August Winkler, 'Vom linken zum rechten Nationalismus. Der deutsche Liberalismus in der Krise von 1878/79,' *Geschichte und Gesellschaft* 4 (1978), 5–28; Hans-Ulrich Wehler, *Nationalismus. Geschichte, Formen, Folgen* (Munich: Beck, 2001); Peter Alter, *Nationalismus* (Frankfurt am Main: Suhrkamp, 1985). Against these positions cf. Hans Peter Herrmann et al. (eds), *Machtphantasie Deutschland. Nationalismus, Männlichkeit und Fremdenhaß im Vaterlandsdiskurs deutscher Schriftsteller des 18. Jahrhunderts* (Frankfurt am Main: Suhrkamp, 1996).

11. This paradigm shift goes back to Dieter Langewiesche's 'Nationalismus im 19. und 20. Jahrhundert: zwischen Partizipation und Aggression' (1994), now in idem., *Nation*, 35–54.

12. Cf. Karen Hagemann, *'Mannlicher Muth und teutsche Ehre.' Nation, Militär und Geschlecht zur Zeit der antinapoleonischen Kriege Preußens* (Paderborn: Schöningh, 2002).

13. Johann Georg Zimmermann, *Von dem Nationalstolze* (Zürich: Heidegger, 1758); Thomas Abbt, *Vom Tode für das Vaterland* (Berlin: Nicolai, 1761), in Johannes Kunisch (ed.), *Aufklärung und Kriegserfahrung* (Frankfurt am Main: Deutscher Klassiker Verlag, 1996), 589–650.

14. Zimmermann, *Nationalstolz*, 210.

15. Cf. Jansen and Borggräfe, *Nation*, 147ff.

16. Zimmermann, *Nationalstolz*, 178–188, 17, 21–22 and 52.

17. Ibid., 95–96 and 210.

18. Abbt, *Vom Tode*, 597–606, esp. 599–600. Cf. Burgdorf, '*Reichsnationalismus*,' 163–164 and 168–169; Planert, *Mythos*, 480–481.

19. Abbt, *Vom Tode*, 600–601. Cf. Eckhart Hellmuth, 'Die "Wiedergeburt" Friedrichs des Großen und der "Tod fürs Vaterland." Zum patriotischen Selbstverständnis in Preußen in der zweiten Hälfte des 18. Jahrhunderts,' *Aufklärung* 10 (1998), 45–47.

20. Abbt, *Vom Tode*, 631, 625 and 594. Cf. Burgdorf, 'Reichsnationalismus,' 163–164.

21. Cf. Christian Jansen (ed.), *Der Bürger als Soldat. Die Militarisierung europäischer Gesellschaften im langen 19. Jahrhundert* (Essen: Klartext, 2004).

22. Abbt, *Vom Tode*, 610 and 616–618. Cf. Burgdorf, 'Reichsnationalismus,' 167–168.

23. Burgdorf, 'Reichsnationalismus,' 163–164.

24. Hellmuth, 'Wiedergeburt,' 52ff.; Linda Colley, *Britons. Forging the Nation 1707–1837* (New Haven: Yale University Press, 1992); Wolfgang Kruse, *Die Erfindung des modernen Militarismus. Krieg, Militär und bürgerliche Gesellschaft im politischen Diskurs der Französischen Revolution 1789–1799* (Munich: Oldenbourg, 2003); David Bell, *The Cult of the Nation in France: Inventing Nationalism, 1680–1800* (Cambridge: Havard University Press, 2001).

25. Often called 'Reichspatriotismus' (referred to the Holy Roman Empire). Due to the reasons mentioned above, 'Reichsnationalismus' appears to be more consistent.

26. His father was Johann Jacob Moser, a famous specialist in constitutional law and publicist, who was held in detention without trial for his leading participation in the opposition against the Duke of Württemberg.

27. Burgdorf, 'Reichsnationalismus,' 170.

28. Friedrich Carl von Moser, *Von dem deutschen National-Geist* (Frankfurt am Main: Schäfer 1765), 5–6, similarly 50–51.

29. Moser, *National-Geist*, 9 and 13 (also the following quotes). It is significant that the French are not mentioned in this listing, although elsewhere (54) the French armies were denounced as destroyers of the 'German freedom.'

30. Ibid., 56, 65f. and 72f.

31. Like all major contemporary states, the Reich did not have a written constitution. When Moser and others mentioned a constitution, they were referring to regulations of common law emerged from tradition and custom with a long history as well as several written basic rights.

32. On Christoph Martin Wieland, who edited between 1773 and 1810 an influential political magazine and offered alternatives to nationalism, see Irmtraud Sahmland, *Christoph Martin Wieland und die deutsche Nation. Zwischen Patriotismus, Kosmopolitismus und Griechentum* (Tübingen: Niemeyer, 1990).

33. *Noth-und Hilfsbüchlein für Bauersleute* (1788), quoted in Reinhart Koselleck et al., 'Volk, Nation, Nationalismus, Masse,' in Otto Brunner, Werner Conze, and Reinhart Kosseleck (eds), *Geschichtliche Grundbegriffe*, vol. 7 (Stuttgart: Klett Cotta, 1992), 315.

34. Herder's work is rather heterogeneous and he never brought his ideas on nation-building into systematic focus. Important are Johann Gottfried Herder, 'Sammlung von Gedanken und Beispielen fremder Schriftsteller über die Bildung der Völker,' 'Über die Bildung der Völker' (both 1769) and 'Idee zum ersten patriotischen Institut für den Allgemeingeist Deutschlands' (1787), in Johann Gottfried Herder, *Werke*, Günter Arnold et al. (eds), vol. 9/2 (Frankfurt am Main: Deutscher Klassiker Verlag, 1997), 212–221, 225–227 and 565–575. Cf. Helmut Walser Smith, *The Continuities of German History. Nation, Religion, and*

Race across the Long Nineteenth Century (Cambridge: Cambridge University Press, 2008), 54–59, who argues that Herder brings about 'a shift from exteriority to interiority, [. . .] from sight to sound' (55–56). See also Hans Kohn, *The Idea of Nationalism. A Study in its Origin and Background* (New York: Macmillan, 1944), 427–451.

35. Johann Gottfried Herder, 'Auszug aus einem Briefwechsel über Oßian und die Lieder alter Völker,' in: *Von deutscher Art und Kunst* (1773) (Stuttgart: Reclam, 1999), 7–62. Herder advocated the systematic collection of 'popular and rural songs, songs from different provinces [. . .] from the streets and alleys and from fish markets' and praised their 'vivacity and rhythm, their naivety and power of language.' This meant a revolutionary breach with literary conventions.

36. Cf. Heinrich Heine, 'Briefe aus Berlin' (1822), in idem, *Werke und Briefe in zehn Bänden*, vol. 3 (Berlin: Aufbau, 1972), 522f., where he refers to a Walter Scott fashion and a masquerade ball with all participants being dressed up like characters from Scott's novels; Christian Jansen, *Einheit, Macht und Freiheit. Die Paulskirchenlinke und die deutsche Politik in der nachrevolutionären Epoche 1849-1867* (Düsseldorf: Droste, 2005), 256–258.

37. Johann Gottfried Herder, 'Ueber die Fähigkeit zu sprechen und zu hören', *Neue Deutsche Monatsschrift* 2 (1795), 57–58.

38. Idem, 'Idee zum ersten patriotischen Institut,' 568–569 and 572–573.

39. Cf. Ute Schneider, 'Die Erfindung des Bösen: Der Welsche,' in Gerd Krumeich and Hartmut Lehmann (ed.), *'Gott mit uns.' Religion, Nation und Gewalt* (Göttingen: Vandenhoeck & Ruprecht, 2000), 35–51.

40. Koselleck, 'Volk,' 283; cf. ibid., 316–318.

41. Elisabeth Fehrenbach, 'Nation,' in *Handbuch politisch-sozialer Grundbegriffe in Frankreich 1680-1820, vol. 7* (Munich: Oldenbourg, 1986), 92–93 and 76; Jörg Echternkamp, *Der Aufstieg des deutschen Nationalismus (1770-1840)* (Frankfurt am Main: Campus, 1998), 495; Hobsbawm, *Nations and Nationalism*, 22; Johann Gottlieb Fichte, *Addresses to the German Nation* (Chicago and London: The Open Court Company, 1922), fourth address.

42. Hagemann, *Mannlicher Muth*, 131ff.

43. Echternkamp, *Aufstieg*, 490.

44. Cf. Dieter Düding, 'Die deutsche Nationalbewegung im 19. Jahrhundert,' in Peter Krüger (ed.), *Deutschland, deutscher Staat, deutsche Nation* (Marburg: Hitzeroth, 1993), 72.

45. Planert, *Mythos*, 383–473 (impressive on the opposition against conscription), 596–613 and 656–657.

46. Düding, 'Nationalbewegung,' 71–73; Echternkamp, *Aufstieg*, 353–355.

47. Cf. Steven Michael Press, 'False Fire: The Wartburg Book-Burning of 1817,' in: *Central European History*, 42 (2009), 621–646.

48. Cf. Echternkamp, *Aufstieg*, 42–44, 483–485 and 493–495; Jansen and Borggräfe, *Nation*, 45–47.

49. Ernst Moritz Arndt, *Blick aus der Zeit auf die Zeit* (n.p. 1814), 190; cf. Smith, *Continuities*, 105.

50. Cf. Smith, *Continuities*, 104–108; Hagemann, *Mannlicher Muth*, 255–270.

51. Jakob Friedrich Fries, 'Über die Ansprüche der Juden an das deutsche Bürgerrecht,' 'Über die Gefährdung des Wohlstandes und des Charakters der Deutschen durch die Juden,' in *Heidelbergische Jahrbücher der Literatur* 16/17 (1816), 248 and 260.

52. Georg Friedrich Hegel, *Rechtsphilosophie* (Frankfurt am Main: Suhrkamp, 1970), §§ 346 ff.

53. Fichte, *Addresses*, 130 (eighth address). Cf. Jansen/Borggräfe, *Nation*, 48. I am discussing Fichte only briefly, because there are quite a few good interpretations of Fichte e.g. Smith, *Continuities*, 58–71.

54. Hagemann, *Mannlicher Muth*, 167; Schneider, 'Erfindung,' 42.
55. Giesen, *Die Intellektuellen*, 227–228.
56. Planert, *Mythos*, 613–619.
57. Düding, 'Nationalismus,' 92–93, 107 and 111–113.
58. Düding, 'Nationalismus,' 180–182 and 225–227.
59. Andreas Biefang, *Politisches Bürgertum in Deutschland 1857–1868. Nationale Organizationen und Eliten* (Düsseldorf: Droste, 1994), 31–33.
60. *Stenographischer Bericht über die Verhandlungen der deutschen Nationalversammlung zu Frankfurt am Main (1848–49)* (Frankfurt am Main: Wigard, 1848–49), 1111.
61. Günter Wollstein, *Das 'Großdeutschland' der Paulskirche. Nationale Ziele in der bürgerlichen Revolution 1848/49* (Düsseldorf: Droste, 1977), 325–326.
62. Cf. Johann Gottlieb Fichte, 'Republik der Deutschen,' in idem, *Gesamtausgabe, Part II, vol. 10: Nachgelassene Schriften 1806–1807* (Stuttgart: Frommann, 1994); *Stenographischer Bericht*, 1160.
63. Ibid., 1141–1148.
64. Ibid., 4621.
65. Here, and the preceding quotations are from Ludwig Bamberger, 'Lettre sur l'unité allemande et le Parlement de Erfurth,' *La Voix du Peuple, Paris*, 4.3.1850 and 11.3.1850.
66. Jakob Venedey, 'Die Diplomatie in der schleswig-holstein'schen Frage,' *Deutsche Monatsschrift für Politik, Wissenschaft, Kunst und Leben* (Stuttgart 1850/I), 8–10 and 30–31.
67. The 'codification struggle' between Anton Thibaut und Friedrich v. Savigny in 1814 was significant for anti-Roman resentments. Cf. Claudia Schöler, *Deutsche Rechtseinheit. Partikulare und nationale Gesetzgebung (1780–1866)* (Cologne: Böhlau, 2004).
68. On the juxtaposition of nationalism and regionalism since 1871 cf. Siegfried Weichlein, *Nation und Region. Integrationsprozesse im Bismarckreich* (Düsseldorf: Droste, 2004).
69. Those still advocating the constitution of 1849 even beyond its failure were called supporters of a 'smaller German solution.' Those demanding an even stronger predominance were supporters of a 'Great Prussian' solution.
70. Cf. Christian Jansen, 'Der Anteil der Liberalen und Demokraten an der deutschen Nations-und Nationalstaatsbildung zwischen Revolution und Reichsgründung,' in *Jahrbuch zur Liberalismusforschung* 16 (2004), 57–73.
71. Cf. idem, 'Bismarck: Modernität und Repression, Gewaltsamkeit und List. Ein absolutistischer Staatsdiener im Zeitalter der Massenpolitik,' in Frank Möller (ed.), *Charismatische Führer der deutschen Nation* (Munich: Oldenbourg, 2004), 63–83.

BIBLIOGRAPHY

BURGDORF, WOLFGANG, '"Reichsnationalismus" gegen "Territorialnationalismus." Phasen der Intensivierung des nationalen Bewußtseins in Deutschland seit dem Siebenjährigen Krieg,' in Dieter Langewiesche and Georg Schmidt (eds), *Föderative Nation* (Munich: Oldenbourg, 2000), 157–190.

DÜDING, DIETER, *Organisierter gesellschaftlicher Nationalismus in Deutschland (1808–1847)* (Munich: Oldenbourg, 1983).

ECHTERNKAMP, JÖRG, *Der Aufstieg des deutschen Nationalismus (1770–1840)* (Frankfurt am Main: Campus, 1998).

GIESEN, BERNHARD, *Die Intellektuellen und die Nation* (Frankfurt a.M: Suhrkamp, 1993)

HAGEMANN, KAREN, *'Mannlicher Muth und teutsche Ehre.' Nation, Militär und Geschlecht zur Zeit der antinapoleonischen Kriege Preußens* (Paderborn: Schöningh, 2002).

HELLMUTH, ECKHART, 'Die "Wiedergeburt" Friedrichs des Großen und der "Tod fürs Vaterland." Zum patriotischen Selbstverständnis in Preußen in der zweiten Hälfte des 18. Jahrhunderts,' *Aufklärung* 10 (1998), 21–52.

HERRMANN, HANS PETER et al. (eds), *Machtphantasie Deutschland. Nationalismus, Männlichkeit und Fremdenhaß im Vaterlandsdiskurs deutscher Schriftsteller des 18. Jahrhunderts* (Frankfurt am Main: Suhrkamp, 1996).

JANSEN, CHRISTIAN and HENNING BORGGRÄFE, *Nation-Nationalität-Nationalismus* (Frankfurt am Main: Campus, 2007).

KLENKE, DIETMAR, *Der singende deutsche Mann. Gesangvereine und Nationalbewußtsein von Napoleon bis Hitler* (Münster: Waxmann, 1998).

KOSELLECK, REINHART et al., 'Volk, Nation, Nationalismus, Masse,' in Otto Brunner, Werner Conze, and Reinhart Kosseleck (eds), *Geschichtliche Grundbegriffe*, vol. 7 (Stuttgart: Klett Cotta, 1992), 141–431.

LANGEWIESCHE, DIETER, *Nation, Nationalismus, Nationalstaat in Deutschland und Europa* (München: C. H. Beck, 2000).

PLANERT, UTE, 'Wann beginnt der "moderne" deutsche Nationalismus?' in Jörg Echternkamp and Sven-Oliver Müller, (eds), *Politik der Nation. Deutscher Nationalismus in Krieg und Krisen 1760–1960* (Munich: Oldenbourg, 2002), 25–59.

—— *Der Mythos vom Befreiungskrieg. Frankreichs Kriege und der deutsche Süden: Alltag-Wahrnehmung-Deutung 1792–1841* (Paderborn: Schöningh, 2007).

SCHULZE, HAGEN, *Staat und Nation in der europäischen Geschichte* (Munich: C. H. Beck, 2004).

SMITH, HELMUT WALSER, *The Continuities of German History. Nation, Religion, and Race across the Long Nineteenth Century* (Cambridge: Cambridge University Press, 2008).

CHAPTER 12

··

GERMAN LITERATURE AND THOUGHT FROM 1810 TO 1890

··

RITCHIE ROBERTSON

APPROACHING nineteenth-century German culture, one needs to free oneself from several misconceptions that have proved surprisingly durable. One is that Germans were devoted to cloudy, theoretical idealism that stayed remote from concrete reality. Heinrich Heine (1797–1856) famously leveled this charge against his fellow-countrymen in *Deutschland. Ein Wintermärchen* ('Germany: A Winter's Tale,' 1844):

> Franzosen und Russen gehört das Land,
> Das Meer gehört den Briten,
> Wir aber besitzen im Luftreich des Traums
> Die Herrschaft unbestritten.[1]

> The land is held by the Russians and French,
> The sea's by the British invested,
> But in the airy realm of dreams
> Our sway is uncontested.[2]

However, Heine was writing polemic, not analysis, inspired by a sense that Germany's political development was lagging behind other European countries. His fragmented nation, suffering under illiberal princely governments, had no counterpart to the July Revolution in France or the Reform Bill of 1832 in Britain. His indictment should no more be accepted at face value than should a group of related misconceptions about German fiction. It is commonly asserted that German authors favored the *Novelle*, rather than the novel; that they practiced a special literary mode called 'poetic realism'; and that in contrast to the realism of Balzac or Dickens, German novelists specialized in an unworldly, introverted form of fiction, focusing on the inner development of the hero, and termed the *Bildungsroman*. These myths, arising from the formation of a national literary canon in the late nineteenth century, have obscured the fact that Germans wrote a vast body of realist fiction, engaging in detail with their society. They have also diverted attention from two aspects of nineteenth-century German literature that can be called distinctive. German writers were some 50 years ahead of such British counterparts as George Eliot or Thomas Hardy in confronting a post-Christian universe. German literature, unlike English or French, continued to excel in tragic drama.

The hallmark of German literature and thought in the nineteenth century is an engagement with reality. Two well-known episodes can serve as emblems of this commitment. One concerns Hegel (1770–1831). Heine, who attended Hegel's lectures in Berlin and knew him personally, tells how he initially thought the philosopher a mere political time-server on the strength of the famous sentence 'Whatever is rational, is real;' but Hegel said to him: 'It could also run: Whatever is rational must become real'—i.e. political systems must be reformed in accordance with the demands of reason.[3] It used to be thought that Heine had invented this anecdote to suggest that Hegel's abstract reasoning should be applied to contemporary politics, but a draft has now been found in which Hegel writes that the rational must *become* real.[4] The relation between philosophy and concrete reality was there in Hegel's thought, although censorship required him to veil his true meaning.

The second emblem of German engagement with reality is the programmatic statement by Leopold von Ranke (1795–1886): 'History has been assigned the task of judging the past and instructing the present for the benefit of the future. The present essay attempts no such lofty tasks. It seeks only to say what really happened.'[5] This is not, as is sometimes claimed, a naïve attempt to recreate the past. Rather, Ranke, the pioneer of historical research based on archival documents, is distancing himself from earlier historians who sought to draw moral or even theological lessons from history. Instead, he sets himself the humbler, but fundamental task of establishing what actually happened, so far as the sources allow. With this approach, one would not ask, for example, whether Martin Luther was divinely inspired, but whether or not he really said at the Diet of Worms, 'Here I stand, I can do no other.' It is only on the basis of established facts that any more ambitious statement about history can hope to be true.

In exploring how nineteenth-century German writers engaged with reality, the conventional literary periods are not particularly helpful. It is customary to call the period from 1815 to the 1848 Revolutions '*Biedermeier*,' a term connoting cozy, domestic, small-scale, unambitious work; the term was rescued from its disparaging implications only by Friedrich Sengle's monumental study of the period. Late Romanticism spills over into this period, and its latter phase turns into the 'Vormärz,' the time of political stirrings leading up to the Berlin revolution of March 1848. After 1848 comes the '*Nachmärz*,' which shades into the '*Gründerzeit*,' the period of sudden economic expansion following the establishment of the German Empire. Insofar as these labels are drawn from external political history, they are unserviceable, even confusing, when imposed on the development of literature, and here they will largely be avoided.

Early in our period, an engagement with the real takes complex and contradictory forms. Hegelian idealism is not supposed to lead away from reality, but rather to reveal the inner structure of reality as a succession of forms in the development of *Geist* (mind/spirit). Hence, it was consistent that Hegel in his later works should trace this development in the specific areas of history, law, and aesthetics. Dealing with the last of these, however, he argues that art must eventually become obsolete. It will be replaced by philosophy as a more direct and appropriate way of understanding the abstract structure of reality. Wilhelm von Humboldt takes a somewhat similar view when contrasting Greek with modern art. The Greeks' concern with the ideal produced a calm and harmonious art, but moderns are concerned with reality, which is hard to get into focus and may even elude the boundaries of art; if so, it is to our credit that we value reality above art: 'if respect for art is the sign of an ascending age, then respect for reality is the hallmark of one that has risen yet higher.'[6]

The writers conventionally called Romantics would not agree that art can be super-seded, but they do retreat from the grandiose ambitions to fuse art and life that were formulated, for example, by the early Romantic poet Friedrich von Hardenberg (*Novalis*, 1772–1801) in such statements as: 'Our life is not a dream, but it should and perhaps will become one.'[7] This retreat is apparent in the finest work of E.T.A. Hoffmann (1776–1822). The story he himself considered his masterpiece, *Der goldne Topf* (The Golden Pot, 1814), is subtitled 'A Modern Fairy-Tale.' Hoffmann takes up the fairy-tale genre popularized by Goethe (*Das Märchen*, 1795) and Ludwig Tieck (1773–1853; *Der blonde Eckbert*, 1797), but transfers it from fairyland to modern Dresden. The student Anselmus, ill-at-ease in bourgeois society and needing a job, is employed by the Archivist Lindhorst to copy documents; but the Archivist is also a salamander, i.e. a nature-spirit, banished from the realm of Atlantis to earth, and permitted to return only when his three daughters have young men with poetic souls—rare creatures in these benighted times. Lindhorst's youngest daughter, Serpentina, who is both a beautiful woman and a snake, guides Anselmus through his trials, until the two are united in Atlantis. In the last chapter, Hoffmann dissolves the boundaries of reality and fiction by making his narrator call on Lindhorst, who tells him that the happiness now enjoyed by Anselmus is available to anyone, for it is 'life in poetry, where the holy harmony of all things is revealed as the deepest secret of nature.'[8] This conclusion is two-sided. While affirming a Romantic utopia of the imagination, it also concedes that this utopia exists *only* in the imagination.

Hoffmann expressed deeper doubts in *Der Sandmann* ('The Sandman', 1816), which hovers between two genres—the fantastic fairy-tale and the realist *Novelle*. Its protag-onist, the poetically-minded student Nathanael, feels pursued by the Sandman, a creature from nursery tales which he identifies with his father's sinister friend, the lawyer Coppelius, and with an Italian peddler called Coppola who sells him a pocket telescope. With this aid to vision Nathanael is deluded into love for Olimpia, an automaton created by the mad scientist Spalanzani, and rejects his loving, but prosaic girl-friend Clara. Even before the catastrophe, the story asks whether the poetic imagination may not serve morbid and self-centered obsessions; whether nursery tales may fatally poison the imagination; and whether the morbid imagination, while often blind to other people, may have an insight into the machinations of dark forces, which it is at the same time unable to resist. The imagination that saved Anselmus destroys Nathanael. The ambiguities of this tale of terror, which Freud analyzed at length in 'The Uncanny' (1919), perennially fascinate readers. It is not surprising that in Hoffmann's later fairy-tales, *Prinzessin Brambilla* (1820) and *Meister Floh* (1822), his protagonists finally reject the fairy-tale world in favor of actual domestic life; while one of his last stories, *Des Vetters Eckfenster* (My Cousin's Corner Window, 1822), shows an invalid, confined to his room, using his imagination to reconstruct the actual lives of the Berlin citizens he sees from his window.

Another way in which Romantics applied the imagination to contemporary reality was through nationalist politics. It was during Germany's subjugation by Napoleon that Achim von Arnim (1781–1831) and Clemens Brentano (1778–1842) published their collection of folk-songs, *Des Knaben Wunderhorn* (The Boy's Magic Horn, 1805–1808), and the brothers Jakob Grimm (1785–1863) and Wilhelm Grimm (1786–1859) their *Kinder- und Hausmärchen* (1812–1814). Following Herder's advocacy of popular literature as the expression of the 'Volksgeist,' these writers claimed to be demonstrating the innate creativity of the German people. Such claims have not worn well. Not only was it hard to collect oral material before the invention of the tape recorder, but Arnim and Brentano took many poems from printed sources, while at least one of the Grimms' informants was of Huguenot descent and told them versions of the fairy-tales written in the seventeenth century by Charles Perrault. Moreover, the Grimms revised their tales in successive editions, creating an artificial fairy-tale style, and introducing a harsh moral message. Thus, in revising *Aschenputtel* ('Cinderella') they invented a punishment in which the wicked sisters had their eyes pecked out by pigeons. They also censored the story of *Sneewittchen* ('Snow White') by changing the original version, in which Snow White's mother tried to kill her, but she was rescued by her father, into one involving a stepmother and a prince, thus leaving the nuclear family intact. The Grimms promoted conservative family values, and the conception of the creative and enduring German people (*Volk*). They were convinced that their folk-tales were linked to ancient Germanic myth. The Grimms had originally studied law under Friedrich von Savigny (1779–1861, brother-in-law of Clemens Brentano) who founded the Historical School of Law, seeing law as the expression not of universal values, but of a specific historical tradition. They moved into German mythology and philology, and are of lasting importance as scholars for their Dictionary, the German equivalent of the Oxford English Dictionary. They were also staunch liberals: in 1837 they were among the 'Göttingen Seven,' a group of professors who resigned from Göttingen University, rather than take an unconstitutional oath of personal loyalty to the King of Hanover. Nationalist enthusiasm was felt by liberals, rather than conservatives: it was liberals who imagined a united Germany in which the petty princes would be swept away, and who in 1848 offered the crown of a united Germany to the King of Prussia.

Late Romanticism becomes laden with pessimism and irony. Heine, who intensely admired the folk-songs collected by Arnim and Brentano and those later written by Wilhelm Müller (1794–1827) (including *Die Winterreise* ['The Winter Journey'] and *Die schöne Müllerin* ['The Miller's Beautiful Daughter'], made famous by Schubert), wrote to Müller: 'How pure and clear your songs are, and they are all folks-songs. In my poems, on the other hand, only the form is in some degree popular, the content comes from conventional society.'[9] The short lyric poems in Heine's *Buch der Lieder* (1827) record gradual recovery from unrequited love (whether this has any biographical basis is unclear); the speaker views his past self with ironic mockery, and thus both affirms romantic desire and laughs at its folly. The poems illustrate the internal division or laceration (*Zerrissenheit*), which became a cliché of the time (satirized especially in Johann Nestroy's Viennese comedy *Der Zerrissene*, 1844). In his prose text *Die Bäder von Lucca* ('The Baths of Lucca,' 1830), Heine defends the notion:

> Alas, dear reader, if you want to complain about this laceration, then complain rather that the world itself is torn down the middle. For, since the poet's heart is the centre of the world, it cannot help being lamentably torn at the present time.[10]

If the world was split, one fault-line ran between religious belief and factual knowledge. The historical study of Christianity, going back to Lessing and the Göttingen school of Bible scholars, had helped to undermine belief in the supernatural claims of religion. Their work was continued by the Tübingen theologians, including David Friedrich Strauss (1808–1874) with his *Life of Jesus, Critically Examined* (1835–1836). Strauss opposes both naïve credulity and the rationalizing explanations of Gospel miracles popular in the previous century. Much in the Gospels must be understood as myth, he says, but that should not undermine the truth of religion, which is founded on spiritual conviction, not historical facts: 'Christ's supernatural birth, his miracles, his resurrection and ascension, remain eternal truths, however much their reality as historical facts may be doubted.'[11] For Strauss's realistic age, however, the Gospels ultimately could not survive without a historical basis. To many readers, Strauss prepared the way for Ludwig Feuerbach (1804–1872), whose *Essence of Christianity* (1841) explained religious belief as a compensation for the actual misery of life: human beings, conscious of their own imperfection and unhappiness, imagined a supreme and perfect being, but ought instead to transfer their energies from heaven to earth and work to improve their own condition. This argument, in the opinion of Karl Marx (1818–1883), provided a basis for socialism. He wrote to Feuerbach: 'The unity of man with man based on the real differences between men, the concept of human species transferred from the heaven of abstraction to the real earth, what is this other than the concept of society!'[12]

Religious skepticism encouraged poets to explore the theme of 'Weltschmerz' or cosmic pain. The poetry of Nikolaus Lenau (1802–1850) expresses the loss of religious faith by repeated images of empty or damaged crosses, but also rejects the Romantic attempt to elevate nature into a religious substitute, evoking many desolate landscapes and scenes of suffering. Even for such a committed Christian poet as the Westphalian Catholic Annette von Droste-Hülshoff (1797–1848), religious faith was now strenuous.

Droste's devotional cycle '*Das geistliche Jahr*' ('The Spiritual Year') reveals a religious life troubled by the conflict between faith and knowledge. Instead of following a clearly lit path, the believer must now either grope through mist or perform daredevil feats of spiritual mountaineering:

> War einst erhellt der schwanke Steg,
> Und klaffte klar der Abgrund auf,
> Wir müssen suchen unsern Weg
> Im Heiderauch ein armer Hauf.
> Des Glaubens köstlich teurer Preis
> Ward wie gestellt auf Gletschers Höhen;
> Wir müssen klimmen über Eis
> Und schwindelnd uns am Schlunde drehen.[13]

[Though once the narrow path was brightly lit, and the abyss yawned clearly, we, a wretched band, have to seek our way amid thick mist. The precious reward of faith has been placed atop a glacier; we must scramble over ice and leap over a dizzying crevasse.]

In the work of the Lutheran clergyman-poet Eduard Mörike (1804–1875), a friend and admirer of Strauss, Christianity features mainly as an attraction to the figure of the child Jesus. Mörike pays homage to the Romantic conception of human life as embedded in nature, but also performs a post-Romantic rejection of it, in the poems *An einem Wintermorgen, vor Sonnenaufgang* ('On a winter morning before sunrise'), where the speaker turns way from the Romantic night to face the day, and '*Mein Fluss*' ('My river'), where the speaker, after a morning swim, extricates himself from the sensuous seduction of the river and is relieved to be back on the firm bank. The Romantic supernatural strongly appeals to him. Yet the sinister and pathetic gypsy girls in the 'Peregrina' cycle and the novel *Maler Nolten* ('Nolten the Painter', 1832) are also destructive. The pagan divinity haunting the grove in *Die schöne Buche* ('The beautiful beech-tree') is an object of awe, while the Christmas rose in *Auf eine Christblume* ('On a Christmas Rose') embodies a complex response to the Christian story of incarnation. Mörike turns in his exquisite poetry to celebrate the concrete details of everyday life: the joys of friendship in *An Wilhelm Hartlaub*, the charms of life in a rural vicarage in the idyll *Der alte Turmhahn* ('The old weathercock'), which is supposed to be uttered by a superannuated weathercock that has been moved from the church spire to the stove in the vicar's study.

For many people, a convincing post-Christian outlook was articulated by Arthur Schopenhauer (1788–1860) in *The World as Will and Idea* (1819). Schopenhauer revised Kant, arguing that the 'thing in itself' concealed behind appearances is a single force, the Will, which makes its presence felt in the growth of trees, the energies of animals, and the desires of men and women, particularly in their sexual appetites. Through these appetites the Will perpetuates itself for no purpose—certainly not in order to make us happy. We become aware of the vanity of life principally through time. Pain and boredom seem to last a long time; pleasure is brief. Pain is so hateful and so frequent that life can never be worthwhile. Non-existence would be better than existence. We can find temporary release from the tormenting pressure of the Will in the contemplation of art, especially music, which Schopenhauer (in contrast to Kant) elevates to the highest form of art because it is the immediate expression of the Will. The highest human value, however, is pity for suffering; and the only solution for life's problems is to renounce the Will, to desire nothing, as the Buddhists do in order to attain Nirvana. Schopenhauer was an important mediator of Buddhist and Hindu thought to the West. However, he wrote too early. For most of his life he was much less well known than his mother, the novelist and salon hostess Johanna Schopenhauer (1766–1838). From the mid-century on, however, he was much read, and his admirers, such as Wagner, Nietzsche, and Thomas Mann, often described their first reading of Schopenhauer as an illumination. 'I am among those readers of Schopenhauer,' announced Nietzsche in 1874, 'who, after reading the first page, know for certain that they will read every page and attend to every word he ever uttered.'[14]

Repression and censorship discouraged writers from addressing major social and political themes; those who attempted it were increasingly forced into exile. The radical journalist Ludwig Börne (1786–1837) moved to Paris, where the July Revolution of 1830 and the installation of the citizen-king Louis Philippe made German liberals hope for similar events at home, and was soon joined by Heine; the latter, however, disliked the exile gatherings in smoke-filled rooms over which Börne presided, and satirized them and him cruelly in *Ludwig Börne: Eine Denkschrift* ('Ludwig Borne: A Memorial,' 1840), published after Börne's death. However, as early as 1831 Heine expressed artistic radicalism by rejecting the classicism associated with Goethe and proclaiming 'the end of the period of art, which began at Goethe's cradle and will end at his coffin.'[15] Although, like Hegel, he contemplated the end of art altogether, he soon announced a new, politically radical art in the work of *Junges Deutschland* (Young Germany), whose writers 'make no distinction between living and writing, never separate politics from scholarship, art and religion, and are at the same time artists, tribunes, and apostles.'[16]

'*Junges Deutschland*' refers not to any organized movement, but to a number of liberal writers, including Karl Gutzkow (1811–1878), Heinrich Laube (1806–1884), and Theodor Mundt (1808–1861), who wanted to discuss society critically in their novels. The best-known of their novels was Gutzkow's *Wally, die Zweiflerin* ('Wally the Sceptic,' 1835), recounting a young woman's relationship with her morally and intellectually emancipated, but cynical lover, which ends in her suicide. The novel caused great offense by its sharp criticism of Christianity and by its sexual boldness, particularly a scene in which Wally, about to marry a man she does not love, allows her lover to see her naked. The scandal gave the Prussian authorities a pretext for banning as immoral the works of the six writers chiefly associated with *Junges Deutschland*, including Heine.

Far more radical was Georg Büchner (1813–1837), most of whose *œuvre* was unpublished when he died prematurely of typhoid. As a medical student in Strasbourg he founded a clandestine semi-communist society, and tried to promote insurrection in his native Hessen with his hard-hitting pamphlet *Der hessische Landbote* ('The Hessian

Country Messenger,' 1834). These plans were betrayed; Büchner's main associate later died in prison; Büchner himself, a political refugee, presently secured a lectureship in anatomy at Zurich. Meanwhile, he was writing astonishing works—*Dantons Tod*, a drama set in the French Revolution; the brilliant ironic comedy *Leonce und Lena*; *Lenz*, a short narrative tracing the descent into madness of the eighteenth-century dramatist J. M. R. Lenz; and the fragmentary social tragedy *Woyzeck*. Büchner included a realist manifesto in *Lenz*, making its protagonist say: 'The writers and artists I like above all are those that most strongly convey the reality of nature, with the result that their work engages my feelings.'[17] Accordingly, Büchner's characters are embodied beings, with powerful erotic urges, and also vulnerable to the squalor of prison and the pain of execution. Their language is direct, ranging from blunt crudity to lyricism, often laden with elaborate historical and literary allusions. With a firm grasp of political machinations, Büchner dramatizes both the corruption of the Revolution in the Reign of Terror, and the urgent need to improve human life that inspired it. Danton, a disillusioned sensualist tired of bloodshed, is set against the priggish Robespierre and his unscrupulous associate Saint-Just, who is prepared to wade through seas of blood towards a better future. If in *Dantons Tod* the common people are still Shakespearean caricatures, in *Woyzeck* an inarticulate, bitterly poor soldier is given a dignity which turns his sadistic commanding officer, and the doctor who subjects him to medical experiments, into authoritarian puppets. Woyzeck's fragmented, lyrical language makes us understand how jealousy drove him to murder his unfaithful partner. These events occur against a background of cosmic emptiness and despair: Danton and his comrades in prison imagine themselves as the playthings of sadistic gods; Lenz, after hard struggles, succumbs to atheism; Woyzeck's fate is indirectly illuminated by a fairy-tale about a deserted universe.

Compared with Büchner, most writers seem tame. Still, the period saw much serious realist fiction, often by women, addressing social issues. The ambitious *Zeitroman* (novel of the times) by Karl Immermann (1796–1840), *Die Epigonen* ('The Latecomers,' 1836), represents present-day Germany as a shallow, insincere sequel to the greater eighteenth century; it criticizes the outdated aristocracy, but questions whether the industrial bourgeoisie, in whom petty rational calculation has replaced aesthetic sensibility, are worthy to succeed them. Louise Otto-Peters (1819–1895) also explores class conflict in *Schloß und Fabrik* ('Mansion and Factory,' 1846), in which a factory-owner calls in debts from an impoverished aristocrat and oppresses his workers. The novel suggests that as the bourgeoisie have supplanted the aristocracy, so they will, in turn, be replaced by the proletariat. Among the latter, there are radicals attracted by Communism, and moderates like the central figure, Franz Thalheim, who is in love with the factory-owner's daughter Pauline. When a workers' uprising does break out, the moderates are its victims. The view of historical change in these novels was radicalized by Marx and Engels in the *Communist Manifesto* (1848), which presents history as class conflict; but since the aristocracy, normally presented in fiction as decadent and debt-ridden, in fact, proved adaptable and powerful throughout nineteenth-century Germany, realist analysis here seems infected by wishful thinking.

Other women writers wrote accomplished fiction on narrower issues. Fanny Lewald (1811–1889), with her own Jewish background in mind, examines issues of conscience in *Jenny* (1843), whose Jewish heroine feels morally and intellectually unable to accept Christianity, and therefore renounces marriage to a clergyman she loves. Droste-Hülshoff in the story *Die Judenbuche* ('The Jew's Beech,' 1842) shows the workings of conscience in a protagonist from a poor, semi-criminal, rural setting, but hedges them about with sophisticated narratorial ambiguities that warn the reader against facile moral judgments. The story also turns partly on the social issue of wood theft, about which Marx wrote in the same year: the villagers see no harm in taking wood from the landowners' forests, since a natural product can be no-one's property, while the landowners redefine this traditional practice as theft.[18]

There was, then, much fictional discussion of social issues outside the radicalism of Junges Deutschland. From 1840 onwards much political poetry was written in the vain hope that the new king of Prussia, Friedrich Wilhelm IV, would introduce liberal reforms. It included the 'Deutschlandlied' by Hoffmann von Fallersleben (1798–1874); the refrain '*Deutschland, Deutschland über alles,*' contrary to a common misapprehension, expresses its author's liberalism by urging readers to place a united Germany—in which the princes would be sidelined or dethroned—above mere regional loyalties. Heine, watching events from Paris, deplored the poetic mediocrity of liberals such as Ferdinand Freiligrath (1810–1876) and Georg Herwegh (1817–75), and replied with *Atta Troll. Ein Sommernachtstraum* ('Atta Troll. A Midsummer Night's Dream,' begun 1841, published in full 1847), in which a dancing bear represents the clumsiness of German would-be revolutionaries, and a world of myth and magic, reflecting Heine's absorption in the Germanic mythology uncovered by the Grimms, relativizes the petty, short-term concerns of political writers. However, Heine soon followed it with its antithesis, *Deutschland. Ein Wintermärchen*, whose protagonist, travelling through Germany, debunks national myths from Father Rhine to Barbarossa, and calls on the German people to liberate Germany without the aid of kings. The rich fantasy of *Atta Troll* and the harsh satire of *Deutschland* together express Heine's discomfort as a writer committed to revolutionary ideals, or at least to the proposition that all should have enough to eat, but fearing that a future egalitarian regime would have no place for the poetic imagination.

Alongside Heine and Büchner, the third great radical writer of the earlier nineteenth century is the comic dramatist Johann Nestroy (1801–1862) who dominated the Viennese popular theatre and was often called a theatrical Dickens. For much of his career Nestroy had to contend with censorship, but he brought contemporary realities on stage in vivid detail. He explored the comic possibilities of railway travel in *Eisenbahnheiraten* ('Railway Marriages,' 1844), of house-hunting in *Eine Wohnung ist zu vermiethen in der Stadt* ('A Flat is for Rent in the City,' 1837), of ruthless social climbing in *Der Talisman* ('The Talisman,' 1840; the talisman is a wig which temporarily transforms the red-haired protagonist's prospects), while in *Der Schützling* ('The Protégé,' 1847) he almost burst the bounds of comedy by letting the main character bitterly denounce the injustice of society in putting a talented person in a social position where his abilities are frustrated. Freed from censorship in 1848, Nestroy dramatized the Revolution in *Freiheit in Krähwinkel* ('Freedom in Sleepy Hollow,' 1848), which upholds liberal ideas (ending with a symbolic marriage between the resourceful radical journalist Ultra and the well-named Frau von Frankenfrey), and expressed a fierce anticlericalism both there and in *Höllenangst* ('Fear of Hell/A Hell of a Fright,' 1849). The realist and radical Nestroy has yet to be fully appreciated.

German literature *is* exceptional in the prominence it gives to tragedy. The tragedies in eighteenth- and nineteenth-century English and French literature are now of historical interest only. Many, as dramatic attempts by lyric poets, attest only to the continuing prestige of the genre. In Germany, however, tragedy flourished from Lessing to Kleist, and was represented in this period above all by Franz Grillparzer, Georg Büchner, and Friedrich Hebbel (1813–1863).

The Austrian Grillparzer stands apart. He differed from Schiller in seeing tragedy not as the assertion of freedom, but as the submission to necessity. Tragic characters come to understand and repent their faults, as Ottokar repents of his self-centered ambition in *König Ottokars Glück und Ende* ('King Ottokar's Fortune and Downfall,' 1825), and gain insight into 'the nullity of earthly things.'[19] The audience should feel pity and fear for them and for their innocent victims, such as Hero in *Des Meeres und der Liebe Wellen* ('The Waves of Love and the Sea,' written 1829, published 1840), who perishes along with her lover through the over-anxious puritanism of her priestly uncle. A more complex, political tragedy is *Ein Bruderzwist in Habsburg* ('Fraternal Strife in the Habsburg Family,' written 1848–1850, published posthumously in 1873), set on the eve of the Thirty Years' War. The apparently irresponsible Emperor Rudolf II claims to be trying through masterly inactivity to stave off the Empire's collapse into religious conflict. He fails, but so do the intriguers around him, who are either out-witted by more ruthless rivals or gain a success that proves bitter.

A different understanding of tragedy was put forward by Hegel. Hegel sees tragedy as the collision of right with right. In his favorite example, Sophocles' *Antigone*, Creon is right to uphold the law by leaving a rebel's corpse unburied, but the dead man's sister Antigone is right to uphold family loyalty by burying the corpse. This is a clash between two equally valid, but irreconcilable expressions of the spirit (*Geist*) whose progress Hegel recounts. There can be no compromise between them. The tragic antagonists must perish, but the values they represent are sublated (*aufgehoben*), transferred dialectically to a higher plane, and reconciled only there.

This conception of tragedy fitted the nineteenth century's fascination with history and historical progress. In historical drama, it helped to produce the recurrent motif of the necessary crime—the result of a conflict between morality and pragmatism. Thus, in Büchner's *Dantons Tod*, the September Massacres are presented as a criminal action undertaken by Danton in order to save the Revolution. For earlier, metaphysical concepts of fate, as in Grillparzer, Büchner substitutes the concept of historical necessity, which makes his characters feel as though they were puppets moved by invisible powers or victims sacrificed for the pleasure of the gods.

Hebbel, who unlike Büchner had read Hegel, sets his tragedies at crucial stages in the historical process. Thus, in *Herodes und Mariamne* (premiered in 1849) the heroine Mariamne represents the dignity of the individual, whereas her husband insists on treating her, like all his subjects, as a possession; the events coincide with the birth of Christ and, thus, anticipate a new conception of human worth. In *Agnes Bernauer* (premiered in 1852), which Hebbel intended as a modern counterpart to Sophocles' *Antigone*, the conflict is between the virtuous Agnes, who is secretly married to the heir of the Duchy of Bavaria, and the reigning Duke Ernst. The humanity of a commoner has to be sacrificed to the demands of the state, and Ernst considers himself obliged to commit a necessary crime by having Agnes executed.

Büchner explores other, thoroughly physical kinds of necessity. Danton speculates about psychological determinism: 'What is it in us that whores, lies, steals, murders?'[20] He and other Büchner characters are driven by their own bodily urges. Woyzeck is refreshingly frank about the natural urges which lead him to scandalize his respectable superiors by urinating against a wall and by fathering a child with his unmarried lover. Hebbel, too, explores necessity, particularly that of insoluble moral dilemmas. In his only piece of contemporary realism, *Maria Magdalene* (premiered in 1846), the heroine, Klara, the daughter of a carpenter in a small town, is forced by her rigidly upright father to promise never to dishonor his name. As she is secretly pregnant, she feels compelled to commit suicide. The abstract demands of an oppressive morality triumph over the sheer urge to enjoy life.

Despite such common themes, Hebbel and Büchner differ widely in the treatment of dramatic material. Hebbel was not interested in history for its own sake. 'For the poet,' he wrote, 'history is a vehicle to embody his opinions and ideas; the poet is not an angel to restore history to life.'[21] Büchner did want to re-present the past, and based his work on close study of sources. For *Dantons Tod* he immersed himself in the history of the French Revolution, and included in the play long speeches actually delivered by his characters' historical prototypes, although he also changed history drastically when it suited his purpose (e.g. Danton's devoted wife Julie commits suicide, rather than outlive him, whereas the historical Madame Danton lived on and remarried). *Woyzeck* is based on an account of a semi-insane soldier called Wozzeck, who was executed in 1824 for murdering a widow, although again Büchner has made crucial changes: the actual Wozzeck was often violent, whereas Büchner's character is inoffensive till driven by grief to murder his unfaithful lover. Nevertheless, Büchner's attention to documents illustrates the respect for historical fact characteristic of the age of Ranke.

Germany's tradition of tragedy was continued in the music-dramas of Richard Wagner (1813–1883). His central work, *Der Ring des Nibelungen* ('The Nibelung's Ring,' premiered in 1876), originated in the 1840s, with Siegfried as a political and erotic revolutionary in the Young German mold. As Wagner developed it, Wotan emerged as a different kind of tragic hero, illustrating, like Hebbel's Duke Ernst, the dilemmas of power. To preserve his rule, he has to sacrifice his beloved son Siegmund. Worse still, the ultimate doom of the gods can only be staved off by Siegmund's son Siegfried, who, unlike Wotan, can regain the ring that bestows power; but Siegfried, representing a new age of human autonomy, spells the gods' doom anyway. We can see here not only a tragic conflict between love and power, which makes criminal actions necessary, but also the narrative of social evolution familiar from realist fiction and Marx's historical philosophy: there, aristocrats are superseded by the lower classes; in Wagner, gods are superseded by humans. A new motif, derived from Schopenhauer, is redemption through annihilation. At the end, Brünnhilde rides her horse into the flames, expecting a mystical reunion with her lover Siegfried, while the gods are consumed in fire. *Tristan und Isolde* (1865) ends with Isolde's love-death, in which she announces her ecstatic absorption into the universe. Wagner, who discovered Schopenhauer in 1854, described his 'central idea, the ultimate rejection of the will to live,' as 'the only redemption.'[22]

German realist fiction needs to be saved from the dismissive account of it given by Erich Auerbach in *Mimesis*.[23] Auerbach uncritically accepted the literary canon formed in the late nineteenth century. This canon privileged the *Novelle* and the *Bildungsroman*, while screening out a large body of realist writing that has consequently been neglected by critics till recently. Among the period's towering realists—Gottfried Keller (1819–1890), Theodor Fontane (1819–1898), and Wilhelm Raabe (1831–1910)—Fontane is particularly disparaged by Auerbach, while Raabe's work was until recently appreciated only by a small number of enthusiasts.

The common conception of nineteenth-century German literature gives disproportionate prominence to the *Novelle*. This is partly because short texts are useful in teaching, and partly because, in the formation of a national canon, the *Novelle* earned admittance by its respectable pedigree in the Romance languages (Boccaccio, Bandello, Cervantes), while the novel was a suspect, popular form without aesthetic pretensions. The *Novelle* gained dignity by complying with German classical aesthetics: it viewed reality through an idealizing lens, and it was often claimed to center on a poetic symbol. From the 1880s it became common to call this approach retrospectively 'poetic realism,' though the term was not used by its supposed practitioners. It was adopted by Otto Ludwig (1813–1865) in his *Shakespeare-Studien*, published only in 1871. Ludwig demanded writing that was true to actual life, while veiling its coarse and gross elements: 'Poetry of reality, hiding life's naked patches behind flowers, and not stressing the intrinsically poetic ones beyond what verisimilitude allows.'[24] Within these limits, German writers produced many masterly *Novellen* whose sophisticated technique, often exploiting the contrast between oral and written story-telling, serves to explore the intrinsic ambivalence of characters' motives and values. Thus the interlocking narrative frameworks of *Der Schimmelreiter* ('The Rider on the White Horse,' 1888) by Theodor Storm (1817–1888) make us wonder whether the protagonist is an enlightened apostle of progress or a ruthless egoist. However, no more will be said here about the *Novelle*, in order to restore the realist novel to prominence.

The other prose genre that was canonized was the *Bildungsroman*. This term again was not current when classic *Bildungsromane* were being written. It was applied retrospectively by the philosopher Wilhelm Dilthey (1833–1911), who wrote in 1870:

'I should like to call the novels that form the school of *Wilhelm Meister* 'Bildungsro-mane.' Goethe's work shows human development in various stages, forms, and periods of life. It fills us with contentment because it does not describe the whole world with its deformities and the struggle of evil passions for existence; the recalcitrant stuff of life is excluded.'[25] For Dilthey, Goethe's *Wilhelm Meisters Lehrjahre* (1795–1796) is exemplary because it shows the hero's successful development and because it abstracts from reality (though one may well feel the thinness of Goethe's fictional world to be a deficiency); and, of course, because Goethe was then being elevated into Germany's national author.

Yet the novels of our period categorized as *Bildungsromane* hardly fit this feel good and abstract model. *Der Nachsommer* ('Indian Summer,' 1867) by Adalbert Stifter (1805–1868) admittedly depicts its hero's conflict-free development, mainly on an Austrian country estate, and screens out ugly and upsetting realities; but its hero describes himself as 'a great friend of the reality of things,'[26] and provides limpid and detailed accounts of the natural and material world. A strange, leisurely, utopian idyll, *Der Nachsommer* is a beautiful anomaly in the history of the novel. Keller's autobiographical novel *Der grüne Heinrich* ('Green Henry,' first version 1854–1855, second version 1879–1880) has a wealth of humor, physical detail, and sharply etched characters that recalls Dickens, along with rich psychological insight. Unlike *Wilhelm Meister*, it is bursting with 'the recalcitrant stuff of life,' and its hero's development ends in failure (only slightly mitigated in the revised version). The term *Bildungsroman* usefully directs us to these masterpieces, but the genre it denotes never existed.

After 1848, influential liberal critics, notably Julian Schmidt (1818–1886) and Gustav Freytag (1816–1895), denounced idealism and called for a realism that should concentrate on representing empirical reality, albeit with some 'transfiguration' (*Verklärung*) of its sordid aspects. Fontane agreed that realism, without getting obsessed with surface detail, should select from reality in order to discover truth: '[Realism] is the reflection of all real life, all true forces and interests, within the element of art.'[27]

Realism accepts the authority of science. This is no longer the *Naturphilosophie* on which Georg Büchner's science was founded, and which sought to comprehend Nature as an aesthetic whole—'the manifestation of a primordial law, a law of beauty.'[28] It is rather the grimly factual positivist and materialist science espoused by his brother Ludwig Büchner in the widely-read treatise *Kraft und Stoff* ('Force and Matter,' 1855). Earlier writers interested in science had often worried about the inhuman picture of the universe it implied. Thus, in Stifter's story *Der Condor* (1840) a young woman who ascends with scientists in a balloon feels that the clouds seen close-up are like cold, clammy grave-shrouds, and in Droste's poem '*Die Mergelgrube*' ('The Marl-Pit,' 1844) vistas of geological time evoke the end of the earth as a burned-out ruin. However, these writers still tried to reconcile natural science with divine Providence, though the strain is palpable in such stories by Stifter as *Abdias* (1843) and '*Bergkristall*' ['Mountain Crystal' in *Bunte Steine* ('Colored Stones'), 1853] and in Droste's agonized poem '*Die ächzende Kreatur*' ('The groaning of creation,' alluding to Romans 8: 22). Positivist science firmly excluded questions of meaning, purpose, and freedom. Organisms are machines, engaged in continual development to which the Darwinian theory of evolution was easily assimilated. Nature is indifferent to suffering. In Storm's *Novelle* '*Im Schloß*' ('In the Castle,' 1862) the heroine hears from her uncle how cruelly insects devour one another, then sees a cat tormenting a mouse, but is saved from despair by learning to understand the organic development of nature as a whole. More pessimistic contemporaries found relief in Schopenhauer's philosophy. One could respond, like Schopenhauer, by making pity the supreme virtue, or, like Nietzsche later, by affirming the struggle for life and the rights of the strongest.

Against this background, some realist novels ambitiously address the social and economic condition of Germany. Friedrich Spielhagen (1829–1911), an immensely prominent novelist till the sudden collapse of his reputation in the 1890s, tackles in his page-turner *Sturmflut* ('Flood-Tide,' 1876) the irresponsible speculation that accompanied economic growth immediately after German unification. A nobleman involved in financial corruption is contrasted with the middle-class hero, who as a ship's pilot is symbolically qualified to guide Germany through these dangerous waters. The engineer Hauke Haien in Storm's *Der Schimmelreiter* is a similar, but more flawed representative of modernization, likewise pitted against the destructive natural power of the sea. Novelists explored conceptions of community. Keller shows in *Der grüne Heinrich* how Swiss national consciousness finds expression in a communal performance of Schiller's *Wilhelm Tell*, while a Nuremberg carnival celebrates an ideal republic of craftsmen, and contrasts both, in an allegorical episode, with the identity of the modern Swiss nation allegedly based merely on money-making.

The realist program also demanded that the German people should be shown at work, as Freytag does by depicting commercial life in *Soll und Haben* ('Debit and Credit,' 1855), though despite his intentions office work comes across as stultifying. Unfortunately this best- and long-selling novel notoriously defines the German people by contrast with un-German Jews and Poles. Freytag, following a common stereotype, portrays the inhabitants of Prussian Poland as backward and shiftless (as the Irish were seen in nineteenth-century Britain), while his stolid German hero has an evil, but much more interesting shadow-self in the villainous jew Veitel Itzig. Raabe has a similar doubling in *Der Hungerpastor* ('The Hungry Pastor,' 1864) where the Jew Moses Freudenstein is also dangerously adaptable: he re-enters the life of his old schoolmate, the hero Hans Unwirrsch, as the fashionable and frenchified Dr Théophile Stein. Yet Freytag and Raabe were sound liberals, who were shocked to be charged with anti-Semitism. This may illustrate how far realism depends on taking the received ideas of its day and passing them off as knowledge about reality.

However, realism also enquired into the condition of women. Women were admitted to university, initially in Switzerland, from the 1870s, and in the 1890s the 'New Woman,' usually a medical graduate from Zurich, enters literature. Before that, however, women writers especially showed that a woman could cope with responsibilities traditionally reserved for men. In *Die letzte Reckenburgerin* ('The Last von Reckenburg,' 1871) by Louise von François (1817–1893), Hardine von Reckenburg successfully runs an estate, and since the novel is set against the French Revolution and the Napoleonic Wars, her competent reforms contrast with the chaotic revolutionary energies unleashed by the ill-starred affair between her plebeian friend Dorothee and the libertine Prince August, who symbolically falls at Valmy, where Prussian forces were repelled by French Revolutionary armies in 1792. Gabriele Reuter (1859–1941) showed in *Aus guter Familie* ('From a Good Family,' 1895) how a conventional upbringing by loving parents could drive a gifted young woman into frustration and madness. The limitations of marriage were explored by Marie von Ebner-Eschenbach in *Unsühnbar* ('Inexpiable,' 1890) and Fontane in *Effi Briest* (1895): in both, a young woman is pressured into marriage with an unloved man and has an affair with a rakish lover which ends tragically. In *Stine* (1890) Fontane allowed a 'kept woman,' Pauline Pittelkow, to defend her questionable lifestyle with robust honesty.

Realism also looks beyond Germany to examine Germany's place in the wider world. Many thousands of Germans emigrated to America, and in fiction America generally appears as the destination of the enterprising – Judith in *Der grüne Heinrich*, the stiff, but worthy Gideon Franke in Fontane's *Irrungen, Wirrungen* ('Errors and Confusions,' 1888)—although American life was denounced in the entertaining, though often absurd, novel *Der Amerikamüde* ('The Man Weary of America,' 1855) by Ferdinand Kürnberger (1821–1879). Africa features especially in Raabe's work, both before and after the beginnings of German colonization in 1884. In *Abu Telfan oder Die Heimkehr vom Mondgebirge* ('Abu Telfan or the Return from the Mountains of the Moon,' 1868), a spell of imprisonment in Central Africa gives the protagonist, on his return to Germany, a satirical perspective on the Germans' enslavement to petty conventions, while in the murder mystery *Stopfkuchen* ('Fatty,' 1891) the narrator is returning to 'Neuteutoburg' in South Africa, a German colony that sounds just as hidebound as the Lower Saxon town where most of the novel is set. The title of Fontane's last and most ambitious novel, *Der Stechlin* (1898), refers to a Prussian lake, which is affected by earthquakes elsewhere on the globe, and from which, on specially significant occasions, a red cock (suggesting revolution) is said to fly up. In many conversations (which in Fontane's late fiction increasingly replace action), Fontane's characters explore German politics (with sympathetic attention to Socialism and the rise of the proletariat), the increasing unity of the world brought about by modern communications, and the place of Germany in this new pattern.

The realist novel even examines the ecological issues whose history David Blackbourn has recently uncovered in *The Conquest of Nature* (2006). Raabe's *Pfisters Mühle* ('Pfister's Mill,' 1884) contrasts old, pre-industrial, idyllic Germany with the new world of industrial prosperity that requires the chemical pollution of natural resources. A central character, the chemist Adam Asche, whose authority earns him a comparison with Bismarck, plays a dual role: he helps to combat the pollution from a factory that has ruined the eponymous mill, but also establishes a factory that cleans clothes, while polluting the River Spree and blasting smoke into the Berlin atmosphere. Raabe's eccentric, jocular, punning, allusive, often sentimental narration serves here to balance the pros and cons of progress.

Yet while realism admits much new subject-matter into literature, it also excludes some. German realism of the late nineteenth century cannot admit those reminders of our bodily condition that Auerbach called '*das Kreatürliche.*' Erotic passion is strongly suggested in Ebner's *Unsühnbar*, but in Fontane's *Irrungen, Wirrungen* it is confined to the gap between two chapters, and the adultery in *Effi Briest* is low-key at best. When passion is present, as in the spell-binding scene in the first version of *Der grüne Heinrich*, where the hero sees a desirable older woman bathing naked, it is overlaid with Romantic associations.

Nor can German realism cope with death. The deaths of Emma Bovary, or of Levin's brother in *Anna Karenina*, find no counterpart. *Der Stechlin* leads up to the death of the kindly and humorous old nobleman Dubslav von Stechlin, but his death is apparently painless, and is accompanied by a beautifully understated symbolic hint of resurrection. A couple of years later, the humiliating death of Thomas Buddenbrook (Thomas Mann, *Buddenbrooks*, 1901) announces the return to fiction of basic creaturely themes.

A bridge between the nineteenth and twentieth centuries can be found in the philosophy of Nietzsche, which exercised wide influence only after Nietzsche's descent into madness in 1889. The nineteenth century's fascination with history and science also dominates Nietzsche's thought, but ambivalently. In early writings he deplored how the historical spirit in German education made the past a source of dead knowledge, rather than an inspiration for life. Yet in his late work *The Genealogy of Morals* (1887) he applied history and prehistory to explain the origin of morality as such, thus undermining its pretensions to supra-historical authority. A keen reader of popular science, Nietzsche envisaged a non-moral view of the universe in which all events were explained by scientific laws. However, his restless skepticism made him question the status of scientific knowledge by arguing that there was no hidden reality—no Platonic forms, Kantian 'thing-in-itself,' or scientific law—behind appearances. Inconsistently, he increasingly sought to explain everything by assuming just such an occult force, which he called the will to power. Whether the will to power would produce a noble and generous master race, or ruthless tyrants, or indeed both, remains the riddle of his philosophy. The multiple ambiguities of Nietzsche's truly radical thought would provide an intellectual agenda for the twentieth century.

Notes

1. Heinrich Heine, *Deutschland. Ein Wintermärchen*, Caput 7, in Klaus Briegleb (ed.), *Sämtliche Schriften*, 6 vols (Munich: Hanser, 1968–76), iv. 592.
2. *The Complete Poems of Heinrich Heine*, trans. Hal Draper (Oxford: Oxford University Press, 1982), 496.
3. Heine, 'Briefe über Deutschland,' in his *Sämtliche Schriften*, v. 197. Cf. 'Preface' in *Hegel's Philosophy of Right*, trans. by T. M. Knox (Oxford: Clarendon Press, 1942), 10.
4. See Jean Pierre Lefebvre, *Der gute Trommler: Heines Beziehung zu Hegel* (Hamburg: Hoffmann und Campe, 1986), 35.

5. Leopold von Ranke, 'Vorrede zu den Geschichten der romanischen und germanischen Völker von 1494 bis 1535' (1824), quoted in Wolfgang Hardtwig (ed.) *Über das Studium der Geschichte* (Munich: DTV, 1990), 45.

6. Wilhelm von Humboldt, 'Geschichte des Verfalls und Unterganges der griechischen Freistaaten' (1807), in Andreas Flitner and Klaus Giel (eds), *Werke*, 5 vols (Darmstadt: Wissenschaftliche Buchgesellschaft 1964), ii. 97.

7. Novalis, *Schriften*, Paul Kluckhohn and Richard Samuel (eds), 5 vols (Stuttgart: Kohlhammer, 1960–88), iii. 281.

8. E. T. A. Hoffmann, *The Golden Pot and Other Stories*, tr. by Ritchie Robertson (Oxford: Oxford University Press, 1992), 83.

9. Letter to Wilhelm Müller, 7 June 1826, in Heine, *Werke, Briefwechsel, Lebenszeugnisse*, Säkularausgabe (Berlin: Akademie-Verlag, Paris: Editions du CNRS, 1970), xx: *Briefe 1815–1831*, 250.

10. Heine, *Die Bäder von Lucca*, in his *Sämtliche Schriften*, ii. 405.

11. David Friedrich Strauss, *Das Leben Jesu, kritisch bearbeitet*, 2 vols (Tübingen: Osiander, 1835–1836), i, vii.

12. Letter to Ludwig Feuerbach, undated (c. 1843), in Karl Marx, *Selected Writings*, ed. David McLellan (Oxford: Oxford University Press, 1977), 113.

13. 'Am zweyten Weihnachtstage (Stephanus),' in Annette von Droste-Hülshoff, *Werke und Briefwechsel*, Winfried Woesler (ed.) (Tübingen: Niemeyer, 1978), iv/1. 161.

14. Friedrich Nietzsche, 'Schopenhauer als Erzieher,' in his *Werke*, Karl Schlechta (ed.), 3 vols (Munich: Hanser, 1966), i. 295.

15. Heine, 'Französische Maler' (1831), *Sämtliche Schriften*, iii. 72.

16. Heine, *Die Romantische Schule* (1836), ibid., iii. 468.

17. 'Lenz' in Georg Büchner, *Complete Plays, Lenz and Other Writings*, trans. John Reddick (London: Penguin, 1993), 150.

18. See 'The Law on Thefts of Wood' (published in the *Rheinische Zeitung*, 1842) in Marx, *Selected Writings*, 20–22.

19. Franz Grillparzer, *Sämtliche Werke*, Peter Frank and Karl Pörnbacher (eds), 4 vols (Munich: Hanser, 1960–1965), iii. 303.

20. *Dantons Tod*, III. 5, in Büchner, *Complete Plays*, 38.

21. 'Mein Wort über das Drama!' (1843), in Friedrich Hebbel, *Werke*, Gerhard Fricke et al. (eds), 5 vols (Munich: Hanser, 1963), iii. 550.

22. Letter to Franz Liszt, 16 December 1854, quoted in Richard Wagner, *Die Musikdramen* (Munich: DTV, 1978), 387.

23. Erich Auerbach, *Mimesis: The Representation of Reality in Western Literature*, tr. by Willard R. Trask (Princeton: Princeton University Press, 1953), p 516–519.

24. Otto Ludwig, 'Dickens und die deutsche Dorfgeschichte,' in William J. Lillyman (ed.) *Romane und Romanstudien* (Munich: Hanser, 1977), 547.

25. Wilhelm Dilthey, *Das Leben Schleiermachers* (1870), quoted in Rolf Selbmann, *Der deutsche Bildungsroman* (Stuttgart: Metzler, 1984), 18.

26. Adalbert Stifter, *Der Nachsommer* (Munich: DTV, 1977), 24.

27. Theodor Fontane, 'Unsere lyrische und epische Poesie seit 1848,' in his *Aufsätze, Kritiken, Erinnerungen*, Jürgen Kolbe et al. (eds), 4 vols (Munich: Hanser, 1969–1973), i. 242.

28. 'On Cranial Nerves' (1836), in Büchner, *Complete Plays*, 184.

BIBLIOGRAPHY

BORCHMEYER, DIETER, *Richard Wagner: Theory and Theatre*, trans. by Stewart Spencer (Oxford: Clarendon Press, 1991).

DEMETZ, PETER, *Formen des Realismus: Theodor Fontane* (Munich: Hanser, 1964).

GÖTTSCHE, DIRK, *Zeit im Roman: Literarische Zeitreflexionen und die Geschichte des Zeitromans im späten 18. und im 19. Jahrhundert* (Munich: Fink, 2001).

HOLUB, ROBERT C., *Reflections of Realism: Paradox, Norm, and Ideology in Nineteenth-Century German Prose* (Detroit: Wayne State University Press, 1991).

KAISER, GERHARD, *Gottfried Keller: Das gedichtete Leben* (Frankfurt a.M.: Insel, 1981).

KONTJE, TODD, *Women, the Novel, and the German Nation 1771–1871: Domestic Fiction in the Fatherland* (Cambridge: Cambridge University Press, 1998).

—— ed., *A Companion to German Realism 1848–1900* (Rochester: Camden House, 2002).

MARTINI, FRITZ, *Deutsche Literatur im bürgerlichen Realismus 1848–1898* (Stuttgart: Metzler, 1962).

PAULIN, ROGER, *The Brief Compass: The Nineteenth-Century German Novelle* (Oxford: Clarendon Press, 1985).

REDDICK, JOHN, *Georg Büchner: The Shattered Whole* (Oxford: Clarendon Press, 1994).

REEVES, NIGEL, *Heinrich Heine: Poetry and Politics* (Oxford: Oxford University Press, 1974).

SAGARRA, EDA, *Tradition and Revolution: German Literature and Society 1830–1890* (New York: Basic Books, 1971).

SAMMONS, JEFFREY L., *Wilhelm Raabe: The Fiction of the Alternative Community* (Princeton: Princeton University Press, 1987).

SENGLE, FRIEDRICH, *Biedermeierzeit*, 3 vols (Stuttgart: Metzler, 1971–1980).

SPRENGEL, PETER, *Geschichte der deutschsprachigen Literatur 1870–1900: Von der Reichsgründung bis zur Jahrhundertwende* (Munich: Beck, 1998).

STERN, J., *Re-Interpretations: Seven Studies in Nineteenth-Century German Literature* (London: Thames & Hudson, 1964), 239–300.

SWALES, MARTIN and ERIKA SWALES, *Adalbert Stifter: A Critical Study* (Cambridge: Cambridge University Press, 1984).

GERMANY: THE NATION STATE

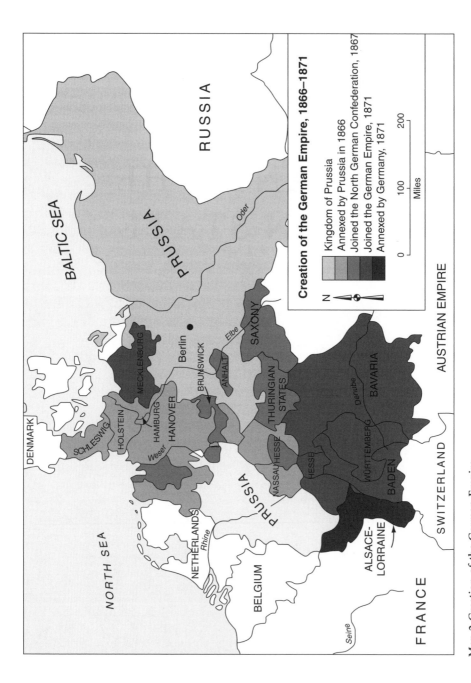

Map 2 Creation of the German Empire

Source: James Retallack (ed.), *Short Oxford History of Germany: Imperial Germany 1871–1918* (Oxford: Oxford University Press, 2008), 313.

CHAPTER 13

NATION STATE, CONFLICT RESOLUTION, AND CULTURE WAR, 1850–1878

SIEGFRIED WEICHLEIN

RITUALS combine past and present. At least this is the intention of their protagonists. During the nineteenth century, this was particularly true for monarchs whose rule had always been symbolically charged. The French king of the restoration, Charles X, had himself crowned like a medieval monarch in the Cathedral of Reims on 31 May 1825. This event was followed by a ceremony of healing the sick in the tradition of the '*rois thaumaturges*,' with Charles X speaking the traditional formula used to cure those suffering from scrofula: '*Le roi te touché, Dieu te guérisse*' ('the king touches you, may the Lord heal you').[1] Charles X possessed, however, as much faith in modern science as in divine assistance, as three of his personal physicians were present at the ceremony to look after the sick. On 18 October 1861, King Wilhelm I of Prussia, who had a monarchic family history of a mere 160 years, similarly employed symbols to emphasize his royal status. On this day, Wilhelm was crowned king in Königsberg, even though he had already been the Prussian king for more than two years. He had begun his reign on 26 October 1858, after his brother had fallen ill. In Prussia, a kingdom since 1701, coronation ceremonies had been uncommon until then. Instead, a ritual act of homage on the part of the estates was traditional. The lavish coronation of 1861, therefore, was an invented tradition introduced because the act of homage could no longer be enforced in the constitutional state.[2]

The Revolutions of 1789 and of 1848 fundamentally changed the way in which symbols of rule were created, making a return to the *status quo ante* impossible. In this sense, the Revolution of 1848–1849 did not end in failure. If unable to create a German nation state, the revolution nevertheless made lasting changes to the political and symbolic landscape. One of the new political symbols was the ritual of the constitutional oath. King Friedrich Wilhelm IV swore an oath to the Prussian constitution in 1851, and his successor, Wilhelm I, did the same on 26 October 1858. Prematurely, but accurately, the liberal Gottfried Rudolf Campenhausen commented on this event of 1851: 'The bird is in the cage, and that is all that matters.'[3]

13.1 LINES OF CONFLICT AND MODELS OF CONSENSUS

The notion that rule requires identity, and that identity has to be based on unity and consensus, derives from assumptions of the liberal historiography of the nineteenth century. Symbols and liturgies, on the other hand, represented actions, differences, tasks, and institutions. The symbolic dispositive always implies more than one protagonist, with the monarch playing one role among others. Coronations, acts of homage, healing rituals, and the monarchic rule were all focused on the king as the main character of a drama. He represented a point at which antagonistic forces intersected, and his power symbolically derived from this convergence.

Working in the liberal tradition, historians, however, have often understood drama and conflict as symptoms of disintegration and division within the nation. The German 'culture war' (*Kulturkampf*) between liberalism and Catholicism has usually been described as an example of this narrative of division, with the existence of political and religious differences, as in the case of Catholics, Social Democrats, and Jews, used to justify the political exclusion of these groups for the benefit of unity. As is well known, Heinrich von Treitschke, for most of his life a National Liberal, took the view in November 1879 that Jews could only be German if they abstained from their 'Jewishness,' an opinion shared by most of the liberal bourgeoisie.[4] Those who were not in line with the National Liberal narrative of homogenization, or who obstructed this process, were denigrated as the 'enemies of the Reich.' The liberals set their hopes in a rational social order without conflict.[5] They also assumed that the nation state, in its ideal form, could only be accomplished when groups assimilated to the canon of liberal values and liberal ideas of progress. Assimilation became the only viable means of conflict resolution, with the result that in Imperial Germany, pluralism existed despite, rather than because of liberal politics.[6]

Between 1850 and 1878, industrialization and nation building were the principal forces generating conflict. Both played a crucial role in politics and society. But in the following chapter, the foundation and formation of the German nation state will be the main focus. The process leading to this state was highly complex, and involved the formation of a political center in contrast to other economic, cultural, and regional centers.[7] In a strict sense, this conflict was premised on a periphery which, in reality and *ex ante*, did not exist. Instead, there were several centers competing with each other for the opportunity to shape politics. Why, then, did a system with several political centers, which was incompatible with the liberal idea of a nation state and went along with the constant threat of secessionism, evolve into a federalist system which was in line with a nation state and tolerated a Prussian dominated political center? This one overarching question implies further questions. When and why did contemporaries deal with conflicts within a German nation state instead of against a nation state? Could Austria have been part of this nation state? Which role could Prussia play in the process of nation building? How could Prussia, which was already a great power in economic and military terms, become part of Germany? And what were the possibilities of democracy and parliamentarianism in a nation state that included the military power of Prussia?

The second conflict over nation building, which was linked to the first one, was the antagonism between the confessional majority and minority: in Germany, this conflict centered on the tension between Catholicism and a Protestant inflected liberalism.[8] This conflict was ideologically charged, but it also had a regional character with Catholicism in the Rhineland and in Bavaria, for instance, also pursuing local interests. However, there were 'culture wars' in other European nation states too. Sometimes these were between Catholics and Protestants, and sometimes between secular liberals and Catholics.[9] Why, and in which way, did German Catholics integrate themselves into a nation state which they had not wanted—particularly one in which the supremacy of Catholic Austria was excluded? How did they benefit from integration? What institutional results did the 'culture war' have?

Both conflicts had in common that liberals in Germany and elsewhere shared the basic logic of assimilation driven by a narrative of progress.[10] This particular narrative considered the Catholic Church as a cultural brake, and the Center Party as a political obstacle, to progress. Neither conflict was decided by an outright defeat or by a clear victory. On the contrary, these conflicts were contained and processed between 1850 and 1878 by institutions such as the monarchical federal state, the Center Party and parliamentary legislation, as well as by federalism and the principle of mutual advantage. The liberal era between 1867 and 1878 was the 'critical juncture' (Gerhard Lehmbruch) of institution building in Germany. During this period, contemporaries developed procedures of conflict resolution that involved the abstraction, transformation, and integration of conflicts. These procedures proved groundbreaking for the future.[11]

13.2 DRAMATIS PERSONAE: NATION BUILDING AND ITS ACTORS 1850–1878

Although the Revolution of 1848–1849 failed to achieve its primary objective—the foundation of the German nation state—it still had a lasting impact on politics and society. If the reaction was successful in military terms, it did not achieve cultural hegemony. Put simply: the counter-revolution was victorious; the political restoration, however, was not. This can be demonstrated in three areas.[12]

a) For one, the experience of coming so close to a German nation state in 1848–1849 was not forgotten afterwards. As the German philosopher Immanuel Kant noted about the Revolution of 1789, a historical phenomenon of this magnitude would always be remembered.[13] The Assembly in the Paulskirche had proved that it was possible to reach a parliamentary consensus on the structure of a nation state, and that the Lesser German Solution (*Kleindeutsche Lösung*) had a political and parliamentary basis. If it failed due to the veto of the Prussian monarchy, the national dynamic of the Paulskirche nevertheless had consequences far beyond the revolution. As the German Confederation urgently required reform from within, the debate about political possibilities began in the 1850s, and, starting in autumn 1858, began to focus on replacing the Confederation with a nation state.[14] What this state would look like, and what role Prussia would play in it, remained unclear, however. More evident was that Metternich's construction of the German Confederation as an institution designed to prevent both democratic, and constitutional development, no longer seemed a viable option. In view of bourgeois demands for political participation, it also no longer seemed possible to base the state solely on the prestige of the monarchy.

b) The second long-lasting change was that in the course of the Revolution of 1848, Prussia evolved into and remained a constitutional state—unlike Austria. On 5 December 1848, the Prussian king imposed a constitution that, with several modifications, remained in force until 1918. In Austria, meanwhile, Emperor Franz Joseph abrogated the forced March Constitution of 1849 with the Sylvester Patent in 1851. Austria and Mecklenburg were now the only states within the German Confederation without a constitution. Mecklenburg went so far as to re-install the political order of the estates (*altständische Ordnung*) of 1755. Generally, however it became clear that monarchs and rulers no longer had absolute power, but instead had to find new roles in order to communicate their status to civil society. Many appealed to the common good to create loyalty, others to 'filial devotion' towards the king. King Ernst August of Hanover, for example, portrayed himself as a father always concerned about the wellbeing of his *Landeskinder* (subjects), implying that only he knew exactly what was good for his immature children. Advocates for a constitution insisted, however, that the common good had to consist of respect for the people and their opinions, and that it required broad political participation. Unlike Ernst August in Hanover, the King of Württemberg, Karl I, represented a modern understanding of his role, inaugurating railway lines and seeing himself as the protector of the constitution.[15] In those states where monarchs opposed modernism and social and political participation, few people missed their rulers after they were deposed by Prussia in 1866.

c) Thirdly and finally, in the course of the Revolution of 1848, the participants learned to think in terms of what, starting in 1853, would be called 'Realpolitik.' Liberals contrasted this 'Realpolitik' to a politics of idealism supposedly endemic to the revolutionaries of 1848. In his eponymous tract, Ludwig Rochau did not advocate anti-revolutionary policies, but a specific form of dealing with the political experiences of the revolution.[16] According to this view, 'Realpolitik' implied an acceptance of Prussia's status and national relevance. Prussia was trying to get out of the German Confederation and its unwieldy regulations in order to expand its status as a great power. During the 1850s, the Prussian envoy in Frankfurt, Otto von Bismarck, became aware that nationalism could be made useful for that political purpose. Bismarck's political view was, in fact, not diametrically opposed to the opinions of the liberal German National Association (Deutscher Nationalverein), an organization for those who championed the Lesser German Solution. Crucially, both the Prussian government and the liberal national movement agreed on the exclusion of Austria from the nation-building plans.[17]

The Liberals, as the heirs of the revolution, perceived themselves as a national constitutional movement. They intended to constitutionally limit, and even reduce, monarchical power. Constitutionalism expressed the bourgeois demand for political participation; it also differentiated liberalism from left-wing republican and democratic ideas while distancing liberals from the forces of political reaction.

Before 1848, the constitutional celebrations in South Germany had symbolically confirmed these ideas. After 1848, however, they became less important, and the nation took over the function of curtailing monarchic power—as became apparent, for instance, on the occasion of the Schiller festivals in 1859, which were lavishly celebrated. Schiller's dramas, especially 'The Robbers' and 'Don Carlos,' represented an emancipatory impulse, opposed to feudal society, and critical of autarchic rulers. The same characteristics also made him a national hero of the socialist workers' movement.[18] The large number of liberal voluntary associations represented this new national emphasis. Turning the cities into crucial platforms for liberal ideas, these associations included the choral and gymnastic societies, physical and geographical associations, natural scientific societies, bourgeois museum associations, and the freemasons.[19] Around 1850, there were 50 different associations in Frankfurt am Main alone, engaging, even before the revolution, 2500–3000 members, or about half of the citizenry.[20] The same happened in the other large cities of the German Confederation. As voluntary associations became a structural element of civic society, they spread bourgeois and secular values, inculcating the principles of self organization, volunteerism, and substantial internal equality.

In these years, liberalism's center of gravity was in the cities, working, in Frankfurt and elsewhere, on local issues such as tax and trade legislation. Due to the census suffrage (votes weighted according to the amount of taxes paid), liberals had an advantage in the city councils, as was the case, for instance, in Cologne or Munich.[21] Liberal mayors, such as Johannes von Miquel (Osnabrück: 1865–1870; 1876–1880; Frankfurt am Main: 1880–1890), represented communal liberalism and to some extent liberalism itself. It was in the cities that liberals put into practice what they had in mind for the whole nation.[22] It was in Germany's urban centers that liberal teachers steadfastly resisted being patronized by clerical supervision, and that Journalists opposed censorship.

In the two decades after the revolution, the liberals widened their organizational and media basis, as well as their level of support. In the Rhineland, liberals addressed their economic demands to the chambers of commerce, which in 1861 joined together to form the German Association of the Chambers of Commerce (*Deutscher Handelstag*).[23] As early as 1858, the Congress of German Economists (*Kongress deutscher Volkswirte*) came into existence and in 1862 the German Congress of Parliamentarians was formed (*Deutscher Abgeordnetentag*).[24] Illustrated magazines, such as the Leipzig-based '*Gartenlaube*,' brought liberal values of society and family into the mainstream.[25] Gustav Freitag's best-selling novel, '*Soll und Haben*' ('Debit and Credit'), published in 1855, represented and idealized, especially in the main character of Anton Wohlfahrt, a liberal model in the spheres of family, business, and public life. In terms of political organization and presence in the public sphere, the liberals were ahead of all other political groups and most notably the conservatives. They began to lose their lead, circa 1863, mainly because of the declining culture of liberal voluntary associations among the lower classes.[26]

Widening the liberal public sphere also altered the shape of liberalism. It was the revolution itself that caused this change. During the second revolutionary wave in the summer of 1848, many liberals had to face a 'social revolution' supported by workers and the lower classes. At this point, the solidarity among the opponents of absolutism, and the unity of the liberal movement, came to an end, and the idealized concept of a 'civic society without classes,' as the German historian Lothar Gall has put it, perished.[27] After 1848, liberalism remained a national constitutional movement, but lost its egalitarian character. In political terms, it no longer advocated a Greater German Solution, even if the idea of a Greater German 'federative nation,' and the sense of cultural affiliation, remained. German Austrians, however, played little or no role in the economic, social, and cultural networks of the nation. The national movements of singers and gymnasts were almost exclusively located outside of Austria. And the Reform Association (*Reformverein*), which advocated a Greater German Solution, lost considerable influence to the German National Association (*Deutscher Nationalverein*), which called for a small German Solution.[28]

By championing the Lesser German Solution, the liberal constitutional movement turned into a political party. In 1861, the conflict between liberals and the Prussian monarchy came to a head, and culminated in the foundation of the Prussian Progressive Party. Joining left-wing liberals and moderate democrats, it became the principal protagonist on the side of the liberals in the conflict with the Prussian king about the character of the Prussian constitution. They were also politically close to the Progressive Parties in South Germany, founded a few years earlier.

Regional differences among liberals soon became apparent. Although all liberals in north and south, east and west, fought to strengthen parliament and the constitution, the conflict was more intense in Prussia than in the South of Germany, where constitutional structures had already been established in Napoleonic times, and where monarchs cooperated with parliaments. Political procedures, which had been practiced for a long time in Bavaria, Württemberg, and Baden, still had to be fought for in Prussia.

Who were these liberals? The traditional differentiation between *Bildungsliberalismus* (the liberalism of the educated classes) and *Wirtschaftsliberalismus* (economic liberalism) marks important social actors within liberalism, but blurs several other differences: the difference between old and new *Mittelstand* (bourgeoisie), the difference between Catholics and Protestants, and the difference between northern and southern Germany. In Baden, for instance, a certain liberal *ésprit de corps*, originating from their years as students together in Freiburg and Heidelberg, prevailed among higher civil servants. Not every bourgeois was liberal, and not every liberal was bourgeois. Some Catholics kept their distance from liberalism; others were oriented to it.[29] First and foremost, the social strata underneath the middle class, predominantly workers, were engaged in liberal organizations. Workers were organized in left-wing liberal associations and only parted with bourgeois democracy in the 1860s or 1870s— the precise timing is controversial.[30] Their separation from bourgeois left-wing liberalism was a result of class formation and, at the same time, a driving aspect of this process.[31] Until the 1870s, the early workers' movement perceived itself as a radical democratic people's movement in the tradition of the March Revolution of 1848.

Unlike liberalism, the Catholic Church, Catholicism and particularly the Catholic laity, emerged strengthened from 1848. The revolution had abolished the paternalism of the state church and state representatives came to see the Catholic Church as an ally in fighting the revolution. The Trier pilgrimage of 1844, a mass pilgrimage to the Seamless Robe of Christ housed in the Cathedral of Trier, had already foreshadowed this development. Social protest was articulated not as politics, but as piety. The closing of ranks did not last long, however, because the Catholic bishops pushed through a strict anti-modernism among the pious. Pius IX turned this anti-modernism into a religious and political doctrine of faith, first with the dogma of the 'Immaculate Conception,' annunciated in 1854, then, more decisively still, with the dogma of Papal infallibility in 1870, promulgated on the eve of the Franco-Prussian war.

After 1848 laymen played a key role in Catholic voluntary associations and in political representation. Liberals were especially sensitive to the fact that lower class Catholics, unlike the Catholics of the *Bildungsbürgertum*, offered no resistance to the two waves of ultramontane dogmatism of 1854 and 1870. The Immaculate Conception of the Virgin Mary and the infallibility of the Pope opposed everything the liberals stood for, including the heritage of the Enlightenment and the French Revolution, and the privileged position of scientific social knowledge. In sociological terms, it offered the benefit of drawing a sharp line between the in-group and the out-group, creating distinct affiliations in times of rapid change.

Patterns of collective interpretations and everyday culture grew further and further apart. Ultramontane Catholics reshaped popular piety. Marian devotions and the Cult of the Sacred Heart offered an attractive language of religious imagery, particularly for the lower classes. Many churches of the Sacred Heart were built, communities established, and brotherhoods founded. The cult of the Sacred Heart was defensive, sorrowful, and anti-modern.[32] This defensiveness was expressed through the activities of its prayer brotherhoods, and several formal and informal spiritual association; it also revealed the significant extent to which rural Catholics, and those from the lower and middle classes in the cities of the Rhineland, felt threatened by Prussia's aggressive religious policies. In addition, liberals and Catholics often stood in direct social contrast to one another. In the Saarland, the Rhineland, and in Westphalia, Protestant employers often employed Catholic workers, with the result that social protest and confessional conflict often reinforced each other. The Bishop of Mainz, Wilhelm Emanuel Freiherr von Ketteler, was the informal leader of the German Catholics, and represented the link between ultramontanism and social-political claims.[33] For bishops like Ketteler, but also for the rural lower classes, devotion to Rome was compelling in social terms.

Conflicts between liberals and ultramontane Catholics had a long tradition. On the political level, these conflicts concerned the relationship between church and state, including mixed marriages, freedom of religion, and religious education. In 1837, the struggle over mixed marriages culminated in the so-called Cologne affair, in which the Archbishop of Cologne, Clemens August von Droste-Vischering, was arrested and held in special confinement in Minden. In 1848, several Catholic members of the National Assembly refused to introduce freedom of religion as a constitutional right, as the liberals demanded. Ultramontane Catholics saw this, and the entire concept of a liberal constitutional state, as an affront to their faith, to the monarchy, and to divine right, if not in fact the divine order itself. They understood sovereignty in theological terms as divine sovereignty, not politically as the people's sovereignty. The same held true for the issue of elementary and religious education, which became a permanent political topic after 1848.[34] The ultramontane Catholic Edmund Jörg from Allgäu, the Hanover-based minister Ludwig Windthorst, and the jurist Hermann von Mallinckrodt became prominent exponents of this view. They formulated a Catholic critique of the state in which the state was not perceived as the definitive measure of the political order, but as an entity derived from the concepts of family and community. In their approach, the family came first, the community second, and the state last, and only in reference to those issues that could not be dealt with in the family or the community. When Edmund Jörg continually criticized the interventionist state, and other Catholics defended the rights of the Church against the state, this ran contrary to the advocates of a liberal nation state guaranteeing freedom of religion and championing the state as a modernizer. On the question of the relationship between state and church, on religious policy, and on political theory, liberals and ultramontane Catholics were diametrically opposed. In the *Syllabus Errorum* of 1864, Pope Pius IX sharpened these pointed differences by anathematizing liberalism. At the end of a long list of errors, Pius IX condemned as error number 80 the sentence: 'The Roman Pontiff can, and ought to, reconcile himself, and come to terms with progress, liberalism and modern civilization.'[35]

This not only concerned religion and the church, but also the order of society and the nation state. According to Edmund Jörg and Franz Joseph Ritter von Buß from Baden, a national society was only possible as a Christian—or more precisely—a Catholic society. But even the representatives of this political orientation understood that religion no longer stood at the center of the political order, and that its importance had subsided. Consequently, the *Katholikentage* (a festival-like gathering organized by and for Catholic laity and their associations) of 1848 and 1849 declared Germany itself a mission country. The task of the Bonifatius Association, founded in 1849, was therefore an inner mission.[36] By worshipping Bonifatius and choosing the city of Fulda, where the English missionary's grave was located, as the venue for the Catholic Bishops' Conference, German ultramontane Catholics underlined their ties to Rome. To them, Germany had only come into existence with the help of Rome, or more precisely with the help of the missionary Winfrit-Bonifatius, who was sent by Rome to bring Christian culture to the territory of *Germania*. For liberals the opposite was true: Germany had come into being in the course of the fight against Rome, and could be traced back to the struggle between Hermann of the Cherusci and the Romans. Luther's break with Rome and the concept of celibacy, as well as the foundation of the Protestant vicarage as a prototype of the bourgeois family, stood in the tradition of this anti-Roman interpretation of history.[37] The worshipping of Bonifatius was a political statement diametrically opposed to the cults of Hermann and Luther.

In political terms, this antagonism distilled into two parties, liberal and Catholic. In the beginning, there was the highly politicized Pius Associations of 1848, which demanded constitutionally protected rights for the Catholic Church. Catholic members of the Prussian Diet constituted the core of a new Catholic party and in 1852 they formed a parliamentary group, which from 1858 on called themselves the 'Center Faction' (*Zentrumsfraktion*). Between 1864 and 1866, around 100 Catholic politicians gathered at nine conferences in Soest in order to found a party with a clear political program. They did so in response to the foundation of the liberal National Association and the Progressive Party. The Soest program of 1870 formulated the slogan: 'For truth, justice and freedom,' and on this basis, in 1871, the Center Party was founded. Its aim was to defend the rights of the Church, and primarily of confessional schools, against the modern state. It advocated a federalist state structure and sought class harmony on the basis of Catholic social teaching.

This liberal-Catholic conflict did not occur in Germany alone. In all European countries, where the process of nation building or reconstruction had started, 'culture wars' emerged between Protestant or lay liberals on the one hand, and ultramontane Catholics on the other.[38] These 'culture wars' were especially fierce in the southern European countries with a nominal Catholic majority, where a minority of laicist liberals sought conflict with a majority society defined by its Catholicism. In Germany, this conflict had an ideological, a political, and a social dimension.

13.3 THE CLIMAX: CULMINATION
AND PERIPETEIA

When Wilhem I assumed the regency in October 1858, the basic parameters of the 'national question' had changed, becoming, in the so-called 'New Era,' the central focus of politics. The political dynamic in the German Confederation was given a new direction due to the Italian War of 1859 between France and Austria. A war involving Austria, as head of the German Confederation, demanded that everyone take a stance. With the exception of a few democrats, and Otto von Bismarck, the matter was clear: the Italian war was also about Germany. In the south of Germany, religious solidarity with Catholic Austria was also a factor. The Italian War thus unified the liberal national movement and closed the gap between advocates of the small and large German Solutions.

Internal conflict followed the Italian War. Prussian Liberals and the government fought from 1860 onward for about six years in an agonizing, but decisive constitutional conflict. Progressive liberals in Prussia, such as Viktor von Unruh, Benedikt Waldeck, and Wilhelm Löwe, challenged the throne in an open conflict in a political field, which the king considered his own preserve: namely, the Prussian military constitution. Since the Napoleonic Wars and the army reform of 1814, the Prussian army had not grown in size; now it was Wilhelm's desire to adapt its size to a Prussian population that had grown from 11 to 18 million people. Three measures were to serve this purpose: increasing the annual conscription of recruits from 40,000 to 63,000, raising the peacetime size of the army from 150,000 to 210,000, and prolonging military service from two to three years. Furthermore, the civil militias (*Landwehren*), which originated from the liberal idea of a citizen-soldier, were to be integrated into the royal army. The liberal majority in the Prussian Diet disagreed vehemently with all three proposals, in particular the extension of military service to three years, and the integration of the *Landwehr* into the royal army.[39] Liberals were, however, willing to support some military reform. Those who favored the Lesser German Solution set their hopes on the military strength of Prussia and its 'German mission,' although they demanded a civil militia and a military service of two years. This conflict became irresolvable because the military reform advocated by King Wilhelm and the War Minister, Albrecht von Roon, required large amounts of money which had to be approved by the Prussian Diet, where the liberals held a majority. The issue of the army reform, therefore, was not only a question of state organization, where the monarch held the prerogative, but also a question of state finances, where the budgetary powers of parliament applied. Liberals found common ground, advancing the motto: 'Parliamentary army or the King's army.' Like the dogma of papal infallibility in 1870, the constitutional conflict provided both political camps with simple phrases to sharply distinguish each other.[40] This conflict was expressed in parliamentary speeches, pamphlets, and in the political press, albeit largely without the participation of ordinary people. Parliament and government were in open, systemic conflict.

Previous strategies of conflict resolution no longer worked in this conflict. A monarchic counter revolution would be against public opinion and was bound to lead to a military dictatorship that was incalculable even for the monarchy. However, Prussian constitutionalism also faced a road block, because the two conflicting constitutional principles could not be aligned. The crisis endangered the entire system. The longer the conflict continued, the slimmer the chance of resolving it. In May 1862, the liberal Diet members Karl Twesten and Heinrich Sybel found a compromise with the War Minister, Albrecht von Roon. The liberals were willing to agree to the overall budget if the length of military service was not extended. The king, well aware of the consequences, refused to compromise, and his intransigence provoked the Diet to reject the entire budget. Discredited by his own government, Wilhelm was ready to abdicate in favor of his son, Crown Prince Friedrich, who was regarded as more liberal.

In the end, however, it was not Crown Prince Friedrich, but Otto von Bismarck, who defined the monarchical response to the liberal challenge. On 22 September 1862, Bismarck was appointed Minister President of Prussia. If he derived his fame as the founder of the German Empire, he was nevertheless more a divisive figure than a unifying one.[41] Born in the year of the congress of Vienna, he stood at the center of every conflict in his tenure as Prussian Minister President and German Chancellor. He started as a diehard anti-liberal in the Prussian constitutional conflict, and then alienated the Prussian conservatives when integrating Prussia in the new Reich. After 1871, he antagonized the Catholics in the 'Kulturkampf,' the Socialists in the anti-Socialist legislation of 1878, and finally the liberals in 1879, when he shifted from free trade to tariffs. He stood at the center of multiple political conflicts as well as conflict resolutions. He became a mythical figure, a trickster, who, following the ethnologist Claude-Levi Strauss, represented at the same time contradictory aspects of old and the new, legitimizing change and making it tolerable.[42]

Starting in 1862 he promised to defend monarchical prerogatives at any cost. In the Prussian Diet he immediately attacked the liberals: 'The great questions of the time will not be decided by speeches and majority decisions—that was the great mistake of 1848 and 1849—but by iron and blood.'[43] Bismarck thereby portrayed as contradictory constitutional parliamentary democracy on the one side, and economic growth and military success on the other.

Supporters of the compromise in both camps lost ground. The constitutional conflict escalated into an institutional crisis. Georg Meyer and Gerhard Anschütz later famously commented on the situation: 'Here public law reaches its limit. The question of how to proceed if no budget law exists is not a legal issue.'[44]

13.4 THE LIBERAL ERA AS CRITICAL JUNCTURE OF INSTITUTION BUILDING, 1867–1878

The Prussian wars against Denmark, Austria, and France transformed the constitutional conflict. These wars—against Denmark over Schleswig and Holstein in 1864, then against Austria over federal reform in 1866, and finally against France in 1870—were national wars of unification only from the perspective of 1871.[45] From the viewpoint of 1850, they could just as well have been called 'national wars of exclusion,' because they ultimately sealed the exclusion of Austria from Germany.

The foundation of the German nation state took place through and amidst war. This was not only true for Germany, but was common to the foundation of most European nation states: France in 1792, Belgium in 1830, and Italy in 1859, with the peaceful separation of Norway and Sweden in 1905 an exception. The connection between war and the foundation of the nation state is based on collective mobilization through fighting an external enemy. The war of 1848, which the Paulskirche fought against Denmark over Schleswig and Holstein, was already characterized by inner national participation and outward aggression.'[46] In Germany, external wars also served an internal purpose: the victory over Catholic Austria, and to an even greater extent the victory against France, was, for example, staged as a victory of Protestant Germany over Catholicism itself and proved the invincibility of Prussia and its military monarchy.

Prussia's military success over Denmark at the battle of Dybbøl (*Düppeler Schanzen*) on 18 April 1864, and, even more so, the victory over the Austrian troops at Königgrätz on 3 July 1866, seemed to legitimize Bismarck's policy of 1862 retrospectively. This was, at least, the view of the predominant part of the national movement, which supported the Lesser German Solution. When he switched sides, Karl Twesten, one of the founders of the Progressive Party and critics of Bismarck and authoritarian rule, was typical of many liberals. He stated that 'an inner conflict in a single German state and a conflict between different German states must be set aside, when it comes to the integrity of the German fatherland.'[47] In other words: the successful wars had opened a new chapter in the relations between the liberals and Bismarck. In autumn 1866, Hermann Baumgarten published his self-criticism of liberalism, in which he went so far as to advocate co-operation with Bismarck.[48]

As a result of the Austro-Prussian War, the world of the German states changed completely. Austria was excluded from the decision-making process regarding the national question. The Kingdom of Hanover, the Electorate of Hessen Kassel, the Duchy of Nassau, and the Imperial city of Frankfurt, were annexed by Prussia as it connected its Western territories with those in the East. Prussia was seemingly on the ascendant, even in financial terms, because the economic boom filled the government's pockets with increasing tax revenues. Baumgarten concluded his self-criticism that the bourgeoisie was meant for work and not for rule. For him, the political consequence of the constitutional conflict was shared liberal bourgeois and aristocratic monarchic rule. This separation of spheres originated from the tradition of compromise and agreement which had been characteristic for liberals in the *Vormärz* period.

The liberal era between 1867 and 1878 saw new institutions that have been characteristic of Germany's political system ever since.[49] The new institutions regulated, contained, and transformed national and confessional conflicts. The first institutional step to pacify the Prussian constitutional conflict was the Indemnity Bill of 26 September 1866. The government admitted having acted illegally in governing without an approved budget since 1862 and was, in return, exempted from punishment; that is to say, it received indemnity. The Indemnity Bill soothed the conflict because a vast majority of 235 members of the Prussian parliament against 75 granted indemnity to the government for its breach of the constitution. In so doing, they legitimized the government's action retrospectively.[50]

Many historians used to consider the Indemnity Bill and the subsequent split of liberalism in 1866 to have been the defeat or the collapse of German liberalism. To them, German liberals were tempted to abandon their liberal principles and succumb to the government in power because they admired Bismarck's political success. In the long-term, this accommodation to power allegedly weakened democratic ideals among Germany's bourgeoisie and subsequently prepared the way for 1933.[51] According to this view, the cooperation between National Liberals and Bismarck meant that the former accepted a system that was only partially parliamentary. But there was another side to it as well. The Indemnity Bill also opened up new possibilities for the liberals, giving them cause to assume that they would be in a position to change circumstances in Prussia. To see only authoritarian solutions and their consequences for the twentieth century does not take into consideration that there were also other institutions of conflict resolution between 1867 and 1871—ones that did not lead to 1933, most importantly those involving democratic suffrage and federalism. These also created new conflicts, which were then transferred to the Reich, but compatible with national co-existence.

Four different developments contained, reworked, and transformed both conflicts: democratic suffrage, which introduced party competition and parliamentary negotiation strategies; federalism, which reorganized the relationship between the individual states and the nation state; a strong monarchy, which could solve conflicts and make decisions from above; and the principles of parity and proportionality. The conflicts of the Revolution of 1848 and of the 1850s were not resolved, as the national enthusiasts perceived them to have been in 1871, but were regulated and contained according to different patterns of action. These patterns were, in fact, contradictory, but could also converge. Some of them, such as the concept of federalism, were old, others, such as democratic suffrage, were new and untested.

13.4.1 Democratic suffrage, Parliamentarianism and party competition in the federal state

On 12 February 1867, democratic elections were held for the first time in the North German Confederation. Every North German man older than 25 years who did not receive any public assistance was entitled to vote for the constituent *Reichstag* of the North German Confederation.[52] There was no electoral boycott as suggested by the Progressive Party, which had denied Bismarck indemnity for his constitutional breach. The turnout in Prussia was, with an average of 65 per cent, substantially higher than in the Diet elections, which were held under the undemocratic three-class voting system. On 25 September 1867, only 1.45 million people in the older Prussian provinces had voted for the Diet. On 12 February 1866, meanwhile, 2.57 million voters showed up for the *Reichstag* elections. Most of them were first time voters. It was no longer the electoral colleges that effectively decided the result, as was the case in the Prussian elections, but the individual voter. The voters themselves had their say in the national elections, and the National Liberals won the elections with 80 mandates, showing particularly strong in the new Prussian territories of Hanover, Kassel, and Nassau.

In that same year electoral reform was also high on the agenda of the House of Commons in London. The Second Reform Act primarily extended suffrage to the urban regions and was perceived as a revolutionary 'leap in the dark' (Lord Derby).[53] This was even truer in the case of Germany's elections where democratic and parliamentary traditions were much less developed. German democratic suffrage was not the result of pressure by socialists and democrats, but by revolution from above. Bismarck had several motives for advocating the suffrage once championed by the Paulskirche. It ultimately excluded Austria from the new national order, because this type of suffrage could not be applied in multi-national Austria. In terms of foreign affairs, its democratic appeal to the nation legitimized Prussian expansion to the other European great powers—first and foremost Great Britain. More importantly, the democratic suffrage, accepted only hesitantly by the National Liberals, curtailed the influence of the liberal bourgeoisie and its electoral colleges, the 'distilled bourgeoisie' (Bismarck). From Bismarck's point of view, it ensured that a liberal parliamentary majority, as had occurred in Prussia, would not occur in the Reich. Liberals had benefited from the census system in the Prussian suffrage. In the Reich, their influence was balanced by the urban and rural lower classes. Bismarck, on the other hand, relied on the conservative and royal mindset of the rural population. Liberals always performed worse in the *Reichstag* elections than in the Prussian elections. However, the winners in the long run were not the conservatives, but the Catholic Center Party and the Social Democrats.

Even contemporaries perceived Bismarck's strategy as a means of rule inspired by Bonapartism. It was designed to weaken liberal leaders in parliament, and even to weaken parliament as an institution.[54] Friedrich Engels equated the foundation of the North German Confederation with Louis Bonaparte's open take-over of power in 1851 and noticed the temptation of the Bonapartist form of rule: 'The period of revolutions from below was concluded for the time being; it followed a period of revolutions from above.... '[55] Napoleon III demonstrated that a monarchic state could exist with, and in spite of, a democratic voting system, and that an authoritarian state government did not contradict the principle of political representation. However, the enthusiasm of the Prussian state ministry for Bonapartism soon flagged. In Prussia, there were candidates from the ranks of the ministry backed by the government. In East Elbia, the typical ministerial candidate was a conservative landowner, in Westphalia and in the Rhineland he was a conservative civil servant. This pattern was still apparent in the elections of 1867, but it could not prevail against the mobilizing effect of party machines and their candidates in the long run. Bismarck took over the democratic voting system, but he was hardly able to appropriate it in a Bonapartist way, because—as he put it— 'Germans cannot be governed in the same manner as the French.'[56]

Seen from a theoretical perspective, the democratic voting system integrated conflicts into parties. Political opponents became parties, which competed for as large a share of the national vote as possible, and no longer attempted to eliminate each other.

This was possible because democratic suffrage legitimized the opposition. No ultimate decision was taken by the democratic franchise. Every three, or since 1888, every five years, voters decided on their political representation. The democratic franchise did not resolutely solve, but rather processed conflicts by periodic elections. Based on the fact that there was more than merely one opinion to every political issue, the democratic franchise engendered in the long run a pluralistic community, where majority and minority were constantly changing.

Prussia's fierce opponents in the process of German nation building organized themselves into parties and stood as candidates. Competing interests and ideas, the elixir of democratic institutions, thereby had an integrative function in the nation state.[57] Only eight months after their defeat at the hands of Prussia, the Saxon patriots took part in the North German elections. In so doing, they accepted the North German Confederation as the basis for their political actions, even while they kept a jealous watch over the independence of Saxony. The royal Hanoverians, the Welfs, and the Bavarian patriots acted in the same way. They all accepted the Reich by taking part in the *Reichstag* elections. The democratic franchise and parties helped foster abstract identities that brought together people from different regions with similar interests. Conflicts between Bavarians and Prussians were not fought against national institutions, but within them. In the words of the historian Margaret Lavinia Anderson: 'As regional and national organizations took on more and more electoral functions, they contributed to a process of abstraction, in which the community was redefined into something trans-local: confession, class, and in most cases party. It was with abstractions such as these that the voters eventually identified.'[58] Voters recognized their own interests in a national party system, which was not built along local or regional lines. Here lies a certain similarity between the foundation of the Reich in 1871, and the German unification in 1990, when the PDS, the successor of the communist SED, stood in the *Bundestag* elections and thereby pragmatically accepted the democratic character of the new order, which the party had steadfastly opposed until then. By contrast, in the Weimar Republic the KPD had refused to stand in the general elections in January 1919.

Democratization could be interpreted either as political participation or as emancipation from older authorities. Political participation gave legitimacy to the political order. Even conservative authors, such as the Saxon minister and law professor Carl Gerber, welcomed democratic institutions in order to foster the monarchy. What he and his like-minded colleagues had in mind was a rather new form of legitimacy indispensable for the monarchical order. Whereas authors like Gerber accepted forms of direct democracy, Bismarck rejected parliamentary government following the English example.[59] Those who understood democracy as a way of political emancipation were to be found on the political left. For Socialists, democracy made their strength public and visible. Even here on the political left, democracy was much more praised than the parliamentary dimension of politics. Whereas parliaments were seen as instruments of bourgeois domination, democracy always had the utopian flavor of a better world. Parliament did not control the German government. The democratic extension of the franchise had not led to a political system with government standing against the opposition, but with government standing against parliament.

In the long run, however, the *Reichstag*, even without the right to elect the *Reichskanzler*, became a key institution in the Reich and a central forum for conflict resolution and the political articulation of interests.[60] In 1873, on the initiative of the Liberal Eduard Lasker, legislative competence for the entire civil, criminal and procedural law—that is, all questions of the rules of procedure and legal equality—were transmitted to the Reich and therefore to the *Reichstag*. Several committees of the *Reichstag* drafted the Civil Code (*Bürgerliches Gesetzbuch*, BGB), which came into effect on 1 January 1900 and had a lasting effect on German society. By 1878, the *Reichstag* had passed 179 bills, many of which extended the regulations of the North German Confederation to the Reich. Democratic suffrage, the *Reichstag* and its legislation shaped the population of the Reich into a political society. East Prussians, Swabians, Rhinelanders, and Silesians all voted under the same suffrage and were subjects of the same law. The *Reichstag* became a symbol of the political nation even in the view of the Reich population. This was shown by a broad media interest in and numerous complaints about any kind of electoral manipulation or fraud.[61]

In a very short period, the democratic voting system made an impact and supported a party system that was essentially similar in all regions. At the *Reichstag* elections in 1871 there were only eight constituencies with a single candidate. All other constituencies saw several candidates, even if it was often clear who would win the mandate. As a result, diversity of opinion prevailed on a broad basis. The unexpected pace of this development becomes clear, when we look to Great Britain, where approximately a quarter of all seats in the House of Commons went uncontested as late as 1910.[62] Democratic suffrage accelerated the development of the German party system whose roots dated back to the Revolution of 1848. The traditional binary party system, which functioned according to the pattern of 'order versus revolution,' made way for a four-party system consisting of liberalism, conservatism, political Catholicism and socialism. These '-isms' usually stood for families of parties. There were several conservative parties—*Reichs- und Freikonservative Partei* (Reich and Free Conservative Party) and *Konservative Partei* (Conservative Party)—next to the two liberal parties (National Liberals and Progressive Party) and the socialists under the lead of August Bebel and Wilhelm Liebknecht (from 1869 *Sozialdemokratische Arbeiterpartei*, Social Democratic Workers' Party; from 1875 *Sozialistische Arbeiterpartei Deutschlands*, Socialist Workers' Party of Germany). In winter 1870/71, the newly established Catholic Center Party nationalized Catholics from all parts of Germany in one Catholic party. In the same way the socialist party nationalized socialists from Berlin and Wuppertal in one party. The national party system created national political interests transverse to regional interests. It also transferred regional conflicts to the national level. The thousands of local religious conflicts, for instance, between the Catholic clergy and liberals were transformed into a national conflict immediately after unification in 1872, when liberal legislation attacked the Catholic church. The local protagonists on both sides looked to the national level for help and assistance.

In the first decade of the Empire, large voting blocks and groups of party supporters were formed. According to the findings of the Catholic electoral researcher Johannes Schauff, between 1874 and 1884, the Center Party succeeded in mobilizing almost the entire Catholic electorate, with eighty percent of all eligible Catholic voters casting their vote in favor of the Center Party.[63] If these figures were in constant decline thereafter, the number of votes for the Center Party was even higher among devout Catholics. The 'culture war' had enabled this development. It emotionally anchored the German party system in the minds of the Catholic electorate. The same was true for the socialists with regard to the Anti-Socialist laws after 1878. For the Catholics, the 'culture war', or *Kulturkampf*, left a deep-seated sense of threat among Catholics, which in turn created emotional cohesion, and enabled a network of voluntary associations and the creation of a political community of conviction. The Catholic social milieu, which shaped the German party landscape until 1928 when it ultimately eroded, originated in the 1860s and 1870s.[64] As in the socialist milieu, Catholic Germany depended on constantly recreating the original sense of threat. Catholic clerics, associations, media, and the *Katholikentage* continually restaged, and thus rendered contemporaneous this primordial moment of threat. Socialist party conventions and anniversaries worked the same way.

The differences between liberals and conservatives gradually faded away after 1871. The political scientist Karl Rohe has even identified a joint 'national camp' arching over both political parties. The parties' common electoral interest in the run-off system, which privileged party coalitions in the second ballot, had enabled this situation. Here, conservatives and liberals often cooperated.[65] The national camp gained in importance when conservatives turned to tariff protection of rye and steel in 1879. Both parties also opposed the socialists after 1878. In terms of the main conflicts of nation building, this realignment between conservatives and liberals finally brought an end to the Prussian constitutional conflict, when both camps had fought a seemingly deadly war. In the 1880s, the national camp took over from the liberals as the informal governing party, becoming in the 1890s the cornerstone of the *Sammlungspolitik* (the policy of 'gathering' all productive forces that sought to 'protect' the state against the Social Democrats).

13.4.2 Federalism and authoritarianism

One of the most significant consequences of the Prussian constitutional conflict for Bismarck was to prevent a parliamentary regime on the national level at any cost. He had faced a liberal majority in the Prussian Diet for years and wanted to prevent that for the Reich. This purpose was served by the Reich's federal construction, which was organized to prevent a showdown as had occurred in Prussia between government and parliament. Unlike the North American model, as codified in the Federalist Papers, federalism in Germany did not organize democracy within a territorial state. By contrast, it organized the permanent acquiescence of the individual German states towards a national state and its institutions to which they had transferred important rights. Bismarck's political objective was to preserve and strengthen the Prussian monarchy, which in 1871 turned into an imperial monarchy. To him, this was most likely to be achieved through the federal structure of an everlasting federation of 25 rulers and city governments—the so called members of the federation (*Bundesglieder*)—and not through democratic elections involving 41 million Germans. The Reich had legislative powers, the German states executive powers. This was the origin of the specific form of federalism in Germany: cooperative federalism. What was signed into law by the national state was set into practice by the states' administration—thereby underscoring the importance of the states. In practice, it meant that the entry of Saxony or Baden into the Reich did not involve a change of elites as it did in 1990 when East and West Germany were reunited. Instead, Saxon postmen turned into Reich postmen. In terms of officials, a surprisingly small number of individuals represented the Reich in the Bismarck period.[66] Instead, it was the familiar authorities of the states which executed Reich legislation. The impact of this fact on the social acceptance of the new national order cannot be emphasized enough.

This was even more pronounced in the seemingly technical field of the imperial finances. The national constitution ensured that the Reich had its own revenues from tariffs and taxes, although they were rather limited until 1879. In the imperial period, it was only in 1896 that the income of the central government covered its budgetary expenditures. In all other years the difference was paid for by the states (*Matrikularbeiträge*), special levies from the states according to their population size, or by the Reich incurring debts. This had lasting consequences for national integration. At least until 1879, the tax officers in the single states virtually funded the Reich, or at least this was the impression most people had. It helped to make the wave of standardization, which swept through German society after 1867 and 1871, socially and politically bearable. Practically, it meant that the German parliament could not shut down the government by rejecting the budget, which Prussian liberals had tried to do in 1862.

Constitutionally, the German Reich was governed by the *Bundesrat*. Next to the *Reichstag*, the *Bundesrat* was the supreme body gathering German rulers and city governments. Unlike the US Senate, which allows the same amount of votes to every state regardless of its size, the different states and cities had votes in the *Bundesrat* according to the size of their population. The exception was Prussia. It comprised about two-thirds of the Reich territory and approximately sixty per cent of the Reich population, but in order to ease the integration of the smaller states, Prussia held merely seventeen out of the entire fifty-eight votes. It therefore depended on the approval of other states—in most cases the kingdoms in South Germany—to get a majority. Prussian diplomats were usually quite successful in doing so. Strategically, the Prussian foreign minister was at the center of this diplomatic web that planned national politics. It was from this position that Otto von Bismarck controlled the *Bundesrat*.

The *Bundesrat* had a dual function. On the one hand, it took part in legislation along with the *Reichstag*. On the other hand, the Reich government was headed by the federal presidium, a position held by the Prussian king as German Emperor. His head of chancellery, the Reich chancellor, was responsible for the executive. At the chancellor's side were state secretaries instead of ministers responsible to the *Reichstag*. This specific structure prevented the *Reichstag* from criticizing or even attacking the Reich government in public. As a monarchical federal state the Reich was not meant to be parliamentarized. At the same time, federalism and *Bundesrat* served as institutions to prevent democracy, because all important decisions—first and foremost all military matters—remained the domain of the executive government. This again was a result of the Prussian constitutional conflict. The federal structure of the Reich was deliberately geared against democratic principles, and this facilitated the integration of Bavaria, Württemberg, Saxony, and all other states into the Reich. Up to the present day, the ability of single state governments to take part in the decision-making process through the *Bundesrat* is still a formative principle of German politics.[67]

However, the profound democratic costs of the political construction cannot conceal the fact that federalism in the medium term had already solved the contradiction between the political center of the Reich and the member states. In Imperial Germany, the solution to the center-periphery conflict involved giving the member states a voice in national legislation. German states were not provinces, being objects of legislation, but instead participants in the work of national legislation. One example, still of relevance today, is civil marriage. In 1875, the liberal Bavarian state government, which was in dispute with the Catholic patriotic majority of the Diet, addressed not only the *Bundesrat*, but also the *Reichstag* and achieved the nationwide introduction of obligatory civil marriage that would never have met with a majority in the Bavarian Diet.[68]

Whereas, federalism encouraged the gradual transition from a constellation characterized by the exclusion of region and nation, to one marked by the inclusion of the two in the 1860s, one was either a Bavarian or a German, in 1890 one was a German because one was a Bavarian. The same mechanism had already become apparent in regard to localism and regionalism. A man from Nuremberg was initially a Franconian, then a Bavarian and finally a German. None of these characteristics was relativized by the others. Loyalties towards community, region, individual state and nation state did not end up in a zero-sum game in which the increasing loyalty towards the nation state would simultaneously imply a declining loyalty towards the region or community. By assuming the position of assimilation, leading representatives of modernization theory and the process of nation building, such as Karl W. Deutsch, supposed that geographically extensive concepts of identity would supersede geographically narrower concepts. In reality, inclusion was based on federalism and on the preservation of local and regional loyalties.[69]

This was also caused by a growing communication and an increase in mobility among the Reich population. Railway companies, conceived within states and tightly controlled by governments until 1920, extended their territorial network. The competition between the railway administrations, which until 1875 were often private, was superseded by the idea of joint accumulation of advantages, and by the understanding that co-operation and mutual permeability for railway traffic would increase profit opportunities for every single railway company. After extending the territorial network, regional networks were condensed by improving local traffic, which connected suburban and rural areas with long-distance transport. Commuters were able to work in town, but live in the countryside where they could carry out subsistence farming and participate in rural life. Hybrid forms of living and co-existence were more common in everyday life than clear separations.

This was not only true for the railway system, but for commerce and communication in general, and for economic and political spaces that recast themselve by networking instead of remaining local. In the entry debate on 21 January 1871, several anti-Prussian Catholic patriots from Bavaria decided in favor of an entry to the Reich. A decision against it would possibly have caused a secession of Franconia and the Palatinate on the left bank of the Rhine. In order to preserve the Kingdom of Bavaria in its form of 1871, it was therefore necessary to join the Reich. A similar connection between preserving autonomy on the one hand, and entering a larger unit on the other, is characteristic for several Eastern European countries in their entry to the European Union.[70]

Federalism was more than just a way of distributing authority throughout the federal states in order to preserve the union. The federalist model deeply affected society. It organized social task sharing, distributed entitlement claims and gave society a federal structure. The German nation state of 1871 did not supersede regions and single states. Instead, regions and nation states reconstituted themselves mutually: partly against each other, partly together in the process of joint accumulation of advantages. At the same time, new regional references emerged, as was shown by the modern terms 'South and West Germany' used in German transport planning during the late nineteenth century. Both nation and region—having previously been antagonists in the fight for the nation state before 1867—changed their self-perception. After 1871, the nation did not mean exclusion of the 'outside,' but 'downward protection' against the socialists. At the same time, the region was modernized once specific 'modern forms of attributing characteristics, exclusions and roles' had found expression through the nation.[71] From now on, to be a Bavarian or a Saxon was the precondition for being a German.

13.5 THE *KAISERREICH* AS A SYSTEM OF CIRCUMVENTED DECISIONS

The *Kaiserreich* was full of contradictions and open from the start as to its long-term possibilities. The Reich was a monarchy, but with a democratically elected parliament. It was a federal state with developed parties operating nationwide. It represented the rule of law (*Rechtsstaat*), but one in which important areas such as the military operated in a legal vacuum and were entirely under royal control. Although the *Reichstag* held budgetary power, most public spending was accounted for by the army and was therefore under the authority of the crown. The approaches of integration were too contradictory and too promising at the same time. What was commonly labeled as a 'dilatory compromise formula' during the foundation period was actually the result of a multitude of previous conflicts.[72] The democratic aspects of the political order were not hard won from below, but granted from above. The two institutions, the *Bundesrat* and the *Reichstag*, represented the dual legitimacy of the *Kaiserreich* based on the sovereignty of the rulers and the people. Tensions between these institutions were bridged more and more frequently by focusing on internal and external enemies, first and foremost through anti-Semitism and anti-socialism.

The high level of integration in the *Kaiserreich* was in no small part the result of co-occurring, but systemically unconnected conflicts. In this way, different forms of appropriation of the *Kaiserreich* emerged: there was a monarchic and authoritarian *Kaiserreich* parallel to a democratic and egalitarian one. When different groups recalled the foundation of the Empire, they meant different things. Many years later, it was the National Socialists who were able to appeal to both: to the authoritarian qualities of the *Kaiserreich* and its promise of democratic participation.

[Translated from German by Christine Brocks.]

NOTES

1. Cf. Achille Darmaing, *Relation complète du sacre de Charles X* (Paris: Communication & Tradition, 1996 [Paris 1825]), 94.
2. Jan Andres and Matthias Schwengelbeck, 'Das Zeremoniell als politischer Kommunikationsraum: Inthronizationsfeiern in Preußen im "langen" 19. Jahrhundert,' in Ute Frevert and Heinz-Gerhard Haupt (eds), *Neue Politikgeschichte. Perspektiven einer historischen Politikforschung* (Frankfurt am Main: Campus, 2005), 27–81.
3. Quoted in: Wolfgang Neugebauer (ed.), *Handbuch der Preußischen Geschichte.* Vol. 3. *Vom Kaiserreich zum 20. Jahrhundert und Große Themen der Geschichte Preußens* (Berlin: de Gruyter, 2000), 277.
4. Cf. Heinrich von Treitschke, 'Unsere Aussichten,' in *Preußische Jahrbücher* 44 (1879), 559–576. Even Treitschke's political opponent Theodor Mommsen advocated assimilation. Cf. Theodor Mommsen, *Auch ein Wort über unser Judenthum* (Berlin: Weidmann, 1880). On the so called 'debate on Anti-Semitism' cf. Uffa Jensen, *Gebildete Doppelgänger. Bürgerliche Juden und Protestanten im 19. Jahrhundert* (Göttingen: Vandenhoeck & Ruprecht, 2005), 197–268.
5. Cf. Armin Heinen, 'Umstrittene Moderne. Die Liberalen und der preußisch-deutsche Kulturkampf,' *Geschichte und Gesellschaft* 29 (2003), 138–160, 149.
6. On the historiography of the culture war cf. the earlier studies of Rudolf Lill, 'Die Wende im Kulturkampf,' *Quellen und Forschungen aus italienischen Archiven und Bibliotheken* 50 (1971), 227–283, 52; 49 (1972), 657–730; id., 'Der Kulturkampf in Preußen und im Deutschen Reich (bis 1878).'; 'Die Beilegung des Kulturkampfes in Preußen und im Deutschen Reich,' in Hubert Jedin (ed.), *Handbuch der Kirchengeschichte*, vol. VI/2 (Freiburg: Herder, 1973), 28–48, 59–78; and Helmut Walser Smith, *German Nationalism and Religious Conflict. Culture, Ideology, Politics 1870–1914* (Princeton: Princeton University Press, 1995); Heinen, 'Umstrittene Moderne.'

7. Cf. Celia Applegate, 'A Europe of Regions. Reflections on the Historiography of Sub-National Places in Modern Times,' *American Historical Review* 104 (1999), 1157–1182.

8. Cf. primarily the studies of Stein Rokkan. Stein Rokkan, *State Formation, Nation Building and Mass Politics in Europe. The Theory of Stein Rokkan, based on his collected Works*, ed. Peter Flora (Oxford: Oxford University Press, 1999).

9. On the European dimension of culture wars cf. Christopher Clark and Wolfram Kaiser (eds), *Culture Wars. Secular-Catholic Conflict in Nineteenth Century Europe* (Cambridge: Cambridge University Press, 2003).

10. Cf. the fundamental study by David Blackbourn, *Marpingen: Apparitions of the Virgin Mary in Nineteenth-Century Germany* (New York: Alfred A. Knopf, 1994).

11. Cf. Gerhard Lehmbruch, 'Der unitarische Bundesstaat. Pfadabhängigkeit und Wandel, *Max Planck Institut für Geschichte*,' Discussion paper 02/2, Cologne 2002.

12. Cf. on this issue Andreas Biefang, *Die andere Seite der Macht. Reichstag und Öffentlichkeit im 'System Bismarck' 1871–1890* (Düsseldorf: Droste, 2009), 38–41.

13. Cf. Immanuel Kant, 'Der Streit der Fakultäten,' in id. *Werke*, vol. 9, *Schriften zur Anthropologie, Geschichtsphilosophie, Politik und Pädagogik*, ed. Wilhelm Weischedel (Frankfurt am Main: Suhrkamp, 1964), 265–393, quote 361.

14. A detailed description in Jürgen Müller, *Deutscher Bund und deutsche Nation 1848–1866* (Göttingen: Vandenhoeck & Ruprecht, 2005).

15. Abigail Green, *Fatherlands. State-building and Nationhood in Nineteenth Century Germany* (Cambridge: Cambridge University Press 2001), 62–92.

16. Cf. August Ludwig von Rochau, *Grundsätze der Realpolitik angewendet auf die staatlichen Zustände Deutschlands* (Stuttgart: Göpel, 1853).

17. Cf. Biefang, *Die andere Seite der Macht*, 38–41.

18. Cf. Thorsten Gudewitz, 'Performing the Nation. The Schiller Centenary Celebrations of 1859 and the Media,' *European Review of History* 15 (2008), 587–601.

19. Cf. Stefan-Ludwig Hoffmann, *Die Politik der Geselligkeit. Freimaurerlogen in der deutschen Bürgergesellschaft 1840–1918* (Göttingen: Vandenhoeck & Ruprecht, 2000).

20. Cf. Ralf Roth, 'Liberalismus in Frankfurt am Main. Probleme seiner Strukturgeschichte,' in Dieter Langewiesche and Lothar Gall (eds), *Liberalismus und Region. Zur Geschichte des deutschen Liberalismus im 19. Jahrhundert* (Munich: Oldenbourg, 1995), 41–86, 64f.

21. Cf. Dieter Langewiesche, '"Staat" und "Kommune". Zum Wandel der Staatsaufgaben in Deutschland im 19. Jahrhundert,' *Historische Zeitschrift* 248 (1989), 620–635.

22. Langewiesche, '"Staat" und "Kommune".'

23. Cf. Beate-Carola Padtberg, *Rheinischer Liberalismus in Köln während der politischen Reaktion in Preußen nach 1848/49* (Cologne: Rheinisch-Westfälisches Wirtschaftsarchiv in Cologne, 1985). On Frankfurt am Main cf. Jan Palmowski, *Urban Liberalism in Imperial Germany 1866–1914* (Oxford: Oxford University Press, 1999).

24. Cf. Hans-Peter Ullmann, *Interessenverbände in Deutschland* (Frankfurt am Main.: Suhrkamp, 1988); Andreas Biefang, *Politisches Bürgertum in Deutschland 1857–1868. Nationale Organizationen und Eliten* (Düsseldorf: Droste, 1994), on the 'Kongress deutscher Volkswirte' 49ff., on the 'Deutscher Handelstag' 207ff., on the 'Deutscher Abgeordnetentag' 221ff.

25. The magazine 'Gartenlaube' has become one of the most popular objects of historical and literary research. Cf. among others Kirsten Belgum, *Popularizing the Nation. Audience, Representation, and the Production of Identity in Die Gartenlaube, 1853–1900* (Lincoln: University of Nebraska Press, 1998); Marcus Koch, *Nationale Identität im Prozess*

nationalstaatlicher Orientierung, dargestellt am Beispiel Deutschlands durch die Analyse der Familienzeitschrift 'Die Gartenlaube' von 1853–1890 (Frankfurt am Main: Lang, 2003).

26. Cf. Biefang, *Politisches Bürgertum*, 15.

27. Cf. Lothar Gall, 'Liberalismus und bürgerliche Gesellschaft Zu Charakter und Entwicklung der liberalen Bewegung in Deutschland,' *Historische Zeitschrift* 220 (1975), 324–356.

28. On the changes of liberalism cf. Karl Rohe, *Wahlen und Wählertraditionen in Deutschland. Kulturelle Grundlagen deutscher Parteien und Parteiensysteme im 19. und 20. Jahrhundert* (Frankfurt am Main: Suhrkamp, 1992), 54ff. On the concept of the "federative nation" cf. Dieter Langewiesche u. Georg Schmidt (eds.), *Föderative Nation. Deutschlandkonzepte von der Reformation bis zum Ersten Weltkrieg* (Munich: Oldenbourg, 2000).

29. On this point see Thomas Mergel, *'Zwischen Klasse und Konfession.' Katholisches Bürgertum im Rheinland, 1794–1914* (Göttingen: Vandenhoeck & Ruprecht, 1994).

30. Cf. on this issue still Gustav Mayer, 'Die Trennung der proletarischen von der bürgerlichen Demokratie, 1863–1870,' in Hans-Ulrich Wehler (ed.), *Radikalismus, Sozialismus und bürgerliche Demokratie* (Frankfurt am Main: Suhrkamp, 1969 [1912]), 108–178; Jürgen Kocka, 'Die Trennung von bürgerlicher und proletarischer Demokratie im europäischen Vergleich. Fragestellungen und Ergebnisse,' in id., Jurgen Kocka (ed.), *Europäische Arbeiterbewegungen im 19. Jahrhundert. Deutschland, Österreich, England und Frankreich im Vergleich* (Göttingen: Vandenhoeck & Ruprecht, 1983), 5–20.

31. On the discussion of this point cf. Thomas Welskopp, *Das Banner der Brüderlichkeit. Die deutsche Sozialdemokratie vom Vormärz bis zum Sozialistengesetz* (Bonn: Dietz, 2000).

32. Cf. Norbert Busch, *Katholische Frömmigkeit und Moderne. Zur Sozial- und Mentalitätsgeschichte des Herz-Jesu-Kultes in Deutschland zwischen Kulturkampf und Erstem Weltkrieg* (Gütersloh: Gütersloher Verlagshaus, 1997).

33. Ursula Nothelle-Wildfeuer, 'Wilhelm Emmanuel von Ketteler, 1811–1877,' in Bernd Heidenreich (ed.), *Politische Theorien des 19. Jahrhunderts*, vol. 3 (Wiesbaden: Hessische Landeszentrale für Politische Bildung, 2000), 275–294.

34. On the alliance between conservative monarchy and ultramontanism cf. Jonathan Sperber, *Popular Catholicism in Nineteenth-Century Germany* (Princeton: Princeton University Press, 1984).

35. Heinrich Denzinger and Peter Hünermann, *Kompendium der Glaubensbekenntnisse und kirchlichen Lehrentscheidungen* (Freiburg: Herder, 1991), 809.

36. Cf. Siegfried Weichlein, 'Religion und Nation: Bonifatius als politischer Heiliger im 19. und 20. Jahrhundert,' *Schweizerische Zeitschrift zur Religions- und Kulturgeschichte* 100 (2006), 45–58.

37. Cf. Siegfried Weichlein, 'Pfarrhaus,' in: Hubert Wolf and Christoph Markschies (eds), *Erinnerungsorte des Christentums* (Munich: Beck, 2010).

38. Cf. Clark and Kaiser, *Culture Wars*.

39. Cf. Wolfgang Petter, 'Die Roonsche Heeresorganization und das Ende der Landwehr,' in Peter Baumgart (ed.), *Die Preußische Armee zwischen Ancien Regime und Reichsgründung* (Paderborn: Schöningh, 2008), 215–228.

40. Dieter Langewiesche, *Liberalism in Germany* (Basingstoke: Macmillan Press, 2000), 91.

41. Cf. Otto Pflanze, *Bismarck. Der Reichsgründer*, trans. Peter Hahlbrock (Munich: Beck, 1997).

42. Cf. Claude Levi-Strauss, *Strukturale Anthropologie*, vol. 2 (Frankfurt am Main: Suhrkamp, 1992), 165f.

43. Wilhelm Schüßler, (ed.), *Otto von Bismarck, Reden, 1847–1869*, in: Hermann von Petersdorff (ed.) *Bismarck: Die gesammelten Werke*, vol. 10 (Berlin: Otto Stolberg, 1924–1935), 139–140.

44. Georg Meyer and Gerhard Anschütz, *Lehrbuch des Deutschen Staatsrechts* (Munich: Duncker & Humblot, 1919), 906.

45. Cf. the summary in Michael Epkenhans, 'Einigung durch "Eisen und Blut". Militärgeschichte im Zeitalter der Reichsgründung 185–1871,' in Karl-Volker Neugebauer (ed.), *Grundkurs deutsche Militärgeschichte Bd. 1: Die Zeit bis 1914. Vom Kriegshaufen zum Massenheer* (Munich: Oldenbourg, 2006), 302–377.

46. Dieter Langewiesche, *Nationalismus im 19. und 20. Jahrhundert: zwischen Partizipation und Aggression* (Bonn: Friedrich Ebert Stiftung, 1994), 13.

47. *Stenographischer Bericht über die Verhandlungen des preußischen Abgeordnetenhauses 1863/1864*, vol. 1, 207; quoted in: Heinrich August Winkler, *Preußischer Liberalismus und deutscher Nationalstaat. Studien zur Geschichte der Deutschen Fortschrittspartei 1861–1866* (Tübingen: Mohr Siebeck, 1964), 44.

48. Cf. Hermann Baumgarten, *Der deutsche Liberalismus. Eine Selbstkritik* (Berlin: Georg Reimer, 1866).

49. Lehmbruch, *Der unitarische Bundesstaat*, 19, 18–21.

50. Details in Erich J. Hahn, *Rudolf von Gneist. Ein politischer Jurist in der Bismarckzeit* (Frankfurt am Main.: Klostermann, 1995), 121ff.

51. Friedrich C. Sell, *Die Tragödie des deutschen Liberalismus* (Stuttgart: Deutsche Verlagsanstalt, 1953).

52. On the elections of the constituent Reichstag of the North German Confederation see Klaus Erich Pollmann, *Parlamentarismus im Norddeutschen Bund 1867–1870* (Düsseldorf: Droste Verlag, 1985), 93–154.

53. Margaret Lavinia Anderson, *Practicing Democracy. Elections and Political Culture in Imperial Germany* (Princeton: Princeton University Press, 2000), 4.

54. Thomas Nipperdey, *Deutsche Geschichte 1866–1918*, 2 vols (Munich: Beck, 1992), 108.

55. Friedrich Engels, Introduction of 'Klassenkämpfe in Frankreich 1848 bis 1850' [1895] in Karl Marx and Friedrich Engels, *Werke*, vol. 22 (Berlin: Dietz, 1972), 509–527, 516.

56. Quote in: Anderson, *Practicing Democracy*, 402.

57. Michael Zürn, 'Die Politik wandert aus,' *Die Zeit*, No. 13 (25 March 2010), 15.

58. Anderson, *Practicing Democracy*, 417.

59. Cf. Christoph Schönberger, *Das Parlament im Anstaltsstaat. Zur Theorie parlamentarischer Repräsentation in der Staatsrechtslehre des Kaiserreichs (1871–1918)*, Ius Commune, Sonderheft 102 (Frankfurt am Main: Klostermann, 1997).

60. Biefang, *Die andere Seite der Macht*.

61. Andreas Biefang, 'Der Reichstag als Symbol der politischen Nation. Parlament und Öffentlichkeit 1867–1890,' in Lothar Gall (ed.), *Regierung, Parlament und Öffentlichkeit im Zeitalter Bismarcks. Politikstile im Wandel* (Paderborn: Schöningh, 2003), 23–42; Robert Arsenschek, *Der Kampf um die Wahlfreiheit im Kaiserreich. Zur parlamentarischen Wahlprüfung und politischen Realität der Reichstagswahlen 1871–1914* (Düsseldorf: Droste, 2003); Anderson, *Practicing Democracy*.

62. Anderson, *Practicing Democracy*, 8.

63. Cf. Rainer M. Lepsius, 'Parteiensystem und Sozialstruktur. Zum Problem der Demokratisierung der deutschen Gesellschaft,' in id., *Demokratie in Deutschland* (Göttingen: Vandenhoeck & Ruprecht, 1993), 25–50; Johannes Schauff, *Die deutschen Katholiken*

und die Zentrumspartei. Eine politisch-statistische Untersuchung der Reichstagswahlen seit 1871 (Mainz: Matthias-Grünewald-Verlag, 1975 [Cologne: Bachem, 1928]).

64. Cf. Siegfried Weichlein, *Sozialmilieus und politische Kultur in der Weimarer Republik. Lebenswelt, Vereinskultur, Politik in Hessen* (Göttingen: Vandenhoeck & Ruprecht, 1996).

65. Cf. Rohe, *Wahlen und Wählertraditionen*, 65.

66. Cf. Rudolf Morsey, *Die oberste Reichsverwaltung unter Bismarck, 1867–1890* (Münster: Aschendorff, 1957).

67. For an overview see Siegfried Weichlein, 'Föderalismus und Bundesstaat zwischen dem Alten Reich und der Bundesrepublik,' in Ines Härtel (ed.), *Handbuch Föderalismus— interdisziplinär. Föderalismus als demokratische Rechtsordnung und Rechtskultur in Deutschland, Europa und der Welt* (Berlin: Springer Verlag, 2011).

68. Cf. Weichlein, *Nation und Region, Integrationsprozesse im Kaiserreich* (Düsseldorf: Droste, 2004), 235ff.

69. Id., *Nation und Region*. 371ff.; Wolfgang Hardtwig, 'Nation-Region-Stadt. Strukturmerkmale des deutschen Nationalismus und lokale Denkmalskulturen,' in Gunther Mai (ed.), *Das Kyffhäuser-Denkmal 1896–1996. Ein nationales Monument im europäischen Kontext* (Cologne: Böhlau, 1997), 54–84.

70. Cf. Alan S. Milward, *The European Rescue of the Nation State* (London/New York: Routledge, 1992); Siegfried Weichlein, 'Europa und der Föderalismus. Zur Begriffsgeschichte politischer Ordnungsmodelle,' *Historisches Jahrbuch* 125 (2005), 133–152.

71. Cf. Rüdiger Gans, 'Das Siegerland zwischen ländlicher Beschränkung und nationaler Entgrenzung. Enge und Weite als Elemente regionaler Identität,' in Rolf Lindner (ed.), *Die Wiederkehr des Regionalen. Über neue Formen kultureller Identität* (Frankfurt am Main.: Campus, 1994), 64–90, 72, 74.

72. Cf. Wolfgang J. Mommsen, 'A Delaying Compromise. The Imperial Constitution of 1871,' in id. (ed.), *Imperial Germany 1867–1918. Politics, Culture and Society in an Authoritarian State* (London: Arnold, 1995), 20–40.

Bibliography

Anderson, Margaret Lavinia, *Practicing Democracy: Elections and Political Culture in Imperial Germany* (Princeton: Princeton University Press, 2000).

Biefang, Andreas, *Die andere Seite der Macht, Reichstag und Öffentlichkeit im 'System Bismarck' 1871–1890* (Düsseldorf: Droste, 2009).

—— *Politisches Bürgertum in Deutschland 1857–1868. Nationale Organisationen und Eliten* (Düsseldorf: Droste, 1994).

Blackbourn, David, *Marpingen: Apparitions of the Virgin Mary in Nineteenth-Century Germany* (New York: Alfred A. Knopf, 1994).

Busch, Norbert, *Katholische Frömmigkeit und Moderne. Zur Sozial- und Mentalitätsgeschichte des Herz-Jesu-Kultes in Deutschland zwischen Kulturkampf und Erstem Weltkrieg* (Gütersloh: Güthersloher Verlagshaus, 1997).

Green, Abigail, *Fatherlands. State-building and Nationhood in Nineteenth Century Germany* (Cambridge: Cambridge University Press, 2001).

LANGEWIESCHE, DIETER, *Liberalism in Germany* (Basingstoke: Macmillan Press, 2000).

—— and LOTHAR GALL (eds), *Liberalismus und Region. Zur Geschichte des deutschen Liberalismus im 19. Jahrhundert* (Munich: Oldenbourg, 1995).

LEPSIUS, RAINER M., *Demokratie in Deutschland* (Göttingen: Vandenhoeck & Ruprecht, 1993).

PALMOWSKI, JAN, *Urban Liberalism in Imperial Germany 1866–1914* (Oxford: Oxford University Press, 1999).

SMITH, HELMUT WALSER, *German Nationalism and Religious Conflict. Culture, Ideology, Politics 1870–1914* (Princeton: Princeton University Press, 1995).

WEICHLEIN, SIEGFRIED, *Nation und Region. Integrationsprozess im Bismarckreich* (Düsseldorf: Droste Verlag, 2004).

WELSKOPP, THOMAS, *Das Banner der Brüderlichkeit. Die deutsche Sozialdemokratie vom Vormärz bis zum Sozialistengesetz* (Bonn: Dietz, 2000).

CHAPTER 14

···

AUTHORITARIAN STATE, DYNAMIC SOCIETY, FAILED IMPERIALIST POWER, 1878–1914

···

HELMUT WALSER SMITH

THE Second German Empire has long been a linchpin for major attempts to make sense of modern German history, with attempts to give structure and meaning to the *Kaiserreich* emphasizing its inner logic, and endogenous social and political processes. Recently, however, historians have come to see as fundamental to the history of the *Kaiserreich* its integration into an international order marked by the competition of empires, heightened mobility, and a degree of economic globalization that Germany did not again attain until the 1970s.[1] In this transnational approach, it is not necessarily domestic struggles—between, for example, liberals for free trade and conservatives for protection—that are decisive, but how the international order framed domestic tensions.[2]

In this chapter, I follow some of the paths suggested by the transnational understanding of the *Kaiserreich*. However, I also take seriously a central insight of the social history of politics (*Gesellschaftsgeschichte*), namely that an adequate interpretation of the *Kaiserreich* has to encompass the totality of this society, and consider, for example, that by far the largest part of it was not made up by the middle classes, but by wage labor (a fact that made the *Kaiserreich* very different from our own societies).[3] What follows is a necessarily incomplete sketch of such an interpretation. As the Oxford Handbook includes separate chapters on economics, religion, intellectual life, nationalism, and imperialism in this period, I will not develop these aspects here. Instead, I concentrate on the relationship between state, society, and democracy, and argue that the essential conflicts of the *Kaiserreich* involved the contradictory integration of a newly-formed, authoritarian national state, with an exceedingly dynamic and mobile society, into a competitive world of overseas empires in the process of imposing white hegemony on large parts of the globe. The interpretive emphasis, which is on the national level, rather than the state or local level, does not presuppose that endogenous structural elements brought about the crisis of the late imperial period. Instead, the interpretation stresses how Germany's troubled integration into the world of imperialist competition opened and closed social and political possibilities. I consider, in turn, the following topics:

1. the Bismarckian turn (the 'second' foundation of the German Empire), which is here stretched from Otto von Bismarck's anti-liberal shift of 1878 to the Congo Congress in Berlin in 1884–1885;
2. the dramatic economic and social changes that made Germany into one of the most dynamic class societies in the world;
3. the constitution of a political sphere that gave democratic expression, but not governing power to the social and cultural differentiation of the Empire;
4. the relationship between *Weltpolitik* and democratization in the age of mass politics;
5. German society as it began to organize itself for war.

14.1 THE BISMARCKIAN TURN

Otto von Bismarck responded to an attempted assassination of Kaiser Wilhelm I, on 11 May 1878, by proposing to ban Socialist meetings, unions, and newspapers. But the Progressives and the majority of the National Liberals rejected the bill, which flagrantly violated even the most rudimentary concept of rights as understood in contemporary civil societies. Here, there might have been a liberal stand on principles. 'The whole world knew,' as the perspicacious Danish reporter, Georg Brandes, wrote, 'that Social Democracy played not the slightest part' in the assassination attempt.[4] However, when a second attempt on the Kaiser's life was made, on 2 June, Bismarck dissolved the *Reichstag* and called new elections. 'Now I've got them,' he famously is supposed to have said, 'The Socialists?,' someone asked, 'No,' Bismark replied, 'The National Liberals.'[5] The subsequent *Reichstag* elections of July 1878 ushered in a new era, with some historians claiming that the political turn constituted a second foundation of the German Empire.

The elections resulted in significant conservative gains and liberal losses, and marked the end of a period of National Liberal ascendancy in the halls of government. In the same year, Pope Pius IX, who had condemned any number of modern heresies in the *Syllabus of Errors*, passed away, thus allowing Bismarck to dismantle some of the *Kulturkampf* legislation, which counted among the most vigorously fought-for liberal programs in the 1870s. The double blow—the loss to the conservatives and the government's negotiation with the Catholics—devastated German liberals, and placed a large question mark on the future of their influence. 'It is a miserable fate to have to figure as a piece of ornament to this regenerating Junker and Clerical state,' wrote a resigned Theodor Mommsen, the Roman historian and liberal *Reichstag* representative.[6]

There was more to come. In November, the historian Heinrich von Treitschke published an article in the prestigious *Preussische Jahrbücher*, in which he declared 'the Jews are our misfortune,' sparking an avalanche of anti-Semitic writings.[7] Soon an anti-Semitic petition circulated, demanding limits on the immigration of foreign Jews, the exclusion of Jews from positions of public authority, a restoration of the Christian character of public schools, and a statistical accounting of the Jewish population. It garnered more than 250,000 signatures, including nearly half the university students in Berlin, and one in four students throughout the Empire.[8] Barely a decade of the new Empire had passed, and Jewish emancipation was placed into question. Then, in July, 1881, violence erupted in the Pomeranian city of Neustettin, with some thirty anti-Semitic riots constituting the most violent anti-Jewish outbreak since 1848.[9] If paling in comparison to contemporaneous anti-Jewish pogroms in the Russian Empire, Neustettin nevertheless suggested new possibilities when race twined with experiments in post-liberal, anti-establishment politics peddled by a new breed of populist politician who claimed not merely to speak for the people, but who fashioned themselves as being of the people.[10]

The larger context of this turn was the beginning of a recession and the turn away from free trade to tariffs. In particular, Hans Rosenberg interpreted the turn as the beginning of a structural shift to the right in central European politics, and the subsequent dominance of a conservative alliance of iron and rye, the captains of industry and the Junkers of the East Elbian *latifundia*, with deleterious consequences for German history reaching all the way to the Third Reich.[11] In Rosenberg's interpretation, the turn became decisive for the constitution of the German *Sonderweg*, defined as a veering away from the liberal west, and emphasizing the stranglehold that pre-modern elites held on political development. However, as Cornelius Torp has recently demonstrated, the economic dimension of the analysis requires significant revision. Many farmers only turned to protection in the course of the 1880s, as the price of grain fell more dramatically, and then against resistance within the hitherto export-oriented agricultural sector.[12] Far from being economically irrational, the new tariffs can be shown to have had significant macro-economic benefits for certain sectors of the imperial economy, such as heavy industry and textiles, and not just for its struggling agrarian sectors.[13] The alliance was the work of Bismarck himself, not backroom agrarian and industrial influence, and Bismarck was, in turn, reacting to fiscal pressures. In fact, the significant context of the turn to protection was not domestic, but international. In addition to the United States and Russia, a whole series of countries, including Austria-Hungary, Italy, Canada, Argentina, Brazil, and eventually France turned to protection in the course of the 1870s and 1880s. By 1890, Great Britain was with its free trade policies largely alone, and the dominant mode of integration into an international economic system, whose proportion of international trade would by 1913 rival the global economy of the 1970s, was, in fact, with guards up and tariffs in place. In this pre-war world of tariffed globalization, German import duties ranged roughly in the middle of the international norm, well behind the United States, Russia, and Spain, and still behind France, Austria-Hungary, Italy, Sweden, and Denmark.[14]

Germany moved closer to the rest in other ways too. In the course of the 1880s, more conservative governments came to power—in England with Lord Salisbury's aggressively imperialist platform and opposition to Irish home rule, introducing, in 1886, a period of nearly uninterrupted conservative ascendancy in Great Britain; in Russia following the assassination of the liberal Czar Alexander II in 1881 and the repressive turn to a policy of 'orthodoxy, autocracy, and nationality;' in Italy, with Francesco Crispi, who fashioned himself an 'Italian Bismarck,' and became Prime Minister in 1887; in Cisleithanian Austria with the cabinet of Eduard Taffe, who likewise followed a Bismarckian combination of higher tariffs, anti-socialist repression and anti-liberal regulation of industry.

The Bismarckian turn involved the renewed repression of ethnic minorities, primarily the Polish population. In the *Kuturkampf*, Bismarck had targeted the Poles, hoping to undermine the position of Polish leaders, primarily the clergy and aristocracy. In the 1870s, Prussian language policy made German the sole official language in government business and in schools, though not in religious instruction. These measures only stirred Polish national activists in Posen, West Prussia, and Masuria, and provided them with significant traction among the Polish population. Between 1883 and 1887, Bismarck expelled some 32,000 Poles without citizenship papers, among them roughly 9000 Jews. A state policy that evoked the religious expulsions of earlier eras, the expulsion inaugurated what would be a long history of anti-Polish population policy.[15] In 1886, the Prussian Diet established the Royal Prussian Settlement Committee, which by 1914 had placed 22,000 German farmers in the eastern areas.[16] It ended with revolutionary expropriations of Polish land, and succeeded mainly in alienating a significant minority from the German Empire.

The wider context of these policies pointed to the increasing prevalence of nationally segregated societies and hardened color lines, crystallizing in a number of anti-centralist ethnicities. Miroslav Hroch has called this 'phase B of national consciousness,' referring to the period when national activists emerge, 'at first without notable success (in one sub-stage), but then later (in another sub-stage) finding a growing reception.'[17] This clash—centralist state with regional identities, ethnicities, and nationalities—intensified throughout Europe in the 1880s and 1890s, bringing to the forefront of politics, in multinational empires and nation states alike, a new, often illiberal politics of the periphery. In east central Europe, Polish, Czech, Ukranian, and Serbian nationalist movements became politicized in this context, while in the west Catalan and Basque movements established political parties in the 1890s, and the Flemish movement gained ground on a Christian-Social platform. In Great Britain, the alliance of Lord Salisbury with liberal unionists precluded the possibility of any kind of home rule for Ireland, which English liberals and conservatives alike equated with 'Rome rule.' The divisions look sharper still when race is taken into consideration, and one considers the battery of segregation laws in the 1890s in the American South and in South Africa, two of the three overtly racist regimes of the twentieth century.[18]

Historians of Imperial Germany have begun to place the empire's eastern policy in a colonial context, and to bring together repressive nationality policies with the turn to direct rule in the colonies, or formal imperialism. The 1880s witnessed the transition to new repertoires of power in the colonial world, utilizing modern technologies of transportation and power—the steamship, the railway, and the machine gun—to dominate vast areas, most dramatically in Africa, but also in southeast Asia. Between 1876 and 1913, a quarter of the globe was formally annexed, putting altogether 42 percent of it under the political rule of Western Europe, the United States, and Japan.[19] Germany, it is sometimes asserted, stood on the sidelines, and colonialism was not central to it. In fact, however, it was third in terms of the amount of new territory gained: behind Great Britain, which increased its territory by 4 million square miles, and France, which gained roughly 3.5 million miles. With more than a million square miles of new territory, Imperial Germany outstripped Belgium and Italy, the United States and Japan, and Portugal and Spain.[20] Germany became a major player in the colonial competition of empire, a very significant third, since the Belgian acquisition of the Congo was essentially allowed to block other powers, and Italy quickly ran into military disaster in Abyssinia (modern day Ethiopia). Bismarck's colonial reluctance notwithstanding, the Berlin Congo Congress of 1884 expressed this strategic position, centered on the triangular relationship between Germany, Great Britain, and France, the major beneficiaries, along with Belgium, of the dissection of Africa.[21] It was in Berlin that the rules for great power domination of Africa were established.

Colonial rule, it is true, never achieved what its supporters wished for. Emigration to German colonies remained miniscule compared with the numbers who left Germany for the United States. By 1914, investment was meager, imports were minor, and exports—mainly of gunpowder, weapons, and alcohol—remained insignificant.[22] Yet central colonial involvement proved an important conduit through which Germans experienced the world, whether through colonial wares, which reached even down to children's games; through exhibitions of exotic peoples; training in the *Pfadfinder* (the German version of boy scouts); or through illustrated journals, which brought the far and away back into the coziness of home.[23] Following the colonial enterprise, replete with missionary societies, trading outposts, and anti-slavery efforts, gave many Germans, if not necessarily Otto von Bismarck, a sense of participating in what it meant to be a great power, a German in the world. It also inculcated a white European identity, at the moment—which people thought would continue indefinitely—of Europe's zenith of power.

14.2 CLASS SOCIETY

There were nearly twice as many Germans in 1914 as in 1850. In the half-century before World War I, Germany became a population powerhouse, second in Europe (not counting colonies) only to Russia in both rate of growth and in absolute terms. The pace of population expansion actually picked up in the two decades before World War I, when German growth rates achieved levels higher than any time in its history. The main driving force behind this was not increased fertility—the number of children born had actually been in steep decline since the 1880s—but a decrease in infant and child mortality. In the first two-thirds of the nineteenth century, infant and child mortality had not changed significantly from the eighteenth century. In the early phases of the industrial revolution, life expectancy may have actually decreased.[24] However, the population explosion, starting circa 1860, signaled a dramatic reversal of life over death. Germany became a country of large families, on average four to five children, with children under fifteen more than a third of the population, and Germany one of the youngest countries in Europe.[25]

The population explosion made Germany into a place of immense human movement. It is impossible to emphasize this fact enough, especially against a nostalgic notion of the *Kaiserreich* as a site of intact hometowns and quaint continuities. At the time of the 'second foundation' of the German Empire, an enormous emigration began, with Germans, mainly from the northeastern states (Pomerania, East and West Prussia), boarding ships in Hamburg and Bremen destined for Ellis Island, and from there to the Great Plains, where the possibility of a five acre homestead beckoned them. Depending on the counting, it was the largest wave of emigration in German history, with nearly two million Germans leaving, making it second in size only to the Irish emigration and compatible in size with the Italian migration. The great emigration hardly exhausted the movement. There was also an immense traversing of Germany by emigrants from the Russian Empire and the Austro-Hungarian Empire. Historians estimate their numbers at roughly five million, as if the whole population of Sweden in the year 1900 moved across Germany. Larger still was the formidable migration within Germany, a process that was especially striking from east to west after 1893, as the poor provinces that had supplied the overseas migrants now sent their indigent to Berlin and to the industrial centers along the Ruhr. The precise numbers are difficult to pin down. However, one tally puts the number of internal migrants over long distances within Germany at 8.7 percent of the population in 1907, while about half of all German subjects no longer lived in the place of their birth.[26] The consequence of this movement is that the world of the German home towns was slipping away, and the gathering *Heimat* movements might be seen not just in the context of regionalism, but also as a reaction to the immense human movement of the period. The demographer Steve Hochstadt has calculated that the years immediately before the outbreak of World War I represented a high water mark of peacetime internal movement.[27] Put differently, Imperial Germany was a far more internally mobile society than the old Federal Republic of Germany, with cities registering mobility rates twice as high in the first decade of the twentieth century as in the 1950s through the 1980s. Finally, the *Kaiserreich* became an immigrant nation—on an international comparison, a very distant second behind the United States. On the eve of World War I there were an estimated 1.2 million foreigners working in Germany, making up close to 2 percent of the population; most of the foreigners were agricultural and industrial workers from the Polish parts of the Russian and Austro-Hungarian Empires, though there were also significant contingents from Italy, the Netherlands, and Switzerland.[28]

The dramatic increase in population and in human circulation corresponded to an equally profound shift that made Germany, once a place speckled by rural villages and small towns, into a country both urban and rural. The large cities represented the most dynamic element; some, like Dortmund, going from small towns to industrial centers almost overnight; others, like Frankfurt am Main, awakening out of a centuries-long slumber; and two, Berlin and Hamburg, emerging as genuine world cities. By 1910, one in five Germans lived in large cities of a population over 100,000, and the number of such cities had increased six-fold. There were, in addition, vast industrial concentrations, as occurred north of the Ruhr along the ancient Hellweg with Duisburg, Essen, Bochum, and Dortmund, whose combined population was already well over a million in 1910. There were also densely populated, never-ending, makeshift industrial towns, like the mining districts along the Emscher, or in the Upper Silesian triangle between Beuthen, Tarnowitz, and Kattowitz.[29]

These cities and industrial concentrations were the sites of immense human movement, prisms refracting vast amounts of coming and going. They also represented a revolution in dwelling, often with baleful consequences in the form of crowding and unhealthy conditions. In Berlin in 1900, 43 percent of all households still had only one heated room, thousands of workers and day laborers lived in barrack-like apartments, and every year, half of the working-class flats changed hands. In cities like Hamburg and Munich, to say nothing of the industrial zones, fluctuation was hardly less dramatic, creating, as one prominent historian has put it, an urban world of 'modern nomads.'[30]

If the industrial revolution enabled immense human movement, it also engendered a significant change in the material possibilities of life. Between 1850 and 1914, net domestic product per person nearly trebled, creating what Wener Sombart called an 'elevator effect,' lifting the living standards of all elements of German society.[31] Even the poor no longer lived constantly on the edge of sustained hunger and malnourishment, as had been the case in the previous century, and was, in fact, exacerbated in the early years of the industrial revolution.[32] Between 1870 and 1910, the consumption of meat doubled, even if, circa 1900, the working poor still drew 90 percent of their caloric intake from bread, potatoes, and lard. However, the days of getting by with rye and vegetable porridge were, for the moment, finished. So too was the era of the fourteen-hour work day. By 1910, the average was down to ten hours.[33] Child labor in the factories was also largely, though not completely, a thing of the past.

Its significant growth notwithstanding, Germany remained a society marked by inequalities in income and in social chances. Despite the 'elevator effect,' the differences between rich and poor widened, rather than narrowed, in this period. It remained the case that in economic power or social prestige a tiny minority stood atop a pyramid with a narrow middle and an extremely wide base.[34] Even in cities with mixed economies, like Trier or Barmen, the various forms of working classes might make up 75 percent of the population, with the upper classes closer to 1 percent, and the middle classes over 20 percent. In terms of wealth, the scissors opened rather than closed. In Prussia, the taxable income of the upper 5 percent generated 21 percent of the total in 1854, but 32.6 percent in 1913. Critical observers certainly noticed the increasing gap in income distribution. Yet it is not clear that Germany lagged behind on this score. In Great Britain, the top 5 percent generated 45 percent of the wealth; in France, according to one estimation, 80 percent.[35]

More than a third of the nearly 18 million people classified as workers in the 1907 census were women, most of them in agriculture, where their importance increased as more and more men migrated to the cities. There were also more than a million domestic servants in Imperial Germany; after agriculture, it was the second largest domain of female employment. Women also predominated in the clothing and textile industries, and constituted the lion's share of workers in hotels and restaurants. In the classic industrial branches, men predominated, although at the lower levels of income, subsistence was only possible if the female head of the household also worked outside the home, often in the many jobs in and around the factories, such as working in kitchens, cleaning, bringing lunch and beer, and taking care of children. Women did, however, have a significant presence in a whole series of modern industries, such as the chemical and electrical industries.[36] In the main and except for agriculture, full time female workers tended to be single or widowed, but increasingly married women joined the regular workforce as well, their numbers increasing from 9 percent in 1882 to 26 percent in 1907.[37] Absent from such global statistics is the large number of women who did piece work at home. Housework too was not counted in the official statistics.

Finally, while Germany was fast becoming an industrialized economy, it retained a strong small town and agrarian base, with roughly 40 percent living in communities of smaller than 2000 in 1910, and the same percentage still tied economically to the land.[38] For a significant number of Germans, then, the world was still mediated through the vizier of such small towns, dominated, as they often were, by local notables, neighbors who knew each other, personalized forms of exclusion, and *Stammtisch* politics. One should not, however, imagine the agrarian sector as a collection of independent farmers, small or large; these made up only the smallest percentage, with roughly a quarter self-employed, and most independent farmers running farms of less than 2 hectares.[39] The large mass of people who worked the land, close to three-quarters in 1907, were wage laborers, and in many ways approximated, as Max Weber argued, the proletariat of the factories. They included more than three million people in 1907, and were increasingly made up of women and foreign workers. They also counted among the least protected workers. The right of the lord of the manor to physically punish his farm hands with a whip or stick was not abolished until 1900. Wages were also significantly lower than in the factories, though payment in kind and foraging in the fields and forests made up some of the difference. For the mass of Germany's agricultural labor, the Romantic notion of a healthy country lifestyle could not have been further from reality. Work was monotonous, and the employer saw his farm as his personal domain. Often, he was a violent figure.

These two groups—industrial and agricultural workers—made up the wide base of Germany's working population. Above them—in material, social, and political possibilities—was the German bourgeoisie, or *Bürgertum*, which one may consider in a narrow and wide sense. The narrow definition encompasses the economic bourgeoisie (*Wirtschaftsbürgertum*) and the educated bourgeoisie (*Bildungsbürgertum*), who together constituted, in a generous calculation, roughly 6 percent of the population.[40] This 6 percent has been the focus of a great deal of controversy and research, since older approaches saw the linchpin of a German *Sonderweg* in a deficit of bourgeois values, or *Bürgerlichkeit*, defined by personal autonomy and political participation. Instead, it was argued, the German bourgeoisie exhibited a high degree of deference to the nobility, a peculiarly German association with the state, and an essentially unpolitical stance. More than twenty years of research have in the meanwhile relativized this characterization. Historians no longer see the German *Bürgertum* as feudal in comparison with English counterparts, or as dependent on the state (if still marked by a tradition of bureaucratic administration), or, indeed, as unpolitical.[41] What has become clear, however, is the degree to which the city, with its highly restrictive communal suffrage laws, became the central arena of bourgeois political activity, the principal site, in fact, of an economic and cultural world of immense power, whose imprint—from steel factories to opera houses, from department stores to museums, and from chambers of commerce to academic *Gymnasia*—has marked our sense of the whole nineteenth century. From Berlin to Jena, Hamburg to Darmstadt, cities were the incubators of a plethora of reform movements that opened German society to modern forms—in art, living arrangements, generational experience, gender relations, new experiences of nature, and much else.[42]

The wider concept of bourgeoisie would include the petite bourgeoisie, consisting of independent shopkeepers, artisans and craftsmen, tavern owners, and retailers (the old *Mittelstand*), as well as subaltern officials and white collar workers (the new *Mittelstand*). Together these two groups made up roughly 8 percent of the population, so that in total numbers the bourgeoisie equaled roughly 15 percent of the population, making the German bourgeoisie, in terms of its size, the rough equivalent of its counterparts in Western Europe.[43] Like the bourgeoisie proper, the *Mittelstand* groups have been the subject of a great deal of research, much of it emphasizing fear in the face of the declining fortunes of artisanal economy, and anxiety at the mounting numerical dominance of the working classes. A similar trajectory may be discerned among the white collar workers and subaltern officials, whose numbers expanded as the paperwork of firms and ever larger government bureaucracies required their services. The socialists derided them as standing-collar proletarians, caught between bourgeois aspirations and worker-like dependency, if usually with easier working conditions and much more job security.[44] In Imperial Germany, the white collar workers organized in the Commercial Employees Association, which in the 1890s and the first decade of the twentieth century was decidedly anti-Semitic. Whether this can be said of most white collar workers is another question. They, like the artisans, were drawn into a politics or resentment, and chauvinistic nationalism was one way they expressed their belonging to a non-proletarian German culture.[45]

At the tip of the social hierarchy was the German aristocracy, dominated, at least in numerical terms by the Prussian Junkers, whose self-understanding centered less on ancient lineage or fabulous wealth, as was the case for the nobility throughout much of central Europe, than on service to the state and military glory.[46] If the Prussian Junkers still personify Imperial Germany in the popular imagination, in fact, they only made up 0.3 percent of the Prussian population in 1880: about 85,000 people belonging to some 20,000 families.[47] Yet they exercised a dominant role in the state apparatus of Prussia, which in turn possessed the key position in the constitutional power structure of Imperial Germany. This predominance was not only at the very top and in the vicinity of the Kaiser. The Prussian nobility also dominated high levels of administration, constituting, prior to 1914, 92 percent of the provincial governors, 64 percent of district governors, and even 57 percent of county prefects. In the upper echelons of the officer corps of the Prussian Army, the predominance was even more striking, with the Prussian nobility constituting 84.1 percent of all generals, 86.2 percent of lieutenant generals, 70.7 percent of major generals, and 68.1 percent of colonels. Nowhere else in Western Europe did the nobility achieve this level of dominance in the apparatus of the state, and in other major states within Germany, like Saxony, Baden, Bavaria, and Württemberg, the presence of the nobility in the bureaucracy and the armed forces was much less striking. Moreover, the Prussian nobility enjoyed an enormous level of social prestige as the creator of the national state in the wars of unification, which, combined with Bismarck's popularity, created a nearly unimpeachable position.

14.3 SOCIAL AND CULTURAL DIFFERENTIATION AND THE POLITICAL SPHERE

Imperial Germany's extremely dynamic public culture existed in considerable tension with the constitutional brake on its developments. This bears emphasis because Germany had developed what Alexis de Tocqueville would have surely recognized as the sinews of a democratic society: Germany had become, as he said of American democracy, a nation of joiners, with the ranks of its associational life, non-political as well as political, full to the brim, and, if not yet egalitarian in outlook, at least in the transition from socially exclusive to socially inclusive. In the first half of the nineteenth century, voluntary associations appear decidedly middle class; by the 1890s, we witness the growth of genuine mass organizations, 'the fourth surge,' as Stefan Ludwig Hoffmann has put it, of 'civic activism.'[48]

Public rhetoric of inclusiveness notwithstanding, this activism was organized along the major fault lines of imperial Germany: social, religious, and national, with not a few organizations focused on an alleged opponent across these lines of division. Generally speaking, there were two essential kinds of organizations: professional organizations or economic lobbies, and public organizations that impacted the lives of its members. The first group included such powerful industrial organizations as the Central Association of German Industry, which pressured the government to introduce iron and steel tariffs, and the Hansa Bund, which served the interests of the export-oriented sections of light industry. It also included a wide array of professional organizations. Blurring the distinction were the trade unions and the Agrarian League, which also shaped the life worlds of their members.

The major public organizations may be divided into three categories—social, religious, and national—with women's organizations an emerging fourth category after 1908, when a new Prussian Association Law significantly eased the participation of women and youth in the public sphere. The divisions in the social sphere are important. If historians in the 1970s perhaps over-emphasized the degree to which that sphere was easily manipulated, later historians saw political style as the decisive issue in the emergence of modern forms of extra parliamentary politics. In both cases, the main question concerned the modalities and styles of political mobilization. Yet the content of political programs also mattered, since these public organizations were also sources of social identity. In Imperial Germany, the public sphere was to a high degree predetermined by major fissures resulting from the double revolution, industrial and national.

A sample of the leading associations (with at least 20,000 individual members) is given in Table 14.1, with dates of foundation and peak memberships.[49]

The extent of social organization, and its principal fissures, is already evident from this incomplete listing. The density is especially apparent among the workers. No working class, save for perhaps in Australia, was as completely organized as in Germany.[50] By 1912, the free trade unions had more than two million members, constituting a giant block of the 4.2 million votes the SPD received in the *Reichstag* election of 1912.[51] Far from encouraging revolutionary politics, however, the free trade unions typically fought for limited gains in the context of imperial labor relations. In fact, they exercised a profound brake on the possibility of radical political action, such as a general strike, which, if unsuccessful, would have shattered the unions' patiently built array of organizations and destroyed the position of many functionaries whose professional lives depended on it. Historians have developed elaborate conceptual insights concerning the negative integration of the workers of imperial Germany into the Empire. Marginalized, so the theory, the workers developed a political culture outside the imperial frame and waited for, rather than pursued, revolution.[52] Newer research emphasizes the positive integration of German workers, and sees the early growth of Social Democracy as an expression less of class consciousness than of a radical democratic tradition, not outside civil society, but in fact one of its most active proponents, insisting, at every turn, on democratic reform and a more just society.[53] 'The right to free elections is the sign,' went the refrain of the most popular worker's song of the Imperial period (the 'Worker's Marseillaise'), 'not hatred against the rich do we preach, but equal rights for everyone.'[54] Economic development, far from bringing Germany to the brink of revolution, legitimized constant pressure to redistribute wealth and to press for democratic reform. In the years before World War I, this meant increased strike activity, centered on a concept of distributive justice within the

Table 14.1 A sample of the leading associations (with at least 20,000 individual members), with dates of foundation, and peak memberships

Association	Peak membership numbers
Social	
Agrarian League (BDL), 1893	330,000 (1914)
Free Trade Unions (SPD oriented), 1890	2,076,000 (1912)
Christian (Catholic) Trade Unions, 1894	343,000 (1913)
Hirsch-Duncker (liberal) Trade Unions, 1869	122,000 (1910)
German Commercial Employee Association, 1896	160,513 (1914)
Political-Religious	
Protestant League, 1887	510,000 (1913)
German (liberal) Protestant Association, 1863	25,000 (1904)
Central Association of German Citizens of Jewish Faith, 1893	36,000 (1913)
People's Association for Catholic Germany, 1890	805,000 (1914)
National	
Pan-German League, 1894	21, 361 (1900)
German Colonial Society, 1887	43,152 (1914)
German Navy League, 1898	320,464 (1912)
German Society of the Eastern Marches, 1899	53,000 (1914)
German Army League, 1912	100,000 (1914)
Kyffhäuser Bund (Veterans associations), 1900	2,800,000 (1913)
German Gymnastics Society, 1868	1,123,000 (1913)
German Singers Association, 1862	205,494 (1914)
Society for Germandom Abroad, 1908	45,272 (1910)

system, and on mass demonstrations for changes to suffrage laws at the state and local level. Moreover, the free trade unions did not encompass all workers, or even all the organized workers. Religion and nationality put up a wall against further organization, but the (Catholic) Christian trade unions, and the (Catholic) Polish unions in the Ruhr and in Upper Silesia also represented a democratic force, if in the former case a less radical one, pushing for the fair distribution of wealth within German society.

A still more significant obstacle to the economic organization of the poor was the giant chasm—demographic, social, and cultural—between city and country. The trade unions and the SPD did not reach the majority of workers because, save for temporary inroads during the elections of 1898 and 1903 in the northeastern parts of the Empire, they were never able to organize agricultural labor. It was not impossible; it happened, to some extent, in the Ukraine, eastern Galicia, Norway, Sweden, and Finland.[55] However, in Imperial Germany, the Social Democrats were a decidedly urban, Protestant party; with a militantly materialist and anti-clerical base (tellingly the *Communist Manifesto* was issued in print runs of a mildly successful academic book, while Otto von Corvin's scurrilous *Pfaffenspiegel*, a book about allegedly licentious, dishonest priests, enjoyed immense popularity among workers).[56] This meant that the possibility of organizing rural labor was ceded to others. In the Catholic south and west, the religious composition and anti-clerical stance of the SPD undermined its ability to win over agricultural laborers. Instead, various peasant leagues and the Center Party competed for an increasingly disgruntled rural vote.[57] In Protestant Prussia, the SPD did have a chance to win this constituency, since the rural areas of the east were more de-Christianized than is often supposed.[58] The conservative Agrarian League, not the SPD, organized and channeled this rural discontent; the League often countered governmental programs and even threatened the pre-eminence of local notables.[59] Yet the Agrarian League remained within the confines of a politics of resentment that funneled into nationalism and anti-Semitism—with the result that one of Imperial Germany's most dispossessed classes, the agricultural laborers, remained within the sphere of influence of their masters (not unlike poor whites in US South, who likewise made common cause with white landowners against a newly-emancipated black population).[60] The same point about political style holds for the German Commercial Employees Association, whose economic-interest politics likewise, if with less vitriol, became conflated with anti-Semitic and anti-Socialist sentiment.

Religion constituted a second *bloc* of social organization giving structure to the public sphere. Pervaded by organizations encouraging different forms of piety, religious organization also powerfully reinforced religious and social differences, alternately encouraging and combating prejudice. The Protestant League was founded in 1886–1887 in order to combat ultramontane Catholicism, which seemed to Protestants to emerge from the *Kulturkampf* with renewed strength. For the men of the Protestant League, the Second Empire was a Protestant Empire, and a return to Protestant virtues—independence, manliness, faith, and loyalty to Kaiser and Reich—would recapture its essential spirit. By 1914, the League emerged as the largest lay organization in Protestant Germany, far outstripping the liberal Protestant Association (*Protestantenverein*), whose influence was confined to academic circles and left liberal politicians.[61] In 1887, the Catholics intended to counter with an anti-Protestant League, but the Center Party leader, Ludwig Windthorst, abhorred religious polemic, and instead set up the People's Association for Catholic Germany, whose intent was to brand Socialism as its principal opponent.[62] The Association also had the effect of reinforcing religious division, which in social organizations ran deep, leading one publicist, from the League to Combat Anti-Semitism, to decry a seemingly ubiquitous religious division, where 'everything has either a Catholic or a Protestant imprint.'[63] Jewish organizations reacted to religious antagonism in similar ways. After a ritual murder accusation in the Rhenish town of Xanten in 1891, liberal Jewish leaders founded the Central Association of German Citizens of the Jewish Faith. It became the largest Jewish organization in Germany, outstripping Zionist competitors by a wide margin, and thereby reinforcing, much like the Catholic People's Association, an underlying message of loyalty to and participation in the new national state—nationalist critics of their alleged disloyalty notwithstanding.[64]

The nationalist public was perhaps the most volatile; it has in any case been at the center of historical controversy concerning the character of the Second Empire. The most socially and religiously inclusive of all the nationalist organizations, the Veterans

Association proved an effective conduit of the military culture of the Empire to the ordinary man on the street, who, like his French counterpart, found in the Veterans Associations a social life centered on patriotic holidays, beer drinking, and camaraderie.[65] During elections, the government often attempted to force the Veterans Associations to agitate for the government's military build-up and anti-Socialist politics, but in practice the many local and regional associations were simply too heterogeneous; and its petty bourgeois, and sometimes even proletarian clientele often remained unmoved by larger issues. The popularity of the Veterans Leagues reminds us that a great deal of patriotism happened, as in the German Singer's Union, outside the cross-fire of party politics, and that the culture of patriotic nationalism on the eve of World War I reached far into the social hierarchy, through Germany's middle classes and perhaps even deeper. Unlike other organizations, the Veterans Organizations also flourished in Catholic areas. The same cannot be said of the other nationalist organizations, which, with the exception of some branches of the Navy League, remained tied to the Protestant middle classes. Here, the essential dividing line was between the world of concentrated, dedicated nationalist activists, as made up much of the numerically small, but tremendously influential Pan-German League, and the socially wider, but in its political style divided Navy League.[66] The tension within the Navy League remained inconclusive, as some leaders insisted on loyalty to the government, and support for national programs, while others adopted a radical nationalist stance that challenged the politics of ruling elites, churned up popular chauvinism, encouraged religious division (both anti-Catholicism and anti-Semitism), and constituted a kind of 'national revolutionary,' 'right wing Jacobinism.'[67]

14.4 WELTPOLITIK AND DEMOCRACY IN GERMANY

The Bismarckian era ended in 1890 with the Chancellor's resignation after a prolonged clash with the new, young monarch, Wilhelm II, who hoped to be a genuinely popular Kaiser and to reach out to the working classes. He had differed with Bismarck over the anti-Socialist laws, which Wilhelm wanted to allow to lapse. This was the manifest issue. The latent issue was the question of who rules, which Bismarck's constitution answered unambiguously in favor of the crown. Thirty-two when he acceded to the throne in 1888, Wilhelm II was a restless monarch. Narcissistic, hating to be contradicted, and in constant need of approval, he was as frenetic and modern as Bismarck seemed steady. Wilhelm criss-crossed Germany by train, attending a ceremony here, leading a military display there, and in the process appearing at one or another time in many of Germany's medium and large cities.[68] His efforts to cement the loyalty of the German people to his own person and to the institution of monarchy hardly struck contemporaries as out of step with time. The decades before World War I witnessed not the withering away, but the seeming permanence of monarchy, with only the United States and France lacking a regent. Suffused with invented traditions, some of which failed (like the attempt to give Wilhelm I the appellation 'the Great'), the late nineteenth century monarchical revival twined nation, populism, and empire, and lent monarchies throughout Europe renewed legitimacy.[69] 'Recognition, by a free democracy, of a hereditary crown, as a symbol of the world-wide dominion of their race'—this is how, for example, a French commentator summed up the coronation of Edward VII in Westminster Abbey in 1905.[70] In Germany, twining monarchy, democracy, and empire would not be as easy—not only because of the challenge of the left, but also because of the drift of the nationalist right, whose middle class leaders took not Wilhelm II, but Otto von Bismarck as their emotive symbol and saw the national state as more important than the Hohenzollern dynasty.

Two other trends also unsettled. One was the twin demographic fact, much discussed at the time, that more Germans now worked in industry than in agriculture, and lived in urban, rather than rural communities.[71] This circumstance had a direct political correlation. In the *Reichstag* election of 1890, the SPD received more votes than any other party, and if demographic trends continued, as they surely would, Socialist expansion seemed inevitable. The steadfast refusal of the government, supported by parties from the center and right, to redraw *Reichstag* districts so as to conform to the altered demographic situation, kept Socialist mandates in check (by comparison, the Center Party, the second most popular party in 1890, had better arrangements in run-off elections and as a result had three times as many mandates as the Social Democrats). Even this skewed system could not, however, keep what seemed like a Socialist deluge indefinitely at bay.

The second fact involved the combined popular vote of the parties that Bismarck had deemed the 'enemies of the Reich'—the Socialists, the Catholics, and the national minorities. In 1890, their combined popular vote was already 45 percent, by 1893, 48.1 percent, and by 1898, 52.1 percent. Thereafter, the 'enemies of the Reich,' as defined in the 1870s, never lost the majority of the popular vote in the first ballot. This second fact is suggestive of wider sentiment, and cautions against blanket generalizations concerning extreme nationalism, which, as a political proposition, never commanded a majority. *Reichstag* mandates had a different arithmetic, and an 'enemy' majority was not obtained until 1912. However, what made the situation precarious is that from 1890 on, the representatives of the 'enemies,' if combined with left liberal mandates, had a permanent majority in the *Reichstag*.

The transition from a nation state in central Europe to a country that embraced world politics in the 'age of empire' occurred as German society underwent momentous transformations, involving the number of people living in Germany, their dwelling places, the pace of their movement, the structure of their work, and their material lives. In one important interpretive tradition, this transition was marked by the inability of the liberal bourgeoisie to claim political power by demanding a government responsible to an elected parliament, a precondition, arguably, for a truly democratic society. The resulting illiberalism derived from the German bourgeoisie's further failure to wrest away from a feudal elite control of essential institutions of political power: in addition to the executive, the upper bureaucracy and the military. A rift then opened between the rapid transformation of society and the control of political power, with power remaining not in the hands of the leading class in the economic sphere, the bourgeoisie, but rather with the Prussian Junkers, the class that resisted change.

This was and remains the high argument of the social history of politics. It has also been productively criticized, with some historians agreeing that the liberal bourgeoisie had more power than previously supposed, but noting that it still lacked the power to decide matters of state.[72] 'Why is it,' one may then still ask (with Ralf Dahrendorf), 'that so few in Germany embraced the principle of liberal democracy?'[73] The answer is surely to be found in part in the structural impediments from 'above.' However, in Germany, these impediments were arguably still stronger from 'below.' After 1878, the great problem of the German liberal bourgeoisie at the imperial level was not its relative position to the aristocracy. Rather, its central dilemma was that it could not come to terms with the fundamental shifts in social hierarchies and their political expression in a competitive field of universal suffrage. The two most important of these transformations involved class and religion, with industrial workers, and many other kinds of workers, seeing Social Democracy as their principal voice, while the great religious minority in Germany, the Catholics, viewed the Catholic Center as their principal expression. The political centrality of these two groups—the one whose influence would grow as a result of a demographic explosion brought about by rapid industrialization, the other whose position remained cemented by a loyalty that was an outgrowth of piety and persecution—meant that starting in the 1880s, and accelerating in the 1890s, there was little room at the Reich level for stable democratic majorities that involved liberal alliances. Put with a sharp point, liberal democracy failed because of democracy. What emerged in Germany instead were other kinds of democratic understandings: social, Catholic (with an extensive social dimension and close alliances with national minorities), and German national. In the 1890s, this latter form of democratic understanding involved a hesitant embrace of populist politics and the hope that colonial expansion and great power politics would deflect social conflict and absorb the Catholic minority in a common imperial project. This was the core of liberal ideology in Imperial Germany as it manifested itself on the Reich level, where universal manhood suffrage obtained. In the individual state parliaments, where class suffrages held, and in the city councils, where the franchise was often even more restrictive, liberals navigated social transformation with greater success.[74]

In the competition of great powers, increasingly conceived in social Darwinian terms as the struggle for existence among great empires, military power was a *sine qua non*, and the military budget the major expenditure of the imperial budget. In 1874, it accounted for 90 percent of the federal budget; in 1913, for 75–80 percent.[75] Calculated in terms of military spending as a percentage of national income (the monetary value of the total flow of goods and services), this amounted to only 4.6 percent in 1914, placing Imperial Germany roughly where the United States is today, but behind contemporary Russia (6.3 percent), Austria-Hungary (6.1 percent), and France (4.8 percent).[76] Seen in light of resource mobilization, Germany hardly appeared especially militaristic, even at the height of its armaments spending. However, for national politics, focused on the federal budget, the figure of military outlays ranging between 75 and 90 percent meant that the military occupied the national public sphere, becoming the central issue on which politics turned. Moreover, at the federal level, there were essentially two sources of revenue: consumption taxes and tariffs, and throughout most of our period the latter constituted the largest source. There were many issues in Imperial Germany—ranging from legal reform to the expansion of a nascent welfare state—but the above facts of the imperial budget and political alignments ensured that the military and how to pay for it assumed center stage.

This was especially so starting in 1897, when the Imperial government began a massive build up of a high seas naval fleet and announced its intention to pursue *Weltpolitk*—in a word, imperialism. The new foreign minister, Bernhard von Bülow, attempted to rally political support for this great power venture by bringing together agrarian and industrial interests, and bourgeois and conservative parties, including the Catholic Center. The new policy, *Sammlungspolitik*, was to be directed against Social Democracy and it was to create a broad base of support for naval build-up.[77] As an economic proposition, it involved considerable, almost New-Deal-like pump priming, since the building program would smooth cyclical fluctuations in heavy industry and eradicate unemployment.

Without doubt the most skillful German politician since Bismarck, Bülow unequivocally embraced a political world view of high imperialism. Subsequently Chancellor from 1900 to 1909, he believed that world politics would soon be dominated by four empires: the United States, Russia, Great Britain, and Imperial Germany. The rest of the world, he reasoned, was in political decay. For Germany, world power, which meant empire, was an absolute necessity. One is either, he said, a hammer or an anvil. Great Britain was in relative decline, but had a large empire. Germany, by contrast, did not have an empire commensurate with its population growth and industrial strength. His whole vision was oriented to what he perceived to be the political realities of global competition. The same may be said of Alfred von Tirpitz, who in 1897 became Secretary of the Reich Marine Office. He was an avid reader of A. T. Mahan's *The Influence of Sea Power on History*, and had the book translated into German and printed in large print runs. Finally, there was the Kaiser, who expressed a child-like enthusiasm about the building of a fleet. In their calculations, Germany would have to increase the German Navy to two-thirds the size of the British, challenging British superiority in the North Sea. In order to protect its wider hegemony, Britain, they supposed, would concede a share of its colonies, thus making the playing field of imperial competition more equal. In fact, the build-up of the German navy set off an arms race and a cold war, and drove Great Britain into the arms of France, its erstwhile imperial rival.[78]

The large navy was also to create enthusiasm for the monarchy and for its imperial mission, and this enthusiasm, the government hoped, would reach deep into the territory of the 'enemies' of the Reich, prying workers away from the Socialists and effecting a Catholic conversion to the national cause. The first of these propositions never worked; whatever sympathy Socialist workers may have had for the spread of

European culture, their pointedly anti-chauvinistic 'alternative culture'—which celebrated separate national holidays and recalibrated national songs—militated against
identification with the great power politics of German imperialism. The Navy League,
founded on Tirpitz's initiative and with the Kaiser as patron, tried to bring workers into
its membership, but the effort was a complete failure. The more realistic target was the
Catholic Center, and bringing it in to support the Navy became one of the principal
tasks of government-sponsored, official patriotism. The Catholic Center, like the Social
Democrats, had an impressive history of opposition to Imperial Germany's military
bills. However, since the end of the official *Kulturkampf*, it had increasingly become a
party whose leaders mediated between its four major constituencies—the church, the
agrarian and *Mittelstand* populists, the bourgeois middle class, and the Christian
workers unions—and principled opposition proved difficult to establish.[79] Moreover,
in exchange for governmental support, the Catholics hoped for further integration and
the repeal of remaining *Kulturkampf* laws, such as the ban on Jesuits.

The government strategy proved a partial success. The Center supported the first
and second naval bills, and for the first time national organizations succeeded, if
unevenly, in organizing Catholics into their ranks.[80] Foremost among them was the
Navy League, whose government-oriented leaders understood that only moderation in
tone kept the Catholics within the national fold. Yet, precisely this moderation proved
untenable to an increasing number of radical nationalists, who saw in Catholic
integration a dilution of the national character and an undermining of Germany's
capacities in the coming Darwinian struggle of empire. The Navy League almost broke
over the issue. In terms of maintaining a stable *Reichstag* majority for naval expansion,
the political-religious dimension of the Navy League crisis of 1906–1907 was as important an issue as the question of radical nationalism's political style.[81]

The impact of these events was perhaps greatest on the political right, encompassing
the Conservative and the National Liberal parties. They increasingly defined their
politics in the terms of the new imperial language of nation and race, demanding
great power politics in the international arena, while resisting democratic change at
home. Historians have seen this as the point where conservative interests precluded the
liberalization of the German Empire. One may well point to the Conservative refusal,
following the protests of the Agrarian League, to accept Bernhard von Bülow's controversial inheritance tax in 1909, highlighting what seemed like a discrepancy between the
right's demand for military build-up and a stingy insistence that it be paid for
disproportionately by the poor through consumption taxes and grain tariffs.[82] The
discrepancy in fact revealed the great fissure in the Conservative party—between its
status as a narrow agrarian interest party driven by the populism of the Agrarian
League, and a pro-government party reluctantly embracing the full implications of
modern imperialism, including radical nationalism, racist thinking, anti-Socialist invective, and anti-Semitic politics. For their part, the National Liberals found themselves
in a similar position, if less torn by the contradictory requirements of an agrarian base.
More than any other party, the National Liberals tied their fate to the imperatives of
great power imperialism and the radical nationalism that came with it—with the result

that in the age of mass politics, from 1890 to 1914, they saw their popular vote steadily dwindle, with only one flicker of hope, in 1907, when Catholics and Socialists criticized colonial abuses, and the government branded them as 'enemies of the Reich.'[83] Even taken together, the Conservatives and the National Liberals, the national camp, never polled more than 30 percent of the popular vote after 1893. In 1912, their combined popular vote did not match the Center party, and their mandates did not equal the SPD, which now emerged with the largest political representation in the *Reichstag*.

The great problem of liberalism was not the preponderance of feudal elites, but democracy itself. Unlike in Great Britain, German liberals in the *Reichstag* had to face the democratic challenges of mass politics head-on, without the benefits of restricted suffrage, or the long transition, buttressed by a gradual widening of suffrage, that marked most European polities. The lack of ministerial responsibility was not irrelevant to this problem. In Germany, it encouraged at the national level a political culture that often made the *Reichstag* into a clearing house for economic interests as opposed to a forum to advance genuine if competing concepts of the public good. At the same time, it became a space where rhetorical excess, not bound to governing responsibility, became the normal stuff of politics, and this, especially in its radical nationalist and racist guises, had a corrosive effect on political understanding more generally.

German liberals also faced two formidable forces, one of which was growing in strength. Starting from 1874, the Center polled 27.9 percent of the votes; in 1912, 16.4 percent, but, save for the very last election, it had achieved a 'dynamic stability' in the 1890s, allowing it to maintain the number of parliamentary mandates at roughly a hundred.[84] The centrality to modern politics of some kind of Christian democracy, typically Catholic, is a democratic feature that imperial Germany shared with a whole array of European countries, but not, alas, with France, England, and the United States, even as religion profoundly marked these countries as well. In any case, democracy more typically includes the complicated exchange between the religious and the secular, with the German story in this case exemplary, rather than an anomaly. A similar case may be made with respect to Social Democracy. It was a growing force, reflecting the profound social changes of the empire, even if many commentators consider it to have reached its electoral limit in 1912, at roughly one-third of the popular vote. It belonged to one of seven pre-war socialist parties, all of which were in central Europe and in Scandinavia, commanding a quarter of the electorate; and to a larger family of socialist parties spreading from the low countries to Czarist Russia, and even into the industrially backwards south of Europe, where anarcho-syndicalist traditions otherwise impeded democratic socialist advance.[85] The weaker parties were in the Anglo-American world, where, in Great Britain, an independent labor party only emerged out of the shadow of a suffrage-protected liberalism in 1906, and in the United States, which in this regard proved such an anomaly that Werner Sombart could legitimately pose the question, '*Why is there no Socialism in the United States?*'[86] Throughout most of the period, Catholic and Socialist parties easily outperformed the combined liberal parties in free elections. They also took more principled stands on crucial questions of minority rights: certainly with respect to the national minorities within the Empire, but also, with the exception of left liberal parties, of Jews. In the question of female suffrage, which by 1913 had been achieved in New Zealand, Australia, Finland, and Norway, all of Germany's democratic parties demurred, the Socialists putting it off for another day, the Catholics leaving it well alone, even though they stood to gain from it.[87] Finally, it was with respect to the great question of the eradication of indigenous peoples in German colonies that Social Democracy and the Catholic Center showed greater fidelity to a normative conception of democracy based on the protection of rights. When in Southwest Africa, German troops slaughtered Herero and Nama, the main voices of opposition were Socialist and Catholic. Left liberals suggested moderation and the consigning of natives to reservations, as was done, they argued, for Indians and wild animals.[88]

14.5 THE MILITARIZATION OF GERMAN SOCIETY

In 1898, the *Reichstag* approved the expansive naval program: the completion of nineteen large battleships, eight armored cruisers, twelve large cruisers, and thirty light cruisers—at a cost of 408 million Marks; thereafter, in 1900, it increased the program to thirty-eight battleships, twenty armored cruisers, and thirty-eight light cruisers. This ambitious program, periodically adjusted thereafter, was to be completed by 1920. In a remarkable act of its own disempowerment, the *Reichstag* also agreed to the replacement of the battleships so that the build-up, once consented to, no longer depended on further appropriations. The passing of the naval bills represented a turn in imperial politics, and it is not too much to say that the central domestic issues of the next decade involved the question of how to pay for it. The Naval Bill also involved acceptance of a wager: that Great Britain, once confronted with the possibility of a naval confrontation in the North Sea, would back down, since, even if Great Britain won, its remaining fleet would not be strong enough to face a third power. Great Britain would then concede colonies and Germany would have its 'place in the sun.'

The strategy brought no such concession. Instead, *Weltpolitik* militarized international relations, and set the antagonists, not unlike the United States and Soviet Union prior to 1989, into thinking about strategy and diplomacy in terms of a military-industrial complex that estimated relative strength in terms of tonnage and gunnery. This was the first consequence of *Weltpolitik*. The second was that it inaugurated a spiral of colonial encounters that in almost all cases ended to Germany's detriment, severely worsening its strategic position, driving Britain into the arms of the French and alienating Russia. In a series of crises, first in Morocco in 1905, then at the subsequent Conference of Algeciras in 1906, then in Bosnia in 1908, and in Morocco again in 1911, Germany found itself increasingly isolated, with only a comparatively weak Austria-Hungary as an ally. As Germany fell into greater isolation, there were no gains to the colonial empire. Since 1900, the salient colonial experience was instead two brutal wars—the Maji Maji War in German East Africa and the Herero Wars in

German Southwest Africa. They involved the loss of fewer than a thousand German soldiers, but the killing of over 200,000 native men, women, and children.

In this context, the radical nationalists experienced what Peter Walkenhorst has called 'cumulative disillusion.' Dismayed by the diplomacy of imperialism, they increasingly concentrated their energies on continental expansion to the east and southeast and on the necessity of armament build-up for a coming war, which seemed the only road to world power. In this conception, they were certainly helped by the illusion—despite good evidence to the contrary—that the next war would be short, and that it would give the upper hand to the offensive.

The immediate years before World War I witnessed in Imperial Germany a palpable militarization, which, following the definition of Michael Geyer, entailed a society 'organizing itself in and for war,' or, in an alternate formulation, 'for the production of violence.'[89] The Army League, founded by self-professed 'national revolutionaries,' quickly recruited over 100,000 members and agitated successfully for the introduction of massive increases in the size of the German Army. That increase was originally to be 300,000 men, which meant increasing the size of the German Army by roughly a third, and *de facto* reshaping Imperial German society as a society in arms.[90] Telling is that the resistance to the bill came from within the army itself, as the quantitative increase meant a dilution of the class character of the Army. Against the demands of an international arms race, even the Prussian army could not prevail, however.[91] In the end, the bill increased the size of the Army by 136,000 men—the largest peace-time increase in the army's history. More importantly, it unleashed a second arms race, one that increased the size of European armies even more.

There was also a militarizing shift in attitudes. General Bernhardi's *Germany and the Next War*, while hardly representative of broader public opinion, signaled a new understanding of the meaning of violence. He saw war as unambiguously positive, a form of regeneration, and a fact of human life that contributed to biological, social, and moral progress. The public sphere itself became militarized, and trafficked in increasingly masculine rhetoric. Pervasive after the Social Democratic victory in the 1912 election, such rhetoric was hardly confined to men alone. Baroness von Spitzemberg, a sensitive seismograph of the pre-war conservative scene, complained that society was becoming 'socialistic, modern, and effeminate.'[92] The reference to gender also reflected a more general reaction to female intrusion into the public sphere encouraged by the Association Law of 1908. This broadened participation, while dramatically raising gendered fears, also occurred in the midst of the militarization of German society, from which women were hardly exempt.[93] In fact, a wide consensus for the army bills obtained, as is evidenced by the broad coalition, reaching through the Center Party and even into the ranks of Social Democracy, to support a further Army Bill in 1913 and to pay for it with a one-time patriotic 'Defense Contribution.' The depth of this support is significant. 'The mass of the workers are not such anti-militarists . . . as we would like,' conceded one SPD leader, hoping still to effect army reform with Socialist support.[94] Significantly, opposition to the bill came from the Conservative Party, whose deputies saw it as opening the door to direct taxation.

Finally, the militarization was especially evident in government circles, where a comparatively weak chancellor, Theobald von Bethmann-Hollweg, was increasingly crowded out by the Kaiser's military advisers. The War Council of 8 December, 1912 revealed this increasing militarization. The major civilian ministers—Bethmann-Hollweg and Alfred von Kiderlen-Wächter of the foreign office—were not present. Chief of the General Staff, von Moltke, insisted that the question was no longer if war, but when, and added the sooner the better. Historians, starting with Fritz Fischer, have used the War Council as evidence that the German government wanted war even before 1914, and cite a directive from the meeting charging ministers with the preparation of Germany for the outbreak of hostilities.[95] The meeting cannot bear the interpretive weight historians have put on it, however. There is no indication that the preparations were carried out. The Army Bill of 1913 was already being drafted; there was no significant stockpiling of foodstuffs; and no acceleration of conscription. It is however significant that in 1912 the Chief of the German General Staff, like the recently recalled head of the Austro-Hungarian General Staff, was advocating preventive war, and thinking more in terms of timetables and windows of opportunity than of diplomatic solutions. The question then became not war or peace, but war or more military buildup.[96]

The responsibility of Germany for the outbreak of the war has constituted one of the most debated propositions in the field of German history. We will not recount this debate, but instead suggest that German responsibility is more precisely understood as a series of propositions. The first involves the question of whether Germany willed war. The preponderance of evidence suggests the contrary. In the July Crisis of 1914, both Bethmann-Hollweg and the Kaiser himself attempted frantically to hold back the full consequences of their diplomacy, with Bethmann-Hollweg desperately sending urgent telegrams on the early morning of 30 July, trying to get Vienna to negotiate.[97] It is, furthermore, not sustainable to see the Reich leadership as taking a conscious leap in the dark, or flight forward, in order to shore up what was becoming an increasingly unsolvable domestic crisis, occasioned by the military build-up and the question of who would pay for it. It remains nevertheless plausible, although not accepted in all quarters, that the military had a disproportionate amount of say in the last weeks of the July Crisis, though the case for confusion at this level is as strong as the case for calculation and design. That the government was in crisis is more difficult to deny.

Between 1900 and 1914 the democratic pressure for parliamentary reform became acute.[98] Historians debate whether the government would have allowed far reaching changes to the constitution. This is a matter of opinion. In the latter half of the twentieth century, we learned that governments with a lot less legitimacy than Imperial Germany can continue costly arms races for a long time—although not indefinitely. The *Reichstag*, the principal outlet for democratic participation, had many limitations and one strength: it held the purse for the national budget, which was in the main a military budget. For this reason, the arms race, and indeed Germany's whole bid for *Weltpolitik*, could not but tear at the foundation of this society. In the period before World War I, the imperatives of *Weltpolitik*, the challenges of radical nationalism, and the militarization of foreign policy shut down alternatives, and gave a disproportionate voice to a nationalism that demanded great power status for a nation state that had palpably failed in its bid to become a great empire. This nationalism, the elixir of a German liberalism's ill starred experience with democratic suffrage, did not force Germany into war. Yet it powerfully contributed to the failure of Germany's integration into a wider world, and was no doubt a contributing factor keeping Germany from stepping away from the precipice.

Notes

1. Sebastian Conrad and Jürgen Osterhammel (eds), *Das Kaiserreich Transnational* (Göttingen: Vandenhoeck and Ruprecht, 2004).
2. Two recent exemplars include Cornelius Torp, *Die Herausforderung der Globalisierung. Wirtschaft und Politik in Deutschland 1860–1914* (Göttingen: Vandehoeck & Ruprecht, 2005); Sebastian Conrad, *Globalisierung und Nation im Deutschen Kaiserreich* (Munich: C.H. Beck, 2006).
3. In this matter, I follow Hans-Ulrich Wehler, *Deutsche Gesellschaftsgeschichte, 1848–1914* (Munich: C.H. Beck, 1995) and Volker Berghahn, *Imperial Germany: Economy, Society, Culture and Politics*, rev. edn (New York: Berghahn Books, 2005). On the historiography of Imperial Germany, the best guides are James Retallack, *Germany in the Age of Kaiser Wilhelm II* (Houndmills, Basingstoke: Macmillan Press, 1996), and Matthew Jefferies, *Contesting the German Empire, 1871–1918* (Malden: Blackwell, 2008).
4. Georg Brandes, *Berlin als deutsche Reichshauptstadt. Erinnerungen aus den Jahren 1877–1883*, trans. Erik M. Christensen and Hans-Dietrich Loock (Berlin: Colloquium Verlag, 1989), 225. In his account, Thomas Nipperdey fudges this fact and emphasizes the reality of the widespread fear of socialism, Thomas Nipperdey, *Deutsche Geschichte, 1866–1918*, vol. 2 (Munich: C.H. Beck, 1992), 383.
5. Cited in James J. Sheehan, *German Liberalism in the Nineteenth Century* (Chicago: University of Chicago Press, 1978), 183.
6. Cited in Stefan Rebenich, *Theodor Mommsen: Eine Biographie* (Munich: Beck, 2002), 169.
7. The text of Treitschke's article is partly reprinted in Karsten Krieger (ed.), *Der Berliner Antisemitismusstreit, 1879–1881. Kommentierte Quellenedition*, 2 vols (Munich: De Gruyter, 2004), vol. 1, 6–16. For an analysis of the debate, see Uffa Jensen, *Gebildete Doppelgänger: Bürgerliche Juden und Protestanten im 19. Jahrhundert* (Göttingen: Vandenhoeck & Ruprecht, 2005), 197–268.
8. The most comprehensive and integrated account of anti-Semitism in the Kaiserreich is now Massimo Ferrari Zumbini, *Die Wurzeln des Bösen. Grunderjahre des Antisemitismus von der Bismarckzeit zu Hitler* (Frankfurt am Main: Vittorio Klostermann, 2003).
9. Christhard Hoffmann, 'Political Culture and Violence against Minorities: The Antisemitic Riots in Pomerania and West Prussia,' in Christhard Hoffmann, Werner Bergmann, and Helmut Walser Smith (eds), *'Exclusionary Violence:' Antisemitic Riots in Modern Germany* (Ann Arbor: University of Michigan Press, 2002), 67–92.
10. On politic style, Carl E. Schorske, *Fin-de-Siècle Vienna* (New York: Vintage Books, 1981), 116–180; David Blackbourn, 'The Politics of Demagogy in Imperial Germany', in David Blackbourn, *Populists and Patricians: Essays in Modern German History* (London:

Allen & Unwin, 1987), 217–245; Margaret L. Anderson, *Practicing Democracy: Elections and Political Culture in Imperial Germany* (Princeton: Princeton University Press, 2000); and James Retallack, *The German Right, 1860–1920: Political Limits of the Authoritarian Imagination* (Toronto: University of Toronto Press, 2006), 76–107.

11. Hans Rosenberg, *Grosse Depression und Bismarckzeit. Wirtschaftsablauf, Gesellschaft und Politik in Mitteleuropa* (Berlin: de Gruyter, 1967), 169–191.

12. Torp, *Die Herausforderung der Globalisierung*, 163–177.

13. Ibid., 117–119.

14. The listing of countries, for 1914, is from Eric J. Hobsbawm, *The Age of Empire, 1875–1914* (New York: Pantheon Books, 1987), 39.

15. William W. Hagen, *Germans, Poles and Jews: the Nationality Conflict in the Prussian East, 1772–1914* (Chicago: University of Chicago Press, 1980), 133; Vejas Gabriel Liulevicius, *The German Myth of the East, 1800 to the Present* (Oxford: Oxford University Press, 2009), 103.

16. Berghahn, *Imperial Germany*, 106.

17. Miroslav Hroch, 'The Nation-Building Process in Europe,' in Geoff Eley and Ronald Grigor Suny (eds), *Becoming National: A Reader* (New York: Oxford University Press, 1996), 63.

18. Georg M. Frederickson, *Racism: A Short History* (Princeton: Princeton University Press, 2002), 105. Nazi Germany was the third.

19. Jane Burbank and Frederick Cooper, *Empires in World History. Power and the Politics of Difference* (Princeton: Princeton University Press, 2010), 288; Hobsbawm, *The Age of Empire*, 59.

20. Hobsbawm, *The Age of Empire*, 59.

21. Paul M. Kennedy, *The Rise and Fall of the Great Powers. Economic Change and Military Conflict from 1500 to 2000* (New York: Random House, 1987), 194.

22. Otto Pflanze, *Bismarck and the Development of Germany*, vol. 3, *The Period of Fortification, 1880–1889* (Princeton: Princeton University Press, 1990), 139–40.

23. There is now a mountain of literature. See, most recently, the essays in: Geoff Eley and Bradley Naranch (eds), *German Cultures of Colonialism: Race, Nation, and Globalization, 1884–1945* (Durham: Duke University Press, 2010); and, for the sustained historiographic argument, Conrad, *Globalisierung und Nation*.

24. Josef Ehmer, *Bevölkerungsgeschichte und historische Demographie, 1800–2000* (Munich: Oldenbourg, 2004), 87.

25. Wolfram Fischer et al. (eds), *Europäische Wirtschafts-und Sozialgescihcte von der Mitte des 19. Jahrhunderts bis zum Ersten Weltkrieg* (Stuttgart: Klett-Cotta, 1985), 22.

26. Gerhard A. Ritter and Klaus Tenfelde, *Arbeiter im Deutschen Kaiserreich* (Bonn: Dietz, 1992), 188; Jochen Oltmer, *Migration im 19. und 20. Jahrhundert* (Munich: Oldenbourg, 2010), 22–3.

27. Steve Hochstadt, *Mobility and Modernity: Migration in Germany, 1820–1989* (Ann Arbor: University of Michigan Press, 1999), 278.

28. Tenfelde and Ritter, *Arbeiter im Deutschen Kaiserreich*, 179.

29. Klaus Tenfelde, *Sozialgeschichte der Bergarbeiterschaft an der Ruhr im 19. Jahrhundert* (Bonn: Verlag Neue Gesellschaft, 1977), 44. Tenfelde and Ritter, *Arbeiter im Deutschen Kaiserreich*, 190.

30. Wehler, *Gesellschaftsgeschichte*, 785–6.

31. Wehler, *Gesellschaftsgeschichte*, 708.

32. Jürgen Kocka, *Das lange 19. Jahrhundert* (Stuttgart: Klett-Cotta, 2001), 45.

33. Ritter and Tenfelde, *Arbeiter im Deutschen Kaiserreich*, 364.

34. Wehler, *Gesellschaftsgeschichte*, 711.

35. Wehler, *Gesellschaftsgeschichte*, 706–712; Kaelble, *Auf dem Weg zu einer europäischen Gesellschaft*, 52.

36. Ute Frevert, *Frauen-Geschichte. Zwischen bürgerlicher Verbesserung und Neuer Weiblichkeit* (Frankfurt: Suhrkamp, 1986), 80–92; Tenfelde and Ritter, *Arbeiter im Deutschen Kaiserreich*, 205–218.

37. Berghahn, *Imperial Germany*, 58–71.

38. Gerd Hohorst, Jürgen Kocka and Gerhard A. Ritter, *Sozialgeschichtliches Arbeitsbuch. Materialien zur Statistik des Kaiserreichs 1870–1914* (Munich: C. H. Beck, 1975), 52.

39. Rita Aldenhoff, 'Agriculture,' in Roger Chickering (ed.), *Imperial Germany: A Historiographical Companion* (Westport, Conn.: Greenwood Press, 1996), 33–61.

40. Wehler, *Gesellschaftsgeschichte*, 712–3.

41. For an entry into this vast research effort, see Thomas Mergel, 'Die Bürgertumsforschung nach 15 Jahren,' *Archiv für Sozialgeschichte* 42(2001), 515–538.

42. For the European context, Peter Gay, *Schnitzler's Century. The Making of Middle-Class Culture, 1815–1914* (New York: W.W. Norton, 2002); for the urban contexts, Maiken Umbach, *German Cities and Bourgeois Modernism, 1890–1924* (Oxford: Oxford University Press, 2009), esp. introduction; Meike G. Werner, *Moderne in der Provinz. Kulturelle Experimente im Fin de Siècle Jena* (Göttingen: Wallstein, 2003).

43. Hobsbawm, *The Age of Empire*, 177.

44. On this class, the classic remains Jürgen Kocka, *Unternehmensverwaltung und Angestelltenschaft am Beispiel Siemens 1847–1914* (Stuttgart: Klett-Cotta, 1969).

45. Ritter and Tenfelde, *Arbeiter im Deutschen Kaiserreich*, 144–147.

46. On the self-understanding of the Prussian Junkers, see Marcus Funck, 'The Meaning of Dying. East Elbian Noble Families as Warrior-Tribes in the 19th and 20th Centuries,' in: Greg Eghigian and Matt Berg (eds), *Sacrifice and National Belonging in the 20th Century*, (Arlington: Texas A & M University Press, 2002), 26–63; Stephan Malinowski, *Vom König zum Führer. Sozialer Niedergang und politischer Radikalisierung im deutschen Adel zwischen Kaiserreich und NS-Staat* (Berlin: Akademie Verlag, 2003), 47–117.

47. Wehler, *Gesellschaftsgeschicht*, 811.

48. Stefan-Ludwig Hoffmann, *Civil society, 1750–1914* (Houndsmills, Basingstoke: Palgrave, 2006), 61.

49. Membership figures are from Dieter Fricke et al. (eds), *Lexikon zur Parteiengeschichte*, 4 vols (Leipzig: Bibliographisches Institut, 1983–1986) and reflect individual, not corporate memberships.

50. Kaelble, *Auf dem Weg zu einer europäischen Gesellschaft. Eine Sozialgeschichte Westeuropas 1880–1980* (Munich: C.H. Beck, 1987), 84. Kaelble's calculation is based on union membership as a percentage of dependent wage earners.

51. Carl Schorske, *German Social Democracy, 1905–1917. The Development of the Great Schism* (New York: Harper & Row, 1972), 13.

52. Guenther Roth, *The Social Democrats in Imperial Germany. A Study in Working-Class Isolation and National Integration* (Totowa: Bedminster Press, 1963); and with especial attention paid to the run-up to World War I. Dieter Groh, *Negative Integration und revolutionärer Attentismus: Die deutsche Sozialdemokratie am Vorabend des ersten Weltkrieges* (Frankfurt am Main: Ullstein Verlag, 1973).

53. Thomas Welskopp, *Das Banner der Brüderlichkeit. Die deutsche Sozialdemokratie vom Vormärz bis zum Sozialistengesetz* (Bonn: Dietz, 2000). See also Richard J. Evans, 'Introduction: The Sociological Interpretation of German Labour History,' in Evans (ed.), *The German Working Class, 1888–1933* (London: Croom Helm, 1982), 18–30.

54. Vernon L. Lidtke, *The Alternative Culture. Socialist Labor in Imperial Germany* (New York: Oxford, 1985), 112–114.

55. Geoff Eley, *Forging Democracy: The History of the Left in Europe, 1850–2000* (New York: Oxford University Press, 2002), 64.

56. Hobsbawm, *The Age of Empire*, 134–5; Lidtke, *Alternative Culture*, 186.

57. Ian Farr, 'Populism in the Countryside: The Peasant Leagues in Bavaria in the 1890s,' in: Richard J. Evans (ed.), *Society and Politics in Wilhelmine Germany* (London: Croom Helm, 1978), 136–159.

58. On the shape of Protestant religiosity, see Lucian Hölscher (with the assistance of Tilmann Bendikowski, Claudia Enders and Markus Hoppe), *Datenatlas zur religiösen Geographie im protestantischen Deutschland. Von der Mitte des 19. Jahrhunderts bis zum Zweiten Weltkrieg*, 4 vols. (Berlin: Walter de Gruyter, 2001).

59. On the Farmer's League, see Hans-Jürgen Puhle, *Agrarische Interessenpolitik und preussischer Konservatiismus im wilhelminischen Reich (1893–1904)*, 2nd edn (Bonn: Verlag Neue Gesellschaft, 1975). See also the criticism of Puhle in Geoff Eley, 'Anti-Semitism, Agrarian Mobilization, and the Conservative Party: Radicalism and Containment in the Founding of the Agrarian League,' in: Larry E. Jones and James Retallack (eds), *Between Reform, Reaction, and Resistance: Studies in the History of Conservatism* (Providence: Berghahn, 1993), 187–228.

60. Shearer Davis Bowman, *Masters and Lords: Mid-19th Century U.S. Planters and Prussian Junkers* (New York: Oxford University Press, 1993).

61. On the Protestant League, Helmut Walser Smith, *German Nationalism and Religious Conflict: Culture, Ideology, Politics, 1870–1914* (Princeton: Princeton University Press, 1995); on the Protestantenverein, and the politics of liberal Protestanism more generally, Gangolf Hübinger, *Kulturprotestantismus und Politik* (Tübingen: Mohr Siebeck, 1994).

62. Margaret Lavinia Anderson, *Windthorst: A Political Biography* (Oxford: Oxford University Press, 1981), 391–3.

63. Cited in Smith, *German Nationalism and Religious Conflict*, 98.

64. Avraham Barkai, *Der Centralverein deutscher Staatsbürger jüdischen Glaubens 1893–1938* (Munich: C. H. Beck, 2002).

65. Jacob Vogel, *Nationen im Gleichschritt. Der Kult der 'Nation in Waffen' in Deutschland und Frankreich (1871–1914)* (Göttingen: Vandenhoeck & Ruprecht, 1997).

66. Geoff Eley, *Reshaping the German Right. Radical Nationalism and Political Change after Bismarck*, 2nd edn (Ann Arbor: University of Michigan Press, 1991). On the question of political style in the national associations and among conservatives, see now James Retallack, *The German Right, 1860–1920: The Political Limits of the Authoritarian Imagination* (Toronto: University of Toronto Press, 2006), 76–107.

67. Eley, 'What Produces Fascism: Pre-Industrial Traditions or a Crisis of the Capitalist State,' in: Eley, *From Unification to Nazism: Reinterpreting the German Past* (Boston: Allen & Unwin, 1986), 265–266.

68. A brief introduction is Christopher Clark, *Kaiser Wilhelm II* (Harlow: Longman, 2000).

69. Eric Hobsbawm, 'Mass-Producing Traditions: Europe, 1870–1914,' in: Hobsbawm and Terrence Ranger (ed.), *The Invention of Tradition* (Cambridge: Cambridge University

Press, 1983), 264. On the revival of Monarchy, Jürgen Osterhammel, *Die Verwandlung der Welt: Eine Geschichte des 19. Jahrhunderts* (Munich: C. H. Beck, 2009), 828–848.

70. Cited in Eric J. Hobsbawm, *The Age of Empire*, 70.

71. Kenneth D. Barkin, *The Controversy over German Industrialization, 1890–1902* (Chicago: University of Chicago Press, 1970).

72. David Blackbourn and Geoff Eley, *The Peculiarities of German History* (Oxford: Oxford University Press, 1984). See the concessions in Wehler, *Gesellschaftsgeschichte*, vol. 2, 712, 714, and David Blackbourn, *The Long Nineteenth Century: A History of Germany, 1780–1918* (New York: Oxford University Press, 1998).

73. Ralf Dahrendorf, *Society and Democracy in Germany* (New York: W. W. Norton, 1967), 14.

74. James J. Sheehan, *German Liberalism in the Nineteenth Century*, 221–230. Two exemplary studies are: Jan Palmowski, *Urban Liberalism in Imperial Germany: Frankfurt am Main, 1866–1914* (New York: Oxford University Press, 1999); Till van Rahden, *Juden und andere Breslauer: Die Beziehungen zwischen Juden, Protestanten und Katholiken in einer deutschen Großstadt von 1860 bis 1925* (Göttingen: Vandenhoeck & Ruprecht, 2000).

75. In terms of total government expenditure (including state and local governments), the figure was closer to 40 percent for 1874, and just over 20 percent in 1913.

76. Quincy Wright, *A Study of War*, vol 1 (Chicago: University of Chicago Press, 1942), 670–671.

77. A god introduction is V.R. Berghahn, *Germany and the Approach of War in 1914*, 2nd edn (New York: St. Martins, 1993), 38–76.

78. On the dynamics of imperial rivalry, Paul M. Kennedy, *The Rise of Anglo-German Antagonism 1860–1914* (London: George Allen & Unwin, 1980).

79. See the influential interpretation of Wilfried Loth, *Katholiken im Kaiserreich* (Düsseldorf: Droste, 1984).

80. Smith, *German Nationalism and Religious Conflict*, 146–153.

81. Peter Walkenhorst, *Nation-Volk-Rasse. Radikaler Nationalismus im Deutschen Kaiserreich 1890–1914* (Göttingen: Vandenhoeck und Ruprecht, 2007), 311–315.

82. Retallack, *The German Right*, 355–360.

83. Sheehan, *German Liberalism in the Nineteenth Century*, 278.

84. Jonathan Sperber, *The Kaiser's Voters: Electors and Elections in Imperial Germany* (Cambridge: Cambridge University Press, 1997), 106.

85. Eley, *Forging Democracy*, 33, 63–64.

86. Cited in Hobsbawm, *The Age of Empire*, 117.

87. Eley, *Forging Democracy*, 99–107; Anderson, *Practicing Democracy*, 127.

88. Helmut Walser Smith, 'The Talk of Genocide, the Rhetoric of Miscegenation: Notes on a *Reichstag* Debate, 1906–1914,' in: Sara Friedrichsmeyer, Sara Lennox, and Susanne Zantop (eds), *The Imperialist Imagination*, (Ann Arbor: University of Michigan Press, 1998), 125–140.

89. Cited in Walkenhorst, *Nation-Volk-Rasse*, 228.

90. Michael Geyer, *Deutsche Rüstungspolitik, 1860–1980* (Frankfurt am Main: Suhrkamp, 1984), 89.

91. Oliver Stein, *Die deutsche Heeresrüstungspolitik 1890–1914. Das Militär und der Primat der Politik* (Paderborn: Schöningh, 2007).

92. Rudolf Vierhaus (ed.), *Das Tagebuch der Baronin Spitzemberg*, 5th edn (Göttingen: Vandenhoek & Ruprecht, 1989), 520.

93. Ute Frevert, *Die Kasernierte Nation. Militärdienst und Zivilgesellschaft in Deutschland* (Munich: C.H. Beck, 2001), 283–286.
94. Cited in Groh, *Negative Integration und revolutionärer Attentismus*, 436.
95. John C.J. Röhl, 'An der schwelle zum Weltkrieg: Eine Dokumentation über den "Kriegsrat" vom 8. Dezember 1912,' *Militärgeschichtliche Mitteilungen*, 21 (1977), 77–134.
96. Michael Geyer, *Deutsche Rüstungspolitik*, 88; Hew Strachen, *The First World War*, vol. 1 (Oxford: Oxford University Press, 2001), 52–55.
97. Strachen, *The First World War*, 87–88.
98. Brett Fairbairn, *Democracy in the Undemocratic State: The German Reichstag Elections of 1898 and 1903* (Toronto: University of Toronto Press, 1997).

BIBLIOGRAPHY

ANDERSON, MARGARET L., *Practicing Democracy: Elections and Political Culture in Imperial Germany* (Princeton: Princeton University Press, 2000).

BERGHAHN, VOLKER R., *Imperial Germany: Economy, Society, Culture and Politics*, rev. edn (New York: Berghahn Books, 2005).

BLACKBOURN, DAVID *The Long Nineteenth Century: A History of Germany, 1780–1918* (New York: Oxford University Press, 1998).

—— and GEOFF ELEY, *The Peculiarities of German History* (Oxford: Oxford University Press, 1984).

CHICKERING, ROGER, *We Men who Feel Most German: A Cultural Study of the Pan-German League, 1886–1914* (Boston: Allen & Unwin, 1984).

——*Imperial Germany: A Histoiographical Companion* (Westport, Conn.: Greenwood Press, 1996).

CONRAD, SEBASTIAN and JÜRGEN OSTERHAMMEL (eds), *Das Kaiserreich Transnational* (Göttingen: Vandenhoeck and Ruprecht, 2004).

ELEY, GEOFF, *Reshaping the German Right. Radical Nationalism and Political Change after Bismarck*, 2nd edn (Ann Arbor: University of Michigan Press, 1991).

HOBSBAWM, ERIC J., *The Age of Empire, 1875–1914* (New York: Pantheon Books, 1987).

KÜHNE, THOMAS, *Dreiklassenwahlrecht und Wahlkultur in Preussen, 1867–1914* (Düsseldorf: Droste, 1994).

NIPPERDEY, THOMAS, *Deutsche Geschichte, 1866–1918*, vol. 2 (Munich: C. H. Beck, 1992), 383.

OSTERHAMMEL, JÜRGEN, *Die Verwandlung der Welt: Eine Geschichte des 19. Jahrhunderts* (Munich: C.H. Beck, 2009).

RETALLACK, JAMES (ed.), *Imperial Germany 1871–1918* (Short Oxford History of Germany) (Oxford: Oxford University Press, 2008).

RITTER, GERHARD A. and KLAUS TENFELDE, *Arbeiter im Deutschen Kaiserreich* (Bonn: Dietz, 1992).

SHEEHAN, JAMES J., *German Liberalism in the Nineteenth Century* (Chicago: University of Chicago Press, 1978).

SPERBER, JONATHAN, *The Kaiser's Voters: Electors and Elections in Imperial Germany* (Cambridge: Cambridge University Press, 1997).

TORP, CORNELIUS, *Die Herausforderung der Globalisierung. Wirtschaft und Politik in Deutschland 1860–1914* (Göttingen: Vandehoeck & Ruprecht, 2005).

WEHLER, HANS-ULRICH, *Deutsche Gesellschaftsgeschichte, vol. 2, 1848–1914* (Munich: C.H. Beck, 1995).

WELSKOPP, THOMAS, *Das Banner der Brüderlichkeit. Die deutsche Sozialdemokratie vom Vormärz bis zum Sozialistengesetz* (Bonn: Dietz, 2000).

CHAPTER 15

....

THE GREAT TRANSFORMATION: GERMAN ECONOMY AND SOCIETY, 1850–1914

....

CORNELIUS TORP

15.1

....

NEVER before had the world changed so dramatically. In the second half of the 'long' nineteenth century, and within only two generations, the part of Central Europe which became Germany in 1871 underwent a fundamental and unprecedented social transformation. Many other forces, such as state building, contributed to this transformation, but arguably, economic development was the most important driving force behind this process. Capitalism was not a totally new phenomenon. Many of its features, such as the production for a market, the individualization of property rights, capital accumulation, or profit orientation can be found in particular contexts of Central European history long before the middle of the nineteenth century—from the long-distance trade of German merchants to proto-industrial enterprises to export-oriented large-scale farming. After 1850, however, capitalism became both industrial and global. At the same time, it left the particular niches and contexts in which it had existed before and started to penetrate the whole society.

Some scholars consider industrialization, the first of the processes mentioned above, as one of the two fundamental revolutions of mankind, comparable only with the 'neolithic revolution' that introduced humankind to the sedentary way of life centered on agriculture.[1] Consequently, the process of industrialization has drawn the attention of generations of historians and economists—among them some of the most outstanding minds, from Karl Marx to Joseph Schumpeter to David S. Landes. In spite of nearly

300 years of empirical research and theoretical reflection, however, there still is nothing like a commonly accepted theory of industrialization.[2] Neither is there a general agreement concerning the very nature of industrialization and its defining features. Nor has a consensus been reached as to the question of whether the 'industrial revolution' represents a more or less sudden breakthrough or an evolutionary process of incremental change.

There are only two points on which the industrialization experts seem to agree.[3] First, the industrialization of the world started in England after the middle of the eighteenth century. Only here, at this time, was there to be found a particular combination of technical and institutional innovations, as well as the political and social preconditions that made a new level of economic development possible. From England, the industrialization spread to continental Europe, roughly following the coal deposits in a north-south and west-east direction, and to North America.[4] In Germany, industrialization gained momentum in the late 1840s. Secondly, industrialization has to be considered not as a national, but as a regional phenomenon. Even if the nation states with their institutions and legal frameworks played an important role, regional factors, such as the existence of raw materials, the population structure, and transportation and communication channels, are decisive for explaining the success or failure of industrialization processes, as well as the particular forms they took. At the turn of the twentieth century, industrialized zones were still surrounded by regions dominated by traditional economic relationships. At the same time, these industrialized regions straddled national borders, such as the industrial macro-region between the Pas-de-Calais and the Ruhr district.[5]

Entangled with industrialization in multiple ways, globalization was the second process that transformed the face of capitalism in the nineteenth century. Again, there had been forerunners of the modern world economy since the sixteenth century, such as the trade and production systems highlighted by Fernand Braudel or Immanuel Wallerstein.[6] After the middle of the nineteenth century, however, technological innovation imparted a new quality to global capitalism, with the extensive use of steamships in overseas trade and the massive expansion of the railroad networks leading to nothing less than a transportation revolution. Concurrently, the establishment of a global telegraph network revolutionized communications. As a consequence, world wide economic integration after 1850 increased so rapidly and steadily that by the eve of World War I a level of global trade intensity had been reached that was comparable to the level achieved in the 1970s and 1980s. Moreover, new world wide investment opportunities boosted international capital mobility to an extent that in some ways has not been arrived at even today. Finally, in the years between 1850 and 1914, transnational mass migration surpassed everything before or since, and tended to establish a world labor market with a global wage nexus. All in all, there is ample evidence of a rapid globalization process in the nineteenth century brought to a halt only by the globalization backlash, which the era of the two World Wars and the Great Depression implied.[7] In this first phase of world wide economic integration, just as in the second wave of globalization after 1950, Germany was one of the most important global players.

In the following pages, I will try to show how both industrialization and globalization transformed the German economy in the second half of the 'long' nineteenth century and how they affected German society. First, the long-term developments of the German economy between 1850 and 1914 will be described based on quantitative indicators (15.2). Then, the main stages of German economic history since 1850 with their characterizing features will be discussed more thoroughly (15.3 and 15.4). Finally, I will try to outline the most important social consequences of the economic transformations Germany went through in the decades before the First World War (15.5).

15.2

Industrialization is often equated with the spread of technological inventions, such as the 'Spinning Jenny' or the steam engine. This story, however, is way too simple. Even if technological inventions played an important role in the process of industrialization, they did not make up more than a necessary precondition. Whether an invention becomes an innovation depends on its economic profitability. Whether the use of a technology is efficient and profitable in turn hinges on a whole set of social, institutional and economic circumstances.[8] In economic history, the complexity of the problem has led to the development of different economic indicators, each focusing on a particular defining feature of industrialization.

Industrialization, first and foremost, means the long-term acceleration of economic growth. Net domestic product (NDP), which measures total economic output (gross domestic product) minus depreciation of capital goods, provides the best gauge of this process. Whereas the NDP of Germany within its 1871 borders increased by around two-thirds between 1800 and 1850, it rose by two-and-a-half from 1850 until 1900.[9] Compared with the middle of the nineteenth century, the NDP on the eve of the First World War had more than quintupled (see Table 15.1). Since economic growth even

Table 15.1 German net domestic product in billion marks (prices of 1913), 1850–1913

1850	1855	1860	1865	1870	1875	1880	1885	1890	1895	1900	1905	1910	1913
9.4	9.7	11.6	13.2	14.2	17.7	17.7	20.4	23.6	27.6	33.2	37.2	43.0	48.5

Source: Walter G. Hoffmann et al., *Das Wachstum der deutschen Wirtschaft seit der Mitte des 19. Jahrhunderts* (Berlin: Springer, 1965), 454 f.

outpaced population increase, the NDP *per capita* rose from 265 Marks in 1850 to 728 Marks in 1914.[10] These figures, it is true, are only rough estimates due to the poor state of the statistical material. The general macro-economic trend, however, is clear enough.

Economic growth, the second characteristic feature of industrialization, did not come at a steady pace, but followed business cycles. In traditional economies, fluctuations in economic development were typically caused by climate changes due to the central importance of weather for the agrarian sector. The resulting random pattern of economic development differs fundamentally from industrial economies that follow a growth path with more or less cyclical variations. These fluctuations vary in duration and are attributed to different causes from over-investment to credit changes. In the German case, it can be shown that at the end of the 1840s, industry had gained such an importance that business cycles began to have a significant impact on the course of economic development.[11] From that time onward, until the First World War, three different main phases can be distinguished. The first lasted until 1873 and was characterized by a continuity of high economic growth rates, only interrupted by the first world wide economic crisis of 1857–1859 and the short recession of 1866. It culminated in the so-called '*Gründerboom,*' the boom period in the years before and, more forcefully still, shortly after the founding of the German Empire. The period between 1873 and 1895 has become known as 'the Great Depression.'[12] However, economic historians today agree that these years were less an enduring depression than a period of retarded growth and of declining prices. Even in the worst years (1874–1883) of the 'Great Deflation' (the proper designation for the period) real NDP increased by 1.22 percent per year.[13] Nevertheless, it is important to bear in mind that contemporaries perceived the decades after 1873 as a sharp and long-lasting depression due to numerous crashes of companies and banks, and due to the radical difference compared with the boom before. From the early 1890s onward the German economy experienced an upswing that lasted until 1913. It was interrupted only by two brief, though serious, slumps in 1900–1902 and 1907–1908. How well the Germany economy did during the two decades before the Great War may be gauged from the fact that the annual growth rate of the NDP from 1895 to 1913 amounted to 3.41 percent and that the production index for all manufactures rose from 48.9 to 100 in the same time period.[14]

A third feature refers to the relation between capital accumulation and economic growth as one of the key mechanisms of industrial capitalism. In order to use the technical innovations of the industrial age economically, a huge increase in the capital stock of the industrializing economies was necessary. This meant a structural change in the organization of production and consumption. A substantial part of the financial resources that otherwise could have been spent for consumption now had to be saved and invested in railroads, iron mills etc. in order to realize profits in the future. This is echoed in Walt W. Rostow's often criticized model of 'The Stages of Economic Growth' according to which the 'take off' stage of an industrializing economy is characterized by a sharp rise in the effective investment rate from around five percent of national income to ten percent or more.[15] Even if this precondition for 'self sustained growth' does not seem to apply to the industrial forerunner England and other countries, it fits quite well in the German case. Table 15.2 shows that the German economy experienced its 'take off' phase in the two decades after 1850. Before mid century, effective invest- ment rates had been much lower; after 1870, with the exception of the early 1880s, they clearly exceeded the critical ten percent line.

A final feature of industrialization is the shifting importance of the diverse sectors of the national economy. In traditional economies, by far the largest part of the workforce is employed in the primary sector, which involves the extraction and production of raw materials, i.e. mainly agriculture and mining. With industrialization picking up steam, the secondary sector, which includes all types of manufactures, quickly gains in importance and finally overtakes the agrarian sector. In Germany, this process set in around the middle of the nineteenth century (Table 15.3). Already in the early 1890s, the secondary sector outperformed the primary sector in terms of both workforce and value added. There was, however, not only a significant shift between the main sectors

Table 15.2 Effective investment rates in Germany, 1850–1913 (five-year averages, current prices)

1850– 1854	1855– 1859	1860– 1864	1865– 1869	1870– 1874	1875– 1879	1880– 1884	1885– 1889	1890– 1894	1895– 1899	1900– 1904	1905– 1909	1910– 1913
9.8	8.1	12.1	9.9	14.1	11.0	9.3	11.5	11.8	14.8	13.9	15.3	15.2

Source: Hoffmann et al., Wachstum, 104.

Table 15.3 Distribution of the workforce among the three major sectors of the German economy, 1825–1907 (in percent)

	Raw material	Manufactures	Services
1825	59.0	22.0	19.0
1846	56.8	23.6	20.4
1855	53.9	25.4	20.6
1861	51.7	27.3	21.0
1871	49.3	28.9	21.8
1882	42.2	35.6	22.2
1895	36.6	38.9	24.8
1907	34.0	40.0	26.0

Source: Toni Pierenkemper, Umstrittene Revolutionen. Industrialisierung im 19. Jahrhundert (Frankfurt: Fischer, 1996), 95.

of the economy, but also within the secondary sector itself. In 1850, only 16 percent of the workforce employed in the manufacturing sector was made up of modern industry whereas the majority was occupied in more traditional branches like handicraft or the proto-industrial putting-out system. In 1913, on the contrary, industrial enterprises accounted for 62 percent of the workforce occupied in the secondary sector, leaving the other subsectors far behind them.[16]

At the same time when industrialization was kicking in, the economies of central Europe increasingly were drawn into the expanding world economy. Unfortunately, even for the dimension of international trade where statistics are much more reliable than for capital export, the available data before the founding of the German Empire are incomplete. For the subsequent period, however, a tremendous increase of German exports can be discerned, as they essentially quadrupled from 1872 to 1913, going from 2,353 million marks in current prices to 10,097 million marks. With this pace of growth, German exports rose even faster than the already quickly increasing world exports and the exports of most other developed countries. As a result, the German Empire before 1914 steadily moved up in the hierarchy of export nations. Of the four most important export nations before the First World War, listed in Table 15.4, only Germany was successful in constantly extending its share of world exports. Only US exports rose at a comparable though more uneven pace, whereas France and the UK continuously lost ground. In the year before the Great War, France actually had dropped out of the league of top exporters. Germany, the United States and the United Kingdom were now more or less equal with around 2.5 billion dollars of exports.[17]

Germany's foreign trade not only rose extremely fast compared with the exports and imports of other countries, but also in comparison with the quickly growing German economy as a whole. Table 15.5 lists the five-year averages of German exports and imports as a percentage of GNP for the decades before World War I. The data show that the German economy increasingly became dependent on its international trade relations. In the years before 1914, imports amounted to almost one-fifth of the German national income, with foodstuff consistently accounting for about one-quarter of

Table 15.4 Shares of world export, 1874–1913 (in percent)

	1874–1878	1879–1883	1884–1888	1889–1893	1894–1898	1899–1903	1904–1908	1909–1913
Germany	9.5	10.0	10.6	10.4	11.0	11.5	11.8	12.2
France	11.7	10.2	9.8	9.4	8.7	8.4	7.8	7.5
UK	17.3	16.7	17.0	15.9	14.7	14.2	13.9	13.5
USA	10.0	12.1	10.9	12.0	12.8	14.3	13.4	12.7

Source: Cornelius Torp, *Die Herausforderung der Globalisierung. Wirtschaft und Politik in Deutschland, 1860–1914* (Göttingen: Vandenhoeck & Ruprecht, 2005), 62.

Table 15.5 German export ratio and import ratio, 1874–1913 (export and import as percentage of GNP, in prices in 1913, five-year averages)

	1874–1878	1879–1883	1884–1888	1889–1893	1894–1898	1899–1903	1904–1908	1909–1913
Export ratio	8.5	9.7	10.5	10.6	11.0	12.0	13.7	15.8
Import ratio	15.2	14.9	14.6	17.1	17.8	17.9	18.6	19.2

Source: Own calculations based on *Statistisches Jahrbuch für das Deutsche Reich*, various volumes; Hoffmann et al., *Wachstum*; William Arthur Lewis, 'The Rate of Growth of World Trade, 1830–1973,' in Sven Grassman and Erik Lundberg (eds), *The World Economic Order. Past and Prospects* (London: Macmillan, 1981), 11–81, here 30 (table 2); Albrecht Ritschl and Mark Spoerer, 'Das Bruttosozial-produkt in Deutschland nach den amtlichen Volkseinkommens- und Sozialproduktstatistiken 1901–1995' *Jahrbuch für Wirtschaftsgeschichte*, no. 2 (1997), 51 (table A.1).

German imports. A third of the wheat consumed in Germany after the turn of the century and almost half of the barley had to be imported from other countries. Yet by far the most important import category concerned raw materials, such as coal, ore, cotton, and wood, needed for Germany's expanding industries. Even more impressive than the rise of imports was the increase in exports. Even during the dismal downturn of the 1870s, the yearly growth rate of exports already amounted to 3.57 percent. In the subsequent decades, it increased steadily, reaching 6.47 percent in 1907–1913. As a result, between the founding of the German Empire and the First World War, German export ratios almost doubled and nearly attained the level later achieved by the highly export-oriented economy of the Federal Republic of Germany at the end of the economic miracle (19.7 percent in 1973). Finally, the structure of exports differed sharply from the composition of imports. Starting as a relative latecomer as compared with Great Britain, Germany before 1914 developed into an exporter of industrial manufactures par excellence. Moreover, the composition of German industrial exports was extremely 'modern' in the sense that it was dominated by the products of engineering, as well as of heavy, electrical, and chemical industry, rather than by textiles as was still the case in Great Britain.[18]

15.3

As to the driving forces of industrialization and the pace of global integration, German economic history between 1850 and 1914 can be divided in two periods. The first stage reaches from the middle of the nineteenth century until the 1880s. It was characterized by the dominance of a set of leading industrial sectors, which turned out to be typical for German industrialization. Stemming from development economics, the term 'leading sector' refers to the strategic core of an industrialization process.[19] Whereas in Great Britain the textile industry functioned as the pacemaker of industrialization, in Germany four different branches—railroads, iron and steel, mining, and engineering—were together of crucial importance. These branches are regularly referred to as a 'complex' of leading sectors, deeply intertwined with various 'forward' and 'backward effects:' the building and maintenance of railroads required large amounts of steel and coal; steel plants were dependent on massive inputs of coal; coal mines and steel works used large scale machines, and transported their products by train.

To understand the sudden breakthrough of the leading sectors in Germany one has to consider the change in economic policy, which took place particularly in Prussia around the middle of the nineteenth century. This change had two major dimensions. On the one hand, the Prussian bureaucracy pursued a pronounced liberalization policy, which eased state control of coal mining, enabling the production of coal in Prussia to more than double between 1850 and 1860, and again in the following decade.[20] A second important field of liberalization involved the German law on stock companies where a far-reaching revision took place in 1870. Liberated from the former restrictions and driven by the 'Gründerboom,' 928 joint stock companies were floated between 1871 and 1873 as compared with the 295 floated over the whole period between 1850 and 1870.[21] On the other hand, Prussia as well as other German states started to mobilize massive financial resources around the mid-century in order to develop their economies. Most of these investments went into railroad building, either in the form of equity participation in railroad stock companies, by subsidies, or in direct investments in the construction of new railway lines. In Prussia, as a consequence of this new economic activity of the state, the national debt between 1848 and 1865 rose by more than 100 percent.[22]

Beyond doubt, railroads constituted the most dynamic and thus most important part of the German industrial core complex, displaying all the decisive characteristics of a 'leading sector.' First, the German railroad sector expanded at a breathtaking speed, far above average as compared with the rest of the national economy. To give only a rough impression, the track length between 1840 and 1880 increased from 469 to 30,125 km, the workforce from 1600 to 272,800 persons, and the volume of freight traffic from 3 million to 13,039 million tons km.[23] Secondly, the railroad sector was of significant and growing importance for the German economy as a whole. From the middle of the 1840s onwards, railroads steadily attracted a substantial part of national effective investments, culminating in a share of more than a quarter of all investments in 1875–1879. Accordingly, the railroad sector's share of German capital stock increased from a mere 3.2 percent in 1850–1854 to 11.4 percent in 1880–1884.[24] Thirdly, technological progress and the increased utilization of capacities allowed for huge productivity gains, which in turn led to decreasing freight rates. Fourthly, there were substantial 'spreading effects,' transcending the railroad sector itself and inducing economic growth in other sectors. As to backward linkage effects, the requirements of the railroads for new inputs of raw materials and machinery were decisive for the expansion of coal mining, and for the development of both the modern iron industry and engineering. Whereas throughout the first years of railroad construction in the 1830s and early 1840s, nearly all the iron products required had to be imported; after a few years a quick import substitution process set in. From the late 1840s onwards, foreign locomotives and rails increasingly were replaced by domestic products.[25] The forward effects of the railroad sector were no less important. A dramatic decline in freight tariffs implied huge cost saving effects for all other industries, giving them access to new markets and setting up incentives for economic growth and modernization.

Other elements of the leading sector complex, interwoven with the railroad sector in multiple ways, also developed at an outstanding pace. The Prussian production of coal, which represented about 90 percent of German production, increased from 4.0 million tons in 1850 to 23.3 million tons in 1870, to 64.4 million tons another twenty years later.[26] In the engineering sector, the demand for locomotives, as well as for all other kinds of machines and engines used in the iron and steel industry and in the mining sector, unleashed new economic activities on an unprecedented scale. In 1862, the statistics of the German *Zollverein* already listed 665 companies. By the end of 1871, this number rose up to 1400. From the 1860s onward, German engineering increasingly became internationally competitive and started to develop its long-term export orientation.[27] The fabulous growth of German heavy industry stands out even more clearly against the background of its British counterpart. Having started as a dwarf compared with the British giant before the middle of the nineteenth century, the German iron and steel industry quickly caught up and finally overtook British heavy industry in 1893 in the volume of steel production, and ten years later in the production of pig iron. Simultaneously, Germany triumphed in the world market for iron and steel and up to World War I surpassed Britain as the leading exporter. Exports in times of economic downturns could take the form of dumping exports in order to discharge overproduction as was the case with the Krupp Company in the depression since 1873 when its export quota climbed up to about three-quarters.[28] In the long run, however, the success of Germany's heavy industry rested on the combination of a set of structural factors: a high degree of vertical integration, strong cartels and tariffs reinforcing each other, and the realization of economies of scale that only could be achieved via large export quantities.[29]

A further backward effect of the leading sector complex as well as one of the most important features of nineteenth-century German economic history was the development of the German banking sector.[30] From the very beginning, German banks had been deeply involved in the industrialization process. Unlike the light-industrial path to industrialization represented by Great Britain, German industrialization, with its dominance of railroads and heavy industry, was extremely capital intensive from the outset. Accordingly, capital market financial institutions, hitherto underdeveloped, were needed to collect existing rent-seeking capital and direct it into the new invest-ment opportunities. Banks, mostly newcomers from the provinces such as the 'Schaaff-hausensche Bankverein,' Sal. Oppenheim JR, or S. Bleichröder, filled this niche. As major shareholders of railroad stock companies, but also as representatives in their decision-making bodies, bankers as early as the 1830–1840s found themselves closely connected to the world of industrial capital. Endowed with these experiences and contacts, it did not come as a surprise that banks again played an important role when capital for the expansion of the iron and steel industry and the mining sector was needed. With the companies of these very sectors increasingly developing into large-scale enterprises listed on the stock exchange, even the banks themselves had to rely on new financial resources and more and more took the form of stock companies (AGs).

There were two main waves of foundations of joint stock banks, both paralleling extreme boom phases. The first took place between 1853 and 1856, the second between 1869 and 1873. By the end of this time, all the major banks that determined German financial affairs until far into the twentieth century had come into existence, among them the four famous D-banks: the 'Deutsche,' the 'Darmstädter,' the 'Dresdner', and the 'Disconto-Gesellschaft.' From the outset, all these banks transcended the traditional British divide between 'investment' and 'commercial' banks and operated along the whole range of banking activities. It is difficult to assess how far the influence of the big German mixed banks (*Universalbanken*) in the German economy actually reached. The often heard claim of an all encompassing dominance of financial capital, already expressed by Rudolf Hilferding in his influential study of 1910,[31] has been convincingly refuted.[32] Collaboration and common interests, rather than domination of one side characterized the relationship between big business and big banks; they were partners on roughly equal terms. That banks played a crucial role in the German industrializa-tion process, however, is hard to deny.

A major driving force behind German industrialization, railroads also transformed space in an unprecedented way. In the historical literature, this aspect is normally dealt with from the perspective of the integration of the domestic market and thus of nation building. There are, however, two other important spatial dimensions of the expansion of the railroad network, which need to be emphasized. First, railroads allowed for a pattern of industrialization, which was characterized by sharp regional differences in economic development.[33] The mining and the iron and steel industry were particularly heavily dependent on the existence of natural resources, especially coal and ore. Heavy industrial centers thus thrived in regions where these factors were abundantly available. In Germany, it was first and foremost the Ruhrgebiet, but also the Saar region and Upper Silesia, which made up the leading regions of industrial development whereas other parts of the country remained widely untouched by industrialization. The railroad, on the one hand, enforced the agglomeration of economic activity by con-necting the leading industrial regions with each other and with other 'industrial islands,' thus providing the necessary market for their products. On the other hand, economic concentration was fostered by the fact that railroads dramatically reduced the transport costs that previously had worked as 'natural tariffs' for regions of traditional industrial activity. Unable to compete with the 'new kids on the block,' these regions often were left bereft of significant economic activity.

Secondly, it has to be stressed that the integration of the national market, brought about by railroads not only in Germany, but everywhere in the second half of the nineteenth century, itself has to be seen as an integral and crucial part of economic globalization. Globalization and territorialization, understood as the increasing penetration of territorially demarcated political entities, therefore need not necessarily be conceived as opposing and historically incongruent processes.[34] Rather, they could interact in a multiplicity of ways, sometimes strongly mutually reinforcing one another. To give just a simple example, the sharp decline of costs for the transport of a bushel of wheat from a farm in Illinois to a German provincial town could be attributed only in part to the improvements in transcontinental shipping. The main decrease in price was made up by falling freight rates of railroads in Germany and the USA. The emerging world economy has to be understood as a result of these intertwining developments in national and international transportation.

For the German economy, the widening of economic space meant not only new chances, but also brought the pressure of new competitors. As everywhere else in western and middle Europe, German agriculture was the first traditional sector severely hit by globalization. From the early 1870s onward, German farmers literally were confronted with a grain invasion from overseas where agrarian exporters, due to cheap and fertile ground, were able to produce at much lower costs.[35] Prices went down dramatically as did the profits of German grain farmers who had been exporters of their goods before. Under the pressure of the new situation, the German Empire in 1879 embarked on a moderate protectionist policy which became more pronounced in the 1880s. Yet even if they were able to improve the situation of agriculture, the tariffs did not uncouple Germany from the international food market. Globalization, therefore, continued to put pressure on German farmers and thus promoted the industrial transformation of the German economy.

15.4

The second stage of the development of the German economy commenced around 1890 and lasted until the war broke out. It was marked by a change in the leading sectors of industrial growth and by a further speeding up of economic globalization, ushering in the *belle époque* of the world economy. During the 1870s and 1880s, the old leading sector complex of railroads and heavy industry increasingly lost its outstanding dynamic. The lead was taken over by 'new' industries, namely the chemical and electrical industry, which depended much more than earlier industries on systematic scientific research.

As to chemicals, industrial production on a large scale did not start until the 1860–1870s. In retrospect, this turned out to be an advantage since there had been little investment in outmoded technologies and German producers could choose the best technologies available. In Germany, for example, and unlike in Great Britain, there was not much capital bound up with the traditional Leblanc process of soda (sodium carbonate) production, which was the basis of many other inorganic chemical processes; German producers since 1880 thus could directly invest in the far more efficient and recently discovered Solvay process. As a result, German soda manufacturers within a few years became highly competitive on the international market. Already in 1884, Germany had switched from being a net importer to being a net exporter of soda, developing into the second largest exporter world wide only ten years later.[36]

Even more remarkable, however, was the success of the German chemical industry in the field of organic chemistry. Insignificant elsewhere, except in Switzerland, the organic branch of the German chemical industry had already by the end of the 1870s covered half of the world demand for synthetic dyestuffs. On the eve of World War I, this share had risen to almost 90 percent. Enjoying a world monopoly, German companies at the same time were heavily dependent on the global market. According to the statistics of three major players, the Badische Anilin-und Soda-Fabrik (BASF), Bayer and Agfa, the export business accounted for 82 percent of their turnover in dyestuffs in 1913. Wherever foreign tariffs or non-tariff barriers hindered the export of dyestuffs, the German chemical industry reacted by founding foreign subsidiaries. Particularly in France and Russia, but also in Great Britain and the United States, German dyestuff producers had launched substantial direct investments since the 1870s in order to circumvent real or expected trade obstacles, so that by 1914 all dyestuff companies had become truly multinational enterprises.[37]

Since laboratory experiments around synthetic dyes had enormous spin-off effects and the manufacture of pharmaceuticals, photographic materials, artificial fibers and explosives developed from there, the German chemical industry not only took the lead in the production of dyestuffs, but also in organic chemistry in general. Particularly in the field of medicinal drugs, besides the big players like Bayer and Hoechst, we find a number of medium size specialized manufacturers such as Schering, Knoll & Co., Merck or C. F. Böhringer. Together they made Germany the 'pharmacy of the world.' How much the other industrial countries were dependent on German chemicals became fully apparent after the outbreak of the First World War. Faced with the absence of the pre-war supply of German chemicals, British chemist William Henry Perkin in his presidential address to the Chemical Society in March 1915 deplored that 'it has long been our habit to import almost all our organic fine chemicals from Germany,' commenting further that 'it may indeed be said that

Germany has no competitor worth considering in the whole domain of organic chemical industry.'[38]

The crucial factor which enabled the chemical industry to meet the rapidly growing world demand in chemical products and to dominate international competition was the systematic planning and organization of large scale laboratory scientific research. The quasi monopoly in the world trade of organic chemicals was first and foremost a monopoly of knowledge, which was both reflected and ensured by the central position that scientists like Carl Duisberg occupied within the management of German firms. The most important advantage, however, that Germany's chemical industry enjoyed in comparison with companies in other countries was the availability of highly-trained scientific personnel. Only in Germany could companies rely on so steady and sufficient a supply of well trained scientific experts as was provided by the German universities and *Technische Hochschulen*.[39]

The amazing success of the German electrical industry in many ways paralleled the development of the chemical industry. Again, we can trace a tremendous growth of both output and people employed within the last decades of the nineteenth century, and see the crucial importance of Research and Development units and of academically educated personnel. Even more than the chemical industry, the German electrical industry up to 1914 experienced a rapid concentration process. In the case of the electrical industry, this development was fostered by the peculiarities of the market for electrical power, which in the beginning comprised mainly municipal lighting systems and municipal transport systems, and involved a huge amount of time and money in each contract, as well as heavy initial investments and a high degree of standardization. By the turn of the century, the German electrical industry was fully dominated by only two big players: Siemens-Schuckert, resulting from a merger of two companies in 1903, and the Allgemeine Elektricitäts-Gesellschaft (AEG), founded in 1883 by Emil Rathenau. Before the First World War, Siemens-Schuckert and AEG together accounted for three-quarters of the output of German electrical industry. Both companies maintained numerous foreign branch offices and in many ways acted like modern multinational enterprises. With 81,745 people employed (18,348 outside Germany), Siemens in 1913 was the largest electrical industry employer worldwide. On world export markets, and again parallel to the chemical industry, the German electrical industry after the turn of the century attained an unchallenged top position. In 1913, German electrical exports accounted for 46 percent of total world exports, twice as much as Britain and three times as much as the United States.[40]

Germany's ever-extending integration in the evolving world market increasingly put pressure on its trade policy. On the one hand, by the turn of the century, Germany had become highly dependent on the global economy. As to imports, a good deal of German industrial production relied on the supply of foreign raw materials and semi-finished products. As to exports, not only the stars of the chemical and electrical industries, but also many companies from the engineering and iron and steel branches sold a substantial share of their products outside Germany, thereby achieving econo-mies of scale which would not have been attainable on the comparatively small domestic market. On the other hand, the world market endangered other, less compet-itive industrial branches and, above all, agriculture. Here, the situation even worsened at the end of the century. Whereas before mainly grain farmers were effected, now large amounts of meat from overseas, which could more easily be transported due to improvements in refrigeration, began to enter the European market. Under these preconditions, the political dilemma of trade was obvious: whereas the maintenance of exports and high speed industrialization demanded a trade regime that was as liberal as possible, the agrarian pressure groups vigorously called for protection from the forces of the global economy. After years of harsh political conflicts, the case was settled with the so called Bülow tariff of 1902, a classic compromise that, however, evoked little enthusiasm on either side. Agriculture was awarded a notable increase in protection, which established German prices for agricultural goods significantly above the world market level. Protectionism, though, was not increased to the point where it could severely hamper German export by provoking retaliatory measures from other countries.[41]

Among historians and social scientists, there has been a long and still ongoing discussion on the question of whether in Germany a distinct model of capitalism had begun to evolve in the 1880s. The proponents of this view claim that in Germany toward the end of the nineteenth century, a new and stable production regime had developed, which in the 1970s was called 'organized capitalism'[42] and is now commonly referred to as a 'coordinated market economy' or 'corporatism'. The German model of capitalism is regularly contrasted with an Anglo-Saxon style 'liberal market economy,' with its strong commitment to the principle of unimpeded competition. Two overriding elements characterize the 'coordinated market economy.' First, it is domi-nated by big economic players—large scale, vertically integrated enterprises and uni-versal banks—who interact less in a spirit of competition, but in one of collaboration and co-operation. To a significant extent, the components of this production system, such as sales syndicates and export cartels emerged as a reaction to the economic crisis since 1873. The same applied to business associations and pressure groups, which gained increasing influence in the realm of politics. On the enterprise level, the German model of capitalism was reflected by the dual structure at the top level of joint-stock corporations. Whereas the management board exerted the operational control, the supervisory board was used to build up networks by appointing external representa-tives, above all from the investing banks, thus facilitating long-term modes of financing. All in all, the German production regime is said to have been 'based on long-term perspective and cooperation.'[43]

The second element of the 'coordinated market economy' is the strong and active state. State influence, however, is less exerted as fairly erratic direct interventions in economic processes, but in the form of a macro-economic frame working through infrastructure and legislation. Again, the economic downturn of the 1870s worked as a trigger here. The swing toward protectionism can be directly related to the depression and the concurring agricultural crisis. In the 1880s, the foundations of the welfare state were laid with the introduction of social insurance schemes for health (1883), accidents (1884), and both invalidity and old age (1889). The nationalization of the railroads in Prussia from the late 1870s onward enabled the Prussian government to open up peripheral regions and thus to pursue classical infrastructure policy. Important parts of the educational system, as already mentioned, were geared toward the requirements of the private economy. According to Werner Abelshauser and others who argue that there was a German model of capitalism, these discrete components fit together tightly and allowed for Germany's tremendous economic success before the First World War. What is more, Abelshauser uncovers strong continuities of German capitalism and makes them an important element in his explanation of the economic miracle after World War II.[44]

This argument, however, has received serious criticism. First and foremost, it has to be asked if the depiction of a corporatist industrial system does not ignore major regional differences and thus falsely reduces German industrialization to only one 'German model.' Gary Herrigel has argued that not one, but 'two distinct, parallel, and internationally competitive systems of industrial organization and practice, located in different regions, have characterized the German experience at all levels of the economy and society since the very onset of industrialization'.[45] The first regional system, which he calls 'autarkic industrial order,' resembles in many ways the model of 'organized capitalism.' It evolved in agricultural regions like the Ruhrgebiet where enterprises had to compensate for the lack of a surrounding infrastructure by incorporating most of the stages of manufacturing and thus developed into large, vertically integrated combines. The second regional system which he refers to as a'decentralized form of industrial order' is based on a dense network of highly specialized small and medium-sized industrial firms, which together with local governments created their own savings, and co-operative banks and institutions. Industry, in this case, could rely on a pre-industrial infrastructure of handicraft and smallholder property. According to Herrigel, both regional distinct patterns of industrial development had paralleled one another throughout the nineteenth and twentieth century, and have to be consistently taken into consideration in the analysis of the German economy.

Even if there were substantial regional differences in the organization of German industrial production, however, this does not deny that the above-mentioned features of 'organized capitalism' earmarked an important part of the German economy and set it apart from other production regimes. It is a rather different question, though, if this is enough to refer to the German system as a particular 'model of capitalism.' A familiar, but nevertheless convincing objection to the *Sonderweg* interpretation of German history seems to apply also here: there are as many particular ways of industrialization or evolving models of capitalism as there are industrializing countries. Moreover, the construction of different models of capitalism runs the danger of obscuring the elements and dynamics which all capitalist economies have in common. Rather than confronting two different models of capitalism, it seems to be more appropriate to understand the German case as one point on the continuum of possible shapes capitalism is able to take.

15.5

The social consequences of the profound transformations the German economy went through in the second half of the nineteenth century are so manifold and far reaching that they can be only superficially touched on here. As in other countries, industrialization in Germany was accompanied by a shift in generative behavior—away from a society with high birth and death rates toward low fertility and mortality. Since this 'demographic transition' took some time—during which mortality decreased, while fertility remained stable—Germany in the decades before the First World War experienced a population boom, boosting the German population from 35.3 million in 1850 to 67.0 million in 1913.[46] The resulting population pressure worked as the most important push factor causing several waves of mass emigration, which drove millions of Germans mostly to North America after the middle of the nineteenth century. Due to Germany's rapid industrialization with its expanding labor demand, this situation changed dramatically in the 1880–1890s. From being a country of emigration, Germany within a couple of years switched to become a destination of immigration for migrants from Eastern Europe. Even more important in terms of quantity was the internal migration that amounted to a mass movement from agrarian eastern Germany to Berlin and the industrial centers in middle and west Germany.[47] The mass migration from the agrarian regions to the cities contributed heavily to Germany's urbanization, which experienced its 'take-off' together with industrialization around the middle of the nineteenth century. Whereas in the newly-founded German Empire, the urban population accounted only for 36.1 percent of the population, this share had risen to 60 percent by 1910. During the same time, the number of large cities with more than 200,000 inhabitants increased from three to twenty-three. However, urbanization did not only mean quantitative growth. It also implied a qualitative change in the life style of the urban population, new social problems, and multiple other unprecedented challenges which the municipal administrations in Germany by and large met by building up effective urban infrastructures.[48]

Turning to the internal structure of the German society, it is evident that economic interests and conflicts became increasingly important. The first and major societal change entailed by industrial capitalism was the advent of class society. According to Max Weber, in contrast to status groups (*Stände*), classes are formed by people who share the same economic position and interests, based on the marketability of their skills or property.[49] More and more, after the middle of the nineteenth century, the income, the living conditions and the prestige of an individual came to depend on his position in economic markets. This is neither to deny the long-lasting legacies of the society of the *ancien régime*, such as the enduring privileges of the nobility. Nor does it mean to underestimate the importance of non-class differences such as gender, confession, or region. In general, however, the trend toward class formation as the dominating principle of society is all too clear. It can be followed in the emergence of classes of urban professionals with their own associations and market strategies, as well as in the countryside where landed gentry and peasants developed into capitalist farmers and the diverse categories of agricultural labor, remaining differences notwithstanding, became increasingly a landed proletariat.

The most important and politically relevant development, though, was the evolving antagonism between the capitalist bourgeoisie and the rapidly growing industrial working class.[50] There is no need to downplay the sharp differences between the diverse groups of industrial workers. In terms of payment, mentality, and lifestyle there was a huge divide between the 'aristocracy' of skilled workers, and the mass of unskilled and day laborers. In the long run, however, the homogenizing effects of class formation prevailed. Among them, the everyday experiences of physically exertive labor and subordination on the factory floor loomed large. The dwelling in particular working-class quarters, sharply segregated from the residential districts of the middle classes, and the emergence of a proletarian subculture with its own clubs, associations, and habits formed another relevant class building force. Most important, however, was the political sphere. Since the mid-1860s, strikes became the dominant form of conflict between industrial employers and workers. Strikes and lockouts massively fostered the politicization of workers and the emergence of a proletarian class consciousness. In strikes, workers became aware of their common interests, practiced proletarian solidarity, and could experience the repressive power of the employer-friendly 'class state.' No less important for class formation as well as its manifestation was the emergence of trade unions and of an extremely well organized Social Democratic Party. Earlier than elsewhere, Germany witnessed the creation and development of a separate working-class party with a Marxist and strictly anti-capitalist ideology. The government reacted with discrimination, exclusion and Anti-Socialist laws remaining in force from 1878 until 1890 and designed to prosecute the 'enemies of the Reich' ('*Reichsfeinde*') with state repression. All this fueled the class consciousness of an ever growing mass of workers and contributed to their identification with the German Social Democratic Party, which, even if its revolutionary potential was limited, remained in strong opposition to the established political system until World War I. It was this social and political situation, which caused the political economist, Johannes Conrad, to deplore in 1906 the 'lamentable class differences which in Germany are sharper than in every other nation of culture.'[51]

To the ruptures of German class society, globalization added two further socio-economic cleavages. In both cases, agrarian producers were pitted against other important segments of German economy and society. The first gap that opened up under the pressure of increasing world wide economic integration was that between agriculture and industry. The 'marriage of iron and rye,' as the alliance of heavy industrialists and agrarians came to be known, had been decisive in the Bismarckian shift to protectionism at the end of the 1870s. However, already by the beginning of the 1890s, it had been shattered in the conflicts over the Caprivi trade treaties, while at the turn of the century efforts to re-establish the old coalition were wrecked in prolonged fights over the Bülow tariff. Neither light industry, nor the likewise export-oriented West-German heavy industry, as it turned out, were ready to support the drastic rise of agricultural protectionism that the agrarian pressure groups vigorously called for and that would have had the potential to ruin German export opportunities by provoking foreign retaliations.[52]

The second socio-economic rift brought upon by globalization emerged between agrarian producers and urban consumers. In the election campaigns for the German *Reichstag* between 1890 and 1903, this latent antagonism of economic interests increasingly became loaded politically. At the same time, tariffs and trade policy moved into the very heart of German politics. More and more, the German government lost its capacity to set agendas, as the propaganda machines on the extreme political right and left came to determine election issues. On the one side of the political spectrum, the still influential agrarian interest groups pounded their drums for walling off German agriculture from the international market; on the other, the Social Democrats launched their powerful protest against the 'hunger tariff' (*'Hungerzölle'*) and thereby succeeded in establishing themselves as the central party of urban consumers.[53]

All in all, due to the forces of industrialization and globalization, the lines drawn by economic interests increasingly structured German society and politics in the decades before the First World War. As a result, an accelerating mutual penetration of the realms of politics and economics can be traced. Deep socio-economic cleavages divided German pre-war society. Why did these growing tensions not have the potential to fundamentally destabilize the German Empire? The answer is two-fold. First, despite the continuing structures of inequality and despite the growing distance between the classes, German society as a whole experienced a significant increase in its standard of living. This trickle-down effect of economic growth can be followed in the rise of real wages, which for industrial workers nearly doubled between 1871 and 1913.[54] Together with the reduction in working hours, this not only meant a considerable material improvement, it also fuelled the expectation of most workers that things were becoming better, albeit slowly, and gave them reason to set their hopes on reforming the existing system. Secondly, the emerging active state played a role in cushioning some of the worst blows of economic development. This applied to the accomplishments of the municipal administrations and to the achievements of the early welfare state, both of which contributed to enhance the lot of the urban working classes. However, it also pertained to protectionism, which curbed the effects of globalization on agriculture, a sector that still employed almost forty percent of the German workforce at the turn of the century. As a result, when Germany went to war in 1914, it did so with a fractured, but stable society.

Notes

1. Carlo M. Cipolla, 'Die Industrielle Revolution in der Weltgeschichte,' in id. and Knut Borchardt (ed.), *Europäische Wirtschaftsgeschichte*, vol. 3 (Stuttgart: UTB, 1985), 1.
2. See also Patrick K. O'Brien, 'Introduction,' in id., *Industrialisation. Critical Perspectives on the World Economy*, vol. 1 (London: Routledge, 1998), XIII.
3. See Jürgen Osterhammel, *Die Verwandlung der Welt. Eine Geschichte des 19. Jahrhunderts* (Munich: C. H. Beck, 2009), 910.
4. See Dieter Ziegler, *Die Industrielle Revolution* (Darmstadt: Wissenschaftliche Buchgesellschaft, 2005), 11.
5. See Sidney Pollard, *Peaceful Conquest. The Industrialization of Europe, 1760–1970* (Oxford: Oxford University Press, 1981); id., (ed.), *Region und Industrialisierung. Studien zur Rolle der Region in der Wirtschaftsgeschichte der letzten zwei Jahrhunderte* (Göttingen: Vandenhoeck & Ruprecht, 1980); Hubert Kiesewetter and Rainer Fremdling, (eds), *Staat, Region und Industrialisierung* (Ostfildern: Scripta-Mercaturae-Verlag, 1985).
6. Fernand Braudel, *Civilization and Capitalism*, 3 vols (New York: Harper & Row, 1981/1984/1982); Immanuel Wallerstein, *The Modern World System*, 3 vols (New York: Academic Press, 1974/1980/1989).
7. Cf. Kevin H. O'Rourke and Jeffrey G. Williamson, *Globalization and History. The Evolution of a Nineteenth-Century Atlantic Economy* (Cambridge, MA: MIT, 1999); Kevin H. O'Rourke and Jeffrey G. Williamson, 'When Did Globalisation Begin?,' *European Review of Economic History* 6 (2002), 23–50; Harold James, *The End of Globalization. Lessons from the Great Depression* (Cambridge, MA: Harvard University Press, 2001); Cornelius Torp, 'Weltwirtschaft vor dem Weltkrieg. Die erste Welle ökonomischer Globalisierung vor 1914,' *Historische Zeitschrift* 279 (2004), 561–609.
8. Cf. Ziegler, *Industrielle Revolution*, 1–5.
9. Jürgen Kocka, *Das lange 19. Jahrhundert. Arbeit, Nation und bürgerliche Gesellschaft* (Stuttgart: Klett-Cotta, 2001), 45; Table 1 and beyond.
10. Ibid.
11. Cf. Reinhard Spree, *Wachstumstrends und Konjunkturzyklen in der deutschen Wirtschaft von 1820 bis 1913. Quantitativer Rahmen für eine Konjunkturgeschichte des 19. Jahrhunderts* (Göttingen: Vandenhoeck & Ruprecht, 1978); id., *Die Wachstumszyklen der deutschen Wirtschaft von 1840 bis 1880* (Berlin: Duncker & Humblot, 1977).
12. Cf. Hans Rosenberg, *Große Depression und Bismarckzeit. Wirtschaftsablauf, Gesellschaft und Politik in Mitteleuropa* (Berlin: de Gruyter, 1967).
13. My own calculations follow Carl-Ludwig Holtfrerich, 'The Growth of Net Domestic Product in Germany 1850–1913,' in Rainer Fremdling and Patrick K. O'Brien (eds), *Productivity in the Economies of Europe* (Stuttgart: Klett-Cotta, 1983), 124–132, here 130.

14. Holtfrerich, 'Growth,' 130; Walter G. Hoffmann et al., *Das Wachstum der deutschen Wirtschaft seit der Mitte des 19. Jahrhunderts* (Berlin: Springer, 1965), 392 f.

15. Walt W. Rostow, *The Stages of Economic Growth. A Non-Communist Manifesto* (Cambridge: Cambridge University Press, 1960).

16. Toni Pierenkemper, *Umstrittene Revolutionen. Industrialisierung im 19. Jahrhundert* (Frankfurt: Fischer, 1996), 96.

17. William Arthur Lewis, 'The Rate of Growth of World Trade, 1830–1973,' in Sven Grassman and Erik Lundberg (eds), *The World Economic Order. Past and Prospects* (London: Macmillan, 1981), 11–81, here 48.

18. For all figures see Cornelius Torp, *Die Herausforderung der Globalisierung. Wirtschaft und Politik in Deutschland, 1860–1914* (Göttingen: Vandenhoeck & Ruprecht, 2005), 85–95.

19. Cf. Walt W. Rostow, 'Leading Sectors and the Take-off,' in id. (ed.), *The Economics of Take-off into Sustained Growth* (London: Macmillan, 1963), 1–21; Toni Pierenkemper, *Wirtschaftsgeschichte* (Munich: Oldenbourg, 2005), 128–132.

20. Cf. Ziegler, *Industrielle Revolution*, 63–71.

21. Hans-Ulrich Wehler, *Deutsche Gesellschaftsgeschichte*, vol. 3 (Munich: C. H. Beck, 1995), 81 f.; Alan S. Milward and S. B. Saul, *The Development of the Economies of Continental Europe 1850–1914* (London: George Allen & Unwin, 1977), 21.

22. Richard H. Tilly, *Vom Zollverein zum Industriestaat. Die wirtschaftlich-soziale Entwicklung Deutschlands 1834 bis 1914* (Munich: dtv, 1990), 49.

23. Ziegler, *Industrielle Revolution*, 53.

24. Hoffmann et al., *Wachstum*, 143, 44.

25. Cf. Rainer Fremdling, 'Railroads and German Economic Growth: A Leading Sector Analysis with a Comparison to the United States and Great Britain,' *Journal of Economic History* 37 (1977), 583–604. Cf. also the input-output table in id., *Technologischer Wandel und internationaler Handel im 18. und 19. Jahrhundert. Die Eisenindustrien in Großbritannien, Belgien, Frankreich und Deutschland* (Berlin: Duncker & Humblot, 1986), 336.

26. Ziegler, *Industrielle Revolution*, 69.

27. Wehler, *Gesellschaftsgeschichte*, vol. 3, 79 f.

28. Wilfried Feldenkirchen, *Die Eisen- und Stahlindustrie des Ruhrgebiets, 1879–1914. Wachstum, Finanzierung und Struktur ihrer Großunternehmen* (Wiesbaden: Steiner, 1982), 232.

29. Torp, *Herausforderung*, 111–120. Cf. Steven B. Webb, 'Tariffs, Cartels, Technology, and Growth in the German Steel Industry, 1879 to 1914,' *Journal of Economic History* 40 (1980), 309–329; Ulrich Wengenroth, *Unternehmensstrategien und technischer Fortschritt. Die deutsche und die britische Stahlindustrie 1865–1895* (Göttingen: Vandenhoeck & Ruprecht, 1986).

30. For the following argumentation see Tilly, *Zollverein*, 59–66; Ziegler, *Industrielle Revolution*, 79–84; Wehler, *Gesellschaftsgeschichte*, vol. 3, 85–91, 628–632.

31. Rudolf Hilferding, *Financial Capital. A Study of the Latest Phase of Capitalist Development (1910)* (London: Routledge, 1981).

32. Volker Wellhöner, *Großbanken und Großindustrie im Kaiserreich* (Göttingen: Vandenhoeck & Ruprecht, 1989).

33. Ziegler, *Industrielle Revolution*, 84–93; Toni Pierenkemper (ed.), *Die Industrialisierung europäischer Montanregionen im 19. Jahrhundert* (Stuttgart: Steiner, 2002); Rainer Fremdling and Richard Tilly (eds), *Industrialisierung und Raum. Studien zur regionalen Differenzierung im Deutschland des 19. Jahrhunderts* (Stuttgart: Klett-Cotta, 1979); Kiesewetter and Fremdling (eds), *Staat*; Pollard (ed.), *Region*.

34. As it is regularly done in the debate on territorialization and globalization, cf. Charles S. Maier, 'Consigning the Twentieth Century to History. Alternative Narratives for the Modern Era,' *American Historical Review* 105 (2000), 807–831.

35. See Kevin H. O'Rourke, 'The European Grain Invasion, 1870–1913' *Journal of Economic History* 57 (1997), 775–801; Thomas Nipperdey, *Deutsche Geschichte, 1866–1918*, vol. 1 (Munich: C. H. Beck, 1990), 203 ff.

36. See Milward and Saul, *Development*, 32 f.; Christian Schallermaier, 'Die deutsche Sodaindustrie und die Entwicklung des deutschen Sodaaußenhandels 1872–1913,' *Vierteljahrschrift für Sozial-und Wirtschaftsgeschichte* 84 (1997), 33–67.

37. See Gottfried Plumpe, *Die I. G. Farbenindustrie AG. Wirtschaft, Technik und Politik 1904–1945* (Berlin: Duncker & Humblot, 1990), 50 ff.; Ludwig Fritz Haber, *The Chemical Industry, 1900–1930. International Growth and Technological Change* (Oxford: Clarendon Press, 1971), 108 ff.; Torp, *Herausforderung*, 104–107.

38. William Henry Perkin, 'The Position of the Organic Chemical Industry,' *Journal of the Chemical Society. Transactions* 107 (1915), 557–578, here 558.

39. See Tilly, *Zollverein*, 95–101; Milward and Saul, *Development*, 32–35; Walter Wetzel, *Naturwissenschaften und chemische Industrie in Deutschland. Voraussetzungen und Mechanismen ihres Aufstiegs im 19. Jahrhundert* (Stuttgart: Steiner, 1991).

40. Wilfried Feldenkirchen, *Siemens 1918–1945* (Munich: Piper, 1995), 44, 456, 647 (table 2), 662 (table 20). Cf. id., 'Foreign Investments in the German Electrical Industry,' in Hans Pohl (ed.), *Transnational Investment from the 19th Century to the Present* (Stuttgart: Steiner, 1994), 117–151.

41. See Cornelius Torp, 'Erste Globalisierung und deutscher Protektionismus' in id. and Sven Oliver Müller (eds), *Das Deutsche Kaiserreich in der Kontroverse* (Göttingen: Vandenhoeck & Ruprecht, 2009), 422–440.

42. Heinrich August Winkler (ed.), *Organisierter Kapitalismus. Voraussetzungen und Anfänge* (Göttingen: Vandenhoeck & Ruprecht, 1974).

43. Werner Abelshauser, *The Dynamics of German Industry. Germany's Path Toward the New Economy and the American Challenge* (New York: Berghahn Books, 2005); Wehler, *Gesellschaftsgeschichte*, vol. 3, 662–680.

44. See Werner Abelshauser, *Deutsche Wirtschaftsgeschichte seit 1945* (Munich: C. H. Beck, 2004), 84.

45. Gary Herrigel, *Industrial Constructions. The Sources of German Industrial Power* (Cambridge: Cambridge University Press, 1996), 1. Cf. Richard H. Tilly, 'Gab es und gibt es ein 'deutsches Modell' der Wirtschaftsentwicklung?' in Jürgen Osterhammel et al. (eds), *Wege der Gesellschaftsgeschichte* (Göttingen: Vandenhoeck & Ruprecht, 2006), 219–237.

46. Hoffmann et al., *Wachstum*, 172–74. See Wehler, *Gesellschaftsgeschichte*, vol. 3, 7–11, 493–503; Peter Marschalck, *Bevölkerungsgeschichte Deutschlands im 19. und 20. Jahrhundert* (Frankfurt: Suhrkamp, 1984).

47. See Friedrich Lenger and Dieter Langewiesche, 'Internal Migration: Persistence and Mobility,' in Klaus J. Bade (ed.), *Population, Labour and Migration in 19th and 20th*

Century Germany (Leamington Spa: Berg, 1987), 87–100; Klaus J. Bade, *Migration in European History* (Malden/Mass.: Blackwell, 2003).

48. See Wehler, *Gesellschaftsgeschichte*, vol. 3, 11–37, 510–545.

49. Max Weber, *Wirtschaft und Gesellschaft. Grundriß der verstehenden Soziologie*, 5th edn (Tübingen: Mohr, 1980), 531 ff.

50. For the following paragraph see Wehler, *Gesellschaftsgeschichte*, vol. 3, 772–804; Jürgen Kocka, *Arbeitsverhältnisse und Arbeiterexistenzen. Grundlagen der Klassenbildung im 19. Jahrhundert* (Bonn: Dietz, 1990); Gerhard A. Ritter and Klaus Tenfelde, *Arbeiter im Deutschen Kaiserreich 1871 bis 1914* (Bonn: Dietz, 1992); Klaus Tenfelde, 'Germany' in Marcel van der Linden and Jürgen Rohjan (eds), *The Formation of Labour Movements, 1870–1914. An International Perspective* (Leiden: Brill, 1990), 243–269; Thomas Welskopp, *Das Banner der Brüderlichkeit. Die deutsche Sozialdemokratie vom Vormärz bis zum Sozialistengesetz* (Bonn: Dietz, 2000).

51. Johannes Conrad, 'Einige Ergebnisse der deutschen Universitätsstatistik,' *Jahrbücher für Nationalökonomie und Statistik* 87 (1906), 433–492, here 484.

52. See Cornelins Torp. 'The "Coalition of Rye and Iron" under Pressure of Globalization. A Reinterpretation of Germany's Political Economy before 1914,' *Central European History* 43 (2010), 401–427.

53. See Jonathan Sperber, *The Kaiser's Voters. Electors and Elections in Imperial Germany* (Cambridge: Cambridge University Press, 1997), 212–40; Brett Fairbairn, *Democracy in the Undemocratic State. The German Reichstag Elections of 1898 and 1903* (Toronto: University of Toronto Press, 1997), 45–68, 209–40.

54. Wehler, *Gesellschaftsgeschichte*, vol. 3, 776.

BIBLIOGRAPHY

ABELSHAUSER, WERNER, *The Dynamics of German Industry. Germany's Path Toward the New Economy and the American Challenge* (New York: Berghahn Books, 2005).

BERGHAHN, VOLKER R., *Imperial Germany, 1871–1914: Economy, Society, Culture, and Politics* (New York: Berghahn Books, 1994).

FREMDLING, RAINER, *Technologischer Wandel und internationaler Handel im 18. und 19. Jahrhundert. Die Eisenindustrien in Großbritannien, Belgien, Frankreich und Deutschland* (Berlin: Duncker & Humblot, 1986).

HERRIGEL, GARY, *Industrial Constructions. The Sources of German Industrial Power* (Cambridge: Cambridge University Press, 1996).

KOCKA, JÜRGEN, *Industrial Culture and Bourgeois Society. Business, Labor, and Bureaucracy in Modern Germany, 1800–1918* (New York: Berghahn Books, 1999).

MILWARD, ALAN S., and S. B. SAUL, *The Development of the Economies of Continental Europe 1850–1914* (London: George Allen & Unwin, 1977).

O'BRIEN, PATRICK (ed.), *Industrialisation. Critical Perspectives on the World Economy*, 4 vols (London: Routledge, 1998).

O'ROURKE, KEVIN H., and JEFFREY G. WILLIAMSON, *Globalization and History. The Evolution of a Nineteenth-Century Atlantic Economy* (Cambridge, MA: MIT, 1999).

PIERENKEMPER, TONI, *Umstrittene Revolutionen. Industrialisierung im 19. Jahrhundert* (Frankfurt: Fischer, 1996).

—— (ed.), *Die Industrialisierung europäischer Montanregionen im 19. Jahrhundert* (Stuttgart: Steiner, 2002).

—— and RICHARD TILLY, *The German Economy during the Nineteenth Century* (New York: Berghahn Books, 2004).

TORP, CORNELIUS, *Die Herausforderung der Globalisierung. Wirtschaft und Politik in Deutschland, 1860–1914* (Göttingen: Vandenhoeck & Ruprecht, 2005).

WEHLER, HANS-ULRICH, *Deutsche Gesellschaftsgeschichte*, vol. 3 (Munich: C. H. Beck, 1995).

ZIEGLER, DIETER, *Die Industrielle Revolution* (Darmstadt: Wissenschaftliche Buchgesellschaft, 2005).

CHAPTER 16

....

RACE AND WORLD POLITICS: GERMANY IN THE AGE OF IMPERIALISM, 1878–1914

....

ANDREW ZIMMERMAN

BOTH transnational processes and national particularities shaped the politics of race in the German *Kaiserreich*.[1] Racism and concepts of race emerged from an unequal, regionally varying, and international division of labor inside Europe and the United States and in those regions around the world over which Europe and the United States came to exercise formal and informal imperial power. In the late nineteenth century, various types of European and American racial thinking came increasingly to influence each other, as certain local racial divisions of labor became paradigms imitated by several imperial and colonial powers, and the racial politics that a state exercised in one region came to influence the racial politics that that state exercised in other regions. Germany developed a unique Central-European politics of race in the contested Polish provinces of the Prussian East, annexed in the eighteenth-century partitions of Poland. Many Germans regarded Poles as deficient in *Kultur*, a concept signifying everything from diligent work habits to a secular rationality supposedly absent among Catholic Poles. Early German racism was thus cultural rather than biological and was promoted by progressive bourgeois, rather than by backward gentry. The liberal self-understanding of Germans as a cultural people, or *Kulturvolk*, engaged in a world-historical struggle for culture, or *Kulturkampf*, also influenced German overseas imperialism. In its empire, Germany further pioneered a colonial adaptation of the unique racial politics of the American New South and took part in the international racial politics of employing Chinese contract, or 'coolie,' laborers. Each of these local and transnational racial politics influenced each other to produce a uniquely German mixture, one that itself in turn further shaped transnational racial politics.

16.1 *KULTURKAMPF* AND *NATURVÖLKER*

The legal campaign that the Kingdom of Prussia undertook in the 1870s against its Catholic subjects constituted the first major instance in which German policy followed the racist logic of specifying and subordinating elements of a population as minorities.[2] These anti-Catholic politics provide an important example of a racism based principally on culture, rather than on biology, and rooted in liberalism, rather than in conservatism or rightist authoritarianism. The common assumption that biological accounts of human difference are racist, while cultural accounts are liberal and anti-racist sets up a series of unwarranted binary oppositions that have clouded historical understandings of racism, culture, and liberalism.[3] Understandings of German history have been especially plagued by these binaries because of attempts, after the Second World War, to create a useable past that would absolve German liberals of responsibility for recent German atrocities, and also, in the Cold War struggle against Communism, absolve European and American liberalism more broadly, of responsibility for racism, imperialism, and nationalism.[4]

The liberal parliamentarian, professor of medicine, and anthropologist Rudolf Virchow declared the Prussian anti-Catholic campaign a *Kulturkampf*, or 'struggle for civilization.' Catholicism, Virchow explained to the Prussian House of Deputies, since it had become 'subservient to the Jesuit spirit,' was, 'absolutely incompatible with the *Kultur* whose bearers we believe ourselves to be.' The 1873 'May laws' that gave the state authority over the choice of priests thus required clergy to pass a 'culture exam' in history, philosophy, and German literature. Virchow described an 'opposition of Papism and the modern world' in which Catholicism opposed 'natural science, with its formalism and its oppression of every free direction of the spirit.'[5] Virchow and other German liberals did not abandon their political principles to support the *Kulturkampf*; the *Kulturkampf* was, as Michael Gross has argued, a realization of their liberal principles.[6] These attempts to subordinate the allegedly unmodern Catholic Church to the supposedly modern German state reconciled many liberals to the project of German unification under the Prussian monarchy.

The German anti-Catholic campaigns differed from similar struggles between the secular state and the Catholic Church in other European nations because of the central role played in Germany by racist anxieties about the Polish portions of the Prussian East.[7] While today most would regard Poles as an ethnicity, rather than a race, it was not uncommon in the years before the First World War to conceive of Poles and other 'ethnic' groups as biological 'races.' Posen and West Prussia, eastern provinces of Prussia that had been part of Poland, had large and, in many areas, majority Polish populations. Bismarck later described his interest in the *Kulturkampf* as related 'overwhelmingly' to 'its Polish aspect.'[8] As Bismarck gradually ended the *Kulturkampf* laws after 1878, he intensified the anti-Polish politics that lay at the heart of his anti-Catholic efforts. Between 1883 and 1885 Bismarck ordered the expulsion of around thirty-two-thousand Poles, both Jewish and Catholic, who did not possess Prussian citizenship.[9] In 1886, the Prussian House of Deputies authorized the Ministry of Agriculture to establish a Settlement Commission (*Ansiedlungskomission*) 'to strengthen the German element in the provinces of West Prussia and Posen against Polonizing efforts.'[10] The Settlement Commission purchased large estates to divide into small plots for German settlers in a program they referred to as 'internal colonization.'[11]

Anti-Polish racism remained a lasting legacy of the *Kulturkampf* because it proved essential to the political economy of German agriculture. Anti-Polish racism both reflected and supported the existence of an especially disempowered Polish rural proletariat, subject to oppression and exploitation by German landlords. By the last decades of the nineteenth century, more than half of these landlords were bourgeois, rather than the rustic *Krautjunker* of popular imagination. The famous *Oktoberedikt* of 1807 had not only ended serfdom, but had also opened land ownership to all social classes.[12] Polish workers had long been important to the agricultural economy of eastern Prussia. With the mass emigration of Germans from this region to the United States and elsewhere in the 1880s, these Polish laborers became even more economically important and, with Bismarck's expulsion of Poles without Prussian citizenship in the same decade, ever more scarce.[13] After 1890, the Prussian government permitted landlords to recruit seasonal laborers from Russian and Austrian Poland. The Prussian state carefully regulated these seasonal migrants to ensure that they did not settle in Germany, and landlords welcomed them as especially '*willig und billig*' (willing and cheap) laborers, especially for the backbreaking work of sugar beet cultivation. The Prussian state created a racially bifurcated situation in the Prussian East, with settled Germans serving as a bulwark against Polish migrants and a counterweight to resident Poles.

Many Germans applied the ideological concepts of the *Kulturkampf*, the 'struggle for civilization,' to their overseas colonial efforts. In part, this is simply because German imperialists, like their European and American counterparts, understood their actions overseas as part of a 'civilizing mission.' Before the turn of the century, however, German understandings of racial and cultural difference did not rest on concepts of gradual evolution, such as those put forth in the anthropology of the British scholar E.B. Tylor, but rather on a fundamental distinction between nature and culture. For German anthropologists, culture was not a universal human property, but rather the exclusive possession of Europeans and other 'historical peoples' or 'cultural peoples' (*Kulturvölker*). Africa, the Pacific Islands, and much of the rest of the world was a static realm of natural peoples (*Naturvölker*) and natural resources. Natural peoples were natural both because they did not change historically and because they could not transform nature with science and technology.[14] The division between what we would call race and culture did not apply to the *Naturvölker*, whose language, customs, and artifacts existed in the same natural register as their flesh and bones. The German colonial *Kulturkampf* did not seek to bring *Kultur* to the natural peoples, but rather to subjugate and control colonial nature for the benefit of European *Kultur*. Even the most obtuse anthropologists recognized that the very contact that made knowledge of supposedly natural peoples possible also changed these societies and made them, by definition, unnatural. Anthropologists preserved the concept of nature by regarding historical change in most societies as pathological, as decline rather than development. Anthropologists normally sought to correct for the signs of historical change by focusing on artifacts and body parts, which they regarded as less susceptible to corruption than customs, mores, or language.

German world politics included not only the colonies in Africa and the Pacific over which Germany claimed formal sovereignty after 1884, but also a longer, broader, and deeper history of German involvement overseas. German physicians served in the Dutch East Indies and in other colonial services. German missionaries evangelized much of the world, well before formal German colonialism and well beyond the later political boundaries of the German empire. Similarly, German merchants and shipping companies, especially operating out of Hamburg and Bremen, played an enormous role in the global economy of imperialism. By 1880, for example, Hamburg alone handled nearly a third of all overseas trade with West Africa.[15] Germany also played a central role in establishing formal European state sovereignty over Africa, beginning with the West Africa Conference held in Otto von Bismarck's Berlin residence in the late fall and winter of 1884–1885, presided over by the German *Reichskanzler*. By the time of this conference, Germany had already established protectorates in Southwest Africa (present-day Namibia), Togo, and Cameroon. On February 27, the day after the Berlin conference closed, the German East Africa Company, headed by the infamously brutal Carl Peters, received imperial status, making present-day mainland Tanzania, Rwanda, and Burundi the fourth German protectorate in Africa. Germany also took Pacific island colonies in the 1880s and after, building, as in Africa, on decades of previous involvement by German merchants. These included northeast New Guinea, the Solomon Islands, the Marshall Islands, Western Samoa, the Caroline Islands, and the Mariana Islands. The German Navy also controlled the Shandong Peninsula of China as a base for its operations in the Pacific Ocean. Germany further pursued an informal empire in the Middle East by cultivating commercial ties with, and offering military training to, the Ottoman Empire, and undertaking the Berlin-Baghdad railroad project.

Germans continued to understand colonialism in terms taken from the *Kulturkampf*, even after they adopted new international racial concepts around the turn of the century. The elections of 1906–1907, called when the Catholic Center Party broke with the German government over colonial scandals, allowed German liberals to resume the rhetoric of the *Kulturkampf*, this time, however, playing on national, colonial, and confessional connotations of the term *Kultur*. By appointing the liberal banker Bernhard Dernburg to head German colonial policy, Kaiser Wilhelm II indicated a new commitment to a colonial civilizing mission, a move rewarded by active political support from the professor of economics Gustav Schmoller and other leading German social scientists in the *Verein für Sozialpolitik*.[16] The largest liberal party, the National Liberals, viewed the struggle over colonies in the 1906–1907 campaign as in part a struggle against an ultramontane 'second government, working through the Center Party and its leaders.'[17] Nonetheless, as Winfried Becker has shown, Catholic critics of colonialism accepted the overseas 'cultural mission' of Germany, as much as the colonial politicians whom they criticized.[18] Only the orthodox Marxists in the Social Democratic Party of Germany, the largest party in the nation, rejected the very premise of a colonial cultural mission. Karl Kautsky, the leading theoretician in the party, explained in 1907 that Social Democrats should never endorse 'the right of peoples of higher culture to "exercise tutelage" over peoples of lower culture' since that was precisely the 'right' that the bourgeoisie claimed justified its own political and economic power over workers in Europe. Indeed, Kautsky explained, the apparent 'lack of culture [*Unkultur*]' resulted, ironically, from the oppression and exploitation carried out by European imperialists under cover of a civilizing mission. The routines of colonialism produced the poverty and misery that—misrepresented as the result of inherent cultural or racial inferiorities—justified these routines in the first place to the metropolitan taxpayers and voters whose support they required.[19]

16.2 GERMAN 'NEGROES' AND AFRICAN FREE LABOR

Early understandings of nature and 'natural peoples' worked most readily with the earliest phase of German overseas ventures, dominated by merchants and based on the simple exchange of European for African commodities. Colonial scientific research in this period focused on collecting from the already existing realm of nature, much as colonial economies revolved around coastal merchants trading within already existing African exchange networks.[20] As German interaction with its colonial empire moved from the distance of trade to the close contact of colonial state formation and the capitalist organization of labor, German authorities borrowed ideologies developed by older racially segregated states and economies, especially the United States. In this period, colonial governments also demanded racial knowledge more specific than the general *Naturvolk/Kulturvolk* dichotomy. The German anthropologist Richard Thurnwald, for example, advocated careful ethnographic study of individual societies in order to employ 'every race according to its ability,' creating an 'orderly symbiosis' of races by transforming 'the chaos of juxtaposition' (*Nebeneinander*) into the 'order of hierarchy' (*Übereinander*).[21] New German imperial efforts employed a variety of racial categories to limit, according to arbitrary laws of biological descent, the claims of individuals to political rights, economic autonomy, and personal dignity.

As a principle of social ordering, race functioned as a colonial kinship system, and thus depended ultimately on the control of sexuality. The racial hierarchies that constituted colonialism brought together races and thus threatened to undo not only these hierarchies, but also the endogamy on which they depended. The mostly male Germans living and working in the colonies, like their counterparts in other nations, engaged in a range of sexual practices with locals of both sexes, ranging from rape to concubinage to marriage. After the turn of the century, colonial officials and politicians began to worry about the status of the racially mixed children that some of the heterosexual unions produced. Inter-racial marriage (although not heterosexual sex) was made illegal in Southwest Africa, German East Africa, and Samoa, and the Reichstag debated a general law prohibiting interracial marriage in all colonies. The concerns of those opposed to 'miscegenation' included the claims of non-whites to German citizenship, the presumption that mixed race individuals were more likely than 'pure' races to challenge white supremacy, and, to a lesser extent, eugenic issues.[22]

As German state authorities and businesses in Africa moved from the assertion of sovereignty and coastal trade to the development of state institutions and capitalist enterprises in the colonial hinterland, they began to reconceptualize their colonial subjects as 'Negroes' (*Neger*), rather than *Naturvölker* or natives (*Eingeborenen*). Central to this new racial concept was the project, as many colonial thinkers put it, of 'educating the Negro to work' (*Erziehung des Negers zur Arbeit*).[23] The racial term 'Negro' reflected the growing German interest in the American New South as a model of a racially divided free-labor economy. The supposed naturalness of Africans and other colonized societies gave way to a supposed capacity for obedience and agricultural labor that could be realized only through authoritarian, but ostensibly benevolent white rule. German colonial authorities, including the famous Colonial Secretary Bernhard Dernburg, visited the American South and consulted with Booker T. Washington, the well-known African American principal of Tuskegee Institute in Alabama, on methods of 'improving' black labor that they could apply in Africa. From 1901 to 1909 Tuskegee graduates even ran a cotton-growing school in the German colony of Togo, initiating a broader European interest in bringing the kind of industrial education developed for African Americans in the New South to colonial Africa. German colonialism, especially in Togo and Tanzania, gained international recognition for its apparent success in reproducing the racialized political economy of the New South in Africa. Colonial luminaries including Frederick Lugard and E. D. Morel, head of the Congo Reform Association, applauded Germany as a model colonizer, and Belgian, English, and French colonial authorities followed the lead of Germany in turning to the Jim Crow cotton South as a colonial model.[24] (The exigencies of propaganda supporting the First World War, the Versailles Treaty, and the League of Nations erased this memory of German colonial rule.) German racial politics in Africa provided a conduit between the American South and transnational colonial empires.

16.3 'COOLIES' AND MIGRANT LABOR

If the 'Negro' of the American New South became the prevalent model of race for the colonial political economies of German Africa, the Chinese contract laborer, or 'coolie,' became the most important model for the political economy of German colonies in the Pacific. Outside of Shandong, whose geopolitical importance as a naval station took priority over political economy, and Micronesia, which remained primarily a trading empire, German exploitation of the Pacific rested primarily on phosphate (guano) mining and on a number of plantation crops, including copra (dried coconut meat and oil, used as cattle feed, as an industrial fat, and for other purposes). As in Africa, German colonial officials and businesses used all means, including taxation, coercive labor contracts, and physical force, to compel workers to serve the colonial economy. Still, labor shortages plagued German businesses in the Pacific even more than in Africa.

The German state took over government in New Guinea only in 1899, and it immediately set about increasing labor recruitment, setting up local stations and urging indigenous political authorities to assist in persuading (often, in fact, forcing) those under their authority to sign labor contracts. Between 1899 and 1914 approximately 85,000 Papuans went to work as indentured laborers for the Germans, but recruitment of indigenous laborers in New Guinea was never sufficient to meet the demands of the New Guinea Company plantations. This was, in part, because of the enormous death rates of indigenous laborers in German colonies, which historian Stewart Firth has estimated to be a staggering 20%, significantly higher than death rates in neighboring Pacific colonies.[25] Not surprisingly, German labor recruiters found few Papuans willing to work for German firms. Only about six-hundred workers could be recruited each year from the New Guinea mainland, so labor agents turned to neighboring islands, especially in the Bismarck Archipelago, and employed increasingly coercive measures. Laborers from New Pomerania (present-day New Britain), for example, had their three-year contracts doubled to six years without their consent.[26] The inhabitants of New Pomerania, in fact, so feared the labor recruiting ships that they hid every time a German ship appeared off shore. Even the rudimentary legal protection that prevented labor recruiters from simply capturing unwilling individuals was often ignored. The government itself soon uncovered evidence of widespread kidnapping in New Pomerania.[27]

The plantations of the German Pacific finally depended on contract laborers recruited from outside the German colonies, principally Chinese 'coolies.' German businesses regarded these Chinese contract workers as better, more civilized workers than Pacific Islanders or Africans.[28] Officials in the German Colonial Office believed, for example, that only the Chinese were competent to work in the phosphate mines of Samoa.[29] (Samoans stood out in their willingness to harvest copra on their own and, as George Steinmetz has shown, enjoyed a highly unusual 'noble savage' status in the colonial world.[30] The Samoan economy, however, like every other plantation economy in the German Pacific, depended upon brutally exploited contract laborers from elsewhere.)

The exceptional brutality of the treatment of laborers by the New Guinea Company, however, limited the amount of labor that could be recruited from China or anywhere else outside the colony. Although Java was one of the models for German New Guinea, the Dutch government would not allow the New Guinea Company to hire Javanese laborers because of the open toleration of the whip. The British forbade recruitment of workers from Singapore, especially because so many laborers died during their contracts in German New Guinea. After the turn of the century, the Chinese government also began vocally opposing the beatings and other abuses to which German planters subjected Chinese 'coolies' with the legal support of the German state.[31] Although the governor of New Guinea recognized that recruiting Chinese laborers would be more difficult if flogging remained a legally sanctioned punishment for workers, he resisted any change, recognizing that 'the New Guinea Company will not wish to cease using the whip on their Chinese coolies.'[32] Only in 1907 did the Governor suspend flogging for Chinese (and then only for two years), after a German consular official in Shanghai informed him that the Chinese government had sent a representative to Samoa to investigate complaints of mistreatment, wage reductions, and forced extensions of labor contracts.[33] After the turn of the century, official Chinese concern for the welfare of Chinese contract laborers caused new difficulties and threatened to ruin the capital investments of the New Guinea Company and a host of other German firms who had set up enterprises with the expectation that they could employ Chinese laborer and increase their output using violence and coercion.[34] Like the image 'Negro,' the image 'coolie' functioned in the colonial political economy not through some occult constructive power of culture, but rather through the routines of violence and coercion implied by these images themselves and authorized by the failure of real workers to correspond to them.

16.4 INTERNATIONAL RACISM AND GERMAN RACISM

German colonial authorities and experts adopted transnational racial categories, especially those of the 'Negro' and the 'coolie,' at a time when racial categories and racist violence had become more important and prevalent than ever around the world. France developed a virulent political anti-Semitism during the Dreyfus affair, beginning in 1894 and dragging on into the early twentieth century. Anti-Semites in the Russian Empire had been carrying out pogroms since the 1880s, encouraged by the anti-Semitism of the Czarist government. Racism also increased its already considerable importance in the United States in the 1890s, as southern states began to enact the 'Jim Crow' laws, which spread segregation from schools and public conveyances to everything from drinking fountains to the Bibles used to swear oaths in court. These laws were not a legacy of the Old South, but rather an innovation of the New South, endorsed by a series of Supreme Court decisions, culminating in the 1896 Plessy vs. Ferguson case.[35] The lynching of blacks by white mobs, already all too common, became in the 1890s increasingly frequent, brutal, and public, with body parts taken as 'trophies' from victims and openly celebratory newspaper coverage.[36]

German authorities participated in this global intensification of racism, taking from, and contributing to, powerful new racist politics in their internal as well as colonial politics. After 1878, anti-Semitism, based on religious and, increasingly, racial hostility, became an important force in German politics. Figures including the Berlin Court Preacher Adolf Stoecker, the professor of economics Adolph Wagner, the professor of history Heinrich von Treitschke, and the journalist Wilhelm Marr, developed anti-Semitism into a potent means of mass political mobilization that brought some success in *Reichstag* elections. In 1880–1881, anti-Semites organized a petition demanding that the state prevent German Jews from occupying higher offices and positions as teachers, restrict further Jewish immigration, and count German Jews separately in the census. Anti-Semites at this time, as historian Massimo Ferrari Zumbini has argued, followed the example of American nativism, especially the anti-Chinese politics that resulted, the year after the anti-Semitic petition, in the first Chinese Exclusion Act of 1882.[37] While the petition did not achieve its stated policy aims, it organized and demonstrated the power of political anti-Semitism in Germany. In the *Reichstag* elections of 1887, 1890, and 1893 voters elected more than a dozen members of parties identifying themselves as anti-Semitic. In 1892, seeking to co-opt these movements, and certainly not adverse to anti-Semitism themselves, the Conservatives adopted anti-Semitism as part of their party platform, seeking to reach beyond their traditional constituency.

Race was a category employed by liberals, as well as conservatives, in discussions of Jews and German nationality. The anthropologist Rudolf Virchow, who, as a liberal candidate, defeated anti-Semite Adolf Stoecker in the Reichstag elections of 1881 and 1884, pursued the racial difference between 'Germans' and 'Jews' more systematically than any anti-Semitic ideologue. Shortly after the unification of Germany, Virchow, as head of the German Society for Anthropology, Ethnology, and Prehistory, directed a statistical study of more than 6.7 million German schoolchildren to determine the prevalent racial characteristics of non-Jewish and Jewish Germans. After exhaustive statistical analysis, the study concluded that Jews were primarily of a dark racial type, with brown eyes, dark skin, and brown hair, while (non-Jewish) Germans were primarily of the a light racial type, with blue eyes, light skin, and blond hair. An opponent of anti-Semitism, Virchow made clear that his interest was not in religious, but in racial difference, and that he did not view this difference as a legitimate basis for creating hierarchies. He noted that Slavs represented another dark racial type, and found evidence of the long process of German colonization of Eastern Europe in the distribution of the two racial types in the East. Virchow consistently opposed anti-Semitism, whether racial or confessional, but perhaps following professional imperatives of anthropology, also gave (pseudo-)scientific credibility and basis to racial conceptions of German nationalism.[38]

Eugenics, which became increasingly popular in Germany, as well as in the rest of Europe and the United States, in the last decades of the nineteenth century, offered a biologistic, although not necessarily racist conception of society. Those concerned with eugenics, or 'racial hygiene,' as it was sometimes known, were at least as likely to concern themselves with alcoholism or syphilis, as they were with the relative superiority and inferiority of various races. Historian Paul Weindling has argued persuasively that physicians promoted eugenics as a means of expanding their own political authority in an increasingly corporatist and anti-individualistic political milieu in Wilhelmine Germany. Eugenic and racist writers gained new outlets in Germany with the journals the *Politisch-Anthropologische Revue*, which began in 1902, and the

Archiv für Rassen- und Gesellschaftsbiologie, which began in 1904. In the course of the early twentieth century, racism and eugenics moved ever closer together and the Nazis managed to merge these two important strains of nineteenth century European thought with catastrophic consequences.[39] However, as Edward Ross Dickenson reminds us, eugenics was only a part—often only a small part—of a larger project of social welfare that functioned at least as well in democracies as it did in totalitarian regimes.[40]

German social theorists and political and economic elites adopted elements of the transnational ideologies of the 'Negro' and the 'coolie' not only in their colonies, but also in the Polish territories of eastern Germany. Primarily out of concern for the chaos unleashed by the growing freedom of labor in nineteenth-century Germany, Gustav Schmoller led other German economists and social scientists in founding the *Verein für Sozialpolitik* (Social Policy Association) in 1872.[41] *Verein* member Georg Friedrich Knapp characteristically lamented that the social science of the eighteenth century had condemned serfdom without finding 'a replacement' (*Ersatz*) for it.[42] Many members of the *Verein für Sozialpolitik* regarded the American New South as a model post-emancipation society. In Germany, as in Africa and the New World, Knapp explained, the psychological motivations promised by free labor ideology could never sufficiently guarantee labor discipline, and thus emancipation required new forms of control. Max Weber's 'Protestant Ethic and the Spirit of Capitalism,' first published in 1904–1905, sought to establish that Protestants in fact possessed the internal compunction required by free labor ideology, so that external coercion was only necessary outside the German imperialist core.[43] The racial political economy of the post-emancipation American South presented a model of labor control, as Gustav Schmoller predicted as early as 1866.[44] The members of the *Verein* applauded and advised the Prussian state policies of internal colonization from their inception in 1886.[45]

The *Verein* had had little to say about the role of racial difference in the Prussian East until Max Weber joined the organization in 1890. In his famous studies of agrarian labor in East Elbian Prussia, Weber worried that what he regarded as the low economic and cultural standards of the Polish workers would degrade those of the German workers who had to compete with them. 'It is not possible,' Weber explained, 'to allow two nations with different bodily constitutions—differently constructed sto-machs...—to compete freely as workers in the same area.' German workers could only compete with Poles, Weber explained, by descending a 'cultural step [*Kultur-stufe*].' Weber thus called for the 'absolute exclusion of the Russian-Polish workers from the German East.'[46] In his now infamous 1895 inaugural lecture at the University of Freiburg, Weber addressed 'the role...that physical and mental race differences [*Rassendifferenzen*] between nationalities play in the economic struggle for existence.' Weber warned his audience that 'the German farmer' was being driven from the land in the East by a 'lower race' (*tieferstehenden Rasse*), the Poles. The Pole succeeded as a farmer in the East, Weber explained, 'not *despite*, but rather *because* of his low physical and mental habits,' which allowed him to flourish in conditions too difficult for Germans.[47] Weber, who later traveled through the American South and visited at

Tuskegee Institute, did more than any other German social scientist to synthesize the racial ideologies of Germany and the American New South.[48]

Chinese contract laborers also played an important role in understandings of labor inside the borders of Germany. Since 1889, with the expulsion of Poles without Prussian citizenship, German agriculturalists had considered employing Chinese contract laborers in Eastern agriculture, as they did in the Pacific. With the abolition of slavery during the nineteenth century, contract laborers from China, as well as India, came to do much of the plantation work around the world, and German discussions of employing 'coolies' in Prussian agriculture were hardly remarkable.[49] In 1892, the government of German East Africa, after much debate, brought at least 700 Chinese 'coolies' to work on plantations.[50] In his earliest discussion of Polish migrant labor, Weber had maintained that, 'from a cultural standpoint' it would be preferable to bring Chinese contract laborers to Germany than to allow Polish migrants, 'since our German workers will not assimilate with coolies.'[51] There followed a lively, although inconclusive, debate about whether the risks to the German race were greater from Chinese, black, or Polish seasonal migrants.[52] The racially subordinate seasonal migrant played an important role in global agriculture, including inside the borders of Germany and in the German colonies.

16.5 TOWARD 1941 OR SETTLER COLONIALISM AS USUAL? THE HERERO GENOCIDE

The Negro, the 'coolie,' and the Pole were racial figures that combined political domination with economic exploitation. Defining groups as racially non-white also tends to categorize them as exceptions to, or at least deviations from, the generalized, unmarked category human and thus, at least in potential, always marked for genocide. The reckless brutality of colonial wars in German and other European colonies indicates this clearly. In the 1905–1907 Maji Maji War in German East Africa, for example, soldiers fighting for the German state employed scorched earth tactics that killed as many as 200,000 Africans, in addition to the approximately 75,000 killed in the fighting.[53] Perhaps the most significant genocidal colonial war was that carried out in German Southwest Africa against the Herero in 1904–1907, both because genocide formed an explicit component of the German strategy and also because, as the first genocide of the twentieth century, and one carried out by Germans at that, it seems to prefigure the Holocaust.[54] It certainly does make sense to see the Holocaust, in part, as a component of a colonial population policy carried out by Germans in re-organizing occupied Europe and, as such, to connect it to the similar efforts in colonial Namibia thirty-five years earlier.[55] The more immediate context in which the Herero genocide should be understood, however, is in the political economy of settler colonies, in which European ranchers or farmers appropriated land held by the local population. In such cases, while there was often a colonial interest in maintaining an indigenous labor force, there was an even greater interest in seizing land and other resources for white settlers. Such a situation, in which colonial whites have no need for a population that they consider in any case not fully human and, indeed, in which this population competes with them for land, has often led to genocides. Victims of such dispossession through genocide have included not only the Herero, but also Native Americans and Tasmanians, who by 1876 were completely wiped out by British settlers.

The war between the Herero and the German colonial state began in January 1904 as the result of growing tensions over competing Herero and German claims to land and cattle. Official reports spoke of a concerted Herero attack, but historian Jan-Bart Gewald has more recently established that a German lieutenant fired the first shots of the war.[56] After six months of fighting, the command of German troops was taken from the governor, Theodor Leutwein, and given to General Lothar von Trotha. Leutwein had fought the Herero with all the brutality common in European colonial wars, but Trotha, a veteran of German East Africa and the suppression of the Boxer Uprising in China, took the war to a new level. As historian Isabel V. Hull has shown, Trotha sought to engage the Herero in the sort of decisive battle recommended by standard military doctrine, encircling and defeating an enemy resolutely enough to destroy their capacity to continue fighting.[57] The entire Herero people, however, and not just their soldiers, had already been defined as the enemy. Thus, Trotha pursued a genocidal campaign against the Herero people even after he had destroyed their military capacity at the Battle of Warterberg in August 1904. In October, after the surviving Herero escaped German pursuit, Trotha issued his infamous 'extermination order,' according to which every Herero man was to be shot down and every Herero woman and child driven into the desert where they were thought sure to die (although a number did, contrary to all expectations, manage to escape to Botswana[58]). Trotha's order was cancelled in December. From this time, surviving Herero were imprisoned in concentration camps, where they continued to die at an alarming rate. The Nama, another society living in Southwest Africa that had risen up against the Germans shortly after the Herero did, found themselves subjected to similar treatment. By the time the state of war ended in 1907 there were less than 20,000 Herero surviving from an original population of between 60,000 and 80,000. The Germans had also killed more than half of the Nama, who had numbered 20,000 before the war. The Germans dissolved Herero political organizations and expropriated their lands. Surviving Herero and Nama were forced to work for German settlers. The genocide of the Herero and the Nama was so extreme and expensive that it cannot be counted as a successful economic policy for settler colonialism, but that hardly makes it any less explicable in terms of economic motives and structures.

Racial categories and racism constituted both an important element of German participation in world politics and a conduit by which world politics shaped German internal politics. The clear temporal continuities between German racism and imperialism in the *Kaiserreich* and the Third Reich should not distract us from the equally clear continuities between German racism and imperialism and other national variants in the United States and Europe. German social thinkers, as well as political and economic elites, combined a liberal project of a struggle for culture against an inferior other with transnational conceptions of race and racial categories to create a global racial politics encompassing German political and economic domination in the Polish East and overseas. It makes little sense to speak of a generic racism, in Germany or anywhere else, for the political economy of racially divided societies differed, it should be obvious, from region to region. Racial categories offered practical guides to managing and exploiting specific populations, whether in phosphate mining, cotton growing, sugar beet cultivation, or, in the case of the Herero, expropriation through genocide. German racism at home and abroad makes sense only in terms of the political domination and economic exploitation from which it emerged, which it helped shape, and for which it provided, after the fact, ideological justification. It is thus not surprising that orthodox members of the Social Democratic Party stood alone in wholesale rejection of, rather than piecemeal calls to improve, imperialism and racism in Germany and abroad.[59] Imperialism and racism remained an important component of liberalism in Germany as in much of the world. Emerging from, and often retaining, the liberal progressive ideology of a *Kulturkampf*, German racism at home and abroad incorporated international racism and racial concepts, making German *Weltpolitik* global both in origins and in outcomes.

Notes

1. For a path-breaking interpretation of German imperialism and racism, see Sebastian Conrad, *Globalisation and Nation in Imperial Germany* (Cambridge: Cambridge University Press, 2010). Christian Geulen offers an especially compelling account of the comparable development of racism in Germany and the United States, in: *Wahlverwandte: Rassendiskurs und Nationalismus im späten 19. Jahrhundert* (Hamburg: Hamburger Edition, 2004).
2. On the *Kulturkampf*, see Siegfried Weichlein and Rebekka Habermas in this volume. Especially helpful for my own understanding of the *Kulturkampf* are Michael B. Gross, *The War Against Catholicism: Liberalism and the Anti-Catholic Imagination in Nineteenth-century Germany* (Ann Arbor: University of Michigan Press, 2004) and Helmut Walser Smith, *German Nationalism and Religious Conflict: Culture, Ideology, Politics, 1870–1914* (Princeton: Princeton University Press, 1995).
3. For a theoretical discussion, see Etienne Balibar, 'Is There a 'Neo-Racism'?' in Balibar and Immanuel Wallerstein (eds), *Race, Nation, Class: Ambiguous Identities*, trans. Chris Turner (London: Verso, 1999). I treat the topic of racism and culture in the German, US, and African context in Andrew Zimmerman, *Alabama in Africa: Booker T. Washington, the German Empire, and the Globalization of the New South* (Princeton: Princeton University Press, 2010).
4. For important critiques of the ways this sanitized liberalism has distorted understandings of German history, see Margaret Lavinia Anderson and Kenneth Barkin, 'The Myth of the Puttkamer Purge and the Reality of the *Kulturkampf*: Some Reflections on the

Historiography of Imperial Germany,' *Journal of Modern History* 54 (1982), 647–686 and Geoff Eley and David Blackbourn, *The Peculiarities of German History: Bourgeois Society and Politics in Nineteenth-Century Germany* (Oxford: Oxford University Press, 1984). I discuss the liberal distortion of Max Weber's racism in 'Decolonizing Weber.' *Postcolonial Studies* 9 (2006), 53–79.

5. Rudolf Virchow in: *Stenographische Berichte über die Verhandlungen des Abgeordneten Haus*, 8 May 1875, 64. Sitzung, Bd. 3, 1797–1801.

6. Gross, *The War Against Catholicism*.

7. For comparative studies of political anti-Catholicism in the nineteenth century, see the essays collected in Christopher Clark and Wolfram Kaiser (eds), *Culture Wars: Secular-Catholic Conflict in Nineteenth-Century Europe* (Cambridge: Cambridge University Press, 2003).

8. Otto von Bismarck, *Gedanken und Erinnerungen*, 2 vols (Stuttgart: Cotta, 1898), 2, 127.

9. See Helmut Neubach, *Die Ausweisungen von Polen und Juden aus Preussen 1885/86: Ein Beitrag zu Bismarcks Polenpolitik und zur Geschichte des deutsch-polnischen Verhältnisses* (Wiesbaden: Otto Harrassowitz, 1967). On this and other anti-Polish measures taken up by Prussia, see William W. Hagen, *Germans, Poles, and Jews: The Nationality Conflict in the Prussian East, 1772–1914* (Chicago: University of Chicago Press, 1980). For a broader survey, see Vejas Gabriel Liulevicius, *The German Myth of the East: 1800 to the Present* (New York: Oxford University Press, 2009).

10. The law is quoted in Georg Friedrich Knapp, 'Landarbeiter und innere Kolonisation' (1893), in Georg Friedrich Knapp, *Einführung in einige Hauptgebiete der Nationalökonomie: Siebenundzwanzig Beiträge zur Sozialwissenschaft* (Munich: Duncker & Humblot, 1925), 124–142, 138.

11. For a detailed account of these laws, naturally from a critical position, see the contemporary account by the leading Catholic Center Party deputy, Matthias Erzberger, *Der Kampf gegen den Katholizismus in der Ostmark: Material zur Beurteilung der Polenfrage durch die deutschen Katholiken* (Berlin: Germania, 1908).

12. See Jonathan Osmond, 'Land, Peasant and Lord in German Agriculture Since 1800,' in Robert W. Scribner and Sheilagh C. Ogilvie (eds), *Germany: A New Social and Economic History*, vol. 3 (London: Arnold, 1996), 82. See also James Brophy, this volume.

13. See Klaus J. Bade, 'German Emigration to the United States and Continental Immigration to Germany in the Late Nineteenth and Early Twentieth Centuries,' *Central European History* 13 (1980), 348–377.

14. See Andrew Zimmerman, *Anthropology and Antihumanism in Imperial Germany* (Chicago: University of Chicago Press, 2001). See also Jürgen Osterhammel, '"Peoples without History" in British and German Historical Thought,' in Benedikt Stuchtey and Peter Wende (eds), *British and German Historiography, 1750–1950: Traditions, Perceptions, and Transfers* (Oxford: Oxford University Press, 2000), pp. 265–287. For a contrasting interpretation of German anthropology in this period, see Glenn Penny, *Objects of Culture: Ethnology and Ethnographic Museums in Imperial Germany* (Chapel Hill: University of North Carolina Press, 2002).

15. Anthony G. Hopkins, *An Economic History of West Africa* (New York: Columbia University Press, 1973), 130.

16. See also Erik Grimmer-Solem, 'The Professors' Africa: Economists, the Elections of 1907, and the Legitimation of German Imperialism,' *German History* 25 (2007), 313–347 and 'Imperialist Socialism of the Chair: Gustav Schmoller and German Weltpolitik,

1897–1905,' in Geoff Eley and James Retallack, (eds), *Wilhelminism and Its Legacies: German Modernities, Imperialism, and the Meanings of Reform, 1890–1930* (New York: Berghahn Books, 2003), 106–22.

17. Centralbureau der Nationalliberalen Partei, *Kolonialpolitik seit der Reichstagsauflösung von 1906* (Berlin: Buchhandlung der Nationalliberalen Partei, 1909), 3, 24.

18. Winfried Becker, 'Kulturkampf als Vorwand: Die Kolonialwahlen von 1907 und das Problem der Parlamentarisierung des Reiches,' *Historisches Jahrbuch* 106 (1986), 59–84.

19. Karl Kautsky, *Sozialismus und Kolonialpolitik: Eine Auseinandersetzung* (Berlin: Vorwärts, 1907), 18–20. Translation by Angela Clifford available at the Marxists Internet Archive: http://www.marxists.org. See also *Internationaler Sozialisten-Kongress zu Stuttgart, 18. bis 24. August 1907* (Berlin: Vorwärts, 1907), 25–39.

20. On this conceptual shift, see Andrew Zimmerman, '"What do you really want in German East Africa, Herr Professor?" Counterinsurgency and the Science Effect in Colonial Tanzania,' *Comparative Studies in Society and History* 48 (2006), 419–461.

21. Richard Thurnwald, 'Die eingeborenen Arbeitskräfte im Südseeschutzgebiet,' *Koloniale Rundschau* 2 (1910), 607–632, 632.

22. On the regulation of interracial marriage in the German colonies, see Pascal Grosse, *Kolonialismus, Eugenik und Bürgerliche Gesellschaft in Deutschland 1850–1918* (Frankfurt am Main: Campus, 2000); Lora Wildenthal, *German Women for Empire, 1884–1945* (Durham, N.C: Duke University Press, 2001), esp. pp. 79–130; and Daniel Joseph Walther, *Creating Germans Abroad: Cultural Policies and National Identity in Namibia* (Athens: Ohio University Press, 2002). See also the discussion of Reichstag debates about interracial marriage in Helmut Walser Smith, 'The Talk of Genocide, the Rhetoric of Miscegenation,' in Sara Friedrichsmeyer, Sara Lennox, and Susanne Zantop (eds), *The Imperialist Imagination: German Colonialism and its Legacy* (Ann Arbor: University of Michigan Press, 1998), 107–124. On male homosexuality in the German colonial empire see Daniel Joseph Walther, 'Racializing Sex: Same-Sex Relations, German Colonial Authority, and Deutschtum,' *Journal of the History of Sexuality* 17 (2007), 11–24 and Heike Ingeborg Schmidt, 'Colonial Intimacy: The Rechenberg Scandal and Homosexuality in German East Africa,' *Journal of the History of Sexuality* 17 (2007), 25–59.

23. See Anton Markmiller, 'Die Erziehung des Negers zur Arbeit,' in *Wie die koloniale Pädagogik afrikanische Gesellschaften in die Abhängigkeit führte* (Berlin: Dietrich Reimer, 1995).

24. See Zimmerman, *Alabama in Africa*. See also Sven Beckert, 'From Tuskegee to Togo: The Problem of Freedom in the Empire of Cotton,' *Journal of American History* 92 (2005), 498–526 and Andrew Zimmerman, 'A German Alabama in Africa: The Tuskegee Expedition to German Togo and the Transnational Origins of West African Cotton Growers,' *American Historical Review* 110 (2005), 1362–1398.

25. Stewart Firth, 'The Transformation of the Labour Trade in German New Guinea, 1899–1914,' *Pacific History* 11 (1976), 51–65.

26. Albert Hahl, Governor of German New Guinea, to the German Colonial Office, 28 September 1911, *Bundesarchiv, Berlin* (hereafter *BArch*), R1001/2313, Bl. 24–25.

27. See the summary report of the Imperial Government of New Guinea to the German Colonial Office, 28 September 1912, *B Arch*, R1001/2313, Bl. 8, as well as the numerous local reports supporting that document contained in that volume.

28. See, for example, Henry Schmidt-Stölting, 'Ein Wort zur chinesischen Kulifrage,' *Der Tropenpflanzer* 11 (1907), 505–538.

29. German Colonial Office to the German Foreign Office, 22 June 1908, *BArch*, R1001/2310, Bl. 168–173.

30. George Steinmetz, *The Devil's Handwriting: Precoloniality and the German Colonial State in Qingdao, Samoa, and Southwest Africa* (Chicago: University of Chicago Press, 2007), 243–358.

31. For a good account of the negotiations between Germany and China over the treatment of Chinese laborers in Samoa, see Stewart Firth, 'Governors versus Settlers: The Dispute over Chinese Labour in German Samoa,' *New Zealand Journal of History* 11(1977), 155–179.

32. Knake, representing the Governor of New Guinea, to the Colonial Section of the German Foreign Office, 16 January 1903, *BArch* R1001/2308, Bl. 52–53.

33. Herr Burt, in Shanghai, to German Chancellor Bernhard von Bülow, 3 May 1907 (copy), *BArch*, R1001/2310, Bl. 21–23.

34. German Colonial Office to the German Foreign Office, 22 June 1908.

35. The novelty of the New South was established decisively in 1951 by C. Van Woodward. See Woodward, *Origins of the New South, 1877–1913*, rev. edn (Baton Rouge: Louisiana State University Press, 1972).

36. Leon Litwack, *Trouble in Mind: Black Southerners in the Age of Jim Crow* (New York: Knopf, 1998), 280–325.

37. Massimo Ferrari Zumbini, *Die Wurzeln des Bösen: Gründerjahre des Antisemitismus: Von der Bismarckzeit zu Hitler* (Frankfurt am Main: Klostermann, 2003), 212–213.

38. The historical significance of these statistics has proven difficult to interpret. The statistics themselves suggest to most modern observers that there was no racial difference between Jewish and non-Jewish Germans. Given Virchow's well known opposition to anti-Semitism, it would seem logical that Virchow would interpret these statistics as pointing to a lack of racial differences. Constantin Goschler, *Rudolf Virchow: Mediziner, Anthropologe, Politiker* (Cologne: Böhlau, 2002), 336–45, makes a strong case for following this interpretation. Virchow himself, however, held that the statistics proved the reality of racial distinctions between Jewish and non-Jewish Germans (although this did not cause him to waver in his opposition to anti-Semitism). Virchow indicated his own interpretation of these statistics clearly in numerous publications. See, for example, Rudolf Virchow, 'Gesammtbericht über die Statistik der Farbe der Augen, der Haare und der Haut der Schulkinder in Deutschland,' *Correspondenz-Blatt der Deutschen Anthropologischen Gesellschaft* 16 (1885), 89–100. I give a detailed account of this study in 'Anti-Semitism as Skill: Rudolf Virchow's Schulstatistik and the Racial Composition of Germany,' *Central European History* 32 (1999), 409–429 and *Anthropology and Antihumanism in Imperial Germany*, 135–146.

39. On developments in German eugenics, racism, anthropology, and medicine in the nineteenth and twentieth centuries, see especially Grosse, *Kolonialismus, Eugenik und Bürgerliche Gesellschaft in Deutschland*; Fatima El-Tayeb, *Schwarze Deutsche: Der Diskurs um 'Rasse' und nationale Identität 1890–1933* (Frankfurt am Main: Campus, 2001); and Paul Weindling, *Health, Race, and German Politics between National Unification and Nazism 1870–1945* (Cambridge: Cambridge University Press, 1989). See also Benoit Massin, 'From Virchow to Fischer: Physical Anthropology and "Modern Race Theories" in Wilhelmine Germany,' in: George W. Stocking, Jr. (ed.), *Volksgeist as Method and Ethic. Essays on Boasian Ethnography and the German Anthropological Tradition* (Madison: University of Wisconsin Press, 1996), 79–154 and Robert Proctor, 'From Anthropologie to Rassenkunde in the German Anthropological Tradition,' in George W. Stocking (ed.), *Bones, Bodies,*

Behavior: Essays on Biological Anthropology (Madison: University of Wisconsin Press, 1988), 138–179.

40. Edward Ross Dickinson, 'Biopolitics, Fascism, Democracy: Some Reflections on Our Discourse About "Modernity",' *Central European History* 37 (2004), 1–48.

41. 1872 was the date of the meeting that founded the organization, which came into official existence in 1873. Especially helpful for my account of the Verein für Sozialpolitik has been Erik Grimmer-Solem, *The Rise of Historical Economics and Social Reform in Germany, 1864–1894* (Oxford: Clarendon Press, 2003).

42. Georg Friedrich Knapp, 'Landarbeiter und innere Kolonisation' (1893), in Georg Friedrich Knapp (ed.), *Einführung in einige Hauptgebiete der Nationalökonomie: Siebenundzwanzig Beiträge zur Sozialwissenschaft* (Munich: Duncker & Humblot, 1925), 124–142, 137.

43. 'Die protestantische Ethik und der 'Geist' des Kapitalismus,' 2 parts, *Archiv für Sozialwissenschaft und Sozialpolitik* 20 (1904), 1–54; 21 (1905), 1–110.

44. Gustav Schmoller, 'Nationalökonomische und socialpolitische Rückblicke auf Nordamerika,' *Preußische Jahrbücher* 17 (1866), 38–75, 153–192, 519–547, 587–611.

45. Verein für Socialpolitik, *Zur Inneren Kolonisation in Deutschland: Erfahrungen und Vorschläge* (Leipzig: Duncker & Humblot, 1886).

46. Max Weber, 'Die ländliche Arbeitsverfassung (1893),' in: *Gesammelte Aufsätze zur Sozial- und Wirtschaftsgeschichte* (Tübingen: J. C. B. Mohr, 1924), 444–469, 456–457.

47. Max Weber, 'Der Nationalstaat und die Volkswirtschaftspolitik' (1895), in: Johannes Winckelmann (ed.), *Gesammelte Politische Schriften*, 3rd edn (Tübingen: J. C. B. Mohr, 1971), 1–25, 2, 12, 8. On Max Weber's work on eastern agriculture, see Cornelius Torp, *Max Weber und die preussischen Junker* (Tübingen: Mohr Siebeck, 1998).

48. I develop this argument in Zimmerman, *Alabama in Africa*.

49. Johannes Nichtweiss, *Die ausländische Saisonarbeiter in der Landwirtschaft der östlichen und mittleren Gebiete des Deutschen Reiches: Ein Beitrag zur Geschichte der preußisch-deutschen Politik von 1890–1914* (Berlin: Rütten & Loening, 1959), 38–40; Ulrich Herbert, *A History of Foreign Labor in Germany, 1880–1980: Seasonal Workers/Forced Laborers, Guest Workers*, trans. William Templer (Ann Arbor: University of Michigan Press, 1990).

50. Juhani Koponen, *Development for Exploitation: German Colonial Policies in Mainland Tanzania, 1884–1914* (Helsinki: Tiedekirja, 1994), 336–337.

51. Weber, 'Die ländliche Arbeitsverfassung,' 457.

52. *Verhandlungen der am 20. und 21. März 1893 in Berlin abgehaltenen General versammlung des Vereins für Socialpolitik über die ländliche Arbeiterfrage und über die Bodenbesitzverteilung und die Sicherung des Kleingrundbesitzes*, vol. 58, *Schriften des Vereins für Socialpolitik* (Leipzig: Duncker & Humblot, 1893), 98–130.

53. There has been much excellent work recently on the Maji Maji War, including Felicitas Becker, 'Traders, "Big Men" and Prophets: Political Continuity and Crisis in the Maji Maji Rebellion In Southeast Tanzania,' *Journal of African History* 45 (2004), 1–22; Jamie Monson, 'Relocating Maji Maji: The Politics of Alliance and Authority in the Southern Highlands of Tanzania,' *Journal of African History* 39 (1998), 95–120; Thaddeus Sunseri, 'Famine and Wild Pigs: Gender Struggles and the Outbreak of the Maji Maji War in Uzaramo (Tanzania),' *Journal of African History* 38 (1997), 235–59; Thaddeus Sunseri, 'Statist Narratives and Maji Maji Ellipses,' *International Journal of African Historical Studies* 33 (2000), 567–584.

54. On the question of continuities in German racism, see especially Helmut Walser Smith, *The Continuities of German History: Nation, Religion, and Race Across the Long*

Nineteenth Century (Cambridge: Cambridge University Press, 2008). Woodruff D. Smith makes a persuasive case for the continuities in German imperialism in *The Ideological Origins of Nazi Imperialism* (New York: Oxford University Press, 1986).

55. See the essays collected in Joachim Zeller and Jürgen Zimmerer (eds), *Genocide in German South-West Africa: The Colonial War (1904–1908) in Namibia and Its Aftermath* (Monmouth, Wales: Merlin Press, 2008).

56. Jan-Bart Gewald, *Herero Heroes: A Socio-Political History of the Herero of Namibia, 1890–1923* (Oxford: James Currey, 1999), 141–191.

57. Isabel V. Hull, *Absolute Destruction: Military Culture and the Practices of War in Imperial Germany* (Ithaca: Cornell University Press, 2005).

58. Gewald, 213ff.

59. Eduard Bernstein and other revisionists dabbled in racism and imperialism, but were soundly rejected by the leaders of their party and by the Socialist International. On those Social Democrats who did embrace imperialism, see Roger Fletcher, *Revisionism and Empire: Socialist Imperialism in Germany, 1897–1914* (London: George Allen & Unwin, 1984). For the international rejection of imperialism, see especially *Internationaler Sozialisten-Kongress zu Amsterdam, 14. bis 20. August 1904* (Berlin: Vorwärts, 1904), 23–39.

BIBLIOGRAPHY

BADE, KLAUS J., 'German Emigration to the United States and Continental Immigration to Germany in the Late Nineteenth and Early Twentieth Centuries.' *Central European History* 13 (1980), 348–377.

CONRAD, SEBASTIAN, *Globalisation and Nation in Imperial Germany* (Cambridge: Cambridge University Press, 2010).

EL-TAYEB, FATIMA, *Schwarze Deutsche: Der Diskurs um 'Rasse' und nationale Identität 1890–1933* (Frankfurt am Main: Campus, 2001).

GEULEN, CHRISTIAN, *Wahlverwandte: Rassendiskurs und Nationalismus im späten 19. Jahrhundert* (Hamburg: Hamburger Edition, 2004).

GROSSE, PASCAL, *Kolonialismus, Eugenik und Bürgerliche Gesellschaft in Deutschland 1850–1918* (Frankfurt am Main: Campus, 2000).

HAGEN, WILLIAM W., *Germans, Poles, and Jews: The Nationality Conflict in the Prussian East, 1772–1914* (Chicago: University of Chicago Press, 1980).

HERBERT, ULRICH, *A History of Foreign Labor in Germany, 1880–1980: Seasonal Workers/ Forced Laborers, Guest Workers*, trans. William Templer (Ann Arbor: University of Michigan Press, 1990).

LIULEVICIUS, VEJAS GABRIEL, *The German Myth of the East: 1800 to the Present* (New York: Oxford University Press, 2009).

SMITH, HELMUT WALSER. *The Continuities of German History: Nation, Religion, and Race Across the Long Nineteenth Century* (Cambridge: Cambridge University Press, 2008).

SMITH, WOODRUFF D., *The Ideological Origins of Nazi Imperialism* (New York: Oxford University Press, 1986).

STEINMETZ, GEORGE, *The Devil's Handwriting: Precoloniality and the German Colonial State in Qingdao, Samoa, and Southwest Africa* (Chicago: University of Chicago Press, 2007).

WEINDLING, PAUL, *Health, Race, and German Politics between National Unification and Nazism 1870–1945* (Cambridge: Cambridge University Press, 1989).

ZELLER, JOACHIM and JÜRGEN ZIMMERER (eds), *Genocide in German South-West Africa: The Colonial War (1904–1908) in Namibia and Its Aftermath* (Monmouth, Wales: Merlin Press, 2008).

ZIMMERMAN, ANDREW. *Alabama in Africa: Booker T. Washington, the German Empire, and the Globalization of the New South* (Princeton: Princeton University Press, 2010).

ZUMBINI, MASSIMO FERRARI, *Die Wurzeln des Bösen: Gründerjahre des Antisemitismus: Von der Bismarckzeit zu Hitler* (Frankfurt am Main: Klostermann, 2003).

CHAPTER 17

GERMANY 1914–1918.
TOTAL WAR AS A
CATALYST OF CHANGE

BENJAMIN ZIEMANN

It is a commonplace to see the First World War as a major caesura in German and European history. Not least, such an interpretation can rely on the perceptions of influential contemporary observers. In Germany, as in other belligerent countries, many artists, intellectuals and academics experienced the outbreak of the war as a cathartic moment. War, conceived as a decisive struggle over life or death between nations, seemed to provide an opportunity to leave the restrictions and ambivalences of bourgeois civilization behind. Instead, intellectuals hoped to usher in a new age where the life of the individual was clearly framed by the superior needs of the national collective. In 1914, theologians of both Christian confessions were not alone in thinking that the war would bring redemption.[1] In a bourgeois culture where the feeling of *ennui* or boredom had gained ground since the turn-of-the-century, the prospect of dying on the battlefield was no reason for dismay or fright, but could offer hope and satisfaction, at least for those intellectuals who were not immediately confronted with it. Even the sociologist Max Weber, usually a very sober mind, reckoned in 1916 that the 'death in the field differs from' simply 'inevitable dying,' as 'only here the individual can believe to know that he dies 'for' something.'[2] War created meaning and offered orientation; that was the gist of this and many other intellectual reflections.

When historians started in the 1970s to investigate the social and cultural repercussions of the First World War in more systematic fashion, they could elaborate on the already well established trope of the conflict as a major caesura. Three examples should suffice to convey how historians conceptualize the place of World War I in the trajectory of modern German history. In his book *Rites of Spring*, published in 1990, Modris Eksteins portrayed the war as the decisive breakthrough of modernist culture. The notion of liberation through sacrifice is one of the key motifs for his argument.

Beginning with the controversial premiere of Stravinsky's ballet 'Sacre du Printemps' in Paris 1913, and moving on to the German soldiers who fought in Flanders fields since 1914, Eksteins aimed to chart how modernism spread beyond the small circles of an artistic elite, and how Germany became 'the modernist nation par excellence,' as the necessity of sacrifice turned into a popular experience. Citing war letters written by students who had volunteered for the war, Eksteins stated that 'the German interpretation' of why the war should be continued was, unlike in Britain or France, 'cloaked in mystical and romantic notions.' Thus, the ground for further political irrationalism and radicalization in the 1920s was prepared.[3]

In another landmark book, also published in 1990, the late George L. Mosse presented his seminal argument about the brutalization of German political culture through the myth of war. Narratives of heroism were 'designed to mask war and to legitimize the war experience.' While such mythological representations of the front-line experiences emerged in all belligerent nations, as Mosse conceded, he insisted that nationalist memories of the war experience 'informed most post-war politics' in Germany, 'which proved most hospitable to the myth.'[4] For Mosse, as well as in slightly different terms for Eksteins, the brutalizing effects of the war were the key to an explanation of the German *Sonderweg*, which ultimately led to the Nazi seizure of power. Whereas Eksteins and Mosse suggest lines of continuity between 1914–1918 and 1933, historian Omer Bartov has even gone one step further. For him, the Holocaust was 'more directly the almost perfect reenactment of the Great War (. . .), with the important correction that all the perpetrators were on one side and all the victims on the other.'[5] This argument, however, is no more than a formal and very superficial analogy, based on the fact that both at Verdun and in Auschwitz some trademark signs of modern military organizations were used, such as 'barbed wire,' 'machine guns,' 'gas,' and 'uniforms.'[6] The context and the intensity of their use, though, differed fundamentally. Poison gas, for example, caused no more than 1.7 percent of all injuries in the German army during World War I.[7]

While it is straightforward to see the mobilization for war and violence as a major caesura for any of the belligerent countries, it is much more complicated to account for causalities and for German peculiarities. Difficult methodological questions arise, which have not always been properly addressed. Taking the alleged 'brutalization' of political culture as an example, we need to distinguish between the unleashing of aggressions as a direct result of front-line service, and the wider repercussions of atrocity stories and violent fantasies, which influenced male (and female?) civilians at the home-front in mediated form through posters, cartoons, and other representations. Whereas severe doubts have been raised with regard to the former argument, the latter is mostly undisputed, but should be further specified with regard to the timing and range of this 'brutalization.'[8] It is equally important to qualify assertions about the war as a caesura with regard to social contexts such as class, gender, confession and regional background, bearing in mind that regional diversity is a key element of German political culture. These qualifications are all the more important as many interpretations have taken the self-descriptions by the small literate elite of the *Bildungsbürgertum* (educated middle class) as indicative of German society as a whole. Historians have also started to attend more carefully to the difference between the change of perceptions up until 1918, and those in the immediate post-war period, when defeat in war, and the loss of territories and colonies resulted in altered political contexts.[9]

These introductory remarks do not intend to diminish the significance of the First World War for modern German history, nor its importance as a moment of rupture and violent discontinuity in the medium and longer term. Rather, it is to insist on a more cautious approach when causality is attributed to certain strands of development, and to flag both August 1914 and November 1918 as pivotal moments of change. These crucial weeks mark, each in their own way, a departure from the political framework of Imperial Germany that had been established in 1871. As such, they deserve specific attention. In the following, we will focus on the ways in which the national community of the Germans was made and unmade during the mobilization for war. We will first examine both the inclusionary and exclusionary effects of a changing mode of political representation, and then chart how mobilization led to increasing claims for participation and paved the way for the revolution. Concluding remarks discuss elements of continuity and consider the Great War as a catalyst of change.

17.1 LONGING FOR UNITY AND THE CHANGING REPRESENTATION OF POLITICS

The journalist Siegfried Jacobsohn was the founder and editor of the journal *Schaubühne*. Since 1918 published under the title *Weltbühne*, it was one of the most important left-wing intellectual journals of the time. Upon the news of German mobilization on 1 August 1914, he noted, while on holiday on one of the small islands in the North Sea: 'If it is time, we will not only mobilize men, but also higher feelings, and we will bash everybody's hat who does not appear to have got plenty of those according to regulations.'[10] With these remarks, Jacobsohn captured the ambivalences of the German 'experience of August 1914,' the complex mixture of emotions and expectations that marked the beginning of the war. The mobilization for war opened up the prospect of national unity, expressed through and accompanied by an outburst of 'higher,' more noble patriotic feelings. However, it was uncertain whether all Germans would join in and celebrate belligerence against Russia, France, and the United Kingdom, and any lack of unanimous support would, as Jacobsohn rightly predicted, soon trigger exclusionary tendencies.

August 1914 was a crucial moment in modern German history, but not because all Germans reacted with exuberant enthusiasm to the declaration of war. Quite to the contrary, public displays of collective enthusiasm for war were only one rather minor element in a much more complicated set of popular attitudes. On 1 August, they were largely confined to the big cities, where mostly middle-class people and members of student fraternities roamed the streets and gathered on inner-city places. The famous photograph of the Odeonsplatz in Munich on 2 August 1914, showing Adolf Hitler among an exuberant crowd celebrating the news of the declaration of war against Russia, is a good example: the crowd is almost exclusively made up of men, and most of them are clearly marked as middle-class by their straw hats, white collars, and suits.[11] Elsewhere in large cities and smaller towns, crowds simply gathered because they were curious to receive the latest news on the rapidly unfolding sequence of diplomatic events, or to participate in 'carnivalesque' events such as hunting down automobiles that were supposed to bring gold from France to Russia. Outbursts of patriotic fervor occurred alongside significant displays of panic, mostly about economic uncertainty, and feelings of outright depression. The latter was the prevalent mood in the countryside, particularly in Catholic regions of the Reich, where uncertainty over the lack of manpower for the harvest and grief about the separation from loved-ones pushed any other concerns aside.[12]

One might argue that it is an 'overly simplistic question' to ask which Germans were supporting the war from the onset, and which were not.[13] However, these differences matter, not least because they indicate early fissures in the German war effort, which had turned by 1916, at the latest, into major cleavages. To be sure, the mobilization of the German war machine commenced without any interruption, as the trains with conscript soldiers made their way to the fronts. However, there is a need to distinguish between the public perception of the *Burgfrieden* (literally: fortress peace), the contemporary term for the suspension of party political strife, and the reality at the grassroots level. When the parliamentary party of the Social Democratic Party (SPD) voted, as all other parties, for the war credits in the *Reichstag* session on 4 August 1914, the party leaders justified their support with the defensive nature of the German war effort and the need to fight against the oppressive Tsarist regime in Russia. However, this was only an ideological smokescreen, used to conceal their deliberate aim to abandon fundamental opposition in favor of national integration. In the days before 31 July, when the state of siege suspended freedom of press and political expression, at least 750,000 rank-and-file members and supporters of the SPD had attended anti-war rallies across the Reich. In early August, Social Democratic workers displayed hardly any enthusiasm, and both as soldiers at the front and in the factories at the home front, they were among the first to note the mendacity of the rhetoric of *Burgfrieden* amidst the deprivations of war. Thus, the seeds for the split of the SPD, which was formally sealed only in April 1917 with the founding of the USPD (Independent Social Democratic Party), were already laid in August 1914, when a sizeable minority in the party was left bitterly disappointed by the Party's opportunistic top-down decision to support the war.[14]

It is thus crucial to distinguish between popular opinion and attitudes in August 1914, and the subsequent mythologized perceptions of the *Augusterlebnis*, representing these days and weeks as a moment of unanimous enthusiasm and national unity. Yet because they wildly exaggerated certain features of the popular *Augusterlebnis*, these mythologies mattered. They are indicative of a substantial recoding and reshaping of the representation of politics. First, August 1914 brought the notion of the *Volksgemeinschaft* or people's community to the fore. One of the characteristic features of the middle-class gatherings on the streets and places of Berlin in late July and early August was the way in which they by-passed the established pageantry of nationalist rituals, which was centered on the army and the Kaiser and side-lined ordinary civilians to the role of mere spectators. Now, as they waited for news and welcomed the declaration of mobilization, middle class Berliners took center stage. Here, they 'could see themselves constituting a nationalist public,' and began to re-enact the nation as a 'less hierarchically bound collectivity.'[15]

These developments on the ground were reflected in the sphere of intellectual debate about the future of the German polity. Academics from all disciplines across the humanities and sciences engaged in a lively discussion about the lessons that had to be drawn from the mythologized *Augusterlebnis* of national unity. These lessons, condensed as the 'ideas of 1914,' are usually interpreted as outlines for a German mission in the wider world, and, in their rejection of universalist values symbolized by the year 1789, as indicative for the German *Sonderweg* or divergence from the West.[16] However, the various public appeals, pamphlets, and petitions by professors neither elaborated on a peculiar mission of the German nation, nor articulated a fundamental opposition to 1789. Rather, the 'ideas of 1914' sought to develop a new, communitarian political framework for the German people that could build on the experience of August 1914. With many differences in detail, two main models were envisaged: a more libertarian *Volksstaat* or people's state, which would turn subjects into citizens, and the harmonizing vision of the *Volksgemeinschaft*, represented by a corporate state and a government of experts above the parties. Crucially, the blueprints of both models transcended the contemporary political system and the valence of the Imperial monarch. In the 'ideas of 1914,' the *Kaiserreich* already came to an end, at least in terms of a substantial intellectual debate on political reform.[17] Not only liberal and national-conservative academics supported these ideas. Reformist Social Democratic intellectuals shared their fascination with the notion of a *Volksgemeinschaft* even as the war dragged on, and were, for instance, ready to see the corporative elements of the Auxiliary Service Law in 1916 as a first step in that direction.[18] The Service Law required mandatory military service and ended the freedom of workers to change jobs.

The shift towards expectations of national community brought, secondly, new modes for the articulation and representation of sociability. In a landmark article 'On the Sociology of World War,' published in 1915, the sociologist Emil Lederer lucidly encapsulated these changes. Part of the 'social transformation' brought about by the war was, he argued, that 'a sense of togetherness' was no longer based predominantly in commercial and legal 'contracts,' as in bourgeois society. Rather, in the wartime community relations based on 'understandings such as in families' created bonds between individuals, framed by the 'state's suggestive power.'[19] Lederer's observation implied that politics were not any longer represented according to a register of compromise and of sober calculations of means and ends. While Germany was facing a 'world of enemies,' as a popular slogan suggested, the semantics of the political shifted to an articulation of emotions, excitements, and promises, contributing to a dramatized narrative centered around the notions of sacrifice and fate.[20] This new accent on the intimate and personal as a site for the expression of emotions of belligerence and community required a new media of political discourse. Until 1918, and even after the armistice, *Feldpostbriefe*, letters sent from the front by the army postal services, were among the most important media for the representation of community and the political meaning of the war. Abundantly reprinted in newspapers and in many edited collections, they seemed to offer authentic voices and emotions from key eyewitnesses of the epic battles between nations. The introduction to one edited collection, published in 1914, praised their qualities like this: 'Reading *Feldpostbriefe* means to feel the pulse of the war (...) The most extreme sacrifice as a matter of course, honesty and uprightness, these are the distinctive features of German *Feldpostbriefe*.'[21]

Apart from the form (community) and the mode (dramatization) we have to consider, thirdly, the range and depth of the changing representation of politics. One common assumption is that propaganda played a vital role. State-sponsored indoctrination had to instill enemy images and to re-interpret acts of aggression that occurred in foreign territories as a defense of the German nation. At first glance, popular visual media, such as picture postcards, seem to support such an interpretation. Since 1914, postcards with patriotic motifs had inundated German stationary shops and department stores. With mottos such as 'Jeder Stoss ein Franzos' ('Each push one Frenchman'), they depicted German soldiers who happily kicked and thrashed cowardly British, French, and Russian troops. With this rather bizarre sense of humor, these postcards seemed typical examples of misguided, but effective German propaganda. However, military censorship in 1914–1915 stopped precisely the distribution of these 'inflammatory' images, as they were deemed to be 'degrading' to the German military and war effort.[22] German mobilization was, as Jacobsohn had noticed, meant to produce 'higher,' more noble feelings. From the iconography of popular media, such as picture postcards and amateur photography we can glean that, at least until 1918, the pictorial representation of death and sacrifice resorted to very traditional, often banal tropes and communicative codes. The impossibility of depicting human agency amidst the emptiness of no-man's-land led to a crisis of the representation of violence. However, during the war itself, only a very few, astute observers analyzed this crisis of representation. Not until the 1920s would fundamental changes in the iconography valorizing war occur, as conservative and Fascist authors and artists selected and rearranged the existing stock of photographs according to a visual code that glorified the machinery of warfare and saw human agency as a mere appendix to technology.[23]

In his reflections on the *Augusterlebnis*, Siegfried Jacobsohn had assumed that those who lacked 'higher' patriotic feelings would soon be at the receiving end of a backlash from the national community. The experience of the Jewish minority in Germany, however, can serve as proof that outsiders were subjected to discrimination even though they supported the war with the very best intentions. The *Centralverein*, the Central Association of German Citizens of Jewish Faith, which represented the large majority of the about 600,000 Jews in the Reich, was hardly alone in adamantly insisting that Jewish Germans had to support the war effort. Taking the rhetoric of the *Burgfrieden* at face value, many male Jewish citizens volunteered for army service or took up important posts in the various bodies that governed the war economy. They clung on to the hope that their service would pay a dividend and would finally bring full acceptance by the Gentile majority population. As censorship curbed anti-Semitic propaganda and the army started to promote Jews to officers, equality seemed to be achieved. However, anti-Semitic associations such as the *Reichshammerbund* rejected the notion of a *Burgfrieden* that would include Jews from the start. They resumed their agitation quickly and filed petitions and memoranda to the authorities, accusing the Jews of being profiteers and shirkers who would avoid front-line service and take advantage of the increasing scarcity of food provision.[24]

This form of anti-Semitic agitation scored its first major success on 11 October 1916, when the Prussian War Minister Adolf Wild von Hohenborn issued the decree for the infamous 'Jew Count,' which ordered all military commanders, through a census to be taken on 1 November, to determine how many Jews who were subject to the draft actually served in the German army. It is difficult to determine the exact motives of the war ministry for this step. However, it was certainly not by chance that Wild von Hohenborn gave in to pressure from anti-Semitic groups exactly at a time when the army was facing a severe manpower shortage, and mobilization for total war had reached its first peak. In this situation, radical nationalist circles and parts of the military believed that 'inner unity could only be achieved by fighting (. . .) the internal enemy.' The Jews were associated with everything that weakened the German war effort.[25] The devastating effects of the *Judenzählung* on the Jews, who felt bitterly disappointed by this symbolic exclusion from patriotic service, have often been described. It is equally clear that the count opened the floodgates for further, ever more vicious anti-Semitic agitation, even though Wild's successor Hermann von Stein declared the issue closed on 22 January 1917, stopping short of issuing a full apology.[26] However, while it is undisputed that the First World War and the Jew Count in particular was important for the radicalization of German anti-Semitism, the exact contours and the pervasiveness of this shift across society at large are still subject to conjecture.[27]

At least three tentative conclusions can be drawn from the existing body of evidence and scholarship. There is, first, hardly any doubt that the encounter of millions of German soldiers with Eastern European Jews during the occupation of vast territories in Russia until 1918 fuelled anti-Semitic stereotypes and informed ideas about a necessary civilizing mission of German 'culture' in the East. However, the long-term repercussions of these contacts with the *Ostjuden* were not straightforward. The sources display also, in perhaps less frequent, but still notable cases, substantial 'expressions of interest and sympathy' with the, at first glance, strange culture of orthodox Polish and Russian Judaism.[28] Secondly, at the level of popular perceptions at the home-front, we have to consider the impact of the rapid deterioration in food supplies since 1915. Food shortages, as we will see below, led to popular protests. Malnutrition and hunger also triggered reflections about the persistence of gross social inequality in German society. A pervasive moral discourse emerged about the discrepancy between those who sacrificed themselves for the war, most prominently the soldiers, and those who gained profit from it. This discourse was effectively the flipside of the rhetoric of the *Burgfrieden*, as it became obvious that not all social groups and strata were equally affected by the war. In this context, Jews who worked as tradesmen, and their presence in the War Corporations that regulated the supply of most raw materials, were starting points for anti-Semitic stereotypes about Jews and usury.[29] The intensity of these emotions and prejudices evoked aggressive comments, as the following letter by someone from Dresden, written in June 1917, demonstrates:

> Unfortunately we have so many Jews who practice usury—certainly it would be the best to string all these up to the next best tree—then, scarcities in food would immediately disappear. These men are our biggest enemies, and one is too weak to kill them. Perhaps this might later be a consequence of the war—it should be wished for.'[30]

However, violent fantasies like this one were not only targeting Jews as usurers and war profiteers. Since 1916, the conflict between rural agrarian producers and urban consumers emerged as *the* major cleavage in German society. As food supplies dwindled, city dwellers took to the countryside every weekend in order to hoard or steal food. In their perception, peasant farmers were the main culprits for the dire state of food supplies, and the ultimate war profiteers. These encounters led to hostility on both sides, and to an increasing number of physical confrontations.[31] Caricatures in satirical journals confirm that the popular iconography of the profiteer and usurer was not simply anti-Semitic, but much more diverse, and also included a mockery of the bureaucratic nature of the highly-regulated war economy.[32] Amidst increasing social inequality and a lack of national cohesion, Jews were, by far, not the only group presented as a scapegoat for these developments.

There is, thirdly, ample evidence for the wartime radicalization of anti-Semitic discourse among nationalist interest and pressure groups such as the Pan-German League and increasing numbers of Protestant, middle-class, teachers, professors, civil servants, and pastors. It seems more appropriate to interpret this trend not as a result of 'brutalization,' but rather as a backlash against the drive towards democratization. It is not by chance that the intensity and the language of the political demonology of *völkisch* anti-Semitism geared up since the spring of 1917, when mass strikes and later the peace resolution of the *Reichstag* signaled first major blows to the authoritarian Wilhelmine system.[33] In this interpretation, only defeat and revolution in 1918 moved anti-Semitism from the fringe to the center of German politics, as an increasing number of those who struggled over the proper representation of the *Volksgemeinschaft* based their vision on the exclusion of Jews. There was, to sum up, no 'direct line' from the Jew Count in 1916 to the Holocaust.[34]

17.2 MOBILIZATION, PARTICIPATION, AND THE ROAD TO REVOLUTION

In its mythologized version, represented in countless poems, sermons, speeches, posters, and postcards, August 1914 was a moment of national recognition. As the bar for the internal cohesion and inclusiveness of the German nation was substantially raised, minority groups such as the Jews—but also the Poles and the people from Alsace-Lorraine, who were constantly harassed by and in the army—failed to qualify as German citizens despite their best efforts. As we have seen, these exclusionary tendencies gained momentum in 1916. The vision of a unified *Volksgemeinschaft*, however, sidelined also those who had no intention of taking part in it. In August 1914, the number of dissenters was small. Even the Social Democratic *Reichstag* deputy Karl Liebknecht, who became the figurehead of the opposition within the SPD once he voted openly against further war credits on 2 December 1914, had—formally—supported them earlier in the *Reichstag* session on 4 August.

However, soon discontent spread widely across the German population, in a process that commenced only weeks after the war had begun. As the casualty lists got longer (and were soon no longer publicized), as the experience of industrial warfare disillusioned even nationalist soldiers who had expected to excel in bravery, and as workers in ammunitions factories were drafted to the front when they voiced minor grievances or engaged in trade union activism, a critical discourse about the war emerged among soldiers and civilians alike. This language of discontent was mostly concerned with petty grievances and personal setbacks, sometimes combined with genuine outrage about experiences of loss and bereavement. However, it was soon summed up in the more general conclusion that the war was only one big 'swindle.' It is important to note that this critical discourse was already firmly established long before extreme material hardship in the form of widespread malnutrition and hunger affected German society since 1916, and turned *Ersatz* into an unpopular codeword for dreaded artificial food of vastly inferior quality. Based on these grievances, average people with no leftist political affiliation started to mock the idea of doing 'the fatherland a good service,' as did a certain Michael Kappelmeier, NCO in a Bavarian regiment and butcher in civilian life, in a letter from the front dated October 1914.[35] Nationalist discourses started to lose their grip on many Germans only weeks after they had been so powerfully reaffirmed and reshaped in August 1914.

Complaints and grievances, to be sure, did not threaten the war effort, at least as long as they did not translate into collective action. However, this happened sooner rather than later. Urban working-class women were the first to challenge the authority of the Wilhelmine state during the war. As the food provision became critical in autumn 1915, long lines in front of grocery stores and market stalls became a regular sight in the big cities. They offered an opportunity to voice collective anger about the rationing system and the inequalities of food provision. In October 1915, the first food riots occurred in Lichtenberg, a working-class suburb of Berlin. Over several days, women protested against the lack of butter, instigated by the rude treatment they had received from shopkeepers. Similar incidents followed in other cities such as Chemnitz, Hamburg, and Nuremberg, where women and youths smashed shop-windows, stormed the city hall, or staged demonstrations demanding 'peace and bread.'[36] The authorities were deeply concerned about these displays of popular unrest. Consequently, they accelerated the shift towards an agricultural policy that was meant to serve, however poorly, the interests of the urban consumers first, thus triggering further discontent in the countryside about the introduction of ceiling prices and delivery quotas. However, participation in food protests did not contribute to a more general discourse of female 'citizenship,' as historians of women have claimed.[37] Some working-class women simply demanded the introduction of a 'food-dictator' who would guarantee the proper and just distribution of groceries. Many others, however, were ultimately overpowered by material hardship, personal bereavement, and the maltreatment they received from male superiors at the shop-floor level. Emancipation or empowerment are inappropriate terms to describe women's experiences at the home front, both in the short-term and with regard to consequences in the post-war period.[38] When the revolution came in 1918, its gender was male. Only in the symbolism of the conservatives who loathed the collapse of the monarchy in 1918 was the revolution female.

At the front, the accumulation of grievances translated into a widely used language that transcended the social and political system of Imperial Germany. This language could draw upon the anti-capitalism and the participatory, democratic aims of the socialist labor movement. While the majority wing in the SPD continued to support the policy of *Burgfrieden*, the minority current quickly established itself as the nucleus of a wider anti-war movement. Already in the first weeks of the war, many rank-and-file members of the party began to unmask the illusion of national unity. At the front, Social Democratic soldiers offered a fundamental critique of the 'human butchery' of war even before the troops started to dig trenches in October 1914. Three leading members of the moderate opposition publicly criticized the *Burgfrieden* in June 1915. The split within the SPD was only formally acknowledged in March 1916, however, when the parliamentary party expelled the most determined proponents of the minority wing. Notions of party discipline, a longstanding feature of the Socialist labor movement, continued to motivate SPD-members at the front to cope with the strains of war, as did their aversion against the authoritarian Tsarist regime. However, the increasing number of soldiers who resented the war used the 20 SPD *Reichstag* deputies, including Karl Liebknecht, who voted against war credits in December 1915, as a symbolic rallying point.

From 1916 onwards, only a minority of the German front-line troops were convinced that they were defending their fatherland against a coalition of enemies, in particular since the ban on any public consideration of war aims was lifted by the Army Supreme Command in the fall of that year. As annexationist fantasies filled the pages of the national-conservative press, even working-class soldiers with no direct affiliation to the SPD aired their disappointment in a language that employed key terms of socialist party discourse. The basket-maker Peter Hammerer from Bavarian Swabia reasoned in November 1916 about the wider causes of 'this misery': 'This must be the payment for the years when we were protecting the Big Capitalists, protecting their stuff. Let them protect it themselves and not send people out who have to go out and make a living. (. . .) I have nothing to defend.' Hearing news about the lack of support for his wife, who was pregnant with their seventh child, Hammerer cursed the hypocrisy of the 'swindle nation.'[39] Written conversations between spouses like these, outlining the causes of the gross inequality and injustice in wartime society, could not be suppressed by censorship efforts. While the private exchange of opinions was perhaps less harmful, outright opposition to the continuation of war was a different matter. Front-line soldiers started in the autumn of 1916 to urge their relatives, in letters or while on furlough, not to sign up for the fifth war loan. This negative impact on the morale of the home front triggered systematic attempts to influence the soldiers by means of propaganda, which finally led to the 'Patriotic Instruction' program, rolled out in the field and replacement army in the summer of 1917. The soldiers, however, simply ignored this form of indoctrination, or used reports and meetings to voice their rejection of any annexationist aims.[40]

Since 1916, a broader anti-war current emerged at the front and at the home front. It coalesced around vaguely defined socialist ideas, identified capitalism as the root cause for the prolongation of the war, and demanded substantial democratic reforms. Not only Protestant industrial and agricultural workers supported these ideas, but also a growing number of Catholics, incidentally turning Matthias Erzberger, who had come out as an ardent supporter of peace in spring 1917, into the most popular politician of the Catholic Centre Party and pushing the party to the left. The leadership of the majority SPD, however, was not yet ready to abandon its support of the German war effort. Only once the USPD was founded in April 1917, did the majority feel forced to publicly express opposition to the Reich leadership, in order to prevent the increasingly intense longing for peace from bolstering support for what had formerly been a competing group within the same party. By adopting the formula produced by the Petrograd Soviet of a peace 'without annexations or reparations' on 19 April 1917, the Majority SPD succeeded in making the term 'Scheidemann peace'—named after Philipp Scheidemann, a leading member of the majority party—synonymous with a peace of understanding.

Support for these aims and the potential for protest was strongest where the impact of the war was most intensively felt, at the front. It was here, among front-line soldiers and NCOs, where mobilization for the war fostered a discourse of participatory citizenship that already anticipated and prepared the revolution in November 1918. When front-line soldiers were polled about their support for an 'immediate peace' without annexations, as in spring 1917 by the Social Democratic newspaper *Munich Post*, their response was overwhelmingly positive. The following quote is just one variation on a theme that was running through all responses: 'The Pan-German League should notice that the broader strata of the people are not backing it. Why should the fighters at the front not turn to that particular party that demands, head held high, those *rights* which also the lower strata of the people (*des Volkes*) are entitled to have?'[41] The outright rejection of aggressive nationalism is not even the most remarkable aspect of this political declaration. Pertinent and crucial for the events to come was the language of rights and entitlements of the ordinary people, making claims that rejected any restrictions on the freedom of political expression and transcended, in Prussia and in the Reich, the political system of Wilhelmine Germany.

It is indicative of the severe impediments for political reform in Imperial Germany that the leaders in the *Reichstag* did not properly seize the opportunity that was presented to them by the upsurge in grassroots support for immediate peace and popular participation. To be sure, Matthias Erzberger managed to push the majority parties in the direction of a more critical stance towards the government. Following a meeting of the *Hauptausssschuss*, the parliamentary budget committee, on 6 July 1917, Majority Social Democrats, Center Party, and the left liberals of the Progressive Peoples Party formed the Interparty Committee, temporarily, but not wholeheartedly also supported by the National Liberals. Working as a steering committee for an informal coalition of the majority in the *Reichstag*, and sometimes meeting on a daily basis, the Interparty Committee scored a first major success when the parliament passed a resolution for a peace of 'understanding' on 19 July 1917. This was, indeed, a significant act of defiance by the parliament against the government of Chancellor Bethmann-Hollweg, who had (secretly) endorsed annexations demanded by the Army Supreme Command, and since February 1917 had supported unrestricted submarine warfare. However, the coalition was based on a fragile compromise. Thus, it did not dare to attack the Army Supreme Command and its Quartermaster General, Erich Ludendorff, who wielded more power than the weak chancellor and was the key obstacle to any substantial political reform. The *Reichstag* majority also did not push for full parliamentarization of the political system and, hence, failed to capitalize on the supportive groundswell of popular unrest.

Consequently, Ludendorff used the opportunity to have the vacillating Bethmann-Hollweg removed by the Kaiser for an even weaker chancellor, Georg Michaelis. Ludendorff also supported a new attempt to rally the masses against any further democratization, and in favor of a peace based on German victory and annexations. The German Fatherland Party, founded in September 1917 by leading members of the Pan-German League and the Conservative party, was a direct backlash against the peace resolution of the majority parties. Many members of the Protestant middle-class, including pastors, teachers, civil servants and officers, were appalled by what they perceived as the power of 'public opinion.' They resented that the 'behavior of the government is dictated by its fear of the clamorers.' From the viewpoint of the conservative elites, the drive towards democracy and a negotiated peace effectively represented only 'political sentimentality, sentimental humanitarianism (*Humanitäts-duselei*) and feebleness.'[42] With its aggressive propagation of wide-ranging territorial war aims and attempts to mobilize the masses for extreme nationalism, the Fatherland Party has sometimes been interpreted as a radical departure from conventional Wilhelmine conservatism and as 'the first pre-Fascist mass movement.'[43]

However, claims for the mass appeal of the party have been vastly exaggerated. In 'early 1918,' it was certainly not 'close to 1,000,000 members.'[44] In February 1918, the party had only around 300,000 members. By September, this figure had increased to 800,000. At least one half of these, though, were not people who had signed up as individuals, but who had been incorporated collectively as members of other nationalist pressure groups such as the *Ostmarkenverein* (Association for the Eastern Marches) or via regional branches of the National Liberal Party. Sociologically, the party utterly failed to meet its declared objectives, extending nationalist mobilization beyond the narrow confines of the middle-class, and attracting workers. Ironically, one of the unintended effects of the Fatherland Party was to boost the political activism and citizenship of patriotic middle-class women, as about one-third of the individual members were female. Public meetings were often well attended, but mostly because a large percentage of the crowd was keen to disrupt the gathering. With its pathetic, incompetent leader, the Prussian conservative Wolfgang Kapp, and its traditional style of *Honoratiorenpolitik*, the Fatherland Party was no departure, but the last gasp of the Wilhelmine *Sammlungspolitik*.[45] At the front and in the rear army, the main success of the party was to dispel any remaining illusions that Germany was fighting a defensive war, and to polarize public opinion even further. In the latter half of the war, it should be stressed, any attempts to propagate aggressive nationalism in Germany backfired.

Already at the beginning of 1918, the bottom-up demand for democratization and immediate peace, together with the deep-felt war weariness and material grievances, had created a potential for revolutionary transformation. The revolution in 1918 was not only, as has often been stated, the result of imminent military defeat. At the home front, working-class unrest had already, in April 1917, led to a first major strike wave, mostly among metal workers in Leipzig, Berlin, and some other cities. In January 1918, about a million workers embarked on a mass strike that was in many ways the 'final rehearsal' for the revolution.[46] The center of gravity of this unprecedented protest was Berlin, where about 400,000 workers went on strike, demanding, as elsewhere, immediate peace, a thorough democratization and parliamentarization both in Prussia and in the Reich, the lifting of the state of siege, and the release of political prisoners. The two last points in particular demonstrate the influence of the USPD, but also the clear aim to overcome the militarization of state and society more generally. The strike was a dress rehearsal for the revolution not only through the radicalism of its aims, but also because the workers learned not to rely on the leaders of MSPD and USPD, who joined the strike committees only in order to facilitate a return to work. When the revolutionary mass movement began in the autumn, it was clearly sympathetic to social democratic aims, but bypassed the two socialist parties and caught their leaders by surprise.

At the front, reactions to the January strike were mixed. Outright resentment was voiced only by a minority. However, even the majority that agreed with the key aim of the strike—peace—tended to compare the dangers of life at the front with the generous wages paid in the armaments industry. More importantly, the soldiers had set their hopes on the imminent final offensive at the Western front, which in their view would bring peace more quickly. When Ludendorff embarked on this final, desperate gamble to win the war and the offensive commenced on 21 March, it was greeted with some optimism among the troops. However, hopes soon turned into disappointment, and, when the Allied troops started their counter-offensive in July, into final resignation. From mid-August to Armistice Day, about 750,000 soldiers on the Western front took their fate and that of the German nation, in their own hands and deserted the front in an unstoppable mass movement, boarding trains for the lightly wounded or simply walking back home. Months before the sailors of the High Sea Fleet in Kiel fired the formal starting shot for the revolution with their refusal to board the ships on 29 October 1918, the 'military strike' in the field army was, in the seminal formulation of the historian Wilhelm Deist, the 'decisive precondition for the revolution and determined its form and content,' as it fatally undermined the army as the 'guarantor of the existing order.'[47]

There is some debate about the exact nature and radicalism of the political aims that were shared by the hundreds of thousands of men who abandoned their military duty in the autumn of 1918.[48] It seems obvious that they did not want to endanger their lives for a regime they perceived as corrupt and fundamentally lacking in legitimacy. There is hardly any doubt that the overwhelming majority of them were in favor of a popular form of democratic representation, widely conceived, which would allow for more social equality and liberty than the authoritarian Wilhelmine state. The revolution differs from August 1914, as no intellectuals waited in the wings to express its meaning in an elaborate set of 'ideas of 1918.' However, as a revolution, this was the moment of the people, not the intellectuals. Its first stage comprised the toppling of the monarchy, the sober recognition and acceptance of defeat in a war that had been prolonged by radical nationalists, and the preparation of a national assembly. In this stage, the revolution found support among its core constituency, the Socialist labor movement. It also found significant support among many Catholic workers and small farmers, white collar workers and other members of the lower middle class—who had shifted to the left during the war. The key points of the 'ideas of 1918' were succinctly summed up by a certain Uhlan Görres, who attended the meeting of the representatives of soldier's councils in the field army, held in Bad Ems on 1 and 2 December, for the 7th Cavalry Division: 'All front-line soldiers demand freedom, truth, justice and bread.'[49] In some respects, November 1918 was a moment of national recognition, as August 1914 had been. Four years of mobilization for total war had unleashed a drive towards participatory democracy. As a consequence, the overwhelming majority of Germans embraced the new republic. There was certainly more to the end of the war than only 'exhaustion.'[50]

Interpretations of the November revolution usually focus on the radicalization of the extreme left and on the bloodshed that was the result when the Majority Social Democrats relied on the Freikorps to crush Communist uprisings in Berlin and Munich in early 1919. Surely, these events polarized German politics and fuelled the more radical second phase of the revolution. It should not be overlooked, however, that the Spartacus Group, the precursor of the Communist Party, played hardly any role in the chain of events which led to the declaration of the republic on 9 November 1918. There was a mismatch between the hysterical reaction of a bourgeois public, which perceived Rosa Luxemburg and Karl Liebknecht as the trailblazers of an imminent Bolshevist revolution in Germany, and the actual power of the Spartacus League, which had never had more than 3000 members. The self-demobilization of the field army in the autumn of 1918, on the other hand, determined the subsequent course of the revolution. When, by the end of December, most of the soldiers had returned home, and the elections to the National Assembly were announced for 19 January 1919, two of their main aims—peace and democracy—had already been achieved, and hence their revolutionary zeal faded. Facilitated by the increasing inflation, which gave a boost to German exports and kick-started the economy, millions of veterans were quickly absorbed back into the labor market and civilian society in the immediate post-war period. Thus, the protest potential which had built up during the war faded away quickly. However, this also posed a problem for the republic. As many veterans tended to gloss over or to forget their previous grievances, they left the commemoration of war to the political right, which was keen to use a heroic, militant discourse about the legacy of the war as leverage against the new political system.[51]

17.3 WORLD WAR I AS A CATALYST OF CHANGE

In this brief overview, we have focused on the making and unmaking of a national community in Germany during the war. We have thus accentuated changes in the symbolic construction and representation of war, violence, and national inclusion. Such an accent on the transitional moments and rituals that defined the meaning of the war—August 1914 and November 1918—and on the semantics of community, victim-ization, and citizenship is bound to miss out on another crucial dimension of the war, its 'materiality': the noise of exploding shells, the pain of the wounds inflicted by them, the bad smell of turnips and *Ersatz* groceries, the very corporeal presence of dismemberment, malnutrition, and starvation as mass phenomena on an unprecedented scale.[52] Even the most dramatic and traumatic physical experiences, however, could only contribute towards social change when they were transformed into meaningful communication. The transformation of experiences and perceptions into symbolic communication en-dowed the war with meaning, and these symbolic representations were perhaps the most important legacy of the war for German society and domestic politics.

Undoubtedly, the Nazi movement tapped successfully into the symbolism of nation-al mobilization, which had emerged since August 1914, and owed its appeal to the fact that it could represent itself as the authoritative representative of the front generation. However, this success required an intensive reworking and medialization of the front-line experiences, and was as such never uncontested throughout the Weimar Republic. There was nothing 'inevitable' about a protracted and complicated process by which the image of the German 'warrior,' filled with 'envy' and 'hatred' of the enemy, came to be the hegemonic representation of the Great War.[53] By no means was this transform-ation accomplished before 1930. During the war, nationalist aims and discourses had not unified the German people, but had rather had a divisive impact and had ultimately undermined the war effort. To be sure, fears about the possible brutalizing effects of four years of industrial warfare agitated many observers. It was widely expected that the return of millions of men who had participated in mass violence would spill over into the domestic political scene and cause an aggressive, confrontational style not only of veteran's politics, but also in public opinion more generally.

Such expectations, however, were not restricted to Germany. In the immediate post-war period, for instance, a wider public in the United Kingdom was terrified about the prospect of wholesale brutalization. This expectation seemed justified through a series of violent riots in various British cities in 1919, and by the behavior of the 'Black and Tans,' mostly ex-servicemen who were drafted into the 'Royal Irish Constabulary' in early 1920, when the Black and Tans committed a string of excesses and atrocities against Catholic civilians and alleged Sinn Fein members in Ireland. However, these fears about brutalization faded as quickly away as they had emerged, when the public reestablished the understanding, shared across the political spectrum, that Britain was the quintessential 'peaceable kingdom.' In comparison with Germany, the crucial difference was not a lack of 'brutalization,' but the shared framework of a political culture that was defined by the rejection and de-legitimization of violence.[54] Ever since the Napoleonic wars, on the other hand, political culture in Germany had been framed around bellicose values and codes of honor. No surprise that the Steel-Helmet and other right-wing paramilitary organizations in Weimar exploited the symbolism of the wars of liberation for the names of their units and their rituals.

As brutalization and political violence put their stamp on German politics since 1919, a clear line of continuity can be established. In an attempt to break up the stalemate of trench warfare, the German army had introduced storm troops in 1916, specially trained and equipped groups of elite soldiers who were meant to penetrate the enemy lines. These were precisely 'the men who after the war were to play a leading role in all the counterrevolutionary attempts' and pursued their 'warrior's creed,' in the *Freikorps*, among the Nazi storm troopers, and in other paramilitary formations. However, the peculiar type of front line fighter who fought in the storm troops was, as the military historian Herbert Rosinski noted already in 1939, 'essentially a volunteer.'[55] The over-whelming majority of the 13.2 million men who were mobilized from 1914 to 1918 remained, both technically, in their mode of recruitment, and socially, in their form of participation, conscripts.

The First World War had had a massive impact on the political imaginary of all political groups in Germany, and fundamentally shaped notions of national belonging, class, and citizenship. Participation emerged as a key issue, and contributed towards the 'two radicalisms' in the post-war period: the radicalism in the socialist camp, where the politics of the *Burgfrieden* left a poisonous legacy of internal fragmentation and bitter in-fighting among moderate Social Democrats and Communists; and the radicalism of the middle class, which struggled to find appropriate forms of political representation in the new setting of the republican system. Both radicalizations were deeply entwined, and ultimately bound to the conflicts that had ensued since 1914, rather than simply reflect-ing long-term cleavages in German society.[56] It is important to accentuate rapid change at the level of political symbolism and representation. On the other hand, the relative stability of institutional forms of sociability even under the strains of total war should not be underestimated. Three brief examples must suffice to make this point.

It has long been assumed, first, that the *Bürgertum* or middle class was further fragmented and ultimately dissolved as a social formation due to the war. Recent empirical studies have, however, put a question mark behind this claim. The family as the key institution of middle class sociability provided stability for men and women of the bourgeoisie who coped with the changes brought about by the war. Core values of the bourgeois mindset and cultural practice or *Bürgerlichkeit*, such as cleanliness, a work ethic centered around notions of duty and performance, and the ideal of *Bildung* or intellectual self-formation, survived the war largely if not fully unscathed. Equally persistent were bourgeois notions of paternalism with regard to the lower classes among higher civil servants, a key reason why the revolution in 1918 caught them by surprise and left them speechless and dismayed.[57] Continuity prevailed, secondly, among the Catholic Church. During the war, it provided pastoral care amidst precarious circumstances and helped to foster 'bonds of Catholic solidarity' between French and Germans in the occupied zone in Northern France.[58] After the war, the moral teaching of the Church continued to command respect among one third of the German population, even though the problem of theodicy—how to reconcile the seemingly futile horrors of war with the idea of an almighty God—had sown doubts in the minds of many faithful believers. Particularly in the countryside, the Catholic Church remained, some lapses in the immediate post-war period notwithstanding, an eminent force of social and mental stability.[59]

One can investigate, thirdly, marriage as one of the core institutions in a civilized society. In Freiburg im Breisgau, for instance, a city with a population of 85,000, exactly thirty couples divorced in 1910. Even in this lovely place in the Black Forest, extended separation since the departure of the troops in 1914 led to some alienation between spouses, and the number of divorces trebled to slightly more than ninety in 1920. However, reflecting a similar trend across the country, at least one-third of these separations occurred in couples bound together through *Kriegstrauungen*, marriages which had been hastily arranged more as a patriotic service than as a heartfelt desire from 1914 to 1918. Still, 'this point was lost on those who viewed the rising divorce-rate' in the post-war period as 'clear evidence of moral decline.'[60] As in many other fields of society and politics during the Weimar Republic, the notion of a 'crisis' of family life was a semantic construct, but nonetheless one that exerted considerable influence on the contemporaries and supported calls for radical change.[61] It would be exaggerated, however, to conclude from these developments that the 'very civil institutions of society were fissuring' during the war.[62]

All in all, it is perhaps best to describe the First World War as a catalyst of change in Germany society and politics, rather than as a fundamental caesura and immediate cause of rapid change. Such an assessment seems to be correct with regard to the radicalization of an extreme form of *völkisch* nationalism, which was well under way in the period since 1900. It is an equally fitting formula for the attempts of the SPD-majority to be accepted and integrated into the national fabric of politics. While the 'negative integration' of Socialist labor into Wilhelmine politics has been previously stressed, recent interpretations have emphasized the incremental positive integration of the Social Democratic labor movement into the Reich.[63] Last, but not least, it is worth mentioning that more radical anti-Semitic ideas had become mainstream among circles of the extreme right already before the war. These blueprints for a solution to the alleged 'Jewish question' combined anti-Semitism with racist ideas and hopes of removing the Jews from German soil altogether. Still, these anti-Semitic fantasies stopped short of contemplating the targeted killing of Jews.[64] It was only after war *and* revolution that anti-Semitism turned from a mere 'cultural code,' elaborated in speeches and printed texts, into the recurring practice of physical violent attacks against Jews on behalf of the *Volksgemeinschaft*.[65]

Notes

1. Roland N. Stromberg, *Redemption by War. The Intellectuals and 1914* (Lawrence: Regents Press of Kansas, 1982).
2. Cited in Bernd Ulrich and Benjamin Ziemann (eds), *German Soldiers in the Great War. Letters and Eyewitness Accounts* (Barnsley: Pen & Sword, 2010), 42.
3. Modris Eksteins, *Rites of Spring. The Great War and the Birth of the Modern Age* (London: Black Swan, 1990), 18, 275.
4. George L. Mosse, *Fallen Soldiers: Reshaping the Memory of the World Wars* (New York/Oxford: Oxford University Press, 1990), 7, 10.
5. Omer Bartov, *Murder in Our Midst: The Holocaust, Industrial Killing, and Representation* (New York/Oxford: Oxford University Press, 1996), 48f.
6. Ibid., 49.
7. For a systematic analysis of methods and contexts of killing in the First World War, see Benjamin Ziemann, 'Soldaten,' in Gerhard Hirschfeld, Gerd Krumeich, and Irina Renz (eds), *Enzyklopädie Erster Weltkrieg* (Paderborn: Schöningh, 2003), 155–168, figure 157.
8. See Benjamin Ziemann, 'Germany after the First World War—A Violent Society? Results and Implications of Recent Research on Weimar Germany,' *Journal of Modern European History* 1 (2003), 80–95.
9. See Moritz Föllmer, *Die Verteidigung der bürgerlichen Nation. Industrielle und hohe Beamte in Deutschland und Frankreich 1900–1930* (Göttingen: Vandenhoeck & Ruprecht, 2002).
10. Cited in Ulrich/Ziemann, *German Soldiers*, 26.
11. For the photo, and a mostly misleading interpretation, see Peter Fritzsche, *Germans into Nazis* (Cambridge, Mass/London: Harvard University Press, 1998), 1–7.
12. See Jeffrey Verhey, *The Spirit of 1914: Militarism, Myth and Mobilization in Germany* (Cambridge: Cambridge University Press, 2000), 58–114, quote 82; Benjamin Ziemann, *War Experiences in Rural Germany, 1914–1923* (Oxford. New York: Berg, 2007), 16–27.
13. Fritzsche, *Germans*, 22.
14. See the detailed account by Wolfgang Kruse, *Krieg und nationale Integration. Eine Neuinterpretation des sozialdemokratischen Burgfriedensschlusses 1914/15* (Essen: Klartext, 1993); compare Verhey, *Spirit*, 156–161.
15. Fritzsche, *Germans*, 25.
16. See, for instance, Wolfgang J. Mommsen, *Imperial Germany, 1867–1918. Politics, Culture and Society in an Authoritarian State* (London: Arnold, 1995), 205–216.

17. Steffen Bruendel, *Volksgemeinschaft oder Volksstaat? Die 'Ideen von 1914' und die Neuord-nung Deutschlands im Ersten Weltkrieg* (Berlin: Akademie Verlag, 2003), 102–141, 313.

18. Gunther Mai, "Verteidigungskrieg' und 'Volksgemeinschaft.' Staatliche Selbstbehaup-tung, nationale Solidarität und soziale Befreiung in Deutschland in der Zeit des Ersten Weltkrieges,' in Wolfgang Michalka (ed.), *Der Erste Weltkrieg. Wirkung-Wahrnehmung-Analyse* (Munich/Zürich: Piper, 1994), 583–602, 589–591.

19. Emil Lederer, 'On the Sociology of War,' *Archives Européennes de Sociologie* 47 (2006), 241–268, 244, 260; translation amended from the original; idem, 'Zur Soziologie des Weltkrieges,' *Archiv für Sozialwissenschaft und Sozialpolitik* 39 (1915), 347–384, 349f., 373.

20. Bernd Weisbrod, 'Die Politik der Repräsentation. Das Erbe des Ersten Weltkrieges und der Formwandel der Politik in Europa,' in Hans Mommsen (ed.), *Der Erste Weltkrieg und die europäische Nachkriegsordnung. Sozialer Wandel und Formveränderung der Politik* (Cologne: Böhlau, 2000), 13–41.

21. Bernd Ulrich, *Die Augenzeugen. Deutsche Feldpostbriefe in Kriegs-und Nachkriegszeit 1914–1933* (Essen: Klartext, 1997), 106–142, quote 109.

22. Christine Brocks, *Die bunte Welt der Krieges. Bildpostkarten aus dem Ersten Weltkrieg 1914–1918* (Essen: Klartext, 2008), 30–32.

23. Brocks, *Die bunte Welt des Krieges*, 53–147, 237–252; on the 'crisis of representation' see Bernd Hüppauf, 'Experiences of Modern Warfare and the Crisis of Representation,' *New German Critique* 59 (1993), 41–76.

24. Christhard Hoffmann, 'Between Integration and Rejection: The Jewish Community in Germany, 1914–1918,' in John Horne (ed.), *State, Society and Mobilization in Europe during the First World War* (Cambridge: Cambridge University Press, 1997), 89–104, here 90–97.

25. Ibid., 103.

26. Werner T. Angress, 'The German 'Judenzählung' of 1916. Genesis—Consequences—Significance,' *Leo Baeck Institute Year Book* 23 (1978), 117–137.

27. See Werner Jochmann, 'Die Ausbreitung des Antisemitismus,' in Werner E. Mosse (ed.), *Deutsches Judentum in Krieg und Revolution 1916–1923* (Tübingen: J. C. B. Mohr, 1971), 409–510; Werner Bergmann and Juliane Wetzel, 'Antisemitismus im Ersten und Zweiten Weltkrieg. Ein Forschungsüberblick,' in Bruno Thoß and Hans-Erich Volkmann (eds), *Erster Weltkrieg—Zweiter Weltkrieg: Ein Vergleich. Krieg, Kriegserlebnis, Kriegserfahrung in Deutschland* (Paderborn: Schöningh, 2002), 437–469. See the qualifications made by Dietmar Molthagen, *Das Ende der Bürgerlichkeit? Liverpooler und Hamburger Bürgerfa-milien im Ersten Weltkrieg* (Göttingen: Wallstein, 2007), 397f., with regard to middle class families.

28. Vejas Gabriel Liulevicius, *War Land on the Eastern Front. Culture, National Identity, and German Occupation in World War I* (Cambridge: Cambridge University Press, 2000), 120; Klaus Latzel, *Deutsche Soldaten—nationalsozialistischer Krieg? Kriegserlebnis-Kriegserfahrung 1939–1945* (Paderborn: Schöningh, 1998), 166–171.

29. Belinda J. Davis, *Home Fires Burning. Food, Politics, and Everyday Life in World War I Berlin* (Chapel Hill: University of North Carolina Press, 2000), 132–135.

30. Excerpt from a letter written in Dresden, 11 June 1917: Bayerische Staatsbibliothek München, Handschriftenabteilung, Schinnereriana.

31. Ziemann, *War Experiences*, 166–176, 191–195; Davis, *Home Fires*, 191–196.

32. Jean-Louis Robert, 'The Image of the Profiteer,' in Jay Winter and Jean-Louis Robert (eds), *Capital Cities at War. Paris, London, Berlin 1914–1919* (Cambridge: Cambridge University Press, 1997), 104–132, 126–131.

33. Jochmann, *Ausbreitung*, 435ff.; Bergmann/Wetzel, *Antisemitismus*, 444f.

34. Gerhard Hirschfeld, 'Germany,' in John Horne (ed.), *A Companion to World War I* (Chichester: Wiley, 2010), 432–446, 440.

35. Ulrich/Ziemann, *German Soldiers*, 128.

36. Davis, *Home Fires*, 80–89, 96–98.

37. Kathleen Canning, 'Between Crisis and Order. The Imaginary of Citizenship in the Aftermath of War,' in Wolfgang Hardtwig (ed.), *Ordnungen in der Krise. Zur politischen Kulturgeschichte Deutschlands 1900–1933* (Munich: R. Oldenbourg, 2007), 215–228, 223.

38. Ute Daniel, *The War from Within. German Working Class Women in the First World War* (Oxford: Berg, 1997), 273–294; Benjamin Ziemann, 'Geschlechterbeziehungen in deutschen Feldpostbriefen des Ersten Weltkrieges,' in Christa Hämmerle and Edith Saurer (eds), *Briefkulturen und ihr Geschlecht. Zur Geschichte der privaten Korrespondenz vom 16. Jahrhundert bis heute* (Vienna: Böhlau, 2003), 261–282.

39. Cited in Ulrich and Ziemann, *German Soldiers*, 106.

40. Ziemann, *War Experiences*, 66–71.

41. Letter excerpt provided by the *Münchener Post*, included in a memorandum by War Ministry press officer von Sonnenburg, 15 June 1917: Bayerisches Hauptstaatsarchiv/Abt. IV, Munich, MKr 2332. Emphasis in the original.

42. From the letter by a lieutenant at the Eastern front, 9 January 1918: Denis Bechmann and Heinz Mestrup (eds), 'Wann wird das Morden ein Ende nehmen?' *Feldpostbriefe und Tagebucheinträge zum Ersten Weltkrieg* (Erfurt: Landeszentrale für politische Bildung Thüringen, 2008), 274.

43. Wolfgang Sauer, 'National Socialism: Totalitarianism or Fascism?,' *American Historical Review* 73 (1967), 404–424, 420; MacGregor Knox, *To the Threshold of Power, 1922/33. Origins and Dynamics of the Fascist and National Socialist Dictatorships*, vol. 1 (Cambridge: Cambridge University Press, 2007), 190f.

44. Roger Chickering, in his otherwise excellent *Imperial Germany and the Great War, 1914–1918* (Cambridge: Cambridge University Press, 1998), 165.

45. See the definitive study by Heinz Hagenlücke, *Deutsche Vaterlandspartei. Die nationale Rechte am Ende des Kaiserreichs* (Düsseldorf: Droste, 1997), 180–187, 192–215, 385–411.

46. Volker Ullrich, *Vom Augusterlebnis zur Novemberrevolution. Beiträge zur Sozialgeschichte Hamburgs und Norddeutschlands im Ersten Weltkrieg 1914–1918* (Bremen: Donat, 1999), 109–157.

47. Wilhelm Deist, 'The Military Collapse of the German Empire,' *War in History* 3 (1996), 186–207, 205, 207. The attempt to revise this argument by Alexander Watson, *Enduring the Great War: Combat, Morale and Collapse in the German and British Armies, 1914–1918* (Cambridge: Cambridge University Press, 2008), 184–231, is fundamentally flawed.

48. Wolfgang Kruse, 'Krieg und Klassenheer. Zur Revolutionierung der deutschen Armee im Ersten Weltkrieg,' *Geschichte und Gesellschaft* 22 (1996), 530–561, 559f.

49. See the document in Heinz Hürten (ed.), *Zwischen Revolution und Kapp-Putsch. Militär und Innenpolitik 1918–1920* (Düsseldorf: Droste, 1977), 17.

50. See Roger Chickering, *The Great War and Urban Life in Germany: Freiburg, 1914–1918* (Cambridge: Cambridge University Press, 2007), 548ff.

51. See Richard Bessel, *Germany after the First World War* (Oxford: Clarendon Press, 1993).

52. See Chickering, *Great War*, 9 (quote), 262–317, 331–351.

53. Quote: Knox, *Threshold*, 194.

54. Jon Lawrence, 'Forging a Peaceable Kingdom. War, Violence, and Fear of Brutalization in Post-First World War Britain,' *Journal of Modern History* 75 (2003), 557–589; Adrian Gregory, 'Peculiarities of the English? War, Violence and Politics 1900–1939,' *Journal of Modern European History* 1 (2003), 44–59; for Germany, see Ziemann, 'Violent Society?'

55. Herbert Rosinski, *The German Army* (London: Pall Mall Press, 1966) [first edition 1939], 149. See Robert G.L. Waite, *Vanguard of Nazism. The Free Corps Movement in Post-war Germany 1918–1923* (Cambridge, Mass.: Harvard University Press, 1952), 23–30; Knox, *Threshold*, 194, fails to make this crucial distinction.

56. See the important article by Helge Matthiesen, 'Zwei Radikalisierungen—Bürgertum und Arbeiterschaft in Gotha 1918–1923,' *Geschichte und Gesellschaft* 21 (1995), 32–62.

57. See Molthagen, *Ende der Bürgerlichkeit?*; Föllmer, *Verteidigung*, 149f.

58. Patrick J. Houlihan, *Local Catholicism as Lived War Experience. Everyday Religious Practice in Occupied Northern France, 1914–1918* (unpublished manuscript, 2010), 27. I am indebted to Patrick J. Houlihan for sending me a copy of his article.

59. Ziemann, *War Experiences*, 240–268.

60. Chickering, *The Great War and Urban Life*, 352–354; quote: Bessel, *Germany*, 232.

61. See, with further references, Benjamin Ziemann, 'Weimar was Weimar. Politics, Culture and the Emplotment of the German Republic,' *German History* 28, (2010) 553–560.

62. Michael Geyer, 'Review of Roger Chickering, The Great War and Urban Life,' *Central European History* 43 (2010), 372.

63. See, in comparative perspective, Marcel van der Linden, 'The National Integration of European Working Classes (1871–1914): Exploring the Causal Configuration,' *International Review of Social History* 33 (1988), 285–311.

64. Helmut Walser Smith, *The Continuities of German History: Nation, Religion, and Race across the Long Nineteenth Century* (Cambridge: Cambridge University Press, 2008), 167–210.

65. Benjamin Ziemann, ''Linguistische Wende' und 'kultureller Code' in der Geschichtsschreibung zum modernen Antisemitismus,' *Jahrbuch für Antisemitismusforschung* 14 (2005), 301–322; Michael Wildt, *Volksgemeinschaft als Selbstermächtigung. Gewalt gegen Juden in der deutschen Provinz 1919 bis 1939* (Hamburg: Hamburger Edition, 2007), 69–100.

Bibliography

BESSEL, RICHARD, *Germany after the First World War* (Oxford: Clarendon Press, 1993).

CARSTEN, FRANCIS L., *War against War. British and German Radical Movements in the First World War* (Berkeley, Los Angeles: University of California Press, 1982).

CHICKERING, ROGER, *Imperial Germany and the Great War, 1914–1918* (Cambridge: Cambridge University Press, 1998).

——, *The Great War and Urban Life in Germany: Freiburg, 1914–1918* (Cambridge: Cambridge University Press, 2007).

DANIEL, UTE, *The War from Within. German Working Class Women in the First World War* (Oxford: Berg, 1997).

FELDMAN, GERALD D., *Army, Industry and Labor in Germany, 1914–1918* (Princeton: Princeton University Press, 1966).

STIBBE, MATTHEW, *Germany 1914–1933. Politics, Society and Culture* (Harlow: Longman, 2010).

ULRICH, BERND and BENJAMIN ZIEMANN (eds), *German Soldiers in the Great War. Letters and Eyewitness Accounts* (Barnsley: Pen & Sword, 2010).

VERHEY, JEFFREY, *The Spirit of 1914: Militarism, Myth and Mobilization in Germany* (Cambridge: Cambridge University Press, 2000).

WELCH, DAVID, *Germany, Propaganda and Total War, 1914–1918. The Sins of Omission* (London: Athlone Press, 2000).

WINTER, JAY, *Sites of Memory, Sites of Mourning. The Great War in European Cultural History* (Cambridge: Cambridge University Press, 1996).

ZIEMANN, BENJAMIN, *War Experiences in Rural Germany, 1914–1923* (Oxford/New York: Berg, 2007).

——, 'Germany after the First World War—A Violent Society? Results and Implications of Recent Research on Weimar Germany,' *Journal of Modern European History* 1 (2003), 80–95 (online at: <http://eprints.whiterose.ac.uk/4748/>).

——, 'Weimar was Weimar. Politics, Culture and the Emplotment of the German Republic,' *German History* 28 (2010), 542–571.

CHAPTER 18

···

THE GERMAN NATIONAL ECONOMY IN AN ERA OF CRISIS AND WAR, 1917–1945

···

ADAM TOOZE

WHEN in 1989 Frances Fukuyama announced his contentious thesis that the developed world had entered the 'end of history,' the country he had specifically in mind was not the United States, but West Germany.[1] Up-dating Hegel he claimed that the Federal Republic of Germany was a polity in which the basic problems of social and political organization had been definitively resolved. West Germany had embraced market capitalism and parliamentary democracy as the only possible modes of social organization. Unlike the USA it had foresworn the temptations of fervent nationalism in exchange for the shared prosperity and peace of the European Community. The underpinning of this state of satisfaction was the relentless growth of the German economy, which meant that, distributional issues aside, the needs of the entire population were met in abundance. Viewed over the long-run, the German economy does, indeed, appear to fit the role that Fukuyama assigned to it as an irrepressible engine of modernization. After each of the great blows dealt to it between 1914 and 1945, it bounced back with remarkable resilience towards the long-run trend line for growth in GDP *per capita*. By the early 1970s West Germany led Europe into a common state of affluence and economic convergence (Fig. 18.1).

Viewed from this angle the history of the twentieth century can be narrated as a quasi natural history, in which the rate or progress was dictated by the accumulation and improvement of the productive forces—labor, capital, natural resources, and technology. In such a history, the most notable developments of the early twentieth century would be technical innovation, improvements in education and the continuing migration of labor from the countryside to the city. Nor, despite its deterministic flavor

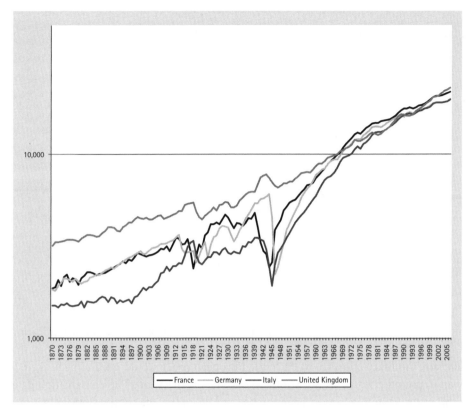

FIG. 18.1 European economic convergence, 1870–2005: GDP measured in comparable dollars of 1990 (Geary–Khamis dollars).

Source: Angus Maddison, OECD.

need this narrative be either depoliticized or dehumanized. The desire, in the face of political upheaval, to maintain the stable functioning of the economic infrastructure and the rhythms of everyday life was a powerful historical force in its own right.

All the time, however, the scope for political control over economic life was on the increase. Between 1900 and 1950 by far the most significant structural change in German economic life was the hugely increased share of national income passing through the accounts of the state. At the same time, however, the sovereignty of the German state, which was relatively untrammelled before 1914, was after the constitution of the FRG in 1949 constrained within a tight mesh of international economic and security networks.

Again, such changes were far from particular to Germany. They, too, can be naturalized as part of a story of modernization. It could be argued, for instance, that as incomes increased and needs became more sophisticated, a greater share of societal resources tended to be allocated to the collective provision of human services through the state.[2] Indeed, from the late nineteenth century social commentators in both Europe and America viewed the public services provided by Germany's municipalities and federal states as exemplary of this trend. Likewise, the tendency of the nation state to become enmeshed in networks of international obligation and responsibility was rationalized by the emerging school of functionalist international relations theory as a basic feature of an increasingly complex international society. In the 1920s such ideas were essential to inspiring the work of the League of Nations and later became the founding ideology of the European Community. It was Germany's enthusiastic embrace of such organizations after 1949, its willingness to surrender sovereignty, its reluctance to assert the power that might have derived from its economic muscle, that marked it out for Fukuyama and others as a society, perhaps the first, to have moved definitively beyond the nation state and the terrible history to which that political form had given rise.

However, history, as Hegel observed, works in cunning ways. The model of Western security and economic co-operation that triumphed in 1989 was originally designed as much to keep 'Germany down' as to keep the 'Soviets out.' NATO and the European Community were built on the ruins left by two vastly destructive bids by Germany to forestall the pacified, materialistic, liberal vision of the end of history that Fukuyama celebrated in 1989. First the Kaiser and then Hitler had violently resisted the logic that dictated that Germany's destiny lay in the common European fate of progressive and peaceful modernization. The principal means of challenging that fate was, of course, the German military, which had won such acclaim in Bismarck's wars of unification. However, after a few months of modern artillery warfare in 1914, it was obvious that Germany's military effort to overturn the European order would need to be backed up by an unprecedented effort at national economic organization. The demarcation dates of this essay, from 1917 to 1945, span the rise and fall of this idea of the German national economy not merely as a vehicle for peaceful social evolution, but as a means by which to violently redirect the course of history.

18.1

In 1916, Germany and the other European combatants evaded President Wilson's offer of a 'peace without victory.' Instead, the Kaiser installed Hindenburg and Ludendorff as the new High Command. With their allies in heavy industry they embarked on the most ambitious of Germany's wartime production efforts—the Hindenburg program—aiming to double armaments output within the year.[3] To gain the trust of organized labor for one more big push, the Wilhelmine regime had for the first time involved the trade unions in the drafting of the so-called Auxiliary Service Law, which conscripted all men between the ages of 17 and 60. The unions' support was all the more important because over the winter of 1916–1917 the cities had begun to starve. Germany, of course, had a blockade weapon of its own, the U Boats. In January 1917 the new High Command took the fateful decision to unleash an all out attack. By the autumn it hoped they would sink enough shipping to bring Britain to its knees. In doing so it accepted the virtual certainty of US entry into the war, with consequences that would be decisive not only for German, but for European, and indeed, world history. How else was Germany to respond? The resources at Hindenburg and Ludendorff's disposal were those of a European workshop economy of somewhat above-average efficiency. Britain, France, and Russia by comparison organized their war effort on a truly global scale.[4] Three-quarters of the shells fired on the German trenches in the awesome preparatory barrage on the Somme in July 1916 had been supplied from North America. This disparity had haunted German strategy since the late nineteenth century. As a nation state how should Germany assert itself against the global hegemony of the British Empire and the emerging continental superpowers of the United States and Russia? One response was, of course, to establish Germany's own empire. As the future foreign Minister of the Weimar Republic, Gustav Stresemann put it in 1915: 'Above all we must aim for a strengthening of our economic position in Central Europe (Mitteleuropa), so that we may have what American industry has, ... a territory of 150 million people ... to satisfying whose consumption industry can direct all its enterprise.'[5] When Russia collapsed in 1917 this and more seemed within reach. By the early summer of 1918 the Kaiser's troops had penetrated as far south as the Caucasus. The grain, oil, and metal ores of the Ukraine and the Caucasus seemed within their grasp.

The military successes of the Kaiser's armies in the first three years of the Great War contributed to the aura of modernity and power that had grown up around the German economy since the 1890s. In far away Japan, conservative commentators wondered whether they had not joined the wrong side. In 1916 London and France came together with their allies in Paris to design a future world economic order specifically aimed at containing the German economic and military threat. To do so the British government—the historic progenitor of global economic liberalism—announced its willingness to adopt protectionism and state sponsorship of technological development. Meanwhile, the young Bolshevik theorist Bucharin, writing from Swiss exile, characterized the German war economy as a horrifying outgrowth of 'organized capitalism.' It was 'an iron organization which envelops the living body of society in its tenacious, grasping paws. It is a new leviathan before which the fantasy of Thomas Hobbes seems child's play. ... there is no power on earth that can compare with it.'[6] Walther Rathenau's War Raw Materials Office was Lenin's inspiration for the kind of planning that might be possible in a transition to socialism, not of course that a Russian overthrow would have any historic legitimacy unless the revolution spread quickly to the heartland of the German proletariat. By 1917 the German economy had thus come to stand as an emblem of the awesome potential of industrial modernity. Ironically, however, the men who managed the German war economy in World War I were highly critical of its achievements and compared it unfavorably with the centralized organization imposed on Britain by the charismatic leadership of Lloyd George. By contrast with the centralized state structures of Britain or France, the decentralized constitution of Bismarckian Germany was an obstacle to the creation of a state-controlled national economy. Prior to 1914 it was the member states, not the Reich that had responsibility for industrial policy.[7] When war broke out it was private industrialists, led by the Walter Rathenau of the AEG group, who took the initiative in launching an improvised system of committees to organize the purchase and allocation of key raw materials. The formation of a more centralized organization, in the autumn of 1916 headed by the Kriegsamt, in fact, resulted from a bitter power struggle between military high command and the Prussian war ministry. The prize program of the new regime, the Hindenburg program was, in fact, a self-serving vehicle for the interests of German heavy industry, which after superficial initial successes unhinged the precarious balance of the German war economy. Even more serious was the failure of the German state to marshal the resources of German agriculture, which was at least as responsible as the blockade for the failure of the food supply.[8] If 1916–1917 is the origin of the myth of the German planned economy, it is also the origin of the recurrent twentieth-century nightmare of mass hunger and deprivation. Combined with the reluctance of Hindenburg and Ludendorff to force their conservative allies to make concessions to the new democratic mood, it was chronic hunger that left the Wilhelmine regime unable to rally the home front. By 1918, the political survival of the Kaiserreich had come to rest on the vain hope of one last, decisive military success. However, in the West, the entry of the United States meant that the material odds against the Kaiser's armies were hopeless. It was not Imperial Germany's self-consciously illiberal militarist industrialism that triumphed in World War I, but the militant brand of capitalist liberalism, trumpeted by Wilson and the Entente.

18.2

The Wilhelmine regime was overthrown in November 1918 and a democratic republican regime established. In early 1919, the new Republican constitution of Germany made the satisfaction of basic material needs into a constitutional foundation of the new state. However, there was no radical reckoning with the old order. Some have argued that the prospects for that democratic political system might have been enhanced if it had been accompanied by a more thorough going social and economic transformation. If the German bourgeoisie had missed its moment in the 'liberal revolution' of 1848, in 1918 it was the German working-class and the SPD who stood accused of shirking their 'historic responsibility.'[9]

However, it is precisely here, amidst the chaos of defeat and revolution that we see the 'economy' in its other role as a powerful force for continuity in national history. One of the most convincing explanations for the unwillingness to gamble on an all-out revolution was the fear of massive disruption to the complex organism of the national economy.[10] Already in October 1918 as the Wilhelmine regime wobbled, the chief employers' organizations and trade unions had bonded together in the so-called Zentrale Arbeitsgemeinschaft (ZAG) to erect a dam against political disorder. Amidst revolution and defeat they would preserve the German economy as the foundation of national survival.[11] It was now not only the German population whose demands needed to be satisfied from its national resources. On signing the Armistice, the German political class managed to convince itself that President Wilson would secure a moderate financial settlement. The peacemakers at Versailles decided to put off the day at which the final bill was presented. However, when the London ultimatum finally came, in May 1921, the shock was terrible: 132 billion Reichsmark, 180 percent of GDP, payable over much of the rest of the century.

Struggling to define Germany's 'capacity to pay,' the Reich's authorities set out for the first time to actually define, measure and govern the German national economy.[12] Statistics had been a tool of European state-building since the seventeenth century. However, now, as Rathenau put it in one of his Delphic essays, 'the economy was Germany's fate.'[13] The Reich's economic statistics were at the center of both national and international attention. By the early 1920s the Reich was issuing a running week by week commentary on the state of the national economy. Even cabinet meetings were scheduled according to the timetable of economic news bulletins.

However, if economic affairs dominated politics, the role of the state in economic life had vastly expanded as well. During the final stages of the war and its immediate aftermath the Reich hastily erected the apparatus of national economic governance that the Bismarckian constitution had lacked. Labor, Food and Agriculture, Transport and the National Economy itself were now defined as spheres of Ministerial responsibility. A huge slice of national income sluiced through the state's budget.[14] However, this did not necessarily make control easier. The state, although expanded in size, had forfeited much of its authority. The private organizations of capital and labor were more assertive than ever before.

Since the turn of the century, revolutionary syndicalists had speculated that in an economy sustained by the labor-intensive processes of coal mining, railway transport, post, and telegraph, the general strike was the ultimate revolutionary weapon. The early history of the Weimar Republic certainly confirmed this intuition. When the paramilitary Freikorps launched the Kapp Putsch in 1920, they were disarmed by a general strike. However, by the same token, big business and the unions also exercised a veto over policies that were not to their liking. Faced with the costs of the war the trade-offs were bound to be painful. After a brief period of respite, from the autumn of 1921, the failure of the fledgling parliamentary regime to master the power play of the interest groups drove inflation ever more rapidly upwards, fanning back into life the apocalyptic politics of the final years of the war. In November 1922, the SPD, the party that had made the revolution, left government. The new right-wing cabinet decided to wager the survival of the Republic on an all out confrontation with the French. In January 1923, after Germany had failed to make timber and coal reparations deliveries, Poincare ordered the French Army to seize the most valuable asset of the European economy, the heavy industrial region of the Ruhr.[15] Once more, the Weimar Republic responded with a deliberate effort to paralyze the economic machine. Berlin paid Ruhr industrialists and workers not to produce for the enemy. However, as was only to be expected, this triggered a comprehensive economic meltdown. Prices spiraled to astronomic levels. Whereas the earlier bursts of inflation could be justified as means of sustaining economic activity, the hyperinflation of 1923 led to collapse. As people sought refuge in alternative currencies the interconnected system of production and exchange that gave the national economy its coherence began to come apart.

18.3

Faced with this disaster, the logic of self-preservation reasserted itself. Too many people both inside and outside Germany had too much to lose to allow a complete collapse of Germany and the disruption of its economic engine. By 1923 Britain had already come to appreciate how much it stood to gain from a recovery of the German economy. The willingness of American private investors to gamble on a recovery of the German currency had been propping up the German balance of payments since 1919. In 1923 the US State Department finally let it be known that if Germany were willing to cooperate, it would seek to moderate French reparations demands, while authorizing Wall Street to offer the long-term credits that Germany needed to finance its foreign payments.[16]

This was the strategic architecture embraced by Weimar's most famous foreign Minister, Gustav Stresemann, and formalized in the Dawes Plan of 1924.[17] Having failed in 1917 to stop the extension of American economic power to Europe by means of the U Boat, Stresemann now welcomed American capital as the foundation for a post-military security strategy. Germany was denied a significant army by the Versailles treaty. The credit of the Reich was exhausted. The Reichsbahn, Germany's gigantic national railway system, was already mortgaged to the reparations creditors. However, Germany's big businesses and bustling industrial cities remained attractive propositions.[18] The lasting ties of economic interdependence would substitute for the dangerous system of military alliances. Wall Street's three billion dollar investment in the Weimar Republic would make America into Germany's protector. In due course America's stake would grow so large Washington would have an interest in seeing to it that the most onerous reparations obligations were lifted.[19]

It is commonly said that US funding enabled the Weimar Republic to buy domestic political stability. It is certainly true that the Weimar Republic built on the legacy of the Bismarckian welfare state. In addition to the existing systems of retirement and invalidity insurance, state-controlled rents and increased investment in public housing provided affordable housing to millions. In 1927 the capstone of the modern welfare state was added with the introduction of unemployment insurance. However, this was not the work of radical Social Democrats. Between 1922 and 1928 the SPD was out of power at the Reich level. Expanding the welfare state reflected a broadly-based social consciousness across much of the German party spectrum. Unemployment insurance was carried by a huge *Reichstag* majority of 355 votes to 47 against with only 15 abstentions. This may appear generous, but in light of the real affluence experienced in the 1920s by much of American society and at least the middle classes in Britain and France, it is worth stressing quite how modest was the living standard of most Germans. Claims about an era of 'mass consumption' in the 1920s should be treated with skepticism.[20] The basics of food, clothing, and shelter accounted for the vast majority of household spending. Although the working class no doubt benefited from the welfare state, they also paid for it through flat rate contributions that imposed a heavy

Table 18.1 Weimar's volatile balance of payments

million Reichsmark	1927			1929			1931			1932		
	Inflows (exports and borrowing)	Outflows (imports and repayment)	Balance	Inflows (exports and borrowing)	Outflows (imports and repayment)	Balance	Inflows (exports and borrowing)	Outflows (imports and repayment)	Balance	Inflows (exports and borrowing)	Outflows (imports and repayment)	Balance
All trade	12455	14975	−2520	15701	15221	480	11249	8021	3228	6997	5680	1317
Reparations	205	1584	−1379	188	2337	−2149	0	988	−988		160	−160
Interest	335	680	−345	400	1200	−800	300	1500	−1200	200	1100	−900
Total current account			−4244			−2469			1040			257
Central bank gold	574	122	452	510	345	165	1653		1653	256		256
Sum of c.a. and gold movements			−3792	510	345	−2304			2693			513
Balance of capital movements			3792	4141	1983	2304			−2693			−513
New long term loans	1345	135	1210	340	11	329	358	232	126	100	136	−36
New purchases/sales of assets	575	20	555	1546	1361	185	512	723	−211	200	150	50
Short-term capital movements	2711	622	2089	2255	611	1644	2682	5555	−2873	486	1013	−527

Source: IfK, Konjunkturstatistisches Handbuch 1936 (Berlin, 1935).

regressive burden, particularly on the less well off. For the overwhelming majority such glamorous items of 'mass consumption' as radios, motorbikes or cars were quite out of the question.

It is undeniable of course that the Weimar Republic exhibited the symptoms of an economy out of balance. The balance of payments statistics regularly compiled by the SRA revealed a large trade deficit and dangerous levels of short-term borrowing (Table 18.1).

Both at the time and since, the state of the Weimar economy has been the subject of bitter recrimination.[21] High wage demands by trade unions, meddlesome state arbitration, and inflated welfare budgets have been blamed for driving up costs, squeezing profits, and stifling German exports. However, to infer causation from such data is notoriously difficult. Under the rules of the international gold standard to which Germany had returned under the Dawes Plan in 1924, as foreign funds flowed into Germany, the additional purchasing power tended necessarily to raise prices and wages, which, in turn, tended to depress exports and raise imports. If we remember the conditions of Germany's stabilization in 1924, then the Republic's use of foreign funds appears less as a political cop out, than as an essential element in Stresemann's strategic gamble to assert his country's national interests. The debts owed to America were the lever with which Germany would secure the removal of French and British forces of occupation in the Rhineland and put an end to reparations. It was a risky strategy both in political and economic terms.

Germany's business community led the charge against the welfare spending and trade union recognition, which underpinned the domestic stability of the Weimar Republic. However, it is also true that much of German big business found the Republic's foreign policy very much to its liking. After re-admission to the League of Nations in 1926, Germany, despite the protectionism of its agrarian lobby, was a consistent advocate of the liberal, multilateral trade regime.[22] In the competition for American funds, German business enjoyed a huge advantage over France, whose government refused to settle its war debts. By the end of the 1920s, Germany's world-beating chemical industry, organized in the gigantic IG Farben group, and its leading electrical engineering conglomerates, Siemens and AEG, had negotiated global market-sharing agreements with their US counterparts.[23] GM had bought Opel. Ford had established a presence in Cologne. German heavy industry not only borrowed on good terms on Wall Street, but joined its Western European neighbors in the formation of a steel cartel that was widely seen as the industrial counterpart to the diplomatic rapprochement at the Locarno Conference of 1925. Of course, the ultra nationalists were never satisfied. However, they had the backing of only a few major industrialists and bankers. Nor was the Reichswehr successful in recruiting big business collaborators for its efforts at clandestine rearmament. The vista of security and prosperity offered by profitable arrangements with both European and American partners was far too attractive. It took the onset of an unprecedented global economic crisis to restore nationalist militarism as a credible, historic option.

18.4

The cyclical downturn that began in Germany in 1928 was not unexpected. Even in 1930, when access to US capital began to dry up and unemployment rose alarmingly, it was no catastrophe. For the center-right cabinet of Chancellor Bruening, which took office after the SPD cabinet refused to agree to cuts in unemployment benefits, the recession provided the opportunity to redress the public sector imbalance by raising taxes and cutting expenditure, thus putting severe downward pressure on wages and prices. Balance of payments adjustment under the rules of the gold standard required nothing less.[24] Furthermore, the formula worked. Despite falling global demand, German exports held up surprisingly well. At the same time, the German import bill was cut in half by plunging domestic demand. Falling world commodity prices shifted the terms of trade in Germany's favor. The trade deficit of -2.5 billion Reichsmarks in 1927 was transformed by 1931 into a surplus of 3.2 billion. At the price of 4 million unemployed, the Weimar Republic was now able to meet its external obligations in full, even without new borrowing.

What Bruening and his supporters underestimated was the risk that shock therapy would trigger a chain reaction, which they could not control and which would undermine their own essentially conservative goals.[25] Already in the summer of 1930, to impose the first round of deflation Bruening had to resort to the infamous emergency powers of Reichspresident Hindenburg. His effort to gain a solid *Reichstag* majority was undercut in September 1930 by a huge surge in support for the Nazis. Bruening responded by shifting dramatically to the right on foreign policy, launching plans for a customs union with the ailing Austrian republic. The revival of such *Grossdeutsch* ambitions in turn undermined confidence in international capital markets, notably in Paris, where Bruening had been earning credit for his painful economic measures.[26] In June 1931, further sabre-rattling combined with the attritional impact of the deflation on balance sheets triggered a panic. Confidence in Germany's commitment to its external creditors collapsed. Funds flowed out of the banks. The DANAT bank was discovered to have made catastrophic losses.[27] Bruening was forced to declare a prolonged bank holiday and suspend convertibility, effectively ending Germany's membership of the gold standard. In a desperate effort to avoid a complete collapse, the Reichsbank imposed comprehensive exchange controls.

It is commonly said that Bruening deliberately bankrupted Germany to force revision of reparations, but this is only part of the story. The success of his strategy really hinged on the leverage that Germany gained through its chief creditor, the US. The key to the solution to the entire complex of post-war financial problems was, as everyone had understood since 1919, for America to make concessions to Britain and France on their war debts. This, in turn, would enable them to reduce their reparations demands. Germany's strategy was to use its indebtedness to America as a lever to unleash this cascade of concessions, forcing the US to choose between Germany servicing its obligations to Wall Street and its reparations debts to Britain and France.

In 1931 the strategy finally paid off. With the American banking system on the edge of collapse, Wall Street could ill afford major losses in Germany. However, as Bruening had loudly proclaimed, if Germany was to continue servicing its debt to the US, it must have relief from reparations. In July 1931, President Hoover intervened to strong-arm London and Paris into accepting a moratorium on all 'political debts' arising from the war, including the war debts owed to America by France and Britain, but also Germany's far larger reparations bill.

At the height of the crisis in 1931 America thus asserted its leadership. However, final agreement on a reparations settlement was not reached for another 12 months, and in the mean time the situation of the German economy continued to deteriorate and its politics to polarize. With the old order collapsing around them the question has never ceased to be asked: why did Bruening and his government not adopt positive counter-measures? In September 1931 the financial panic spread to London and Britain responded by departing from the gold standard, creating the flexibility they needed to launch a successful revival strategy. Why did Germany not follow suit? The short answer is that relying on the US to gain freedom from reparations came at a price. America remained firmly attached to the gold standard and Washington made clear that it disapproved of any attempt to follow Britain. However, not devaluing in line with sterling left the Reichsmark overvalued and German exports at the mercy of the implosion in worldwide trade. In a desperate bid to regain competitiveness, Bruening took further emergency powers, enabling him to force compulsory cuts in wages, prices and interest rates. *The Economist* magazine in London described these measures as the most draconian ever seen outside the Soviet Union. However, all was in vain. Unemployment mounted relentlessly to the headline figure of 6 million over the winter of 1931–1932. The jobless flocked into the ranks of the Stalinist Communist Party. For much of the rest of the population the NSDAP established itself as the nationalist alternative. What united the extremes was their hostility to the Republic and their rejection of the bankrupt system of international economics on which Weimar's stabilization had so fundamentally relied.[28]

Between 1917 and 1923 the German state and its relation to the national economy had been reshaped by its realignment within the international economy and the assertion at home of the power of organized labor and capital. By crippling the US economy and splitting Europe into competing economic blocs, the depression created a vacuum of international power. At the same time mass unemployment knocked the fight out of the trade unions. Big business, which had once leveraged its relationship to Wall Street, now found itself as the desperate recipient of state aid. The force-field within which the Weimar Republic had been stabilized in 1923–1924 had been changed beyond recognition. In the spring of 1933 just as Hitler took power, FDR took the momentous decision to unhook even the dollar from gold.

It was in the context of this general, international collapse that a pillar of corporate liberalism, such as IG Farben, could lose its political compass.[29] The system of multilateral free trade and the free flow of capital, in which German big business had prospered, no longer existed. The stage was set for a dramatic return to the nationalist militarism of 1917. With the trade unions enfeebled, the challenge from the German left would be broken once and for all. Hitler's Nazi party would provide the mass base that the Kaiser had lacked. In the vacuum of both domestic and international power created by the disaster of the Great Depression Hitler's regime and its collaborators set about realizing the fantasy of a unified, national military-economic machine. To do so the Third Reich drew on the new structure of national economic governance bequeathed to them by the Weimar Republic, reinforced by the organizational talent of the German military, the enthusiasm of professionals and technical experts and the resources of certain key elements of German big business.

18.5

It used to be commonplace to divide the economic history of Hitler's regime into a phase of civilian recovery from the great depression followed by a phase of overt militarism. If full employment and the Autobahnen were emblematic of the civilian achievements of the regime, Goering's Four Year Plan announced the second phase in 1936.[30] This distinction, always apologetic in its implications, is no longer tenable.[31] The money spent in the first six months of 1933 came largely from schemes devised in the autumn of 1932 that were always intended as cover for clandestine rearmament. However, credit is due to Chancellors Papen and Schleicher not Hitler. The only significant 'civilian' projects unambiguously attributable to the new regime were the First and Second Reinhardt programs launched in the summer and early autumn of 1933.[32] The first of these was hedged around with secret commitments to the military. When the engineer Fritz Todt touted his vision of the *Autobahnen* to Hitler in the summer of 1933, he made sure to equip them too with a military rationale. It was not until 1935 that Todt's building sites employed any significant numbers of workers. In the mean time, already in December 1933, only ten months after Hitler came to power, a decision was taken to stop the allocation of any new funds to civilian work-creation schemes. By 1934, rapidly increasing military spending already dominated the Reich's spending. In the years to come it became all-consuming.

Inevitably, surging economic activity created tension at the weak point of the national economy, the balance of trade. German demand for imported food and raw materials soared. The performance of overpriced exports was lackluster at best. The foreign exchange controls of the Reichsbank prevented an open currency crisis. However, with hard currency reserves plunging to truly dangerous levels, Hitler's economic miracle, seen from the inside, resembled a continuous exercise in crisis management. During the worst moments in the summer of 1934 the Reichsbank lived hand to mouth, doling out what little foreign exchange it could scrape together from one day to the next. In the summer of 1933, Berlin took advantage of the isolationist turn in the first months of Roosevelt's presidency to suspend payment to Germany's foreign creditors. Though this provided relief, it could not redress the underlying problem. In 1934, the foreign exchange controls improvised by Bruening in the summer of 1931 were turned into a comprehensive system of exchange rationing. The once-powerful network of German business associations was reorganized by order of the Reich and tied to what Hjamar Schacht, head of the Reichsbank and acting Economics Minister, dubbed the 'New Plan.' In 1935 a heavy turnover tax was imposed on the beneficiaries of the domestic boom to subsidize ailing exports. In 1936 Goering agglomerated a variety of schemes to boost domestic production of synthetic textiles, oil, rubber and iron from domestic iron ore to form the Four Year Plan. However, his long-term investment program was immediately called into question, when in 1937 the scarcity of foreign exchange forced the restrictive rationing of steel.

The drive to organize and discipline extended beyond the industrial economy. In 1933–1934 the great mass of peasant households were brought into a national system of farm management (RNS) designed to raise output and restrict dependence on imported inputs.[33] In World War I food rationing had not begun until 1916. Hitler's regime began surreptitious rationing already in 1935. Farm labor was subject to state discipline as of the harvest of 1934. By 1938 a year before the outbreak of war, hundreds of thousands of German workers were tied to their workplaces by military discipline.

Nor was this merely administrative accretion. While Britain and America experienced the 'Keynesian revolution' in the 1930s, the Third Reich devised its own organic, macro-economic vision. The Weimar Republic had already made an unprecedented investment in national economic accounting. In 1937 vast charts on display at the exhibitions staged to celebrate four years of Hitler's regime illustrated for the public the central role of the state in regulating the workings of the national economic organism. In staff discussions within the Ministerial bureaucracy and the military-economic apparatus, questions of national finance, foreign exchange allocation, and raw materials planning were now routinely considered in holistic, macro-economic terms. Driven by this demand for information, the Reich's Statistical Office expanded to gargantuan size. The statisticians even began work on an Input-Output table, a tool of state planning devised by Soviet economists and borrowed by the Germans when they passed through en route to exile in the United States.[34]

As is well known, this organizational effort never cohered into a single monolith.[35] The Third Reich was riven with factional infighting. In 1933–1934 Schacht asserted himself as economic supremo, overcoming the opposition of both the SA brown-shirts and the agrarian wing. However, in the autumn of 1935 the forces of the Party rallied against Schacht and in the spring of 1936 they were taken under Goering's capacious wings. The German Army also aligned itself against Schacht. Goering himself, of course, presided over the rapidly-expanding military-industrial complex of the Luftwaffe. However, despite Goering's victory, Schacht was not finally forced out of the Presidency of the Reichsbank until January 1939 and the Four Year Plan was never a true national economic command center. Nor did Fritz Todt, appointed Munitions Minister in the spring of 1940, or Albert Speer, his celebrated successor in February 1942, ever achieve total control of every aspect of the national economy. The result, undeniably, was a degree of administrative confusion and duplication of effort. However, if the economic organization of the Third Reich was not the mega machine of totalitarian fantasy, this observation begs the question of what historical standard the Nazi regime is being measured against. As we have seen, it was a fantasy to imagine that the Kaiser's war effort had been underpinned by a coherent economic organization. Though the Weimar Republic did at least create the necessary national ministries, their relations were far from harmonious. If we compare the Third Reich to the United States, where FDR was mounting a similarly energetic interventionist effort, we find there too an 'alphabet soup' of competing agencies.[36]

However, aside from the superficiality of mere administrative disorganization, a truly important insight concerns the position of the state itself in the Third Reich. Extending the state's influence into the economic sphere everywhere had the effect of blurring the demarcation between state and civil society, rendering problematic any simplistic notion of 'state control' and calling into question the distinct identity of the state. The Nazi party furthermore consciously encouraged this undermining and hollowing out of the state. Egged on by Hitler himself, the most clear-headed exponents of Nazi ideology regarded the German fixation with the state as an enfeebling inheritance of liberalism. Lawyers and civil servants were their enemies. Of course, the Nazi anti-state ideal did not imply less government, or a return to archaic political organization, but an attempt to institute modern government unconstrained by legal formality.[37] Teams of technical experts, engineers, and officers, guided by the Fuehrer's vision, would exercise direct command over the resources of the Volk. One of the earliest and most perceptive accounts of Nazi political economy, by Franz Neumann, bears the significant title—Behemoth, or 'unstate.'[38]

It might, of course, be suspected that the real profiteers of such a blurring of public and private boundaries would be major private corporations that would thereby be enabled to colonize the governmental apparatus. Goering's Four Year Plan created in the autumn of 1936 to unify all the regime's synthetic materials projects could easily be taken as a front for IG Farben, the mighty chemicals conglomerate. It was on that basis that the US Justice Department took the lead in prosecuting IG at the Nuremberg tribunal, along with Krupp and a number of other heavy industrialists.[39] However, although the charges of slave labor and spoliation were made to stick, wider evidence of conspiracy proved harder to come by. The best recent scholarship argues that although IG executives and technicians occupied key positions in Goering's organization, in the same process the priorities of the corporation became blurred with those of the regime. Though there were, of course, instances in which the regime forcibly imposed its will against business opposition—most flagrantly with regard to the development of inferior-grade German iron ore by the Reichswerke Hermann Goering—the more common pattern was for a productive and mutually profitable partnership.[40] Comparing the Third Reich to the Weimar Republic one might say that if what Stresemann had needed German business for was their international credit, what Hitler needed was their technology and productive expertise.

Certainly, the honors and treasure heaped on Germany's corporate executives stand in stark contrast to the treatment meted out to the leadership of Germany's labor movement. The first generation of concentration camps set up in 1933–1934 were used to destroy the KPD and the social democratic labor movement. Not, of course, that a party that proudly proclaimed itself the National Socialist German Workers Party had any intention of merely repressing the German worker. The destruction of the free trade unions created the space for the formation of a single, gigantic German Labor Front (DAF).[41] This organization was by no means supine in the face of German employers. It had its own national socialist vision for labor, in which individually calibrated performance wages would be combined with improved social provision and working conditions.[42] Against uncooperative and anti-social employers, the DAF could mobilize intimidating political pressure. It also had considerable funds looted from the trade union and cooperative movement with which it underwrote unprecedented organized leisure programs and the enormous investment required to launch the VW project.[43] At the same time, it served the purposes of rearmament by putting a lid on collective wage claims.

For ordinary Germans the chief material benefits of Hitler's regime, therefore, were the rapid return to full employment and from the late 1930s, the prospect of considerable, individual wage increases.[44] Furthermore, despite the sexist rhetoric of the regime, these opportunities extended to women—even married women. If truly long-range social mobility remained an illusion, the armaments boom, and the regime's vision of national social progress, unquestionably assisted millions of German workers in rising upwards within the blue-collar hierarchy. By the late 1930s, virtually all male adolescents were enrolled in one or other form of training scheme.[45] The 'skills machine' that was such a defining feature of German society after 1945 had been set in motion. Meanwhile, as promises of the new living standard to come, the regime selectively promoted certain key symbols of modern consumption, notably the people's radio.[46] The Volkswagen was promised for sometime in the early 1940s. What the regime could not admit, of course, was that a far richer array of consumer goods was available on world markets, if only the foreign exchange had not been reserved for armaments-related imports. Synthetic fibers made a poor substitute for imported cotton and wool. Likewise, as the DAF well understood, the main need of the ordinary working-class household was not a VW, but affordable, good quality housing. The Nazi social engineers devised a program that would have made apartments with indoor plumbing and electricity available to all the Volksgenossen. However, this was costed at 65 billion, almost exactly the amount that the Fuehrer boasted of spending on rearmament in the first six years of his regime.

The construction of Hitler's Volksgemeinschaft was hedged around by painful trade offs. However, we must beware the assumption that 'ordinary' Germans, if given the choice, would have prioritized their material self-interest over national rearmament. When Goering posed the choice between 'guns and butter,' he certainly did not mean to imply that the German people were concerned only with their bellies. As Goering demonstrated in person, the desire for both guns and butter could easily dwell within a single breast. Though the subject cries out for greater investigation, there can be little doubt that the remilitarization of Germany was greeted with huge enthusiasm by a large part of German society. To that extent, the costs were willingly born. Militarization was a spectacular act of collective mass consumption.

18.6

By 1939 the Third Reich had taken full advantage of the economic crisis to accomplish the single most dramatic transfer of resources ever realized by a capitalist state in peacetime. Its armed forces were up to date and at least partially modernized. The mood in the Third Reich certainly did not match the supposed euphoria of August 1914, but it is reasonable to credit Hitler's regime with having achieved a considerable degree of mass support. What was also beyond question, however, was that the huge surge of rearmament spending had profoundly destabilized the economy. As Schacht warned in the weeks before his dismissal in January 1939, Germany was heading towards a foreign exchange crisis.[47] State controls were struggling to hold back the threat of inflation. And this was all the more ominous in light of the global arms race. Using purchasing power parity adjusted comparisons of military spending in relation to GDP, Wehrmacht experts concluded in the spring of 1939 that unless Germany could further increase its efforts it would soon lose whatever lead it had gained since 1933. The implied message seems to have been one of caution. However, though Hitler's regime was guided by military and economic expertise, in the final analysis, it was not ruled by it. As at the earlier moment of decision in January 1917, in 1939 the interpretation of the military-economic data was colored by a heightened rhetoric of historical drama. Since the autumn of 1938, Hitler had become firmly convinced that the forces of international Jewry were converging against him. The string-pullers in the City of London and Wall Street were orchestrating a gigantic trans-Atlantic coalition against Germany. The data from the experts confirmed Hitler's conviction that the Third Reich had no option, but headlong aggression.

The military victories achieved up to the summer of 1941 seemed to vindicate Hitler's gamble. New weapons, notably tanks and dive bombers, played an eye-catching role in every campaign. However, we should guard against any simple assumption that military victory was the result of deliberate military-industrial preparation. The Wehrmacht's greatest victory, the defeat of France and its Allies in 1940, certainly cannot be explained in this fashion, since despite the rearmament effort, the German Army, both in quantity and quality of equipment, was inferior to its enemies. Furthermore, in the early months of 1940 as Germany braced for the assault on France, Hitler's main concern was not with tanks, but with ensuring a sufficient supply of ammunition. His priorities were those of the Hindenburg program of 1917, not the Blitzkrieg. It was only after the lightening victories in Poland and France that a new vision of rapid, highly mobile warfare began to exercise a formative influence on economic planning. Only in the summer of 1940 did the possibility of eliminating a major power in a matter of weeks provide the license for the Nazi leadership to attempt something even bolder, namely the simultaneous preparation of two wars at once. The immediate priority was the build-up for the invasion of the Soviet Union, this time concentrated on the mobile forces. However, at the same time, the Luftwaffe began preparing for the longer range war against Britain and America. The scale of the challenge facing Germany was made clear by the announcement of Lend-Lease in the spring of 1941, which provided a staggering $25 billion in assistance for Britain. It was, the German embassy in Washington reported to Berlin, a sure sign that the Jewish conspiracy was in control of FDR. The German answer came in a succession of gigantic new aircraft and aero-engine plants. To feed them with rubber and fuel, the Four Year Plan, in close collaboration with IG Farben, set in motion a major expansion in annexed Polish territory, the most monumental instance of which was the gigantic synthetic rubber plant sited at Auschwitz.[48] By 1945 it was to become the single largest investment project of the Third Reich.

It is worth singling out 1941 for closer attention because this was the long-aspired to moment of grand synthesis, the only moment in which the competing agencies of the Nazi government formulated something akin to an overall strategic conception in which the entire resources of the national economy were consciously conceived and directed towards a coherent multi-dimensional 'war plan,' however unrealistic that military design may have been.[49] It was also the moment at which the Reich conceived in most encompassing terms the harnessing of the occupied European economies. One element of that planning was the profoundly pessimistic assessment of Europe's food balance, which in the spring of 1941 led to the decision that, following the occupation, the entire urban population of the Soviet Union should be starved to death.[50] At the same moment, in January 1941 Reinhard Heydrich received his order from Goering to put together a draft conception for the Europe-wide solution of the 'Jewish Question.' In the first six months of 1941, early ideas about long-term German settlement of occupied Poland metastasized into the grandiose vision of the *Generalplan Ost*. This envisioned that the territory from the Baltic to the Black Sea, the territory first occupied in 1918, was to be cleared of its native population and opened up for German investment and settlement. The massive expansion of the SS prison camp at Auschwitz, to which a large extermination facility was later added, was originally intended to serve the labor needs of the *Generalplan Ost*.

Through its stunning military success, confirmed in the summer of 1941 by the early gains in the Soviet Union, the Nazi regime had opened up an unprecedented space for the imagination of power. In their sheer scale and monolithic comprehensiveness, in the literal-minded deliberation with which violence was harnessed towards the attainment of ideological, economic, and social goals the plans hatched in this phase of the Hitler regime's history were more ambitious than anything contemplated up to that point by any state in recorded history. However, they were in their single-minded brutality, not the vision of a multi national empire, but essentially a racialized vision of the nation state writ on a grotesquely large scale.[51]

At this point the trajectory we have sketched since 1917 reaches its apex, only for any semblance of coherence to collapse as the invasion of the Soviet Union ground to a disastrous halt in the autumn and winter of 1941. Not, of course, that all coherence was lost immediately. In 1942 the Wehrmacht's deep strike into the South of the Soviet Union revived hope. Up to Stalingrad, the seemingly contradictory projects of starving

Table 18.2 Outproduced: Axis and Allies armaments production 1942–1944

	000s								1990 PPP $		000 tons	
	Rifles	Machine pistols	Machine guns	Guns	Mortars	Tanks	Combat aircaft	Major naval vessels	1941 GDP	1944 GDP	Steel prod. 1939	Steel prod. 1944
USA	10714	1685	2291	512	61.6	86	153.1	6755	1094	1499	55731	81321
UK	2052	3682	610	317	65.3	20.7	61.6	651	344	346	13716	12337
SU	9935	5501	1254	380	306.5	77.5	84.8	55	359	495	18796	16350
Allies	22701	10868	4155	1209	433.4	184.2	299.5	7461	1797	2340	88243	110008
Germany	6501	695	889	262	66	35.2	65	703	412	437	21528	24218
Italy			83	7	11.3	2	8.9	218	144	137	2283	1025
Japan	1959	3	341	126	4.3	2.4	40.7	438	196	189	6693	6366
Axis	8460	698	1313	395	81.6	39.6	114.6	1359	752	763	30504	31609
Allies/Axis	2.7	15.6	3.2	3.1	5.3	4.7	2.6	5.5	2.4	3.1	2.9	3.5
Allies/ Germany	3.5	15.6	4.7	4.6	6.6	5.2	4.6	10.6	4.4	5.4	4.1	4.5

Sources: Statistisches Handbuch, 292
Harrison, *The Economics of World War II*, 17

the population of the East, extracting foreign labor, and murdering the entire Jewish population of Europe could still somehow be reconciled as part of a grand plan.[52] As Himmler made his fateful trip around Poland in July 1942 he carried orders designating Auschwitz as the killing center for West European Jewry. However, he also commanded a ruthless sequestration of the Polish harvest. He urged the accelerated extermination of the Jewish population of Warsaw in the gas chambers of Treblinka to free up food and to dry up the black market. Finally, he gave the go ahead for the clearance and first German settlement in the Zamosc region of Poland. Meanwhile, food from Western Europe was ruthlessly redirected to restore the rations of the German population and to feed the millions of forced laborers being drafted by Gauleiter Sauckel from all over the continent.[53] This was enough to provide Albert Speer, Hitler's new armaments minister, with the launch pad for his so-called 'Armaments Miracle.' Unlike the Hindenburg Program of 1917, which relapsed within months in a morass of recrimination and ration cuts, Speer's achievement was to turn the armaments effort into a true pillar of the regime. Though the military situation was far less promising than it had been in 1917–1918, the home front held together to the bitter end. Coercion, of course, played its part. Speer welcomed Himmler's spies into his factories. However, the triumph of production, as such, came to provide a *raison d'être* for the dogged continuation of a war, a token that all was not yet lost, that the *Endsieg* might yet still be achieved. The human and moral cost was enormous. As late as the summer of 1944 peak output for fighter aircraft was achieved under the hail of allied aerial bombardment in improvised underground factories, in which German workers lorded it over the emaciated remnants of the Jewish population of Hungary, supplied to Speer directly from the Auschwitz railway yard.

However, the rhetoric of national salvation through ever greater production at whatever price was ultimately as solipsistic in 1944 as it had been in 1917. German armaments production relative to that of its enemies mirrored exactly the pre-war ratio of the output of steel and GDP. The final outcome was written in the data (Table 18.2).

18.7

Since the nineteenth century, Germany's ideologues had been haunted by fantasies of national triumph or utter annihilation. In 1945 amidst the rubble of Germany's ruined cities and faced with the slaughter of an entire generation, it must have seemed as though the talk of *finis Germaniae* had finally been realized. In human and cultural terms the losses were indeed irreparable. In political terms the German nation was never to regain full and untrammelled sovereignty. However, the terrible irony is that within months of the end of the war, years before the political structure of a new Germany had been resolved; efforts to restart its economic motor had begun. By 1950 the demands of the Cold War made the complete unfettering of the Ruhr essential to America. It was this, in turn, which forced the French into launching the European

Coal and Steel Community. Europe was given an entirely new political architecture to contain the economic power of Germany.

Through all the extraordinary turbulence of German history in the first half of the twentieth century the significance of the self-sustaining dynamic of economic development thus stands dramatically confirmed. However, if the pacified, post-historic, contentment of Germany at the end of the twentieth century is in some sense a confirmation of the basic model of modernization, it is far from being its mechanical or inevitable outcome. It was rather the result of a struggle, a struggle which twice exploded the confines of the German nation state, to involve virtually the entire rest of the world.

NOTES

1. Frances Fukuyama, *The End of History and the Last Man* (New York: Free Press New York, 1992).
2. Gerald A. Ambrosius, *A Social and Economic History of Twentieth-Century Europe* (Cambridge: Harvard University Press, 1989).
3. Gerald D. Feldman, *Army, Industry and Labor in Germany 1914–1918* (Oxford: Berg, 1992).
4. Stephen Broadberry and Mark Harrison (eds), *The Economics of World War I* (Cambridge: Cambridge University Press, 2005).
5. Manfred G. Berg, *Stresemann und die Vereinigten Staaten von Amerika* (Baden-Baden: Nomos, 1990.), 43.
6. Stephen F. Cohen, *Bukharin and the Bolshevik Revolution* (Oxford: Oxford University Press, 1980), 30.
7. Volker Hentschel, *Wirtschaft und Wirtschaftspolitik im wilhelminischen Deutschland: Organisierter Kapitalismus und Interventionsstaat?* (Stuttgart: Klett-Cotta, 1978).
8. Jürgen Kocka, *Facing Total War: German Society, 1914–1918* (Oxford: Berg, 1984) and Belinda J. Davis, *Home Fires Burning: Food, Politics and Everyday Life in World War I Berlin* (Chapel Hill: University of North Carolina Press, 2000).
9. Hans Mommsen, *The Rise and Fall of Weimar Democracy* (Chapel Hill: University of North Carolina Press, 1996).
10. Heinrich August Winkler, *Germany: The Long Road West 1789–1933* (Oxford: Oxford University Press, 2006), 340–350.
11. Gerald D. Feldman, *The Great Disorder Politics, Economics, and Society in the German Inflation, 1914–1924* (Oxford: Oxford University Press, 1996).
12. J. Adam Tooze, *Statistics and the German State 1900–1945* (Cambridge: Cambridge University Press, 2001).
13. A sense of Rathenau's thinking can be gleaned from Walther Rathenau, *New Society* (New York: Harcourt, 1921), 145–146.
14. Harold James, *German Slump: Politics and Economics 1924–1936* (Oxford: Oxford University Press, 1986).
15. Conan Fischer, *The Ruhr Crisis 1923–1924* (Oxford: Oxford University Press, 2003).

16. Patrick Cohrs, *The Unfinished Peace after World War I* (Cambridge: Cambridge University Press, 2006).

17. Jonathan Wright, *Gustav Stresemann. Weimar's Greatest Statesman* (Oxford: Oxford University Press, 2002).

18. William C. McNeil, *American Money and the Weimar Republic* (New York: Columbia University Press, 1986).

19. Albrecht Ritschl, *Deutschlands Krise und Konjunktur 1924–1934* (Berlin: Akademie Verlag, 2002).

20. Konrad H. Jarausch and Michael Geyer, *Shattered Past. Reconstructing German Histories* (Princeton: Princeton University Press, 2003), 269–316.

21. Knut Borchardt, *Perspectives on Modern German Economic History and Policy* (Cambridge: Cambridge University Press, 1991) and Theo Balderston, *Economics and Politics in the Weimar Republic* (Cambridge: Cambridge University Press, 2002).

22. Reinhard Neebe, *Grossindustrie, Staat und NSDAP 1930–1933* (Göttingen: Vandenhoeck und Ruprecht, 1981).

23. Adam Tooze, *Wages of Destruction: The Making and Breaking of the Nazi Economy* (London: Penguin, 2006), 99–117.

24. Barry Eichengreen, *Golden Fetters: The Gold Standard and the Great Depression, 1919–1939* (Oxford: Oxford University Press, 1992).

25. William I. Patch, *Heinrich Brüning and the Dissolution of the Weimar Republic* (Cambridge: Cambridge University Press, 1998).

26. Tom Ferguson and Peter Temin, 'Made in Germany: The German Currency Crisis of July 1931,' *Research in Economic History* 21 (2003), 1–53.

27. Gerald D. Feldman, *The Deutsche Bank 1870–1995* (London: Weidenfeld, 1995), 240–276.

28. Avraham Barkai, *Nazi Economics: Ideology, Theory and Practice* (New Haven: Yale University Press, 1990).

29. Peter Hayes, *Industry and Ideology: IG Farben in the Nazi Era* (Cambridge: Cambridge University Press, 2001).

30. Richard Overy, *The Nazi Economic Recovery. 1932–1938* (Cambridge: Cambridge University Press, 1996).

31. Adam Tooze, *Wages of Destruction*, 37–98.

32. Dan P. Silverman, *Hitler's Economy: Nazi Work Creation Programs, 1933–1936* (Cambridge: Cambridge University Press, 1996).

33. Gustavo Corni, *Hitler and the Peasant: Agrarian Policy of the Third Reich, 1930–1939* (Oxford: Berg, 1990).

34. Tooze, *Statistics*, 177–214.

35. Richard J. Overy, *War and Economy in the Third Reich* (Oxford: Oxford University Press, 1994).

36. J.A. Garraty, 'The New Deal, National Socialism and the Great Depression,' *American Historical Review* 78 (1973), 907–944.

37. Jane Caplan, *Government without Administration. State and Civil Service in Weimar and Nazi Germany* (Oxford: Clarendon Press, 1988).

38. Franz Neumann, *Behemoth: The Structure and Practice of National Socialism 1933–1944* (New York: Oxford University Press, 1942, 1944).

39. Joseph Borkin, *The Crime and Punishment of IG Farben* (New York: Pocket, 1979).

40. Mark Spoerer, 'Industrial Profitability in the Nazi Economy,' in Christoph Buchheim and W. R. Garside (eds), *After the Slump. Industry and Politics in 1930s Britain and Germany* (Frankfurt am Main: Lang, 2000), 112–137.
41. Ronald M. Smelser, *Robert Ley: Hitler's Labor Leader* (Oxford: Berg, 1988).
42. Tim Mason, *Social Policy in the Third Reich. The Working-Class and the National Community* (Oxford: Berg, 1990); Tilla Siegel 'Whatever was the Attitude of German Workers?' in Richard Bessel (ed.), *Fascist Italy and Nazi Germany. Comparisons and Contrasts* (Cambridge: Cambridge University Press, 1996), 61–77.
43. Shelly Baranowski, *Strength Through Joy: Consumerism and Mass Tourism in the Third Reich* (Cambridge: Cambridge University Press, 2004). Hans Mommsen and Manfred Grieger, *Das Volkswagenwerk und seine Arbeiter im Dritten Reich 1933–1948* (Duesseldorf: Econ, 1997).
44. Detlev Peukert, *Life in the Third Reich* (Oxford: Oxford University Press, 1991).
45. Alf Luedtke, 'The "Honour of Labour",' in David F. Crew (ed.), *Nazism and German Society 1933–1945* (London: Routledge, 1994), 67–109; and John Gillingham, 'The "Deproleterianization" of German Society: Vocational Training in the Third Reich,' *Journal of Social History*, 19 (1986), 423–432.
46. Corey Ross, *Media and the Making of Modern Germany: Mass Communications, Society and Politics from the Empire to the Third Reich* (Oxford: Oxford University Press, 2008), 266–291.
47. For the following see Tooze, *Wages of Destruction*, 244–367.
48. Robert Jan van Pelt and Deborah Dwork, *Auschwitz: 1270 to the Present* (New Haven: Yale University Press, 1996).
49. A perspective shared by Andreas Hillgruber, *Hitlers Strategie. Politik und Kriegsfuehrung 1939–1941* (Frankfurt am Main, Bernard & Graefe, 1965) and Goetz Aly and Susanne Heim, *Architects of Annihilation. Auschwitz and the Logic of Destruction* (Princeton: Princeton University Press, 2006).
50. Alex J. Kay, *Exploitation, Resettlement, Mass Murder: Political and Economic Planning for German Occupation Policy in the Soviet Union, 1940–1941* (Oxford: Berg, 2006).
51. Mark Mazower, *Hitler's Empire: How the Nazis ruled Europe* (London: Penguin Press, 2008).
52. Christian Gerlach, *Krieg, Ernährung, Völkermord: Deutsche Vernichtungspolitik im Zweiten Weltkrieg* (Hamburg: Hamburger Edition, 1998).
53. Ulrich Herbert, *Hitler's Foreign Workers* (Cambridge: Cambridge University Press, 1997).

BIBLIOGRAPHY

BORCHARDT, KNUT, *Perspectives on Modern German Economic History and Policy* (Cambridge: Cambridge University Press, 1991).
CORNI, GUSTAVO, *Hitler and the Peasants* (Oxford: Berg, 1990).
FELDMAN, GERALD D., *Army, Industry and Labor in Germany 1914–1918* (Oxford: Berg, 1992).
——, *The Great Disorder Politics, Economics, and Society in the German Inflation, 1914–1924* (Oxford: Berg, 1996).
GERLACH, CHRISTIAN, *Krieg Ernährung, Völkermord: Deutsche Vernichtungspolitik im Zweiten Weltkrieg* (Hamburg: Hamburger Edition, 1998).

HAYES, PETER, *Industry and Ideology: IG Farben in the Nazi Era* (Cambridge: Cambridge University Press, 2001).

HERBERT, ULRICH, *Hitler's Foreign Workers* (Cambridge: Cambridge University Press, 1997).

JAMES, HAROLD, *The German Slump: Politics and Economics 1924–1936* (Oxford: Oxford University Press, 1986).

KERSHAW, IAN, *Weimar: Why did German Democracy Fail?* (London: Weidenfeld, 1990).

KOCKA, JÜRGEN, *Facing Total War: German Society, 1914–1918* (Oxford: Berg, 1984).

MCNEIL, WILLIAM C., *American Money and the Weimar Republic* (New York: Columbia University Press, 1986).

OVERY, RICHARD J., *War and Economy in the Third Reich* (Oxford: Oxford University Press, 1994).

RITSCHL, ALBRECHT, *Deutschlands Krise und Konjunktur 1924–1934* (Berlin: Akademie Verlag, 2002).

TOOZE, ADAM, *Wages of Destruction: The Making and Breaking of the Nazi Economy* (London: Penguin, 2006).

TURNER, HENRY, *German Big Business and the Rise of Hitler* (New York: Oxford University Press, 1985).

CHAPTER 19

DICTATORSHIP AND DEMOCRACY, 1918–1939

THOMAS MERGEL

19.1 INTRODUCTION: DICTATORSHIP AND DEMOCRACY AS NEW CONCEPTS AFTER WORLD WAR I

BOTH dictatorship and democracy were essentially new concepts of political rule in Germany after World War I. It was true that suffrage had been increasingly extended after the revolution of 1848–1849, and more citizens (male citizens, that is) were entitled to vote in Imperial Germany than, for instance, in Great Britain. Without doubt, the process of politicization, which had begun in the late 19th century, had created a certain mindset of political participation.[1] Yet, despite this, Germany was a long way away from being a democracy. The Reich had remained a monarchy until 1918, and the equally monarchic German states and their administrations had considerable control over its decision-making structure. Neither the chancellor (*Reichskanzler*) nor his secretaries were allowed to be members of parliament, a fact that provides a striking illustration of how different this form of government was compared with parliamentary democracy. However, the first 'total' war of modern history involved all citizens, and these participants now expected to benefit from their sacrifices by being awarded more political participation. In this respect, the war furthered democracy.

Dictatorship, too, was a new form of political control, at least in Germany. In France, Napoleon III had installed a dictatorship backed by the military as early as 1851. In reference to this new form of power, Karl Marx had coined the term 'dictatorship of the proletariat' in 1852, a phrase that for a long time remained far more widespread than the concept of political dictatorship. Lenin and Trotsky adopted it for the Russian

Revolution and, in turn, the German political philosopher Carl Schmitt carried the notion of dictatorship into the mainstream after the First World War.[2] There was a second reason for this, apart from its associations with Bolshevism: during the First World War Germany had been governed by a military dictatorship. Established in 1916 by Erich Ludendorff, the quartermaster-general, and Paul von Hindenburg, the head of army supreme command, this regime, while nominally under the roof of the monarchy, had systematically undermined the power of the Emperor and marginalized regular governmental institutions. Field Marshal Hindenburg's immense popularity, which even led to a second career in the democratic Weimar Republic after the revolution, is a clear indication that dictatorship—at least in the immediate memory of the German people—was not so much associated with brutality and repression, but instead perceived as a political system above party lines that was resilient, capable of making decisions and protecting German honor. The interwar period was a testing ground for new forms of political rule, all of which made explicit reference to the people.

19.2 FORMATION OF NEW CONCEPTS OF CONTROL DERIVING FROM WAR EXPERIENCES

The term 'people' was to become a standard formula for the self-understanding of German politics after 1918. In its shades of meaning, it saw the people as a social organism, rather than as an ethnic community. 'People' referred to the many. It described the social commitment with which a good community was supposed to be built.[3] The Weimar Republic regarded itself as a 'social people's state' and almost all party names contained terms such as 'democratic,' 'social,' or 'people.' The notion of the *Volksgemeinschaft* (people's community), which became widely used during the Weimar period, had an impact far beyond the right-wing parties. This was because the concept of community was added to the notion of *Volk*. 'Community' was, as political scientist Kurt Sontheimer put it, 'one of the magic words of the Weimar period.'[4] All parties from both the right and the left appealed to the community of the German people, to their unity, and to social harmony. The reasons for this were, on the one hand, the memory of the mythically inflated war community (*Kriegsgemeinschaft*) and, on the other, the inner conflict suffered by Germany, which became apparent in the diverse party landscape of the Weimar Republic, in never-ending political quarrels, and in growing violence. The concept of the *Volksgemeinschaft* was one of the most powerful terms in this discourse. For a long time, it by no means had solely ethnic or racist connotations. Not only conservative and *völkisch*, but also socialist and Christian authors employed it. For the Young Socialists (*Jungsozialisten*), who were influenced by the *bündisch* Youth Movement, it signified the intertwining of national and social unity. Catholics used the term in connection with the overcoming of confessional divisions, and Gustav Stresemann, who became Chancellor in 1923 and served as foreign secretary from 1923 to 1929, saw national community primarily as a means of calming the atmosphere of class struggle in industrial relations and of achieving cross-party cooperation in foreign policy.[5] Social reformers, on the other hand, saw the *Volksgemeinschaft* as a differentiated system of social and political intervention.[6] It was not until 1930 that the term increasingly focused on the ethnic and ultimately the racial community.[7]

This was one side of the political mentalities that emerged during the war. The other was the new role ascribed to violence as a political means. For Erich Ludendorff, leading figure of the third Army Supreme Command since 1916 and participant in the Beer Hall Putsch in 1923, war was the father of all things. Even the more astute political theorists, such as Carl Schmitt, conceived of politics from the perspective of war. Many political issues were portrayed as 'vital matters,' political opponents were labeled as the 'enemy,' and there was a sharp separation between 'us' and 'them.' These labels were born out of war and initially referred to external enemies yet increasingly bled into the sphere of domestic politics. Coming from the political fringes, both on the Left and the Right, they confronted moderate politicians with a conception of politics whose consequences they were unable to cope with. For a long time, the widespread disposition for violence in the interwar period was presumed to have been an immediate result of the brutalization of the soldiers in the war. However, it is now generally accepted that most German soldiers were sick and tired of war, and tended to belong to the vast majority in Weimar who preferred peaceful politics.[8] The approximately 400,000 soldiers (out of a total of about 13 million) who were determined to continue the struggle were an exception. As members of the *Freikorps* (free corps), they continued fighting in the Baltic States and in Upper Silesia. Among them were a striking number of officers who felt humiliated and whose military careers had collapsed—a plight they blamed on the defeat and, to an even greater extent, the peace terms of the Treaty of Versailles. Predominantly, however, it was young people who were willing to participate in the violence. They had not fought in the war, but were told stories of self-sacrifice and heroism time and time again. The myths about the 'war community' in the trenches took on a life of their own after the war, and glorified the bravery, determination, and sacrifices of the soldiers. These terms also infected the political discourse of democracy. Even among the democrats themselves, the political sphere in Weimar was, on the one hand, characterized by a desire for community and the perception that political conflicts represented unwelcome discord and disunity. On the other hand, ideas of war-like behavior contaminated even the political arena and led politicians to view the rules of the democratic system as technical issues, rather than matters of principle. This created a dual paradox with regard to parliamentary democracy, a system defined as a society of conflict, but which is supposed to address these conflicts according to regulations and in a peaceful manner. Weimar Democracy was unable to endure conflict and, wherever conflicts were inevitable, they tended to culminate in violence. Germany was, however, not the only war-torn country shaped by violence.[9]

On 29 October 1918, sailors in Wilhelmshaven revolted against the suicidal intentions of their naval officers who, despite being vastly outnumbered, were planning to set sail for another sea battle in order to restore the navy's honor. The conflagration quickly turned into a revolution. Initially, the rebellion was directed against the war, but it very soon evolved into a political revolution spearheaded by the Majority Social Democrats. Workers' and Soldiers' Councils were formed, depriving local rulers and military authorities of their power. A few days later, on 9 November, the Emperor abdicated. In this short period, all options were open. The parties of the reform coalition—the Center Party, the left-wing Liberals and the Social Democrats—demanded immediate elections of a constituent National Assembly and attempted to gain control of the government. The radical left-wing Spartacus League was also active, fighting for a revolution modeled on the Bolshevik example. Philipp Scheidemann, the Social Democratic member of the *Reichstag*, only just managed to forestall the Communists when he proclaimed the republic from the window of the *Reichstag* building at midday on 9 November. Nonetheless, Communists and parts of the Workers' Councils tried to force a revolution following the Russian example, whereupon the Social Democratic leaders summoned the aid of the radical right-wing *Freikorps* who brutally suppressed left-wing workers and their attempts at an uprising. The Social Democrats, and in particular their Secretary of Defense (*Reichswehrminister*) Gustav Noske, were blamed for the murder of Karl Liebknecht and Rosa Luxemburg, both leaders of the Spartacus League. Noske felt compelled to suppress the rebellion because the Social Democrats strove for parliamentary democracy and opposed the Bolshevik dictatorship, as did the bourgeois parties and the vast majority of the Workers' and Soldiers' Councils.[10] Nevertheless, in the final days of the Republic, the Right constantly accused them of being a community of interest with the Communists.

In the elections for the constituent National Assembly in January 1919, the republican parties obtained an overwhelming majority. Almost three-quarters of the electorate voted for the 'Weimar coalition' comprised of the Catholic Center Party (*Zentrum*, Z), the left-wing liberal German Democratic Party (*Deutsche Demokratische Partei*, DDP) and the Social Democratic Party (*Sozialdemokratische Partei Deutschlands*, SPD). It was the first democratically elected government in the Reich with Social Democratic participation. The consultations over the constitution were relocated to the small town of Weimar in Thuringia, not primarily because it had been the home of Goethe and Schiller, but because here the continuing threat of civil war was less menacing than in Berlin. The meetings took place in the town's theatre, and were characterized by provisional arrangements and poor working conditions. Beyond this, they were further influenced by the ongoing peace negotiations with the Allies. Right from the outset, the burdensome conditions imposed by the Allies put considerable pressure on the constitutional proceedings, forcing concessions in foreign affairs. This pressure was intensified by the threat of invasion if the Germans were to oppose the conditions set by the Allies. Philipp Scheidemann, the Social Democratic Prime Minister (*Reichsminister-präsident*), refused to sign the Treaty of Versailles and resigned in June 1919. Gustav Bauer became his successor. Only a narrow majority in favor of the peace treaty was achieved in the National Assembly, and even those who voted for the treaty criticized it sharply for its war-guilt clause. From the Social Democrats to the politicians of the far Right, all were opposed to Article 231 of the Treaty of Versailles. In this sense, the first

German democracy was characterized from the very beginning by the desire to revise precisely those conditions which had enabled its existence in the first place.

19.3 DICTATORSHIP AND DEMOCRACY IN THE CONSTITUTION OF THE WEIMAR REPUBLIC

Debates on the war, war guilt, and in particular on the question of whether the war could have been ended sooner and with fewer casualties, emerged time and again during the proceedings of the National Assembly. At times they were marked by moments of drama, for instance when Matthias Erzberger, a member of the Center Party, presented official documents proving that the government of the Reich and the Conservatives had spurned numerous opportunities to begin peace negotiations. Apart from these rare situations, the members of the National Assembly were surprisingly cooperative and worked out what could be considered an exemplary constitution by republican and democratic standards.[11] It introduced sovereignty of the people and an extremely fair system of proportional representation for the *Reichstag* elections, and for the first time, women were also entitled to vote. Parties suggested their representatives as candidates and the government was based on the confidence of the majority of the *Reichstag*.

On the other hand, this constitution contained elements that secured it against what contemporaries called a 'parliamentary absolutism.'[12] One of these elements was the position of the president, who was elected in direct elections just as the members of parliament. The president had extensive constitutional rights even in everyday politics: he assigned the task of forming a government and had the power to dissolve the *Reichstag*. Due to his long, seven-year term in office, he enjoyed a far greater degree of independence than the chancellor. However, he gained even more power through his right to take 'emergency measures.' Article 48 allowed him to govern using the so-called 'emergency decrees' (*Notverordnungen*); that is, to suspend the legislative power of parliament as long as the *Reichstag* did not actively object. The Social Democratic president Friedrich Ebert frequently used emergency decrees to govern during the early period of the Weimar Republic, which was marked by civil war. However, this method was also used later in Weimar's history. Paul von Hindenburg, an old monarchist who was elected president in 1925, also resorted to rule by decree under Article 48 during the final phase of the Weimar Republic. Particularly during the global economic crisis, Article 48 was used not only in the case of national emergency, for which it was originally designed, but also in the context of ordinary economic policy. With the right to implement an emergency decree, the president was predestined to become not only an ersatz-monarch, but also a dictator in times of need, a dictator who was not seriously restricted by legislative or judiciary bodies. He was legitimized directly by the people and, in this respect, was as much an expression of the sovereignty of the people as the *Reichstag*. This emergency dictator represented the 'state' above the 'parties,' as well as the organic leader of the people who were supposed to mesh into a unified body under his leadership. Even at the time, many considered this dual embodiment of the sovereignty of the people problematic. What if parliament and the president contradicted each other? Can the sovereign contradict himself? Article 48 granted decisive power to a dictatorship legitimized by plebiscite. In practical terms, the dictatorial presidency—initially a form of emergency rule—gradually evolved into a normal method of exercising power after 1925. This development was justified by the fact that the majority of citizens and political philosophers regarded the president as a leader by plebiscite, and one who was supposed to counterbalance parliament with his charisma. Because parties were suspected of pursuing particular interests instead of the public good, it was the president, rather than the parties, who was thought to embody the unity of the people.

Indeed, the unity of the people was a recurring subject of debate in the Weimar Republic, since its government, elected by majority, was combated by extremists from the political fringes from the beginning.[13] As early as January 1920, parts of the *Reichswehr* under the leadership of General Lüttwitz marched on Berlin and proclaimed Wolfgang Kapp, an East-Prussian agricultural official, as chancellor. There was considerable anxiety in the *Reichswehr* because the Treaty of Versailles reduced the army to 100,000 men, which meant a tremendous decline in social status for many of the officers who were summarily dismissed. The government escaped the putschists, who were supported by elements of the right-wing parties, and fled first to Dresden, then to Stuttgart. The putsch was, however, stopped in its tracks by a general strike, in which many workers participated, and by the refusal of large parts of the state administration to co-operate with the putschists. A few months later, however, general elections showed that many Germans did not fully support the government, as voting for anti-republican parties suggests. The right-wing DVP and DNVP (*Deutschnationale Volkspartei*; German National People's Party) emerged as clear winners, doubling their votes. Left-wing fringe parties such as the USPD (*Unabhängige Sozialdemokratische Partei Deutschlands*; Independent Social Democrat Party of Germany) and the KPD (*Kommunistische Partei Deutschlands*; Communist Party of Germany), which ran for the first time, even tripled their share of the vote. The Weimar coalition was already outnumbered only a short time after the constitution had come into effect. Parties that opposed parliamentary democracy, meanwhile, gained the majority. At no point during the entire history of the Weimar Republic were the parties that had voted in favor of the Weimar constitution able to obtain an absolute majority.

Right-wing violence continued to be a daily occurrence. The *Freikorps* were the bedrock of a movement that intended to punish the 'November criminals'—that is, those who allegedly bore the blame for the defeat in World War I and those who supported the Treaty of Versailles. On 26 August 1921, Matthias Erzberger, a Center Party politician, was shot dead. He had been the architect of a comprehensive system of federal taxation and one of the four signatories of the Treaty of Versailles. A few months later, on 24 June 1922, the German foreign secretary, Walther Rathenau, who had advocated the fulfillment of reparations payments, was murdered.[14] In both cases, the assassinations were carried out by Operation Consul, a secret terrorist group comprised of former *Freikorps* soldiers. 'The enemy stands on the right,' proclaimed Chancellor Joseph Wirth (Center Party) in front of the *Reichstag*. This was a fitting description of the circumstances in terms of the scale of the danger posed by the right; however, it was not quite accurate when looking at the entire political spectrum. The extreme left was in turmoil because the Bolshevik Communist Party in Germany had carefully observed the example of the October Revolution in Russia (1917) and intermittently conducted a putschist policy, albeit with limited success. There were attempted uprisings in Thuringia and Saxony in 1921 and, in March 1923, the militant KPD in Hamburg launched a militarily hopeless rebellion. Objectively speaking, the danger emanating from the left was less than the danger from the right. However, the general strike against the *Kapp-Lüttwitz Putsch* had demonstrated that it was possible to mobilize the workers. This, in turn, lent credence to the idea that a genuinely successful upheaval had to be based on the people and would come from the Left. In its opposition against political violence, the bourgeoisie primarily focused on left-wing violence. Violence from the Right, on the other hand, enjoyed the sympathy or even the participation of the military; it could always successfully claim to be establishing order, and this also meant it could claim to be acting against the alleged anarchy of the lower classes.

Within these conflicts, and to an even greater extent during the economic crisis of hyperinflation, when parliamentary structures of decision-making were largely paralyzed, the president often acted as a quasi-dictator. Friedrich Ebert governed by emergency decree between 1920 and 1924, as did his successor Paul von Hindenburg in the crisis from 1930 onwards.[15] This followed from the logic of the Weimar constitution and did not mean that Weimar democracy was bankrupt. Political philosophers such as Max Weber and Carl Schmitt also conceived of the political system from the perspective of the state of emergency. In everyday political life, the parliamentary form of government was supposed to be the appropriate instrument of control. In times of crisis, however, dictatorial and quasi-dictatorial means were considered to have greater and more resounding impact. This, in turn, fuelled the exuberant expectations hoisted onto a dictatorial leader at a later stage, namely during the global economic crisis.

19.4 POLITICAL EXPECTATIONS AND EVERYDAY LIFE IN WEIMAR DEMOCRACY

Weimar democracy had started with high expectations.[16] Germans understood that the Western democracies had won the war and the Central and Eastern European monarchies—such as Russia, Austria-Hungary, and Germany—were, in fact, the defeated states. President Ebert had concluded his opening statement in the Weimar National

Assembly by citing Fichte: 'We seek to build an empire of justice and truth, based on the equality of all beings with a human face.'[17] These high expectations were themselves a legacy of the war. Germans perceived the war as an enormous sacrifice, and this was particularly the case for workers and for the bourgeoisie, whose financial position suffered the most from the inflation that followed. All subsequent governments faced the general expectation that these sacrifices be justified; in mundane terms, everyone expected some form of gratification, and greater social and political equality. This placed increasing demands on the state that had a wider jurisdiction during the war than ever before and that now, as a republic, claimed to be a 'social people's state,' capable of guaranteeing justice and happiness. The political language reflected this by creating a mood of promise, encouraging citizens to expect the political sphere to deliver everything. The negative expectations, too, were highly exaggerated. There was talk of downfall, of huge dangers and, of a struggle for existence: The high expectations led to an all-or-nothing rhetoric, which systematically overburdened the state. Disappointment was inevitable. Arduous political reality stood in a dialectical relationship with exceedingly high expectations of politics, politicians, and members of parliament, which were bound to be disappointed. An overwhelming desire and intensive search for a genuine leader can be observed throughout the entire Weimar period. On the one hand, this leader was supposed to be a man of the people. On the other, he was expected to be different and special, at a distance from the political classes and thus uncorrupted.[18] This search for the leader was promoted primarily by right-wing groups. Initially, they did not search among their own ranks, but rather among the left wing, as they assumed that the left had closer ties to the people, that is, to the workers. Carl Severing and Gustav Noske, both Social Democrats, also attracted the attention of the Right. In this respect, Hitler managed to channel expectations that initially had not been specifically anti-republican. These expectations arose from the much regretted fact that all politics in the republic's everyday life was necessarily routine, procedural, in a certain sense automatic, and heavily influenced by special interests.

The Weimar Republic represented, for the first time in German history, a political system based on political parties.[19] Suffrage, which was now extended to citizens of both sexes twenty-one years of age and older, rested on proportional representation. Instead of individual candidates, the electorate voted for lists compiled by the parties for each constituency. As these constituencies were extremely large (there were only thirty-six constituencies in Weimar Germany), the candidates' personal profile was not a criterion for the election. Rather, the parties were responsible for selecting the candidates in an anonymous process. Furthermore, proportional representation ensured that votes would not be wasted as is the case in a winner-take-all system. There was no electoral threshold—that is, no clause stipulating a minimum percentage required for a party to enter parliament—which would prevent the smallest parties from entering the *Reichstag*. The main intention here was not to ensure parliament's decision-making ability, but to mirror the structure of society as accurately as possible. A fair result for political groups, rather than trust in specific individual politicians, was the basis of this voting system. This reflected the belief that had grown during the war, namely that social collectives—a conglomerate of major groups, gathering in different parties—constituted a people, with social and economic motives overriding political motives when it came to choosing a political party. Therefore, interest groups and occupational groups played a significant role in the composition of candidates. A major issue for all parties was the number of workers' and employers' representatives they nominated as candidates, which in turn depended on the level of activity of special interest groups. Conversely, there was a perception, quite common even among right-wing parties, that a people's party should have some industrial workers among its ranks. Behind these discussions was also a question as to which kind of representation was preferable. Should representatives of the people be outstanding individuals, exceeding the average, or should they be more like the people themselves, sharing in their experiences and personal situation? Increasingly, the latter took precedence, and this implied distrust toward professional politicians. As party politicians became increasingly professionalized during the Weimar period, they were forced to counter suspicions that they had no genuine interest in the common good.

Characterized by routines and procedures, democratic life often led to compromises and only rarely presented large political spectacles. People observing politics were easily under the impression that Germany's vital matters were drowning in a sea of technical political procedures, influenced by profiteering and selfishness without any sense of responsibility or of the common good. According to this common view, alienation between the people and the political class was inherent to democracy. Therefore, the public paid great attention to corruption and constantly made scandals of politicians' behavior, accusing them of exploiting the political system for their own benefit. Although the Weimar Republic was not particularly corrupt by international standards—in fact, the opposite was the case—politicians always faced the question of how they themselves benefited from the system.

Apart from its initial chaotic phase, Weimar's political system, nevertheless, functioned and was capable of integration. Even the anti-democratic parties of the far right and the far left participated in elections and in the practical process of decision-making in parliament. After 1923, the parties, including the Communists and the Nazis abstained from violence— at least until the early 1930s. The DNVP in particular, with its broad political spectrum ranging from manifest right-wing extremists to conservative democrats, excelled at anti-republican rhetoric, yet remained open to compromise in many areas.

Although the details of innumerable political issues of the Weimar Republic were highly controversial, most of the parties nevertheless agreed on some basic principles. The Peace of Versailles was perceived as a humiliation and reparations and the losses of territory were to be revised sooner or later. Furthermore, it was agreed that Weimar democracy had to focus on the man in the street, people like workers, pensioners, and small farmers, and that Weimar should therefore be turned into a welfare state. This consensus became most obvious in the fact that the establishment of unemployment insurance—Weimar's most important achievement in terms of social policy—was not introduced by the Social Democrats, as one might expect, but under the aegis of the

DNVP. Indeed, references to the 'people's community' and the responsibility of the state had the potential to create consensus on a practical level.

The understanding that representatives had of their own role was equally undisputed. They saw the everyday tasks of government as a job for ministerial bureaucracies, rather than parliament. The latter was considered to be responsible for the establishment of guidelines and the formulation of political principles. Ministerial officials took it as a matter of course that they could pre-formulate bills which the members of Parliament then merely had to approve. Civil servants preferred to formulate their regulations as decrees, which did not require parliamentary approval and, in so doing, were able to disregard parliament entirely. Compared with bills, the number of decrees experienced a boom, particularly during times of crisis, as was the case during 1923 and also after 1930. This was a relic of a constitutionalist understanding of government that sought to limit the role of parliament to a mere controlling function that was rather vague. It was, on the other hand, the government (and the bureaucracy alongside it), which was supposed to be in charge of actual political practice. Nonetheless, the *Reichstag* became much more active after 1924. It not only prevailed over the bureaucracy by outnumbering its decrees, but also over the government by introducing considerably more bills than the latter. This development during the quieter years of the Weimar Republic demonstrated the emancipation of the members of parliament, and the beginnings of a new political mindset that was less passive and reactive than that seen in the era of the monarchy.

The basic consensus, procedural rather than programmatic, regarding the roles of institutions was actually quite surprising given recent German history, marked, as it was, by war, defeat, revolution, and postwar trauma. This consensus clashed, however, with a completely different mood in the mass media and among the parties' grass roots, where the prevalent experience was social fragmentation.[20] The mass media, and especially the print media, addressed party followers, rather than the broader public. The system of voluntary associations (*Vereine*), which had been a pillar of civil society from the 19th century onwards, was divided along ideological lines. Even the sporting arena offered, for instance, separate Catholic and workers' sport clubs, and workers' clubs, in turn, competed at exclusively workers' Olympic games. Economic and ideological lobbying groups from the *Reichslandbund* (Reich Agrarian League; Germany's largest agrarian association), to the Homeowner Association, to the major industrial lobbies, emphasized the divergent interests of the people. They gained substantial influence because the insufficiently funded parties depended on their financial contributions. This meant that the lobbying groups were not only able to influence individual policies, but also the list of candidates. In this sense, the Weimar Republic can be described not only as a party state, but also as a lobby state.[21] Contemporaries perceived this form of pluralism as group-led egotism and as damaging to the unity of the people. Moreover, those who were not engaged in these lobbies, such as the Communists or the Nazis, were able to advertise the fact that they were not participating in the fragmentation of the people.

The perception of pluralism, then, was controversial. On the one hand, the people were seen as a conglomerate of major collectives, each attempting to gain influence. On the other hand, the German people suffered from a clash of interests that allegedly disunited it. Initially, only nationalism seemed to effectively transcend these divisions. In referring to terms such as *Volksgemeinschaft*, German honor, or *Schützengrabengemeinschaft* (trench community), nationalism promised that the German people would find themselves and that a true German identity would be restored. It offered utopian ideas in terms of social justice and contained elements of a 'third way,' which was to avoid the Western European form of class society, as well as the aberration of Bolshevism. Religious ideas of national rebirth, some with anti-Semitic content, also played a role that is not to be underestimated. These ideas tended to interpret the German defeat as a punishment, and by corollary saw Germany's reascent as a sign of providence. In the end, the Weimar Republic included many different types of nationalism, and nationalism was to be found in almost all political camps, even Social Democracy, as became evident in conflicts with the Socialist parties of other nations.

19.5 DEMOCRACY IN CRISIS AND THE ASCENT OF DICTATORSHIP

In this respect, the ascent of the Nazi movement, beginning in the second half of the 1920s and accelerating at a breathtaking pace after 1930, echoed mentalities and collective desires in Germany that transcended political camps.[22] In the specific German process of coming to terms with the past, German historians have tended to perceive National Socialism as something that came from the outside, with Hitler, Goebbels, and Himmler appearing as political desperados who were otherwise socially marginalized. Yet these men were far from typical for the Nazi movement, and the movement itself was, likewise, not an indication of the 'panic among the bourgeoisie,' as the sociologist Theodor Geiger described it with reference to the global economic crisis. Rather, two aspects are to be stressed. For one thing, the ascent of the Nazis began before the global economic crisis and before the crisis of democracy had begun, although it benefited from both. Secondly, the National Socialist movement was neither a movement of outsiders nor of specific strata or classes. It was, instead, a people's party of protest, which could attract members of all social groups, including the workers.[23] Contemporaries appreciated the fact that the movement was politically radical, as they perceived this as an indication of its determination to replace the failing political classes and to reunite the people.

In 1920, a veteran of the First World War, Adolf Hitler, had joined a sectarian, radical nationalist group called the '*Deutsche Arbeiterpartei*' (German Workers' Party). After only a short time he held the party under his sway and renamed it the '*Nationalsozialistische Deutsche Arbeiterpartei*' (National Socialist German Workers'

Party).[24] In the atmosphere of crisis during the early 1920s, the party propagated a right-wing extremist putschism. Influenced by Mussolini's successful 'march on Rome' in October 1922, it launched a putsch attempt in Munich in 1923. The putsch was quickly brought to an end by the Bavarian police force and its ringleader, Hitler, was sentenced to *Festungshaft* (a confinement that excluded forced labor, offered comfortable cells, and allowed visitors almost on a daily basis). Hitler ordered his party to adopt a new and legal course of action. The ersatz-organizations newly founded after the ban of the NSDAP, such as the '*Deutschvölkische Freiheitspartei*' (German Völkisch Freedom Party), subsequently entered German state parliaments and even the *Reichstag*. Josef Goebbels, an unemployed literary scholar, who was leader of the district of Berlin (Gauleiter) from 1926 and head of party propaganda from 1930 onward, provided publicity for the party by exploiting the violent conflicts with Communist groups in 'red Berlin.' Under the direct control of Hitler as charismatic Führer, the centralist party organization and its wide range of sub-organizations, appealed to young men in particular; the SA (*Sturmabteilung*; storm troopers) was more than a mere paramilitary organization, offering a home, comradeship, and hot meals in its SA-hostels.[25] However, it was not only young men who were interested in war games and brawls. The promise of overcoming the 'humiliation of Versailles' and of restoring the German 'people's community' also appealed to respected notables, especially in the countryside.[26] Here, Nazism did not present itself as a manipulative propaganda movement, as is often maintained, but as a movement that attracted 'the many,' funded primarily by admission fees to rallies and merchandizing.[27] There was little trace of Josef Goebbels' modern propaganda in the Hessen countryside or the remote Black Forest. People from the countryside were not so much attracted by Hitler, who was a distant figure, but by the promise of overcoming social and political divisions among the German people, and by the movement's offer of community building. National Socialists could benefit from the decline of the system of voluntary associations, as well as that of the liberal milieu, by penetrating the vacuums both had left behind.

By 1928 the party already had over 100,000 members. One year later it won 900,000 votes in the local Prussian elections. In 1930 Wilhelm Frick was the first National Socialist member of a federal state government when he became interior minister in the state of Thuringia. The party's dramatically improved performance in the *Reichstag* general elections in 1930 was, therefore, not unexpected, although its scale surprised all observers—the NSDAP won 18.2 percent of the vote and turned from a political splinter party into the second largest party after the Social Democrats. In the elections of July 1932, the Nazis doubled their vote to 37.3 percent, leaving the Social Democrats far behind with 21 percent. Even though it appeared in the November 1932 elections as if the party had exhausted its potential—it won 33 percent of the vote—the NSDAP was still the most successful party in German history, given the speed of its ascent. It benefited mainly from mobilizing those who had been non-voters, those who were generally dissatisfied with Weimar Germany and those who had little enthusiasm for politics. In addition, the Nazis were able to benefit from swing voters from all parties, primarily from the liberal center and from smaller interest parties, although voters also switched from the Social Democrats to the NSDAP on a large scale.[28] As intensive research activity since the 1980s has shown, the party drew voters from all strata. Forty percent of its voters were workers, which shows that this group was slightly underrepresented (the proportion of workers in the entire population was 45 percent).[29] Compared to the general strata of German society, the Nazi party was a people's party with a middle-class belly (Jürgen Falter), but in absolute terms it was, nonetheless, a workers' party, comprising more workers than any other political party. One has to assume that the ascent of the party was no mishap.

The propaganda that made this success possible was, however, quite ambiguous.[30] It consisted of a form of political advertisement that told whomever it addressed what they wanted to hear. National Socialists promised to take care of the business worries of small and medium-sized companies, and assured farmers that they would also deal with their concerns over prices of agricultural products and global competition. To workers, they made promises of high employment and fair salaries, while mothers were promised cheap bread. Nazi propaganda was radically nationalist in character, but that was nothing remarkable for a right-wing party, particularly during the late 1920s.

In the last partially free elections on 5 April 1933, the Nazis were able to win only 44 percent of the vote, despite a large-scale propaganda effort, violent clashes between the SA and its political enemies, and a remarkable mobilization of non-voters—the turnout of nearly 89 percent would not be reached again until the 1970s. This meant that the National Socialists were unable to win over the majority of the German people in free elections, even though they made every effort to do so and had all kinds of advantages. However, if we include the 8 percent won by the DNVP—the coalition partner of the Nazis which was associated with the right-wing paramilitary organization 'Stahlhelm'— the result also shows that in spring 1933 there was a clear majority on the right that voted against parliamentary democracy. For a long time, research has used the term 'seizure of power' to signify the government takeover by Hitler on 30 January 1933. It was, in fact, a handing over of power, not only on the part of the old elites who brought Hitler into government, but also on the part of the electorate.[31] To a large extent, Hitler's dictatorship was based on the approval of the people he governed, a fact which led the historians Karl-Dietrich Erdmann and Hagen Schulze to coin the term 'surrender of democracy.'

19.6 WEIMAR DEMOCRACY IN INTERNATIONAL COMPARISON

When looking at the characteristics of Weimar democracy, the strikingly high level of technical and juridical perfectionism on the part of those who created the Weimar Constitution and the instruments of democratic rule initially becomes apparent. However, these regulations, although intricately balanced, collapsed like a house of cards when the crisis began and determined opponents dismantled the republic. The

Weimar case shows that democracy requires not only good laws, but also, and to an even greater extent, a certain willingness to apply these laws in a democratic way. This was not always the case in the Weimar Republic. The reason for this was, as I have tried to demonstrate, not a 'betrayal' by the elites, but the realization of a widely shared mindset that preferred the decisiveness of dictatorial control over the compromise achieved by discourse.

For far too long, the Weimar Republic has been judged by the standards of the Atlantic democracies. It has been forgotten that Anglo-American societies, in particular, already had a long history and experience of democratic systems. Even the Third Republic in France could look back on 60 years of history and had survived a world war by the time Hitler took power in Germany. But if instead we focus on the other new democracies founded in Central and Eastern Europe after the First World War, it is rather surprising that the Weimar Republic survived as long as it did. Most of the other states became dictatorships much earlier. Even in those countries that remained democratic in a general sense, quasi-dictatorial instruments of control had been introduced, as was the case, for example, in Czechoslovakia. Dictatorship, and specifically the type of dictatorship that referred to the people, was the most successful and most popular form of political rule in the inter-war period. Even the Third Republic was on the brink of dictatorship in 1934, and the pace at which Marshal Petain was able to establish the dictatorial Vichy Regime reveals that, even in France, democracy had a hard time. In this respect, the Weimar Republic was no exception. From an American perspective, it might have appeared surprising that the European states did not accept the gift of democracy. Yet, in many countries, resentment towards democracy was, among other reasons, due to the fact that it came from the outside. It was a widespread view, fostered by authoritarian regimes, that democracy did not match the unique character of the nation in question. In Austria in 1933, Engelbert Dollfuß established a clerical *Ständestaat* (state based on estates), which referred heavily to the Catholic legacy and strongly sympathized with Mussolini, who also acted as the regime's patron. Regardless of Wilson's doctrine of national self-determination, Czechoslovakia was not a nation state, but a multiethnic state with a Czechoslovakian majority. Here, an aggressive form of nationalism ruled the country, feeding off the fact that the Czechs had fought for their independence for such a long time. Now, they harassed the German and the Hungarian minority, returning the persecution they had once felt themselves. In Poland, the national hero Jozef Pilsudski overthrew the republic—which had been built in 1921 on the French example—in a 1926 putsch supported by many sides. He established a popular dictatorship that was driven by Polish nationalist and socialist ideas alike. Despite Hitler's disdain for Poland, the German Führer was a pronounced admirer of the left-leaning Polish dictator, whose memoirs were published in German with a preface by Hermann Göring in 1935.[32] Such ideas of a distinct national path were also echoed in Germany, where the search for a third way between 'Western' democracy and 'Eastern' despotism, which would mirror the specific structure of German society, spawned not only *ständestaatliche* (estate-based) and authoritarian concepts, but also programs, such as Oswald Spengler's 'Prussian Social-ism,' which emphasized order and justice.

The waves of democratization after the Second World War, the end of the Latin-American and European dictatorships in the 1970s and after, and the end of Eastern European communism have taught us that democracy has to be learned and that this process takes time. Even Spain, Portugal, and Greece, and particularly the former GDR and Hungary, experienced long transitional periods in which the future political direction remained unclear. However, a number of conditions can be identified that applied to these states, but not to the Weimar Republic or, indeed, to other failed democratic states in the interwar period. First, Spain, Portugal, and Hungary met with a favorable international environment willing to admit the new democracies as quickly as possible into institutions of international cooperation. European integration in particular provided an obvious boost to the new democracies. Germany, on the other hand, met with an international environment in 1918 that was dominated by French fears that it's major neighbor would grow too quickly, and by attempts to keep this opponent as small as possible. A second significant aspect is closely related to the first. International integration after the Second World War was interlinked with the promise of prosperity.[33] Democracy as a political system clearly gains a lot of support if it promises wealth and prosperity, as was possible in the case of the German 'economic miracle' after the Second World War. This was not the case during the crises of the interwar period. Thirdly, and finally, democratic culture implies alternating govern-ments. In Spain, Greece, and Hungary, it seems to have been helpful that parties which had previously sympathized with or had even been hand in glove with the earlier dictators eventually entered government after a few years. This paved the way for integrating opponents of the democratic system into the republic. This model could also be observed in the case of the early Third Republic. In the Weimar republic, on the other hand, it was perceived as almost contrary to the system that the DNVP twice became part of the government. Over the years, the political classes of the Weimar right became increasingly prepared to cooperate with this development.[34] Yet the radical supporters of the right-wing parties, alongside an equally radical party press, refused to take part in the process of republicanization and despised their elites for compromising. This takes us back to a crucial point: the sphere of politics was an area ruled by enmity, and this inner enmity—paradoxically combined with an almost pathological desire for community—was shared by all political camps in the republic. In this respect, collective political attitudes hindered the process of inner republicanization.

19.7 CONSENSUS AND TERROR. THE NATURE OF NAZI RULE 1933–1939

On 30 January 1933, Adolf Hitler was appointed chancellor of a coalition government that was composed of members of previous presidential cabinets that had failed. This government was precisely the type of alliance between fascist mass movements and the conservative bourgeois camp that was already well-proven in Italy.[35] By July 1933 all other parties had been abolished and the NSDAP had become a monopoly party. Unions were banned and German Federalism was destroyed in favor of a centralist structure. Basic rights were abolished and 27,000 political prisoners were detained in concentration camps. More than a half century later, it is still remarkable how quickly Hitler and the Nazis established a totalitarian rule strikingly different in terms of its extent from all other dictatorial regimes in Europe.[36] It took Stalin roughly six years before his position was similarly beyond dispute. Mussolini needed even more time and never fully achieved the degree of unrestricted power that Hitler had been able to gain within half a year. The old elites around Franz von Papen had hoped to 'encircle' Hitler in a coalition government, but these hopes soon evaporated. Although initially only two other ministers were National Socialists—Wilhelm Frick as minister of the interior, and Herman Göring as minister without portfolio and also as provisional Prussian minister of the interior—it took Hitler only a short time to dismantle the republic's protective mechanisms. The most important bastion, Prussia, with its effective police force led by Social Democrat Carl Severing, had already fallen victim to a coup in July 1932 and was ruled by a quasi-dictatorial Reich commissar. In taking over the Reich and the Prussian home office, Hitler had secured access to powerful authorities such as the police force and criminal prosecutors, who would now serve as instruments of terror against political opponents. Yet the administration, the unions, the parliament, diets, parties, and finally the *Reichswehr* also surrendered across the board shortly thereafter. There is no doubt that fortune and coincidence played an important role in the speed with which Hitler gained power. However, Hitler's tactical skills and his ability to react quickly are not to be underestimated. Already during the course of forming the cabinet, Hitler enforced the dissolution of parliament and the calling of new elections. In their campaign, the Nazis used all the means of power at their disposal, ranging from the visibility bonus held by the incumbent party of government ('*Regierungsbonus*'), to their privileged access to means of communication, to the terror tactics of the SA. Deploying SA thugs as an auxiliary police force, Hermann Göring made it known from the start that he would support the use of firearms against political opponents. Then, on 27 February 1933, right in the middle of the election campaign, the *Reichstag* building was set on fire. Much speculation then arose—and some still exists today—that the Nazis themselves had been behind the arson attack, because the event undoubtedly suited their intentions. However, there is considerable evidence that Marinus van der Lubbe, a Communist from the Netherlands, was indeed the lone perpetrator. Meanwhile, the new incumbents reacted remarkably quickly. As early as the following day they issued a decree 'for the protection of people and state,' the so called '*Reichstag* fire decree,' which suspended political rights and basic liberties 'until further notice.' It imposed a state of emergency that remained in place until the end of the Third Reich. The political scientist, Ernst Fraenkel, rightly described this decree as the 'constitutional charter of the Third Reich.'[37] Thus, only four weeks after coming into power, Hitler was able to govern by emergency decree. It was used to terrorize political opponents, to muzzle the media and political institutions, and to manipulate public opinion through a major propaganda campaign. According to Josef Goebbels, the new minister for 'people's enlightenment and propaganda,' it was not the task of National Socialism to terrorize the remaining 48 percent of the population who did not stand behind the regime with the help of the 52 percent who did. Quite the opposite; this strong minority was to be turned into loyal followers. Goebbels' directive highlighted a key element in the Nazi technique of rule: the dual character of terror and consensus with which National Socialists penetrated every pore of German society. This penetration, deeper than some scholars have assumed, was only possible because of a certain openness to it within society.

On 23 March 1933 the *Reichstag* passed the Enabling Act (*Ermächtigungsgesetz*), which allowed the government to pass laws without requiring the assent of the *Reichstag*—even laws that were not in accordance with the constitution! Now Hitler did not even have to suspend the Weimar constitution to govern without and against it. President Hindenburg was thus degraded to a political figure with a merely ornamental function, while the chancellor became the sole authority in Germany. All political parties of the *Reichstag*, apart from the Social Democrats (and the Communists, who were, however, now outlawed), assented to the Enabling Act, which was limited to four years, but was promptly extended each time it expired. Based on this emergency decree, German federalism was abolished one week later by dissolving the remaining German states, where other parties predominantly held power in state parliaments. Within a few months, unions and parties were dissolved; a law from 14 July banned their reestablishment, as well as the formation of new parties and the NSDAP was declared to be the only German party. Thus, discord and self-destruction, which many Germans associated with the party system, had come to an end. The Nazi party was to become a symbol of national unity for all Germans. Indeed, within three months, party membership figures increased from 700,000 to just less than 2.5 million. From 1 May 1933 onward, new members were no longer admitted. Not only was it remarkable that about 95 percent of all members were men—that is, one in ten German males was a member of the Nazi party—but also that the NSDAP was a party of the publically active parts of society: only 5 percent of all party members were pensioners, housewives, or school pupils, although these groups constituted more than 50 percent of the entire population. Every fourth teacher and every sixth self-employed person was a party member, and a third of all Nazi party members belonged to the working class.

Opportunism definitely played an important role in motivating the masses to join the Nazis, as did the desire to participate in a radical reorganization of society. The party attempted to penetrate, control, and organize the people and place it under permanent surveillance. It established and organized a system of blocs and cells penetrating day-to-day life in Germany. A '*Blockwart*' (block attendant, the lowest official in the NSDAP) was in charge of about 80 households. A fifth of all party members acted as volunteers. In the National Socialists' penetration of German society, many people were given responsibilities and this created a system of omnipresent denunciation and observation. It equally presented an opportunity for many people to participate in establishing Nazi rule in German everyday life.

The scholarly debate in the 1970s and 1980s centered on a dispute over whether the Nazi dictatorship was an autocracy built solely on Hitler's power or a chaotic polycracy. This debate was, however, largely based on an outdated conception of dictatorship. After Paul von Hindenburg's death in 1934, Hitler made himself president by holding a plebiscite to officially legitimize this position. From then on, he was both head of government and head of state, ruling absolutely as a charismatic leader. His word was law. Hitler was anything but a weak dictator, and he was able to achieve and maintain this strength as a leader because there were many who were willing to 'work towards the Führer' (Ian Kershaw). These supporters anticipated his intentions and put them into practice on their own accord, radicalizing them even further in the process in order to present themselves as particularly loyal followers. This was only possible because they shared many of Hitler's views. Hitler's dictatorship was built on consensus and periodically demanded a reaffirmation of this consensus. A charismatic leader constantly has to prove himself, and Hitler managed to do so by proceeding to transform German society at an extremely rapid pace. He repeatedly confronted the German population with surprising turns, new objectives, and unexpected successes, which were especially remarkable in foreign affairs, in particular with respect to reparations, restrictions on armaments, and territorial revision. Hitler's pace in dealing with foreign affairs was as fast as it was in the Nazification of German society—much to the surprise of the public, who soon expected him to be able to cut through the same Gordian knot, which had previously given republican politicians such a hard time.

Acts of terror were one side of the National Socialists' attempts to enforce their power. Especially in the early stages, these were endemic and rather unspecific in many cases. The SA, which was founded by Ernst Röhm in 1921, had grown to an army of 400,000 men by the end of the Weimar Republic. During the early period of the Hitler regime, membership figures exploded, reaching a total of 2.5 million. The SA became the main instrument of enforcing rule during the early Nazi period. Röhm planned to build up a people's militia, which could compete with the *Reichswehr*. The activist SA served as a reservoir for social revolutionaries. After the seizure of power, they demanded a 'second revolution:' the elimination of the old elites and the formation of a people's state based on the concept of a 'people's community' with socialist elements. In so doing, Röhm—who had known Hitler since 1919 and was one of a select few who were allowed to address him informally—opposed the Führer. In contrast to Röhm, Hitler declared the end of the revolution on 6 July 1933. Instead of a socialist reorganization of society, Hitler championed national revisionism and imperialist expansion. For this purpose, he needed a professional army, rather than a gang of brutal thugs. On 30 June 1934, in a cloak and dagger operation, he ordered the assassination of the SA leaders and of representatives of the conservative elites who opposed his dictatorship. Neither the *Reichswehr*, nor the conservative nobilities, nor members of the *Reichstag* thwarted these measures or even protested against this course of action, despite the fact that two generals of the *Reichswehr* had been amongst its victims. The *Reichstag*, still in existence, passed a law introduced by Hitler to legitimize this act of state terrorism retroactively. President Hindenburg, himself a general, even congratulated Hitler on his actions. Indeed, a palpable sense of relief swept the country. Hitler had demonstrated that he was neither a social-revolutionary desperado, nor somebody who intended to radically change the order of German society.

From then on, the SA was no longer an instrument of Nazi terror. Its former functions were taken over by the regular police force, but even more often by the SS. This elite unit was founded as a paramilitary organization and perceived itself as the advocate of a 'rational' enforcement of Nazism. It attracted many young academics and other ambitious people. Under Heinrich Himmler's leadership, it was responsible for the construction and administration of a large number of concentration camps and later, during the war, the extermination camps. The SS was meant to become the nucleus of a new male elite fanatically committed to National Socialism, which would ruthlessly and impassively implement German rule all over Europe.

After Himmler became leader (*Reichsführer*) of a small guard of a few hundred stewards in 1929, he expanded the SS into a special task force of about 250,000 men at the beginning of the war. Alongside the SS, there was the security service (*Sicherheitsdienst*, SD), the secret state police (*Geheime Staatspolizei, Gestapo*), and the criminal investigation services (*Kriminalpolizei, Kripo*)—all of which were combined in 1939 in the Reich Main Security Office (*Reichssicherheitshauptamt*) under Himmler's control. Himmler erected a totalitarian surveillance system, which was widely used to persecute and later to murder Jews. However, the 'SS-state' (Eugen Kogon) was not simply based on a high density of surveillance. The *Gestapo* had relatively few officers, yet it was so efficient in detecting and persecuting Jews and political dissidents that it came to attain mythical status. The cooperation of ordinary citizens was crucial to its success; by voluntarily acting as informants, the Gestapo created a surveillance system which was, in a sense, self-perpetuating.

These institutions are examples of the characteristics of Nazi rule for which the German political scientist, Ernst Fraenkel, coined the term 'dual state,' consisting of the 'normative' and the 'prerogative' state.[38] The 'normative state' was still in operation and in charge of all those who were neither victims nor opponents of the state. For these people, the state was in working order as usual. For the others, the 'prerogative state' was in charge, and this did not have to concern itself with issues of legality. Even respectable citizens without a criminal record could be taken into 'protective custody' (*Schutzhaft*) by the *Gestapo*—a euphemism for detention without legal basis—which was used when there was no legal means for prosecution. It was not possible to appeal against 'protective custody.' Ever since the seizure of power, the system of concentration camps expanded precipitously. In 1933 they were placed under the control of the SS, which carried out its acts of terror there without restriction. In the end, there were several thousand concentration camps: huge central and small local camps, as well as camps affiliated with businesses. Their existence was hardly a secret. A large concentration camp such as Dachau attained considerable economic importance for the city.[39] Those living under the 'normative state' knew very well what to expect if they strayed from the permitted path. A vague fear of unnameable consequences did its bit to uphold compliance.

In so doing, the Nazis effectively hollowed the state out from within. Although most of the former institutions continued to exist, they became less important because parallel institutions emerged that took over their functions. These new institutions had grown out of the network of Nazi organizations. They were linked to the Führer personally, either under his direct control or personally connected to him. Consequently, the network of political and administrative institutions turned into an empty shell. At the same time, para-state institutions conducted the actual political and administrative tasks, unhindered by regulations. Thus, the 'prerogative state' systematically undermined the 'normative state.'

This notwithstanding, Hitler's rule was not merely a reign of terror. Rather, he perceived himself as an instrument of divine providence accountable to the German people. Periodically staged rituals legitimized the plebiscitary power of the Führer and evoked his affiliation with the people. The annual party rallies in Nuremberg were spectacles of party power, which demonstrated that party, people, and state were merging together. At a huge financial cost and with an impressive mastery of cinematic technique, director Leni Riefenstahl captured the 1934 party rally on film. Hitler approached Nuremberg by plane, symbolically descending from the heavens. On the Zeppelinfeld—an area larger than twelve football pitches—he took the salute of the military parade of the German people which was symbolized through Nazi organizations differentiated by generation, region, gender, and profession. Thus, every single person in the audience could imagine him or herself as part of the party rally—and consequently of the new Germany.

The referendums Hitler used to legitimize his policies also shared the same publicly representative character. By using the same means, he made himself head of state after President Hindenburg's death (although with a disappointing result: more than 5,000,000 of the electorate either voted openly against Hitler or destroyed their ballot paper). There were plebiscites on the withdrawal from the League of Nations (1933), on the return of the Saarland to Imperial Germany (1935), and on the annexation of the Rhineland (1936) and Austria (1938). These were little more than symbolic performances, evidence of a desire to legitimize the dictatorship through the people and to turn this political act into a performative event. Clearly, Hitler did not need (or want) the political conflict that is always implied by free elections. However, he did need mass acclamation to demonstrate the affiliation between him and his people.

These forms of legitimization were the coatings of a popular consensus, albeit one exaggerated by the regime. There is, however, no doubt that this consensus existed and that Hitler enjoyed a popularity achieved by few German politicians before or after him.[40] He created a consensus around a system of rule that seemed to represent the consummation of German history and the overcoming of trauma. Only a minority perceived it principally as a regime of terror. Obviously, we know much more about the public mood in societies with an unregulated public sphere than about the mood in dictatorial states. Yet the regime monitored its citizens with a thoroughness that came close to scientific opinion polls, if not in terms of its methodology, then at least in terms of the range of its findings.[41] Naturally, the observers who wrote the reports for the SD had an interest in presenting a favorable picture, yet the reports unequivocally suggest that acceptance for Hitler's policies grew continually until the Munich Agreement of 1938. Had Hitler held free general elections in the summer of 1938, he would have won approval ratings undreamt of by democratic politicians. Germans were also monitored from the outsider. The exiled leaders of the Social Democrats had installed a system of informal observers delivering relatively reliable information about everyday life and the mood in Germany.[42] Even though, as undercover Social Democrats, their local observers were biased as well, their reports also show a high degree of approval for Hitler and his policies. Private records recently examined by historians point in the same direction.[43] How can we explain this public approval for a dictatorship which brutally suppressed everyone not to its liking?

First of all, the regime was extremely effective at mobilizing German citizens. Many of them were involved in Nazi organizations and were assigned tasks. This type of involvement had consequences in terms of integration. Life became increasingly de-privatized and de-individualized, a process, that emphasized equality not in terms of equal opportunities, but in terms of the equal value of all citizens. This integration of all 'Volksgenossen' (comrades of the people) was more extensive the more it was combined with the exclusion of others: Jews, Communists, the homeless, and so-called 'Gemeinschaftsschädlinge' (people 'damaging' to the community). The exclusion of these people effectively confirmed the cohesion of the others, who now imagined themselves as a society of unambiguous mutual affiliation, a homogeneous community, even a society of equals. It goes without saying that in the 1930s this form of social order was highly attractive to many Germans.

Secondly, Nazi promises did not remain mere propaganda. Within a short period after his seizure of power, Hitler managed to tackle the main problem caused by the global economic crisis: unemployment. Hitler had learned his lesson from the defeat of the First World War, and he knew that he had to win over the loyalty of the workers and of those on the 'Heimatfront' (home front) for the next war. Hitler's strategies to overcome the global economic crisis did not differ much from those implemented in other countries, whether it was dictatorial states, such as Italy and Portugal, or democratic ones, such as Great Britain and the United States. The state became an active agent in the field of labor and investment. It raised money, either through loans, through restricting consumption, or through reassigning other funds (such as the reparations that were no longer paid after 1931). These funds financed job-creation measures, which predominantly focused on investments in infrastructure and, consequently, improved conditions for private enterprise.[44] From as early as the last years of the Weimar Republic, motorways had been planned for the newly-developing automobile traffic. The 'Autobahn' was not Hitler's idea, nor was it a uniquely German one. The construction of motorways was also a means of government-funded job-creation in the United States, and it was a means of creating a demand for industrial products through public investment. In contrast to these other countries, however, investment in

Germany was closely linked to preparations for war. The *Reichsarbeitsdienst* (RAD, Imperial Labor Service), established in 1931 on a voluntary basis, was in 1935 turned into a six-month-long official duty for young men and was, in fact, a paramilitary organization. There were labor services in other countries, too, for instance in the USA.[45] There, however, these organizations were designed to deploy cheap human labor wherever expensive machine work was not profitable enough. The American 'Civilian Conservation Corps' (CCC), for instance, was focused on practical environmental preservation and also offered members the opportunity to learn job skills.

Due to these measures, and the slowly improving global economic situation, unemployment could be reduced within a short period of time.[46] Furthermore, the growing armaments production required so many workers that full employment was achieved in 1935–1936 and even a shortage of labor was soon reported. Subsequently, there was a substantial rise in wages so that the real wage level of 1928, at the end of the good times of the Weimar Republic, was reached again in 1937.[47] Much of this money was later recovered by the state, for example, through donations and compulsory membership fees, and this funded a form of public social policy. Even though making a donation was sometimes perceived as a nuisance, people still felt that they were making a symbolic contribution to the community, not least because organizations such as the *Winterhilfswerk* (winter welfare organization) or '*Kraft durch Freude*' (KdF; literally: 'strength through joy,' a leisure organization and part of the German Labor Front) fulfilled the functions of a welfare state. The KdF was a national holiday service that, for the first time in German history, enabled even the working class to go on holiday.[48] Purchasing a cheap radio receiver (a 'people's radio set' produced from 1933 onwards in large quantities and at a highly affordable price) or even the hope of buying a '*Volkswagen*' (people's car) in a few years' time, gave ordinary people the feeling of social advancement and the sense of an emerging consumer society after the subsiding global economic crisis. All this was seemingly thanks to the Führer. In this respect, the brown 'social revolution' (David Schoenbaum) was much more than propaganda.[49] Many people rightly perceived a significant improvement in their standard of living.

On the other hand, it was obvious to well-informed people that the system was largely built on sand. The German way out of the crisis was funded by loans, and these were not used for productive investments in the usual sense.[50] Most of the money did not fund social policy projects, but war preparations, and the planners came to expect a rich bounty from the war that would cover the debt at a later stage. In plain language: the defeated nations of the next war were expected to settle German debt. In 1933 Germany spent almost 2 billion Reich Marks on armament. By the time the war started, this expenditure had increased eighteen-fold. In the years up to 1939, more than 60 billion was spent on armaments in total—this amounted to two-thirds of the entire public spending of the Reich.[51] It was impossible to raise these sums through taxation or by taking out regular loans, which is why those responsible conjured up cunning methods of taking on debt without appearing to do so. Nonetheless, by 1938–1939 Germany was up to its ears in debt, and national bankruptcy was only a matter of time. This was another reason why Hitler urged going to war. However, to argue that the war derived solely from a financial crisis and was merely a form of ravenously-funded social policy—as the historian Götz Aly has done—is to reverse cause and effect.[52] Warfare was the vital principle of National Socialism, and not only because it was a means of reclaiming lost territories or gaining the status of a world power. Warfare was, in fact, perceived as a form of existence and was therefore at the core of Nazi ideology. Those lacking a belligerent nature were doomed. In this respect, Hitler imagined his 'people's community' as a war community from the outset. The world war, which Hitler had planned systematically from the beginning and which he precipitated on 1 September 1939, was a war aimed at the conquest, enslavement, and colonization of Europe.

19.8 National Socialist dictatorship in comparison with other European dictatorships

When comparing Hitler's dictatorship with other European dictatorships that developed after 1918, we can identify a large number of differences despite several similarities. The conservative dictators in central-eastern and south-eastern Europe during the interwar period differed significantly from the Nazi dictatorship. Granted, most of them perceived themselves as right-wing and anti-democratic, often as racist and anti-Semitic, and at the very least nationalist. However, neither Metaxas in Greece, nor Horthy in Hungary, nor Pilsudski in Poland, nor Franco in Spain, nor Salazar in Portugal ever achieved the same extent of totalitarian control over society as Hitler. None of them constituted a dictatorship of a movement aiming at the reorganization of an entire society, and none of them came even close to radically reshaping their societies as the Nazis did. Moreover, most of these governments relied on the use of armed forces to a greater extent than the Nazis. There are two other regimes that can, and often have been compared with Nazi Germany. Hitler compared himself with Mussolini several times and they shared a cordial relationship.[53] It has even been suggested that the Duce was Hitler's only friend. Mussolini provided the concept of fascism as a dictatorship of a movement with the two elements of consensus and coercion that served as a veritable blueprint for Hitler, even though the German Führer was not only incomparably more brutal in attaining and retaining power, but also more successful in doing so. Despite what his perception of himself suggested, Mussolini was never a totalitarian ruler. He had to accept compromises with the old elites throughout the entire duration of his dictatorship. The monarchy was never abolished and the King still played an active role in politics. It was these old liberal elites, along with the King, who finally deposed him from office and placed him under arrest. The fact that this was possible lays bare the difference between Mussolini's and Hitler's rule. Moreover, while Italian fascism was indeed belligerent and there were only a few years when Italian troops were not deployed somewhere in the world, it was never part of Mussolini's agenda to plan and conduct a world war in order to enslave Europe and ultimately conquer the entire world, as Hitler had attempted. The historian Wolfgang Schieder rightly described Italian fascism as a prototype from which German National Socialists learned and which they emulated. Sometimes, however, students outgrow their teachers.[54]

Stalinism, the second type of dictatorship often compared with National Socialism, is a slightly different story, because Nazism and Stalinism perceived themselves as completely different from each other in ideological terms.[55] This notwithstanding, there are some similarities between both ideologies in their totalitarian control of society, their mixture of consensus and terror, and their militant self-characterization. Both forms of rule attached little value to human life when it came to achieving their aims. Stalinism, like National Socialism, was a concept that worked on the principle that the end justified the means. This became evident in the detention of millions of people in Soviet labor camps, sometimes for highly trivial reasons, or even for no reason at all. It also became evident in the Russian process of industrialization with its penchant for consuming human resources and in the methods of Russian warfare. By all available means, both regimes pursued the goal of establishing a society characterized by clearly defined affiliations, where similar individuals lived similarly, and right and wrong were easily definable, as the historians Jörg Baberowski and Anselm Doering-Manteuffel have recently argued.

Baberowski has however also raised questions about the similarities of the two regimes. In his view, Stalinism differed considerably from Nazism due to the different personalities that incarnated both regimes. Baberowski ascribes the specific brutality of Stalinism not so much to a reckless modernity, as is often asserted, but much more to the archaic provenance of its leader. Originally from Georgia, Stalin established a system of sadistic despotism the mindset of which was based around ideas of tribal feuds and vendettas. Stalin almost always preferred terror over consensus, relying on raw violence, intimidation and personal dependencies. Under Stalinist circumstances, Bolshevism lost its Leninist rationale that calculated terror was helpful in order to build a new society (according to the role model of French Jacobinism). One should not however overestimate this difference, as Stalin cannot be equated with Stalinism any more than Hitler can be equated with Nazism. Indeed, there were many in Russia who aspired methodically and systematically towards a new social ideal; Stalin's terror was by no means undirected insofar as it helped build a loyal Communist *nomenclatura* and constructed a new, industrialized and proletarianized society.

Pointing out the difference between Stalin and Hitler rightly stresses the diverging contexts of the two dictatorships. Germany, an important country in the center of Europe, a world leader in economic, scientific and cultural terms, chose as its leader a man who was little more than an unemployed, rabble-rousing politician with a criminal record, a threadbare education, and a history of involvement in a coup d'état. With little formal military training, he led the country to war, and to a genocide in which hundreds of thousands took part as perpetrators and bystanders. These circumstances were substantially different from the context in which Stalin came to power. The latter was a Georgian Apparatchik and professional revolutionary. He led a revolutionary cadre party that had taken control of an enormous and backward country that had just a small bourgeoisie and even smaller proletariat. That Hitler, an outsider, could achieve the position he did, cannot be explained solely by his talents, which he undoubtedly had, or by categories like 'manipulation,' or 'propaganda.' Nor can the functioning of his regime be explained with an emphasis on terror. One has to instead consider the message of National Socialism, and the ways in which the style of Hitler's politics met the desires of a great many people in Germany in the 1930s.

19.9 CONCLUSION: CLOSENESS BETWEEN DEMOCRACY AND DICTATORSHIP DURING THE INTERWAR PERIOD

In 1918 German society was highly unsettled. After a long-running war with many victims, a war that for a long time had been expected to be successful, a large nation had been deeply humiliated and branded a pariah on the international stage. The trauma of inner discord and controversy, the unfulfilled promise of a social people's state—which was, in fact, little more than a conflict between corporate, party, and lobbying-group cliques—made democracy appear terminally inadequate. The antagonism between the desire for community, on the one hand, and the deep political cleavages and inability to compromise, on the other, bolstered the myth of the 'community of the trenches' even further. Political semantics infected by the spirit of war served the concepts of community and the exclusion of the enemy. Germans longed for homogeneity instead of pluralism. The leader as the expression of this concept of community, which legitimized him at the same time, had in this respect already become an idealized figure during the democratic period. The presidents of the republic had never been able to fulfill public expectations, not least because they appeared as symbols of party quarrels and cliquish behavior. Hindenburg, rather than Ebert, was able to meet expectations. His broad electoral base promoted the concept of a leader elected by the people. However, Hindenburg was a remnant of a bygone past. Hitler represented youth, social mobility, and the unity of all Germans, even of those who lived outside the territory of Weimar Germany. Essentially, he promised catharsis: he promised that all Germans would come to terms with themselves in a process of self-discovery within an ethnically and socially egalitarian society. At that time, most people were not yet aware that Hitler wanted war. However, after Hitler's successful domestic and foreign policy, they were willing to follow him even that far, albeit with limited enthusiasm. In this respect, Hitler promised to heal the wounds inflicted by World War I and the Treaty of Versailles, as well as the conflicts of democracy. The people followed him into war—initially rather hesitantly, as it had become clear how much could have been achieved without going to war and because the fear of war was still widespread. However, the spectacular victories made even this war popular—at least up until Stalingrad.

In summary, this would mean that the caesura of 1933 should be drawn less sharply. The years from 1918 to 1939 can be understood as a coherent historical period, because, during this time, 'the people' were the dominant principle of politics. Yet 'the people' preferred to be represented by someone with whose political actions they could identify—which was not the case when it came to quarrelling political parties. The lesson that the people are not a harmonious entity and that modern societies are always societies characterized by conflict remained to be learned, even after 1945. Even the early Federal Republic of Germany perpetuated the ideal of a harmonious society—which had by then transformed into a middle class society characterized by the 'economic miracle'— and remained suspicious of and aggressive towards those who were different. It was, in fact, not until the 1960s that it was widely recognized that modern societies are comprised of differences and that the harmonious ideal hidden behind the concept of a leader and a 'people's community' was, at the same time, profoundly violent.

[Translated from German by Christine Brocks.]

NOTES

1. Cf. Margaret Lavinia Anderson, *Practicing Democracy. Elections and Political Culture in Imperial Germany* (Princeton: Princeton University Press, 2000).
2. Cf. Ernst Nolte, 'Diktatur,' in Otto Brunner, Werner Conze, and Reinhart Koselleck (eds), *Geschichtliche Grundbegriffe*, vol. I (Stuttgart: Klett Cotta, 1972), 900–924.
3. Cf. Thomas Mergel, 'Führer, Volksgemeinschaft und Maschine. Politische Erwartungsstrukturen in der Weimarer Republik und im Nationalsozialismus 1918–1936,' in Wolfgang Hardtwig (ed.), *Politische Kulturgeschichte der Zwischenkriegszeit 1918–1939* (Göttingen: Vandenhoeck & Ruprecht, 2005), 91–127; Jeffrey Verhey, *The Spirit of 1914. Militarism, Myth, and Mobilization in Germany* (Cambridge: Cambridge University Press, 2000).
4. Kurt Sontheimer, *Antidemokratisches Denken in der Weimarer Republik. Die politischen Ideen des deutschen Nationalismus zwischen 1918 und 1933* (Munich: DTV, 31992), 251.
5. Larry Eugene Jones, *German Liberalism and the Dissolution of the German Party System 1918–1933* (Chapel Hill: University of North Carolina Press, 1988), 136, 195.
6. Alice Salomon, *Die deutsche Volksgemeinschaft* (Leipzig: B. G. Teubner, 1926).
7. Cf. Michael Wildt, *Volksgemeinschaft als Selbstermächtigung. Gewalt gegen Juden in der deutschen Provinz 1919 bis 1939* (Hamburg: Hamburger Edition, 2007).
8. Cf. Benjamin Ziemann, *War Experiences in Rural Germany 1914–1923* (Oxford/New York: Berg Publishers, 2007); Richard Bessel, *Germany after the First World War* (Oxford: Oxford University Press, 1993).
9. According to Volker Berghahn, it was even this special type of 'men of violence' who dominated Europe in the time between the wars; Volker Berghahn, *Europe in the Era of Two World Wars. From Militarism and Genocide to Civil Society 1900–1950* (Princeton: Princeton University Press, 2006), 4. Gunther Mai talks about 'reconciliation through violence' (Versöhnung durch Gewalt), Gunther Mai, *Europa 1918–1939, Mentalitäten, Lebensweisen, Politik zwischen den Weltkriegen* (Stuttgart: Kohlhammer, 2001), 7.

10. Eberhard Kolb, *Die Weimarer Republik* (Munich: Oldenbourg, 2002), 170ff.

11. Cf. Heiko Bollmeyer, *Der steinige Weg zur Demokratie. Die Weimarer Nationalversammlung zwischen Kaiserreich und Republik* (Frankfurt am Main: Campus, 2007); Mergel, *Parlamentarische Kultur.*

12. Christoph Schönberger, *Das Parlament im Anstaltsstaat. Zur Theorie parlamentarischer Repräsentation in der Staatslehre des Kaiserreiches 1871–1918* (Frankfurt: Klostermann, 1997), 381.

13. Cf. on violence in general Dirk Schumann, *Political Violence in the Weimar Republic 1918–1933. Fight for the Streets and Fear of Civil War* (New York: Berghahn, 2009).

14. Martin Sabrow, *Die verdrängte Verschwörung. Der Rathenau-Mord und die deutsche Gegenrevolution* (Frankfurt am Main: Fischer, 1999).

15. Cf. data in Mergel, *Parlamentarische Kultur*, 223; for the years up until 1925 revised data in Thomas Raithel, *Das schwierige Spiel des Parlamentarismus. Deutscher Reichstag und französische Chambre des Députés in den Inflationskrisen der 1920er Jahre* (Munich: Oldenbourg, 2005), 586.

16. Cf. Thomas Mergel, 'High Expectations—Deep Disappointment: Structures of Public Expectations Towards Politics in Weimar Germany,' in Kathleen Canning et al. (eds), *Weimar Publics/Weimar Subjects. Rethinking the Political Culture of Germany in the 1920s* (New York: Berghahn, 2011).

17. Friedrich Ebert, *Schriften, Aufzeichnungen, Reden II* (Dresden: Reissner, 1926), 156.

18. Mergel, *Führer.*

19. Cf. Mergel, *Parlamentarismus*, 155–229, 362–398.

20. Detlef Lehnert, 'Die unterschätzte Republik. Ein fragwürdiger Negativkonsens über das Scheitern von "Weimar" in zeitgenössicher Sicht der politischen Gegner des Nationalsozialismus,' in Peter Steinbach and Johannes Tuchel (eds), *Widerstand gegen den Nationalsozialismus* (Bonn: Bundeszentrale für politische Bildung, 1994), 85–96.

21. Fritz Blaich, *Staat und Verbände in Deutschland zwischen 1871 und 1945* (Wiesbaden: Steiner, 1979).

22. Hans-Ulrich Wehler, *Deutsche Gesellschaftsgeschichte. Vom Beginn des Ersten Weltkrieges bis zur Gründung der beiden deutschen Staaten*, vol 4 (Munich: Beck, 2003), 542–580. Martin Broszat, *Die Machtergreifung. Der Aufstieg der NSDAP und die Zerstörung der Weimarer Republik* (Munich: DTV, 1994).

23. On the analysis of the electorate of the NSDAP: Jürgen W. Falter, *Hitlers Wähler* (Munich: Beck, 1991); id., 'The Social Bases of Political Cleavages in the Weimar Republic, 1919–1933,' in Larry Eugene Jones and James Retallack (eds), *Elections, Mass Politics, and Social Change in Modern Germany* (Cambridge: Cambridge University Press, 1992), 371–397; Dirk Hänisch, *Sozialstrukturelle Bestimmungsgründe des Wahlverhaltens in der Weimarer Republik. Eine Aggregatdatenanalyse der Ergebnisse der Reichstagswahlen, 1924–1933* (Duisburg: Sozialwissenschaftliche Kooperative, 1983); Peter Manstein, *Die Mitglieder und Wähler der NSDAP 1919–1933. Untersuchungen zu ihrer schichtenspezifischen Zusammensetzung* (Frankfurt am Main: Lang, 1990).

24. On the history of the NSDAP and on Hitler's biography see: Ian Kershaw, *Hitler*, 2 vols (London: Allen Lane, 1998; 2000); Richard J. Evans, *The Coming of The Third Reich* (London: Penguin, 2004).

25. Sven Reichardt and Armin Nolzen (eds), *Faschismus in Italien und Deutschland. Studien zu Transfer und Vergleich* (Göttingen: Wallstein, 2005).

26. Wolfram Pyta, *Dorfgemeinschaft und Parteipolitik 1918–1933. Die Verschränkung von Milieu und Parteien in den protestantischen Landesgebieten Deutschlands in der Weimarer Republik* (Düsseldorf: Droste, 1996).

27. The idea that Nazism was funded predominantly by big industrialists is a myth. See Henry A Turner, *Faschismus und Kapitalismus in Deutschland. Studien zum Verhältnis zwischen Nationalsozialismus und Wirtschaft. Der Weg zum Aufstieg* (Göttingen: Vandenhoeck & Ruprecht, 1972).

28. Conan Fischer (ed.), *The Rise of National Socialism and the Working Classes in Germany* (Providence R.I./Oxford: Berghahn, 1996); Jürgen W. Falter and Dirk Hänisch, 'Die Anfälligkeit von Arbeitern gegenüber der NSDAP bei den Reichstagswahlen,' *Archiv für Sozialgeschichte* 26 (1986), 179–216. Jürgen W. Falter: 'The First German Volkspartei. The Social Foundations of the NSDAP,' in Karl Rohe (ed.), *Elections, Parties and Political Traditions. Social Foundations of German Parties and Party Systems, 1867–1987* (New York, Munich: Berg, 1990), 53–81.

29. Ibid.

30. Thomas Childers, 'The Social Language of Politics in Germany. The Sociology of Discourse in the Weimar Republic,' *American Historical Review* 95 (1990), 331–358; Dieter Ohr, *Nationalsozialistische Propaganda und Weimarer Wahlen. Empirische Analysen zur Wirkung von NSDAP-Versammlungen* (Opladen: Westdeutscher Verlag, 1997); Gerhard Paul, *Aufstand der Bilder* (Bonn: Dietz, 1990).

31. Norbert Frei, '"Machtergreifung". Anmerkungen zu einem historischen Begriff,' *Vierteljahreshefte für Zeitgeschichte* 31 (1983), 136–145.

32. Jozef Pilsudski, *Erinnerungen und Dokumente*, selected by Waclaw Lipinski, with a preface by Hermann Göring, 2 vols (Essen: Essener Verlagsanstalt, 1935).

33. Berghahn, *Europe in the Era*.

34. Mergel, *Parlamentarische Kultur*, 323–331; Thomas Mergel, 'Das Scheitern des deutschen Tory-Konservatismus. Die Umformung der DNVP zu einer rechtsradikalen Partei 1928–1932,' *Historische Zeitschrift* 276 (2003), 323–368.

35. Henry A. Turner, *Hitler's Thirty Days to Power. January 1933* (London: Bloomsbury, 1996).

36. Cf. on this still Karl-Dietrich Bracher, et al., *Die nationalsozialistische Machtergreifung. Studien zur Errichtung des totalitären Herrschaftssystems in Deutschland 1933–1934* (Cologne: Westdeutscher Verlag, 1960); Martin Broszat, *The Hitler State. The Foundation and Development of the Internal Structure of the Third Reich* (London: Longman, 1981), Wehler, *Gesellschaftsgeschichte*.

37. Ernst Fraenkel, *The Dual State* (New York: Oxford University Press, 1941), 3.

38. Ibid.

39. Sibylle Steinbacher, *Dachau: Die Stadt und das Konzentrationslager in der NS-Zeit* (Frankfurt: Peter Lang, 1993).

40. Kershaw, *Hitler*.

41. Heinz Boberach (ed.), *Meldungen aus dem Reich. 1938–1945. Die geheimen Lageberichte des Sicherheitsdienstes der SS*, 17 vol. (Herrsching: Pawlak, 1984).

42. Klaus Behnken, *Deutschland-Berichte der Sopade 1934–40*, 7 vol. (Salzhausen: Nettelbeck, 1980). These were not the only investigations conducted by Socialists, cf. Bernd Stöver, *Volksgemeinschaft im Dritten Reich. Die Konsensbereitschaft der Deutschen aus der Sicht sozialistischer Exilberichte* (Düsseldorf: Droste, 1993).

43. Peter Fritzsche, *Life and Death in the Third Reich* (Cambridge: Harvard University Press, 2008); Götz Aly (ed.), *Volkes Stimme. Skepsis und Führervertrauen im Nationalsozialismus* (Bonn: Bundeszentrale für politische Bildung, 2006).

44. Wolfgang Schivelbusch, *Entfernte Verwandtschaft: Faschismus, Nationalsozialismus, New Deal 1933–1939* (Munich: Hanser, 2005).

45. Kiran Klaus Patel, *Soldiers of Labor. Labor Service in Nazi-Germany and New Deal America 1933–45* (Cambridge: Cambridge University Press, 2005).

46. Adam Tooze, *The Wages of Destruction. The Making and Breaking of the Nazi Economy* (London: Allen Lane, 2006).

47. Bernd Jürgen Wendt, *Deutschland 1933–1945. Das Dritte Reich. Handbuch zur Geschichte* (Hanover: Fackelträger-Verlag, 1995).

48. On KdF see Götz Aly, *Hitlers Volksstaat. Raub, Rassenkrieg und nationaler Sozialismus* (Frankfurt am Main: Fischer, 2005); Timothy Mason, *Social Policy in the Third Reich. The Working Class and the 'National Community'* (Providence, Oxford: Berg 1993); Hasso Spode, 'Fordism, Mass Tourism and the Third Reich. The "Strength through Joy" Seaside Resort as an Index Fossil,' *Journal of Social History*, 38 (2004), 127–155.

49. David Schoenbaum, *Hitler's Social Revolution. Class and Status in Nazi Germany 1933–1939* (Garden City: Doubleday & Co., 1967).

50. Willi Boelcke, *Die Kosten von Hitlers Krieg. Kriegsfinanzierung und finanzielles Kriegserbe in Deutschland 1933–48* (Paderborn: Schöningh, 1985); Fritz Blaich, *Wirtschaft und Rüstung im 'Dritten Reich'* (Düsseldorf: Schwann, 1987); Hans-Erich Volkmann, 'Die NS-Wirtschaft in Vorbereitung des Krieges,' in Militärgeschichtliches Forschungsamt (ed.), *Das Deutsche Reich und der Zweite Weltkrieg*, vol I, (Stuttgart: Deutsche Verlagsanstalt, 1979) 177–368.

51. Data in Blaich, *Wirtschaft und Rüstung*, 83; Boelcke, *Kosten*, 28.

52. Aly, *Hitlers Volksstaat*.

53. Cf. Wolfgang Schieder, *Faschistische Diktaturen. Studien zu Italien und Deutschland* (Göttingen: Wallstein, 2008).

54. Schieder, *Diktaturen*.

55. Alan Bullock, *Hitler and Stalin. Parallel Lives* (London: HarperCollins, 1991); Jörg Baberowski and Anselm Döring-Manteuffel, *Ordnung durch Terror* (Bonn: Dietz, 2006), especially for the following. On the parallels and divergences of Nazi and Soviet Society, see also Ian Kershaw and Moshe Lewin, *Stalinism and Nazism. Dictatorships in Comparison* (Cambridge: Cambridge University Press, 1977); Michael Geyer and Sheila Fitzpatrick, *Beyond Totalitarianism. Stalinism and Nazism Compared* (Cambridge: Cambridge University Press, 2008).

BIBLIOGRAPHY

ANDERSON, MARGARET L., *Practicing Democracy. Elections and Political Culture in Imperial Germany* (Princeton: Princeton University Press, 2000).

BESSEL, RICHARD, *Germany after the First World War* (Oxford: Oxford University Press, 1993).

EVANS, RICHARD J., *The Coming of The Third Reich* (London: Penguin, 2004).

FALTER, JÜRGEN, *Hitlers Wähler* (Munich: Beck, 1991).

FRITZSCHE, PETER, *Life and Death in the Third Reich* (Cambridge: Harvard University Press, 2008).

KERSHAW, IAN, *Hitler*, 2 vols (London: Allen Lane, 1998; 2000).

MAI, GUNTHER, *Europa 1918–1939. Mentalitäten, Lebensweisen, Politik zwischen den Weltkriegen* (Stuttgart: Kohlhammer, 2001).

MERGEL, THOMAS, 'Führer, Volksgemeinschaft und Maschine. Politische Erwartungsstrukturen in der Weimarer Republik und im Nationalsozialismus 1918–1936,' in Wolfgang Hardtwig (ed.), *Politische Kulturgeschichte der Zwischenkriegszeit 1918–1939* (Göttingen: Vandenhoeck & Ruprecht, 2005), 91–127.

——, *Parlamentarische Kultur in der Weimarer Republik. Politische Kommunikation, symbolische Politik und Öffentlichkeit im Reichstag* (Düsseldorf: Droste, 2005).

REICHARDT, SVEN and ARMIN NOLZEN (eds), *Faschismus in Italien und Deutschland. Studien zu Transfer und Vergleich* (Göttingen: Wallstein, 2005).

SCHIEDER, WOLFGANG, *Faschistische Diktaturen. Studien zu Italien und Deutschland* (Göttingen: Wallstein, 2008).

SCHIVELBUSCH, WOILFGANG, *Entfernte Verwandtschaft. Faschismus, Nationalsozialismus, New Deal 1933–1939* (Frankfurt am Main: Fischer, 2008).

SCHUMANN, DIRK, *Political Violence in the Weimar Republic 1918–1933. Fight for the Streets and Fear of Civil War* (New York: Berghahn, 2009).

WILDT, MICHAEL, *Volksgemeinschaft als Selbstermächtigung. Gewalt gegen Juden in der deutschen Provinz 1919 bis 1939* (Hamburg: Hamburger Edition, 2007).

CHAPTER 20

....

PIETY, POWER, AND POWERLESSNESS: RELIGION AND RELIGIOUS GROUPS IN GERMANY, 1870–1945

....

REBEKKA HABERMAS

MANY citizens of the Wilhelminian Empire believed they were seeing an increasing decline in the importance of religion. This view was also shared by scholars at the time including August Comte and Max Weber. Weber thought it possible to identify at least four distinct factors in such a process: first, a growing separation of church and state; secondly, a decline in the importance of religion in everyday life; thirdly, a demystification of the world; and fourthly, a general decrease in piety that could be measured by indicators such as church attendance. Moreover, he viewed the secularizing process as a fundamental component of modernization. Not only Weber and his contemporaries held this view; subsequent generations of sociologists and historians likewise adhered to the notion that modernity was secular; indeed, this alone sufficed to make it 'modern.' Only in recent decades have doubts been expressed about this general secularizing trend on the one hand, and about the link between a decline in religious faith and modernization on the other. American sociologists of religion were forced to admit that in North and South America alike, daily life and official politics are deeply imbued with religious structures.[1] As a result, at least among American sociologists, the theory of secularization—and above all, the close connection drawn between modernity and secularization—lost a considerable amount of its persuasive power. It followed logically that it was Anglo-Saxon historians who first dared to reexamine the theory of secularization in reference to the nineteenth century. Their findings were striking: while to some extent a growing separation between church and state could be observed, the historians found neither a decline in piety nor a demystification of the world. On the contrary: as early as 1972, Emmet Larkin noted such a sharp increase in religious practices, particularly beginning in the second half of the nineteenth century, that he called it a veritable 'devotional revolution.'[2]

The stronger the critique of the secularization theory became, the more intently people searched for alternative ways to explain the perceived changes in piety and religious institutions from the nineteenth century onward. In the German debate, for example, the so-called reconfessionalization theory (*Rekonfessionalisierungsthese*) enjoyed brief popularity: according to this theory, individual denominations grew in importance between the Congress of Vienna and 1968, a period that also saw an increased emphasis on the differences between individual denominations.[3] In view of the current importance of religion, the problems with this curious periodization quickly became evident.[4]

However we may judge individual arguments against the theory of secularization and redominalization, and aside from the fact that some aspects of this master narrative are still very much part of the ongoing discussion, they no longer serve as foundational, guiding principles for research on the sometimes downright tumultuous changes in the religious sphere at the close of the nineteenth and beginning of the twentieth century. They have been retired for several good reasons. First, both are based on a theory of modernization now considered obsolete: no one today, for instance, contends that simply because American society is deeply religious, it is not at the same time a highly modern society. Secondly, both theories incorporate statements and perceptions of the time all too uncritically. The notions of religion as vestige or trace (*Schwundstufe*) found in Comte and Weber, Durkheim, and Troeltsch were not, for example, considered as concepts reflecting these thinker's social standing, religious denomination, gender, status as experts, or other shared characterizing features. Instead, their theses about secularization, which obfuscated the religious upheavals of their own time, were elevated to the status of a universally valid explanatory pattern. The theory of redenominalization likewise tends to simply follow the interpretations of the time, rather than make them the object of analysis; after all, it was the writings of Weber and Troeltsch that played a major role in the codification of denominational differences and helped to invent them in the first place.

Rather than follow nineteenth-century leads, I would like to take a cue instead from the twentieth-century social anthropologist Talal Asad. Asad asks what was even understood by such terms as profane and sacred, secular and religious, religion and superstition. In other words, Asad suggests a historicization of precisely those categories that had been uncritically adopted as the self-evident starting point of an analysis in earlier theories. He thus draws attention to the constructedness of these categories, and by focusing on the categories as constructs opens up new avenues of inquiry for the history of both religious and secular practices and norms. Asad shows that these terms first came into use in the Early Modern Period precisely at the moment of contact between Europeans and non-Europeans, when the one group became defined as 'Nature Folk' believing in fetishes, the other as 'Culture Folk' who had religion.[5] Finally, in the eighteenth century a secular concept of superstition developed: no longer defined as 'heresy' using canonical terminology, superstition was now regarded as a state of being that deserved to be pitied, a state of 'illusion and oppression before people could be liberated from them.'[6] As recent studies in the history of science show, during the nineteenth century religion itself became the object of research, the study of religion developed into a scholarly discipline, and what are now considered the autonomous spheres of the religious and the secular came into being.[7] The following pages will explore how different concepts, practices, and norms in the conceptualization of the secular and the religious developed at the end of the nineteenth and the beginning of the twentieth century.

20.1 THE SECOND GERMAN EMPIRE 1870–1918

20.1.1 Topographies of the religious and the secular

Germany differed fundamentally from many other European countries because of its denominational heterogeneity. It contained Catholic, Protestant, and Jewish segments of the population, and within Protestantism in particular, a number of different strands also existed: Lutherans, Reformed, Awakened, Pietists, and so-called Cultural Protestants, some of whom were divided by virtual 'barriers of disgust,'[8] while others even attended church services together. At times, however, this happened only with the greatest reluctance; hence, the report of a Lutheran missionary in a Reformed church service closes with the relieved exclamation: 'God be praised that we are Lutheran Christians!'[9]

Approximately one-third of the population was Catholic, just under two-thirds were Protestant, and the Jewish segment of the population stood at one to two percent.[10] This denominational distribution changed very little during the time of the Wilhelminian Empire. In the Weimar Republic some shifting did occur, in that for the first time, the proportion of people who claimed no religious affiliation rose to several percent; noteworthy here is that during the 1920s, disproportionately high number of Protestants left the church. In addition to the growing number of people without denomination, a slight growth in sects can also be observed beginning at the end of the nineteenth century, particularly in the Protestant segment of the population. This relative constancy in the distribution of the denominations' quantitative size until the mid-1930s should not, however, disguise the fact that the importance of the church as an institution, its societal and political influence, the form and the intensity of religious belief in the public and private spheres, and religious commitment as measured by church attendance all underwent profound changes.[11] What sorts of changes were these?

The most important change can be seen in the enormous amount of public attention that issues concerning people's religious commitment increasingly attracted during the last third of the nineteenth century. Of key importance here was the repeated claim, already voiced in *Vormärz* discussions, of a 'decline in faith' among the lower classes, which in turn was viewed as the main cause of material hardship and, more importantly, of moral and spiritual poverty. This poverty was considered so dire a threat that people warned repeatedly, with a mixture of fascination and horror, about alcoholism, promiscuity, filth, and the loss of all moral restraint. The reports also assumed that all of these ills were especially acute in the slums of the urban underclasses and underscored the 'decline in faith' as a fundamental cause. Slowly, but surely, this link between a decline in religious faith and moral, material, and spiritual poverty became a certainty, propagated in hundreds of brochures, as well as in social topographies constructed with the latest scientific means. If this change of religious life seemed clear and indisputable in the public debate, something also echoed in the social scientific debate at the time. In empirical reality religious life had many different facets.[12]

We can only speculate about many things such as changes in religious practices in private life.[13] Other things, however, such as membership in religious organizations, the public practice of religion—pilgrimages, for instance—and religious commitment as documented by church attendance, can be measured numerically.[14] If we focus on church attendance as an indicator of religious commitment, we notice the following: in many regions of the empire barely any changes at all can be seen. In Franconia, parts of the former kingdom of Hanover, Württemberg, and Old Bavaria, the Protestant population both in rural areas and cities attended church regularly. Catholics almost everywhere attended Mass with great regularity. In Münster, for instance, well above half of the Catholic population attended church on Easter, and did so consistently until after World War I.[15] While church attendance in Catholic regions remained by and large unchanged, regardless of whether we look at workers or lawyers, serving maids or women of the nobility, people's active involvement in Catholicism through associations or participation in retreats or pilgrimages actually increased considerably.[16] After 1848 church associations enjoyed a veritable 'boom,' so that by 1914 between one-quarter and one-third of all Catholics belonged to at least one such group.[17] In addition, during this period so many congregations were founded, especially for women, that contemporaries spoke of a 'springtime of religious orders.'[18] Finally, a Catholic media empire arose slowly, but with increasing force that included thousands of association pamphlets and even interregional daily newspapers.[19]

If there was little evidence of the much bemoaned 'decline in faith' in Catholicism, in Protestant regions the situation looked different. Here, we see a decline in church attendance, or more precisely, attendance was already quite low during the Second German Empire.[20] Up until 1900, this applies much more to males than females, and to a large extent remains independent of social status. Not only male factory workers, as reports from that time would have us believe, but also doctors and factory owners attended church less frequently than their wives.[21] Only at the beginning of the twentieth century does a tendency become evident that is specific to class: now the numbers of people leaving the church began to rise especially in urban working-class neighborhoods. Yet here, according to Berlin's Protestant circles, it was not the impoverished occasional workers, the truly poor, but qualified 'metalworkers [. . .]

mechanics, masons, and painters [...]' who turned their back on the church.[22] As a bewildered Berlin district synod notes, 'in the apartments of those leaving the church it usually looks quite orderly and comfortable; if there is no ill will, one can talk to them quite reasonably; they apparently wish to be counted among the "intelligent," who even without the church wish to live a decent, virtuous life.'[23] Although Protestant males in general attended church less frequently, and some—especially workers—left the congregation altogether, female Protestants continued to attend religious services as in the past, and their active involvement in church associations even increased. Despite decreasing religious commitment among male congregation members, in Protestantism as a whole we see an increase in religious commitment. Here too, it was primarily women who sought new forms of religious life, in deaconesses' houses for example,[24] and they did so with such fervor that for a long time researchers spoke about the development of a specifically female religiosity.[25]

As contradictory as the findings sketched out here may be when compared with those aspects of religious life that can be easily quantified (in contrast to private religious devotion), they do help to correct the widespread impression of the time that a threatening decline in faith was underway, especially among the lower classes. Such a decline began only very slowly in the next century, and not until after World War I did it reach noteworthy proportions. These findings also correct the perceptions of those who espouse the theory of secularization. If during the Second German Empire we see not so much a widespread decrease in religious commitment, or even a more narrowly defined class-specific decline, but instead a partial increase in religious commitment, we need to ask what the crucial determining factors might be in this by no means unambiguous empirical finding. This question brings us to a different level of change, namely, the changing relationship between church and state, and it also brings us back to Talal Asad's proposal that the notions 'secular' and 'religious' always be considered together.

20.1.2 Reconfigurations of the secular and the religious

How were the secular and the religious organized and conceptualized in the Wilhelminian Empire? The answer has many levels. At the institutional level we find a complex combination of church and state responsibilities in all twenty-five states that comprised the Empire; as a result, the secular, and the religious were closely intertwined. A saying of the time refers to so-called 'mixed things,' which were understood to be everything for which church and state were jointly responsible: the education sector; social, charitable, and ethical or moral issues, which involved hospitals and reformatories, for instance; and the domain of marriage and family. While there was broad consensus that these 'mixed things' should be the shared affairs of church and government institutions, representatives of the bourgeoisie in particular favored a clear separation of the secular and the religious in all other areas. Beyond the 'mixed things,' the church alone should be responsible for managing its internal affairs, and everything else, especially the legislature and executives, should be solely in government hands. In reality, however, no such sharp distinctions existed. The church clearly intervened in areas that were supposed to be regulated by the government alone. For instance, a substantial number of seats in the upper chambers of individual *Länder* parliaments had always been reserved for representatives of the clergy so that the church might have a voice in political decisions and legislative procedures. Conversely, the state was also involved in the internal affairs of the church. The Prussian king had a voice in the composition of synods, for example, and the Bavarian king nominated bishops.[26] In short, at the beginning of the Second German Empire the secular and religious spheres were anything but clearly separated, and if we limit our focus to the judicial level, this remained almost unchanged until 1914. Only the introduction of civil marriage in 1874 marked a dramatic change; similarly, the laws passed during the *Kulturkampf* were intended to exclude the churches from the area of education and prevent clerics from using the pulpit to voice their political views. For the most part, however, these laws were quickly repealed.

In spite of the fact that there was sometimes confusing overlap and co-mingling of church and state responsibilities at the institutional level beyond the 'mixed things,' during the Wilhelminian Empire the notion developed that the secular and the religious were clearly separated. At the same time, what was understood by the terms 'secular' and 'religious' was gradually changing. Protestant educational institutions, for example, were considered less religious than Catholic ones. At state-supported public universities, genuinely Protestant interpretations of history were taught, then tested in state-sponsored exams, and ultimately conveyed to pupils in state-supported public schools, whereas Catholic stories of origin were denounced as misleading and were supposed to be kept out of state-supported educational institutions. Stated very broadly, during the course of the Second German Empire a development took place that resulted in the Catholic Church, awakened and Pietist groups, and also Orthodox Jewry all becoming associated with a concept of the religious that had predominantly negative connotations.[27] 'Religious' was a negative category insofar as it included everything that ran counter to a modern bourgeois notion of society: superstition, adherence to traditions, religious practices such as pilgrimages that were denounced as 'irrational,' and other public forms of prayer, processions, or spiritual exercises.[28] At best, these stigmatized forms of religiosity could find a legitimate place in the private sphere, newly redefined as a site of religious freedom. In contrast, the Protestant church in general and liberal theology and assimilated Jewry in particular, became associated with the secular and, hence, did not have to be restricted to the private sphere. Protestantism found expression in partially governmental religious services—at coronation jubilees, for instance—and even became a central component of new disciplines that claimed scientific objectivity, such as the study of religion.[29]

This reconceptualization of the secular and the religious, as curious as it was consequential, can be traced in an entire range of developments and events. The founding of the Second German Empire, the anti-Semitism debate (*Antisemitismusstreit*), the

Kulturkampf, and the development of liberalism all played a role. The process of empire foundation shows with particular clarity how the Protestant church became identified with the German state and thereby became part of the secular realm. Regardless of how closely this equation of all things German with Protestantism actually corresponded to reality, the enthusiastic invention of traditions and histories through monumental dedications, banquets, holidays, and parades that conveyed this image had far-reaching consequences. An exclusive Protestant pantheon developed around Schiller, Goethe, Bach, and Luther together with the developing culture of commemoration days (*Gedenktagekultur*) that began in the nineteenth century. Protestant ministers, but also many citizens tirelessly invoked the unity of Bismarck, Luther, and the Hohenzollern dynasty, even as a veritable sacralization of the nation was taking place.[30] Recent research has rightfully stressed that this equation of all that was German with Protestantism served to overcome considerable denominational, historical, economic, and mental differences as well as dynastic loyalties among the many individual *Länder* that were now to form a nation.[31] A second consequence should also be emphasized, however: this equation meant that mainstream Protestantism was now firmly situated in the realm of the secular.

More or less parallel to this 'Protestantization of the national,' a process of resituating or reinterpreting the concept 'Jewish' also took place that can be seen most clearly by following the anti-Semitism dispute (*Antisemitismusstreit*). In the course of this dispute a clear distinction was drawn between those Jews considered part of the German nation and those marginalized. The controversy was sparked by an article entitled 'Our Views,' published in 1879 by the renowned and widely respected historian Heinrich von Treitschke. Treitschke drew on anti-Semitic stereotypes to denounce the Jewish population, which had achieved legal equality only in 1871, as foreigners and undependable nationals who 'are nothing more than German-speaking Orientals.'[32] Only those Jews who, by means of perfect mimicry, could bridge the 'chasm between the Occidental and Semitic character' could become part of the nation, which in Treitschke's view meant first and foremost becoming assimilated into the Protestant bourgeoisie.[33] If the 'Protestantization of the national' served as an important backdrop for the new mental map of the religious and the secular and created a special intimacy between the Protestant Church and the state, at times even equating the two, the anti-Semitism dispute shows that only those Jews who entered into a symbiosis with the Protestant German majority culture could view themselves as part of the new German nation, and as such as part of the secular realm.[34] All others, and especially *Ostjuden*, whose membership in the underclass also defined them in Treitschke's view as a 'band of ambitious trouser-selling youths,' year after year forcing their way 'across our eastern border from the inexhaustible Polish cradle,' were placed under the notion of the religious with all its negative connotations, including proximity to superstition.[35] During the Wilhelminian Empire not only Orthodox Jews, but also Catholics were considered part of the religious sphere, and were even seen as the epitome of all that was negative about the religious. There were a number of reasons for this view: both Bismarck and the emperor were Protestant, and only two of the twenty-five *Bundesländer* had a Catholic ruler; in other words, in political representation at the national level there was, in fact, a Protestant majority. A development within the Catholic Church also played a role: in the nineteenth century, the Catholic Church further centralized its worldwide, supranational organization. The 1871 dogma of infallibility, issued over considerable protest by German bishops, was only the most visible sign of this policy of centralization, a policy that also served as a response to liberal notions about the modern state and the subordinate role of the church in that state.[36] Thus, parallel to the formation of the German nation state, the Catholic Church designed a new image for itself as a mighty bastion steeped in tradition, whose primary task was to preserve Catholic religious teaching and expand its institutions.

With the *Kulturkampf*, the process that had begun with the Protestant infusion of 'the national' and the centralization of the Catholic Church now gained momentum.[37] Several laws passed in Prussia between 1871 and 1875 might still give the impression of creating a sharper division between church and state, such as the 1872 edicts designed to ensure government oversight of all schools, including denominational ones, or the ordinance that placed the education and appointment of clerics under state control. But the true directional thrust became clear in 1872 at the latest with the successful expulsion of Jesuits, Redemptorists, Lazarists, and priests of the Holy Spirit. When all non-charitable religious orders and congregations were finally forbidden in 1874, the reconfiguration of the secular and the religious revealed itself *in nuce*: what was Catholic should be marginalized, and things Catholic increasingly took on all the negative characteristics now associated with the concept of the religious, while Protestantism was, in effect, divested of its religious character.

This process was reinforced by an outright polemic against religion that developed in the course of the *Kulturkampf*, but which had actually started several years earlier in liberal circles, and denounced everything Catholic. At issue here are attributions described by Michael Gross as classic forms of liberal anti-Catholicism.[38] In his impressive study, Gross contends that at the very heart of liberal identity was a view of Catholicism as anti-modern and anti-rational, and, as such, a hostile force that was diametrically opposed to both of the sacred cows of liberalism: modern rationalism and bourgeois individualism. According to this liberal logic, which had a strong affinity to cultural Protestantism, constitutionalism, the free market, education, science, and individualism, stand opposite a Catholicism that seemed to be full of superstition, obscure practices, and militant subordination.[39] Protestantism in contrast appeared to be free of all these irrational elements—a conviction that led a scientist like Rudolf Virchow to even demand in a lecture for the prestigious Society of German Natural Scientists and Physicians (1874) that the Catholic belief in miracles 'be placed completely under scientific control.'[40]

By 1914 at the latest, liberal ideology together with Catholic centralism, the 'Protestantization of the national,' the *Kulturkampf*, and the anti-Semitism dispute had altered perceptions of the secular and the religious so extensively that large parts of Protestantism were now located in the secular realm, whereas the Catholic Church together with Orthodox Judaism, Pietists, and Awakened were allocated to 'the religious' with its lingering hints of the irrational, the superstitious, and the traditional.[41]

20.1.3 Religion in national and global context

Running counter to this reconfiguration of the religious and the secular, and their peculiar attributes, religious views played a surprisingly large role particularly in public life, although admittedly, at the time they were not perceived as religious, let alone derided or dismissed as mere superstition. Both on a national and global level, the religious views at work were ones whose Christian origin was barely perceptible at the time, since they were presented more as general ethical or moral concepts than as specifically religious ones, whether Catholic or Protestant. Here, I am referring to the discourses mentioned earlier in which a 'hostility toward God' of 'epidemic' proportions was directly linked with the 'current . . . terrible spiritual disease of the masses,' a condition that included 'neglected children, . . . fornication in the countryside . . . the economic and moral state of rural workers and day workers living there,' as well as the devastating influence of dance halls.[42] In this way, serious social, economic, mental, and political changes were described primarily in terms of individual ethical behavior, on the one hand, while on the other, a 'decline in faith' was deemed the cause. These views, thoroughly imbued with Christian ideas, played a determining role in the broad sector of social work and in debates about the so-called 'social question' in the Empire, and they did so without their religious content being recognized, since they seemed to be the expression of generally applicable moral truths.

The power of these views can be seen in the tremendous growth in denominational clubs or associations. These groups were particularly active in the area of charity work, and understood the purpose of their work in precisely the sense described above: to help groups of people deemed materially and spiritually needy—usually members of the underclass—work toward religious faith, morality, and material well-being, by combining offers of material aid with the Divine Word. These associations set up soup kitchens, established kindergartens, founded hospitals, and held Bible readings and edifying lectures.[43] There was barely a city in Germany without a home for wayward girls (*Magdalenenasyl*) or an 'association for the elevation of morality,' usually run by middle-class women and aimed directly at women of the lower classes.[44]

While the growth in Catholic associations was downright explosive, the Protestant realm also experienced a wave of club formations, though with a smaller influx of members, and the number of Jewish associations increased as well.[45] All of these initiatives were extremely effective. In addition to the actual social work they performed, they acted as important catalysts and disseminators.[46] Almost all of these associations had their own newspapers, and they supplied a broad public with religious views through lectures and celebrations. Their influence was enormous, particularly regarding social and ethical issues that included (among other things) the need for adequate housing; passing judgment on what was 'good' and what was 'bad' sexuality; debates about alcohol consumption; and deciding which reading matter was offensive and which was edifying. Even feisty atheists like Friedrich Engels were caught up in such religious interpretive patterns or paradigms, although Engels himself did not recognize the identical cause-and-effect *modi* at work, as we see if we glance at his best-seller of 1845, *The Condition of the Working Class in England*.[47] In Engels' work we find exactly the same terms as in the leaflets or *'Fliegende Blätter'* published by a group of Protestant associations that had joined forces in the Inner Mission of Johann Hinrich Wichern. Like the flyers, Engels speaks about the dangers of taverns and houses of ill repute, about a 'moral obligation to marriage', and about the demoralizing influences of 'need, filth, and bad surroundings.'[48] His conclusions might just as easily be found in a tract from the homes for wayward girls: 'next to intemperance in the enjoyment of strong spirits, licentiousness in sexual relations represents a major vice of many English workers.'[49]

In addition to the importance of local religious initiatives for understanding and addressing the so-called Social Question, religious views also played a role at the global level. Here, too, they were not always easily recognizable as religious, but instead had the character of general, non-religious truths. I am referring to the important role—widely underestimated even today—of missions, missionary societies, and missionary associations, together with the image of life outside of Europe that they produced and disseminated, an image that indirectly also helped construct people's perceptions and interpretations within Europe, as Germans and as Europeans.[50] Beginning in the 1820s, long before Germany became a colonial power, Awakened and Pietist circles had founded a large number of Protestant missionary societies where young men were trained to become missionaries so that they might spread Christianity in Africa and Asia.[51] As the *Kulturkampf* waned, it also became possible for Catholic missionary orders to train missionaries.[52] In a parallel development, Protestant and Catholic missionary associations were established in many cities both large and small, and even in some villages.[53] These associations grew rapidly, and they gradually assumed precisely the same function as charitable organizations: they oversaw the production and distribution of missionary journals, sponsored mission collections, mission church services, and mission festivals, and even founded mission museums.[54] In this way, missionary associations, just like the charitable organizations of specific religious denominations, became important catalysts and disseminators in the marketplace of public opinion. Focusing less on social questions than on global issues presented in a religious way, they played a crucial part in ensuring that the work of the missionaries, their reports about 'the kaffir' and 'our Zulus,' as well as pictures—photographs at first, and later large-scale images projected in slide shows—reached even remote parts of rural society.[55] Missionaries appeared in every village, no matter how small, and from their missionary's suitcases they produced photographs of dancing heathens, remnants of objects used in magic rituals, and even testimonies they had written themselves about the devotion of freshly converted 'Negro children.' With the aid of these sometimes bizarre objects and their often dramatic reports, missionaries structured perceptions of what lay outside Europe: it was they who reported on the dubious practice of polygamy in both rural and urban areas, told of ostensibly brutal Arab slave traders and the pressing 'African Brandy Issue,' and repeatedly invoked the 'indescribable misery' of the heathens.[56] It was also the missionaries who brought black children with them when they returned to Europe to prove with living examples just how urgently these people needed the civilizing superiority of Europe.

Thus, in addition to the images of foreigners, a firm belief in their own ethical and moral goodness, racial valuations, and denominational judgments were also conveyed. It goes without saying that missionary work also just happened to provide an important legitimizing basis for colonialism, since colonialism could also be presented as the salvation of poor heathen souls.[57] But like social-charitable initiatives, the main contribution of the missions lay in their introduction of religious perspectives into debates about social and extra-European issues, views that were perceived not as religious, but as general moral attitudes.

20.2 Weimar Republic and National Socialism

A conflicted reconceptualization of the secular and the religious; the incomplete separation of church and state; intensified religious commitment, which subsequently declined among Protestants; and at the same time the tremendous if often obscured presence of the religious in central aspects of life—this complex and interrelated state of affairs remained basically unchanged until after World War I. Some shifting did occur before this time of course. But it was only in the Weimar Republic that the situation changed fundamentally. The growth of alternative religious offerings led to a pluralization of religious options, the Catholic Church found a way out of its defensive position (the way having been paved by its vociferous enthusiasm for the war), and anti-Semitic conflicts became increasingly acute.[58]

20.2.1 Pluralization, crises and conflicts: reconfiguring the religious

The pluralization of religious options has many facets, one of which is the decision to forgo any religious affiliation whatsoever. It was not until the Weimar Republic that a sizable number of people chose this option. Between 1919 and 1932, almost three million people left the Lutheran Church. In contrast, between 1919 and 1926 the Catholic Church lost only 250,000 members, i.e. only 0.2 percent. As at the beginning of the century it was primarily men who left the church; they often belonged to the working class, and tended to be from the north, rather than the south of the Republic.[59] The situation was particularly radical in cities like Berlin, where in 1933 a good 14 percent of the population were without religious affiliation.[60]

Another indicator of pluralization is an increased number of religious groups and alternative lifestyles that distanced themselves for the most part from ties or commitments to a specific church. The first signs of this type of pluralization can be seen already in the nineteenth century. For example, spiritualistic séances that reflected a combination of scientific and religious interest, especially in the bourgeoisie, took place at the homes of the von Arnims, and the Göttingen scientist and professor Wilhelm Weber.[61] But séances offered by associations only became a widespread phenomenon in late nineteenth- and early twentieth-century Saxon guesthouses. Quasi-religious groups like the Salvation Army had a considerably stronger attraction. Like most religious groups at the beginning of the twentieth century, the Salvation Army had its roots in Anglo-Saxon Protestantism. Baptists and Mennonites were among the other groups of dissenters that had originated in England and began to attract an increasing number of followers. By 1925, for instance, the New Apostolic Church already had 140,000 members.[62] The majority of the people who were attracted to these new religious groups came from the Protestant underclass. If we also include the non-Conformist churches (*Freikirchen*), established already in the nineteenth century, we are looking at half a million Protestants who turned to these new communities in protest against their own churches and in search of new public forums, greater solidarity, and a firmer moral footing, or simply spirituality. In any case, these groups were by no means a simple collecting bin for the losers of modernization. Rather, as Christoph Ribbat notes, 'exalted religiosity offered one of a number of cultural options that people deliberately selected.'[63] One could just as easily choose to join one of the quasi-religious groups that were part of the larger *Lebensreform* movement: vegetarians, nudists, or the *Wandervogel* movement.

The fact that it was predominantly Protestants who searched for new options has to do with the singular location of Protestantism on the map of the secular and the religious. As we have seen, in the course of the Wilhelminian Empire, Protestantism became increasingly associated with the worldly realm; in the words of the Jena publisher Eugen Diedrichs, it appears to be something 'sober and reasonable' in a 'godforsaken time that calls itself realistic.' At least according to Diedrichs, by situating itself thus, Protestantism also brought out 'an instinctive, unexpressed yearning for religious renewal, since ecclesiastical Protestantism in its present form has become barren for the life of the people (*Volksleben*) and, hence, also barren for the coming people's community (*Volksgemeinschaft*), which cannot be created without a religious ethos.'[64]

Writing in 1929, Diedrichs refers to feelings of loss typically experienced by those people who had seen the downsides of modernity. Urbanization, the acceleration of time, and the destruction of family ties and social traditions are just a few of the phenomena widely viewed as symptoms of crisis and impending decline, and which did not end with World War I as many people had hoped. Instead the symptoms of crisis tended to become even more pronounced, and were only reinforced by the disillusionment that set in quickly after the euphoria of August 1914. At the end of the war people found themselves in a situation that brought not the hoped for all-encompassing renewal of Germany, but instead real territorial losses, millions maimed and dead, material privation and radical political changes. Middle-class Protestants in particular felt the full impact of this 'crisis of classic modernity' (Detlev Peukert). In 1919 the new Republic granted suffrage to both men and women, adopted a constitution that made no reference to a Christian God, and abolished the patronage of local rulers over Protestant *Landeskirchen*, spelling the final, definitive separation of throne and altar, and thereby a massive loss of power. That a 'yearning for renewal,' like the one described by Eugen Diedrichs, developed in such a situation seems completely understandable.

It was, however, by no means a foregone conclusion that people turned to sometimes quite obscure quasi-religious groups to satisfy this yearning, rather than looking to the *Landeskirchen* or to the Mennonites or Baptists. Some of these quasi-religious groups were strongly anti-Semitic, *völkisch*, and full of magical and heathen borrowings. They represented a radical alternative to the Judeo-Christian traditions of universalism, and thereby signaled a clear break with the Protestant church hierarchy, as well as with Protestant dissenters. The groups in question here are those coalitions and orders, leagues, and associations that appeared in increasing numbers after Germany lost World War I. These groups liked to emphasize the importance of the land or soil (*Scholle*), and it was not uncommon for them to demand proof from their members that they had neither black nor Jewish ancestors. This, in turn, enabled the groups to link up with a number of regional communes (*Landeskommunen*) from the Lebensreform movement that saw themselves as rooted in 'Germandom.' Almost all of these small esoteric, theosophical groups were openly anti-Semitic.[65] It therefore comes as no surprise that we can draw a straight line from some of them directly to National Socialism: from the 'Coalition for the German Church' established in 1921, for instance, to the subsequent founding in 1932 of the 'Faith Movement of German Christians,' a group known for its open support of National Socialism.[66]

While the Protestant church had been suffering already since the beginning of the twentieth century due to various forms of modernization, it was only in the mid-1920s that Catholicism made its first more concerted effort to address two problems: people leaving the church, and the ostensible erosion of morals and decency that had also been diagnosed among Catholics, primarily in large cities. It was in this connection that the *Zentrum*, the Center, the partisan-political arm of German Catholicism, proposed a law in 1928 'for the protection of youth from trashy and smutty writings.' A whole new group of associations also formed such as *Quickborn*, the Catholic branch of the *Wandervogel* movement. It aspired to fundamental renewal in a sense very similar to that envisioned by small Protestant groups: here, too, the power of faith was seen as a way to link the notions of 'home' (*Heimat*) and 'the people' (*Volk*), and 'renewal' meant a return to purity, nature, and simplicity.

Though the 'crisis of classical modernity' in Catholicism had a different face, it was also not nearly as threatening as in Protestantism, since the rates of Catholic church attendance and the concentration of church associations remained nearly as high as ever.[67] Moreover—and herein lies the decisive difference—Catholic reform movements took place within the Church, so Catholics did not abandon the church and turn to ever new sects and quasi-religious groups. In some respects, the Catholic Church even profited from these developments, since it was able to improve its status in the Empire. Having occupied a far from enviable position in the arrangement of the secular and the religious, Catholicism was viewed now less and less as part of a religious sphere with decidedly negative connotations that had to be denounced as a seat of superstition and obscurantism, particularly when it extended its reach into the public domain. An important contributing factor was that in the summer of 1914, Catholic religious leaders had greeted the war with at least as much national enthusiasm as their Protestant colleagues, for whom nationalism had become routine since 1870. Now the message resounded from Catholic pulpits as well, of how 'organic' the unity of church and authority actually was, and that the war represented a path of renewal, providing a 'gripping drama for angels and humans' that would lead to the 'healing of our people in the profoundest depths of the people's soul.'[68] The war was even declared 'a holy war, a battle for God and our people, for humanity and Christianity! For the foundational pillars of divine world order.'[69] The extent of the new closeness between the state and the Catholic Church can be seen in the fact that Mathias Erzberger, leader of the Catholic Center Party when the war began, was placed in charge of foreign propaganda, where he quickly employed an entire group of Jesuits who were ideally suited for the job. Something comparable would have been unthinkable during the 'Jesuit paranoia' of the 1880s, in 1890, or even as late as 1900. Once the previously close ties between the state and the Lutheran Church had been severed by the Weimar Constitution, which for the first time contained no explicit references to anything Christian, Catholics moved into high government posts. The symbolic order of the sacred and the religious shifted as a result, with the borders between these realms becoming more porous. Catholicism was seen as more than simply a model form of superstition loyal to Rome. The unity of state and *Landeskirchen* had begun to unravel and new quasi-religious forces came into being.

Jewish life had also changed. Despite ongoing discrimination, a growing proportion of the Jewish population benefited from legal equality, even if this did not always lead automatically to social equality. All efforts to assimilate were still rewarded similarly with integration, as noted repeatedly by many liberals and, hence, many Jews.[70] Yet, closer ties developed with increasing frequency between the Jewish and Christian populations, both at the level of clubs or associations and in the form of marriages— a development that even something like the anti-Semitic riots provoked by Adolf Stoecker's agitation and their echoes in Berlin and rural areas could not stop.[71]

At the same time a Zionist movement arose, in no small part out of the contradictions between the liberal promise of participation in the Christian majority society and the day-to-day experience of discrimination. The movement attracted primarily young Jewish intellectuals and fought for an independent state that was supposed to make the mimicry required in Germany superfluous. The First World War also saw an increasing number of Orthodox Jews, many of whom had fled the pogroms in Eastern Europe, entering Germany. It was not only the Christian majority society that often viewed this group with suspicion. At times they aggravated tensions that flared up repeatedly within Jewish communities over such questions as: how modern or Jewish or German should a person be? Is it possible to be Jew and a German simultaneously? What should we think about Palestine?[72]

It was precisely this uneasy coexistence of integration and assimilation, adherence to and reinvention of Orthodox traditions, covert and overt anti-Semitism, and the more or less openly expressed requirement that Jews become integrated into the Christian majority society, that began to erode with World War I. The Jewish population experienced growing discrimination, frequent marginalization and sometimes violent harassment, and anti-Semitic riots increased. Even in areas where Jews and Christians had lived for a very long time in close proximity—in rural society, for instance, and in so-called Jewish villages, as well as the Catholic part of the Black Forest—conflicts were clearly on the rise.[73]

In the Weimar Republic, many things contributed to this gradual erosion of the delicate balance in the coexistence of Christian denominations and Jewish communities: the drastic economic situation, which was more difficult for unemployed Jews to bear than for Christians due to anti-Semitism; the considerable physical, but also emotional suffering generated by the large number of war dead, as well as the constant presence of hundreds of thousands of cripples (the term used at that time); growing nationalizing tendencies; and brutalization that could be seen daily on Weimar streets.[74] Last, but not least, Jews began to appear increasingly in journals, caricatures, and films transformed into anti-Semitic distortions of modernity.[75] They were equated everywhere with the downsides of modernism: whether it be a capitalist economy gone awry, blatant materialism, even socialism, rapid change, or the new cigarette-smoking femininity with its bobbed hair and wild dance parties in the evil big city—all these phenomena became linked with the notion of 'the Jewish as such.'

20.2.2 Denominations and churches under National Socialism

In 1933, when the NSDAP had attracted over 40 percent of the vote, basic rights had been revoked by means of the *Ermächtigungsgesetz* (Enabling Act), and the first official boycott of Jewish businesses had been announced, people found themselves in different situations depending on their denomination and the strength of their ties to their respective religious communities. For German Jews, National Socialism began with legal forms of discrimination that reached a first culmination point in the Nuremberg Race Laws of 1935; it then led to mass migrations, and ultimately to the Wannsee Conference of 1942, where the 'Final Solution' was organized. Along the way were many futile hopes, but also political resistance and numerous Jewish self-help initiatives.[76] It was a different situation for Christian denominations: while Protestants suffered from a feeling of great loss, many Catholics drew newfound strength from their confrontation with the National Socialist state. Quite a few people who belonged to quasi-religious coalitions and small esoteric groups felt that the renewal, of which Eugen Diederichs had already spoken in 1929, was at last at hand.

How did the situation look for church institutions and for church members at the individual level?[77] Let us begin with the Catholic Church, whose membership even during the 'Third Reich' remained noticeably stable.[78] Although Hitler signaled to the churches that existing contracts would be honored, the Catholic Church responded with guarded reserve and, in some cases, open rejection. The Bavarian bishops' conference, for instance, had warned against the National Socialists already in 1931. Even so, Catholicism's political arm, the Center Party, had voted for the Enabling Act, and the pastoral message in the spring of 1933 contained the following statement: 'We do not wish to divest the new state of its powers at any cost, and we may not do so, for only the power of the people and the power of God that streams, invincible, from religious life can redeem and raise us up. A wait-and-see attitude, or worse, church hostility toward the state, would have serious consequences for church and state.'[79] A number of groups, such as the Catholic apprentices' association, some of whose members joined the SA as a group, began to adopt National Socialist ideas. Others, however, including the Catholic workers' association, remained as critical as the union and Social Democratic organizations. Many Catholics were relieved when on 20 July 1933 the *Reichskonkordat* was signed. This agreement between the German state and the Catholic bishops of Germany, represented by the Pope, guaranteed freedom of religious practice, the autonomy of the Catholic Church, the right of religious orders to exist, parental freedom of choice in selecting schools for their children, and the rights of Catholic organizations. Cardinal Faulhaber of Munich is said to have reacted with the statement: 'it comes sincerely from our souls: may God preserve our *Reichskanzler* for our people.'[80] The relief was all the greater since Catholics felt they were the victims of widespread persecution. Consequently, they also tended to ignore the situation of those men and women—Jews and other persecuted people—whose existence was truly threatened. The oversight proved fateful. It derived in part from Catholics' view of themselves as victims. This feeling came easily: it had been nurtured by an entire series of identical martyr legends that kept alive the memories of decades-long persecution during the *Kulturkampf*, and almost any action of the state taken against the church was viewed as part of this tradition. People also misjudged both their own situation and that of the Jewish population because of strong anti-Jewish tendencies that still existed within Catholicism. This Catholic anti-Judaism had gained strength in the *Kulturkampf*, when Liberals and Jews were often seen as identical, and it found fresh sustenance in numerous statements made by some of the highest-ranking representatives of the Catholic Church.[81] In 1939, for example, the bishop of Limburg wrote in his Lenten message: 'The Jewish people is guilty of the death of God and has been cursed since the day of the crucifixion.'[82] This overt anti-Judaism, taken together with the Catholics' focus on their own circumstances, helps explain why the Catholic Church remained largely silent about anti-Semitic attacks and ultimately about the Holocaust. The Church failed to protest in April 1933, when civil servants of 'non-Aryan' descent were removed from their posts, or in 1935, when the Nuremberg Race Laws were promulgated. Even the *Reichskristallnacht* of 1938 drew only isolated individual reactions from within the Church.[83]

Only in 1937, when the Pope demanded in his encyclical 'With Burning Concern' that the freedom of 'Christian mission of salvation' be defended against a multitude of onslaughts, was more at stake than the Church's own interests; this is particularly clear in the passage that reads: 'Whoever removes 'race' or 'the people' or 'the state'...from this, its earthly scale of values, makes it into the highest norm for all values including religious ones, and worships it as a false idol, reverses and falsifies the order of things that was created and ordained by God.'[84] In 1941, several bishops including those from Osnabrück and Meißen finally became involved in protecting Catholic 'non-Aryans' (but only them) against deportation. The Catholic Church behaved more effectively and decisively in 1939 in the wake of widespread protest against the euthanasia initiative of the National Socialists.

For the Protestant Church, which under National Socialism was initially slower to lose members and only in the second half of the 1930s began to lose them in greater numbers, the situation was more complicated.[85] Already in 1932 a 'Faith Movement of German Christians' (*Glaubensbewegung Deutscher Christen*) had split off from the Church and had declared its goals as 'racial purity,' the destruction of 'Marxism which is hostile to the people,' and the 'dejudiazation' of the church's message. To some extent, this group represented the collected 'yearnings' for renewal spoken of by Eugen Diederichs, and it rapidly gained the support of the majority of Protestant congregations in some regions such as Prussia. The 'Young Reformist Movement' of Martin Niemöller emerged in 1933 as a countermovement and quickly developed into the 'Bekennende Kirche,' (Confessing Church) which distanced itself from National Socialism and at times even openly criticized it. Invoking the Gospel, members protested against the 'false teaching as if there were areas in our life in which we should not serve Jesus Christ, but other masters.'[86] In 1936, the 'Bekennende Kirche' published a memorandum against 'de-Christianization,' anti-Semitism, concentration camps, and Gestapo despotism. Aside from the 'German Christians' and 'Bekennende Kirche' there were many Protestants that conformed, and many others that were internally split. In some cases, churches close to the 'Bekennende Kirche' stood immediately next to churches decorated with National Socialist symbols, flags, and swastikas where 'German Christians' preached 'liberation from all things Jewish' and where public burials of SA men were staged with great pomp.[87]

When, at the end of 1933, Hitler appointed the 'German Christian' Ludwig Müller as *Reichsbischof*, it looked as if the 'German Christians' had gained the support of the majority of the *Landeskirchen*. But it was not only the *Landeskirchen* in Württemberg and Bavaria that refused to become incorporated into a *Reichskirche*. Over time, many of those who had converted to the 'German Christians' when Hitler came to power began to distance themselves from this group.

What did daily life look like for Catholics and Protestants under National Socialism? Can we really speak of a specifically Catholic resistance, on the one hand, and of an equally specific or recognizable Protestant conformity, on the other, as researchers have long claimed?[88] First, it should be emphasized that there were many forms of open co-operation between the National Socialist state and Catholic, as well as Protestant Christians. Many people doing forced labor in church institutions, for instance, worked under conditions marked by overt racism.[89] Also noteworthy is the support for the National Socialist regime evidenced by denunciations: accusing neighbors of living in a state of 'racial defilement,' for example, or claiming that a colleague had made a critical remark about Hitler.[90] Here, too, no denominational differences can be found, nor can it be proven that church members tended to denounce others less than people who had no church affiliation. Finally, it is remarkable just how calmly the loyal churchgoing population—regardless of denomination—accepted the deprivation of people's rights, terror, and ongoing discrimination. In short, neither Catholics nor Protestants distinguished themselves particularly through dissent, let alone resistance.[91]

Despite the fact that Protestants and Catholics supported, or simply endured, National Socialism, we also do find occasional instances of individual religious or faith-based resistance, dissent, and even opposition, and here denominational differences do exist. Writing about Catholicism, Cornelia Rauh-Kühne concludes that 'no other large group in society . . . was able to mount a comparable defense against its destruction or infiltration by the National Socialist state.'[92] Still, defending Catholic identity, the milieu, and Catholic religious practices was not the same as offering genuine resistance. Above all it meant that a strong Catholic milieu continued to exist as before and, while this milieu no longer represented an anti-modern stance, it also by no means represented a specifically anti-Fascist position.[93] In defending its own identity and the rights of the Church against the National Socialist state, Catholicism did, indeed, distinguish itself, but this defense should not be confused with systemic resistance, let alone opposition. Rather, this position remained part of a tradition of conceptualizing the secular and the religious in a way that had become firmly entrenched during the Wilhelminian Empire, a time when Catholicism existed in tension with the state. For this reason, as Rauh-Kühne concludes, 'the defensive stance of the Catholic milieu vis-à-vis National Socialism cannot be deemed the expression of a fundamentally democratic disposition; on the whole, it was not a conscious effort to uphold the constitution of the Weimar Republic.'[94]

In Protestantism under the Third Reich there was no such comparable closed milieu—and none had existed in the Second German Empire, either.[95] Instead, there were a large number of 'milieu circles,' which generally did not, however, claim independence from the state, in part because Protestantism as a whole was too much a part of the secular realm for that to happen. On the contrary: especially for 'German Christians' and a large number of conformist Protestants, a particular closeness continued to exist between church and state. It would nonetheless be wrong to speak of a specific affinity between Protestantism and National Socialism, which would have made all forms of dissent difficult. Because of pluralization, Protestantism actually had many different forms (this had also been evident in the way the secular and the religious were configured in the Second German Empire, in that some trends were located in the negatively charged field of 'the religious' and, hence, far away from the state). These forms also included the '*Bekennende Kirche*' that invoked the word of Christ to turn against the National Socialist state.

Hence, when discussing Protestantism we need to differentiate very carefully according to individual city and state (*Land*), gender, social status, and denominational orientation if we wish to make any assertions about dissent. Even then we may arrive at surprising conclusions. For instance, a study of Franconia revealed that already in 1930 over 70 percent of the predominantly Protestant villages voted for the NSDAP, yet there was bitter protest when the SA attempted to change the *Kirchenstuhlordnung*, an ordinance governing seating order.[96] Here, in rural Franconia, open hostility toward 'German Christians' prevailed, and people fought persistently against efforts to incorporate the Bavarian *Landeskirche* into the *Reichskirche*. Yet resistance directed toward groups that were considered Prussian imports did not necessarily mean protest against the deportation of Jewish citizens. Manfred Gailus concludes that in Protestantism there was at best detachment. Struggle was reserved for one's own identity, which Gailus describes as 'the struggle to realign one's own identity under the overwhelming influence of the National Socialist upheaval in 1933.'[97] This struggle was not directed primarily against a National Socialism that saw its own *raison d'etre* in its frontal assault on Christian faith. In Gailus' view it was more a matter of maintaining a balance of power within the framework of an increasing number of claims to total domination.

As different as the stances of the two Christian churches were under National Socialism, their official statements after 1945 contain accounts of themselves that, despite differences in specific content, were equally deceptive and powerful. In 1945 representatives of the Lutheran Church in Germany released a statement in which they claimed: 'We have indeed fought long years in the name of Jesus Christ against the spirit that found its terrible expression in the National Socialist regiment of violence; but we admonish ourselves for not having professed more courageously, prayed more stalwartly, believed more joyously and loved more fiercely.'[98] Guilt was acknowledged, yet at the same time the impression was generated that the Lutheran Church had fought valiantly, but simply not hard enough, against National Socialism.

The first official publication of the Catholic Church in August 1945 claimed that in the preceding twelve years the majority of Catholics had taken a laudable stance against National Socialism, and that the failure to be lamented was not of the church itself, but at most of individual Christians. In order to prove this assertion, all dioceses were instructed to research and document the resistance of priests and members of religious orders as quickly as possible.[99] This publication does more than conjure up a misleading picture of a church offering resistance to National Socialism. At a time when the concentration camp gates had barely been opened, it also evokes a highly idiosyncratic culture of remembrance.

With this interpretation, still in effect today, a final reconceptualization of the secular and the religious began.[100] At first both the Catholic and Lutheran Church placed themselves firmly in the religious sphere and insisted on their detachment from the secular, although in fact the connections between church and state remained as strong as ever. Now, after 1945, however, the religious sphere was seen in a completely positive light, as a place beyond all worldly temptations to evil, to the irrational, and to all that was power-hungry and base. At the same time in postwar Germany, after every Jewish community had been destroyed, Judaism was defined for the first time as an equally legitimate part of this field with its now entirely positive connotations. While the study of religion in the nineteenth century had already begun to explore the shared roots of Christianity and Judaism, the discussion stopped short of actually recognizing a common history; it was now precisely this shared history that became a given for the Christian churches.[101]

In Germany today, the denomination considered 'religious' in the same negative sense of traditionalist and full of archaic irrationalism that applied to Catholicism, Awakened, and Orthodox Jews in the Wilhelminian Empire, is a faith that at the time of that empire was known only from the reports of missionaries: Islam.

[Translated from German by Elizabeth Bredeck.]

NOTES

1. I would like to thank Michael Schwarzbach, Karolin Oppermann, Christina Templin, and Merve Lühr. For a good, but short survey of the problem, see José Casanova, 'Secularization Revisited: A Reply to Talal Asad,' in David Scott and Charles Hirschkind (eds), *Powers of the Secular Modern. Talal Asad and His Interlocutors* (Stanford: Stanford University Press, 2006), 12–30.
2. Emmet Larkin, 'The Devotional Revolution in Ireland,' *American Historical Review* 77, 3 (1972), 625–652.
3. Olaf Blaschke, 'Das 19. Jahrhundert: Ein zweites konfessionelles Zeitalter?,' *Geschichte und Gesellschaft* 26 (2000), 38–75.
4. If one calls the period from 1818 to 1968 an age of redenominalization, which reasonable concept could then be found for the last twenty years, during which the importance of religion increased, not only on the American continent and in many Muslim countries?
5. Talal Asad, 'What Might an Anthropology of Secularism Look Like?' in Talal Asad, *Formations of the Secular. Christianity, Islam, Modernity* (Stanford: Stanford University Press, 2003), 21–66, 35.
6. Ibid., 35.
7. Arie L. Molendijk and Peter Pels, (eds), *Religion in the Making. The Emergence of the Sciences of Religion* (Leiden: Brill, 1998).
8. Gangolf Hübinger, *Kulturprotestantismus und Politik. Zum Verhältnis von Liberalismus und Protestantismus im wilhelminischen Deutschland* (Tübingen: Mohr, 1994). With regard to the nineteenth century, see Lucian Hölscher, *Geschichte der protestantischen Frömmigkeit in Deutschland* (Munich: Beck, 2005).
9. R. Hobis, '*Africa,*' *Hermannsburger Missionsblatt* 23 (1876, January), 9–16, 16.
10. See also the excellent study of Simone Lässig, *Jüdische Wege ins Bürgertum. Kulturelles Kapital und sozialer Aufstieg im 19. Jahrhundert* (Göttingen: Vandenhoeck & Ruprecht, 2004).

11. With regard to the difficult classification of the different levels of involvement in church, piety, public and private practices cf. Lucian Hölscher, 'Die Religion des Bürgers. Bürgerliche Frömmigkeit und protestantische Kirche im 19. Jahrhundert,' *Historische Zeitschrift* 250 (1990), 595–630.

12. The development of Max Webers 'Säkularisierungsthese' must also be seen in this context.

13. With regard to the religious practices in private spheres during the first half of the century cf. Rebekka Habermas, 'Rituale des Gefühls. Die Frömmigkeit des protestantischen Bürgertums,' in Manfred Hettling and Stefan-Ludwig Hoffmann (eds), *Der bürgerliche Wertehimmel. Innenansichten des 19. Jahrhunderts* (Göttingen: Vandenhoeck & Ruprecht, 2000), 169–192.

14. See also the studies by: Antonius Liedhegener, *Christentum und Urbanisierung, Katholiken und Protestanten in Münster und Bochum 1830–1933* (Paderborn: Schöningh, 1997); Lucian Hölscher, *Datenatlas zur religiösen Geographie im protestantischen Deutschland. Von der Mitte des 19. Jahrhunderts bis zum Zweiten Weltkrieg*, 4 vols. (Berlin: de Gruyter, 2001); Hugh McLeod, *Secularisation in Western Europe, 1848–1914* (Basingstoke: Macmillan Press, 2000).

15. Liedhegener, *Christentum*, 236.

16. Ruth Harris, *Lourdes. Body and Spirit in the Secular Age* (London: Penguin, 1999); David Blackbourn, *Marpingen. Apparitions of the Virgin Mary in Nineteenth-Century Germany* (New York: Alfred A. Knopf, 1994).

17. Liedhegener, *Christentum*; Jospeh Mooser, 'Das katholische Milieu in der bürgerlichen Gesellschaft. Zum Vereinswesen des Katholizismus im späten Kaiserreich,' in Olaf Blaschke and Frank-Michael Kuhlemann (eds), *Religion im Kaiserreich. Milieus—Mentalitäten—Krisen* (Gütersloh: Gütersloher Verlagshaus, 1996), 59–92, 75.

18. With regard to the Congregations cf. Relinde Meiwes, *'Arbeiterinnen des Herrn.' Katholische Frauenkongregationen im 19. Jahrhundert* (Frankfurt am Main: Campus, 2000).

19. With regard to the media of both denominations see Bernd Sösemann, 'Die konfessionelle Publizistik des 19. Jahrhunderts in der zeitgenössischen Auseinandersetzung und als Gegenstand der Forschung,' in Kaspar Elm and Hans-Dietrich Loock (eds), *Seelsorge und Diakonie in Berlin. Beiträge zum Verhältnis von Kirche und Großstadt im 19. und beginnenden 20. Jahrhundert* (Berlin: de Gruyter, 1990), 385–412; Friedrich Weichert, 'Die evangelische Kirchenpresse Berlins. Ein Rückblick auf ihre Geschichte,' in ibid., 413–426; Jürgen Michael Schulz, 'Katholische Kirchenpresse in Berlin,' in ibid., 427–449.

20. See the exemplary study by Lucian Hölscher and Ursula Männich-Polenz, 'Die Sozialstruktur der Kirchengemeinde Hannovers im 19. Jahrhundert. Eine statistische Analyse,' *Jahrbuch der Gesellschaft für niedersächsische Kirchengeschichte* 88 (1990), 159–211; see also Hölscher, *Datenatlas*.

21. Hugh McLeod, *Piety and Poverty. Working-Class Religion in Berlin, London and New York 1870–1914* (New York: Holmes & Meier, 1996).

22. 'Bericht über die Austritte aus der Kapernaumkirchengemeinde, sowie über die Rück- und Übertritte im Jahre 1913,' in: Markus Reitzig, *Berlin-Wedding in der Zeit der Hochindustrialisierung (1885–1914)* (Ph.D. Dissertation, Humboldt University, Berlin, 2006), 27–28.

23. 'Bericht über den weiteren Verlauf der Austrittsbewegung in der Kapernaumgemeinde,' cited in: Reitzig, *Berlin-Wedding*, 27.

24. With regard to the debate on female religiousity, which was initiated in the 1970s by Barbara Welter, cf. Hugh McLeod, 'Weibliche Frömmigkeit—männlicher Unglaube? Religion und Kirche im bürgerlichen 19. Jahrhundert,' in Ute Frevert (ed.), *Bürgerinnen und Bürger. Geschlechterverhältnisse im 19. Jahrhundert* (Göttingen: Vandenhoeck & Ruprecht, 1988), 134–156; Lucian Hölscher, '"Weibliche Religiosität?" Der Einfluss von Religion und Kirche auf die Religiosität von Frauen im 19. Jahrhundert,' in Margret Kraul and Christoph Lüth (eds), *Erziehung der Menschengeschlechter. Studien zur Religion, Sozialisation und Bildung in Europa seit der Aufklärung* (Weinheim: Deutscher Studien-Verlag, 1996), 45–62; Rebekka Habermas, 'Weibliche Religiosität oder: Von der Fragilität bürgerlicher Identitäten,' in: Klaus Tenfelde and Hans-Ulrich Wehler (eds), *Wege zur Geschichte des Bürgertums* (Göttingen: Vandenhoeck & Ruprecht, 1994), 125–148.

25. In the meantime it has become quite obvious that a discussion about 'female religiosity' has to take in account the denominational boundaries and different 'religious cultures,' particularly in relation to 'male religiosity.' See also: Monika Mommertz and Claudia Opitz-Belakhal, '"Religiöse Kulturen" und "Geschlecht". Einige Konzeptionelle Überlegungen,' in Monika Mommertz and Claudia Opitz-Belakhal (eds), *Das Geschlecht des Glaubens. Religiöse Kulturen zwischen Mittelalter und Moderne* (Frankfurt: Campus, 2008), 7–48.

26. Thomas Nipperdey, *Deutsche Geschichte 1800–1866*, vol. 1, *Arbeitswelt und Bürgergeist* (Munich: Beck, 1990), 432 pp.

27. See Michael B. Gross, *The War against Catholicism. Liberalism and the Anti-Catholic Imagination in Nineteenth-century Germany* (Ann Arbor: University of Michigan Press, 2004).

28. Professor Gerland, 'Die Mission im Leben der Gegenwart,' *Zeitschrift für Missionskunde und Religionswissenschaft* 1 (1886), 8–22, 21.

29. For a the formation of religious studies as a genuine Protestant science (in Germany) against the background of the rearrangement of the secular and the religious, see Suzanne L. Marchand, *Down from Olympus. Archaeology and Philhellenism in Germany, 1750–1970* (Princeton: Princeton University Press, 1996) and in regard to the colonial context David Chidester, *Savage Systems. Colonialism and Comparative Religion in Southern Africa* (Charlottsville: University Press of Virginia, 1996).

30. Frank-Michael Kuhlemann, 'Pastorennationalismus in Deutschland im 19. Jahrhundert—Befunde und Perspektiven der Forschung,' in Heinz-Gerhard Haupt and Dieter Langewiesche (eds), *Nation und Religion in der deutschen Geschichte* (Frankfurt am Main: Campus, 2001), 548–586. Haupt and Langewiesche (eds), *Nation und Religion in Europa.*

31. With regard to the 'Antisemitismusstreit' see the excellent analysis of Uffa Jensen, *Gebildete Doppelgänger. Bürgerliche Juden und Protestanten im 19. Jahrhundert* (Göttingen: Vandenhoeck & Ruprecht, 2005), 219. See Heinrich von Treitschke '"Unsere Aussichten"' printed in *Der 'Berliner Antisemitismusstreit' 1879–1881. Eine Kontroverse um die Zugehörigkeit der deutschen Juden zur Nation. Kommentierte Quellenedition*, Karsten Krieger, Vol. 1 (Munich: Sauer, 2003), 6–16, 15.

32. Treitschke, 'Aussichten,' 15.

33. On the impact of the Kulturkampf on the process of the construction of a nation state, see Helmut Walser Smith, *German Nationalism and Religious Conflict. Culture, Ideology, Politics, 1870–1914* (Princeton: Princeton University Press, 1995), 20. Offering a

different view, Olaf Blaschke sees the *Kulturkampf* in a classical way, as a 'fundamental conflict between liberalism and Catholicism.' See Olaf Blaschke, *Katholizismus und Antisemitismus im Deutschen Kaiserreich* (Göttingen: Vandenhoeck & Ruprecht, 1997), 59.

34. Heinrich von Treitschke, 'Unsere Aussichten,' 6–16, 11.

35. Martin Greschat, 'Der deutsche Protestantismus im Kaiserreich,' in Jaques Gadille and Jean M. Mayeur (eds), *Die Geschichte des Christentums. Religion-Politik—Kultur*, vol. 11, *Liberalismus, Industrialisierung, Expansion Europas (1830–1914)* (Freiburg: Herder, 1997), 656–681.

36. Ronald J. Ross, *The Failure of Bismarck's Kulturkampf. Catholicism and State Power in Imperial Germany, 1871–1887* (Washington D.C.: Catholic University of America Press, 1998); Margaret L. Anderson *Windthorst. A Political Biography* (Oxford: Oxford University Press, 1981); Christopher Clark and Wolfram Kaiser (eds), *Culture Wars. Secular-Catholic Conflict in Nineteenth-century Europe* (Cambridge: Cambridge University Press, 2003).

37. Gross, *The War against Catholicism*.

38. Hübinger, *Kulturprotestantismus und Politik*, 307.

39. Rudolf Virchow, 'Über Wunder' (1874), in Hans-Jochem Autrum (ed.), *Von der Naturforschung zur Naturwissenschaft. Vorträge, gehalten auf Versammlungen der Gesellschaft Deutscher Naturforscher und Ärzte (1822–1958)* (Berlin: Springer-Verlag, 1987), 91–108, 105.

40. On these common Catholic and Protestant stereotypes in rural communities, see Tobias Dietrich, *Konfession im Dorf. Westeuropäische Erfahrungen im 19. Jahrhundert* (Cologne: Böhlau, 2004).

41. Friedrich Siegmund-Schultze 1912, cit. in Rolf Lindner, *Walks on the Wild Side. Eine Geschichte der Stadtforschung* (Frankfurt am Main: Campus, 2004), 101. 'Das Studium der socialen Frage,' *Fliegende Blätter* 1 (1877), 27–28, 27.

42. Historians have discussed these activities in connection with the social doctrine of both denominations. See Helga Grebing (ed.), *Geschichte der sozialen Ideen in Deutschland. Sozialismus, Katholische Soziallehre, Protestantische Sozialethik. Ein Handbuch* (Essen: Klartext-Verlag, 2000).

43. With regard to the Protestant commitment to women see Ursula Baumann, *Protestantismus und Frauenemanzipation in Deutschland 1850 bis 1920* (Frankfurt am Main: Campus, 1992); Iris Schröder, *Arbeiten für eine bessere Welt: Frauenbewegung und Sozialreform 1890–1914* (Frankfurt am Main: Campus, 2001).

44. See Rainer Liedke, 'Jüdische Identität im bürgerlichen Raum: Die organisierte Wohlfahrt der Hamburger Juden im 19. Jahrhundert,' in Andreas Gotzmann, Rainer Liedtke and Till van Rahden (eds), *Juden, Bürger, Deutsche. Zur Geschichte von Vielfalt und Differenz 1800–1933* (Tübingen: Mohr Siebeck, 2001), 299–314; Schröder, *Frauenbewegung und Sozialreform*.

45. See Norbert Busch, *Katholische Frömmigkeit und Moderne. Die Sozial- und Mentalitätsgeschichte des Herz-Jesu-Kultes in Deutschland zwischen Kulturkampf und Erstem Weltkrieg* (Gütersloh: Gütersloher Verlags-Haus, 1997); Steffi Hummel, *Der Borromäusverein 1845–1920. Katholische Volksbildung und Büchereiarbeit zwischen Anpassung und Bewahrung* (Köln: Böhlau, 2005); Jeffrey Zalar, '"Knowledge Is Power." The Borromäusverein and Catholic Reading Habits in Imperial Germany,' *Catholic Historical Review* 86, 1 (2000), 20–46; Jeffrey T. Zalar, 'The Process of Confessional Inculturation. Catholic

Reading in the "Long Nineteenth Century,"' in Helmut Walser Smith (ed.), *Protestants, Catholics and Jews in Germany*, (Oxford: Berg, 2001), 121–152.

46. Engels himself made extensive use of the accounts of the Statistical Societies and Sanitary Maps (like the ones by Edwin Chadwick). Lindner, *Walks*, 28. Engels also cited verbatim accounts of local pastors. See Friedrich Engels, 'Die Lage der arbeitenden Klasse in England. Nach eigener Anschauung und authentischen Quellen' (1845), in: *Marx-Engels-Werke*, vol. 2 (Berlin: Dietz Verlag, 1974), 229–506, 261. He also cited from the 'Bettler Fürsorge-Vereinigung' (266) and from medical reports (267).

47. Engels, *Lage*, 239, 260.

48. Ibid., 355, 369.

49. See Rebekka Habermas, 'Mission im 19. Jahrhundert. Globale Netze des Religiösen,' *Historische Zeitschrift* 287 (2008), 1– 51.

50. Thorsten Altena, *Ein Häuflein Christen mitten in der Heidenwelt des dunklen Erdteils. Zum Selbst- und Fremdverständnis protestantischer Missionare im kolonialen Afrika 1884–1918* (Münster: Waxmann, 2003).

51. Klaus J. Bade (ed.), *Imperialismus und Kolonialmission. Kaiserliches Deutschland und koloniales Imperium* (Wiesbaden: Steiner, 1982).

52. Much research remains to be done. See Siegfried Weichlein, 'Mission und Ultramontanismus im frühen 19. Jahrhundert,' in Gisela Fleckenstein and Joachim Schmiedl (eds), *Ultramontanismus. Tendenzen der Forschung* (Paderborn: Bonifatius, 2005), 93–109, 94, note 4. With regard to Switzerland, see Patrick Harries, *Butterflies and Barbarians. Swiss Missionaries and Systems of Knowledge in South-East Africa* (Oxford: Currey, 2007), 11ff.

53. Bernard Arens, *Die katholischen Missionsvereine. Darstellung ihres Werdens und Wirkens ihrer Satzungen und Vorrechte* (Freiburg: Herder, 1922), 28. Even though the museums of the different mission societies made great contributions to the representations of the non-European world, hardly any historical research has been done. See Altena, 'Ein Häuflein Christen,' 89pp.

54. With regard to the 'lantern shows,' see Harries, *Butterflies and Barbarians*. With regard to the photos, see Jens Jäger, 'Bilder aus Afrika vor 1918. Zur visuellen Konstruktion Afrikas im europäischen Kolonialismus,' in Paul Gerhard (ed.), *Visual History. Ein Studienbuch* (Göttingen: Vandenhoeck & Ruprecht, 2006), 134–148; Paul Jenkins, 'Land und Arbeit als vergessene Werte in der Mentalität von Baseler MissionarInnen um 1900: ein Essay mit Bildquellen,' in Inge Mager (ed.), *Christentum und Kirche vor der Moderne. Industrialisierung, Historismus und die Deutsche Evangelische Kirche. Zweites Symposium der deutschen Territorialgeschichtsvereine, 9. bis 11. Juni 1995* (Hanover: Rihn, 1995).

55. All citations are from D. Buchner, D. R. Grundemann, and D. Gustav Warneck (eds), *Allgemeine Missionszeitschrift* (Berlin: Verlag von Martin Warneck, 1874–1923).

56. A large amount of research shows that the phenomenon of missionary work certainly cannot be reduced to this aspect alone. See the classical description of John und Jean Comaroff, *Of Revelation and Revolution*, vol. 1, *Christianity, Colonialism and Consciousness in South Africa* (Chicago: University of Chicago Press, 1991), and John and Jean Comaroff, *Of Revelation and Revolution*, vol. 2, *The Dialectics of Modernity on a South African Frontier* (Chicago: University of Chicago Press, 1997).

57. Christoph Ribbat, *Religiöse Erregung. Protestantische Schwärmer im Kaiserreich* (Frankfurt am Main: Campus, 1996); Ulrich Linse, *Geisterseher und Wunderwirker. Heilssuche im Industriezeitalter* (Frankfurt am Main: Fischer, 1996). Heinrich Missalla, *'Gott mit*

uns.' Die deutsche katholische Kriegspredigt 1914–1918 (Munich: Kösel, 1968) und Wilhelm Pressel, *Die Kriegspredigt 1914–1918 in der evangelischen Kirche Deutschlands* (Göttingen: Vandenhoeck & Ruprecht, 1967). On anti-Semitic conflict, Helmut Walser Smith, *The Butcher's Tale: Murder and Anti-Semitism in a German Town* (New York: W. W. Norton, 2002).

58. Rainer Hering, 'Säkularisierung, Entkirchlichung, Dechristianisierung und Formen der Rechristianisierung bzw. Resakralisierung in Deutschland,' in Stefanie von Schnurbein and Justus H. Ulbricht (eds), *Völkische Religion und Krisen der Moderne. Entwürfe 'arteigener' Glaubenssysteme seit der Jahrhundertwende* (Würzburg: Königshausen & Neumann, 2001), 120–164. Lucian Hölscher, *Datenatlas*, 120–21. See, for example, the villages in the region of Dransfeld and Einbeck, in the north of Göttingen, where until the 1930s 40–60% of the Protestant population were active Protestants.

59. Manfred Gailus, *Protestantismus und Nationalsozialismus. Studien zur nationalsozialistischen Durchdringung des protestantischen Sozialmilieus in Berlin* (Köln: Böhlau, 2001), 34.

60. Diethard Sawicki, *Leben mit den Toten. Geisterglauben und die Entstehung des Spiritismus in Deutschland 1770–1900* (Paderborn: Schöningh, 2002); Linse, *Geisterseher*.

61. See Hölscher, *Geschichte der protestantischen Frömmigkeit in Deutschland*; Ribbat, *Religiöse Erregung*.

62. Ribbat, *Religiöse Erregung*, 24.

63. Cit. in Justus H. Ulbricht, '"...in einer gottfremden, prophetenlosen Zeit"... Aspekte einer Problemgeschichte "arteigener" Religion um 1900,' in Stefanie von Schnurbein and Justus H. Ulbricht (eds), *Völkische Religion und Krisen der Moderne.* (Würzburg: Königshausen & Neumann, 2001), 9–39. On Eugen Diederichs and the 'Serakreis' in Jena, see Meike G. Werner, *Moderne in der Provinz. Kulturelle Experimente im Fin de Siècle Jena* (Göttingen: Wallstein, 2003).

64. With regard to these groups see Ulrich Nanko, 'Das Spektrum völkisch-religiöser Organisationen von der Jahrhundertwende bis ins "Dritte Reich",' in Stefanie von Schnurbein and Justus H. Ulbricht (eds), *Völkische Religion und Krisen der Moderne*, 208–226.

65. See Karla Poewe, *New Religions and the Nazis* (New York: Routledge, 2006).

66. With regard to Münster see Liedhegener, *Christentum*, 243.

67. August Huber, *Die göttliche Vorsehung* (Freiburg: Herder, 1915), 108 cit. in Heinrich Missalla, *Gott mit uns*, 52; Norbert Peters, *Heldentod. Trostgedanken für schwere Tage in großer Not* (Paderborn: Bonifacius-Druckerei, 1914), 41, cit. in Ibid., 59.

68. Norbert Peters, *Heldentod*, 38, cit. in Ibid., 85. Certainly it has to be said that the sermons of the Protestant Church were exactly as nationalistic and martial as the Catholic ones, see Pressel, *Kriegspredigt*.

69. Till van Rahden, *Juden und andere Breslauer. Die Beziehungen zwischen Juden, Protestanten und Katholiken in einer deutschen Großstadt von 1860 bis 1925* (Göttingen: Vandenhoeck & Ruprecht, 2000), 95.

70. Ibid., 145. In the years, 1911 to 1915, 34 of 100 Jewish weddings were interfaith. See Michael Imhof, *'Einen besseren als Stöcker finden wir nicht.' Diskursanalytische Studien zur christlich-sozialen Agitation im deutschen Kaiserreich* (Oldenburg: BIS-Verlag, 1996).

71. The conflicts between 'modern' and 'orthodox' Jews also intensified on behalf of the question whether or not women were allowed to vote in their community—the so-called *Geschlechterfrage*.

72. With regard to Königsberg see Stefanie Schüler-Springorum, *Die jüdische Minderheit in Königsberg, Preußen: 1871–1945* (Göttingen: Vandenhoeck & Ruprecht, 1996), 189ff.

73. Ulrich Baumann, *Zerstörte Nachbarschaften. Christen und Juden in badischen Landgemeinden 1862–1940* (Hamburg: Dölling und Galitz, 2000), 185 pp.

74. Schüler-Springorum, *Jüdische Minderheit*.

75. Anke-Marie Lohmeier, 'Propaganda als Alibi: Rezeptionsgeschichtliche Thesen zu Veit Harlans Film Jud Süß (1940),' in Alexandra Przyrembel and Jörg Schönert (eds), *'Jud Süß.' Hofjude, literarische Figur, antisemitisches Zerrbild* (Frankfurt am Main: Campus, 2006), 201–220; Armin Nolzen, '"Hier sieht man den Juden, wie er wirklich ist . . .": Die Rezeption des Filmes Jud Süß in der deutschen Bevölkerung,' in ibid., 245–261.

76. Recently, historians have emphasized that the history of Jewish life in the Third Reich cannot be reduced to persecution. See Sylvia Rogge-Gau, 'Jüdische Selbstbehauptungsstrategien zwischen nationaler Identität und Diskriminierung', in Detlef Schmiechen-Ackermann (ed.), *Anpassung, Verweigerung, Widerstand. Soziale Milieus, Politische Kultur und der Widerstand gegen den Nationalsozialismus in Deutschland im regionalen Vergleich* (Berlin: Hentrich, 1997), 193–220.

77. Research concerning National Socialism and churches has since moved from an exclusively 'church history' perspective. See Gailus, *Protestantismus*, and the microhistorical study of Cornelia Rauh-Kühne, *Katholisches Milieu und Kleinstadtgesellschaft. Ettlingen 1918–1939* (Sigmaringen: Thorbecke, 1991).

78. Kurt Meier, 'Deutschland und Österreich,' in Jean-Marie Mayeur (ed.), *Die Geschichte des Christentums. Politik—Religion—Kultur, vol. 12, Erster und Zweiter Weltkrieg. Demokratien und totalitäre Systeme* (Freiburg: Herder, 1992) 681–772.

79. Guenther Lewy, *Die Katholische Kirche und das Dritte Reich* (Munich: Piper, 1963), 113 pp., cit. in Alexander Groß, *Gehorsame Kirche—ungehorsame Christen im Nationalsozialismus* (Mainz: Matthias-Grünewald-Verlag, 2000), 17.

80. Ibid., 19. Today, historians consider this agreement controversial: either it was a step too far towards the acceptance of the Nazi-government or it offered it political warranties for the much-in-need church.

81. See Blaschke, *Katholizismus und Antisemitismus*.

82. Lewy, *Katholische Kirche*, 303, cit. in Groß, *Gehorsame Kirche*, 30.

83. Kurt Meier, *Deutschland und Österreich*, 701.

84. *Acta Apostolicae Sedis* 29 (1937), 145–167, 149.

85. Lucian Hölscher, *Datenatlas, vol.1: Norden* (Berlin: de Gruyter, 2001), 16.

86. Barmer 'Theologische Erklärung der Bekennenden Kirche, 2,' These-Gerd Niemöller (ed.), *Arbeiten zur Geschichte des Kirchenkampfes, vol. 6: Die erste Bekenntnissynode der Deutschen Evangelischen Kirche zu Barmen. II. Texte-Dokumente-Berichte* (Göttingen: Vandenhoeck, 1959), 196–202, 199.

87. Gailus, *Protestantismus*, 179ff.

88. Winfried Becker, 'Christen und der Widerstand. Forschungsstand und Forschungsperspektiven,' in Karl-Joseph Hummel and Christoph Kösters (eds), *Kirchen im Krieg. Europa 1939–1945* (Paderborn: Schöningh, 2007), 473–492.

89. Uwe Kaminsky, 'Zwangsarbeit in Evangelischer Kirche und Diakonie,' in Karl-Joseph Hummel and Christoph Kösters (eds), *Kirchen im Krieg Europa*, 343–362; Jochen-Christoph Kaiser (ed.), *Zwangsarbeit in Diakonie und Kirche 1939–45* (Stuttgart: Kohlhammer, 2005); Baldur Hermans (ed.), *Zwang und Zuwendung. Katholische Kirche und Zwangsarbeit im Ruhrgebiet.* (Bochum: Kamp, 2003).

90. Alexandra Przyrembel, *'Rassenschande.' Reinheitsmythos und Vernichtungslegitimation im Nationalsozialismus* (Göttingen: Vandenhoeck & Ruprecht, 2003).

91. The debate, which began in the 1970s with the large project of Martin Broszat (Zeithistorisches Institut in Munich) on NationalSocialism in Bavaria about the terms of 'Widerstand,' 'Dissenz,' and 'Resistenz' is still going on.

92. Cornelia Rauh-Kühne, 'Anpassung und Widerstand? Kritische Bemerkungen zur Erforschung des katholischen Milieus,' in Detlef Schmiechen-Ackermann (ed.), *Anpassung, Verweigerung, Widerstand. Soziale Milieus, Politische Kultur und der Widerstand gegen den Nationalsozialismus in Deutschland im regionalen Vergleich* (Berlin: Hentrich, 1997), 145–164, 153. See also Werner K. Blessing, '"Deutschland in Not, wir im Glauben...".' Kirche und Kirchenvolk in einer katholischen Region 1933–1949,' in: Martin Broszat, Klaus-Dietmar Henke, and Hans Woller (eds), *Von Stalingrad zur Währungsreform* (Munich: Oldenburg, 1988), 3–112, 37.

93. See the study on the archdiocese Bamberg by Thomas Breuer, *Verordneter Wandel? Der Widerstreit zwischen nationalsozialistischem Herrschaftsanspruch und traditionaler Lebensführung im Erzbistum Bamberg* (Mainz: Matthias-Grünewald-Verlag, 1992).

94. Rauh-Kühne, *Katholisches Milieu*, 422.

95. See Dietmar von Reeken, 'Protestantisches Milieu und "liberale" Landeskirche? Milieubildungsprozesse in Oldenburg 1849–1914,' in: Olaf Blaschke and Frank-Michael Kuhlemann (eds), *Religion im Kaiserreich*, 290–315.

96. Hans Otte, 'Evangelische Kirchengemeinden als resistentes Milieu? Einige Beobachtungen anhand der vorliegenden Regionalstudien,' in Detlef Schmiechen-Ackermann (ed.), *Anpassung, Verweigerung, Widerstand*, 165–192.

97. Gailus, *Protestantismus*, 637.

98. 'Stuttgarter Schulderklärung 19.10.1945—Erklärung des Rates der Evangelischen Kirche in Deutschland gegenüber den Vertretern des Ökomenischen Rates der Kirche,' in Karl Kupisch (ed.), *Quellen zur Geschichte des deutschen Protestantismus von 1945 bis zur Gegenwart*, Part 1, (Hamburg: Siebenstern, 1971) 56–57, 56.

99. See 'Erster gemeinsamer Hirtenbrief nach dem Krieg, Fulda, 23. August 1945,' in Günter Baadte and Anton Rausche (eds), *Dokumente deutscher Bischöfe, vol. 1: Hirtenbriefe und Ansprachen zu Gesellschaft und Politik 1945–1949*, prepared by *Wolfgang Löhr* (Würzburg: Echter, 1986), S. 40–45.

100. See Björn Mensing, 'Über "braune" Protestanten und protestantische "Märtyrer": Erinnerungskultur und Geschichtspolitik im deutschen Protestantismus,' in Karl-Joseph Hummel and Christoph Kösters (eds), *Kirchen im Krieg*, 493–506, and Franziska Metzger, 'Diskurse des Krieges. Komparative Thesen zu katholischen Erinnerungsdiskursen des Zweiten Weltkrieges in Österreich und der Schweiz,' in ibid., 569–592.

101. See Uffa Jensen, *Doppelgänger*, 81–97, 89.

BIBLIOGRAPHY

ASAD, TALAL, *Formations of the Secular. Christianity, Islam, Modernity* (Stanford: Stanford University Press, 2003).

BLACKBOURN, DAVID, *Marpingen. Apparitions of the Virgin Mary in Nineteenth-Century Germany* (New York: Alfred A. Knopf, 1994).

BORUTTA, MANUEL, *Antikatholizismus. Deutschland und Italien im Zeitalter der europäischen Kulturkämpfe* (Göttingen: Vandenhoeck & Ruprecht, 2010).

CLARK, CHRISTOPHER and WOLFRAM KAISER (eds), *Culture Wars. Secular-Catholic Conflict in Nineteenth-century Europe* (Cambridge: Cambridge University Press, 2003).

GROSS, MICHAEL B., *The War against Catholicism. Liberalism and the Anti-Catholic Imagination in Nineteenth-century Germany* (Ann Arbor: University of Michigan Press, 2004).

HAUPT HEINZ-GERHARD and DIETER LANGEWIESCHE (eds), *Nation und Religion in der deutschen Geschichte* (Frankfurt am Main: Campus, 2001).

HARRIS, RUTH, *Lourdes. Body and Spirit in the Secular Age* (London: Penguin, 1999).

MEIWES, RELINDE, *"Arbeiterinnen des Herrn." Katholische Frauenkongregationen im 19. Jahrhundert* (Frankfurt am Main: Campus, 2000).

VAN RAHDEN TILL, *Juden and Andere Breslauer. Die Beziehungen zwischen Juden, Protestanten und Katholiken in einer deutschen Großstadt von 1860 bis 1925* (Göttingen: Vandenhoeck & Ruprecht, 2000).

RAUH-KÜHNE, CORNELIA, *Katholisches Milieu und Kleinstadtgesellschaft. Ettlingen 1918–1939* (Sigmaringen: Thorbecke, 1991).

SCHÜLER-SPRINGORUM, STEFANIE, *Die jüdische Minderheit in Königsberg, Preußen: 1871–1945* (Göttingen: Vandenhoeck & Ruprecht, 1996).

SMITH, HELMUT WALSER (ed.), *Protestants, Catholics and Jews in Germany: 1800–1914* (Oxford: Berg, 2001).

CHAPTER 21

....

THE PLACE OF GERMAN
MODERNISM

....

STEPHEN D. DOWDEN AND MEIKE G. WERNER

WHAT is the place of German modernism? The question pulls in two directions. First, it points toward the problem of how German modernism ought to be situated in literary and art history. No doubt the simplest, most efficient answer is that German modernism finds its place within the larger setting of European modernism. The larger European context can shed light on the specificities of the German situation, and perhaps the details of German modernism may sharpen our sense of certain aspects of European modernism. Though modernism is a pan-European phenomenon, the shifts in historical circumstances that precipitated aesthetic modernism were experienced more acutely in Germany and Austria than elsewhere in Europe: the rise of science and the culture of technology, rapid industrialization and its accompanying social changes, sudden national unification, a rapid demographic shift from a rural to an urban culture, but above all defeat in the Great War and then the economic turbulence that followed the Treaty of Versailles.[1]

The war was catastrophic in itself for all participants, but all the more so in Germany and Austria, because—apart from the unprecedented carnage and the human suffering—their very worlds came to an abrupt end. The Habsburg Empire and its failed tradition disappeared, and the newly founded German Reich collapsed along with the monarchy into the chaos of Weimar Germany's disorientation, hyperinflation, and sense of apocalyptic transition. The Great War and its catastrophic aftermath created a crisis for the German world that was not different from elsewhere, but it was—not the least because of the lost war—more acute than in France, England, and the United States. This war led to the Russian Revolution, the rise of totalitarianism in the Soviet Union, Germany, and China, the manifold crises of the Second World War, the Shoah, the Cold War, the founding of Israel, and the crisis in the Middle East. The aesthetic response to these ruinous historical circumstances—modernism—marks the German setting as a special case within the European context; special because it is more intense, more chaotic, more disturbingly *modern*.

Still, there is a second way of placing German modernism, one that implies a narrower, more concrete understanding of place. Do certain sites carry special and revealing meaning for understanding German modernism? Berlin, for example, often figures in critical discussions of German modernism, both as a crucial theme and setting—Döblin's *Berlin Alexanderplatz* is the classic example—but also as the site of important work. The modern metropolis, especially Paris and London, but also Petersburg and Weimar-era Berlin (in 1920 the third largest city in the world after London and New York), is where much modernist art unfolds. The urban experience itself is a conspicuously strong modernist theme. However, are there not, perhaps, a number of other significant German places, *lieux de mémoire* (in the phrase made famous by Pierre Nora and his colleagues) that might help define the specificity of modernist Germany and Austria? Is a concentrated focus on the 'German nation,' the German tradition, and its historical exigencies—in that same sense that Nora insists on the French nation as a framework—perhaps the more appropriate way to place German modernism?[2] How German is German modernism? How European is it?

Certainly classic German modernism appears to offer many 'memory sites.' Yet, tellingly, they are often not German at all. We might think of the eponymous Grodek of Trakl's poem, the Italian-Slovenian castle of Rilke's *Duino Elegies*, the Venice of Mann's *Death in Venice* or the Rome of Koeppen's *Death in Rome*, the China, London, and Thirty Years War of Brechtian displacements, the cosmopolitan unfolding of Dada at the Café Voltaire in Zurich and its expansion across Europe. *Der Zauberberg* (1924), Thomas Mann's crucial Weimar novel, is emphatically not German, but takes a cosmopolitan Swiss sanatorium as its setting. His novel of German fascism, *Doktor Faustus*, does accentuate German settings—mostly pastoral—yet its protagonist is shunned by German culture.[3] The audience for Leverkühn's music lies outside of Germany. His compositions would have met the criteria for 'degenerate art' under National Socialism, as did so many Expressionist and other modern works purged from the 1937 exhibit 'German Art' at the *Haus der Kunst* in Thomas Mann's Munich. Leverkühn compositions would have been discredited as too international, too abstract, too modern and, hence, insufficiently 'German.' Like many other German modernists, Mann emigrated and never returned to Germany as a German national. Should Pacific Palisades, where Mann composed *Doktor Faustus*, be reckoned among the German *lieux de mémoire*? Uwe Johnson's New York? Günter Grass's Gdansk? Paul Celan's Czernowitz?

So many of these places are not on German soil at all. Among them Auschwitz looms largest, both in and apart from Paul Celan's poetry. Guernica is also a site of German memory, though the work of art that has burned the Basque village into modern memory is Picasso's, not the work of a German artist. We may think of Prague as Kafka's city, and Kafka is surely the central figure of modernist German fiction, yet somehow multi-ethnic Prague would not seem to qualify as a site of German memory in Nora's sense, which emphasizes the concept of positive national identity.[4] The same is true for Wittgenstein's Vienna, and Freud's, each a crucial modernist who ended up in England and whose particular achievements in any case did not draw on the spirit of place—the popular tourist destination at Berggasse 19 nothwithstanding.

The most misleading implication commonly drawn from the myth about Freud's cases is 'the conviction that psychoanalysis is somehow characteristically, inescapably Viennese.'[5] Freud was a cosmopolitan child of the Enlightenment, Europe's last *philosophe*. His classic work of modernism—*The Interpretation of Dreams* (1900)— takes as its motto Virgil's *Acheronta movebo*, 'I shall stir the infernal depths,' a twentieth-century complement to the *Sapere aude!* of Kant's classic essay 'Answering the Question: What is Enlightenment?' (1784). Like Kant's, Freud's *'Aufklärung'* is disinterested and aims at unvarnished truth. Daring to know, Freud's thought draws on reason and is not meant as an expression of cultural identity, local knowledge, or rootedness in place.[6] Like Nietzsche and Marx, Freud demonstrated that domestic appearances—the happy face of family life—can mask patricidal rage and incestuous desire. His aims were not to shock, but to enlighten. The much-vaunted modernist aim to 'shock the bourgeois' is, more accurately seen, a matter of the modernist attempt in art as elsewhere to reveal truths, not to cultivate the sense of place.

Similarly, the great music of Viennese modernism is not Viennese in its purport. In obvious contrast to the music of Johann Strauss, Franz Lehár, and (in some works) Richard Strauss, Schoenberg's atonal and serial compositions have little about them that is Austrian or Viennese or even German in any sense of being at home in a place. Schoenberg's music is never at home and does not invite its listeners to feel at home in the world. It is news that stays news. Not only *unheimlich*, this music is even unearthly. It breathes 'luft von anderem planeten,' air from some other planet, not from Vienna.[7] In some very early compositions Schoenberg set works by Peter Altenberg and Hugo von Hofmannsthal, the most Viennese of all modernist-era writers. However, from his breakthrough composition of 1912—the atonal song cycle *Pierrot Lunaire* (with text translated from the French)—to his late, unfinished opera *Moses und Aron* (begun in 1933), Schoenberg's modernism is above all cosmopolitan. Wagner's music had claimed for itself a specifically, even heroically German national identity. In the era of the first German unification, he had a national theater built at Bayreuth to glorify his creation of German national myth in works such as the Ring cycle and *Parsifal*. They played out the spiritual drama of German *Innerlichkeit* on a colossal, nationalized scale and with monumental intent. By contrast Schoenberg's severe formal beauty, however much it owes technically to the traditions of both Wagner and Brahms, claims universality, much as Bach's and Mozart's music did.

Schoenberg saw himself as an isolated figure, not as a part of the mainstream of Viennese or German culture of his day, but a prophet in the wilderness, maintaining the greater cosmopolitan tradition of German music that reached back to Bach. The second act of *Moses und Aron*, for which Schoenberg also wrote the libretto, concludes in a powerfully modernist gesture. Moses, the true prophet, lacks the power of language to make himself understood: 'O word, thou word that I lack!' This opera is an emphatically Jewish work, composed during and against the rise of National Socialism. But it is Jewish in the sense that Bach's work is Christian: the music speaks a language that transcends divisive boundaries of national, ethnic, and religious identity. Bach's music models the power of art to gather a fragmented community into a whole.

Schoenberg's Moses embodies the modernist artist—elevated to a prophet crying in the wilderness of European war and decadence—unheeded while the people dance around the golden calf. His power to form and speak the true word has failed. His brother Aron, like many lesser writers and composers, has the gift of easy communication, but mere communication is not the same as the power of giving to spiritual truth a compelling, intelligible form that can create genuine community.

The unheeded prophet wandering in exile is a basic trope of modernism, and Nietzsche's Zarathustra is its prototype. Nietzsche himself, the great progenitor of German and European modernism, gave up being German altogether. He renounced his citizenship to teach in Switzerland and became stateless for the rest of his life. The final years were spent wandering between the Swiss Alps and northern Italy while thinking of himself not as a German at all, but as a 'good European.'[8] In *The Gay Science* Nietzsche prides himself, as Adorno observed, on not being a homeowner. With this passage in mind Adorno further observes that it has become a moral imperative 'not to be at home in one's home.'[9] Like his widely misunderstood remark that writing poetry after Auschwitz is barbaric, this one too could be set aside as a pretentiously sanctimonious exaggeration. However, Adorno pinpoints a simple truth about modernist art, in particular, but one that also holds true for the place of art in general. Between the world as it is represented in art (even in the most affirmative representation) and the vicissitudes of living experience, tensions and contradictions inevitably arise. Art simultaneously distances us from life as it brings us closer to it. Hermann Broch's novel of poetry, homecoming, and political tyranny—*The Death of Virgil*—embodies this paradox in one way; the final words of Samuel Beckett's *The Unnamable* in another: 'I can't go on, I'll go on.' It is the fate of Schoenberg's Moses, of Robert Walser's Jakob von Gunten, and maybe in even more complicated ways of Else Lasker-Schüler's and Gertrud Kolmar's poetry. K.'s fate in *The Castle* is one of being at home and not at home simultaneously. Literature is a way of being at home in the world that at the same time keeps us distant from the world. This is true not only of modernism, but is especially clear in modernism.

If literature is a process of coming home that never ceases, so is publishing. The publishing programs of modernist houses such as Albert Langen, Anton Kippenberg, Kurt Wolff, and most notably Samuel Fischer and Eugen Diederichs are instructive.[10] They were not only a new type of publisher, the so-called 'Kulturverleger,' but they also constituted 'interpretative communities' distinctly associated with places. Samuel Fischer, originally from a small town near the Tatra Mountains in Slovakia, made Berlin the home of what then became the most important publishing house of German high modernism. Founded in 1886 when Fischer was only twenty-six years old, the S. Fischer Verlag published the young revolutionary movement of literary naturalism, with Gerhart Hauptmann as its most prominent proponent. Fischer's approach was to place the German modernists within the context of other modern European writers such as Zola, Tolstoy, Dostoevsky and, most notably, Ibsen. With his commitment to *avant-garde* literature, Fischer became the leading publisher of literary modernism. Besides Hauptmann, his publishing list included Hermann Bahr, Hugo von

Hofmannsthal, Arthur Schnitzler, Hedwig Dohm, Gabriele Reuter, Thomas Mann, Jakob Wassermann, and Hermann Hesse.

Eugen Diederichs founded his publishing house ten years later in Florence and Leipzig, and settled in Jena in 1904. His vision contrasted sharply from that of S. Fischer's urban modernism yet was no less emphatically modernist and international.[11] He combined in his publishing house all literary and cultural movements attempting to transcend Wilhelmine reality, and re-enchant a disenchanted modern world. Whereas Fischer published the literary avant-garde with metropolitan Berlin at its center, Diederichs promoted Jena with its classical and romantic traditions as an alternative, more radically modern '*Kraftzentrum*' (center of energy) for the formation of a modern German culture. 'Jena is the center of the world. For the center of the world is Europe, the center of Europe is Germany. In the middle of east and west, north and south, however, lies Jena,'[12] he wrote, rather unironically. In his attempt to de-differentiate the modern differentiated world, or—as his, his authors' and readers' intellectual mentor Nietzsche once formulated it—of '*reshaping of the world* in order to be able to endure it,'[13] Diederichs not only published contemporary neo-romantic and neo-idealistic German literature. He also collected, translated, and promoted French philosophy (Bergson), English politics (Fabians), American Transcendentalists (Emerson and Thoreau), Russian literature (Tolstoy, Chekhov), the complete works of Ruskin and Kierkegaard, Chinese religion and philosophy, fairy tales from across the world, Nordic sagas, writers of the Italian Renaissance, Greek antiquity, and German Romanticism, as well as protagonists of modern European reform movements. In addition, he represented medieval and contemporary religious heretics, dissidents, and outsiders across the political and ideological spectrum. While his ambition in assimilating related and foreign cultures was universalistic and international, his program was decidedly national. To appropriate Fichte's terms, a new German culture was to be forged from mixing and friction with other cultures. There is no denying the cultural-imperial gesture of his Jena program, because much like Fichte, Diederichs believed that only the Germans could give ultimate form to world literature and culture. Fischer died in 1934 in Berlin, but his son-in-law and successor Gottfried Bermann (like Fischer, Bermann was Jewish) left Nazi Germany with the publishing rights and printed books of Fischer's now 'undesirable' authors, finding a new home in Vienna, Stockholm, and finally New York. Diederichs died in 1930 in Jena; however, his two sons Niels and Peter together with Diederichs's second wife Lulu von Strauss und Torney successfully established a place for their—now less cosmopolitan and more *völkish*—Jena program in the 'Third Reich.'

The tension between metropolitan center and outlying province finds its classic formulation in Georg Simmel's essay 'The Metropolis and Mental Life' (1902–1903).[14] But the dynamic tension often congealed into the misleading cliché of urban progress versus rural stasis, of the modern versus the pre-modern. In some instances the opposition Berlin-versus-province became the expression of conservative protest against the perceived ills of modernization associated with metropolitan centers, especially Berlin. With its rejection of industrialization, capitalism, socialism, intellectualism, and Jews, the literature of the so-called *Heimatkunst*-movement, most prominently 'Bauernromane', or peasant novels, such as Gustav Frenssen's *Jörn Uhl* (1901), presented to the reader a loving image of the German rural *Heimat* with its attendant way of life and values, its German soil and German customs.[15] However, in the 1920s, the tension between the pastoral image of the countryside and the nightmarish vision of the city took a radical turn, politicizing an initially literary juxtaposition and making the opposition between Berlin and the provinces part of the ideological formulas exploited to define who belonged and who did not: city versus country, civilization versus culture, writer versus poet, intellect versus feeling, Americanization versus the cultivation of national custom, cosmopolitan versus national, Jewish versus German, rootlessness versus rootedness in place. As Jochen Meyer writes: 'The contrasting pair, Berlin and the province, could stand in for all these.'[16]

Still, the tension between metropolitan center and province was more than an ideological battleground. For example, in Marieluise Fleißer's dramas and novellas, as well as in her novel *Mehlreisende Frieda Geier* (1931) (and after the Second World War in Martin Walser's and Uwe Johnson's novels), the contrast can be fruitful. Walter Benjamin in his review of her Ingoldstädter novellas admires Fleißer's easy-going pride in provincial life: 'She simply believes that you can have experiences in the provinces on a par with those available to large lives carried on in big cities. In fact, Fleißer considers these experiences important enough to stake her life and her work as a writer on them.'[17] Unlike most regional writers, Fleißer includes in her works 'what is happening in Europe.'

Yet Fleißer is not a well-known figure outside of Germany. Her position even within German cultural history, like virtually all women who wrote, painted, or were active as intellectuals is 'verstellt,' skewed.[18] Curiously enough, there is no Virginia Woolf or Gertrude Stein in German modernism. However, there is a remarkable increase in numbers of women writers—from 323 between 1700 and 1820 to 3617 between 1820 and 1900—and their sheer number and in some cases success seem to have posed a threat to male writers.[19] We think of Hedwig Dohm, Lou Andreas-Salomé, Isolde Kurz, Ida Boy-Ed, Ricarda Huch, Gabriele Reuter, Else Lasker-Schüler, Franziska zu Reventlow, Bertha von Suttner, Ina Seidel, Agnes Miegel, Annette Kolb, Margarete Susman, Emmy (Ball-)Hennings, Gertrud Kolmar, Marieluise Fleißer, Irmgard Keun, and Vicky Baum to name only a few.[20] As writers, poets, and thinkers these women successfully challenged the traditional confinement of women to the private sphere, while claiming a more public or independent role, even 'a room of their own.' This greater independence was evident in education (women were admitted to German universities in the years after 1900), in politics (one thinks of Bertha von Suttner and Rosa Luxemburg), and in the realm of literary culture, especially prose, dramas, and poetry. The argument has been made that the re-definition of gender roles, the battle of the sexes, is at the center of the modernist movement and even more radically that it paradoxically inspired male writers, 'fueling the innovations of the avant garde in order to ward off the onslaughts of women.'[21] This male fear of and fascination with women, femininity, and sexuality produced an endless variety of literary representations, most notably through female figures, such as the helpless, sickly, and dependent *femme fragile*, like Christine Weiring in Schnitzler's *Liebelei*, or the seductive, animalistic, dangerous *femme fatale*, epitomized by Lulu in Wedekind's *Erdgeist*. Muse, saint, virgin, wife, mother, hetaera, Medusa, Sphinx, Lilith, Salomé are all variations of male projections onto the (literary) body of women. Of the women writers—themselves often active participants in the battle of the sexes over the word, space, and construction of femininity—only very few made it in the canon of modernist literature, itself a product of often male categories.[22] Among them are certainly Else Lasker-Schüler, Marieluise Fleißer, and more recently Gertrud Kolmar. Ricarda Huch, too, is often mentioned, but not really read. And Franziska zu Reventlow, Lou Andreas-Salomé and Emmy (Ball-)Hennings might be on their way to being 'rescued' from the exclusionary realm of 'mere' women's literature.[23]

However, another decisive but underexplored constellation deserves mention, namely that of intellectual women as collaborators, co-authors, partners in dialogue, and addressees of male writers and intellectuals. Such constellations of living speech undermine or escape easy integration in (patri)linear narratives or traditions of authorship. Lou von Salomé and Nietzsche were the first ones to dare the modern experiment of a 'writing friendship.'[24] Sixteen days of intense conversations with remarkable 'philosophical openess'—as Nietzsche wrote to a friend about his encounter with Lou Andreas (-Salomé) in August 1882.[25] This was the constellation of a man and a woman, a philosopher and an intellectual, two books, *Wort* and *Antwort*, word and counterword: *Thus Spoke Zarathustra*, written frantically in early 1883 and brandishing the concept of the spoken word in the title, and Andreas-Salomé's *Friedrich Nietzsche in seinen Werken*, begun in fall 1882 and published as a book in 1894, a work that has yet to find its readers. Another major constellation: Franz Rosenzweig's *Star of Redemption* (1921), as we know now, was written day by day to a friend, a lover, Margit Rosenstock, the wife of his friend Eugen Rosenstock. And Margarete Susman, author of *Frauen der Romantik* (1929), *Das Buch Hiob und das Schicksal des jüdischen Volkes* (1946), *Deutung einer grossen Liebe: Goethe und Charlotte von Stein* (1951)—was the 'mistress of thinking in conversation.'[26] The constellations of her friendships with Simmel, Lukács, and Ernst Bloch, and her role as their addressee, interlocutor, and co-thinker, raise unsettling questions about the modern process of writing and thinking, of authorship and gender.[27]

Conversation—living speech—may well be the true home of German modernism, rather than any particular setting. Yet not all modernists felt ambivalent about the idea of home. Nietzsche's most important philosophical successor did not follow him into cosmopolitan homelessness. Martin Heidegger scarcely ever left Germany, though many of his most prominent colleagues and students, most of them Jewish, found deracination from German ground either expedient or necessary: Karl Jaspers, Hannah Arendt, Karl Löwith, Leo Strauss, Hans Jonas, Herbert Marcuse, Günther Anders. In his *Theory of the Modern Novel* (1916), itself a classic of German modernism by another non-German, Georg Lukács famously describes the characteristic modern condition as 'transcendental homelessness.' For many German writers, artists, and intellectuals this condition, metaphorical before 1914, became literal in the aftermath of the Great War with the rise of Nazism. Apart from Nietzsche, the precursors to German modernism were other misfits who wrote about the condition of being without a place in the world: Rahel Levin Varnhagen, Heinrich von Kleist, Friedrich Hölderlin, and Georg Büchner. Marginal, spiritually homeless, and unintelligible in their own time, Levin Varnhagen, Kleist, Hölderlin, and Büchner were figures in whom German modernists discovered themselves and the disenfranchized conditions of their own existence. Together with other precursor figures—including especially Baudelaire, Dostoevsky, Whitman, and Kierkegaard—a counter-tradition emerged. It opposed the spiritually hollow myth of scientific and technological progress and the economic systems and political ideologies, left and right, that this myth fueled. The books that emerged from Eugen Diederichs's publishing house—also called a 'laboratory of religious modernity'—focus this trend in revealing ways.[28]

Estrangement, as from home, and estrangement as detachment from the conventional idiom—of language, of painting, or of music (indeed, from the normative gender)—is a key feature of aesthetic modernism in general and German modernism in particular. Nor does it affect creative artists alone. Novalis describes philosophy as a nostalgic feeling of 'homesickness,' *Heimweh*. The German modernists' preoccupation with themes of alienation, disenchantment, and homelessness is not a sudden tear in the fabric of culture. It reaches back past Marx to Schiller and Novalis, and as Lukács makes plain in his theory of the novel as an alienated form, to Don Quixote and Robinson Crusoe. Lukács appeals directly to Novalis: 'Philosophy is really homesickness,' says Novalis: 'it is the urge to be at home everywhere.'[29] If taken literally, however, the German word *Heimweh* becomes estranged and ambiguous. One may ache with longing for a place or, on the other hand, some virulent place might inflict misery. There is continuity between the modernist period in philosophy and criticism and the global present in criticism and literature. Edward Said is the crucial voice in this continuity of modernist criticism. He emphasizes the 'figure of exile' in his critical writing and draws repeatedly in his work on Erich Auerbach in Turkish exile as an exemplary embodiment of it.[30] Many such German and Austrian figures come to mind linking the practice of criticism not with attachment to place, but with the experience of estrangement from it: Walter Benjamin, Hannah Arendt, Erich Auerbach, Leo Spitzer, Gershom Scholem, Hans Mayer, Peter Demetz, Erich Heller, Peter Szondi, George Steiner, Peter Gay, Geoffrey Hartman, Gershon Shaked, Walter Sokel, Bertha Badt-Strauss, Margarete Susman, Käte Hamburger, Ruth Klüger, Marjorie Perloff, Heinz Politzer, Leo Löwenthal, and many others. Even within German culture, being Jewish (and all of these critics were or are Jews) places the critic in the outsider's perspective. The obverse side of homesickness is the bracing estrangement that sharpens the listening ear, focuses the critical eye, and quickens the intellect.

The site of memory associated with Heidegger is Todtnauberg, the rustic setting of his cottage in the Black Forest. Heidegger's homesickness, his nostalgia for rootedness in place, comes uncomfortably close to the nationalistic cultural perspective of Nora.[31] As a prophet-like thinker, renowned lecturer, university rector, and former member of the Nazi party, Heidegger met there with Paul Celan in 1967. The German poet—a Jew born and raised outside of Germany and only at the outermost provinces of the

Austrian world—did not have a home or homeland in the sense of romantic nationalism that Nora and Heidegger to some degree have in common. Celan's wandering homelessness and Heidegger's picturesquely rustic rootedness: two extremes in the modernist sense of place and placelessness. After the war, after the Shoah, Celan lived out his posthumous life in post-war Paris. Following a public reading of his poetry at the University of Freiburg, the great poet once paid a visit to the great philosopher at his Black Forest cottage, to walk and talk with Heidegger on the philosopher's home ground. The memory of this morally ambiguous place and uneasy meeting are held fast in Celan's poem 'Todtnauberg,' written in 1967 shortly after the visit it describes. It was first published in 1970, the year of Celan's suicide in Paris.[32] Still, the feeling for home stubbornly persists, even in exile—especially in exile. It is not something one has much control over. The tension between home and not-home can be productive. Modernism is the expression of that productivity.

Given the exigencies of German modernism—so many of its places are not German at all, so many of the modernists themselves were both transcendentally and literally homeless, so many of the actual sites on German soil lay in rubble by 1945 (Berlin's central ruin, the Church of Remembrance, is emblematic for many such destroyed places)—it may be useful to think of literature itself as the place of German remembering. Literature is portable, readily available, and ubiquitous. In this, the crucial link to modernism is plain. Because the early and middle twentieth century was so massively violent, so full of cruel reversals and unprecedented national and individual catastrophes, literature plays a conspicuous role in interpreting them, making them available for reflection and exploration. Walter Benjamin pointed out that German soldiers returning from the First World War did not have much to say for themselves upon their return home.[33] The things they saw, the scarcely intelligible events that engulfed them, seemed to lay beyond the reach of the accustomed patterns of speech and tale. Their experiences were so new, the character of violence and suffering so out of scale and unprecedented that the tradition of narrative did not readily accommodate a truthful accounting of what had really happened. A rift opened up between lived experience and the means of expression at the disposal of writers and artists.

This crisis of representation is the crux of modernism itself: the modern world had changed so quickly and radically—the shock of the First World War being only an intensely dramatic moment in the much larger unfolding of a great many historical transformations—that the means of expression available to the imagination appeared to have become inadequate. To write about the unique and protracted horror of the First World War, for example, in the narrative templates established in the novels of Tolstoy or Stendhal or Fontane, would have meant to domesticate, to falsify that experience. Storytelling's old coherencies of diction, structure, and sensibility seemed no longer to apply to changed circumstances: 'The days when people knew, really knew, how to tell stories,' as Rilke's Malte ruefully observes in *The Notebooks of Malte Laurids Brigge* (1910), 'must have been before my time.'[34] In the *Duino Elegies* Rilke speaks of deed without word or image, 'Tun ohne Bild.' The broken and estranged character of modern experience—desultory wandering in Paris is Malte's window on it—calls for new, or at least more tentative, defamiliarized forms of articulation. This writing occurs as 'notebooks,' in Malte's case, not narrative storytelling, just 'Aufzeich-nungen,' a literary equivalent of flâneury. Just as confidence in methodical philosoph-ical systems disintegrates for figures as different as Wittgenstein and Heidegger, so also does confidence in larger coherencies of storytelling.

Traditional narrative and prosody give way to new forms that aim to capture the truths that elude the received techniques. Unprecedented circumstances require un-precedented modes of expression to give them form and so make the accessible, manageable. The term 'modernism' describes the search for expressive forms adequate to the interpretive task that an era of unprecedented experiences imposes on art. The task for art and literature is not, strictly speaking, mimetic, the imitation of outward appearances and actions. Rather the task is to make the world intelligible by giving it articulate form: new kinds of poetry (Trakl and Celan), a new musical language (Schoenberg), a new vocabulary of form in art (Kandinsky, Schwitters, the Expression-ists). Finding one's way in the world is predicated on a truthful view of how things are. This dialogue between the familiar and the alien is basic to art, but is especially obvious in modernism. 'To recognize one's own in the alien, to become at home in it, is the basic movement of the spirit, whose being consists only in returning to itself from what is other,' writes Hans-Georg Gadamer in his classic study of hermenutics.[35] Gadamer lived through the era of the First World War and the catastrophes that followed. He was intensely aware of its art in relation to the strangeness of modern experience. His hermeneutic philosophy and literary criticism—especially on the poetry of Paul Celan—turn on this dialectic between the strange and the familiar, and are of a piece with modernism. Above all he emphasizes the relation of art to truth.[36] Artistic innovation for its own sake has always been a distraction in modernism.[37] The decisive feature in modernist art is art for the sake of truth.

Moreover, no aspect of the cultural life is exempt from the modern, including that which is most conservative and most traditional. Like any other artistic activity translation, too, bears the marks of history. Consider the Bible translation undertaken by Franz Rosenzweig and Martin Buber.[38] The first volume of *Die Schrift* appeared in 1925, and it was ultimately completed in 1961—in Jerusalem, the scene of Buber's post-Shoah exile. It belongs among the most significant achievements of literary modernism in German. The translators' aim was, in part, to shock the bourgeoisie, but not gratuitously. Rather, they intended to restore to German Jews and Christians alike—and to the German language itself—a sense of Hebrew Scripture's claim on and challenge to the modern mind.[39] The Luther Bible had become too complacently unquestioned a cultural possession, they argued, its language eroded through famil-iarity. In order to bring modern readers into a living dialogue with the Bible, estrange-ment was necessary. In modernism, estrangement is always the basic tactic of renewal. To achieve a productive defamiliarization, Buber and Rosenzweig crafted an idiosyn-cratic, highly literal and etymologically informed German idiom that suggested the Bible's voice was different from the easy intelligibility of everyday speech. This lan-guage was and remains 'difficult', and calls upon the reader to work for understanding, to enter into active dialogue with the Bible. In their view, Holy Scripture is not a receptacle for historical or universal truths, the way a shoe box might contain a pair of shoes. Instead, the Bible is the place at which an encounter occurs, and this engagement has the temporal character of a two-way conversation. Consequently, the oral and aural dimensions of the German language—which is to say its poetry—takes on crucial importance for Buber and Rosenzweig. This Bible is not a repository of inflexible written laws and commandments, but an open-ended tradition of living, breathing speech that *speaks* to the present and responds to its questions. The emphasis on truth as a matter not of settled fact, but of fluid mobility is a motif that recurs in modernism from its earliest defining moments.

The trajectory of European and German modernism begins, at the latest, with Baudelaire's *Les Fleurs du Mal* (1855). The purport of his modernism is succinctly glossed in his essay, 'On the Painter of Modern Life' (1859–1860). Baudelaire saw that modern life was on the cusp of radical changes and would require of poetry and painting an acute sense of the unprecedented transformations underway: 'By 'modernity' I mean the ephemeral, the fugitive, the contingent, the half of art whose other half is the eternal and the immutable.'[40] Such art is not, strictly speaking, mimetic in the nineteenth-century's sense that Rilke regarded as no longer viable for the new century. It does not imitate fixed appearances. Rather, it seeks to estrange appearances and in so doing to open to view an underlying, ephemeral truth.

One of the German-language modernists to think most searchingly about this reformulation is Robert Musil. Every *thing*, as he frames this basic thought in *The Man without Qualities*, is a petrified variant of its own manifold possibilities. 'Any order, he says, if you take it too seriously gets to be somehow absurd and like a wax figurine. Any thing is a frozen, individual instance of all its possibilities. But these are not doubts. Rather, they are a dynamic, elastic indeterminacy capable of anything.'[41] Musil saw the task of fiction as finding a way to express the fluid, dynamic nature of underlying reality without reifying and so falsifying it. 'Truth,' as Ulrich, his man without defining characteristics says, 'is not a crystal that you can slip into your pocket. Instead, it is an endless fluid that you fall into.'[42]

How is the endlessly fluid mobility of life to be expressed in fixed words of a novel or a poem? For Musil the answer lay in the nature of language. If language has the power to fix thoughts, feelings, and experiences in a permanent shape, then Musil also seeks an element or function within language that militates against its Medusan power to fossilize living experience into a caricature of itself, something that gives narrative a life of its own instead of reiterating a predetermined meaning. He found this element in the unstable character of metaphorical and other figurative language. The living reality of the ethical, in Musil's view, is the reality of the soul. Metaphor—because of its unfixed nature—is able to follow what he thought of as 'die gleitende Logik der Seele' (the gliding or floating logic of the soul). For Musil the task of fiction and poetry is not to illustrate some already established and accepted moral or psychological norm. Law, custom, convention, psychiatry, philosophy, and codes of behavior all do a more or less adequate job of this already. Why duplicate in art what has already been established with great and perhaps excessive clarity and force elsewhere? It demotes art to mere illustration and superfluity.

For the modernist, art and literature have cognitive force and should not merely duplicate other forms of cognition. The common thought that stories are simply a roundabout way of inculcating (i.e. teaching) ideas and morals radically underestimates the place of narrative in our lives. Poetry is elementally cognitive, a way of exploring the world and seeing it anew, and perhaps of grasping some things that can in no other way be apprehended—not by science, law, philosophy, religion, or mathematics. In Musil's view at least, art and narrative should hold themselves apart from the institutions that codify knowledge. Rather, the task of art is truthfully to explore and express those aspects of living that are inchoate, the undefined experiences, formless thoughts, and ephemeral moments that cannot be made visible or intelligible in any other way.

Nineteenth-century realism sought to produce the verisimilar illusion of concrete events. The modernist imagination seeks an art that reveals the ephemeral and the spiritual as well. Art makes estranged experience emotionally, intellectually, and morally available. It is the task of language and, especially of literature, to give shape and definition to human experience. Hence the importance of a work such as James Joyce's *Ulysses* (1922), which appeared to define a new path of expression.

Joyce's *Ulysses* remains the defining masterpiece of European modernism in literature. Or is it Kafka's *Castle* (1922, published posthumously in 1926)? The choice is difficult, which is strange: apart from the basic theme of exile the two works have practically nothing in common. Moreover, the contrast is revealing when it comes to understanding the particularity of German modernism vis-à-vis European modernism in general. Joyce's confident appeal to myth and epic, to eternal recurrence and timelessness, to the power of the word to express self and world is steeped in tradition. It is reflected in his manifold styles, his traditional symbolism, and above all in the sheer exuberance of his verbal imagination. This language takes hold of the world and shakes it, never doubting its grip. Joyce not so much makes a turn away from the great realist tradition of nineteenth-century European fiction as offer a grand culmination of it, one that extends the reach of fiction into inward life and to every aspect of outward life that had previously been excluded. Indeed, Joyce's place in the realist tradition is so understood even in Erich Auerbach's crucial study *Mimesis*, though the critic focuses on Virginia Woolf's related achievement, rather than directly on Joyce's *Ulysses*. Joyce and Woolf are easy to place: in Dublin and London, *and* in the realist tradition. Joyce and Woolf, with Proust the last great novelists of the nineteenth century, do not question the power of language to reproduce both inner and outer life. Theirs is an exploration of plenitude, an art of recovery, an apotheosis of the word. Joyce, the Irish exile, recovers Dublin in *Ulysses*; Proust's Marcel, narrator of *In Search of Lost Time*, recovers his rich past in the telling of his tale as orderly narrative. Woolf's Clarissa Dalloway is nothing if not at home in the cozy world the novelist celebrates.

Kafka can take no such place in Auerbach's vision. He explores not plenitude, but the nooks and crannies of defeat, loss, and what his nearest kindred spirit in English and French, Samuel Beckett, has called 'lessness.' Beckett gave *Losigkeit* as the German equivalent.[43] No past is regained, no place reconstituted, no home restored. Still, this approach must be recognized for what it is, and it is not a passive collapse into despair. It is active *exploration*, a pressing forward by the means of art into *terra incognita*. Unlike Pound and Yeats, Eliot and Joyce, Proust and Woolf, the German modernists wonder critically about what the limitations of language might be. Here is one of W. G. Sebald's stunningly articulate protagonists pondering a sentence of his own composition:

> All I could think was that such a sentence only appears to mean something, but is in truth at best a makeshift expedient, a kind of unhealthy growth issuing from our ignorance, something which we use, in the same way as many sea plants and animals use their tentacles, to grope blindly through the darkness enveloping us.[44]

The larger passage from which this sentence is excerpted plainly alludes to Hofmannsthal's classic *The Lord Chandos Letter* of 1902, which concerns a writer paralyzed by the realization of how much crucial human experience will always exceed the grasp of language. Moreover, Sebald is not simply responding to the German modernist tradition; he is participating in it. The world always exceeds language. In the tradition of German modernist narrative there are no Joycean mythic patterns, no Nietzschean eternal recurrences, no Freudian or Jungian psychological constants, no falling back on religious or philosophical doctrine, received wisdom, or conceptual certainties of any sort. Instead, there is a modest, but intensely powerful concentration on the specific, the singular, the immediate, 'the half of art of which the other half is the eternal and the immutable.' The most strikingly original German-language modernists—including Kafka and Trakl, Walser and Musil and Celan, Benn and Lasker-Schüler, Handke, Bachmann, Jelinek, and Thomas Bernhard—focus more on the unrepeatable strangeness of the unique here-and-now. This desire to affirm the singular moment, even when it is very dark, belongs to that part that Baudelaire stakes out as the truest terrain of modernism.

Notes

1. For scholarship that attempts a larger integration of German or other national modernism into the larger context see bibliography.
2. Pierre Nora and Lawrence D. Kritzman (eds), *Realms of Memory: Rethinking the French Past. European Perspectives* (New York: Columbia University Press, 1996), 1, xii. See also Nora's comments on the ways in which the three-volume German follow-up to the successful French undertaking is different: Pierre Nora, 'Nachwort,' in Etienne François and Hagen Schulze (eds), *Deutsche Erinnerungsorte*, 3 vols (Munich: Beck, 2001), 3, 681–687.
3. Hans Rudolf Vaget, 'Kaisersaschern als geistige Lebensform: Zur Konzeption der deutschen Geschichte in Thomas Manns *Doktor Faustus*,' in Wolfgang Paulsen (ed.), *Der deutsche Roman und seine historischen und politischen Bedingungen* (Berne and Munich: Francke, 1977), 200–235.
4. Emphasizing geographic space over national identity, see the different approaches by Peter Demetz, *Prague in Black and Gold* (New York: Hill and Wang, 1997); Derek Sayer,

The Coasts of Bohemia (Princeton: Princeton University Press, 1998), and Scott Spector, *Prague Territories* (Berkeley: University of California Press, 2000).

5. Peter Gay, *Freud, Jews, and other Germans* (New York: Oxford University Press, 1978), 31.

6. It is a point Gay has made often, see for example his essay, 'The Last Philosophe: "Our God Logos,"' in *A Godless Jew: Freud, Atheism and the Making of Psychoanalysis* (New Haven: Yale University Press, 1987), 35–68.

7. 'Ich fühle luft von anderem planeten' is the first line of Stefan George's 'Entrückung,' a poem from his lyric cycle *Der siebente Ring* (Berlin: Blätter für die Kunst, 1907). Schoenberg sets this unearthly poem in the fourth, vocal movement of his Second String Quartet (Op. 10) of 1907–1908.

8. David Ferrell Krell and Donald L. Bates, *The Good European: Nietzsche's Work Sites in Word and Image* (Chicago: University of Chicago Press, 1997).

9. Theodor Adorno, 'Refuge for the Homeless,' in *Minima Moralia: Reflections from a Damaged Life*, trans. E. F. N. Jephcott (London: Verso, 1978), 39.

10. For the most recent comprehensive overview see Gangolf Hübinger and Helen Müller, 'Politische, konfessionelle und weltanschauliche Verlage im Kaiserreich,' in Georg Jäger (ed.), *Geschichte des deutschen Buchhandels im 19. und 20. Jahrhundert*, vol. 1, *Das Kaiserreich 1871–1918*, part 1 (Frankfurt am Main: Buchhändler-Vereinigung, 2001), 347–405, as well as Reinhard Wittmann, *Geschichte des deutschen Buchhandels* (Munich: Beck, 1999), 295–359.

11. Helmut von den Steinen, *Das moderne Buch* (Heidelberg: Unger, 1912), 26–30, as well as Celsus's (i.e. Carl von Ossietzky) obituary, 'Eugen Diederichs,' in *Die Weltbühne* 26, No. 38, 16 September 1930.

12. Eugen Diederichs, *Lebensaufbau. Skizze zu einer Selbstbiographie 1920/21.* Typescript (Deutsches Literaturarchiv Marbach, NL Eugen Diederichs), 47. For Diederichs with extensive references to current scholarship see also Meike G. Werner, *Moderne in der Provinz. Kulturelle Experimente im Fin de Siècle Jena* (Göttingen: Wallstein, 2003), 63–193 and id., 'Provincial Modernism. Jena as Publishing Program,' in *Germanic Review* 76, no. 4 (2001), 319–334.

13. Friedrich Nietzsche, *Nachgelassene Fragmente 1884–1885. Kritische Studienausgabe*, ed. Giorgio Colli and Mazzino Montinari, vol. 11 (Munich: DTV, 1999), 33; cited in Stefan Breuer, 'Kulturpessimist, Antimodernist, konservativer Revolutionär? Zur Position von Eugen Diederichs im Ideologiespektrum der wilhelminischen Ära,' in Justus H. Ulbricht and Meike G. Werner (eds), *Romantik, Revolution & Reform. Der Eugen Diederichs Verlag im Epochenkontext 1900–1949* (Göttingen: Wallstein, 1999), 36–59, here 41.

14. Georg Simmel, 'The Metropolis and Mental Life,' in Simmel, *On Individuality and Social Forms: Selected Writings, ed.* with an introduction by Donald N. Levine (Chicago and London: University of Chicago Press, 1971), 324–339.

15. Peter Zimmermann, *Der Bauernroman. Antifeudalismus—Konservatismus—Faschismus* (Stuttgart: Metzler, 1975); Helmuth Kiesel, *Geschichte der literarischen Moderne: Sprache, Ästhetik, Dichtung im zwanzigsten Jahrhundert* (Munich: C.H. Beck, 2004), 53–64.

16. Jochen Meyer, 'Berlin Provinz: Literarische Kontroversen um 1930,' in *Marbacher Magazin* 35 (Marbach: Deutsche Schillergesellschaft, 1985), here 4.

17. Here and the following Walter Benjamin, *Kritiken und Rezensionen*, ed. Hella Tiedemann-Bartels, vol 3, *Gesammelte Schriften*, (Frankfurt am Main: Suhrkamp, 1991), 189–191, cited in Kiesel, *Geschichte der literarischen Moderne*, 57.

18. Bettine Menke, 'Verstellt—der Ort der "Frau." Ein Nachwort,' in Barbara Vinken (ed.), *Dekonstruktiver Feminismus. Literaturwissenschaft in Amerika* (Frankfurt am Main: Suhrkamp, 1992), 436–476.

19. Susanne Kord, *Sich einen Namen machen. Anonymität und weibliche Autorschaft 1700–1900* (Stuttgart and Weimar: Metzler, 1996).

20. For a detailed presentation of their works, see the essays by Chris Weedon and Sabine Werner-Birkenbach in Jo Catling (ed.), *A History of Women's Writing in Germany, Austria and Switzerland* (Cambridge: Cambridge University Press, 2000), 111–145; Karin Tebben (ed.), *Deutschsprachige Schriftstellerinnen des Fin de Siècle* (Darmstadt: Wissenschaftliche Buchgesellschaft, 1999); Gisela Brinker-Gabler (ed.), *Deutsche Literatur von Frauen*, vol. 2, *19. und 20. Jahrhundert* (Munich: Beck, 1988).

21. Sandra M. Gilbert and Susan Gubar, *No Man's Land. The Place of the Woman Writer in the Twentieth Century*, vol. 1, *The War of the Words* (New Haven and London: Yale University Press, 1987), 130–131.

22. Very instructive are Renate von Heydebrand and Simone Winko, 'Geschlechterdifferenz und literarischer Kanon. Historische Beobachtungen und systematische Überlegungen,' in *Internationales Archiv für Sozialgeschichte der deutschen Literatur* 19 (1994), 96–172.

23. A critical anthology like Bonnie Kime Scott's *The Gender of Modernism* (Bloomington: Indiana University Press, 1990)—dedicated to the 'forgotten and silenced makers of modernism'—could be an interesting and inspiring project of rethinking and redefining the canon of German modernism.

24. Here and the following Barbara Hahn, 'Freundschaft schreiben. Intellektuelle Konstellationen nach Nietzsche,' in Ulrike Bergermann and Elisabeth Strowick (eds), *Weiterlesen. Literatur und Wissen* (Bielefeld: transcript, 2007), 31–44.

25. Nietzsche to Franz Overbeck, September 9, 1882, cited in Hahn, 'Freundschaft schreiben,' 31.

26. Hahn, 'Freundschaft schreiben,' 39.

27. For more such constellations of writing and thinking between intellectual women and male writers see Barbara Hahn, *Unter falschem Namen. Von der schwierigen Autorschaft der Frauen* (Frankfurt am Main: Suhrkamp, 1991).

28. Friedrich Wilhelm Graf, 'Das Laboratorium der religiösen Moderne. Zur "Verlagsreligion" des Eugen Diederichs Verlags,' in Gangolf Hübinger (ed.), *Versammlungsort moderner Geister. Der Eugen Diederichs Verlag—Aufbruch ins Jahrhundert der Extreme* (Munich: Diederichs, 1996), 243–298; and Heinz Dieter Kittsteiner, 'Romantisches Denken in der entzauberten Welt,' ibid, 486–504.

29. Georg Lukács, *Theory of the Novel*, trans. Anna Bostock (Cambridge: MIT Press, 1990), 29.

30. Edward Said, 'Erich Auerbach, Critic of the Earthly World,' *Boundary* 2, 31.2 (2004), 11–34; see also Edward Said, 'The Mind of Winter: Reflections on Life in Exile,' *Harper's Magazine* (September 1984), 49–55.

31. Cf. the classic critique by Robert Minder, 'Heidegger und Hebel oder die Sprache von Messkirch,' in his *Dichter in der Gesellschaft: Erfahrungen mit deutscher und französischer Literatur* (Frankfurt am Main: Insel, 1966), 210–264.

32. Paul Celan, *Lichtzwang* (Frankfurt am Main: Suhrkamp, 1970), 29–30. Cf. Hans-Georg Gadamer, *Philosophical Apprenticeships*, trans. Robert R. Sullivan (Cambridge: MIT Press, 1985), 52–54. Cf. also John K. Lyon, *Paul Celan and Martin Heidegger: An Unresolved Conversation, 1951–1970* (Baltimore: Johns Hopkins, 2006), 159–191.

33. Walter Benjamin, 'Erfahrung und Armut,' in *Illuminationen: Ausgewählte Schriften*, ed. Siegfried Unseld (Frankfurt am Main: Suhrkamp, 1955), 313–318.

34. Rainer Maria Rilke, *The Notebooks of Malte Laurids Brigge*, trans. Stephen Mitchell with an introduction by William Gass (New York: Vintage, 1985), 146.

35. Hans-Georg Gadamer, *Truth and Method*, trans. Joel Weinsheimer and Donald Marshall, 2nd edn (London: Continuum, 1989), 13. See also the essays collected in his *Gadamer on Celan: Who Am I and Who Are You? and Other Essays*, trans. Richard Heinemann and Bruce Krajewski (Albany: State University of New York Press, 1997).

36. On Gadamer in the context of his philosophical, intellectual, and artistic era see esp. Donatella Di Cesare, *Gadamer—Ein philosophisches Porträt* (Tübingen: Mohr Siebeck, 2009).

37. Empty originality is the flipside of kitsch. Kitsch is a problem that comes to the fore in the era of modernism. The comforting flight into banal conventions of the past is kitsch when and because it fails to reveal truth. However, artsy, spuriously 'progressive' work is also a form of kitsch when it reveals nothing but ambition, or supposedly sophisticated taste, or novelty for its own sake, or the desire to secure a place in the market of art and celebrity. See esp. Hermann Broch, 'Einige Bemerkungen zum Problem des Kitsches,' in *Hermann Broch. Schriften zur Literatur*, ed. Paul Michael Lützeler (Frankfurt am Main: Suhrkamp, 1975), 158–176. Cf. Karsten Harries, *The Meaning of Modern Art: A Philosophical Investigation* (Evanston: Northwestern University Press, 1968), 74–83.

38. Klaus Reichert, *Die unendliche Aufgabe. Zum Übersetzen* (Munich: Hanser, 2003), esp. 151–198. Also Siegfried Kracauer's very critical review 'Die Bibel auf Deutsch' in *Frankfurter Zeitung*, April 27, 1926, reprinted in Siegfried Kracauer, *Das Ornament der Masse. Essays* (Frankfurt am Main: Suhrkamp, 1977), 173–186; and Margarete Susman's positive response, 'Eine neue Übersetzung der Heiligen Schrift,' in *Basler Nachrichten*, February 18–19, 1928 (literary supplement to no. 49), n.p.

39. Martin Buber and Franz Rosenzweig, *Die Schrift und ihre Verdeutschung* (Berlin: Schocken, 1936), trans. Lawrence Rosenwald with Everett Fox as *Scripture and Translation* (Bloomington: Indiana University Press, 1994).

40. Charles Baudelaire, *The Painter of Modern Life and Other Essays*, trans. and ed. Jonathan Mayne (New York: Da Capo, 1986), 13.

41. Robert Musil, *Gesammelte Werke* (Reinbek bei Hamburg: Rowohlt, 1978), 5:1509.

42. Musil, *Gesammelte Werke*, 2:533–34.

43. E. M. Cioran, *Anathemas and Admirations*, trans. Richard Howard (New York: Arcade, 1991), 131.

44. W. G. Sebald, *Austerlitz*, trans. Anthea Bell (New York: Modern Library, 2001), 124.

Bibliography

Beller, Steven (ed.), *Rethinking Vienna* (New York: Berghahn, 2001).

Belting, Hans, *Art History after Modernism*, trans. Caroline Saltzwedel and Cohen Mitch, with additional translation by Kenneth Northcott (Chicago: University of Chicago Press, 2003).

——, *The Germans and their Art: A Troublesome Relationship*, trans. Scott Kleager (New Haven and London: Yale University Press, 1998).

BILSKI, EMILY D. (ed.), *Berlin Metropolis. Jews and the New Culture 1890–1918* (Berkeley, Los Angeles, London: University of California Press, 1999).

BRADBURY, MALCOLM and JAMES MCFARLANE (eds), *Modernism. A Guide to European Literature 1890–1930* (London: Pelican, 1976, reprinted with a new preface in Penguin Books, 1991).

BRINKER-GABLER, GISELA (ed.), *Deutsche Literatur von Frauen*, vol. 2, *19. und 20. Jahrhundert* (Munich: Beck, 1988).

BUTLER, CHRISTOPHER, *Early Modernism: Literature, Music and Painting in Europe, 1900–1916* (Oxford: Clarendon Press, 1994).

CALINESCU, MATEI, *Five Faces of Modernity: Modernism, Avant-Garde, Decadence, Kitsch, Postmodernism* (Durham: Duke University Press, 1987).

CATLING, JO (ed.), *A History of Women's Writing in Germany, Austria and Switzerland* (Cambridge: Cambridge University Press, 2000).

CLARK, T. J., *Farewell to an Idea: Episodes from a History of Modernism* (New Haven: Yale University Press, 1999).

DEMETZ, PETER, *Prague in Black and Gold. Scenes from the Life of a European City* (New York: Hill and Wang, 1997).

DI CESARE, DONATELLA, *Gadamer—Ein philosophisches Porträt* (Tübingen: Mohr Siebeck, 2009).

DOWDEN, STEPHEN D., *Sympathy for the Abyss: Study in the Novel of German Modernism— Kafka, Broch, Musil and Thomas Mann* (Tübingen: Niemeyer, 1986).

——, *Kafka's The Castle and the Critical Imagination* (Columbia: Camden House, 1995).

EVERDELL, WILLIAM R., *The First Moderns: Profiles in the Origins of Twentieth-Century Thought* (Chicago: University of Chicago Press, 1997).

FRISCH, WALTER, *German Modernism: Music and the Arts* (Berkeley: University of California Press, 2004).

GAY, PETER, *Modernism. The Lure of Heresy* (New York: W.W. Norton, 2007).

GRIMMINGER, ROLF, MURAŠOV JURIJ and STÜCKRATH JÖRN (eds), *Literarische Moderne. Europäische Literatur im 19. und 20. Jahrhundert* (Reinbek bei Hamburg: Rowohlt, 1995).

HAHN, BARBARA, *Unter falschem Namen. Von der schwierigen Autorschaft der Frauen* (Frankfurt am Main: Suhrkamp, 1991).

JANIK, ALLAN and STEPHEN TOULMIN, *Wittgenstein's Vienna* (New York: Simon and Schuster, 1973).

JELAVICH, PETER, *Berlin Alexanderplatz. Radio, Film, and the Death of Weimar Culture* (Berkeley: University of California Press, 2006).

KIESEL, HELMUTH, *Geschichte der literarischen Moderne: Sprache, Ästhetik, Dichtung im zwanzigsten Jahrhundert* (Munich: C. H. Beck, 2004).

LORENZ, DAGMAR, *Wiener Moderne* (Stuttgart, Weimar: Metzler, 1995).

PARET, PETER. *German Encounters with Modernism: 1840–1945* (New York: Cambridge University Press, 2001).

SCHLÖGEL, KARL, *Jenseits des Großen Oktober. Das Laboratorium der Moderne. Petersburg 1909–1921* (Berlin: Siedler, 1988).

SCHORSKE, CARL E., *Thinking with History: Explorations in the Passage to Modernism* (Princeton: Princeton University Press, 1998).

——, *Fin-de-Siècle Vienna. Politics and Culture* (New York: Vintage, 1981).

SCHUTTE, JÜRGEN and PETER SPRENGEL (eds), *Die Berliner Moderne 1885–1914* (Stuttgart: Reclam, 1987).

SPECTOR, SCOTT, *Prague Territories. National Conflict and Cultural Innovation in Franz Kafka's Fin de Siècle* (Berkeley: University of California Press, 2000).

TEBBEN, KARIN (ed.), *Deutschsprachige Schriftstellerinnen des Fin de Siècle* (Darmstadt: Wissenschaftliche Buchgesellschaft, 1999).

WERNER, MEIKE G., *Moderne in der Provinz. Kulturelle Experimente im Fin de Siècle Jena* (Göttingen: Wallstein, 2003).

WILLIAMS, RAYMOND, *The Politics of Modernism: Against the New Conformists* (London: Verso, 1989).

WUNBERG, GOTTHART and JOHANNES J. BRAAKENBURG (eds), *Die Wiener Moderne. Literatur, Kunst und Musik zwischen 1890 und 1910* (Stuttgart: Reclam, 1981).

CHAPTER 22

NATIONALISM IN THE ERA OF THE NATION STATE, 1870–1945

PIETER M. JUDSON

UNDER the first German nation state (1870–1945), nationalism became a more potent and, occasionally, a destabilizing force in politics and social life than it had previously been in German society. With the creation of a German nation state, governments and administrators began to treat nationalism as a legitimate tool for the promotion of their official policies at the same time that all manner of activists, politicians, journalists, and reformers used nationalist rhetoric to legitimate their diverse programs for Germany and claims on the state. Although nationalists' programs sought to forge social stability by unifying Germans divided by region, class, and confession in a national community, their activism could produce the opposite effect. Issues such as the national interest, membership in the nation, or the state's effectiveness at pursuing the national interest became at times the subjects of heated public debate with a potential to produce political instability. Debates such as these were hardly new to German society, but after 1870 issues such as the character of the German nation or membership in the national community became legal and administrative questions, not simply subjects of political or philosophical discussion. Germany's rulers often found themselves walking a fine line between encouraging a nationalist activism they believed could help to unify the new German society and dampening nationalism's more radical manifestations. This balancing act became especially apparent around 1900 as nationalists increasingly used mass appeals tinged with ideological radicalism to question the ability of Germany's conservative rulers to represent the interests of the national community adequately and effectively.

For many years historians viewed nationalism as a tool wielded largely by Germany's highly conservative rulers for the purpose of manipulating political life in a rapidly industrializing society. Nationalist and patriotic enthusiasm in Imperial German society, it was believed, had papered over growing differences among interest groups by deflecting popular attention away from social and economic complaints.[1] This argument saw Germany's pursuit of an ambitious colonial policy in the 1880s and 1890s, and its increasingly aggressive foreign policy choices after 1900, as products of a dangerous attempt by the elite to incite nationalist feeling and thereby master the domestic political opposition. There are two obvious disadvantages to viewing German nationalism in this framework. In the first place, while it may be tempting to see nationalism largely in terms of the policies and practices of the nation state, doing so would hide from view the vitality of social movements in an age of mass politics that wrapped their own claims against the state in the mantle of nationalism. Popular nationalism in Germany was far more a product of the imaginative rhetorical and organizational strategies devised by activists than it was a product of state manipulation. In the second place, viewing nationalism as a product of elite manipulation forces us to view it as a fundamentally unifying force in society, rather than seeing its often unpredictable and destabilizing dynamic qualities.

The proclamation of the German Empire in 1871 transformed the challenges Germany's small and relatively elite groups of nationalists had recently faced. With the birth of the federal German state nationalists transferred their efforts from the achievement of political unification to the creation of a unified national society. They continued to justify their programs by claiming to speak for the national community even as their key goal was to create such a community in the first place. From the start, the project of nationalizing Germany's citizens faced several unexpected obstacles. At first, existing regional loyalties and popular devotion to familiar symbols, rituals, and practices of local politics (not necessarily to local regimes) continued to provide many educated Germans with a more compelling sense of identification than did an unfamiliar German nation state dominated by Prussia. To local observers, the dimensions and qualities of the new Germany often seemed more abstract than real. Despite aggressive nationalist propaganda churned out by reputable historians, writers, and journalists, segments of the educated population in parts of Baden, Saxony, Bavaria, or Württemberg viewed the German nation state with skepticism, often precisely because the new state broke so dramatically with familiar practices and traditions.[2]

The challenge to nationalists was to produce and popularize a unifying idea that would attract German citizens of diverse backgrounds, religions, and regional practices. However, in the early years after 1871, most nationalists produced relatively narrow and triumphalist understandings of the German national community. The qualities that defined Germanness for these early activists derived largely from their own Protestant religious affiliation and bourgeois class experience.[3] Most nationalists had belonged to National Liberal parties in the various federal states; they were men who had agitated for small-German (*kleindeutsch*) unification under Prussia for two decades. Their efforts tended to reach a limited public for whom bourgeois and Protestant narratives of nationhood already held a kind of common sense persuasiveness.[4] In their efforts the National Liberals profited enormously from their political collaboration with the Prussian leader Otto von Bismarck, architect of unification and Chancellor of the new

Germany. In the 1870s Bismarck's policies directed against the Catholic hierarchy (the so-called *Kulturkampf*) appeared to lend government support to a particular liberal and Protestant conviction about what constituted German nationhood. It encouraged the National Liberals to question openly whether Germany's Catholics could ever legitimately be considered part of the national community. The government's persecution of clerics, newspaper editors, and laymen, who had allegedly defied the new laws, not only produced a popular Catholic backlash, but also confirmed for many Germans that the new nation was in fact a narrowly partisan Liberal and Prussian creation.[5]

Their desire to diminish the influence of political Catholicism, especially in the Southern German states and among Polish-speakers in the East, was only one concern that animated the liberals to support the *Kulturkampf*. Liberal enthusiasm for the *Kulturkampf* ultimately derived less from questions of Church state relations than from deeper presumptions about the nation's fundamental values. Liberal Protestant writers habitually associated Catholicism with a culture of feminine dependence unworthy of a nation of independent citizens because it allegedly subjected people to an absolutist form of belief and political rule. By contrast, the liberals' vision of the new Germany rested on a middle-class masculine ideal of personal independence and active citizenship that they explicitly associated with their Protestant beliefs. Liberals also accused Catholicism of fostering international loyalties at the expense of national ones, loyalties that they also associated with Germany's linguistic minorities, most of whom also happened to be Catholics. Along with the taint of their alleged indifference to the national community, liberal writers also associated both Catholicism and linguistic diversity with ignorance, superstition, economic backwardness, and untoward foreign influence. Some liberals like historian Heinrich von Treitschke doubted that a society troubled by religious and ethnic diversity could ever succeed as a national society.[6] As an illustration of this fear they pointed to the Habsburg Monarchy whose Catholic status and linguistic diversity allegedly required the imposition of absolutist forms of rule that they considered unworthy of Germany's free citizens.[7]

National liberal efforts to forge a more unified nation of Germans that rejected religious and ethnic diversity merely intensified ideological division at every level of society. In political terms, the *Kulturkampf* helped create a mass-based Catholic Center Party that sought to unite German Catholics of all classes and regions in defense against state persecution. In social and cultural terms the *Kulturkampf* also produced popular irritation and some suspicion against the very idea of nation. To some Germans the public invocations of the 'nation' in local rituals implied the Liberals' particular version of nationhood, and this is reflected in accounts of failed local celebrations of national unity in the 1870s and early 1880s. While specific commemorations of the war against France appealed to most Germans, for example, they tended to view annual Sedan day celebrations as National Liberal events.[8]

Over time, the end to the *Kulturkampf* policies, and the increasing experience of living in a German nation state made nationalism a more popular phenomenon throughout Germany. By the 1890s nationalists had more successfully linked inclusive concepts of nation to familiar local traditions and loyalties.[9] With the waning of the

Kulturkampf in the 1880s, the goals of the state in propagating nationalist values and ideologies had also parted company from the efforts of the early nationalist activists. Reversing course, the state gradually sought to integrate Germany's Catholics more fully into the national community. Official state nationalism sought to stabilize society by minimizing the confessional and regional conflicts of an earlier era and by unifying different social forces around policies that appealed specifically to nationalist or patriotic sentiment. Some versions of this *Sammlungspolitik* tried to unify differing groups on the basis of their common support for German colonialism, or, more frequently, on the basis of their common hostility to internationalist socialism. By the 1890s, the rhetorical challenges posed by the Social Democratic Party (SPD) to the regime offered Germany's chancellors promising new opportunities to build coalitions among a broad array of groups whose joint antipathy to socialism purchased a tenuous nationalist unity.

Despite the ideological attractions of this *Sammlungspolitik*, many nationalist activists and organizations refused to follow the lead of the state, treating such initiatives with caution and even with cynicism and suspicion. Those activists who had seen Catholicism as a fundamental danger to the German nation, for example, did not simply abandon their anti-Catholicism just because Bismarck had done so. At issue for them was not national unification, but rather the *terms* under which it would be accomplished; not the national community as a fact, but the *way* that this community was to be imagined.[10] Many Protestant liberals continued to assert their highly specific vision of the nation for Germany, warning that accommodation with Catholicism would undermine precisely those qualities that made the German nation distinctive and strong. In 1887, for example, the founders of an organization designed to build support for this perspective, the Protestant League, typically asserted that while government concessions to Catholics might purchase a degree of national unity, it would be at the cost of subverting the very character and identity of the nation.

In the 1880s, thanks largely to Bismarck's enormous personal prestige in nationalist circles, this kind of rivalry between proponents of state and more narrowly defined forms of nationalism had remained muted. Another issue that rallied nationalists behind the state and where both appeared to share a more ethnic definition of nation was in their common desire for a Germanization of Prussia's Eastern provinces in the 1880s. In 1871 Germany's Polish-speakers had comprised around 6% of the population of the new state.[11] This seemingly small percentage masked the fact that in several Prussian districts, Polish speakers constituted over 80% of the population.[12] Bismarck's pursuit of the *Kulturkampf* in the 1870s had derived in part from his concern about potential resistance to the new state from Polish-speaking Catholics. Many of Bismarck's subsequent policies, including limiting the use of Polish language in the public sphere and weakening the influence of the Catholic Church, constituted forcible attempts to assimilate Germany's Polish-speaking citizens into a German national community.[13] When these measures failed over time to produce the desired results, however, Bismarck sought to diminish the size of the Polish-speaking population through even harsher measures that included the outright deportation of (non-citizen) migrant laborers to Russia. To support these ends the Prussian government had long pursued a small-scale policy of German ethnic land colonization in the East, founding a Royal Prussian Settlement Commission in 1866 that bought land held by Polish estate owners, divided it up, and sold parcels at subsidized rates to German farmers from the West.[14] Over time, however, the colonization policy had aggravated relations between the more radical nationalists and traditional conservatives in Prussia. Conservatives—especially large estate owners—relied on cheap Polish-speaking migrant labor from Russia and opposed nationalist demands to end this practice. Radical nationalists meanwhile, dissatisfied with the small-scale efforts of the colonization commission, demanded an end to the migration of cheap labor into Germany and the forcible division of more Polish estates into family-sized plots to benefit German settlers.

The government's ambivalent policies—what nationalists would call half measures—reflected its attempt to balance its concerns about the potentially subversive activities of Polish nationalist activists against the need for agricultural labor on the great estates. However the nationalist presumption (German or Polish) that use of the Polish language somehow expressed an individual's Polish national loyalty or rejection of Germany reflected a fundamental misreading of local conditions. Whether or to what extent Poles (those with a sense of Polish national identity) and Polish-speakers in Prussia identified with any nation is a question that cannot easily be answered, as several local studies have demonstrated. The very idea of understanding Germany's Eastern borderland regions primarily in terms of a war to the death between Poles and Germans was more often a projection by German and Polish nationalists of their own thinking onto events in these regions. Many Polish speakers, for example, considered themselves to be loyal citizens of Imperial Germany, and daily life in Silesia or Posen bore little resemblance to the stories of eternal nationalist struggle propagated by activists. Nor did long-term voting patterns in the East betray fundamental or authentic national loyalties. The degree to which Polish-speaking Prussians gave their votes to Polish nationalist parties or to the (German) Catholic Center Party in Silesia, for example, depended more on the situational ability of one or the other party to represent issues of local concern, than on the national identification of their voters.[15]

The government's periodic bans on Polish language schools or the use of Polish in public suggested that the government believed that Germany's Polish-speakers could *become* Germans over time, and that this would essentially solve what both nationalists and the government saw as a national problem in the East. Nationalists in turn supported the government's harsh language policies, but they often held different beliefs about the possibilities of assimilating Slavic peoples to the German nation. Their ambivalence on this issue was itself a product of their own activism: the more activists emphasized the distinctive nature of German ethnicity in the East, the less they could imagine the successful Germanization of other peoples. If, indeed, Germans and Poles fundamentally differed from each other, then policies of assimilation could hardly resolve the national struggle.

After Bismarck's resignation in 1890, his successors had appeared to relax many of the regime's harsher anti-Polish measures. With the iconic Bismarck gone, the more radical of the nationalist activists were far less reluctant to pressure, criticize, and occasionally to attack the German government more openly. They organized several nationalist associations designed to mobilize popular support for their diverse causes and to lobby the government on a broad range of nationalist interests, not simply its Eastern policies. The most successful and popular of these new organizations were the General German School Association (1881) (later the Society for Germandom Abroad or VDA), the Colonial Society (1887), the Pan German League (1891), the Society for Germandom in the Eastern Marches (1894), and the Navy League (1898).[16]

The Society for Germandom in the Eastern Marches, also known as the H-K-T after its founders' initials (von Hansemann, Kennemann, and von Tiedemann), agitated for tougher policies against Polish speakers in Germany's East. Within a year of its founding the organization already boasted a membership of 20,000.[17] The association raised money to support the work of the Royal Settlement Commission, and to furnish needy towns and villages in the East with German language libraries, books, and periodicals. It also disseminated virulently anti-Polish and anti-Catholic propaganda framed as common-sense German nationalist arguments in its journal, *Die Ostmark*.[18] Along with the *Alldeutsche Blätter* published by the Pan German League, *Die Ostmark* played a dominant role in shaping radical nationalist opinion about Germany's eastern frontiers in other parts of the country as well. To the west in neighboring Saxony, for example, the *Alldeutsche Blätter* attempted, albeit with little success, to raise the alarm about migrant Czech industrial workers from Bohemia who were allegedly intent on founding colonies in Dresden and Leipzig and slavicizing this border region as well.[19]

Despite their growing influence on nationalist opinion in the rest of Germany, the Pan Germans and the Society for Germandom in the Eastern Marches did not attract significant support from most German-speakers who actually lived in Germany's East. In Posen, West Prussia, or Upper Silesia, for example, it was largely peripatetic representatives of the local or state administration from elsewhere in Germany—mid-level civil servants, teachers, Protestant pastors—who joined these nationalist associations in the greatest numbers. Estate owners in the region, as we have seen, strongly disapproved of the Eastern Marches' Society's anti-immigrant stance, given their dependence on seasonal labor from Russia.[20] Similarly, German-speaking farmers, industrial workers, and small business owners expressed little interest in the organization. 'H-K-T' stood for a radical Germanizing politics that, unlike the Catholic Center Party's program, was explicitly anti-Polish. Many German-speakers in the East assessed the national situation in more moderate terms than the radical H-K-T-ers and their outside agitators, as one example from nineteenth century Posen suggests: 'A recently arrived civil servant who was as yet inexperienced in the 'Polish Question' didn't see things through quite the same lens as did a local merchant who, although a convinced [German] patriot, nevertheless found it necessary to treat his Polish clients with care.'[21]

By the turn of the century the nationalist associations enjoyed considerable success throughout Germany in attracting members and in shaping middle-class popular opinion about domestic and foreign issues, from Polish policy to colonial settlements in Africa. Their leaders were usually local notables, generally Protestant, high-level civil servants, businessmen, and academically educated professionals. Originally, each of these associations sought to influence policy by cultivating a close relationship to the government, and most governments between 1895 and 1914 had reciprocated by making resources available to nationalist organizations and by turning to them for help in building public support for policy initiatives. Ideally, as we have seen, the associations sought to add a kind of popular legitimacy to broad political coalitions (*Sammlungen*) around popular nationalist issues, anti-Socialism, or both. This working relationship had led some historians to characterize the relationship between government and popular associations as a specific example of the governing elite's manipulation of mass politics.[22] Yet this seamless picture of synergy between a powerful government and an abject civil society hid the combustible threat these organizations actually posed to the ruling elite if things ever got out of hand. Some members who took the expansive ideological missions of these associations seriously did not want to fall into line when the government pursued policies they considered to be too moderate. Furthermore, the expanding social, confessional, and regional memberships of many of these organizations brought frequent challenges to the elite national leadership.[23]

The most conspicuous example of the threat that these mass-based nationalist associations could pose to government stability involved the campaign to expand Germany's navy. Starting in 1897, Admiral Alfred von Tirpitz had pursued a strategy of increased funding for the navy that sought both to minimize the provocation to other naval powers (Britain) on the one hand, while cementing a nationalist parliamentary coalition around increased support for the Navy at home. The Navy League was meant to popularize Tirpitz's growing budgetary requests. As with nationalist criticism of the government's allegedly halfhearted Polish policy in the East, a group of radicals managed to gain temporary control of the Navy League by criticizing the Tirpitz plan for its moderation in the face of international threats to the nation. Demanding a more rapid and expensive naval build-up, the radicals explicitly questioned Tirpitz's (and by extension the Kaiser's) judgment about Germany's national interests, implying that neither man was adequately addressing Germany's military needs. In 1908 the Kaiser himself found it necessary to intervene in the ongoing crisis, threatening to withdraw lucrative government patronage from the Navy League to force the resignation of the offending radicals.[24]

During the same period, the Pan German League also challenged official state and dynastic forms of nationalism. The government had already angered the League at the time of the Boer War (1899–1902) by not aiding the allegedly ethnic German Boers whose cause many German nationalists had embraced. During the 1905 Moroccan crisis the Pan Germans again criticized the government harshly for failing to obtain tangible colonial concessions for Germany. At that time Chancellor Bernhard von Bülow had responded by deriding the Pan Germans' ignorance of complex policy issues. The last straw for many in the Pan German League, however, came with the publication by the *Daily Telegraph* in 1908 of an interview with the Kaiser. In a rambling monologue Wilhelm II disavowed his alleged support for the Boers a decade earlier and even referred to a secret German contingency plan to help to defeat the very

Boer insurgents that the Pan Germans had idolized. This revelation set in motion a rejection by the Pan Germans of the dynasty and the government. The League had traditionally opposed all democratic reform of Germany's political system, but it now found itself arguing that ultimate authority in national questions should be vested in the nation rather than in the Monarch.[25]

These challenges to the government posed by nationalist associations demonstrate how easily mass mobilization around nationalist issues might threaten the very legitimacy of the state and monarchy it was meant to reinforce. Since 1871 Germany's governments had repeatedly deployed nationalist rhetoric as a means to achieve greater political unity and social stability. More recently, governments had seen in the nationalist associations a useful tool with which to influence elections and forge useful political coalitions. Yet their mass quality made these organizations increasingly unpredictable allies for the state, and after 1900 they frequently embarrassed governments and even occasionally produced political instability.

Radical forms of nationalism in Germany diverged from state-based nationalism over other divisive issues as well. Decades of statehood had made official forms of nationalism into a generally accepted civic religion in Germany, one whose basic symbols, such as the flag or the monarchy enjoyed nationalist significance thanks to their close association with the state. Not surprisingly, however, given activists' emphasis on the conflict with Slavs in the East, a radical fringe of nationalists parted company with this state-based understanding of nationhood in the 1890s to define the nation and its interests more in ethnic or even racial terms. In this view, not the citizens of the German nation state, but rather a German *Volk* spread among several states formed the national community. For these pan-German ethnic nationalists, 1871 had constituted not an end point—the final unification of a German nation state—but rather a first step toward the ambitious unification of all ethnic Germans in Europe into a vaguely defined continental empire that might someday include much of the Habsburg Monarchy and parts of Russia. This kind of radical ethnic pan-Germanism developed in tandem with a counterpart movement in Habsburg Austria starting in the 1880s. There, the followers of the volatile radical German nationalist and anti-Semitic demagogue Georg von Schönerer had proclaimed their treasonous adherence to the vision of a greater (Protestant) Germany. Schönerer's followers never made up more than a tiny, if vocal minority among German nationalists in Imperial Austria and Schönerer himself was brought down by scandal, imprisonment, and the loss of his noble title.[26] Clearly, this pan-German emphasis on culture and ethnicity as the determining factors in nationhood, rather than statehood or citizenship, demanded a radical transformation of Germany's borders and its citizenship laws, aims whose attempted realization could radically destabilize both German society and the European balance of power.

Ironically, however, as radical activists defined Germanness in more geographically expansive terms, they explicated their cultural understanding of Germanness far more narrowly. Even as they claimed national membership for the millions of alleged Germans who lived outside Germany's borders, some pan-Germans sought to strip German citizens who were not ethnic Germans by their exacting standards, including

Polish-speakers and Jews, of their citizenship rights.[27] As an idiom of nineteenth-century peasant and artisanal protest, anti-Semitism had often framed local social and economic issues in specifically cultural or religious terms. The Conservative Party's Tivoli Program of 1892, for example, had proclaimed its intention to: 'combat the widely obtruding and decomposing Jewish influence on our popular life' and demanded, 'a Christian authority for the Christian people and Christian teachers for Christian pupils.'[28] Yet this invocation of anti-Semitism that rested on the alleged victimization of a Christian population by Jews had little to do with ideas about the German nation as such. Instead, this popular form of anti-Semitism invoked more traditional explanations for the perceived ills of German society in an age of profound economic, social, and cultural transformation. The political appeal of this anti-Semitism—to the minimal extent that it did appeal to voters—rested on the recognizable religious and economic images it conjured.

When factions in the Pan German League rejected the monarchy and the state in the decade before 1914, however, their leaders turned increasingly to a new and decidedly racial form of anti-Semitism, finding in it a coherent worldview on which to found their radical activism.[29] If they failed to expand Germany's borders or to change the legal status of Germany's Jews, these radical nationalists could at least impose a racially anti-Semitic definition of nationhood on their own organizations. Their own practices of membership discrimination and boycott may have had few practical effects on German society in 1900, but their insistence on defining the nation ideologically in racial terms and their relentless focus on purifying its membership positioned them for greater influence after the First World War when even the state began to pursue policies that favored a more ethnic definition of nationhood.[30]

Racially anti-Semitic thinking, while hardly shared by the majority of the population, or even majorities within nationalist associations, nevertheless entered into public debate about citizenship and what it meant to be German, thanks also to Germany's developing overseas colonial empire. When German rule over other peoples came to include the creation of significant settlements in Southwest and East Africa, race became a pressing issue. Settlers themselves increasingly raised practical questions of property ownership in racial terms as a way to assert their interests both against indigenous peoples and against the power of colonial and military administrators. However, when it came to the legal status of children of so-called mixed-race marriages in the colonies, for example, newer racial arguments designed to underwrite German power within colonial societies clashed unexpectedly with traditional gauges of German citizenship based on patrilineal descent.

Both settlers and local colonial administrators increasingly sought to outlaw racially mixed marriages among Germans and to deny claims of citizenship to the offspring of such unions in the early twentieth century.[31] The courts inside Germany, however, refused to follow this practice, often siding with the German men who sought citizenship status for their descendants of whatever race. This situation posed two different concepts of national citizenship against each other, both based on theories of descent. The new German citizenship law of 1913 made no mention of this racial question, although issues about Germans and race in the colonies had been raised during debates both in public and in the Reichstag. The law did formalize a right to citizenship based on descent, but it did not explicitly answer the question of whether German men could claim citizenship for their mixed-race descendants. Nevertheless, the debates around colonial practices clearly contributed to the racialization of the concept of German nationhood in both its global and European context among some nationalists.[32]

When Germany entered the war in August of 1914, the Kaiser proclaimed that he 'knew no parties, only Germans,' offering an official wartime image of a unified German national community. War soon offered nationalists of many different stripes the opportunity to dream expansively about Germany's future in Europe, but also to delineate just what cultural qualities and characteristics they believed differentiated Germans from their enemies in the West and the East. As the war ground on, however, the extreme sacrifices demanded by the state of its citizens, both at the front and at home, produced a political radicalization of German society, which also found expression in competing visions of the nation. As in the past, however, the question for nationalists was not so much whether Germany was unified, but rather the terms on which this unity should be forged.

During the war, new issues also influenced competing visions of the nation. Women gained increasing public visibility and influence, especially women of the working classes and the *Mittelstand*, with men at the front and children at home who vigorously protested the increasing difficulty of procuring basic foodstuffs. During the war, such women came to demand government aid as a core right of national citizenship, owed them because of their extreme sacrifice to the national community.[33] This link between wartime sacrifice and expanded rights of national citizenship constituted a new way to understand both the national community, and its obligation to its members. Would workers gain recognition of their unions and a role in determining industrial policy in return for their cooperation in the war effort? Would the restrictive suffrage system that elected the Prussian Diet finally be broadened?

Conflict about the meaning of nation also centered on the issue of war aims, fueled by a protracted political debate of the issue in the *Reichstag* in 1917. Should Germany seek an immediate peace with its enemies, or should it continue to seek a victory that would guarantee it territorial expansion and increased global power? In July 1917, in the shadow of the Russian Revolution, a *Reichstag* majority made up of deputies from the SPD, the Catholic Center Party, and the Progressive Liberals passed a so-called peace resolution that demanded a cessation of hostilities that would forego territorial annexation or financial reparations. In direct response, radical nationalist activists founded the German Fatherland Party in Königsberg in September 1917 to lobby for a victorious peace (*Siegfriede*) that would include annexations in western and Eastern Europe, as well as in Africa. 'For the government to carry out a strong *Reichspolitik*,' claimed the party's manifesto, 'it needs a strong instrument. Such an instrument must be a large party resting on the support of a broad majority in the Fatherland.' Seeking to 'mobilize all patriotic forces without respect to political position,' the organizers scoffed at the weak nerves of the *Reichstag* deputies who had passed the peace resolution, claiming that only they reflected the will of the nation.[34] With Admiral Tirpitz as its national chair and civil servant Wolfgang Kapp (future leader of a failed Putsch against the Weimar Republic in 1920) as second in command, the Fatherland Party swiftly gained a remarkable following.

The organizers of the Fatherland party remained purposefully vague about their specific war aims precisely because they, as Tirpitz wrote, worried 'that the average German will become fearful when he hears the words Ireland or Egypt, and our opponents will have an easy time portraying us as wanting to prolong the war.'[35] While the party's rapid growth was indeed impressive, Roger Chickering's study of wartime Freiburg demonstrates, not surprisingly, that the new party often created more conflict than unity even among its own supporters. The founding of a local Fatherland Party branch in Freiburg undermined the existing fragile consensus among the other parties on the legitimacy of the war there. 'The city's leading patriots,' writes Chickering, 'had attempted to revivify national solidarity, to recommit loyalties to the great common cause of the fatherland.' Instead, they poisoned the local discourse and so saddled the symbols of national community with their own aggressive political designs that national solidarity strained along its many fault lines.'[36] One local Catholic politician warned against stirring up the masses in the name of nationalism, arguing, that were 'this [same] kind of agitation [to] be imitated by the Independent Social Democrats . . . we should have revolution in Germany.'[37]

The eventual end to the war in the West, however, was preceded by significant events in the east that played a critical role in shaping German nationalist attitudes in the period that followed. The collapse of the western front in October 1918 was all the more shocking to most Germans because Germany had recently celebrated an overwhelming victory in the east. The Treaty of Brest Litovsk, signed on 3 March 1918, had substantially changed the map of the East, assigning territory as far East as Rostov on the Don to Germany, and creating German client states in the western regions of the former Russian Empire. Brest-Litovsk stripped Russia of half of its industry and a third of its population, offering hope that massive food supplies would soon reach starving Germans back home. The treaty also underscored the degree to which the border regions to Germany's East had become sites where nationalists might play out fantasies of colonial expansion and radical Germanization. The *Oberost*, an occupied region stretching from the Baltic to northern Poland, served the wartime Hindenburg/ Ludendorff regime specifically as the site of such colonial experimentation. As Vejas G. Liulevicius has argued, the *Oberost* command was far more than an occupying regime. It attempted to Germanize land and peoples through wide-ranging policies that rigidly controlled population movement and sought to transform indigenous peoples by subjecting them to cultural Germanization.[38]

With defeat in the West, and revolution at home, bands of nationalist volunteers led by military veterans, the so-called *Freikorps*, organized both to battle socialists at home and to defend Germany's borders in Silesia, Posen, and in the Baltic region of the *Oberost* Command. In this latter goal their efforts were reinforced by the allies' desire to use the *Freikorps* as a temporary bulwark against the Bolsheviks whose forces were intent on recapturing the Baltic region for Russia. The dual efforts of the *Freikorps* as they saw it—to defend Germany from Slavs in the East and Communists at home—often became mutually constitutive in their nationalist propaganda. In the Baltic, *Freikorps* units sought to hold 'Slavic or Jewish Bolshevism' at bay, and to protect the German national community from incurring this ideological 'infection.'[39] Increasingly during the war, right-wing nationalists had already attempted to write Jews out of the national community, baselessly accusing them, for example, of avoiding military service or open treachery.[40] After the Russian Revolution many German and Russian nationalists openly equated Bolshevism with Jews, arguing that a rising tide of foreign Jewish influence in German society had produced the German Revolution in 1918–1919. This concept of political ideological infection conveyed an increasingly racial and medicalized construction of national differences in the East, based in part, as Paul Weindling has eloquently argued, on wartime and postwar efforts to limit immigration, seeing in it a major cause of the spread of infectious diseases in Germany.[41]

Yet another indirect legacy of Brest-Litovsk was the popularization of conspiracy theories to explain Germany's sudden defeat in the West. Some believed that since the war had largely been fought on foreign territory, and because Germany and its allies had won a great victory against Russia, the German military could not actually have been defeated in the field, a presumption that military leaders themselves and especially Ludendorff helped to promote. The collapse, they believed, must have resulted from betrayal by traitorous foreign elements (generally Jews and Communists) on the home front.

During this violent and confusing period after the end of the war, a German National Assembly met at Weimar from February to August 1919 to draw up a constitution for the new Republican Germany. This liberal document declared that power emanated from the people, although in earlier drafts deputies had debated whether power should emanate from the German people. This statement did little to settle the issue of membership within the national community and national community became an even more important part of general political thinking and rhetoric following the wartime defeat. Under the new Republic almost every political party constantly reminded Germans in one way or another of what was called their humiliation—indeed their national martyrdom—at the hands of their enemies. The inexplicable defeat along with Germany's unfair treatment by the victors at the Paris Peace Settlement remained central to different nationalist complaints in the 1920s and 1930s. At the same time, German nationalists also began to popularize a very different concept of German national community than the state-oriented one that had dominated most thinking under the *Kaiserreich*. By eliding Germany's political humiliation with the dismemberment of its ally Austria-Hungary, German nationalists implied that the ethnic Germans who had formerly been citizens of Austria-Hungary somehow shared the same relationship to the German state, as did the former German citizens who now lived under Polish, Belgian, French, or Danish rule. The equivalence nationalists asserted between these very different populations and their experiences popularized the kind of ethnic understanding of German nationhood that some Pan Germans had touted before the war, suggesting that all of these people suffered similar fates as victims, and that all ultimately belonged to the German nation state.

This new vision effectively answered the allies' promotion of a peace settlement allegedly founded on democratic principles that favored the self-determination of nations. Some on the left understood German claims to more territory and people in terms of a republican vision of nationhood that hearkened back to *grossdeutsch* traditions first articulated in 1848.[42] Like German nationalists on the right, they argued that the Paris Settlements had ignored democratic principles when they placed millions of German speakers under the rule of Polish or Czech nationalists. As with the allies' justifications of the settlement, this argument too rested on questionable logic, presuming as it did that the common use of the German language somehow made these different German-speaking groups in Central Europe members of a single national community. German nationalists increasingly referred to such popula-tions—ranging in size from 6 million Germans in Austria or 3 million Germans in Czechoslovakia to smaller enclaves of German speakers in Poland, Romania, and Yugoslavia—as *Streudeutsche* (literally 'scattered Germans') or *Sprachinsel* ('language island') Germans.[43] The use of such terms implied that the allies had forcibly dispersed the German national community among its hostile neighbor states, thereby creating a German diaspora of minority communities.

The idea of a German diaspora—of German populations scattered among alien rulers—had never been particularly popular before the war, except among radical fringe elements in Germany and Imperial Austria. It had never carried much weight because before 1918 most of the populations in question had been citizens of Germany's close ally, Austria-Hungary. Perceptions of profound religious, regional, and cultural differences also meant that most of the peoples in question did not view themselves as potential citizens of Germany. Even in Austria or Bohemia many nationalists saw themselves as only distantly related to Germans in Germany, and few favored joining the Reich except perhaps in a loose federal arrangement. Some community leaders in these states were happy to receive financial or moral support from Germany, but this did not make them future citizens of Germany or even beholden to Germany's interests.

Many nationalists in Weimar Germany, however, claimed these Germans for their nation state, and increasingly asserted Germany's right to protect and foster their cultural survival. This consideration alone—the ability to pose as protector of orphan *Streudeutsche* communities in Czechoslovakia, Poland, Yugoslavia, or Romania—even justified Germany's entry into the despised League of Nations for nationalists who otherwise abhorred the institution. It also underlay the logic of Gustav Stresemann's foreign policy initiatives through the 1920s that sought accommodation in the West, while leaving border questions in the East open. Should the map of Europe be redrawn at a later date, many nationalists also believed that the continued existence of strong German enclaves across the border in Poland, for example, would help to justify territorial revision in Germany's favor. It was therefore critical to support the continued existence of those minorities and to prevent them from emigrating to Germany. Not surprisingly, perhaps, Weimar Germany became for a time the acknowledged champion of the rights of European minorities, and it frequently sponsored minority petitions to the League.[44]

Forced decolonization in Africa and Asia after the war also produced a tendency among nationalists to define their nation in cultural, rather than political terms, and to re-imagine German's global role in terms closer to home. In the past, the exercise of political power over territories in Africa and Asia had defined Germany's relationship to its colonies. With Germany's colonies parceled out to the victors, however, post-war nationalists turned increasingly to culture as the measure of a territory's German identity. Some argued, for example, that the presence of German cultural practices in agriculture, husbandry, schooling, in short in all aspects of life, meant that Southwest Africa remained fundamentally German in character, even if it was now ruled by Britain.[45] More frequently, however, nationalist activists applied these cultural arguments to claim territories and populations in Eastern Europe for Germany. In the fall of 1918 Gustav Stresemann had written that: 'Perhaps in the future Germany will turn rather more to the east and we will find there some substitute for what we will not be able to obtain for the time being in competition overseas.'[46] Many nationalist organizations within Germany followed this new colonial logic, taking up so-called *Volkstumsarbeit*, or cultural work on Germany's eastern frontiers, in order to recover or protect German culture from the alleged threat of denationalization. *Volkstumsarbeit* became a particularly important form of activism in communities where German speakers on either side of the new frontier constituted a local minority of the population. In such places, often rural villages, activists distributed periodicals, founded small libraries, built Kindergartens, schools, and daycare facilities, and sought to create employment, job education, or apprenticeships for German youth. They also tried to create a greater sense of national community among locals by involving them together in holiday rituals or creating associations to promote local music, dance, or crafts.[47]

But, what were the signs of a local German cultural presence in the East? In theory, they ranged from exacting domestic habits, the production of tasteful (not kitschy or Slavic) domestic crafts or the ability to transform unfriendly rural landscapes into productive gardens. Building on nineteenth-century tropes that had made German culture recognizable in the whiteness of a German woman's linens or the 'laughing meadows and flourishing fields [German farmers] have wrested from a wild nature,' (as opposed to the sordid mess—*polnische Wirtschaft*—they claimed characterized the fields of their Slavic neighbors), German nationalists sounded the alarm. Nationalists warned the public that Germans everywhere in the East found themselves in mortal danger of losing their cultural distinctiveness to the hostile nationalization policies of enemy nation states.[48] They researched histories (*Ostforschung*) that documented and justified a German presence in the East, wrote literature that praised the historic accomplishments of German colonists there, drew maps that constantly reminded the public of the Eastern territories where German culture might be found, and produced tourist literature that extolled the cultural German qualities of Eastern destinations.[49] Nationalists constantly reminded their readers in Germany that, as Bohemian poet Wilhelm Pleyer's 1932 poetry collection '*Deutschland ist größer!*'

(Germany is bigger!) suggested, there was more to the German nation than just the people who lived within the borders enforced by the victors at Versailles. The map on the cover of Pleyer's poetry volume served as a typical graphic example of these claims. Here, both the lost territories (Alsace Lorraine, Eupen-Malmedy, Schleswig, Danzig, Upper Silesia, the Polish Corridor, and Memel) were shaded in the same tone as were all of Austria and the allegedly German-speaking regions of Czechoslovakia, Italy, Poland, Yugoslavia, Romania, and the Baltics. Together these regions constituted the true and legitimate territorial span of the German nation.[50]

Both the republican government and later the Nazi regime subsidized nationalist cultural organizations that claimed to support ethnic German communities in the borderlands, starting in 1920–1921 when the radical Pan German League—now re-named the *Verein für das Deutschtum im Ausland* (VDA)—and the new *Deutscher Schutzbund für das Grenz- und Auslandsdeutschtum* mobilized voters for plebiscites in East and West Prussia, and in Silesia.[51] There is less evidence that German-speaking inhabitants of these frontier regions necessarily saw themselves as threatened in a specifically national sense. In Upper Silesia, for example, the democratization of Prussia after the revolution of 1918, the increased influence of the Catholic Center Party in Germany, and a plebiscite regime that guaranteed the region meaningful local autonomy, helped to produce a surprise majority vote for Germany in several Polish-speaking districts. Although activists interpreted this outcome as something of a victory for German nationalism, local studies of the region demonstrate that in 1921 many voters believed that inclusion in Germany might better protect the region's religious, cultural, and economic interests. Despite the best efforts of German and Polish nationalists (and their media) to paint the region as a hotbed of nationalist unrest after the plebiscite, most Silesians, whatever languages they might speak, remained indifferent to the blandishments of the more radical nationalists on either side. This did not mean that they paid no attention to what the nationalists said and did. Instead, the decisions of Silesians' to support one nationalist side against the other, or indeed to support neither side, often rested on their evaluations of their particular interests in a given situation and not, as the nationalists would have wished, on the basis of a long-term nationalist commitment that overrode all other considerations.[52]

In the early years of the economic depression, both government and bourgeois Germans turned increasingly to nationalist commitment as the solution for reviving Germany's fortunes. Although the Reich government had already proposed special borderland economic aid for East Prussia in 1926, with the onset of economic depression, nationalists elsewhere in Germany increasingly sought such funds for their own regions, which they now designated as threatened borderlands. Regional and local authorities in Prussia, Saxony, and even in Bavaria, invoked nationalist fears of creeping Slavicization in their bids for funding from the central government. Their applications to subsidize public works projects or to expand welfare or tourism facilities increasingly invoked threats of Slavic infiltration and German denationalization. In 1930 Reich legislation designed specifically to improve conditions along Germany's border with Poland called for the greater protection of Germany's threatened border areas in general. Almost immediately Bavaria and Saxony invoked the wording of this law to apply for similar borderland funds to protect German culture along their frontiers with Czechoslovakia.[53]

A consensus in German bourgeois circles about the importance of nationalism as somehow above the polarized and sordid political conflicts of the day eventually helped the Nazi party to build an impressive electoral constituency in the 1930s. Before the onset of the depression, Germany's diverse and traditionally nationalist middle-classes frequently viewed Nazism with mistrust and concern. The party's extreme nationalist rhetoric may have pleased such voters, but its socially radical image usually did not. And on social issues the Nazi's uncompromising rhetoric could sound dangerously revolutionary and sometimes indistinguishable from that of the hated Communists. The Nazi party was only one of several whose campaign rhetoric promised national regeneration through the pursuit of ultra-nationalist foreign policies. Nevertheless, as economic conditions deteriorated from 1930 to 1932, many came to see the Nazi's revolutionary edge in a more positive light. While many bourgeois Germans had viewed the Nazi SA storm troopers as dangerous rowdies in the 1920s, by 1930 they often saw in them the only force willing to battle the Communists and Socialists, in the streets if necessary. As regional and national Nazi vote totals soared between 1928 and 1932, the Party also transformed its rhetoric to feature even more of a unifying nationalist patriotism and a celebration of the military. In this way the Nazis hoped to add voters who feared the possibility of communist revolution, who resented the Weimar Republic's social egalitarianism, and who longed for a revival of German national greatness.

The electoral success of the Nazis in 1932 should not blind us to the ideological differences that, nevertheless, still separated them from more traditionalist nationalists whose parties they defeated. The Nazi vote that reached a high of 37% in the July parliamentary elections did not necessarily reflect an unbridled enthusiasm even among radical German nationalists for the Nazi party program as much as it reflected an exhausted rejection of an impotent political establishment largely incapable of pursuing the nationalist interests of its voters.[54] An older organization like the Pan German League, whose radicalism was rooted in the Wilhelmine period and that had survived the First World War, had not engaged in the new street politics at which the Nazis excelled. Moreover, despite their recourse to racial anti-Semitism, the Pan Germans had traditionally defined German culture and national identity specifically in terms of *Bildung* or academic education and cultural achievement. It was, after all, this traditionally German quality that gave Germans a right to colonize others, and that entitled educated men to lead the nationalist movement. Both in *Mein Kampf* and in countless public pronouncements, however, Hitler openly rejected this link between *Bildung* and national leadership, often demonstrating contempt for precisely the class of men that had led the radical nationalists before the war.[55] The focus on racial struggle produced a socially leveling quality in Nazi ideology that recognized no traditional distinctions of cultural or class status within the national community. This potential egalitarianism, which offered countless opportunities for social advancement to people who in earlier nationalist associations would have had to defer to their social betters, made Nazism worrisome to more traditional nationalists. By 1932, however, many of these more traditional German nationalists nevertheless voted for the Nazis, hoping that they would crush the threat of communism for good, replace class conflict with national unity, and restore Germany's rightful position in international affairs.

Once in power, the new regime justified these hopes immediately, moving swiftly and harshly against its political opponents on the left and using an aggressive nationalist rhetoric of unity to justify almost every other policy. In particular, the Nazis made the realization of *Volksgemeinschaft* or national community their explicit goal. Although the term *Volksgemeinschaft* can be translated to mean a 'people's community,' the regime made no secret of its view that the people in question was a racially defined German nation. The Nazis characterized the implementation of this vision as a return to an earlier, traditional social unity that allegedly predated the German Revolution of 1918 and the Weimar Republic. In its outlines, however, this *Volksgemeinschaft* symbolized a radical departure from earlier forms of national community. Members of this community, it was claimed, would relate to each other primarily in terms of a shared racial identity and not in terms of their differing professions, geographic regions, or confessions. This unity would replace a republican order that had promoted unhealthy social divisions and an artificial class conflict among Germans.

The Nazis swiftly altered many elements of traditional administrative, institutional, and legal practice to help to produce—or according to many nationalists, to revive—the national community. Domestically, this meant the abandonment of the legal *Rechtsstaat* and an outright manipulation of law and the judiciary to favor the interests of the national community against those it defined as outsiders. The proclamation of the Nuremberg laws in 1935 explicitly outlined a new racial standard for citizenship that defined just who constituted the nation and who was now an outsider. The racial definition of citizenship and nation also strengthened the view that Germany's legitimate foreign policy interests included the well being of Germans elsewhere in Central and Eastern Europe. In the eyes of the Reich, they too were members of the nation and, as such, should be considered potential citizens of Germany. Moreover, some nationalists asserted that the territories these Germans inhabited could also legitimately be claimed for the German state.

If the domestic promises of national renewal—of a true *Volksgemeinschaft*—rested on what appeared to be an egalitarian vision of racial citizenship, they nevertheless encouraged professional Germans to hope that the new order would counter the threat of democratization they had experienced under the hated Republic. Many white-collar professionals, for example, hoped that the new regime would limit access to their professions and restore to them a degree of social privilege and respect that they believed they had lost under the Republic. At the same time, however, the regime also promised a greater measure of respect and nationalist privilege to racial Germans of all classes, combining vigorous propaganda with its racial policies to navigate the potential contradictions lodged in these varied promises. All of this produced an impression among much of the public that the regime was, indeed, changing the German national community by restoring lost privileges to legitimate Germans, while removing Jews and other non-desirables from the national economy.

The racial concept of national community turned out to be flexible in practice. Because structurally the regime fostered an unregulated competition among its many agencies and institutions, activists in different sectors of the regime could simultaneously pursue competing initiatives, while using nationalist ideology to justify their particular ends. In terms of policing, the regime publicized the first concentration camps widely as sites where political enemies (generally Communists) were allegedly subjected to political re-education. A stay at such a camp should remind Germans of their loyalties and duties to the nation, often by reacquainting them with the values of hard physical labor. After 1933–1934 and the decline of political opposition to the regime, the inmate populations dwindled considerably. A few years later, however, the camps revived again, this time by detaining people the regime labeled in racial terms as asocials, rather than in political terms: repeat criminal offenders, the homeless, addicts, homosexuals. These were all people who it was assumed regularly violated social norms for reasons of heredity. The regime and its opportunistic supporters increasingly defined such marginal populations in racialist and eugenic terms that excluded their possible re-education and made their banishment to the camps permanent, rather than temporary in nature for the protection of the nation.[56]

The increasing use of racial reasoning to explain what was considered deviant social behavior in German society also produced potential contradictions in the ongoing definition of national community. If heredity explained chronic social deviance in an individual, then to protect its health, the nation must prevent those individuals from reproducing. Eugenic practices—especially forced sterilization—became a standard means to accomplish this attempt to breed certain threatening characteristics out of the community. The logic behind such policies rested on an unrecognized yet typical ideological contradiction frequently found in nationalism that balances awkwardly between assertions of superiority, on the one hand, and fears about vulnerability and victimization, on the other. Just as nineteenth-century anti-Semitism had limited the numbers of people one could count as Germans at the very time when activists sought to increase the number of Germans in frontier regions, for example, so too did this turn to eugenic policies—from sterilization to euthanasia—contradict the Nazi attempts through other policies (marriage loans) to increase the size of the German population.[57]

The centrality of a race to the national community produced myriad professional opportunities for many Germans, since it demanded both new experts qualified to diagnose hereditary qualities that made people asocial, as well as a growing bureaucracy required to police racially dangerous asocials. However, whether the majority of Germans shared such extreme racial beliefs about the national community is doubtful. Peter Fritzsche has recently argued that at the very least, Nazi pronouncements and policies forced average Germans to engage with concepts of race and nation in daily life situations, whether or not race held any significance for them personally. As citizens of a racial state, most Germans, for example, found it necessary at some point to construct family trees to confirm their Aryan identity (and their suitability for marriage).[58] Others encountered race in the context of local economic boycotts, signs banishing Jews from using public accommodations, in Nazi media, or in the open violence of the November pogrom in 1938.

Many bourgeois and politically conservative German groups praised the new regime—and the new *Volksgemeinschaft*; they appreciated order in the streets, the disappearance of the Communists, and the frequent nationalist rituals. Many more Germans remembered the period 1933–1939 in positive terms.[59] The regime did, however, make greater demands on some citizens than on others in its efforts to realize national community. Formerly Socialist, Communist working-class or unemployed Germans often had little choice, but sullenly to accept the regime. Although Nazi propaganda suggests that the regime sought constantly to mobilize Germans for nationalist goals in their daily lives, the evidence shows that the regime aimed more to demobilize those social groups least likely to accept Nazi rule. Nazi programs, such as the German Labor Front's 'Strength Through Joy,' attempted to co-opt working-class Germans through consumer oriented policies that would both make them more effective workers and ensure the regime a minimum of cooperation among the populations most likely to resent Nazi rule. The 'Strength Through Joy' programs created opportunities for tourism and travel for workers who had little access to leisure travel of any kind, allowing them a chance to experience their place in the larger national community personally by getting to know other parts of Germany. A select few workers even gained the chance to travel abroad on cruises, often to destinations where they might experience Germany's global racial superiority for themselves.[60]

Nazi foreign policy victories in the 1930s, from the return of the Saar to Germany (1935) to the remilitarization of the Rhineland (1936), offered German nationalists the perception of a steady revision of the unfair terms of the 1919 treaties. For many jubilant nationalists these victories presaged potential future border revisions and the annexation of more of Europe's Germans to Germany. Despite some fears about the possible outbreak of war, Germans welcomed *Anschluss* with Austria and annexation of the German-speaking regions of Czechoslovakia (1938). These victories could be understood in traditional German nationalist terms as redressing iniquities of the 1919 settlement and restoring Germany's position in Europe, as could war against Poland, and the occupation of Bohemia and Moravia in 1939. However, most German nationalists did not envision world conquest on the global scale that Hitler envisioned it. They were, in a sense, far less imaginative and ambitious than were the Nazis and far more focused on redressing the injustices of 1919 through specific territorial revision. Hitler's conception of empire was also was rooted in German nationalist visions largely inherited from the nineteenth century, and based on ideologies about the East that dated at least to the Revolutions of 1848. However, in Hitler's view territorial revision merely constituted a minor prelude to achieving control over vast territories and resources in Eastern Europe that would enable Germany not simply to unite all Germans inside a national and continental empire, but also to become the world's leading imperial power.[61]

With the outbreak of war in 1939, and especially with the invasion of the Soviet Union in 1941, Nazi ambitions turned out to be far more difficult to realize than expected, thanks largely to Germany's lack of preparedness to fight a long war on several fronts. Problems with the pursuit of the war also derived from the regime's expenditure of valuable resources on ambitious nationalist population politics: first, the immediate resettlement of so-called ethnic Germans (*Volksdeutsche*) in newly acquired Polish territories, and later the extermination of Europe's Jews. Both of these policies sought to realize different aspects of the broader Nazi vision of national community, and the importance assigned by Hitler to both policies shaped occupation practices in the East, and made prosecution of total war significantly more difficult from the standpoint of the military.

As with their rule over German society, the Nazis' wartime command structures introduced several competing sites of authority (the SS, the *Wehrmacht*, the individual *Gauleiter* or provincial chiefs in the East, the East Ministry in Berlin, the various institutions of experts on Eastern matters). The infighting among these authorities produced very different approaches to officially shared goals, such as the Germanization of annexed territory or the exploitation of local Slav populations. All of them justified their policies and their use of scarce resources in terms of the racial ideology of nationhood, and all produced profoundly contradictory administrative practices.[62]

Although Nazi administrators arrived in the Sudetenland and later in the Protectorate of Bohemia Moravia seeking to restore German national power and to destroy the Czech nation, they soon modified their original intentions. Nazi racial policy when applied to Czechs in Bohemia and Moravia, for example, looked very different indeed from its application to Poles or Ukrainians.[63] In the newly annexed *Reichsgau* Sudetenland, deliverance by the Reich from Czech oppression and union with the larger German national community produced ambivalence and uncertainty among many German speakers. While their new Nazi rulers attempted to win over local Germans (and Germanizable Czech speakers) with generous funding for municipal projects, schools, and welfare payments, Sudetenland Germans were in no mood to sacrifice for their new homeland by serving in the *Wehrmacht*, or paying higher German prices for essential goods and services. German nationalists in the Sudetenland had long complained that Czechs dominated the civil service and school teaching positions. This, they believed, would not change if German men left for the front or to labor in Germany. Sudeten Germans also wanted the Nazis to treat Czechs with much greater severity, something their new rulers were loath to do, since they valued the highly-skilled industrial Czech labor force. The resulting resentments produced regional sentiments easily capable of undermining the feelings of national community that the Nazis sought to realize. It also, ironically, meant that the Nazis were willing to tolerate a certain amount of Czech nationalism, as long as it was not directed against the Reich.[64]

In Poland, meanwhile, a very different situation obtained. In the annexed regions, Himmler sought to remove Polish and Jewish populations to the East, dumping them in the General Government territory with no regard to food supplies, overcrowding, or medical conditions. Ideally, after the systematic destruction of the Polish leadership—the intelligentsia and the political classes—the surviving Poles would serve somehow as a flexible labor supply. Local and regional Nazi administrators sought to Germanize the territories under their control using varying strategies. In Poland the Nazis imposed a German *Volksliste* that divided potential Germans in the region into hierarchic categories with different degrees of privilege, depending ostensibly on their nationalist credentials, but often enough on their political reliability. In order to realize its vision of nationhood that united all ethnic Germans, the regime also drew up agreements with the Soviet Union to resettle ethnic Germans from Bukovina, Volhynia, and the Baltics (all newly annexed by the USSR) in the annexed regions of Poland.

Although Himmler believed that the resettlement process could be accomplished swiftly; in fact, most of the ethnic Germans who trekked westward to build a new life in the Reich found themselves living in camps for the duration of the war. To keep them docile in the camps, where their frustrated expectations of land produced growing complaints, the regime withheld full citizenship from the settlers until after the war, when their record of politically loyal behavior would confirm their membership in the national community. Here, as in the late nineteenth century or in the 1920s, expectations among nationalists in Germany about the racial and national characteristics that allegedly separated Slavs and Germans on the borderlands produced confusion and uncertainty when activists encountered real ethnic Germans in the occupied territories.[65] Young, often female nationalist activists who were sent during the war to do *Volkstumsarbeit* or welfare work in the newly-annexed territories in the East, anticipated that they would play an important role in a nationalist drama that pitted German civilization against Slavic chaos on the frontier. What they actually encountered, however, were profoundly ambivalent situations that confounded their expectations about national community. Among the local Germans, as well as the *Volksdeutsche* settlers, young activists might encounter bilingualism, strong Catholic loyalties, a deplorably low degree of civilization, and a profound indifference to the National Socialist revolution—much less to the concept of nation. Female volunteers in the Wartheland assigned to help the SS clear out Polish families from their farms and replace them with *Volksdeutsche* families often noticed that settlers from Volhynia often spoke better Polish than German. The ethnic German settlers appeared to share more with local Polish speakers than they did with the middle-class nationalist activists from Germany.[66] In regions occupied by Germany, but neither annexed nor slated for resettlement, the concept of ethnic German became even more elastic. From the Baltics to the Ukraine it was increasingly those who were most fully Nazified and who collaborated most enthusiastically with the invader, who might earn the coveted status of *Volksdeutsche*. Anyone who sought ethnic German status to gain local privileges needed to demonstrate his Germanness palpably, usually by inflicting violence on his Jewish neighbors or at least betraying them to the Nazi occupiers.[67]

In the spring of 1945, as the Third Reich finally collapsed, German speakers were on the move across Eastern Europe, often fleeing the Red Army or retribution from local partisans. Thanks to policies of imperial expansion pursued by the Nazi regime, those who had been resettled by the Nazis also found themselves again forced to abandon their homes and to flee to the West. Less than a century after the founding of a German nation state, the proponents of the most radical form of German nationalism had gained the power to convert their ambitious visions into practice. With the full force of the state behind them, they had driven Europe and their own society into catastrophe, thanks in large part to their insistence on bending the rule of law to the ideological demands of their nationalism. Whether it was in the eugenic policies they applied to members of the nation or in the genocidal policies with which they targeted its alleged enemies like the Jews, the Nazis completely abandoned the rule of law for an order that instead made nation (as their functionaries defined it) into the highest good.

The dynamics of an expansionist nationalism that sought ever more ways to purify the national community, on the one hand, and ever more territorial acquisitions on the other, had in part produced this catastrophe. It was the particularly nationalist components of these aggressive policies that shaped both their imperial and genocidal characters. However, was *German* nationalism to blame for the catastrophes brought about by Nazism? How exceptional was German nationalism? In fact, during this period German nationalism looks remarkably similar to other forms of nationalism in Europe, even taking into account the specificities of the German case. Racialized forms of nationalism could be found across Europe, from Ireland to Romania. In June 1932, for example, a Polish nationalist Silesian newspaper welcomed the strict separation of the races promised by the Nazis, 'in the interest of the purity of both cultures.' Polish activists believed that separation would finally end the national indifference that characterized many Poles in the region.[68] Other elements of German nationalism, such as the dynamic sense of victimization German nationalists had cultivated after 1918 or the assertion that the peace had unjustly consigned co-nationals to the oppression of hostile neighbors, constituted critical components of Hungarian and Italian nationalism as well. However, perhaps the most important characteristic shared by German nationalism with its European counterparts was its tendency to conceive of the national community in cultural/ethnic, rather than in political terms, even in societies traditionally associated with more civic forms of nationalism. In recent years scholars have effectively demolished the older dichotomous view—itself a product of the wars of the 20th century—that contrasted a western civic nationalism with an eastern ethnic nationalism. Wherever we encounter it in mid-twentieth-century Europe, nationalism rested on the idea of a prior national community defined by shared culture if not ethnicity, whether in Germany, France, Hungary, or Serbia. It was, after all, the French in 1918 who found it necessary to engage in expulsions from Alsace, not on the basis of loyalty or even language use, but on the basis of descent. The nationalist impulse to realize this kind of nation in practice created all manner of dangerously oppressive practices across Europe in the twentieth century.[69]

If the Nazis were highly nationalistic, the character and murderousness of their particular and extreme vision of national community were also no more German than were other, competing visions of the German nation. This is not to say that there is or was a good nationalism and a bad nationalism, the way some scholars have argued since the 1950s.[70] All twentieth-century nationalisms contain by definition at least the seeds of what the Nazi variety produced, from the concentration camp to more benign institutions like the flag or the anthem. To paraphrase Hannah Arendt's insightful observation from over a half century ago, the nationalization of European society that produced national minorities and stateless people in significant numbers after the First World War largely succeeded in replacing the rights of man with the rights of nations.[71] This development did not have to produce genocide or ethnic cleansing, but it certainly made those outcomes in Germany and elsewhere all the more possible.

Notes

1. For the classic statement of this argument, Hans-Ulrich Wehler, *The German Empire 1871–1918*, trans. Kim Traynor (Dover NH: Berg Publishers, 1985). For the argument with greater detail and force, focused on social imperialism, see Hans-Ulrich Wehler, *Deutsche Gesellschaftsgeschichte, 1849–1914*, vol. 3 (Munich: C. H. Beck, 1995), 1138–1140.

2. Nikolaus Buschmann, 'Between the Federative Nation and the National State: Public Perceptions of the Foundation of the German Empire in Southern Germany and Austria,' in Laurence Cole (ed.), *Different Paths to the Nation. Regional and National Identities in Central Europe and Italy 1830–1870* (New York: Palgrave Macmillan, 2007), 157–179.

3. Helmut Walser Smith, *German Nationalism and Religious Conflict. Culture, Ideology, Politics, 1870–1914* (Princeton: Princeton University Press, 1995), 33.

4. Smith, *German Nationalism*, 33.

5. For a brief summary of the literature on the Kulturkampf, see Christopher Clark, 'Religion and Confessional Conflict,' in James Retallack (ed.), *Imperial Germany 1871–1918* (New York: Oxford University Press, 2008), 83–105.

6. Michael B. Gross, *The War Against Catholicism: Liberalism and the Anti-Catholic Imagination in Nineteenth-Century Germany* (Ann Arbor: University of Michigan Press, 2004); Smith, *German Nationalism*, 40, 54–55.

7. This charge ignored the liberal constitutional arrangements that characterized both Austrian and Hungarian systems following the 1867 Compromise. Pieter M. Judson, *Exclusive Revolutionaries. Liberal Politics, Social Experience, and National Identity in the Austrian Empire, 1848–1914* (Ann Arbor: University of Michigan Press, 1996), 117–143.

8. Erwin Fink, 'Symbolic Representations of the Nation: Baden, Bavaria, and Saxony, c. 1860–80,' in Cole (ed.), *Different Paths to the Nation*, 200–219, especially pp. 202–208.

9. Celia Applegate, *A Nation of Provincials: The German Idea of Heimat* (Berkeley: University of California Press, 1990); Alon Confino, *The Nation as Local Metaphor. Württemberg, Imperial Germany, and National Memory, 1871–1918* (Chapel Hill: University of North Carolina Press, 1997), especially pp. 52–93.

10. Smith, *German Nationalism*, 118. See also pp. 140–156 for further examples of conflicts between the state and more radical nationalists.

11. The German census for 1900 reported the following figures for mother tongue: 92.05% German, 5.48% Polish, 0.38% French, 0.25%, Danish, 0.19% Lithuanian, 0.18% Kashubian, 0.16% Sorb, 0.14% Dutch. From *Statistik des Deutschen Reichs. Band 150: Die Volkszählung*

am 1. Dezember 1900 im Deutschen Reich (Berlin: Verlag für Sozialpolitik, Wirtschaft und Statistik, 1903).

12. At least twenty-three districts in Posen, Silesia, and West Prussia counted over 80% Polish speakers, and in another thirty districts the percentage of Polish speakers was 50–80%. From *Statistik des Deutschen Reichs. Band 150.*

13. The nationalists' identification of Poles with Catholicism did not fully reflect social and cultural realities, since German-speaking Catholics and Polish-speaking Protestants could be found in Germany's Eastern territories. James Bjork, *Neither German Nor Pole. Catholicism and National Indifference in a Central European Borderland* (Ann Arbor: University of Michigan Press, 2008), 13–14; Smith, *German Nationalism*, 170–191.

14. Richard Timms, *Germanizing Prussian Poland: The H-K-T Society and the Struggle for the Eastern Marches in the German Empire* (New York: Columbia University Press, 1941); Sabine Grabowsky, *Deutscher und polnischer Nationalismus: Der deutsche Ostmarken-Verein und die polnische Straz 1894–1914* (Marburg: Verlag Herder Institut, 1998); William Hagen, *Germans, Poles, and Jews: The Nationality Conflict in the Prussian East, 1772–1914* (Chicago: University of Chicago Press, 1980).

15. James Bjork, *Neither German nor Pole.*

16. The Navy League was founded in part by initiatives from within the Government's Naval Office. For membership statistics for the Society for the Eastern Marches, the Navy League, the Pan German League, the Colonial Society, and the Society for Germandom Abroad; see Geoff Eley, *Reshaping the German Right. Radical Nationalism and Political Change After Bismarck* (New Haven: Yale University Press, 1980), 366–367.

17. Although membership numbers fluctuated considerably in its first decade of existence, by 1906 the organization had doubled its membership to 40,500 and in 1914 the number stood at 54,000. Eley, *Reshaping the German Right*, 366–367.

18. On the HKT Association, see Wehler, *Deutsche Gesellschaftsgeschichte*, 1849–1914, vol. 3, 1075–1076.

19. Caitlin Murdock, *Changing Places. Society, Culture, and Territory in the Saxon-Bohemian Borderlands, 1870–1946* (Ann Arbor: University of Michigan Press, 2010), especially 68–76. In 1909, for example, the *Alldeutsche Blätter* complained bitterly that mail from Bohemia was being sent to Dresden and Zwickau allegedly addressed to 'Drazd'any' and 'Cvikava.'

20. The Pan Germans also supported the imposition of strict limits on the size of landed estates, a position that did not endear them to Conservatives in the region. Roger Chickering, *We Men Who Feel Most German. A Cultural Study of the Pan German League, 1886–1914* (Boston: George Allen & Unwin, 1984), 280.

21. Thomas Serrier, *Provinz Posen, Ostmark, Wielkopolska. Eine Grenzregion zwischen Deutschen und Polen 1848–1914* (Marburg: Verlag Herder Institut, 2005), 53. See also Serrier, 'Deutsche Kulturarbeit in der Ostmark. Der Mythos vom deutschen Vorrang und die Grenzproblematik in der Provinv Posen (1871–1914)' in Michael G. Müller and Rolf Petri (eds), *Die Nationalisierung von Grenzen. Zur Konstruktion nationaler Identität in sprachlich gemischten Grenzregionen* (Marburg: Verlag Herder Institut, 2002),13–34.

22. The locus classicus of this position was Hans-Ulrich Wehler, *The German Empire 1871–1918*, 83–88. In his later *Deutsche Gesellschaftsgeschichte*, vol. 3, 942–945, 1074, he writes, however, of the nationalism of Imperial Germany as a 'political religion,' and of 'a new opposition from the right' with respect to the Pan-German League. Conversely, he insists that *Welt-politik* had 'primarily domestic motives' (p. 1140).

23. Eley, *Reshaping the German Right*; Chickering, *We Men Who Feel Most German.*

24. Eley, *Reshaping the German Right*, especially 267–290.

25. Chickering, *We Men Who Feel Most German*, 213–223.

26. Andrew Whiteside, *The Socialism of Fools. Georg Ritter von Schönerer and Austrian Pan Germanism* (Berkeley: University of California Press, 1965); Lothar Höbelt, *Kornblume und Kaiseradler, Die deutschfreiheitlichen Parteien Altösterreichs 1882–1918* (Wien: Verlag für Geschichte und Politik, 1993).

27. By rejecting Jews from the nation in both Germany and Imperial Austria, radical German nationalists rejected people who in linguistically mixed regions often provided key support to Germans in the census and in local elections.

28. Peter Pulzer, *The Rise of Political Anti-Semitism in Germany and Austria*, rev. edn (Cambridge: Harvard University Press, 1988), 112.

29. Chickering, *We Men Who Feel Most German*, 232–245; James Retallack, *The German Right 1860–1920. Political Limits of the Authoritarian Imagination* (Toronto: University of Toronto Press, 2006), 273–324.

30. Dieter Gosewinkel, *Einbürgern und Ausschliessen: die Nationalisierung der Staatsangehörigkeit vom Deutschen Bund bis zur Bundesrepublik Deutschland* (Göttingen: Vandenhoeck & Ruprecht, 2001).

31. Lora Wildenthal, 'Race, Gender, and Citizenship in the German Colonial Empire,' in Frederick Cooper and Ann Laura Stoler (eds), *Tensions of Empire: Colonial Cultures in a Bourgeois World* (Berkeley: University of California Press, 1997), 263–283.

32. Rogers Brubaker, *Citizenship and Nationhood in France and Germany* (Cambridge: Harvard University Press, 1992), especially 114–137; Howard Sargent, 'Diasporic Citizens. Germans Abroad in the Framing of German Citizenship Law,' in Krista O'Donnell, Renate Bridenthal, Nancy Reagin (eds), *The Heimat Abroad. The Boundaries of Germanness* (Ann Arbor: University of Michigan Press, 2005) 17–39; Gosewinkel, *Einbürgern und Ausschliessen*; Markus Lang, *Grundkonzeption und Entwicklung des deutschen Staatsangehörigkeitsrechts* (Frankfurt am Main: Verlag für Standesamtwesen, 1990).

33. Belinda Davis, *Home Fires Burning. Food, Politics, and Everyday Life in World War I Berlin* (Chapel Hill NC: University of North Carolina Press, 2000).

34. 'Aufruf der Deutschen Vaterlandspartei' reproduced in Heinz Hagenlücke, *Deutsche Vaterlandspartei. Die nationale Rechte am Ende des Kaiserreichs* (Düsseldorf: Droste Verlag, 1997). On the founding of the party, 143–163.

35. Quoted in Hagenlücke, *Deutsche Vaterlandspartei*, 212–213.

36. Roger Chickering, *The Great War and Urban Life in Germany. Freiburg, 1914–1918* (New York: Cambridge University Press, 2007).

37. Chickering, *Freiburg*, 537. The local efforts of the Fatherland Party also appear inadvertently to have helped the local SPD to remain united.

38. Vejas Gabriel Liulevicius, *War Land on the Eastern Front. Culture, National Identity and German Occupation in World War I* (New York: Cambridge University Press, 2000). Liulevicius argues that the experience of occupation in the East prepared the attitudes that underlay Nazi colonial efforts there during the Second World War. Isabel Hull cautions that the *Oberost* regime, while brutal, was more the product of traditional German military logic than of nationalist-völkisch ideology. Isabel V. Hull, *Absolute Destruction. Military Culture and the Practices of War in Imperial Germany* (Ithaca: Cornell University Press, 2005), 248.

39. Annemarie H. Sammartino, *The Impossible Border: Germany and the East, 1914–1922* (Ithaca: Cornell University Press, 2010), especially chapter 2; Hagen Schulze, *Freikorps*

und Republik, 1918–1920 (Boppard am Rhein: H. Boldt, 1969); Hagen Schulze, 'Der Oststaatplan 1919,' *Vierteljahresheft für Zeitgeschichte* 18, no. 2 (1970), especially 123–130.

40. On the Jewish census, Sven Oliver Müller, *Die Nation als Waffe und als Vorstellung: Nationalismus in Deutschland und Großbritanien im Ersten Weltkrieg* (Göttingen: Wallstein, 2002), 144.

41. Liulevicius, *War Land*, especially 227–246; Robert Waite, *Vanguard of Nazism: The Free Corps Movement in Postwar Germany, 1918–1923* (New York: W.W. Norton, 1953); Paul Weindling, *Epidemics and Genocide in Eastern Europe 1890–1945* (New York: Oxford University Press, 2000).

42. Claudia Klemm, *Erinnert—umstritten—gefeiert: Die Revolution von 1848/49 in der deutschen Gedenkkultur* (Göttingen: V&R unipress, 2007); Erin Hochman, 'Staging the Nation, Staging Democracy: The Politics of Commemoration in Germany and Austria 1918–1933/34' (PhD dissertation, University of Toronto, 2010); Eric Bryden, 'In Search of Founding Fathers: Republican Historical Narratives in Weimar Germany' (PhD dissertation, University of California Davis, 2008); Robert Gerwarth, 'The Past in Weimar History,' *Contemporary European History* 15, no. 1 (2006), 1–22.

43. A leading example from the enormous literature that promoted this idea is Erwin Barta and Karl Bell, *Geschichte der Schutzarbeit am deutschen Volkstum* (Dresden: Verein für das Deutschtum im Ausland, 1930).

44. Carol Fink, *Defending the Rights of Others: the Great Powers, the Jews, and International Minority Protection, 1878–1938* (New York: Cambridge University Press, 2004).

45. Wildenthal, *German Women for Empire, 1884–1945* (Durham: Duke University Press, 2001), 176–178.

46. Jonathan Wright, *Gustav Stresemann, Weimar's Greatest Statesman* (Oxford: Oxford University Press, 2002), 107; quoted in Liulevicius, *The German Myth of the East: 1800 to the Present* (New York: Oxford University Press, 2009), 148.

47. Elizabeth Harvey, *Women and the Nazi East. Agents and Witnesses of Germanization* (New Haven: Yale University Press, 2003), 28–43.

48. Erich Gierach, quoted in David Blackbourn's insightful essay, 'The Garden of our Hearts: Landscape, Nature, and Local Identity in the German East,' in David Blackbourn and James Retallack, *Localism, Landscape, and the Ambiguities of Place. German-Speaking Central Europe, 1860–1930* (Toronto: University of Toronto Press, 2007), 149–164.

49. Liulevicius, *German Myth*; Michael Fahlbusch, *Wissenschaft im Dienst der nationalsozialistischen Politik? Die 'Volksdeutschen Forschungsgemeinschaften' von 1931–1945* (Baden Baden: Nomos, 1999); Michael Burleigh, *Germany Turns Eastward: A Study of Ostforschung in the Third Reich* (London: Pan, 2002); Nancy Reagin, *Sweeping the German Nation: Domesticity and National Identity in Germany, 1870–1945* (New York: Cambridge University Press, 2007); Harvey, *Women and the Nazi East*.

50. Wilhelm Pleyer, *Deutschland ist größer! Gedichte eines Grenzlanddeutschen*, 2nd edn (Weimar: Alexander Duncker Verlag, 1932). On inter-war nationalist cartography, Henrik Herb, *Under the Map of Germany: Nationalism and Propaganda, 1918–1945* (New York: Routledge, 1996); Kristin Kopp, 'Cartographic Claims: Colonial Mappings of Poland in German Territorial Revisionism' in Gail Finney (ed.), *Visual Culture in Twentieth-Century Germany: Text as Spectacle* (Bloomington: University of Indiana Press, 2006) 199–213.

51. Sammartino, *The Impossible Border*, chapter 2.

52. Bjork, *Neither German Nor Pole*, 244–266, disputes the claim that Polish speakers who voted for Germany were in fact becoming Germans. On the dynamics of indifference in daily life, see also Brendan Karch, 'Nationalism on the Margins: Silesians between Germany and Poland, 1848–1945,' (PhD dissertation, Harvard University, 2010); Tara Zahra 'Imagined Non-Communities: National Indifference as a Category of Analysis,' *Slavic Review* 69 (Spring 2010), 93–119.

53. Murdock, *Changing Places*, 158–162; Harvey, *Women and the Nazi East*, 46–47.

54. Thomas Childers notes, 'If the [Nazi] party's support was a mile wide, it was at critical points an inch deep,' *The Nazi Voter. The Social Foundations of Fascism in Germany 1919–1933* (Chapel Hill: University of North Carolina Press, 1983), 268.

55. Hermann Beck, *The Fateful Alliance. German Conservatives and Nazis in 1933. The Machtergreifung in a New Light* (New York: Berghahn Books, 2008); Chickering, *We Men Who Feel Most German*, 299–300.

56. Robert Gellately, *Backing Hitler: Consent and Coercion in Nazi Germany* (Oxford: Oxford University Press, 2001), 66.

57. Michael Burleigh and Wolfgang Wippermann, *The Racial State. Germany 1933–1945* (New York: Cambridge University Press, 1991), 136–182.

58. Peter Fritzsche, *Life and Death in the Third Reich* (Cambridge: Harvard University Press, 2008) 76–142.

59. Eric A. Johnson, *Nazi Terror. The Gestapo, Jews, and Ordinary Germans* (New York: Basic Books, 2000) 253–301; Fritzsche, *Life and Death*, 19–75; Detlev J. K. Peukert, *Inside Nazi Germany. Conformity, Opposition and Racism in Everyday Life*, trans. Richard Deveson (New Haven: Yale University Press, 1987).

60. Shelley Baranowski, *Strength through Joy: Consumerism and Mass Tourism in the Third Reich* (New York: Cambridge University Press, 2004), 75–76, 120.

61. Mark Mazower, *Hitler's Empire. How the Nazis Ruled Europe* (New York: Penguin Press, 2008).

62. Mazower, *Hitler's Empire*, 144.

63. Tara Zahra, *Kidnapped Souls. National Indifference and the Battle for Children in the Bohemian Lands, 1900–1948* (Ithaca NY: Cornell University Press, 2008) 169–251; Karel Berghoff, *Harvest of Despair. Life and Death in Ukraine Under Nazi Rule* (Cambridge MA: Harvard University Press, 2005); Wendy Lower, *Nazi Empire Building and the Holocaust in Ukraine* (Chapel Hill: University of North Carolina Press, 2005), especially 162–179; Mazower, *Hitler's Empire*, 78–101; 179–222; Götz Aly, *Final Solution: Nazi Population Policy and the Murder of the European Jews* (London: Arnold Press, 1999), 59–81.

64. Ralf Gebel, *'Heim ins Reich!': Konrad Henlein und der Reichsgau Sudetenland (1938–1945)* (Munich: Oldenbourg, 1999); Volker Zimmermann, *Die Sudetendeutschen im NS Staat: Politik und Stimmung der Bevölkerung im Reichsgau Sudetenland 1938–1945* (Essen: Klartext, 1999), Zahra, *Kidnapped Souls*, 180–186 and 231–251.

65. Markus Leniger, *Nationalsozialistische 'Volkstumsarbeit' und Umsiedlungspolitik 1933–1945: Von der Minderheitenbetreuung zur Siedlerauslese* (Berlin: Frank & Timme, 2006).

66. Harvey, *Women and the Nazi East*, 72; 147–190.

67. Doris L. Bergen, 'The Nazi Concept of 'Volksdeutsche' and the Exacerbation of Anti-Semitism in Eastern Europe, 1939–1945,' *Journal of Contemporary History* 29 (1994), 569–582.

68. From *Nowiny Codzienne*, quoted in Brendan Karch, 'Nationalism on the Margins,' 223.

69. Rogers Brubaker, 'Civic' and 'Ethnic' Nationalism,' in Brubaker, *Ethnicity Without Groups* (Cambridge MA: Harvard University Press, 2004), 132–146. On Alsace, Laird Boswell, 'From Liberation to Purge Trials in the 'Mythic Provinces:' Recasting French Identities in Alsace and Lorraine, 1918–1920,' *French Historical Studies* 23, no. 1 (2000), 129–162; Tara Zahra, 'The 'Minority Problem' and National Classification in the French and Czechoslovak Borderlands' *Contemporary European History* 17, no. 2 (2008), 137–165.

70. For example, Liah Greenfeld, *Nationalism: Five Roads to Modernity* (Cambridge: Harvard University Press, 1992).

71. Hannah Arendt, *The Origins of Totalitarianism* (Cleveland; The World Publishing Company, 1958), especially 290–292.

Bibliography

Applegate, Celia, *A Nation of Provincials: The German Idea of Heimat* (Berkeley: University of California Press, 1990).

Bjork, James, *Neither German Nor Pole. Catholicism and National Indifference in a Central European Borderland* (Ann Arbor: University of Michigan Press, 2008).

Breuilly, John, 'Sovereignty, Citizenship, and Nationality: Reflections on the Case of Germany' in Malcolm Anderson and Eberhard Bort, *The Frontiers of Europe* (London: Pinter, 1998) 36–67.

Brubaker, Rogers, *Ethnicity Without Groups* (Cambridge: Harvard University Press, 2004).

——, *Nationalism Reframed: Nationhood and the National Question in the New Europe* (New York: Cambridge University Press, 1996).

Chickering, Roger, *We Men Who Feel Most German. A Cultural Study of the Pan German League, 1886–1914* (Boston: George Allen & Unwin, 1984).

Confino, Alon, *The Nation as Local Metaphor. Württemberg, Imperial Germany, and National Memory, 1871–1918* (Chapel Hill: University of North Carolina Press, 1997).

Eley, Goeff and Jan Palmowski (eds), *Citizenship and National Identity in Twentieth-Century Germany* (Stanford: Stanford University Press, 2008).

Gosewinkel, Dieter, *Einbürgern und Ausschließen: Die Nationalisierung der Staatsangehörigkeit vom Deutschen Bund bis zur Bundesrepublik Deutschland* (Göttingen: Vandenhoek & Ruprecht, 2001).

Hagen, William W., *Germans, Poles, and Jews. The Nationality Conflict in the Prussian East, 1772–1914* (Chicago: University of Chicago Press, 1980).

Liulevicius, Vejas G., *War Land on the Eastern Front. Culture, National Identity and German Occupation in World War I* (New York: Cambridge University Press, 2000).

Mazower, Mark, *Hitler's Empire. How the Nazis Ruled Europe* (New York: Penguin Press, 2008).

Müller, Michael G. and Rolf Petri (eds), *Die Nationalisierung von Grenzen. Zur Konstruktion nationaler Identität in sprachlich gemischten Grenzregionen* (Marburg: Verlag Herder-Institut, 2002).

Sammartino, Annemarie H., *The Impossible Border: Germany and the East, 1914–1922* (Ithaca, NY: Cornell University Press, 2010).

Smith, Helmut Walser, *German Nationalism and Religious Conflict. Culture, Ideology, Politics, 1870–1914* (Princeton: Princeton University Press, 1995).

CHAPTER 23

TODESRAUM: WAR, PEACE, AND THE EXPERIENCE OF MASS DEATH, 1914–1945

THOMAS KÜHNE

In May 1945 Germany's total war ended with total capitulation and with total devastation throughout most parts of Europe. Only a few weeks before Nazi Germany crumbled, an ordinary soldier in Hitler's army, Kurt Kreissler, was full of optimism and in the best mood. In a letter to his relatives in Baden, he boasted about his deeds on the Eastern Front. Kurt, a thirty-three-year-old NCO, did not hide the fact that the nation's future was not rosy; mass death covered the earth, and most of his comrades had fallen. Kreissler knew also about the ravage of Germany's cities. But there were other things which counted more. Social life made up for physical death. Kreissler's battalion was reduced to 150 men. Yet only recently it had successfully defeated a Soviet detachment of 1000 men. The mood of his unit 'couldn't be better,' he wrote. They got along splendidly even if they had been assembled only shortly before with men from various parts of Germany. Immediately becoming 'the best of friends' with men one had never known before proved to be a daily experience in the German army, and such feeling of great community became stronger the longer the devastation endured. Kreissler's conclusion in February 1945 was: 'We want to stick together, we want to fight together, or want to get wounded together—that's what we are longing for.'[1]

Hoping to cheer his parents at home, Kreissler may have suppressed the depressive moments that he and his comrades suffered from amidst the destruction. Yet, the spirit of his letter captures a key feature of the mood of Germans in early 1945. They stuck together—and not only Hitler's army or some units within it. Notwithstanding the devastation of their homeland, the death of millions of their comrades and loved ones, and an overall climate of social and moral dissolution, the German nation did not fall apart. By no means was this a matter of course. Once before, at the beginning of the

First World War, German Emperor William II had envisioned a nation united by war and proudly announced, 'I no longer recognize parties, I recognize only Germans.'[2] But the communal spirit of 1914, conjured as *Burgfrieden* (domestic peace), soon evaporated; in the November Revolution of 1918 it crashed momentously. The trauma of 1918, Germany's defeat and dissolution, would not stop haunting nationalist Germans until the Third Reich collapsed; many Germans took the legend of the stab in the back as a matter of fact, according to which a Jewish-communist conspiracy had betrayed the national cause and sold out the otherwise victorious army. But there was no repeat of 1918. No revolution against the Nazi regime took place. Nor was it ever planned on any broader social basis. In a grand public speech in the Berlin Sportpalast on 30 September 1942, Hitler, not without reason, announced that '1918' was overcome. The divisions between lower and upper classes were concealed; men and women thought, felt, and acted uniformly; and home front and battlefront were no longer divided, but united. This, in any case, is what Hitler thought, celebrating that 'what we National Socialists envisioned when we came out of the First World War' had come into being: 'the great Reich of a *Volksgemeinschaft* [people's community] bound together by suffering and by joy.'[3] Eventually, in his political testament, given on 29 April 1945 shortly before he committed suicide, Hitler could praise the war 'as the most glorious and valiant demonstration of a nation's life purpose.'[4] At that time, the *Volksgemeinschaft* was about to be destroyed physically, and it would be defeated militarily, but it had remained intact as a cohesive and united nation. This chapter is to explore how, from 1914 to 1945, the perpetration of mass violence structured national solidarity. I shall argue that it was exactly the dynamic of destruction that glued the German nation *in extremis*.

23.1 THE DOMINANCE OF THE CIVILIAN: WORLD WAR I

World War I was the 'great seminal catastrophe' of the 20th century, wrote George F. Kennan, suggesting a continuity that encompasses war enthusiasm in August 1914, the battlefields at Verdun and at the Somme, the October Revolution in Russia and Stalinist terror, the Nazi 'seizure of power,' the genocide of the European Jews, and finally total war and near total destruction in Europe.[5] Indeed, the mass killing in the First World War initiated an epoch of unforeseen barbarity, terror, and destruction. At the same time, this narrative blanks those forces, actions and reactions that enhanced peace, obstructed violence, recalled the values of the civilian society, and showed alternative paths into the twentieth century. This is true, beginning with the initial event of that sequence of catastrophes: World War I.

From 1914 to 1918 more people than ever before in Europe were killed as a result of human intention; never before was the destruction of soldiers and civilians carried out so methodologically; and never before had human brutality convulsed the symbolic and moral order of mankind so rapidly and so massively. Worldwide more than 60 million men served as soldiers; nine million died, 6000 per day on average. The Central Powers (Germany, Austria, Bulgaria, and Turkey) deployed 25 million soldiers, the Allied Powers 40 million. Between 10 and 13 percent of them lost their lives. Germany, Austria, and France conscripted about 80 percent of those considered fit for military service, the bulk of the adult male population. The infamous battles in 1916 saw millions of soldiers firing against each other on single huge battlefields, 2.5 million Allied against 1.5 million Germans at the Somme, with 1.1 million men killed, injured, or taken prisoner.[6] Over the course of that entire year and on all fronts, the Germans lost nearly 1,500,000 men. For what? At the end of these battles, the Germans had moved three miles forward. The soldiers who survived did so amidst pure destruction. 'Everywhere deep shell holes, usually filled,' wrote a German medical officer on the Somme battlefield in his diary in fall 1916. 'One feels one's way past the edge, wading through mud. Then there are tree-trunks, shot to pieces and laying across the ground, which one has to climb over. Then a group of corpses, [the sight of which] makes your flesh creep, about six of them, their bodies torn apart, covered with blood and mud. The head of one of them has been half shot away, and some distance away there is a severed leg, and some of the bodies have been so intertwined that one can no longer distinguish the individual corpses.'[7] War propaganda responded to the horrors of mass death by glorifying a steely, cold-blooded, male super-warrior, who had rid himself of his previous civilian identity, stoically accepted his destiny, and was ready to kill or to sacrifice himself on the altar of his fatherland. As the soldiers' private letters and diaries reveal, only a few of them were ready to buy into these images, however. Most of them tried to secure their civilian visions, identities, and morals. Their most basic law said: 'Thou shalt not kill.' Ubiquitous fear of getting killed was enmeshed in the horror of being forced into committing 'mass murder,' as soldiers, terrified of their own 'brutalization,' had already come to realize.[8]

Whereas all sides were horrified by mass death in battles and trenches, the Germans and the Austrians were unable to compensate from the losses and were outnumbered by the Allied Powers. Even more than the number of soldiers, it was the number of weapons that decided the war. Although the Hindenburg Program of August 1916 increased the production of tanks, artillery, machine guns, and munitions, the Central Powers could not match the output of the enemies. In 1917, when 10.6 million actives and reserves of the Central Powers faced 17.3 million of the Entente, the relation of machine guns was 20,042 to 67,276; in 1918 the Allied (including America) produced 57 million tons of steel, Germany only 12 million.[9]

Neither the 'war materiel' nor the destructive dynamic unfolded by soldiers was limited to Germany. What made Germany particular, although not singular, was its tendency to transgress legal and moral restrictions of warfare. When the war started in 1914, Germany's economic imbalance was not as apparent as it became when the USA entered the war on the side of the Allied Powers. But another decisive strategic imbalance had frightened German war planners for some time: Germany's encirclement by enemy powers and war on two fronts. To counter its geographic and economic disadvantage, Germany developed and then radicalized a military doctrine that left international laws of war and standards of ethics behind. Seeking to attack France by surprise from the North and then to defeat it by encirclement, the infamous Schlieffen plan was clearly built on violating Belgium's neutrality. When the plan failed, the German army further developed a military doctrine fueled by an ideology of 'absolute destruction' (I. Hull). No longer was the goal just to disarm the enemy, but to 'to bring about a gradual exhaustion of his physical and moral resistance' by devastating his territory and by abusing its people.[10] The unexpectedly strong resistance the Germans faced in northern France at the beginning of the war propelled not only spontaneous over reactions, but systematic terror on the civilian population. The destruction of Louvain with its famous library went far beyond what could be excused as collateral damage. So too did the deportation of at least 10,000 French and 13,000 Belgian civilian men, women, and children in 1914. Contrary to international law, civilians were forced to dig trenches, build fortifications, and railways for the Germans, and thus to work against their own country. When the Germans retreated in 1917 and again in 1918, they devastated areas with a 'scorched earth' policy; they flooded coalmines, removed industrial factories, and robbed museums. In the East, German occupation went even further by installing a military state called 'Ober Ost,' a laboratory of colonization, exploitation and 'Germanization' of huge territories and populations, including most of today's Belarus, Poland, and the Baltic states. In the South of Europe, German officers advised the Young Turks carrying out genocide against the Armenian people. On the Atlantic Ocean, the German navy pursued 'unrestricted submarine warfare,' destroying 6000 ships and causing the death of almost 15,000 civilian seamen.

Why did the German military entangle itself in criminal warfare? It was not only the wish to counter geographic and economic imbalances. Less rational motives mattered even more. An aura of distinctiveness and a climate of autism disconnected the military from the civilian world and even from reality. The three glorious Prussian wars from 1864 to 1871, in particular the defeat of France in 1871 (which cleared the way for the foundation of the German Empire) granted the military enormous social prestige and a privileged position within the political realm. Military affairs were a prerogative of the Emperor and exempt from civilian control. Thus, the Prussian General Staff had discussed the Schlieffen plan since the 1890s with various Reich Chancellors being informed, but none of them intervened, the apparent moral and legal abysses of the plan notwithstanding. The predominance of the military in Imperial Germany climaxed in August 1916 when Generals Paul von Hindenburg and Erich Ludendorff took over the Supreme Command, and installed a quasi-military dictatorship. Facing their country's defeat in fall 1918, the Supreme Command, supported by rightist nationalists, turned to martial visions of a terminal battle to the point of self-destruction, an *Endkampf* that the German people should fight in order to acquire eternal honor and national redemption.[11]

Exorbitant prestige and constitutional exemption did not protect the military from traumatic fears. Having faced the Paris Commune of 1871, the military elite was, as most conservatives, obsessed with the fear of a domestic socialist upheaval; once operating outside of Germany's borders by occupying France and Belgium, the military feared guerilla fighters (*franc-tireurs*), that is, uprisings of enemy civilians. Apotheosizing a cult of honor that demanded violent and even brutal responses to any challenge in order to avoid the slightest impression of weakness, the symbolic world of the German military left no space for compromises or reluctance. In 1914 and later, *franc-tireurs* never seriously threatened the German occupiers, but served to justify terror, deportations, and devastation as retributive acts or as preventive measures against possible guerilla movements. The myth of the *franc-tireurs* camouflaged a 'war of annihilation' that aimed to destroy enemy countries like France politically, socially, and economically.

However, Imperial Germany's 'war of annihilation' never reached the genocidal dimensions of the war Nazi Germany carried out three decades later. Despite all the tendencies toward unleashing mass violence, despite all the atrocities and inhumanities, some basic humanitarian boundaries remained intact in Germany's first total war. Germany's eastern occupational regime did not draw explicitly on the colonial experience; no comprehensive policy of ethnic resettlement, no systematic murder of entire peoples was yet considered within continental Europe. The Belgian atrocities remained an episode, although a particularly cruel one. Massive international embarrassment sufficed to make the German political and military leadership back off, at least in the West. The *Endkampf*, the national self-sacrifice on the altar of eternal honor, never went beyond the fantasies of military leaders and rightist nationalists. The German nation was not ready yet to either commit suicide or to murder an entire enemy people.

In fact, the Germans did not place the nation above other loyalties. As their private war letters show, ordinary soldiers refrained from concepts such as 'nation,' 'fatherland,' or 'Germany' when it came to making sense of fighting or dying. Nor did they dwell on hatred of their enemies. They rather referred to their close comrades, to religious ideas of sacrifice, to their local homelands, and even more to protecting their families. Throughout the war, they yearned to return home, to their lives as civilians. Already in August 1914, when mass marches in favor of the war had spilled onto streets and throngs of volunteers joined the army, it was panic, anxiety, and lethargy that had caught the majority of Germans; they just didn't dare to display their fear of the war machine publicly.

The official propaganda conjured a truly united nation, but could not undo the deep social, religious, and political antagonisms. The *Burgfrieden* was a chimera. When nationalist intellectuals and politicians indulged in the rhetoric of a true national community, they envisioned an authoritarian state that would tame the socialist movement, overcome the ideals of democracy and parliamentarism, and suffocate class struggle. But the longer the war went on and the more the lower classes suffered from its consequences, the stronger the dissenters became. At home, the middle and upper classes were rumored to be war-profiteers, whereas lower class women, children and men suffered from insufficient food supply, and many of them from extreme exhaustion from working in armament factories. Social fairness also eluded the working class at the battlefront. Access to the rank of officer remained limited to upper middle-class people and aristocrats. Officers enjoyed privileged cuisine. Mass death in the trenches treated all of them equally, but the soldiers wanted to survive, individually and physically, rather than merely as an anonymous piece of an abstract nation that fought a seemingly senseless war. From 1916 on, working class soldiers embraced the vision of a socialist revolution. After strikes and protest marches of men and women at the home front, increasing hatred of the officers in the army, mass desertion, and the mutiny of the sailors, the revolution broke out in November 1918. In the end, the war did not bear a united nation, but led to national dissolution.

In the First World War, civilian visions and values persisted—in three regards. First, Germans, even in the government, shrank from radicalizing warfare into the extremes of mass crime; ruthless exploitation of enemy civilians and brutal war atrocities did not merge into genocide within German dominated Europe. Secondly, it was class conflicts, that is, civilian social identities that first blocked and then disabled the military's unifying maelstrom. Thirdly, soldiers craved for physical survival in order to return to their civilian careers and their families; they refused to trade their individual lives for the honor of a warrior nation.

23.2 WAR, PEACE, AND MORAL CONFUSION: THE INTER WAR PERIOD

In late 1918 Germany's war against other nations was over, but not the war within Germany. Most decisively, after 1918, the gap between socialist, left-liberal, and left-wing Catholic advocates on the one side, and various strands of conservative and nationalist opponents of the Weimar Republic on the other side. The former were proud of their political achievements. The Revolution of 1918 had ended the war and replaced the monarchy, which they considered responsible for the sufferings caused by the war, with a democratic and parliamentary model state, the first in German history. 'Never Again' was the lesson they took from the experience of mass death. The League of Nations and the idea of reconciliation between former enemy countries seemed to lead into the future. The anti-republican forces, however, spread the legend of the stab-in-the-back to denounce democracy and to save the reputation of the German army. They wanted to revise the Treaty of Versailles, avenge Germany's humiliation (or what they saw as such), regain Germany's territorial losses, and annul its reparations. To reestablish Germany's grandeur, some were even willing to fight, and some quarters—civilian and military—prepared a 'future war.'[12]

As is well known, these anti-democratic, nationalist, and militarist revisionists needed less than fifteen years to destroy the democracy. But as historians have often argued, this result was not foreseen before the 1929 depression precipitated Germany into economic, social, and political turmoil that the young democracy proved too weak to fight. There was no one-way road from the First to the Second World War or from Germany's defeat in 1918 to the rise of Nazism in 1933. Right after the war, the militarists were put on the defensive, not only through the restrictions of the Treaty of Versailles that limited the army to 100,000 men. To be sure, civil war at Germany's borderlands allowed the Freikorps movement to preserve and even radicalize a martial way of life. In 1920, Ernst Jünger published *Storm of Steel*, the literary monument to the eternal warrior, who enjoys the pleasure of war and rids himself of any scruples about killing. Neither this book nor similar literary products became bestsellers before 1933, however. They remained at the margins of German society. In 1920, roughly 400,000 Freikorps fighters confronted almost twice as many war invalids organized by the Social Democratic *Reichsbund der Kriegsbeschädigten und ehemaligen Kriegsteilnehmer*, the National Association of Disabled Soldiers and Veterans. The war invalids made only a small part of an impressive peace movement that mobilized hundreds of thousands of Germans to march against any further war. Already at the end of the war, the traditional war veterans' associations, the *Kriegervereine*, had lost almost a quarter of about the 2.8 million they had before 1914. Even supporters of newly-established militarist associations, such as the *Stahlhelm* (Steel Helmet), doubted whether they would ever gain substantial popularity. When the Germans searched for lessons to be drawn from the experience of mass death, most of them were looking for peace and normality, rather than belligerence and turmoil.

Although organized pacifism lost its mass support in the 1920s, the moderately pacifist *Reichsbanner Schwarz-Rot-Gold*, the Social Democrats' veterans' association, grew to one to two million members, including left liberals and supporters of the Catholic Center Party, more than the nationalist *Stahlhelm* and some other newly created militarist associations together. Around 1930, pacifist war novels that denounced the 'shame of a criminal and murderous frenzy' and the 'predatory virtues' ingrained through war revitalized the 'Never Again' movement. Erich Maria Remarque's novel *All Quiet on the Western Front* (1929) sold almost a million copies within a year. Preprinted in a major newspaper and filmed right after publication, it reached all segments of the German youth. Its public impact can be measured not least by the embarrassment of militarist and nationalist politicians in Germany, who feared that the future generation of soldiers would become infected by pacifism, anti-militarism, and the idea of reconciliation. In fact, pacifist war literature around 1930 aimed for exactly this: to deepen popular support of and thus to animate the 'spirit of Locarno,' even after its initiator in Germany, Gustav Stresemann, had died. The left-wing veterans' organization had always worked on approaching their French counterparts, in order to establish a dialogue between war veterans of both countries, and to popularize the visions of the League of the Nations.

Why did pacifism fail in Germany's interwar period? For a full answer one must engage in a complex historical analysis of the failure of Weimar democracy and the rise of the Nazi movement, which goes far beyond the scope of this chapter. It is worth noting, though, that what was called and understood to be 'pacifism' in Weimar Germany became more and more entangled in the ideological, psychological, and moral world of belligerent activism and paramilitary movements. Prominent pacifists in Germany did not justify desertion from the army, but rather stressed that they too had done their duty on behalf of the fatherland. They confirmed a militarized ideal of 'tough' masculinity that left no chance for men who condemned war not only rhetorically, but had actually abandoned it. The hero of popular pacifist war literature was not the deserter or the coward, but the maltreated and misused front-line soldier who did his duties, obeyed orders, and sacrificed himself on behalf of his fatherland and his comrades. This is what united anti-war and pro-war movements in interwar Germany: though setting different accents, they paid homage to a myth of the comradeship of frontline soldiers that helped Germans to cope with the horrifying experience of mass death and, at the same time, leveled the ground for a future war. Militarists and pacifists were working on a collective memory of war that, whilst not always glorifying war, made it bearable.

In the myth of comradeship, the soldier did not appear as an agent of destruction, but rather as a human being who longs for home, security, and harmony. The typical soldier had been, said a speaker at a veterans' meeting of 10,000 people in August 1925 at Lake Constance, 'sneered at by the horror of all the mass deaths, despised, and degraded.' But he had been pulled from this hell by 'the supporting, compensating, alleviating counterweight of his comrades.' The 'secret of comradeship,' so the Catholic vicar added, lay in the 'enduring awareness of what is human.' Returning from the firing line, 'soldiers were able in the company of dear comrades to properly recover their sense of what it means to be a human being.'[13]

Similar stories were told all over Germany, mostly by nationalist authors and agencies, above all by the popular veterans' movement as represented by the *Stahlhelm* and the *Kriegervereine*. The majority of Germans yearned for stories that reconciled the horrors of mass death with the normality of a civil society. The myth of comradeship provided exactly this bridge over the abyss between civility and war. The message of the myth was that whoever had practiced comradeship in war had saved humanity from the inhumanity of war. As the *Kyffhäuser*, the news magazine of the oldest and most popular German veterans' organization, put it in 1929: 'Practicing comradeship' invalidates the 'thoughtlessly spread untruth according to which the past war had brutalized people and had dismissed them as being something like robbers and murderers.'[14]

The myth of comradeship responded to the moral burden of Germans that was engendered by the piles of corpses the war had left behind. That burden had been stressed by the guilty verdict the Treaty of Versailles had returned. The experience of the horror of an industrialized war and one's own participation in the immense violence of the war could no longer be 'categorized' as individual guilt and responsibility. The collective memory of these orgies of destruction concealed the 'I' in the 'Us.' In that 'Us' individual responsibility was dissolved. Communities of comrades, resigned to their fate, neutralized their aggression toward those outside of the community through altruism and harmony within it.

Such stories were advocated primarily by, but not limited to, the right-wing, nationalist milieus in Germany. The socialist camp also adopted them, although with different accents. Refusing the right-wing myth of a true comradeship between officers and privates, the *Reichsbanner* and authors such as Remarque praised a comradeship that denoted standing shoulder to shoulder against your superiors. But even in such anti-war stories comradeship operates as the motor of military violence, by carrying the individual soldier along and thus relieving him of personal responsibility. Nobody mutinies, nobody deserts. Killing was presented, in both revisionist and pacifist remembrance of the war, as a collective act determined by fate. Comradeship produced, in the accounts of veterans on both Right and Left, a pull from which the individual could not escape. Remarque's anti-heroes, once in battle, act outside of individual responsibility. 'If we were not automata at that moment we would continue lying there, exhausted, and without will. But we are swept forward again, powerless, madly savage and raging; we will kill, for they are still our mortal enemies . . . and if we do not destroy them, they will destroy us.'[15] The socialists, as well as the rightists, held on to the idea that whoever had performed comradeship in war was morally sacrosanct and not contaminated by responsibility for mass death.

The myth of comradeship went even a decisive step further to provide relief from the onuses the German nation was loaded with after 1918 by answering to the longings for national community that were frustrated by class struggles and ideological fights since the nineteenth century and even more by the revolution of 1918. In the comradeship of front soldiers, all civil struggles—between poor and rich, worker and employer, conservatives and socialists, Protestants and Catholics—were overcome, according to the myth. The group of comrades in the trenches represented the ideal of a nation, and namely a peaceful, not an aggressive nation. In presenting such idealized remembrance of the war, which in fact was shaped by class struggle even in the trenches, the myth of comradeship came also with a demand and with a promise. If the Germans did reorganize their nation according to the model of frontline comradeship, then society would be healed of all its wounds, its inner clashes, conflicts, and confusions. In fact, in bringing people of different social backgrounds together, the veterans' meetings anticipated a truly united nation. 'One day, the Stahlhelm's frontline community will give birth to the *Volksgemeinschaft*,' announced the *Stahlhelm* in January 1925.[16]

To be sure, it was primarily the rightist, revisionist, and militarist political camp that advocated and popularized this decisively nationalist version of the myth of comradeship. The Social Democrats, the left wing of the Catholic Center Party, and the Left Liberals—the three major columns of the Weimar democracy—and the *Reichsbanner* did not easily join in the utopia of a national rebirth through vitalizing front-line comradeship. Popular antiwar novels, though, published around 1930 and addressed to both veterans and youth, supported the myth of a trench community that had overcome civilian antagonisms. At the same time not only veterans' organizations, but also a broad range of youth associations bought into the conformist ingredients of the myth of comradeship. Contrary to friendship, a self-chosen relationship, comradeship was the epitome of a community of fate, into which you were thrown and to which you had to adjust. Comradeship was about joining in, about conforming. It left no space for individualists, for individual favors and lifestyles, let alone for deserters or shirkers. The same held true for the culture of the German youth movement before 1933, whether of the left or of the right. Beside the many egos united around the campfire a collective

'We' held sway in the leagues of youth. The community—this was the threat implied in the youth movement or in the military—'spots the outsider and knows how to defend itself.'[17] In 1920, such youth groups engaged in spontaneous hiking trips; ten years later, they marched like soldiers in closed formations. Until 1933 nobody was forced into this community life. But young people from all political and social backgrounds wanted to be pressed into a comradeship which compeled a 'mother's boy' to curtail his private demands. It was left to the Nazi state to fulfill the longing for such community and to utilize it for making Germans join in a total war that went beyond the scope of criminal warfare as hitherto known.

23.3 NATION-BUILDING THROUGH GENOCIDE: THE NAZI 'WAR OF EXTERMINATION'

For decades, and still in the 1980s, historians of the Third Reich examined separately two sides of their topic, the state and the society *within* the German territory (the home front during the war) on the one hand, and the war carried out from 1939 on *outside* of the territory of Germany, including the Holocaust, the occupation, and exploitation of Europe, on the other hand. Only since the late 1980s have scholars agreed that Nazi Germany found its identity only through a gigantic war unquestionably linked to genocide. Although no 'master plan' for the murder of the Jews may have existed before the summer of 1941, the Nazi state was built on a terrorist utopia that from the beginning bore the potential of genocide. According to this utopia, the German nation, humiliated in 1919, would resurrect itself and survive only through a brutal war against supposed foreign and domestic 'racial' enemies. Taking the Nazi utopia seriously enables us to examine what made Nazi Germany, its state and its society, 'work.' What, in other words, held Nazi society together, given its obvious inner ideological, social, and cultural ruptures and differences? What kept its governmental and administrative machinery running, given the ubiquitous rivalry between party and state institutions and the resulting '"structurelessness" of the regime'?[18] Why was there no substantial resistance against the regime or against the perpetration of the Holocaust? Why did the Germans keep fighting a total war at a time when they could have realized, and did indeed realize that there was no chance to win it? Gestapo terror on German citizens certainly mattered. So did Hitler's charisma and the quasi-religious belief of many Germans in the supposedly supernatural talents of the Führer. But Hitler's prestige evaporated the more Germany's downfall loomed; and yet the Germans nevertheless stuck to the regime. Notwithstanding Himmler's terror apparatus, private letters, diaries, and many other sources reveal that probably a majority of Germans supported the Nazi agenda not because they were forced to, but because they wanted it and because they had, through violence, participated in it. Assuming widespread compliance or even consensus with the regime, however, does not imply ignoring different attitudes within German society. The working class, formerly mostly Socialist or Communist, kept some distance from the economic promises of the Nazis and their vision of an egalitarian *Volksgemeinschaft* spreading harmony and happiness. Although Nazi propaganda fought continuously against class divisions, Nazi policy never came close to eliminating the gap between the middle and the working classes.

It would be a mistake to see the Nazi *Volksgemeinschaft* as merely a motor for individual advancement and economic satisfaction. In the Nazi utopia, the Promised Land was not the land of milk and honey. Instead, that land would be liberated from the selfish dynamic that burdened modern societies with endless internal conflicts. Rooted in social-Darwinist obsessions of history as a constant struggle between people for superiority and in the dogma that other nations never had the same right as Germany, the Nazi *Volksgemeinschaft* would be the result of a racial rather than an economic revolution; millions of people seen as racially inferior were to be annihilated or enslaved. One may well ask, what kind of revolution would have changed class hierarchies more dramatically? In the Nazi utopia, the destruction of the other was inevitably linked to the 'construction' of the 'us.' The *Volksgemeinschaft* would come into being only through, and can be understood only by fathoming, its two poles— construction and destruction. Neither can be isolated, both existed only in relation to each other. Hitler had elaborated this rationale long before he came in power. In 1927, he dwelled on the mythical past, 'where there was no class division.' According to Hitler: 'This was in the platoons at the front line. There must be a chance to establish such kind of unity also at home. Why did it work at the front line? Because opposite laid the enemy, because you were aware of the threat he constituted.' Hitler's conclusion was: 'If you want to amalgamate our people into a unity, the first thing you have to do is to create a new front line, with a mutual enemy, so that everybody knows: We have to be united, because this is the enemy of all of us.'[19]

No community, no social harmony, no belonging can exist without the 'other,' without those who do not belong, who threaten the community, in reality or supposedly, physically or just by looking different, by pursuing different ways of life, by harboring different experiences and visions—thus by challenging the identity of those who belong. If there is no enemy, one has to be invented. The larger and the more complex the in-group (as in industrial societies), the more difficult it is to guarantee uniformity and to create a needed negative that can be shared on a common basis. Carl Schmitt, whose political philosophy offered a defense for the Nazi dictatorship, outlined in 1932 what a nation had to do to reach 'internal peace.' It had to decide 'upon the domestic enemy,' the enemy within. 'Whether the form is sharper or milder,' he explained, 'explicit or implicit, whether ostracism, expulsion, proscription, or outlawry are provided for in special laws or in explicit or general descriptions, the aim is always the same, namely to declare an enemy.'[20]

Statements like these suggest an orderliness and straightness of history that did not exist or was at least not visible to ordinary people, apart from very few exceptions. What made Nazi society work was not so much certainty, but ambiguity. While Hitler, in a secret meeting with military leaders in February 1933, had made clear that

Germany was to be rearmed to wage a ruthless war of conquest in the East, he prepared and in 1934 signed a pact with Poland that renounced violence between the two countries. Similar treaties were signed with other countries as well; in summer 1936 the Berlin Olympics staged Nazi Germany's will to peace more than anything else. What the left-wing, pacifist veterans' association in Weimar Germany had longed for, but never achieved, the Nazis made happen: a spectacular mass meeting of both German and French veterans was celebrated at Verdun in 1936.[21] Only from 1938 on, and even more so in early 1939, when Germany annexed Czechoslovakia, people inside and outside of Germany could no longer have any doubts of Hitler's real intentions; in November 1938, he had informed a group of German journalists that his peace rhetoric had served only one goal: to dupe the Allied powers and to allow Germany to rearm— and to dupe Germans too, as he might have added. For many Germans were afraid of a new war and thus willing to buy into Hitler's peace rhetoric. When Germany invaded Poland in the fall of 1939, there was no resistance and no protest among Germans, to be sure. But as secret reports on the mood of ordinary Germans both by Nazi spies and by spies of the exiled Social Democratic Party (SoPaDe) clearly show, there was not much enthusiasm either. Germans obeyed and performed loyalty to the regime, but it was a 'reluctant loyalty,' as historians have argued.[22]

Reluctance also shaped the attitude of many Germans toward the Nazis' racial politics in the 1930s. Combining older anti-Semitic traditions, popular eugenic discourse, and anti-communist resentments, the Nazis chose 'the Jew' as the racial paradigm of a 'domestic enemy' and painted a frightening picture of a Jewish conspiracy being planned, and executed inside and outside of Germany. But 'ostracism' *and* 'outlawry' of fellow citizens, who were marked as enemies or as 'aliens,' harassment and boycott of the Jews and other outsiders did not create the *Volksgemeinschaft* as fast as the Nazis may have hoped. Many Germans inconspicuously or even demonstratively ignored the Nazi appeals to boycott Jewish shops, doctors, and lawyers. As historian David Bankier writes, 'The public was polarized on the handling of the Jewish question: party circles and their periphery gave full support, while the large majority condemned it.'[23]

It was only through the 'war of extermination' that the *Volksgemeinschaft* came into being. Its gigantic and methodic destructiveness, both regarding the range and number of victims and the unconceivable brutality of the perpetrators, are well known. The crucial point is the consequence with which a completely new kind of warfare was planned and executed. War atrocities and massacres had happened throughout history, just as enemy peoples had been enslaved and their homelands exploited; even genocides had happened before. What was new from 1939 on was, first, the intended confusion of traditional notions of war and murder in such a way that even the perpetrators unlearned the distinction between military violence against soldiers and the large scale murder of civilians; secondly, the widening of the genocide of a defined group, the Jews, into a program of indiscriminate mass murder of numerous other peoples; thirdly, paralleling the widening of genocide, the expansion of a defined group of perpetrators, such as the SS Einsatzgruppen, and concentration and extermination camp staff, into a huge group of people, consisting of millions and comprising a society of perpetrators including masses of conscripted soldiers and innumerous local collaborators across an entire continent; and finally, that the mission of mass death eventually did not halt in front of that perpetrator society, but victimized this society as well—in order to, paradoxically, provide their society with a special kind of social life and to guarantee its eternal symbolic life.

Poland was Germany's laboratory for experiments in brutality, killing, enslavement, and exploitation of entire peoples, and at the same time it served as a training field making 'ordinary' people complicit in mass crimes. By 1940, more than 300,000 Poles were expelled from their homeland in the western parts of the country and sent to barren territories of the eastern General Government to make place for some 200,000 ethnic Germans, whom Hitler called 'home' into the Reich. At the same time, the SS started murdering Jews and the Polish elite systematically; over half a million Polish Jews died in newly-established labor camps and ghettos of starvation, diseases, or because they were openly murdered. Thousands of Roma were also dumped in Polish ghettos. The Nazis' 'euthanasia program,' the murder of handicapped people (or whoever the Nazis took as such) was not limited to Poland, but nevertheless constituted a crucial part of the 1939–1940 take-off in genocidal politics: in January 1940, gassings of people were concluded successfully for the first time. Concealment was not possible, neither of the murder of Poles or Jews nor of the 'euthanasia.' Remarkably, though, it was only the latter that provoked social action of Germans or, more precisely, by church circles. Their outcry against the killing of innocent persons with mental and physical defects, as Pope Pius XII put it, was taken seriously by the Nazi leadership (although it did not stop the program); it showed that the German people had choices and the option to stop mass murder. They used such chances when their loved ones were threatened, but did not care when it was 'only' the Jews whose lives stood at risk.

Although the murder of Polish civilians was assigned to the SS, once in Poland, ordinary Wehrmacht soldiers often willingly joined in to torture or even kill civilians— Jews in particular. In Poland, German soldiers could rape and pillage as they had never dared on the Rhine or the Mosel, as Marcel Reich-Ranicki, deported as a young German Jew to Poland in 1938, remembered. 'There was no one to spoil the fun of those German troops, no one to stop them from maltreating Jews.'[24] Yet, not all parts of the Wehrmacht supported murder and torture of civilians. Numerous leading officers despised what their troops and the SS were doing, and some even intervened, such as Colonel General Johannes Blaskowitz, who in February 1940 prophesized a 'tremendous brutalization and moral profligacy that will spread like a pest in precious German manpower.' Soldiers like Blaskowitz were isolated, however, and they became so even more when Hitler booked victories all over Europe in 1940 and early 1941, occupying Denmark, Norway, the Netherlands, Belgium, France, Serbia, and Greece. What Blaskowitz criticized, was exactly what the Nazi leaders wanted: a moral revolution through genocidal warfare to create the merciless *Volksgemeinschaft*. Already on 4 October 1939, Hitler had issued a secret blanket amnesty for crimes committed by Germans against Poles during the campaign—and given a clear signal to expand and intensify the new style of warfare, rather than to stop it.[25]

What this meant became apparent when the war on the Soviet Union was planned from late 1940 on and then executed from 22 June 1941 on. The *Einsatzgruppen* were massively expanded and trained to murder anyone suspected of not complying with the German occupiers, which by Nazi definition included Jews. During the initial occupation of Poland, from 1939 to 1941, numerous orders and provisions made sure that SS and *Wehrmacht* coordinated their efforts and that the troops did 'their share in the ideological struggle of the Eastern Campaign,' as Franz Halder, Chief of the General Staff of the Army, said in May 1941.[26] Indeed, without the Wehrmacht's support, the Einsatzgruppen could not have killed more than a million Jews in the Soviet territory in just a few months. In some regions, for instance in Belarus (or in Serbia), the Wehrmacht executed the Holocaust largely on its own—without the SS.

The Wehrmacht's 'share' went far beyond mere co-operation in mass murder, however. The military and the Nazi leadership had decided that the army would not just live off the occupied land, but send massive amounts of foodstuff back home to Germany. What that meant for Russia was that millions of people starved to death, as the Nazi war planners rightly anticipated. A similar disaster of unthinkable proportions was anticipated for and happened to the Soviet prisoners of war. They would not only be sent to forced labor in Germany, they were also to be simply shut up in huge, overcrowded compounds where they would be without shelter and without sufficient food. By the end of the war, more than half of all Soviet POWs were dead, whereas not even one out of twenty-five American and British POWs died in German captivity.[27]

What gave the most cruel distinction to Germany's 'war of extermination' on the Soviet Union was initiated by the two later so-called criminal orders, authorized by Hitler and issued by the High Command of the Armed Forces on 13 May and 6 June 1941. Whereas the Commissar Order required the troops to hand over commissars of the Red Army, who actually were in charge of political indoctrination, to the SS or to 'liquidate' them right away, the Courts-martial Decree went much further.[28] It not only suspended any jurisdiction for the subjugated population, but asked the troops to kill 'guerillas' 'ruthlessly' even after their capture and ordered 'collective punitive measures' against villages from which the Wehrmacht was 'insidiously and maliciously attacked.' As there was no clear definition of what was to be considered a guerilla or a malicious attack, the decree allowed German soldiers to do whatever they liked to enemy civilians; it also guaranteed amnesty in advance. *De facto*, the two orders declared open season on both prisoners of war and the civilian population of the occupied areas of the USSR.[29]

These and other orders were embedded in anti-Semitic and anti-Slav propaganda that denigrated the enemy population in the East as inferior, but fanatically angry, and capable of sabotage and other vicious attacks, while denouncing Jews in particular as born or hidden partisans to be 'exterminated' even before they had a chance to attack Germans. Minor or alleged partisan attacks, as well as the discovery of massacres of local Poles committed by the Soviet NKWD before retreating, stimulated a climate of fear and nervousness, a 'guerilla-psychosis,' among the troops. The occupiers could not accept resistance that questioned alleged racial superiority, but learned to subsume most brutal reaction to the slightest incident of defiance as 'military necessity' and to condemn compassion for the enemy as a sin against one's own comrades. Already on 16 July 1941, Hitler had welcomed the first Russian partisan attacks, which were still minor: 'This partisan war...has some advantage for us. It enables us to eradicate everyone who opposes us,' he said to his military entourage.[30]

Invading East Europe, German soldiers encountered a reality that seemed to verify and even to trump the propaganda. Often, for the first time, they saw the unusual appearance of orthodox East European Jews and 'understood the need of a radical solution of the Jewish question,' as a private wrote during the Polish campaign. 'Everyone who was not already a radical anti-Semite would necessarily become one there,' he concluded.[31] As their private letters and diaries show, soldiers across all military ranks, social classes, and ideological backgrounds approved German terror on Jews. Occupying Riga in summer 1941, Private Helmut Wißmann, son of a left-wing working-class family, wondered in a letter to his 'little cherub' whether it might be 'possible to ever exterminate this pest?' He had just learned that 'in Lithuania they had hanged all Jews with no exception.'[32] Not all soldiers who applauded the murder of the Jews joined in murder personally, however. A few soldiers even protested against the blatant crimes the German army committed or supported. But these were rare exceptions. As Wehrmacht Private Jochen Klepper, a conservative-Christian writer whose wife was Jewish, realized in September 1941, there was an almost undivided consensus among his comrades. 'The propaganda has been almost completely successful. Nobody spends any more thoughts about it. "The Jews have to go."'[33] From December 1941 on, the SS opened the death camps at Chelmno, Belzec, Treblinka, Sobibor, Majdanek, and Auschwitz-Birkenau to 'industrialize' the murder of the Jews in order to conclude the 'final solution' as decided upon at the Wannsee Conference in January 1942. Whereas, at that time, 75 percent of the Jews who would eventually be killed were still alive, only one year later, 4.5 million Jews, precisely this share, were dead. Face-to-face murder of Jews and other groups of civilians still went on at all parts of East Europe and also at other theaters, usually disguised as retaliation for alleged partisan attacks. Although the Wehrmacht now faced a real partisan movement and a strong military enemy in the East, the front remained relatively stable and allowed the Germans to put the grandiose plans for creating *Lebensraum* into practice, which, first of all, meant to exploit the conquered territories. From spring 1942, millions of Russian civilians were forced into abusive labor service for Germans; Wehrmacht soldiers supporting colonial slave hunting, took part in destroying families, societies, and lives all over the occupied territories.

Starting with the defeat of the Sixth Army at Stalingrad, the tide turned at the Battle of Kursk in July 1943 even more obviously than ever before. On a battlefield as large as Connecticut, the Soviets assembled 1,300,000 men (two-fifths of the entire Red Army) to defeat 900,000 German soldiers. The Germans lost half of their men and were driven far back; a fortnight after Kursk, the Red Army could read a signpost: '1209 miles to Berlin.' While the Wehrmacht in 1940 suffered from 'merely' 83,000 dead or missing soldiers, the beginning of the Russian campaign initiated much higher death tolls: 357,000 in 1941, 572,000 in 1942, and 812,000 in 1943, with roughly four out of five (or even more) occurring on the Eastern front. But in summer 1944, casualty figures outran any previous dimension. In one month, August 1944, 277,000 German soldiers lost their lives on the Eastern front, and 349,000 on all fronts. During the last five months of the war, casualty figures increased again exorbitantly, with the absolute peak of 451,000 in January 1945. During each of the following three months, almost 300,000 soldiers were killed.[34]

Suffering from mass death did not stop Germans from inflicting it on others. On the contrary. Retreating, from 1943 on, the German troops covered the rest of East Europe with marauding, murder, and plunder. The policy of 'scorched earth' concluded the destruction of half of a continent.[35] Approximately three million Soviet citizens lost their homes and all their belongings. An estimated 300,000–500,000 people were killed during the Wehrmacht's anti-partisan war in the Soviet Union. Whether they were Jews, partisans or just strange looking civilians no longer intrigued the executioners. 'Russia was turning into a depopulated, smoking, burning, wreckage-strewn desert,' Private Willy Reese stated in early 1944 in a distressed 'Confession' of his own complicity in devastation, terror, and murder. 'The war had become insane, it was all murder, never mind whom it affected,' he wrote. As the Germans were forced to retreat further and further, a new sense of collective identity emerged, a camaraderie fueled by pure cynicism. 'Two hanged men swayed on a protruding branch,' noted Reese, 'One soldier took their picture; another gave them a swing with the stick. We laughed and moved off.' In 1942 he had written in a poem about a huge gang of soldiers, guzzling and whoring, boasting and lying, cursing and triumphing. 'As a bawling crowd,' they had 'marched to Russia, gagged people, butchered blood,' and 'murdered the Jews . . . We wave the banners of the Aryan ancestors, they suit us well . . . We rule as a band.'[36] The band was the Wehrmacht, the spearhead of the Aryan Volksgemeinschaft, the German nation.

As much as they sank into collectively performed cynicism, soldiers still worried about what they had become involved in. It was these very worries that Hermann Goering and other Nazi leaders addressed, when they reminded the Germans publicly what the entire German people and not only the SS or the Nazi elite had done to the Jews. 'The Jew,' Goering stated in a radio speech on 4 October 1942, 'is behind all, and he has declared to kill all of us. And nobody [he meant no German] should think, he might say afterwards: "I always have been a good democrat against these mean Nazis." The Jew will treat all [Germans] equally. He will take revenge on the whole German people.'[37] The soldiers got the message. 'We have to win the war,' stated a private, 'otherwise we would be badly off. Foreign Jewry would take horrible revenge on our people, given the fact that here hundreds of thousands of Jews had been executed in order to establish calm and peace in the world.' The somber visions charged fighting morale. The Germans were exactly where the Nazi elite wanted to have them. Considering the disaster of Stalingrad in March 1943, Goebbels agreed with Göring, 'On the Jewish question in particular we are so committed that there is no escape for us at all,' Goebbels noted in his diary, 'and that is good. Experience shows that a movement and a *Volk* that have burned their bridges fight much more unconditionally than those who still have the chance of retreat.'[38] Goebbels was right. Not only the Nazi movement or just the SS, but the entire German nation would adopt the pariah role Hitler had envisioned long before and fought for unconditionally. As Private Franz Wieschenberg wrote in August 1944 in a letter from the Eastern front, 'We Germans are the nation that has gone for this war enthusiastically and we will have to bear the consequences.' Three years before, in August 1941, this same soldier had reported to his wife, then fiancée: 'I just saw how the Jews in a town we previously conquered had to move out of their party offices and march through the streets on their way to the stake, carrying photos of Stalin in front of them—that was a sight for sore eyes, what fun!'[39]

Both messages, that of 1941 and that of 1944, were addressed to the women at home. From the beginning of Operation Barbarossa in summer 1941, Germans at home learned about the murder of the Jews in the Soviet Union through soldiers' letters, oral accounts, gossip, and rumor. How did they react? Many of them were shocked by the rumors of mass shootings of civilians behind the Eastern Front from 1941 on. They knew that they were not supposed to openly talk about what they he had heard. They did so anyway. In December 1941, a woman in a bakery in Rhenish Emmerich spoke compassionately about the Jews in Russia whom, as she had heard, the Germans drove into the woods to gun them down. She did so in front of various clients, one of whom denounced her to the Gestapo. The cult of secrecy radiated monstrosity, uneasiness, qualms—and curiosity. In January 1942 during a vacation in Austria, a staff judge from Berlin mentioned to a waitress in a coffee shop that the Jews in Germany would be notified of their deportation and would then be shipped to Poland where their graves were already prepared. Asked not to talk about such things, he said, 'this is an open secret, any intelligent person knows about it, only the fools do not.'[40]

It is impossible to estimate how many Germans, whether men or women, whether at the battle front or on the home front, knew about the Holocaust, and what exactly they knew. Probably only a few Germans knew about the entire monstrous dimensions of the death machinery of Auschwitz or Majdanek. Multifaceted research, though, into a broad variety of different sources, ranging from Gestapo files and reports to private letters, diaries, and memoirs, has left little doubt that Germans who wanted to know were able to acquire at least rough knowledge of the ongoing mass murder. Some Germans knew even more. Victor Klemperer, who as a Jew living in Dresden in a mixed marriage was always afraid of deportation, was one of them. On 24 October 1944 he noted in his diary that 'six to seven million Jews . . . have been slaughtered (more exactly: shot and gassed).' It is worth noting to whom Klemperer owed his knowledge: the 'reports of Aryans.'[41]

There is no reason to disavow the massive and manifold inner frictions that shaped the German society at the end of the war. Social isolation in the rubble, loss of faith in Hitler, and collapse of war morale spread all over Germany. What united soldiers or civilians, men or women, young or old, war enthusiasts and war resisters, Nazis and anti-Nazis, the hangmen of the Gestapo and the few hidden or open opponents of the regime was a new sense of national belonging, the knowledge of being part of a grand community of crime. There was no belonging outside of the perpetrator society. The

German nation had shackled itself to mass crime, and the Germans knew it. It was the knowledge of the nation's responsibility for the murder of the Jews that fueled the sense of belonging to a community of fate that left no choices. Germans understood: the only choice left was to fight into the abyss. The fear of revenge united home front and battle front, just as rumors of the murder of the Jews had done from 1941 on or even before.

Establishing a new society, a racially purified nation, was the Nazis' utopian promise. It became much more than a mere fiction of the propaganda machine. In fact, genocidal warfare from 1939 to 1945 made Germans feel as if they were such a unified nation. A nation is an 'imagined community,' as Benedict Anderson has explained, that is, a community not based on face-to-face contacts like a family or a neighborhood, but on a multiplying system of communication, which is administered by central powers as mass media and fueled by certain symbols, overall on ideas of common ground. It was the knowledge of having supported or being involved in the Holocaust that constituted a completely new kind of nation building in Germany during the Second World War—the national brotherhood of mass murder.

Notes

1. Letter of Kurt Kreissler to his parents, 19 February 1945, copy owned by author.
2. Quoted in Gordon A. Craig, *Germany 1866–1945* (New York: Oxford University Press, 1978), 340.
3. Max Domarus, *Hitler. Speeches and Proclamations 1932–1945 and Commentary by a Contemporary. The Chronicle of a Dictatorship*, 4 vols (Wauconda: Bolchazy-Carducci, 1992), vol. 4, 2681f.
4. *Nazi Conspiracy and Aggression*, 8 vols and 2 supplements (Washington, DC: U.S.G.P.O., 1946–1948), vol. VI, 259–263, Doc. No. 3569–PS.
5. George F. Kennan, *The Decline of Bismarck's European Order. Franco-Prussian Relations, 1875–1890* (Princeton: Princeton University Press, 1979), 3.
6. Rüdiger Overmans, 'Kriegsverluste,' in Gerhard Hirschfeld et al. (eds), *Enzyklopädie Erster Weltkrieg* 2nd edn (Paderborn: Schoeningh, 2004), 664f.
7. Cited in Alan Kramer, *Dynamic of Destruction. Culture and Mass Killing in the First World War* (New York: Oxford University Press, 2007), 216.
8. Benjamin Ziemann, *Front und Heimat. Ländliche Kriegserfahrungen im südlichen Bayern 1914–1923* (Essen: Klartext, 1997), 185 fn 728 (soldier's letter, 12 April 1917).
9. Roger Chickering, *Imperial Germany and the Great War, 1914–1918*, 2nd edn (New York: Cambridge University Press, 2004), 93, 171, 177.
10. John Horne and Alan Kramer, *German Atrocities. A History of Denial* (New Haven: Yale University Press, 2001), 237f.
11. Michael Geyer, 'Endkampf 1918 and 1945. German Nationalism, Annihilation, and Self-Destruction,' in Alf Lüdtke and Bernd Weisbrod (eds), *No Man's Land of Violence. Extreme Wars in the 20th Century* (Göttingen: Wallstein, 2006), 44–47.

12. Michael Geyer, *Aufrüstung oder Sicherheit. Die Reichswehr in der Krise der Machtpolitik 1924–1936* (Wiesbaden: Felix Steiner Verlag, 1980).

13. Quotes in Thomas Kühne, *Kameradschaft. Die Soldaten des nationalsozialistischen Krieges und das 20. Jahrhundert* (Göttingen: Vandenhoeck & Ruprecht, 2006), 27.

14. *Kyffhäuser*, 5 May 1929, 337f.

15. Erich Maria Remarque, *All Quiet on the Western Front* (New York: Fawcett Books, 1982), 115.

16. *Stahlhelm*, 18 Jan 1925.

17. *Das Reichsbanner*, 17 October 1931, 336f.

18. Ian Kershaw, 'Hitler and the Nazi Dictatorship,' in Mary Fulbrook (ed.), *German History since 1800* (London: Arnold, 1997), 331.

19. *Adolf Hitler in Franken. Reden aus der Kampfzeit* (Nuremberg: n.p., 1938), 83.

20. Carl Schmitt, *The Concept of the Political* (New Brunswick: Rutgers University Press, 1976), 46f and 27.

21. Claire Moreau-Trichet, 'La propagande nazie a l'égard des associations françaises d'anciens combattants de 1934 a 1939,' *Guerres mondiales et conflits contemporains*, no. 205 (2002/1), 55–70. Holger Skor, 'Inszenierte Kriegserinnerung. Das deutsch-französische Frontkämpfertreffen in Freiburg 1937 als nationalsozialistischer Propagandacoup,' in Christian Geinitz et al. (eds), *Kriegsgedenken in Freiburg. Trauer-Kult-Verdrängung* (Freiburg: J. Haug, 1995), 170–206.

22. Wilhelm Deist, 'Überlegungen zur 'widerwilligen Loyalität' der Deutschen bei Kriegsbeginn,' in idem, *Militär, Staat und Gesellschaft* (Munich: R. Oldenbourg, 1991), 355–368.

23. David Bankier, *The Germans and the Final Solution. Public Opinion under Nazism* (Oxford: Blackwell, 1992), 86f. Michael Wildt's in many regards inspiring book, *Volksgemeinschaft als Selbstermächtigung. Gewalt gegen Juden in der deutschen Provinz 1919 bis 1939* (Hamburg: Hamburger Edition, 2007), overestimates the degree to which the *Volksgemeinschaft* supported and perpetrated violent antisemitism before 1939.

24. Marcel Reich-Ranicki, *The Author of Himself* (Princeton: Princeton University Press, 2001), 123, 127, 129.

25. Gerd R. Ueberschär (ed.), *NS-Verbrechen und der militärische Widerstand gegen Hitler* (Darmstadt: Wissenschaftliche Buchgesellschaft, 2000), 159f. Helmut Krausnick and Hans-Heinrich Wilhelm, *Die Truppe des Weltanschauuungskrieges. Die Einsatzgruppen der Sicherheitspolizei und des SD 1938–1942* (Stuttgart: Deutsche Verlagsanstalt, 1981), 82.

26. Charles Burdick and Hans-Adolf Jacobsen (eds), *The Halder War Diary* (Novata: Presidio Press, 1988), 384 (6 May 1941).

27. 3.3 million of 5.7 million (57 percent) Soviet POW in Germany captivity died, but only 8300 of the 231,000 British and American POWs (3.6 percent), Christian Streit, *Keine Kameraden. Die Wehrmacht und die deutschen Kriegsgefangenen 1941–1945*, new edn (Bonn: J. H. W. Dietz Nachf., 1997).

28. *Nazi Conspiracy and Aggression*, vol. III (Washington, DC: U.S.G.P.O., 1946), 637–639.

29. Geoffrey P. Megargee, *War of Annihilation. Combat and Genocide on the Eastern Front, 1941* (Lanham: Rowman & Littlefield, 2006), 19–41.

30. Minutes of a meeting at Hitler's Headquarters, 16 July 1941, Nuremberg Document 221-L, translated in *Documents on German Foreign Policy, 1918–1945* (Washington, DC: U.S.G.P.O., 1964), Series D, Vol. 13, Document 114, 149–156. Cf. Ben Shepherd, *War in the Wild East. The German Army and Soviet Partisans* (Cambridge: Harvard University Press, 2004); Mark Mazower, *Inside Hitler's Greece. The Experience of Occupation, 1941–44* (New Haven: Yale University Press, 1993).

31. Quoted in Jochen Böhler, *Auftakt zum Vernichtungskrieg. Die Wehrmacht in Polen 1939* (Frankfurt: Fischer Taschenbuch Verlag, 2006), 48.
32. Quoted in Kühne, *Kameradschaft*, 185.
33. Jochen Klepper, *Überwindung. Tagebücher und Aufzeichnungen aus dem Kriege* (Stuttgart: Deutsche Verlagsanstalt, 1958), 206 and 213, diary entries, 20 and 25 Sept 1941; see also 160, entry from 23 Aug 1941.
34. Rüdiger Overmans, *Deutsche militärische Verluste im Zweiten Wektkrieg* (Munich: R. Oldenbourg, 1999), 237–240, 276–284.
35. Shepherd, *War in the Wild East*, 129–218.
36. Willy Peter Reese, in Stefan Schmitz (ed.) *A Stranger to Myself. The Inhumanity of War: Russia, 1941–1944*, ed. (New York: Farrar, Straus and Giroux, 2005), 135, 51–53 (Russia); idem, in Stefan Schmitz (ed.), *Mir selber seltsam fremd. Die Unmenschlichkeit des Krieges. Russland 1941–44* (Berlin: List Taschenbuch, 2004), 242f. (Poem, not in the English edition.)
37. Goering speech, 4 Oct 1942, in Walter Roller and Susanne Höschel (eds), *Judenverfolgung und jüdisches Leben unter den Bedingungen der nationalsozialistischen Gewaltherrschaft*, vol. 1, *Tondokumente und Rundfunksendungen, 1930–1946* (Potsdam: Verlag für Berlin-Brandenburg, 1996), 217f; Jeffrey Herf, *The Jewish Enemy. Nazi Propaganda during World War II and the Holocaust* (Cambridge: Harvard University Press, 2006), 168f.
38. Elke Fröhlich (ed.), *Die Tagebücher von Joseph Goebbels*, part II, vol. 7 (Munich: R. Oldenbourg, 1993), 454 (2 March 1943).
39. *Kempowski-Archiv Nartum*, Nr. 3386.
40. Bernward Dörner, *Die Deutschen und der Holocaust. Was niemand wissen wollte, aber jeder wissen konnte* (Berlin: Propyläen, 2007), 336–340.
41. Victor Klemperer, *I Will Bear Witness. A Diary of the Nazi Years, 1942–1945* (New York: Random House, 1999), 371 (24 Oct 1944), 377 (26 Nov 1944).

BIBLIOGRAPHY

ANGRICK, ANDREJ, *Besatzungspolitik und Massenmord. Die Einsatzgruppe D in der südlichen Sowjetunion 1941–1943* (Hamburg: Hamburger Edition, 2003).

BARTOV, OMER, *Hitler's Army. Soldiers, Nazis, and War in the Third Reich* (New York: Oxford University Press, 1991).

FRITZSCHE, PETER, *Life and Death in the Third Reich* (Cambridge: Harvard University Press, 2008).

HULL, ISABEL V., *Absolute Destruction: Military Culture and the Practices of War in Imperial Germany* (Ithaca: Cornell University Press, 2005).

KLEE, ERNST, WILLI DRESSEN, and RIESS VOLKER (eds), *'The Good Old Days.' The Holocaust as Seen by Its Perpetrators and Bystanders* (New York: Free Press, 1991).

KRAMER, ALAN, *Dynamic of Destruction. Culture and Mass Killing in the First World War* (New York: Oxford University Press, 2007).

KÜHNE, THOMAS, *Kameradschaft. Die Soldaten des nationalsozialistischen Krieges und das 20. Jahrhundert* (Göttingen: Vandenhoeck & Ruprecht, 2006).

——, *Belonging and Genocide. Hitler's Community, 1918–1945* (New Haven: Yale University Press, 2010).

LIULEVICIUS, VEJAS GABRIEL, *War Land on the Eastern Front: Culture, National Identity, and German Occupation in World War I* (Cambridge: Cambridge University Press, 2000).

MÜLLER, SVEN OLIVER, *Deutsche Soldaten und ihre Feinde. Nationalismus an Front und Heimatfront im Zweiten Weltkrieg* (Frankfurt: S. Fischer, 2007).

POHL, DIETER, *Die Herrschaft der Wehrmacht. Deutsche Militärbesatzung und einheimische Bevölkerung in der Sowjetunion 1941–1944* (Munich: R. Oldenbourg, 2008).

ROSSINO, ALEXANDER B., *Hitler Strikes Poland. Blitzkrieg, Ideology, and Atrocity* (Lawrence: University Press of Kansas, 2003).

Verbrechen der Wehrmacht. Dimensionen des Vernichtungskrieges 1941–1944. Ausstellungskatalog (Hamburg: Hamburger Edition, 2002).

VERHEY, JEFFREY, *The Spirit of 1914: Militarism, Myth and Mobilization in Germany* (New York: Cambridge University Press, 2000).

ZIEMANN, BENJAMIN, *War Experiences in Rural Germany, 1914–1923* (Oxford: Berg Publishers, 2007).

....

CHAPTER 24

THE THREE HORSEMAN OF THE HOLOCAUST: ANTI-SEMITISM, EAST EUROPEAN EMPIRE, ARYAN FOLK COMMUNITY

....

WILLIAM W. HAGEN

Two interpretive traditions have, since Hitler's day, commanded scholarly efforts to understand the Holocaust. One emphasizes *ideas*, recounting the intellectual history of anti-Semitism and the aims and political actions of those gripped by its poisoned talons. Its motto might be Heinrich Heine's dictum: 'thought precedes act as lightning thunder.'[1] Paired with this approach is the conviction that history is made by human beings' conscious choice: beliefs inspire purposive behavior seeking their realization. Historical actors are aware of their actions and responsible for them.

In Holocaust historiography, this widespread understanding of history and human behavior has yielded the 'intentionalist' argument. This holds that (1) anti-Semitic ideology of a uniquely aggressive type flourished in late nineteenth-and early twenti-eth-century Germany; (2) Adolf Hitler and other National Socialist leaders embraced it and crafted it into a political program; and (3) the anti-Jewish policies (*Judenpolitik*) of Hitler's 'Third Reich' led, if perhaps by a 'twisted path,' to a mass murder which the Nazis' anti-Semitic ideas, and the dictator Hitler's in particular, authorized and even commanded.

The second interpretive approach, no less venerable than intentionalism, figures in historiographical debate as 'functionalism' or 'structuralism.' It sees complex historical phenomena such as the Holocaust as the outcome of intersecting supra-personal political and social developments, of which individuals—including the the powerful dictator Hitler—are both creations and embodiments. Actors' intentions are important, but they must be understood as responses to configurations of power and culture over which no one exercises guiding control. Thus, where intentionalists have stressed Hitler's beliefs and commanding will, and the clear-eyed, cold-hearted purposiveness of other National Socialist perpetrators, 'functionalists' have sought to grasp the Holocaust as the expression in Germany of mighty—if dark and pitiless—trends in modern history: the formation of ethnically and culturally homogenized nation states, imperialism, political mass mobilization (driven by utopian, sometimes biologized, visions of modernity), and the emergence of amoral, bureaucratized and militarized states, especially totalitarian states, warring among each other and riddled internally with self-aggrandizing political factions and other institutional struggles. From the interaction of such developments events crystallize, such as the Holocaust, which, though they result from the aggregation of individual thoughts and actions, are only comprehensible in their structural, supra-individual complexity.[2]

The historical literature on the Holocaust, whether intentionalist or functionalist, has in recent decades focused fixedly on the origins of the comprehensive mass murder of which Auschwitz, as the largest and deadliest of the National Socialist death camps, is the chilling symbol. How did the German leadership arrive at the *decision* to 'annihilate' (*vernichten*) or, in an even more inhuman idiom, 'exterminate' (*ausrotten*) the millions of Jews it held captive? While, as we shall see, a historiographical consensus has emerged that the *implementation* of a *policy* of comprehensive mass murder evolved from the interaction of Hitler, the chief Nazi agencies, and the military and economic situations prevailing after the outbreak of World War II, the *causes* of its gradual adoption remain controversial. Many historians, of an intentionalist cast of mind, view the transition to mass murder as the triumph of Hitler's will, breaking through in the midst of apocalyptic war the shackles of restraint which pre-war circumstances had forged. Other, structuralist-inclined historians emphasize the unpredictable, step-by-step unfolding of a process of 'cumulative radicalization,' driven by 'bureaucratic Darwinism' among National Socialists high and low for the support of a dictator who contented himself with conjuring up desired outcomes—the 'removal' (*Entfernung*) of Jews from the Nazi realm, or their 'annihilation'—without specifying precisely how.[3]

This debate is necessary and productive. It forces both intentionalists and structuralists to marshal the concrete empirical evidence, and to construct the chronologically framed narratives, without which their approaches remain philosophical-methodological manifestos. This chapter aims, however, to focus interpretation of the Holocaust and its origins, not on the decision-making process of 1941–1942, but on a wider-ranging interplay of factors. The first of these is the ideology and political program of anti-Semitism, especially in its National Socialist form. The second is Germany's drive to establish in conquered eastern Europe a 'Greater German Racial'—or Living-Space (*Lebensraum*)—Empire. The third is the Nazi project of building, among the 'racially' designated 'Aryan' German population—and on an imperial scale—a prosperous, socially mobile, harmonious, and politically alive 'people's or folk community' (*Volksgemeinschaft*). I propose that only by a linked analysis of these three dimensions can the Holocaust, both as a National Socialist deed and as an object of our own contemporary knowledge, begin to come adequately into focus.

Nazi anti-Semitism aggressively demanded the 'exclusion' of Jews from German society, and often even—if by unspecified means—from life itself. Yet in the absence of German conquest and attempted empire-building in Eastern Europe, the Holocaust could never have occurred. For the great majority of its victims were east European Jews: among a total of some six million dead, there were roughly 2.7 million Polish Jews, 2.1 Soviet Jews (mostly inhabitants of the historic Polish-Lithuanian-Belarusian-Ukrainian borderlands), 500,000 Hungarian Jews, and about 150,000 Jewish citizens of Czechoslovakia. Those who were German or Austrian inhabitants numbered, respectively, some 165,000 and 65,000. In Western Europe the genocidal machinery engulfed 200,000 people, not a few of them refugees from the German lands and Eastern Europe.[4]

To radically simplify: no anti-Semitism, no Holocaust. But also: no east European Nazi empire, no Holocaust. Yet anti-Semitism as an ideology did not always mandate German empire, nor did empire in Eastern Europe inescapably entail lethal anti-Semitism, as German practice in World War I shows. *It is the convergence of these two projects, neither necessarily entailed by the other, that generated the Holocaust.* As for the 'people's community' or *Volksgemeinschaft*, I hold, with other present-day historians, that its creation was the National Socialist regime's foremost promise to its 'Aryan' German subjects. The degree of its realization was the decisive test of Hitlerism's legitimacy, both in the eyes of Nazi rulers and Nazi-inclined 'Aryan' subjects.

Crucially, however, *Volksgemeinschaft* at the Germanic center depended, in the theory and practice of Hitler and the National Socialist governing elite, on the extension of racially exclusivist empire into its eastern periphery. For the 'American-style' prosperity and modernity the Nazis sought for their favored subjects could only, they believed, be attained through the ruthless, colonial exploitation of conquered Eastern Europe. Thus, *Volksgemeinschaft* entailed eastern empire which, as projected by its anti-Semitic conquerors, demanded the 'removal' of its Jewish population, eventually by means of mass murder. In this way, the three factors this essay highlights—anti-Semitism, eastern imperialism, and the promise of social modernization on the domestic front—interlocked to bring forth, in a process the following pages will sketch, the Holocaust.[5]

24.1 ANTI-SEMITISM: THE INTERPRETIVE DILEMMAS OF PRIVILEGING BELIEF

The history of religiously inspired Christian anti-Judaism and secularly grounded modern anti-Semitic ideology serves in many (perhaps most) minds as proof that the Holocaust was a premeditated crime. Yet the religious line of thought commonly concluded that Jews should convert to Christianity, whereupon they would be embraced. If they refused, they should be segregated and ghettoized, or forced into renewed exile. In extreme form, modern anti-Semitism, born of the late nineteenth century and grounded in the newly emergent 'science of race,' rejected Enlightenment liberalism's strategy of Jewish civil emancipation and acculturation within the democratic nation state. As a biologically-defined separate race, anti-Semites argued, Jews were unassimilable; their inclusion in the nation blocked its healthy development, saddling it with pathologies of modernity (notably predatory capitalism and bomb-throwing, anti-bourgeois revolutionism), which—whether because of God's curse, or biology's—Jews allegedly propagated. In self-defense, anti-Semites held, the European peoples must reverse liberal emancipation, strip Jews of citizenship, and otherwise exclude them from national life.[6]

In his ponderous manifesto *Mein Kampf* (1925), Adolf Hitler celebrated the ideal of a 'folkish state' (*völkischer Staat*). This meant, for the Germans, political unification in one state of all of central Europe's contiguously settled German-speakers—some eighty-five million, as Hitler thought. The collective 'people's body' (*Volkskörper*) required ennoblement through state-guided 'selective breeding' of racially positive human types (hard and war-like, unshakably fraternal, resistant to Christianity's 'slave morality'). This entailed the exclusion—through prohibitions on child-bearing and marriage and even through 'euthanasia' (medical murder)—of 'life unworthy of living' (a flexible concept, as National Socialist practice would show). As a vast organism, the nation or *Volk* must expand geographically on an imperial scale, or wither into world-historical insignificance. Germany's future 'living space'—its *Lebensraum*—lay in eastern Europe, where the enormous Soviet Union (dominated, in Hitler's view, by Jewish influences inimical to stable state-formation) would become, as Hitler later said, 'Germany's India.'[7]

Germany's Slavic-speaking and other ethnically distinctive neighbors in central, southeastern, and Eastern Europe could claim no inherent right to occupation of their lands or even to existence. 'The stronger man,' as Hitler told his generals on the eve of the 1939 invasion of Poland, 'is right.'[8] As for the German Jews, Hitler's prescription before 1933 (and until 1939) was legal segregation and cultural humiliation paired with a punishing policy of economic marginalization and dispossession that would encourage Jewish 'self-removal' through emigration. Although the implication of biologically grounded racism may be genocidal, it must not necessarily be acknowledged or acted on, as caste-like arrangements and systems of slavery and *apartheid* suggest. In Hitler's case, obsessive and hyper-aggressive anti-Semite though he was, the empirical record does not support a long-standing genocidal intent, nor do present-day historians assert it. There was, Saul Friedländer writes, 'no predetermined enactment of a demonic script.'[9]

Anti-Semitism, even in its pseudo-scientific racialized form, has always lacked plausibility and credibility except in the eyes of true believers, learned and unlearned alike. Its adherents commonly embraced it as righteous justification of ethnic and religious prejudices whose egregiousness and arbitrariness were evident to independent-minded outsiders. Scholars have thus usually interpreted it in its functionality, rather than its literal claims. Above all, they have understood anti-Semitism as an irrational response to the disquieting 'disembedding effects' of social-political-cultural 'modernization.' It appears too as a millenialist creed, promising in place of received religion (under siege by rationalist modernity) utopian fulfillment on earth, should allegedly baleful 'Jewish influences' finally be defeated, so as to enable the 'people's body' (under appropriate political traineeship) to splendidly flourish. Hitler's 'folkish state' was the most clearly limned and consistently blueprinted of all anti-Semitic visions.

Because anti-Semitism incorporates irrational anxieties and longings, it is impossible to avoid regarding its adherents as subjects, in some degree, of psychic disturbance: imperfect ego formation, projected self-hatred, paranoia—conditions that social discrimination and disabilities, as well as political shocks, can engender among even considerable segments of a large population. Yet historians rarely push this point, for not only did Hitler and his colleagues display considerable political and technological-managerial prowess, but to judge them as psychologically deranged risks absolving them of moral competence.[10]

Doubtless the interpretation of National Socialism most widely accepted, both among scholars and the western public, holds that it embodied and enacted the most extreme form of anti-Semitism. The outstanding recent formulation of this argument is conveyed in Saul Friedländer's magisterial two volumes on *Nazi Germany and the Jews* (1997–2007). Here, National Socialism figures 'as a political religion, commanding the total commitment owed to a religious faith.' Nazi anti-Semitism was 'redemptive.' It synthesized a 'murderous rage'—above all, Hitler's own— 'and an "idealistic" goal, shared by the Nazi leader and the hard core of the party, [leading] to the ultimate decision to exterminate the Jews.'[11] The broad German public was drawn into the vortex of genocidal complicity, because 'for a regime dependent on constant mobilization, the Jew served as the constant mobilizing myth.' Altogether, 'Nazism confronts us with some kind of "sacralized modernism,"' proving that 'modern society does remain open to—possibly in need of—the ongoing presence of religious or pseudoreligious incentives within a system otherwise dominated by thoroughly different dynamics,' that is, economic self-interest, amoral political logic and bureaucratic rationality.[12]

Friedländer dwells far more on National Socialist *Judenpolitik* than he does on the Nazis' 'idealistic goal'—doubtless the racial-imperial *Volksgemeinschaft* enjoying 'American' living standards. Yet, *from his narrative*, and from the empirical record in general, it is evident that Nazi anti-Semitism did *not* drive Hitler's central political *actions*. Rather, the regime's anti-Jewish policies (as distinct from its anti-Semitic impulses and enthusiasms) were largely subordinated to—that is, they were *functions of*—its feverish pursuit of economic recovery and rearmament, subjugation of Austria and Czechoslovakia, military defeat and violent Germanization of Poland and, finally, conquest and exploitation of the Soviet Union.

The National Socialist regime's far-reaching exclusion in 1933–1934 of Jewish Germans (along with defiant republicans and outspoken leftists) from public sector employment, including academia, as well as from medicine, law, and the arts and entertainment branches certainly sent a powerful anti-Semitic message. Yet such purges also rewarded Hitler's followers in the middle classes with vacated jobs, while terrorizing adherents of the fallen Weimar Republic, and so helped consolidate the new populist dictatorship. Grass-roots anti-Jewish violence, to which rank-and-file Nazis, SA storm troopers, and Hitler Youth were drawn, found regime approval in the pre-war years only to a limited, strategic degree, and was as often suppressed from above so as not to interfere with higher priorities. In the 1930s communist activism and other forms of anti-Nazi resistance, not Jewish identity, led to Gestapo jail-cells and the new concentration camps.[13]

The 1935 Nuremberg Laws stripped Jewish Germans of citizenship, segregating them from 'Aryan' Germans on 'racial grounds'—if grandparents' religious practice of Judaism (the Nazis' identity test) can be called racial. This would establish, Hitler hypocritically proclaimed, 'tolerable relations with the Jewish people,' enabling them, through government-sanctioned, specifically Jewish social-cultural institutions, to pursue 'their own *völkisch* life' more freely than in other European countries.[14] This policy, alongside continued toleration of Jewish Germans' private-sector business enterprise, aimed to 'normalize' and 'legalize' segregated Jewish life in Hitler's Germany, and defuse foreign criticism and reprisals against National Socialist anti-Semitism, emanating especially, as the Nazis feared, from Jewish organizations in western Europe and America. The short-term aim, largely attained, was to avoid obstacles on the road to German economic recovery.

When, after 1936, the regime began expropriating—'aryanizing'—Jewish business, it did so principally to seize assets whose further sale or nationalization allowed the regime to significantly offset rearmament's colossal costs. Yet the politically ill-steered 'wild aryanization,' pursued to the accompaniment of severe anti-Semitic street violence in Austria following Hitler's veiled subversion and annexation of that country in March 1938, accelerated anti-Jewish radicalism within the National Socialist party in Germany itself. This culminated amid anxieties over renewed European war triggered by Hitlerian aggression against Czechoslovakia—superficially assuaged at the October 1938 Munich conference—in the 'Crystal Night' pogrom of November 9, 1938. Its nation-wide grass-roots (but Nazi-directed) violence—hundreds of synagogue-burnings, innumerable shop-plundering, beatings, some one hundred immediate deaths by murder, police razzias brutally imprisoning twenty thousand and more Jewish men—inaugurated a government-managed terminal confiscation of Jewish assets in Germany and a massive wave of Jewish emigration from the land.

In this way, by the time of Hitler's September 1939 Polish invasion, the religiously marked German Jewish population, which in 1933 had stood at about a half million, had declined by 60 percent, leaving a remnant of largely impoverished and elderly people, and a disproportionate number of women, to face gradual extinction through material deprivation and 'social death.' This state of affairs came close to constituting a 'final solution' of the 'Jewish problem' in Germany itself, preceding the outbreak of mass murder in Eastern Europe. It fulfilled Hitler's pre-1933 hopes of Jewish 'removal' from the 'Aryans' midst, with the additional advantage of its having, through 'aryanization' of Jewish property, substantially aided German economic recovery and rearmament.

It was a successfully fulfilled anti-Semitic program, *but* also one that was *subordinated* to the attainment of Hitler's fundamental objectives: eastern conquest through rearmament, and social appeasement and modernization through government spending programs (including better wages paid and confiscated Jewish housing redistributed). Friedländer acknowledges the dimension of 'economic rationality' in National Socialist *Judenpolitik*, especially the linkage in 1938–1939 between 'economic expropriation and expulsion of the Jews.' He adds, though, that two years later, 'another "logic"' was to appear.[15]

Anti-Jewish policy following the 1939 war's outbreak consisted primarily in the effort to expel Polish Jews from the 'incorporated eastern territories,' that is, the large part of defeated Poland annexed directly into what had become the 'Greater German Reich' (*Grossdeutsches Reich*). In this conquest German occupation authorities and ethnic German vigilantes executed some 45–65,000 Polish citizens, about 7000 of them Jewish, the rest members of the Polish political and intellectual classes, as well as soldiers and ordinary people. Among 50,000 prisoners of war, roughly 25,000 classified as Jewish died in winter 1939–1940 from a deliberately applied maltreatment that was a harbinger of worse things to come. In the German-annexed major industrial city of Łódź and in occupied central and eastern Poland—that is, in the colonially conceived and administered 'General Government' (*Generalgouvernement*)—Nazi policy began forcing the millions of Polish Jews into ghettos, sealed in 1940, where rampant death through malnutrition and disease set in.[16]

Friedländer views this state of affairs in occupied Poland, which lasted into 1941, as a 'holding pattern' on the 'Reich model.'[17] But it was much worse—indeed, arguably, the beginning of the Holocaust, understood as mass death induced by state violence and abuse. As Götz Aly and Susanne Heim have shown, in 1939–1941 National Socialist *Judenpolitik* confronted impasses whose implications were ominous. Nazi authorities, above all SS leaders Heinrich Himmler and Reinhard Heydrich—Himmler's second-in-command responsible for operationalizing Jewish policy—sought feverishly to deport Poles and Jews from the newly-acquired 'incorporated eastern territories' so as to settle in their place ethnic Germans from east European minority communities, especially those under Soviet control (whose emigration Stalin had agreed with Hitler to allow).[18]

The German–Polish ethnic frontier had, since the late nineteenth century, been a site of embittered nationalist competition for predominance in population and land-holding.[19] The National Socialists now inaugurated what they intended to be a 'final solution' to this 'nationality struggle' (*Nationalitätenkampf*) by the most ruthless decimation of the Polish political leadership class, uprooting of Polish farmers, and rapid-fire settlement of German colonists, pushing the German ethnic boundary far eastward in the course of but a few years. German policy in subjugated Poland meant cultural genocide for the Poles.[20] Friedländer writes that 'the ongoing violence in occupied Poland created a blurred area of murderous permissiveness that, unplanned as it was, would facilitate the transition to more systematic murder policies.'[21] The violence, however, was planned—aimed at the Poles (3000 more political leaders, among 30,000 fresh arrestees, were shot in May 1940), though raging local ethnic German militias, SS death squads and army units plundered and murdered individual Poles and Jews at will.

Meanwhile, it intensely frustrated the Nazi authorities that the captive Polish Jews especially, but also German, Austrian, and Czech Jews, could not be successfully 'removed' through deportation to somewhere in occupied eastern Poland, as the abortive 1939 'Nisko Reserve' plan had foreseen. Ghettoization in Poland amounted to human warehousing pending shipment to a still-unknown destination. After Germany's military defeat of France in spring 1940, hopes arose among National Socialist leaders, Hitler included, that the large East African island of Madagascar (today's Malagasy Republic), hitherto ruled by France, could be acquired as a destination for Nazi-deported Jews (who would live—and perish—there under German SS rule). But Britain's refusal to capitulate and its continued naval domination of the high seas doomed this malevolent idea.

Thus, in the first two years of the war, National Socialist *Judenpolitik* depended on a course of events driven by Hitler's pursuit of *Lebensraum* through war and *Volksgemeinschaft*-expansion through German colonization in 'the East.' If, in occupied Poland, extensive Jewish death was commencing, this was the consequence of the German effort to build an east European racial empire, while plundering a shattered Poland for food and other assets with which to offset the cost of war and maintain, and possibly raise, living standards in Germany. If such an outcome gratified Hitler and other anti-Semites, it nevertheless represented 'collateral damage' more than achievement of official *Judenpolitik*'s objectives (which, so far as captive Jews were concerned, still focused on deportation).

Instead, the burden of policing and minimally sustaining millions of Jewish hostages appeared to National Socialist planners as a deficit whose continued weight 'German society' could not be expected to bear. It had been clear to Nazi officials responsible for food supply that war would require replacement of lost overseas imports at Eastern Europe's expense, where crops and livestock would be seized for German consumption. There was no place in this calculus for captive Jews. In Germany itself, the question whether the residual Jewish community should even continue to have a beggarly claim on now scarcer food and other consumer goods grew ominous.

The June 1941 invasion of Stalin's Russia promised Hitler world-power, perhaps world-domination, through extension of German *Lebensraum* far eastward, to the Ural Mountains, if not beyond. The dictator foresaw the German population soon swelling to 125 million and more, and the German language conquering Europe. British resistance would buckle, and a German imperium from Atlantic and Mediterranean to Black Sea and Arctic would begin its thousand-year sway. This was, too, a 'war against the Jews,' for Hitler understood the Bolshevik political class as 'racially' Jewish or Jewish-controlled. Hence, his notorious 'Commissar Order' on the invasion's eve, mandating summary execution of captured Communist political-administrative functionaries. To this end, and to murderously suppress anti-German subversion and partisan resistance, which Soviet Jews were, according to anti-Semitic formulas, expected to launch *en masse*, the SS-commanded Task Forces (*Einsatzgruppen*), which had already performed execution duty in Poland, were greatly expanded and sent into action on Soviet soil. By the end of 1941 they had shot a half-million Jews, eliminating, among others, the entire Jewish population—man, woman, and child—of the occupied Lithuanian-Baltic region.

On 31 July 1941 Hermann Göring commissioned Reinhard Heydrich to draft a plan for 'the final solution of the Jewish Question in Europe.' Friedländer interprets this as an 'overall extermination plan of all European Jews.' Certainly it registered the deadly escalation that the anti-Soviet war inaugurated. Food-supply planners, led by the SS's Herbert Backe, intended systematic starvation of captured or besieged Russian cities, and in plundered Soviet, mainly Ukrainian, agricultural districts. Nazi authorities accepted that the victims would number in the tens of millions: the greatest mass death, Göring complacently observed, since the seventeenth-century Thirty Years War.[22]

Since spring 1940 Himmler and his staff had been elaborating plans for the Germanization of the Polish provinces incorporated into the Reich in 1939 through colonization and eastward deportation of non-Germans. These culminated in the 'General Plan for the East' (*Generalplan Ost*), which Hitler approved—as Himmler reported of 'the happiest day of my life'—in July 1942. This document in its several drafts foresaw the reduction, in thirty or even twenty years, of the mainly Slavic population—from the Polish General Government eastward into Russia—of between thirty to fifty million people. They would perish from the rigors of hard labor, aggravated by undernourishment, deportation, and medical neglect. Millions of selected children would be kidnapped and Germanized. Millions of others, children and adults, would be kept alive as servile workers. Polish, Russian, and the tongues of other doomed cultures would survive, if only into the mid-range future, as helot-languages. Hitler favored an analogy between *Lebensraum* colonization in Eastern Europe and the nineteenth-century conquest by white settlers of the North American west. As he lectured his dinner-guests in October 1941, 'we eat Canadian corn [i.e., wheat] and don't think of the Indians.' Some four million Soviet prisoners of war fell into German hands in the 1941 invasion. They were, under the regular German army's guard, mostly starved to death in their camps, though some half-million died by firing squad. By February 1942 but one million remained alive, of whom fewer than half were deployable in forced labor.[23]

The captive Jews' fate remained unresolved. In the Polish General Government, National Socialist ghetto administrators steered toward short-term 'productivization,' keeping able-bodied workers alive to render useful wartime services, while the 'useless eaters' perished through deliberate neglect. In Berlin, where most of the remaining German and many Austrian Jews had huddled together, some 40,000 young adults were dragooned into munitions and other war industries. This violated Hitler's and other high-ranking Nazis' conviction that Jews embodied subversive revolt in the making, on analogy with what they remembered as the 'Jewish-bolshevik'-led strikes and anti-war demonstrations—the 'stab in the back'—which in 1917–1918 had undermined (as they thought) an otherwise triumphant Germany.

The Jews in German hands had seemed politically useful as pawns in gaining the western powers,' especially the United States,' toleration of Hitler's empire-building. But as President Roosevelt deepened his commitment to British resistance and German defeat, such considerations—in any case delusive in view of Nazi abuse of the captive Jews—faded. Yet the idea of deportation persisted. In February 1941 Hitler, speaking confidentially to Nazi leaders, said that 'originally he had only thought of breaking the power of the

Jews in Germany, but now his goal had to be the exclusion of Jewish influence in the entire Axis sphere . . . If only he knew where to put several million Jews, there were not so many after all.' But he would not risk German ships to deliver them to Madagascar. 'He was thinking of many things in a different way, and not exactly more friendly.'[24] Ominously, in mid-October 1941 Heydrich blocked any further Jewish emigration from Nazi-occupied Europe, even when foreign entry visas and external economic support were on offer.

Friedländer, like many other historians, sees Auschwitz's shadow arising out of the anti-Soviet war's violence. By fall 1941, genocidal killing was issuing from the barrels of SS guns, already broken in to mass executions earlier in Poland. Other SS men were adapting the technique of gas-chamber murder—previously employed in the 'T-4' euthanasia program to kill tens of thousands of German and, later, Polish mental hospital inmates—for use against east European Jews. But however murderous the drift of Nazi policy, Hitler's 'final decision,' Friedländer holds, was only made 'as a result of the American entry into the war.' It was on December 12, 1941, one day after his declaration of war against the United States—in solidarity with his Japanese ally—that Hitler, addressing a broad audience of top National Socialist leaders and regional NS-Party Gauleiters, announced that 'the world war is here, the extermination'—that is, destruction (*Vernichtung*)—'of the Jews must be its necessary consequence.' This was a reference to his oft-cited Reichstag speech of 30 January 1939, in which he had threatened 'destruction' of the European Jews should 'international finance Jewry'—from their supposed British and American bastions of influence—provoke a new world war. On December 18, Himmler noted of a private meeting with Hitler: 'Jewish Question [:] exterminate as partisans;' in other words, all Soviet Jews, at least, were to be murdered on the pretext of eliminating partisan resistance.[25]

In January 1942 the Wannsee Conference near Berlin gathered, at Heydrich's invitation, a wide array of key German government ministerial officials. They readily agreed to commit resources, including the railroad systems, to Jewish 'deportations to the East,' where the able-bodied would be put to hard labor which, if it did not kill them, would be followed by 'appropriate treatment.' It was understood, but left unspoken that, for the Jewish masses unable to 'build roads,' camps were under construction equipped with gas chambers and massive crematoria. Doubtless the previous smooth operation of the T-4 euthanasia program, which by 1942 claimed 70,000 victims, had proven that German officialdom was prepared to co-operate in the dictatorship's murderous programs, if only so as not to appear indifferent to the regime's bureaucratic imperative of 'working toward the Führer,' that is, attempting to anticipate Hitler's will and satisfy its demands by means of maximally hard measures. Mass death was, by winter 1942, becoming Nazism's familiar accompaniment: as the Wannsee participants toasted each other, millions of Soviet prisoners of war were already dead or dying, while the guns of the SS *Einsatzgruppen* continued to blaze.

Poor harvests and food shortages in 1941–1942 prompted SS officials, backed by Himmler, to mandate by the end of 1942 the 'liquidation' of the General Government's ghettos. The productivization strategy saved a core of workers in the Białystok ghetto until the fall of 1943 and in the larger Łódź ghetto until 1944. But otherwise the German regime, reassured by fulsome harvests in summer and fall 1942, undertook to nourish better its non-Jewish slave laborers from east Europe and elsewhere (notably France), so as to send the captive Jews—including the politically suspect German Jews—to perish in the death camps. This was a process to a large degree completed in 1943, although the deportation of Hungarian Jews and other victims to Auschwitz in 1944 raked the lethal coals back into flame.

It corresponds to Friedländer's emphasis on 'redemptive anti-Semitism' that Hitler and other leading Nazis, notably Joseph Goebbels, celebrated—sometimes very publicly and bluntly—the Jewish mass murder. In a speech on 30 January 1942 at the Berlin Sportpalast, Hitler exulted that 'the hour will strike when the most evil world enemy of all time will have ended its role at least for a thousand years.' In a self-styled political testament, dictated shortly before his suicide on 29 May 1945, Hitler blamed 'international Jewry' for the war and the sufferings it imposed on Germany, justified his fight ('by humane methods') with the Jewish arch-enemy, and called for 'the strictest keeping of the race laws' and 'merciless struggle' in the future 'against the universal poisoner of all people.' Since 1919, Friedländer concluded, 'nothing seems to have changed in Hitler's innermost ideological landscape.'[26]

As for the dictator's German subjects' co-operation in the 'redemptive final battle for the salvation of Aryan humanity,' it was, Friedländer writes, their 'frenzied devotion,' their 'hysterical adoration and blind faith,' which cemented the tie to the charismatic Führer (*Führer-Bindung*), guaranteeing their acquiescence in all his commanded works. This was less an anti-Semitic bond than a pseudo-religious one, whereby defeat of the 'universal poisoner' was the precondition of folkish felicity. But Friedländer concedes, too, the strength of historian Götz Aly's insistence on the popularity of plundering Jews and other victims for the benefit of the 'Aryan' *Volksgemeinschaft*. 'Robbing the Jews,' Friedländer writers, 'contributed to the upholding of the *Volksstaat*; murdering them and fanning the fears of retribution became the ultimate bond of Führer and *Volk* in the collapsing *Führerstaat*.'[27]

If the Holocaust fulfilled an ideological program entailing belief that world salvation required 'removal' of 'the Jews,' it appears in this light far more clearly *after its occurrence* than before or during it. For prior to the Wannsee Conference and the subsequent inauguration of the death-camps, *Judenpolitik* figured in contemporaries' minds, as we may see it too, as a function or concomitant of objectives independent of narrow anti-Semitic postulates. That is, the Greater German East European Empire and its corresponding *Volksgemeinschaft* were the goals for which the Third Reich fought and died. If, officially, their realization entailed Jewish exclusion, or even mass murder, it was nonetheless these objectives that beckoned to Nazi enthusiasts as the great positive destinations lying on the far side of the solution to the 'Jewish question' (and also the 'questions' posed by biologically 'unworthy' existences at home and in non-German eastern Europe). It was in large measure because National Socialists could view the world in this racialized and totalitarian manner that they accepted with no moral scruples the human destruction their actions wrought.

We have seen, however, that the 'path to Auschwitz' did not proceed directly from *Mein Kampf,* but rather that it opened up on the roads to Warsaw and Moscow, especially once Hitler had burned his bridges to the West. Recent scholarship emphasizes that, however comprehensive Hitler's murderous intent, the mass murder's scope was never firmly fixed, and so consisted of a series of decisions, rather than following from a single dictatorial death sentence. The Holocaust amounted to an unfolding process, dependent on circumstance—especially capture of Jewish populations, such as the Hungarian, outside Nazi control (in this case, until mid-1944), or loss of control over Jewish fate, as occurred when, after 1943, the once pro-Hitler Romanian government retreated from further murder of its multitudinous Jewish subjects.[28]

Had Europe and America managed to halt German expansion in the borders of summer 1939, the Holocaust in the sense of Jewish mass murder would never have occurred, even if central European Jewry could not have avoided disappearance through forced emigration and brutal maltreatment. A *grossdeutsche Volksgemeinschaft*—confined to Germany, Austria, and the Czech lands—would have focused Nazi energies, including such murderous eugenic impulses as propelled the T-4 program. The fate of the east European Jewish millions—though perhaps hard—would not have been mass death under the auspices of pseudo-scientized anti-Semitism. But could the Third Reich have survived without external war? Would it have consumed itself in mad internal 'cleansings' and purges? Could it have persuaded other, friendly authoritarian or fascist regimes to adopt its ruthless anti-Jewish policies? Might it have ossified into an inward-turned authoritarianism? Would domestic rebellion have upended it?

24.2 IMPERIAL VIOLENCE THE HOLOCAUST'S PROGENITOR

Although, like many other historians, Friedländer traces the Holocaust to anti-Semitic beliefs, he recognizes that, as a process of mass murder, it grew from the soil of Nazi-occupied western and central Poland and Nazi-assaulted Soviet or Soviet-controlled lands: the Baltic countries, Belarus, Ukraine, and eastern Poland. It was a response to German capture of millions of east European Jews. This was, as these pages emphasize, the consequence, not of anti-Semitism, but of German imperialism. Yet National Socialist racism, not imperial domination, prescribed Holocaust murder. In World War I, the Kaiser's Germany held sway over roughly the same east European lands as Hitler had conquered by 1941–1942. Toward the Jews of the region German World War I policy was in part protective, in part economically exploitative, certainly not without anti-Jewish prejudice, yet not driven by anti-Semitism and not aimed at anti-Jewish violence. Similarly, the Kaiser's government sought to create friendly, conservative-ruled satellite-dependencies of the Poles and other peoples transferred from tsarist to German rule, and not to enslave and obliterate them, as the National Socialist *Generalplan Ost* forecast.

A multifarious literature has found synthesis and analysis in Mark Mazower's *Hitler's Empire: Nazi Rule in Occupied Europe* (2008). Deepening an earlier furrow in British historiography, Mazower finds the roots of the National Socialist imperium 'not in anti-Semitism, nor in the blind lust for conquest, but rather in the quest to unify Germans within a single German state,' a project traceable to the liberal-democratic revolution of 1848.[29] Yet, in fact, this quest found *fulfillment* in 1938 through annexation of Austria and the Sudeten region of Czechoslovakia. Hitler's subsequent program of eastward expansion and ruthless Germanization flowed from other sources: above all, the ideological fusion of eugenicist racism, anti-Semitism, German nationalism, and the geopolitical postulate that the twentieth-century future belonged, not to mere nation states, but to nations raised to continental/imperial scale.

Mein Kampf blueprinted the bio-political, folkish empire, but Mazower does not pause long over its lineaments. Instead, he underscores the enthusiasm Hitler displayed, in his unpublished 1928 'Second Book,' for the United States. There 'the best Nordic forces' had subjugated a rich continent and its indigenous inhabitants. Racial segregation and post-World War I blockage of immigration by ethnically stigmatized people ensured the future of a dominant white society, characteristic of European settler colonies. Hitler celebrated, Mazower writes, 'the geopolitical potency of a state that had overcome both food scarcity and threats to its racial purity'.[30] This was his goal for Germany, as he repeatedly told his generals in coaching them for a war for *Lebensraum*, self-sufficiency in food-supply, and overall economic autarchy. These could only be gained in eastern Europe, not—as he told them in November 1937—'on the basis of liberal-capitalist conceptions about the exploitation of [overseas] colonies' (although Hitler never lost his admiration for the British Empire, whose racist and extractive features he praised while dismissing its 'civilizing mission' as obfuscation and cant).[31]

Hitler's empire was more modern than Mazower's stress on continuity with the *grossdeutsch* nationalism of 1848 allows. Likewise, emphasis on the 'intense nostalgia for the past' that Mazower discovers in Nazi conceptions of east European empire (with their visions of a sturdy Aryan peasantry and SS nobility) distracts from Hitler's and other Nazi planners' enthusiasm to plunder east European resources, including its labor-power, to rapidly catch up with or even outstrip 'American' modernity in the future *Volksgemeinschaft*—in industry and technology, population growth, living standards, and social mobility.[32] The future Germanized eastern Europe would be dotted with technologically and architecturally cutting-edge cities, criss-crossed by freeways, enabling visitors from the Reich to comfortably drive to the Crimea on the Black Sea— in Hitler's mind, Germany's future 'California.' The question has often arisen: might not the east European Jews, who as Yiddish-speakers were easily assimilable to German-language culture, and whose urban occupations could have been useful to German purposes, have been desirable recruits into the *Volksgemeinschaft*? Yet in Nazi eyes, the eastern Jews in a great majority were far too poor and backward in their socio-economic practices to qualify for such a role, leaving aside the pro-Bolshevism and other defects anti-Semitic ideology attributed to them.[33]

Of the Holocaust, Mazower writes, consistent with these pages' argument, that 'the "war against the Jews" essentially grew out of Hitler's "war for the Germans."' Granted Hitler's anti-Semitic aggressiveness, the fate of captive Jews, nevertheless, 'grew out of the circumstances of the war and fluctuated according to its fortunes.' Because the 'Final Solution' emerged from 'even more ambitious Nazi plans for the racial reorganization of much of eastern Europe, the boundaries of the killings were always unclear.' The Nazis targeted other groups for extinction. A German official in the General Government generals was not wrong to attribute the Poles' underground armed resistance to their fear that the Jews' fate conjured 'an atrocious picture of their own destiny.' Mazower cautiously evokes the 'ever wider horizons of annihilation' that might have opened beyond the Holocaust.[34] Yet such horizons had dawned before the Jewish mass murder began.

Hitler's New Order occupies the far right wing of a stage on which Europe's other modern empires stand. If it seems to contrast jarringly with the Dutch, French, and British imperiums, remembering their foundations in slave-economies and the demographic decimation they wrought among their non-white populations, by violence or disease, reduces the distance between them. In the twenty years of its existence, Belgian king Leopold II's rapacious Congo Free State halved its large African population through brutal exploitation and murder. Nor, as Hitler self-servingly emphasized, can such white-settler colonies as the Spanish and Portuguese American empires, British North America, Australia, and South Africa escape their own semi-genocidal shadows. Stalinist Russia worked at the 'liquidation' of 'enemy nations' within its vast boundaries, while militarist Japan ruthlessly occupied China, targeting Manchuria (like Korea before it) for settlement as the Nazis did Poland.

Mazower may go too far, then, in holding that other European empires never dealt with 'the power of numbers'—that is, those of the colonially dominated, slated for cultural eclipse—as violently or hastily as the National Socialists. But he is right to emphasize that, in their assault on the Soviet Union, they overreached themselves, creating shortages of food and other vital materials, which 'turned their cult of force and racial geopolitics . . . into a programme of extermination'—foreshadowed, it may be added, in the Nazi-occupied Poland of 1939–1940—'on a scale which had no precedent.'[35]

24.3 VOLKSGEMEINSCHAFT: 'PEOPLE'S STATE,' 'PEOPLE'S COMMUNITY,' 'PEOPLE'S BODY,' 'FOLK-ALIENS'

An accelerating current in historiography on National Socialism has swept away from the political and social-structural history of Hitler's regime toward the *Volksgemeinschaft* as Nazi theory and practice. Enthusiasts for this reorientation include those who, like the influential senior historian Hans-Ulrich Wehler, stress the importance of ordinary

Germans' yearnings for prosperity and social mobility in sparking their consent to Hitler's rule (though Wehler emphasizes no less the politics of charismatic totalitarianism). Götz Aly has provoked debate, but won much qualified support with his reading of National Socialism as a 'favor-bestowing dictatorship' (*Gefälligkeitsdiktatur*): the Nazis were 'classic feel-good politicians' (*Stimmungspolitiker*), who 'on a daily basis bought themselves public backing or anyway indifference' through crowd-pleasing improvements in social welfare benefits, wage and tax advantages, and egalitarian undercutting of elite privileges and pretensions.[36]

The National Socialists, Aly argues, delivered their populist gifts at the cost of the murdered Jews and their 'aryanized' property—which in the aggregate across central and eastern Europe possessed an enormous value—and through the plunder of the occupied territories in general. Nazi 'extermination-policy (*Vernichtungspolitik*)' drew its energy less from intellectualized ideological anti-Semitism than from this program of social redistribution: 'it oriented itself to the people's well-being (*Volkswohl*).' Hence, Aly charges, the weakness of anti-regime opposition, and even the widespread lack in the German population of a later sense of guilt.[37]

Doubtless Aly exaggerates, but his argument's thrust finds support in the scholarly consensus that expropriation of Jews and economic exploitation of both eastern and Western Europe served vitally to sustain living standards in wartime Germany and so undergird the Nazi regime's popular acceptance. If the 'favors' National Socialism bestowed in the way of living standards and social mobility were lower than advertised, the effect of their half-delivery and future promise did, indeed, elicit an enthusiasm that only Allied bombing, which in 1943 began to destroy German big-city life, gradually diminished. Yet in the war's final years, Eastern Europe—and France too—went hungry to the German consumer's advantage, and comprehensive misery only struck Germany *after* the 1945 defeat.

Industrial society's shaping as ethnically homogeneous, nationally integrated and politically mobilized—and as raised to maximal biological health and reproductive vigor by means of state-guided programs of citizenship-formation, secularized public education, and eugenics-informed medical and mental-health programs—figures as the central dynamic of 'modernization' or 'modernity' in historically-contoured social theories, in part inspired by Michel Foucault, which in recent decades have flowed from the pens of Zygmunt Bauman, Detlev Peukert, Peter Wagner and others.[38] Many research historians have shown concretely how the Nazi *Volksgemeinschaft* was meant to embody this social utopia, and how especially its pursuit consigned Jewish Germans to exclusion on supposedly scientific racial grounds. The fact that gas-chamber technology was developed and first applied to inmates of psychiatric institutions reveals, before the onset of Holocaust violence, the murderous potentiality of bio-political utopianism (and the amoral potential of modern science and technology).

Ultimately, the eugenic-racist stigmatization of Jews in particular could only occur because of the earlier history of anti-Judaism and anti-Semitism. Yet very many Nazis, especially degree-holding SS and Nazi party planners and functionaries, but also Hitler and Goebbels, dismissed old-fashioned 'bourgeois' anti-Semitism in favor of the 'racial science' inspiring their vision of eugenic modernity. To the considerable extent that the Holocaust served the realization of this social Darwinist dream, the emergence of modern right-wing nationalism underpinned by racist eugenics figures as a fundamental cause of the Jewish mass murder. Its triggering power was, arguably, more potent than that of the older anti-Semitism which, had it not undergone reformulation (however untenable) in modern scientific discourse, would likely have gradually disappeared (as has happened in Western Europe and North America) in the interstices of religious obsession and crank politics.

24.4 GERMAN PUBLIC OPINION AND THE HOLOCAUST: INDIFFERENTISM, COMPLICITY PASSIVE OR WILLING, FOREBODINGS, GUILT

The enormity of National Socialist murder raises the question of the German population's knowledge of the regime's genocidal actions, the degree of their active complicity, and the depth of their assent. On one side stand those who underscore the Nazi regime's 'consensualist' nature. They argue that support for Hitler's dictatorship skyrocketed from a near majority in 1932 to massive acclamation of its, in certain respects, stunningly successful accomplishments by the eve of the war in 1939. Whether for reasons of material self-interest, political conviction, or quasi-religious self-immersion in the sea of collective belief, most Germans—so this view holds—accepted National Socialism. They regarded its iron-fisted repression of Communists and Social Democrats, its antagonism to the Catholic church and liberal Protestantism, its eugenic program (including forced sterilizations), and its persecution of Jewish Germans as justifiable and necessary to the attainment of the yearned-for *Volksgemeinschaft*.

Consensualist historians point to the absence of effective resistance to National Socialist rule (while underestimating resistance *attempts*) and to the regime's own confidential soundings of public opinion in concluding, so far as official *Judenpolitik* was concerned, that most Germans either actively embraced the anti-Semitic program or viewed it with the indifference of bystanders for whom everything else was more important. Nazi indoctrination of youth was indeed, by all accounts, widely effective, so that many young NS party activists and recruits into the armed forces and SS showed little hesitation in acting as 'Hitler's willing executioners.' The scruples of those of their elders still bound to the allegedly fading sub-cultures of liberalism and Christian morality encountered contemptuous dismissal among regime functionaries and zealous youth alike.[39]

Two clouds trouble the consensualist skies. One is cast by the ultra-repressive character of Hitler's dictatorship, and especially its judicial-administrative and police powers. Opposition and regime-criticism were from the start serious crimes, frequently punished by imprisonment or death. Monthly Gestapo arrests of Germans as late as October 1941 numbered 544 for 'Communism and Marxism,' 1518 for 'opposition,' 531 for 'prohibited association [often sexual] with Poles or prisoners of war,' and 7729 for 'stopping work.' This amounted to some 65 arrests daily throughout the Reich for often severely penalized political offenses. During the war, the German armed forces staged three million court-martials, including 400,000 against civilians and prisoners of war. Thirty-thousand German soldiers received death sentences, of which two-thirds were carried out (in contrast to forty-eight soldiers put to death during World War I). The civil criminal courts imposed on German citizens 16,000 wartime death penalties, three-quarters actually carried out (amounting to six executions daily in a six-year period, usually widely reported in the press as warnings to others). In 1944, the Justice Ministry began drafting a law empowering the courts and police to eliminate 'community aliens' (*Gemeinschaftsfremde*), an omnibus term encompassing defeatists, critics, misfits, outsiders, 'failures' (*Versager*), and 'folk-pests' (*Volksschädlinge*).[40] Of jailed Germans deemed physically unsightly, a 1944 Justice Ministry conference concluded: 'they look like miscarriages of hell . . . It is planned that they too shall be eliminated. Crime and punishment are irrelevant.'[41]

Under such circumstances, Germans—as much evidence testifies—widely enacted the script attributed to them by a clandestine informant of the exiled Social Democratic Party in March 1940: 'The comprehensive terror compels 'national comrades' [*Volksgenossen*] to conceal their real mood, to hold back from expressing their real opinions, and instead to feign optimism and approval. Indeed, it is obviously forcing ever more people to conform to the demands of the regime even in their thinking; they no longer dare to bring themselves to account. The outer shell of loyalty that forms in this way can last a long time yet.'[42]

This psychologically insightful report points to the second cloud casting shadows on consensualism. In the fullest and most sophisticated study of German attitudes on National Socialist anti-Jewish policy so far undertaken, Peter Longerich has shown that the dictatorship suppressed 'public opinion' in any meaningful sense.[43] It was, instead, the task of Nazi propaganda, notably press and radio, but even also of the regime's own confidential internal reports on the public mood, to *create* and *mold* opinion. This was vital to imposing assent to anti-Jewish policy both within officialdom and on a population that was widely suspected by the political leadership of inclining against it—for example, in deploring the violence and cruelty of the 1938 *Kristallnacht-Pogrom*, or in observing with disquiet and alarm the fatal deportation of the German Jews beginning in October 1941, or in (rightly) fearing, as the war turned toward defeat, that mass murder in Eastern Europe would spell disaster for German society. The regime's opinion-formation figured also as a step in the implementation of successively more radical stages of official anti-Jewish policy, in that it simulated—through periodic blaring press campaigns, distribution of posters and other advertisements, or release of anti-Semitic films—public support for new steps, aiming simultaneously to repress such dissent as they might otherwise elicit.

Longerich shows that anti-Semitic violence in pre-1939 Germany, and even such important events as issuance of the 1935 Nuremberg Laws and the November 1938 pogrom, were downplayed or suppressed in the official media. After the war began, substantive factual information on violence against Jews in Eastern Europe rarely found official expression. With the regime's turn in 1941 and 1942 to systematic genocide, proclamations of the 'final solution,' of the Jews' 'total destruction' or 'extermination' were accompanied by news blackouts concerning the Holocaust's details. In spring 1943, Goebbels's Propaganda Ministry undertook a two-month campaign in which, while attacking the Soviet Union for mass murder at Katyń of captive Poles, it brazenly acknowledged that Jewish populations under Nazi command had largely ceased to exist.

This revelation aimed to stiffen German resistance to the Soviet offensive by making it clear that the entire society must stand behind the Holocaust. Grim warning of Soviet reprisals, often (self-projectively) depicted as 'Jewish death squads,' induced an un-nerved and fear-ridden reaction in the German population, encouraging denial of knowledge and complicity. Already in October 1942 Göring bullied his listeners in a nation-wide radio broadcast: 'This war is not the Second World War, it is the Great Racial War (*grosser Rassenkrieg*).' It was a life-and-death struggle between 'German and Aryan and Jew . . . Let no one fool himself into believing he can come forward later on and say: I was always a good democrat among those terrible Nazis.'[44]

The effect of Nazi opinion-molding was to destroy alternative public spheres at home from which the German population could gain information and understanding about *Judenpolitik* and the unfolding Holocaust. While many grasped that the deported Jews were being transported to their doom, and while rumors of death by gas circulated, the scale of the death-camp slaughter was rarely understood. This was also true even in the West, where credible, eye-witness reports on the genocide arrived from Polish under-ground sources. Locked in private isolation, many people continued anachronistically and deludedly to conceptualize the 'Jewish question' in pre-1933 or pre-1939 terms, revolving about legal disenfranchisement, economic dispossession, and forced emigra-tion. Among Nazi true believers, the regime's messages concerning anti-Jewish policies were doubtless complacently accepted or welcomed. Yet there is also evidence that relatively well-educated and serious-minded NSDAP members preferred to block infor-mation and rumors about the nightmarish mass murder from their minds.[45] So too did masses of ordinary people, for whom—as Longerich concludes—*Judenpolitik* and anti-Semitism *troubled*, rather than solidified their relationship to Hitler's regime. He, too, sees *Volksgemeinschaft* as the mobilizing force, but war shattered it.

24.5 CONCLUSION

A certain analytical disposition will ask: 'what was German National Socialism a case of?' A brief answer, leaving depths unplumbed, would say that it was an extreme example of nation state-formation shading off, as happened in many European countries, into an imperialist expansion entailing ethnic cleansing of minorities in-habiting borderlands and other conquered spaces. It was an anti-liberal, anti-socialist, anti-communist fascism that, like many other right-wing mobilizations in Europe, stigmatized 'the Jews' as partisans and even creators of the hated ideologies of capitalist democracy and Marxist revolution. It was a utopian project promising the blessings of technological modernity on an imperial scale, rivaling those on offer by Soviet and Anglo-American competitors. It orchestrated a backlash against the ambiguities, sub-jectivities, relativisms, and incomprehensibilities of cultural and scientific modernity.[46]

It is not surprising that Germany, recovering from defeat in World War I, should have renewed its bid for European hegemony and east European empire. Britain and France emerged weakened from their seeming victory of 1918, while in Russia a regime far more menacing to German interests and values than vanished tsarism had arisen under Stalin's rule—which yet also seemed, to Hitler, easy prey to his soldiers, tanks, and artillery. But there was no place in his empire for the millions of mostly poor, Yiddish-speaking, economically old-fashioned Jews the German armies captured on their march eastward, any more than there was for supernumerary Slavic captives and subjects.

The Holocaust's 'industrial' or 'factory-like' efficiency and bureaucratic rationality have sometimes been, for philosophically understandable reasons, exaggerated. In part, the mass murder was a succession of terrible bloodbaths, executed with guns and horses. Although not the first or last of genocides, it is especially hard to contemplate because of the helplessness, innocence, and abandonment of the Jewish victims, the pitilessness, arrogance, and ideological self-delusion of the murderers, and the deploy-ment of modern science and technology in Auschwitz's and the other death camps' terrible enterprise. In our eyes, neither empire, nor *Volksgemeinschaft*, nor ideologically promised redemption could ever justify it. Yet in other eyes, they did.

Author's note

This essay represents an interpretive response to current and recently published broad-gauged synthetic literature. The works highlighted here, both in text, notes, and bibliography, comprise a dialogue and debate, so that on issues of interest to readers, it is recommended that they compare the relevant studies.

Notes

1. 'Der Gedanke geht der Tat voraus, wie der Blitz dem Donner.' Heinrich Heine, 'Zur Geschichte der Religion und Philosophie in Deutschland,' in Heinrich Heine, *Historisch-kritische Gesamtausgabe der Werke*, Manfred Winfuhr (ed.), vol. 8, 1 (Düsseldorf: Hoffmann and Campe, 1979), 118.

2. For historiographical orientation, see Dan Stone, *Histories of the Holocaust* (New York: Oxford University Press, 2010). This valuable survey and critique of Holocaust historiography of recent decades abstains from advancing a large-scale interpretation of its subject such as this chapter offers. It neglects the interplay of east European empire and Aryan folk community highlighted here, as it does National Socialist repression and terror directed toward German society, which I underscore. Essential too are Ian Kershaw, *The Nazi Dictatorship: Problems and Perspectives of Interpretation* (London: Arnold, 2000) and Michael R. Marrus, *The Holocaust in History* (Hanover, NH: Brandeis University Press, 1987). See also Nicolas Berg, *Der Holocaust und die westdeutschen Historiker. Erforschung und Erinnerung* (Göttingen: Wallstein-Verlag, 2003) and Ulrich Herbert (ed.), *National Socialist Extermination Policies: Contemporary German Perspectives and Controversies* (New York: Berghahn, 2000 [German original: 1998]), 1–52 and passim.

   Valuable recent accounts and interpretations of National Socialist anti-Jewish policy and violence are Peter Longerich, *Holocaust: The Nazi Persecution and Murder of the Jews* (New York: Oxford University Press, 2010 [German original: 1998]) and Saul Friedländer, *Nazi Germany and the Jews: The Years of Persecution, 1933–1939* (New York: HarperCollins, 1997); idem, *Nazi Germany and the Jews, 1939–1945: The Years of Extermination* (New York: HarperCollins, 2007). The pioneering master-work, first published in 1961, still unrivaled in empirical depth, and stamped by structuralist-determinist emphasis on bureaucratic process, is Raul Hilberg, *The Destruction of the European Jews*, 3 vols, 3rd edn (New Haven: Yale University Press, 2003). In *The Third Reich in Power* and *The Third Reich at War* (London: Penguin, 2006–2008) Richard J. Evans integrates anti-Jewish policy and violence into a larger account of the National Socialist regime. See also Michael Wildt, *Geschichte des Nationalsozialismus* (Göttingen: Vandenhoeck & Ruprecht, 2008); Alan E. Steinweis, 'Judenverfolgung und Holocaust,' in Dietmar Süss and Winfried Süss (eds), *Das 'Dritte Reich': Eine Einführung* (Munich: Pantheon, 2008), 287–310; Doris Bergen, 'Occupation, imperialism, and genocide, 1939–1945,' in Jane Caplan (ed.), *Nazi Germany* (New York: Oxford University Press, 2008), 219–245; Hans-Ulrich Wehler, *Deutsche Gesellschaftsgeschichte*, vol. 4, *Vom Beginn des Ersten Welkriegs bis zur Gründung der beiden deutschen Staaten, 1914–1949* (Munich: Beck, 2003).

3. Christopher R. Browning, *The Origins of the Final Solution. The Evolution of Nazi Jewish Policy September 1939–March 1942* (Lincoln: University of Nebraska, 2004), as well as Longerich, *Holocaust*; Friedländer, *Nazi Germany and the Jews*; and Stone, *Histories* ch. 2; on 'cumulative radicalization,' cf. Hans Mommsen, *Von Weimar nach Auschwitz* (Stuttgart: Deutsche Verlags-Anstalt, 1999).

4. Süss and Süss (eds), *Das Dritte Reich*, 303. Cf. Wolfgang Benz, *Dimension des Völkermords. Die Zahl der jüdischen Opfer des Nationalsozialismus* (Munich: DTV, 1996). The National Socialists also murdered some 130,000 Greek, Yugoslavian, and Bulgarian-Macedonian Jews. Of the 200–275,000 Jewish victims under Romanian rule, most died at the hands of their own militarist-fascist government. In *Bloodlands: Europe Between Hitler and Stalin* (New York: Basic Books, 2010), Timothy Snyder offers a new assemblage of numerical data on Jewish and non-Jewish loss of life resulting from politically driven mass murder under Stalinism and German National Socialism, but without altering the order of magnitudes expressed in the text above. See also Snyder's 'Holocaust; The Ignored Reality,' *New York Review of Books*, LVI:12 (July 16, 2009), 14–16, an essay which, like *Bloodlands*, emphasizes the Holocaust's east European locus and its genesis

out of Hitler's anti-Soviet war, launched in June 1941. Snyder posits a mutually reinforcing dynamic between German and Soviet political violence, though without holding that the anti-Jewish genocide depended on it. In harmony with Mark Mazower's *Hitler's Empire: Nazi Rule in Occupied Europe* (London: Penguin, 2008), Snyder's narrative highlights the Nazi project of *Lebensraum*-empire. But neither author proposes the present chapter's causal linkages and interdependencies.

5. On the National Socialist economy and its relation to war and imperial expansion: Adam Tooze, *The Wages of Destruction: The Making and Breaking of the Nazi Economy* (New York: Viking, 2007). Cf. Tooze, 'The Economic History of the Nazi regime,' in Jane Caplan (ed.), *Nazi Germany* (New York: Oxford University Press, 2008), 168–195.

6. For a broad-ranging history of anti-Semitic politics and ideology in German central Europe, emphasizing the transposition of anti-Semitic modernization anxieties into racialized terms, see Massimo Ferrari Zumbini, *Die Wurzeln des Bösen. Gründerjahre des Antisemitismus: Von der Bismarckzeit zu Hitler* (Frankfurt am Main: Klostermann, 2003). Cf. Shulamit Volkov, *Germans, Jews, and Antisemites: Trials in Emancipation* (Cambridge: Cambridge University Press, 2006); Helmut Walser Smith, *The Continuities of German History: Nation, Religion, and Race across the Long Nineteenth Century* (New York: Cambridge University Press, 2008); Christhard Hoffmann, Werner Bergmann, and Helmut Walser Smith (eds), *Exclusionary Violence: Antisemitic Riots in Modern German History* (Ann Arbor: University of Michigan Press, 2002); William W. Hagen, 'Before the "Final Solution:" Toward a Comparative Analysis of Political Antisemitism in Interwar Germany and Poland,' *Journal of Modern History* (July 1996), 1–31.

7. Hitler to Otto Abetz, September 1941, quoted in Mazower, *Hitler's Empire*, 558.

8. From Hitler's briefing on 22 August 1939, cited in ibid., 64.

9. Friedländer, *Nazi Germany and the Jews*, I, 5. Cf. Hilberg's judgment: 'The bureaucracy had no master plan, no fundamental blueprint, no clear-cut view of its actions.' Hilberg, *Destruction*, I, 1064. For interpretations of Hitler, see Ian Kershaw, *Hitler, 1889–1936: Hubris* (New York: Norton, 1999) and *Hitler, 1936–45: Nemesis* (New York: Norton, 2000), esp. I: xix–xxx and II, chapters 3, 10; Wehler, *Gesellschaftsgeschichte*, IV, 598–917, and passim.

10. For interesting psychoanalytic analysis, see Jacques Sémelin, *Purify and Destroy: The Political Uses of Massacre and Genocide* (London: Hurst, 2007); Ernst Simmel (ed.), *Anti-Semitism, a Social Disease* (New York: International Universities Press, 1946). Writing in the Holocaust's immediate aftermath, German pedagogue and Weimar-era activist against anti-Semitism Michael Müller-Claudius, in *Der Antisemitismus und das deutsche Verhängnis* (Frankfurt am Main: Verlag Josef Knecht, 1948), stressed the post-1914 interaction of German anti-Semitism as an ego-wounded and paranoid society's defense mechanism with authoritarian-militarist traditions. Cf. David Redles, *Hitler's Millenial Reich. Apocalyptic Belief and the Search for Salvation* (New York: New York University Press, 2005).

11. Friedländer, *Nazi Germany and the Jews*, I, 3, 71–72.

12. Ibid., II, xix (italics removed), 656–657.

13. Michael Wildt, *Volksgemeinschaft als Selbstermächtigung: Gewalt gegen Juden in der deutschen Provinz 1919 bis 1939* (Hamburg: Hamburger Edition, 2007). Cf. Peter Longerich, *'Davon haben wir nichts gewusst!' Die Deutschen und die Judenverfolgung 1933–1945* (Munich: Pantheon, 2007).

14. Quoted in Friedländer, *Nazi Germany and the Jews*, I, 141.

15. Ibid., I, 247–248.
16. Figures from Evans, *The Third Reich at War*, 15, 21, 53. Cf. Alexander B. Rossino, *Hitler Strikes Poland: Blitzkrieg, Ideology, and Atrocity* (Lawrence, Kan.: University Press of Kansas, 2003); Gustavo Corni, *Hitler's Ghettos: Voices from a Beleaguered Society, 1939-1944* (New York: Oxford University Press, 2002).
17. Friedländer, *Nazi Germany and the Jews*, II, 188.
18. Götz Aly and Susanne Heim, *Vordenker der Vernichtung. Auschwitz und die deutschen Pläne für eine neue europäische Ordnung* (Frankfurt am Main: Fischer, 1993). Isabel Heinemann deepens the ideological-racial dimension of Aly and Heim's argumentation in her *'Rasse, Siedlung, deutsches Blut.' Die Rasse-und Siedlungshauptamt der SS und die rassenpolitische Neuordnung Europas* (Göttingen: Wallstein, 2003).
19. William W. Hagen, *Germans, Poles and Jews: The Nationality Conflict in the Prussian East, 1772-1914* (Chicago: University of Chicago Press, 1980).
20. Philip T. Rutherford, *Prelude to the Final Solution. The Nazi Program for Deporting Ethnic Poles, 1939-1941* (Lawrence: University Press of Kansas, 2007).
21. Friedländer, *Nazi Germany and the Jews*, II, 187–188.
22. Ibid., 237; Mazower, *Hitler's Empire*, 147.
23. Quotations in Mazower, 205, 385. Czesław Madajczyk (ed.), *Vom Generalplan Ost zum Generalsiedlungsplan* (Munich: Saur, 1994); Mechthild Rössler and Sabine Schleiermacher (eds), *Der 'Generalplan Ost': Hauptlinien der nationalsozialistischen Planungs-und Vernichtungspolitik* (Berlin: Akademie Verlag, 1993); Wendy Lower, *Nazi Empire-Building and the Holocaust in Ukraine* (Chapel Hill: University of North Carolina Press, 2005); Alex J. Kay, *Exploitation, Resettlement, Mass Murder: Political and Economic Planning for German Occupation Policy in the Soviet Union, 1940-41* (New York: Berghahn, 2006); David Furber, 'Near as Far in the Colonies: The Nazi Occupation of Poland,' *International History Review*, 26 (2004), 542–579.
24. Hitler quoted in Browning, *The Origins of the Final Solution*, 101.
25. Quoted in Friedländer, *Nazi Germany and the Jews*, II, 279–81.
26. Ibid., II, 322, 645, 660.
27. See Longerich, *Holocaust*, 422–435, and idem, *The Unwritten Order: Hitler's Role in the Final Solution* (London: Tempus, 2005). Götz Aly speculates that resistance within the German civil government to the Wannsee's genocidal blueprint might have stilled the machinery of the death camps, or slowed it, forcing Nazi *Judenpolitik* to continue in its emphases on ghettoization, 'productivization,' and attrition. Aly, *Endlösung: Völkerverschiebung und der Mord an den europäischen Juden* (Frankfurt am Main: Fischer, 1995), 398–389.
28. Friedländer, *Nazi Germany and the Jews*, 656–8. Cf. Aly, *Volksstaat*.
29. Mazower, *Hitler's Empire*, 30.
30. Ibid., 556.
31. Quotation from notes on Hitler's briefing of 5 November 1937 ('Hossbach Memorandum'), www.ns-archiv.de/krieg/1937/hossbach. Cf. Mazower, *Hitler's Empire*, 58, 259.
32. Mazower, *Hitler's Empire*, 180–181. Cf. Götz Aly, *Hitler Volksstaat. Raub, Rassenkrieg und nationaler Sozialismus* (Frankfurt am Main: Fischer, 2005).
33. Cf. Aly and Heim, *Vordenker*.
34. Mazower, *Hitler's Empire*, 12, 412–415. On Polish perceptions of their fate under National Socialist occupation, see Klaus-Peter Friedrich, *Der nationalsozialistische Judenmord und das polnisch-jüdische Verhältnis im Diskurs der polnischen. Untergrundpresse (1942-1944)* (Marburg: Verlag Herder-Institut, 2006).

35. Mazower, 588. On European imperialism: C. A. Bayly, *The Birth of the Modern World 1780–1914* (Oxford: Blackwell, 2004), chapter 12 and passim. On the Holocaust-like plunder of the Congo: Adam Hochschild, *King Leopold's Ghost* (New York: Houghton Mifflin, 1998). Cf. Pascal Grosse, 'What does German colonialism have to do with National Socialism?' in Eric Ames et al. (eds), *Germany's Colonial Pasts* (Lincoln: University of Nebraska Press, 2005), 115–135; Philip Ther, 'Imperial Instead of National History: Positioning Modern German History on the Map of European Empires,' in Alexei Miller and Alfred J. Rieber (eds), *Imperial Rule* (Budapest: Central European University Press, 2004), 47–66; Benjamin Madley, 'From Africa to Auschwitz: How German Southwest Africa Incubated Ideas and Methods Adopted and Developed by the Nazis in Europe,' *European History Quarterly*, 35 (2005), 429–464.

36. Aly, *Volksstaat*; Wildt, *Volksgemeinschaft*; Wehler, *Gesellschaftsgeschichte*, v. 4. Cf. Jill Stephenson, 'Inclusion: Building the National Community in Propaganda and Practice,' in Caplan (ed.), *Nazi Germany*, 99–121. Frank Bajohr and Michael Wildt (eds), *Volksgemeinschaft: Neue Forschungen zur Gesellschaft des Nationalsozialismus* (Frankfurt am Main: Fischer, 2009).

37. Aly, *Volksstaat*, 36–38, and passim.

38. Zygmunt Bauman, *Modernity and the Holocaust* (Ithaca: Cornell University Press, 2000); Peter Wagner, *A Sociology of Modernity: Liberty and Discipline* (London: Routledge, 1994); Detlev Peukert, 'The Genesis of the 'Final Solution' from the Spirit of Science,' in David Crew (ed.), *Nazism and German Society, 1933–45* (London: Routledge, 1994), 274–299. On the political multivalence of eugenic and other bio-scientific projects: Edward Ross Dickinson, 'Biopolitics, Fascism, Democracy: Reflections on Our Discourse Concerning "Modernity,"' *Central European History* 37 (2004), 1–48.

39. See Robert Gellately, *Backing Hitler: Consent and Coercion in Nazi Germany* (Oxford: Oxford University Press, 2001); Peter Fritzsche, *Life and Death in the Third Reich* (Cambridge: Harvard University Press, 2008); Stone, *Histories*. Cf. the ultra-consensualist argument by Daniel Jonah Goldhagen, *Hitler's Willing Executioners: Ordinary Germans and the Holocaust* (New York: Knopf, 1996).

40. See, including for figures on court-martials, Evans, *Third Reich at War*, 365, 501, 513–514, 537–538. Evans offers a persuasive appraisal of the Nazi regime's consensual and coercive dimensions. See also the second volume of his trilogy, *The Third Reich in Power* (London: Penguin, 2005) and his 'Coercion and Consent in Nazi Germany,' *Proceedings of the British Academy*, 171 (2007). Cf. Nicholas Wachsmann, 'The Policy of Exclusion: Repression in the Nazi State, 1933–39', in Caplan (ed.), *Nazi Germany*, 122–145.

41. Quoted in Hilberg, *The Destruction of the European Jews*, III, 1067.

42. Quoted in Evans, *Third Reich at War*, 560–61.

43. Longerich, '*Davon haben wir nichts gewusst!*' (see note 13, above). In harmony with Longerich's line of analysis is also Ian Kershaw, *The 'Hitler Myth': Image and Reality in the Third Reich* (Oxford: Oxford University Press, 2001).

44. Longerich, '*Davon haben wir nichts gewusst!*', 204.

45. Müller-Claudius (see note 11) clandestinely elicited and recorded the views of 61 NS party members on the November 1938 'Crystal Night' pogrom and later, in fall 1942, as awareness spread of Jewish mass murder in eastern Europe, of 41 NS party members on their appraisal of official *Judenpolitik*. In both cases, he encountered firm or vociferous support for radical violence among only a small minority, while willingness to criticize it, high in 1938, declined precipitously. He concluded that only a few by 1942 had freed

themselves from National Socialism's anti-Semitic world-view, while somewhat more were inclined—unrealistically—to imagine an end to anti-Jewish persecution at war's end. He reckoned that some five percent had actively surrendered themselves to Nazism's murderous postulates. The majority, though professing regime loyalty, were reluctant to express opinions on the 'final solution.' Such a guarded, morally and emotionally paralyzed posture does not seem identical with 'indifference.' Müller-Claudius, *Antisemitismus*, 162–172.

46. Benjamin Liebermann, *Terrible Fate: Ethnic Cleansing in the Making of Modern Europe* (Chicago: Dee, 2004); Norman M. Naimark, *Fires of Hatred: Ethnic Cleansing in Twentieth-Century Europe* (Cambridge: Harvard University Press, 2001); Eric D. Weitz, *A Century of Genocide: Utopias of Race and Nation* (Princeton: Princeton University Press, 2003); Jörg Baberowski and Anselm Doering-Manteuffel, *Ordnung durch Terror. Gewaltexzesse und Vernichtung im nationalsozialistischen und im stalinistischen Imperium* (Bonn: Dietz, 2006); Christophe Charle, *La crise des sociétés impériales: Allemagne, France, Grande-Bretagne, 1900–1940: essai d'histoire sociale comparée* (Paris: Seuil, 2001); Enzo Traverso, *Im Bann der Gewalt: Der europäische Bürgerkrieg, 1914–1945* (Munich: Siedler, 2008).

BIBLIOGRAPHY

This list excludes titles cited in the accompanying endnotes, among which are many works of prime importance, to which interested readers should turn without fail.

BARTOV, OMER. *Mirrors of Destruction: War, Genocide, and Modern Identity* (New York: Oxford University Press, 2000).

—— (ed.), *Studies on War and Genocide* (New York: Berghahn Books, 2000).

BENZ, WOLFGANG, HERMANN GRAML and HERMANN WEISS (eds), *Enzyklopädie des Nationalsozialismus* (Stuttgart: Klett-Cotta, 2007).

BREITMAN, RICHARD (ed.), *Nazi Germany (1933–1945)*, Part IV of *German History in Documents and Images* (Washington, DC: German Historical Institute: www.ghidc.org).

BROWNING, CHRISTOPHER R., *Ordinary Men: Reserve Police Battalion 101 and the Final Solution in Poland* (New York: HarperPerennial, 1998).

HILBERG, RAUL. *The Destruction of the European Jews*. 3 vols (New Haven: Yale University Press, 2003).

Holocaust and Genocide Studies (New York: Pergamon, 1986ff.).

Jahrbuch für Antisemitismusforschung (Frankfurt: Campus Verlag, 1992ff.).

KAPLAN, MARION A. *Between Dignity and Despair: Jewish Life in Nazi Germany* (New York: Oxford University Press, 1998).

MEYER, MICHAEL A. and MICHAEL BRENNER et al. (eds), *German-Jewish History in Modern Times*, 4 vols (New York: Columbia University Press, 1996).

NS-Archiv. Dokumente zum Nationalsozialismus. www.ns-archiv.de.

Polin: A Journal of Polish-Jewish Studies. (Oxford: Blackwell, 1994ff.).

PULZER, PETER, *Jews and the German State: The Political History of a Minority, 1848–1933* (Oxford: Blackwell, 1992).

——, *The Rise of Political Anti-Semitism in Germany and Austria* (Cambridge: Harvard University Press, 1988).

SLEZKINE, YURI. *The Jewish Century* (Princeton: Princeton University Press, 2004).

SOFSKY, WOLFGANG. *The Order of Terror: The Concentration Camp* (Princeton: Princeton University Press, 1997).

WILDT, MICHAEL. *Generation of the Unbound: The Leadership Corps of the Reich Security Main Office* (Jerusalem: Yad Vashem, 2002).

YAD VASHEM (ed.), *Documents of the Holocaust* (Jerusalem). yadvashem.org/about_holocaust/documents/home_documents, 2004.

Yad Vashem Studies (Jerusalem: Yad Vashem Martyrs' and Heroes' Remembrance Authority, 1976).

CHAPTER 25

....

ON THE MOVE: MOBILITY, MIGRATION, AND NATION, 1880–1948

....

SEBASTIAN CONRAD AND PHILIPP THER

SINCE the late nineteenth century, Germany was on the move. Railways, the tourism industry, and seaside resorts were evidence of the mobility of the middle classes. Permanent and seasonal labor migration was on even higher levels. Population growth, the increasing pull of the cities, and economic opportunities in the industrial centers all contributed to a flight of people from rural areas. Migration from the countryside to the urban centers was often just the first stage of a longer journey that brought millions of Germans abroad (and frequently back again). Germany was not merely a point of departure for migrants, however; it was also the destination of many immigrants, seeking either permanent or temporary work. The national economist Werner Sombart compared Imperial Germany with an ant-heap into which a passer-by had pushed his walking-stick.[1] This was only the beginning. The end of the First World War triggered post-imperial population movements on a large scale—labor, political, but also a new type of 'ethnic' migration. Finally, the cataclysm of National Socialism resulted in forced exile, forced labor, flight, expulsion, and 'transfer' of more than 12 million ethnic Germans from Central and Eastern Europe.

These massive and frequently overlapping forms of mobility demonstrate the degree to which German history was embedded in transnational processes. Migration was one of the forms through which large segments of the population experienced global entanglement first hand. In the following chapter, we will chart the trajectories of this cross-border mobility, both inward and outward-bound, keeping three general issues in mind. It will become clear, first, that these movements responded to particular German, and sometimes more local, predicaments, while at the same time being linked to larger conjunctures. Mobility connected different levels of experience and tied the local and regional to the national and the global. Secondly, migration was framed in a context in which material concerns, and the logic of economic order and labor markets were negotiated with shifting regimes of racial discourse and exclusionary practices. Finally, mobility operated in a contested field in which the dynamics of cross-border movement constantly undermined, and at the same time dialectically reinforced, senses of nationality. Indeed, it was one of the foundational tensions of mobility that the transnational processes of labor and ethnic migration were negotiated in national terms.

25.1 'National energies,' colonial settlement, and race: *Auswanderung* in imperial Germany

In imperial Germany, spatial mobility was a mass phenomenon that transformed whole cities and regions. For a long time, scholarship has treated the three waves of German migration in the nineteenth century as chapters of a continuing process. The third wave of trans-Atlantic migration between 1880 and 1883 that brought more than two million people overseas was not just the sequel to earlier movements, however. It was the result of very specific circumstances, related to the effects of industrialization, to the long economic slump of what used to be called the 'Great Depression,' and to the pressures of the world market.[2]

As a result, migration emerged as a central field of public debate. The alleged 'loss of national energies' was pitted against the advantages of migration as a 'safety valve' that rid the Empire of 'revolutionary elements.' For many decades the discussion centered on the benefits and costs that the German states incurred through this outward movement. This changed at the end of the century when migration was seen as a natural phenomenon accompanying industrialization and modernization. Now the focus of debate shifted to issues of geography—not least because emigration was seen as the concomitant of German influence in the world, and thus as a precondition of *Weltpolitik*. Among the explicit goals of the colonial movement, for example, was the redirection of population flows to the colonies—so that Germans would remain Germans, albeit overseas, and not deteriorate into a 'fertilizer of the peoples' (*Völkerdünger*), a term that in contemporary parlance referred to the allegedly rapid assimilation of Germans in the United States.

As Bradley Naranch has suggested, the shift in the meanings associated with outward mobility can be observed through shifts in terminology. While German migrants overseas had for a long time been referred to as *Auswanderer* (emigrants), this began to change in the last third of the nineteenth century. Supplementing the centrifugal overtones of emigration, the term *Auslandsdeutsche* (diaspora Germans) became predominant in the *Kaiserreich* as its use was extended from the German diaspora in Central Europe to overseas migrants. The term expressed social and cultural fears that were aroused by increasing mobility. In light of the fact that notions of belonging in the German states were deeply influenced by a concept of territorial rootedness, emigration was associated with the danger of losing one's national identity. The modified terminology stressed the timelessness and stability of belonging to a nation defined by culture and language. The perceived gap between *Heimat* and overseas settlements was here translated into the conviction that a national identity that presupposed a cultural (and soon *völkisch*) essence could not be cast away.[3] The new sense of national identity was mainly to be found on the nationalist fringe and among those who reported on the diaspora Germans. Here, there was a booming nationalist print culture, a sustained discourse of Germanness (*Deutschtum*), and a call for a politics of Germanization in places of German settlement.

The overwhelming majority (more than 90%) of the German emigrants—six million between 1820 and 1913—settled in the United States. Most of the emigrants left for economic reasons, although the promise of a life relatively free of state and religious interference also played a role. It was not the poorest part of the population that departed, but rather those who had the energy and means to seek improvement of their social situation. The frequent letters to their families and home communities further enticed the chain migration that was so typical for European migrants.[4]

The social advancement and subsequent assimilation of a large number of emigrants contributed to the negative reception of the North American 'melting pot' in the *Kaiserreich*—compared, for example, with the Germans in Russia (the most important destination of German emigration in the late eighteenth and early nineteenth century, and where the census of 1897 listed more than 1.8 million citizens of German descent). This negative reception eventually led to attempts to redirect the flow of German emigrants elsewhere. Colonial Africa, albeit in the political spotlight, was never home to more than 16,000 Germans. More important were South America (in particular Brazil, with 200,000 German emigrants over the course of the nineteenth century and Argentina with about 120,000 Germans emigrants), Canada (about 145,000 emigrants), Australia and South Africa (40,000–50,000 each), and parts of the Habsburg and Ottoman Empires. Here, the reasoning went, Germans did not dissolve into the majority population, but were able to retain and even foster their German national characteristics. The ideology of diaspora Germanness was shaped by these different contexts, but the general thrust of the rhetoric exhibited many similarities.[5]

In the late nineteenth century, public attention focused, in spite of the small number of emigrants, on the settlement projects in the newly acquired African colonies where migration was supported by state subsidies. German Southwest Africa, in particular, was envisioned as a settler colony, and the first governor, Theodor Leutwein, initiated a series of measures to establish large planter and settler communities there. The large colonialist associations, like the German Colonial Society (*Deutsche Kolonialgesellschaft*), supported these projects, which were fuelled not only by considerations of power politics and international competition, but also by visions of a reconstruction of Germanness. The idea was to found a new Germany that was not riven by internal conflicts of class, region, and confession, and thus to go beyond the political unification of the *Kaiserreich* in 1871, which nationalist and *völkisch* milieus considered to be incomplete.

Long debates ensued in governmental and colonialist circles in a quest for the ideal settler, who was not only to be manly and productive, but was to assume the role of a bearer of German culture. As recruitment of migrants proved difficult, a number of different schemes were developed, including attempts to establish tuberculosis sanatoriums in the colonies.[6] In the end, however, the politics of colonial settlement proved unsuccessful. Before 1914, scarcely more than 20,000 Germans lived in all the overseas possessions combined.

Three aspects of these long-lasting debates about outward mobility deserve particular attention.

First, discussions about mobility were at the center of political concerns, and they could have very palpable effects. A good example, reminiscent of the shift from *Auswanderer* to *Auslandsdeutsche*, is the revision of German citizenship law in 1913. The law of 1870 had foreseen that citizenship would end ten years after leaving the country; but this stipulation was revoked in 1913, and from this point on, citizenship could not expire and was even transferred to descendants. Simultaneously, the law was restrictive vis-à-vis 'non-German' immigrants, especially Jews and Poles, who were supposed to be prevented from acquiring German citizenship. Hence, immigration policy steered toward an ethnic definition of German nationhood. So too did emigration. In particular, the provision concerning the *Auslandsdeutsche* represented a reaction to changing conditions of mobility. During the nineteenth century, the vast majority of emigrants had moved to the United States, most of them permanently, and were considered a loss to the national substance. The acquisition of colonies since 1884 was motivated, to large extents, by the intention to provide emigrants with opportunities without severing their ties with the German nation. In the face of political support for the colonial project, it seemed expedient to enable Germans to settle in the colonies without risking their legal status. The modification of the durability of citizenship thus was a direct outcome of the debates about global mobility. This was no mere legal cosmetic, rendered insignificant by the dissolution of the colonial empire just shortly thereafter; rather, it concerned central dimensions of belonging and participation. It is instructive to note that the effects of this legal adaptation survived the end of empire. When, in the 1990s, large groups of descendants of former emigrants (*Aussiedler*) 'returned,' as it came to be called, from the Soviet Union, they still benefited from this early twentieth-century redefinition of Germanness under global and colonial conditions.[7]

Secondly, it is important to note that debates about the German diaspora in South America, about the German colonial possessions, and about the political dynamics of the *Kaiserreich* were not neatly separated. Instead, social actors frequently operated within a framework in which these spheres of action overlapped and influenced each other. For example, at about the same time as the settlement project in Southwest Africa, the Prussian government initiated its policy of demographic Germanization in the Polish-speaking areas of the Reich. In 1886, the Royal Prussian Colonization

Commission (*Königlich Preußische Ansiedlungskommission*) was established to buy up large Polish estates. It subsequently sold them in smaller plots to German farmers that were lured to the East by state subsidies. The Commission was supported by the Eastern Marches Society (*Ostmarkenverein*), founded in 1894 to supply both the political lobby and the publicity for the project. Largely composed of state servants, especially petty bureaucrats and school teachers, the Society counted among the most important pressure groups for a redefinition of Germanness along ethnic lines. By 1914, its members even argued for a population policy that included the forced movement and relocation of large groups, albeit within the state of Prussia. Typically, these proposals are read as part of a prehistory of the genocidal measures of National Socialism. It is also instructive, however, to see the correspondences with similar population policies in the overseas colonies, such as Governor Lindequist's call to move 'the whole tribe of Witboois to Samoa' in order to stabilize colonial rule in German Southwest Africa. Racial segregation and ethnic separation, but also deportation of large populations after the turn of the century, was common practice in the colonial arena before it became a political strategy that was also employed in Europe.[8]

This brings us to our third point, namely the role of categories of race. German migration overseas was always accompanied by a discourse of racial difference. In the United States, people of 'German stock' were long a privileged group of immigrants, especially when compared with Irish settlers, the Eastern European migrants of the turn of the century, or the Chinese who since 1882 were subjected to harsh politics of exclusion. This changed only at the beginning of the twentieth century, and in particular during the First World War, when a surge of anti-German sentiment and violence forced many German schools and newspapers to close and German-Americans to abandon the hyphen.[9] The dynamic was similar in South America. The Brazilian government, for example, saw immigration from Europe as a racial tool that contributed towards *embranquecimento* (making the population more white). It particularly promoted and facilitated immigration from Germany, a policy that was backed by intellectuals who, following Gobineau, stressed the advantages of Germans over 'Romans' on racial grounds. After 1900, and more obviously during World War I, this ideology gradually gave way to a popular discourse of the 'German peril' (*perigo alemão*) that contributed to Brazilian nationalism.[10]

In Germany, too, *Auswanderung* was a central element in debates about the racial composition of the nation. In the diaspora and most conspicuously in the colonies, the specter of racial mixing, of going native, and of degeneration appeared to loom large, if one believed the nationalist rhetoric. In Southwest Africa and East Africa, along with Samoa, German colonial governments introduced a legal ban on interracial marriage in order to impede miscegenation. The prohibitive measures were complemented by a large-scale campaign to bring German women to Southwest Africa. Some of them were trained specifically in colonial women's schools in order to inculcate the virtues of *Deutschtum*, femininity, and domesticity. Eventually, over 2,000 women settled in the colony, where colonial activists hoped that German women would be bearers of German culture and keep the predominantly male colony from going native.[11]

It is interesting to note, finally, that the racialization of discourses of belonging played out not only overseas, but in Germany as well. It has long been recognized that the final decades of the nineteenth century saw the emergence of biological racism, most notably in the case of anti-Semitism. It remains an open question to what extent this internal European form of racism was linked to the racist practice in the overseas colonies. It is striking, however, that synchronous with the acquisition of colonial territories in Africa, the notion of racial difference became increasingly important for delimitations between Germans and Poles. In 1885, the *völkisch* ideologue Paul de Lagarde was the first to suggest, if parenthetically, that Jews be forcefully removed to the island of Madagascar.[12] As mobility spanned the globe, and the global dimension of migration was anchored in public consciousness, the discourse of race, likewise, was applied to a situation in which Germany could not neatly be separated from the larger global context. One of the expressions of this global consciousness was the emergence of the concept of *lebensraum*, first coined as a scholarly term without political aspirations by the geographer Friedrich Ratzel. As Woodruff Smith has argued, the subsequent political call for *lebensraum* emerged as one of the answers to overcome various dangers to the nation, such as immigration from the East, the narrowing of Germany's sphere of economic interests, the closing of the colonial frontier, and the rivalry of the world powers. Since the 1920s, the concept gained broad public acceptance as an ideological template that allowed for the articulation of a discourse on Germanness under the conditions of global mobility.[13]

25.2 Imported labor

In 1897, after long years of lobbying and discussion, the Prussian government passed an emigration law that was intended to channel a process that for a century had flourished without government control. Ironically, this law came at a moment when emigration was essentially already a thing of the past. After 1893, the number of Germans venturing overseas dwindled to a minimum, never again surpassing the threshold of 40,000 migrants per year. At the same time, immigration figures soared, and from the mid-1890s, Germany had in fact turned into a country importing cheap labor on a scale second only to the United States.

A large part of this labor was agricultural labor, as the Prussian countryside was affected by the flight from the land and to the industrialized centers. To counter the shortage of workers, Prussian landlords began to recruit workers from the Polish speaking parts of Russia, and from Austrian Galicia. By 1914, an estimated 500,000 foreigners were employed in agriculture in Germany, almost half of them women. Most of them spoke Polish and this created a huge stir and provoked protests from nationalist quarters who feared a 'Polonization' of the Prussian provinces. Even the trade unions were torn between their internationalist doctrines and a form of labor protectionism that frequently drew on cultural stereotypes. As the Prussian government was also suspicious of the rise of Polish nationalism, it introduced a singular measure unknown in any other European country at the time: the 'restricted period' (*Karenzzeit*). It obliged foreign workers to return home for the winter in order to prevent them from settling permanently in Germany.

In 1905, the German Central Office For Field Workers (*Deutsche Feldarbeiterzentralstelle*) was set up to tackle contract-breaking and the activities of agents and more fundamentally to allow closer control of immigration. At the border stations, each worker was issued an identity card that he or she had to hand over to his or her employer, making it impossible for workers to change employer without permission. This gradual increase in state control over the labor market marked a new stage of institutionalized state discrimination against foreign workers. It is no coincidence that these measures were introduced in the period following the Russian Revolution in 1905, when the mobility of workers from Eastern Europe was seen as a potentially revolutionary influence.[14]

Even larger than in agriculture was the influx of foreign workers into the centers of German industry—almost 700,000 by the outbreak of the First World War. The largest group, totaling more than 120,000 people, were Italians who frequently found employment in the construction industry; the second largest cohort came from the German-speaking regions of Austria-Hungary; large groups also came from Russia and the Netherlands. The foreign workers were frequently unskilled, and they were typically employed in the lowest ranks of the industrial enterprises, thus effectively serving as a buffer of workers easily laid off in times of economic contraction. While recruitment of foreign workers was clearly economically driven, political concerns were also at work in the industrial sector: recruitment of Poles, in particular, was limited to Eastern Prussia, while their employment in the industrial centers in Western Germany was prohibited by the state administration. These provisions, too, were a response to the prevalent fears of 'Polonization.' In the Rhine-Ruhr region, these fears were exacerbated by the influx of about 500,000 Poles and Masurians from Eastern Prussia who held Prussian citizenship, but were nevertheless perceived by the local population and authorities as the core of a Polish nationalist movement.[15]

The public concern about Polish immigration was reinforced by the fact that it was linked, in nationalist rhetoric, to an entirely different process, namely the huge transit movement of people migrating from Eastern Europe to the Americas. More than five million people travelled through Germany to embark on their trans-Atlantic journey in Hamburg and Bremerhaven. Their temporary sojourn had repercussions in Germany on both the local and the national level: on the local, for example, there was a separate train station built in 1890 in Ruhleben west of Berlin for the sole purpose of channeling incoming laborers to the outbound sea ports; on the national level, the high proportion of Jewish migrants particularly aroused public suspicion in a climate increasingly dominated by anti-Semitism. Although only 78,000 of the more than two million Jewish migrants eventually settled in Germany, they provoked a heated debate in the nationalist press. In the popular imagination, Eastern European Jews were linked with radicalism, poverty, trafficking in women from Eastern Europe, unhygienic conditions, and the importing of infectious diseases, such as the major cholera epidemic of the early 1890s. Anti-Semitic stereotypes were thus reinforced by fears of the 'East' and of 'Asian' influences, while, conversely, the debate about the threat of 'Polonisation' acquired anti-Semitic features. These links were not limited to rhetoric: an example of their real effect is the joint expulsion in 1885 of 32,000 Poles and Jews who did not have Prussian citizenship. Although this spectacular action remained a single incident and was overtaken by the new regulations on the admission of seasonal workers, discrimination against Poles and Jews as a single group continued, for example, in the restrictive way naturalization was managed. Massimo Ferrari Zumbini has thus argued that increasing migration in the 1890s led to 'a merging of anti-Slavism and anti-Semitism that was understood in expressly racial terms.'[16]

The First World War put an abrupt end to these large-scale cross-border movements. A few days after the outbreak of the war, the Prussian war ministry ordered the borders closed and henceforth prohibited the return of workers to enemy countries. This implied that about 300,000 workers from Polish Russia were forced to stay in Germany under the status of civilian prisoners of war. They were not allowed to change employer (mostly in agriculture), or to leave their place of residence, let alone return to their place of origin. Rigid regulations, including a curfew at night, were enforced in order to curtail resistance and flight. Under wartime conditions, further recruitment on Russian territory drove the number of Polish-Russian workers in Germany up to about 600,000. Forced recruitment was not limited to the Eastern front. In occupied Belgium, too, German authorities began with a deportation program that was, however, relaxed after massive protests in the public, both in Germany and internationally. In 1919, about 130,000 Belgian forced laborers lived in Germany. A final component of military interventions in the wartime economy concerned prisoners of war. About one million prisoners were employed forcefully, the large majority of them, mainly from Russia and Serbia, in the countryside.[17] Even if, in economic terms, forced labor proved largely inefficient, in many ways it inaugurated a slide into the altogether different universe of inhumane treatment and exploitation of prisoners of war and civilians that characterized World War II, especially on the eastern front.

The end of the war and subsequent demobilization changed all this. Most foreign workers, voluntary and involuntary recruits, returned to their countries of origin. In 1924, under the impact of recession and hyper-inflation, only about 170,000 foreign workers were left in Germany, and their numbers continued to decrease. Unlike during the *Kaiserreich* or amidst the major upheavals of the Second World War and its aftermath, the troubled years of the Weimar Republic were not characterized by massive population movements. This is not to say that mobility entirely ceased. Overseas migration continued after the war, and more than 600,000 people moved to the United States between 1919 and 1932. More important than the quantitative dimension of migration were two general trends that would shape the dynamics of cross-border mobility in the years to come.

First, migration was increasingly caused by political events and followed a political rather than an economic logic. This was true for about 250,000 Polish-speaking

Germans who used the option they were given by the Versailles treaty and then by the Geneva Convention to leave the Weimar Republic. About half of them moved to the newly-founded Polish nation-state, while the other half sought employment in the industrial centers in Northern France. Conversely, one million Germans from territories ceded to France and Poland migrated to the Germany of the Weimar Republic. They were accompanied by political refugees from Russia, by Eastern European Jews, and by former prisoners of war refusing to return to the Soviet Union. The fall of the three European continental empires and the establishment of nation states after the war led to massive population movements that also deeply affected the Weimar Republic. This is especially true for the influx of Eastern European Jews that in some ways changed the character and focus of anti-Semitism.

Secondly, one can observe a tendency toward increasing state control of mobility. The nationalization of trans-national migration had begun in the 1890s, but it was above all the First World War that led to a marked increase in border controls, issuance of passports, and the deployment of biometrical devices, such as fingerprinting and picture identification. The transformation of nation-states into interventionist states was particularly visible in the labor markets where access and exclusion were more and more governed by protectionist logics. 'The migration economy of the world is currently moving from liberalism to a state-directed economy,' as the German economist Karl C. Thalheim observed as early as 1918.[18] This shift corresponded to a fundamental discursive reconfiguration of the labor market whose control and maintenance was now seen as the responsibility of the state. As both the protection of national labor and government expenditures on welfare increased, trans-border mobility was subjected to a series of restricting measures with the aim of driving down migration figures.[19]

25.3 THE RISE OF NATIONAL SOCIALISM AND SUBSEQUENT POLITICAL AND ETHNIC MIGRATION

The rise of National Socialism changed once more the character of migration to and from Germany. Already in 1933, tens of thousands of Social Democrats, Communists, and other adversaries of National Socialism left Germany. This wave of political migration was not a novelty in German history, especially in view of the emigration of the revolutionaries of 1848. The scale of persecution and subsequently political emigration was unprecedented, however. Around 16,000–19,000 political refugees fled from Germany in the first two years of the Nazi regime alone; by 1939, their numbers rose to approximately 30,000. Initially, most political refugees migrated to neighboring European countries such as France, Belgium, the Netherlands, Czechoslovakia, and Austria.

Thereafter, they increasingly migrated to Great Britain and the Americas, some to the Soviet Union.

These initial migrations were based on political, not economic motives. In fact, many exiled Germans lost their previous social status and had to live in poverty. This was bearable as long as there was some hope of toppling the regime from outside or of supporting internal resistance. The consolidation of the regime through the purge of the left wing of the National Socialist party in 1934 (the so-called 'Röhm-Putsch'), the occupation of the demilitarized zone of the Rhineland in 1936, and the economic recovery destroyed those hopes, however. Moreover, there was a growing acceptance of National Socialism, not only in Germany, but also in international politics. All major neighboring countries tried to conclude either treaties like the Polish-German Non-aggression Pact of 1935 or to accommodate the Nazi regime. This affected the treatment of political refugees who were increasingly perceived as a burden to international relations. Those refugees who had gone to Czechoslovakia and contributed to the cultural blossoming of pre-war Prague faced an even worse fate. When England, France, and Italy sacrificed the most stable democracy of Central Europe in the Munich Agreement of 1938, more than 10,000 political refugees who had come from Germany had to run and hide under miserable circumstances.

This was also true for the desperate political refugees who were caught by the sudden and unexpected defeat of France. Only some managed to cross the Atlantic and to escape detention in the French camps or concentration camps upon delivery to the German Security Service. The reason was the very restrictive immigration policy of the United States at this time, which was, however, countered by many private initiatives. Many Communists escaped to the Soviet Union, which turned out to be the opposite of a safe haven. The political refugees in Moscow were caught in inner party feuds and purges. Only the most reliable or simply lucky Stalinists survived well, and were able to return after World War II. The deterioration of the situation of political refugees in Europe also changed the patterns of migration. Once more, the Americas became the most prominent area of destination. As in the nineteenth century, the United States was the most important country of arrival, but many émigrés also chose to go to Argentina or to Brazil. Another pivotal change, especially among Jewish émigrés, was that they perceived their political exile not as temporary, but as permanent.

Political émigrés nevertheless had a major advantage compared to other refugees who fled Germany based on ethnic and racial persecution. Political émigrés could rely on pre-existing networks or the help of previous migrants. Moreover, their flight had a high level of political legitimacy. Adversaries of Hitler were initially welcomed in neighboring countries, even in Austria, which was ruled by an authoritarian, clerical-fascist regime. Especially the first wave of refugees received asylum and material help either from state or private resources. Many of the political émigrés were well educated and thus managed get jobs after an initial phase of adaptation.

In contrast, Jewish refugees were mostly unwanted.[20] Even where the political elites adopted favorable attitudes towards Jews, such as France or Czechoslovakia, countries were reluctant to take in a large number of the more than 250,000 German Jews who fled Germany between 1933 and the outbreak of World War II.[21] The emigration directly after the National Socialists had taken power in 1933 featured a disproportionate number of political activists, intellectuals, and civil servants. The racist Nuremberg laws passed in 1935 added economic pressure to leave, and widened the social bases of emigrants. Thereafter, the pogroms of 'Reichskristallnacht' in November 1938 led to a dramatic increase in Jewish emigration at all levels of Jewish society. In November and December of 1938, between 33,000 and 40,000 Jews left Germany; in the following year, 1939, 75,000–80,000 managed to escape.[22] Those who were stranded in Western Europe, and did not have French, Belgian, or Dutch citizenship often perished during the German occupation, whereas 'indigenous' Jews had a much higher rate of survival. Jews who had escaped to Central and Eastern Europe had only a chance of survival, if they managed to get to the Near East or the United States.

The main problem for 'ethnic' or 'racial' emigrants, as Jews were defined, was that the doors for them were mostly closed. The United States and other immigration countries overseas had introduced ethnic quota for immigrants already in the 1920s. The small neighbors of Germany such as Belgium, Switzerland, or Czechoslovakia were afraid that a large scale influx of Jewish refugees would unsettle their social balance, burden their welfare systems, and provoke future conflicts with Nazi Germany. Together with the high level of anti-Semitism all over Europe this created the paradoxical situation that Germany could not push out as many Jews as it aspired to.

25.4 MASS MIGRATION DURING AND AFTER WORLD WAR II

The racist policy of the Nazis did not only aim to make Germany 'free of Jews' (Judenrein), but also had the goal to further Germanize the population by homeland migration. In 1939 and 1940, Nazi Germany concluded treaties with Italy, the Baltic States, the Soviet Union, Romania, and other countries to resettle German speaking minorities, the so called 'Volksdeutsche,' to Germany.[23] The slogan for these resettlements was to come 'back to the Reich' (Heim ins Reich), but in fact many of the 770,000 homeland migrants were settled in regions annexed by Nazi Germany in Western Poland (especially the so-called 'Warthegau'). The Nazi authorities created a central administration for immigration in Łódź, which was renamed Litzmannstadt. The policy of settlement had many similarities with the work of the Ansiedlungskommission in Royal Prussia, but there was one key difference: the population policy not only relied on settling groups to homogenize a given territory; it also began to remove existing populations. Upon the arrival of the 'repatriates' from the East, parts of the Polish population were expelled to the General Government (Generalgouvernement), forming the main part of occupied Poland. If one includes internal deportations within the enlarged Reich, 840,000 Poles were uprooted from the Warthegau, the province of

West Prussia, and other annexed parts of Poland. The Jews inhabiting these areas were soon transported to ghettos and extermination camps, where the vast majority were killed. The policy vis-à-vis the Poles was also genocidal, if not in the literal sense of killing every man, woman, and child. The intellectual elite, priests, and political activists were murdered in large numbers in order to turn the Poles into an uneducated slave nation.[24]

Other populations affected by the National Socialist expansion and ethnic cleansing included more than 200,000 Czechs, especially from the borderlands annexed in 1938 (they are rarely mentioned in the literature on ethnic cleansing), and around 70,000 Slovenes from the northern, annexed parts of Slovenia. Although it was a great strain on the war economy, the German occupiers expelled more than 100,000 people in the eastern Polish region of Zamość in 1942 to create a racial German population bridge that reached from East Prussia to the Carpathians. After the destruction of Warsaw in the fall of 1944, the Germans ordered the deportation of its surviving 800,000 inhabitants. Beside the ethnic cleansing carried out by Germany itself, the Nazis oversaw and directed a chain of unilateral, bilateral, and even multilateral schemes of ethnic cleansing in co-operation with its wartime allies in Central and South-Eastern Europe. The various ethnic cleanings under Nazi domination affected a minimum of two million people. The goal was to create a system of homogenous nation-states; only the priorities of war kept it from being fully realized.

In many places ethnic cleansing was turned into genocide. This is, of course, true for the Jews, of whom approximately six million were killed, many by Wehrmacht units, the special 'Einsatzgruppen,' or local militias, others in the ghettos of Eastern Europe and the system of concentration and extermination camps.

While the ethnic cleansing and genocide in Central and Eastern Europe permanently transformed the ethnic structures of Europe and had a clearly ideological basis, other forms of forced migrations and mass killings followed more pragmatic motives. This is true for the over eight million forced laborers who were deported to Germany in order to support the war economy.[25] The Nazi leaders had a vivid memory of the breakdown of the home front during World War I and wanted to avoid any economic hardship for Germans as long a possible. As in World War I, the forced laborers were employed in the agricultural sector and in industry. Although the heartlands of Germany had never seen such a numerous influx of people of foreign origin, the National Socialists tried to seal off the 'racially' cleansed *Volksgemeinschaft* from the forced laborers as much as they could. This was not possible anymore after the defeat of Nazi Germany, when millions of 'Displaced Persons' wandered through Germany trying to return home or to migrate to other countries. Although Nazi ideology ceased to be propagated, the attitudes towards the former '*Fremdarbeiter*' remained mostly hostile. Traces of this ideological mindset could still be observed in the 1960s in the attitudes of the older generations towards the 'guest workers' who came to Germany from Southern Europe. The premise of this migration was still that these workers of foreign origin would only come for a limited period of time like the seasonal workers in late Wilhelmine Germany and the forced laborers in both world wars.

The defeat of Germany and the retreat of the Wehrmacht in 1944–1945 created another unprecedented wave of migration, now mostly ethnic Germans. The advance of the Red Army motivated hundreds of thousands of Germans to leave their home-lands in the fall and winter of 1944–1945. By spring 1945, around half of the civilian population in the Eastern Territories of the German Empire had fled from their homelands. Extremely traumatic, the flight happened during winter, and often under attack of the Red Army. The 3.5 million war refugees from Germany were the first cohort of what came to be termed as 'expulsion' in post-war West Germany. When World War II ended, the refugees were not allowed to return to their homelands, as had been the case in previous European wars. The Red Army, together with Polish and Czech authorities, continued to drive Germans from their homes after the capitulation of Nazi Germany. For Poles, Czechs, Russians, and other nations affected by Nazi occupation it was unimaginable to live with Germans in the same country. The Allies had already decided at the conferences of Teheran and Yalta in 1943, and in early 1945 that Poland should be moved westward around 200 km, incorporating large stretches of territory that had, until then, belonged to Germany. The idea was still to establish an order of homogenous nation states in Central and Eastern Europe, or as Winston Churchill had declared in his speech about the future of Poland in December of 1944: 'There will be no mixture of populations to cause endless trouble . . . A clean sweep will be made.'[26] The population policy of the late nineteenth century, which mostly depended on settling contested areas with co-nationals, was driven to the other extreme. Large swaths of Europe were homogenized by driving out ethnic minorities, and sometimes even the majority population. The terms for this redrawing of nations were euphemistic and were called 'transfer' in the case of the Germans, and 'repatriation' in the case of Poles, and other nations affected by the ethnic cleansing during and after World War II.[27]

According to the Potsdam treaty concluded in August of 1945, all German citizens and ethnic Germans remaining in the post-war territory of Poland, Czechoslovakia, and Hungary were to be 'transferred' to occupied Germany. By 1948, around 3.5 million Germans still located in the Eastern territories of the German Empire, as well as 3 million Sudeten Germans and more than 200,000 ethnic Germans from Hungary were removed, often under miserable circumstances. All in all, around 12 million people arrived in post-war Germany. It is impossible to establish exactly how many perished on their way. The official number of two million victims is exaggerated, but probably between half a million and one million people died, many of them still as civilian victims of war. The 12 million refugees amounted to almost one-quarter of the population in the Soviet Zone of Occupation, the later GDR, whereas they made up one-sixth of the population in West Germany. In paradoxical ways, the Nazi utopia to create an ethnically and racially clean German nation had never been achieved as fully as in 1948 when most DPs, including the Jewish survivors of the Holocaust, had left, and the Germans from the East had arrived. In the first post-war years, the refugees were a heavy burden for the welfare system. They were, moreover, often mistreated by the local German population, who even questioned the Germanness of the disliked

'*Flüchtlinge*,' another proof that the Nazi idea of a '*Volksgemeinschaft*' kept together by mutual solidarity was nothing more than a negative utopia.

The post-war migration from third countries was followed by an internal mobility on very high levels. In 1945–1946, most of the refugees had been settled in rural areas, where housing was more readily available than in the bombed-out cities. In the countryside, however, there were few jobs, and many refugees chose to go to the cities and other industrial areas after 1947–1948. By the end of the 1950s, at least every second refugee family moved at least once from their original place of settlement. They usually had to accept work that was below their standard of education and thus formed a new lower stratum of society. This changed only in the 1960s. By then, some of the refugees had experienced upward social mobility, while the guest workers from southern Europe now took the less prestigious and lower paid jobs in industry and services.

The lives of many refugees were radically transformed in the course of their external and internal migration, but their presence also had palpable consequences for post-war German society.[28] The 'economic miracle,' in particular, depended on the availability of cheap labor provided by the refugees. Moreover, for some agrarian regions, especially in Bavaria, the economic miracle also brought about a first wave of industrialization. The impact of the migration transcended the economic sphere, however. As the refugees came from different religious denominations (mostly Protestant from the former Eastern territories of Germany, almost exclusively Catholic from Czechoslovakia, Hungary, Yugoslavia, and Upper Silesia), their settlement contributed to the dissolution of Protestant and Catholic enclaves in post-war Germany, and weakened what had hitherto constituted relatively cohesive social-religious milieus.

In the public consciousness, however, the history of the refugees and their rather successful integration was not perceived in economic terms or as an experience of immigration. The refugees were seen as victims of ethnic nationalism, and in the context of the Cold War, of Communism. This was undoubtedly an important dimension of the experience of the refugees, but again contributed to an interpretation of migration in national and nationalistic terms. One way of overcoming the internal gaps between indigenous and immigrant Germans was to construct a national martyrology centered on the victimhood of the 'expellees.' This victimology was particularly prominent in the agenda of the so called '*Vertriebenenverbände*,' the expellee organizations that retained considerable political influence as a lobby until the advent of the Chancellorship of Willy Brandt in 1969.[29] The very term '*Vertriebener*' (expellee) encompassed a moral and legal condemnation of the 'expulsion' (*Vertreibung*) from Central and Eastern Europe, blaming Poles and Czechs for crimes against humanity and condemning Communists and in particular Stalin. Although solidarity with the expellees on a daily level was very limited, the anti-Polish, anti-Czech and anti-Russian stance worked as a political cohesion for conservatives and parts of the Social Democrats in the context of the Cold War. This ideological interpretation of the expulsion also explains why the expellees were not seen as migrants, but as victims only until the détente with Eastern Europe in the 1970s. Although the two Germanies, both East and West, had *de facto* become countries of immigration, and quite successfully managed the resulting social policy challenges, they never perceived themselves as migration societies. This state of affairs did not change until the 1980s, and then more dramatically when the bipolar division of Europe ended in the 1990s. The political denial of immigration during the long post-war decades was deeply connected to constructing the nation in narrow, ethnic terms. Thus, the discourses about migration and the nation in ethnic terms remained connected over this long period of German history and beyond.

NOTES

1. Werner Sombart, *Die deutsche Volkswirtschaft im 19. Jahrhundert und im Anfang des 20. Jahrhunderts*, 7th edn (Berlin: Georg Bondi, 1927), 408.

2. Klaus Bade, *Europa in Bewegung. Migration vom späten 18. Jahrhundert bis zur Gegenwart* (Munich: C. H. Beck, 2000).

3. Bradley D. Naranch, 'Inventing the Auslandsdeutsche. Emigration, Colonial Fantasy, and German National Identity 1848–71,' in Eric Ames, Marcia Klotz, and Lora Wildenthal (eds), *Germany's Colonial Pasts* (Lincoln: University of Nebraska Press, 2005), 21–40.

4. See Klaus J. Bade (ed.), *Deutsche im Ausland—Fremde in Deutschland. Migration in Geschichte und Gegenwart* (Munich: C. H. Beck, 1992).

5. K. Molly O'Donnell, Renate Bridenthal, and Nancy Reagin (eds), *The Heimat Abroad: The Boundaries of Germanness* (Ann Arbor: University of Michigan Press, 2005).

6. Birthe Kundrus, *Moderne Imperialisten: Das Kaiserreich im Spiegel seiner Kolonien* (Cologne: Böhlau, 2003), 43–119.

7. Howard Sargent, 'Diasporic Citizens: Germans Abroad in the Framing of German Citizenship Law,' in O'Donnell, Bridenthal and Reagin (eds), *Heimat Abroad*, 17–39.

8. See Eric D. Weitz, 'From the Vienna to the Paris System: International Politics and the Entangled Histories of Human Rights, Forced Deportations, and Civilizing Missions,' *American Historical Review* 113 (2008), 1313–1343.

9. Michael Ermarth, 'Hyphenation and Hyper-Americanization. Germans of the Wilhelmine Reich View German-Americans, 1890–1914,' *Journal of American Ethnic History* 21 (2002), 33–58.

10. On this subject see R. A. Hehl, *Die Entwicklung der Einwanderungsgesetzgebung in Brasilien* (Leipzig: Duncker & Humblot, 1896); Thomas E. Skidmore, 'Racial Ideas and Social Policy in Brazil, 1870–1940,' in Richard Graham (ed.), *The Idea of Race in Latin America, 1870–1940* (Austin: University of Texas Press, 1990), 7–36; Nancy S. Stepan, *The Hour of Eugenics: Race, Gender, and Nation in Latin America* (Ithaca: Cornell University Press, 1991), 155.

11. Krista O'Donnell, 'Home, Nation, Empire: Domestic Germanness and Colonial Citizenship,' in O'Donnell, Bridenthal and Reagin (eds), *Heimat Abroad*, 40–57.

12. See Magnus Brechtken, '*Madagaskar für die Juden.*' Antisemitische Idee und politische Praxis 1885–1945* (Munich: Oldenbourg, 1997), 16.

13. Woodruff D. Smith, *The Ideological Origins of Nazi Imperialism* (New York: Oxford University Press, 1986).

14. Johannes Nichtweiß, *Die ausländischen Saisonarbeiter in der Landwirtschaft der östlichen und mittleren Gebiete des Deutschen Reiches. Ein Beitrag zur Geschichte der preußisch-deutschen Politik von 1890 bis 1914* (Berlin: Rütten & Loening, 1959).

15. See Ulrich Herbert, *Geschichte der Ausländerbeschäftigung in Deutschland 1880 bis 1980. Saisonarbeiter, Zwangsarbeiter, Gastarbeiter* (Bonn: Dietz, 1986), 46–81. On the Poles in the Ruhr region, see Christoph Kleßmann, *Polnische Bergarbeiter im Ruhrgebiet 1870–1945. Soziale Integration und nationale Subkultur einer Minderheit in der deutschen Industriegesellschaft* (Göttingen: Vandenhoeck & Ruprecht, 1978).

16. Massimo Ferrari Zumbini, *'Die Wurzel des Bösen'. Gründerjahre des Antisemitismus: Von der Bismarckzeit zu Hitler* (Frankfurt: Klostermann, 2003), 556. See also Jack Wertheimer, *Unwelcome Strangers. East European Jews in Imperial Germany* (New York: Oxford University Press, 1987).

17. See Herbert, *Geschichte der Ausländerbeschäftigung*, 82–113; Jochen Oltmer, 'Zwangsmigration und Zwangsarbeit: Ausländische Arbeitskräfte und bäuerliche Ökonomie im Deutschland des Ersten Weltkriegs,' *Tel Aviver Jahrbuch für deutsche Geschichte* 27 (1998), 135–168; Leo Lucassen, 'The Great War and the Origins of Migration Control in Western Europe and the United States (1880–1920),' in Anita Böcker (ed.), *Regulation of Migration: International Experiences* (Amsterdam: Het Spinhuis, 1998), 45–72.

18. Karl C. Thalheim, 'Gegenwärtige und zukünftige Strukturwandlungen in der Wanderungswirtschaft der Welt,' *Archiv für Wanderungswesen* 3 (1930), 41–47, quote: 45.

19. Jochen Oltmer, *Migration und Politik in der Weimarer Republik* (Göttingen: Vandenhoeck & Ruprecht, 2005).

20. This is also the title of Michael Marrus, *The Unwanted. European Refugees in the Twentieth Century* (Oxford: Oxford University Press, 1985).

21. For the most exact estimate, see Herbert A. Strauss, 'Jews in German History: Persecution, Emigration, Acculturation,' in Herbert A. Strauss and Werner Röder (eds), *International Biographical Dictionary of Central European Emigrés 1933–1945*, vol. 2 (Munich: K.G. Sauer, 1983), xi–xvi.

22. See for the emigration the overview by Wolfgang Benz, 'Die Jüdische Emigration,' in Claus-Dieter Krohn et al. (eds), *Handbuch der deutschsprachigen Emigration 1933–1945* (Darmstadt: Wissenschaftliche Buchgesellschaft, 1998), 6–16; and in detail Marion Kaplan, *Between Dignity and Despair: Jewish Life in Nazi Germany* (New York: Oxford University Press, 1998), 62–73 and 129–144.

23. See Pertti Ahonen et al., *People on the Move. Forced Population Movements in Europe in the Second World War and its Aftermath* (Oxford: Berg, 2008), 14–20.

24. See for the National Socialist occupation of Poland the older overview by Czesław Madajczyk, *Die Okkupationspolitik Nazideutschlands in Polen 1939–1945* (Köln: Pahl-Rugenstein, 1988). Recently, a number of excellent regional studies have been published. Among them are Jacek Mlynarczyk, *Judenmord in Zentralpolen. Der Distrikt Radom im Generalgouvernement 1939–1945* (Darmstadt: Wissenschaftliche Buchgesellschaft, 2007); Michael Alberti, *Die Verfolgung und Vernichtung der Juden im Reichsgau Wartheland 1939–1945* (Wiesbaden: Harrassowitz, 2006).

25. On forced laborers, see Alexander von Plato, Almut Leh, and Christoph Thonfeld (eds), *Hitlers Sklaven. Lebensgeschichtliche Analysen zur Zwangsarbeit im internationalen Vergleich* (Wien: Böhlau, 2008); Ulrich Herbert, *Hitler's Foreign Workers: Enforced Foreign Labor in Germany Under the Third Reich* (New York: Cambridge University Press, 1997);

Mark Spoerer and Jochen Fleischhacker, 'Forced Laborers in Nazi Germany: Categories, Numbers, and Survivors,' *Journal of Interdisciplinary History*, 33, 2 (Autumn, 2002), 169–204.

26. Winston Churchill, 'The Future of Poland. A Speech to the House of Commons, December 15, 1944,' in Charles Eade (ed.), *The Dawn of Liberation. War speeches by the Right Hon. Winston S. Churchill C.H., M.P.* (London: Cassell, 1945), pp. 290–300, quote: 296.

27. See for a comparative perspective Philipp Ther, *Deutsche und Polnische Vertriebene. Gesellschaft und Vertriebenenpolitik in der SBZ/DDR und in Polen 1945–1956* (Göttingen: Vandenhoeck & Ruprecht, 1998).

28. See Andreas Kossert, *Kalte Heimat. Die Geschichte der deutschen Vertriebenen nach 1945* (Munich: Siedler, 2008); Ther, *Deutsche und polnische Vertriebene*, 110–257.

29. See Pertti Ahonen, *After the Expulsion. West Germany and Eastern Europe 1945–1990* (Oxford: Oxford University Press, 2003).

BIBLIOGRAPHY

AHONEN, PERTTI, et al., *People on the Move. Forced Population Movements in Europe in the Second World War and its Aftermath* (Oxford: Berg, 2008).

BADE, KLAUS J. (ed.), *Deutsche im Ausland—Fremde in Deutschland. Migration in Geschichte und Gegenwart* (Munich: C. H. Beck, 1992).

—— (ed.), *Population, Labor and Migration in 19th and 20th Century Germany* (New York: Berg, 1987).

——, PIETER C. EMMER, LEO LUCASSEN, and JOCHEN OLTMER (eds), *Enzyklopädie Migration in Europa: Vom 17. Jahrhundert bis zur Gegenwart* (Paderborn: Schöningh, 2007).

BENZ, WOLFGANG, 'Die Jüdische Emigration,' in Claus-Dieter Krohn et al. (eds), *Handbuch der deutschsprachigen Emigration 1933–1945* (Darmstadt: Wissenschaftliche Buchgesellschaft, 1998), 6–16.

CONRAD, SEBASTIAN, *Globalisierung und Nation im Deutschen Kaiserreich* (München: C. H. Beck, 2006).

HAGEN, WILLIAM W., *Germans, Poles and Jews: The Nationality Conflict in the Prussian East, 1772–1914* (Chicago: University of Chicago Press, 1980).

HERBERT, ULRICH, *Geschichte der Ausländerbeschäftigung in Deutschland 1880 bis 1980. Saisonarbeiter, Zwangsarbeiter, Gastarbeiter* (Bonn: Dietz, 1986).

HOERDER, DIRK and JÖRG NAGEL (eds), *People in Transit: German Migrations in Comparative Perspective, 1820–1930* (Cambridge: Cambridge University Press, 1995).

KOSSERT, ANDREAS, *Kalte Heimat. Die Geschichte der deutschen Vertriebenen nach 1945* (Munich: Siedler, 2008).

KULISCHER, EUGENE M., *Europe on the Move: War and Population Changes, 1917–1947* (New York: Columbia University Press, 1948).

MADAJCZYK, CZESŁAW, *Die Okkupationspolitik Nazideutschlands in Polen 1939–1945* (Köln: Pahl-Rugenstein, 1988).

MARRUS, MICHAEL, *The Unwanted. European Refugees in the Twentieth Century* (Oxford: Oxford University Press, 1985).

O'DONNELL, K. MOLLY, RENATE BRIDENTHAL, and NANCY REAGIN (eds), *The Heimat Abroad: The Boundaries of Germannness* (Ann Arbor: University of Michigan Press, 2005).

OLTMER, JOCHEN, *Migration und Politik in der Weimarer Republik* (Göttingen: Vandenhoeck & Ruprecht, 2005).

——, *Migration im 19. und 20. Jahrhundert* (Munich: Oldenbourg, 2009).

PLATO, ALEXANDER VON, ALMUT LEH, and CHRISTOPH THONFELD (eds), *Hitlers Sklaven. Lebensgeschichtliche Analysen zur Zwangsarbeit im internationalen Vergleich* (Vienna: Böhlau, 2008).

STRAUSS, HERBERT A., 'Jews in German History: Persecution, Emigration, Acculturation,' in Herbert A. Strauss and Werner Röder (eds), *International Biographical Dictionary of Central European Emigrés 1933–1945*, vol. 2 (Munich: K. G. Sauer, 1983), xi–xvi.

THER, PHILIPP, *Deutsche und Polnische Vertriebene. Gesellschaft und Vertriebenenpolitik in der SBZ/DDR und in Polen 1945–1956* (Göttingen: Vandenhoeck & Ruprecht, 1998).

——, 'A Century of Forced Migration: The Origins and Consequences of Ethnic Cleansing,' in Philipp Ther and Ana Siljak (eds), *Redrawing Nations: Ethnic Cleansing in East-Central Europe 1944–1948* (Lanham: Rowman and Littlefield, 2001), 43–72.

PART IV

·····································

GERMANY
1945–1989

·····································

Map 3 Germany after World War II

Source: Martin Kitchen, *A History of Modern Germany, 1800–2000* (Oxford: Blackwell Publishing, 2006), xvi.

CHAPTER 26

GERMANY IS NO MORE: DEFEAT, OCCUPATION, AND THE POSTWAR ORDER

STEFAN-LUDWIG HOFFMANN

In the fall of 1945, the writer Alfred Döblin returned as an officer of the French occupation army to Germany, the country he had been forced to leave twelve years earlier. Like many other observers from the West, he was shocked by the sight of destroyed German cities, but even more so by the strange callousness with which people walked among the ruins as if nothing had happened.[1] The return to a peaceful everyday life amid the ruins appeared unreal and incomprehensible after Nazi Germany's genocidal war, which had cost more than forty million lives in Europe alone.

More people died in the Second World War than in any other conflict before or since. Unlike in the First World War, civilians, most of them Soviet and Polish citizens, constituted almost half of the war dead. Particularly between the Elbe and the Volga, the Nazi war of extermination had left a wasteland of death. In this land of death, the Nazis killed five to six million European Jews. The question asked by contemporary observers like Döblin is still relevant for present day historians: How did Germans and Europeans after 1945 emerge from the horrors of Nazism and mass killings? To what extent did wartime violence leave its mark on postwar societies?

26.1 GERMANY'S ZERO YEARS

In order to understand this transition from war to peace, two premises have to be kept in mind. First, it is necessary to focus not just on the actual moment of the Third Reich's collapse in spring 1945. There was no 'zero hour' (*Stunde Null*) in international politics. Instead, Europe's mid-1940s should be seen as a transition period of its own. In only five years historical events forcibly, suddenly, and irreversibly changed political and social configurations on the continent. This transition began in 1942–1943: Nazi genocidal policies in the East reached their zenith, Germany's defeat became a certainty, and the Allies began to draft plans for a postwar order. It ended in 1947–1948 when the postwar settlement turned into a new conflict among the victorious powers, which ultimately split the continent and the German lands into two halves, the Capitalist West and Communist East. The Cold War constellation, which lasted in Europe until 1989/90, emerged from this short transition period between war and peace.

Second, the nature of this violent transition implies that these events cannot be explained merely from the perspective of German history. 'The Second World War, the culmination of nearly a century of growing violence between European powers inside and outside the continent—was really several wars in one,' as Mark Mazower has noted.[2] It was a war started by Nazi Germany for imperial hegemony in Europe, which developed into a global conflict and had global consequences, such as the Universal Declaration of Human Rights in 1948 and the beginning of decolonization. The Second World War not only ended German imperial ambitions in Europe, but also led to a (further) decline in Europe's global importance and to the disintegration of its colonial empires. As a result, the United States and Soviet Union emerged as the new global hegemons. And the Second World War was in many ways an ideological civil war. Fascism and Communism were international movements. In spring 1945 the Red Army was greeted with red flags in the working class neighborhoods of Berlin and Vienna (however deceptive the hopes associated with these flags were to prove). Among the last defenders of the Reich Chancellery, on the other hand, were French soldiers, remnants of the Waffen-SS Charlemagne division and units of the Nordland Division, among them many Danish and Norwegians. The ideological nature of this civil war helps to explain the extent of collaboration, which occurred in all European societies, with Nazi Germany. It also explains the intensity of hatred which postwar societies found difficult to contain. These hatreds, anti-Fascist and anti-Communist sentiments principal among them, were transmuted by the geo-political realignments of the Cold War, turning former enemies into strategic partners of a new conflict. In the shadows of this realignment, evident as early as 1947–1948, liberal democracies emerged in the post-Fascist societies of Western Europe and Japan.

In short, the demise of Nazi rule in Europe constituted a global moment. Within only a few years, the international order changed radically. Hardly anyone in Europe went unaffected by the changes, and the political shockwaves were noticeable all around the world. The impact was not unified, however. The end of the Second World War had different meanings for different people according to their experiences, whether as victors or as vanquished, or as recently liberated. These different meanings subsequently translated into incommensurable perspectives on the same events—conflicting memories, but no single history.[3]

In spring 1945, only one thing was certain: the Germans were the defeated of this war. Even though there was no 'zero hour' in terms of a sharp separation between wartime and peacetime, and even though it makes more sense to see the transition period from war to peace as a distinctive realm of experiences, it was beyond doubt for contemporary observers like Alfred Döblin that '1945' was a breach of continuity in German national history. '"Germany" has become a word without meaning,' wrote Döblin: 'It is a case of finished history. The territory once called Germany, once occupied by the Nazis and now administered by the allied victors, has become a No Man's Land, a sort of ownerless property. Newspapers, stamps, and public buildings bear only the adjective "German"—for instance, "German mail"—but never the noun "Germany."'[4]

After the 'unconditional surrender' of 8 May, 1945—the formulation was initially coined for the defeated Southern states in the American Civil War—German territories came under the control of the four Allied Powers, creating an ambiguous legal status unprecedented in the history of modern international law. According to Articles 42–56 of the Hague Convention, this was neither the *occupatio bellica* (belligerent occupation)—that is, the occupation of a sovereign state, which concedes certain rights to the occupied population granted by international law—nor the *occupatio imperii* (imperial occupation), which would have turned the Germans into subjects of the victorious powers.[5] Instead, Germany was conquered, but not annexed—apart from the Eastern territories. In principle, Germany's status was that of a colonial protectorate. Divided into four zones by the victorious powers, German territories were under foreign occupation for the very first time since the Napoleonic Wars. Ending a chapter in German history that began with the founding of the German Empire in 1871, Germany was now no longer a sovereign nation state.

26.2 DISSOLUTIONS

Total war was unleashed by Nazi Germany in 1939; it returned there five years later with numbing ferocity. For Germans, the last year of the war was the most lethal. What had started as a *blitzkrieg* to subject and colonize Europe evolved in the East into a fierce life-or-death struggle, a war without limits between two dictatorships.[6] As Joseph Goebbels declared in the Sportpalast in Berlin on 30 January 1943, it was the Führer's will that, in total war, there would be neither victor nor vanquished, but only survivors and annihilated. Nazi Germany's conduct of war in the East deliberately aimed at eliminating any hope of peace for the defeated. The 'barbarization of warfare' had hardly any strategic impact on the outcome of the war, but served the Nazi choreography of German defeat as catastrophic downfall.[7] Contrary to Nazi propaganda, Hitler and the other Nazi leaders did not believe in an 'ultimate victory' during the last two years of the war. Instead, the allegedly heroic sacrifice of the German people was supposed to prevent a peace through negotiations (as in 1918) and to enable the return of Nazism as a myth. Like a Wagner opera, the Third Reich was to end in memorable bloodshed. This was the basic rationale behind Nazi killing policies in the final years of war. The more war crimes German soldiers committed, the more they were forced into a guilt collective, which had burned all potential bridges toward the Allies, and therefore toward peace. Nazi propaganda itself hinted at these war crimes (and at the Judeocide) more and more frequently for this purpose.

This might help explain why the violence at the end of the war escalated to such an extent, even though it did not make much sense in military terms. Entire cities such as Warsaw were completely razed, their populations killed or deported before the German retreat. In 1944, spontaneous massacres, conducted in particular by SS units, which had become common practice in German warfare in Eastern Europe and in the Balkans, occurred also in France and Italy, notably in the villages of Oradour-sur-Glance and Civitella, where nearly the entire local population was killed. In the last year of the war, the SS concentration camp system on German territory expanded dramatically once again. Some 300,000 people are thought to have been killed in the death marches of concentration camp inmates during the last months of the war. Many victims died from physical exhaustion even after they were liberated. The horrifying pictures of the liberated concentration camps in Bergen-Belsen, Dachau, and Buchenwald shocked the British and American public in the spring of 1945, and continue (unlike the Soviet photographs of the abandoned extermination camps in Auschwitz and Majdanek) to shape the visual imagery of the Second World War in the West.[8]

At the end of the war, the terror of the regime also turned against the majority of the German population, not least against its own soldiers. More *Wehrmacht* soldiers died during the last ten months of the war, when German defeat was inevitable, than during the four years prior to July 1944. In other words, more than half of the 5.3 million German soldiers who died in the war could have been saved had the 20 July 1944 plot against Hitler succeeded.[9] In January 1945, when the offensive of the Red Army brought its troops from the Vistula to the Oder in just a few weeks, the *Wehrmacht* lost more soldiers in one month (450,000) than either the British or the American army during the entire war. Every third German male born between 1910 and 1925 did not survive the war.

The death rate of German soldiers was twice as high in relative terms in the Second World War compared with the First. The large number of losses also changed the gender ratio in postwar society. The group aged between 20 and 35 years was affected the most. After the First World War, women outnumbered men by a ratio of 5:4. In 1946, that ratio was 2:1. The number of deserters was also considerably higher than in the First World War. More than 100,000 *Wehrmacht* soldiers deserted during the Second World War. Some 15,000 German soldiers were executed during the war for desertion, and it is probable that more than half of these were carried out in the final year. In comparison, 40 British soldiers and 146 GIs were sentenced to death during the entire war. Only the Red Army imposed more death sentences on deserters than the *Wehrmacht*.

Still, historians are struggling to explain why most German soldiers continued to fight even though all was lost. The fear of revenge, especially by the Red Army, was surely an important motive. The brutality of German warfare and occupation not only undermined the stability of the Nazi regime in Europe, but also radicalized the plans of the Allies for the postwar order. The Nazis wanted to subjugate Europe and liked to think of themselves as the 'new Rome' or as the heirs of the British Empire. However, they were lacking a political vision of how to govern this Empire peacefully. The moral legitimacy and military furor of the Allied campaign against Nazi Germany grew with every year of the war. As early as January 1943, the Allies concurred that the war had to end with Germany's unconditional surrender. Hate campaigns against Nazi Germany had been conducted since 1942–1943, particularly in the Soviet Union. The brutality of German occupation constantly fueled these emotions. As they retreated, the Germans left a terrible wake of violence and devastation in Eastern Europe, first and foremost in the labor and extermination camps. The importance of these camps in shaping the perceptions of the Red Army soldiers pursuing the *Wehrmacht* as it retreated cannot be overestimated. More than a million Soviet soldiers returned to the attack units of the Red Army after they had been liberated from German camps.

When the Red Army reached German territory in East Prussia in October 1944, and when, shortly afterwards, Aachen became the first larger German city to surrender without a fight to US troops, German society was already in a process of complete social dissolution. By that time at the latest, the Nazi regime lost most of its popular support. During the Allied bombing campaigns, approximately 600,000 German civilians were killed, the majority in the last year of the war (up to 25,000 alone in the bombing of Dresden between February 13 and 15, 1945). Here and elsewhere in the collapsing Nazi Empire, and later in the postwar societies of Europe, the dissolution of government structures forced individuals to rely for survival on local and family networks in the bombed-out cities. Black markets and petty crime were as much expressions of a growing distance from the imperatives of the Nazi state as were sexual relations, for example, between German women and foreign laborers, or later Allied soldiers. These were particularly provocative for a regime obsessed with racial purity. Across wartime Europe, and in the immediate postwar years, 'the unheroic mentality of "getting by" and a strange sense of individual freedom and personal uncertainty' were the most common reactions to social dissolution and despair.[10]

The Nazi regime responded with legal terror against 'ordinary' Germans who uttered defeatist comments, engaged in plunder or black market activities, or surrendered prematurely to the Allies.[11] More and more Germans were found guilty of economic offenses, dissent, or illegal contacts with prisoners of war. As a consequence, the number of German women behind bars rapidly increased. Previously, women had made up only a small portion of the prison population.[12] Reports in the Nazi media on harsh sentences against Germans served as an instrument of deterrence. 'Let this punishment be a warning to you' was the straightforward message of the Nazi regime, on street posters or in the press, to anyone who did not comply with the politics of destruction.

Another important social consequence of the rise and demise of Nazi rule in Europe was the dislocation of millions of people.[13] The Nazis had not only robbed Jewish property and looted the occupied countries for the benefit of the German population, but brought forced laborers from all parts of Europe to Germany. Paradoxically, Hitler's Germany became a country of migrants, particularly during the final years of the war. In September 1944, there were 7,487,000 foreign laborers (and at the end of war almost 10 million foreigners) in Germany, most of whom were there against their will.

In Berlin and Nuremberg, they made up 20 percent of the population in 1944. In the last months of the war, the Gestapo or SS killed in desperate 'revenge' against Allied air raids at least 10,000 to 30,000 foreign laborers.[14]

After the war, the western European forced laborers returned to their home countries. The vast majority of eastern Europeans remained as displaced persons in the German territories occupied by the Western Allies and waited for a chance to leave. Among them were former POWs, survivors of concentration camps, refugees from the Soviet Union (among them many Jews who had reached safety behind the front lines and who wanted to emigrate to Palestine) and Nazi collaborators in hiding. By 1947, the number of displaced persons had declined to about one million. Of more than 500,000 German Jews who had lived in Germany in 1933, only 15,000 were left in 1946–1947 after forced emigration and extermination by the Nazi regime. Jewish survivors often faced German resentment and Allied ignorance about their suffering during the Holocaust, as has been described, for example, in Ruth Klüger's memoir *Still Alive* (2001).[15]

For survival in the last months of the war, racial or national categories were often more important than class, but fundamental differences existed between urban and rural experiences of war. The German countryside remained remarkably well-off and untouched by the war—much to the consternation of Allied, especially Soviet troops, who had witnessed the scorched earth retreat of the *Wehrmacht* in Eastern Europe. Most German cities were, however, in ruins. By the end of the Second World War, more than half of Germany's urban residents were dead or on the move. More German civilians (over 50,000) died during the Battle of Berlin in the last three weeks of the war than during the entire Allied bombing campaign against the city (approximately 20,000) since November 1943. Before the war, Nuremberg was a city of 420,000 inhabitants. After the war it housed only 180,000. The figures for Cologne were even more dramatic (1939: 772,221; and 1945: 45,000) and the trend was repeated in Kassel (1939: 211,624; and 1945: 35,000), Stettin (1939: 275,000; and 1945: 20,000) and Königsberg (1939: 372,164; and 1945: 47,000). Shortly before the end of the war, Breslau was one of the few undestroyed large cities in Germany. The number of inhabitants had grown during the war from 630,000 to more than one million. The city was declared a fortress in the last months of the war and was razed to the ground, mainly by German troops. Only 150,000 inhabitants were still in the city when the Red Army conquered Breslau in May 1945 and when, shortly afterwards, the city was handed over to the Polish authorities.[16]

Other undestroyed cities, such as Leipzig and Göttingen, were crowded with refugees, and the number of inhabitants was greater than before the war. Although probably seven million Germans were killed in the war—about a tenth of the Reich population in 1937 (69.32 million)—the three Western occupied zones were filled to the bursting point with people due to territorial losses and the flight from the Red Army (this population increase, it is less well-known, was one of the preconditions for the later 'economic miracle'). In the German territories east of the Oder (Silesia, West Prussia, and East Prussia), in contrast, the population had shrunk to approximately 20 or 30 percent of pre-war numbers. Many German refugees had returned home after the end of war, but were ultimately removed by 1947–1948 or died from epidemics and malnutrition. For instance, almost 30 percent of the German population who had remained in the Königsberg area died between September 1945 and November 1946.

Even though the Allies officially rejected the idea of German collective guilt, the treatment of Germans at the end of the war told a different story. When fourteen million Germans were evacuated and expelled from Central and Eastern European countries, at least half a million perished, most of them women and children.[17] 3.5 million German prisoners of war were kept as forced laborers by the Soviet Union (the last 10,000 only returned home ten years later). At least 330,000 German civilians were deported to the Soviet Union in the GULAG camps. Soviet authorities regularly kidnapped Germans between 1945 and 1947 (also in West Berlin) for political reasons or, as in the case of a few thousand highly-skilled engineers, for 'human' reparations (the engineers were transported to the Soviet Union to work in the Soviet armaments industry). By as early as January 1945, 75,000 young men and women of the German minority in Romania had already been deported for forced labor to the Soviet Union, as has been described in Herta Müller's novel, *Everything I Possess I Carry With Me* (2009).

There are no accurate figures on the number of rapes by soldiers of the Red Army.[18] According to contemporary estimates, in spring 1945 alone, at least every second woman in Berlin aged sixteen to sixty was sexually assaulted. The situation was similar in Vienna and Budapest, but less excessive in cities such as Belgrade and Prague, which had been liberated by the Red Army. (Rapes also occurred during the French occupation of southwest of Germany, although to a much lesser extent). The fear of revenge by the Red Army was the most important motive for the suicide epidemic in 1945—which, according to official statistics, reached 3881 cases in Berlin in April 1945 alone (and the real figure was presumably much higher.)[19] It was not only soldiers of the Red Army who exacted vengeance. Everywhere in Europe, acts of revenge against Germans and Nazi collaborators occurred. While Red Army violence was apparently not planned (although tolerated) by the authorities, the retributions against Germans in East Central Europe were not merely the result of spontaneous explosions of hatred, but were strategically employed to reduce the number of those who had to be deported later.[20] After the so-called *Volksdeutsche* had supported Nazi occupation, it was unimaginable for Czechs or Poles (and for the Allies) to rebuild East Central European societies with the presence of a German minority.

For most Germans, the end of the Second World War was more catastrophic than the war itself. Despite initial relief that the war was over, many Germans felt that the tables had been turned, that the Germans would now pay for Nazi and *Wehrmacht* crimes, perpetrated not only, but primarily, in Eastern Europe. 'The shock of violence' (Richard Bessel) at the end of war, and the completeness of defeat, served to de-Nazify, and demilitarize Germans far more effectively than subsequent Allied re-education programs.[21] At the same time, the very different German encounters with the British, American, French, and Soviet Allied troops in the wake of war and during the early occupation prefigured the geo-political realignments of the Cold War. In only five years since 1942–1943, Nazis had turned into Germans again and ultimately—much to their amazement—into Allies.

26.3 Occupiers and occupied

Almost all continental European nations experienced regimes of occupation between 1939 and 1949 (some, like Poland, were occupied three times) and these experiences varied greatly. Nazi rule in Eastern Europe was much more brutal than in the West, and Soviet (and French) rule in Germany and Austria was more coercive than the British and American occupation regimes. In some cases, as with the Germans and the French since 1914, there was a recurring reversal of roles between occupiers and occupied, which shaped subsequent perceptions and policies. One of the unintended consequences of all occupations was, however, an unprecedented mixing (and later unmixing) of peoples, not only in German territory, but all over Europe. As part of the social dissolutions and political reconfigurations in the wake of war, the problem of how to police encounters between occupiers and occupied was considered to be of fundamental importance by all occupation powers.

The paradox for the Allies in postwar Germany was that they had expected a population of fanatical Nazis and violent insurgents, but in reality encountered a people sick of war, contemptuous of the ruling elite that had led them into disaster, and initially complacent about the realities of occupation.[22] 'One could understand the people being relieved at our coming; one could understand the old warriors from the trade unions of pre-Hitler days, the staunch anti-Nazis who had escaped the concentration camps, coming out to welcome us,' reported Leonard Mosley, a war correspondent who accompanied the British occupation army into the Ruhr, 'but the noisy, demonstrative greeting of so many, the obvious happiness of all who saw us, was a phenomenon that I find hard to explain; yet there it was.'[23] In fact, in the months following the defeat of Nazi Germany, occupiers and occupied alike were struck by the high incidence of fraternization between Allied troops and German civilians. Black GI's, for example, were surprised by the apparent absence of racism in their relations with Germans. In striking contrast to racial segregation at home, African American soldiers enjoyed more civil liberties in occupied Germany and were able to move about without undue restrictions.[24] Similarly, during the summer of 1945, Jewish Red Army officers recorded their astonishment at their cordial relationships with Germans, in particular German girls and their families, and a general sense of newly-gained freedom.[25] Conversely, the Russians became an object not only of terror, but of intense fascination and bewilderment for fellow occupiers and occupied alike.[26] After all, for many Germans and most contemporary Western observers, this was their first encounter with the Soviet system that had prevailed over Nazism.

The problem of postwar intercultural contact captures the different trajectories of the western and Soviet occupations in Germany. When the Americans came to Germany, fraternization was strictly forbidden. As early as the summer of 1945, however, even the threat of punishment was unable to deter American soldiers from relinquishing resentments against German women and children. As a result, the ban on fraternization was lifted, and in 1948 inter-marriages were allowed. During the four years of occupation, American GIs fathered 94,000 children with German women. The French authorities attempted to bring the children of German women and French soldiers back to France for adoption in order to balance the losses in population during the World War, though the affinities of this program to Nazi population policies ultimately undermined it.[27]

There are no official data about the so called 'Russian children,' (and, significantly, no historical studies on consensual relations between Red Army soldiers and German women), but their number was presumably more than twice as high. According to the testimony of Soviet deserters, almost every Soviet officer based in Berlin lived in the flat of his German mistress in the period immediately after the war. Many of these deserters fled to West Berlin with their German girlfriends and were later interrogated by US intelligence. Initially, Soviet authorities did not issue any regulations on the relationship between Russian soldiers and German civilians. It was not until contacts in everyday life began to take on more cordial forms that Soviet policies changed. The Stalinist regime distrusted all contacts with foreigners, and for this reason sent many western-liberated Soviet nationals who had been forced laborers on German territory straight to the GULAG. Beginning in the fall of 1946, Soviet troops were completely separated from the civilian population, and all private contact with Germans was prohibited.[28] Red Army officers, who had been a common presence in East Germany and Austria after the war, essentially disappeared from civilian life. The propagated ideology of German-Soviet friendship never corresponded to an everyday experience until the end of the GDR.

Recent historical accounts have corrected the image so prevalent in German political and intellectual life that most Nazi criminals were never punished. The Americans, at the outset, were particularly strict and arrested more than 100,000 individuals (mostly men) whom they suspected of being Nazis, including many industrialists and representatives of the old elites. Up to the end of the 1950s, more than 95,000 Germans and Austrians were sentenced in Nazi trials throughout Europe, most of them in the immediate postwar period. It is no surprise that more than half of these convictions were imposed in Eastern Europe. Ironically, the expulsion of the Germans made impossible a more comprehensive legal retribution based on individual guilt, since many of the Germans suspected or convicted of war crimes escaped to West Germany as they were collectively pushed out of East Central Europe.

The four major Allied powers together convicted 8812 Germans or Austrians in occupation courts on German soil, the Nuremberg Trials in 1945–1946 being merely the most prominent example. The Germans themselves convicted nearly 20,000 people of Nazi crimes, almost twice as many in the East as in the West. Naturally, the number of those investigated or indicted was much higher, according to recent estimates at least three times higher.[29] As with the rest of Europe, where revenge against and severe punishment of collaborators ceased by 1947–1948, the vigor with which Nazi criminals were prosecuted, and of de-Nazification policies in general, diminished with the advent of the Cold War and the search for political and economic stability.

In the Soviet zone of occupation, as everywhere in East Central Europe, the war was followed by a social revolution 'from above.' The old elites were removed from their positions in the judiciary, the education system, the economy, and state administration, and superseded by young socialist cadres who were hastily trained. For them, social mobility was politically linked to the communist project.[30] According to official statistics, by the end of 1946 more than 390,000 former members of the Nazi Party had already been dismissed. Many more Nazis and representatives of the old elites had escaped from Soviet controlled territory. However, Soviet retributions against Germans aimed not only at de-Nazification, but also at the establishment of Communist rule. By expropriating the East Elbian *Junker* (members of the landed nobility of Prussia) and distributing land to so-called new farmers, both ends were served. Much the same applies to the expropriation of many German companies (and the takeover of management by former workers). By these means, the Soviets wanted to break the power of the old German industrial elites who had supported Hitler's war. Unlike today, many contemporaries blamed unbridled capitalism for the rise of Nazism. Even those who supported nationalizing the economy were put off by the extent of lawlessness shown by the Soviets during this process.

In order to achieve their objectives, the Soviet Military Administration in Germany used Stalinist methods of rule: terror, coercion, and show trials, all of which contributed to the growing estrangement between the Allies.[31] Between 1945 and 1950, one third of all newly-arrested prisoners (155,000) died in GULAG camps on German territory. Often erected on the site of former Nazi concentration camps, such as Buchenwald or Sachsenhausen, these camps held more Social Democrats than Nazi leaders. In other words, Stalinist terror was not primarily directed against Nazi criminals, but against political opponents or, more generally (and arbitrarily), against anyone who was perceived as a threat to the imperatives of Soviet occupation. This included German youths (half of all inmates were under 20 years old), who were interned for minor offenses such as petty theft or alleged collaboration with the Western Allies. Postwar purges and the establishment of Communist rule were closely intertwined and kept the local population in the Soviet zone of occupation in Germany (and Austria) in a state of terror.[32]

Hence, Soviet lawlessness against the defeated—rape, kidnapping, requisitions, shootings, deportations—turned military victory into moral defeat. To be sure, the Western Allies initially also sought to restore state authority in postwar Germany with draconian penalties. The anti-fascist committees founded at the end of the war by former unionists, Social Democrats and Communists were dissolved as early as the beginning of summer 1945. In the same way, all forms of spontaneous revenge were prevented (after twelve years of Nazi rule there were many scores to settle among Germans). In the immediate postwar period, British and American military courts often imposed death sentences, for instance for possession of a weapon and for any form of violence such as robberies by organized groups of refugees. As a result, British military courts sentenced to death for such offenses more displaced persons, who had been forced laborers or concentration camp inmates under the Nazis, than Germans.[33]

It was, however, recognizable that the objective in the Western zones of occupation was the restoration of the rule of law. In contrast, the large degree of lawlessness of Soviet rule in Central Europe was a sobering experience even for those who had sympathized with Soviet Russia, and explains why Communism rapidly lost its constituency in postwar (West) Germany and Austria.[34]

26.4 Embracing democracy

Contrary to conventional wisdom, the immediate postwar years were not only a time of social exhaustion and apathy, but also of political promise and activism. Once elections were allowed, the turn-out was high. The electorate, predominantly female as a result of the war, initially gave the most support to forces perceived as being the antithesis of Nazism: namely Communism, Social Democracy, and Christian Democracy. In 1946, in the first free local and regional elections, Social Democrats and Christian Parties mostly prevailed in the Western occupation zones. In the Soviet zone (but not in Berlin or Vienna, former communist strongholds still under shock by the behavior of the Red Army) the new Socialist Unity Party of Germany (*Sozialistische Einheitspartei Deutschlands*, SED) founded under Soviet pressure by Social Democrats and Communists often took the majority of votes. The SED won 47.5 percent of the vote in the first regional elections in the Soviet occupation zone in 1946—not enough by Stalinist standards, but almost twice as much as the Christian Democrats (24.5 percent) or the Liberals (24.6 percent). In other words, in these early elections we can already discern the divergent Cold War trajectories of the two Germanies: liberal democracy in the West, Communist rule in the East.

However, the immediate postwar period was, all in all, the hour of the Left. Even the 'Ahlen program' (1947) of the newly-founded conservative Christian Democratic Party, for example, held capitalism to be responsible for the end of the Weimar Republic and the rise of Nazism, and demanded central economic planning as a remedy. Coalition governments of Christian Democrats, Socialists, and Communists were extremely popular, as was the case in Austria since the first free National Assembly elections in November 1945 (after 1949 without the Communists). In the GDR there was—until its very end in 1990—the so called 'government of the national front' (*Regierung der nationalen Front*), which included all parties and could be conveniently controlled by the SED. Still, it is remarkable to what extent government by consensus became the preferred model of postwar German politics in marked contrast to the civil and political strife of the 1920s and 1930s.

As Martin Conway has argued, this embrace of democracy in postwar Europe was a struggle between competing concepts of democracy, including ideologies of the left and right, which one might not automatically associate nowadays with democratic practices.[35] In occupied Germany, for example, practicing democracy could imply opposition to Allied rule—in the Soviet, but also in the Western zones. While the Allies in

1945 had been surprised by the docile and complacent nature of the Germans, this attitude changed during the course of the occupation. Regardless of Allied censorship, the authoritarian regime of the occupation powers was more and more criticized, especially by those who had not been Nazi members and who now claimed political rights for Germans, in particular the right to self-determination.[36] When the Social Democrat Kurt Schumacher, who had been a concentration camp inmate during most of the Third Reich, demanded that democracy should be defended if necessary against Allied occupation regimes, he summarized a striking sense of political entitlement among Germans in the early Cold War.[37]

Germans were not only passive spectators, but had some agency in the conflicts between the Allies. During the Berlin crisis in June 1948, more than 300,000 people gathered in front of the destroyed Reichstag building to protest against the blockade of the city by the Soviets. This was only one of many instances in which popular protest manifested itself during the immediate postwar period. The Soviets had feared that West Germany would become part of a political and military block against the USSR, and not without reason. The conflict intensified only because each side expected the other side not to resort to violence. In 1948–1949, there was never a real danger of a Third World War, despite popular fears of a final war of annihilation, which continued for most of the 1950s and 1960s. Unlike in June 1953 during the workers' uprising against the GDR regime, the Soviet occupation army was not even mobilized.[38]

When it became clear that the majority of Germans wanted to embrace democracy as a way out of the Nazi past, it was impossible for the Allies to continue to treat them as 'if they were an extraordinarily intelligent tribe of Bedouin' (Noel Annan).[39] This shift in American and British perceptions of postwar Germany was also stirred by the realization that the dire state of postwar Germany had turned into a burden for the Allies. Britain, for example, had to deliver many more goods to its occupation zone than it was able to extract as reparations. 'A few months ago criticism of inhuman and unreal conceptions of a Carthaginian peace were still regarded as some sort of heresy,' noted Isaac Deutscher as early as December 1945 in the British *Observer*. 'Even mild and decent people seemed to breathe revenge. Now the pendulum has swung almost to sentimental sympathy for defeated Germany. "We must help Germany to get back on her feet," has become a fashionable phrase.'[40]

British and American media coverage of Germany shifted from pictures of Nazi concentration camps to images of destroyed cities and of German desolation, hunger, social chaos, and austerity, which was common all over postwar Europe. The fate of children in particular became a dominant theme of reportage, photojournalism, and films about life in occupied Germany—for instance, in Roberto Rosselini's 'Germania anno zero' (1946–1947). The newly-founded UN relief organizations sent humanitarian aid and social workers to Europe where millions of children still remained homeless.[41] Particularly in the American media, the humanitarian crisis in postwar Europe gained much attention and included, if at first reluctantly, images of German hardship.

For the Western Allies, this postwar sense of humanitarian emergency made it increasingly difficult to reconcile their wartime commitment to crush Nazi Germany and make Germans pay for their crimes. The quasi-colonial power of the military governments increasingly lost its legitimacy, not least thanks to the pressure of the British and American media, which described social dissolution in occupied Germany as a humanitarian disaster. By the summer of 1946 at the latest, even neutral observers, like the Swedish writer Stig Dagerman, criticized the Allied occupation. By demanding that postwar Germans no longer be viewed as 'one solid block, irradiating Nazi chill,' but as 'a multitude of starving and freezing individuals,' Dagerman summarized the moral dilemma, particularly of American occupation policies in postwar Germany.[42] The longer the state of occupation lasted, the more it lost its political legitimacy in the eyes of occupied Germans, American (and British) occupiers, and neutral observers.

26.5 COLD WAR RECOVERY

After 1945, the economic recovery of Europe seemed even less likely than the return of democracy. The First World War had been followed by a period of economic chaos and depression. Why would it be any different after a second, even more devastating war? One of the Allied war goals was the complete dismantling of the German armaments industry, particularly of those big corporations which had enabled Hitler's 'New Order' in Europe. The Krupp Corporation (like most of the Ruhr industry) was expropriated and put under Allied control; the steel works in Essen were dismantled. Alfried Krupp von Bohlen und Halbach himself, as well as his managers, were arrested and sentenced by an Allied court in 1948—only to be released in the early 1950s. Likewise, the managers of the largest European chemical corporation, IG Farben, were arrested and sentenced by the Allies, but later amnestied in the Federal Republic. IG Farben had, among other things, colluded with the SS, setting up in Auschwitz a chemical plant and labor camp, which was supplied with inmates of the adjacent concentration camp, and whose atrocious conditions Primo Levi described in his *Survival in Auschwitz*, first published in Italian in 1947. The IG Farben Corporation was confiscated and dissolved by the Allies, its foreign assets expropriated. The imposing headquarters in Frankfurt upon Main had to be cleared—the American military government moved into these premises.

German industry was demilitarized and weakened not just in order to render impossible future revenge, but also so that Germany paid for the war in the form of reparations. Here again, there was a significant difference between the East and the West, due to previous wartime experiences with Nazi Germany. In the Western occupation zones, only the French urged larger reparations, whereas East Germany was burdened with consequential costs of the war for years to come. (In 1946 48.8 percent of the East German GNP went as reparations to the Soviet Union, in 1953 it was still 12.9 percent.) In the immediate postwar period, almost half of the industrial facilities in East Germany were dismantled by the Soviet Union, most of which were never reassembled and put to use. (In the late summer of 1945, trains with dismantled industrial facilities were backed up more than 60 miles at the Soviet border station of Brest.) Around half of all rail tracks in the East of Germany were dismantled, but few of them were ever laid again in the Soviet Union. Part of the industrial production was directly sent to the Soviet Union during the first postwar years. A quarter of all companies were expropriated on site to the benefit of Soviet stock corporations (*Sowjetische Aktiengesellschaften*, SAG), among them the large chemical plants in Buna and Leuna, and the uranium mines in the Ore Mountains.[43]

Given the substantial dismantling (not only in the Soviet zone) it is even more surprising that Germany's industrial production grew initially after the war. There were several reasons for this. The German armaments industry had reached its highest level of production in the last two years of the war, far above the pre-war level. War damage was, furthermore, less than expected. Aerial bombing had destroyed the historic centers of most German cities; however, the industrial facilities were hit less severely. Even according to the Allies' own calculations, seven times more bombs were dropped on civilian housing and traffic infrastructure than on plants of the war industry. Thanks to high investments in the armaments industry during wartime, Germany's economy had more investment capital available than before the war, while German refugees offered a large potential labor force. Moreover, first the Nazis and then the occupation authorities had essentially stymied organized labor in wartime and postwar Germany. Thus Germany's industrial production recovered quickly during the first postwar year (whereas basic supplies for the population remained scarce)—in the Western zones, but, surprisingly enough, also in the East, where central planning initially proved to be successful in coping with the postwar situation. It was not before the disastrous winter of 1946–1947 that the German and subsequently the entire Western European economy collapsed.

This raised the question of how to deal politically with German reparations, an issue which subsequently led to the ultimate break-up of the Allies. Considering the deplorable humanitarian situation in postwar Germany, the Americans in particular pressed for an end to high reparations, the more so as postwar Europe was a potentially important market for US industrial production that had grown throughout the war. The Soviet Union, on the other hand, was in a completely different situation. The Nazi war of extermination had left a devastated country, which was to be reconstructed and developed with the help of the reparations. Postwar famine was a far more serious problem in the USSR than in occupied Germany. Unlike the USA (and Great Britain), the Soviet Union had experienced first hand the exploitative brutality of the German occupation. It is no surprise that the Soviets interpreted American sympathy for postwar Germans as an attempt to reconcile prematurely with the former enemy, an enemy who only recently had conducted a fierce racial war against the Soviet people. In other words, behind the Cold War American-Soviet rift lay the enormous gulf in their wartime experiences.[44]

Moreover, the brutality of German warfare in the East and the Soviet state terror were closely intertwined. It has been argued that the barbarization of warfare during the Second World War was both conditioned by and integral to the Soviet ethos.[45] For witnesses of the war in the East like the writer Vasily Grossman, it was clear that 'a severe peace is coming after the severe war,' as he noted in spring 1945 in his diaries.[46] One year later, the nature of Soviet rule in Central Europe was perceived by the Western Allies increasingly as a threat. Soviet lawlessness in postwar Germany (which paled in comparison to the Nazi killing policies in the Soviet Union) was one reason why Americans viewed Soviet and Nazi rule in Europe increasingly as two sides of the same 'totalitarian' coin.[47] Consequently, the imperatives of the occupation in the West quickly shifted from political and moral cleansing and demilitarization to the stabilization of their own zones of occupation. Germany was supposed to become independent from American aid and thereby politically armed against communism, the new challenge to liberal democracy.

In this context, a strict occupation regime to disarm the former enemy economically and politically became less imperative. By spring 1947, the American government decided to support the economic recovery of Germany (and Europe) 'to make democracy safe for capitalism.'[48] Even if the economic significance of the so-called Marshall Plan (the European Recovery Program, named after the American secretary of state) is disputed among historians, its political importance can hardly be overestimated. US engagement proved to West Germans that their integration into the West was beyond dispute. This had already been demonstrated in 1948–1949 when the Soviets had blocked all access to West Berlin. In response, the Western Allies organized the so-called Berlin Airlift from 24 June 1948 until 12 May 1949, to carry supplies to the people in West Berlin. The currency reform on 20 June 1948, which had ignited the Soviet blockade of West Berlin, cemented economically the separation of the two German states and the integration of both German societies into the sphere of influence of the respective superpowers. The promise of American aid and prosperity led to a change in the political expectations of occupied and occupiers alike.[49] In West Germany as elsewhere in Western Europe, the Socialist parties suffered greatly from the rhetorical separation of politics from economics, bolstered by the American emphasis on aid as business.[50] By 1948/49, the postwar moment of the Left had passed. West Germany, Japan, and Italy became, ironically enough, in the 1950s and 1960s the centers of the most sustained economic boom in modern history.

26.6 CONCLUSION: FROM WAR TO PEACE

'The war had changed everything,' as Tony Judt has summarized the postwar sentiment in Europe.[51] The conservative materialism and quietism of 1950s West German families that had so enraged its children, the generation of 1968, was only the antidote to the social dissolutions of the 1940s forged by Nazism, war, and occupation. Between 1942–1943 and 1947–1948, the everyday lives of ordinary Germans were marked by a permanent state of emergency which generated new social norms and popular expectations.[52] After 1949, Germans embraced liberal democracy and the promise of prosperity in the West, or to a lesser extent, the welfare dictatorship in the East, as a way to transcend wartime experiences.

This is not to say that the immediate months and early postwar years were a moment of silence about Nazism, as is conventionally assumed. When the war was over, Germans were debating, in private or (under Allied censorship) in public, problems of sexuality, family, morality, juvenile delinquency, urban housing, educational reform or, more generally, the dangers of capitalism, secularism, mass culture, and totalitarian rule, all connected with an explicit or implicit reference to the Nazi past.[53] As Dolf Sternberger would write in July 1945 in his diaries (published in the first issue of the journal *Die Wandlung*), many Germans initially viewed themselves as forced accomplices (*erzwungene Mitschuldige*) in Nazi crimes, not necessarily as innocent victims, despite 1950s narratives of German victimization that have gained much attention recently by historians.[54] The postwar embrace of democracy would have been impossible without the awareness of bearing part of the guilt. Distancing from the Nazi past ('anti-fascism' in Communist parlance) became the *raison d'être* of both postwar Germanies, each accusing the other of being the dangerously potent successor to Nazism. In truth, however, after 1945 German power was no longer a problem in international politics.

The most striking change that the war entailed was the end of the German Reich (and in 1947 of Prussia) as an imperial nation state and, simultaneously, of the class antagonisms that had dominated its political life for over a century. The loss of the German territories in the East and the demise of the conservative, land-owning Junker class east of the Elbe turned out to be irreversible. The German Junkers, until 1939 a significant element in German politics, lost their land and their livelihood within a few years. The Prussian aristocracy never regained political power. Likewise, the propertied and educated German *Bürgertum* lost much of its social and political capacity in the 1930s and 1940s, not least because its Jewish members were forced to emigrate or were killed by the Nazis. The transformative power of Nazism, war and occupation, also eroded the class and political cohesion of German workers, who had been strongly organized in Imperial and Weimar Germany, providing the heartbeat of European socialism.

By contrast, West Germany became a moderately conservative middle-class society during the economic miracle years, managed by supposedly nonpartisan experts. As in Japan, where the representatives of the old bureaucracy were not dismissed under American occupation, parts of the Third Reich's economic and administrative elites were able to regain positions in semi-sovereign West Germany in the beginning of the 1950s and to make liberal democracy their cause. ('I vacillate a great deal,' Victor Klemperer noted in his diaries in 1957, 'but my hate turns instinctively against Bonn with its Nazi and Jew-murderer ministers.'[55]) East Germany was governed in the name of the working class by a handful of hardened Communists as a welfare dictatorship, racing behind similar ideals of material improvement and social harmony while depriving workers of their basic social and political rights.[56] For different reasons, confessional antagonism, which had been so significant for Imperial and Weimar Germany, essentially disappeared from political life (though not altogether from social life). Both postwar Germanies aimed to be comparatively egalitarian societies, more homogeneous than ever before.

The end of total war had also crushed German nationalism and militarism. As in Japan, pacifism became a salient feature of German political culture. Postwar Germans had to be convinced of the necessity of rearmament in the 1950s by the Cold War rivals. Moreover, the idea of reclaiming the German lands in the East never attracted any serious political consideration, much to the frustration of expellee organizations in West Germany. On the contrary, the mid-1940s profoundly changed the mental maps of Germans. Imperial and Weimar Germany might have been more a part of the West than British and American re-education programs after 1945 were willing to concede. Still, since the mid-nineteenth century the German frontier that stirred colonial fantasies had been in the East.[57] After the Second World War, it was not only one fifth of pre-war Germany that was severed from the country and its German population removed. In 1946 Konrad Adenauer, who would become Chancellor in 1949, declared that Asia stood on the Elbe, thus cutting off from Europe the vast zone of death and destruction that the Germans had left in the East. The fact that the Federal Republic until 1970—and formally even until 1990—did not acknowledge the German-Polish border at the Oder and Neisse rivers was just a symbolic concession to German expellees. More than anything else, postwar Germans wanted to belong to the West.

The return to semi-sovereignty in 1949 created two German states, albeit with the continuing presence of the occupation armies and integration into the two political blocs. Unlike after the First World War, there was no final peace treaty after 1945 to end the conflict—initially there was no sovereign German state and no representatives who could have signed such a treaty, and later the Cold War dominated all else. East Germany essentially remained an occupied country. Only after the return to a unified German nation state in 1990, and after concluding a peace treaty, did the Soviet army retreat. This marked the formal end of the Second World War, but more fundamentally it signaled the dissolution of the postwar order.

[Translated from German by Christine Brocks.]

NOTES

1. Alfred Döblin, 'Germany is No More: Life among the Ruins,' *Commentary* 2 (Sept 1946), 227–232, here 230.
2. Mark Mazower, *Dark Continent. Europe's Twentieth Century* (London: Allen Lane, 1998), 212.
3. Dan Diner, *Gegenläufige Gedächtnisse. Über Geltung und Wirkung des Holocaust* (Göttingen: Vandenhoeck & Ruprecht, 2007); Reinhart Koselleck, 'Der 8. Mai in der

deutschen Erinnerung,' in Reinhart Koselleck, *Vom Sinn und Unsinn der Geschichte* (Frankfurt am Main: Suhrkamp, 2010), 254–268.

4. Döblin, 'Germany is No More,' 227.

5. Austria was also occupied by the Allies, but was regarded as a 'liberated nation,' the foundation myth of the Second Republic. As in the rest of Europe, Nazism was soon considered a strictly German phenomenon.

6. Mark Edele and Michael Geyer, 'States of Exception. The Nazi-Soviet War as a System of Violence, 1939–1945,' in Michael Geyer and Sheila Fitzpatrick (eds), *Beyond Totalitarianism. Stalinism and Nazism Compared* (Cambridge: Cambridge University Press, 2009), 345–398.

7. Bernd Wegner, 'Hitler, der Zweite Weltkrieg und die Choreographie des Untergangs,' *Geschichte und Gesellschaft* 26 (2000), 493–518.

8. Dagmar Barnouw, *Germany 1945. Views of War and Violence* (Bloomington: Indiana University Press, 1996); Cornelia Brink, *Ikonen der Vernichtung. Öffentlicher Gebrauch von Fotografien aus nationalsozialistischen Konzentrationslagern* (Berlin: Akademie Verlag, 1998).

9. Rüdiger Overmans, *Deutsche militärische Verluste im Zweiten Weltkrieg* (Munich: Oldenbourg, 1999), 318, 321.

10. Martin Conway, 'The Rise and Fall of Western Europe's Democratic Age 1945–1973,' *Contemporary European History* 13 (2004), 67–88, here 75–76; Robert Gildea et al. (eds), *Surviving Hitler and Mussolini: Daily Life in Occupied Europe* (New York: Berg, 2007); Rainer Gries, *Die Rationen-Gesellschaft. Versorgungskampf und Vergleichsmentalität: Leipzig, München und Köln nach dem Kriege* (Münster: Westfälisches Dampfboot, 1991).

11. Neil Gregor, 'A Schicksalsgemeinschaft? Allied Bombing, Civilian Morale, and Social Dissolution in Nuremberg, 1942–45,' *Historical Journal* 42 (2000), 1051–1070, here 1069.

12. Nikolaus Wachsmann, *Hitler's Prisons. Legal Terror in Nazi Germany* (New Haven: Yale University Press, 2004), 384.

13. See also Chapter 25 in this volume.

14. Ulrich Herbert, *Hitler's Foreign Workers. Enforced Foreign Labor in Germany under the Third Reich* (Cambridge: Cambridge University Press, 1997).

15. Anthony D. Kauders, *Democratization and the Jews: Munich, 1945–1965* (Lincoln: University of Nebraska Press, 2004); Atina Grossmann, *Jews, Germans, and Allies: Close Encounters in Occupied Germany* (Princeton: Princeton University Press, 2007).

16. Gregor Thum, *Die fremde Stadt. Breslau 1945* (Munich: Siedler, 2003); Per Brodersen, *Die Stadt im Westen: Wie Königsberg Kaliningrad wurde* (Göttingen: Vandenhoeck & Ruprecht, 2008).

17. The often quoted number of nearly two million dead seems highly inflated. It encompasses all persons that were declared missing in the postwar West German census. This might have included, for example, persons who declared themselves to be Germans in 1939 and Poles after 1945. Rüdiger Overmans, 'Personelle Verluste der deutschen Bevölkerung durch Flucht und Vertreibung,' *Dzieje Najnowsze* 24 (1994), 51–63; more generally Michael Esch, 'Gesunde Verhältnisse.' *Deutsche und polnische Bevölkerungspolitik in Ostmitteleuropa 1939–1950* (Marburg: Herder-Institut Verlag, 1998).

18. Atina Grossmann, 'A Question of Silence. The Rape of German Women by Occupation Soldiers,' *October* 72 (1995), 43–63; Norman Naimark, *The Russians In Germany: The History of The Soviet Zone of Occupation, 1945–1949* (Cambridge: The Belknap Press at Harvard University Press, 1995), chapter 2.

19. Christian Goeschel, 'Suicide at the End of the Third Reich,' *Journal of Contemporary History* 41 (2006), 153–173.

20. Benjamin Frommer, *National Cleansing. Retribution against Nazi Collaborators in Post-war Czechoslovakia* (Cambridge: Cambridge University Press, 2005), 40; Andreas R. Hofmann, *Die Nachkriegszeit in Schlesien. Gesellschafts- und Bevölkerungspolitik in den polnischen Siedlungsgebieten 1945–1948* (Cologne: Böhlau, 2000); David Curp, *A Clean Sweep? The Politics of Ethnic Cleansing in Western Poland 1945–1950* (Rochester: Rochester University Press, 2006).

21. Richard Bessel, *Germany 1945. From War to Peace* (London: Simon & Schuster, 2009).

22. Similarly for Japan: John W. Dower, *Embracing Defeat. Japan in the Wake of World War II* (New York: W.W. Norton & Co., 1999).

23. Leonard O. Mosley, *Report From Germany* (London: Gollancz, 1945), 28. See also Frances Rosenfeld, *The Anglo-German Encounter in Occupied Hamburg, 1945–1950* (PhD dissertation, Columbia University, 2006).

24. Heide Fehrenbach, *Race After Hitler. Black Occupation Children in Postwar Germany and America* (Princeton: Princeton University Press, 2005).

25. Oleg Budnitskii, 'The Intelligentsia Meets the Enemy: Educated Soviet Officers in Defeated Germany, 1945,' *Kritika. Explorations in Russian and Eurasian History* 10 (2009), 629–682; Vladimir Gelfand, *Deutschland Tagebuch 1945–1946. Aufzeichnungen eines Rotarmisten*, ed. Elke Scherstjanoi (Berlin: Aufbau Verlag, 2005).

26. Grossmann, *Jews, Germans, and Allies*, 55.

27. Fabrice Virgili, *Naître ennemi: Les enfants des couples franco-allemands nés pendant la Seconde Guerre mondiale* (Paris: Éditions Payot, 2009).

28. See the memoirs by M.I. Zemiryaga, *Kak my upravlyali Germanii. Politika i zhizn* (Moscow: Rosspėn, 1995), 320.

29. Norbert Frei, 'Nach der Tat. Die Ahndung deutscher Kriegs-und NS-Verbrechen in Europa-eine Bilanz,' in Norbert Frei (ed.), *Transnationale Vergangenheitspolitik. Der Umgang mit deutschen Kriegsverbrechern in Europa nach dem Zweiten Weltkrieg* (Göttingen: Wallstein Verlag, 2006), 30–31; and Devin Pendas, 'Seeking Justice, Finding Law: Nazi Trials in Postwar Europe,' *Journal of Modern History* 81 (2009), 347–368.

30. Jan T. Gross, 'War as Revolution,' in Norman Naimark and Leonid Gibianskii (eds), *The Establishment of Communist Regimes in Eastern Europe, 1944–1949* (Boulder: Westview Press, 1997).

31. Western powers in Nuremberg allowed incriminating evidence against the Soviet Union to be introduced and read in open court, whereas British, French, and US war crimes were kept out of the courtroom. This confirmed Stalin's view that international law first and foremost served international power politics. Francine Hirsch, 'The Soviets at Nuremberg: International Law, Propaganda, and the Making of the Postwar Order,' *American Historical Review*, 113, no. 3 (2008), 701–730.

32. Mark Pittaway, 'Making Peace in the Shadow of War. The Austrian-Hungarian Borderlands 1945–1956,' *Contemporary European History* 17 (2008), 345–364.

33. Richard J. Evans, *Rituals of Retribution. Capital Punishment in Germany 1600–1987* (Oxford: Oxford University Press, 1996), 752.

34. Naimark, *The Russians in Germany*, 470; Jill Lewis, *Workers and Politics in Occupied Austria, 1945–55* (Manchester: Manchester University Press, 2007).

35. Conway, 'The Rise and Fall of Western Europe's Democratic Age,' 88.

36. Lora Wildenthal, 'Rudolf Laun and the Human Rights of Germans in Occupied and Early West Germany,' in Stefan-Ludwig Hoffmann (ed.), *Human Rights in the Twentieth Century* (New York: Cambridge University Press, 2011), 125–144.

37. Jeffrey K. Olick, *In the House of the Hangman. The Agonies of German Defeat 1943–1949* (Chicago: University of Chicago Press, 2005), 237–246.

38. Norman Naimark, 'Stalin and Europe in the Postwar Period, 1945–1953: Issues and Problems,' *Journal of Modern European History* 2 (2008), 28–57; Thomas Lindenberger et al. (eds), *Sterben für Berlin? Die Berliner Krisen 1948 bis 1958* (Berlin: Metropol, 2000); Paul Steege, *Black Market, Cold War. Everyday Life in Berlin 1946–1949* (New York: Cambridge University Press, 2007).

39. Quoted in Riccarda Torriani, 'Des Bédouins particulièrement intelligents? La pensée coloniale et les occupations française et britannique de l'Allemagne (1945–1949),' *Histoire & Sociétés: Révue européenne d'histoire sociale* 17 (2006), 56–66.

40. Peregrine [Isaac Deutscher], 'European Notebook: 'Heil Hitler!' Password for a Flat in Germany,' *The Observer*, 9 December 1945.

41. Tara Zahra, 'Lost Children: Displacement, Family, and the Nation in Postwar Europe,' *Journal of Modern History* 81 (2009), 45–86.

42. Stig Dagerman, *German Autumn* [Swedish 1946]. Translation and introduction by Robin Fulton (London: Quartert Books, 1988), 9–10 and 12–13.

43. André Steiner, *The Plans that Failed. An Economic History of the GDR* (New York: Berghahn Books, 2010).

44. Mazower, *Dark Continent*, 242–243.

45. Amir Weiner, 'Something to Die For, A Lot to Kill For: The Soviet System and the Barbarisation of Warfare,' in George Kassimeris (ed.), *The Barbarisation of Warfare* (London: Hurst & Co., 2006), 101–125.

46. Vasily Grossman, *A Writer at War. Vasily Grossman with the Red Army 1941–1945*, ed. and trans. Antony Beevor and Luba Vinogradova (London: Harvill Press, 2005), 333.

47. Indicative was that the two most vivid reports on Red Army violence both appeared first in English. See Ruth Andreas-Friedrich, *Berlin Underground*, trans. Barrows Mussey, with an introductory note by Joel Sayre (New York: Henry Holt & Co., 1947); and *A Woman in Berlin*, trans. James Stern (New York: Harcourt, 1954, new edn trans. by Philip Boehm (New York: Metropolitan Books/Henry Holt, 2005).

48. Geoff Eley, *Forging Democracy: The History of the Left in Europe, 1850–2000* (Oxford: Oxford University Press, 2002), 302.

49. Charles S. Maier, 'The Two Postwar Eras and the Conditions for Stability in Twentieth Century Europe,' *American Historical Review*, 86 (1981), 327–352, here 341.

50. Carlo Spagnolo, 'Reinterpreting the Marshall Plan. The Impact of the European Recovery Programme in Britain, France, Western Germany, and Italy 1947–1952,' in Dominik Geppert (ed.), *The Postwar Challenge 1945–1958* (Oxford: Oxford University Press, 2003), 288.

51. Tony Judt, *Postwar. A History of Europe since 1945* (New York: Penguin Press, 2005), 63.

52. Friedrich H. Tenbruck, 'Alltagsnormen und Lebensgefühle in der Bundesrepublik,' in Richard Löwenthal and Hans-Peter Schwarz (eds), *Die zweite Republik. 25 Jahre Bundesrepublik-eine Bilanz* (Stuttgart: Seewald, 1974), 293.

53. Dagmar Herzog, *Sex after Fascism. Memory and Morality in Twentieth Century Germany* (Princeton: Princeton University Press, 2005); Svenja Goltermann, *Die Gesellschaft der Überlebenden Deutsche Kriegsheimkehrer und ihre Gewalterfahrungen im Zweiten Weltkrieg* (Munich: DVA, 2009); Daniel Fulda et al. (eds), *Demokratie im Schatten der Gewalt. Geschichten des Privaten im deutschen Nachkrieg* (Göttingen: Wallstein Verlag, 2010).

54. Dolf Sternberger, 'Tagebuch. Reise in Deutschland-Sommer 1945,' *Die Wandlung* 1:1 (1945–1946), 107. On 1950s West German narratives of victimization see, for example, Elizabeth Heineman, 'The Hour of the Woman. Memories of the German's "Crisis Years" and West German National Identity,' *American Historical Review* 101 (1996), 354–395; Robert G. Moeller, *War Stories: The Search for a Usable Past in the Federal Republic of Germany* (Berkeley: University of California Press, 2001); Frank Biess, *Homecoming. Returning POWs and the Legacies of Defeat in Postwar Germany* (Princeton: Princeton University Press, 2009).

55. Victor Klemperer, *The Lesser Evil. The Diaries of Victor Klemperer 1945–1959* (London: Weidenfeld & Nicholson, 2004), 500 (entry for 6 Nov. 1957), quoted in Richard Bessel, 'Hatred after War. Emotion and the Postwar History of East Germany,' *History & Memory* 17, no. 1 (2005), 210–211.

56. Christoph Kleßmann, *Arbeiter im 'Arbeiterstaat' DDR. Deutsche Traditionen, sowjetisches Modell, westdeutsches Magnetfeld* (Stuttgart: Verlag J.H.W. Dietz Nachf., 2007).

57. For an overview, see Vejas Gabriel Liulevicius, *The German Myth of the East. 1800 to the Present* (Oxford: Oxford University Press, 2009).

BIBLIOGRAPHY

BESSEL, RICHARD, *Germany 1945. From War to Peace* (London: Simon & Schuster, 2009).

—— and DIRK SCHUMANN (eds), *Life after Death. Approaches to a Cultural and Social History of Europe during the 1940s and 1950s* (New York: Cambridge University Press, 2003).

BIESS, FRANK and ROBERT G. MOELLER (eds), *Histories of the Aftermath. The Legacies of the Second World War in Europe* (New York: Berghahn Books, 2010).

BOEHLING, REBECCA, *A Question of Priorities. Democratic Reform and Economic Recovery in Postwar Germany* (New York: Berghahn Books, 1996).

BROSZAT, MARTIN et al. (eds), *Von Stalingrad zur Währungsreform. Zur Sozialgeschichte des Umbruchs in Deutschland* (Munich: Oldenbourg, 1987).

ENZENSBERGER, HANS MAGNUS (ed.), *Europa in Ruinen. Augenzeugenberichte aus den Jahren 1944–1948* (Munich: DTV, 1995).

FEHRENBACH, HEIDE, *Race After Hitler. Black Occupation Children in Postwar Germany and America* (Princeton: Princeton University Press, 2005).

FOITZIK, JAN, *Sowjetische Militäradministration in Deutschland (SMAD). Struktur und Funktion* (Munich: Oldenbourg, 1999).

GOEDDE, PETRA, *GIs and Germans. Culture, Gender, and Foreign Relations 1945–1949* (New Haven: Yale University Press, 2002).

GROSSMANN, ATINA, *Jews, Germans, and Allies: Close Encounters in Occupied Germany* (Princeton: Princeton University Press, 2007).

HEINEMAN, ELIZABETH D., *What Difference Does a Husband Make? Women and Marital Status in Nazi and Postwar Germany* (Berkeley: University of California Press, 1999).

HENKE, KLAUS DIETMAR, *Die amerikanische Besetzung Deutschlands* (Munich: Oldenbourg Verlag, 1995).

HERBERT, ULRICH and AXEL SCHILDT (eds), *Kriegsende in Europa. Vom Beginn des deutschen Machtzerfalls bis zur Stabilisierung der Nachkriegsordnung 1944–1948* (Essen: Klartext Verlag, 1998).

JARAUSCH, KONRAD H. and MICHAEL GEYER, *Shattered Past: Reconstructing German Histories* (Princeton: Princeton University Press, 2003).

JUDT, TONY, *Postwar. A History of Europe since 1945* (New York: Penguin Press, 2005).

KARNER, STEFAN and BARBARA STELZL-MARX (eds), *Die Rote Armee in Österreich. Sowjetische Besatzung 1945–1955*, 2 vols (Vienna: Oldenbourg, 2005).

KLESSMANN, CHRISTOPH, *Die doppelte Staatsgründung: Deutsche Geschichte 1945–1955* (Göttingen: Vandenhoeck & Ruprecht, 1991).

MAZOWER, MARK, *Dark Continent: Europe's Twentieth Century* (London: Allen Lane, 1998).

MÜLLER, ROLF-DIETER (ed.), *Der Zusammenbruch des Deutschen Reiches 1945*, 2 vols (Munich: DVA, 2008).

NAIMARK, NORMAN, *The Russians In Germany: A History of the Soviet Zone of Occupation, 1945–1949* (Cambridge: Belknap Press at Harvard University Press, 1995).

NAUMANN, KLAUS (ed.), *Nachkrieg* (Hamburg: Hamburger Edition, 2001).

OLICK, JEFFREY K., *In the House of the Hangman. The Agonies of German Defeat 1943–1949* (Chicago: University of Chicago Press, 2005).

SCHIVELBUSCH, WOLFGANG, *In a Cold Crater. Cultural and Intellectual Life in Berlin 1945–1948* (Berkeley: University of California Press, 1998).

SHEEHAN, JAMES J., *Where Have All the Soldiers Gone? The Transformation of Modern Europe* (Boston: Houghton Mifflin Harcourt, 2008).

WEHLER, HANS-ULRICH, *Deutsche Gesellschaftsgeschichte*, vol. IV: *1914–1949* (Munich: C. H. Beck, 2003).

CHAPTER 27

....

DEMOCRACY AND DICTATORSHIP IN THE COLD WAR: THE TWO GERMANIES, 1949–1961

....

ANDREW I. PORT

THE 'long 1950s' was a decade of conspicuous contrasts: a time of dismantling and reconstruction, both economic and political, as well as cultural and moral; a time of Americanization and Sovietization; a time of upheaval amid a desperate search for stability.[1] But above all, it was a time for both forgetting *and* coming to terms with the recent past. It could be argued, in fact, that no subsequent period witnessed as much *Vergangenheitsbewältigung* as the early years of the two new German states—depending, of course, on how one defines that term. Although a public preoccupation with the Holocaust would not come until almost two decades after the Berlin Wall had been built, almost every aspect of public and private life in the 1950s was, directly or indirectly, a reckoning with the tumultuous events of the two previous decades. The parallels between the two states in this respect, as well as in many others, were as important as the obvious differences.

In terms of the purely political, the long 1950s began with the official founding of the two German states in 1949 and climaxed with the erection of the Wall in August 1961. These were the years that cemented the division of the former Reich, both literally and figuratively. As such, it was a time in which the concept and meaning of the nation state were reappraised, as both halves of Germany inexorably drifted away from each other and became integrated—politically, economically, militarily, socially, and culturally— into two hostile camps, the capitalist West and the communist East. Yet, there was never a complete separation and certainly no 'zero hour'. The continuities were as many, and as important, as the obvious ruptures, making it perhaps more appropriate to speak of a 'fresh start'—for Germany itself, a nation state that no longer existed, and for those Germans who had survived the ravages of the Third Reich and the recent war that its leaders had unleashed.[2]

When did the division of Germany begin? The original sin was surely Adolf Hitler's decision to launch another major war. But what exactly sealed Germany's postwar fate, and when did this occur? Whether the wartime meetings of the Big Three, especially the one held at Yalta in February 1945, the London Conference that convened exactly three years later, or the Berlin Blockade that began in June 1948 as a result of the 'recommendations' made in the British capital to introduce a currency reform and create an independent West German state—the growing tensions between the victorious Allied powers were clearly determinative. And once those frictions had heated up into a Cold War, the task of drafting new constitutions began on both sides of the Elbe.

This first step on the path to statehood—and formal division—was first taken in the West, and the drafters of the document that would become known as the 'Basic Law' (*Grundgesetz*) clearly bore the weight of Weimar on their shoulders. At pains to avoid those shortcomings of the Republic's constitution that had helped pave the way to dictatorship, the authors of the new constitution diminished the role of the president (heretofore an ersatz Kaiser of sorts) and, instead, augmented that of the government, parliament (now known as the *Bundestag*), and political parties. They reduced the power of the central state in favor of a federalist model that gave the new states (*Länder*) extensive competencies (as well as greater representation at the federal level in the newly created Federal Council, or *Bundesrat*), and they eliminated the Weimar constitution's plebiscitary elements. The adoption of a so-called 'constructive vote of no confidence,' which required the members of parliament to form a new working majority before toppling the current government, was an innovative and highly effective measure intended to forestall another rapid succession of governing coalitions—something that had made Weimar so unstable. The adoption of a hybrid voting procedure that helped obviate the pitfalls of proportional representation by combining it with the majority system—coupled with the introduction in 1953 of a rule requiring a party to receive at least 5 percent of the vote (or win direct mandates) in order to enter the parliament—similarly aimed to prevent another of Weimar's failings: the presence of large numbers of extremist splinter parties that not only called into question the very right of the Republic to exist, but also made it exceedingly difficult to forge viable coalitions.[3]

For analogous reasons, the Basic Law gave the Federal Constitutional Court (*Bundesverfassungsgericht*), another institutional novelty for Germany, the authority to declare unconstitutional those political parties that sought 'to undermine or abolish the free democratic basic order or to endanger the existence of the Federal Republic' (Art. 21). The new Court first used its power to declare a party unconstitutional in its 1952 ruling against the *Sozialistische Reichspartei*, a group of unrepentant Nazis whose message and propaganda clearly conformed to that of the National Socialists. This marked the first time in German history that a party had been outlawed for supposedly being unconstitutional; four years later in 1956, the West German Communist Party (KPD) suffered a similar fate. These decisions—especially the one regarding the KPD, the first political party banned by the Nazis in 1933—were not uncontroversial.

Anticipating the objections of those who argued that, in a democracy, only the voters should have the right to consign a party to oblivion, the Social Democratic jurist Carlo Schmid declared at the opening ceremony of the constituent assembly in September 1948 that one must have the courage to be intolerant toward those who wish to use the tools of democracy to destroy it. Like his colleagues, whose average age was fifty-six, Schmid had experienced Weimar, its failure, and the *consequences* of that failure firsthand and desperately wished to avoid a repeat performance.[4]

The same was true of German communist leaders in the East, who—in what would become a long series of playing catch-up—convened their own constituent assembly in late May 1949, just three weeks after the West German one had completed its work and just days after all of the new federal states (except Bavaria) had ratified the Basic Law. The constitution of the German Democratic Republic (GDR), which was founded that October—less than five months after the Federal Republic had come into being—had all the trappings of a democratic document in the tradition of 1848 and the spirit of Weimar. Like the Basic Law, it enshrined the traditional catalogue of basic civil rights and liberties for all of its citizens. In both instances, this was an unmistakable statement about, and rejection of, the atrocities committed by the state against the individual under the Third Reich. But there were not-so-subtle differences as well. The infamous Article 6 of the East German constitution, ostensibly another rebuff to the crimes of the recent past, took with one hand what it gave with the other. In the same breath that it reaffirmed the *Rechtsstaat* by guaranteeing equality before the law, it criminalized a wide range of activities imprecisely described as *Boykotthetze, Mordhetze*, and *Kriegshetze*. State and security officials would subsequently interpret this provision broadly in order to quash whatever behavior was deemed somehow inimical to the socialist state.[5]

Would it be entirely misleading to draw a parallel between Article 6 of the East German constitution and Article 21 of the Basic Law? Although the former would be used against *individuals* and in an incomparably more indiscriminate manner than the latter, they nevertheless shared a number of similarities. Both reflected a keen desire to protect and defend the two newly-created states against (real or imagined) foes from within and without, and were thus products of the Cold War hysteria of the period—be it anti-communist or anti-capitalist. But that was not all: they also bore witness to the trauma of Weimar and the Third Reich. To that extent, and in not entirely dissimilar ways, the two constitutions represented real efforts—at least on paper, and under the watchful eyes of the occupation authorities—to come to terms with the recent past. The mantra of antifascism became the GDR's unofficial hymn, in fact—no surprise, of course, given the biography of the early East German leadership. The communist rank-and-file, as well as those who had suffered under the Nazis, may have sincerely embraced the regime's anti-fascist rhetoric. The extent to which 'ordinary' East Germans did so remains less clear, especially as the methods of the new regime increasingly came to resemble those of the last dictatorship.[6]

The foundational myth was quite different in the West, where the Berlin Blockade and the Korean War helped forge an 'anticommunist consensus' by the early 1950s—one shared by leading politicians, as well as by a populace predisposed to do so by the rhetoric of the Nazis and graphic reports about the brutal behavior of marauding Soviet troops in the East. That antipathy toward 'Bolshevism' helped explain the appeal of the newly-formed Christian Democratic Union (CDU), but only in part. A direct descendant of the Catholic Center Party, the CDU dominated the political stage during the 'long 1950s' and well into the 1960s—as did its counterparts in many other West European states at this time. By emphasizing its Christian *and* anti-Marxist credentials—which clearly distinguished it from the National Socialists, the Communists in the East, as well as the rival Social Democrats (SPD) at home—the CDU was able to expand beyond its precursor's traditional base and become a catch-all 'people's party' of sorts that attracted Protestants along with Catholics from across the social and geographical spectrum. It even managed in 1957 to win—along with its associate party in Bavaria, the Christian Socialist Union (CSU)—an absolute majority in the parliament, another first in German history.[7] The party owed much of its popularity to its economic and foreign policy successes: with some obvious qualifications, this was one of the very few things—along with some questionable personnel appointments—that it had in common with the Nazis.

Those successes, as well as that of the party itself, were inextricably linked to two individuals: Konrad Adenauer, the septuagenarian Rhinelander who led the CDU and became the first chancellor of the Federal Republic on 15 September 1949, and Ludwig Erhard, a little known economist from the Franconian provinces who served as the architect of the social market economy and then presided over the so-called 'economic miracle.' After winning a bitterly fought campaign against the reconstituted SPD under the leadership of Kurt Schumacher, Adenauer went on to head the West German government until 1963, i.e. for a longer period than all of the almost two dozen Weimar cabinets put together. At the time, few would have predicted such longevity—political or otherwise. Almost the same age that Otto von Bismarck had been when the Iron Chancellor left office, Adenauer was not a well-known figure at the end of the war. Born in 1876, he joined the Catholic Center Party after studying law, and then served as Lord Mayor of his hometown, Cologne, until the Nazis forced him out of office in 1933. After spending most of the Third Reich in the proverbial 'inner emigration' (or in jail), Adenauer re-entered politics at the end of the war: he became chairman of the CDU in the British zone of occupation in 1946, and then served as president of the assembly that drafted the Basic Law three years later.[8]

The system of government created by that document has often been described as a *Kanzlerdemokratie* ('chancellor democracy'), a designation that refers, first and foremost, to the considerable powers that the West German constitution bestows upon the office of chancellor. It is he or she who appoints and dismisses cabinet ministers, he or she who alone determines and assumes responsibility for government policy. But it was Adenauer's personal governing style itself that first gave the term its true meaning. Thanks to his great political gifts, mental acuity, pragmatism, and cunning, he completely dominated the West German political stage during his tenure. His calm Rhenish disposition and disarming sense of humor helped disguise the unscrupulous political methods he occasionally used to achieve his goals, while his ability to explain complex issues in relatively simple (and sometimes simplistic) terms made him an avuncular father figure who inspired trust and confidence.[9] During the long 1950s, the patriarchal Adenauer personified the Federal Republic at home and abroad.

Walter Ulbricht, Adenauer's communist counterpart, had a similar political standing in the GDR, where he was the dominant—and domineering—figure. But that was where the similarities ended. Ulbricht was born into a working-class milieu in the central Saxon city of Leipzig in 1893, apprenticed as a cabinetmaker, and became a member of the SPD in 1912. After serving in the First World War, he joined the German Communist Party soon after its founding and rapidly ascended its ranks during the Weimar period. A member of the Reichstag and Central Committee of the KPD, he quickly went into exile after the Nazis came to power and spent the war years in the Soviet Union, returning to Germany in 1945 to help re-establish the KPD. He oversaw the creation, a year later, of the Socialist Unity Party (SED)—a shotgun marriage of sorts between the KPD and its bitter working-class rival, the SPD. As its General Secretary (later First Secretary), Ulbricht effectively became the most powerful political figure in the GDR.[10]

With the backing of Soviet authorities, the SED began introducing key aspects of the USSR's political and economic system in the late 1940s. This included fundamental economic reforms such as centralized planning, land redistribution, and the nationalization of major industries; the build-up of repressive paramilitary and state security organs; the removal of potentially disruptive individuals from positions of public influence and their replacement with reliable cadres; the taming and subordination of other political parties and the so-called 'mass organizations' (including the unions and youth groups) through terror, personnel purges, and political justice. The SED also transformed itself into a so-called 'party of a new type' at this time, which meant that it not only slavishly adopted the program and organizational model of the Soviet Communist Party, but also purged its own ranks of thousands of supposedly unreliable members, above all former Social Democrats. In 1950, it formally adopted the model of 'democratic centralism,' which tightened the party hierarchy—on top of which sat the Politburo, the locus of real power in the GDR—by enforcing strict discipline on the part of the rank and file, and by obliging lower-level party organs to adhere strictly to all orders issued by superior bodies.[11]

For all intents and purposes, the SED was able to establish a one-party dictatorship by the early 1950s. But that did not mean that its power—or the position of its leader Walter Ulbricht—went uncontested. Unlike Adenauer and the CDU, the feisty Saxon and the party he was instrumental in creating did not enjoy great popular support. This became most clear on 17 June 1953, when hundreds of thousands of East Germans took to the streets to protest in force against the ruling party and its leaders. Initiated by angry construction workers in Berlin three months after Stalin's death, the first state-wide insurrection in the Soviet bloc was set off by a series of highly unpopular policies adopted over the past year in a rash attempt to 'construct socialism.' These measures, which were not unlike similar ones introduced in the other 'people's democracies' at the time, included a palpable increase in state repression, the beginning of agricultural collectivization, and, most fatefully, an across-the-board hike in production quotas for workers.[12]

Acting on orders from Moscow, East German authorities announced in early June that they would rescind all of the unpopular measures *except* for the one specifically affecting workers—and it was that omission that ignited the revolt. Though primarily concentrated in the urban industrial areas of the south, the protest involved disgruntled East Germans from almost all regions and social groups, and could only be quelled with the forceful assistance of Soviet occupation troops—testimony to the embryonic state of the East German security apparatus at that time, even though the infamous Ministry for State Security, or Stasi, had doubled in size over the course of 1952 alone. With now over 10,000 officials, it was even larger than an earlier security organization that had more successfully maintained control of a more sizeable population, namely the Gestapo.

That was only one of several ironies associated with the events of June 1953—and one that suggested, incidentally, that terror and repression were not in themselves sufficient to hold the East German population in check. Another irony was the fact that the upheaval had helped salvage Ulbricht's increasingly precarious position as head of the SED. The escalating number of East Germans who fled to the Federal Republic because of the unpopular reforms he introduced, along with the economic chaos caused by those measures, had seriously eroded his standing in Moscow and led to growing criticism within the party's uppermost echelons of his imperious style of leadership. But because his removal after the uprising might have been perceived as a sign of political weakness, he managed to stay on and even topple his main critics in the Politburo.

Ulbricht's position was challenged once again later that decade as a result of the de-Stalinization campaign launched by Soviet Premier Nikita Khrushchev in early 1956. This brief political thaw sparked a vigorous debate in the GDR about the necessity of internal reforms that would help make East Germany a more viable state. While prominent members of the so-called intelligentsia called for greater economic decentralization, more open discussion, and increased democracy within the SED, several members of the Politburo itself voiced criticism behind closed doors of the party's rigid dogmatism, cult of personality, and lack of a truly collective leadership. Once again, it was popular upheaval that saved the day for Ulbricht, for the disturbances that took place in Poland and especially Hungary in late 1956 cut short the de-Stalinization process. In the GDR itself, officials cracked down on those so-called 'revisionists' who had recently clamored for reform. Many of them were imprisoned, while Ulbricht's most critical colleagues on the Politburo were accused of 'factionalism' and unceremoniously removed from power. That marked the effective end of the movement for a more 'democratic socialism,' as well as a missed opportunity for possibly salutary renewal in the GDR.[13]

It should be emphasized that the alleged 'factionists' in the Politburo, as well as intellectual 'revisionists' such as the philosopher Wolfgang Harich, remained committed socialists to the core—members of the loyal opposition, in effect. Socialists on the other side of the Elbe who endeavored to reform *their* party enjoyed more success at the time, and the vastly different result of their efforts spoke volumes about the vastly dissimilar nature of the two rival political systems. After losing to the CDU in the 1949 election, the SPD settled into the role of the Federal Republic's main opposition party. That loss was tied in no small measure to the personal qualities of its leader, Kurt Schumacher, whose abrasive behavior—which included bitter and sometimes even coarse verbal attacks against political opponents, as well as against the Catholic Church—alienated many voters. So, too, did his very physical appearance. An invalid since the First World War, Schumacher had spent much of the Third Reich in concentration camps; as a result, the pain of that period was inscribed in his body and face, a visible and uncomfortable reminder of the recent barbarization.[14] But it was above all the SPD's program that the majority of the electorate rejected in 1949—and then again in 1953 and 1957. It was not until the CDU/CSU had won an absolute majority in that last federal election (running on the reassuring slogan 'No experiments!') that the SPD finally began to reconsider in earnest its stubborn rejection of the two most successful and popular policy pillars of the Adenauer government: the social market economy and the Federal Republic's integration into the Western camp.

That wake-up call in 1957 ultimately led to the fundamental programmatic reform adopted two years later at an SPD party congress held just outside Bonn, West Germany's provincial capital in the Rhineland. The famous Godesberg Program was an important turning point on a number of levels. Most fundamentally, it marked the SPD's formal break with its Marxist past, now in theory as much as in practice. That meant, more concretely, that the party now rejected state economic planning, pacifism, and anti-confessional *Kulturkampf* in favor of marketplace competition, Western integration (military, as well as political and economic), and co-operation with both churches—all in an attempt to expand beyond its traditional working class constituency and become a party of the entire people.[15]

In extremely different ways, then, the Social Democrats had been more or less sidelined in both the GDR and the Federal Republic during the long 1950s, though those in the West would enjoy a much different fate the following decade. There were other parallels as well, however superficial, between the party landscapes of the two postwar German states. In the first place, both were clearly dominated by a single party, the CDU in the West, the SED in the East. The former had managed to achieve that position by the force of its program and policies, the latter by force alone. At the time of the 1949 election, there were more than a dozen political parties in the Federal Republic. The splinter parties had more or less vanished by the end of the decade as a result of the 'five-percent clause,' Article 21 of the Basic Law, and, most important, the successful way in which the CDU's popular policies had gradually weaned voters away from those parties with more specialized constituencies, such as the Federation of Expellees (BHE), which represented the interests of refugees from the East. The Free Democratic Party (FDP) was the only middle-class party to escape that fate. It was not so much its advocacy of traditional liberal values, such as the rule of law and the sanctity of private property, that distinguished it from the CDU, but rather its unreserved belief in the gospel of the free market and its anticlericalism. Its consistent ability to surpass the five-percent hurdle not only assured its continual presence in the parliament, but also bestowed upon it the role of kingmaker: except in 1957, its support would remain essential for the formation of a working parliamentary majority.[16]

The same could not be said, of course, for any of the so-called 'block parties' in the GDR. A number of Christian Democrats and members of the Liberal Party (LPD, later LDPD) in the East offered some early resistance to the SED's gradual imposition of one-party rule. But by the early 1950s, these middle class parties had been rendered more or less impotent through the co-optation, flight, or arrest of their more renitent members and leaders. The two other East German parties had offered almost no challenge to the SED since their founding, on Soviet initiative, in 1948: the Democratic Farmers Party (DBD), which ostensibly represented the interests of those who worked the land, and the National Democrats (NDPD), a puppet organization founded with an eye to winning the support of nominal ex-Nazis and conservative craftsmen for the new regime. Organized together in a so-called 'National Front,' the parties were elected by single lists according to a predetermined formula that guaranteed the predominance of the SED.[17] The point is that by the end of the 1950s, and for strikingly different reasons, smaller parties had become politically insignificant in both states—a development that, in greatly different ways, contributed to the very *stability* of those states.

The economic performance of the Federal Republic and the GDR arguably played an even more important role in determining their long-term viability. Both faced similar challenges at the outset: wartime destruction, a ruined infrastructure, severe shortages of housing and basic consumer goods, hunger, unemployment, and poverty, all made worse by the need to care for and integrate millions of returning soldiers, evacuees, and uprooted refugees from the East.[18] Yet, many of those early challenges proved beneficial in the long term: refugees helped replenish the ranks of a labor force decimated by total warfare, for example. More modern factories and machinery eventually came to replace the old and often obsolete ones destroyed during the war—although sooner in the West than in the East.

The Federal Republic enjoyed a more advantageous starting point, of course, having escaped the type of plundering visited by the Soviets upon the Eastern zone. But that alone did not explain the so-called *Wirtschaftswunder*, i.e. the unprecedented economic growth and prosperity that followed reconstruction in the 1950s. Full employment, stable prices, rising real wages and salaries, new export records—the figures spoke for themselves, especially in the industrial sector. This was not really an 'economic miracle,' however, for miracles cannot be explained and the *Wirtschaftswunder* certainly could. After Marshall Plan aid and the currency reform of 1948 had provided a jumpstart, the Korean War, an undervalued currency, and a new global system dedicated to free trade all led to a subsequent boom in exports. Just as essential were pent-up consumer desires at home following the 'hunger years' of the 1940s, the willingness of an extremely well-trained labor force to advance moderate demands for the time being in return for promises of future abundance, as well as German production quality and traditions—combined with the new and reinvigorating influence of American managerial and marketing methods.[19]

The economic upswing was not just limited to the Federal Republic, but it did seem to confirm, after some initial economic turbulence following the founding of the new state, the merits of the 'social market economy' advocated so forcefully by Adenauer's Minister of Economics, Ludwig Erhard.[20] Though not its intellectual father, he was certainly the most energetic prophet of this seemingly paradoxical term, which referred to an economic system that allowed for the relatively unbridled play of market forces, free trade, and competition, while at the same time protecting individuals against excessive exploitation and ensuring them economic and social security. It was a system, in other words, that promoted economic freedom and the pursuit of profit while guaranteeing social justice and responsibility. It was one in which the state played an active role in promoting both sets of goals.

Building on established German traditions—and promising 'Wohlstand für alle' (affluence for all), as the title of a bestseller by Erhard put it—the Federal Republic adopted a wide array of programs aimed at providing its citizens with more than just a modicum of social protection. The original focus was on those *Germans* who had suffered most directly because of the war: refugees and other so-called 'war victims,' such as the widows and children of fallen soldiers or those who had lost their homes.[21] The most important measure in this respect was the 1952 *Lastenausgleichgesetz* ('Equal-ization of Burdens Law'), which oversaw the largest transfer of funds in German history before unification in an attempt to compensate those individuals who had suffered materially because of the war by those who had remained relatively unscathed. Other significant social welfare measures included massive investment in new housing pro-jects, which led to the construction of more than five million apartments in the 1950s alone; the disbursement of *Kindergeld* ('child support money'), a practice first begun during the Third Reich; and, most controversially, the passing in 1957 of a novel reform that tied pension levels to increases in the earnings of those still active in the workforce.[22]

It was the very success of the West German economy that allowed for such largesse, of course. The situation was much different in the GDR, even if the aspirations on this score were just as, if not more, ambitious. The regime's vaunted social welfare benefits included subsidized foodstuffs, low-cost housing, cheap transportation, free childcare, as well as a variety of public and workplace facilities designed to lighten the load of working men and women. But the lackluster performance of the command economy, which slavishly followed the Soviet example, made it extremely difficult for the regime to satisfy demand and thus make good on its promises. As a result, severe shortages of even the most basic foodstuffs, consumer durables, housing, and kindergarten spots were not only common, but also frustratingly recurrent throughout the 1950s and well beyond. Prices were also high that decade—especially in special state-run stores where rationed goods could be acquired at an elevated cost—and pensions woefully inad-equate. Access to items that were in short supply usually involved long waits on line, or reliance on personal connections through informal social networks of mutual assist-ance that often involved barter.[23]

What accounted for the poor showing of the East German economy? Was it the unpropitious starting point of the late 1940s or poor decision-making by East German authorities later on? In other words, was the economy doomed from the outset because of wartime destruction, Soviet dismantling, the overzealous nationalization of key industries, and the adverse effects of national division? Or did it ultimately fail instead because of bureaucratic ineptitude, rigid centralized planning, the absence of self-correcting market mechanisms, the gradual elimination of private business and manufacturing, and, last but not least, the loss of the more than three million persons who fled to the Federal Republic for personal, political, or economic reasons from 1950 to 1961 alone?[24] All of these factors obviously played some role. Economic planning—which was also embraced by the pre-Godesberg SPD in the West, and which had so successfully, though at great human cost, turned the Soviet Union into a major industrial power in the 1930s—proved to be highly inefficient: as a result, the series of multi-year economic 'plans' hammered out by ministerial officials on high uniform-ly failed to achieve their goals and satisfy consumer demand. The most famous example of this was the dismal disappointment of the infamous Seven-Year Plan of 1959, which vowed with considerable hubris that *per capita* consumption in the GDR would surpass that of the Federal Republic by 1961. Instead, quality remained poor and productivity low, with the latter persistently being outstripped by increases in wages.

The SED failed to solve, in short, a major dilemma of its own making: how to boost economic efficiency without relinquishing central control of the economy. This, along with the single-minded, Stalinist emphasis on heavy industry and raw quantity as the measure of all things, were among the main reasons for the failure to satisfy consumer demand, and also among the most important factors behind the June 1953 uprising. The so-called 'New Course,' tardily introduced by the SED earlier that month as a correct-ive, did not lead to long-term fundamental changes. Nor did the modernization campaign unveiled in the second half of the 1950s: provisioning improved to some extent, but the 'scientific-technological revolution' proclaimed with great fanfare at this time would not bear any real fruit until the following decade (and even then, the results were modest).[25] To some extent, that was true in the Federal Republic as well, for the iconic images of overflowing shop windows immediately following the currency reform of 1948 misleadingly suggested a sudden affluence that did not really materialize until the late 1950s and especially the 1960s.[26]

The Federal Republic's founding decade nevertheless witnessed an unmistakable rise in the living standard of most West Germans, as real wages increased, on average, more than 5 percent annually. This allowed for greater and more demonstrative consump-tion practices that helped put behind the deprivations of the 1940s. The so-called *Freßwelle* ('eating frenzy') of the early 1950s was followed by the *Reisewelle*, or 'traveling craze'—especially to warmer climes abroad: originally an interwar phenomenon, the latter was facilitated by the spread of mass tourism, as well as a fourfold increase in car ownership that decade. The five millionth Volkswagen Beetle—perhaps *the* symbol of the 'economic miracle'—rolled off the assembly line, in fact, just months after the mortar holding the Berlin Wall together had hardened.

A more intense pursuit of leisure activities was another hallmark of this new 'consumer society,' which was marked by an increasing homogenization of leisure and purchasing habits—and made possible, as elsewhere in the West, by higher disposable incomes, the gradual introduction of a shorter five-day working week, as well as the advent of time-saving appliances in the household. Although radio and cinema remained popular, television was well on its way to becoming the preferred pastime of many West Germans by the late 1950s. It was all of these media that helped contribute to the growing 'Westernization' of West German society in terms of tastes, lifestyles, outlooks, and sensibilities. But what did that mean exactly and how far-reaching was it? Most obvious, in this respect, was the influence of Hollywood, jazz, and rock-and-roll music, especially on youths. Older Germans, for their part, remained partial to the domestic (in more than one sense) *Heimatfilme* and sentimental *Schlager* popular at this time, which reflected the persistence of established tastes and style. More to the point, even the so-called 'Americanization' of the Federal Republic was mediated by and filtered through traditional German practices and conventions. If the latter was more than just slavish emulation, it was also more than just limited to the cultural realm. Besides the changes in business practices mentioned earlier, politics itself also became more 'Anglo-American' in form and substance: from campaigning style to the very institutions of a federal democracy dominated by political parties. A number of factors contributed to this: the media, the return of those emigrants who had spent the Third Reich in Western exile, the policies and very presence of the occupation forces, and, more generally, the political, economic, and military integration into the Western alliance—by far one of Adenauer's most significant accomplishments.[27]

The reaction to this 'Americanization' was ambivalent, just as it had been since the inter-war period: admiration and enthusiasm on the one hand, wariness, condescension, and even resentment on the other. The fervor for jazz, for example, provoked the same type of racist criticism common before the war—on both sides of the iron curtain. As the cultural expression of downtrodden 'negroes,' blues music eventually enjoyed the imprimatur of East German ideologues, but all things American, from jeans to rock-and-roll, remained highly suspicious to authorities in the GDR as subversive imperialist exports. They were, nevertheless, embraced by many young people, as in the West.[28] The counterpart to creeping Americanization in the Federal Republic was formal Sovietization in the East in the political, economic, and cultural realms. But there was a major difference: the majority of the population there never became convinced by the catchy slogan 'To learn from the Soviet Union means to learn victory'—just as those in the East who compared Ulbricht to Stalin clearly meant something quite different from those in the West who referred to Willy Brandt, the charismatic mayor of West Berlin and a rising star in the SPD, as the German version of John F. Kennedy. Whatever the feelings of ambivalence toward the United States, most West Germans responded positively, even enthusiastically, to Westernization, especially given the alternative. For their part, the majority of ordinary East Germans remained hostile to, or at the very least highly skeptical of, Sovietization in its various manifestations.[29]

Even if one of the keys to Adenauer's popularity was the successful integration of the Federal Republic into the Western camp, tensions remained pronounced there between a lingering wish for national unity and a strong desire to re-enter the comity of democratic nations as an equal and sovereign member. This issue was *the* Gordian knot of the 1950s. Adenauer's priority was clearly the latter, even if his desire for reunification was more than mere lip service, as his critics charged (above all those in the SPD, an ostensibly internationalist party that remained vociferously committed, until 1960, to national unification *before* Western integration). It was true that the chancellor, by most accounts, felt great personal antipathy toward Prussia and, hence, the East—no surprise, given his Rhenish biography. But that did not mean that he was opposed in principle to unification on terms favorable to the Federal Republic, or that he purposefully sabotaged *genuine* chances to bring it about.[30]

The best known (if not necessarily genuine) 'missed opportunity' was the series of so-called Stalin notes of 1952, in which the Soviet dictator offered the prospect of German unity in return for strict neutrality. There was nothing truly novel about the proposals presented to the Western powers, who, along with the Bonn government, dismissed them as an insincere and cynical maneuver intended to forestall the planned rearmament and military integration of the Federal Republic in the Western alliance— which is surely what they were. Moscow had long been calling for a single German state, in fact, and a steady stream of appeals for unity had flowed from the Soviet zone and later the GDR—beginning with the so-called 'People's Congress' movement of the late 1940s, and most energetically in response to moves that threatened to tie the Federal Republic even closer to the West.[31] In point of fact, the SED leadership was extremely chary of unity, even as it swore an unwavering commitment to achieving it. This was something else that it had in common with the CDU, but the primary reason for its wariness was quite clearly different, namely the justifiable fear that unification would lead to a loss of communist power.[32]

Whatever the actual commitment to unity on the part of their leaders, both states, as products and expressions of the growing conflict between the two superpowers, moved further and further away from each other. Their inexorable integration into the two rival Cold War blocs was a process that went hand-in-hand with the gradual recovery of sovereignty over the course of the long 1950s. Even if the latter was more formal than real in the case of the GDR, the international constellation limited the room for maneuver of both states, both domestically, as well as in terms of their foreign policy.[33] That had been especially true for the Federal Republic under the terms of the Occupation Statute of September 1949, which reserved a number of essential prerogatives to the Western powers, from questions of security to control of the Ruhr industrial region.

A series of international agreements in 1955 abrogated the statute and thus marked the formal acquisition of sovereignty, yet West Germany had already been well on its way to becoming more of a subject than a mere object in the international arena. The first major steps in this direction, as well as on the path to West European integration, were its memberships, since 1949 and 1952 respectively, in the Organization for European Economic Co-operation (OEEC), which oversaw the distribution of Marshall Plan aid, and then in the European Coal and Steel Community (ECSC), which placed the production of these two essential commodities under the control of an international authority. This supranational institution was significant because it gave the Federal Republic a more equal standing vis-à-vis the other major West European states, whose economic sovereignty was now similarly restricted. The signing of the Treaty of Rome five years later, which created the European Economic Community (EEC), marked the crowning moment of West Germany's incorporation into the Western alliance as an (almost) equal partner.

The GDR continued to play a game of catch-up that decade—without ever catching up in the areas that truly mattered: popular support, political legitimacy, and economic success. It joined the COMECON, the East European trading bloc, in September 1950, less than a year after the Federal Republic had joined the OEEC, and it became a founding member of the Warsaw Pact less than two weeks after West Germany had gained sovereignty and joined the North Atlantic Treaty Organization (NATO) in early May 1955. The GDR was granted formal sovereignty itself just a few months later in September. Its leaders nevertheless remained completely subservient to Moscow, even if they habitually worried that the Kremlin might abandon them by striking some sort of disadvantageous deal with the West—a concern shared, incidentally, by Adenauer and other wary politicians in Bonn with respect to Washington, London, and Paris.[34]

Krushchev allayed such fears in the East when he proclaimed in the spring of 1955 that unification was an issue to be determined by the Germans themselves—only to create new concerns the following year with his de-Stalinization campaign, which disquieted East German leaders because of its potentially destabilizing effects. The unrest in Poland and Hungary confirmed such fears, but the Soviet Union did not seriously plan on abandoning the GDR, not least because its economy had already become the most productive in Eastern Europe—*despite* the many disadvantages of membership in the COMECON, where economic benefits (unlike those of the EEC) accrued primarily to a single state, the USSR.

Moscow's steadfast commitment to its German ally became even more pronounced with the beginning of a new crisis in the winter of 1958: increasingly alarmed about the sustained exodus of East Germans via West Berlin, the Soviet premier threatened that November to alter unilaterally the postwar status of the former German capital. East Germans—faced with the very real possibility that the most popular exit route to the West was about to be cut off, as well as with a new collectivization campaign in the countryside—now swarmed to the Federal Republic in unprecedented numbers. High-level officials responded to this massive flight by adopting an extraordinary measure that grabbed international headlines in August 1961: the construction of a twelve foot high, ninety-six mile long concrete and barbed wire barrier that hermetically sealed off West Berlin from the GDR. The Wall effectively stanched the heavy flow of migrants to the West—almost 50,000 during the first two weeks of August 1961 alone—and put the final touch, literally and figuratively, on the division of Germany.[35] It also put to rest, of course, any lingering doubts about East Germany's unequivocal integration into the Eastern bloc, a process that had begun in the late 1940s when its political, institutional, and economic structures first began to closely resemble those of the other 'people's democracies.'

The Cold War was without doubt the main reason for the rapid rehabilitation and integration of the two German states, which more or less took place within a decade following the end of the Second World War.[36] It was also why their new partners (some to a greater extent than others) were willing to countenance their rearmament—especially following communist aggression on the divided Korean peninsula, in the case of the Federal Republic. After the failure to create a so-called European Defense Community—a French initiative aborted in the end by the French themselves, who understandably felt threatened by the prospect of any German rearmament—West Germany was permitted to join NATO in 1955. The Federal Republic formally pledged not to produce atomic, biological, or chemical weapons, but the creation of a West German military and the stationing of atomic weapons on German soil still unleashed a torrent of domestic protest by a broad coalition that included the churches, the SPD, the unions, as well as youths and a number of leading scientists and intellectuals.[37] The protest movement may have failed to achieve its goals (despite the coining of a number of catchy slogans such as 'Ohne mich' [without me] and 'Kampf dem Atomtod' [fight atomic death], but it was nevertheless a foretaste of what would come in the late 1960s. Just as importantly, it attested to an evolution in the German mentality after, and largely as a result of, the Second World War: the experiences of the last major conflagration, along with the strong likelihood that the next military conflict would be fought against their own people on the other side of the Elbe, had apparently helped exorcise lingering militarist demons.

The same was true of many ordinary East Germans as well, especially those men who steadfastly refused to join the various paramilitary organizations created in the 1950s, such as the so-called Barracks Police or the factory 'combat units' (*Kampfgruppen*) that were set up to defend the new state against all enemies. Anger about the diversion of essential resources toward the military was, in fact, one of the main grievances voiced during the June 1953 upheaval. The young were particularly resistant to the massive enlistment campaigns launched that decade, especially following the creation of the National People's Army in 1956, and the pacifist sentiments that many expressed were not unlike those voiced by their counterparts in the Federal Republic.[38] This draws attention to an important parallel in both states, where youths tended to be especially critical of official policy. In fact, so-called *Halbstarke* ('hooligans'), as well as disillusioned, dispassionate, and largely conformist youths—unideological and individualistic members of the 'skeptical generation' identified that decade by the West German sociologist Helmut Schelsky—lived on both sides of the Elbe (as well as outside of the two Germanys).[39] But that was where the similarities ended: there would be no equivalent in the GDR to the youth rebellion that rocked the Federal Republic in the late 1960s—even if many state security officials in that decade nevertheless seemed to believe that their own 'beatnik' and 'rowdy' youths posed one of the greatest domestic threats to regime stability. The failure of that generation to erupt in the East as it did in the West spoke volumes about the differences between the two systems, above all with respect to the possibilities for expressing discontent publicly—and thus, indirectly, with respect to the repressive nature of the GDR.[40]

As this example suggests, the trajectories taken by the two postwar German societies exhibited important differences as well as similarities, although the former were usually more apparent than the latter. Whereas the old economic and educated middle-class elites lost their power and position in the GDR—to cite the most obvious example—those in the Federal Republic were largely able to weather the half-hearted de-Nazification efforts of the late 1940s.[41] Another case in point was the position of women: the East German constitution, and a flurry of other official decrees proclaimed early on the principles of equal rights and equal pay for women. They were strongly encouraged to enter the labor force for ideological reasons, as well as for practical economic considerations tied to severe manpower shortages and the challenges of reconstruction. Women nevertheless faced a good deal of everyday discrimination in the GDR in terms of pay, possibilities for promotion, and sexist hazing by male colleagues. The situation was much different for women living in the Federal Republic—but not because of more sexually progressive policies or mores. Rather, traditional gender roles quickly re-emerged in the West, where women were forced out of the workforce at the end of the war—to make room for returning soldiers and 'de-Nazified' civil servants—and back into the role of homemaker. Some conservatives even praised this cult of domesticity as an example of the Federal Republic's superiority to the GDR, where women were supposedly forced to work against their will. In any event, women on both sides of the Elbe continued to confront the same types of sexist treatment common before 1945—an important sign of historical continuity, as well as another parallel between the two postwar societies.[42]

That said, the general characters of those two societies were utterly dissimilar, at least on the surface: on the one hand, a proletarian order in which the working classes supposedly set the tone and were given pride of place; on the other, a consumer-oriented, 'leisure' society dominated by the middle classes. While 'class warfare' was the order of the day in the GDR—especially during the first half of the 'long 1950s', when members of the middle classes were targets of official persecution—class-based antagonism seemed to be dissipating in the Federal Republic, which Schelsky memorably referred to as a 'nivillierte Mittelstandsgesellschaft' ('leveled middle class society'). What he meant by this was that West German society was becoming more equal, more homogeneous, and more 'middle class' thanks to a variety of developments: the social and political disenfranchisement of the nobility, the loss of wealth suffered by many members of the propertied middle classes in the 1930s and 1940s, the massive expansion of the white-collar sector, and the improved position of the working classes. Many workers came to enjoy a significant rise in their standard of living as a result of higher wages, full employment, heightened social security, and greater social mobility. As a whole, West Germans may have been becoming more and more alike, especially in terms of their living standards, leisure activities, and other daily pursuits, yet—as Schelsky's critics pointed out—continuing disparities in the distribution of wealth and the absence of members of the lower classes in leadership positions clearly relativized such claims.[43]

The situation was much different in the GDR, where the regime courted the manual working classes, in whose name its leaders claimed to rule, by giving them preferential treatment with respect to educational opportunities and professional advancement. The newly created Worker-and-Farmer Faculties did make it possible for members of previously underprivileged classes to gain access to higher-level education, for example. But in the end, 'sociopolitical' engagement, politically acceptable behavior, and loyalty to the party undoubtedly counted more than one's social pedigree when it came to getting ahead. More to the point, official propaganda about the replacement of capitalism with new forms of socialist ownership was, in many respects, just that: propaganda. The means of production might have now belonged to the 'people' after the mass expropriation of private property in the late 1940s, and many 'ordinary' workers did advance to positions of influence in many factories. But it was still clear who gave and who followed orders, and who made and who carried out important policy decisions. Traditional hierarchies more or less survived the war, and the shop floor did not experience any absolute zero hour in 1945—notwithstanding the introduction of supposedly superior Soviet production methods and other schemes aimed at raising productivity, such as the brigade movement and organized industrial competition.

To give workers the impression that they had an important say in the running of their factory, East German authorities held regularly-scheduled production meetings and even introduced so-called *Betriebskollektivverträge* in the spring of 1951: workers and management made a variety of mutual pledges regarding production levels, as well as working conditions and social benefits in these 'collective factory labor contracts'— which were, in essence, the GDR's answer to West German *Mitbestimmung* ('factory co-determination'). The latter was first introduced that spring in the coal and steel industry, and gave workers more control of their factories by allowing them to delegate representatives to the highest levels of management. Along with the relatively moderate demands of the unions in the 1950s, this helped significantly reduce class antagonism in the Federal Republic that decade. In the GDR, for its part, workers were often handled with kid gloves by functionaries concerned about maintaining domestic peace and satisfying the almighty Plan—especially following the 'learning shock' of June 1953. That was why factory functionaries often kept production quotas artificially low and why, in turn, increases in wages regularly outpaced those in productivity.

But East German workers did not necessarily feel as if they were especially well treated. In fact, most continued to complain bitterly about the same types of issues that had perennially soured industrial relations in Germany and elsewhere: insufficient earnings, poor working conditions, and long hours. The many material benefits given to members of the so-called *Intelligentsia* (i.e., highly trained specialists and other professionals who performed non-manual tasks) were a major source of anger and resentment as well, especially given the regime's egalitarian rhetoric and its official ideology about the privileged position of the proletariat. The irony of all this is that the position of workers in the capitalist West was, in many respects, superior to that of their brethren in the Workers-and-Farmers state across the Elbe.[44]

What about the lot of those in the primary sector? Like elsewhere across the globe after 1945, the relative importance of farming in the East and West German economies declined significantly—as did the percentage of the population that toiled the land. The desire for higher earnings in the industrial sector, as well as the yearning for more 'modern' amenities and lifestyles, spurred a massive flight from the land to urban centers on both sides of the Elbe, especially on the part of many youths. This was a global phenomenon, of course, yet some East German officials characteristically placed the blame on supposedly hostile forces intent on undermining the economy. While it is doubtful that 'class enemies' were unwittingly serving as the agents of modernity, there was clearly one major difference between the similar demographic shifts taking place in both postwar German states: it was only in the GDR that discontent about forced agricultural collectivization was driving many young people away from the land and toward the towns and cities—not only because of the poor performance of the new collective farms, but also because of the loss of independence that collectivization entailed.

The abiding desire for independence on the part of many East German farmers reflected the persistence of traditional mentalities in the countryside and thus the clear limits of 're-education.'[45] The latter held true for both the Soviet *and* Anglo-American varieties, for old norms, behavioral practices, and ways of thinking did not simply disappear overnight. There was no mental 'zero hour,' and earlier forms of socialization reaching back to the imperial period endured in both postwar states, which faced the formidable task of eradicating years of Nazi indoctrination while integrating millions of 'true believers.' Wariness of democracy and parliamentarian institutions, a relic of Wilhelm and Weimar, proved easier to overcome in the West than anti-Bolshevik sentiment did in the East—and vice versa. That was not necessarily the case for East German leaders and the committed rank-and-file.[46] Yet, the extent to which the ten new Socialist Commandments (*Gebote*) proclaimed by Ulbricht in 1958 reshaped mentalities and created a new 'socialist consciousness' remained unclear. The same was true of the new type of worker collective also introduced at this time: the so-called *Brigaden der sozialistischen Arbeit*, whose members pledged to 'work, learn, and live' in a socialist manner. Formal interviews conducted that decade with refugees from the GDR nevertheless suggested that communist ideology was leaving a mark and trans-forming social values, from a heightened sense of social responsibility, for instance, to a greater acceptance of communal forms of property.[47]

In the Federal Republic, for its part, popular enthusiasm for the West, increasing faith in democratic institutions, as well as the vocal opposition to remilitarization discussed earlier, suggested an important change in mentality. So, too, did the strong reaction elicited by the 1962 '*Spiegel* Affair': in response to a critical article by the Hamburg weekly about the supposedly inadequate military preparedness of the West German army, Minister of Defense Franz Josef Strauss ordered the search and seizure of the magazine's offices, the confiscation of thousands of documents, as well as the arrest of several editors and journalists, including Editor-in-Chief Rudolf Augstein. Some may have interpreted the strong-arm tactics used by the West German govern-ment against the *Spiegel's* allegedly 'treasonous' act as a dangerous sign of backsliding, but the large-scale public protests that erupted in defense of press freedom attested to just how far many Germans had left the Nazi past behind them—and were yet another prelude to the greater liberalization that would take place later that decade.[48]

The desire to leave that past behind (in a much different sense, of course) was a comprehensible one, even if it eventually prompted many young West Germans to accuse their elders of trying to sweep the Nazi era under the proverbial rug. Such recriminations, which had already surfaced in the Federal Republic during the 1950s, were not entirely accurate. It was true, on the one hand, that many former Nazis had quickly returned to their prior positions and were thus able to 'reintegrate' rapidly into society after an uneven and rather lackadaisical de-Nazification effort. This included 'active' ones whose behavior during the Third Reich was not, to put it mildly, beyond reproach.[49] The most notorious example of this was the appointment of Hans Globke as a secretary of state under Konrad Adenauer, who considered him to be one of his closest confidants and advisors. In the mid-1930s, Globke had co-authored the legal commentary on the infamous Nuremberg Race Laws.

As a rule, the Nazi period and the Holocaust itself were passed over in silence in classrooms and textbooks. The Adenauer government agreed to pay Israel compensation in the early 1950s to 'make up' for the mass murder of the European Jews, but only over the vocal opposition of the chancellor's own party and the majority of the West German population, which continued to believe that Nazism was a 'good idea' in principle, but one that had been carried out poorly. There was little sense of personal responsibility for what had occurred, but rather a focus on German 'victimization,' i.e. on what the Germans had suffered themselves as a result of the Third Reich and the war—something that Hannah Arendt acerbically commented on during her first visit to Germany shortly after 1945. The German Jewish émigé was later equally dismissive of those young Germans who felt expiatory guilt for crimes they themselves had not committed, but their sense of anger about the crass escapist materialism of an elder generation that ostensibly refused to 'come to terms' with the recent past was certainly understandable.[50]

It would nevertheless be incorrect to conclude that the tragic events of the 1930s and 1940s were simply ignored or conveniently forgotten about, for there are different types and levels of memory. In the first place, some of the most important measures and decisions taken during the long 1950s—from the adoption of important constitutional corrections to the concerted efforts aimed at rebuilding and strengthening the economy, providing for the social and material needs of the population, and integrating the Federal Republic into the West—represented a not-so-indirect attempt to avoid the mistakes of Weimar and prevent a repetition of the National Socialist nightmare. Auschwitz and other atrocities may not have been on many lips, but a few public figures did have the courage and moral probity to speak openly about German crimes. The July 20 conspiracy to assassinate Hitler, as well as leftist opposition to the Nazis, were publicly snubbed—at the same time that disingenuous claims were cultivated about supposedly widespread resistance on the part of the churches. But serious efforts to explain the inexplicable did get underway at this time in academic circles, above all in newly-established research institutions, such as the Institute for Contemporary History in Munich.

Many of the conclusions that were drawn at the time by the intellectual elite were somewhat exculpatory, e.g., that Hitler had been a mere 'glitch' (*Betriebsunfall*) without precedent in German history, and that National Socialism was the product of a larger global phenomenon associated with the onset of modernity and the rise of 'mass' society. But to suggest that *Vergangenheitsbewältigung* first began in 1968 is misleading. In fact, the type of 'coming to terms with the past' usually associated with this unwieldy word had arguably begun a decade earlier with the creation in 1958 of a 'Central Office' in Ludwigsburg to investigate Nazi crimes, as well as the adoption of new guidelines shortly thereafter for teaching more in depth about the Third Reich in schools (the latter came largely in response to a recent wave of shocking anti-Semitic acts).[51] That said, an earnest public discussion of the so-called 'final solution' itself would not begin until the late 1970s, i.e., a decade *after* the youth revolt of the late 1960s.[52]

How did the East German response to the Nazi past compare? To begin with, the GDR's entire *raison d'etre* was ostensibly rooted in opposition to the fascist experiment. As a result, the horrors of National Socialism were ever present in public discourse, and its leaders were strongly committed to preventing a resurgence of fascism—something they shared with their rivals in the West. In the GDR, however, where anti-fascism was the regime's foundational myth, that desire was instrumentally used to justify the SED's more controversial policies as well as its very monopoly on power. It also accounted for the more thoroughgoing de-Nazification process—even if many former Nazis *did* manage to achieve positions of influence in the GDR, as well. There may have been no East German 'Globkes' (officials there even tried and condemned the West German secretary of state in absentia for his role during the Third Reich), but the necessity of integrating and winning the support of large numbers of former fascists (as well as the need for their technical and administrative 'know-how') meant that their checkered pasts were frequently forgiven or, at the very least, conveniently overlooked.[53]

As in the Federal Republic, there was a widespread sense of victimization as well, but one in which officials exclusively emphasized the suffering of communists and the working classes. The fate of the Jews received precious little attention as a result. Besides, as East German officials speciously argued, there was no reason for the GDR to make amends for the crimes of the Nazi period because all of the fascists had absconded to the Federal Republic anyway. There were others reasons besides ideological ones for this selective take on the past, however: in the early 1950s, the GDR witnessed a shameful wave of anti-Semitic persecution largely directed against supposedly 'suspicious' SED functionaries—Jewish as well as non-Jewish ones like Paul Merker, who had dared to speak out in favor of material compensation for the Jews. All of this came on the heels of the Soviet bloc's 'anti-Zionist' shift at the close of the 1940s—and less than a decade after the 'liberation' of the German death camps.[54]

One may rightly criticize, in retrospect, the incomplete and imperfect ways in which the Federal Republic and the GDR dealt with and chose to recollect the recent past. It could, nevertheless, be argued that this very imperfection helped account for the stability of these two states during the long 1950s. Far too many guilty individuals were insufficiently punished, but the magnitude of their numbers, as well as the need for their valuable expertise, helped explain why pragmatism all too often trumped morality. The successful integration of these individuals, as well as of the millions of refugees from the former territories in the East (who were often one and the same), was the *sine qua non* of postwar reconstruction *in all its guises*. More to the point, it played an essential role in shoring up and stabilizing the two postwar states, whose provisional nature at the time of their founding cannot be emphasized enough. The 1950s was essentially the story of how both became both permanent and stable.

Despite serious concerns at the time, it turned out that Bonn was *not* Weimar,[55] and a number of factors made this so: the Federal Republic's strong economic performance, which helped sustain its generous welfare state and significantly reduce social and class antagonism; its successful economic, cultural, political, and military integration into the community of Western nations; the gradual emergence of a stable political system dominated by a handful of moderate and mainstream parties working under the provisions of a new and improved constitution; and, last but certainly not least, a gradual change in mentality that allowed for the growing identification of ordinary citizens with their new state, and with its largely peaceful policies and democratic institutions. All of this was abetted by the very existence of the Federal Republic's fraternal rival in the East, which helped rally many West Germans to their state by forging an anti-communist consensus grounded in fear.

There were different reasons for the stability of the German Democratic Republic, whose lackluster economy often failed to satisfy even the most basic needs of the populace, whose leadership could not make good on its generous social welfare promises, and whose citizens, for the most part, remained cool—if not outright hostile—toward their country's exploitative economic integration into the Eastern bloc, and toward a government that lacked democratic legitimacy. The regime nevertheless managed to weather somehow the severe crises of the 1950s, above all the statewide upheaval of 1953 and the human hemorrhage that eventually led to the construction of the Berlin Wall. What, despite overwhelming evidence of widespread dissatisfaction, held East Germany together—or at least prevented it from falling apart? Repression, fear, and obedience certainly played a role, even if they failed to stop East Germans from taking to the streets *en masse* in June 1953. Apathy and withdrawal, the flight of the more disgruntled to the West, the efforts by many low-level officials to try, to the best of their ability, to appease those under their charge by responding to their demands and grievances—all of this played a significant role as well. But there was another important factor: while 'class warfare' was abating in the Federal Republic, it was encouraged by authorities in the GDR—either explicitly in their official pronouncements against 'class enemies,' such as large farmers and private businessmen, or unwittingly in the format of divisive policies that caused social frictions by rewarding some select segments of society over others. Such cleavages were important because they effectively promoted stability by hindering East Germans from presenting a united front to authorities when mounting opposition or pressing for change.[56]

In the end, however, East German officials resorted to more vigorous measures in order to keep their state intact—just at the time that Adenauer's star was beginning to wane in the West because of his own desperate attempts to hold on to power. The erection of the Berlin Wall in August 1961 marked the final division of postwar Germany, as well as the end of the 'long 1950s.' It may have shored up the stability of the GDR, but the price for that, at least for the time being, was the German nation itself.

Notes

1. Although there are many fine overviews of this period, this essay relies most heavily on the following works for their innumerable insights, as well as for the 'basic facts' and general lines of development: Edgar Wolfrum, *Die geglückte Demokratie. Geschichte der Bundesrepublik Deutschland von ihren Anfängen bis zur Gegenwart* (Stuttgart: Pantheon, 2006); Manfred Görtemaker, *Geschichte der Bundesrepublik Deutschland. Von der Gründung bis zur Gegenwart* (Munich: C. H. Beck, 1999); Dietrich Staritz, *Geschichte der DDR*, 2nd edn (Frankfurt am Main: Suhrkamp, 1996); Christoph Kleßmann, *Die doppelte Staatsgründung. Deutsche Geschichte 1945–1955* (Bonn: Bundeszentrale für politische Bildung, 1991); idem, *Zwei Staaten, eine Nation. Deutsche Geschichte 1955–1970* (Bonn: Bundeszentrale für politische Bildung, 1997).

2. For an assessment of 1945 as a major caesura, see the essays in Hans-Erich Volkmann (ed.), *Ende des Dritten Reiches—Ende des Zweiten Weltkrieges. Eine perspektivische Rückschau* (Munich: Piper, 1995). For a more sympathetic view of the term 'zero hour,' see Richard Bessel, *Germany 1945: From War to Peace* (New York: HarperCollins, 2009), 395–396.

3. Superb overviews of the West German political system include Manfred G. Schmidt, *Political Institutions in the Federal Republic of Germany* (Oxford: Oxford University Press, 2003); Klaus von Beyme, *Das politische System der Bundesrepublik. Eine Einführung*, 10th edn (Wiesbaden: Verlag für Sozialwissenschaften, 2004).

4. Görtemacher, *Geschichte*, 66. Also see Patrick Major, *The Death of the KPD: Communism and Anti-Communism in West Germany, 1945–1956* (Oxford: Oxford University Press, 1998); Henning Hansen, *Die Sozialistische Reichspartei. Aufstieg und Scheitern einer rechtsextremen Partei* (Düsseldorf: Droste, 2007).

5. A good place to begin on repression during this period is Falco Werkentin, *Politische Strafjustiz in der Ära Ulbricht. Vom verdeckten Terror zur verdeckten Repression*, 2nd edn (Berlin: Ch. Links, 1997). On the creation of the GDR, see Dietrich Staritz, *Die Gründung der DDR. Von der sowjetischen Besatzungsherrschaft zum sozialistischen Staat*, 3rd edn (Munich: DTV, 1995).

6. Compare Sigrid Meuschel, *Legitimation und Parteiherrschaft. Zum Paradox von Stabilität und Revolution in der DDR 1945–1989* (Frankfurt am Main: Suhrkamp, 1992), 29–40, with Manfred Agethen, Eckhard Jesse, and Ehrhart Neubert, *Der Missbrauchte Antifaschismus. DDR-Staatsdoktrin und Lebenslüge der deutschen Linke* (Freiburg: Herder, 2002); Antonia Grunenberg, *Antifascismus, ein deutscher Mythos* (Reinbek bei Hamburg: Rowohlt, 1993). Also see Andrew I. Port, *Conflict and Stability in the German Democratic Republic* (New York: Cambridge University Press, 2007), 3, 60–61, 117.

7. See, for example, Frank Bösch, *Die Adenauer-CDU. Gründung, Aufstieg und Krise einer Erfolgspartei 1945–1969* (Stuttgart: DVA, 2001).

8. Hans-Peter Schwarz, *Konrad Adenauer*, 2 vols (Providence: Berghahn Books, 1995, 1997) should be read in conjunction with Henning Köhler, *Adenauer. Eine politische Biografie*, 2 vols (Frankfurt am Main: Propyläen, 1994).

9. Görtemacher, *Geschichte*, 88–94; also see Arnulf Baring, *Im Anfang war Adenauer. Die Entstehung der Kanzlerdemokratie*, rev. edn (Munich: DTV, 1991). More generally, Karlheinz Niclauß, *Kanzlerdemokratie. Regierungsführung von Konrad Adenauer bis Gerhard Schroeder*, rev. edn (Paderborn: Schöningh, 2004).

10. See Carola Stern, *Ulbricht: A Political Biography* (London: Pall Mall Press, 1965); Mario Frank, *Walter Ulbricht, Eine deutsche Biografie* (Berlin: Siedler, 2001); Norbert Podewin, *Walter Ulbricht, Eine neue Biografie* (Berlin: Dietz, 1995).

11. Useful overviews of this period include Staritz, *Gründung*; idem, *Geschichte*; Kleßmann, *Staatsgründung*; Norman Naimark, *The Russians in Germany: A History of the Soviet Zone of Occupation, 1945–1949* (Cambridge: Belknap Press of Harvard University Press, 1995); Dierk Hoffmann, *Die DDR unter Ulbricht. Gewaltsame Neuordnung und gescheiterte Modernisierung* (Zurich: Pendo, 2003).

12. For an extremely useful overview of the most recent literature on the uprising, see Jonathan Sperber, '17 June 1953: Revisiting a German Revolution,' *German History* 22 (2004): 619–643.

13. See the essays in Siegfried Prokop (ed.), *Zwischen Aufbruch und Abbruch. Die DDR im Jahre 1956* (Berlin: Homilius, 2006).

14. See Peter Merseburger, *Der schwierige Deutsche. Kurt Schumacher. Eine Biografie* (Stuttgart: DVA, 1995).

15. See Kurt Klotzbach, *Der Weg zur Staatspartei. Programmatik, praktische Politik und Organisation der deutschen Sozialdemokratie 1945–1965* (Bonn: Dietz, 1996).

16. On the early years of the FDP, see Theo Rütten, *Der deutsche Liberalismus 1945 bis 1955. Deutschland- und Gesellschaftspolitik der ost- und westdeutschen Liberalen in der Entstehungsphase der beiden deutschen Staaten* (Baden-Baden: Nomos, 1984).

17. See Gerd-Rüdiger Stephan et al. (eds), *Die Parteien und Organisationen der DDR. Ein Handbuch* (Berlin: Dietz, 2002).

18. See the essay by Stefan-Ludwig Hoffmann in this volume.

19. See Werner Abelshauser, *Wirtschaftsgeschichte der Bundesrepublik Deutschland 1945–1980* (Frankfurt am Main: Suhrkamp, 1993); Herbert Giersch, Karl-Heinz Pacqui, and Holger Schmieding, *The Fading Miracle: Four Decades of Market Economy in Germany* (New York: Cambridge University Press, 1992), 45–124; Hans-Ulrich Wehler, *Deutsche Gesellschaftsgeschichte. Bundesrepublik und DDR 1949–1990*, vol. 5 (Munich: C. H. Beck, 2008), 48–73.

20. See Alfred C. Mierzejewski, *Ludwig Erhard: A Biography* (Chapel Hill: University of North Carolina Press, 2006).

21. West Germany refused to recompense slave laborers until the signing of a peace treaty.

22. See Anthony J. Nicholls, *Freedom with Responsibility: The Social Market Economy in Germany, 1918–1963* (Oxford: Clarendon Press, 1994).

23. See Manfred Schmidt, *Sozialpolitik der DDR* (Wiesbaden: Verlag für Sozialwissenschaften, 2004); Annette Kaminsky, *Wohlstand, Schönheit, Glück. Kleine Konsumgeschichte der DDR* (Munich: C. H. Beck, 2001); Philipp Heldmann, 'Negotiating Consumption in a Dictatorship: Consumption Politics in the GDR in the 1950s and 1960s,' in Martin Daunton and Matthew Hilton (eds), *The Politics of Consumption: Material Culture and Citizenship in Europe and America* (Oxford: Berg, 2001), 185–202.

24. For an overview of this debate, see Corey Ross, *The East German Dictatorship: Problems and Perspectives in the Interpretation of the GDR* (London: Arnold, 2002), 69–96.

25. On the East German economy, see Jeffrey Kopstein, *The Politics of Economic Decline in East Germany, 1945–1989* (Chapel Hill: University of North Carolina Press, 1997); André Steiner, *Von Plan zu Plan. Eine Wirtschaftsgeschichte der DDR* (Munich: DVA, 2004).

26. See Michael Wildt, *Am Beginn der 'Konsumgesellschaft.' Mangelerfahrung, Lebenshaltung, Wohlstandshoffnung in Westdeutschland in den fünfziger Jahren* (Hamburg: Ergebnisse, 1994).

27. For a succinct but superb overview of consumption practices and cultural developments in the Federal Republic at this time, see Wolfrum, *Demokratie*, 153–169. Also see the essays in Hanna Schissler (ed.), *The Miracle Years: A Cultural History of West Germany, 1949–1968* (Princeton: Princeton University Press, 2001).

28. Uta Poiger, *Jazz, Rock, and Rebels: Cold War Politics and American Culture in a Divided Germany* (Berkeley: University of California Press, 2000), 137–205.

29. See, for example, Port, *Conflict and Stability*, 117–119, 121, 167–168.

30. In addition to the relevant sections in the two biographies cited in note 8, see the colorful anecdotes about Adenauer's feelings toward Prussia in Arnulf Baring, *Außenpolitik in Adenauers Kanzlerdemokratie* (Munich: R. Oldenbourg, 1969).

31. See Gerhard Wettig, *Stalin and the Cold War in Europe: The Emergence and Development of East-West Conflict, 1939–1953* (Lanham: Rowman & Littlefield, 2008), 158–166, 174–177, 216–221; Wilfried Loth, *Die Sowjetunion und die deutsche Frage. Studien zur sowjetischen Deutschlandpolitik von Stalin bis Chruschtschow* (Göttingen: Vandenhoeck & Ruprecht, 2007).

32. On the SED's tortured relationship with unification, see Dirk Spilker, *The East German Leadership and the Division of Germany: Patriotism and Propaganda, 1945–1953* (Oxford: Oxford University Press, 2006).

33. For a general overview, see Helga Haftendorn, *Coming of Age: German Foreign Policy since 1945* (Lanham: Rowman & Littlefield, 2006), 1–156.

34. See Loth, *Sowjetunion;* Ronald Granieri, *The Ambivalent Alliance: Konrad Adenauer, the CDU/CSU, and the West, 1949–1966* (New York: Berghahn, 2003).

35. See Hope Harrison, *Driving the Soviets up the Wall: Soviet-East German Relations, 1953–1961* (Princeton: Princeton University Press, 2003).

36. Traumatic memories of the disastrous consequences of the Treaty of Versailles played a significant role as well.

37. See David Clay Large, *Germans to the Front: West German Rearmament in the Adenauer Era* (Chapel Hill: University of North Carolina Press, 1996); Hans Karl Rupp, *Außerparlamentarische Opposition in der Ära Adenauer. Der Kampf gegen die Atombewaffnung in den fünfziger Jahren* (Cologne: Pahl-Rugenstein, 1970).

38. See Port, *Conflict and Stability*, 128–133.

39. See Poiger, *Jazz*, 71–136.

40. See the essay by Uta Poiger in this volume.

41. See Norbert Frei, *Adenauer's Germany and the Nazi Past: The Politics of Amnesty and Integration*, trans. Joel Golb (New York: Columbia University Press, 2002).

42. See Donna Harsh, *Revenge of the Domestic: Women, Family, and Communism in the German Democratic Republic* (Princeton: Princeton University Press, 2007); Robert Moeller, *Protecting Motherhood: Women and Family in the Politics of Postwar West Germany* (Berkeley: University of California Press, 1993).

43. See Wolfrum, *Demokratie*, 144–151; Görtemacher, *Geschichte*, 174–182.

44. See Kopstein, *Politics;* Port, *Conflict and Stability;* Christoph Kleßmann, *Arbeiter im 'Arbeiterstaat' DDR. Deutsche Traditionen, sowjetisches Modell, westdeutsches Magnetfeld (1945 bis 1971)* (Bonn: Dietz, 2007); Josef Mooser, *Arbeiterleben in Deutschland 1900–1970. Klassenlagen, Kultur und Politik* (Frankfurt am Main: Suhrkamp, 1984); idem, 'Die

Arbeiterbewegung in der Bundesrepublik und DDR in den fünfziger Jahren,' in Arnd Bauerkämper et al. (eds), *Doppelte Zeitgeschichte. Deutsch-deutsche Beziehungen 1945– 1990* (Bonn: Dietz, 1998), 142–157.

45. See Arnd Bauerkämper, *Ländliche Gesellschaft in der kommunistischen Diktatur. Zwangs- modernisierung und Tradition in Brandenburg 1945–1963* (Cologne: Böhlau, 2002); Port, *Conflict and Stability*, 226–227.

46. See, for example, Catherine Epstein, *The Last Revolutionaries: German Communists and their Century* (Cambridge: Harvard University Press, 2003).

47. See Staritz, *Geschichte*, 171–172, 178, 180–181. The Socialist Commandments were reminis- cent of the Bible *and* the Boy Scout movement, e.g. 'II. Thou shalt love your Fatherland and always be prepared to use all of your power and ability for the defense of the Worker- and-Farmer Power (*Macht*).' All ten are listed in the entry on 'socialist morals' in Hartmut Zimmermann (ed.), *DDR Handbuch*, vol. 1, 3rd edn (Cologne: Verlag Wis- senschaft und Politik, 1985), 918.

48. See David Schoenbaum, *The Spiegel Affair* (Garden City: Doubleday, 1968).

49. See Frei, *Nazi Past*.

50. See Hannah Arendt, *Besuch in Deutschland* (Berlin: Rotbuch, 1993), 28; idem, *Eichmann in Jerusalem: A Report on the Banality of Evil* (New York: Penguin, 1994), 251.

51. See Edgar Wolfrum, 'Die beiden Deutschland,' in Volkhard Knigge and Norbert Frei (eds), *Verbrechen erinnern. Die Auseinandersetzung mit Holocaust und Völkermord* (Munich: C. H. Beck, 2002), 134–139; Jeffrey Herf, *Divided Memory: The Nazi Past in the Two Germanies* (Cambridge: Harvard University Press, 1997), 201–333; Ulrich Broch- hagen, *Nach Nürnberg. Vergangenheitsbewältigung und Westbindung in der Ära Ade- nauer* (Hamburg: Junius, 1999). For a useful overview of recent literature on Vergangenheitsbewältigung during this period, see Kay Schiller, 'The Presence of the Nazi Past in the Early Decades of the Bonn Republic,' *Journal of Contemporary History* 39, no. 2 (2004): 285–294.

52. A case in point: Raul Hilberg's monumental study from 1961 about the destruction of the European Jews was not published in German translation until the early 1980s—and then by a little-known West German publishing house. See Raul Hilberg, *The Politics of Memory: The Journey of a Holocaust Historian* (Chicago: Ivan R. Dee, 1996), 171–173.

53. See Olaf Kappelt, *Die Entnazifizierung in der SBZ sowie die Rolle und der Einfluss ehemaliger Nationalsozialisten in der DDR als ein soziologisches Phänomen* (Hamburg: Kovac, 1997); Timothy Vogt, *Denazification in Soviet-occupied Germany: Brandenburg, 1945–1948* (Cambridge: Harvard University Press, 2000).

54. See Wolfrum, 'Die beiden Deutschland,' 141–147; Herf, *Divided Memory*, 106–161.

55. Fritz René Allemann, *Bonn ist nicht Weimar* (Cologne: Kiepenheuer & Witsch, 1956).

56. This is one of the main arguments in Port, *Conflict and Stability*.

BIBLIOGRAPHY

BENDER, PETER, *Deutschlands Wiederkehr. Eine ungeteilte Nachkriegsgeschichte 1945–1990* (Stuttgart: Klett-Cotta, 2007).

CREW, DAVID (ed.), *Consuming Germany in the Cold War* (Oxford: Berg, 2003).

FULBROOK, MARY, *The People's State: East German Society from Hitler to Honecker* (New Haven: Yale University Press, 2006).

FREI, NORBERT, *Adenauer's Germany and the Nazi Past* (New York: Columbia University Press, 2002).

GÖRTEMAKER, MANFRED, *Geschichte der Bundesrepublik Deutschland. Von der Gründung bis zur Gegenwart* (Munich: C. H. Beck, 1999).

HAFTENDORN, HELGA, *Coming of Age: German Foreign Policy since 1945* (Lanham: Rowman & Littlefield, 2006).

HERF, JEFFREY, *Divided Memory: The Nazi Past in the Two Germanies* (Cambridge: Harvard University Press, 1997).

JARAUSCH, KONRAD, *After Hitler: Recivilizing Germans, 1945–1995* (Oxford: Oxford University Press, 2006).

MAJOR, PATRICK and JONATHAN OSMOND (eds), *The Workers' and Peasants' State: Communism and Society in East Germany under Ulbricht, 1945–71* (Manchester: Manchester University Press, 2002).

MOELLER, ROBERT (ed.), *West Germany under Construction: Politics, Society and Culture in the Adenauer Era* (Ann Arbor: University Of Michigan Press, 1997).

NICHOLLS, ANTHONY, *The Bonn Republic: West German Democracy, 1945–1990* (London: Longman, 1997).

POIGER, UTA, *Jazz, Rock and Rebels: Cold War Politics and American Culture in a Divided Germany* (Berkeley: The University of California Press, 2000).

PORT, ANDREW, *Conflict and Stability in the German Democratic Republic* (New York: Cambridge University Press, 2007).

SCHISSLER, HANNA (ed.), *The Miracle Years: A Cultural History of West Germany, 1949–1968* (Princeton: Princeton University Press, 2001).

STARITZ, DIETRICH, *Geschichte der DDR*, 2nd edn (Frankfurt am Main: Suhrkamp, 1996).

TURNER, HENRY, *Germany from Partition to Unification* (New Haven: Yale University Press, 1992).

WEHLER, HANS-ULRICH, *Deutsche Gesellschaftsgeschichte, 1949–1990* (Munich: C. H. Beck, 2008).

WINKLER, HEINRICH AUGUST, *Germany: The Long Road West. Vol. 2: 1933–1990*, trans. Alexander J. Sager (Oxford: Oxford University Press, 2007).

WOLFRUM, EDGAR, *Die geglückte Demokratie. Geschichte der Bundesrepublik Deutschland von ihren Anfängen bis zur Gegenwart* (Stuttgart: Pantheon, 2006).

CHAPTER 28

....

GENERATIONS: THE 'REVOLUTIONS' OF THE 1960S

....

UTA G. POIGER

THE 'Sixties'—as a set of associations including greater autonomy of youth, anti-imperialist and anti-war activism, leftist aspirations to political revolt, sexual revolution, and women's emancipation—continue to elicit strong reactions in Germany. '1968,' in particular, functions as a myth, or a set of competing myths, fostered by the participants in rebellion, their detractors, and the media. Central to the resonance of 'the sixties' and '1968' is the international, even global character of rebellions that took place in cities from Paris to Chicago, Mexico City to Tokyo, and from Berkeley to Prague in the form of demonstrations, strikes, counter cultures, and liberation movements. Both international connections and national politics shaped 1960s rebellions—and the efforts to assess them ever since. In West Germany, identifying as a '68er' has been a claim to political courage and historical conscience, suggesting that one had worked successfully to overcome Nazi and other authoritarian legacies. Around the twentieth anniversary of 1968 and in the immediate aftermath of German unification in 1990, the moral caché of this position was so great that the question of whether East Germans could lay claim to their own 68er generation was much debated.[1] In the 1970s and 1980s, attempts of the political right to discredit as terrorist the rebellions of the 1960s and the social movements that followed were not successful. More recently, however, criticism of 1960s rebels has again gained traction, especially in assertions of the political immaturity of the 68ers, their narcissism, their totalitarian affinities, or their general ineffectiveness.[2]

In Germany, the 1960s looked quite different depending on whether one was east or west of the Iron Curtain. During these key years of the Cold War and the division of Germany, two rival ideologies, liberal democracy and communism, vied for transformations of society and for interpretations of Europe's violent and traumatic past. As

East and West Germany sought to complete the process of integrating into the two opposing political and military systems, the rebels of the 1960s demanded change. They operated in two different public spheres: in the West, reform and, at times, even revolution could be debated; in the East, the regime understood itself to be in the process of achieving a socialist society and debate was severely curtailed. The global context also shaped agendas. By the 1960s, anti-colonial and other liberation movements around the world challenged a sense, already damaged in two world wars, of European 'civilizational superiority.'

This chapter asks about the different manifestations of rebellions in East and West, and about the longer historical trajectories and international linkages that they forged. It focuses on the relationship between reform and rebellion as a way of understanding the transformations and upheavals of the 1960s, especially in such areas as youth cultures and the entertainment industry, shifts in gender and sexual norms, challenges to the workings of political and educational institutions, and anti-colonialism. In these overlapping arenas, rebels pursued four not always compatible goals: emancipation, transparency, authenticity, and community. It is the contention of this chapter that rather than being *initiators* of political and cultural reform, the multifaceted 'revolutions' or rebellions of the 1960s took place in a *context* of reform. State socialism, too, was reformed in the 1960s, but here rebels experienced more restrictions and as a result had less direct impact on institutional transformations.[3]

Cold War battles and competing visions of the German past also shaped the rebellions of the 1960s, with attempts to come to terms with the Nazi past imparting a particular valence to events in Germany. However, other aspects of the German past were also subject to debate, especially the longer histories of German imperialism and authoritarianism reaching back into the nineteenth century. At the same time, East and West German reformers and rebels built affiliations beyond the borders of Germany and criticized international power relations. Imperialism, neo-colonialism, and war became key issues of concern. The existence of labels such as 'Maoist' or 'Tupamaro' in 1960s West Germany, and of Che Guevara posters in both states, reveals the concrete and imagined international links that protest movements forged. In the course of the 1960s, these imaginative links were the basis of competing moral geographies, of cognitive maps and affiliations.[4] Within these transnational coordinates, rebels debated the shape of society in East and West Germany.

28.1 YOUTH AND CULTURE INDUSTRIES

In the GDR and FRG of the 1950s, educators, social scientists, and politicians regularly expressed anxieties about the cultural styles of youth and their alleged political implications. Following the tradition of Catholic social critique, West German conservatives saw American cultural influences, such as rock 'n' roll dancing or western movies as a threat to a 'Christian West.' Concerns about a lack of respectability among rock musicians and fans were grave enough that West German radio stations, in this period state-controlled, would not play rock music until the mid-1960s. For their part, East German politicians worried that rock or westerns were part of the 'psychological warfare of the West:' they therefore restricted Western musical imports and prohibited the 'dancing apart' of rock 'n' roll. Both East and West German cultural conservatives frequently used terms common in eugenic thought and Nazi ideology, such as 'degenerate.'

In the West, a more liberal attitude toward adolescent consumption and associated musical styles took hold in the second half of the 1950s. Jazz, which numerous commentators had seen as threatening in the early 1950s, was now seen as modern, youthful, and respectable—and as the proper musical form for a democratic West Germany. By 1964, West German Goethe Institutes, in charge of fostering German culture and cultural understanding abroad, even sent West German jazz groups into several Asian countries. Ambivalence persisted nevertheless. Educators founded state-run jazz and film clubs whose offerings included 'hot rhythms,' but also urged adolescents to shed controversial styles such as the wearing of jeans.[5]

In spite of, or perhaps also because of concerns about the youth's health, youthfulness became increasingly a part of marketing consumer goods and popular culture in the prosperous 1960s. By the middle of the 1960s, the United States had lost to Great Britain its status as the main exporter of controversial products for youth, as parents, educators, and politicians on both sides of the iron curtain worried about the music of British bands, such as the Rolling Stones and the Beatles, and about the casual clothing and long hair of male rock fans. Such concerns no doubt fostered a sense that authoritarian attitudes were still pervasive in Germany. However, in 1965 the state-run West German television began broadcasting a music show for adolescents called *Beat-Club* in which rock bands and controversial artists like Jimi Hendrix found a nation-wide German audience. International musical tastes became more widespread: if at the beginning of the 1960s, it was still a minority of West German adolescents that preferred American or Western popular music, by the end of the decade it was a majority. Increasingly, the press treated adolescents as trendsetters ahead of older generations in opinions and styles, while promoters of such changes in cultural consumption positioned these as tangible expressions of social and political reform.[6]

Throughout the 1960s, East German party and youth leaders struggled even more with Western influences and adolescent autonomy. With the drain of workers to the West closed off by the Berlin Wall, East German leaders were willing to undertake some reforms. As part of its efforts to foster more individual initiative in the economy and in culture, the SED Politburo, in a 1963 Youth Communiqué, gave youth 'trust and responsibility' in the building of socialism. 'Which tact or rhythm the youth selects is up to it,' the Politburo announced, but demanded right away: 'The main thing is that it remains tactful!'[7] These statements, along with the continuous attacks on the 'psychological warfare' of the West, showed how difficult it was for the SED leadership to find a balance between its own calls for self-definition, on the one hand, and its demands for a constant commitment to the socialist system on the other.

Officials, adolescents, and the producers of movies, music, concerts, and literature made use of these openings after 1962. Adolescents and even party leaders danced the twist, while rock bands sprang up all over the GDR. Movies such as *Don't think I'm crying* ('*Denk bloß nicht ich heule*,' GDR, 1965) took up the issue of adolescent alienation under socialism. In 1965, the state-owned record company issued an LP by the Beatles, while press reports claimed that the Beatles' music, like jazz earlier, was protest music in the West. In 1964, officials founded a radio station, 'dt64,' which catered to its adolescent audience with music by Western, as well as domestic rock and beat bands. And with two special stations the GDR also provided beat music for West German adolescents, who after all could not find such music on West German stations until 1965.[8]

Soon, however, the SED and the state youth organization FDJ (Free German Youth) reined the youth culture in again. By the fall of 1965 East German officials withdrew the licenses for GDR rock bands and stopped an FDJ guitar contest when too many of the entries showed American and British influences. In October, the police arrested participants of a so-called 'beat demonstration' in Leipzig, where 2500 fans protested repressive measures. After this event the FDJ endorsed actions where classmates cut the long hair of their peers. Some fans were sentenced to prison or forced labor.[9] In December 1965, the infamous 11th Plenum of the SED Central Committee widened the crackdown. Future party chief Erich Honecker gave a speech, in which he accused movies, television shows, and literary works of propagating brutality and sexual drives, and complained that many were not defending the GDR against 'American immorality and decadence.' The party and FDJ leadership railed against 'skepticism,' which 'questions everything,' against 'objectivism,' 'which positions itself between two fronts,' and against the 'bourgeois theories of man's loneliness.' These were facile attacks on the ideas of a 'skeptical generation,' an 'end of ideology,' and the 'loneliness of the crowd' that West German and American Cold War liberals, such as Helmut Schelsky and David Riesman, had introduced in their efforts to come to terms with consumer culture. Party leaders rejected the calls for self-definition that some of them had endorsed earlier as foreign-produced and as dangerous. Instead they recommended ideological education and the raising of class-consciousness among the East German youth. In the wake of the 11th Plenum, party leaders prohibited numerous movies that showed adolescent alienation, and cracked down on singers and writers, including the singer-songwriter Wolf Biermann.[10]

Psychology, which played an important role in making consumer culture both understandable and acceptable in West Germany in the 1950s, was long repressed in East Germany. In West Germany, psychological models of adolescent development assigned consumption an increasingly important function, although this embrace coexisted with uneasiness about consumer culture. In 1966 the SED leadership authorized a new Central Institute for Youth Research (*Zentralinstitut für Jugendforschung*). The researchers investigated the attitudes of young men with long hair, and concluded that, contrary to public denunciations, these young people were not socially deviant high-school dropouts. Nor were they fully committed to the goals of socialism. Another study found that more and more adolescents found nothing wrong with listening to Western radio stations. Needless to say, such complex findings could not be made public. The East German regime encouraged its citizens to formulate their identities primarily as workers, soldiers, socialists, and anti-fascists, even as consumer culture increasingly undercut such allegiances.[11]

28.2 Radicalization and Internationalization of Activism in West Germany

West of the Iron Curtain, critiques of authoritarian structures became more and more vehement among the West German public and raised the question of continuities with the authoritarianism of Wilhelmine Germany or Nazi practices and personnel. Early in the decade the sociologists Ralf Dahrendorf, from a liberal perspective, and Jürgen Habermas, from a Marxist perspective, questioned the state of democratization in mentalities and social relations in West Germany and suggested continuities with the hierarchical organization of Germany during the Wilhelmine era. Their texts were both indicators and initiators in a burgeoning debate on the democratization of society in West Germany, a debate that soon raised questions about methods of childrearing and education, and about the workings of key institutions such as universities and schools, the media, churches, and the military.[12] In 1962, the Spiegel Affair, caused by the effort of Defense Minister Franz-Josef Strauss to intimidate the press over unfavorable coverage of his ministry, led to mass demonstrations against overreaching state authority and resulted in Strauss's resignation. Press coverage of the Eichmann Trial in Jerusalem in 1961 and of the Auschwitz Trial in Frankfurt from 1963 to 1965 also triggered expanded public interest in German responsibility for Nazi crimes and specifically the genocide of Jews. The integration of many Nazi party members into West German institutions (which was probably important for achieving West German stability) came to be seen as an accommodation of the extreme right. Persistently brought to the public eye in East German publications, especially the so-called *Brown Book*, revelations about the Nazi involvements of figures such as the sociologist Helmut Schelsky, the chancellor Georg Kiesinger, or the West German president Heinrich Lübke became a staple of critical West German press coverage in the course of the 1960s.

As the West German press provided a broader forum for debates over authority, transparency, and emancipation, as some West Germans protested nuclear armament, and as critiques of US and European involvement in wars of decolonization became more audible, a new and more radical movement emerged. In 1961, the West German SDS (Socialist German Student Federation) expressed solidarity with liberation and anti-colonial movements 'against political dependence and economic exploitation.'

Arguing that the Federal Republic was implicated in these conflicts through its membership in NATO, SDS especially attacked US policies against the Cuban Revolution, Portugal's 'genocidal war' in its African colonies, the actions 'of Belgian capital' against the Congolese liberation movement, and the French government's 'colonial war' in Algeria. Until its expulsion that same year in 1961, SDS had been the student organization of the Social Democratic Party; now it became one of the main building blocs of a West German New Left that sought new forms of political action and new Marxist analysis as distinct from state socialism and what it perceived as the accommodations policies of Social Democracy.[13]

Protests against an official visit of Congolese leader Moishe Tshombe to West Germany in December 1964 introduced new tactics, such as a sit-in organized by self-proclaimed anti-authoritarians, and further crystallized a radical student movement. German and African students cooperated (with black and white men marching in suits, neckties, and short hair). In 1966 the willingness to battle with West German state authorities increased as groups of German and African students tried to shut down showings of the Italian movie *Africa Addio*, which many commentators in Germany and abroad saw as an apology for European colonialism and racism in Africa. In a West Berlin theater, black and white protestors used civil disobedience tactics pioneered by the civil rights movement and the free speech movement in the United States and by anti-apartheid protestors in South Africa (who, in turn, drew on Gandhi and others), so that the police dragged them out of the theater. Two days later, the West Berlin police chief prohibited a rally in front of the theater, because 'Communist demonstrators' might 'use it for their purposes.' Further clashes with police ensued, resulting in the prosecution of some protestors.[14]

Protests against imperialism in Africa or soon the Vietnam War were, of course, not merely a West German phenomenon; West German students knew through press reports that stressed such simultaneity that they were part of international protests. Conferences with international participation, as well as the translation and circulation of radical texts, also fostered a sense of internationalism. Particularly important in West Germany was the journal *Kursbuch*, at once analyst of and voice for radical positions in West Germany, and understood by its editor Hans Magnus Enzensberger as a guide 'to connections.' The second issue of the journal in August 1965 was devoted to the Third World and featured an excerpt of Frantz Fanon's *The Wretched of the Earth*, in which Fanon emphasized the global contexts of local liberation movements.[15]

Personal contacts between German and foreign students further contributed to a sense of internationalism. For example, as an exchange student in the United States, Michael Vester, later an important figure in SDS, participated in activities of the American Students for a Democratic Society. Full accounts remain to be written of the impact of foreign exchange students on the West German rebellions. Throughout the 1960s, ca. 23,000 foreign students studied in West Germany (close to 10 percent of the entire student body), many of them brought by government-financed exchanges that were part of development programs in the Third World. While turnover made personal continuity difficult to maintain, some like Nigerian Adekunle Ajala in the *Africa Addio* protests gained prominence and many more provided information and encouragement for the international visions of young Germans. Other foreign students, like the American Angela Davis, who studied philosophy with Theodor Adorno at the University of Frankfurt from 1965 to 1967, saw their involvement in West German student activism as important to their own political formation.[16]

The radicalization of protests in West Germany received an additional push in 1966 with the so-called 'Grand Coalition' government, formed by the Christian Democrats and Social Democrats in response to an economic downturn and electoral gains by the right-wing NPD. Since 1955, West Germany's Hallstein Doctrine had held that West Germany was the only legitimate representative of the German people and prohibited diplomatic relations with any country, save for the Soviet Union, that recognized East Germany. Yet by the late 1960s, West German politicians like Willy Brandt had begun to soften the doctrine. As foreign minister in the Grand Coalition, Brandt negotiated a guest worker agreement with Yugoslavia in 1967 in order to bring in workers from a region where Germany had played a particularly violent role during World War II, and to signal greater co-operation with Communist countries. Such reformist tendencies in West German foreign policy hardly satisfied the radical critics of the West German government, however.[17]

Suspicion against the Grand Coalition grew quickly when it agreed in 1966 to bring before parliament the so-called 'Emergency Acts' (*Notstandsgesetze*) that provided for the contingency of a state of emergency. (Until the passage of such laws, emergency powers rested with the Allies.) Intellectuals like the philosopher Karl Jaspers protested against the proposed measures, and SDS in conjunction with anti-armament activists and defenders of civil liberties formed an Extra-Parliamentary Opposition (APO). The radical adherents of APO came from a variety of political directions, but were increasingly united by a suspicion of 'the system' and the manipulative powers of the media as well as mistrust of 'the bourgeoisie.' Both orthodox and unorthodox Marxist critiques of liberal democracies gained in urgency. Increasingly, radicals believed that they were living in a pre-fascist state, while student protests convinced many SPD politicians and trade unionists who had earlier opposed such legislation that a state of emergency could in fact occur in West Germany.[18]

By 1967, radical protests against U.S. involvement in the Vietnam War overshadowed concerns about decolonization, neocolonialism, and racism in Africa. The West German demonstrations against the Vietnam War began in the spring of 1965. That year the Berlin chapter of SDS organized a panel discussion about the war and put together an exhibit designed to show that the United States had allied with South Vietnamese villains in a civil war. Vietnam protests were another example of the international links of German protest movements; however, they also took on particular German characteristics, when Vietnam became another venue to talk about the Nazi past, and West German politicians and protestors struggled over 'controlling political analogies.' Whereas leading West German politicians claimed that the Vietnam War was a fight against communism and therefore a fight to defend West

Germany and West Berlin, student rebels suggested that those who supported the United States in Vietnam were just as guilty as those who had remained silent in the face of Nazism.[19]

When protests against US intervention in Vietnam met largely with silence in West Germany, activists saw their suspicions of a moral abdication of the West German bourgeoisie confirmed, and many of them perceived this conflict in generational terms—of having to fight against a generation silent in the face of the Nazis in the 1930s and now silent again. Following Herbert Marcuse, student rebels, especially in SDS, came to think of themselves as a 'marginal group' who in collaboration with Third World liberation movements could change the capitalist world system. At the first West Germany-wide conference of protesters against the Vietnam War in Frankfurt in March 1966, Marcuse (himself a refugee from Nazism and then sociology professor at UC San Diego) called for 'solidarity of reason and sentiment' between protestors in the First and Third World.[20] Marcuse and many German commentators perceived the naked bodies of Vietnamese victims of napalm and Jewish victims at Auschwitz as equivalent. Moreover, Marcuse's concept of 'repressive tolerance' fostered the notion that liberal democracies and consumer capitalism had authoritarian tendencies—and stressed the responsibility of the intellectual for creating possibilities for mental and social transformation.

In East Germany, identification with Third World Liberation movements took place under very different conditions. Like the Soviet rulers, the East German government saw itself as a supporter of radical liberation movements. East German media sought to link the Federal Republic to racism, fascist continuities, and neo-colonialism in Congo, producing a book and a TV documentary called *The Laughing Man* (*Der lachende Mann*, GDR, 1966), on Siegfried 'Congo' Müller, a German who had fought in the Wehrmacht during World War II and was a member of Tshombe's mercenary armies. For radicals and the liberal press in West Germany such a figure raised the specter of West German continuities with the Nazi past, an issue that the East German press reinforced by speaking in sensationalist terms of Tshombe's 'SS executioners.' West German authorities responded by preventing importation of *The Laughing Man*. The East German state youth organization was able to draw on young Germans' enthusiasm for liberation movements, organizing a number of events and soliciting donations of money and of blood for Vietnam. Whereas in West Germany even left liberal politicians did not dare voice criticisms of Tshombe or the Vietnam War, East German protests were officially sanctioned, indeed they were organized by party and state.[21]

28.3 CHANGES IN LIFESTYLES AND MORES

1967, more than 1968, proved a transformative year in West Germany. The changing appearances of demonstrators, more dramatic for men than for women, were indicative of broader changes in lifestyles and mores. West German men demonstrators replaced suits and ties with jeans, casual jackets, longer hair, and sometimes beards, while women demonstrators sported skirts and high boots or sometimes jeans (but not the miniskirts or baby doll dresses that were also fashionable in East and West).[22] Rebels affirmed the notion that authoritarian forms of socialization in family, school, and society were central to the functioning of authoritarian political systems. At the same time they expressed strong belief in the transformative capacities of individuals and societies, and saw style as an expression of mental-social changes.

While diverging music and fashion tastes had already pointed to a gap between generations, no other development fostered a sense of generational conflict as much as the emergence of communes. In West Berlin, Kommune 1 (whose founding members included five men, including Fritz Teufel and Dieter Kunzelmann, and two women, Dagmar Seehuber and Dorothea Ridder) consciously constituted itself in early 1967 as an alternative living arrangement and a public spectacle in opposition to bourgeois society. Kommune 1 members (the personnel changed over the less than three years of the commune's existence) played with the notion of generational conflict ('we are the people our parents warned us against') and quickly succeeded in grabbing the attention of the mainstream media. Dieter Kunzelmann in particular was influenced by the international Situationist movement that sought to undermine existing mental and political power structures through spectacular action. He initiated numerous 'happenings'—from having members photographed in the nude from behind while leaning against a wall; to burning effigies of US president Johnson and SED leader Ulbricht on Berlin's *Kurfürstendamm*; to a foiled 'pudding attack' on US vice president Hubert Humphrey. The idea was to shock 'saturated' fellow citizens out of their complacency, by condoning, for example, a department store fire in Brussels, in which 300 people died, as 'an attack on King Consumer' to be emulated in West Germany and 'to reveal that crackling Vietnam feeling (being there and burning along).' Kommune 1 members were among the first to sell propaganda material from the Cultural Revolution underway in Mao's China (which *Der Spiegel* described as part of an international youth revolt). The anti-authoritarians of Kommune 1 were by no means representative of a broader radical movement, however, and in spring 1967, the Berlin SDS ejected members of Kommune 1 for their unorthodox activities.[23]

The breaking of sexual taboos in verbal and photographic self-representations was one of the ways in which Kommune 1 was able to gain media attention. The fantasies that members of the commune at once fostered and satirized were thoroughly heterosexual and sexist. In one magazine, a male member of the Kommune 1 claimed that commune men tried to convince women to change male partners regularly and to see sex as an expression of lust not love. 'Whoever sleeps twice with the same woman, already belongs to the establishment,' was how one slogan put it. Accusations that Kommune 1 established new forms of sexual coercion soon surfaced among its leftist critics. (Apparently members also received a personal reminder from Marcuse on a visit to the commune that sexual liberation did not mean promiscuity.)[24] Yet their activities and media reception were part of a broader change that took place in societies East and West of the Iron Curtain. Pre- and extramarital heterosexual relations and pleasure became far more acceptable, at a time when what contemporaries began to call a sex wave or a sexual revolution played out in the media. Women in poses that suggested 'sexiness' had already become a staple of magazines such as *Twen* by the second half of the 1950s and the mid- to late 1960s saw a veritable explosion of female nudity on the covers of magazines, including the leftist *Konkret*. By the late 1960s, films, usually under the guise of reportage or education, likewise showed nudity and sex, and gave advice on enhancing heterosexual pleasure. Radicals and left liberals alike now interpreted National Socialism as having repressed sexuality, and by extension understood the conservatism of the 1950s as a holdover of fascist values. It was in this context that the photo of the nude Kommune 1 from May 1967 ('nude Maoists in front of a nude wall,' as *Der Spiegel* popularized it) resonated.[25]

A coalition from younger and older generations fostered new attitudes towards sexuality in a number of institutions. By the late 1960s numerous voices within the Protestant Church argued for greater tolerance of premarital sex, more liberal divorce laws and the significance of sex within marriage. Catholics too began to call for a revision of anti-sex attitudes in Christian morality, and in 1968 the Catholic bishops of West Germany articulated the possibility, against guidelines issued by the Vatican, that spouses in a Catholic marriage could, if their conscience required, use birth control. For many voices in Germany, sexual expressiveness guaranteed a better life, as well as a successful overcoming of National Socialism and more generally of authoritarian structures.[26]

This sexual revolution was primarily a heterosexual revolution, but, within narrow limits, attitudes towards homosexuality changed as well. Liberal lawyers and social scientists pushed for the reform of Paragraph 175, which had criminalized male homosexuality since 1871 and which the Nazis radicalized in 1935. Yet efforts to make sex between men over 21 legal, which succeeded in West Germany in 1969, were accompanied by extensive testimony about the dangers of seduction for younger men and the potential for social deviance among homosexual men. In East Germany, the more stringent Nazi regulations were rejected in 1950 and the law was no longer enforced for sexual relations between adult men from the late 1950s onward. In 1968, a new criminal law made sexual relations between adult men and women and adolescents under sixteen illegal. Here legal reform co-existed with severe sanctions against homosexual men in many GDR institutions, such as the army or police.[27]

The changing legal and rhetorical frameworks for abortion reveal another dynamic of reform in the arenas of sexuality and reproduction in the East Germany of the 1960s. It was the 'experts,' doctors and health officials, favoring easier access to abortions, who quietly pushed through a change in policy, without public debate, but in conversation with arguments about a female right to self-determination made by East German women petitioners (these arguments were also made by Western experts and exchanged at international conferences). While governmental concern over births never disappeared, the 1960s saw a temporary turn away from worries about shrinking population size that had dominated anxieties in numerous industrialized countries. Larger, rather than smaller populations now seemed a liability for prosperity, and well-educated working women a key to progress. The East German abortion law was liberalized in 1965, and first-trimester abortions became freely available in 1972. It would take the Federal Republic four more years and public action by a new women's movement to make first-trimester abortions broadly available, if with more restrictions than in East Germany. Changes in abortion laws show that greater self-determination was a goal experts and common citizens expressed in both East and West Germany, but that in this case, the East German system was quicker to respond with reform than the West German one—and much slower than its communist Eastern allies.[28]

In West more than East Germany, leftists and liberals also debated childhood, parenting, and education in the 1960s. Kommune 1 and its sister Kommune 2 became known for unconventional childrearing methods. Taking children out of the nuclear family, and distributing the tasks of caring for them and for the household equally among men and women, *Kommune* members sought to shape new humans. From 1967 onward, New Left women and men also founded new independent and alternative childcare centers in West Germany that were designed to put the anti-authoritarian theories of Wilhelm Reich and the Scottish educator Alexander Sutherland Neill (founder of the famous Summerhill School) into practice. The childcare centers allowed children to explore the world and their sexuality independently, rejected coercive toilet-training, and sought to expunge the authoritarian patterns of mothers and fathers. For many on the left, these centers were part of revolutionary practice.

Changing behavioral boundaries for children led to much debate among experts and the parents involved, and to sensationalist portrayals of disobedient or dirty children in the mainstream press. In less radical versions, however, these changing practices also influenced reform in early childhood and elementary school education in the 1970s. As West Germans sought to reorganize the disciplining of children, they debated and then abolished corporal punishment in schools in 1973. Polls show that in the minds of more and more Germans, 'discipline and diligence' lost importance, while 'self-determination and free will' gained in significance. While self-determination (*Selbständigkeit*) was a goal for 28 percent of West German respondents in 1954, twenty years later it had become the most often given educational aim, voiced by 53 percent of the respondents.[29]

In the GDR of the 1960s, experts debated the effects of institutional care on children when, as was expected, both parents worked; in the end mothers held prime responsibility for high standards of parental involvement in children's development and many mothers insisted on part-time work as long as children lived at home. Corporal punishment in schools was prohibited in the GDR since 1949, but unlike in West Germany, no broad public debate existed about authoritarianism in families.[30]

Yet East Berlin too saw the forming of a commune. K 1 Ost was founded in 1968 after the Soviet invasion in Czechoslovakia by the children of fairly privileged parents, such as Frank Havemann, son of East German chemist and dissident Robert Havemann, and Erika Berthold, the daughter of a high-level government official. (Berthold, Frank Havemann, and his brother Florian were among those who protested the violent end of the Prague Spring in August 1968, and were arrested for their actions.) The commune existed until 1973 with revolving membership and in different apartments.

Its goals were similar to those of the anti-authoritarians in the West: to find new paths of self-discovery and thereby to change society. Members sought to transform gender roles, and engaged intensely with Marxism and psychoanalysis, as well as with anti-authoritarian child rearing literature smuggled in from the West. Like their West Berlin counterparts, Kommune 1 and 2 (some of whose members actually visited them over the years), the commune was shaken by conflicts over living arrangements and by debates over whether to work for change within official institutions. Unlike its West Berlin counterparts, Kommune 1 Ost could not access a public sphere in the GDR and for fear of reprisal avoided media attention from the West; necessarily it had much more limited impact.[31]

The communes of the late 1960s were part of an effort to find fundamentally democratic forms of self-determination. Living according to the maxim 'the personal is political,' members tried to create relationships unburdened by traditional social boundaries, and made this effort part of their critique of the social and economic system of the FRG and of the GDR. Fan mail to Kommune 1 is testimony that many young people perceived its members as models to emulate.[32] Communal living arrangements became common for young West Germans, especially students, over the next decade, as the law that prohibited giving shelter to unmarried couples was first no longer enforced and then abolished in 1973. Neither in East nor in West Germany, nor in other countries, did the counter culture constitute a unified movement, but because of the considerable media attention that youth and alternative forms of living received it influenced popular culture and everyday life.

Many East and West German rebels in the 1960s engaged in a search for authenticity in cultural forms and personal expression, interpreting authenticity as a condition for political transformation. Experimentation with drugs was one manifestation of this search, the attraction to folksongs another. Any claim to purely aesthetic experiences met with great suspicion. Yet those searching for the authentic saw themselves in a constant battle with the forces of commodification, which were indeed very quick to capitalize on the cultural caché of international rebellion. In 1967, a West German advertisement promoted suits in the 'Mao-Look,' 'the fashion style of the young guards' for the bourgeois woman customer. From 1965 onward, advertising pioneer Charles Wilp used black female models in a number of successful advertizing campaigns for West German companies to sell soda, for example. Wilp drew on traditions of exoticism *and* deployed icons of black glamour and black pride, such as the afro hairstyle. Iconographically his commercial imagery was actually more challenging than the soft-porn or primitivist representations of black bodies found in the leftist journal *konkret*. At once playing with and countering narrow visions of black authenticity, Wilp's adverts commercially expressed a multi-faceted West German 'Afro-Americanophilia' that manifested itself also in valorizations of soul, Black Power, or interracial sex. Often German 'Afro-Americanophilia' hinged on a construction of authentic 'black culture,' in which music, aesthetics, politics, and everyday style formed a unity—in contrast to the experiences of alienation and sexual narrow-mindedness in 'German' or 'Western culture.'[33]

28.4 ON THE PATH TO REVOLUTION?

Before June 1967 was over, depictions of nudity in commune living competed with the image of the most famous victim of state repression, the photo of the dying student Benno Ohnesorg. Shot in the head by a plain-clothes police detective during a demonstration against a visit by the Shah of Iran to West Berlin, Ohnesorg died on 2 June 1967. As the police tried to disperse demonstrators at the anti-Shah demonstration, small units of policemen beat up young men and women. The West Berlin mayor subsequently put responsibility for Ohnesorg's death not on the police, but on the demonstrators, whom the police had beaten up. The right-wing Springer tabloid *Bild* even compared the demonstrators to Nazi stormtroopers intent on destroying the public peace. As a result, Ohnesorg became a martyr for the rebellion, and demonstrators now believed themselves to be in a situation similar to the Nazi rise to power in 1933, when communists were among the first victims of the Nazis.

At a convention organized by SDS the day after Ohnesorg's funeral, a telling rift manifested itself: student leader Rudi Dutschke, himself an unorthodox Marxist and anti-Stalinist, attacked the critique of the 'authoritarian meritocracy' (*Leistungsgesellschaft)* made at the same event by Frankfurt philosophy professor Jürgen Habermas. Accusing Habermas of 'clubbing to death the emancipatory subject' with his 'formless objectivism,' Dutschke demanded 'direct action' in the form of sit-in strikes at universities, at a time 'when the productive forces had reached a point where it is possible to abolish hunger, war, and tyranny.' In turn, Habermas responded to Dutschke's attack, and a lack of clarity about whether violence should be employed in the service of radical transformation, by accusing the student rebels of 'leftist fascism'—a provocative and devastating attack on anti-authoritarians who saw themselves as anti-fascists and victims of a renewed fascism.[34]

Ohnesorg's death at the hand of a policeman, a West Berlin court's failure to convict Ohnesorg's killer, and trials of demonstrators reinforced a more general suspicion of the 'emissaries' of the liberal welfare state—not merely in the police and the judiciary, but also in schools and universities, in psychiatric hospitals, and in other institutions. A few weeks later at a conference of SDS delegates in Frankfurt in the summer of 1967, Dutschke, by now anointed the leader of the radical movement by the mainstream media, spoke of an 'urban guerilla' who 'is the organizer of complete irregularity as a means of destroying the system of repressive institutions.' The SDS conference approved a 'Resolution for the Fight against Manipulation and for the Democratization of the Public,' which demanded that the media be brought under public ownership and control and that 'consumer propaganda' be replaced 'with factual information for the consumer.' At the same time, SDS also committed itself to critical, alternative universities on American models. Revolution was on the agenda, but the path remained unclear.[35]

By summer 1968, about half of German students, around 150,000, had participated in strikes or demonstrations, with intense media attention contributing to a sense among participants that they were motors of historic change. At the end of an international Vietnam convention in West Berlin in February 1968, 12,000 people demonstrated in strong identification with the Vietcong, whose 'fight for the Vietnamese Revolution [was] part of the liberation of all humans from oppression and exploitation.' The New Left saw itself under the moral obligation to support liberation movements in the Third World and thereby also to foster radical change, perhaps even revolution in the metropole.[36]

Some now drifted towards violence. In early April 1968, Gudrun Ensslin, Andreas Baader, and two other founding members of what would in 1970 become the terrorist group Red Army Faction (RAF) planted bombs at two Frankfurt department stores, which caused damage to goods and structures. In explicit emulation of the Black Panthers in the United States, the future RAF members sought to deploy 'guerilla tactics' to 'protest the indifference with which the people watch the genocide in Vietnam.' This act put leftist terrorism into the spotlight, but it also revealed the lack of cohesion within the student rebellion. Kommune 1 distanced itself from the bombing, explicitly questioning the implied equivalence of blacks in the United States and students in West Germany. In turn, Baader's defense attorney, Horst Mahler, and Ensslin's estranged partner, the radical writer Bernward Vesper, characterized the action as a generational battle against a parents' generation inactive in the face of Nazi crimes, and still in positions of judicial and political power.[37]

Political mobilization and demonstrator violence in West Germany reached a high-point in April 1968 when Dutschke was shot and almost killed by a laborer who had articles from the Neo-Nazi press in his pockets. Students made the Springer media responsible for inciting the assassination attempt, which came on the heels of the assassination of Martin Luther King, Jr in Memphis. The West German so-called Easter riots engulfed several West German cities. Unlike in France, where May 1968 saw a short-lived alliance of workers and students, such an alliance never materialized in West Germany. Yet even in France those who thought they were on a path to revolution clearly overestimated their power.

By the summer break, West German students seemed exhausted. The Great Coalition had passed the Emergency Laws in May 1968 (thereby taking another step toward West German sovereignty) and students were further disappointed in August 1968 when the Soviet invasion of Czechoslovakia put a violent end to the Prague Spring. Kommune 1 dissolved in 1969 due to internal conflict and drug addiction. The disbanding of the SDS in 1970 completed what had been clear much earlier; that the rebellions of the 1960s did not have uniform goals and that they did not have the power to effect political revolution.

Arguably many participants shared the conclusion formulated by Habermas in 1968 that they had witnessed a political '*Scheinrevolution*'—a 'pretend revolution'—and embarked on one of three paths. A minority engaged in terrorism, while others organized in vocal Marxists groups ranging from Trotskyites to the newly founded German Communist Party (DKP).[38] Many more sought to work for transformation 'through a long march through the institutions.' For some that meant entering state institutions, especially academia, for many others it meant work as writers, intellectuals, or as activists in a host of groups. Often described as new social movements, these groups addressed a range of issues from the environment to women's rights and the reform of psychiatric hospitals.[39]

In West Germany a newly organized feminist movement also had its roots in the ferment of the 1960s. Identification with the term feminist was more difficult in West Germany than in France or in Anglo-Saxon countries, and nearly unthinkable in communist East Germany. Whether they called themselves feminist or not, women in West and East made the particular social position of women and their roles in families, workplaces, politics—and history—an explicit issue. The main West German political organizations of the 1960s rebellions were, without a doubt, male dominated, even if women like Sigrun Fronius and Sigrid Rüger became important elected leaders of West Berlin students by the second half of the 1960s. In the public portrayals of communes and political actions men also dominated, while some women, like Kommune 1 member and model Uschi Obermaier, appeared in glossy photographs as sex symbols. Ever increasing numbers of women students began meeting in West Berlin in late 1967 in an action council (*Aktionsrat*) to discuss the problems of mothers' and women's position in society more generally, and to work on the founding of new anti-authoritarian children's centers. At a September 1968 SDS convention, film student Helke Sander gave an unscheduled speech as a representative of the *Aktionsrat*, demanding that male comrades examine themselves critically and make the social position of women an explicit topic. When the SDS leadership refused a discussion of Sander's speech, a visibly pregnant Rüger famously threw tomatoes at the podium. These women's actions showed that they, like so many who associated with the New Left, believed in the 'clarifying effect of provocation.'[40] Thus, the Frankfurt women's council (*Weiberrat*) demanded at an SDS conference, 'Liberate the socialist pricks from their bourgeois dicks,' while in a Hamburg courtroom, women activists bared their breasts to use sexuality as a means in the fight for emancipation and to withdraw it from the abusive use in advertising. Several independent groups had formed to study the situation of women and they came to understand themselves as part of a new women's movement, whose radicalism was 'in distinction' to an earlier 'bourgeois' women's movement. Some of the arguments formulated by women's groups aimed at transformation within a splintering revolutionary movement, in which the anti-authoritarians were losing dominance in 1968 and 1969; others called for female separatism. Thus, the women's groups that had emerged as part of the New Left were likewise shaken by disagreement: about the significance of motherhood, and about the relationship between women's emancipation and revolution. Like SDS, these groups disbanded soon, but the networks established around the New Left would be an important foundation for 1970s feminist activism in West Germany. Their activities would also be watched with a critical eye by East German writers like Brigitte Reimann who discussed the situation of women with renewed vigor in their fiction in the 1970s.[41]

By 1969, more West German fringe groups styled themselves as 'urban guerillas' engaged in an armed anti-imperialist struggle. Among the most controversial was

'Tupamaros Berlin-West,' which was modeled on the 'Tupamaros' in Uruguay and founded after some of its members, including Kunzelmann, pursued military training in a Palestinian camp in Jordan. The organization attempted to explode the Jewish Community Building in Berlin on 9 November, 1969, when Jewish community members had gathered to commemorate the Night of Broken Glass. A technical defect kept the bomb from exploding, but the attack, had it been successful, would have resulted in a huge loss of life. Scholars differ about what the botched attack says about anti-Semitism among the West German New Left of the 1960s.[42] Early in the decade Israeli *kibbutzim* had found many admirers among New Leftists. But after the 1967 War between Israel and its Arab neighbors, a radicalized student movement applied a very broad definition of fascism—as an expression of capitalism that necessarily manifested itself in imperialist expansion—also to Israel. Seeing Israel as imperialist led to increasing solidarity with Palestinians, and a new fashion code of Palestinian scarves around the necks of many West German youth, but not to widespread support for terrorism. This interpretation of fascism also failed to recognize the significance of racism for National Socialism and the frequent proximity of anti-Zionism and anti-Semitism.[43]

In East Germany, much less room existed for public critique of political institutions—and there was no temporary softening similar to the Prague Spring. At the occasion of a protest against the demolition of the church at Leipzig University in May 1968, the singer and poet Bettina Wegner, who would later leave the GDR, wrote a poem directed against the regime. It equated the suppression of rebellious youth as *Gammler* (do-nothings) and the forced haircuts administered by state youth or police as a continuation of practices at Auschwitz. 'Twenty years ago in Auschwitz, we found hair in masses, well, raise your glasses, Karl Marx as barber, an army's on the move, ... armed with sheers, the bloody German hair-collectors, beat the *Gammler*! Hurrah, the *Gammler*!'[44] In East Germany too, activists constructed rhetorical equivalences between the Nazi past and their present, but in contrast to West Germany, such a critique had little chance to find broad public airing.

Whereas West German students were more likely than workers to be involved in protests, East German students tended to have strong allegiances to the regime and were less likely than workers to voice discontent. When a few hundred of them participated in painting graffiti or distributing leaflets against the Soviet invasion of Czechoslovakia (in which East German troops participated by securing the border), their actions were likely indicative of their distance to the East German state, rather than a sign of engagement for the reform of socialism. East German authorities reacted with arrests and by making alleged enemy actions, including the distribution of Western music, responsible for a harmful 'depoliticization' of youth.[45]

Meanwhile, the relationship of West German rebels to state socialism was a consistent bone of contention. Many, like Rudi Dutschke who himself hailed from the GDR, were quite critical of state socialism. The lack of enthusiastic support for the Prague Spring on the part of SDS and the New Left more generally suggested ambivalence. Some found themselves drawn to the model of the Chinese Cultural Revolution, willfully ignoring the reports about the immense human suffering it brought about.

Only after the collapse of East Germany would it become clear how close the links to state socialists at times were. SDS organizers of an anti Vietnam-War exhibit in 1965 got much of their material from the North Vietnamese embassy in East Berlin. The left magazine *Konkret* received financial support from East Germany. The shooter of Benno Ohnesorg, as we now know, was a Stasi spy. By the 1980s some of the RAF terrorists retired in the GDR. Of course, such links do not mean that the GDR successfully steered West German radicalism.

28.5 CONCLUSION: GENERATIONAL POSITIONS

As we have seen, many West German participants in 1960s rebellions thought of themselves as members of an international movement that sought fundamental transformations of personality and political structures in the name of democracy. A contemporary understanding of the simultaneity of international rebellion fostered by the media and travel contributed to a sense of generational cohesion. While there is little doubt that many contemporaries (and commentators since) saw the West German 1960s as a conflict between a generation ready to break authoritarian mental and institutional structures, and an older generation tainted by National Socialism, the situation is clearly more complex. To take generational conflict as an explanation for change in the 1960s can obscure as much as it clarifies.

In the West, many of those interested in university or sexual reform spanned generations. Particularly influential were members of the so-caller '45er generation' who, born in the 1920s and 1930s, had reached positions of public influence at a relatively young age by the 1950s and 1960s. Jürgen Habermas can be taken as one representative of the 45er generation of reformers, and his interactions with the student revolt and especially Rudi Dutschke were in a sense paradigmatic for tensions in the relationship of reform and revolt. Although a mere eleven years separated Habermas's and Dutschke's years of birth (1929 and 1940), their disagreements were understood by contemporaries as a political and generational rift. However, just as Dutschke found vocal supporters among older generations of leftists, among them Martin Niemoeller, Wolfgang Abendroth and Herbert Marcuse, there were critics of a revolutionary *habitus* in both its anti-authoritarian and more orthodox Marxist versions among Dutschke's age group.[46]

If one can, nevertheless, speak of an experience of 'generational warfare' for many in West Germany, as well as in other European countries and in the United States, it did not exist in East Germany. A 1969 survey revealed little conflict among East German adolescents and their parents. In contrast to West German autobiographies, which are filled with disappointment and rejection of parents, especially fathers, East German autobiographies by the same age group express solidarity with their parents whom sons and daughters perceived as victims or at least objects of external control.[47]

1960s rebellions were heterogeneous, they sometimes had contradictory goals, and they led to multifaceted outcomes. To see 1968 as having been dealt a 'crushing defeat' is thus exaggerated.[48] In the West 1968 failed as a revolution in the sense of over-throwing a political system, but helped speed up reform and social change. In West Germany in 1969, Willy Brandt attracted voters almost 25 years after the end of World War II with the slogan 'dare more democracy' and became chancellor. Over the next years, the stakeholders in many West German institutions would look critically at decision-making processes and structures of authority, even as the state reacted with repression to the threat of terrorism. In East Germany too calls for self-determination were part of changes in matters such as abortion rights and sexual relations. However, Honecker's 1971 promise 'When one proceeds from the position of socialism . . . there can be no taboos,' remained largely unfulfilled.[49]

As the press stylized youth as a trendsetter in matters of consumption and politics, youth movements in East and West broke down conservative obstacles to consumption a process that had already begun in the first decades of the twentieth century.[50] Lasting changes in East and West included transformations in gender relations and less supervision of premarital relations between the sexes. Among the positive outcomes of sixties rebellions were also greater and safer possibilities for expression in subcul-tures and new social movements, which regularly looked and worked across national boundaries, but which had far fewer opportunities for institutionalization in East than in West Germany. The events of the late 1960s were part of longer-term processes of reform, but one should recognize that many in the West experienced the public presence of a commune, the liberalization of sexual mores, the proliferation of 'under-ground' publications, the challenging of authority in schools and universities, the sudden increase in conscientious objectors for military service, or the founding of women's centers as a positive (or negative) break with the past.[51]

No doubt the 1960s revolts fostered in East and West Germany, as elsewhere, a more critical examination of corporate, military and political power, as well as skepticism about the terms in which scientific knowledge and cultural canons were produced and used to govern. The multifaceted rebellions in Germany and around the world in the 1960s resulted in a Western world more willing to examine itself critically, but efforts of questioning for example sexual norms in Germany or 'the West' often relied on reductionist, or even racist and imperialist visions of other cultures.[52] In West Germany, an expansion of the university system was among the motors and outcomes of rebellion. In some sense the 1960s protest movements were most successful in the academy and in the world of publishing and the media, where they succeeded in redefining research agendas and in pushing new ideas about social change into the mainstream. These developments help explain the unusual drive and ability of the West German 1960s cohort to participate in the sixties meaning-making through autobiographical narratives.[53]

Even if the effort to find a generation of politically engaged 68ers in the GDR says more about the pressures of the 1990s than about political engagement in the 1960s, one can nonetheless speak of a generation of 'cultural 68ers' and similarities in the cultural orientations and lifestyles of East and West Germans.[54] Because of the fear of reprisal and the restrictions of expression, coming of age in the GDR of the 1960s meant being disciplined more tightly by school, party, and state than in the West. Yet evidence of more insistence on self-determination exists in East Germany as well, visible in petitions to authorities, divorce proceedings, or in music scenes in village restaurants.[55] Overall, however, the late 1960s meant less of a caesura for East than for West Germans.

NOTES

1. Bernd Lindner, 'Zwischen Integration und Distanzierung: Jugendgenerationen in der DDR in der sechziger und siebziger Jahren,' *Aus Politik und Zeitgeschichte* B45 (2003), 33–39; Timothy S. Brown, '"1968" East and West: Divided Germany as a Case Study in Transnational History,' *American Historical Review* 114 (February 2009), 69–96. For their helpful suggestions on earlier drafts, I would like to thank Ruth Feldstein, Robert Moeller, and especially Helmut Walser Smith.

2. Recent examples include Götz Aly, *Unser Kampf: 1968—Ein irritierter Blick zurück* (Frankfurt am Main: Fischer, 2008); Hans-Ulrich Wehler, *Deutsche Gesellschaftsgeschichte Bd. 5: Bundesrepublik und DDR 1949–1990* (Munich: Beck, 2008).

3. Christina von Hodenberg and Detlef Siegfried (eds), *Wo '1968' liegt: Reform und Revolte in der Geschichte der Bundesrepublik* (Göttingen: Vandenhoeck & Ruprecht, 2006); Norbert Frei, *1968: Jugendrevolte und Globaler Protest* (München: Deutscher Taschenbuch Verlag, 2008); Sven Reichardt, 'Authentizität und Gemeinschaftsbindung, Politik und Lebensstil im linksalternativen Milieu vom Ende der 1960er bis zum Anfang der 1980er Jahre,' *Forschungsjournal NSB* 21, no. 3 (2008): 118–130; Donna Harsch, *Revenge of the Domestic: Women, the Family, and Communism in the German Democratic Republic* (Princeton: Princeton University Press, 2007); Dorothee Wierling, *Geboren im Jahr Eins: Der Jahrgang 1949 in der DDR: Versuch einer Kollektivbiographie* (Berlin: Links, 2002).

4. On this concept, see Michael J. Shapiro, 'Moral Geographies and the Ethics of Post-Sovereignty,' *Public Culture* 6, no. 3 (1994), 41–70.

5. Uta G. Poiger, *Jazz, Rock, and Rebels: Cold War Politics and American Culture in a Divided Germany* (Berkeley: University of California Press, 2000).

6. Detlef Siegfried, *Time Is on My Side: Konsum und Politik in der westdeutschen Jugendkultur der 60er Jahre* (Göttingen: Wallstein, 2006); Michael Rauhut, *Beat in der Grauzone: DDR-Rock 1964 bis 1972, Politik und Alltag* (Berlin: BasisDruck, 1993).

7. Kommuniqué des SED-Politbüros, September 17, 1963, reprinted in excerpts in Ulrich Mählert and Gerd-Rüdiger Stephan, *Blaue Hemden, Rote Fahnen: Die Geschichte der Freien Deutschen Jugend* (Opladen: Leske & Budrich, 1996), 150–152.

8. Mählert and Stephan, *Blaue Hemden*, 152–160; Rauhut, *Beat*, chapter 2; Siegfried, *Time*.

9. Rauhut, *Beat*, chapter 3; Dorothee Wierling, 'Youth as Internal Enemy: Conflicts in the Education Dictatorship of the 1960s,' in Katherine Pence and Paul Betts (eds), *Socialist Modern: East German Everyday Culture and Politics* (Ann Arbor: University of Michigan Press, 2008), 157–181; Mark Fenemore, *Sex, Thugs and Rock 'n' Roll: Teenage Rebels in Cold-War East Germany* (New York: Berghahn Books, 2007).

10. 'Stenographische Niederschrift,' December 15–17, 1965, SAPMO-BArch DY30 IV 2/1 336 cited in Poiger, *Jazz*, 216–217; Rauhut, *Beat*; Marc-Dietrich Ohse, *Jugend nach dem Mauerbau: Anpassung, Protest und Eigensinn (DDR 1961–1974)* (Berlin: Links, 2003).

11. Rauhut, *Beat*, 212–216; Wierling, *Geboren*.

12. Moritz Scheibe, 'Auf der Suche nach der demokratischen Gesellschaft,' in Ulrich Herbert (ed.), *Wandlungsprozesse in Westdeutschland: Belastung, Integration, Liberalisierung 1945–1980* (Göttingen: Wallstein, 2002), 245–277; especially Ralf Dahrendorf, *Gesellschaft und Freiheit: Zur soziologischen Analyse der Gegenwart* (München: R. Piper, 1961); and Jürgen Habermas, *The Structural Transformation of the Public Sphere: An Inquiry into a Category of Bourgeois Society* (Cambridge: MIT Press, 1989, published in German in 1962).

13. SDS quoted in Niels Seibert, *Vergessene Proteste: Internationalismus und Antirassismus 1964–1983*, 1st edn (Münster: Unrast, 2008), 21. See also Katrina Hagen, 'Internationalism in Cold War Germany' (PhD Dissertation, University of Washington, 2008); Ingo Juchler, *Die Studentenbewegungen in den Vereinigten Staaten und der Bundesrepublik Deutschland der Sechziger Jahre: Eine Untersuchung hinsichtlich ihrer Beeinflussung durch Befreiungsbewegungen und -theorien aus der Dritten Welt* (Berlin: Duncker & Humblot, 1996).

14. Seibert, *Vergessene Proteste*, 27–49, quote on 39; Hagen, 'Internationalism,' chapters 2–4; Nick Thomas, *Protest Movements in 1960s West Germany: A Social History of Dissent and Democracy* (Oxford: Berg, 2003), 94–97.

15. Henning Marmulla, 'Das Kursbuch: Nationale Zeitschrift, internationale Kommunikation, transnationale Öffentlichkeit,' in Martin Klimke and Joachim Scharloth (eds), *1968: Handbuch zur Kultur-und Mediengeschichte der Studentenbewegung* (Stuttgart: J. B. Metzler, 2007), 37–47.

16. See Seibert, *Vergessene Proteste*; Hagen, 'Internationalism;' Brown, '"1968" East and West.'

17. Kaja Shonick, *Émigrés, Guest Workers, and Refugees: Yugoslav Migrants in the Federal Republic of Germany, 1945–1995* (PhD dissertation, University of Washington, 2008); William Glenn Gray, *Germany's Cold War: The Global Campaign to Isolate East Germany, 1949–1969* (Chapel Hill: University of North Carolina Press, 2003); Jeremi Suri, *Power and Protest: Global Revolution and the Rise of Detente* (Cambridge: Harvard University Press, 2003).

18. Michael Schneider, *Demokratie in Gefahr: Der Konflikt um die Notstandsgesetze: Sozialdemokratie, Gewerkschaften und intellektueller Protest (1958–1968)* (Bonn: Neue Gesellschaft, 1986).

19. 'Controlling political analogies' in Wilfried Mausbach, 'Auschwitz and Vietnam: West German Protest Against America's War During the 1960s,' in Andreas W. Daum, Lloyd C. Gardner, and Wilfried Mausbach (eds), *America, the Vietnam War, and the World: Comparative and International Perspectives* (New York: Cambridge University Press, 2003), 279–298, 287; see also Seibert, *Vergessene Proteste*.

20. Mausbach, 'Auschwitz und Vietnam,' 289.

21. Hagen, 'Internationalism,' introduction and chapters 2–4, 'SS executioners' in chapter 2; Mählert and Stephan, *Blaue Hemden*, 187–188, 196.

22. Sabine Weißler, 'Unklare Verhältnisse: 1968 und die Mode,' in Klimke and Scharloth, *1968*, 305–310.

23. Uta G. Poiger, 'Imperialism and Consumption: Two Tropes in West German Radicalism of the 1960s and 1970s,' in Axel Schildt und Detlef Siegfried (eds), *Between Marx and Coca-Cola: Youth Cultures in Changing European Societies, 1960–1980* (New York: Berghahn Books, 2006), 161–172, 164–165; Frei, *1968*, 110–111; Brown, '"1968" East and West;' 'Übertriebene Generation,' *Der Spiegel*, October 2, 1967, 154–170.

24. Ulrich Enzensberger, *Die Jahre Der Kommune I: Berlin 1967–1969* (Cologne: Kiepenheuer & Witsch, 2004), 186–187.

25. Dagmar Herzog, *Sex After Fascism: Memory and Morality in Twentieth-Century Germany* (Princeton: Princeton University Press, 2007), chapter 4; Pascal Eitler, 'Die "sexuelle Revolution" ': Körperpolitik um 1968,' in Klimke and Scharloth, *1968*, 235–246.

26. Herzog, *Sex after Fascism*.

27. Robert G. Moeller, 'Private Acts, Public Anxieties, and the Fight to Decriminalize Male Homosexuality in the Federal Republic of Germany,' *Feminist Studies* 36,3 (Fall 2010), Jennifer Evans, 'Decriminalization, Seduction, and 'Unnatural Desire' in the GDR,' *Feminist Studies*, 36,3 (Fall 2010).

28. Harsch, *Revenge*, chapter 7.

29. Herzog, *Sex after Fascism*, 162–174; Dirk Schumann, 'Legislation and Liberalization: The Debate About Corporal Punishment in Schools in Postwar West Germany, 1945–1975,' *German History* 25, no. 2 (April 2007), 192–218; Miriam Gebhardt, *Die Angst vor dem kindlichen Tyrannen: Eine Geschichte der Erziehung im 20. Jahrhundert* (Munich: DVA, 2009); polls cited in Scheibe, 'Auf der Suche,' 259–260.

30. Harsch, *Revenge*, especially 297–303.

31. Timothy S. Brown, 'East Germany,' in Martin Klimke and Joachim Scharloth (eds), *1968 in Europe: A History of Protest and Activism, 1956–1977* (New York: Palgrave Macmillan, 2008), 189–198; Ute Kätzel, 'Erika Berthold und die Kommune 1 Ost,' in Kätzel (ed.), *Die 68erinnen: Porträt einer rebellischen Frauengeneration* (Berlin: Rowohlt, 2002), 220–237.

32. Brown, ' "1968" East and West.'

33. Reichardt, 'Authentizität und Gemeinschaftsbindung;' Mao fashion in Weißler, 'Unklare Verhältnisse,' 306; Moritz Ege, *Schwarz Werden: 'Afroamerikanophilie' in den 1960er und 1970er Jahren* (Bielefeld: Transcript, 2007).

34. See Frei, *1968*, especially 112–121, quotes on 120.

35. Frei, *1968*, 123–125.

36. Frei, *1968*, on student participation 148, quote on 129.

37. Poiger, 'Imperialism and Consumption,' 165.

38. Frei, *1968*, 148.

39. Frei, *1968*; Thomas, *Protest Movements*.

40. Kristina Schulz, 'The Women's Movement,' in Martin Klimke and Joachim Scharloth (eds), *1968 in Europe: A History of Protest and Activism, 1956–1977* (New York: Palgrave Macmillan, 2008), 281–294, 285.

41. Kristina Schulz, *Der lange Atem der Provokation: Die Frauenbewegung in der Bundesrepublik und in Frankreich, 1968–1976* (Frankfurt am Main: Campus, 2002), quote on 88.

42. Wolfgang Kraushaar, *Die Bombe im Jüdischen Gemeindehaus* (Hamburg: Hamburger Edition, 2005).

43. Frei, *1968*, 223–225; Christina von Hodenberg and Detlef Siegfried, 'Reform und Revolte: 1968 und die langen sechziger Jahre in der Geschichte der Bundesrepublik,' in Hodenberg and Siegfried, *Wo '1968' liegt*, 7–14, 11.

44. Robert-Havemann-Gesellschaft, *Archiv Heiko Leitz*, HL 160/2, quoted in Brown, "1968' East and West,' 87–88.

45. Wierling, *Geboren*, 295–316; Rauhut, *Beat*, 217–218; Poiger, *Jazz*, 218.

46. Hodenberg and Siegfried, 'Reform und Revolte,' 10–11; Herzog, *Sex after Fascism*; A. Dirk Moses, 'The Forty-Fivers: A Generation Between Fascism and Democracy,' *German Politics and Society* 17, no. 1 (1999), 105–127; Frei, *1968*.

47. Wierling, *Geboren*, 329–332.
48. For the emphasis on defeat, see Philipp Gassert, 'Narratives of Democratization: 1968 in Postwar Europe,' in Klimke and Scharloth, *1968 in Europe*, 307–324; Tony Judt, *Postwar: A History of Europe Since 1945* (New York: Penguin Press, 2005); for an emphasis on transformative power in the Cold War order, see Suri, *Power and Protest*.
49. Frei, 1968; Harsch, *Revenge*; Mary Fulbrook, *The People's State: East German Society from Hitler to Honecker* (New Haven: Yale University Press, 2005); Honecker quoted in Mary Fulbrook, *A History of Germany, 1918–2008: The Divided Nation*, 3rd edn (Chichester: Wiley-Blackwell, 2009), 246.
50. Stephan Malinowski and Alexander Sedlmaier, '"1968" als Katalysator der Konsumgesellschaft: Performative Regelverstöße, kommerzielle Adaptionen und ihre gegenseitige Durchdringung,' *Geschichte und Gesellschaft* 32, no. 2 (2006), 238–267; Siegfried, *Time*.
51. Hodenberg and Siegfried, 'Reform und Revolte,' 12.
52. Ege, *Schwarz Werden*; Eitler, 'Die 'sexuelle Revolution."
53. Christina von Hodenberg, 'Der Kampf um die Redaktionen: "1968" und der Wandel der westdeutschen Massenmedien,' in Hodenberg and Siegfried, *Wo '1968' liegt*, 139–163; Frei, 1968.
54. Wierling, *Geboren*, 332.
55. Ibid., 334; Harsch, *Revenge*; Fulbrook, *The People's State*.

BIBLIOGRAPHY

BROWN, TIMOTHY S., '"1968" East and West: Divided Germany as a Case Study in Transnational History,' *American Historical Review* 114 (February 2009), 69–96.

FENEMORE, MARK, *Sex, Thugs and Rock 'n' Roll: Teenage Rebels in Cold-war East Germany* (New York: Berghahn Books, 2007).

FINK, CAROLE, PHILIPP GASSERT, and DETLEF JUNKER (eds), *1968, the World Transformed.* (Cambridge: Cambridge University Press, 1998).

FREI, NORBERT, *1968: Jugendrevolte und globaler Protest* (Munich: DTV, 2008).

GILCHER-HOLTEY, INGRID, *1968: Eine Zeitreise* (Frankfurt am Main: Suhrkamp, 2008).

HARSCH, DONNA, *Revenge of the Domestic: Women, the Family, and Communism in the German Democratic Republic* (Princeton: Princeton University Press, 2007).

HERBERT, ULRICH (ed.), *Wandlungsprozesse in Westdeutschland: Belastung, Integration, Liberalisierung 1945–1980* (Göttingen: Wallstein, 2002).

HERZOG, DAGMAR, *Sex After Fascism: Memory and Morality in Twentieth-Century Germany* (Princeton: Princeton University Press, 2007).

HODENBERG, CHRISTINA VON and DETLEF SIEGFRIED (eds), *Wo '1968' liegt: Reform und Revolte in der Geschichte der Bundesrepublik* (Göttingen: Vandenhoeck & Ruprecht, 2006).

KLIMKE, MARTIN and JOACHIM SCHARLOTH (eds), *1968 in Europe: A History of Protest and Activism, 1956–1977* (New York: Palgrave Macmillan, 2008).

KNOCH, HABBO (ed.), *Bürgersinn mit Weltgefühl: Politische Moral und solidarischer Protest in den Sechziger und Siebziger Jahren* (Göttingen: Wallstein, 2007).

OHSE, MARC-DIETRICH, *Jugend nach dem Mauerbau: Anpassung, Protest und Eigensinn (DDR 1961–1974)* (Berlin: Links, 2003).

SCHILDT, AXEL, DETLEF SIEGFRIED, and KARL CHRISTIAN LAMMERS (eds), *Dynamische Zeiten: Die 60er Jahre in den beiden deutschen Gesellschaften* (Hamburg: Christians, 2000).

SIEGFRIED, DETLEF, *Time Is on My Side: Konsum und Politik in der westdeutschen Jugend-kultur der 60er Jahre* (Göttingen: Wallstein, 2006).

THOMAS, NICK, *Protest Movements in 1960s West Germany: A Social History of Dissent and Democracy* (Oxford: Berg, 2003).

....

CHAPTER 29

INDUSTRIALIZATION, MASS CONSUMPTION, POST-INDUSTRIAL SOCIETY

....

DONNA HARSCH

FRAMED by the postwar crisis and early Cold War rivalry, debate about the future of German class society began almost as soon as the war ended. Americans assured despairing Germans that the 'free market' would generate prosperity and foster social fairness. Communists promised the hungry masses that expropriation and nationalization of industry would create social equality and forge economic expansion. The former Allies and their German allies hotly disputed the meaning of economic prosperity and social equity, and how to attain them. Yet each side insisted that its system would deliver both and criticized old Germany for having failed to do so. Americans blamed its national peculiarities, while Communists condemned its class nature, but their critiques overlapped: German society was stratified, hierarchical, and loaded in favor of birthright. In the eyes of Americans and their German acolytes, the solution was to generate a wide, deep middle-class. Communists planned to fix class society by smashing the bourgeoisie and elevating the working-class.[1]

After 1949, the two Germanys continued to embody competition between capitalism and Communism. The fate of class society in each state always provoked debate, with several points of consensus emerging from a discussion increasingly centered on social and economic data, not crude propaganda. Both societies experienced an attenuation of socially-distinctive life styles. Germany's richly articulated 'workers' culture,' for example, never completely revived after National Socialist repression.[2] Scholars attribute these cultural changes to postwar economic prosperity. While the standard of living eventually rose in both societies, its increase in the Federal Republic (FRG) was astonishing. West Germany's national income quadrupled between 1950 and 1980, a steeper rise than in any other Western economy. Prosperity generated impressive income benefits for all sectors of society. There occurred, in the words of Rainer Geißler, an 'explosion in prosperity.'[3]

Beyond these conclusions, scholarly opinion divided along the earlier line of dispute: prosperity versus equality. Scholars debated whether the extraordinary increase in the West German standard of living was the main protagonist, indeed, the hero of postwar social development in *both* Germanys. Yes, answered one school of interpretation: the rising tide lifted all boats, drowning class society—and finally swamping East German socialism as well. Its adherents accepted, if with qualification, the claim by the sociologist Helmut Schelsky that a 'leveled middle-class society' was emerging in West Germany and other market-industrial societies by the mid-1950s.[4] No, responded members of the counter-interpretive school: the size of the boats still mattered despite prosperity. Social inequalities persisted, its adherents argued, and shaped the evolution of West German society after 1945.[5] Working in the tradition of critical societal analysis, they drew on Max Weber's understanding of class as an 'interest-camp' related to a 'way of life' and a porous sense of belonging. To interpret cultural milieus, they turned to Pierre Bourdieu's notion of socially-grounded 'fine distinctions.'[6]

East German society has been studied less than society in the FRG, although recent research has partially closed the gap. East Germany, studies have agreed, experienced a massive initial compression of vertical social divisions. Most Western scholars criticized this sudden, repressive equalization for creating a 'de-differentiated' society or a 'society leveled toward below.' They recognized that, nonetheless, the economy grew and the standard of living rose significantly before stagnation set in after 1970. The West German 'rising tide,' acknowledged scholars of all persuasions, influenced the social-cultural history of the German Democratic Republic (GDR).[7]

This chapter assesses change and continuity in German society between 1945 and 1990. Adopting the critical societal perspective, it treats disparities based on income, occupation, gender, and ethnicity as integral to the story. It is a comparative in two senses: it compares the social development of West and East Germany, and, where the data permit, it also considers the Germanys in relation to other industrial societies, especially in Western Europe. Structural similarity justifies comparison between the Germanys despite their different economic and social systems. It also justifies comparison between the Germanys and Western Europe despite their different war-time histories. In both Germanys, as well as throughout Western Europe, the form and function of the family, for example, tended to converge on the model of the nuclear family. All of these economies, moreover, experienced intense industrialization and, as a consequence, mobilized major new sources of labor. Not only Western Europe, but East Germany made the transition into mass consumption. Each country also had to adapt to the end of the industrial boom after 1970. In sections on the postwar crisis, the family, economic trends, the remaking of the working class, social inequalities, and mass consumption, this chapter explores the interactions between dynamic structural conditions, social homogenization, and social differentiation. It ends with a brief consideration of the fate of class society in re-unified Germany.

29.1 SOCIAL CONSEQUENCES OF THE SECOND WORLD WAR

The most significant social novelty for defeated Germany in 1945 was the massive influx of German refugees and expellees from the Sudetenland, Poland, and further east. Four million refugees settled in the eastern zone of occupation, while eight million migrated directly to the western zones. Eventually, a significant minority of those in the GDR moved westward (as part of the migration of three million people from East to West in the 1950s). Initially, though, both societies experienced a major infusion of non-native, German-speaking settlers who had to be integrated as workers and citizens. In 1950, these displaced, dispossessed people comprised about 20 percent of the East German and 17 percent of the West German population. What began as a gigantic burden became, however, a demographic advantage that fed industrial expansion and urbanization in the FRG and the GDR.[8] In 1960, 40 percent of the West German workforce was comprised of German-speaking immigrants, including expellees, refugees, and migrants from the GDR.[9] They manifested, according to the many studies of them, a distinctive mix of social behaviors. To regain former levels of income, refugees formed interest-groups that demanded state resources to 'balance' their losses. They also worked hard to 'make it' and fit in. Nonetheless, it took two generations for the majority of immigrants to pull even with native-born Germans. Parents cultivated in their children bourgeois values such as obedience, order, and 'decency.' Yet, far from elitist, refugees were perceived as scrappy and 'striving.' They nurtured customs from their 'Heimat,' even as they intermarried with natives at a steady clip.[10]

We know little about refugees in the GDR, for the SED did not treat them as a separate statistical category. It is clear that in the East, as in the West, large numbers of refugees quickly left rural areas where many were initially settled and took jobs in expanding industries in growing towns. Indirect evidence suggests that refugees who stayed in the GDR were well-integrated into the wider society by the 1960s—perhaps even better than in the West, for they could not form identity-cultivating refugee associations and lived in a society where everyone with wealth had lost it.[11]

A lopsidedly female adult population was a major demographic consequence of the war. The percentage of female-headed households remained high into the mid-1950s, especially in the GDR. All zones of occupation experienced a decline in fertility, a surge in infant mortality, and a leap in divorce, all of which prompted alarm and natalist policies in both states. As postwar turmoil subsided, the divorce rate declined, the birth rate rose, and many more babies survived in both Germanys—and elsewhere in Europe. To summarize, the war, postwar crisis, and emerging economic expansion unleashed significant demographic trends which generally moved in tandem in the 1950s.[12] There was an important exception to these parallels: the population of the FRG grew not only from natural increase, but also from the continuing immigration of German-speakers, while the GDR's natural increase was annulled by emigration to the

West. FRG gains from this infusion of skilled and educated laborers were impressive, but nothing like the demographic and economic losses experienced by the much smaller GDR.[13]

29.2 THE FAMILY

In addition to early crises, East and West Germany shared the enduring social formation of the nuclear family. Popular attachment to the family ran high after the war, nurtured by its extraordinary contribution to members' survival during upheaval and dearth. The family's hierarchical structure also emerged more or less unscathed. During the crisis women often constituted the bulwark of this 'vital community of solidarity,' yet this accomplishment did not translate into egalitarian gender relations inside the revitalized family. In both Germanys, as generally in the Western world, wives enjoyed less leisure time than husbands because they performed the lion's share of child care and household work.[14]

Certainly, the war and postwar crisis left marks on the family. Home became, for example, more central to male socializing, especially in working-class households, where husbands and fathers had earlier spent their scant free time in pubs or workers' organizations. The 'retreat into the family,' argues Josef Mooser, narrowed the social disparities of everyday life. The retreat is harder to perceive in East Germany. In the 1950s, when family advancement rested on the husband's shoulders, many men engaged in the political activity necessary for political and occupational success. Pressure to take part in public rituals, as well as shortages that placed a premium on family-based 'organization,' fed a tendency in the East, however, to depend on the family and withdraw into it to escape politicized activities.[15]

Meanwhile, changes in the 'who' and 'how' of domestic labor narrowed differences in the private routines of socially disparate women. Throughout Europe the percentage of families with a live-in servant fell after World War I and collapsed after World War II. Middle-strata women now performed much of their own housework and, in this regard, became more like worker-women.[16] As the era of full-time servants ended, the age of the mechanized household began. Before 1945, the rationalization of housework reached only solidly bourgeois homes in Europe, in contrast to wider expansion in the United States. The trend widened, however, in the 1950s and took off in the 1960s, including in *East* Germany (in contrast to most other socialist states). As the use of labor-saving devices spread down the social ladder, the domestic life of the working-class woman became more like that of her middle-class counterpart.[17]

These homogenizing tendencies were related to a major change with leveling effects across social groups and inside the family: the rise in married women's workforce participation. In 1970, East Germany had the highest rate of female employment in the industrialized world. Especially indicative of a break with the past was the high rate of employment among mothers. In 1967, 55 percent of women with three or more children at home worked for wages.[18] While the GDR (along with Norway and the USSR, for example) was ahead of a curve that has profoundly affected society in the postwar era, the FRG lagged behind it. Married mothers moved into paid employment much more slowly than in the GDR or than in the United States, and many countries in Europe. Given the durable myth that West German wives retreated to the kitchen, it is important to emphasize that their participation in the workforce did increase. In 1950, 25 percent of wives worked for wages; in 1960, 32.8 percent did; in 1970, 35.2 percent did.[19] Both societies experienced several developments that weakened the pre-war correlation between women's employment and their marital status as single women or their comparatively low economic status. These included increasing part-time work by wives, educated women's tendency to work at a high rate combined with rising levels of female education, and a decline in the birth rate after 1965. It became more common for women of every social group, marital status, and maternal situation to work outside the family. Along with these trends came a shift in the meaning of women's waged labor: an employed wife or mother did not necessarily signify low status and/or an inadequate male provider, but might denote individual inclination or a cultural value (such as commitment to women's equality or to family mobility). These changes happened gradually, accompanied by tensions inside the family and, especially in the FRG, public agonizing over the cultural dangers associated with (married) mothers' employment.[20]

The rise in women's employment was associated with greater gender equality inside the family, if not to the degree feared by conservative opponents or hoped by Commun-ist, Social Democratic, or feminist supporters. The 'partnership marriage' became the norm—spouses consulted each other about important family decisions, and there occurred some, if not much, redistribution of household labor and childrearing responsibilities. These trends went further in the GDR, but not dramatically so. When a husband was violent, obstructive, or otherwise inadequate in an employed wife's eyes, she often got a divorce, another trend that was more common in the GDR than the FRG, although not more so than in the USSR, United States, or Sweden.[21]

These social trends accompanied growing prosperity. The lure of mass consumption motivated wives' employment, especially in West Germany. Higher levels of workforce participation also motivated women to buy labor-saving devices, especially in East Germany. Whether consumption nudged female employment forward or the other way around, the data show that appliances were the first 'big ticket' items purchased by households in both Germanys—and in France and the UK. German interviewees often recall the exact date when they bought their first refrigerator or washing machine and also remember the purchase as a postwar caesura, according to Michael Wildt. Women's family-based labor, thus, shaped consumer habits that were trend-setting and memory-making in the early phase of postwar consumerism—and no wonder given that in the early 1950s women spent from eight (GDR) to twelve (FRG) hours a day doing housework.[22]

Social and economic changes (and state policies) in West and East took place to different degrees and at different paces, gradually shaping an East German family different from its West German counterpart. In 1989, East German families were likelier to have an employed wife, be headed by a single mother, and include more children. Still, the typical family was not strikingly different in East and West. Key trends ran in the same direction, especially in the 1950s and in the 1980s. The nuclear family, with a married couple and children at its core, remained the form of the family in which most people lived at every social level.[23] The small family was a major site of socialization and acculturation, as well as a place of work and fun. It was a driving force behind the (desire for) mass consumerism that distinguishes postwar society.

29.3 THE INDUSTRIALIZATION BEFORE DE-INDUSTRIALIZATION

People on both sides of the Atlantic associate the postwar era with de-industrialization, yet in Europe it began with two decades of intensive industrialization. The postwar industrial expansion was without historical precedent.[24] Industrialization was especially extensive in the two Germanys. Germany had an industrial economy, of course, before the First World War and over time became more industrial, with breaks during the Great Depression and postwar crisis. In late 1948, the West and East German economies entered a period of reconstruction that by 1952–1953 had become an industrial boom, concentrated (especially in the GDR) on heavy and basic industry, but also on other 'producer goods' such as metals, chemicals, and electronics. As measured by contribution to GDP, the secondary sector reached its pinnacle in both states in the 1960s. The GDR had hands-down the most industrialized economy in the Eastern Bloc. The FRG was 'by far the most industrially oriented of all states in the European Economic Community in 1965.' In West Germany, argues Werner Abelshauser, the boom was accompanied by a 'deep change in attitudes toward industrialization.' As the American occupiers anticipated, virtually everyone applauded a process that before 1933 alarmed not only landowners, but shopkeepers and civil servants. In East Germany the same change in attitude occurred instantly. Leaders of the ruling Socialist Unity party (SED) believed profoundly in the power of socialized industry to transform society.[25]

Postwar agrarian employment shrank even more in the Germanys than in most other European countries. As rural laborers entered industrial employment, they contributed to a rise in the percentage of urban dwellers. The rise in the dependent (wage-earning) labor force looks even more dramatic if white-collar employment is added in. The service sector developed in tandem with industry. The expansion of tertiary employment was considerably smaller in the GDR than the FRG, although the West German service sector too employed relatively fewer workers than did many other Western industrial economies. Criss-crossing adjustment in employment by sector was a decline in the number of independent retailers and producers (Fig. 29.1).

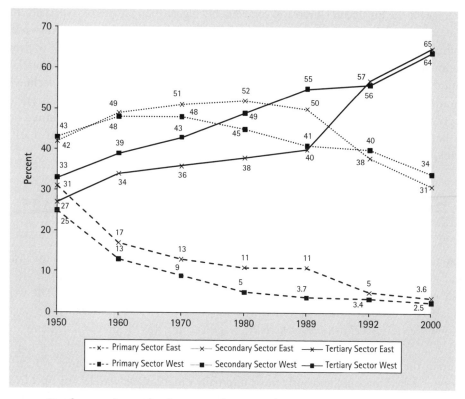

FIG. 29.1 Employment by production sector (1950–2000).

Sources: Statistical Yearbook FRG 1960, 142 (West 1950); 1990, 20 (West 1960–89); 1994, 116 (1992); Statistical Yearbook GDR 1990, 19, 125, 128 (East 1949–89); Federal Office of Statistics (2000).
Cited in: Rainer Geißler, Die Sozialstruktur Deutschlands. Die gesellschaftliche Entwicklung vor and nach der Vereinigung, 3rd ed.

In the GDR, expropriation and collectivization forced a precipitous, politically-fraught decline of the 'old *Mittelstand*' and, somewhat later, of the family farm. As *social* processes, however, the reduction in rural employment, expansion of dependent labor, and increase in urbanization ran in parallel in West and East into the 1960s.[26]

After 1970, sector development diverged in the two Germanys. In West Germany, as the postwar boom came to an end, the size of the industrial workforce decreased absolutely and relatively.[27] Service employment topped industrial employment, while the agricultural sector continued to shrink. In 1973, West Germany officially entered the age of 'de-industrialization,' alternatively called the 'service economy' or 'post-industrial society.' The shift, registered when industrial production accounted for less than 50 percent of GDP, occurred around the same time as in France and Italy, West Germany's fellow big boomers. In contrast, the UK, Germany's 'early industrial' counterpart, did not become officially post-industrial until the 1980s. The United States, of course, had long had a service economy. In 1990, the relative size of the West German industrial sector, concentrated as it was on exports, was slightly above average for the European Union and considerably bigger than Japan's or, especially, the United States.' Its service sector remained smaller than in many West European countries and much smaller than in the United States. In the GDR, the socialist boom also ended at the end of the 1960s, but de-industrialization did not occur. The industrial workforce did not shrink nor did the service sector grow, and the decline in rural employment ground to a halt. The GDR entered, in other words, an era of economic stagnation that was more all-encompassing and long-lasting (It turned out to be permanent!) than the comparable 'stagflation' that afflicted Western market economies in the 1970s.[28]

29.4 THE RE-MAKING OF THE WORKING CLASS

Capitalist or socialist, European lands hummed with industrial production in the 1950s and 1960s, creating, according to Hartmut Kaelble, a 'world of workers.' In the 1960s, half of all employed people in the FRG, and around 55 percent in the GDR were industrial workers.[29] Whether called a 'work society' (*Arbeitsgesellschaft*) or 'wage-earner society' (*Arbeitnehmergesellschaft*), wage-earning was the predominant employment category, with blue-collar industrial workers the main wage-dependent group.[30] During the boom, the composition and self-perception of the expanding industrial workforce became simultaneously more internally differentiated *and* less distinct from other social groups in both East and West. These trends contributed to the demise of workers' culture and, especially in the FRG, the dissolution of the proletarian milieu. These intersecting declines weakened, but did not sever the connection between social identity and occupational stratum in either society.

Early on, expanding industries in East and West hired heavily from the same 'new' categories: refugees and expellees, rural laborers, and non-employed or 'family-assisting' women. After initially converging, the gender and ethnic composition of the working class in the Germanys gradually diverged in the 1960s. A high percentage of women entered the industrial workforce in the GDR, whereas in the FRG women's employment did not increase appreciably until the 1980s. In West Germany, moreover, two groups joined the labor force in massive numbers: Germans who fled the GDR, and foreigners from Spain, Italy, Portugal, Yugoslavia, and Turkey who came to the FRG as 'guest workers.' Typically, the newly-mobilized groups entered industrial and/or blue-collar work, although many women took low-level white-collar jobs. Other European industrial workforces were also remade during the postwar boom. Virtually every economy mobilized rural labor for industry. Large numbers of women entered wage labor in many countries, but before 1960, no other European workforce integrated such large numbers of immigrants as did the Germanys—above all, the FRG. For decades, the FRG held first place in employment of immigrants.[31]

The majority of employed refugees/expellees in East and West ended up in the working-class, although less than two-fifths were so employed before 1945. In 1950, almost three-quarters of them in the FRG labored as workers, mainly in industry. In their homelands one-third had been independently employed or assisting family members, but in 1955 only 8 percent were so engaged. Compared with West German natives, they worked disproportionately for wages and as blue-collar workers into the 1970s. In industry, many (male) refugees or their children moved into skilled work in the 1960s. The occupational structures of refugees and natives converged only around 1980.[32]

In both economies, women moved into industrial manual labor out of domestic service and, especially, family-helper status. Women's 'rate of employment' hides this transfer from family labor into waged labor and, thus, masks a significant transition. It became much less likely for women to work under conditions of classic patriarchy as was the case in family businesses and in the agricultural sector, and as a result women's experience of manual labor became more like men's. Nevertheless, continuities in women's experience of work prevailed, mainly in the type of industrial work they performed. With the exception of the electronics industry, women tended to concentrate in the same industrial branches as before 1945: textiles/garments, food and drink, and chemicals. In the GDR, gender segregation by industry and industrial occupation was definitely less pronounced than in the FRG, but not radically so. In both economies (as in other industrial economies) women worked overwhelmingly in unskilled or, later, semi-skilled positions.[33] They earned from 30 to 40 percent less than male industrial workers, and they faced discrimination not only from employers and managers, but also from male workers. Considerable evidence on gender tensions on the East German shop floor reveals that male workers colluded with low-level trade union and SED functionaries to resist the feminization of the better-paid industrial branches and, above all, to oppose women as supervisors over men. Women's 'intrusion' presumably generated similar conflicts in the FRG, for analogous kinds of opposition have arisen wherever women move into 'male' jobs.[34]

In later decades, the profile of women's work diverged in East and West. Not only did more married mothers work for wages in the socialist East, but many more female workers gained skills. Forty-one percent of employed women in the GDR had a skilled diploma or educational degree by 1970. In West Germany, female blue-collar workers remained overwhelmingly unskilled or semi-skilled. As late as the year 2000, in united Germany, two-thirds of German female workers labored in unskilled and semi-skilled positions, in comparison to one-quarter of German male workers. In both societies, women's work in the home undermined their ability to advance occupationally or even hold a full-time job. Neither state nor economy effectively addressed, much less overcame, this fundamental social distinction whose significance is often discounted or even trivialized. The GDR's desperate need for women's wage labor did spur the SED to expand policies, if belatedly and inadequately, to decrease the double burden on women workers. Most significantly, the GDR expanded kindergartens to cover virtually all children aged three to five and extended crèches to encompass 80 percent of infants and toddlers.[35]

The number of foreign workers in the West German workforce began to increase after the economy reached full employment around 1955. This practice took off after the construction of the Berlin wall stopped the flow of East German migration. In 1970, foreign workers, the great majority of whom were men, comprised 16 percent of the wage-earning workforce. When the 'oil shock' sent industrial employment into a tail spin in 1973–1974, the state enacted a (gradually circumvented) 'stop' to foreign recruitment. After that, many guest workers brought their families to the FRG. The vast majority of guest workers came from rural backgrounds and had no skills relevant to their employment in Germany. They rarely attained such skills, due to language barriers, the structure of apprenticeship programs, discrimination, and huge barriers to them attaining citizenship.[36]

Booming industry created a world of workers, but did not forge a unified workers' world in either Germany. Divisions had long existed between skilled and unskilled, heavy industrial and light industrial, factory and small shop workers, while structural differences intersected with culturally-constructed categories such as 'women's work.' In the postwar era, the spread of assembly lines, shift work, and piece work meant that the experience of manual labor became increasingly similar across industries, just as differences between skilled and unskilled or semi-skilled labor widened.[37] As native male workers and, later, male refugees moved into the ranks of skilled, supervisory, and even managerial labor, this division between skilled and unskilled labor came to part more clearly along gender and ethnic lines, especially in the FRG, where the influx of guest workers allowed German male workers to move en masse into skilled labor and salaried work.[38] Taken together, these developments created a West German industrial working class that by the 1970s was a 'fully different ensemble of social formations' than in 1933.[39]

The new ensemble made sense of 'wage labor' in notably heterogeneous ways.[40] Refugees were bunched in the working class, but did not tend to interpret their situation in class terms. Indeed, they were notably anti-Communist. In the FRG, many joined trade unions and voted Social Democratic, but their status as refugees carried more emotional resonance than did workplace identity. Their marked orientation toward self- and family-advancement percolated into the wider shop floor culture.[41] Women workers too did not fit the classic mold of workplace culture. Due to their experience of laboring *for* and *in* the family, they were much likelier than men to harbor a dual commitment to paid and unpaid labor. Men saw themselves as the family breadwinner, but labor *in* the family shaped their identity very little. Women's employment, in contrast, was often subject to their labor in the family. They were less likely than men to identify waged work as their life mission, although female workers cared about compensation and conditions. Male workers often discouraged female participation in shop floor organizations, but then criticized women as apathetic and lacking solidarity. Even wider was the distance between the social milieus of West German workers and *foreign* workers. The wide gulf was exposed when native workers cried 'Ausländer raus!' as unemployment rose during the recession of 1966–1967.

Antagonism flared again during the long downturn of the 1970s—and periodically ever after.[42]

Native male workers had formed the core of Germany's organized workers' culture and broader proletarian milieu. Elements of this working-class world survived Nazi repression and war. In the GDR, industrial strongholds of pre-Nazi *Arbeiterkultur* were the centers of the massive strike wave in June 1953 against SED labor and consumption policies.[43] Militancy and shop floor culture in West German mines and foundries in the early 1950s demonstrated traditional forms of solidarity.[44] By the 1960s, 'classic' shop floor culture had eroded in both states in part due to the decline of *Arbeiterkultur*. In the West, Social Democrats decided not to revive workers' cultural organizations. In the East, the SED suffocated autonomous forms of sociability and 'encouraged' participation in its 'mass organizations.' In contrast, oppositional Communist parties in postwar Italy and, especially, France constructed an elaborate workers' culture that looked a lot like pre-1933 *Arbeiterkultur*. This difference may illuminate why West German workers and unions called fewer and less militant strikes than French and Italian workers during the economic troubles that affected all of Europe around 1970. Unlike French and Italian workers, West German workers also did not join student protesters during '1968,' although students in West Berlin were as rebellious as in Paris and Milan.[45]

By the late 1970s, organized workers' culture and the proletarian milieu were in decline throughout Western Europe. They deteriorated, Kaelble posits, because workers no longer needed physical, psychological, or cultural sustenance from the workers' movement.[46] Full employment, rising wages, improved benefits, and the 'safety net' of social policies overcame their sense of vulnerability, isolation, and inferiority, contributing to a 'deproletarianization' of the working class. As the ratio of workers decreased relative to white-collar employees, European society became less proletarian from a social-structural perspective as well. Of course, one could argue that white-collar work was becoming proletarianized. By 1960, most low-level white-collar employees were female, meaning that the status of retail and clerical work had declined. Their pay was low and many worked in factory-like offices. Yet, if this meant they were proletarians, they did not want to know about it. White-collar female employees looked down on their blue-collar counterparts.[47]

In the GDR, a version of the traditional proletarian milieu survived into the 1980s, in part because industrial workers remained a huge block of the employed population and in part because the SED lionized industrial workers and manual labor, and the production brigade, the GDR's ubiquitous work-unit collective, nurtured a workplace identity.[48] Countervailing trends, however, altered the proletarian milieu. The movement of large numbers of workers into skilled labor enhanced job satisfaction, social policies benefited workers, full employment created security and better living standards directed attention toward consumption.[49] As in the west, the East German worker's milieu did not respond adaptively to a feminizing workforce. However, there were also conditions particular to socialism that undermined a milieu whose classic form was intertwined with oppositional workers' organizations—which the SED had repressed or brought 'into line.' As production brigades forged small-group solidarity (and higher quotas) through production competitions, worker loyalties tended to fragment, and dissent was atomized and strongly inflected by *Eigen-Sinn* (self-constructed meaning). The absence of major strikes after 1953 signified this waning of the classic proletarian milieu. In socialist Poland, in contrast, industrial protest and cooperative dissent by workers and students became more public and better organized over time. Effective repression in the GDR only partially explains the difference. In autumn 1989, when demonstrations swept the GDR and brought down the wall, industrial workers participated as individuals, not as members of a self-conscious group.[50]

If the social identity of East German industrial workers weakened more than one might have predicted in a 'labor society,' the group identity of West German workers paled less than one might have expected in a 'social-market society.' In 2001, a poll found that 70 percent of skilled workers and 80 percent of unskilled and semi-skilled workers identified themselves as members of the 'worker-stratum' (*Arbeiterschicht*). The participation of former East Germans probably influenced these numbers. Yet in the old Federal Republic, too, workers articulated a labor-associated identity. In 1972, two out of three workers still voted for the SPD; and in the late 1970s, a majority of workers found the division of wealth in the FRG 'unjust.[51] The trend was not nationally specific, however. Throughout Europe, argues Kaelble, compensation, safety, promotion, work climate, and 'voice' remained of great concern to workers and employees. Increasingly, though, workers and employees are articulating workplace interests through individual complaints more than by organized conflict—suggesting, ironically, that western workers are following a path carved by workers in the GDR.[52]

29.5 EVIDENCE OF SOCIAL DIVISION: COMPARING BOATS

The degree and meaning of social inequality in the GDR and FRG (and other rich industrial countries) are contested issues. Critics of the panglossian cheerleaders for either the East or the West have gathered data on income, social mobility, and education that reveal both surprising internal inconsistencies and German-German similarities. In both societies income gaps narrowed and social mobility accelerated somewhat in the 1950s and 1960s, but not later. Neither state addressed class-based educational disparities as effectively as supporters asserted. After the 1960s, both made major strides toward closing the gendered educational gap. Each society had its elites. Beneath the sharp contrasts in their composition and wealth, one can identify a unifying trend: educated elites gained status and influence relative to propertied elites in East *and* West.[53]

The rising tide of prosperity has distracted public and scholarly attention, according to Hans-Ulrich Wehler and others, from an 'astounding' and 'striking' stability in the gap between rich and poor in West Germany. In 1950, the top quintile of households earned 45 percent of the national income; in 1985, they earned 44 percent. In 1950, the bottom quintile earned 5.4 percent, while in 1985, they received 7.4 percent. The distribution of wealth showed an even steeper slope. In 1986, the top 12 percent of households owned 60 percent of national property/assets, while the bottom 30 percent owned only 1.5 percent of wealth. Monetary assets rose among all groups, but the uneven distribution of assets between top and bottom, on the one hand, and between dependent and independent labor, on the other, shifted little between 1949 and 1989. Studies conclude that the rich grew richer from the late 1970s on, erasing most of the relative gains made by the lower quintiles in the 1950s and 1960s. The concentration of wealth was associated with an increasing concentration of business ownership. The Federal Republic's distribution of income and wealth stands in the middle of the spectrum whether the comparative pool is Western economies or members of the European Union. Many post-industrial economies saw the 'scissors' close somewhat up to 1975, only to open again since then. The income gap is less yawning in the FRG than in the US or Canada, yet German ownership of assets is more concentrated at the top of the pyramid than in Sweden, the UK, *or* the US.[54]

In the GDR, expropriation of property and businesses of all types and sizes dramatically flattened the distribution of wealth. The allocation of income was also much more equal than in the West. The state tilted wages toward industrial workers relative to white-collar employees, on the one hand, and slanted tax and social benefits to wage-earners relative to the small number of independently employed East Germans, on the other. East German workers earned 64 percent of what West German blue-collar workers did, whereas East German white-collar employees earned only 47 percent of their West German counterparts.[55]

As did virtually all of Europe, East and West Germany significantly expanded universities and other institutions of higher learning between 1949 and 1989, and in the process became massively better educated. Both societies equalized access to secondary education, if at different points and to different degrees, and the expansion of tertiary education delivered major pay-offs in income and social standing in both states, so that strong correlations developed between higher education, distribution of income, social mobility, and the definition of elites. In the FRG, all social layers benefited from the expansion of education, but the middle and upper strata benefited more. Access to higher education for working-class children made a significant leap in the 1960s in the wake of reforms in secondary education. Since then, worker-children's access to college-prep high schools has expanded, but not as rapidly as in the 1960s, especially in contrast to that of the children of white-collar employees and civil servants. In 1950, the percentage of worker-children at university was 6 percent; it rose to 16.9 percent in 1970 and has since stagnated at around 15 percent. By some measures of international comparison, educational achievement in the Federal Republic remains unusually socially stratified. In 2000, the gap in the reading achievement of fifteen-year-olds from the lowest and highest quarters of the population was wider in the FRG than any other OECD country. The gap in reading scores of children from immigrant and native families was second widest in the FRG.[56]

The GDR expanded higher education to train a 'socialist intelligentsia.' In 1950, only 6 percent of the employed population had a higher degree, while in 1989, 22 percent did. The SED moved from two directions to level the expanding educational field. In the 1950s, the party made it easier for working-class children to enter university. At the same time, it discriminated heavily against children from 'bourgeois' backgrounds. The percentage of worker-children among students rose impressively. As early as the 1960s however, children of the new socialist intelligentsia and of old 'bourgeois' families shot ahead in university attendance. In 1988, only 7 percent of university students in the GDR were worker-children. This reversal took place after the state stopped actively promoting 'affirmative action.' As in the FRG, teacher bias hurt the chances of worker-children. Blue-collar parents tended to accept teacher evaluations of their children while educated parents in both states insisted on university education for their children. In the GDR, from 1970 onward, university attendance was highly correlated with an educated mother—and East German mothers were likelier than West German mothers to have a university degree. In the GDR, the university system as a whole stagnated in the 1980s. Whereas in 1960, 10 percent of East German youth versus 6 percent of West German youth studied at a university or advanced technical school, in 1988 the ratio was 20 percent in West Germany and 14 percent in the GDR.[57]

The GDR addressed educational discrimination against girls earlier and more aggressively than did the FRG. Girls' rate of graduation from Eastern college-prep schools (*Erweiterte Oberschule*) topped the male rate by the 1960s. In the FRG girls surpassed boys' rate of graduation from gymnasium only in the early 1980s. East German women's attendance at university drew even with men's in the 1970s and moved ahead in the 1980s. In the 'old' FRG, enrollment at universities was still less than 50 percent female in 2000, in contrast to most other European countries, the United States, *and* the 'new federal states.' In both the West and the East, young women at university were even likelier than young men to have parents who were already educated. Working-class parents tended to discourage girls' education more than they did boys.'[58]

Occupational opportunity within and across generations in the FRG was quite dynamic. Still, upward social mobility was not as common in the 1950s as the trope of the 'self-made man' would suggest. The data are difficult to evaluate, but suggest that social mobility was most widespread in the 1960s. Correct in the stereotype of the 'self-made-man' was, however, the gender of mobility: it was predominately male. As the boom came to an end and educational reform stalled, occupational and income mobility slowed. Yet the shift from the industrial to the service economy drew the next generation heavily into white-collar employment—and society overall was 're-stratified' upward. The typical step in the 1950s and 1960s was by unskilled male Germans into skilled positions, while in the 1970s and 1980s skilled workers typically moved into low-level management, higher-level office jobs, and the civil service. Family background molded children's chances in many ways, including, but not limited to financial means. Social circles too swayed ambitions and provided connections. Sociability was quite closed, as two-thirds of worker-children married worker-children. Despite structural and cultural obstacles to mobility, the FRG was, Rainer Geißler concludes, a society with 'notably high upward generational mobility' for native men, due to full employment and demand for skilled labor and, later, to the shift toward higher education and service jobs.[59]

The GDR was characterized by high levels of both upward and downward mobility in the 1950s. Workers and employees trained to move into the thousands of skilled and professional positions left open by doctors, teachers, engineers, and all that migrated to the West. After 1960, the GDR experienced a general rise in education and qualification levels and, thus, the whole society re-stratified upward. The economy did not, however, enter the service phase after 1970 and so the upward rotation of society as a whole stopped. A stagnant social structure reproduced itself—thus, blocking upward mobility for lower social groups and younger people. In 1977, three-quarters of workers came from a family in which the father was a worker. As in the FRG, women did not fare as well as men, even though the gendered gap in social mobility was less wide because women gained higher levels of skill and education. Communism in Eastern Europe, concludes Göran Therborn, improved the equality of opportunity relative to Western Europe, but not to either North America or Japan.[60]

Elites in the FRG experienced modification within stability, whereas East German elites evinced resilience within transformation. Gentile elites survived the war, shaken, but not undone by material and human losses. The FRG revived the career civil service with more or less the same personnel as before 1945. Many lawyers and almost all doctors (re)founded private practices. Three-quarters of the pre-1945 membership of company boards and other leading business institutions stayed in the same positions. Nonetheless, elite *political* loyalties evolved quickly and quite dramatically. The anti-democratic, anti-republican revanchism that characterized bourgeois circles after World War I did not revive. Employers negotiated with trade unions; academics forgot their earlier disdain for industry and commercialism, and professional and employer associations tenaciously represented group interests, but did so within the give-and-take of parliamentary deal-making. Elites, in summary, embraced the 'Bonn republic.' Culturally, the bourgeois milieu adapted less rapidly. German liberal values of education and self-improvement became only gradually less patriarchal, exclusive, and parochial as lower social strata adopted them and as they took on some of the freer spirit of Anglo-American liberalism. Rather than express itself so blatantly as earlier, elite taste articulated itself as fine distinctions in dress, leisure, and opinion. Socially, the *bürgerliche* milieu changed quite slowly. Initially, even the economic and academic elites comingled little, not to speak of recruiting from the lower orders. As the size of the business and educational elites expanded, though, they began to draw members from other elites and even from 'lower' circles.[61]

In the East, the leadership of the Communist party—the new political elite—imprisoned or drove out the old propertied and political elites. It needed, however, the expertise of physicians, accountants, scientists, engineers, and professors; thus, the old academic elite survived and, even after a socialist intelligentsia arose, maintained a place in East Germany's 'niche society.' The SED did not like the bourgeoisie, but it greatly respected and cultivated pre-twentieth-century bourgeois culture. For these and other reasons, recent scholarship suggests, East German society was not truly 'de-differentiated' or atomized, but maintained social distinctions and milieus.[62]

29.6 SOURCES OF SOCIAL COHESION: THE RISING TIDE

Given the persistence of social inequality, why have West German social relations been calm since 1945 in contrast to earlier? The societal perspective concedes the cushioning effects of prosperity, but also notes the impact of redistributive tax and social policies.[63] The optimist school squarely credits the rising tide, arguing absolute prosperity trumped social comparison. The vast majority of West Germans earned enough money, benefits, and free time to partake of an ever increasing quantity and variety of goods, services, and leisure activities. Mass consumption of goods and mass-produced culture nourished, in turn, a convergence of tastes and even life styles. Convergence did more than deflect social comparison, according to the optimists. It actually diminished the usefulness of social position as a standpoint from which to evaluate society. Throughout Western Europe life styles were simultaneously individuated and 'nationalized' or even internationalized as options expanded in all senses of the word.[64]

West German prosperity had the opposite effect on East Germans. It provoked them to social comparison—with West Germans. East German sensitivity to the German-German gap in prosperity irked the SED leadership, for it acted as a quite literal magnet before the construction of the Berlin wall and remained psychologically mesmerizing afterwards. Under Erich Honecker, the Politburo tried, but failed to meet popular consumption needs and desires, at least in part to counteract this pull. The widening gap in the standard of living after 1980 fostered an ever sharper consciousness of social imbalance between East and West. This consciousness, many studies have argued, contributed to the most stunning upheaval in postwar German history: the Revolution that brought about the fall of the Berlin Wall in 1989. Although not wrong, the claim concerning East German consciousness of disparity is incomplete. It focuses exclusively on the rough beginning and declining end of GDR living standards, and it considers the GDR only in comparison to the FRG, rather than also to itself. An internally-focused, longer-term perspective shows that the standard of living and, in its wake, consumption increased significantly for several decades.[65] It suggests, moreover, that mass consumption bolstered social and political stability between the mid-1950s and mid-1980s.

West Germany's national income increased thirteen times faster between 1950 and 1980 than it had in the same region of Germany between 1900 and 1950. Confirming that people toward the bottom of the income scale benefitted from this rise, the net earnings of worker/employees rose 3.2 times between 1950 and 1979. Even scholars who adopt the critical societal perspective recognize that unprecedented prosperity not only improved people's lives, but colored their perception of society and their social prospects. In the GDR, the glass of prosperity looks different depending on the angle of observation. The rise in the standard of living was very impressive there too, especially compared with the immediate postwar era. Yet, as we all know, the glass looks half empty if compared with the much greater rise in West Germany. In 1960, the difference in average household income was 30 percent; in 1970, it was 40 percent; in the early 1980s, it stood at 55 percent. If measured in cash assets, the distribution of wealth was even more unequal.[66]

Studies of postwar consumption often employ the metaphor of the wave, especially in reference to West Germany. They describe progressive 'waves' of food, fashion, consumer durables and interior design, automobiles, and travel.[67] The wave imagery, the historian Michael Wildt argues, evokes a natural phenomenon, rather than pointing to social decisions—and family negotiations—about how to spend hard-earned wages. Along with Mooser, Wildt dates the shift from inelastic need toward elastic need later than do most scholars. Workers were eating more and better food before 1955, certainly, but only around 1960 did they begin to redefine 'need' to encompass goods once considered luxuries.[68] This redefinition was the critical cultural shift that, in turn, altered social perceptions, according to Kaelble. Mass consumption, he suggests, began to reshape class society in Europe when many high-value goods, like televisions and cars, crossed from status symbol to ordinary commodity. This process occurred throughout Western Europe, but at different paces. Although Germany was famous for its automobiles, for example, many fewer Germans than Englishmen or Frenchmen owned a car before 1945. The gap did not close until the late 1960s when workers' car ownership jumped upward. According to Eric Hobsbawm, the automobile was the signature commodity in the cultural redefinition of luxury as need, for the car was an expensive, ostentatious product that saved time, provided comfort, and allowed physical mobility, under conditions of privacy and autonomy.[69] One could conclude, then, that West Germany made the cultural transition out of 'class society' slightly later than France or the UK.

Scholars have long debated the impact of the 'Americanization' of West European consumption. Its level and patterns became more American, Kaelble posits, as European economies became more like the American one. Yet, he adds, the types, design, and provenance of many preferred products continued to reflect a distinctive European taste despite the popularity of Coca-Cola, Levis, and Hollywood movies.[70] Many students of West Germany see the 'American model' as a significant arbiter of cultural and social trends, including adolescent habits, decision-making in boardrooms, and marketing. Mary Nolan, by contrast, resists sweeping generalizations about Americanization in the FRG, conceding that it influenced consumer preferences and cultural trends in the 1950s, but arguing that its sway diminished over time.[71]

A major divergence between Western European and American social experience was in the amount of leisure available to employees and the ways in which they spent free time. Leisure increasingly defined workers' lives as the number of working hours per week and, even more, days per year declined. The spread of the two-day weekend made European free time more like the US version, but the rise of the long summer holiday shaped a uniquely European world of leisure and tourism.[72] By the 1960s, West Germany stood at the pinnacle of comparative measures of workers' free time. Like workers throughout Europe, West Germans were ever more likely to spend their leisure imbibing mass culture, rather than participating in homegrown cultural clubs (with the exception of football leagues!). Initially, they listened to radio at home or went to the movies with spouse or friends; later, they watched TV with the family or read the daily press, especially tabloids, with the West German especially taking to the new, sensationalistic, politically conservative *Bild-Zeitung*, which captured almost a quarter of the newspaper market. For their ever longer vacations, workers, like middle-strata Germans, were ever likelier to pack up the family and head for a Mediterranean resort or, later, Disney World.[73]

Mass consumption in the GDR lagged behind the FRG (Table 29.1). For both ideological and economic reasons, the SED leadership disliked individual, private consumption or, indeed, much consumption at all. The gradual shift of more investment into private consumption reflected Cold War competition for German hearts and minds. It was also a response to popular unrest and workers' rebellion in 1953. The leadership was responding, last, but not least, to the needs and demands of the nuclear family—and especially wives and mothers whom the party needed to mobilize for employment. The state expanded socialized services, but catered increasingly to private consumption. For about three decades, East Germans saw their standard of living improve, if fitfully, relative to their past and, especially, compared with the Eastern

Table 29.1 Households equipped with consumer goods, 1962–2000 (in percent)

	West					East				
	1962	1973	1983	1988	2000	1960	1970	1983	1988	2000
Passenger car	27	55	65	68	75	3	16	42	52	70
Washing machine[1]	34	75	83	86	94	6	54[1]	87[1]	66	96
Freezer	3	28	65	70	72	0	19	29	43	68
Dishwasher	0	7	24	29	52					33
Telephone[2]	14	51	88	93	97		6	12	16	95
Mobile or car phone					30					28
Color TV	0	15	73	87	96	0	0	38[3]	52	98
Hi-fi stereo	0	0	38	42	65					55
Personal computer					56					51

1. West—Washing fully automatic. The 1970 and 1983 figures for the East include other washing machines
2. GDR—Number of main connections in residences for every 100 households
3. 1985

European or Soviet cities to which they could travel. Their sense of plenty was, certainly, strongly tempered by intermittent absolute shortages and by constant comparative shortage vis-à-vis West Germany. Nonetheless, East Germans experienced the 1960s and, especially, 1970s as good years. Their consumption followed a wave-like pattern whose contents looked exceedingly like the West German and wider West European waves. There too family negotiations defined need, suggesting that worker families in East and West set strikingly similar priorities. Western tastes influenced preferences, especially in the case of 'elastic needs' such as fashion and youth culture. East Germans always enjoyed much less (official) free time than did West Germans or other West Europeans, but their leisure expanded in amount and variety. As in the West, most free time was spent at home, listening to the radio and, later, watching TV, but also reading, sleeping, visiting, and gardening. Over time, an East German leisure culture emerged that was different from the West and the rest of Eastern Europe. It encompassed summer camping colonies, a nudist sub-culture along the Baltic coast, and group travel to resorts on the Black Sea or Yugoslav Adriatic coasts.[74]

Mass consumption and mass culture encouraged homogenization (or nationalization) of daily experience in the West and probably even more in the East, where choices were fewer and the standard of living more compressed. They also generated an intersecting trend toward individuation as people, even in the East, used disposable income and the assortment of wares to craft personal variations in their style of life. Homogenization and individuation did not eliminate social position as a determinant of fine distinctions. Hobbies, fashion, manners, and automobile model expressed social background, although they were also influenced by generation, gender, and ethnicity. Studies show, for example, that worker families in France, the UK and the FRG watched more television than middle-strata families, and watched it differently. For them, TV programs provided cultural knowledge and functioned as a substitute for travel and reading.[75]

29.8 THE END OF CLASS SOCIETY

In the comparative history of postwar society, West German prosperity emerges as a commanding force with tranquilizing and transformative social effects. This version of the story captured the popular imagination for decades. It also shaped Western scholarly research on society in the two states. It reached its persuasive apogee in 1989–1990 as the wall came down, currency union went through, and unification took the fast track, all under the influence of the emotional allure and very real resources of West German wealth. Any remaining vestiges of a class mentality seemed swept away by the peaceful revolution and East Germans' moving cry, '*Wir sind das Volk!*'

Western prosperity's greatest triumph soon turned, however, into its greatest test. The GDR economy was in considerably worse shape than even its harshest critics expected. Rather than bolstering the economy, however, the introduction of competitive conditions precipitated rapid de-industrialization. A 'virtual structural collapse' intensified a new wave of migration to the West as two million easterners moved to the old Federal states in the 1990s. Unemployment surged in the new Federal states and unskilled and semi-skilled workers saw their jobs evaporate and their status plummet. Comparative 'winners' in the East were service-sector employees and, especially, professionals such as physicians, pharmacists, engineers, and chemists. Single parents—most of them women—suffered disproportionate losses in income, while pensioners made relative gains. In the 1990s, female unemployment was higher than male, although they reversed positions after 2000. Intergenerational downward mobility was pronounced. The gap between educational opportunity in East and West was wide in 2000: university study encompassed 24 percent of former West Germans, but only 15 percent of East Germans of the relevant age. Although the standard of living improved, social inequalities in eastern Germany rose substantially. Still, Rainer Geißler emphasizes, post-unification divisions reproduced disparities that existed in the GDR.[76] Unification also entailed major costs for West Germans, including rising taxes and higher unemployment than in the US, UK, and other Western economies. The development of global capitalism after the fall of Communism contributed to a continuing, if gradual, process of de-industrialization in the 'old' Federal states.

West German prosperity lost a measure of its material power and its cultural glamour after 1990. In 1999, 75 percent of 'West' Germans and 86 percent of 'East' Germans believed that the poor were ever poorer and the rich were ever richer in Germany. Scholarship on society too shifted with the sands. The critical societal approach to postwar social history—which this chapter has adopted—gained considerable steam. Reality, adherents of this perspective recognize, is 'dually constituted' by 'objective social structures' and their cultural construction.[77] They argue, on the one hand, that social milieus still reflect societal conditions in Germany today: social groupings adhere to social divisions, including background, income, occupation, and education. Pointing especially to its notable concentration of wealth and the determination of the rich to maintain their position, societal studies conclude that unified Germany is not yet moving 'beyond class society.'[78] They acknowledge, on the other hand, that after 1945 social milieus became less sharply delineated and social groups less self-conscious. Vertical social hierarchies were crisscrossed by gender and ethnic divisions that influenced social position and its perception. These simultaneously homogenizing and differentiating trends took partially different forms in the two Germanys, not surprisingly, given the important economic and social distinctions between these Cold War rivals. Nonetheless, a similar combination of social blending and demarcation characterized societal development in these advanced industrial states, for they held significant economic and social structures in common. They both moved beyond, or at least out of, the 'traditional' or 'classic' German class society disdained by their respective American and Russian liberators. The merger of East and West since 1990 has proven to be unexpectedly divisive, accompanied by regional tensions, economic resentment, political struggles, and incidents of racist violence. Yet one sees no evidence of a revival of traditional German class society. Instead, the contradictory process of homogenization and differentiation continues to reproduce the societal distinctions that Germany shares with other post-industrial lands.

Notes

1. Konrad Jarausch, *Die Umkehr. Deutsche Wandlungen 1945–1995* (Munich: Deutsche Verlags-Anstalt, 2004), 209–210; Greg Castillo, 'Domesticating the Cold War: Household Consumption as Propaganda in Marshall Plan Germany,' *Journal of Contemporary History* 40,2 (April, 2005), 261–288; Mark Landsman, *Dictatorship and Demand: The Politics of Consumerism in East Germany* (Cambridge: Harvard University Press, 2005), 29. Also see Paul Steege, *Black Market, Cold War: Everyday Life in Berlin, 1946–1949* (Cambridge: Cambridge University Press, 2007); Norman M. Naimark, *The Russians in Germany: A History of the Soviet Zone of Occupation, 1945–1949* (Cambridge: Harvard University Press, 1995).

2. See, e.g. Klaus Tenfelde, 'Ende der Arbeiterkultur: Das Echo auf eine These?' in Wolfgang Kaschuba, Gottfried Korff, and Bernd Jürgen Warneken, *Arbeiterkultur seit 1945—Ende oder Veränderung? 5. Tagung der Kommission Arbeiterkultur in der Deutschen Gesellschaft für Volkskunde in Tübingen 1989* (Tübingen: Tübinger Vereinigung für Volkskunde, 1991); Axel Schildt, *Die Sozialgeschichte der Bundesrepublik Deutschland bis 1989/90* (Munich: Oldenbourg Wissenschaftsverlag, 2007), 31–32, 74, 84, 87–89; Hartmut Kaelble, *Sozialgeschichte Europas. 1945 bis zur Gegenwart* (Munich: C. H. Beck, 2007), 187; Rainer Geißler, *Die Sozialstruktur Deutschlands. Die gesellschaftliche Entwicklung vor and nach der Vereinigung*, 3rd edn (Wiesbaden: Westdeutscher Verlag, 2002), 112–115, 117–119, 125–126, 134–136; Hans-Ulrich Wehler, *Deutsche Gesellschaftsgeschichte 1949–1990* (Munich: C. H. Beck, 2008), 110–113.

3. Wehler, *Gesellschaftsgeschichte*, 122; Geißler, *Sozialstruktur*, 81–82, 84; Schildt, *Sozialgeschichte*, 23, 41.

4. See e.g., Arnold Sywottek, 'Wege in die 50er Jahre,' in Axel Schildt, Arnold Sywottek (eds), *Modernisierung im Wiederaufbau. Die westdeutsche Gesellschaft der 50er Jahre* (Bonn: Dietz, 1993), 18; Schildt, Sozialgeschichte, 19–21; Tenfelde, 'Ende,' 19–21.

5. See, e.g. Michael Wildt, 'Konsumbürger. Das Politische als Optionsfreiheit und Distinktion,' 255–283, in Manfred Hettling and Bernd Ulrich (eds), *Bürgertum nach 1945* (Hamburg: Hamburger Edition, 2005), 272–273; Wolfgang Kaschuba, 'Arbeiterkultur heute: Ende oder Transformation?,' in Kaschuba et al., *Arbeiterkultur seit 1945*, 44; Everhard Holtmann, 'Flüchtlinge in den 50er Jahren: Aspekte ihrer gesellschaftlichen und politischen Integration,' in Schildt and Sywottek (eds), *Modernisierung im Wiederaufbau*, 349; Wehler, *Gesellschaftsgeschichte*, 114–117; Geißler, *Sozialstruktur*, 115, 137–138.

6. Wehler, *Gesellschaftsgeschichte*, 115–116; Christoph Klessmann, *Arbeiter im 'Arbeiterstaat,' DDR. Deutsche Traditionen, sowjetisches Modell, westdeutsches Magnetfeld (1945 bis 1971)* (Bonn: Dietz, 2007), 654 –655; Michael Wildt, 'Privater Konsum in Westdeutschland in den 50er Jahren,' in Schildt and Sywottek (eds), *Modernisierung im Wiederaufbau*, 288; Geißler, *Sozialstruktur* 125–126, 134.

7. First quote: Sigrid Meuschel, 'Überlegungen zu einer Herrschafts- und Gesellschaftsgeschichte der DDR,' *Geschichte und Gesellschaft* 19 (1993), 5. Second quote: Wehler,

Gesellschaftsgeschichte, 223. Also see Hartmut Kaelble, 'Die Gesellschaft der DDR im internationalen Vergleich,' in Hartmut Kaelble, Jürgen Kocka, and Hartmut Zwahr (eds), *Sozialgeschichte der DDR* (Stuttgart: Klett-Cotta, 1994).

8. Geißler, *Sozialstruktur*, 69; Werner Abelshauser, *Deutsche Wirtschaftsgeschichte seit 1945* (Munich: C. H. Beck, 2004), 315; Wehler, *Gesellschaftsgeschichte*, 35–36; Holtmann, 'Flüchtlinge,' 351.

9. Josef Mooser, *Arbeiterleben in Deutschland 1890–1970. Klassenlagen, Kultur und Politik* (Frankfurt am Main: Suhrkamp, 1984), 110.

10. Holtmann, 'Flüchtlinge,'351–354, 357–358; Abelshauser, *Wirtschaftsgeschichte*, 315; Schildt, *Sozialgeschichte*, 17–18; Wehler, *Gesellschaftsgeschichte*, 157.

11. Geißler, *Sozialstruktur*, 69.

12. Donna Harsch, *Revenge of the Domestic: Women, the Family, and Communism in the German Democratic Republic* (Princeton: Princeton University Press, 2007), 135, 137, 142; Ralf Rytlewski and Manfred Opp de Hipt, *Die Bundesrepublik Deutschland in Zahlen 1945/49–1980* (Munich: C. H. Beck, 1987), 53, 55; Lothar Mertens, *Wider die sozialistische Familiennorm. Ehescheidungen in der DDR 1950–1989* (Opladen: VS Verlag für Sozial-wissenschaften, 1998), 12, 25.

13. Wehler, *Gesellschaftsgeschichte*, 43–45. Geißler, *Sozialstruktur*, 53, 67. Almost 400,000 people emigrated from the West to the East in the 1950s.

14. Mooser, *Arbeiterleben*, 151–152; Abelshauser, *Wirtschaftsgeschichte*, 323–324. Göran Therborn, *Die Gesellschaften Europas 1945–2000* (Frankfurt am Main: Campus, 2000), 79. Also see Elizabeth D. Heineman, *What Difference Does a Husband Make? Women and Marital Status in Nazi and Postwar Germany* (Berkeley: University of California Press, 1999); Harsch, *Revenge.*

15. Mooser, *Arbeiterleben*, 148, 151–52, 155; Harsch, *Revenge*, 210–216; Sabine Haustein, *Vom Mangel zum Massenkonsum. Deutschland, Frankreich und Grossbritannien im Vergleich 1945–1970* (Frankfurt am Main: Campus, 2007), 203; Schildt, *Sozialgeschichte*, 40–41.

16. Sywottek, 'Wege,' 18.

17. Haustein, *Mangel*, 199.

18. Harsch, *Revenge*, 247. The great majority of East German women with three or more children were married.

19. Haustein, *Mangel*, 32.

20. Eva Kolinsky, *Women in West Germany: Life, Work, and Politics* (Providence: Berg, 1989), 174–178; Gisela Helwig and Hildegard Maria Nickel (eds), *Frauen in Deutschland 1945–1992* (Berlin: Akademie Verlag, 1993); Kaelble, *Sozialgeschichte*, 74; Harsch, *Revenge*, 246–261; Mooser, *Arbeiterleben*, 33; Wehler, *Gesellschaftsgeschichte*, 157–58; Schildt, *Sozialgeschichte*, 18, 36–39; Haustein, *Mangel*, 29, 32–34; Merith Niehuss, 'Kontinuität und Wandel der Familie in den 50er Jahren,' in Axel Schildt and Arnold Sywottek (eds), *Modernisierung im Wiederaufbau. Die westdeutsche Gesellschaft der 50er Jahre* (Bonn: Dietz, 1993), 325–326; Wehler, *Gesellschaftsgeschichte*, 157–158. Also see Christine von Oertzen, *Teilzeitarbeit und die Lust am Zuverdienen: Geschlechterpolitik und gesellschaftlicher Wandel in Westdeutschland 1948–1969* (Göttingen: Vandenhoeck & Ruprecht, 1999); Carola Sachse, *Der Hausarbeitstag. Gerechtigkeit und Gleichberechtigung in Ost und West 1939–1994* (Göttingen: Vandenhoeck & Ruprecht, 2002).

21. Mooser, *Arbeiterleben*, 38; Harsch, *Revenge*, 284–297. Also see Michael Wagner, *Scheidung in Ost- und Westdeutschland. Zum Verhältnis von Ehestabilität und Sozialstrucktur seit den 30er Jahren* (Frankfurt am Main: Campus, 1997).

22. Haustein, *Mangel*, 28–31; Wildt, 'Konsum,' 281, 283. Also see Erica Carter, *How German is She? Postwar German Reconstruction and the Consuming Woman* (Ann Arbor: University of Michigan Press, 1997); Jennifer A. Loehlin, *From Rugs to Riches: Housework, Consumption, and Modernity in Germany* (Oxford: Berg Publishers, 1999).

23. Mooser, *Arbeiterleben*, 159; Harsch, *Revenge*, 198–200.

24. Sywottek, 'Wege,' 18, 24; Gerold Ambrosius, 'Wirtschaftlicher Strukturwandel und Technikentwicklung,' in Schildt and Sywottek (eds), *Modernisierung im Wiederaufbau*, 107–108; Kaelble, *Sozialgeschichte*, 62; Geißler, *Sozialstruktur*, 198.

25. Abelshauser, *Wirtschaftsgeschichte*, 305 (quote), 318; Klessmann, 'Arbeiterstaat', 770.

26. Ambrosius, 'Strukturwandel,' 107–108; Schildt, *Sozialgeschichte*, 19, 28; Kaelble, *Sozialgeschichte*, 67; Therborn, *Gesellschaften*, 90; Abelshauser, *Wirtschaftsgeschichte*, 309–311; Geißler, *Sozialstruktur*, 200.

27. Geißler, *Sozialstruktur*, 198; Schildt, *Sozialgeschichte*, 30; Mooser, *Arbeiterleben*, 28.

28. Geißler, *Sozialstruktur*, 198; Therborn, *Gesellschaften*, 90; Kaelble, *Sozialgeschichte*, 81; Stefan Hradil, *Die Sozialstruktur Deutschlands im internationalen Vergleich* (Wiesbaden: VS Verlag, 2004), 185–187.

29. Geißler, *Sozialstruktur*, 230, 238; Klessmann, 'Arbeiterstaat', 654–55.

30. Martin Kohli, 'Die DDR als Arbeitsgesellschaft? Arbeit, Lebenslauf und soziale Differenzierung,' in Kaelble et al., *Sozialgeschichte der DDR*. Rainer Lepsius called the FRG an 'Arbeitnehmergesellschaft.'

31. Schildt, *Sozialgeschichte*, 33–34, 56–58; Kaelble, *Sozialgeschichte*, 187.

32. Mooser, *Arbeiterleben*, 111; Schildt, *Sozialgeschichte*, 17; Holtmann, 'Flüchtlinge,' 353–54.

33. Mooser, *Arbeiterleben*, 33–35; Harsch, *Revenge*, 91–100; Schildt, *Sozialgeschichte*, 18, 36–39; Haustein, *Mangel*, 33; Wehler, *Gesellschaftegeschichte*, 157–58, 172; Rachel Alsop, *A Reversal of Fortunes? Women, Work and Change in East Germany* (New York: Berghahn Books, 2000), 30–35.

34. Harsch, *Revenge*, 44–53, 115–23; Andrew I. Port, *Conflict and Stability in the German Democratic Republic* (Cambridge: Cambridge University Press, 2007). Also see Sachse, *Hausarbeitstag*. On wage differential, Wehler, *Gesellschaftsgeschichte*, 121–22.

35. Harsch, *Revenge*, 248–49; Gisela Helwig, 'Frauen im SED-Staat,' in *Materiellen der Enquete-Kommission 'Aufarbeitung von Geschichte und Folgen der SED-Diktatur in Deutschland.'* Vol. III/2 (Frankfurt am Main: Suhrkamp, 1995), 1265.

36. Wehler, *Gesellschaftsgeschichte*, 160, 157; Schildt, *Sozialgeschichte*, 40, 33–34; Geißler, *Sozialstruktur*, 67–8; Mooser, *Arbeiterleben*, 40.

37. Mooser, *Arbeiterleben*, 62–63.

38. Schildt, *Sozialgeschichte*, 33–34, 235–236; Mooser, *Arbeiterleben*, 43, 53, 61–64; Burkart Lutz, 'Integration durch Aufstieg. Überlegungen zur Verbürgerlichung der deutschen Facharbeiter in den Jahrzehnten nach dem Zweiten Weltkrieg,' in Manfred Hettling and Bernd Ulrich (eds), *Bürgertum nach 1945* (Hamburg: Hamburger Edition, 2005), 307–3208.

39. Wehler, *Gesellschaftsgeschichte*, 153.

40. Mooser, *Arbeiterleben*, 43–44, 111.

41. Holtmann, 'Flüchtlinge,' 351–354, 357–358; Abelshauser, *Wirtschaftsgeschichte*, 315. Schildt, *Sozialgeschichte*, 17–18; Wehler, *Gesellschaftsgeschichte*, 157.

42. Sachse, *Hausarbeitstag*; Mooser, *Arbeiterleben*, 35, 45, 42; Schildt, *Sozialgeschichte*, 33–34.

43. Klessmann, *Arbeiterstaat*, 659–660.

44. Joachim Radkau, '"Wirtschaftswunder" ohne technologische Innovation? Technische Modernität in den 50er Jahren,' in Schildt and Sywottek (eds), *Modernisierung im Wiederaufbau*, 141–142.

45. Mooser, *Arbeiterleben*, 11; Wehler, *Gesellschaftsgeschichte*, 162.

46. Kaelble et al., *Sozialgeschichte der DDR*, 186–187.

47. Geißler, *Sozialstruktur*, 230–233; Mooser, *Arbeiterleben*, 211, 227–228; Schildt, *Sozialgeschichte*, 36–39.

48. Schildt, *Sozialgeschichte*, 238–40; Klessmann, *Arbeiterstaat*, 654–55; Jörg Roesler, 'Die Produktionsbrigaden in der Industrie der DDR. Zentrum der Arbeitswelt?' in Kaelble et al. (eds), *Sozialgeschichte der DDR*; Peter Hübner, *Konsenz, Konflikt und Kompromiß. Soziale Arbeiterinteressen und Sozialpolitik in der SBZ/DDR 1945–1970* (Berlin: Akademie Verlag, 1995), 212–218, 223–230.

49. Schildt, *Sozialgeschichte*, 238–40.

50. Hübner, *Konsenz*, 241–44; Klessmann, *Arbeiterstaat*, 769–72; Michael Hofmann and Dieter Rink, 'Vom Arbeiterstaat zur de-klassierten Gesellschaft? Ostdeutsche Arbeitermilieus zwischen Auflösung und Aufmüpfigkeit,' in Helmut Bremer and Andrea Lange-Vester (eds), *Soziale Milieus und Wandel der Sozialstruktur* (Wiesbaden: VS Verlag für Sozialwissenschaften, 2006), 262–294.

51. Geißler, *Sozialstruktur*, 233; Wehler, *Gesellschaftsgeschichte*, 16; Mooser, *Arbeiterleben*, 127, 137, 140. Kaschuba, 'Arbeiterkultur,' 48.

52. Kaelble, *Sozialgeschichte*, 129–30.

53. Geißler, *Sozialstruktur*, 313; Manfred Hettling, 'Bürgerlichkeit im Nachkriegsdeutschland,' in Hettling and Ulricht (eds), *Bürgertum nach 1945*, 10.

54. Schildt, *Sozialgeschichte*, 23, 31–32, 98; Wehler, *Gesellschaftsgeschichte*, 121–123, 118; Geißler, *Sozialstruktur*, 92–93, 96–97; Abelshauser, *Wirtschaftsgeschichte*, 358–359.

55. Geißler, *Sozialstruktur*, 100–101, 233; Lutz, 'Integration,' 288.

56. Hradil, *Sozialstruktur*, 153–156, 159; Wehler, *Gesellschaftsgeschichte*, 195–196; Geißler, *Sozialstruktur*, 95, 335–336, 347–348.

57. Mooser, *Arbeiterleben*, 127; Geißler, *Sozialstruktur*, 336, 347, 352–357.

58. Geißler, *Sozialstruktur*, 359; Wehler, *Gesellschaftsgeschichte*, 172; Hradil, *Sozialstruktur*, 150–52; Mooser, *Arbeiterleben*, 116; Karin Zachmann, *Mobilisierung der Frauen. Technik, Geschlecht und Kalter Krieg in der DDR* (Frankfurt am Main: Campus, 2004).

59. Schildt, *Sozialgeschichte*, 32–33; Geißler, *Sozialstruktur*, 313, 321; Mooser, *Arbeiterleben*, 114–116, 127, 138; Wehler, *Gesellschaftsgeschichte*, 161, 155, 179.

60. Geißler, *Sozialstruktur*, 322, 324, 326; Therborn, *Gesellschaften*, 210.

61. Thomas Großbölting, 'Entbürgerlichte die DDR? Sozialer Bruch und kultureeller Wandel in der ostdeutschen Gesellschaft,' in Hettling and Ulricht (eds), *Bürgertum nach 1945*, 415–416; Jarausch, *Umkehr*, 206, 209; Wehler, *Gesellschaftsgeschichte*, 136–39, 141–45; Volker R. Berghahn, 'Recasting Bourgeois Germany,' in Hanna Schissler (ed.), *The Miracle Years: A Cultural History of West Germany, 1949–1968* (Princeton: Princeton University Press, 2001); Hettling, 'Bürgerlichkeit,' 9–10, 18–21; Geißler, *Sozialstruktur*, 147–148, 150.

62. Geißler, *Sozialstruktur*, 156–8; Wehler, *Gesellschaftsgeschichte*, 217–18, 220–221, 227–229; Hettling, 'Bürgerlichkeit,' 8, note 4; Großbölting, 'DDR,' 408–410, 422–426.

63. Schildt, *Sozialgeschichte*, 23, 31–32; Wehler, *Gesellschaftsgeschichte*, 121–123, 118; Geißler, *Sozialstruktur*, 92–93, 96–97; Abelshauser, *Wirtschaftsgeschichte*, 358–359.
64. Haustein, *Mangel*, 193.
65. See, e.g., Port, *Conflict*, 244–253.
66. Wehler, *Gesellschaftsgeschichte*, 122, 233; Geißler, *Sozialstruktur*, 81–84; Mooser, *Arbeiterleben*, 73–74; Schildt, *Sozialgeschichte*, 23, 41.
67. Ambrosius, 'Strukturwandel,' 113.
68. Wildt, 'Konsum,' 281, 275–278, 287–288.
69. Kaelble, *Sozialgeschichte*, 90; Haustein, *Mangel*, 125, 135, 137; Sywottek, 'Wege,' 18.
70. Kaelble, *Sozialgeschichte*, 111–114.
71. Uta G. Poiger, *Jazz, Rock and Rebels: Cold War Politics and American Culture in a Divided Germany* (Berkeley: University of California Press, 2000); Mary Nolan, 'Varieties of Capitalism und Versionen der Amerikanisierung,' in Volker R. Berghahn and Sigurt Vitols (eds), *Gibt es einen deutschen Kapitalismus?* (Frankfurt am Main: Campus, 2006). Also see Konrad Jarausch and Hannes Siegrist (eds), *Amerikanisierung und Sowjetisierung in Deutschland 1945–1907* (Frankfurt am Main: Campus, 1997).
72. Haustein, *Mangel*, 28.
73. Wehler, *Gesellschaftsgeschichte*, 156; Schildt, *Sozialgeschichte*, 23–28, 183; Mooser, *Arbeiterleben*, 214.
74. Ina Merkel, *Utopie und Bedürfnis. Die Geschichte der Konsumkultur in der DDR* (Cologne: Böhlau, 1999); Annette Kaminsky, *Wohlstand, Schönheit, Glück. Kleine Konsumgeschichte der DDR* (Munich: C. H. Beck, 2001); Katherine Pence and Paul Betts (eds), *Socialist Modern: East German Everyday Culture and Politics* (Ann Arbor: University of Michigan Press, 2008).
75. Geißler, *Sozialstruktur*, 233; Haustein, *Mangel*, 193, 139–141.
76. Hoffmann and Rink, 'Arbeiterstaat;' Geißler, *Sozialstruktur*, 357, 242–43, 102–107, 327–330.
77. Wehler, *Gesellschaftsgeschichte*, 207–209.
78. Quote from Abelshauser, *Wirtschaftsgeschichte*, 358–359. Also see Geißler, *Sozialstruktur*, 96–97; Hradil, *Sozialstruktur*, 278.

BIBLIOGRAPHY

Geißler, Rainer, *Die Sozialstruktur Deutschlands. Die gesellschaftliche Entwicklung vor and nach der Vereinigung*, 3rd edn (Wiesbaden: Westdeutscher Verlag, 2002).

Harsch, Donna, *Revenge of the Domestic: Women, the Family, and Communism in the German Democratic Republic* (Princeton: Princeton University Press, 2007).

Haustein, Sabine, *Vom Mangel zum Massenkonsum. Deutschland, Frankreich und Grossbritannien im Vergleich 1945–1970* (Frankfurt am Main: Campus, 2007).

Hettling, Manfred and Bernd Ulrich (eds), *Bürgertum nach 1945* (Hamburg: Hamburger Edition, 2005).

Hradil, Stefan, *Die Sozialstruktur Deutschlands im internationalen Vergleich* (Wiesbaden: VS Verlag, 2004).

JARAUSCH, KONRAD, *Die Umkehr. Deutsche Wandlungen 1945–1995* (Munich: Deutsche Verlags-Anstalt, 2004).

KAELBLE, HARTMUT, JÜRGEN KOCKA, and HARTMUT ZWAHR (eds), *Sozialgeschichte der DDR.* (Stuttgart: Klett-Cotta, 1994).

——*Sozialgeschichte Europas. 1945 bis zur Gegenwart* (Munich: Beck, 2007).

KASCHUBA, WOLFGANG, GOTTFRIED KORFF, and BERND JÜRGEN WARNEKEN, *Arbeiterkultur seit 1945—Ende oder Veränderung?* (Tübingen: Tübinger Vereinigung für Volkskunde, 1991).

LANDSMAN, MARK, *Dictatorship and Demand: The Politics of Consumerism in East Germany.* (Cambridge: Harvard University Press, 2005).

MOOSER, JOSEF, *Arbeiterleben in Deutschland 1890–1970. Klassenlagen, Kultur und Politik* (Frankfurt: Suhrkamp, 1984).

——*Die Sozialgeschichte der Bundesrepublik Deutschland bis 1989/90* (Munich: Oldenbourg Wissenschaftsverlag, 2007).

SCHILDT, AXEL and ARNOLD SYWOTTEK (eds), *Modernisierung im Wiederaufbau. Die westdeutsche Gesellschaft der 50er Jahre* (Bonn: Dietz, 1993).

THERBORN, GÖRAN, *Die Gesellschaften Europas 1945–2000* (Frankfurt and New York: Campus, 2000).

WEHLER, HANS-ULRICH, *Deutsche Gesellschaftsgeschichte 1949–1990* (Munich: Beck, 2008).

CHAPTER 30

RELIGION AND THE SEARCH FOR MEANING, 1945–1990

BENJAMIN ZIEMANN

ON July 29 1945, Victor Klemperer, a professor of Romance languages and literatures who had been forced out of his position in 1935 by the Nazi regime, listened in Dresden to the radio broadcast of a service celebrated by the Lutheran bishop of Berlin-Brandenburg, Otto Dibelius. Klemperer was a Jew who had converted to Protestant Christianity in 1912, but nonetheless survived World War II and the Holocaust only due to his marriage to an 'Aryan' woman. He was impressed and captivated to hear Dibelius talking about Paul in Athens (Acts of the Apostles, 17, 16–34), where the apostle had tried to convert some philosophers who only knew about an 'unknown god.' In line with the apostle, Dibelius insisted that 'one had to find HIM, had to get to know him.' But then, Klemperer noted in his diary, came the 'disappointment that always comes when one entrusts himself to the pastors.' As Dibelius demanded that people had to change their ways and to acknowledge Jesus, a disillusioned Klemperer expressed scorn at the opportunity 'to believe in the loving kindness of the heavenly father, in spite of all the cruelties of these years' since 1933. And he concluded: 'Every day it is ever more mysterious to me how people can believe in the gracious, loving etc. God. I intend to leave the church, which has let me down in such a shameful manner, right now and particularly now.'[1]

This episode encapsulates some of the problems that are under scrutiny in this chapter: the ongoing relevance of religion in the search for meaning in postwar Germany, amidst growing discontent with the churches as organized bodies and their professional representatives; the ways in which their lack of resistance against the anti-Jewish policies of the Nazi regime haunted the Christian churches after 1945; and secularization, understood as the flight from the churches, exemplified in Klemperer's intention to give up his membership. We will discuss these developments in three steps:

first, with a survey of the quantitative and qualitative evidence for secularization; then by considering the changing forms and sites of piety and the impact of theological debates on the active rank-and-file members of the Christian churches; and finally, by looking at the changing social configurations of religious beliefs, especially in the context of tensions between a pluralized 'invisible religion' and the inertia and attempts at reform within organized religion.

30.1 SECULARIZATION

Germany in 1945 was still a country with a predominantly Christian population, but it was less Protestant than the unified nation state founded in 1871 had been. As a result of the expulsion of millions of Germans from territories east of the Oder-Neisse line and from Eastern European countries, such as Hungary, Czechoslovakia, and Romania, the confessional map of Germany was redrawn. Whereas only one-third of the population had been Catholic up till 1945, 44.3 percent of the population in the Federal Republic was Catholic, compared with 51.5 percent Protestants. One in five Catholics in West Germany was an expellee from the East. The higher number of Protestants leaving their church in the following decades, discussed below, ultimately turned the advantage in favor of the Catholics, who outnumbered Protestants in the Federal Republic from the late 1970s on. The expulsion also affected the territory of the GDR; already in 1946, East Germany comprised a considerable proportion of Catholics—12.2 percent.

Amidst the rubble of the society of the immediate postwar period, bishops, priests, and theologians of both Christian churches agreed that a rebuilding of the moral and political order could only succeed through a reaffirmation of Christian values. In their perception, the barbarism and the mass crimes of the Nazi regime were the result of a break with God and the secularization of public life, which had created a moral vacuum and, hence, left the German people vulnerable to the temptation of totalitarianism. Rebuilding the moral compass and the international authority of the Germans would, hence, require a rechristianization of society. The terms and practical implications of this rechristianization were never spelled out in detail, but it was apparently based on an anti-Communist political agenda, the vague conservative ideological tradition of a 'Christian occident,' and hopes for a unification of western Europe along these lines. Both churches, and the Catholic church in particular, could justify this reasoning with the claim that they were the only public institutions that had not been brought under the control of the Nazi regime. They had also shown their moral responsibility, for instance with public protests against the program of euthanasia in 1940. Both the powerful symbolism of Catholic processions held in the ruins of cities such as Münster or Cologne in the summer of 1945, and widely reported figures showing that people rejoined the churches in droves seemed to support these claims for a rechristianization of German society.

Yet already by the late 1940s, some contemporary observers noted the huge discrepancy between the far-reaching expectations for a wholesale rechristianization of German society and the realities on the ground. Those who rejoined as church members are a good case in point. When the return to Christian church affiliation in the western occupation zones peaked in 1946, 75,000 people had joined the Protestant churches again. But already in 1949 the overall balance of joiners and leavers was negative, with a net loss of 43,000 people who exited the Protestant churches. This very moderate success has to be seen against the backdrop of a massive exodus during the 'Third Reich,' when one million people had left the Protestant churches from 1937 until 1939 alone, responding to the aggressive policies of a regime bent on curbing the influence of organized Christianity. As astute priests noted, many of those Protestants and Catholics who joined again in 1945 were driven by opportunistic motives, hoping simply to improve their chances for a lenient sentence in their individual de-Nazification procedure (Fig. 30.1).[2]

Quite contrary to the hopes for a rechristianization, the figures of those who gave up their church membership in the Federal Republic show a cyclical increase, with every new cycle commencing on a higher plateau. The lower absolute figures for Catholics prove that their commitment to the church was stronger, whereas the largely parallel developments in the two Christian churches indicate that external, rather than internal reasons motivated those who ultimately left the church. A crucial factor in this respect was the church tax, which is automatically deducted as a percentage of the income tax in the Federal Republic. Increases in the income tax level and a worsening of the

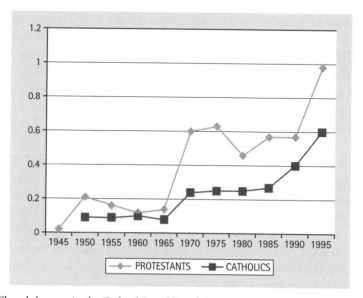

FIG. 30.1 Church leavers in the Federal Republic of Germany, 1945–1995 (in percent)

Source: Religion in Geschichte und Gegenwart. Handwörterbuch für Theologie und Religionswissenschaft, vol. 4, 4th edn (Tübingen: Mohr Siebeck, 2001), 1055.

economic situation, as in the early 1970s and after reunification in 1990, tipped the balance in favor of exit for those whose bonds with the church had already loosened. Although the 1960s and again the 1980s were marked by relatively low levels of exits, the accumulation of exits over the decades and the rapidly increasing numbers of leavers since 1990 have left about 12 percent of all West Germans in 1998 without any church affiliation.[3]

Even after reunification, however, the overwhelming majority of all Germans living in the West were at least formally members of one of the Christian churches. The GDR, however, experienced a radically different trajectory: a massive de-Christianization of both the population and of public life. Already from 1950 to 1964, the number of Protestant church members in the GDR dropped from 80.5 to 59.4 percent, while the share of those without any church affiliation quadrupled to a staggering 31.9 percent.[4] Crucial for the rapid secularization of East German society were not modernizing social trends, but rather the aggressive church policies of the SED, the state-supporting Socialist Unity Party. Already since the founding of the GDR in 1949, the communist regime had tried to curb the public presence of the churches by resorting to polemical press campaigns, threatening or arresting individual parish priests, and launching a major attack on the *Junge Gemeinde*, a Protestant youth group. After the shock of the uprising on June 17, 1953, the Communist regime developed even more intensive and systematic attempts to break the Christian monopoly on the rites of passage, such as baptism, confirmation, and even burial. The introduction of the *Jugendweihe* in 1954, a state-organized ceremony marking, at the age of fourteen, the transition from child-hood to maturity, represented a particularly bold attempt to curb the social reproduc-tion of Christian beliefs. The Protestant church tried to counter its impact through a mobilization of its members and negotiations with the SED. When these conflicts reached a climax in 1958, the church was finally forced to give in and declare its loyalty to the socialist state. The *Jugendweihe* was not made compulsory, but the confirmation as a crucial rite of passage for the reproduction of the Protestant *Volkskirche*, a popular church which represented the majority of the population, was irreparably damaged. The percentage of youths opting for confirmation dropped rapidly from three-quarters in 1956 to a mere one-third in 1959, and decreased further to about 15 percent by the mid-1970s.[5]

Relations between the Communist state and the Protestant church did not always remain as hostile as during the late 1950s and most of the 1960s. Since 1975, in line with the obligations to respect human rights enshrined in the Helsinki Accords, and in an attempt to boost the legitimacy of the regime, the SED held talks with the church at all levels and tried to support those Protestant currents that understood themselves as a 'church within socialism.' Subsequently, small, emerging independent groups of peace activists and environmentalist campaigners sought shelter in the framework of some urban parish communities. As the mushrooming opposition groups were accommo-dated by the Protestant church, tensions with the regime resurfaced during the 1980s, and the regime increased attempts to infiltrate the church with the help of *Stasi* snitches. These developments ultimately led to the exaggerated claim that the opening of the wall in 1989 was the result of a 'Protestant revolution.'[6]

It would be misleading, however, to infer from these political developments that the Protestant church regained a crucial role in East German society. Quite to the contrary, the 1970s and 1980s saw a further acceleration in the fundamental de-Christianization of the GDR. When the collapse of the GDR-regime in 1990 made reliable surveys possible, only thirty percent of all East Germans still belonged to a Christian church, whereas the number of unaffiliated people had reached a whopping 70 percent. At the same time, only 17 percent of all newborn babies were baptized, and the attendance figure for Sunday services had fallen to a mere 4 percent.[7] Taking all quantitative and qualitative criteria into account, the GDR in its final decade was by far the most secularized of all European societies. It was a place where, for a large majority of the population, Christian religion had ceased to have any ritual functions and biographical relevance, or offer any relevant cognitive orientation. Yet these striking facts were not only the result of systematic and sustained state repression, which had successfully broken the 'chain of memory' in families and local communities so vital for a continuation of Christian beliefs.[8] On top of that, the thorough secularization of East German society since 1945 had other, long-term roots.

Already in 1900, the territories east of the river Elbe had had considerably lower rates for attendance at Communion services than most of the Protestant regions in the south and west of Germany. This was partly due to the higher degree of urbanization in the East, in connection with the existence of socialist working-class strongholds in Saxony, Thuringia, and Sachsen-Anhalt, but also due to the lack of Pietist traditions, which placed a premium on active forms of piety.[9] Another reason was the impact of scientism, the belief in the superior explanatory power of the modern sciences as a coherent worldview. Scientism provided a substitute for the religious claim to answer the 'ultimate' questions of life, death, and human destiny, and it was deeply rooted in the scientific socialism of the Marxist labor movement. In the GDR, it was actively promoted by the Urania, a 'society for the dissemination of scientific knowledge' founded in 1954. With an avalanche of public lectures and printed materials, the Urania reached out to millions of GDR citizens and successfully promoted a scientific and atheistic system of ethics. It is one of the consequences of this secularization through scientism that even after German reunification in 1990, far fewer non-affiliated Germans in the East believe in God than their counterparts in the West.[10]

If we consider the trajectory of secularization in the Federal Republic, attendance figures for Sunday services provide further crucial quantitative evidence. They shed light on the ability of the churches to sustain a milieu of active Christians who often not only attended services on a regular basis, but were also members in religious associations or took part in a whole raft of church-related activities at the parish level. For Catholics, attending Sunday services and receiving communion at Easter was a part of the five Commandments of the Church (which included holy days of obligation, the confession of mortal sins, and abstinence before lent), established since the Council of Trent and providing a yardstick for what a 'good' Catholic ought to do.

Compiled by a separate statistical office for the Catholic church, the statistical aggregation of data on Catholic observance provided vivid evidence of secularization, and played a central role in internal debates about church policy. For the very same reason, however, we also need to interpret these figures with caution. As attendance and communion figures were a benchmark for pastoral success, the hierarchical structure and organizational logic of the Catholic church provided parish priests with good reasons to inflate their counts artificially, and the bishops with good reasons not to investigate this (Fig. 30.2). At least until the 1960s, the attendance figures were, hence, to some extent exaggerated.[11]

Nonetheless, they allow a provisional assessment of the continually decreasing relevance of traditional acts of practical piety. At a glance, we can see that the percentage of active Catholics has shrunk to roughly one-fifth within four decades. In addition, we see that the pace of this downhill trend has accelerated markedly since the late 1960s, a reason why many conservative Catholics attributed the decline to the liberal and participatory attitudes which many younger Catholics adopted in the wake of the 1968 student revolt. Especially for the 1950s, where the aggregate figures still seem to suggest a remarkable stability of the Catholic milieu, additional evidence needs to be taken into account, in particular attendance figures stratified according to sex, age, and profession. These data, which were established for many urban areas, show that the notion of a coherent Catholic milieu was already in the mid-1950s a mere façade. Among the churchgoers, gainfully employed men in their thirties and forties were grossly under-represented, and housewives, children, and pensioners provided the bulk of the flock gathered in the church. Whereas middle-class males, in particular civil

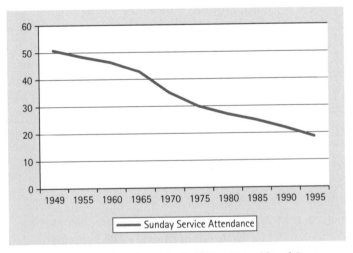

FIG. 30.2 Catholic Sunday service attendance in the Federal Republic of Germany, 1949–1995 (in percent)

Source: Kirchliches Handbuch. Statistisches Jahrbuch der Bistümer. Vol. xxxv, 1997–1998.
(Cologne: J. P. Bachem, 2003), 182.

servants and white-collar employees, still turned out in considerable numbers, industrial workers, the largest group of urban Catholics, showed much less inclination to attend services. Even in strongholds of the Christian labor movement such as the Ruhr-district, where a dense network of Catholic professional and religious associations had, until 1933, formed a stable milieu, less than 20 percent of the workers attended mass in the mid-1950s.[12]

The quantitative evidence on church-goers shows a substantial erosion of the number of active Catholics in the Federal Republic, in a process that had already begun in the 1950s. Hence, it cannot simply be blamed on the excessive adaption to modern society demanded by the Second Vatican Council (1962–1965), or the implosion of moral values since 1968, as conservative critics of both events have claimed. Two qualifications are, however, necessary. One reason for the dramatic nature of the decline of the Catholic milieu in postwar Germany was its very stability until 1945, when it was still able to bind the large majority of all Catholics in a dense network of religious forms of sociability. In comparison, Protestantism started from a much lower level of active, organized piety, with attendance figures in the Federal Republic never higher than 7 percent.[13] Secondly, after four decades of decline, celebrating mass on Sunday remains the most widespread form of collective religiosity. With six million Roman Catholics attending on an average Sunday in 1990, it is the single most widely practised form of organized sociability in reunified Germany, by far outnumbering those who attend professional soccer in the *Bundesliga* (first division) or other team sports.[14]

30.2 CHANGING FORMS OF PIETY
AND THEOLOGY

The considerable impact of secularization on both Protestants and Catholics should not obscure the fact that both churches developed, adopted, and embraced new forms of piety and theology since 1945. Some of these developments were driven by the need to come to terms with the moral and theological legacy of the Nazi past. Others responded to the challenges of a rapidly modernizing society and aimed to provide a platform for the encounter with this complex modernity. Traditional forms of piety were superseded in the process and quickly lost their relevance. One prominent example involves pilgrimages. As public mass demonstrations, they had been a crucial part of the ultramontane revival of Catholic piety from the 1840s into the 'Third Reich.' Apart from some examples in the immediate postwar period, however, they quickly lost both participants and publicity in the Federal Republic. A striking feature of the changing forms of piety and theology is their implicit ecumenical nature. The confessional divide of the nineteenth century had effectively led to an increasing divergence between the demonstrative, public forms of Catholic piety and the more private and intimate forms with which Protestants expressed their faith. As they were facing the prospects and perils of modernization, both churches focused on a set of similar platforms for religious encounters and an exchange of views about contemporary society.

Before they could embrace modern society, Protestants first had to deal with the legacy of a tradition that had identified the cause of the German nation with that of the Protestants, and had led to widespread active support for the Nazi regime both among ministers and the laity. These issues had practical implications particularly with regard to the de-Nazification of the clergy. From the beginning, leading Protestant bishops such as Theophil Wurm (1868–1953) in Württemberg and Hans Meiser (1881–1956) in Bavaria agreed with their flock in an outright and wholesale rejection of the de-Nazification measures taken by the Allies. Their resentment was triggered by the bureaucratic impracticalities of the procedures, but rested also on the perception that the sworn ideological enemies of conservative Protestants, namely Social Democrats and Communists, were the main beneficiaries of de-Nazification. Even more crucial was the fact that the Protestant churches were themselves affected by the measures. According to the criteria of the March 1946 law, which assigned the task of de-Nazification to German tribunals (*Spruchkammern*), 226 out of 645 active pastors in Hesse, 143 of 341 in Baden, and even 51 of 55 in the small Protestant church in Bremen were incriminated. Problematic were also the large numbers of ministers who had been members of the Nazi party, even more so as there were apparently no significant differences in de-Nazification prosecutions between regional strongholds of the *Deutsche Christen*, who had wholeheartedly supported the regime, and those of the *Bekennende Kirche* (confessing church), which had stood up against the Nazification of the Protestant churches since the famous 1934 Barmen declaration, opposed the German Christians, and rejected the subordination of church to state.[15] Protestant bishops, pastors, and laypersons were also united in their unanimous rejection of the Allied accusation of a collective German guilt for the deeds of the Nazi regime. This accusation was, in fact, a postwar invention of the vanquished, as the Allies had never published an official document in which they postulated a collective guilt of the Germans.[16] But this fact did not stop Protestants and also many Catholics from resenting the gross injustice of this invented verdict and to put in a word for the defendants in many of the postwar trials against *Wehrmacht* officers and other Nazi perpetrators.[17]

The recognition of their own complicity in and guilt for the Nazi regime was, hence, a very protracted and complicated process for the overwhelming majority of German Protestants. Neither the prospect of repentance nor a critical examination of the intellectual traditions of national Protestantism—with its idea of the Germans as a chosen people and its strong conservative inclination—appealed to them in the immediate postwar period. The *Evangelische Kirche in Deutschland* (EKD), an umbrella body representing both Lutheran and Reformed regional churches, and those where the two had been merged in a union during the nineteenth century, agreed on the text of the 'Stuttgart declaration of guilt' in October 1945. This, however, was 'not simply an act of conscience,' but the result of pressure from representatives of the World Council of Churches, who had met with the twelve members of the EKD council in Stuttgart. The declaration included the admission that 'through us has endless suffering been brought to many peoples and countries,' and indicated remorse in the words 'we accuse ourselves for not witnessing more courageously, for not praying more faithfully, for not believing more joyously.'[18]

The document failed to single out the genocide against the European Jews as the most crucial element of German guilt, even while a small number of Jews were trying to rebuild their lives in Germany.[19] Not until 1950 did the EKD issue a 'word on the Jewish question.' If it still used an anti-Semitic turn of phrase in the document's title, the pronouncement nevertheless acknowledged for the first time that Protestants had been 'complicit' (*mitschuldig*) in the 'heinous deed' against the Jews.[20] The Stuttgart declaration, however, had not even been published by its authors, so that the laity only got to know it when the German press printed the text following up on reports in British newspapers. Laypersons reacted with a storm of objections and furious comments, and many conservative leaders of the EKD were firm in diluting any political implications of the text.[21] It was only after a process of introspection and recognition of the new realities of a democratic society that West German Protestants abandoned their national-conservative mentalities. Gradually, they learned to accept the realities of German defeat and the positive relevance of values, such as pluralism, religious and political tolerance, and democracy. There is some controversy among scholars about the extent and speed of this value-change and the significance of continuities in the postwar period, as shown by the grassroots protests against the Stuttgart declaration. The empirical evidence, particularly opinion polls with data on the dwindling of positive reminiscences about the Nazi past, suggests that a majority of the West German Protestants had not abandoned the national Protestant mindset until the late 1950s.[22] The ground for this substantial shift in mentalities, however, had already been laid in 1947, when the Fraternal Council (*Bruderrat*) of the EKD, which represented the remnants of the confessing church, issued the so-called *Darmstädter Wort*. This brief text displayed the convoluted prose of Protestant theologians, but was nonetheless unequivocal in its condemnation of the former 'dream of a peculiar German mission,' and labeled the wholesale rejection of Marxism by the church until 1945 as a 'mistake' and an 'aberration' (*Irrweg*).[23] This document was subsequently a crucial point of reference for all those Protestants who wanted to disentangle their church from its long-established ties with political conservatism and German nationalism.

As both Protestants and Catholics were increasingly ready to engage with a pluralistic society, confessional academies were one important forum both for religious spirituality and for a dialogue between Christians and the social and political tendencies of the time. They were meant to be 'centers for the radiation of Christian ideas' in society. In addition, the academies were responding to the widespread demand for a church that would not pontificate from the pulpit, as Victor Klemperer had complained in 1945, but rather listen to the spiritual, intellectual and theological questions of the believers and their search for meaning. The academies also fostered open discussions based on partnership rather than deference.[24] Pastor Eberhard Müller had initiated the idea of academies, which had no real precedent in German church history, when in October 1945 he invited leading figures from the economy and the legal professions in Württemberg to an 'academy conference' in Bad Boll. Gathering for a fortnight, the 120 participants started every day with a contemplation on biblical themes provided by a theology professor, followed by a mixture of talks and discussions. Stressing the religious component, a devotional was also part of the daily routine at this and subsequent meetings.[25] The success of this conference soon led to a regular institution, the *Evangelische Akademie* Bad Boll, which commenced its work in April 1946. Within a year, several other academies had opened, and the annual number of conferences in all these houses increased to 1000 in 1961, drawing in no less than a total of 51,000 participants. Many of them were members of the professional elites, physicians, journalists, or teachers who discussed the ethical implications of their work. Another type of academy conference discussed topical political issues with participants from all walks of life. 'Social ethical' topics, such as the relations between industrial employers and their workers, were a third focus of the meetings. Adopting the Protestant example, the Catholic church opened its first *Akademie* in 1950, establishing sixteen further houses by 1960. Both in their range of topics and in the mixture of discussion and religious contemplation, Catholic academies followed the pattern set by the Protestants. The Catholics accentuated and taught, however, the social doctrines of the church, as in the 'social seminars' offered by the Franz Hitze-house in Münster since the 1950s. Catholic academies were also the site of trailblazing initiatives, for instance when the *Katholische Akademie Bayern* in Munich invited for the first time major Social Democratic politicians to a Catholic venue in January 1958 and thus kick-started an increasingly intensive dialogue between the Catholic church and the SPD.

Both Protestant and Catholic academies catered predominantly to the laity with an advanced educational degree, with the aim of preparing an academically-trained elite for the encounter between the church and the secular world. Both churches, however, also had an established forum for displaying a broad variety of lay initiatives and associations and for gathering the masses. These were the *Kirchentage*, or biannual church conventions, which alternated between different cities, and until 1961 also between East and West, thus linking the churches in the Federal Republic and the GDR at least symbolically together. During the 1950s and most of the 1960s, both Protestant and Catholic church conventions were carefully choreographed mass events, aiming to occupy the public space in a large and hence often secular city with explicitly Christian symbols, gatherings and rituals. Thousands of Christians sang together and marched through the streets, aiming to convey a sense of the missionary zeal and the might of the churches, as well as showing the spiritual qualities, and the discipline of a voluntary and peaceful mass gathering. The Protestant *Kirchentag* in Leipzig in July 1954 was the epitome of this disciplined, top-down approach. Held in an officially atheist town, the final manifestation displayed the cheerful Christianity of its 650,000 participants and their hopes for a German reunification.[26]

The character of these conventions began to change gradually in the 1960s, when purely proclamatory public events gave way to working meetings with open discussions. Then the Catholic *Katholikentag* held in Essen in September 1968, at the height of the student protests, brought participation and lay representation as key elements of these gatherings to the fore. Following the publication of the encyclical '*Humanae Vitae*,' not only the activists of the left-wing group 'Critical Catholicism,' but also ordinary middle-class laypersons engaged in an intensive debate on contentious issues such as birth control, the proper implementation of the reform decrees of the Second Vatican Council (1962–1965), and the intellectual, spiritual, and organizational crisis of the church. Instead of being a carefully choreographed mass event, the Catholic *Katholikentag* in 1968 was a place of contestation and unrest. The laity attacked the hierarchical structures of the Catholic church and demanded an open dialogue and responsiveness from the bishops. This demand was at least symbolically met by the implementation of a comprehensive opinion poll, the distribution of a questionnaire to all 21 million Catholics in the Federal Republic.[27] Essen inaugurated a fundamental change in the character of the *Kirchentage* of both churches. From a public demonstration of a strong faith, these mass conventions turned into an information and communication hub for both the spiritual and the worldly activities and themes of the various lay groups and initiatives. The Protestant conventions formally subscribed to this development since the *Kirchentag* in Frankfurt in 1975. For the first time it included a separate 'market of possibilities,' which accentuated this transformation to a religious fair.[28] Although the church conventions are only temporary events, they have continued to attract large numbers of participants and huge public interest with their amalgamation of participation, spirituality, and elements of modern pop culture.

The *Kirchentage* made a significant contribution to the changing forms of piety in postwar Germany, as they provided a platform for momentary, if popular religious mass encounters. Their continuing appeal in the 1970s and 1980s, however, was also a side-effect of the student revolt of 1968, which created resonance for new, participatory forms of expressing religious beliefs. The search for new social configurations, beyond the parish, in which faith could be lived and experienced was accompanied by an experimentation with new liturgical forms. One crucial example was the political night prayer (*Politisches Nachtgebet*), an ecumenical initiative first practised in Cologne in October 1968 in the aftermath of the *Katholikentag* in Essen; it then swiftly spread to other cities in West Germany, the Netherlands, and Switzerland. As an attempt to create new liturgical forms, the political night prayer aimed to overcome the privacy and subjectivity of conventional prayers, and to replace them with a collective appeal against injustice and exploitation in the capitalist world system as exemplified by the war in Vietnam or hunger and starvation in Africa. In practice, however, the political night prayer more resembled seminars devoted to a collective interpretation of Karl Marx, Herbert Marcuse, and Theodor W. Adorno, the staple diet of student protesters, than any form of Christian church service. They consisted mainly of readings from prepared texts, presentations on political themes, and appeals. Prayers were rare, and singing and personal contributions strictly unwanted, as they were reminiscent of the subjective piety of Pietist conventicles. When the political impetus of the student movement faded away, the remaining faithful still sought closeness, joy, and a current of warmth in the liturgy, and the regular practice of the night prayers came to an end in 1972.[29]

The political aims of this experiment were bound up with the New Leftist ideologies of the student revolt, which found their religious counterpart in the proponents of a 'political theology.' This theological current was prominently represented by the Catholic theologian Johann Baptist Metz (1928– present) and the Protestant theologian Dorothee Sölle (1929–2003), who quickly rose to public fame far beyond church circles after 1968, not least through her leading role in the preparation of the political night prayers in Cologne. During the 1970s and 1980s, Sölle was undoubtedly the most prominent theologian in the Federal Republic. In her writings on political theology, she aimed 'to rediscover the political relevance of the Gospel,' particularly by a recognition of the social radicalism of the 'historical Jesus.' Against subjective, existentialist readings of the bible, Sölle stressed the inherent 'political dimension of existence' and the need to consider this in theological reflection. A crucial case in point was the concept of sin. Conventional interpretations of sin, salvation, and other key categories of Christian doctrine had reduced them for Sölle to 'privatistic categories.' Privatistic (*privatistisch*)—this neologism of 1970s progressive talk was meant to denote, in a critical perspective, an attitude which exaggerates privateness and individuality as values in their own right. Instead, sin had to be seen as a form of 'collaboration,' not depending on the conscience of the individual, but rather on the collective complicity of people in the Western world in globalized forms of injustice.[30]

Political theology was not the only new and important departure in Christian thinking since the 1960s. While today, as historian Dagmar Herzog has rightly stated, 'religious renewal' in the late twentieth century is most often associated with the rise of evangelical fundamentalism or with New Age spiritualism, it was 'a form of Marx-inspired liberation theology adapted to western European context from its Latin American' origins that 'decisively rescued' the credibility of Christianity amidst the apparent secularization and inner contestation in the churches around 1970.[31] Liberation theology is a broad label, denoting both the leftist reinterpretation of Christian dogmas by prominent theologians, such as Gustavo Gutiérrez from Peru or Leonardo Boff from Brazil, and the vibrant grassroots movements for a reform of the church through 'base communities' and a fight against exclusion and poverty, endeavors which are often associated with the names of their most prominent supporters among the bishops in Latin America such as Oscar Romero (1917–1980) from El Salvador or Dom Hélder Câmara (1909–1999), the bishop of Recife in Brazil. As a theological current, liberation theology was predicated on assumptions that bore close resemblance with ideas from political theology, not surprisingly as, for instance, Gutiérrez was strongly influenced by Johann Baptist Metz, and all liberation theologists were well acquainted with the European new theologies of the postwar period through their studies in universities such as Munich, Lyon and, most importantly, the Catholic University of Leuven in Belgian Flanders. They developed the notion of a God suffering with the human beings, of solidarity as an important prerequisite for an experience of God, and of the preeminence of the immanent social reality for the lived faith.[32]

Although most liberation theologists were Catholic, their ideas found a wide reception in the Federal Republic in the late 1960s among Protestants, not least through the intellectual translation and adaption provided by Dorothee Sölle. Liberation theology was the most important transnational encounter of German Christians in the postwar period, and its impact on the religious field during the 1970s and 1980s can hardly be overestimated. Not only Christian student associations, youth groups and related reform initiatives, but also the mushrooming Third-World groups and the many professionals working in *Diakonie* and *Caritas*, the Protestant and Catholic social welfare organizations, embraced ideas and slogans from liberation theology. This widespread and enthusiastic reception process, however, was only partly a result of the intellectual significance of the ideas developed by Boff, Gutiérrez, and others. Much more important was the perception of the vibrant and optimistic lay initiatives in the Latin American churches influenced by liberation theology. They appeared to be in a stark contrast to the increasing desolation of lay activists in the Federal Republic, particularly once the hopes for a democratic reform of the churches were dashed in the early 1970s. Against the backdrop of a 'church without confidence,' liberation theology promised hope and 'trust' in the continuous power of faith. And amidst widespread discontent with the perceived ossification and bureaucratic habits of the 'official church' (*Amtskirche*) and its leaders, the leftist bishops from Latin America, with their lack of decorum, modest if not Spartan lifestyle and their open, direct rhetoric seemed to embody a positive alternative and were hence hailed as 'prophets.' Dom Hélder Câmara particularly attracted huge audiences at public appearances in Germany, and the hype around his person reached a climax in 1973, when he was nominated for a Nobel Peace Prize.[33]

The widespread reception of liberation theology in the West German churches and the symbolic significance of its figureheads for the hopes and expectations of the laity indicate the increased standing and importance of progressive currents in organized Christianity since the late 1960s. For the Catholic church, this was partly a side-effect of the Second Vatican Council, which had nurtured hopes for a thorough reform of the church and had provided them with legitimacy. More generally, this was a result of the political and cultural experiments associated with the symbolic date of 1968. Although this is rarely acknowledged in the growing literature on the student revolt, faithful young Catholics and Protestants were part and parcel of the rebellion of '68, and their ideas and beliefs helped to shape less authoritarian and more pluralistic attitudes in the churches.[34] When Elisabeth Rickal paid her first visit as newly elected head of the 'League of German Catholic Youth' (BDKJ) to Bishop Franz Hengsbach in Essen in 1968, he stretched out the hand with his bishop's ring for her to kiss. She refused this deferential gesture, and pointedly shook his hand.[35] These progressive religious and theological currents after 1968 had not only a short-term impact on the churches, but also long-term significance for German society, as the churches provided a reservoir for leftist and anti-capitalist ideas during the neo-liberal attack on the welfare state in the 1980s and after the demise of Communism in 1990.

As left-liberal and progressive currents gained ground in the churches, their advance was not uncontested. A conservative backlash had already developed in the late 1960s, comparable to developments in other western European countries and the USA. It was, however, much weaker than the burgeoning evangelicals in the UK and USA or the traditionalist revolt of the schismatic Catholic archbishop Marcel Lefebvre in France. Those Protestants in the Federal Republic who rejected the perceived leftist dilution of core beliefs were more diverse and less well connected than the Anglo-Saxon evangelicals and fundamentalists. They also did not forge an alliance with conservative Catholics, as the neofundamentalists in the USA have done since the 1980s. Rather, Catholic fundamentalists rejected the post-Vatican reforms as a 'protestantization' of their church, thus flagging their eagerness to stress the distinctive profile of their faith. They tried to re-establish a monopoly on the articulation of religious truth in- and outside the Catholic church, and resented the increasingly precarious position of the sacred in society. But Catholic fundamentalists remained a small fringe group.[36] More significant was a minority of Catholics who could arrange themselves with many of the decrees of the Second Vatican Council in principle, but lamented the dubious results of their implementation. Instead of ushering into a renewal of the faith and a strengthening of the church, they argued, it had rather led to noisy, but superfluous participatory experiments, growing internal strife, and a weakening of the Catholic cause. These critics, however, lacked any coherent institutional core or public voice and hence had only an indirect influence on the workings of the church. Consequently, some conservative bishops and theologians portrayed them as a 'silent majority' in order to raise their profile.[37]

In the Protestant church, the term 'evangelical' was for the first time used in 1966 and gained currency only a couple of years later. Since 1966, when a group of ministers founded the Confession of Faith-Movement 'No other Gospel' (*Bekenntnisbewegung 'Kein anderes Evangelium'*) and attracted 19,000 people at a first mass gathering in Dortmund, Protestant evangelicals had their own institutional core.[38] The complicated title of the group indicated both it roots in the Pietist awakening movement and an attempt to tap into the symbolism of the *Bekennende Kirche* during the Third Reich. Evangelicals thus understood themselves as victims of a totalitarian aggression and the rise of a critical theology that had diluted and falsified the sole truth of the gospel, as it applied the historical-critical method to biblical texts and followed the progressive Zeitgeist in the form of political theology. It was not by chance that these public outpourings of discontent followed the 1965 *Kirchentag* in Cologne, where lectures by Dorothee Sölle had left the evangelicals aghast and shell-shocked. But although the evangelicals maintained a vociferous presence in the 1970s, they failed to gain a foothold in the institutional structures of the church. Since 1969, they henceforth aimed to establish an alternative institutional presence, for instance in missionary work or with their own press outlets. But these attempts faltered quickly, too.[39] The crux for an understanding of the different trajectory of post-1968 evangelicalism and fundamentalism in Germany, in comparison with the USA and the UK, is thus the hegemony and inertia of the mainstream religious organizations. As a separation in form of a free church seemed to be too risky, the evangelicals had to acknowledge the dominance of the established church apparatus and thus sealed their own insignificance.

30.3 CONTINUITIES AND PERILS OF RELIGIOUS ORGANIZATIONS

The fate of the evangelical revolt against a modernist theology that seemed to dilute revelation is only one example for the relevance and prevalence of formal organizations in the search for religious meaning. Whether secularization, religious crisis, or changes in the form of piety—these developments all occurred in and depended upon the churches as organized bodies, with the contestations after 1968 pitting the laity against the *Amtskirche* and the decisions made by the bishops. But they in turn were also affected by the decisions of laypersons, who decided, for instance, that 'voice' was no longer a viable reaction to the decline of the church and opted for 'exit,' i.e. gave up their church membership.[40] Search for transcendence and for religious meaning happened in, with, and then often also against the churches. Religiosity was thus to a large extent an organized religiosity.[41] A peculiarity of the German constitutional law since the Weimar constitution from 1919, which had been incorporated also in the 1949 Basic Law (*Grundgesetz*), contributed crucially to the hegemony of established, organized religion in the Federal Republic. According to Article 140 of the Basic Law, the Christian churches were corporations under public law, which provided them with a very beneficial legal status. It gave them autonomy for the regulation of their internal affairs, but required the state to collect church taxes on their behalf, to provide regular subsidies, and to protect the sanctity of Sunday and other church holidays. It also acknowledged religion, taught by teachers educated at theological departments under church supervision, as a proper subject in all state schools. Building upon their status as corporations under public law, the churches have also secured the regular presence of their representatives in the supervisory boards of public broadcasters and welfare state bodies, and in committees which give policy advice on issues such as health care, families, and education at the federal level.[42]

The Protestant and Catholic churches in the Federal Republic are not a state church as is, for example, the Church of England. But as organized bodies, they are in a much more advantageous position than religious communities in countries with a strict separation of state and church, such as the USA or France since 1905. One crucial example is the finances. Churches in France and the USA have to make continuous fundraising efforts and rely heavily on the voluntary contributions of their members to balance their budget, which in turn makes them much more responsive to the pastoral needs of their client-customers. Their counterparts in the Federal Republic can rely on a constant revenue stream from the church tax, which is levied as a percentage of the income tax. Although this increased the number of those who exited the church in the 1970s, as we have seen above, it also ushered in a period of unprecedented church spending power and provides the hidden curriculum of West German religious history in the decades since 1945. For example, in the short period from 1963 until 1978, the Catholic church almost quadrupled—in nominal terms—its income. The diocese authorities, not the parishes, now managed this revenue, which was as a consequence only partly used in the parishes, and was often instead put into a large-scale construction program of new church and administrative buildings. A substantial effect of the increased spending power was a further bureaucratization and professionalization of the diocesan authorities themselves. In the Catholic diocese of Münster, for example, the personnel of the *Generalvikariat*, the head administration led by the vicar-general, expanded massively from only 31 clerics and laypersons in 1948 to 417 employees in 1974.[43]

Throughout the period from 1945 to 1990, most Christians put a premium on the continuation of the churches as organized bodies and a diversification of their administrative apparatus. Longing for continuity had already characterized the situation in 1945, when the Protestant regional churches had to respond to the collapse of the unified national body that had been created by the *Deutsche Christen* in July 1933. Martin Niemöller (1892–1984), the figurehead of the confessing church, had spent the years since 1937 in a concentration camp and was thus a highly regarded moral authority. But he was quite alone in his insistence on rebuilding the Protestant church from the bottom-up, based on the spiritual principles of the Barmen declaration and by replacing an administrative apparatus with large-scale autonomy of the individual parish, in an analogy to the free churches in the USA. Even in a meeting of the *Reichsbruderrat* in Frankfurt in late July 1945, which represented the remnants of the confessing church, Niemöller's proposals were not rejected, but simply ignored, as everyone recognized the continuing role of the *Landeskirchen* and their apparatus. When Niemöller reiterated his proposals at a conference of Protestant church leaders in Treysa (August 27–31, 1945), he met fierce resistance from Lutheran bishops. Consequently, the conference paved the way for the slightly modified continuation of the *Landeskirchen* in a league of separate churches, the EKD.[44]

Continuity is, paradoxically, also the keyword for the attempts to reform the Protestant churches and to respond to the dwindling attractiveness of a *Volkskirche* that meant to represent in principle all baptized Protestants at the level of the local parish community. Since the mid-1960s, a growing number of proposals were demanded to supplement the parochial parish community with functionally defined services offered at a regional level, such as pastoral work for tourists or pastoral counseling. In the newly-built districts of larger towns in the 1970s, a large variety of pastoral offerings could thus be bundled in a 'church forum.' In an ecumenical fashion, these fora often combined Catholic and Protestant parish offices, and could, as an astonished observer noted in 1978, deliver everything from Christian education for families, diaconate, and *Caritas* services to student parishes. 'In between,' not audible, but visible through the glass walls of the multifunctional concrete building, the observer could even watch 'Dorothee Sölle talking about Christian anarchism in the USA,' exemplifying a pastoral work situated between the local level and ecumenical perspectives in a global horizon.[45] In the course of the reform initiatives of the 1960s and 1970s, older organizational patterns such as works (*Werke*) or services for specific strata or estates (*Stände*) such as women, youths or workers were not simply set aside. Fueled by the constant stream of tax revenue, the reform of pastoral services up until the 1990s rather followed the 'principle of structural addition,' which added further layers to the existing bureaucratic structures, but thus enabled the church machinery to absorb the impetus for a democratization of the church and leftist contestation after 1968.[46]

Our interpretation has stressed both the continuities and the perils of religious organizations, as the inflexibility of the highly bureaucratic churches tended to stifle the motivation of many of their members. Data from several opinion-polls conducted in the late 1960s confirm this point. They show that 90 percent of all West Germans still believed either in God or in a higher being. A considerable percentage even of the active church members, however, criticized the traditional structures and attitudes in the church as an institution and its reliance on church tax. Catholics in particular struggled to accept the papal policy with regard to contraception, and members of both denominations resented church interference in politics and the mass media, and demanded a stronger focus on pastoral activities, which they perceived to be the core function of the churches. In addition, Catholics perceived a cognitive dissonance between the values held by the church and those of the wider society, particularly with regard to the persistence of authoritarian attitudes and the lacking potential for autonomous self-realization.[47]

These and other data show also, by implication, that the religious field in the Federal Republic from the 1960s to the 1980s was not yet influenced by what the sociologist Thomas Luckmann in a seminal book, first published in 1963, has called 'invisible religion.' Based on his own empirical surveys in various parish communities, Luckmann was able to forecast the subsequent decline in *Kirchlichkeit*, i.e. the decreasing participation in organized forms of piety and church-related activities. He rightly predicted an increasing privatization of religiosity, when individuals started to pick and mix from the available pastoral services and forms of piety. But Luckmann was wrong with his assertion that the religious field would be dominated by what he called 'small transcendencies,' i.e. settings such as the family, in which the individuals would transcend their consciousness and built up a 'holy cosmos.'[48] Rather than ushering into a period of invisible religion—invisible in society as it is not expressed and represented in stable structures and institutions—the churches remained the key players in the religious field in Germany until German reunification in 1990. Even when individualized patterns of Christian religiosity were increasing since the 1980s, forms of spirituality beyond the confines defined by the churches remained pretty marginal. Less than 5 percent of all West Germans have experienced and experimented with Buddhism and Zen meditation, New Age-spirituality, or other forms of mysticism and magical healing. Where the percentage is slightly higher, as with fortunetelling or astrology, the experiences were mostly negative.[49]

CONCLUSION

The concept of secularization has come under sustained attack from historians who perceive it as a mere Procrustean bed for the history of religion.[50] But it remains a vital analytical tool for an understanding of the trajectory of organized religion in Germany after 1945. Both Protestant and Catholic churches were confronted with the empirical consequences of a dwindling *Kirchlichkeit*. Those who stopped attending services, receiving communion or even left the church for good not only created adverse consequences for the remaining active members, but finally, since the 1990s, also major financial problems, particularly for the Protestant churches. Secularization was, however, not only an effect of the lacking attractiveness of traditional church related activities. It was also a result of the increasing attempts of both churches to observe the rapid modernization of society, and of the forms in which politics, education, and the mass media no longer followed religious imperatives.[51] The validity of secularization as a conceptual tool for religious change in postwar Germany does not, however, imply that this was basically a story of decline. Quite to the contrary: as the Christian churches tried to cope with the strains of secularization, they experimented with new forms of piety, adapted the church apparatus to societal change and encountered new forms of thinking about the place of God in life, such as liberation theology. These were important and highly significant endeavors. They not only mattered for the faithful, but also contributed to the liberalization of West German society and to the potential for civil unrest, which was building up in the GDR during the 1980s. Secularization also did not lead to the death of Christian Germany, in analogy to the point made about the 'death of Christian Britain' by the historian Callum G. Brown.[52] While the GDR has been effectively dechristianized since the 1960s, West Germany continued to be a dominantly Christian country even after reunification. Christianity provided a widely accepted framework for public morality and the practice of rites of passage, even for those who had severed most of their links with the church.

NOTES

1. Victor Klemperer, *So sitze ich denn zwischen allen Stühlen. Tagebücher 1945–1949* (Berlin: Aufbau, 1999), 59–60.
2. Franz zu Löwenstein SJ, 'Religiöse Einkehr in Internierungslagern,' *Frankfurter Hefte* 2 (1947), 463–470.
3. For extensive data on secularization in the Federal Republic compare Michael N. Ebertz, *Erosion der Gnadenanstalt? Zum Wandel der Sozialgestalt von Kirche* (Frankfurt am Main: Knecht, 1998), here 103; Detlef Pollack, *Säkularisierung—ein moderner Mythos? Studien zum religiösen Wandel in Deutschland* (Tübingen: Mohr Siebeck, 2003).

4. Detlef Pollack, 'Von der Volkskirche zur Minderheitskirche. Zur Entwicklung von Religiosität und Kirchlichkeit in der DDR,' in: Hartmut Kaelble, Jürgen Kocka and Hartmut Zwahr (eds), *Sozialgeschichte der DDR* (Stuttgart: Klett-Cotta, 1994), 271–294, 272.

5. See Detlef Pollack, *Kirche in der Organisationsgesellschaft. Zum Wandel der gesellschaftlichen Lage der Kirchen in der DDR* (Stuttgart: W. Kohlhammer, 1994), 125–175.

6. For a thorough assessment see ibid., 293, 333–370, 446–455.

7. Pollack, 'Volkskirche,' 272, 284, 280.

8. See Danièle Hervieu-Léger, *Religion as a Chain of Memory* (New Brunswick: Rutgers University Press, 2000).

9. Lucian Hölscher, *Geschichte der protestantischen Frömmigkeit in Deutschland* (Munich: C. H. Beck, 2005), 182–189.

10. Thomas Schmidt-Lux, 'Das helle Licht der Wissenschaft. Die Urania, der organisierte Szientismus und die ostdeutsche Säkularisierung,' *Geschichte und Gesellschaft* 34 (2008), 41–72, 59, 71.

11. Benjamin Ziemann, *Katholische Kirche und Sozialwissenschaften 1945–1975* (Göttingen: Vandenhoeck & Ruprecht, 2007), 59–75.

12. Benjamin Ziemann, 'Auf der Suche nach der Wirklichkeit. Soziographie und soziale Schichtung im deutschen Katholizismus 1945–1970,' *Geschichte und Gesellschaft* 29 (2003), 409–440, here 422–429.

13. See Pollack, 'Säkularisierung,' 163.

14. *Kirchliches Handbuch. Statistisches Jahrbuch der Bistümer und ihnen gleichgestellten kirchlichen Gebietskörperschaften im Bereich der Deutschen Bischofskonferenz*, vol. XXXIV (Bonn: Sekretariat der Deutschen Bischofskonferenz, 1996), 156.

15. Clemens Vollnhals, 'Die Hypothek des Nationalprotestantismus. Entnazifizierung und Strafverfolgung von NS-Verbrechen nach 1945,' *Geschichte und Gesellschaft* 18 (1992), 51–69, here 57.

16. Norbert Frei, 'Von deutscher Erfindungskraft oder: Die Kollektivschuldthese in der Nachkriegszeit,' *Rechtshistorisches Journal* 16 (1997), 621–634. Many studies get this important point wrong. See for example Matthew D. Hockenos, *A Church Divided: German Protestants Confront the Nazi Past* (Bloomington: Indiana University Press, 2004), 72; Karen Riechert, 'Der Umgang der katholischen Kirche mit historischer und juristischer Schuld anlässlich der Nürnberger Kriegsverbrecherprozesse,' in Joachim Köhler and Damian van Melis (eds), *Siegerin in Trümmern. Die Rolle der katholischen Kirche in der deutschen Nachkriegsgesellschaft* (Stuttgart: W. Kohlhammer, 1998), 18–41, here 19.

17. Vollnhals, 'Hypothek,' 59–66. For Catholic reactions, see Riechert, 'Umgang,' 25–41.

18. Hockenos, 'Church,' 77, 187.

19. See Michael Brenner, *After the Holocaust. Rebuilding Jewish Lives in Postwar Germany* (Princeton, NJ: Princeton University Press, 1997).

20. Siegfried Hermle, 'Die Auseinandersetzung mit der nationalsozialistischen Judenverfolgung in der Evangelischen Kirche nach 1945,' in: Ursula Büttner (ed.), *Die Deutschen und die Judenverfolgung im Dritten Reich* (Hamburg: Christians, 1992), 321–333, here 327.

21. Hockenos, 'Church,' 84–99.

22. Too optimistic is the interpretation by Detlef Pollack, 'Abbrechende Kontinuitätslinien im deutschen Protestantismus nach 1945,' in: Manfred Gailus and Hartmut Lehmann (eds), *Nationalprotestantische Mentalitäten. Konturen, Entwicklungslinien und Umbrüche eines*

Weltbildes (Göttingen: Vandenhoeck & Ruprecht, 2005), 453–466. For a nuanced account see Frank–Michael Kuhlemann, 'Nachkriegsprotestantismus in Westdeutschland. Religionssoziologische und mentalitätsgeschichtliche Perspektiven,' in: Bernd Hey (ed.), *Kirche, Staat und Gesellschaft nach 1945. Konfessionelle Prägungen und sozialer Wandel* (Bielefeld: Luther-Verlag, 2001), 23–59.

23. Martin Greschat, 'The Potency of "Christendom." The example of the Darmstädter Wort 1947,' in Hugh McLeod and Werner Ustorf (eds), *The Decline of Christendom in Western Europe, 1750–2000* (Cambridge: Cambridge University Press, 2003), 130–142, here 134–5.

24. Axel Schildt, *Zwischen Abendland und Amerika. Studien zur westdeutschen Ideenlandschaft der 50er Jahre* (Munich: R. Oldenbourg, 1999), 120. See ibid., 111–165 for an exemplary account of the work of two important academies in Bad Boll and Münster.

25. Martin Greschat, *Die evangelische Christenheit und die deutsche Geschichte nach 1945. Weichenstellungen in der Nachkriegszeit* (Stuttgart: W. Kohlhammer, 2002), 212–215.

26. Harald Schroeter-Wittke, 'Der Deutsche Evangelische Kirchentag in den 1960er und 70er Jahren-eine soziale Bewegung,' in Siegfried Hermle, Claudia Lepp, Harry Oelke (eds), *Umbrüche. Der deutsche Protestantismus und die sozialen Bewegungen in den 1960er und 70er Jahren* (Göttingen: Vandenhoeck & Ruprecht, 2007), 214.

27. Benjamin Ziemann, 'Opinion Polls and the Dynamics of the Public Sphere. The Catholic Church in the Federal Republic after 1968,' *German History* 24 (2006), 562–586.

28. Schroeter-Wittke, 'Kirchentag,' 219.

29. Peter Cornehl, 'Dorothee Sölle, das "Politische Nachtgebet" und die Folgen,' in: Hermle et al. (eds), *Umbrüche*, 277.

30. Dorothee Sölle, *Political Theology* (Philadelphia: Fortress Press, 1974), 36–37, 59, 42, 89.

31. Dagmar Herzog, 'The Death of God in West Germany. Between Secularization, Postfascism and the Rise of Liberation Theology,' in: Michael Geyer and Lucian Hölscher (eds), *Die Gegenwart Gottes in der modernen Gesellschaft. Transzendenz und religiöse Vergemeinschaftung in Deutschland* (Göttingen: Wallstein, 2006), 431–466, 435.

32. On liberation theology, see Michael Dodson, 'Liberation Theology and Christian Radicalism in Contemporary Latin America,' *Journal of Latin American Studies* 11 (1979), 203–222; on the Belgian and German connections see Andrea-Isa Moews, *Eliten für Latein Amerika. Lateinamerikanische Studenten an der Universität Löwen in den 1950er und 1960er Jahren* (Cologne, Weimar, Vienna: Böhlau, 2000).

33. Benjamin Ziemann, 'Zwischen sozialer Bewegung und Dienstleistung am Individuum: Katholiken und katholische Kirche im therapeutischen Jahrzehnt,' *Archiv für Sozialgeschichte* 44 (2004), 357–393, 378–9.

34. For a succinct analysis see, however, Hugh McLeod, *The Religious Crisis of the 1960s* (Oxford: Oxford University Press, 2007), 141–161; Christian Schmidtmann, *Katholische Studierende 1945–1973. Ein Beitrag zur Kultur- und Sozialgeschichte der Bundesrepublik Deutschland* (Paderborn: Ferdinand Schöningh, 2006), 316–367. As an example for the neglect of progressive Christians in the historiography on 1968, see Timothy S. Brown, '"1968" East and West: Divided Germany as a Case Study in Transnational History,' *American Historical Review* 113 (2009), 69–96.

35. Personal communication with Elisabeth Rickal in Bochum, December 9, 2002.

36. Ebertz, 'Erosion,' 239.

37. Ziemann, 'Polls,' 583–4.

38. Siegried Hermle, 'Die Evangelikalen als Gegenbewegung,' in: Hermle et al. (eds), *Umbrüche*, 334–337.

39. Ibid., 342–344.
40. For these categories see Albert O. Hirschman, *Exit, Voice and Loyalty. Responses to Decline in Firms, Organizations and States* (Cambridge: Harvard University Press, 1970). For context, see Ziemann, 'Katholische Kirche,' 212–215.
41. See Benjamin Ziemann, 'Die Katholische Kirche als religiöse Organisation. Deutschland und die Niederlande, 1950–1975,' in: Friedrich-Wilhelm Graf and Klaus Große-Kracht (eds), *Religion und Gesellschaft. Europa im 20. Jahrhundert* (Cologne: Böhlau, 2007), 329–351.
42. Frederic Spotts, *The Churches and Politics in Germany* (Middletown: Wesleyan University Press, 1973), 183–207.
43. Ziemann, 'Katholische Kirche als religiöse Organisation,' 348–349; Wilhelm Damberg, *Abschied vom Milieu? Katholizismus im Bistum Münster und in den Niederlanden 1945–1980* (Paderborn: Ferdinand Schöningh, 1997), 166.
44. Greschat, 'Christenheit,' 105–124.
45. Cited in Jan Hermelink, 'Einige Dimensionen der Strukturveränderung der deutschen evangelischen Landeskirchen in den 1960er und 1970er Jahren,' in: Hermle et al. (eds), *Umbrüche*, 285–302, here 289.
46. Ibid., quote 300; for similar developments in the Catholic church see Ziemann, 'Zwischen sozialer Bewegung,' 382–388.
47. See Werner Harenberg (ed.), *Was glauben die Deutschen? Die Emnid-Umfrage. Ergebnisse und Kommentare* (Munich: Christoph Kaiser, 1969), 38, 62; Gerhard Schmidtchen, *Zwischen Kirche und Gesellschaft. Forschungsbericht über die Umfragen zur Gemeinsamen Synode der Bistümer in der Bundesrepublik Deutschland* (Freiburg: Herder, 1972), 8–9, 37, 58–59.
48. Cf. Thomas Luckmann, *The Invisible Religion* (New York: Macmillan, 1967). The English edition was based on an earlier German version published as *Das Problem der Religion in der modernen Gesellschaft. Institution, Person und Weltanschauung* (Freiburg: Rombach, 1963). I cite from a revised German edition, *Die unsichtbare Religion* (Frankfurt am Main: Suhrkamp, 1991), 156, 168.
49. Detlef Pollack, 'Religion und Moderne. Zur Gegenwart der Säkularisierung in Europa,' in Graf and Große-Kracht (eds), *Religion und Gesellschaft*, 73–103, here 94–95.
50. See David Nash, 'Reconnecting Religion with Social and Cultural History: Secularization's Failure as a Master Narrative,' *Cultural and Social History* 1 (2004), 302–325.
51. For this argument, see Ziemann, 'Katholische Kirche und Sozialwissenschaften.'
52. Callum G. Brown, *The Death of Christian Britain: Understanding Secularization 1800–2000* (London: Routledge, 2001).

BIBLIOGRAPHY

BECK, WOLFHART, *Westfälische Protestanten auf dem Weg in die Moderne. Die evangelischen Kirchengemeinden des Kirchenkreises Lübbecke zwischen Kaiserreich und Bundesrepublik* (Paderborn: Fedinand Schöningh, 2003).
HERMLE, SIEGFRIED, CLAUDIA LEPP and HARRY OELKE (eds), *Umbrüche. Der deutsche Protestantismus und die sozialen Bewegungen in den 1960er und 70er Jahren* (Göttingen: Vandenhoeck & Ruprecht, 2007).

HEY, BERND (ed.), *Kirche, Staat und Gesellschaft nach 1945. Konfessionelle Prägungen und sozialer Wandel* (Bielefeld: Luther-Verlag, 2001).

JEANROND, WERNER G., 'From Resistance to Liberation Theology: German Theologians and the Non/Resistance to the National Socialist Regime,' *Journal of Modern History* 64 (1992), supplement, 187–203.

MCLEOD, HUGH, *The Religious Crisis of the 1960s* (Oxford: Oxford University Press, 2007).

POLLACK, DETLEF, *Kirche in der Organisationsgesellschaft. Zum Wandel der gesellschaftlichen Lage der Kirchen in der DDR* (Stuttgart: W. Kohlhammer, 1994).

—— *Säkularisierung—ein moderner Mythos? Studien zum religiösen Wandel in Deutschland* (Tübingen: Mohr Siebeck, 2003).

RENDTORFF, TRUTZ (ed.), *Protestantische Revolution. Kirche und Theologiein der DDR: Ekklesiologische Voraussetzungen, politischer Kontext, theologische und historische Kriterien* (Göttingen: Vandenhoeck & Ruprecht, 1993).

SCHÄFER, BERND, 'State and Catholic Church in Eastern Germany, 1945–1989,' *German Studies Review* 22 (1999), 447–461.

SCHMIDTMANN, CHRISTIAN, *Katholische Studierende 1945–1973. Ein Beitrag zur Kultur-und Sozialgeschichte der Bundesrepublik Deutschland* (Paderborn: Ferdinand Schöningh, 2006).

THOMAS, MERRILYN, 'The Evangelical Church in the German Democratic Republic,' in Patrick Major and Jonathan Osmond (eds), *The Workers' and Peasants' State. Communism and Society in East Germany under Ulbricht 1945–71* (Manchester: Manchester University Press, 2002), 210–226.

VOLLNHALS, CLEMENS, 'Die Evangelische Kirche zwischen Traditionswahrung und Neuorientierung,' in Martin Broszat, Klaus-Dietmar Henke and Hans Woller (eds), *Von Stalingrad zur Währungsreform. Zur Sozialgeschichte des Umbruchs in Deutschland*, 3rd edn (Munich: R. Oldenbourg, 1990), 113–167.

ZIEMANN, BENJAMIN, *Katholische Kirche und Sozialwissenschaften 1945–1975* (Göttingen: Vandenhoeck & Ruprecht, 2007).

——'The Gospel of Psychology: Therapeutic Concepts and the Scientification of Pastoral Care in the West German Catholic Church, 1950–1980,' *Central European History* 39 (2006), 79–106.

CHAPTER 31

....

CULTURE IN THE SHADOW OF TRAUMA?

....

LUTZ KOEPNICK

In the immediate aftermath of the Franco-Prussian War of 1870–1871, Friedrich Nietzsche had felt a deep need to challenge his contemporaries' triumphalism. In contrast to dominant views, which celebrated military victory as a seedbed for great artistic achievements, Nietzsche emphasized the strained relationship between the realms of the political and of cultural expression in modern Germany. Historical periods of political triumph, he argued, could not but produce mediocre art, whereas vibrant cultural production necessitated a certain ailing of political affairs. In section eight of *Human, All Too Human*, Nietzsche summarized this inverted reciprocity of culture and politics as follows: '*Resurrection of the spirit*—A nation rejuvenates itself on the political sickbed and rediscovers its spirit, which it gradually lost in its seeking for and assertion of power. Culture owes this above all to the ages of political weakness.'[1]

Although Nazi ideologues sought to fold isolated elements of Nietzschean philosophy into their patchwork of ideological positions, Nietzsche's rather cynical views about the possibility of a truly German *Kulturstaat* had no real appeal to the Third Reich. Nazi Germany pursued both at once: the resurrection of great politics, understood as a project of unfettering political leadership from democratic deliberation; and the construction of a unified national culture that would level critical distinctions between high art and popular taste, while erasing the alleged ills of modernist experimentation, Bolshevist internationalism, and Judaism. Contrary to Nietzsche, the Nazi state considered determined acts of leadership as signs of cultural achievement themselves, thus seeking to fuse the political and the aesthetic, power and art, into one mobilizing dynamic. It is not beyond the stretch of the historical imagination that the catastrophic breakdown of the Nazi regime in 1945 could have led to a potent return of Nietzsche's thoughts on the asymmetry of power and culture, the bankruptcy of German political affairs being seen as a unique opportunity for processes of artistic, literary, and intellectual resurrection. However, now partitioned into various and shifting zones of political governance and cultural identity formation, what Germany initially witnessed instead was a variety of efforts to restore the principal autonomy of cultural expressions, and thus unhinge both Nietzsche's critical and the Nazis' affirmative coupling of good art and self-confident politics. In the ruins of World War II, culture was meant to mend the spiritual wounds and traumatic losses of everyday life by providing meanings and orientations unscathed by the functionalization of aesthetic culture during the Nazi era. Politics, in turn, for some years to come, was to stay free of any aesthetic ambition and avoid the public use of affective symbols and choreographed expressions of power. Art, literature, theater, film, and music, in both emerging Germanys, were no doubt embraced as conduits for a resurrection of the spirit. However, the traumas left by the immediate past led artistic practitioners and their recipients alike to believe that such a resurrection could only succeed if aesthetic experience was allowed to unfold in relative distance to postwar politics. The felt task, in the first years after 1945, was not only to reconstruct art and culture as realms independent from the course of political action. As importantly, the perceived task among many was to protect the political from its own former aesthetic excesses and thus warrant the possibility of self-restrained, sober, and unassuming forms of government.

In more recent decades, the figure of trauma has provided a key trope in order to chronicle the resurrection of culture after the Nazi era, trauma here being understood as the result of harrowing events that deny the very possibility of experience, of coherent stories, and meaningful interpretations. Because traumatic events are not really registered or experienced in the first place, they cause the individual to seal off certain emotional or intellectual sectors, while at the same time forcing this individual to displace the repressed past into static patterns of perception, thought, and behavior. However, to recall the postwar years as times of traumatic arrest and displacement, and forgetting, in many cases raises more questions than it can answer. While it potentially erases the difference between perpetrators and victims, it also often fails to distinguish adequately between different forms of torment and their cultural effects after 1945, be it those of concentration camp survivors, former exiles, refugees from the East, air war victims, or returning soldiers shell-shocked about their own violence. Postwar German culture, in each of its initial four occupational zones and later in both of its Cold War incarnations, cannot be subsumed under one rubric, let alone be retold with the help of one master narrative. The true trauma of German postwar culture, in fact, might be seen in the fact that this culture splintered into a variety of narratives and structures of symbolization, yet that only a few were willing or able to recognize this multiplicity as more than merely an expression of loss. This essay will first reconstruct some of the plots and patterns postwar German culture developed over the years to cope with the afterlife of its violent past and the fundamentally unsettled site of aesthetic expression after Auschwitz. In a second step, however, I will also detail a number of critical emplotments of postwar German culture pivoting not around the rupture of 1945, but rather around the break of 1989 and around how cultural expressions prepared the ground for the undeniable success story of late twentieth-century Germany, namely its astounding transition from totalitarian rule to democratic civility, from staunch nationalism to international responsibility, from the Nazi's total mobilization of German society, and the near annihilation of Jews and other persecuted minorities to a society second to none in its efforts to contain the catastrophic impact of technology and power on human and natural environments.

31.1 CULTURE AFTER AUSCHWITZ

31.1.1 Representing what defies representation

No phrase has been quoted more frequently in order to assess the state of German culture in the immediate aftermath of World War II than Theodor W. Adorno's 1949 dictum that, 'To write poetry after Auschwitz is barbaric.'[2] For the exile Adorno, the systematic extinction of European Jewry marked the final moment of a fatal dialectic of culture and barbarism. Far from understanding Auschwitz as antithetical to enlighten- ment culture, Adorno considered the Nazi death camps as the catastrophic outcome of a society in whose hands advanced rationality had corroded the foundation of reason, thus not only enabling the possibility of industrial mass killing, but also obstructing any postwar attempt to cast the horrors of this destruction into communicable forms and representations. Contrary to what many of his readers assumed, Adorno's point was certainly not to bar future poets, artists, or thinkers from engaging with Auschwitz. Rather, what Adorno sought to suggest was that artistic production after Auschwitz had to reckon with the fact that German culture not only had not helped to prevent, but had actively produced Nazi barbarism, and that therefore neither high art nor any form of cultural activity after 1945, in their possible efforts to address the traumas and torments of the Nazi period, could legitimately return to the aesthetic languages, poetic tropes, and formal inventories of earlier ages. Romantic metaphors of mourning, in the eyes of Adorno, were as inadequate a means to represent the lethal dialectic of culture and barbarism during the Third Reich, as rhymed stanzas, linear narrative arrange- ments, figurative paint strokes, or harmonic tonality.

Adorno's ponderings about the challenges of representing the Nazi death camps, one might argue, deeply penetrated the fabrics of German postwar culture, yet not for the reasons Adorno himself had envisioned, but simply for the fact that poets, writers, painters, and composers shied away from explicitly addressing the horrors of Ausch- witz in their work in the first place. Whereas the official anti-fascism of the GDR left little room for considering the murder of millions of Jews as a central axis of Nazi politics and warfare, the focus of West-German writers and artists in the early decades of the postwar period was less on finding new aesthetic languages to communicate the incommunicable than on restoring the viability and integrity of the aesthetic *in spite of* the shadows of Auschwitz. The overall absence of work trying to find images, words, and narratives to represent the Nazi death machine is more than remarkable. Al- though the allied forces forced civilian Germans to face the horrors of neighboring concentration camps in the immediate days after the capitulation, such experiences rarely caused poets or artists to reflect on the complicity of culture and barbarism during the Nazi period, and the resulting corrosion of existing vocabularies of aesthetic expression. Outstanding exceptions in this case tend to confirm the pattern. The poetry of Paul Celan, a German-speaking Jew from Romania whose work during the postwar years found equal admirers in Adorno and Adorno's philosophical arch-enemy Martin Heidegger, may be considered as one example. First published in 1948, Celan's *Death Fugue*, with the help of enigmatic metaphors, paradoxical images, and a profound fracturing of grammar and syntax, encoded the horrific experience of concentration camp inmates, culminating in the oft-quoted line:

> Death is a master from Germany his eye is blue
> he shoots you bullets of lead his aim is true.[3]

Another exception might be found in Peter Weiss's 1965 *The Investigation*, a play written in the immediate aftermath of the Eichmann and Auschwitz trials in Jerusalem and Frankfurt respectively and, with a neo-Brechtian gesture, restaging the systematic killing of the death camps in the deeply unsettling form of an oratorio. Both authors, in their attempt to voice Adorno's dialectics of barbarism and culture, left no doubt about the impossibility of using established poetic languages to write about and after Auschwitz. Yet, not least of all because both saw no possibility of living in or returning to Germany after the war (Celan resided in Paris, Weiss in Stockholm), their interventions largely remained at the cultural fringes. Although Celan's 'Death Fugue' eventually became a common reference, the larger public's canonization and quotation of the poem ended up neutralizing much of its disturbing power. Even though *The Investigation* played to wide audiences in the second half of the 1960s, the perception of Weiss remained that of an outsider whose formal experiments and provocations could not but remain external to what mattered most to German postwar audiences, West and East.

It is one of the vexing ironies of postwar German culture that it took Adorno's least respected medium, television, and a mini-series designed by commercially-oriented American producers, the NBC drama *Holocaust*, in order to pierce the wall German art and literature had more or less built around the representation of the death camps in the 1940s and 1950s. Broadcast in West Germany in January 1979, the show triggered an unprecedented public outpouring of formerly repressed memories and affects. In screening Nazi atrocities on what high-brow critics continued to condemn as the principal medium of postwar complacency and forgetting, *Holocaust*—unlike any other cultural artifact before it—caused Germans of all ages and social strata to face the horrors of the death camps and find their own languages to speak about the unspeakable. *Holocaust* certainly neglected Adorno's plea to shun existing forms, tropes, and formulae in the effort to represent the deadly dialectic of modern German rationality. It repackaged Nazi gas chambers as sites of melodramatic intensity and thus, as various critics insisted, potentially turned traumatic events into consumable objects. However, in relying on rather conventional forms to touch upon the minds and emotions of millions of viewers, this imported television series finally succeeded in what German art and literature in the previous thirty-four years had failed to accomplish: to render Auschwitz communicable, no matter how much the actual horror of the Nazi death camps exceeded and continue to exceed the limits of communication.

31.1.2 Zero hour

Myths are shared stories whose purpose is to stitch the social fabric together; they offer symbols, narratives, and images that provide orientation and advance the individual's sense of belonging. No myth was more powerful in the immediate postwar era than the one considering May 1945 as a blank slate, a zero hour that defined cultural activity as the primary realm of rebooting the German mind and soul. Yet, no myth also had more conflicting interpretations, meanings, and consequences than the one that regarded the end of the war as a cataclysmic tabula rasa, a ground zero of the symbolic. To be sure, within days and weeks of VE-day, German civilians eagerly frequented whatever cultural events specific local conditions and occupational authorities permitted, in particular music concerts and theater performances on makeshift stages. While Soviet, American, British, and French military officials often differed about how to respond to and regulate this startling desire for culture, the everyday reality of hunger and death, of devastated cityscapes and geographical displacement seemed to spur, rather than contain deep-seated needs for diversion and contemplation. However, to describe and recall May 1945 as a moment of radical cultural rebirth would, nevertheless, miss the point, given not only that people were eager to reconnect to older cultural traditions unscathed by Nazi oversight, but also that many cultural institutions (e.g. symphonic orchestras, the film industry, publishing houses) were far from willing to dismiss the personnel that had run their operations during the 1930s and early 1940s. For some, to speak of 1945 as a zero hour meant to express hope for a resurgence of cultural production independent of wartime suffering and political control. For others, it either served as a screen masking existing continuities or as an open invitation to repress troubling memories of the most immediate past. For a third group, finally, it provided a key word at once to proclaim new ideological directions and to restrict the space for dissenting voices or alternative visions. Myths are shared stories, but there is no need for everyone to understand them in one and the same way. One of the most effective aspects of the myth of the zero hour was its ability to provide different meanings to different constituencies. It helped suture the social fabric in spite of—or, in fact, precisely because of—its inherent function of expressing contrasting perspectives on how to regenerate German culture after the war.

Recalling his own role as an emerging writer in the immediate aftermath of the war, later Nobel-laureate Heinrich Böll, in 1952, considered the rubble of Germany's cities as sites of spiritual cleansing obligating poets and artists to decontaminate their perception and develop unassuming forms of aesthetic representation: '[I]n truth, the people about whom we wrote lived in rubble, emerged from the war damaged, men and women to an equal degree, and children too. They had a keen vision: they saw things.'[4] The literature and art produced amid the rubble of the war, as exemplified in the writing of Böll himself, the dramas of playwright Wolfgang Borchert, or the drawings and paintings of Werner Heldt, Wilhelm Rudolph, and Karl Hofer, pursued muted formal arrangements and quasi-minimalist aesthetic registers. While often recalling the language of 1920s expressionism, German rubble literature and art after 1945 displayed none of the artistic frenzy, the violent outbreaks, and the avant-gardist energies that German culture had witnessed after World War I. Rubble writing instead was largely driven by self-effacing linguistic constructions, a controlled use of metaphor and metonymy, an aversion to formal excess, and a strong emphasis on the material concreteness of the everyday; rubble visual art, by contrast, often 'fell back on Christian images of the Passion, martyrdom, and apocalypse, rendered in an expressive realist style close to allegory.'[5] Although much of the work of literary and visual artists from this period looks derivative and tedious in retrospect, it no doubt aimed at finding appropriate—which in this context primarily meant relatively transparent, restrained, and rather unpretentious—means to depict an atmosphere of existential destitution, of despair and depravation, of guilt and desolation. Content clearly dominated form, the experience of moral defeat calling for an at times self-restrained, at time pathos-ridden ethics of aesthetic representation. Rather than to reframe the war's violence through *avant-garde* interventions, the principal ambition of zero hour literature and art was to move the postwar subject somewhere beyond the violent ambitions of the past; to take stock of one's catastrophic present and find solace in the sheer fact of survival.

Yet, it is this focus on the sheer challenges of life amid ruins that in much of German rubble art often results in a spectral return of repressed history, with artists appropriating expressive languages that in their deliberate simplicity appeared symptomatically haunted by the violence of the past. Nowhere does this perhaps become more evident than in the opening minutes of Wolfgang Staudte's 1946 DEFA-film *Die Mörder sind unter uns* ('Murderers Among Us'), produced in the Soviet occupational zone. This very first feature film of the postwar period commences with a shot in which the camera slowly ascends from a grave so as to show us an image of a devastated street in Berlin. A man in black approaches our view. His movements express the disorientation of a man shell-shocked by the experience of war. The film's soundtrack strangely adds to the man's strangeness, for what we hear is the clatter of honky-tonk music whose origin will be shown to us only somewhat later. Postwar German cinema thus immediately confronts the viewer with a profound destabilization of the cinematic frame. Already utterly out of place within the narrative space itself, the soundtrack's lighthearted honky-tonk music produces an unsettling sense of displacement in the spectator as well. It situates our act of viewing in a rather undefined perceptual non-place, and in doing so it questions cinema's ability to frame reliable views of the present. To live among ruins is to live in a world in which the visual and the auditory no longer add up to a whole anymore. It is to inhabit a present in whose context the dream of perceptual synthesis and fulfilled self-presence—so central to narrative cinema—has come to naught. The first shot of postwar German cinema thus directly reveals the whole complexity of what, in the months and years following May 1945, it meant to speak of a zero hour. While the ubiquity of rubble embodied the total political, social, and cultural collapse of the Third Reich, and called for a radical new beginning, no artistic form—even when simply trying to capture the bleakness of postwar existence—was really able to mask the continued impact of the war not only on the minds and lives of people, but also on the way in which certain artistic techniques sought to assemble their materials within the unity of an art work.

31.1.3 Late starts, early beginnings

Even in the eyes of those actively engaged in proclaiming the degree zero of German culture in the immediate aftermath of the war, it was quite clear that the Nazi period had ushered German society into an often unsettling multiplicity of temporal experiences and historical trajectories. When, it is more than rhetorical to ask, did postwar German culture actually start? Did it commence in May 1945? Do we need to locate its true origins in 1948 or 1949, with the institutionalization of two different German states and two distinct frameworks of cultural production and consumption? The second question is how to deal with the literature, art, and thought produced by exiles throughout and after the Nazi period, some of whom were eager to return to their homeland right after the war, some of whom prolonged their exile all the way through the 1950s or even longer, and some of whom—like Thomas Mann—would eventually return to Europe, but take up residence in countries other than Germany? *Dr. Faustus*, Mann's allegorical tale of German aesthetic hubris and catastrophic downfall, was first published in 1947, but are we really prepared to consider it as a contribution to postwar German culture? How, one might ask, are we to accommodate the fact that Germany, West and East, in the first years after the war was a society of highly itinerant cultural producers and consumers, with millions of refugees seeking new homes for years to come and hundreds of thousands of soldiers not returning from captivity until the mid-1950s? How does their sense of prolonged displacement and delay figure into our retrospective attempt to identify a clear historical beginning of the postwar period?

While it is tempting to single out a whole variety of starting points for German postwar culture in the second half of the 1940s and early 1950s, among contemporaries it was equally appealing to explore much earlier moments of cultural productivity and meaning, in particular the putative timelessness of literary classicism, as a departure date for moral rejuvenation. Friedrich Meinecke's much-read *Die deutsche Katastrophe* ('The German Catastrophe'), published in 1946, provides a good case in point. A historian who since the early decades of the twentieth century had argued for the importance of cultural traditions in the formation of the modern nation state, Meinecke viewed Nazism as representing a fatal swerving away from the richness of German classical education, aesthetics, and cultural refinement. What postwar Germany needed, in turn, were new cultural institutions able to inspire Germans to return to the past, in particular the writings of Johann Wolfgang von Goethe. For Goethe's dramas and poems, as Meinecke believed, were 'perhaps the most essentially German parts of our literature. He who steeps himself in them will detect something indestructible—a German *character indeliblis*—in the midst of all the destruction and misfortune of our Fatherland.'[6] Goethe's voice, in Meinecke's understanding, had the power to move Germans beyond the ruins of the immediate past back into a brighter future. True German culture was indelible—an enduring and eternal value. Its strength and calling could be temporarily forgotten or obscured, but in essence it knew of neither beginning nor end. Similar to many others who denied Adorno's troubling association of culture and barbarity, Meinecke therefore hoped for nothing less than to restart German postwar culture somewhere circa 1800. *Faust*, not *Dr. Faustus*, provided the most salient model of finding meaning and orientation amid the physical and metaphysical debris of the war.

Although the trope of the zero hour suggested a shared German need to leave the past behind, and inhabit one and the same new present, German culture in the shadow of the Nazi period, in fact, was often marked by conflicting recollections and anticipations, by contradictory temporalities that resisted any attempt to be synthesized within the single space of the present. The belated and uneven reception of early twentieth-century modernism during the 1950s is as much part of this masking of multiple historicities as the rather deferred acknowledgment, from the 1960s onwards, that modernism may have run its course and been replaced by post-modern sensibilities. Repressed and defamed as degenerate during the Nazi period, modernist literature and the art of the Weimar period witnessed a rediscovery in the 1950s in the West (whereas cultural authorities in the East often continued to censor modernist experimentation as a sign of bourgeois formalism and a violation of the tenets of socialist realism). However, modernist literature and art in the 1950s was rarely read, in all its negativity, as a critical destabilization of traditional forms of aesthetic representation. Instead, it offered universal expressions encoding the existential condition of the modern mind and soul: Kafka's prose, for 1950s readers, was all about the ineluctability of alienation in modern bureaucratic society, whereas the legacy of abstraction in painting was indicative of modern man's inalienable will to freedom, an affirmative plea for unrestricted self-expression and, hence, a powerful argument against the rigorous dictates of socialist realism in the East.

The late 1950s are often considered as a decisive turning point, not only in how German literary culture sought to address the past and, in so doing, disturb postwar materialism and complacency, but also in how a host of younger writers on either side of the Iron Curtain began to experiment with more unruly poetic forms and questioned dominant paradigms of realist story telling. All published in or around 1959, such novels as Heinrich Böll's *Billard um Halbzehn* ('Billiards at Half-Past Nine,' 1958), Günter Grass's *Die Blechtrommel* ('The Tin Drum,' 1959), Uwe Johnson's *Mutmassungen über Jakob* ('Presumptions about Jakob,' 1959), Martin Walser's *Halbzeit* ('Halftime,' 1960), Peter Weiss's *Abschied von den Eltern* ('Leavetaking,' 1961) and Christa Wolf's *Der geteilte Himmel* ('The Divided Heaven,' 1963) finally seemed to reconnect

German literature to the kind of modern writing that Nazi authorities had deemed debased and banned as decadent. Although each of these writers engaged different formal repertoires and structures of narration, what they all—in true modernist fashion—shared was a concerted effort to probe how language and literature could render the past present in the first place. Whether authors recalled the Nazi period through the eyes of a three-year-old who refuses further growth, or whether they satirically mapped the hypocrisies and repressions of middle-class life during the economic miracle, German literature around 1960 aspired to break away from an earlier hope that narratives could contain even the most painful pasts and that controlled acts of storytelling could situate their narrators firmly in the present. The opening of Grass's *Tin Drum* is perhaps the most symptomatic example for this. We read: 'Granted: I am an inmate of a mental hospital; my keeper is watching me, he never lets me out of his sight; there's a peephole in the door, and my keeper's eye is the shade of brown that can never see through a blue-eyed type like me.'[7] Far from providing an operative answer to the ongoing crises of identity and meaning, the act of storytelling here itself has become the true problem. No longer transparent to themselves, the narrators and narrative arrangements of German literature circa 1959 abound with fractured recollections and decentered visions of the present. Like Grass's Oskar Matzerath, the boy drummer, this new literature employed formal reflexivity— the legacy of aesthetic modernism—as a powerful means to undercut postwar desires to fuse past or present into one coherent narrative, be it Meinecke's ambition to use the classical tradition as a resource for moral rejuvenation or the widespread hope simply to restart culture from scratch again.

A product of the displaced, belated, and bifurcated materialization of aesthetic modernism in Germany, the impact of how German authors circa 1959 shook up literary culture cannot be underestimated. Yet, it is important to note that the work of Grass, Johnson, Wolf, and Walser, in spite of its quest for literary and poetic innovativeness, remained dominantly bound to a rigorous ethics of public responsibility and self-inspection. Unlike the work of many literary modernists and avant-gardists during the Weimar period, the belated modernism of Germany's postwar writers avoided uncontained gestures of aesthetic playfulness and—cautioned by the systematic manipulation of the aesthetic during the Nazi period—instead understood literary innovation as part of a deeply moral enterprise, namely the poet's task to speak as the divided and disgraced nation's true conscience. It therefore should come as no surprise that German intellectual and literary culture often violently rejected the advent of post-modern styles so typical for other Western contexts since the late 1960s. Though it might be intriguing to think about the divisions of German culture after 1945, 1949 or 1961 as post-modern instance of multiplicity,[8] post-modernism in literary and artistic practice—with its stress on ambiguous strategies of double-encoding; its blurring of elite culture and the popular; and its irreverent fusion of incompatible historical materials—was largely decried as a crude violation of the ethical task and moral responsibility of writing after Hitler. In the best case, post-modern playfulness was seen as a sign of both political and aesthetic (and, at heart, American) superficiality; in the worst case, post-modernism all the way through the 1980s was condemned as a practice not only violating the progressive legacy of the Enlightenment, but also allowing fascist residues to re-enter German culture through the (mostly French) backdoor. Just as future generations of scholars will no doubt continue to quarrel about determining the actual beginning of the postwar period, so, due to the unsettled paths of German culture in the shadow of the Nazi era—it will remain virtually impossible to agree on the historical timeline according to which modernist sensibilities during the postwar era first witnessed a second spring and later were to vanish from public awareness.

31.1.4 Repressed guilt and the inability to mourn

The trope of Germans' inability to mourn has been one of the most influential concepts to describe how postwar German culture sought to displace the catastrophic outcome of the Nazi past by embracing the burgeoning sites of modern consumer culture. The term was coined by Alexander and Margarete Mitscherlich in their 1967 eponymous publication, but it had circulated already in various versions over the preceding twenty years, not least of all in a number of late 1940s debates about the concept of collective guilt and the degree of responsibility for the crimes committed by the Nazis.[9] Arguing from a psychoanalytic perspective, the Mitscherlich thesis rested on the assumption that German culture, after the downfall of the Hitler regime, should have been struck by a massive wave of despair, melancholia, and disorientation, whereas in actual fact Germans were eager to entertain fantasies of social upward mobility and to pursue unprecedented forms of material reconstruction, industrial productivity, and economic prosperity. Rather than to work through pain and guilt, German postwar culture of the late 1940s and 1950s, in the eyes of the Mitscherlichs, was marked and marred by rampant desires to escape the past, to flee into alluring visions of a different future, and to find a home in a present of apolitical consumption and complacent privacy, of local happiness, rather than historical responsibility.

West German film-making of the 1950s, as it emerged in the wake of the often uneasy images and narrative constellations of the late 1940s, is often seen as one of the principal engines of historical displacement and forgetting in the early postwar era. While West German films addressing the horrors of the Nazi period primarily recalled the war as a conflict between corrupt military leaders, and largely innocent and dutiful soldiers, and made no mention of the Holocaust, the decade's main entertainment staple was the so-called *Heimatfilm* and its stress on the seemingly timeless and, hence, ahistorical integrity of rural life. *Heimatfilms* offered postcard images of breathtaking alpine settings. They engaged viewers in sweeping romantic love stories and celebrated traditionalist moral values as a bulwark against the corrupting influence of urban modernity. Although the narrative economy of these genre films, in their effort to show off the pristine beauty of the countryside, often tended to suspend the dominant logic of teleological storytelling and identification in commercial cinema, their plots, images, and sounds nevertheless seemed to provide a safe haven for all those hoping to escape any troubling memories of the past. Yet, it is not difficult to see that West German *Heimatfilms*, in their very endeavor to displace the burden of the past and circulate timeless meanings, often failed to erase the signatures of history. The generic conflict between good foresters and evil poachers, for instance, clearly mimicked the increasing tensions between the cold war super powers during the 1950s, whereas the seemingly dogmatic juxtaposition of the rural and the urban, the traditional and the modern, often could not but result in a certain leveling of the divide, a conservative vision of heedful modernization and a compassionately paternal remodeling of unset-tled communities.[10] The *Heimatfilm*'s locations were never as stable and timeless as popular fantasy might have wanted them to be, the films' formal shapes and narrative arrangements being haunted by the very history they so determinately sought to leave behind. In this, the *Heimatfilm* can be seen as indicative of the fact that 1950s popular culture, in spite of its concerted efforts to displace mourning, reflection, and guilt, was far from as homogenous and successful as many postwar critics have made it out to be.

In postwar West-German culture, the popular dimension, in particular after the introduction and proliferation of television in the second half of the 1950s, no doubt often served as an anesthetic numbing painful memories and deflecting from the need to actively work through the burdens of the past. However, as the example of the *Heimatfilm* genre at least partially suggests, and contrary to the fears of many a high-brow intellectual, commercial popular culture did not necessarily always function as a site of subjecting the individual into blind submission and mindless complacency. In particular, the import and reception of American popular music, of jazz and even more so of rock and roll, offered meanings, pleasures, and forms of happiness that not only ran counter to dominant tastes and middle-class values of self-restriction, but in doing so also opened up a breach between different generations, a space in which ever more critical questions about the role of the parent generation during the Holocaust were raised and gestures of dissent could be articulated. Born only a few days after the end of the war, filmmaker Wim Wenders has described this unruly and counter-hegemonic potential of postwar popular culture perhaps most emblematically when recalling that American rock and roll, during the 1950s, was 'the only alternative to Beethoven (and I'm really exaggerating here)—because I was very insecure then about all culture that was offered to me, because I thought it was all fascism, pure fascism; and the only thing I was secure with from the beginning and felt had nothing to do with fascism was rock music.'[11]

Similar arguments can be made about the role of mass cultural elements in East Germany, even though it is important to emphasize not only the way in which the rhetoric of anti-fascism was built into the ideological self-positioning of East German culture from its inception, but also that it took a good number of additional years before rock and pop (and punk) were able to insert disruptive energies into the fabric of GDR culture. Official culture in postwar East Germany was driven by the belief that neither public expressions of guilt nor extensive acts of mourning were necessary in order to come to terms with the past: the very inauguration of a socialist state and its international alliances was seen as a compelling proof for the fact that the burdens of the Nazi era had been left behind. While the aesthetic doctrines of socialist realism claimed to overcome the modernist divide of high and low and integrate the divergent paths of modern cultural activity into one single post-bourgeois dynamic, they at the same time hoped to charge artistic practice in all domains of cultural life with a political mission, namely the task of strengthening the coherence of the post-fascist collective and provide happiness from above, as it were. One element of this cultural doctrine, one might in fact argue, constituted the other, each in need of one another. As a consequence, within the horizon of official GDR ideology, neither historical memory nor the popular dimension really constituted a problem, the development of post-fascist attitudes and popular happiness went hand in hand, and—therefore—the Mitscherlichs' thesis had no relevance for the East at all.

Needless to say, historical reality gravely differed from this ideological framework. East German culture, art, and literature were as much as their western counterparts often structured by petit-bourgeois sentiments of complacency, conservatism, and withdraw-al, by a resistance against experimentation and a carefully cultivated sense of private amnesia, by industriousness, rather than reflection. Choreographed rituals of public integration and commitment did not do away with a private sphere longing for protect-ive warmth, ahistorical quiescence, escapist fantasy, and pleasurable consumption. Regime leaders, in fact, were highly concerned about the role of mass cultural meanings and pleasures, whether such popular intensities were secretly or not so secretly imported from the West, or whether they emerged from homegrown sources. Though at times, in particular between 1958 and 1964, the SED regime allowed for greater cultural openness in matters of popular taste, in retrospect it is hardly possible to overlook the govern-ment's profound failure in regulating popular memory, futurity, happiness, and pleasure from above and in containing the people's appetite for consumption, privacy, and leisure. As Konrad Jarausch and Michael Geyer summarize, 'Ubiquitous and repressive as it was, . . . [the SED regime's] entire huge apparatus of mass culture and surveillance also became oddly irrelevant. It was singularly incompetent in organizing and providing meaning for the quotidian life, which it so desperately attempted to orchestrate. The masses, in turn, proved to be cunning consumers who put together their own everyday culture. If their world was for the most part work oriented, it nonetheless became increasingly defined by the creative appropriation of goods.'[12]

In the mid-1960s, DEFA films such as *Die Spur der Steine* ('The Trace of Stones,' dir. Frank Beyer, 1966), were temporarily able to stress the discrepancies between the regime's and ordinary people's notion of pleasure and happiness, before new cultural policies tightened this sense of permissiveness again. In the late 1970s and early 1980s, in turn, rock and punk became active media to deviate both from ideological demands and the prevailing desire for privacy and quiescence, thus not simply displaying the regime's failure to provide happiness and fulfillment for all, but revealing the extent to which the goal of postwar GDR culture—the construction of post-fascist identity by means of mandating the popular from above—had missed its goal and produced a similar sense of historical repression and forgetting as in the West. The strength of right-wing extremism in the former GDR after 1990 might be seen as a product not only of the impossibilities of constructing an anti-fascist popular culture from above, but of the fact that the GDR's official rhetoric of anti-fascism had simply displaced any serious attempt to work through painful memories of the past, and that the Mitscherlich thesis therefore may have applied even more so to the East than to the West.

31.2 Culture before the fall of the wall

When seen in retrospect, as part of a society trying to re-emerge from the barbarism of Auschwitz, postwar German culture might dominantly appear as a culture of uncertain beginnings and missed opportunities, of symptomatic displacements and repressive amnesia, of ahistorical longings and mindless acts of retreat. Konrad Adenauer's (in)famous slogan of the 1957 election, 'No Experiments!,' might as well be seen as describing many aspects of literary and artistic production in the postwar period, whether they entail popular or more high-brow forms of expression and reception, or whether we recall the cultural formations of East or of West Germany. Implicit taboos and outspoken proscriptions, calls for unassuming modesty and aesthetic self-restraint, loomed large over many aspects of postwar cultural exchange. Such calls even emerged from the scenes of progressive liberal and left-wing literary production, most vividly perhaps embodied by the demands of authors such as Victor Klemperer and the so-called *Gruppe 47* hoping to purge the German language of every word possibly tainted by the legacy of Nazi discourse. In this respect, the Nazis' systematic use of the aesthetic as a source of manipulating people's minds and emotions led to a clear mistrust of the aesthetic and its affective registers in the postwar era, even where aesthetic material did not try to make a larger claim on the political public sphere.

However, German unification in 1989–1990 has given us also some cause to rethink the overall trajectory of postwar culture, to recall this culture not simply as one struggling with the traumas of the Nazi era, but also as one quite effectively preparing the ground for the successful and—given its speed and its international reputation—rather astonishing transformation of German society from Nazi totalitarian rule to democratic civility, from authoritarian submissiveness to critical dissent and post-nationalist responsibility, and from the lethal instrumentalization of inner and outer nature to a unique ethos of environmental activism. To be sure, it is difficult to ignore how many taboos in the postwar period limited artistic experimentation out of fear that uncontained aesthetic practice could trigger a violent return of the past. In the wake of the peaceful revolution of 1989, however, it has become equally difficult to overlook the extent to which some of the historical groundwork for Germany's new political culture of civility, dispute, internationalism, and ecological concern was carried out precisely by artists and writers challenging the postwar consensus and its call for artistic modesty so as to explore the truly transformative power of the aesthetic. In the remainder of this essay, I would like to identify a few positions within this alternate history of postwar

German culture after Auschwitz as it, to some degree, has become visible only in hindsight after unification.

Consider the literary and essayistic work of both Uwe Johnson and Alexander Kluge. Having begun his writing career in the GDR, Johnson moved to the West in 1959, first to West Berlin, later to New York, and finally to Sheerness on Sea, a small island off the eastern English coast, where Johnson died in 1984. As a writer who seemed to embody differences and similarities between the literary worlds of East and West, Johnson throughout his life nevertheless polemically resisted any attempt to utilize his persona for any Cold War agenda and instead insisted on the principal autonomy of literary and artistic production. An unsteady wanderer between the worlds, Johnson's most memorable achievement became his monumental four-volume *Jahrestage* (*Anniversaries*), published between 1970 and 1983 and providing a fractured account of the life of the novel's heroine Gesine Cresspahl. Uncompromising in its formal gestalt and thematic complexity, *Jahrestage* chronicles Gesine's identity as one being suspended somewhere between past and present, between the East-German province and her new home New York, between remembering the impact of political exigencies onto the German hinterland and reading daily reports about the violence of the Vietnam War in the *New York Times*. The particular and local stories of German life in the twentieth century, in Johnson's at once rigorous and deeply humanistic perspective, cannot be told in isolation of the pressures of political and international history, and yet the bond between memory and history, the personal and political, the local and the (inter) national is a precarious one; it resists narrative integration or ideological totalization. Born two years prior to Johnson in 1932, Alexander Kluge's work shares a similar hostility against synthetic narratively and teleological history, but contrary to Johnson's formal exactitude and purity Kluge's work is driven by over-abundance, excess, and indefatigable transgressions of dominant boundaries between discourses and media. Kluge's recurrent obsession has been with the nature of obsession, of how the violence of twentieth-century German history has produced ever-changing structures of affect, emotion, passion, and pain. In marked difference to W. G. Sebald's infamous thesis that German literature failed to address the civilian traumas caused by air raids during World War II, Kluge's work—whether we consider prose texts such as *Schlachtbeschreibung* ('The Battle,' 1964) and *Neue Geschichten* ('New Histories,' 1977), films such as *Abschied von Gestern* ('Yesterday Girl,' 1966) and *Die Macht der Gefühle* ('The Power of Emotions,' 1983), or theoretical interventions, co-authored with Oskar Negt, such as *Öffentlichkeit und Erfahrung* ('Public Sphere and Experience,' 1972)—has repeatedly sought to chart the impact of Nazi warfare on the sensory, psychic, and intellectual infrastructure of postwar Germany.[13] In this, however, Kluge's point has never been simply to play out tropes of German (self-)victimization against the German responsibility for World War II. Through multifaceted and often unruly aesthetic and theoretical mediation, Kluge instead has sought to disrupt the bipolar oppositions and ideological certainties that have structured much of postwar discourse, thus exposing the limitations of a solely national perspective on World War II and stressing the fact that the German history of the Nazi era is by no means only a German story.

Similarly, in the realm of visual culture and film, the work of Anselm Kiefer and Werner Herzog come to mind, the first—in the late 1960s—traveling across various European countries in order to have his image taken, his right arm assuming the pose of the Hitler salute; the second—starting in the early 1970s—sending actor Klaus Kinski twice into the Amazonian jungle in order to produce thinly-veiled allegories of totalitarian realities, of ambiguous fusions of the aesthetic and the political, and of megalomaniac personalities whose narcissistic desire to control fate and make history resemble that of the erstwhile painter Hitler. Because of their blatant disregard for discursive taboos, and their predilection for the sublime and the monumental, both Kiefer and Herzog were often seen as being in close proximity to the very object they represent; both, it was argued when their early work became distributed, toyed with a problematic reawakening of Nazi mentality. Yet, with historical hindsight, a clearly different picture has emerged allowing us to understand the degree to which both Kiefer and Herzog were engaged in a project of reiterating and reframing the symptomatic expressions of historical traumas, of restructuring the narratives about the Nazi era, so as to change their symptomologies. The realm of aesthetic expression and experience here served as a conduit, not to reinstate the past, but to find some traction in the present again. Kiefer's Hitler poses in *To Genet* (1969), as much as Herzog's images of delusional aesthetic power in *Aguirre, Wrath of God* (1972) and *Fitzcarraldo* (1982) rested on no less than the assumption that Germany's recovery from the traumas of the past should be considered as a homeopathic process, one in which the subject needs to take in controlled doses of what afflicted the body in the first place so as to learn how to move beyond pain and guilt by learning how to move with it.[14] Probing the limits of representation, both Kiefer and Herzog thus also critically probed the place of contentious thought and material in a post-fascist public sphere. Their polemical stances and intense aesthetic gestures became crucial mechanisms to strengthen the degree of civility, of meaningful debate and controversy, in a culture overshadowed by trauma and taboo.

Finally, let us remember how West Germany from the late 1950s onwards, served as a base for international media artists and avant-garde operations, such as Nam June Paik and the Fluxus movement, making active use of state-sponsored cultural programs and institutions in order to establish network-like landscapes of international collaboration and artistic experimentation; and of how unorthodox visual and performance artists, such as Joseph Beuys were able, not only to convert private war mythologies into inclusive projects of aesthetic education, but to charge artistic practice with the task of making urban and natural landscapes more livable and us more responsive to the repressed language of nature. While systematically challenging dominant postwar standards of respectability and taste, Fluxus and Beuys, on the one hand, helped redefine (West) Germany as a cultural topography eager to serve as a crossroads for international artistic positions and thus to suspend the fateful coupling of culture and nation that had so troubled Nietzsche and enthused the Nazis. The cosmopolitan sensibilities of West German culture, at times, may have helped consolidate either Cold War agendas or the ever-growing prospects of the West-German tourist industry. However, in the long-run, they also infused German postwar culture with a fundamental and, arguably, quite unique interest for otherness, for constituting identity in face of and in active negotiation with what is different. On the other hand, in their very stress on post-national connectivity, on dismantling older hierarchies of artistic practice and exploring links between the local and the global, artists such as Beuys became key figures in relating the realm of art to the grass-root movements of the late 1970s—movements that protested the increasing exploitation and demolition of nature in the late-capitalist society. Contemporary art and aesthetic experience, in Beuys' boisterous visions, was to demand more reflexive, more reciprocal, more responsible interactions between humanity and its environments. Art's task was to empower forms of ecological activism, of stewardship for the future of the planet, that became most vividly exemplified in Beuys's own public forays: his famous 7000 oak project at Documenta 7 in Kassel in 1982 as much as his active involvement in the historical formation of the Green Party in West Germany around 1980 and, hence, in paving the way for the unique role of unified Germany as an international spokesperson for sustainability and clean energy use today.

The examples given here are no doubt sketchy, mere probes into the jagged landscapes of pre-unification German culture. Many more projects and positions could and should be named in order to map this landscape in all its richness and diversity. In spite of their sketchiness, however, these positions allow us to draw a number of important conclusions about how to approach and think about German culture in the shadow of the Nazi era and the Holocaust, and how to complicate the kind of accounts that have dominated the writing of German cultural history until the 1990s. First and foremost, the history of German culture cannot be written in the singular. German postwar culture is a dynamic that unfolds in the plural, entails multiple stories and histories, conflicting memories and emplotments, dissimilar institutional and discursive frameworks. It cannot be reduced to one teleological trajectory, whether we trace its departure from the Nazi era or its anticipation of our own present. Contrary to the postwar notion of the zero hour, German culture in the shadow of the Holocaust might best be understood in terms of its heterogeneous layers of often incompatible temporalities, memories, anticipations, and durational extensions—an unsteady space in which competing narratives of past, present, and future often appeared in close, albeit irreconcilable, proximity.

Secondly, there are many good reasons to insist that the framework of the nation state and the more recent scholarly fixation on questions of national identity, are simply too narrow in order to account for the many (hi)stories that make up German culture after 1945. On both sides of the Iron Curtain, cultural and aesthetic practice unfolded in close interaction with and, at times, in polemical opposition to international trends and materials. Similar to the way in which the history of the Holocaust, with its nearly universal effects and echoes, cannot be confined to the pages of German history books, we cannot understand the history of German culture in the wake of the Holocaust as simply a German affair, but need to conceptualize it also as an intersection of various inter-, trans-, and post-national voices, visions, and itineraries.

Thirdly, although trauma has served as a central keyword in many critical analyses in recent years, the multiplicity of narratives that constitute postwar German culture provides ample evidence not to overextend this concept and its clinical implications. For each writer, artist, filmmaker, and musician trying to encode the traumatic ruptures of German twentieth-century history with the help of modernist languages of disruption and fragmentation, we find many others whose idioms dodged normative expectations about how to produce art after Auschwitz and how to signify the silence of experience after the losses of World War II. German postwar culture was void of one single master narrative, including the seemingly splintering and, hence, pluralistic master narrative of trauma or traumatic recovery.

Fourth and finally, in its various efforts to move beyond the shadow of the Nazi era and anticipating our own increasingly global present, the developments of postwar German culture can be seen as putting to rest Nietzsche's concern about the reciprocity (and inverted relationship) of culture and politics. While aesthetic materials continue to play important roles in the construction of German identity and of civil networks of interaction, the fractured course of postwar German history effectively diffused wider claims for a stalwart unity of culture and great politics. Culture did not (re)flourish after the war merely because politics was ailing. Culture also didn't simply go downhill when German politics gained national confidence and international recognition again. In spite of its often bad reputation, postwar German culture instead provides important perspectives on how to envision and conceptualize more relaxed relationships between art and the political. In marked contrast to the legacy of the nineteenth- and early twentieth century, the history of German culture after 1945 invites its student neither to consider the aesthetic as a privileged site of political redemption nor to think of state and government as the principal custodians of cultural affairs. Given the disastrous fusion of art and politics during the Nazi era, it is difficult to deny the importance of such perspectives and insights.

NOTES

1. Friedrich Nietzsche, *Human, All too Human*, trans. R. J. Holingdale (Cambridge: Cambridge University Press, 1999), 169. For more on Nietzsche's as well as modern Germany's negotiation of culture and politics, see, among many others, Wolf Lepenies, *Kultur und Politik: Deutsche Geschichten* (Frankfurt am Main: Fischer, 2008).
2. Theodor W. Adorno, 'Cultural Criticism and Society,' *Prisms*, trans. Samuel and Shierry Weber (Cambridge: MIT Press, 1983), 34.
3. Paul Celan, 'Death Fugue,' trans. Joachim Neugroschel, *Paul Celan: Speech-Grille and Selected Poems* (New Work: E. P. Dutton & Co., 1979), 29.
4. Quoted. in William Rasch, 'Looking again at the Rubble,' in Wilfried Wilms and William Rasch (eds), *German Postwar Films: Life and Love in the Ruins* (New York: Palgrave MacMillan, 2008), 1.

5. Andreas Huyssen, 'Figures of Memory in the Course of Time,' in Stephanie Barron and Sabine Eckmann (eds), *Art of Two Germanys/Cold War Cultures* (New York: Abrams, 2009), 229.

6. Friedrich Meinecke, *The German Catastrophe: Reflections and Recollections*, trans. Sidney B. Fay (Cambridge: Harvard University Press, 1950), 120–121; also quoted in Stephen Brockmann, *German Literary Culture at the Zero Hour* (Rochester: Camden House, 2004), 131.

7. Günter Grass, *The Tin Drum*, trans. Ralph Manheim (New York: Vintage International, 1990), 15.

8. Wolfgang Welsch, 'Modernity and Postmodernity in Post-war Germany (1945–1995),' in Reiner Pommerin (ed.), *Culture in the Federal Republic of Germany, 1945–1995* (Oxford: Berg, 1996), 109–132.

9. Alexander and Margarete Mitscherlich, *Die Unfähigkeit zu trauern: Grundlagen kollektiven Verhaltens* (Munich: Piper, 1967).

10. Johannes von Moltke, *No Place Like Home: Locations of Heimat in German Cinema* (Berkeley: University of California Press, 2005).

11. Jan Dawson, *Wim Wenders*, trans. Carla Wartenberg (New York: Zoetrope, 1976), 12.

12. Konrad H. Jarausch and Michael Geyer, *Shattered Past: Reconstructing German Histories* (Princeton: Princeton University Press, 2003), 301.

13. W. G. Sebald, 'Air War and Literature,' *On the Natural History of Destruction*, trans. Anthea Bell (New York: Random House, 2004), 1–104.

14. For more on the homeopathic in German cinema, see Eric L. Santner, *Stranded Objects: Mourning, Memory, and Film in Postwar Germany* (Itahca: Cornell University Press, 1990), 19–26; and Caryl Flinn, *The New German Cinema: Music, History, and the Matter of Style* (Berkeley: University of California Press, 2004), 1–25.

Bibliography

Adorno, Theodor W. 'Cultural Criticism and Society.' *Prisms*, trans. Samuel and Shierry Weber (Cambridge: MIT Press, 1983), 19–34.

Barnouw, Dagmar. *Germany 1945: Views of War and Violence* (Bloomington: Indiana University Press, 1997).

Barron, Stephanie and Sabine Eckmann (eds), *Art of Two Germanys/Cold War Cultures* (New York: Abrams, 2009).

Brockmann, Stephen, *German Literary Culture at the Zero Hour* (Rochester: Camden House, 2004).

Demetz, Peter, *After the Fires: Recent Writing in the Germanies, Austria and Switzerland* (New York: Harcourt Brace Jovanovich, 1986).

Fehrenbach, Heide, *Cinema in Democratizing Germany: Reconstructing National Identity after Hitler* (Chapel Hill: University of North Carolina Press, 1995).

Glaser, Hermann. *Kulturgeschichte der Bundesrepublik Deutschland: Zwischen Kapitulation und Währungsreform 1945–1948* (Munich: Hanser, 1985).

Herf, Jeffrey. *Divided Memory: The Nazi Past in the Two Germanys* (Cambridge: Harvard University Press, 1997).

HERMAND, JOST, *Kultur im Wiederaufbau: Die Bundesrepublik Deutschland, 1945–1965* (Munich: Nymphenburger, 1986).

HORKHEIMER, MAX and THEODOR W. ADORNO, *Dialectic of Enlightenment*, trans. John Cumming (New York: Continuum, 1995).

KAPCZYNSKI, JENNIFER M., *The German Patient: Crisis and Recovery in Postwar Culture* (Ann Arbor: University of Michigan Press, 2008).

KLEMPERER, VIKTOR, *Kultur: Erwägungen nach dem Zusammenbruch des Nazismus* (Berlin: Neues Leben, 1946).

LEPENIES, WOLF. *Kultur und Politik: Deutsche Geschichten* (Frankfurt am Main: Fischer, 2008).

MEINECKE, FRIEDRICH, *The German Catastrophe: Reflections and Recollections*, trans. Sidney B. Fay (Cambridge: Harvard University Press, 1950).

MITSCHERLICH, ALEXANDER and MARGARETE, *Die Unfähigkeit zu trauern: Grundlagen kollektiven Verhaltens* (Munich: Piper, 1967).

PICARD, MAX, *Hitler in Our Selves*, trans. Heinrich Hauser (Hinsdale: Henry Regnery, 1947).

POIGER, UTA G., *Jazz, Rock, and Rebels: Cold War Politics and American Culture in a Divided Germany* (Berkeley: University of California Press, 2000).

SCHIVELBUSCH, WOLFGANG, *In a Cold Crater: Cultural and Intellectual Life in Berlin, 1945–1948*, trans. Kelly Barry (Berkeley: University of California Press, 1998).

SEBALD, W.G., *On the Natural History of Destruction*, trans. Anthea Bell (New York: Random House, 2003).

SHANDLEY, ROBERT R., *Rubble Films: German Cinema in the Shadow of the Third Reich* (Philadelphia: Temple University Press, 2001).

WILMS, WILFRIED and WILLIAM RASCH (eds), *German Postwar Films: Life and Love in the Ruins* (New York: Palgrave MacMillan, 2008).

CHAPTER 32

THE TWO GERMAN STATES
IN THE INTERNATIONAL
WORLD

ANDREAS W. DAUM

32.1 HALF WAY: DÉTENTE 1972

THE year 1972 seemed to be promising, certainly for the Germans. A decade had passed since the Cuban Missile crisis, the last climax of the old Cold War. A decade later, as we know today, West Germany would be torn in a heated debate over the deployment of NATO missiles; a new Cold War cast its shadow over Europe. In 1972, however, détente—the period of relaxation, openness, and communication between the two antagonistic superpowers and their allies—had reached its height. The United States and the Soviet Union practiced a dialogue. In February, American president Richard Nixon visited China. In spite of heavy domestic opposition, the Federal Republic consolidated its relationship with the neighboring states in the East, including the German Democratic Republic (GDR). Many in the West no longer saw the border that separated the Germans into antagonistic political blocs as an insurmountable 'Iron Curtain.' The building of the Berlin Wall in August 1961 had been a brutal act. However, Germans had to become accustomed to the reality of the Wall. Ironically, its existence also opened new opportunities for encounters between West and East.

Dialogue, openness, and transparency were values that many in the Federal Republic cherished in 1972. These, too, were values that West Germans wanted others and the world at large to associate with their country. They were meant to articulate—at home and abroad—that West Germany had developed into a knowledge-based, technologically advanced, internationally minded, and peaceful consumer society. Already in the early 1960s, even moderate conservatives had begun to feel the need to move beyond the thinking of Konrad Adenauer, who stepped down as chancellor in 1963 after almost fourteen years in office. By this point, hardly anyone—not even the Social Democratic Party (SPD)—questioned Adenauer's seminal achievements. They ranged from the integration of expellees, to the Federal Republic's alignment with the United States and its active role in the process of Western European integration. However, Adenauer himself and the policies he advocated had clearly reached their limits. Contrary to many stereotypes, West German society was anything but encrusted or marked by immobility in the Adenauer years. Still, these years appeared increasingly as *muffig*— musty like the air in a room whose windows had not been opened for a long time. The election of the SPD chairman Willy Brandt as chancellor in October 1969 was an important event, but hardly the first act of opening. After all, since 1948 the SPD had ruled almost continuously in West Berlin, the Cold War's frontline city. Most important, the Social Democrats had been a partner in the federal government since 1966, when they embarked on a grand coalition with the Christian Democrats (CDU) and its Bavarian counterpart, the Christian Social Union (CSU).

Like no chancellor before him, Brandt found the right words to embrace what many West Germans—especially of the middle and younger generation—hoped for. He put into words the desire that German politics would respond creatively to the fundamental social, generational, and cultural transformations in the last third of the century. In his inaugural address as chancellor to the federal parliament, the *Bundestag*, Brandt set a new tone and drafted a new vision. His government would promote more freedom and 'more democracy' (the formula that was later most cited and most derided). The new coalition between the SPD and the liberal Free Democratic Party (FDP) would work toward creating a greater sense of individual and collective responsibility, more access to education, more scientifically-based policy planning, more efficiency and legal security, more social stability, and a better partnership with the so-called Third World. 'We want to be and become,' concluded Brandt, 'people who are good neighbors, at home and toward the outside world.'[1]

The year 1972, when the city of Munich hosted the twentieth Summer Olympic Games, offered West Germans a unique opportunity to show themselves as 'good neighbors.' Almost a generation after the Nazi-controlled Olympics in Berlin in 1936, Germans once again invited the world, this time to a city the Nazis liked to call the 'capital' of the National Socialist movement. In 1972, everything was meant to be different from Germanic monumentalism, Prussian classicism, and the Nazis' uniform fetishism. The Munich Games combined high-tech modernity with Bavarian folklore. The values of openness, modernity, and international understanding materialized spectacularly in the architecture of the central stadium. It was only partially covered with a transparent, steel and glass ceiling that extended in curved lines into the surrounding Olympic park. Softness and openness were expressed, too, in the light colors and pastels that tinted flags, decorations, and the officials' dress. The Federal Republic's team ultimately won thirteen gold medals and thus ranked fourth in the medals list. This was just the right amount of success to avoid any impression of hubris. The West German audience, too, demonstrated good-will and fairness. It did not hesitate to cheer Soviet track-and-field sprinter Valerie Borsov, East German back-stroke swimmer Roland Matthes, and the Cuban boxer Teofilo Stevenson. Patriotic vernacularism and Cold War narrow-mindedness seemed *passé*.

The spectacle of the Munich Summer Olympics was still in the minds of the West German populace when, a few moths later, the SPD under the leadership of Willy Brandt won an astonishing 45.8 percent of the votes in the election for a new *Bundestag*. The mixture of relaxed self-confidence and openness toward the world, which the Munich Olympics had exhibited, mirrored Willy Brandt's remarkable campaign slogan: 'Germans, we can be proud of our country.' These few words implied that the Federal Republic's achievements—not the longing for an imagined, larger nation—provided the West Germans with a collective identity. Both the Olympic Games of 1972 and Brandt's electoral campaign thus bore a post-national imprint.

The GDR, too, arrived in Munich freed from the ballast of the 1950s and 1960s. Walter Ulbricht, the epitome of Cold War East Germany, had been ousted from the most important political positions during the previous year. His successor as first secretary of the Socialist Unity Party (SED), Erich Honecker, promised to lead the country toward technological modernization and the Socialist version of a more consumer-oriented society. Like Willy Brandt, Honecker was interested in détente, although for different reasons—and less so than Ulbricht had been.[2] Honecker was keen to legitimize the GDR as a state in its own right, both in legal and political terms. Moreover, he wanted the GDR to gain economically from a closer relationship with the West. Honecker's aim was to secure the existence of a Socialist society at the cost of confirming the division of the European continent. Brandt, on the other hand, hoped to overcome Germany's division in the long run by engaging the other side in a dialogue. In the meantime, Brandt's politics toward Eastern Europe (known as *Ostpolitik*) aimed at making Germany's division bearable for people on both sides of the border and allowing them to communicate with each other. According to the logic of *Ostpolitik*, the East German rulers would gradually reduce the internal pressure on their population once external, that is Western, pressure was reduced: the GDR would liberalize because it was stabilized. This concept had grown out of a formula that Egon Bahr, Brandt's closest advisor, had coined already in 1963. The German-German relationship and especially the conditions for those Germans living in the GDR would change for the better if the two sides came closer to one another (*Wandel durch Annäherung*).[3]

As the preparations for the Munich Olympics entered their final stage, the two German states intensified direct negotiations. They had already closely followed the Quadripartite negotiations on Berlin, which the four Allied powers of World War II—the United States, Great Britain, France, and the Soviet Union—signed in September 1971. The Berlin Agreement confirmed the security of West Berlin and the Allies' responsibility for the whole of Berlin. Complementing the Quadripartite Berlin Agreement, the GDR concluded a so-called Transit Agreement with the Federal Republic in December 1971; it further facilitated traffic between East and West. For the first time, both German states entered a direct contractual relationship. The Transit Agreement was topped by the comprehensive *Verkehrsvertrag*, signed in May 1972. It expanded the possibilities of mutual travel. A few days earlier, the *Bundestag* passed—only after heated debates, though—the treaties with the Soviet Union and Poland with which the Brandt government had launched *Ostpolitik* in 1970. Both treaties confirmed that West Germany accepted the territorial status quo in Europe and sought more dialogue with its eastern neighbors. When the Munich Olympics were officially opened on 26 August, the two German states were in the midst of negotiating an even more fundamental Basic Treaty (*Grundlagenvertrag*). This was signed shortly before Christmas. Both parties were thus committing themselves to respecting the inviolability of their borders, each other's independence, and the principles of the Charter of the United Nations.

32.2 PASTELS AND BLACK: GERMAN DILEMMAS

Détente was visible, tangible, and audible in Munich. Each German team carried its respective national flag.[4] The GDR team performed well and ended one notch above the West German team in the overall medals table. The actual surprise came before the competitions started. For over twenty years, Western observers had depicted life in East Berlin and the GDR as shabby, gloomy, and literally gray. On 26 August, the GDR sent its team into the opening ceremony dressed not in less, but in more colors than its West German counterpart. Soft blue, orange, green, pink, and yellow clothes dominated— exactly the spectrum the Munich designers had chosen to depict the 'cheerful Games,' as the slogan ran.

Contemporaries and historians have debated heatedly whether and to what extent détente falsely assumed—so the critique—a willingness on the part of the Socialist world to allow more freedom within its borders. However, was pursuing détente not the only realistic strategy left to soften the Cold War stalemate and achieve improvements for the people living in the East?[5] The Munich Olympics cast a slightly different light on the promises as well as the fragility of détente. On 5 September 1972, the pastel colors were covered with blood and overshadowed by a group of militant Palestinians who called themselves 'Black September.' They entered the Olympic village, stormed the quarters of the Israeli team and took nine hostages after having shot two team members. The Games were interrupted. After intense negotiations, the hostage-takers were flown with their victims to a nearby airport under the pretext of being transported out of the country. German sharpshooters opened fire, aiming to eliminate the kidnappers. In the ensuing wild shooting, all Israeli hostages, most of their kidnappers, and one policeman died.

The synchronicity of the cheerful imagery of the Munich Olympics and the cruel attack on Israel's team reflected the precarious position of divided Germany in the Cold War's international world. Munich's post-national imprint and the emphasis on openness were not simply an expression of naivety. Certainly, together with the alarmingly lax security measures, these features can be seen as a sign of *Machtvergessenheit*, a lost awareness of power, violence, and realpolitik that can be partly explained by an overreaction against the obsession with power politics and military postures in previous German regimes, in particular Wilhelminian and Nazi Germany.[6] But the emphasis on transparency corresponded to a larger foreign policy concept that served West Germany's political and economic interests. Since the Federal Republic was allowed to establish a ministry of foreign affairs in 1951 (the GDR had had its own since 1949, although dominated by the SED), West Germany's overarching foreign policy aim was to establish itself as a trustworthy international partner, to avoid the impression of any aggressive intentions, and to frame its public representations in multilateral terms that signaled openness to the world. The 'posture of moderation' in international relations was meant to be an integral part of West Germany's realpolitik.[7]

The Munich Massacre, however, catapulted divided Germany into an arena beyond the 'German Question,' demonstrating the limits of West Germany's approach to securing a well-respected position in the world. Over the course of the past two decades, the two German states had been overly fixated on issues related to military security, the East-West conflict, and legal as well as political sovereignty. This focus had led them to believe that security along the borders in Central Europe would, indeed, secure their peace. To a large degree, both viewed the world outside Europe as a bipolar one, torn between the superpowers and thus indirectly or even directly opting for one of the German states. In the Federal Republic, this view had generated the so-called Hallstein Doctrine in the late 1950s. The doctrine did not allow for diplomatic relations with states that recognized the GDR (with the notable exception of the Soviet Union) and was only gradually given up after 1967. In the GDR, the Third World was primarily seen as a turf where it could gain symbolic capital and counteract the Federal Republic.

The Munich events, however, showed that Germany was exposed to an increasingly complicated world marked by regional conflicts and centrifugal forces. 'Black September' brought the conflict between Palestinians and Israel, and non-state terrorism, to Germany. Interestingly, the first major deployment of the special task force called GSG 9 ('Border Protection Group'), which the Federal Republic's government constituted as a consequence of the Munich massacre, took place outside Europe. It was once more connected to the conflict between Israel and the Palestinians. In 1977, the GSG 9 successfully stormed a German airplane, which had been hijacked by Palestinians, in Mogadishu, Somalia.

The Munich events thus pointed to the dual necessity of protecting Israel and of developing better contacts with Arab states. Unlike the GDR, which reacted coldly to the Munich massacre, the Federal Republic had accepted the idea that support for Israel was a historical responsibility; it had developed a 'special relationship' with Israel.[8] West Germany had begun reparation payments for Israel in 1952, delivered arms to the country since 1957, and commenced diplomatic relations in 1965 (which the GDR never did). The murder of eleven Jewish men during the Olympic Games in Munich revealed yet another side of the 'German Question:' West Germany's attempts to position itself in the world needed to factor in the German past. Willy Brandt embraced this idea in the most convincing way. He was well aware that all of Germany's neighbors, partners, and opponents had a legitimate desire to suppress any potential for renewed German aggression, coming from whatever source. Brandt's *Ostpolitik* contributed to a politics of history that explicitly acknowledged the victims of the Nazis' genocidal wars in Europe. The image of one of the Palestinian terrorists looking down from the balcony of Israeli Olympic team's apartment building in 1972 demonstrated in a bizarre and unforeseen way how vulnerable this politics of history remained. It stands in stark contrast to an image of Willy Brandt during his visit to Poland in December 1970. In Warsaw, Brandt went down on his knees in front of the Polish monument that commemorates the insurrection in the Warsaw Ghetto in 1943.

32.3 ALLIANCES AND INTERESTS: 1949–1972

Détente and *Ostpolitik* did not simply mean a radical break with the past. Both were embedded in larger trends in international politics. Détente as a strategy allowing for communication across the Iron Curtain derived from the stabilization of the status quo in Europe in the mid-1950s, although it was not pursued as a main foreign policy imperative at that time. The year 1955 was a watershed. The Soviet Union officially declared that the state of war with Germany was over. The Western Allies terminated the occupation regime on the territory of what had become the Federal Republic and established embassies in Bonn. The Federal Republic also established diplomatic relations with the Soviet Union in exchange for the release of the remaining German prisoners of war. The two blocs consolidated their position further with the Federal Republic's incorporation into NATO and the founding of an eastern military alliance, the Warsaw Pact, which included the GDR as a member. *Wiedervereinigung*, reunification of Germany, would be possible only if all parties *and* all alliances involved in Europe would agree. All sides tried to accommodate themselves to the newly-confirmed status quo. Neither of the two German states fundamentally questioned the hegemonic power of the United States and the Soviet Union, respectively. They had no interest in doing so; after all, the superpowers guaranteed their existence. Instead, the international positioning of both German states was characterized by attempts to gain more leeway within their respective hegemonic systems.

As Wolfram Hanrieder has pointed out, West German foreign policies in the Cold War era embraced a 'territorial mode of thinking' in one context and rejected it in another.[9] His statement holds true, too, for the unequal sibling in the East. Neither of the two German states aimed at any territorial gains; the Saar Region's incorporation into the territory of the Federal Republic in January 1957 was a special case.[10] Reunification would have meant—and ultimately did mean—that a unified Germany was territorially larger than each of the two existing states alone. However, neither the Federal Republic (which understood itself as the legal successor of the German Reich in its borders of 1937) nor the GDR sought to include further territories into a unified Germany. Still, and for understandable reasons, Germany's eastern neighbors and Poland in particular harbored concerns. West Germany remained hesitant to recognize formally the German-Polish border or *Oder-Neisse-Linie*. Even the Western allies increasingly saw this attitude as outdated and detrimental to a peaceful international order in Europe. West Germany's position also stood in contrast to that of the GDR, which had officially accepted the border with Poland in the Görlitz Treaty of July 1950. West Germany's contortions regarding the *Oder-Neisse-Linie* continued until 1990. They can be partially explained by the fear of losing the votes—and also giving up the restitution claims—of the expellees. The hesitation to recognize fully the Polish-German border also had to do with the ethnic Germans in the East who wished to emigrate. Most important, all West German governments maintained that a final territorial agreement grounded in international law could only be achieved through a peace treaty involving the four major allies of World War II. Even the *Ostpolitik* treaties left a tiny door open. They fully recognized the 'territorial integrity' of all existing borders and emphasized that the Federal Republic pursued 'no territorial claims at all.' Still, these treaties spoke of the 'inviolability' of borders, which did not exclude, in principle, changes based on mutual agreements.[11]

The territorial mode in which the two Germanies positioned themselves in the world also became obvious in their main geopolitical orientations. For the Federal Republic, a firm anchor in the West served its interests best. It remained the seminal achievement of the Federal Republic's first chancellor, Konrad Adenauer, to have dropped this anchor. American hegemony meant military security, nuclear protection against the Soviet Union, and economic support. A good relationship with Great Britain reinforced the integration into the North Atlantic world and was necessary to overcome lingering British resentment against Germany. The attempt to seek a close alignment with France generated at times considerable conflicts with the United States and Britain. This became clear during the presidency of Charles de Gaulle (1958–1969). Adenauer's own party, the CDU, mirrored these conflicts. The so-called Atlanticists favored close co-ordination with the United States. The Gaullists rallied behind CSU-leader Franz Josef Strauß, who favored a German-French alliance. Both groups got their share in the Federal Republic's foreign policy. To the chagrin of the United States, the Federal Republic concluded a friendship treaty with France in January 1963. Yet, the *Bundestag* ratified it only after having added a preamble that emphasized West Germany's commitment to the Atlantic alliance and the United States. Ultimately, the picture of Adenauer and de Gaulle standing next to each other during a service in the cathedral of Reins in July 1962 co-existed as one of the iconic images of the Federal Republic's history with that of US president John J. Kennedy delivering his *Ich bin ein Berliner* speech in front of West Berlin's city hall in June 1963.[12]

In the 1960s, West Germany sought to pursue its interests more flexibly by using its limited maneuvering space. This strategy also translated into the Federal Republic's role in those Western European communities it had joined in the previous decade: the European Council in 1951, the European Coal and Steel Community in 1952, the Western European Union in 1955 as well as the European Economic Community (EEC) and the European Atomic Energy Community (EURATOM, both in effect in 1958). Vis-à-vis France, Adenauer's successors Ludwig Erhard (1963–1966), Kurt Georg

Kiesinger (1966–1969), and Willy Brandt (1969–1974) did not back de Gaulle's veto against Britain's admission to the European Economic Community. They also insisted on maintaining the Federal Republic's high export rate. At the same time, the West Germans wanted to keep the French troops on their soil after France had left the military structure of NATO in 1966. In their relations with the United States, problems mounted in the 1960s. The United States pressured the Federal Republic to help financially in light of a growing deficit in its balance of payments, especially given the high costs incurred through the deployment of troops in Germany. Erhard's attempt to provide some relief by purchasing US military equipment ultimately contributed to his failure as chancellor in 1966. However, West Germany also wanted to keep US troops as a security guarantee against the Soviet Union and tried to prevent all plans, regularly discussed in the United States, for a troop withdrawal. Finally, the Federal Republic did not want to get involved in America's war in Vietnam, which triggered unprecedented waves of protest against the United States at home, as elsewhere, and fueled anti-American outbursts.

Distinctly German interests also surfaced in controversial discussions about the political and military strategy of NATO. For a while, Adenauer and especially Strauß pursued the idea of obtaining access to nuclear weapons, an attempt that met staunch American opposition. As a lukewarm compromise, the United States suggested establishing a multilateral nuclear force (MLF), but the idea evaporated in the mid-1960s. Nevertheless, in 1966 the Federal Republic became a member of NATO's newly established Nuclear Planning Group. Equally controversial was West Germany's initial skepticism toward the military strategy of 'flexible response'—that is of gradual escalation—which the Kennedy administration favored over that of 'massive retaliation.' A strategy that factored in conventional warfare was financially costly for the Federal Republic. It also triggered fears that the German territory could constitute an isolated battle field in a future war; Germany's security interests would thus be decoupled from those of the United States. The Federal Republic insisted on a strategy that (theoretically) assumed a quick escalation toward nuclear war in order to ensure that the United States realized that the survival of America was at stake. Obviously, however, no German government was interested in any war, certainly not one involving the nuclear devastation of German territory. West Germany's security politics was thus 'rational' *and* 'absurd' at the same time.[13] Still, NATO adopted a new tone toward the East that corresponded to specific German interests. In 1967, the Western alliance passed the Harmel Report, which called for a dual strategy: military security should be complemented by a willingness to seek actively détente with the East.[14]

Toward the East, the Christian Democratic chancellors Erhard and Kiesinger demonstrated much more flexibility than Adenauer had. They sought more exchange, primarily in the field of economics and trade. Gerhard Schröder, foreign minister from 1961 to 1966, pursued a *Politik der Bewegung* (policy of movement), which created a network of trade missions with eastern European states. Willy Brandt, who succeeded him as foreign minister in the Grand Coalition, accelerated this course. Kiesinger, the Coalition's chancellor, accepted direct contacts between the two German governments in Bonn and East Berlin. Pragmatism began to prevail over adherence to old principles, although the CDU chancellors stopped short of designing a coherent *Ostpolitik*. Brandt himself had set a successful example in his previous position as ruling mayor of West Berlin. Two years after the GDR had erected the Wall around the western sectors of the city, and in full consultation with the Federal Republic's government, Brandt's municipal administration reached an agreement with East Berlin. Over the Christmas holidays of 1963, West Berliners were allowed to obtain special passes (*Passierscheine*) to cross the border and visit the eastern sector. Almost 800,000 West Berliners queued for the passes and unexpected opportunity to meet friends and family members in East Berlin.[15]

The Wall gave the GDR new room to maneuver on the international stage. Walter Ulbricht had insisted on walling West Berlin in against initial Soviet reservations.[16] A continuous flight of East Germans westward, especially highly trained ones, would have also undermined the GDR's ability to perform in the world as an independent actor. The GDR stretched the political limits within the eastern bloc in the early 1960s. It made overtures to China, whose confrontation with the Soviet Union had just reached a first climax. The Soviet Union brought the GDR back on course, in this case as in others. However, Moscow could not control East Germany's foreign policy completely. In 1967, the GDR went again on the political offensive, in order to counter West Germany's attempt to reach out to Eastern Europe without recognizing the GDR. East Germany concluded a series of bilateral treaties with Warsaw Pact allies and introduced a nominal East German citizenship (West Germany claimed that there was only one German citizenship, represented by the Federal Republic). The so-called Ulbricht Doctrine, adopted at a meeting of the Warsaw Pact's foreign ministers in February 1967, was meant to deal the deathblow to West Germany's Hallstein Doctrine: Warsaw Pact states seeking diplomatic relations with the Federal Republic, as Romania had just established, were committed to insisting that the Federal Republic recognize the GDR and the *Oder-Neisse-Linie*. When Moscow decided to suppress the Prague Spring in the Czech Republic in 1968, the GDR did not join the military invasion, but provided logistical and political support.

Undoubtedly, Ulbricht tried to pursue a distinctly East German path to modernity and in the international world. Already in 1963, he had launched the New Economic System of Planning and Management, which tried to introduce more flexibility into the national economy. Ulbricht wanted to lead the GDR toward becoming an achievement-oriented career society. The attempt to turn the GDR into a socialist model state continued to cause concerns in the Soviet Union. They were fueled by Ulbricht's emphasis on the GDR as a Socialist state 'of the German nation,' as the new GDR constitution claimed in 1968,[17] and his ideas about a new *Westpolitik* in response to Brandt's *Ostpolitik*. These concerns were shared by internal opponents guised as modernizers, such as Honecker, and they contributed to the ousting of Ulbricht from power in 1971.

Beyond the geographical realm of their respective alliance systems, both German states began to strengthen their presence in Africa, Asia, and South America. The

Federal Republic invested heavily outside of Europe, politically as well as financially. Adenauer had already kicked off a massive program of capital lending to the so-called Third World in 1960, and created a Ministry for Economic Cooperation (with the developing world) one year later. In 1963, the German Development Service, modeled after the Unites States' newly-created Peace Corps, was launched. Like the GDR, however, the Federal Republic tended to see the Third World through the lens of the 'German Question.' The fierce competition for the right to solely represent Germany abroad was cemented in the Federal Republic by the Hallstein Doctrine, even though the later was not truly coherent and often led to hasty decisions. On the other side, the GDR tried to gain a foot in the door of newly-independent states. The peak of its reputation among the non-aligned states was reached in 1965, when Egypt's president Gamal Abdel Nasser received Ulbricht with highest honors. Over-all, the GDR's success was limited. In 1954, the Federal Republic maintained diplo-matic relations with fifty-three states around the world, the GDR with only eleven, all of which were associated with the socialist world. Nine years later, the corresponding numbers were ninety-eight and thirteen. None of the sixteen African states that gained independence in 1960 recognized the GDR.[18] More and more states did so from 1969 on, when the Brandt government gave up the Hallstein Doctrine. This trend culminated in the establishment of East German diplomatic relations with the United States in 1974.

32.4 PRINCIPLES AND PRACTICES: MODES OF INTERNATIONALISM

The geopolitical orientations of German foreign policies were themselves parts of a larger framework that continued to exist until 1989—and even beyond. It can be captured in five categories that help to explain the positioning, goals, and leeway of the two German states in the international arena, as well as the striking differences between the two:

1. *Continuity and reliability:* Both German states performed on the international stage with a high degree of continuity. As a democratic political system, the Federal Republic generated changing coalitions and governments. Most notable were the changes in 1969, when the new SPD–FDP government began to launch *Ostpolitik*, and in 1982, when this coalition gave way to the conservative-liberal government of the CDU and FDP under Chancellor Helmut Kohl. In both cases, West Germany's foreign policy remained committed to the basic international orientation that previous govern-ments had established, i.e., the alignment with the West and *Ostpolitik*, respectively. The remarkable degree of continuity in foreign policy rested upon the consensus shared by all democratic parties that the Federal Republic needed to remain

predictable, reliable, and trustworthy in its dealings with the world. Not surprisingly, the terms 'community,' 'contract,' and 'loyal' were key for the leading Social Democrat Herbert Wehner when he, in a legendary speech of June 1960, signaled the SPD's full commitment to respecting the western alliances in which Adenauer had anchored the Federal Republic.[19] In the case of the GDR, change was not inherent since the country was continuously dominated by the SED. As a result, the GDR remained, in international terms, remarkably predictable—though, ironically enough, less so under the Cold War veteran Ulbricht than under his successors.

2. *Sovereignty and entanglement:* Europe's post-World War II order, remaining legal constraints, and the interests of the superpowers continued to restrict the sovereignty of the two German states until 1990. Neither was granted access to nuclear weapons. Neither could have decided the fate of Berlin alone—or jointly, for that matter. Both states had foreign troops stationed on their soil, and the Federal Republic desired nothing more than this to retain security guarantees from its Western military partners. Both were integrated in collective political, economic, and military structures, both accepted that this entanglement meant, in effect, their containment. The continuous efforts to contain Germany became clear when the United States pressured the Federal Republic to sign the Test Ban Treaty in 1963 (and thereby also tolerate the GDR as an independent signatory) and the Non-Proliferation Treaty five years later. Both states operated in an asymmetrical power relationship with their respective superpower. Still, West Germany's relationship with the United States was one among democratic powers and thus based on a very different legitimacy—plus, unlike the GDR's relationship with the Soviet Union, it was open to public debate. The Federal Republic, as well as the GDR, declared *and* practiced entanglement out of conviction, as well as to pursue best their respective interests. Remarkably, both states also wrote a commitment to international law into their constitutions, so in Article 25 of the West German Basic Law and in Articles 5 and 8, respectively, of the East German constitutions of 1949, 1968, and 1974.[20]

Demographic and cultural orientations were affected by a sort of entanglement across borders that was specific to the Federal Republic. In 1955, the Bonn government signed, with Italy, its first labor recruitment treaty. Over the next few years, West Germany established the largest labor recruitment program of all Western European nations. In 1964, the one-millionth 'guest worker' arrived in the Federal Republic. The numbers continued to climb. The percentage of foreigners rose from 1.2 percent in 1961 to over 8 percent in 1990. Most guest workers initially came from Italy, which was later surpassed as the country of origin by Turkey and Yugoslavia.[21] The Federal Republic thus began to add a southern—and a Muslim—dimension to its society.

3. *Multilateralism and transnational networks:* Entanglement as principle and practice meant for both German states—in spite of very different ideological goals—a preference for co-operation over aggression, in whatever form. Both states avoided risks (with Ulbricht in the early and late 1960s, and Brandt in the early

1970s coming closest to being regarded suspiciously by their partners abroad). As far as the Federal Republic was concerned, the 'softness' of its power was a necessary feature in order to achieve its goals.[22] It also meant paying much attention to symbolic politics, as in the case of the Munich Olympics. Almost ostentatiously, the Federal Republic tried to display a 'gesture of national restraint'[23] and invested significantly in cultural diplomacy. This gesture corresponded to a fundamental multilateral orientation. It reinforced the Federal Republic's rise to the status of a 'civilian power' that sought co-operation in order to pursue international objectives, used non-military means to secure national security goals, and opted for integration in supranational structures.[24]

Multilateralism was not confined to the realm of state actors. The Federal Republic promoted institutions that mediated between culture, educational activities and politics, as well as between Germany and the international world. Early examples are the Goethe Institute (1951) and the Alexander von Humboldt Foundation (1953). Additionally, societies devoted to cultivating bilateral relations—such as the German-French Office for the Youth (1963)—were founded; universities established student exchange programs; cities embarked on partnerships across borders; foundations sponsored by the major political parties reached out to other countries, etc. West Germany thus established a broad network of transnational contacts that helped to solidify West Germany's role as a reliable, culturally attractive, and technologically advanced international actor. In the GDR, membership in the Society for German-Soviet Friendship was almost obligatory; important, too, was the League for International Friendship.

Cultivating transnational contacts also meant for the Federal Republic generating qualified personnel whose training and career advances now required experiences in inter-, supra-, and transnational institutions. This effect was strengthened by the involvement in the European Community's administration and—for aspiring military officers—through stints at the NATO Defense College in Rome. West Germany was particularly successful in its game of one-upmanship with the GDR at the United Nations. More than twenty years before both German states joined in 1973, the Federal Republic had begun lobbying the UN, had sent a permanent observer to New York, and contributed financially ($430 million between 1960 and 1973).[25] The Federal Republic also joined the United Nations' special organizations, while preventing the GDR from taking any of the these steps.

4. *The 'economization' of foreign policy:* As far as the Federal Republic was concerned, increasing economic strength, and growing prosperity added considerable weight to its international position. These factors created a setting in which international and economic goals became closely linked with one another. By the early 1970s, West Germany had become Europe's economic powerhouse and most important export nation. The Federal Republic had the second largest share, after the United States, in world exports, exporting more than twenty percent of its gross national product. In 1979, the trade volume with the Soviet Union was six

times as high as in 1969.[26] West Germany's attractiveness for the so-called Third World was not least grounded in the fact that the Federal Republic could offer developing countries significantly more aid and stronger economic incentives than the GDR. West Germany's monetary and trade interests also served distinctly German-German interests, with the Federal Republic successfully pushing for special GATT (General Agreement of Tariffs and Trade) and EEC regulations that protected its trade with the GDR. The later was exempt from EEC customs so that the GDR became a silent member of the Western European customs union. *Ostpolitik* and Chancellor Schmidt's tenure from 1974 to 1982 further contributed to tightening the close linkage between economic, monetary, and foreign policies. Against this background, one may say that the Federal Republic's foreign policy—as its international standing at large—became increasingly 'economized.'

5. *The public sphere of international politics:* Another fundamental difference between the Federal Republic's and the GDR's positioning in the international world derived once again from the character of West Germany as a pluralistic society and the GDR's imprint as a dictatorial regime. Foreign, security, and economic policies were issues of public debate in the Federal Republic. They could—and did at times—trigger heated debates. All West German governments needed to seek domestic consensus for their international role. Publicity also meant that fundamental international orientations, especially the alignment with the West, could mobilize the population in an affirmative way and thus generate a process of transnational community-building.[27] Interestingly, in the early eighties, the incipient opposition in the GDR against East Germany's military imprint and the arms race planted seeds that would help force the regime's collapse in 1989.

32.5 FROM DISENCHANTMENT TO THE END OF THE SECOND COLD WAR: 1972–1989

Divided Germany's place in the international world and the domestic situation in both German states seemed to be consolidated by the end of the Olympic year 1972. In the Federal Republic, Willy Brandt—decorated with the Nobel Peace Prize a year earlier—had survived an attempt by the parliamentary opposition to topple him with a vote of no-confidence (*konstruktives Mißtrauensvotum*). He had also scored, as mentioned, a spectacular win in the federal elections. After turbulent debates, his government had pushed the treaties of *Ostpolitik* through parliament. They were complemented the following year by the Prague Treaty, which normalized relations with the Czech Republic. At the end of 1972, East Germany, too, had reasons to be proud. It maintained diplomatic relations with fifty-eight states around the world and had become a member of UNESCO. The GDR now allowed more than three times as many travelers from the Federal Republic and West Berlin to its territory than three years earlier (altogether over 3.6 million). Led by Honecker, the GDR also signaled more tolerance in domestic affairs, a clever move to disguise the continuously repressive character of the regime. It declared an amnesty for some so-called political criminals, 171 of whom were released to the Federal Republic in November.[28]

When the United Nations admitted both German states officially as members in September 1973 (a parallel application to the organization had been agreed upon in the Basic Treaty), the vision that John F. Kennedy had drafted a decade earlier seemed to have come true. In June 1963, Kennedy had used his speech at Berlin's Free University to describe Germany's new role in the world: pragmatism, a spirit of co-operation, and communication across the East–West divide would replace old dogmatism. The right of self-determination would need to be seen as a universal right, rather than as a 'special privilege' of the Germans. The issue of reunification would be subordinated to global détente, and the West would be well advised to rely more on its economic attractiveness than on military deterrence alone.[29] Along these lines, the road to Helsinki seemed to be marked out by the early 1970s. The Finish capital provided the platform, on August 1, 1975, for representatives of almost all European states, the United States and Canada to sign the final accords of the Conference on Security and Cooperation in Europe (CSCE). This act sealed the post-World War II order, guaranteed the territorial integrity of all states, and committed all participants to respecting human rights and fundamental freedoms, the so-called third basket of the principles. In Helsinki, Helmut Schmidt and Erich Honecker met for the first time in person; it was a polite, business-like encounter. Both states acted as formally equal, international partners. They did so, too, in Vienna, where countries from NATO and the Warsaw Pact began to convene in 1973 to negotiate 'mutual and balanced force reductions' (MBFR) in the realm of conventional arms.

However, disenchantment was already tangible everywhere. Like other European countries, the Federal Republic was haunted by domestic terrorism. The Munich Massacre of 1972 had already demonstrated that West German society was not only 'penetrated,' as political scientists had long put it, by the specific East-versus-West setting that had followed the Second World War. It had also become part of a larger world that was too complicated to conform to the rules of the Cold War order. More than anything else, the international economy now set new parameters. The unequal promise of both German states to lead their societies toward a well-respected position in the world—cushioned by prosperity in the West and based, in the East, on the claim to provide just living conditions—relied not only on military security. The realization of this promise also depended heavily on favorable trading conditions and a stable economy. Yet, the 'limits to growth'—the soon-to-be famous diagnosis by the Club of Rome in 1972—suddenly became obvious. In 1973, and ostensibly motivated by Western support for Israel in the Yom Kippur War, the oil-exporting countries began to raise dramatically the price of petroleum, which was so badly needed to sustain the illusion of an ever-growing consumer society. In addition, the international monetary system, drafted in Bretton Woods in 1944, collapsed; it was formally abandoned in 1973. The system of fixed exchange rates, with the US dollar tied to the gold standard, was replaced by a new floating-rate system. This contributed to increased inflation, now coupled, however, with an economic slowdown—a new economic phenomenon known as 'stagflation.' Constraints in purchasing oil became even more pronounced with a second price explosion in 1979–1980.

The GDR's answers to the turbulence in the international economy were not merely insufficient, but disastrous in the long run. COMECON, the Soviet-dominated economic and trading community in Eastern Europe, seemed to shelter the GDR from collapse. However, Honecker made things worse by reintroducing policies of centralized planning under the slogan of the 'Unity of Social and Economic Policy.' The GDR misdirected priorities, emphasized an ultimately weak high-tech industry, and continued to subsidize consumer prices and social services. In addition, the GDR began to rely on West German loans, which amounted to two billion (West) German Marks in 1983–1984 alone. The GDR's budget deficit assumed dramatic dimensions. By the fall of 1989, the GDR had accumulated a foreign debt of over $ 26 billion.[30]

Under Chancellor Helmut Schmidt, the Federal Republic responded to the international recession by insisting on its multilateral commitments and by maintaining its status as an export nation. Furthermore, the Federal Republic worked toward establishing new forms of co-operation with its western partners that allowed for the sharing of economic, as well as political responsibilities. Like his predecessors Kiesinger and Brandt and later followed by his successor Helmut Kohl (1982–1996), Schmidt did not give in to American pressure in moments of crisis nor did he cancel lucrative treaties with the Soviet Union that secured gas supplies. This was one angle of *Ostpolitik* and prudent energy policy alike. He reinvigorated the Franco-German relations and put them, together with French President Valéry Giscard d'Estaing, on a strong economic footing. The two leaders introduced to Western Europe a new 'European Currency System' that tried to eliminate uncertainties by regulating exchange rates. Schmidt firmly established the Federal Republic in the club of the world's leading economic—and thus also political—nations. Together with Giscard d'Estaing he founded in 1975 an annual meeting of the most potent industrial nations, which was soon referred to as the world economic summit. The Federal Republic reached the height of its international standing in the midst of the 1970s crises, not at least due to the fact that Bonn followed the core values of predictability and reliability that had characterized its foreign policy since the 1950s. The newsmagazine *Spiegel* pointed out in January 1975 that West Germany—an economic giant with Western Europe's largest conventional army—had become a *Weltmacht wider Willen*, a 'world power against its own will.'

The acceptance of West Germany as a power player, but also the limitations of this player were obvious when the East–West relations began to deteriorate massively and a new Cold War took shape. The last two years of Jimmy Carter's tenure as US president, 1978–1980, coincided with a hardening of Soviet policies both on the domestic scene and in international relations. The Soviet invasion of Afghanistan in 1979 troubled the United States as much as Ayatollah Khomeini's return to Iran, the taking of American hostages in Teheran later that year, and the revolution of the Sandinistas in Nicaragua. The intransigence and aggressiveness of the Soviet Union and Carter's turn away from détente, accompanied by a reorientation toward military deterrence, created a huge dilemma for both German states. As in the past, the Federal Republic could not risk losing American support. Bonn thus succumbed to some—though not all—of the countermeasures that Carter and, after 1981, his conservative successor, Ronald Reagan, demanded from their allies. This was why West Germany joined the United States in boycotting the Moscow Olympic Games in 1980.

The dilemmas of West German foreign policy and the particular, yet ambivalent meaning of détente for both German states once again became abundantly clear. Since 1977 Schmidt was worried that one of the main achievements of American-Soviet détente, i.e., the negotiations on limiting strategic nuclear arms (SALT), would 'impair the security' of NATO's European members if the ensuing limitations remained confined to the two superpowers and if NATO did not react to the Soviet deployment of new missiles (SS 20) that were aimed exclusively at Western Europe.[31] Schmidt feared that the United States would be decoupled from Western and particularly German security interests. He was even invited to join the leaders of the United States, Great Britain, and France at an intimate (though inconclusive) meeting held on the island of Guadeloupe in January 1979 to discuss the issue. At this meeting Schmidt opened the Pandora's Box of NATO's response to Soviet missile build-up. What followed was a long and thorny experience of unintended consequences and multiple misunderstandings. NATO reacted in December 1979 by offering to negotiate with the Soviet Union. However, the alliance also threatened the Soviet Union with the deployment of its own intermediate-range missiles (Pershing II and Cruise Missiles) if Moscow did not withdraw the SS 20s. NATO's so-called Double-Track Decision polarized the West German public in an unprecedented way. A mass peace movement protested against the *Nachrüstung*, the stationing of new US missiles, and against US foreign policy in general. What was intended as a security measure turned out to be, in the eyes of many contemporaries, a risky threat to NATO's own population.

Still, the two German states now insisted on maintaining their special relationship—in spite of all their ideological differences and pressures from their hegemonic powers. Schmidt, Kohl, and Honecker tried to rescue as much détente as possible. For them, détente was divisible: it could co-exist with tensions in other parts of the world. When Helmut Kohl welcomed Honecker in Bonn in September 1987 with the highest of honors, his official remarks spoke volumes. Kohl did not hesitate to address the issue of reunification and the Berlin Wall. However, he explicitly called on both sides to 'concentrate on the possible' and emphasized distinctly German-German interests, including opportunities for East Germans to travel to the Federal Republic.[32] Both German states felt that they were parts of a *Verantwortungsgemeinschaft*, a community of responsibility. At that time, Reagan and the Soviet Union's new leader, Mikhail Gorbachev, were already on their way to ending the nuclear arms race and, indeed, the Cold War as such. In December 1987, they signed a treaty that eliminated, in the East as in the West, the intermediate-range nuclear missiles that had angered large parts of the German public only a few years earlier. This was yet another reminder that the German position in the world continued to depend on the decisions of others.

Around 1987, most outside observers completely overestimated the economic stability and domestic legitimacy of East Germany. To many in the West, the GDR appeared as a respectable international actor trying to muddle through economic crises as it continued to literally sell to the Federal Republic citizens who had been imprisoned for political reasons, altogether more than 30,000 since 1963.[33] On the other side, the Federal Republic stabilized once again its position as a reliable ally partner and export nation, accumulating a substantial trade surplus. The conservative government of Kohl and his foreign minister from the FDP, Hans-Dietrich Genscher, continued to do what their predecessor had done. They accepted that the 'German question cannot, and must not, have priority over peace' in Europe, as Schmidt had once put it.[34] However, like the Brandt and Schmidt governments, they sought to maintain as much leeway in pursuing German interests toward the East as the United States would tolerate. This approach continued to generate conflicts within the Western alliance. They surfaced in 1988–1989 when the Federal Republic opposed both a complete elimination and a deployment of new short-range nuclear missiles on German soil. Still, West German foreign policy was also able to build on the trust it had created through its interactions with partners all over the world. The Federal Republic's economic, political, and cultural investments, as well as the fact that its transnational networks spanned the globe, now paid off.

When Gorbachev visited the Federal Republic in June 1989, there were many indications that this trust also extended to the Soviet Union. Under Honecker, the GDR was alienating itself more and more from its reform-oriented hegemonic power in the East. The aging SED leader even supported the brutal suppression of protesters in Beijing in June 1989. Ultimately, not even the Soviet Union was willing to stand up for the very existence of the East German state. The Federal Republic, on the other hand, managed to gain the full support of the United States when the unexpected happened, and the people of Eastern Europe and in the GDR demanded their freedom in 1989. There was initially some international opposition to allowing the GDR to join the Federal Republic as a state. Ultimately, however, unification happened as it could only have happened: on the basis of unanimous international agreements and based on credible checks and balances that allowed the unified Germany to remain what the old Federal Republic had been, that is a reliable, predictable, and peaceful actor in the world.

Notes

1. 'Regierungserklärung Bundeskanzler Willy Brandt, 28. Oktober 1969,' *Verhandlungen des Deutschen Bundestages. 6. Wahlperiode. Stenographische Berichte*, vol. 71 (Bonn 1969–1970), 34; author's translation.
2. Mary Elise Sarotte, *Dealing with the Devil: East Germany, Détente, and Ostpolitik 1969–1973* (Chapel Hill: University of North Carolina Press, 2001).

3. '15. Juli 1963: Vortrag des Leiters des Presse-und Informationsamtes des Landes Berlin, Bahr, in der Evangelischen Akademie Tutzing,' in Bundesministerium für innerdeutsche Beziehungen (ed.) *Dokumente zur Deutschlandpolitik*, IV. Reihe, Band 9, Zweiter Halbband (1.7.1963–31.12.1963) (Frankfurt am Main, 1978), 572–575.

4. From 1956 to 1964 the two German states were represented at the Olympics as a unified team with a special flag; see Martin H. Geyer, 'On the Road to a German Postnationalism? Athletic Competition between the Two German States in the Era of Konrad Adenauer,' *German Politics & Society*, 25, No. 2 (June 2007), 140–167.

5. For opposing conclusions, see Timothy Garton Ash, *In Europe's Name: Germany and the Divided Continent* (London: Cape, 1993) and Peter Bender, *Die 'Neue Ostpolitik' und ihre Folgen: Vom Mauerbau bis zur Vereinigung*, 4th edn (Munich: DTV, 1996).

6. So Hans-Peter Schwarz, *Die gezähmten Deutschen: Von der Machtbesessenheit zur Machtvergessenheit* (Stuttgart: DVA, 1985).

7. Johannes Paulmann (ed.), *Auswärtige Repräsentationen: Deutsche Kulturdiplomatie nach 1945* (Cologne: Böhlau, 2005), 1.

8. Lily Gardner Feldman, *The Special Relationship Between West Germany and Israel* (Boston: Allen & Unwin, 1984).

9. Wolfram F. Hanrieder, *Germany, America, Europe: Forty Years of German Foreign Policy* (New Haven: Yale University Press, 1989), XIII.

10. After the Second World War, the Saar Region (Saarland) enjoyed a special international status and was closely associated in economic terms with France. In 1955, however, the overwhelming majority of the Saar population voted against a Europeanization of the territory. France and the Federal Republic ultimately agreed on the incorporation of the region into the latter's territory.

11. The first quote is from Article 3 of the Moscow Treaty of August 12, 1970, between the Federal Republic and the Soviet Union; the second and third from Article I of the Warsaw Treaty concluded between the Federal Republic and Poland on December 7, 1970. Both in Bender, '*Neue Ostpolitik*', 300 and 303; author's translation.

12. Andreas W. Daum, *Kennedy in Berlin*, trans. Dona Geyer (New York: Cambridge University Press, 2008), 61–65, 136–156.

13. Peter Graf Kielmannsegg, *Das geteilte Land. Deutschland 1945–1990* (Munich: Pantheon, 2004), 176.

14. 'The Future Tasks of the Alliance: Report of the Council—'The Harmel Report',' North Atlantic Treaty Organization: http://www.nato.int/cps/en/natolive/official_texts_26700.htm (27 December, 2010).

15. Bender, '*Neue Ostpolitik*', 130–131, 285–290.

16. Hope M. Harrison, *Driving the Soviets up the Wall: Soviet-East German Relations, 1953–1961* (Princeton: Princeton University Press, 2003).

17. Hans-Ulrich Evers and Rudolf Schuster (eds), *Alle deutschen Verfassungen*, 2nd edn (Munich: Goldmann, 1989), 243.

18. William Glenn Gray, *Germany's Cold War: The Global Campaign to Isolate East Germany, 1949–1969* (Chapel Hill: University of North Carolina Press, 2003), 21, 87, 148.

19. Herbert Wehner, 'Rede vor dem Deutschen Bundestag nach dem Scheitern der Paiser Gipfelkonferenz, 30. Juni 1960,' in Wehner, *Wandel und Bewährung: Ausgewählte Reden und Schriften 1930–1967* (Frankfurt am Main: Ullstein, 1968), 239, 240, 242.

20. Evers, *Alle deutschen Verfassungen*, 145, 190, 220.

21. Kielmansegg, *Das geteilte Land*, 398–99.

22. Peter J. Katzenstein (ed.), *Tamed Power. Germany in Europe* (Ithaca: Cornell University Press, 1997), 4.

23. Paulmann, *Auwärtige Repräsentationen*, 17.

24. Hanns W. Maull, 'Germany and Japan: The New Civilian Powers,' *Foreign Affairs*, 69, no. 5 (Winter, 1990), 91–106.

25. Klaus Hüfner, *Peanuts für die UNO: Das deutsche Finanzengagement seit 1960* (Frankfurt am Main: Peter Lang, 2008), 182.

26. Kielmansegg, *Das geteilte Land*, 214–15; Jost Dülffer, *Europa im Ost-West Konflikt 1945–1991* (Munich: Oldenbourg, 2004), 90.

27. Daum, *Kennedy in Berlin*.

28. Bender, *'Neue Ostpolitik'*, 359–60; Hermann Weber, *DDR: Grundriß der Geschichte 1945–1990*, rev. edn (Hanover: Fackelträger, 1991), 317.

29. John F. Kennedy, 'Address at the Free University of Berlin. June 26, 1963,' *Public Papers of the Presidents of the United States. John F. Kennedy: Containing the Public Messages, Speeches, and Statements of the President, January 20 to November 22, 1963* (Washington, DC: United States Government Printing Office, 1964), 528.

30. Charles S. Maier, *Dissolution: The Crisis of Communism and the End of East Germany* (Princeton: Princeton University Press, 1997), 59.

31. Helmut Schmidt, 'The 1977 Alastair Buchan Memorial Lecture,' *Survival*, 20 (January/February 1978), 4.

32. 'Ansprache von Bundeskanzler Helmut Kohl [. . .],' in Eckart Conze and Gabriele Metzler (eds), *50 Jahre Bundesrepublik Deutschland: Daten und Diskussionen* (Stuttgart: DVA, 1999), 150.

33. Gregor Schöllgen, *Die Außenpolitik der Bundesrepublik Deutschland* (Munich: Beck, 1999), 122.

34. Schmidt, 'Memorial Lecture,' 5.

BIBLIOGRAPHY

BANCHOFF, THOMAS, *The German Problem Transformed: Institutions, Politics, and Foreign Policy, 1945–1995* (Ann Arbor: University of Michigan Press, 1999).

BENDER, PETER, *Die 'Neue Ostpolitik' und ihre Folgen: Vom Mauerbau bis zur Vereinigung*, 4th edn (Munich: DTV, 1996).

DAUM, ANDREAS W., *Kennedy in Berlin*. trans. Dona Geyer (New York: Cambridge University Press, 2008).

GARTON ASH, TIMOTHY, *In Europe's Name: Germany and the Divided Continent* (London: Cape, 1993).

HAFTENDORN, HELGA, *Coming of Age: German Foreign Policy since 1945* (Lanham: Rowman & Littlefield, 2006).

HANRIEDER, WOLFRAM F., *Germany, America, Europe: Forty Years of German Foreign Policy* (New Haven: Yale University Press, 1989).

JUNKER, DETLEF (ed.), *The United States and Germany in the Era of the Cold War, 1945–1990*. 2 vols (New York: Cambridge University Press, 2004).

KIELMANNSEGG, PETER GRAF, *Das geteilte Land. Deutschland 1945–1990* (Munich: Pantheon, 2004).

MAIER, CHARLES S., *Dissolution: The Crisis of Communism and the End of East Germany* (Princeton: Princeton University Press, 1997).

McADAMS, A. JAMES, *Germany Divided: From the Wall to Reunification* (Princeton: Princeton University Press, 1993).

PART V

CONTEMPORARY GERMANY

Map 4 Contemporary Germany

Source: Martin Kitchen, *A History of Modern Germany, 1800–2000* (Oxford: Oxford University Press, 2006), xvi.

CHAPTER 33

ANNUS MIRABILIS: 1989 AND GERMAN UNIFICATION

DAVID F. PATTON

IN 1989–1990, the two Germanies underwent a series of remarkable changes that would signal the end of the postwar division of Europe. East Germans peacefully toppled the hard-line Socialist Unity Party (SED) that had ruled with an iron fist for forty years. In so doing, they staged the first successful democratic revolution in modern German history and opened the door to national unification. Those that challenged the communist regime in 1989 had little in common with those that crafted unification the following year. The East German citizen movement operated at the grass roots in the dilapidated cities and towns of East Germany; West German political leaders conducted high politics behind the scenes in the chancellery and in the grand halls of international conferences. After the Berlin Wall was breeched on 9 November 1989, a gradual shift occurred toward national unification. The familiar call at East German demonstrations 'We are the people,' in essence an appeal for democratic self-determination in a dictatorship, increasingly gave way to a new slogan, 'We are one people!,' underscoring the right to national self-determination. The debate over unification would dominate politics in East and West Germany in the months to come. The GDR's peaceful revolution, at least according to many of its protagonists, had prematurely run its course.

33.1 THE TRANSNATIONAL CONTEXT

In 1989, popular movements brought down communist governments throughout eastern Europe. How 'German' was the peaceful revolution, or, as it came to be known, the turning point (*Wende*)? There is little question that the broader context of waning Soviet dominance in the region set the stage for fall 1989.

During the Cold War, the Soviet Union asserted its hegemony over eastern Europe by maintaining security (Warsaw Pact) and economic (COMECON) pacts for itself and its satellites. In 1985, Mikhail Gorbachev assumed power in the USSR and embarked on ambitious reforms. At home, he sought to reinvigorate an ailing economy through *perestroika* (i.e. economic restructuring and decentralization) and *glasnost* (i.e. greater openness). In foreign relations, Gorbachev no longer enforced the Brezhnev doctrine by which the USSR had come to the rescue of its client states at times of domestic upheaval. Soviet military intervention had preserved hard-line regimes in the GDR in 1953, in Hungary in 1956 and in Czechoslovakia in 1968. Yet Gorbachev, the reformer, not only kept Soviet troops in the barracks in the late 1980s, even as rising domestic opposition threatened unpopular communist regimes, but he implicitly urged his allies to begin domestic reforms of their own. The importance of the Soviet Union's newfound reluctance to police its sphere of influence in eastern Europe cannot be overstated. Suddenly, failing governments faced, without the cover of Soviet tanks, an emboldened domestic opposition.

In the United States, the Reagan Administration's military build-up in the 1980s, including its Strategic Defense Initiative, may have convinced Soviet leaders to pursue accommodation with the West since they struggled to keep up in a high-tech arms race.[1] Writing in 1987, Paul Kennedy described the dilemma facing the Soviet Union: 'it must also try to keep up with the United States in rocketry, satellite-based weapons, space exploration, and so on. Thus, the USSR—or, better, the Marxist system of the USSR—is being tested both quantitatively and qualitatively in the world power stakes; and it does not like the odds. However, those odds (or "correlation of forces") would obviously be better if the economy were healthier, which brings us back to Russia's long-term problem.'[2] The Soviet retreat from east-central Europe stemmed in part from the consequences of imperial overstretch, whereby the country's military commitments could no longer be sustained by its economic capabilities. This was a fate common to great powers throughout history.[3]

The Helsinki Accords (Conference on Security and Cooperation in Europe, CSCE process) served to hollow out the moral authority of communist regimes in eastern Europe that signed a treaty to which they did not adhere. These governments committed themselves to basic human rights and civic rights, such as free speech, open airwaves, and freedom of travel. 'What this meant,' according to the historian John Lewis Gaddis, 'was that the people who lived under these systems—at least the more courageous—could claim official permission to say what they thought.'[4] Throughout the eastern bloc, dissidents, such as the Charter'77 movement in Czechoslovakia, justified their actions, and embarrassed their governments, by pointing out the gap between what the regimes claimed and what they actually allowed. Moreover, by reducing tensions and encouraging cultural and economic exchange, the CSCE process arguably set the stage for a reformer such as Gorbachev to come to power with a vision of a 'common European home' that was very much in the spirit of the Helsinki

Accords. Dissidents in the GDR and throughout the eastern bloc in turn looked to Gorbachev's *glasnost* to legitimize their own demands on their governments.

In the early 1970s, a new West German *Ostpolitik* resulted in Bonn's de facto acceptance of the GDR and postwar central European borders, increased inter-bloc trade, and non-use of force agreements. Its critics claimed that the policy would stabilize communist dictatorships and harden the postwar division of Europe, while its proponents argued that theirs was a policy of 'change through rapprochement' (*Wandel durch Annäherung*) that created more favorable conditions for liberalization in eastern Europe. Egon Bahr, an architect of the new *Ostpolitik* and close associate of Chancellor Willy Brandt, proposed 'overcoming the status quo by not changing the status quo in the short term.'[5] The new policy promised to dispel lingering concerns about West German revanchism that had helped knit together the eastern bloc countries, many of which had experienced German expansionism first hand in World War II.

As trade with the West grew, so did the appetite of eastern consumers and producers for high-quality western goods. To meet this demand, Warsaw Pact countries increasingly borrowed from the West and, in so doing, amassed enormous debts that added to their considerable economic and political woes. Excessive planning, bloated welfare states, and rigid political structures proved inefficient at managing the transition from heavy industry to emerging knowledge-based industries. Fateful decisions in the 1970s contributed to the systemic failure of communism in eastern Europe by the late 1980s. Whereas advanced industrial societies in East and West both confronted a difficult international economic environment in the early 1970s, Western economies, gradually adjusted to the logic of the changing global market economy. In contrast, the eastern European states, among them the USSR, Czechoslovakia and the GDR, rejected limited market reforms and instead returned to a rigid communist orthodoxy that offered no solution to a worsening situation.[6] Under Erich Honecker's leadership, the East German regime promoted the unity of economic and social policy, which had the effect of greatly increasing spending for social programs. This was something that the GDR could ill afford by the 1980s.

In short, the long-term roots of the 1989 crisis in the GDR—whether economic stagnation, political immobility, or lacking legitimacy—closely resembled those throughout the Warsaw Pact. Developments in the USSR, Poland, and Hungary shaped the GDR's peaceful revolution as communist regimes fell like dominoes in 1989. As Timothy Garton Ash observed at the time, what took approximately ten years to transpire in Poland, took ten months in Hungary, ten weeks in the GDR, and might proceed in but ten days in Czechoslovakia.[7] The triumphant return of Solidarity in 1989 emboldened democrats throughout eastern Europe and disproved the theory that totalitarian governments—in contrast to authoritarian ones—were incapable of gradually transforming themselves into democracies. In Hungary, reform communists began dismantling their country's heavily fortified border with Austria. This in turn opened a hole in the Iron Curtain through which vacationing East Germans fled en route to West Germany in summer 1989. The resulting exodus set in motion events that culminated in the end of the GDR.

Forms of protest and conflict resolution, as practiced throughout east-central Europe, appeared in the East German context in 1989. For instance, civic groups in the GDR invoked the spirit of Helsinki as they demanded peaceful, democratic change. They spearheaded a mass movement that mobilized hundreds of thousands in an impressive display of non-violent people power. In this regard, they resembled civic groups that had formed in Hungary, such as the Hungarian Democratic Forum and the Alliance of Young Democrats (FIDESz), and in Czechoslovakia, such as Civic Forum and Public Against Violence. As had the Catholic church in Poland and Czechoslovakia, the East German churches played an important role in the *Wende*. Lutheran churches provided a sanctuary for pro-democracy activists; civic group leaders were often pastors; and some scholars went so far as to describe fall 1989 as a 'Protestant revolution.'[8]

The East German revolution, like others in east-central Europe, eschewed violence and instead demanded, and eventually commanded, the cooperation of communist authorities. In the GDR, the autumn protests led to round tables, an institutional innovation used in Poland in early 1989, and inclusive governments, as practiced in Poland, Hungary and Czechoslovakia, that brought together reform-minded communists and the opposition during the democratic transition. Garton Ash coined the term 'refolution' to describe an approach in Poland and Hungary that mixed peaceful reform with revolutionary change. 'There is, in both places, a strong and essential element of voluntary, deliberate reform led by an enlightened minority (but only a minority) in the still-ruling Communist parties . . . . Their advance consists of an unprecedented retreat: undertaking to share power, and even—*mirabile dictu*—talk of giving it up altogether, if they lose an election.'[9] While revolution required the removal of the SED old guard in fall 1989, the communists that followed them did reach out to the opposition. In this regard, the GDR also experienced a brokered transition away from communist dictatorship toward representative democracy.

33.2 PECULIARITIES OF THE EAST GERMAN REVOLUTION

Vladimir Lenin famously mocked the Germans' inability to effect revolutionary change. 'If the Germans staged a revolution at the train station, they would buy tickets for the platform first,' he once remarked.[10] Yet hundreds of thousands confronted a repressive regime in 1989 and brought it to its knees in non-violent fashion. While the East German revolution bore striking similarities to those in neighboring countries, several features, such as the relationship between intellectuals and workers, the size of the opposition, and its politics, set it apart.

Unlike in Poland, Hungary and Czechoslovakia, where intellectuals and industrial workers joined forces within Solidarity, pro-democracy groups, and Civic Forum, the masses and intellectuals largely worked apart in the GDR. In August 1989, vacationing East Germans managed to cross from Hungary into Austria on their way to West Germany, while others bided their time in provisional camps in the hope that they would be released to the Federal Republic. Despite East Berlin's demands that they be sent back to the GDR, the Hungarian government eventually sided with the Federal Republic, rather than its Warsaw Pact ally, and allowed thousands to leave for the West. Others crowded into West German embassies in Budapest, Czechoslovakia and Poland. In late September, the Federal Republic arranged with East Berlin for those camped out in its Prague embassy to travel through the GDR by train en route to a safe haven in West Germany. Upon word of the arrangement, desperate East Germans stormed the Dresden train station on 4 October in an attempt to board the westbound trains; violent clashes with police ensued.

The mass exodus plunged East Germany into crisis by creating acute labor shortages in key sectors, such as health care. Frustrated citizens, unable to get out of the country, took to the streets to demand a relaxation of travel restrictions, which had been further tightened after the GDR closed its border to Czechoslovakia and barred travel to Hungary. 'We want out of here!' was a common refrain as angry East Germans demanded that they be allowed to leave. At the Nikolai Church in Leipzig, which later became know as the city of heroes for its part in the revolution, weekly Monday evening demonstrations grew in size throughout late summer and fall. On 4 September, an estimated 1000 citizens took part in the first Monday demonstration. In the coming weeks, participation at the rallies soared despite efforts by the secret police, the Stasi, to hinder the movement. On 25 September, 6,500 people took to the streets and by 2 October, it was approximately 20,000. Prior to 9 October, the *Leipziger Volkszeitung* ominously warned of a crackdown: 'We are prepared and willing to actively protect what we have created with our own hands in order to eliminate finally and effectively these counter-revolutionary activities. If necessary, with gun in hand!'[11] Notwithstanding such threats and a massive police presence, more than 70,000 citizens courageously gathered in Leipzig to call for freedom of travel and democratic change. In the end, the SED chose to allow the demonstration, rather than impose a 'Chinese solution' (i.e. blood bath). This 'day of decision' eased the way for the spread of democratic protests throughout the country.[12]

As East Germans fled in summer 1989, pro-democracy activists formed civic groups calling for reform. The first, and arguably most important, was New Forum, which was founded on 9 September by a group of doctors, natural scientists, clergy, and other intellectuals. Its most prominent co-founder was the artist and dissident Bärbel Bohley who has been described by a fellow activist as the 'Joan of Arc of the German Democratic Revolution.'[13] A New Forum co-founder, the Berlin molecular biologist Jens Reich, explained, with passing reference to Lenin, why the group chose to register as an association rather than as a political party: 'We wanted to act legally (revolutionaries who first buy a platform ticket) and there was only a law for associations, but not one for parties.'[14] In its opening manifesto, New Forum linked the GDR's crisis to the faulty communication between state and society that stifled creative solutions to the country's problems. New

Forum underscored its commitment to democracy, justice, peace and the environment and called upon East Germans to join its ranks to reshape the GDR.[15] By late October, around 200,000 had signed the founding proclamation, even though the state had declared New Forum illegal on 21 September. New Forum attracted disproportionately middle class professionals, the middle aged, and women.[16] Other civic groups, such as Democracy Now and Democratic Awakening, soon formed. The burgeoning citizen movement (*Bürgerbewegung*) showed the vitality of East German civil society and provided protesters with an agenda for non-violent transformation.

In contrast to Solidarity and Civic Forum, the East German civic groups generally lacked close ties to the East German working class, many of whom were more interested in leaving the country than reforming it. As a challenge to both hardliners in power and those running away, demonstrators asserted that 'we are staying put!' The economist Albert O. Hirschman highlighted the crucial coincidence of interests among those choosing 'exit' (We want out of here!) and those activists exercising 'voice' (We are staying put!). Whereas the East German regime had allowed more emigration (exit) in the 1980s as a way to weaken the opposition (voice), the two were now 'confederates' in a 'joint grave digging act.'[17] 'The "Vacation Revolution" [*Urlaubsrevolution*] from without was accompanied by the "After-Hours Revolution" [*Feierabendrevolution*] from within the GDR.'[18] Together, those leaving the country and those rallying to reform it presented the SED with a powerful challenge. Over 120,000 East Germans left the GDR for the Federal Republic between July and October, with an additional 133,000 refugees in November.[19] All the while, many more demonstrated for reform.

This one-two punch left the GDR's leadership reeling. On 18 October, Egon Krenz replaced the aging Erich Honecker as general secretary of the ruling party and promised reforms. His credibility was limited, though, since he had faithfully served the SED and even praised the Chinese government crackdown in Tiananmen Square. On 8 November, Prime Minister Willi Stoph and the entire GDR government resigned as the country's crisis deepened. Hans Modrow, a more credible reform figure, was nominated to head the government. On 9 November, Günter Schabowski, a Politiburo member, had conveyed to journalists at an international press conference the mistaken impression that the GDR had decided to allow East Germans to travel directly and without delay to the West. That very evening, amidst a good deal of confusion at border crossings in East Berlin, the Berlin Wall was suddenly opened, allowing millions of East Germans to visit the Federal Republic in the coming days. This was a moment of great joy and happiness for East Germans and West Germans alike.

In the GDR, the organized opposition formed later and was smaller than in Poland, Hungary, and Czechoslovakia. This stemmed in part from the highly repressive character of the SED-regime, whose feared secret police, the Stasi, tracked potential dissidents through a vast network of informants. The GDR allowed very little in the way of independent civil society, encouraging disaffected citizens to focus on their private lives in what has been described as a 'niche society.' Under pressure from the state, even the Protestant church would call itself the 'church in socialism' as it came to terms with communism to a far greater degree than had the Catholic church in Poland.

The GDR further held the opposition in check by expelling dissidents and allowing others to leave. Together, repression, expulsion, and emigration kept the East German opposition fragmented and weak. Nonetheless, dissidents did manage to oppose the regime at great personal risk prior to fall 1989. In spring 1989, for instance, they documented clear evidence of fraud in local elections.

Unlike Solidarity and pro-democracy movements in east-central Europe, the East German civic groups had not broken as decisively with socialism. Instead, they envisioned a democratic, socialist GDR that charted a third way between communism and capitalism. Democracy Now declared that 'Socialism must now discover its true, democratic form if it is not to be lost forever. It cannot be allowed to disappear because humanity, faced with its extinction and in the search for lasting forms of co-existence, needs alternatives to western consumer society whose prosperity is paid for by the rest of the world.'[20] Democratic Awakening indicated that although it 'takes a critical view of much in real-existing socialism, this does not mean that it rejects in principle the vision of a socialist social order.'[21] Jens Reich later reported that well-known intellectuals had refused to sign New Forum's founding proclamation because it did not refer to socialism.[22]

Why were East German dissidents, on the whole, less critical of socialism than their counterparts elsewhere? According to Freya Klier, a former GDR dissident, the earlier exodus of 'critical intelligentsia' to West Germany had thinned the ranks of the 'Vaclav Havel generation of the GDR.'[23] Many intellectuals that did stay in the GDR in the 1950s and early 1960s, at a time when they could have moved to the FRG, either supported, had made peace with, or hoped to reform East Germany.

A related peculiarity of the East German *Wende* was that nationalism did not comprise as central a component of the democratic movement. In Poland, Solidarity promised democracy, a functioning market economy and liberation from Soviet hegemony. At the start of the Velvet Revolution, students, who had gathered to mark the fiftieth anniversary of the killing of a Czechoslovakian student by the occupying Germans, then proceeded to lead a protest against the communist party, a longstanding ally of the USSR, which, like Germany in 1939, represented foreign domination. The Velvet Revolution asserted national self-determination rights that the Soviet Union had denied brutally in 1968. In Hungary, over 100,000 people attended a funeral service in 1989 for the former Prime Minister Imre Nagy, who had been secretly executed in 1958 after the Soviet-led quelling of the 1956 uprising. In so doing, they laid claim to national sovereignty at a time when Hungary was trying to break free of the Soviet sphere of influence.[24] Yet in the GDR, pro-democracy groups refrained from presenting their cause as part of a broader national movement. They initially declared 'We are the people,' rather than 'We are one people,' a rallying cry that resounded only after the fall of the Berlin Wall. As Christian Joppke notes, 'National symbols and sentiments fueled and accompanied the victorious revolutions in eastern Europe. When the German flag appeared in the streets of Leipzig, the East German revolution had reached its inglorious end—or so it seemed to the leaders of the citizen movement.'[25] Intellectuals in particular avoided nationalist appeals. This had to do with the Third Reich's discrediting of German nationalism and with the civic groups' project of renewing East

Germany from the bottom-up rather than having someone else unify it from the top-down. Some felt betrayed by calls for unification that grew louder at Leipzig Monday marches in late 1989.[26]

The prominence of western actors represented another distinctive feature of the East German revolution. While developments in Moscow provided the backdrop for the 1989 uprising in the GDR and elsewhere, a western country, the Federal Republic, had a major effect on the *Wende*. Prior to November 1989, it was not the federal government in Bonn, which had been caught off guard, but rather longstanding West German policies that conditioned the peaceful revolution. While the Federal Republic had come to terms with the second German state, and even supported East Berlin with financial credits and *de facto* recognition, it was constitutionally committed to unification. To some, the Federal Republic was living a lie (*Lebenslüge*), since it had grown comfortable with the postwar territorial status quo in central Europe. All the same, West Germany still extended automatic citizenship, as well as offered considerable assistance, to East German refugees entering the country. This open door encouraged East Germans to try to resettle in the Federal Republic—a country that was at once much freer and richer than the GDR—and contributed to the 1989 crisis.

The West German media played its part as well. Except for those living in remote areas, East Germans received and watched West German television broadcasts. As a result, they knew about Hungary's decision to remove fortifications along its border to Austria, the summer exodus, and the chaos at the Dresden train station in early October, when crowds of East Germans desperately tried to board overfilled trains heading for the west. They also knew about the Monday evening marches in Leipzig, and the pro-democracy groups. Knowledge of the exodus prompted others to leave as they witnessed the successful flight of fellow citizens on television. Knowledge of the citizen movement made it easier for reform-minded East Germans to participate in demonstrations and to join civic groups. Following Schabowski's muddled press conference, West German television reported on 9 November that the wall was opening, leading East Berlin residents to gather at the border and demand from perplexed border guards permission to cross. Without access to western television and radio broadcasts, East Germans would have experienced fall 1989 through the lens of GDR propaganda to a greater degree.

By early 1990, the federal government in Bonn was directly involved in East German affairs as Chancellor Kohl actively pursued unity. Unification, for which there was nothing comparable throughout eastern Europe, save perhaps the nascent and soon aborted attempt to unify Moldova with Romania, would set the East German experience apart from those of its neighbors.

33.3 UNIFYING GERMANY

By February 1990, something like a consensus was forming in the two German states in favor of unification. Several factors brought the issue to the fore. After the Berlin Wall opened, the Monday evening demonstrations revealed a changed GDR. Whereas intellectuals and young people had disproportionately taken to the streets in the early demonstrations, it was now workers and older East Germans that predominated.[27] 'We are one people' and 'Germany, United Fatherland'—a verse taken from the GDR's national hymn, but banned once it no longer matched official East German policy—became rallying cries. Protesters angrily denounced the privileged lives that the leaders of the 'worker and farmer state' had secretly led in the Berlin suburb of Wandlitz and demanded retribution for the regime's crimes. They waved the West German flag and showed little interest in the citizen movement's project to salvage the second German state.

For the most part, it was not a chauvinistic nationalism, but rather a pragmatic one.[28] Timothy Garton Ash described the mood at a Monday evening demonstration in Leipzig in November: 'Yet one already felt, instinctively, that the voices for reunification would prevail. Not because of the power of nationalism. Just because of the power of common sense.'[29] A speaker at the rally received much applause when he pointed out that socialism had not delivered on its promises, and a new socialism would fall short as well. 'We are not laboratory animals' and 'Our compatriots in the Federal Republic are not foreigners.' Loud chants of 'Germany, United Fatherland' resounded.[30] To the chagrin of civic group leaders that held out hope for a democratic, socialist GDR, East Germans increasingly favored unification as the surest path to prosperity. As one historian observed, 'When they regained their voice, the silent masses spoke out against the Third Way.'[31]

On 1 December, the leading role assigned to the communist party was struck from the GDR constitution. Two days later, Egon Krenz resigned as party general secretary, while the SED's entire central committee and politburo stepped down, not to be replaced. On 7 December, the central round table convened for the first of many times in East Berlin with the SED, former 'bloc' parties that had faithfully served the SED (but were now hastily distancing themselves from the ruling party), church representatives, and opposition civic groups. Despite high hopes on the part of the civic groups, the round table did not stabilize the GDR. Although Prime Minister Modrow reached out to the opposition, agreed to hold democratic elections, and appealed to West Germany for financial assistance, he was unable to halt the ongoing exodus. In December, 43,000 East Germans left for the Federal Republic; by January the number had risen to more than 73,000, adding to the GDR's economic plight.[32] By December, East German industry was losing eighty million GDR marks a day, while the GDR economy posted a balance of payment deficit of nearly 2.5 billion dollars and an overall debt in hard currency of over 20 billion dollars.[33] In the first quarter of 1990, GNP dropped by 3.4 percent, while unemployment shot upward.[34]

By early 1990, concerns were mounting that a power vacuum would leave the GDR ungovernable. Civic groups had shown great courage in confronting the communist regime in the fall, but demonstrated neither the will nor the ability to lead the country. All the while, the discredited SED was struggling to reinvent itself as hundreds of thousands quit its ranks. Eventually, the Party of Democratic Socialism (PDS) arose out of the wreckage of the SED, yet lacked broad appeal. The Modrow government lost public trust by mishandling the issue of East Germany's secret police, the Ministry for State Security (MfS or Stasi). The Stasi had committed countless human rights abuses, overseeing a massive espionage network that ruined careers, relationships and in many cases the lives of those deemed to be hostile to the regime. The Modrow government proposed transforming the Stasi into a smaller Office for National Security (ANS), yet its efforts were met with deep suspicion on the part of the opposition and public. On 15 January, despite Modrow's reversal on the ANS, angry crowds stormed the former MfS headquarters in East Berlin, signaling that neither the civic groups nor the government had control of an increasingly volatile situation. The deteriorating situation strengthened the hand of those calling for unification.

Pro-unification sentiment grew in West Germany as well. Chancellor Helmut Kohl delivered his 10-point plan for overcoming the division of Germany and Europe on 28 November. While it proposed a gradual unification process embedded in international institutions, the plan was widely viewed as the start of the federal government's push to unify the two German states. Unification was now on the policy agenda at home and abroad. By early 1990, West Germans noted the deteriorating situation in the GDR and worried about the consequences of unchecked refugee flows. Just as many East Germans viewed unification as a practical solution to the grave problems that they faced, West Germans, concerned about prolonged crisis in the GDR, saw it as potentially effective crisis prevention.

33.4 FORGING UNITY: RIVAL CONCEPTIONS

The growing support for unification did not however produce anything resembling a consensus on how to achieve it. By February 1990, there was fundamental disagreement on both its 'national' and 'social' dimensions.[35] The national question revolved around when and how to unify. Should formal unity be achieved rapidly or should it follow a more gradual process? Should unification extend the institutions of the Federal Republic eastward, or should the two German states come together to draft a new constitution? West Germany's Basic Law laid out two paths to unity. Article 23 listed the federal states where the jurisdiction of the Basic Law applied and stated that 'in other parts of Germany it shall be put into force upon their accession.'[36] This held open the option that eastern federal states would accede to the Federal Republic. This is how the Saar region, a western territory that had been separated from Germany after 1945, joined the FRG in 1957. In contrast, Article 146 foresaw a new constitution for unified Germany: 'The Basic Law shall cease to be in force on the day on which a constitution adopted by a free decision of the German people comes into force.'[37]

Chancellor Kohl and the center-right government in Bonn favored Article 23 as their preferred path to unity. Kohl's East German allies, such as the Christian Democratic Union (East-CDU), and West German business, also favored this approach. Its proponents pointed to the advantages of extending the stable and prosperous West

German model to the east, rather than possibly ending up with something much worse. They maintained that the East German exodus demanded a fast process and that favorable international conditions might not last forever. The speedy accession of eastern Germany to the Federal Republic further promised to check the influence of SED cadres in the eastern bureaucracy, industry and universities since they would have less time and opportunity to become entrenched.

Proponents of a gradual process warned of *de facto* annexation and subordination of the east. They reasoned that two sovereign states should negotiate a common future after so many years apart. This would in theory allow positive features of both systems to be adopted and new reforms to be incorporated. Some critics of a rapid unification believed that Helmut Kohl was driving the issue in order to win re-election in fall 1990, while others worried that a rush to unity might endanger stability in Europe. The West German Social Democratic Party (SPD) and its chancellor candidate Oskar Lafontaine, the churches, the trade unions, East German civic groups, and the East German reform communists, urged a more deliberate pace than the one favored by Kohl and his allies.

How would the burdens of unification be distributed? This social component represented a further contested dimension. The Kohl government deemphasized costs and focused on how unification would benefit everyone. Kohl promised that neither higher taxes nor extra sacrifice would be needed. He argued that the center-right West German parties were best equipped to achieve economic success since they had presided over the economic miracle of the 1950s. 'The coalition of FDP, CSU and CDU has already achieved great things in the formative years of the Federal Republic. ... We are determined to draw upon these experiences and upon this spirit in the time ahead.'[38] West German industry representatives generally downplayed concerns about costs and argued that currency union would bring prosperity to the east.[39]

Oskar Lafontaine, in contrast, demanded a frank and open appraisal of unity's costs and warned against unifying on the backs of the economically vulnerable. This tapped into West German fears about costs. The trade unions and churches also voiced concern about how the burdens of unification were shared. In the GDR, the reformed communist party (Party of Democratic Socialism) and the civic groups warned of the damaging social consequences of unbridled market capitalism. They too viewed unification as a social issue as well as a national one.

33.5 CHANCELLOR DEMOCRACY AND THE INTERNAL FRAMEWORK FOR UNITY

To unify Germany in 1990, Chancellor Kohl would need domestic and international backing. In fact, these two processes—building domestic support and securing external approval—were tightly interconnected. External support was predicated on the assumption that the Germans wanted unity, while domestic support was conditional on the good will of Germany's allies and neighbors. Without strong international backing, most Germans would have viewed an aggressive unification policy as too risky.

How did Chancellor Kohl forge the necessary domestic and international coalitions to effect rapid unification? After all, he was operating within a domestic political system well known for policy incrementalism. In 1983, Kohl had come to office as the head of a center-right coalition after promising a 'spiritual-moral change' (*eine geistig-moralische Wende*) in the Federal Republic. Yet with its ample institutional checks and powerful societal interests, the political system hindered sweeping changes and policy incrementalism prevailed. In 1990, however, Kohl did implement a bold new course in a manner that bore little resemblance to the gradual, consensual policy-making that had often defined West Germany.

While the Basic Law grants chancellors authority to determine the overall policy direction of the federal government (*Richtlinienkompetenz*), leading some political scientists to describe the political system as a 'chancellor democracy,' chancellors are restrained by federalism, powerful parapublic institutions, coalition governments, and influential, well-organized interest groups.[40] On occasion, however, chancellor democracy has flourished in the Federal Republic, with chancellors dominating the political process and spearheading far-reaching policy changes. This pattern arose at times when international change created an opening for a new foreign policy.[41] As controversial foreign policy debates emerged, and cut across established partisan lines, the chancellor has been in a position to transcend politics-as-usual and rally support behind a major policy revision. In the early 1950s, as cold war tensions mounted, Konrad Adenauer actively pursued West German membership in the European Coal and Steel Community and the European Defense Community. While critics feared that the Federal Republic's *Westbindung* would deepen the division of Germany, Adenauer took full advantage of the powers of the office of chancellor to implement his foreign policy. Twenty years later as cold war tensions eased, Chancellor Willy Brandt embarked upon a controversial Eastern policy (*Ostpolitik*) to normalize relations with the eastern bloc and the GDR. Like Adenauer, he demonstrated that the chancellor held a strong hand in foreign policy making, even when confronting strong domestic opposition.

In 1990, Chancellor Kohl took a page from his two predecessors' playbook and pushed ahead with rapid unification. Much like the cold war's rise in the late 1940s and thaw in the late 1960s had created opportunities for Adenauer and Brandt, respectively, the coming end of the cold war made possible a bold unification policy (*Deutschlandpolitik*) that was inconceivable just months earlier. Like Adenauer and Brandt, Kohl dispensed with well-established policy-making practices, such as broad consultation, and instead dominated the unification process in 1990. He defined the debate along national, rather than social lines; he relied upon informal committees that planned and oversaw the unification process; he excluded the domestic opposition at key junctures; and he impressively managed the external aspects in a way that not only reassured international skeptics, but also went far to allay domestic fears that rapid unification would damage the Federal Republic's foreign relations. At three key moments, Kohl triumphed: in parliamentary elections in the GDR on 18 March; in determining the timing and terms of currency union; and in the '2 + 4' negotiations between East Germany, West Germany, and the four wartime allies.[42]

In early 1990, the East German government moved forward the date for parliamentary elections to 18 March in the hope of stabilizing the country. In February, the Kohl government began planning a currency union to extend the *Deutschmark* to the GDR. The promise was that if the DM flowed eastward, East Germans would no longer stream westward. Since the next East German government would likely be negotiating currency union and unification with Bonn, much depended on the outcome of the Volkskammer election. Unification was the overriding concern of parties and voters alike during the historic election campaign.

In the GDR, three conservative eastern parties—the East German CDU, the citizen group Democratic Awakening, and the CSU-backed German Social Union—formed the center-right 'Alliance for Germany' and called for speedy unification by way of Article 23. They favored rapid currency union with West Germany, a popular position among East Germans whose own currency, the GDR mark, plummeted in value on the open market, while their appetite for western goods, especially cars, increased. The leading center-left party, the East-SPD, also supported unification, yet cautioned against too rapid a course. An early electoral favorite, the SPD struggled to combat conservative attempts to link it to communism. The heroes of fall 1989, New Forum, Democracy Now, and the Initiative for Peace and Human Rights, banded together as 'Alliance'90' and opposed any 'annexation' of the GDR by West Germany. They instead favored a gradual unification process. While many of its members rejected unification outright, the PDS in principle favored a slow process, provided that unified Germany incorporated the virtues and values of East Germany.

During the 1990 Volkskammer campaign, Helmut Kohl threw his full weight behind Alliance for Germany, a partnership he had helped forge. Alliance for Germany had a solid organization, a clear electoral strategy of calling for rapid currency union while tying the SPD to socialism, and the formidable presence of Helmut Kohl on the campaign trail. At six rallies, Kohl addressed nearly a tenth of the East German electorate.[43] He was introduced as a modern-day Bismarck: 'Once so far, some 120 years ago a German chancellor—Otto von Bismarck—brought about the unity of Germany. Today it is Helmut Kohl who will bring us unity.' The chancellor stirred crowds, amidst a sea of black-red-gold flags, by invoking the benefits of national unity: 'We are one Volk and one Fatherland and we belong together!'[44] He pushed hard for unification via Article 23 and promised prosperity ('blossoming landscapes') in the east. At a campaign rally in mid-March, Kohl said that small savings would be swapped at the highly favorable rate of one DM for one GDR mark. The announcement came after polling showed the SPD poised for victory.[45] 'The chancellor brought his authority,' the historian Manfred Görtemaker observed, 'and the financial power of the Federal Republic, into play in order help his party win the election.'[46]

On 18 March, the center-right Alliance for Germany won a decisive victory. The CDU alone received over 40 percent of the vote, while the Alliance fell just short of an absolute majority. Despite high expectations, the SPD stumbled badly to finish a distant second with 21.9 percent. The post-communist PDS received 16.4 percent of the vote after warning against rapid unification and capitalism. An alliance of three liberal parties won 5.3 percent. Alliance'90 and the Greens, which had rejected Kohl's unification course, settled for 2.9 and 2 percent, respectively. This stood in stark contrast to the triumphant performance of Solidarity in the 1989 parliamentary elections in Poland and that of Civic Forum in the 1990 democratic elections in Czechoslovakia, and it provided further proof of the relative weakness of the East German civic groups. After the Volkskammer election, a grand coalition of Alliance for Germany, the SPD and the liberals, elected Lothar de Maizière (CDU) minister president. Henceforth, the Kohl government would have a friendly negotiating partner in East Berlin. The SPD emerged divided with its eastern party in government and its western party in opposition.

The powerful allure of the DM on favorable terms had helped the East-CDU to victory. Yet West German economic experts questioned the wisdom of a parity exchange rate in light of inflationary pressures and rising eastern unemployment, as labor costs, augmented by currency union, outpaced productivity. The Bundesbank's president, Karl Otto Pöhl, emerged as an outspoken critic of parity exchange and instead favored a 2:1 rate for wages and pensions, while exchanging small savings at 1:1. Its board of directors recommended 2:1 as the general rate, a position broadly shared by the leading economic research institutes in West Germany.[47] As the Kohl government weighed its options, East Germans took to the streets to demand parity exchange. Sensing an opening, the West German opposition criticized the chancellor for breaking his word, while Kohl's political allies in East Berlin pressed for parity conversion. With eastern opposition swelling, the Kohl government in late April settled on a compromise that would exchange wages and pensions at 1:1, while converting most savings beyond 4000 Marks at the less favorable 2:1 rate. East Germans generally were satisfied with Kohl's offer and handed the CDU victory in local elections in May.

In implementing the state treaty establishing monetary, economic and social union, the Kohl government had bypassed established policy-making practices, relying instead on informal teams of experts. The SPD complained in late April that it had no meaningful role in drafting the historic policy, while the leading trade union federation, the DGB, lamented the Kohl government's minimal consultation.[48]

Currency union bolstered Kohl's reputation in the east, but did little to reassure West Germans about unification's costs. On 14 May, the SPD won a state election in the populous western region of North Rhine-Westphalia, and thereby acquired a majority in the Bundesrat, the upper house that would have to approve the state treaty. Lafontaine, the designated SPD chancellor candidate, now urged his party to oppose a treaty that he regarded as a grave mistake. Yet Lafontaine himself admitted that it was too late to block the treaty. In subsequent negotiations with the SPD, the Kohl government made changes to the treaty that ensured greater Social Democratic support and the treaty's subsequent passage in parliament.

On 1 July, the state treaty establishing economic, monetary, and social union went into effect. Much like the currency union of 1948, which had preceded West German statehood the following year, it set the stage for German unification. This pattern of economic union preceding political union had antecedents in the 19th century *Zollverein* in Germany. Oskar Lafontaine later put forth another model, betraying his Saar roots. The region, after being separated by France in 1945, rejoined Germany in 1957, yet kept the weaker Saar franc as its currency for nearly two and a half years while its economy adjusted.[49] However, by spring 1990, the deteriorating eastern economy and growing calls for the DM made this approach difficult and politically unattractive.

The state treaty awarded West Germany effective control of economic and social policy in the east, stripping the GDR of sovereignty in key policy areas. It also mandated the establishment of a functioning market economy in the GDR. To this end, East Berlin passed a law in mid-June 1990 that empowered a Trusteeship (*Treuhandanstalt*) to privatize state-owned industries. After unification, this agency would struggle to find buyers for unproductive eastern firms and, as it grappled with whether to continue to subsidize or to shut them down altogether, became a focal point of eastern opposition to unification policy.

The East German economic crisis deepened once the coveted new currency arrived. East Germans spurned GDR-made products in favor of western ones; eastern labor costs and unemployment spiraled upwards; and the country's trade with eastern bloc neighbors collapsed. Pressure for a speedy political unification mounted.

In summer 1990, West Germany and East Germany negotiated a second state treaty that regulated key aspects of the GDR's accession. The 'unification treaty,' for instance, incorporated and clarified a recent agreement on the issue of contested property in the east. While not reversing land expropriations undertaken in the Soviet occupational zone, it asserted the general principle of 'return over compensation' of private property that had been seized in the GDR after 1949. This principle, strongly supported by the West German FDP, allowed former owners, many of whom had fled to West Germany prior to the Berlin Wall in August 1961, to file claims for the return of property.[50] This added to regional tension as it was often westerners attempting to recover houses in which easterners lived. While in principle it upheld ownership rights, the settlement had the practical effect of increasing uncertainty over property rights and complicated efforts to privatize state-owned businesses and attract investment. In the words of the economists Gerlinde Sinn and Hans-Werner Sinn, 'Natural restitution has brought not clarity, but uncertainty, ambiguity, and confusion. It has manacled the invisible hand.'[51]

The unification treaty allowed for the dismissal of redundant or politically compromised eastern public workers after unification.[52] Newly formed eastern federal states would have the option of closing university departments, such as sociology, economics, philosophy, history, and Marxism-Leninism, and establishing new ones, with new personnel, modeled after West German counterparts. While arguably necessary to create a uniform public administration at short notice, the forced retirement, demotion and in some cases purging of SED cadres, who were often replaced by incoming westerners, left eastern elites numerically underrepresented in unified Germany.

Under time pressure, the negotiating partners put off a final decision on the controversial matter of abortion. In the GDR, women had a general right to abortion during the first trimester of the pregnancy, while in the Federal Republic women had access to abortion when specific circumstances, such as health concerns, social hard-ship, or rape or incest, were present. The unification treaty allowed the former West Germany and former GDR to maintain their current practices until a new law was passed. The treaty also left undecided the fate of Berlin or Bonn as governmental seat. Despite these issues, which when later resolved resulted in tangible change, the unification treaty overall reaffirmed the general direction of the Kohl government's unification policy that extended the western political, economic and administrative model eastward. Wolfgang Schäuble (CDU), the West German interior minister who led the unification treaty negotiations, had left little doubt about this: 'my set speech went as follows: Folks, it is about the accession of the GDR to the Federal Republic, not the reverse operation. We have a good constitution that has proven itself. We will do everything for you. You are heartily welcome. We do not want to ride roughshod over your wishes and interests. However, a union of two equal states is not taking place. We are not beginning afresh with equal starting positions.'[53]

East Germans soon enjoyed the benefits of the functioning administration that the Federal Republic had transferred eastward. This 'ready-made state' provided a smooth bureaucratic transition and was a privilege that the GDR's neighbors in east-central Europe did not have.[54] Since institutions, such as the legal code, court system, and public administration, were extended to a region where residents had scant direct experience with the Federal Republic, incoming western civil servants, experienced in public administration, were arguably better suited to promote eastern interests than were less seasoned homegrown actors. The Federal Republic had ample civil servants able and willing to assume leadership in the former GDR until a new, less compromised generation had arisen. Yet this came at a cost that became apparent once the afterglow of unification dimmed. Easterners took less pride in something that was handed to them by others rather than achieved on their own. Lothar de Maizière, the first and last democratically elected prime minister in the GDR, later explained: 'The Czechs designed their new system themselves, and they feel personally responsible for both its failure and its successes. Here it is different. Everything is imposed from Bonn. Even if the end result looks better on paper, people have the sense that they were not and are not the masters of their own destiny.'[55] This contributed to a widespread feeling among former East Germans that they were second-class citizens in the Federal Republic.

33.6 Chancellor democracy and the external framework for unity

While Helmut Kohl skillfully forged a domestic coalition in favor of rapid unification in 1990; he also played a central role in securing international support. By mastering the diplomatic challenges of the process, Kohl and the foreign minister Hans-Dietrich Genscher allayed concerns at home that rapid unification would damage the Federal

Republic's international standing. In late November 1989, Horst Teltschik, a foreign policy advisor to Kohl, had noted that 'the chancellor's lofty international reputation must be better utilized, and that the German Question could serve as a bridge to an improved [domestic] image for the federal chancellor.'[56] In the coming months, Kohl managed just this feat by deftly overcoming foreign policy obstacles on route to national unity, while enhancing his domestic reputation in the lead-up to national elections in late 1990. To do so, he took full advantage of the opportunities that foreign policy-making may offer a chancellor. On 28 November 1989, Kohl placed national unity on the policy agenda with his 10-point plan, which he had drafted unbeknownst to Hans-Dietrich Genscher and West Germany's closest allies.[57] While Genscher played a key part in regulating the external dimensions of unification, Kohl assumed the more prominent position as the process advanced, culminating in his landmark meeting with Gorbachev in the Caucasus in July 1990.[58] Yet because Kohl took the lead on foreign policy, and proceeded without meaningful opposition involvement, he would be held responsible for setbacks.

One miscue involved the issue of when and how the Federal Republic would formally recognize the Oder-Neisse line as its eastern frontier. What was not at issue was West Germany's commitment to the postwar German-Polish border. In late 1989 and early 1990, however, Kohl balked when pressed by Poland and others to settle the matter conclusively and without conditions. A border guarantee had been the missing 'eleventh point' in Kohl's 10-point plan of November 1989.[59] The chancellor maintained that only a united, fully sovereign German state possessed the legal authority to relinquish definitively former German lands in the east. West Germany had accepted the Oder-Neisse line in the early 1970s and Kohl had no intention of challenging the existing border. However, he did hope that final recognition might be coupled with issues such as Polish reparations claims and the treatment of the ethnic German minority in Poland. Kohl also hesitated out of concern that refugees and German nationalists would abandon the CDU in the coming federal election once it signaled closure on the border issue. Eventually, the chancellor yielded as domestic and international opposition mounted. On 21 June, the Bundestag and the Volkskammer passed a joint resolution recognizing the eastern frontier and backing a border treaty with Poland following unification. On the issue of its border, Poland took part in the international negotiations that preceded German unity. After unification, the Federal Republic and Poland concluded a formal treaty that established the Oder-Neisse line as Germany's eastern boundary, thereby settling the matter once and for all.

As German unification became a real possibility in late 1989, leaders in Israel, Poland, the United Kingdom, France and the Soviet Union all showed initial misgivings through either words or diplomatic actions. The former wartime allies' reservations were especially serious, since they retained rights regarding Germany as a whole and Berlin. In late 1989, François Mitterrand traveled to Moscow, Warsaw, and East Berlin in what was widely seen as a sign of French opposition to unification. Margaret Thatcher expressed concern that a precipitous German unification might upset the balance of power in postwar Europe and destabilize the region. The United States, in contrast, emerged as an early backer of unification, yet indicated that the Federal Republic should remain part of NATO, a position that the USSR strongly rejected. With its commanding economic, military, and political position in the GDR, the USSR posed the biggest threat to quick unification. Not only did this former wartime ally have a formal say in matters relating to Germany as a whole, but its boots on the ground—i.e. approximately 380,000 stationed troops in the GDR—lent it added weight.[60] Without Soviet backing, a rapid unification was effectively a non-starter. It was therefore significant that Gorbachev in February signaled to Kohl that the Soviet Union would respect the Germans' right to self-determination in peace.

The two German states and the four wartime powers soon settled upon a framework of meetings, the so-called 2 + 4 talks, to regulate unification's external dimension. The Federal Republic did its best to reassure Moscow that the USSR stood to benefit from unification and the easing of inter-bloc hostilities in Europe. Kohl and Genscher were careful to embed unification in the CSCE process and the European Community, while avoiding a settlement that would punish or humiliate the USSR as the cold war's loser. The primary stumbling block to a settlement remained the USSR's opposition to a newly unified Germany remaining in NATO, which on the surface would erase the strategic gains made by the USSR, and paid for at great cost, in 1945. The Federal Republic, backed by the United States, sought to make its continued NATO member-ship as palatable as possible for the Soviets. In the London Declaration, the NATO summit in July stressed East-West co-operation in Europe and conveyed a less adver-sarial approach toward the Soviet Union, anticipating that 'in a transformed Europe, they [the Allies] will be able to adapt a new NATO strategy making nuclear weapons truly weapons of last resort.'[61] By adjusting its military doctrine, and underscoring common purpose between the blocs, the NATO summit helped Soviet reformers sell Germany's NATO membership to party hardliners at home.[62] (Years later, Russia would assert that the West had broken its word by admitting former Warsaw Pact countries into NATO. Mary Elise Sarotte has concluded however that while the United States at no time gave the USSR any official assurance that NATO would not subse-quently spread eastward, Helmut Kohl had in fact intentionally cultivated ambiguity on this matter in a critical meeting with Gorbachev in February 1990.[63])

In July, Kohl, Genscher and other West German officials traveled in July to Moscow in an effort to settle outstanding business. After talks in the capital, Gorbachev and Kohl then flew to the Soviet leader's hometown region of Stavropol in the Caucasus and continued negotiations there. In dramatic fashion, they proceeded to reach agreement on a number of key points. The USSR would accept unified Germany's NATO membership and its full sovereignty, while the Federal Republic agreed to limit its troop totals to 370,000, not pursue atomic, biological or chemical weapons, and not extend non-German NATO troops or nuclear weapons to the former GDR. West Germany would provide financial support to the Soviet Union for troop withdrawal from the former GDR, which was to be completed within four years. The Federal Republic offered the USSR a bilateral pact on good neighborly relations, partnership, and co-operation.

The Caucasus breakthrough cleared the way for a successful conclusion of the 2 + 4 talks. On 12 September 1990, the two German states and the four powers signed the Treaty on the Final Settlement with Respect to Germany (2 + 4 Treaty). Even though the treaty had not yet been ratified, the four powers agreed to suspend their reserved rights and responsibilities on the day the two German states formally unified. This unfolded on 3 October 1990 when the five newly-constituted eastern states acceded to the Federal Republic under the terms of article 23.

The following month in Paris, the CSCE conference praised unification as 'an important contribution to a just and lasting order of peace for a united, democratic Europe aware of its responsibility for stability, peace and co-operation.'[64] In late 1990, the Soviet Minister of Foreign Affairs, Eduard Shevardnadze, underscored the historic nature of the settlement: 'The German question, this great and classical problem of world politics that yesterday seemed insolvable, was solved peacefully and with satisfaction on all sides.'[65] Chancellor Kohl earned accolades at home and abroad for his handling of the external aspects of unity. Even Oskar Lafontaine acknowledged that 'the result from the Caucasus was a great success for your government because it laid the tracks to the benefit of the people in Germany.'[66] On 2 December, voters went to the polls in the first democratic, all-German national election in nearly six decades. Although the costs of unification were already becoming apparent, voters in east and west generally remained optimistic and returned the governing CDU/CSU-FDP to power. This was Kohl's triumph; in just over a year after his 10-point plan, he had overcome domestic and international opposition to unify the country, and win an election, on his terms.

While many had feared a return of the German Question—with a newly unified and resurgent Germany upsetting the balance of power in post-cold war Europe—the events of 1989–1990 in fact conclusively settled, in a peaceful, democratic and internationally recognized manner, previously contested and potentially disruptive business. No longer would Germans argue over the number of legitimate German states, Germany's eastern frontiers, or its western commitment. Unification ended an era that had commenced in the 19th century when Germans began debating the boundaries of a future nation state. Some demanded that Germany house all ethnic Germans, while others accepted more than one state within the nation. Whether in the Kaiserreich, the Weimar Republic or the Federal Republic, Germans did not agree on the answer to a most basic question: What is Germany and what are its final frontiers? In 1990, unification answered the question in its cold war iteration and established a long elusive consensus.[67]

Notes

1. John Lewis Gaddis, *The Cold War: A New History* (New York: Penguin, 2005), 226–233.
2. Paul Kennedy, *The Rise and Fall of the Great Powers: Economic Change and Military Conflict from 1500 to 2000* (New York: Random House, 1987), 512–513.

3. Kennedy, *The Rise and Fall of the Great Powers*.

4. Gaddis, *The Cold War: A New History*, 190.

5. Quoted in Peter Pulzer, *German Politics: 1945–1995* (Oxford: Oxford University Press, 1995), 77–78.

6. Charles S. Maier, *Dissolution: The Crisis of Communism and the End of East Germany* (Princeton: Princeton University Press, 1997), 89–93.

7. Timothy Garton Ash, *The Magic Lantern: The Revolution of '89 Witnessed in Warsaw, Budapest, Berlin and Prague* (New York: Random House, 1990), 78.

8. Detlef Pollack, 'Der Umbruch in der DDR—eine protestantische Revolution?' in Trutz Rendtorff, *Protestantische Revolution? Kirche und Theologie in der DDR: Ekklesiologische Voraussetzungen, politischer Kontext, theologische und historiche Kriterion* (Göttingen: Vandenhoeck & Ruprecht, 1993), 41–72.

9. Timothy Garton Ash, *The Uses of Adversity: Essays on the Fate of Central Europe* (New York: Random House, 1989), 309–310.

10. Quoted in Rafael Seligmann, 'Revolution, Made in Germany' *The Atlantic Times*, December 2005: http://www.atlantic-times.com/archive_detail.php?recordID=371.

11. Quoted in Tobias Hollitzer, '15 Jahre Friedliche Revolution,' *Aus Politik und Zeitgeschichte*, 41–42/2004 (October 4, 2004), 3.

12. Hollitzer, '15 Jahre Friedliche Revolution,' 4.

13. Erhart Neubert, *Geschichte der Opposition in der DDR 1949–1989*, 2nd edn (Bonn: Bundeszentrale für politische Bildung, 2000), 837.

14. Jens Reich, *Rückkehr nach Europa. Bericht zur neuen Lage der deutschen Nation* (Munich: Hanser, 1991), 187.

15. Reich, *Rückkehr nach Europa*, 187–190.

16. Reich, *Rückkehr nach Europa*, 186.

17. Albert O. Hirschman, 'Exit, Voice and the Fate of the German Democratic Republic: An Essay in Conceptual History,' *World Politics* 45, no. 2 (January 1993), 185–190.

18. Michael Gehler, 'Die Umsturzbewegungen 1989 in Mittel und Osteuropa. Ursachen—Verlauf-Folgen,' *Aus Politik und Zeitgeschichte*, 41–42 (October 4, 2004), 41.

19. Konrad H. Jarausch, *The Rush to German Unity* (New York: Oxford University Press, 1994), 62.

20. Democracy Now, 'Appeal for intervention in our own affairs,' reprinted in Gert-Joachim Glaeßner (ed.), *The Unification Process in Germany: From Dictatorship to Democracy* (New York: St. Martin's Press, 1992), 139.

21. 'Democratic Awakening—social, ecological (DA), Association of Democratic Initiatives,' in Glaeßner, *The Unification Process in Germany*, 141.

22. Reich, *Rückkehr nach Europa*, 186.

23. Freya Klier, 'Stapelweise Modrow, Gysi, Kant und Genossen,' in Eckhard Jesse, *Eine Revolution und ihre Folgen: 14 Bürgerrechtler ziehen Bilanz* (Berlin: Ch. Links Verlag, 2000), 161.

24. Karl P. Benziger, 'The Funeral of Imre Nagy: Contested History and the Power of Memory Culture,' *History & Memory* 12, no. 2 (Fall/Winter 2000), 142–164.

25. Christian Joppke, *East German Dissidents and the Revolution of 1989: Social Movement in a Leninist Regime* (New York: New York University Press, 1995), 165.

26. Joppke, *East German Dissidents and the Revolution of 1989*, 166–167.

27. Joppke, *East German Dissidents and the Revolution of 1989*, 166.

28. Helmut Walser Smith, 'Socialism and Nationalism in the East German Revolution,' *East German Politics and Societies* 5, no. 2 (1991), 234–246.

29. Garton Ash, *The Magic Lantern*, 71–72.

30. Garton Ash, *The Magic Lantern*, 71.

31. Jarausch, *The Rush to German Unity*, 93.

32. Jarausch, *The Rush to German Unity*, 62.

33. Mike Dennis, '"Perfecting" the Imperfect: The GDR Economy in the Honecker Era,' in Gert-Joachim Glaeßner and Ian Wallace (eds), *The German Revolution of 1989: Causes and Consequences* (Oxford: Berg, 1992), 71–72.

34. Dennis, '"Perfecting" the Imperfect,' 77, 79.

35. David F. Patton, *Cold War Politics in Postwar Germany* (New York: Palgrave, 2001), 111–123.

36. *The Basic Law* (Bonn: Press and Information Office of the Federal Government, 1981), 24.

37. Perfecting *'The Basic Law,'* 93.

38. *Verhandlungen des Deutschen Bundestages*, 15 February 1990, 15110.

39. Patton, *Cold War Politics in Postwar Germany*, 122.

40. Peter J. Katzenstein, *Policy and Politics in West Germany: The Growth of a Semisovereign State* (Philadelphia: Temple University Press, 1987).

41. Patton, *Cold War Politics in Postwar Germany*.

42. Ibid.

43. Jarausch, *The Rush to German Unity*, 124.

44. Hans-Ulrich Kempski, 'Stunden, die nicht wiederkommen,' *Süddeutsche Zeitung*, March 12, 1990, 3.

45. Manfred Görtemaker, *Unifying Germany, 1989–1990* (New York: St. Martin's Press, 1994), 144–145.

46. Ibid., 145.

47. Ibid., 146–9.

48. Patton, *Cold War Politics in Postwar Germany*, 130.

49. 'Die schnelle Währungsunion hat die Einheit stark verzögert,' Interview with Oskar Lafontaine,' *Berliner Zeitung*, 1 July 2000.

50. Peter E. Quint, *The Imperfect Union: Constitutional structures of German Unification* (Princeton: Princeton University Press, 1997), 127.

51. Gerlinde Sinn and Hans-Werner Sinn, *Jumptstart: The Economic Unification of Germany* (Cambridge: MIT Press, 1992), 92.

52. Quint, *Imperfect Union*, 166–193.

53. Wolfgang Schäuble, *Der Vertrag: Wie ich über die deutsche Einheit verhandelte* (Munich: Knauer, 1993), 131.

54. Richard Rose and Christian Haerpfer, 'The Impact of a Ready-made State,' in Helmut Wiesenthal, *Einheit als Privileg: Vergleichende Perspektiven auf die Transformation Ostdeutschlands* (Frankfurt: Campus, 1996), 105–140.

55. Quoted in Jennifer A. Yoder, *From East Germans to Germans: The New Post-communist Elites* (Durham: Duke University Press, 1999), 204.

56. Horst Teltschik, *329 Tage. Innenansichten der Einigung* (Berlin: Siedler, 1991), 41.

57. Stephen F. Szabo, *The Diplomacy of German Unification* (New York: St. Martin's Press, 1992), 39.

58. Ibid., 81–2.

59. Karl Kaiser, 'German Unification,' *Foreign Affairs* 70, no. 1 (1991), 201.

60. Jarausch, *The Rush to German Unity*, 35.

61. Szabo, *The Diplomacy of German Unification*, 92.
62. Ibid., 95–7.
63. Mary Elise Sarotte, 'Enlarging NATO, Expanding Confusion,' *New York Times*, 29 November, 2009, http://www.nytimes.com/2009/11/30/opinion/30sarotte.html?_r=1.
64. CSCE, 'Charta of Paris for a new Europe,' November 1990, www.osce.org/documents/mcs/1990/11/4045_en.pdf.
65. Quoted in Szabo, *The Diplomacy of German Unification*, 112.
66. *Verhandlungen des Deutschen Bundestages*, 23 August, 1990, 17444.
67. Patton, *Cold War Politics in Postwar Germany*, 154–155.

BIBLIOGRAPHY

GADDIS, JOHN LEWIS, *The Cold War: A New History* (New York: Penguin, 2005).

GARTON ASH, TIMOTHY, *The Magic Lantern: The Revolution of '89 Witnessed in Warsaw, Budapest, Berlin, and Prague* (New York: Random House, 1990).

——*The Uses of Adversity: Essays on the Fate of Central Europe* (New York: Random House, 1989).

GLAEßNER, GERT-JOACHIM, *The Unification Process in Germany: From Dictatorship to Democracy* (New York: St. Martin's Press, 1992).

GÖRTEMACHER, MANFRED, *Unifying Germany, 1989–1990* (New York: St. Martin's Press, 1994).

HIRSCHMAN, ALBERT O., 'Exit, Voice and the Fate of the German Democratic Republic: An Essay in Conceptual History,' *World Politics*, 45, no. 2 (January 1993), 173–202.

JARAUSCH, KONRAD H. *The Rush to German Unity* (New York: Oxford University Press, 1994).

JOPPKE, CHRISTIAN, *East German Dissidents and the Revolution of 1989: Social Movement in a Leninist Regime* (New York: New York University Press, 1995).

KATZENSTEIN, PETER J., *Policy and Politics in West Germany: The Growth of a Semisovereign State* (Philadelphia: Temple University Press, 1987).

MAIER, CHARLES S., *Dissolution: The Crisis of Communism and the End of East Germany* (Princeton: Princeton University Press, 1997).

NEUBERT, ERHART, *Geschichte der Opposition in der DDR 1949–1989*, 2nd edn (Bonn: Bundeszentrale für politische Bildung, 2000).

PATTON, DAVID F. *Cold War Politics in Postwar Germany* (New York: Palgrave, 2001).

PULZER, PETER, *German Politics: 1945–1995* (Oxford: Oxford University Press, 1995).

QUINT, PETER E., *The Imperfect Union: Constitutional Structures of German Unification* (Princeton: Princeton University Press, 1997).

SCHÄUBLE, WOLFGANG, *Der Vertrag: Wie ich über die deutsche Einheit verhandelte* (Munich: Knauer, 1993).

SINN, GERLINDE and HANS-WERNER SINN, *Jumpstart: The Economic Unification of Germany* (Cambridge: MIT Press, 1992).

SZABO, STEPHEN F. *The Diplomacy of German Unification* (New York: St Martin's Press, 1992).

YODER, JENNIFER A., *From East Germans to Germans: The New Postcommunist Elites* (Durham: Duke University Press, 1999).

CHAPTER 34

··

GERMANY AND EUROPEAN INTEGRATION SINCE 1945

··

KIRAN KLAUS PATEL

FINDING its place in Europe and defining what its Europe should be is a *leitmotif* of Germany's history. Long before the twentieth century, its central position and size raised the question of how both Germany and Europe could be organized in a constructive, stable, and peaceful way that would work for Germans, as well as for their neighbors. Following national unification in 1871, the *Kaiserreich* was tempted to pursue a policy of competitive penetration and expansion, particularly vis-à-vis its eastern neighbors and non-European territories. After initial failure and the ambivalent interlude of Weimar, Nazi aggression further radicalized this policy. At its zenith, Hitler's empire spanned most of Europe, bringing terror, war, and genocide to the continent and other parts of the world.

In a basically chronological manner, this chapter analyzes the sea-shift in Germany's relationship to Europe since 1945, understanding 'Europe' not as a vague cultural or geographical entity, but rather as institutionalized forms of political and economic integration with a European focus. I argue that German history in the course of the second half of the twentieth century has been inextricably linked to the creation of such Europe(s) and their subsequent changes. To fully capture its history, these integration steps and their Europeanizing effects on the political and legal realm, as well as on society, have to be taken into account.

34.1 DIVIDING GERMANY, MAKING EUROPE(S), 1945–1968

···

By 1945, the most important attempts to define Germany's relationship to Europe and the world had utterly failed. Internationally, there was a consensus that no successor should ever get a third chance to unleash the country's destructive potential. Clearly, this goal was unattainable through nineteenth-century balance-of-power politics, while attempts to neutralize or curtail the Reich had sparked radicalism and revisionism in Germany, and thus planted the seeds of future trouble. But *laissez-faire* and non-involvement were not viable options either. So the daunting challenge of finding a practical path for the unsettled heart of central Europe remained a central litmus test for the postwar order.

At the same time, it was quite unclear what 'Europe' actually stood for and whether Germany should become part of it. Two of the three most important pro-European initiatives of the early postwar years excluded the country: the treaties of Dunkirk (1947) and Brussels (1948), paving the way for military co-operation in Western Europe, saw Germany not as a new partner, but as a former and potentially also future enemy. Containing Germany was as important as the idea of counterbalancing the Soviet Union and its emergent Eastern Bloc, and this motive also found its way into NATO (1949) of which the Brussels pact was a precursor. Secondly, the Council of Europe, instituted in 1949, which some hoped would become the central motor of a broad European integration, did not include Germany amongst its original members. Only the American-driven Marshall Plan opted for a different strategy: even if the OEEC was initiated before the creation of a West German state, the three Western occupation zones participated, and the Federal Republic became a regular OEEC member soon after its formation. For Washington, the economic reconstruction of Western Europe was quite inconceivable without German participation, while in Europe, reluctance to treat the remnants of the Reich as an equal partner still predominated after two world wars launched by Germany in the previous 35 years.[1]

These three initiatives also demonstrate how vague and volatile European integration projects still were. Clearly, they were all designed to gather together the non-communist countries of Western European. But their geographical reach varied hugely—with the OEEC bringing together seventeen European countries including Greece, Turkey, and even authoritarian Portugal as partners of the United States; the Council of Europe originally involving ten states with a heavy focus on western and northern Europe; and the Treaty of Brussels encompassing only five Western European democracies. Questions of neutrality, democratic stability, and specific need decided who was to be part of each of these Europes—and whether they were framed as purely European enterprises or as transatlantic projects.

All these organizations started as forums for a wide range of activities—from political and military to economic and cultural integration. NATO, for instance, was by no means only conceived as a military organization; it took the Korean War to galvanize its member states into creating a truly military structure. The ensuing heated discussion concerned not only the size and purpose of these institutions, but also their organizational set-up and particularly the degree to which member states were to surrender sovereignty. Many continental pro-Europeans had hoped that the Council of Europe in particular would pave the way for a federal, supranational Europe—a perspective that the Scandinavian states and Britain made sure to efface. In the end,

NATO, the OEEC, and the Council of Europe turned into rather traditional international organizations whose members were formally equal nation states that did not abandon sovereignty to a higher body.

Particularly in this first period, no country defined the trajectory of Germany's role in European integration as much as the United States. At least from 1947 onwards, Washington insisted on the western zones of occupation being treated as equals in European matters. The American foreign policy elite saw integration as a way of keeping Germany under control while creating an equal partner and a strong pillar of the Western bloc. This approach also implied the division of Germany—integration into 'Europe' with the United States as a benevolent hegemon was only plausible if the eastern extremities of both Germany and the continent were amputated. So the foundation of the two German states in 1949 was the precondition for real steps integrating Germany's western parts into the nascent European structures under American auspices. By the late 1940s, France had also learnt that it needed Germany's economic power; that any plan to liquidate its eastern neighbor once and for all as a European power would face insurmountable American resistance; and that it had to take the initiative unless it wanted to allow Britain and the United States to define the postwar order in Western Europe.[2]

This was the backdrop to the Schuman Plan of 1950, proposing co-operation in coal and steel production. Here, France blended economic arguments with the idea of making war impossible by ensuring shared access to key resources. Negotiations on this plan led to the European Coal and Steel Community (ECSC), which was the first successful initiative to give Franco-German co-operation pride of place. Also it was the first international organization with strong supranational elements. From this starting point, France, Germany, and the other four founding members of the ECSC (Italy, the Netherlands, Belgium and Luxembourg) soon embarked on new and even more audacious projects: the European Defence Community (EDC) and the European Political Community were conceived as further steps towards supranational co-operation, this time extending beyond the economic realm—until the veto of the French National Assembly brought these soaring hopes crashing down in 1954.[3]

Obviously, Germany was more a plaything of larger forces and powers than a strong actor in its own right in all these projects. Even after its foundation in September 1949, the Federal Republic was not a proper sovereign state: under the Occupation Statute, 'supreme authority' continued to lie with the Western Allies.[4] Particularly in the field of foreign policy, there was no room for independent and uncoordinated initiatives. However, important parts of ruling West German elites, particularly Chancellor Konrad Adenauer and his Christian Democratic Union, endorsed basically the same agenda as the United States and other Western partners, even though a majority of the population would have given priority to national unification. *Westintegration*, however, stood for a close alliance with the United States, and for a Western European integration built on Franco-German reconciliation. This strategy was seen as the best way to protect West Germany from Soviet aggression, as well from its own violent and ultranationalist past. This broad consensus between Bonn and the Western Allies on the overall political direction and the aptitude of the key actors were the main reasons why Germany's path into Europe was able to unfold quite smoothly, peacefully, and harmoniously—and why this specific Europe would turn into a powerful and meaningful category. It also explains why the marginality of Germany in these first steps of European integration is sometimes overlooked.[5]

If anti-Communism and *angst* over the country's past were motives that united Germany and its Western partners in their choice for Europe, there was also a factor that was unique to the Federal Republic: paradoxically, it could regain sovereignty by surrendering it. Rearmament is the obvious example. In the negotiations over the European Defence Community Chancellor Adenauer insisted that in exchange for the deployment of troops, Germany should have its equal international status restored. During the negotiations the Allies basically accepted this proposal. The EDC project failed in 1954, but the promise had been made, and in 1955 a similar, in its details even more advantageous package deal for Germany arrived—full membership of NATO and the pre-existing Western European security structures in return for the General Treaty (*Deutschlandvertrag*), which gave it most of the rights of a sovereign state. Thus, West Germany only regained sovereignty because it was willing to integrate into Western European and transatlantic structures.

Other motives played a role, too, such as the hope of winning access to new markets and fostering economic growth. This was particularly true in 1957, when the six ECSC members overcame the impasse caused by the failure of the EDC by signing the Treaties of Rome. Although this brought European integration down to earth— planning the scrupulous continuation of sectoral and economic integration rather than a quick leap to a federal political structure—it did create two fascinating projects: Euratom to promote co-operation in the sphere of atomic energy and the European Economic Community (EEC) to create a common market. In an institutional sense, both had substantial supra-national elements.

Due to its strong and export-oriented industry, Germany was particularly interested in the common market. The economic dimension should not be over-emphasized, however. Important segments of German society would have preferred a different European or global arrangement instead of the *kleineuropäisch* approach of the Europe of the Six. Ludwig Erhard, Adenauer's minister of economics, was an outspoken proponent of such a position. On the day the German parliament first discussed the Treaties of Rome, he called the whole project 'nonsense from a macroeconomic point of view.'[6] Indeed, he feared that an insulated and protectionist common market of six economies with an uncontrollable bureaucracy in Brussels would cut Germany off from its largest traditional trading partners. This objection was by no means unfounded— 75 percent of West Germany's exports went to countries outside the future EEC and in a purely economic sense a 'more European' approach (e.g. including Britain and Denmark) or a global free trade line would have been more beneficial to the country.

This position was quite strong in the late 1950s. For example, there was a lot of support in Germany for the British plan to create a free trade area around the EEC, and the acceptance of the Treaties of Rome can, to a great extent, be explained by the hope of putting *kleineuropäisch* protectionism into a broader and more liberal framework. That idea was not to be—or, more precisely, turned into an alternative model of European integration, however, when Britain and six other European states created the European Free Trade Association (EFTA) in 1960. These unexpected twists left Germany stuck in an economically-defined Europe that many of its business leaders found rather problematic.

Quite generally, the choice of Europe—and of the specific Europe of the EEC— remained contested in Germany. Social democrats were not against integrating Europe. Their Heidelberg program of 1925 already included a strong plea for a 'United States of Europe.' But they certainly disliked the projects marching under that banner in the postwar period. With their towering leader Kurt Schumacher, the SPD feared that a *kleineuropäisch* solution would override their prime objective of German reunification. To them, the ECSC smelled too much of Catholicism, conservatives, and cartels, and the defense project was seen as a new escalation of the Cold War. The Treaties of Rome were then the first initiative that found their agreement—among the major German parties, only the liberals voted against them, prioritizing national unification instead.[7]

Much worse than this unexceptional political squabbling was that most Germans simply did not care about the EEC and Euratom. In January 1957, just weeks before the Treaties of Rome were signed, opinion polls showed that only 49 percent of West Germans had even heard the terms 'Common Market' or 'European Economic Community'—and only 17 percent could explain adequately what they stood for. One year later, only about one-quarter of the population knew that the treaties had already been concluded. Most Germans were unaware of the quantum leap in the country's foreign policy and 73 percent thought that German unification was more urgent than European integration. The Europe that the EEC stood for was the project of a small elite, while most Germans continued to live in the mental container of the nation state.[8]

But why was there no larger interest? Germany, like other countries, saw a flurry of activity by intellectuals and pro-European movements in the second half of the 1940s and the early 1950s. Europe was always a minority project, but in the early postwar years this group was quite significant. Still, Europe meant very different things to different people, and only some associated the idea with democracy, the rule of law, or pluralism, whereas other groups wanted to give it a confessional, monarchist, socialist, racist, or imperialist slant—thus continuing the threads of German history. The only common denominator that can be identified in the debate is that most hoped to establish Europe as a 'third force' between the two superpowers—an idea that the Catholic Walter Dirks, the Protestant Martin Niemöller, the social democrat Richard Löwenthal, and the conservative Jakob Kaiser found equally appealing. For Germany, such an approach could have been an elegant way of synthesizing German unity and European integration—had not the dynamics of the Cold War forbidden such a solution. From summer 1948 on, most of the supporters of the 'third force' model therefore switched to *Westintegration. Realpolitik* prevailed.[9]

In the early 1950s, 'Europe' was still cool, however. In 1950, for example, young pro-Europeans burnt dozens of barriers along the German-French border, and did not neglect to invite the press to document their activities. Bewitching and overwhelming customs officers with pretty girls pretending to faint was one thing, wielding real political influence another. Even if hundreds of thousands were active, and many hoped to achieve a federal Europe quickly, these aspirations did not translate into much political action. Europe was built not from below, but by elderly statesmen, well-versed in power politics and with little interest in a complete abandonment of the nation states that were their own power base.

More precisely for the German case, the Adenauer government had a problematic way of managing the path into Europe. Certainly, there was considerable PR activity by the government—partially funded by the CIA, but when it came to decision-making, Adenauer preferred the arcane style of nineteenth-century diplomacy and remained suspicious of the people he had to rule. Considering the country's brown past, this was not entirely beside the point; but social democracy, for example, was also bypassed as long as possible. Also after 1957, the technocratic and opaque style of negotiations in the EEC did not help. From the second half of the 1950s onwards, Europe did not have the glitzy gleam of the agora, but smelled of the dusty corridors of Bonn and Brussels. Interest in European matters also ebbed because of other factors, such as the easing of the Cold War after Stalin's death, the security that NATO membership brought, the new sovereignty of the Bonn Republic and internal problems of the pro-European grassroots movements. Ironically, Europe thus became aloof from the German people during the very years in which many Germans dumped important parts of their authoritarian ideological baggage and began to associate Europe with democracy and pluralism.[10]

So indifference and resignation were quite strong from the second half of the 1950s onwards and the consensus to opt for the Europe of the Six remained superficial. Critical potential, however, was hamstrung by the fact that there was no popular vote on the choice for Europe: decision-making took place in the steady waters of parliamentary structures. Apart from a marginal fringe on the extreme right and left, critics of *Kleineuropa* also did not offer a true alternative. Besides, positive talk of EEC-Europe abounded—it was one of the standard phrases of politicians' Sunday speeches. Indeed, on a discursive level West German democracy did not allow for any real alternative to a pro-European stance. The best example for this is agriculture. The Common Agricultural Policy was an integral part of the EEC. In Germany, this key project of European integration met fierce resistance by farmers and their central lobbying group. However, they always framed their opposition in pro-European language. Generally, the absence of a German discourse of 'national interests' concerning European policy is quite remarkable. Both on the national and international levels, Germany's past and its weak international position set clear discursive boundaries.[11]

The talk of Europe thus trickled down from the top and was re-energized by earlier enthusiasm and by discussions that had nothing to do with the EEC, but rather with the Europe of Christianity, the Enlightenment or other cultural formations. And, even more importantly, there were the concrete material effects of European integration. With the ECSC and Euratom not being very successful and no other major project of European integration launched during the 1960s, Europe basically became an economic project. According to some calculations, incomes in the Six in the years from 1959 to 1969—when the EEC came into being—would have been about 4 percent lower without the Common Market.[12] European integration was thus part of the potion that explains the enormous wealth generated in Germany and other member states during the *'trente glorieuses.'*

Still, most people on the ground did not see direct links between their daily lives and this Europe. Granted, thousands of homes for industrial workers were built with ECSC funds—but it is unclear how many of them felt grateful to Europe because of this. The *kleineuropäisch* Europe was administered by a distant bureaucracy and German politicians made sure to take credit for concrete economic successes while leaving Europe in a hazy rhetorical *Überbau*. More than any material gain, the main legitimization for European integration was reconciliation, close co-operation (particularly with France), and peace after a sequence of bloody wars.

All in all, 'Europe' was primarily a political choice for West Germany. Economic integration was seen through this lens and, similar to the days of the Weimar Republic, Germany regained international recognition primarily by economic means. But this is probably the only parallel to the inter-war years—Franco-German rapprochement, American hegemony and a supranational institutional framework signified a new trajectory. At the same time, the *gestalt* of Europe was quite unclear in the 1950s, and the EEC continued to be a fragile creature in the following decade. Sharp shifts in global constellations (such as the Korean War that killed most of the hopes for the ECSC) or inner-European conflicts (most notably the Gaullist challenge to the Community in the 1960s) could have drowned it quite easily.

It is sometimes argued that the GDR was the hidden, seventh founding member of the EEC. It is true that due to the conflicted situation, the eastern part of the country was not treated as completely external in some of the trade regulations. Still, it would be completely over-rated to perceive it as a proper member state: the GDR never signed any of the treaties, opposed its capitalist design, and openly fought against this concept of Europe. The East German regime perceived the EEC as an aggressive American satellite, furthering the Cold War division of Europe. Inconsistently, European integration was often also seen as a tool of German imperialism and hegemony. By and large, an ideologically charged view prevailed, and due to these blinkers, the GDR joined the Soviet Union in refusing to recognize the EEC as an international body (unlike Hungary or Czechoslovakia, for instance).[13]

The GDR did not develop any viable idea of its own concerning political, economic, or cultural integration focusing on a notion of Europe, nor was it part of any such plan. Soviet-style internationalism with varying degrees of German nationalism blended in ruled the day, even if COMECON, as the Eastern answer to 'European' integration, was primarily geared towards the USSR's East European partners. The socialist countries ceded most of the discursive field of Europe to their Western foes, and did not counter the bravado of the *kleineuropäisch* EEC and the similarly small EFTA with any comparable 'European' rhetoric of their own. Instead, COMECON had the tendency to globalize itself. Mongolia joined in 1962, Cuba in 1972, and Vietnam in 1978. Thus, the Eastern answer to European integration was not a direct counter-model, but a vision based on socialist internationalism.

34.2 West Germany as a post-national democracy in Europe, 1968–1990

There is, of course, no precise date at which this first phase of Germany's post-1945 Europeanization came to an end. However, the removal of customs duties within the EEC in 1968, creating the world's biggest trading group; the Hague summit in 1969 that opened the way to the first enlargement of the Community and to new integrated policies; the end of a sequence of three conservative chancellorships in the Federal Republic in 1969; as well as the general political, economic, and cultural shifts of the late 1960s and early 1970s mark important changes. By now, European integration had started to become a defining factor on the European landscape, and the German question had been stabilized and shelved through a division of the country into two sovereign states and through détente.

It is during this period that for the first time, West Germany's role in Europe became more active and independent. Most obviously, the new *Ostpolitik* of change through rapprochement went beyond the hitherto dominating strategy of *Westintegration*. Its ultimate goal was to redraw the political map of Europe by normalizing West Germany's relationship to the GDR and other Eastern European states. Having taken shape since the early 1960s, *Ostpolitik* became a core issue during Willy Brandt's chancellorship from 1969 on. Another example of Bonn's more self-reliant role was the way it pushed for an enlargement of the European Community after the resignation of de Gaulle, who had blocked this process throughout the 1960s. Also on some other issues, such as the discussions about the creation of a common monetary policy, the Bonn Republic was less compliant during the 1970s than before.[14]

To some extent, these changes were an effect of West Germany's new role in Europe—its growing economic power and its increasing self-confidence. Also, the general trajectory of European integration and the global context were different than in the first twenty-five years after World War II. Enlargement demonstrated the attractiveness of the European Communities (EC), which had been created in 1967 through the fusion of the executives of the ECSC, Euratom, and the EEC. At the same time, the amplified heterogeneity of an expanding number of member states made decision-making more difficult; particularly plans to embark on new, maybe even supra-national projects stood a smaller chance. This was also true because Western European nation states were (and, more importantly, were considered by their contemporaries) much less vulnerable and dependant on each other now, after their postwar reconstruction. Not least due to its growing internal problems, US support for European integration dwindled, too. Détente diminished the external pressure to unite and the turbulent economic situation of the 1970s took its toll, reducing optimism, belief in progress, and trust in European solutions during a phase of intensifying globalization and economic insecurity. All these reasons explain why Germany's room for maneuver looked somewhat different than in the first two postwar decades.[15]

However, it is easy to over-estimate the magnitude of change in Germany's stance on Europe. In all important dimensions, continuity prevailed. *Ostpolitik* was always preceded and balanced out by attempts to deepen *Westpolitik*, so the fears of some of Bonn's partners that Germany was heading for a new Rapallo were quite unfounded. Even if West Germany played an important role in opening the door to the European Communities for Britain, Denmark, and Ireland, it preferred to leave the center stage to France during the entry negotiations—as well as generally. During the 1980s, Germany accepted the role of France's junior partner in the Franco-German engine, at least symbolically. In European and international politics, the economic Gulliver of Western Europe voluntarily kept its shackles.

Monetary policy—one of the hottest political topics in the Europe of the 1970s—exemplifies the new nuances and overall continuities. Since the late 1960s, when economic turbulence started to destabilize the Western world, Germany's hard-nosed insistence on monetary discipline several times demonstrated to France and other EC partners their humiliating dependence on the largest member state. In 1978, however, Chancellor Helmut Schmidt and his French counterpart Valéry Giscard d'Estaing agreed on the creation of the European Monetary System (EMS) linking—but not fully integrating—European currencies to prevent large fluctuations relative to one another. Fears of the German Bundesbank that this would turn Germany into the financer of an inflationary community were subordinated to political concerns. Considering the strength and stability of the *Deutschmark*, and the German successes in limiting inflation over the course of the decade, this step was quite a big concession, all the more because the *Deutschmark* was not only economically key, but had developed into a German *ersatz* symbol of national pride—of wealth, stability, and democracy—in a country devoid of strong national symbols.[16]

However, multilateralism and generosity did not just have inner-German roots. There was little room for alternatives. Germany's EEC partners were no longer worried about totalitarian tendencies or aggressive onslaughts emanating from Germany—their updated version of *angst* focused on the country's colossal economic power and saw integration as the best way of taming the Teutonic giant. Therefore, the German government could never have pushed its concerns to the extent that for example its British or later on also its Greek counterparts have done. Admittedly, German diplomatic language of the 1970s saw increasing use of the formula 'national interest.' But the way in which Germany framed these interests was still predominantly pro-*communautaire* and consensus-oriented.

The EMS, which was created in 1979 and included all EC members with the exception of Britain, also encapsulates a certain change regarding decision-making mechanisms. The project had a longer prehistory, but the breakthrough was reached in private, clandestine discussions between Schmidt and d'Estaing in their living rooms. Not surprisingly, the EMS was primarily tailored according to the needs of the 'Franco-German engine.' Integration was to remain sectoral and limited, frustrating the federalists' hopes for a strengthening of the community bodies. During this period the German political elite increasingly opted for an intergovernmental Europe in place of a supranational form of integration. Instead of pooling sovereignty, member states were to retain their power. Already in 1966, when the Gaullist challenge to the EEC had led to the Luxembourg Compromise that reinforced the role of the member states vis-à-vis supra-nationality, there had been little protest in Germany. During the 1970s, Bonn placed more emphasis on the European Councils—the intergovernmental meetings of the heads of states and governments—than on strengthening Community bodies. The congenial partnerships between the social democrat Schmidt and the center-right Giscard d'Estaing and later on between the Christian democrat Helmut Kohl and the socialist François Mitterrand symbolize this tendency, and the European Councils in general developed into a new engine of European integration. This more intergovernmental choice, however, was not specific to German European policy; similar tendencies can be found in the other member states, too. And yet, the institutional arrangements of the Europe of the 1940s and 1950s were not abandoned or substituted by the new frameworks. Rather, they were complemented and customized according to the new realities and needs.[17]

On the one hand, the EC thus became more central in Europe. EFTA had already lost a good part of its attraction in 1961, when Britain, as its main protagonist, applied for EEC membership. The OECD, superseding the OEEC since 1961, as well as the Council of Europe remained rather technical organizations for the remainder of the Cold War. Equally important, no new, permanent, and powerful organizations were conceived. The European Community turned into Western Europe's prime institutional body—and due to the further rounds of enlargement after 1973 (Greece in 1981, Portugal and Spain in 1986, plus several applications during the 1980s including Austria and Turkey) this 'Europe' also grew far beyond its original *kleineuropäisch* scope.

On the other hand, the 1970s also saw a major initiative that transcended the boundaries of the Cold War and put a different Europe on the agenda. The Conference on Security and Co-operation in Europe (CSCE) opened in Helsinki in 1973, based on a Soviet initiative. The Helsinki Accords of 1975 seemingly brought a major diplomatic boost for the Eastern bloc through its clauses on the inviolability of national borders, which consolidated the territorial regime of the Cold War. In the medium term the civil rights portion of the agreement proved to be more important, however, because it gave Eastern European dissidents a decisive point of reference in their claims for human rights. Less in the GDR than among intellectuals *in* or even more importantly *from* other Central and Eastern European Countries—like Milan Kundera, Václav Havel, Adam Michnik or Czesław Miłosz—a new debate on 'central Europe' emerged, claiming the Europeanness of their countries vis-à-vis Soviet domination. In the long run, the CSCE process not only created a new 'European' institutional framework with subversive implications, but also contributed to peaceful change and the end of the East-West conflict in Europe. At the same time, it saw the strengthening of the EC's Europe: at least during the final round of CSCE negotiations, the EC member states co-ordinated so closely that many perceived them as a single entity; and they spoke with a slightly different voice than the Americans. Hence, several Europes continued to co-exist, but the EC consolidated its pivotal place in the landscape of European institutions.[18]

Generally, US influence on European integration was not as strong in this period as it had been during the first two postwar decades. No longer did it take Washington to ensure that Germany was treated as an equal partner by its neighbors. European plans for monetary integration in Western Europe were partially meant as an alternative and remedy for the problems caused by the American economy and economic policy. Even if the United States continued to be an 'empire by integration,' the tectonic shifts in the transatlantic relationship were considerable.[19]

Although there were tentative forays into foreign and security issues, the Europe of the EC primarily remained an economic creature with a mixture of intergovernmental and supranational traits. This was too much federalism for those who believed in sovereign nation states and too little for ardent partisans of the 'United States of Europe.' Still, integration was accepted by a large majority of Germans. As before, this sentiment was based on a permissive consensus and not on active support. When, in 1979, direct elections to the European parliament were introduced, voter turnout in Germany only reached 66 percent; by 2009 it had fallen to 43 percent—whereas Bundestag elections attracted 89 percent (in 1980) and 71 percent in 2009. The EC provided insufficient or only indirectly tangible answers to most of the salient questions of the late 1970s and early 1980s—such as economic insecurity and rising unemployment after the '*trente glorieuses*,' growing environmental concerns, or the fight for civil liberties. In the early 1980s, it was unable to come up with shared and convincing reactions to the reawakening of Cold War tensions, be it the Soviet invasion of Afghanistan, martial law in Poland, or the new round of rearmament. For the first time, a discussion about the artificiality of this institutional framework arose, later condensed in the ugly term 'Eurosclerosis' to characterize the period from the mid-1970s to the mid-1980s. Although the EC held a paramount place in Europe, it remained vulnerable.[20]

This is quite ironic because during the very same two decades, many West Germans started to identify themselves with the Bonn Republic as a 'post-national democracy amongst nation states.'[21] This implied that the goal of German unification had lost in importance. Even if Adenauer's landmark decision of *Westbindung* had already implied that the re-establishment of a united German nation state did not have top priority, most Germans had continued to dwell in the mental framework of national sovereignty and grandeur. Indeed, even during the 1980s a clear majority of West Germans still hoped for unification—but an opinion poll in 1986 showed that 76 percent no longer believed they would witness such an event during their lifetime. The younger generation, especially, felt little national attachment to Germans in the GDR—or beyond, as some of their grandparents still did.[22] Post-national identity therefore implied several things at the same time: sub-national in the sense of an attachment to the Bonn *provisorium*; European and Western more in a vague cultural or civilizational sense than in a concrete institutional vein; and forms of cosmopolitanism oscillating between starry-eyed idealism and economically potent *savoir-vivre*.

Concrete effects of European integration on everyday life in Germany remained patchy. Certainly, farmers became completely dependent on the regulations emanating from Brussels; German connoisseurs of liqueur could praise the European Court of Justice for its famous Cassis de Dijon ruling of 1979, which allowed for the importation of the famous French liqueur against claims that its alcohol content was too low to qualify as a liqueur; exporters and lawyers could do likewise, because this decision turned into a gateway for the abolishment of non-tariff barriers to trade between the member states and thus to market liberalization. For the one group this meant business, for the other publications.[23] Aside from the effects for these small segments of society, the 1970s and 1980s saw a dramatic increase in the presence of lobbyists and of the German *länder* in Brussels—furthering the transnationalization of careers of civil servants, experts, and activists. And, more generally, the economic interdependence of member states rose sharply. As a result of the customs union, the Common Agricultural Policy, and the EMS, the share of exports remaining within the original six EEC member states grew from 35 to 56 percent between the late 1950s and 1980.[24]

For most people, however, ramifications remained elusive. There is economic evidence that the EC reduced the economic crises of the 1970s, but this was not an easily marketable success story. In the early 1980s, the Community's economic and technological development lagged behind other regions of the world; the recovery of the US and the apparently unstoppable rise of Japan caused serious worries. To many observers, the EC seemed incapable of tackling these problems. Also, the very effects of integration changed the way in which German media reported on the EC. Instead of commenting on or supporting abstract idealistic goals, they fulfilled their critical function of following concrete political processes. In a 1985 survey, 81 percent associated the EC with the future and 74 percent with peace—but 92 percent associated it with 'butter mountains' as the symbol of the expansive production of agricultural surpluses.[25] What at first glance can be read as criticism of the integration process might also be interpreted as a sign that Europe had become part of the normal political environment of Germans, below the special, almost transcendent status it had been granted in earlier years.

Even if the level of knowledge and satisfaction in Germany remained low in the second half of the 1980s, change was around the corner. Shifts in the macro-economic situation, an easing of Cold War tensions coupled with the advent of Mikhail Gorbachev, the energetic Delors Commission, together with a change of heads of government in several European capitals, facilitated agreement on the Single European Act of 1986. The first major revision of the 1957 Treaty of Rome pushed for more market liberalization, some institutional reforms, and initiatives that led the EC further beyond the economic sphere. Germany very much supported these new initiatives, particularly the completion of the single market. The agenda of liberalization was more in line with the country's economic interests than the original trajectory of the EEC, and at the same time, Bonn saw this project as a lever for opening up some of its own hitherto tightly regulated markets, for example, telecommunications. Again, Germany was happy to act multilaterally; supporting European integration in order to win a more prominent foreign policy role, generate wealth, and stabilize its international environment.[26]

34.3 TOWARDS AN EVER CLOSER UNION? DEVELOPMENTS SINCE 1990

The fall of the Berlin Wall and the end of the Cold War led to a re-opening of the German and, hence, the European question, at least from the perspective of many contemporaries. Margaret Thatcher epitomized the fear that unification could overturn the power balance in Europe. In the breathtaking months between November 1989 and February 1992, the Federal Republic allayed these concerns by continuing a policy of self-restraint. Vis-à-vis the crumbling Soviet Union, it agreed to a severe reduction of its combined armed forces and affirmed its renunciation of weapons of mass destruction as a contribution to a new international security structure. In its Western and global contexts, it continued its multilateral course, with a firm commitment to the UN, to NATO, and its other international memberships. The same holds true for the EC, where Germany again took a pro-integrative stance with Franco-German co-operation as a core element.

Sacrificing its currency was the main European price Germany paid for national unification. France, in particular, insisted on this point. In February 1992, twelve member states agreed on the Maastricht Treaty that stipulated the creation of a common currency by 1999. The Maastricht Treaty also reorganized the Community and strengthened pre-existing policy structures that had developed incrementally outside EC institutions since the 1970s, most importantly in the fields of foreign policy, justice, and home affairs. The newly created European Union (EU) thus propelled institutional Europe far beyond its previous preoccupation with economic issues, and brought about the biggest changes and amendments to the original treaties since 1957.[27]

Chancellor Kohl and his government supported this process unambiguously, driven by a belief that a united Germany should be anchored deeply in European institutions. At the same time, this German stance was boosted by external pressure: Maastricht was part of a parcel that made German unification acceptable to the former allies of World War II. Had Bonn not agreed to commence negotiations on further European integration in 1990, national unification would probably have been inconceivable for its Western partners. Two technical details are important in this context: the EC was only able to agree on such a dramatic deepening so quickly because discussions of further monetary integration beyond the existing EMS had already started in the mid-1980s. Secondly, Germany could still have vetoed the road to monetary integration after Maastricht, in the course of the 1990s—had its political elite not been so pro-integrationist. Hence, unification depended on further integration, but even more on the trust that Germany's partners in the end had in Bonn's commitment to stand by its word.[28]

Besides the crucial, but also somewhat weak link in the negotiations on the German and the European tier, unification left a deep mark on the EC. For the Community, it was a first step beyond the Cold War division: through the Unification Treaty of 1990, the former GDR became part of the Federal Republic and hence of the Community. Considering the enormous sums that Germany was willing to invest in its eastern provinces, it was quite easy for the EC to swallow this chunk. Still, the procedure was quite remarkable: without special negotiations or a particular treaty, sixteen million people entered the Community. Also, unification conspicuously expanded Germany's role in the EC—it now accounted for 30 percent of the EC's GDP and 23 percent of its population.[29]

Unlike in Denmark, France, and Britain, where ratification met severe difficulties, the Maastricht Treaty sailed through the German Bundestag quite smoothly. Generally, the inextricably linked processes of German unification and the creation of the EU polarized the German public much less than Adenauer's *Westintegration* or Brandt's *Ostpolitik*—the two other key phases of Germany's (European) foreign policy—had done in their times. Apart from heated discussions among professors and other experts on the merits of monetary integration, with comparably little public impact, a certain ambivalence was only added when in 1993, the Federal Constitutional Court decided that the EU Treaty was in line with the German Basic Law, but that the European Union could not broaden its jurisdiction without the consent of the states concerned.[30] This decision was reinforced in 2009 when the Federal Constitutional Court confirmed that the Lisbon Treaty was in accordance with the Basic Law, but again stressed the sovereignty of the German state, particularly the legislative role of the national parliament.

Many arguments support this reading of the German constitution, but had such interpretation already been applied in the 1950s, the dramatic integration steps of the first decades would have been seriously impeded. It is revealing that the 2009 decision of the Federal Constitutional Court uses the terms 'sovereign' or 'sovereignty' almost fifty times, while these terms are not found at all in the German Basic Law. Another example for changed perceptions in Germany can be found in the European policy of Kohl's successor Gerhard Schröder who—in a mixture of pragmatism and populism—had phases in which he emphasized defense of Germany's 'national interests' against Brussels more than his predecessors.[31]

In the early 1990s, particularly among Christian democrats, another atmosphere ruled the day. Infected by the winds of change that had blown away fundamental political constellations that dated as far back as 1945 and even 1917, the pro-European elites aimed for an ambitious reorganization of European structures with strong federal elements as a solid platform for future challenges. Already during the negotiations on the Maastricht Treaty they had stressed this need—also to compensate and consolidate monetary integration and prepare the Community for further enlargements beyond the Cold War divide. Another example of this specific form of Euro-enthusiasm is the Schäuble-Lamers paper of 1994, written by two top CDU politicians and advocating a 'hard core' Europe. But such positions also found unexpected support at the other end of the political spectrum when in 2000, Green foreign minister Joschka Fischer pressed for the establishment of a European federation as the final goal of the integration process. It bespoke a new German self-confidence that some of these ideas—in that sense resembling the reflections of Oskar Lafontaine and others during the 1980s—aimed to forge this Europe very much after the model of the German federal state and idealized Germany as a potential driving force in such a process.[32]

Obviously, not very much came out of these pleas, and taken together, the federalist and the more intergovernmentalist positions led into completely different directions. Apart from the usual political conflicts, they demonstrate that Germany was still trying to find its political identity in a world after the Cold War. It remained unclear how to blend its European policy with a tendency to greater national reassertion and the need to face global challenges. Still, all of these views also signified the further shift to a more proactive and at times even stubborn role in Europe without challenging the basic constellations and institutions created since the postwar years. This tendency was reinforced by budgetary constraints. Due to the costs of unification and economic problems, Germany was now much less able and willing to make financial concessions to its population and its partners to facilitate compromises. These tendencies became fully visible in the 2010 Euro crisis, when Germany's policy was criticized by many of its partners as close-fisted, short-sighted, and egoistic.

These changes in the German position can also be explained by generational shifts and the effects of migration: fifteen years after unification, a woman became chancellor who had grown up on the eastern side of the Iron Curtain and for whom 'European integration' was not a major part of her own biography—and Angela Merkel shared this experience with roughly one fifth of all Germans. Considering that in 2005, about another fifth of the population belonged to migrant communities (roughly half of them ethnic Germans from Eastern Europe and the former Soviet Union, the others from all parts of the world) life experiences in Germany had become dramatically more disparate.[33] The choice of Europe as a fundamental experience of the postwar generation in West Germany thus loses its firm grip on the historical narratives and identity formations in Germany, and considering these changes, the predominant continuities are quite surprising. They bespeak of the Federal Republic's political stability, its smooth-running institutions, and a prevailing pro-European consensus among its elites.

A lot of this also holds true for many other European countries, and therefore Germany can now be seen as a 'post-classical democratic nation state amongst others.'[34] Yet, these more reassured member states could not agree in which direction they wanted to take the EU, leading to the awkward negotiations about the treaties of Amsterdam (1997), Nice (2001), and Lisbon (2007). The main difference to other member states is that at least up to the end of the first decade of the new century, Germany did not witness a relevant and outspokenly Euroskeptic political formation. To some extent, this can be explained by the country's past; it also stems from the fact that all key decisions on Europe have been ratified by parliament. Referenda are not provided for by the constitution. This held at bay not only populism, but also a form of thorough politicization. If the German people had been able to vote on vital questions of European policy directly, the outcome would be quite open. The permissive consensus that supported European integration in Germany during the Cold War has foundered. According to the Eurobarometer survey of fall 2008, for instance, 58 percent of all Germans (and 61 percent of all EU citizens) believed that their voice did not matter in Europe and only 48 percent (45 percent in the whole EU) had a positive overall image of the EU—whereas during the 1970s and 1980s, roughly 80 percent still thought that European unification was a good thing.[35]

Frustrations with the opaqueness and democratic deficits of the Union are important explanations for this, as well as the fact that Germany itself did not perform as hoped in the new EU. The fiscal problems of some member-states in the world financial crisis after 2007 as well as the subsequent Euro crisis have nourished these forms of skepticism, and have made it easy to overlook how much Germany itself has profited from integration. Moreover, many Germans felt increasingly frustrated about continuous waves of enlargement. In the early 1990s, Bonn was still pushing for a widening of the EU, by accepting the Scandinavian countries and Austria, and throughout the decade it very much supported the entry of Eastern European countries—to overcome the Cold War, frame Germany more broadly, and win additional markets. Things looked quite different in the case of Turkey. Germany witnessed a heated debate on the merits of its entry and a majority of the population did not want to see Turkey as a member state—partly because they thought that the EU was not yet ready to digest this vast country, partly because they felt Turkey still had to do its homework, and partly for xenophobic reasons.[36]

The public discomfort with the European Union stands in stark contrast with the level to which the EU has started to impact on everyday life in Germany since the 1990s. For the first time since 1945, the attribute 'European' is more than geographical hyperbole. On an economic level, this became particularly visible with the Commission's interventions regarding mergers and state subsidies for companies. With the Euro, the EU has reached the pockets of average citizens, and the Euro crisis of 2010 poses a much larger direct threat to citizens than any previous crisis in European integration. In any German city center, European flags are impossible to miss on public buildings. Even if it does not reflect the political weight of the EU, press coverage of European matters is broader in the German media than in those of comparable member states. Between its creation in 1987 and 2007, more than 260,000 German students participated in the EU's Erasmus program, allowing them to study in another European country.[37] Still neither hard currency, nor symbols, nor the Erasmus-Europe built on Sartre, sangria, and sex has managed to raise support for institutional Europe significantly. Again, this is quite ironic, because on many levels, including social, cultural, and technological aspects, convergence and interdependence between European societies are higher than ever before.[38] But, maybe these entanglements are the very reason why Germans and other Europeans are not more passionate about the EU. Direct participation and democratic legitimacy are low in this political system. Also, its main original motivations—to preserve peace and create wealth—do not necessarily depend on this framework any more. Due to its sheer successes, integration might not be necessary any more as an answer to the German question. On the other hand, the EU is better equipped to cope with globalization than its member states would be on their own—but it is difficult to demonstrate this.

Despite 11/9 and 9/11, the United States loomed large in European integration during this period. Although less visible than in the early postwar years, it still left its imprint on all crucial moments and issues. Germany had Washington's full support on the road to unification, thus also quieting the concerns of other allies. America bailed the Europeans out when they proved unable to end the wars in former Yugoslavia. In 1999, strong support from President Bill Clinton and Secretary of State Madeleine Albright helped to gain Turkey candidacy status in the EU. And in 2004, all new Eastern European EU member states were first granted NATO membership as a security guarantee facilitating their transition into institutional Europe. Thus—and despite serious transatlantic turbulences during the Iraq war—Germany and the Europe of the EU have remained parts of a larger transatlantic framework.[39]

All in all, Germany has found its secure place in a stabilized Europe. In 1943, Thomas Mann—like many of his contemporaries—was horrified by Hitler's plan 'to make Europe German.' Instead, he 'wanted Germany to become European'—a wish that in the meanwhile has turned into a political reality.[40] Today, this Europe is predominantly associated with the EU. Its exact shape and size remain utterly imprecise and volatile, giving it room to develop in new directions in a period in which the German question does not form a big challenge any more. On a day-to-day level, Germany has played an increasingly more assertive role in this forum since the late 1960s. Until recently, it has rarely flexed its muscles, considering its sheer size and its economic strength. A consensus-oriented and co-operative style has prevailed and the choice for Europe is solidly grounded in the political and legal culture and institutions. But contrary to earlier decades, this EU is not the *ersatz vaterland* for Germans any more—as in most other member states, *vernunftliebe* and indifference are the main bridges to this institutional entity.

Notes

1. Dieter Krüger, *Sicherheit durch Integration? Die wirtschaftliche und politische Integration Westeuropas 1947 bis 1957* (Munich: Oldenbourg, 2003).

2. See Charles S. Maier (ed.), *The Marshall Plan and Germany: West German Development within the Framework of the European Recovery Program* (New York: St. Martin's Press, 1991); Beate Neuss, *Geburtshelfer Europas? Die Rolle der Vereinigten Staaten im europäischen Integrationsprozeß 1945–1958* (Baden-Baden: Nomos, 2000).

3. John Gillingham, *Coal, Steel, and the Rebirth of Europe, 1945–1955: the Germans and French from Ruhr Conflict to Economic Community* (Cambridge: Cambridge University Press, 1991).

4. *Foreign Relations of the United States*, vol. 1949, III (Washington DC: U.S. Government Printing Office, 1979), 179.

5. See Mareike König and Matthias Schulz (eds), *Die Bundesrepublik Deutschland und die europäische Einigung, 1949–2000. Politische Akteure, gesellschaftliche Kräfte und Internationale Erfahrungen* (Stuttgart: Steiner, 2004); Ludolf Herbst, *Option für den Westen: Vom Marshallplan bis zum deutsch-französischen Vertrag* (Munich: DTV, 1989); Ronald J. Granieri, *The Ambivalent Alliance: Konrad Adenauer, the CDU/CSU, and the West, 1949–1966* (New York: Berghahn Books, 2003).

6. 'Kritische Äußerungen Erhards,' *Neue Zürcher Zeitung*, 21 March 1957. See also Alan S. Milward, *The European Rescue of the Nation-State*, 2nd edn (London: Routledge, 2000); Reinhard Neebe, *Weichenstellung für die Globalisierung. Deutsche Weltmarktpolitik, Europa und Amerika in der Ära Ludwig Erhard* (Cologne: Böhlau, 2004).

7. William E. Paterson, *The SPD and European Integration* (Farnborough: Lexington Books, 1974); Dietmar Ramschukat, *Die SPD und der europäische Einigungsprozeß: Kontinuität und Wandel in der sozialdemokratischen Europapolitik 1949–1955* (Niebüll: Videel Verlag, 2003).

8. See Elisabeth Noelle and Erich Peter Neumann (eds), *Jahrbuch der öffentlichen Meinung 1958–1964* (Allensbach: Verlag für Demoskopie, 1965), 542–50; Elisabeth Noelle and Erich Peter Neumann (eds), *Jahrbuch der öffentlichen Meinung 1957* (Allensbach: Verlag für Demoskopie, 1957), 342.

9. Wilfried Loth, 'Von der 'Dritten Kraft' zur Westintegration: Deutsche Europa–Projekte in der Nachkriegszeit,' in: Franz Knipping and Klaus–Jürgen Müller (eds), *Aus der Ohnmacht zur Bündnismacht: Das Machtproblem in der Bundesrepublik Deutschland 1945–1960* (Paderborn: Schöningh, 1995), 57–83; Vanessa Conze, *Das Europa der Deutschen. Ideen von Europa in Deutschland zwischen Reichstradition und Westorientierung (1920–1970)* (Munich: Oldenbourg, 2005).

10. Conze, *Europa der Deutschen*, 385–403.

11. Kiran Klaus Patel, *Europäisierung wider Willen: Die Bundesrepublik Deutschland in der Agrarintegration der EWG, 1955–1973* (Munich: Oldenbourg, 2009), 123–128, 156–165.

12. See Barry Eichengreen, *The European Economy since 1945. Coordinated Capitalism and Beyond* (Princeton: Princeton University Press, 2007), 181; for a more skeptical interpretation, see e.g. Werner Plumpe and André Steiner, 'Dimensionen wirtschaftlicher Integrationsprozesse in West- und Osteuropa nach dem Zweiten Weltkrieg,' *Economic History Yearbook* (2008), 21–38.

13. Jana Wüstenhagen, *'Blick durch den Vorhang.' Die SBZ/DDR und die Integration Westeuropas 1946–1972* (Baden-Baden: Nomos, 2001).

14. Eckart Conze, *Die Suche nach Sicherheit: Eine Geschichte der Bundesrepublik Deutschland von 1949 bis in die Gegenwart* (Munich: Siedler, 2009), 418–58.

15. Desmond Dinan, *Europe Recast: A History of the European Union* (London: Palgrave, 2004), 125–166.

16. Eichengreen, *European Economy*, 225–293; Carl–Ludwig Holtfrerich, Harold James and Manfred Pohl, *Requiem auf eine Währung: die Mark, 1873–2001* (Stuttgart: DVA, 2001).

17. See König and Schulz, *Bundesrepublik Deutschland*, particularly the contributions on Schmidt (185–220) and Kohl (221–37); Haig Simonian, *The Privileged Partnership. Franco-German Relations in the European Community 1969–1984* (Oxford: Clarendon, 1985).

18. On CSCE see Wilfried Loth and Georges–Henri Soutou (eds), *The Making of Détente: Eastern and Western Europe in the Cold War, 1965–1975* (London: Routledge, 2008); on the dissidents' debate see e.g.: Rainer Schmidt, *Die Wiedergeburt der Mitte Europas: Politisches Denken jenseits von Ost und West* (Berlin: Akademie–Verlag, 2001); José M. Faraldo, Paulina Gulińska–Jurgiel and Christian Domnitz (eds), *Europa im Ostblock. Vorstellungen und Diskurse (1945–1991)* (Cologne: Böhlau, 2008).

19. Lundestad, Geir, *The United States and Western Europe since 1945. From 'Empire by Invitation' to Transatlantic Drift* (Oxford: Oxford University Press, 2003); Matthias Schulz and Thomas A. Schwartz (eds), *The Strained Alliance: US-European Relations from Nixon to Carter* (New York: Cambridge University Press, 2010).

20. Dinan, *Europe Recast*, 145–85.

21. Karl Dietrich Bracher, *Die deutsche Diktatur: Entstehung, Struktur, Folgen des National-sozialismus*, 5th edn (Cologne: Kiepenheuer & Witsch, 1976), 544. This afterword was only added in the 1976 edition.

22. Elisabeth Noelle-Neumann and Renate Köcher (eds), *Allensbacher Jahrbuch der Demos-kopie 1984–1992* (Munich: Verlag für Demoskopie, 1993), 432–437.

23. On farmers see Patel, *Europäisierung*, 470–494; on the Cassis de Dijon decision: Paul P. Craig and Gráinne De Búrca, *EU Law, Text, Cases, and Materials*, 4th edn (Oxford: Oxford University Press, 2008), 677–681.

24. Eichengreen, *European Economy*, 336.

25. Elisabeth Noelle-Neumann and Edgar Priel (eds), *Allensbacher Jahrbuch der Demoskopie 1978–1984* (Munich: Verlag für Demoskopie, 1984), 599.

26. Dinan, *Europe Recast*, 185–231; Peter J. Katzenstein (ed.), *Tamed Power. Germany in Europe* (Ithaca: Cornell University Press, 1997).

27. Frédéric Bozo, Marie-Pierre Rey, N. Piers Ludlow and Leopoldo Nuti (eds), *Europe and the End of the Cold War: A Reappraisal* (London: Routledge, 2008); Frédéric Bozo, *Mitterrand, the End of the Cold War, and German Unification* (New York: Berghahn, 2009).

28. Chris Mulhearn and Howard R. Vane, *The Euro. Its Origins, Development and Prospects* (Cheltenham: Edward Elgar, 2008); Andreas Wirsching, *Abschied vom Provisorium: 1982–1990*, vol. 6 (Geschichte der Bundesrepublik Deutschland) (Munich: DVA, 2006), 673–694; Simon Bulmer, Charlie Jeffery and William E. Paterson, *Germany's European Diplomacy: Shaping the Regional Milieu* (New York: St Martin's Press, 2000).

29. E.g. see Gerhard Brunn, *Die Europäische Einigung von 1945 bis heute* (Stuttgart: Reclam, 2002), 269.

30. See the contributions of Franz C. Mayer, 'The European Constitution and the Courts' and for the wider background Philipp Dann, 'The Political Institutions' in: Armin von Bogdandy and Jürgen Bast (eds), *Principles of European Constitutional Law* (Oxford: Hart, 2008), 281–333 and 229–36; on Lisbon, see the special section in the *German Law Journal* 10 (2009), 1201–1308 with its various contributions.

31. Daniel Göler and Mathias Jopp, 'Deutschlands konstitutionelle Europapolitik: Auswir-kungen veränderter innen- und außenpolitischer Rahmenbedingungen,' in: Thomas Jäger, Alexander Höse and Kai Oppermann (eds), *Deutsche Außenpolitik. Sicherheit, Wohlfahrt, Institutionen und Normen* (Wiesbaden: Verlag für Sozialwissenschaften, 2007), 462–484; the decision of the Federal Constitutional Court: www.bundesverfas-sungsgericht.de/entscheidungen/es20090630_2bve000208.html.

32. See Oskar Lafontaine, *Die Gesellschaft der Zukunft: Reformpolitik in einer veränderten Welt* (Hamburg: Hoffmann und Campe, 1988), particularly 185–197; Schäuble-Lamers paper: *CDU/CSU-Fraktion des Deutschen Bundestages, Überlegungen zur europäischen Politik* (Bonn, 1 September 1994); Joschka Fischer, *Vom Staatenverbund zur Föderation: Gedanken über die Finalität der europäischen Integration. Talk at Humboldt University*, 12 May 2000, online as: http://www.hu-berlin.de/documents/fischer.pdf.

33. Statistisches Bundesamt (ed.), *Statistisches Jahrbuch 2007 für die Bundesrepublik Deutsch-land* (Wiesbaden: Bundesamt, 2007), 64–65.

34. Heinrich August Winkler, *Germany, the Long Road West*, vol. 2, *1933–1990* (Oxford: Oxford University Press, 2007), 571.

35. European Commission, *Eurobarometer 70. Nationaler Bericht: Deutschland* (Brussels: Office for Official Publications of the EC, 2009), 11, 30–31; European Commission,

Eurobarometer 29. Complete Report (Brussels: Office for Official Publications of the EC, 1988), 4. Note that the set of questions has changed to some extent during this period.

36. Esra LaGro and Knud Erik Jørgensen (eds), *Turkey and the European Union: Prospects of a Difficult Encounter* (Houndmills: Palgrave, 2007); Claus Leggewie, *Die Türkei und Europa: die Positionen* (Frankfurt: Suhrkamp, 2004).

37. European Union, Press Release IP/08/736, 13 March 2008; Ainhoia de Federico de la Rúa, 'How do Erasmus Students Make Friends,' in Susanne Ehrenreich, Gill Woodman and Marion Perrefort (eds), *Auslandsaufenthalte in Schule und Studium: Bestandsaufnahmen aus Forschung und Praxis* (Münster: Waxmann, 2008), 89–104.

38. Hartmut Kaelble, *Sozialgeschichte Europas. 1945 bis zur Gegenwart* (Munich: Beck, 2007).

39. Lundestad, *United States*, 249–293.

40. Thomas Mann, 'Broadcast, 29 January 1943,' in Walter Lipgens (ed.), *Documents on the History of European Integration*, vol. 2 (Berlin: de Gruyter, 1986), 591.

BIBLIOGRAPHY

BULMER, SIMON, CHARLIE JEFFERY, and WILLIAM E. PATERSON, *Germany's European Diplomacy: Shaping the Regional Milieu* (New York: St. Martin's Press, 2000).

CONWAY, MARTIN and KIRAN KLAUS PATEL (eds), *Europeanization in the Twentieth Century: Historical Approaches* (Houndmills: Palgrave, 2010).

CONZE, VANESSA, *Das Europa der Deutschen. Ideen von Europa in Deutschland zwischen Reichstradition und Westorientierung (1920–1970)* (Munich: Oldenbourg, 2005).

CONZE, ECKART, *Die Suche nach Sicherheit: Eine Geschichte der Bundesrepublik Deutschland von 1949 bis in die Gegenwart* (Munich: Siedler, 2009).

DINAN, DESMOND, *Europe Recast: A History of the European Union* (London: Palgrave, 2004).

EICHENGREEN, BARRY, *The European Economy since 1945. Coordinated Capitalism and Beyond* (Princeton: Princeton University Press, 2007).

KATZENSTEIN, PETER J., *Tamed Power. Germany in Europe* (Ithaca: Cornell University Press, 1997).

KNODT, MICHÈLE and BEATE KOHLER-KOCH (eds), *Deutschland zwischen Europäisierung und Selbstbehauptung* (Frankfurt: Campus, 2000).

KÖNIG, MAREIKE and MATTHIAS SCHULZ (eds), *Die Bundesrepublik Deutschland und die europäische Einigung, 1949–2000. Politische Akteure, gesellschaftliche Kräfte und internationale Erfahrungen* (Stuttgart: Steiner, 2004).

MILWARD, ALAN S., *The European Rescue of the Nation-State*, 2nd ed. (London: Routledge, 2000).

MORAVCSIK, ANDREW, *The Choice for Europe. Social Purpose and State Power from Messina to Maastricht* (Ithaca: Cornell University Press, 1998).

PATEL, KIRAN KLAUS, *Europäisierung wider Willen: Die Bundesrepublik Deutschland in der Agrarintegration der EWG, 1955–1973* (Munich: Oldenbourg, 2009).

WINKLER, HEINRICH AUGUST, *Germany, the Long Road West*. vol. 2, *1933–1990* (Oxford: Oxford University Press, 2007).

WIRSCHING, ANDREAS, *Abschied vom Provisorium: 1982–1990 (Geschichte der Bundesrepublik Deutschland, vol. 6)* (Munich: DVA, 2006).

CHAPTER 35

TOWARD A MULTICULTURAL SOCIETY?

WILLIAM A. BARBIERI, Jr.

35.1 SOCCER NATIONALISM

35.1.1 Is twenty-first century Germany a multicultural society?

Let us consider two images associated with one fairly reliable barometer of the state of the nation in Germany: the national game, soccer. In hosting the World Cup of 2006, Germany presented a new face to the world. The widely circulated image of the Afro-German footballer Gerald Asamoah in the publicity campaign '*Du bist Deutschland*' advertised a Germany comfortable with its diversity and optimistic about its future prospects.[1] In the build-up to the tournament, the German national team, trained by an Americanized expatriate, fielded players with Turkish, Brazilian, and Nigerian roots. Once the tournament began, the team rode the attacking exploits of players of Polish, Swiss, and Ghanaian heritage to an unexpectedly successful showing. The prominent displays of the German flag and other manifestations of national pride at the euphoric celebrations surrounding the games were hailed by German President Horst Köhler as 'something beautiful . . . a sign that the country is increasingly returning to normal.'[2] The conjunction of suddenly unabashed German patriotism and enthusiastic support of its diverse roster of representatives on the soccer pitch helped create the impression of a country that had transcended its dark history to find a new identity as a tolerant and inclusive society affirmative of its immigrant character.

At the same time, however, Germany was experiencing something of a backlash with respect to gains made in the direction of a multicultural society. Against the backdrop of fear elicited in the preceding months by the Madrid and London bombings, and the murder of Theo van Gogh in Amsterdam, sobering descriptions of the eroding socio-economic status of Germany's own migrant minorities prompted a spate of writings about the failure of multiculturalism. The new German Chancellor, Angela Merkel, declared it time to relinquish the failed utopian dream of the multicultural society. Meanwhile, in the world of soccer, a former government spokesman named Uwe-Karsten Heye caused a furor by suggesting that non-white soccer fans could not travel to the eastern German state of Brandenburg without risking life and limb. Meanwhile, another Afro-German player on the national team, Patrick Owomoyela, sought a court injunction against the country's largest extreme-right party, the NPD, after the group launched a campaign for an all-white national team using the image of his jersey with the slogan, 'White. It's more than just a jersey color. For a *real* national team.'[3]

These two snapshots reflect some of the divergent sensibilities and political forces in play as German society kicks off the twenty-first century amidst controversies over how best to come to terms with the ethnic diversity bequeathed by the 'guest worker' policies and various other migrations of the past fifty years. The extent to which Germany has become a multicultural society is a complex and, indeed, politicized question, one that stretches in its implications from the soccer field to foundational debates over German identity. Investigating it requires engaging a number of topics, including the meaning of multiculturalism, the history of ethnic diversity in modern Germany, the current demographic constitution of German society, the politics of ethnic and religious identity and the institutional response of the state, the position of Germany with respect to broader historical processes such as European integration and de-secularization, and contemporary ethical debates about the rights and wrongs of patriotism and tolerance. I will address each in turn. How Germany is dealing with cultural diversity and the challenge of integration is, as I will show, a '*Schlüsselfrage*,' a key question for German society as it confronts the historical challenges of a new century.

35.2 Conceptions of multiculturalism

In approaching the topic of multiculturalism, there is no way around the task of confronting some of the ambiguities associated with the term itself. The checkered career of the ideal of the 'multicultural society'—which was imported to Germany from Australia by the churches in the 1970s, fashioned into a progressive mantra in the 1980s, largely ignored in the wake of German Unification in the 1990s, and castigated in the tense years following September 11, 2001—should not distract from the continuous trajectory of underlying questions about how best to respond to an evolving picture of diversity within German society. But multiculturalism can mean different things in different contexts, and distinguishing some of these meanings may assist in identifying what is truly at stake in the debate.

For some, the central issue has been the *descriptive* question of whether German society is essentially heterogeneous, or whether it may still be properly thought of as the preserve of a singular German cultural entity. Because definitions of who counts as a member of German society vary depending on whether one links belonging to citizenship, or to legal residence, or simply to long-term presence and integration into the economy, descriptions on this point are not a purely empirical matter. Still, it is hard to deny the proposition that Germany, with a foreign-born population of roughly 13 percent and half again as many native-born children of migrants, presently encompasses a significant variety of cultural identities. By comparison, the foreign-born population of France in 2003 was 7.8 percent; of Spain, 8.8 percent; of the UK, 8.9 percent; of the Netherlands, 10.7 percent; of Sweden, 12.0 percent; and of the USA, 12.6 percent.[4] In this sense, it is hard to contest that Germany is a multicultural society.

Beyond the descriptive issue, however, we quickly encounter the *normative* question of whether existing cultural diversity is to be affirmed, in the sense of being taken into account in an active and constructive way in the institutional structuring of social and political life. After all, it is a central realization of modern political life that cultures are malleable, and hence the cultural makeup of a state society can be altered and adjusted through means ranging from the subtle to the draconian. German politics, marked indelibly by the Holocaust, operates under certain constraints with regard to the treatment of religious and national minorities. Still, these limits did not impede an effort by the government in the 1980s to provide financial incentives for emigration in an attempt to prevent the establishment of a settled minority of primarily Turkish, largely Muslim 'guest workers.' Such efforts notwithstanding, however, few would contest that on the basic normative issue of whether or not to accept diversity, multiculturalism has won the day.[5] At least in liberal democratic states, the principle that established minorities are entitled to some basic protections is well established. Consequently, the question for Germany, one could say, has become not whether to pursue a multicultural society, but how to deal with one.

But what counts as a culture in a multicultural society? Obvious candidates include national minorities, linguistic groups, ethnic groups, and race-based communities. But what of religious communities? Or, for that matter, the gay community, or women, or the disabled? It may be, as some political thinkers maintain, that the German philosophical tradition stretching back to Herder nurtures an affinity for the idea of cultures as the forms of life of collectivities or 'peoples,' yet German history provides good grounds for looking skeptically at any conception of culture that appears to be essentialist in nature and risks reproducing the dehumanizing effects of Nazi ideology.[6] Sociological accounts, too, are problematic, because of the way in which internal diversity and various types of hybridity militate against the drawing of neat boundaries among social groups. Culture is more aptly construed, perhaps, in political terms, as a certain kind of framework for corporate, minority action in response to group-related disadvantage, inequality, or exploitation. Political theorists have suggested that *recognition* (of group difference) serves as a key term for conceiving of the purpose linked to the agenda of multiculturalism.[7] In modern societies, language, nationality, race, and ethnicity can serve as markers for both discrimination and organization for collective action. The dangers of speaking of cultures have prompted some to argue for the 'multi-ethnic' society as a more apt ideal than the multicultural one in Germany's case. Indeed, how to define culture remains one of the contested aspects of the overall question of multiculturalism.

The issue of how to define culture is related in turn to the crucial problem of how to conceive of the agenda of multiculturalism. There are, indeed, different ways of envisaging how desirable relations among culturally diverse social groups might look, a circumstance reflected in the metaphors often used: 'a melting pot,' 'a salad,' 'a mosaic.' As a result we must speak in this connection of different and contending multiculturalisms.[8] For example, on one version, multiculturalism is a matter of individuals with diverse backgrounds living together ('*miteinander*') in a society with no official preference for any one national culture, enriched by all; it was this sort of vision that enjoyed currency in the West Germany of the 1980s. For a contrasting version, the goal is equal rights and respect for group differences in a manner enabling diverse groups to co-exist ('*nebeneinander*'), while maintaining their cultural integrity within a common basic framework of rights. Many of the recent barbs in German political debates have been directed at yet another view that posits a society in which subcultures exist in largely autonomous enclaves ('*auseinander*') in which, for example, distinct religious norms and law might apply. These broad visions take on more specific outlines in connection with the particular policy questions attending the task of integrating immigrant and other non-mainstream groups, involving religious freedoms, group rights, affirmative action, political representation, bilingual education, and so on. In any event, though, the issue of multiculturalism remains a 'Gretchen question,' one that calls for a statement of political, ethical, and even religious conviction in response.

35.3 THE DIALECTIC OF MULTICULTURALISM

The rise of the question of multiculturalism, for Germany, has accompanied the steady increase in the number of non-ethnically German members of German society following the initiation of foreign worker recruitment policies in 1955. When the immigrant population nearly doubled in the early 1990s under the cumulative effects of family reunifications for guest workers and increased flows of refugees, asylum seekers, and ethnic German repatriates, the issue increased in urgency. Yet, in point of fact, Germany, like any modern state, has since its inception been consistently confronted with the issue of how to integrate non-German populations, and the German population has been distilled over time from a brew including, at various times, many different nationalities.[9] Indeed, an earlier chapter of German integration concerned thousands of Turkish prisoners of war—the so-called *Beutetürken*—who were brought home as forced labor in 1683 following the Battle of Vienna and who, in many cases, were converted to Christianity and eventually assimilated. In the same period, roughly one-third of the population of Berlin was made up by French-speaking Huguenots who arrived following the Edict of Potsdam of 1685, which authorized them to conduct church services in French. Later, in the early days of the German nation state, an influx of hundreds of thousands of Polish laborers played an important role in the industrializing economy in the Ruhr region. While subject to official Germanization policies, the Poles of the Ruhr enjoyed minority rights arrangements persisting into the twentieth century, and their presence continued to be felt, among other places, in the procession of footballers with Polish names who helped account for the glory days of clubs such as FC Schalke 04. Another chapter in the history of Germany's multicultural society, of course, concerns the Jewish population, which numbered over half a million before the Nazis came to power. Although subject in many respects to official restrictions, the Jewish minority was also accorded occasional accommodations. In nineteenth-century Prussia, for example, testing students on Saturdays was prohibited in acknowledgment of the Jewish Sabbath. In this light, the challenges posed by the various groups of newcomers in German society are only the latest episode in an ongoing process of migration and integration.

The present episode has its origins in the labor needs associated with the *Wirtschaftswunder* of the 1950s. When the influx of ethnic Germans following the end of World War II proved unable to blunt the need for more labor as the postwar economy took wing, workers were recruited beginning in 1955 from Italy, Spain, Greece, Turkey, Portugal, Tunisia, Morocco, and Yugoslavia. The original intent, shared with other recruiting countries such as Austria and Switzerland, was to import short-term laborers—'guest workers'—who would return to the sending countries after a couple of years in exchange for replacements, but in practice the needs of employers favored longer stays, which in many cases became indefinite. When the West German government terminated the recruitment programs in 1973, many workers—especially those from Turkey—stayed on, in spite of the fact that there was no official policy supporting immigration. A subsequent series of court cases not only established a legal basis for the migrants' continued presence, but recognized their right to be joined by family members. This process reflected a tacit acknowledgment that, as the novelist Max Frisch famously put it, 'We sent for workers, but human beings came.' By the close of the 1970s it was clear that a sort of existential process of settling had occurred, and the Social Democratic government began to debate whether the worker population should be assimilated or otherwise integrated. Legally, however, the guest worker community remained 'denizens' as opposed to citizens, and the fact that divided Germany remained an 'incomplete nation' worked against any efforts to modify German citizenship laws to include non-ethnic Germans.[10] In the 1980s, despite the aforementioned initiative of the governing Liberal-Christian Democratic coalition to use financial incentives to induce the migrants to repatriate themselves, the new minority instead consolidated its presence through an extensive process of family reunification.[11] At the end of that decade, the peculiar 'family reunification' experienced by the German nation itself brought with it an adopted child in the form of a residual Vietnamese minority from East Germany, also the progeny of a foreign worker program. The case can be made that German reunification and the host of issues surrounding the integration of East Germans effectively delayed the process of redefining the meaning of Germanness so as to include these new migrant minorities.[12] In the early 1990s, refugee movements became the engines of diversity, as hundreds of thousands of migrants arrived from the Balkans and elsewhere to lay claim to the right to asylum affirmed in Article 16 of the Basic Law.[13] The end of the Cold War also released massive flows—peaking at just fewer than 400,000 in 1990—of ethnically German migrants, primarily from the former Soviet Union, who were able to lay claim to German citizenship under Article 116 of the Basic Law. Ironically, in that period, even as the German government persistently repeated that Germany was 'not a country of immigration,' the country was a greater target of migration than any other European land, receiving over a million migrants per year through 1995.[14] This situation, which strengthened the hand of far-right parties, quickly prompted legislative action to trim the constitutional right of asylum and place caps on the number of repatriates, thus ensuring that migration would return to minimal rates.

By this point, the die had been cast for a culturally diverse Germany, and the chief political questions shifted from matters of admissions for new migrants to 'membership debates' regarding the inclusion of those already present. The guest worker population, occasionally referred to euphemistically as 'foreign co-citizens' (ausländische Mitbürger), enjoyed a broad range of rights and protections under Germany's 1990 Aliens Act, but remained culturally marginalized, socioeconomically disadvantaged, and politically disenfranchised. This latter circumstance in particular prompted advocates of the migrants—including the churches, labor unions, welfare organizations, and the more left-leaning political parties—to initiate a series of efforts to promote means of political and institutional inclusion for the new minority. Initial attempts to provide local voting rights for non-EU nationals or to facilitate naturalization by allowing dual citizenship were rebuffed in the early 1990s, but gradual reforms in the laws affecting the rights of foreigners over the course of that decade were capped by legislative steps that heralded major shifts in German attitudes toward migration and inclusion. A new citizenship law that went into effect in 2000, replacing the previous law—the Reichs- und Staatsangehörigkeitsgesetz—of 1913, took the symbolically important step of expanding the traditional rule of nationality through parentage (ius sanguinis) to include a limited provision for nationality based on place of birth (ius soli), thus opening up dual citizenship automatically to children born to long-term residents. The new law also eases naturalization requirements for those residents themselves.[15] Of comparable symbolic significance was an immigration law that went into effect in 2005 which finally cast Germany as a country of immigration willing both to welcome and to attempt to steer the growth of its population through migration and, just as important, to integrate newcomers.[16] Beginning in 2006, the government also initiated a twin series of sometimes contentious summits on the topics of integration and Islam in Germany, with the purpose of drawing representatives of various minority communities into a consultative policymaking process. Taken together, these changes mark something of a sea change in Germany's official stance toward migration, membership, and minorities.

The new focus on integration within Germany has been paralleled by, and in certain respects is inseparable from, the rather different process of integration occurring on the European level. In several respects, there has even been an Europeanization of Germany's approach to the structuring of a multicultural society. Many of the concerns that confront Germany with respect to its cultural minorities are shared by other European countries, many of which also have acquired sizable Muslim immigrant populations in recent decades. As countries like the Netherlands have retrenched from strong regimes of minority rights and other countries have recognized that assimilation alone will not suffice, there has been a convergence toward a model matching limited accommodations of cultural difference with demands that foreigners acquire competence in the local language, and demonstrate knowledge of and a commitment to the local legal culture.[17] For their part, European Union policy and law have placed certain restrictions on the German government's latitude in defining rights and protections for foreign workers and other minorities. At the same time, Germany, in the wake of the Schengen Agreement and the Treaty of Amsterdam, has benefited from European measures designed to establish a zone of free movement among most member states and, consequently, to develop collective policies to regulate migration and asylum applications from non-EU countries. This process also produced a framework designed to harmonize immigrant integration measures both at the national and EU levels.[18] On another front, the politics of Turkey's bid to join the European Union has meshed with the fortunes of the German Turkish minority in a complex way. It is hard to overlook the irony of a Germany pursuing a program of integration at the national level designed to give Turks a greater stake in society, even as it continues to oppose the full inclusion of the Turkish homeland within Europe.[19] This incongruity, moreover, is wrapped in a further irony: that of a German polity wrestling with the question of the degree of cultural diversity it can tolerate within its own society even as it strives to preserve its own traditions and distinctiveness in the negotiations surrounding the construction of the European Union.

35.4 CULTURAL DIVERSITY IN GERMANY

Which identities constitute the cultural mix that has come to characterize twenty-first century Germany? The German social landscape presently incorporates several kinds of groups that might be thought of as culturally distinct and that, in various ways, have laid claim to official acknowledgments of difference. There are, to begin with, several comparatively small, territorially settled autochthonous non-German nationalities that enjoy official protection of their language and traditions under the Council of Europe's Framework Convention for the Protection of National Minorities of 1995: the Sorbs, Danes, Frisians, Roma, and Sinti peoples. Then there are ethnicities produced largely by migration, which as of 2005 comprised roughly 15 million people or about 20 percent of the population in Germany.[20] Of these, the Turkish minority is the most prominent, but this group in turn has substantial internal divisions among subgroups including Kurds, Sufis, and Alevis. Other prominent communities nurture identities as Croatians, Serbs, Russians, Greeks, Italians, and Vietnamese. If, by comparison to the United States, race plays a comparatively small role in the politics of cultural identity, it is by no means absent in Germany. The rise of the category of *Afrodeutsche*, applied to progeny of black Americans, as well as Africans, betrays a shift in conceptions of race in Germany; and some have argued as well that a racialization of the Turkish minority is underway.[21] A religious divide separates Germany's over three million Muslims from the three large and roughly equal populations of Catholics, Protestants, and those with no religious affiliation. Although the category of Muslims tends indiscriminately to lump together members of the Turkish and Arab minorities, many of whom are non-practicing, it has been a notable feature of the migration experience in Germany that religious sentiment and identification has strengthened with time. To the list of cultural groups defined in terms of nationality, ethnicity, race, and religion, we can add another that is distinct in all these respects: the Jewish community actively recruited from abroad from the early 1990s on and over 100,000 strong. Moreover, although they do not show up in the statistics as foreigners, ethnic German repatriates from Russia and Eastern Europe—a group larger even than the Turkish minority—have also tended to build up their own subcultures.

Alongside the various linguistic groups living in Germany, there have also been significant divisions created, in a sense, by language—the language of law and bureaucracy employed to mark differences between members of the German *Staatsvolk* and others of lesser status. But because the broad distinctions between Germans and 'aliens' (*Ausländer*) or between citizens and migrants no longer adequately reflect the fault lines in German society—nor the hybridized identities emerging from recent history—the German government has recently found it necessary to deploy a new category, that of 'persons with a migration background,' to designate the fifth of the state's residents who come from elsewhere or were born to parents who did. This designation encompasses, for example, guest workers who are 'German' in the sense of having naturalized; third-generation migrants who still do not possess German citizenship; and ethnic Germans who migrated from Eastern Europe or the former Soviet Union, but do not speak German. One of the most significant features of this group is that, in demographic terms, it constitutes the primary force countering the overall trend toward an aging and shrinking population. Indeed, almost two-fifths of the children born in Germany in recent years belong to this category.[22] Just as strikingly, eleven of the twenty-three members of the German national team at the 2010 World Cup in South Africa—that is, roughly half—were from migrant families.

35.5 MEASURES OF INTEGRATION

The investigative journalist Günter Wallraff's popular 1985 book *Ganz Unten*, chronicling his misadventures after he disguised himself as a Turkish worker, carried two lessons: that members of the migrant minority faced severe discrimination and disadvantage, and that it took the voice of a non-migrant to expose their situation. Since then, there have been clear signals that groups such as the Turkish German minority are well on their way to establishing themselves as full-fledged members of German society. Over time, members of the population of foreign workers have made their way forward economically, with a recent study showing, for example, that 582,000 'foreign' entrepreneurs have created roughly two million jobs. Since the Citizenship Law of 2000 eased naturalization requirements, nearly a million migrants have become German citizens, a development which, in turn, has opened up the political process to their respective communities. Although initially, progress was halting in this sphere, migrant groups have slowly been able to place members in public office at all levels, ranging from local government to the German and European Parliaments. In the realm of the arts, the rise of a '*Migrantenliteratur*' preoccupied with the problems of dislocation and integration has given way, in some cases, to the work of artists who consider their migrant background largely immaterial to their work.[23] As a consequence, the German literary firmament now contains the Arab German writer Rafik Schami, the Italian German Gino Chiellino, and numerous Turkish Germans including Aras Ören, Zafer Şenocak, and Emine Sevgi Özdamar. Much the same development can be seen in the cinematic evolution from Tevfik Başer's 1986 film *40 Quadratmeter Deutschland* to the sophisticated intercultural themes of Kutluğ Ataman's *Lola und Bilidikid* or Fatih Akin's *The Edge of Heaven*. Meanwhile, in daily life, interactions between migrants and ethnic Germans have increased; thus, recent surveys have found that people of Turkish descent increasingly have German friends, that bi-national marriages are on the increase, that mosque associations have vastly increased their engagement with German conversation partners: and that over half of the Turkish minority participate in clubs which, in most cases, are actively involved with German organizations.[24] In the world of soccer, integrated teams have become commonplace, rather than the exception.[25] One opinion poll produced a strong testament to the idea that migrants and Germans have come to terms with the prospect of co-existence, as 81 percent of Turks and 76 percent of Germans affirmed the proposition that Turks should consider themselves part of Germany.[26]

35.6 CULTURAL FAULT LINES

If it is clear that Germany's minorities with 'migration backgrounds' have in many respects carved out a place for themselves in German society, there undeniably remains an abundance of neuralgic points at which the issue of multiculturalism continues to be contested.

There is, to begin with, the persistence of xenophobic attitudes and violence against members of migrant communities. Hoyerswerda, Rostock, Mölln, and Solingen lead the litany of sites of major attacks against foreigners that welled up in the early 1990s in the wake of German unification and played a much-debated role in the government's subsequent abridgment of the right of asylum.[27] These actions, stemming as they did from extremists, could not be taken as representative of the public at large. Indeed, large numbers of Germans turned out in demonstrations against violence and in solidarity with the victims. Still, these violent events nonetheless contributed to a climate of hostility toward foreigners that exacerbated the alienation accompanying their precarious legal state. It was symptomatic of this development that in 1991 the term '*ausländerfrei*,' denoting an area cleansed of all foreigners, earned the designation of '*Unwort des Jahres*.'

Mirroring this choice, in a sense, was the runner-up for Word of the Year in 2004, '*Parallelgesellschaft*.' The controversial idea of a 'parallel society' served as the focal point for a debate about the degree to which immigrant minorities in France, Holland, the United Kingdom, or Germany were forming independent subcultures immune to the influence of mainstream culture and political values, and within which intolerance and extremism might flourish. The notion is instructive because, in the politics of identity, it cuts in two ways. On the one hand, it implies a process of self-segregation marked by an unwillingness on the part of migrants to make the requisite concessions to adapt themselves to the norms of the host society or to take action against the potential terrorists in their midst. On the other hand, it suggests a process of ghetto-ization arising from discrimination, structural inequalities, and legal and political disadvantages imposed by the dominant social order.

On the first count, participants in debates regarding multiculturalism have some-times appeared to subscribe to the view endorsed in the German Parliament by Alfred Dregger in 1982, namely that Turks, Asians and Africans are in principle not assimila-ble in German society.[28] Former Chancellor Helmut Schmidt added partial support to this outlook in a 2004 interview, commenting that 'the concept of multiculturalism [*Multikulti*] is difficult to reconcile with a democratic society . . . In this respect it was a mistake to bring guest workers from foreign cultures into the country in the early 1960s.'[29] The notion that particular minorities are inherently resistant to integration draws on certain well-publicized markers of difference for support. The proportionally high rate of foreigners involved in criminality, including domestic abuse, is one such marker. Others include cultural practices such as female genital mutilation, forced marriages, polygamy, and most sensationally, the phenomenon of 'honor killings'— murders of kinfolk, usually women, held to have dishonored their families.[30] To these can be added, finally, the alarming image of the potential homegrown Muslim terrorist.

With regard to the process of ghettoization implied by the notion of a 'parallel society,' there have been plentiful indicators regarding the subordination and isolation of cultural minorities, chief among them the Turkish community. At some level, xenophobic discrimination doubtless plays a role in the subordinate status of Ger-many's migrants, though empirical assessments of the degree vary.[31] Underneath daily experiences of face-to-face discrimination, however, lurk weightier structural diver-gences associated with cultural groups. Unemployment rates for non-German migrants have consistently been double the national average in recent years, and general economic prosperity measurably lower for minority populations.[32] These trends are related to pronounced deficits in measures of educational attainment, such as high school diplomas, university places, and positions in job training programs, a state of affairs which has not been helped by the formation of public schools in some urban areas with overwhelmingly high percentages of students with migration back-grounds. At the root of the situation are language skills, which in bi-national children are frequently substandard in both languages.[33] Compounding the entire situation is the overall political exclusion of the migrants, who still, for the most part, remain foreign nationals and hence lack voting rights.

35.7 INTEGRATION MEASURES

Acknowledgment of these deficits has prompted vigorous policy debates on a range of remedial measures, and over time the German political establishment has begun to piece together a co-ordinated response to the set of challenges posed by cultural diversity. The federal government, which for many years resisted calls to enact anti-discrimination laws, finally moved somewhat reluctantly in this direction in 2006 in response to obligations incurred through the Europeanization process. From a public discussion of federal integration policy and a restructuring of the federal authority responsible for integration emerged a strategy emphasizing the importance of (and in some cases requiring) German language training for migrants, as well as a primer in German history and culture. Early childhood education likewise became a focus of government efforts. Interestingly, the German debate has scrupulously avoided the notion of affirmative action or 'positive discrimination' that has been employed in other countries, such as the USA and India; however, in light of an increasing trend toward the segregation of public schools, recently proposals for busing students have begun to be aired.[34] Appropriate models for intercultural education, including bilingual instruction, remain under discussion, but sports has been given a prominent role in the federal program of integration; here again, we see the changing face of soccer national-ism. On the crucial question of political representation, the campaign to naturalize long-term resident migrants and extend citizenship to the younger generation has addressed the matter of enfranchisement, although the question of acceptance of dual citizenship continues to simmer, and a recent decision to institute a test for applicants for citizenship also sparked controversy.[35]

Particularly in the wake of September 11, 2001, the religious dimensions of cultural difference have moved to the forefront of negotiations of multiculturalism. Muslim associations in Germany have periodically encountered friction with their surround-ings by probing the limits of religious freedom and toleration. Efforts to build mosques and minarets that would add visible markers of their presence to German cityscapes have frequently met with local resistance resulting in public hearings and court cases.

Similar controversies have concerned the impact of muezzin calls to prayer in the middle of the day and the treatment of animals subjected to *halal* butchering practices. Next to these issues of the free exercise of religion, crucial matters regarding the establishment of religion have also arisen. One is the question of institutional parity with the Catholic, Protestant and Jewish religious organizations, which enjoy the privileged status of 'bodies of public law' (*Körperschaften des Öffentlichen Rechts*); a difficulty in this regard, however, has been posed by the lack of a single centralized authority for the Muslim community. A related issue concerns the provision of Islamic education. In the interest of promoting integration, the case has been made that to offset private Koran courses, which in some cases may expose students to extremist strands of Islam, Islamic religion courses should be offered in public schools on the same terms in which courses on Christianity and Judaism are offered. Further proposals have suggested that teachers of Islam and, indeed, imams should be trained in German institutions of higher learning, and that professorships in Islam should be built up in the university system.

Some of the most penetrating debates about Islam and multiculturalism revolve around the status of women. As with France's discussion of *le foulard*, Germany has experienced a vibrant controversy initiated by the court case involving the Afghan German Fereshta Ludin's claim that she should be allowed to wear a headscarf as a teacher in public school.[36] The issue of how the state should respond to head coverings is a complex one, not least because the headscarf can symbolize divergent meanings ranging from assertions of 'girl power' to the subjugation of women. For some prominent feminist social critics, such as Necla Kelek and Seyran Ateş, the headscarf is to be viewed as of a piece with Muslim efforts in the migrant communities to exclude girls from swimming classes or sex education classes. For them, multiculturalist respect for religious-cultural difference is pernicious if it refuses to challenge patriarchal violations of gender equality. On the other side, even such a conservative thinker as the former judge Ernst-Wolfgang Böckenförde has defended the right of Muslim women to wear headscarves in public settings. This is one instance of how the positions staked out in debates on multiculturalism do not map neatly onto the chief differences defining the German political spectrum.

35.8 Ethics of integration

Disagreement over the issue of headscarves and other questions arising from Germany's cultural diversity is linked, fundamentally, to underlying theoretical issues that involve some genuine ethical challenges. The reality of cultural diversity requires a stance in response to the legacies of German history, political culture, and institutions of belonging. There are several facets to the overarching problematic here. I will address four broad areas of discourse and disagreement, concerning, in turn, the political foundations of different approaches to dealing with migrants, the philosophical commitments brought to the project of integration, the religious issues at stake in the structuring of modern societies, and the historical task of bringing the meaning of the past to bear on what some have called the 'new Social Question' of the twenty-first century.[37]

In the political sphere, one way to put the central normative question raised by the diversification of German society is as a sort of *quid pro quo*: what are fair accommodations to cultural minorities, and what can properly be required as adaptations on their part? Over the past decade or so much of the public discussion of this broad issue has revolved around the opposing catchphrases of '*Leitkultur*' and '*Verfassungspatriotismus.*' The notion of a German *Leitkultur*—a set of normative attributes and values associated with Germanness to which migrants should conform as a precondition for inclusion in society—was advanced by Christian Democratic politicians such as Friedrich Merz and Jörg Schönbohm in the context of their opposition to Social Democratic proposals for integration.[38] Their suggestion that familiarity with German language, history, and culture provided a necessary foundation for social harmony constituted an argument in favor of conformity to a monocultural model—some would even say *Germanisierung*—rather than integration on a culturally pluralistic basis. This claim has at times produced more heat than light—for example, in Turkish Prime Minister Tayyip Erdogan's statement during a visit to Cologne that 'assimilation is a crime against humanity.'[39] Yet the *Leitkultur* thesis has helped focus the question of the relation between culture and politics and the difference between integration and assimilation. An alternative position has been staked out by thinkers such as Dolf Sternberger and Jürgen Habermas in the shape of the ideal of *Verfassungspatriotismus* or 'constitutional patriotism.' According to this notion, the proper basis for belonging in a modern state such as Germany is not a particular ethnic identity, but rather an engaged commitment to the values of a free and democratic constitutional order—a commitment that, within limits fixed by the human rights enshrined in the constitution—is compatible with a broad range of cultural or ethnic identities.[40] Rather than ethnonationalism, on this view, it is republicanism that provides the basis for the successful integration of subcultures.[41]

As the German case makes clear, facing up to the reality of cultural diversity necessitates reflection and debate on some rather elemental questions of political philosophy. What are the implications of perceived conflicts between the enlightened liberal democratic order of the *Bundesrepublik* and the mores and traditions of Turkish, or Arab, or Vietnamese, or African communities? In philosophical terms, disputes over multiculturalism turn in part on competing moral theories. On the one hand, arguments for placing strict limitations on the more controversial practices of migrants in the name of human rights tend to be associated with a universalistic ethical outlook. On the other hand, claims of unfettered autonomy for members of minority cultures smack of a thoroughgoing moral relativism. The middle ground in this debate is occupied by varying recognitions of moral pluralism. It is within this context that the longstanding Western philosophical discourse of toleration has taken root in present discussions.[42] The issue of toleration concerns the terms under which practices and modes of life that are held to be objectionable—but not beyond the pale—may coexist with the greater good of society. In the German setting, the question of the limits of toleration crops up regularly in discussions about the degree to which elements of Muslim culture in particular are to be accommodated.[43] Where a place for difference is acknowledged, further questions of a philosophical-anthropological cast—but with clear legal implications—arise: should the requisite acknowledgments or accommodations be cast in terms of the rights and freedoms of individuals, or should the law take into account the existence of groups in the form of collective rights and corporate protections?[44]

In taking on the issue of cultural diversity, some commentators have also been attuned to the complex religious dimensions that are involved. Habermas, for example, has recognized that the multicultural society faces challenging questions about the proper scope of religious freedom and appropriate relations between church and state. Yet he also argues that it must confront even deeper questions about the character of secularization and the relationship between faith and reason. In writing about the notion of the 'post-secular society,' he describes the contest between 'Enlightenment fundamentalism' and radical multiculturalism as a 'new *Kulturkampf.*' As the resurgence of religion in Europe has belied the more ambitious predictions associated with the secularization thesis, it has become increasingly clear that secularists and members of religious subcultures alike must engage in a mutual coming to terms in which they accept, from their varying perspectives, a *modus vivendi* for incorporating religious speech into civic culture.[45] With respect to Islam in particular, the fears surrounding the events of September 11 and the rise of Islamism have lent urgency to the task of distinguishing the roots of radicalism—which can include the sort of humiliation that may accompany persistent disadvantaging and disrespect—from the conditions for the nurturing of a moderate Islam that affirms the compatibility of Muslim religion with a secular and democratic political order. This undertaking, led elsewhere by figures such as Tariq Ramadan, Abdullahi An-na'im, and Fethullah Gülen, has been spearheaded in Germany by the work of Bassam Tibi, who has given special attention to the manner in which Europe and Islam have shaped and informed one another through a long-standing history of interaction and inculturation.[46]

Tibi's placing of the present tensions between Islamization and Europeanization within the context of a long history of 'threat and fascination' invokes the question of the specter of the past that hangs over German multiculturalism. As Germany tries to triangulate its way toward an effective balance of social cohesion, equality, and respect for difference, historiographical questions inevitably arise about the ways in which history informs present developments—and vice versa. What are the implications of the *Sonderweg* idea for Germany's attempts to affirm cultural pluralism? Can a modern—and modernizing—German republicanism overcome the historical tendency to emphasize the *Kulturnation* or even the ethnic *Volk* as the basis of German identity? The evidence is mounting that a shift is underway in this direction. As the principle of *ius sanguinis* gives way to *ius soli* in citizenship law, as politicians with 'migration backgrounds' enter the Bundestag and the European Parliament, and as the language of the government bureaucracy comes to include naturalized migrants as 'Germans,' it becomes clear that changes are being wrought in the constitution of the nation and what it means to be German. Still, this development is not close to leaving behind the long shadow of Nazism and the Holocaust. In an interview in 1995 published under the title 'May One Compare Turks and Jews, Mr. Şenocak?' the Turkish German author Zafer Şenocak noted that

> One can immigrate to a country, but not to its past. In Germany, history is read as a diary of the 'community of fate' [*Schicksalsgemeinschaft*], the nation's personal experience, to which Others have no access. This conception of history as ethnic, collective memory was tied to the question of guilt after the crimes of the Nazis . . . Can immigrants participate in shaping the German future without having access to a shared history with the native population? Is it possible to weld peoples with different histories together into one nation?[47]

It was perhaps a measure of the degree to which the Turkish migrants have become integrated into the project and pitfalls of German history when Faruk Şen, one of the foremost authorities on the Turkish minority in Germany and an immigrant himself, was unceremoniously fired in 2008 for comparing the situation of Turks in Europe to that of the Jews under the Nazis.

35.9 MULTICULTURALIST GOALS

In 2008 another milestone on the road to integration in Germany was reached during the European soccer championship, which put on display the evolution of ethnic, national, and cultural identities in contemporary Europe. During the tournament the German striker Miroslav Klose, pressed about his loyalties to his two countries of Germany and Poland, earned headlines when he responded that he simply preferred to be called European. Later, as a semifinal matchup between Germany and Turkey approached and politicians somewhat nervously denied that they were concerned about the possibility of violent conflicts during and after the game, the German media interviewed Turkish residents who proclaimed they would be happy whichever side won. *Hürriyet*—a Turkish daily that publishes a weekly insert in German for Turks who cannot read Turkish—ran a large friendship poster featuring both teams, and the match formally began with pointed statements about tolerance delivered by both team captains. The German team had been led into the match by a native German trainer who established his coaching credentials in Turkey's professional league; the game itself featured a star turn for Turkey by Hamit Altintop, a player who was born in Germany and had played his entire career there. The broadcast of the tense match on German television was disrupted during the decisive final minutes of the game when an Alpine storm broke off the transmission of the Swiss feed. In the multicultural society, however, not a minute was missed by those Germans of foreign extraction who were watching the game on Al-Jazeera.

Notes

1. Much to the embarrassment of the designers of Germany's most expensive publicity action at the time, photographic evidence soon turned up that the similar slogan 'Denn Du bist Deutschland' had been prominently employed at a National Socialist party convention in the mid-1930s in Ludwigshafen.
2. 'German Politicians Hail New Patriotism,' *Deutsche Welle* (dw-world.de), 18 June 2006.
3. A transcript of Heye's interview is at www.dradio.de/dkultur/sendungen/interview/ 501431; on the Owomoyela case, see the *International Herald Tribune*, 25 March 2008.
4. OECD, *International Migration Outlook 2008*. Among OECD countries, Germany was surpassed only by Canada (19.0 percent), New Zealand (19.2 percent), Switzerland (23.1 percent), Australia (23.4 percent), and Luxembourg (33.0 percent). However, immigrants account for over 10 percent of the population in more than half of the thirty OECD countries.
5. Christian Joppke and Steven Lukes quote Nathan Glazer on this point in their *Multicultural Questions* (Oxford: Oxford University Press, 1999), 1–2.
6. Lutz Hoffmann, *Die unvollendete Republik* (Köln: PapyRossa, 1990), 145–157. See also Joseph Carens, *Culture, Citizenship, and Community* (Oxford, Oxford University Press, 2000); Seyla Benhabib, *The Claims of Culture: Equality and Diversity in the Global Era* (Princeton: Princeton University Press, 2002); Brian Barry, *Culture and Equality: An Egalitarian Critique of Multiculturalism* (Cambridge: Harvard University Press, 2002); Anne Phillips, *Multiculturalism Without Culture* (Princeton: Princeton University Press, 2007); and Roland Hsu (ed.), *Ethnic Europe: Mobility, Identity, and Conflict in a Globalized World* (Stanford: Stanford University Press, 2010).
7. Charles Taylor et al., *Multiculturalism and the 'Politics of Recognition'* (Princeton: Princeton University Press, 1992); Axel Honneth, *Kampf um Anerkennung*, 4th edn (Frankfurt am Main: Suhrkamp, 2003). See also Iris Marion Young, *Inclusion and Democracy* (Oxford: Oxford University Press, 2000).
8. Cf. Amartya Sen, 'A Freedom-Based Understanding of Multicultural Commitments,' Acceptance Speech for the Meister Eckhart Prize, University of Cologne, 28 November 2007.
9. As Wolfgang Zank notes in his *The German Melting Pot: Multiculturality in Historical Perspective* (New York: Palgrave, 1998), 'Ethnically, the Germans of today are of Celtic, Roman, Saxon, Frankish, Alaman, Danish, Frisian, Obodrite, Polbic, Pomeranian, Kashubian, Sorbian, Old-Prussian, Mazurian, Polish, French Huguenot, Jewish, Czech, Italian, Spanish, Portuguese, Yugoslav, and Turkish origin' (243).
10. The term is Tomas Hammar's, from his *Democracy and the Nation-State: Aliens, Denizens, and Citizens in a World of International Migration* (Aldershot: Avebury, 1990). For an argument characterizing the panoply of rights enjoyed by non-citizen immigrants in Germany and other European countries as "postnational membership," see Yasemin Soysal, *Limits of Citizenship: Migrants and Postnational Membership in Europe* (Chicago: University of Chicago Press, 1994).

11. Karin Hunn, *'Nächstes Jahr kehren wir zurück . . . :' Die Geschichte der türkischen 'Gast-arbeiter' in der Bundesrepublik* (Göttingen: Wallstein, 2005).

12. Rita Chin, *The Guest Worker Question in Postwar Germany* (Cambridge: Cambridge University Press, 2007), 246.

13. Although only roughly 5 percent of asylum applications were approved, in many other cases applicants were granted a provisional right to stay in Germany.

14. Germany, followed closely by Spain and the UK, remained the largest target of migration in Europe through 2005, even as all of the original members of the European Union except the Netherlands continued to receive positive migration flows. *Migrationsbericht des Bundesamtes für Migration und Flüchtlinge im Auftrag der Bundesregierung*, 2006.

15. The measure was adopted only after stiff resistance by the CDU and CSU, in the form of a massive petition drive, succeeded in leading to the scrapping of the proposed unlimited acceptance of dual citizenship. The current provision requires that children who receive dual citizenship through birth in Germany must choose one citizenship by the age of 23 and renounce the other.

16. The significance of this step is somewhat tempered by the government's insistence on calling the new measure a 'Zuwanderungsgesetz' ('Migration Law') as opposed to 'Ein-wanderungsgesetz' ('Immigration Law'). It is an irony, moreover, that in the period in which Germany has edged toward an official acceptance of the designation of a country of immigration, it has succeeded—through limitations on family reunification and the repatriation of ethnic Germans—in largely drying up the stream of migrants.

17. Steffen Angenendt, 'Migrations- und integrationspolitische Entwicklungen, Herausfor-derungen und Strategien in ausgewählten EU-Staaten,' in Rosemarie Beier-De Haan (ed.), *Zuwanderungsland Deutschland: Migrationen 1500–2005* (Wolfratshausen: Edition Minerva, 2005), 134–147.

18. See *Common Basic Principles for Immigrant Integration Policy in the EU* (Council Document 14615/04) and *A Common Agenda for Integration* (COM [2005] 389).

19. Chancellor Merkel has proposed the more limited arrangement of a 'privileged partner-ship' instead.

20. Interestingly, prior to 2005 the federal German government did not track ethnicity or nationality in its census data.

21. Fatima El-Tayeb, ' "The Birth of a European Public:" Migration, Postnationality, and Race in the Uniting of Europe' *American Quarterly* 60, no. 3 (2008), 649–670.

22. As of 2008, 34.4 percent of all children under five years old living in Germany had a 'migration background.' *Bevölkerung und Erwerbstätigkeit: Bevölkerung mit Migrations-hintergrund—Ergebnisse des Mikrozensus 2008* (Wiesbaden: Statistisches Bundesamt, 2010), 8.

23. Chin, *The Guest Worker Question*; Azade Seyhan, *Writing Outside the Nation* (Princeton: Princeton University Press, 2001); and 'From Istanbul to Berlin: Stations on the Road to a Transcultural/Translational Literature,' in Günter H. Lenz et al. (eds), *Toward a New Metropolitanism: Reconstituting Public Culture, Urban Citizenship, and the Multicultural Imaginary in New York and Berlin* (Heidelberg: Universitätsverlag Winter, 2006), 383–398.

24. Faruk Şen and Dirk Halm, 'Wanted: The Chance to Become German,' *Atlantic Times*, (2008), 4; *Berliner Zeitung*, 7 June 2007, 25.

25. Frank Kalter, *Chancen, Fouls, und Abseitsfallen* (Wiesbaden: Westdeutscher Verlag, 2003).

26. Oddly, however, a 2008 poll commissioned by *Die Zeit* (http://zelos.zeit.de/2008/12/Bevoelkerung-Migration-2008.pdf) revealed that an overwhelming percentage of 'Deutschtürken' (78 percent overall, and 85 percent among Turks with German citizenship) do not subscribe to Angela Merkel's recent claim that she is also the Chancellor for Turks living in Germany. In the same poll, just over half of those surveyed said they feel like Turks when in Germany, and Germans when in Turkey.

27. At the peak of the wave of violence, the month of June 1993 saw 1307 attacks against foreigners, including 161 involving arson or explosives. See Rene Del Fabbro, 'Germany: A Victory of the Street,' in Bernd Baumgartl and Adrian Favell (eds), New Xenophobia in Europe (Boston: Kluwer, 1995), 132–47, at 144.

28. *Verhandlungen des Deutschen Bundestages* from 4 February 1982, 4891–95. Dregger's view was echoed by the Heidelberg Manifesto of 4 March 1982.

29. 'Wieviel Anatolien verträgt Europa?' *Hamburger Abendblatt*, 24 November 2004.

30. German asylum law recognizes that the threat of female genital mutilation constitutes grounds for asylum. On the various ways in which Muslim men are construed to be unassimilable see Katherine Pratt Ewing, *Stolen Honor: Stigmatizing Muslim Men in Berlin* (Stanford: Stanford University Press, 2008).

31. Richard Alba et al., *Germans or Foreigners? Attitudes Toward Ethnic Minorities in Post-Reunification Germany* (New York: Palgrave Macmillan, 2004).

32. In 2008, for example, the unemployment rate for persons with a migration background was 12.4 percent, while for those without a migration background the rate was 6.5 percent. *Beauftragte der Bundesregierung für Migration, Flüchtlinge und Integration, 8. Bericht über die Lage der Ausländerinnen und Ausländer in Deutschland.*

33. Hartmut Esser, *Sprache und Integration: Die sozialen Bedingungen und Folgen des Spracherwerbs von Migranten* (Frankfurt am Main: Campus, 2006).

34. Alke Wierth, 'Mit Rütli ging es wieder los,' *Die Tageszeitung*, 30 June 2007.

35. As critics were quick to point out, for at least one of the questions included in an early version of the test—'At which agency must one register one's dog in Germany'—there is no single correct answer.

36. Although the Federal Constitutional Court ruled in favor of the plaintiff (docket number 2BvF 1436/02 from 24 September 2003, at www.bundesverfassungsgericht.de), the decision led to the adoption in individual German states of legislation forbidding the wearing of prominent religious symbols by teachers in public school classrooms.

37. See, e.g., Armin Laschet, *Die Aufsteigerrepublik: Zuwanderung als Chance* (Köln: Kiepenheuer & Witsch, 2009).

38. In so doing, they appropriated a notion originally developed by Bassam Tibi with specific reference to European society as a whole. See his *Europa ohne Identität?* (Munich: C. Bertelsmann, 1998).

39. David Crossland, 'Erdogan's Visit Leaves German Conservatives Fuming,' 12 February 2008, www.spiegel.de/international/germany/0,1518,534724,00.html.

40. Jürgen Habermas, *Die Einbeziehung des Anderen: Studien zur politischen Theorie* (Frankfurt am Main: Suhrkamp, 1999), and Habermas, *Die postnationale Konstellation* (Frankfurt am Main: Suhrkamp, 2006).

41. See William A. Barbieri, Jr., 'The Many Faces of Republicanism, Or, What's in a Name?' in Jan-Werner Müller (ed.), *German Ideologies since 1945* (New York: Palgrave Macmillan, 2002).

42. See Rainer Forst, *Toleranz im Konflikt: Geschichte, Gehalt und Gegenwart eines umstrittenen Begriffs* (Frankfurt am Main: Suhrkamp, 2003). On this question as with others, German political theory has been influenced by Anglo-American debates. See, e.g. Michael Walzer, *On Toleration* (New Haven: Yale University Press, 1997); James Bohman, 'Deliberative Toleration,' *Political Theory* 31, no.6 (2003), 757–779; Melissa Williams and Jeremy Waldron (eds), *Toleration and Its Limits: Nomos XLVIII* (New York: NYU Press, 2008).

43. A considerable amount of fuel for these debates has been provided by the Danish 'cartoon controversy' and, in the United Kingdom, the Archbishop of Canterbury's comments about the advisability of integrating certain aspects of shariah with British law.

44. Jutta Limbach has argued that the jurisprudential culture of Germany should be adapted to make room for group rights in 'Multikultur und Minderheit: Das Toleranzgebot des Grundgesetzes,' *Blätter für deutsche und international Politik* 50, no. 10 (2005), 1221–1229. On this question in general with regard to liberal democracies see Will Kymlicka, *Multicultural Citizenship* (Oxford: Oxford University Press, 1995).

45. Habermas, 'Die Dialektik der Säkularisierung,' *Blätter für deutsche und international Politik* 53, no. 4 (2008), 33–46. See also Joseph Ratzinger and Jürgen Habermas, *The Dialectics of Secularization: On Reason and Religion* (Ft. Collins: Ignatius Press, 2007). Cf. Tariq Modood, *Multiculturalism* (Oxford: Polity, 2007), especially Chapter 4.

46. See Bassam Tibi, *Political Islam, World Politics, and Europe* (London: Routledge, 2007).

47. Zafer Şenocak, *Atlas of a Tropical Germany: Essays on Politics and Culture, 1990–1998*, ed. and trans. Leslie A. Adelson (Lincoln: University of Nebraska Press, 2000), 53.

BIBLIOGRAPHY

ADELSON, LESLIE A., *The Turkish Turn in Contemporary German Literature: Toward a New Critical Grammar of Migration* (New York: Palgrave Macmillan, 2005).

ARGUN, BETIGÜL ERCAN, *Turkey in Germany: The Transnational Sphere of Deutschkei* (New York: Routledge, 2003).

ATEŞ, SEYRAN, *Der Multikulti-Irrtum: Wie wir in Deutschland besser zusammenleben können* (Berlin: Ullstein, 2007).

BADE, KLAUS J., *Die multikulturelle Herausforderung: Menschen über Grenzen—Grenzen über Menschen* (Munich: C. H. Beck, 2000).

—— et al. (eds) *Enzyklopädie Migration in Europa: Vom 17. Jahrhundert bis zur Gegenwart* (Munich: Ferdinand Schöningh, 2007).

BIELEFELDT, HEINER, *Menschenrechte in der Einwanderungsgesellschaft. Plädoyer für einen aufgeklärten Multikulturalismus* (Bielefeld: Transcript, 2007).

BÜCKING, HANS–JÖRG, and JESSE ECKHARD (eds), *Deutsche Identität in Europa* (Berlin: Duncker & Humblot, 2008).

CHIN, RITA, *The Guest Worker Question in Postwar Germany* (Cambridge: Cambridge University Press, 2007).

FETZER, JOEL S. and J. CHRISTOPHER SOPER, *Muslims and the State in Britain, France, and Germany* (Cambridge: Cambridge University Press, 2004).

GEDDES, ANDREW, *The Politics of Migration and Immigration in Europe* (London: Sage, 2003).

GÖKTÜRK, DENIZ, et al. (eds), *Germany in Transit: Nation and Migration, 1955–2005* (Berkeley: University of California Press, 2007).

HABERMAS, JÜRGEN, 'Equal Treatment of Cultures and the Limits of Postmodern Liberalism,' *Journal of Political Philosophy* 13, no. 1 (2005), 1–28.

HERBERT, ULRICH, *Geschichte der Ausländerpolitik in Deutschland: Saisonarbeiter, Zwangsarbeiter, Gastarbeiter, Flüchtlinge* (Munich: C. H. Beck, 2001).

JOPPKE, CHRISTIAN, 'Multiculturalism and Immigration,' *Theory and Society* 25, no. 4 (1996), 449–500.

KASTORYANO, RIVA, *Negotiating Identities: States and Immigrants in France and Germany* (Princeton: Princeton University Press, 2002).

KELEK, NECLA, *Die fremde Braut: Berichte aus dem Inneren des türkischen Lebens in Deutschland* (Cologne: Kiepenheuer & Witsch, 2005).

KLAUSEN, JYTTE, *The Islamic Challenge: Politics and Religion in Western Europe* (New York: Oxford University Press, 2008).

KLOPP, BRETT, *German Multiculturalism: Immigrant Integration and the Transformation of Citizenship* (Westport: Praeger, 2002).

KLUSMEYER, DOUGLAS B., and DEMETRIOS G. PAPADEMETRIOU, *Immigration Policy in the Federal Republic of Germany: Negotiating Membership and Remaking the Nation* (New York: Berghahn, 2009).

LEVY, DANIEL, and STEFAN LUFT, *Abschied von Multikulti. Wege aus der Integrationskrise* (Gräfelfing: Resch, 2006).

LUCASSEN, LEO, *The Immigrant Threat: The Integration of Old and New Migrants in Western Europe* (Chicago: University of Illinois Press, 2005).

MALLOY, TOVE H., *National Minority Rights in Europe* (Oxford: Oxford University Press, 2005).

MANDEL, RUTH, *Cosmopolitan Anxieties: Turkish Challenges to Citizenship and Belonging in Germany* (Durham: Duke University Press, 2008).

MEIER-BRAUN, KARL-HEINZ, *Deutschland, Einwanderungsland* (Frankfurt am Main: Suhrkamp, 2002).

MILICH, KLAUS J. and JEFFREY M. PECK (eds), *Multiculturalism in Transit: A German-American Exchange* (New York: Berghahn, 1998).

NOWAK, JÜRGEN, *Leitkultur und Parallelgesellschaft. Argumente wider einen deutschen Mythos* (Frankfurt am Main: Brandes & Apsel, 2006).

OLTMER, JOCHEN, *Migration steuern und verwalten: Deutschland vom späten 19. Jahrhundert bis zur Gegenwart* (Göttingen: Vandenhoeck & Ruprecht, 2003).

TIBI, BASSAM, *Europa ohne Identität? Die Krise der multikulturellen Gesellschaft* (Munich: BTB Verlag, 2002).

VERTOVEC, STEVEN, and SUSANNE WESSENDORF, *The Multiculturalism Backlash: European Discourses, Policies, and Practices* (New York: Routledge, 2010).

YURDAKUL, GÖKCE and Y. MICHAL BODEMANN (eds), *Citizenship and Immigrant Incorporation: Comparative Perspectives on North America and Western Europe.* (New York: Palgrave Macmillan, 2007).

INDEX